Contemporary
Literary Criticism

Guide to Gale Literary Criticism Series

When you need to review criticism of literary works, these are the Gale series to use:

If the author's death date is:

You should turn to:

After Dec. 31, 1959
(or author is still living)

CONTEMPORARY LITERARY CRITICISM

for example: Jorge Luis Borges, Anthony Burgess,
William Faulkner, Mary Gordon,
Ernest Hemingway, Iris Murdoch

1900 through 1959

TWENTIETH-CENTURY LITERARY CRITICISM

for example: Willa Cather, F. Scott Fitzgerald,
Henry James, Mark Twain, Virginia Woolf

1800 through 1899

NINETEENTH-CENTURY LITERATURE CRITICISM

for example: Fedor Dostoevski, Nathaniel Hawthorne,
George Sand, William Wordsworth

1400 through 1799

LITERATURE CRITICISM FROM 1400 TO 1800
(excluding Shakespeare)

for example: Anne Bradstreet, Daniel Defoe,
Alexander Pope, François Rabelais,
Jonathan Swift, Phillis Wheatley

SHAKESPEAREAN CRITICISM

Shakespeare's plays and poetry

Antiquity through 1399

CLASSICAL AND MEDIEVAL LITERATURE CRITICISM

for example: Dante, Homer, Plato, Sophocles, Vergil,
the Beowulf Poet

Gale also publishes related criticism series:

CHILDREN'S LITERATURE REVIEW

This series covers authors of all eras who have written for
the preschool through high school audience.

SHORT STORY CRITICISM

This series covers the major short fiction writers of all nationalities
and periods of literary history.

ISSN 0091-3421

Volume 57

Contemporary Literary Criticism

Excerpts from Criticism of the
Works of Today's Novelists, Poets,
Playwrights, Short Story Writers, Scriptwriters,
and Other Creative Writers

Roger Matuz
EDITOR

Cathy Falk
Sean R. Pollock
David Segal
Bridget Travers
Robyn V. Young
ASSOCIATE EDITORS

 Gale Research Inc. · DETROIT · NEW YORK · LONDON

STAFF

Roger Matuz, *Editor*

Cathy Falk, Sean R. Pollock, David Segal, Bridget Travers, Robyn V. Young, *Associate Editors*

John P. Daniel, Rogene M. Fisher, Mary K. Gillis, Susanne Skubik, Debra A. Wells, *Assistant Editors*

Jeanne A. Gough, *Production & Permissions Manager*
Linda M. Pugliese, *Production Supervisor*
Jennifer Gale, Suzanne Powers, Maureen A. Puhl, *Editorial Associates*
Donna Craft, David G. Oblender, Linda M. Ross, *Editorial Assistants*

Victoria B. Cariappa, *Research Supervisor*
Karen D. Kaus, Eric Priehs, Maureen R. Richards, Mary D. Wise, *Editorial Associates*
H. Nelson Fields, Judy L. Gale, Jill M. Ohorodnik, Filomena Sgambati, *Editorial Assistants*

Sandra C. Davis, *Permissions Supervisor (Text)*
H. Diane Cooper, Kathy Grell, Josephine M. Keene, Kimberly F. Smilay, *Permissions Associates*
Maria L. Franklin, Lisa M. Lantz, Camille P. Robinson, Shalice Shah, Denise M. Singleton,
Permissions Assistants

Patricia A. Seefelt, *Permissions Supervisor (Pictures)*
Margaret A. Chamberlain, *Permissions Associate*
Pamela A. Hayes, Lillian Quickley, *Permissions Assistants*

Mary Beth Trimper, *Production Manager*
Marilyn Jackman, *External Production Assistant*

Art Chartow, *Art Director*
C. J. Jonik, *Keyliner*

Laura Bryant, *Production Supervisor*
Louise Gagné, *Internal Production Associate*

Since this page cannot legibly accommodate all the copyright notices,
the Acknowledgments section constitutes an extension of the copyright notice.

Copyright © 1990
Gale Research Inc.
835 Penobscot Bldg.
Detroit, MI 48226-4094

Library of Congress Catalog Card Number 76-38938
ISBN 0-8103-4431-9
ISSN 0091-3421

Printed in the United States of America

Contents

Preface   vii

Acknowledgments   xi

Authors Forthcoming in *CLC*   xvii

Preface

Literary criticism is, by definition, "the art of evaluating or analyzing with knowledge and propriety works of literature." The complexity and variety of contemporary literature makes the function of the critic especially important to today's reader. The critic assists the reader in identifying significant new writers, recognizing trends, understanding the importance and implications of particular works, and mastering new terminology. Until the publication of the first volume of *Contemporary Literary Criticism (CLC)* in 1973, there existed no ongoing digest monitoring scholarly and popular sources of critical opinion and explication. *CLC,* therefore, has fulfilled an essential need.

Scope of the Work

CLC presents significant passages from published criticism of works by today's creative writers. Each volume of *CLC* includes excerpted criticism on about thirty authors who are now living or who died after December 31, 1959. More than 2,000 authors have been included since the series began publication. Since many of the writers covered by *CLC* inspire continual critical commentary, authors frequently appear in more than one volume. There is, of course, no duplication of reprinted criticism.

Authors are selected for inclusion for a variety of reasons, among them the publication or dramatic production of a critically acclaimed new work, the reception of a major literary award, revival of interest in past writings, or the dramatization of a literary work as a film or television screenplay. For example, the present volume includes John Krizanc and Robert Kroetsch, recipients of Canada's Governor General's Literary Award; André Malraux, an influential force in contemporary French art, politics, and philosophy; and Isabel Allende and Bruce Chatwin, whose recent novels, *Eva Luna* and *Utz,* respectively, received much attention from critics and readers. Perhaps most importantly, works that frequently appear on the syllabuses of high school and college literature classes are represented by individual entries in *CLC; Waiting for Godot,* by Samuel Beckett, and *The Waste Land,* by T. S. Eliot, are examples of works of this stature covered in the present volume. Attention is also given to several other groups of writers—authors of considerable public interest—about whose work criticism is often difficult to locate. These include mystery and science fiction writers, literary and social critics, foreign writers, and authors who represent particular ethnic groups in the United States.

Format of the Book

Altogether there are about 500 individual excerpts in each volume—with approximately seventeen excerpts per author—taken from hundreds of book review periodicals, general magazines, scholarly journals, monographs, and books. Entries include critical evaluations spanning from the beginning of an author's career to the most current commentary. Interviews, feature articles, and other published writings that offer insight into the authors works are also presented. Emphasis has been placed on expanding the sources for criticism by including an increasing number of scholarly and specialized periodicals. Students, teachers, librarians, and researchers will find that the generous excerpts and supplementary material provided by *CLC* supply them with vital information needed to write a term paper, analyze a poem, or lead a book discussion group. In addition, complete bibliographical citations facilitate the location of the original source and provide all of the information necessary for a term paper footnote or bibliography.

A *CLC* author entry consists of the following elements:

- The **author heading** cites the author's full name, followed by birth date, and death date when applicable. The portion of the name outside parentheses denotes the form under which the author has most commonly published. If an author has written consistently under a pseudonym, the pseudonym will be listed in the author heading and the real name given on the first line of the biographical and critical introduction. Also located at the beginning of the introduction to the author entry are any important name variations under which an author has written. Uncertainty as to a birth or death date is indicated by question marks.

- A **portrait** of the author is included when available.

- A brief **biographical and critical introduction** to the author and his or her work precedes the excerpted criticism. However, *CLC* is not intended to be a definitive biographical source. Therefore, *cross-references* have been included to direct readers to these useful sources published by Gale Research: *Contemporary Authors*, which includes detailed biographical and bibliographical sketches of more than 92,000 authors; *Children's Literature Review*, which presents excerpted criticism on the works of authors of children's books; *Something about the Author*, which contains heavily illustrated biographical sketches of writers and illustrators who create books for children and young adults; *Dictionary of Literary Biography*, which provides original evaluations and detailed biographies of authors important to literary history; *Contemporary Authors Autobiography Series*, which offers autobiographical essays by prominent writers; and *Something about the Author Autobiography Series*, which presents autobiographical essays by authors of interest to young readers. Previous volumes of *CLC* in which the author has been featured are also listed in the introduction.

- The **excerpted criticism** represents various kinds of critical writing, ranging in form from the brief review to the scholarly exegesis. Essays are selected by the editors to reflect the spectrum of opinion about a specific work or about an author's literary career in general. The excerpts are presented chronologically, adding a useful perspective to the entry. All titles by the author featured in the entry are printed in boldface type, which enables the reader to easily identify the works being discussed. Publication information (such as publisher names and book prices) and parenthetical numerical references (such as footnotes or page and line references to specific editions of a work) have been deleted at the editors' discretion to provide smoother reading of the text.

- A complete **bibliographical citation** designed to help the user find the original essay or book follows each excerpt.

Other Features

- A list of **Authors Forthcoming in *CLC*** previews the authors to be researched for future volumes.

- An **Acknowledgments** section lists the copyright holders who have granted permission to reprint material in this volume of *CLC*. It does not, however, list every book or periodical reprinted or consulted during the preparation of the volume.

- A **Cumulative Author Index** lists all the authors who have appeared in *CLC*, *Twentieth-Century Literary Criticism*, *Nineteenth-Century Literature Criticism*, *Literature Criticism from 1400 to 1800*, *Classical and Medieval Literature Criticism*, and *Short Story Criticism*, with cross-references to these Gale series: *Children's Literature Review, Contemporary Authors, Contemporary Authors Autobiography Series, Contemporary Authors Bibliographical Series, Dictionary of Literary Biography, Something about the Author, Something about the Author Autobiography Series, Yesterday's Authors of Books for Children*, and *Authors & Artists for Young Adults*. Readers will welcome this cumulated author index as a useful tool for locating an author within the various series. The index, which lists birth and death dates when available, will be particularly valuable for those authors who are identified with a certain period but whose death date causes them to be placed in another, or for those authors whose careers span two periods. For example, Ernest Hemingway is found in *CLC*, yet a writer often associated with him, F. Scott Fitzgerald, is found in *Twentieth-Century Literary Criticism*.

- A **Cumulative Nationality Index** alphabetically lists all authors featured in *CLC* by nationality, followed by numbers corresponding to the volumes in which they appear.

- A **Title Index** alphabetically lists all titles reviewed in the current volume of *CLC* followed by author's name and the corresponding page numbers where they are discussed. English translations of foreign titles and variations of titles are cross-referenced to the title under which a work was originally published. Titles of novels, novellas, dramas, films, record albums, and poetry, short story, and essay collections are printed in italics, while all individual poems, short stories, essays, and songs are printed in roman type within quotation marks; when published separately (e.g., T.S. Eliot's poem *The Waste Land*), the title will also be printed in italics.

- In response to numerous suggestions from librarians, Gale has also produced a **special paperbound edition** of the *CLC* title index. This annual cumulation, which alphabetically lists all titles reviewed in the series, is available to all customers and will be published with the first volume of *CLC* issued in each calendar year. Additional copies of the index are available upon request. Librarians and patrons will welcome this separate index: it saves shelf space, is easily disposable upon receipt of the following year's cumulation, and is easy to use.

Suggestions Are Welcome

The editors welcome the comments and suggestions of readers to expand the coverage and enhance the usefulness of the series. Please feel free to contact us by letter or by calling our toll-free number: 1-800-347-GALE.

Acknowledgments

The editors wish to thank the copyright holders of the excerpted criticism included in this volume, the permissions managers of many book and magazine publishing companies for assisting us in securing reprint rights, and Anthony Bogucki for assistance with copyright research. We are also grateful to the staffs of the Detroit Public Library, the Library of Congress, the University of Detroit Library, Wayne State University Purdy/Kresge Library Complex, and University of Michigan Libraries for making their resources available to us. Following is a list of the copyright holders who have granted us permission to reprint material in this volume of *CLC*. Every effort has been made to trace copyright, but if omissions have been made, please let us know.

COPYRIGHTED EXCERPTS IN *CLC*, VOLUME 57, WERE REPRINTED FROM THE FOLLOWING PERIODI-CALS:

Africa Report, v. 32, July-August, 1987. Copyright © 1987 by The African-American Institute. Published by permission of Transaction, Inc.—*The American Book Review,* v. 10, March-April, 1988. © 1988 by *The American Book Review.* Reprinted by permission of the publisher.—*The American Poetry Review,* v. 15, January-February, 1986 for "Soundings: Zaum, Seriality, and the Recovery of the 'Sacred' " by Marjorie Perloff; v. 16, November-December, 1987 for an interview with Yehuda Amichai by David Montenegro; v. 17, May-June, 1988 for "Working Time" by Jane Miller; v. 18, January-February, 1989 for "Not Life So Proud to Be Life: Snodgrass, Rothenberg, Bell, and the Counter-Revolution" by Larry Levis. Copyright © 1986, 1987, 1988, 1989 by World Poetry, Inc. All reprinted by permission of the respective authors.—*The American Spectator,* v. 20, November, 1987. Copyright © *The American Spectator* 1987. Reprinted by permission of the publisher.—*Américas,* v. 24, August 24, 1972. © 1972 *Américas.* Reprinted by permission of the publisher./ v. 34, March-April, 1982. Reprinted by permission of the publisher.—*Analog Science Fiction/Science Fact,* v. XCVII, June, 1977 for "Man and Beast" by Sonya Dorman Hess. Copyright © 1977 by the Condé Nast Publications, Inc. Reprinted by permission of the author./ v. CVII, August, 1987 for a review of "Aegypt" by Tom Easton. © 1987 by Davis Publications, Inc. Reprinted by permission of the author.—*The Antioch Review,* v. 37, Spring, 1979. Copyright © 1979 by the Antioch Review Inc. Reprinted by permission of the Editors.—*Australian Book Review,* v. 6, December, 1966 & January, 1967.—*Belles Lettres: A Review of Books by Women,* v. 3, May-June, 1988; v. 4, Winter, 1989. Both reprinted by permission of the publisher.—*Best Sellers,* v. 37, December, 1977. Copyright © 1977 Helen Dwight Reid Educational Foundation. Reprinted by permission of the publisher.—*The Bloomsbury Review,* v. 7, March-April 1987 for "The Heart of Memory & Ferment of Displacement" by Donald Revell; v. 8, September-October, 1988 for "A Preference for Strange Stories" by Steve Rasnic Tem. Copyright © by Owaissa Communications Company, Inc. 1987, 1988. Both reprinted by permission of the respective authors. *Book World—The Washington Post,* June 9, 1968. © 1968 Postrib Corp. Reprinted by permission of *The Washington Post.*/ November 12, 1978; March 23, 1980; October 4, 1981; March 29, 1987; April 19, 1987; August 2, 1987; November 8, 1987; November 29, 1987; April 13, 1988; October 9, 1988; January 22, 1989; February 26, 1989. © 1978, 1980, 1981, 1987, 1988, 1989 *The Washington Post.* All reprinted by permission of the publisher.—*Booklist,* v. 79, August, 1983; v. 83, October 1, 1986. Copyright © 1983, 1986 by the American Library Association. Both reprinted by permission of the publisher.—*Books,* London, n. 4, July, 1987. © Gradegate Ltd. 1987. Reprinted by permission of the publisher.—*Books Abroad,* v. 39, Summer, 1965. Copyright 1965 by the University of Oklahoma Press. Reprinted by permission of the publisher.—*Books and Bookmen,* n. 321, June, 1982 for "Wit and Terror" by Roz Kaveney; n. 358, August, 1985 for a review of "Separate Checks" by Nigella Lawson. © copyright the author 1982, 1985. Both reprinted by permission of the respective authors.—*Books in Canada,* v. 12, October, 1983 for "No Excuses" by Alberto Manguel; v. 15, January-February, 1986 for "From Bath to Verse" by Lesley Choyce; v. 16, March, 1987 for "To Tell the Truth" by John Gilbert. All reprinted by permission of the respective authors./ v. 17, March, 1988 for an interview with John Krizanc by Ann Jansen. Reprinted by permission of John Krizanc and Ann Jansen.—*Boston Review,* v. XI, August, 1986 for "The Emperor's New Fiction" by Rosellen Brown. Copyright © 1986 by the Boston Critic, Inc. Reprinted by permission of the author.—*British Book News,* April, 1985; August, 1985. © *British Book News,* 1985. Both courtesy of *British Book News.*—*The Cambridge Quarterly,* v. XV, 1986 for "The Seriousness of Samuel Beckett" by Geoffrey Strickland. Copyright © 1986 by the Editors. Reprinted by permission of the author.—*Canadian Literature,* n. 102, Autumn, 1984 for "Double Vision" by Linda Hutcheon; n. 115, Winter, 1987 for "Discourse of the Other" by Paul Hjartarson; n. 119, Winter, 1988 for "Roses Are Read" by Manina Jones; n. 119, Winter, 1988 for "Endings Be Damned: Robert Kroetsch's 'Gone Indian' " by Margaret E. Turner; n. 118, Autumn, 1988 for a review of "Prague" by Viviana Comensoli. All reprinted by permission of the respective authors.—*Canadian Slavonic Papers,* v. XXIX, December, 1987. Copyright ©, *Canadian Slavonic Papers,* Canada, 1987. Reprinted by permission of the publisher.—*Canadian Theatre Review,* n. 56, Fall, 1988 for a review of "Prague" by Vaclav Taborsky. Copyright © 1988, by the author. Reprinted by permission of the author.—*Chicago Review,* v. 20, 1968; v. 22, January-February, 1971. Copyright © 1968, 1971 by *Chicago Review.* Both reprinted by permission of the publisher.—*Chicago Tribune—Books,* April 19, 1987. ©

Authors Forthcoming in *CLC*

Contemporary Literary Criticism, Vol. 59: Yearbook 1989 will be devoted to an examination of the outstanding achievements and trends in literature during 1989. Along with entries on major new writers, prizewinners, and notable authors who died during the year, *CLC-59* will feature commentary on literary events and issues that generated extensive public interest and media coverage. Volumes 58 and 60 will contain a number of authors not previously covered as well as criticism on newer works by authors included in earlier volumes.

To Be Included in Volume 58

Fernando Arrabal (Moroccan dramatist and novelist)—Influenced by the Surrealist movement, Arrabal is best known for his macabre plays written in the tradition of the Theater of the Absurd. His works often examine human brutality and sexuality through the perspectives of children.

Cyrus Colter (American novelist and short story writer)—In his fiction, Colter attempts to bridge the gap he perceives between the experiences of black Americans and the ways in which they have been represented in literature. His deterministic plots emphasize the universality of his middle-class characters and their problems with loneliness, alienation, guilt, and communication.

Douglas Crase (American poet and critic)—A poet whose first collection, *The Revisionist*, earned high praise, Crase focuses upon the American landscape and such concerns as history and ecology. Critics often compare Crase's bold style to those of Wallace Stevens and Walt Whitman.

William Golding (English novelist and short story writer)—Winner of the 1983 Nobel Prize in literature, Golding is best known for his novel *The Lord of the Flies*. Commentary in his entry will focus on this allegorical work, which is widely regarded as a powerful psychological and sociological fable about the primal savagery underlying civilized behavior.

Chester Himes (American short story writer and novelist)—Perhaps best known for *Cotton Comes to Harlem*, one in a series of highly regarded detective novels set in New York that combine irony with biting humor, Himes is considered a valuable contributor to the American tradition of black protest fiction for his vehement portraits of racial oppression and black resistance.

Joyce Johnson (American novelist, short story writer, and autobiographer)—In her fiction, Johnson often relates her involvement with various members of the 1950s Beat generation, providing a rare female perspective on the era and movement. *Minor Characters*, a revealing, candid memoir of her romance with Jack Kerouac, won the National Book Critics Circle Award.

Maxine Hong Kingston (American autobiographer, short story writer, and novelist)—In her memoirs, Kingston blends myth, legend, and history to examine her dual heritage as a Chinese American. Kingston's entry will include commentary on *The Woman Warrior: Memoirs of a Girlhood among Ghosts*, a standard text in women's studies courses, as well as *Tripmaster Monkey*, her recent first novel.

Michael Moorcock (English novelist and editor)—Moorcock is associated with the British "New Wave" literary movement of the 1960s that introduced experimental techniques and a wider range of subject matter to fantasy and science fiction literature.

Christopher Nolan (Irish poet, short story writer, and autobiographer)—Nolan won wide acclaim for his first collection of poetry, *Dam Burst of Dreams*, and his autobiographical work, *Under the Eye of the Clock*. Nolan often describes his experiences as a paralyzed mute in an exhilarating prose style, which has been compared to that of James Joyce for its use of Celtic-styled alliteration and invented words.

Alice Walker (American novelist, poet, and essayist)—Regarded as an important chronicler of African-American life, Walker is best known for her novel *The Color Purple*, for which she received the Pulitzer Prize in fiction. Commentary in this entry will focus on Walker's recent novel, *The Temple of My Familiar*, which concerns the multiple lives of a reincarnated woman.

Douglas Adams (English novelist)—In his popular series of satirical novels beginning with *The Hitchhiker's Guide to the Galaxy,* Adams uses the devices of science fiction to lampoon modern culture. Adams blends slapstick and fantasy in his recent novels, *Dirk Gently's Holistic Detective Agency* and *The Long Dark Tea Time of the Soul,* to portray the unusual adventures of a private investigator.

Erskine Caldwell (American novelist and short story writer)—The author of such controversial Depression era novels as *Tobacco Road* and *God's Little Acre,* Caldwell blended realism and comic pathos in his work to portray the desperate existence of poor Southerners.

Annie Dillard (American essayist and poet)—Dillard is best known for *Pilgrim at Tinker Creek,* her Pulitzer Prize-winning meditation on nature that critics have compared to Henry David Thoreau's *Walden.* She has also earned praise for her works of literary criticism, poetry, and autobiography.

Umberto Eco (Italian novelist and semiotician)—Acclaimed for his international best-seller *The Name of the Rose,* Eco has generated widespread interest with his recent mystery novel, *Foucault's Pendulum.* Spanning several centuries and exploring the nature of language and words, this work combines intrigue, autobiography, political commentary, and esoteric motifs.

Carlos Fuentes (Mexican novelist and essayist)—In his internationally acclaimed works, Fuentes often employs myth, legend, and history to examine Mexico's past and contemporary social and cultural issues. This entry will focus on his recent novel, *Christopher Unborn,* and *Myself with Others: Selected Essays.*

Shirley Jackson (American novelist and short story writer)—A prolific author, Jackson is generally known for such Gothic horror tales as "The Lottery" and *The Haunting of Hill House.* In lucid prose juxtaposing humor with intense psychological states and an atmosphere of foreboding, Jackson explores the dark side of human nature.

Harper Lee (American novelist)—Lee's Pulitzer Prize-winning novel *To Kill a Mockingbird,* which examines racial attitudes in the Deep South through the experiences of a young girl in a small Alabama town, will be the focus of this entry.

Anaïs Nin (French-born American diarist, novelist, and short story writer)—Nin is best known for the erotic pieces she wrote during the 1930s and 1940s and for her numerous books containing excerpts from her diaries. This entry will emphasize recent analyses of her work.

Molly Peacock (American poet)—In such collections as *Raw Heaven* and *Take Heart,* Peacock uses humor, unusual rhyme schemes, and contemplative tones to examine sexuality.

Kurt Vonnegut (American novelist and short story writer)—Widely regarded as a masterful contemporary writer, Vonnegut uses satire, irony, and iconoclastic humor to explore social values and the meaning of life. This entry will focus on *Slaughterhouse-Five; or, The Children's Crusade,* Vonnegut's absurdist novel about his experiences as a prisoner of war during the firebombing of Dresden, Germany, in World War II.

Robert (Fordyce) Aickman

1914-1981

English short story writer, novelist, autobiographer, critic, editor, and nonfiction writer.

Considered a prominent author of contemporary horror fiction, Aickman composed what he termed "strange stories" in which disturbing supernatural events occur within the context of commonplace situations. Like such early twentieth-century writers as M. R. James and Walter de la Mare, Aickman employed a detached narrative voice to portray a seemingly ordinary environment subtly manipulated by the subconscious of its inhabitants. While some critics have faulted his ambiguous conclusions as unsatisfying, most contend that Aickman transcends the sensationalism of standard horror fiction through his ability to coolly evoke an atmosphere of menace. Steve Rasnic Tem commented: "Aickman eschews the rather specific conventions of ghostly fiction and folklore for a much more ambitious task: offering his readers a glimpse into an entire unconscious world, a world at once more terrible, and more beautiful than our own, and yet alarmingly very much the same."

In several of Aickman's stories, the unacknowledged fears and desires of his protagonists emerge as independent, ghostly entities. In "The Fetch," for example, a story which appeared in *Intrusions: Strange Tales* (1980) and the posthumously published *The Wine-Dark Sea* (1988), a withdrawn Scotsman is haunted by a fetch, a silent figure who bears the face of a person who is soon to die. After witnessing the spectre prior to the deaths of his wife and mother, the Scotsman attempts to escape it by locking himself in a room in his isolated mansion. However, his sanctuary becomes a prison when the fetch returns, hovering eternally outside the door and windows. In 1975 Aickman received a World Fantasy Award for Best Short Fiction for "Pages from a Young Girl's Journal," a tale included in *Cold Hand in Mine: Eight Strange Stories* (1976). This story concerns an early nineteenth-century woman who is transformed into a vampire after dancing with a dark stranger. In "The Stains," a story first published in *Night Voices: Strange Stories* (1985) and later in *The Wine-Dark Sea,* a widower falls in love with an ethereal woman whose malignant birthmarks slowly migrate from her body to his, presaging his approaching death. Colin Greenland observed that in this piece, "the deftly-intensified claustrophobia is transcended in an expressly operatic gesture. Death is a consummation. It is the rest of the blemished world that must go on suffering, mouldering."

In many stories, Aickman evokes a sense of unease by exploring the relationship of the surrounding environment to the psyche of his characters. An isolated heath, for instance, plays a significant role in "The Trains," published in *We Are for the Dark: Six Ghost Stories* (1951), a collection of tales by Aickman and Elizabeth Jane Howard. In this story, the landscape of the moor ominously metamorphosizes to reflect the growing terror of two female hikers who, after following train tracks to a secluded farmhouse, attempt to discover why a woman has frantically waved to passing engineers for twenty years. "Ringing the Changes," collected in *Dark Entries* (1964) and *Painted Devils: Strange Stories* (1979), also de-

scribes the horrifying transformation of a seemingly innocuous setting in its portrayal of a couple who learn that the church bells of the peaceful English village they have chosen for their honeymoon wake the dead. "Into the Wood," published in *Sub Rosa: Strange Tales* (1968) and *The Wine-Dark Sea,* centers upon an Englishwoman who checks into a Swedish hotel that also functions as a sanatorium for insomniacs. At night she is drawn to the labyrinthine woods that surround the building, where she discovers her inner self. Unable to return to her former life, she continues to wander the forest in an eternally sleepless state. Peter Straub observed that in this story "all of Aickman's themes come together in an act of self-acceptance which is at once dangerous, enigmatic, in narrative terms wholly justified, and filled with the reverence for the imaginative power demonstrated by Aickman's work in general."

In addition to his short fiction, Aickman wrote two novels: *The Late Breakfasters* (1954), about a modern woman who discovers a community living an eighteenth-century existence in an isolated castle, and *The Model,* published posthumously in 1987. He has also published *The Attempted Rescue: An Autobiography* (1966), which centers upon his eccentric family, and edited *The Fontana Book of Great Ghost Stories* (1964-1972).

(See also *Contemporary Authors*, Vols. 5-8, rev. ed.; and *Contemporary Authors New Revision Series*, Vol. 3.)

NANCY MICHELL

Those who enjoy an oddity, a quirkiness, an obliquity of vision in their fiction will find Robert Aickman's *The Late Breakfasters* very much their cup of tea. Utterly improbable from start to finish, this story of Griselda de Reptonville who starts her career at a wildly funny house-party of eccentrics in Surrey and ends—by way of an extremely dubious if accommodating bookshop near Piccadilly—in a Welsh Gothic castle where life is lived as in the eighteenth century, is a delight for those who can appreciate an allusive sophistication and malicious observation. Oddly enough the atmosphere of the novel is very vaguely reminiscent of *Zuleika Dobson*—and this should be recommendation enough.

> *Nancy Michell, "People and Attitudes," in* The Tablet, *Vol. 218, No. 6482, August 15, 1964, p. 918.*

THE TIMES LITERARY SUPPLEMENT

Mr. Aickman has clearly taken to heart one of the great axioms of the ghost storywriter's art: that there is no horror quite so horrid as that left to the reader to conjure up for himself. Unfortunately in this volume of macabre tales [*Dark Entries*] he sometimes carries things a bit far: in the opening story, **"The School Friend"**, for example, so much is left to the reader's imagination that even after two readings he may find it difficult to work out what happens, let alone derive the desirable frisson of horror from the events partially chronicled. Other stories, particularly **"Ringing the Changes"**, generate a suitably eery atmosphere and Mr. Aickman writes stylishly in an amiable, slightly old-fashioned way.

> *A review of "Dark Entries," in* The Times Literary Supplement, *No. 3276, December 10, 1964, p. 1121.*

BRIGID BROPHY

I have never before reviewed a book without reading the whole of it. I trust Mr Aickman will forgive me for doing so now, because my excuse pays him a compliment. The first of his ghost stories [in *Dark Entries*] left me cold. The second left me goose-fleshed. I have no intention of reading the remaining four, because I don't enjoy being frightened in this particular way; but I hope those who do will read the same amount of recommendation as usually goes into 'I couldn't put it down' in my solemn declaration about *Dark Entries* that I could never again take it up.

> *Brigid Brophy, "Great Man," in* New Statesman, *Vol. LXIX, No. 1768, January 29, 1965, p. 170.*

ELIZABETH MAVOR

"My father remains the oddest man I have ever known," declares Mr Aickman in the opening sentence of [*The Attempted Rescue: An Autobiography*]. There follows his own brilliant version of the Aeneas-Anchises story. But Mr Aickman not only piggy-backed an aged and wildly eccentric father but a repressed and embittered mother, as well as a grotesque great-aunt and great-uncle together with the formidable genetic dowry which disposed him to pessimism and disgust with the age.

He writes about his horrible childhood with extraordinary detachment, inducing tears of shocked laughter. Yet the tears should not blind one to the underlying hopelessness of his message. We are doomed, according to Mr Aickman, to be reduced from homo sapiens to homo mechanicus. Perhaps in the less objective and not quite so amusing second half of his book he harps a little too loud and long upon the theme of universal degeneration (rising prices, poor food, bad theatre, vulgarity, vandalism, etc., etc.), which gives him an air of querulous garrulity. Nevertheless, he not only detests but, like a true Erewhonian, he fights the machine.

> *Elizabeth Mavor, in a review of "The Attempted Rescue: An Autobiography," in* The Observer, *May 22, 1966, p. 27.*

DAVID WILLIAMS

The special forms of eccentricity prevalent among the English well-to-do are a gift to any writer. . . . Robert Aickman hacks away at this rich seam in *The Attempted Rescue*. In the main he concentrates on his father, an architect of some distinction, who died in 1941 "from loss of luxuries." Aickman specialises in a sort of gawky, angular comedy which makes excellent reading. The spirit of the times—roughly the late 'twenties and 'thirties—is splendidly caught, and his ability to convey the exasperations, the passionate magnifications and private lunacies of family life is real enough to earn him (I hope) many delighted readers.

> *David Williams, "Papa, You're Impossible," in* Punch, *Vol. CCL, No. 6562, June 15, 1966, p. 893.*

THE TIMES LITERARY SUPPLEMENT

Mr. Aickman is a writer of ghost stories in the classic, urbane tradition of M. R. James: his view of the familiar world about us is clear and often coolly witty, and the things that go bump do so all the more intimidatingly for their precise placing in the surroundings least conducive, it would seem, to eerie imaginings. The telephone, admittedly, has frequently proved a useful prop of modern horror-stories, but seldom so effectively as in **"Your Tiny Hand is Frozen"** [in *Powers of Darkness*]. And in other stories Mr. Aickman finds something nasty lurking on the fringes of a cultural conference in Birmingham, off a sunny Greek island, behind the scenes in a provincial rep, in **"The Mastodon Palace of Westminster"** and down an abandoned lead mine. Perfect reading for some quiet corner. . . .

> *A review of "Powers of Darkness," in* The Times Literary Supplement, *No. 3381, December 15, 1966, p. 1178.*

HENRY J. STAUFFENBERG

To encounter striking variety of style, setting, and characterization in an eight-story anthology devoted to a single generic mode is unusual; to find a high narrative standard sustained throughout is even more surprising. Yet Robert Aickman has accomplished in [*Cold Hand in Mine: Strange Stories*] variety in form, unity in "spirit" (the pun is warranted!), quality in execution.

As its subtitle implies, this collection of bizarre tales explores virtually every aspect of traditional (and neo-traditional) gothic horror. With one exception, all stories are written in the first person. But don't be misled! Diversity abounds. The characters, for instance, range from an obscure German prince ("Albrecht von Allendorf, known as Elmo to his associates") to an equally obscure grocery salesman. . . .

Stylistically, Aickman *loves* language. "Alembicated," "bedizened," "boskage," "conurbation," "pantechnicon," and "feral habitude" are balanced by such phrases as "the usual fuss and schemozzle." Thus, the average reader who might wish "to take Aickman to bed" had best make it a threesome—with a dictionary.

The reviewer has chosen at random two examples indicative of Aickman's versatility. The first is taken from **"The Hospice":** "Falkner had appeared. To bed, all, he cried genially, subduing the crepitation on the instant." Contrast this with the chilling simplicity of the passage from **"A Young Girl's Journal,"** in which the heroine meets some "huge, gruzzled" creatures with tongues "flopping and lolling . . . in the silvery light":

> I smiled at the wolves. Then I crossed my hands on my little bosom and curtsied. They will be prominent among my new people. My blood will be theirs and theirs mine.

Bram Stoker and Sheridan Le Fanu notwithstanding, gothic terror-narrative may well achieve its perfection in the twentieth century largely through Aickman's efforts.

A final word of advice: The lover of classic horror fiction would do well to begin with the second tale. If the first offering (**"The Swords"**) is worth reading at all, it should be reserved for last. But then, seven successful stories out of eight isn't a bad record.

> *Henry J. Stauffenberg, in a review of "Cold Hand in Mine: Strange Stories," in* Best Sellers, *Vol. 37, No. 9, December, 1977, p. 258.*

T. J. BINYON

No one is better at raising the hairs on the back of the neck, or causing perspiration to run cold, than Robert Aickman. Yet he employs no spectacular effects, there are no excesses of style or emotion, none of the stock in trade of the gothic school. Some of his stories, indeed, are closer to Kafka than to Mrs Radcliffe; they begin with a seemingly ordinary situation, transmogrified by degrees into something strange and enigmatic, and preserve throughout a limpid and objective narrative tone. The seven stories in this collection [*Tales of Love and Death*] range in mood from the light to the macabre; the best are the two longest, one of which deals with a mother's attempts to control her peculiarly unruly twin sons, while the other has as its ostensible subject the proceedings of the Open Spaces and Cemeteries Committee of a local council, but the other five are by no means frisson-free.

> *T. J. Binyon, "Criminal Proceedings," in* The Times

Literary Supplement, *No. 3952, December 23, 1977, p. 1513.*

KIRKUS REVIEWS

Nine more "strange stories" from the very British Mr. Aickman—who [in *Painted Devils*] often seems to be apologetic, even embarrassed, when his engaging and elegantly moody tales slip again and again into supernatural clichés. An uneasy honeymoon couple in a rundown resort hotel besieged by the clanging of nearby bells: marvelous situation . . . till the bells wake the local dead for a The-Zombies-Walk finale. A Rosemary's Baby is revealed, ghosts appear in an abandoned house or a deserted railway station or the Houses of Parliament—these occult punchlines, though delivered with far more subtlety than is usual in the genre, are the weakest elements in otherwise beguiling, suggestive stories. Aickman does better when the strangeness is less clearly supernatural, more blended with hallucinations and psychological insecurities. . . . [Best] of all is **"Marriage,"** a story that never leaves its down-to-earth groundings as its quiet, ordinary hero slides into a surreal arrangement with two women, best friends Helen and Ellen, who complement each other in providing him with all the conjugal services. But even this graceful parable has a twist tacked on—a Freudian one. Aickman is too fine a stylist, too natural a storyteller to be relying on gimmicky codas, supernatural or otherwise; fans of ghostly doings may appreciate the good writing here, but fans of good writing will probably want to wait till Aickman settles into stories worthy of his talent. (pp. 73-4)

> *A review of "Painted Devils," in* Kirkus Reviews, *Vol. XLVII, No. 2, January 15, 1979, pp. 73-4.*

JULIA BRIGGS

"Alive" can hardly be the *mot juste* for the ghost story, but it is certainly well and being written by Robert Aickman, whose latest collection *Intrusions* is the best yet, and arguably the best since Walter de la Mare's *A Beginning*, nearly thirty years ago. Its centrepiece, **"The Breakthrough"**, certainly invites comparison with that great (greatest?) master of the form, in its combination of supernatural events with a deeply felt human tragedy that unfolds slowly, subtly, and with unremitting intensity. The horrors—brilliantly described—that come up from the church's broken pavement are, in the end, subordinated to the drama of the inadequate rector, the uncommitted narrator, and the outcast Lizzie.

All the stories in *Intrusions* seem to benefit from a new-found freedom and expansiveness, as well as a cavalier disregard for the conventional formulae. **"The Next Glade"** and the extraordinary fantasy, **"No Time is Passing"** are imaginative inventions of a particularly high order, but there are no makeweights here. Robert Aickman's gifts, always considerable, have now matured to the point where he has unquestionably become the leading writer in the field.

> *Julia Briggs, "Brief Hauntings," in* The Times Literary Supplement, *No. 4057, January 2, 1981, p. 19.*

PAUL KINCAID

[*Night Voices: Strange Stories*] is the last collection of stories by the late Robert Aickman, a writer it is impossible to categorize. To call him a writer of horror stories is somehow to broaden and coarsen what he does. He writes a precise and elegant prose, full of sharp perceptions of the ordinary, so sharp that a niggling sense of unease slowly develops without anything out of the ordinary actually happening. That is his strength, and when he writes to it he produces work of chilling effect. In **"The Stains"**, for instance, a lonely widower meets a beautiful girl in remote moorland and settles into what would be a rural idyll were it not for the stains that begin to appear everywhere. In **"The Trains"** two girls hike across another stretch of moorland, with the constant passage of trains acting as a signpost directing them to a horrific end.

The wild moorland setting seems to suit his work best; **"Just a Song at Twilight"** has all the qualities of these other two stories, except that it is set on an imprecisely realized Mediterranean island, and that very lack of precision weakens the story almost fatally. And, when Aickman resorts to more overt strangeness, as in **"Rosamund's Bower"** or the poor retelling of the Sweeney Todd story, **"Mark Ingestre"** he is definitely at his weakest. When he *tells,* these stories just fail to work, but, when he *suggests,* they are very good indeed.

Paul Kincaid, in a review of "Night Voices: Strange Stories," in British Book News, *August, 1985, p. 489.*

COLIN GREENLAND

Night Voices brings together the five remaining uncollected stories of Robert Aickman, one of them previously unpublished, together with **"The Trains"**, his first publication, from the 1951 volume *We Are for the Dark.* The subtitle "Strange Stories" was the author's preferred term for his work, whose ghosts and apparitions are not imaginary monsters created for their *frisson,* nor vengeful violators of the natural order, but "creatures we once knew, . . . things within us which we have, as psychologists say, projected outside us". These intimate strangers, we are to understand, await us all just beyond the limits of the everyday, because we have put them there.

And how quickly those limits may be reached, in Aickman's topography. A hiking holiday in the Pennines, an overgrown footpath at Godstow, a Fleet Street cellar, a corner of the Parc Monceau: one step further, and the pedestrian is precipitated into the psychic abyss. . . . Civilization, conformity, consciousness are no more than a thin membrane of custom. In **"Rosamund's Bower"** a spectral Seneschal tells the questing undergraduate Aylwin-Scott that "properly speaking", the Law is "like a veil. Like the veil of the temple." It covers the mysteries; and it may be swiftly rent.

It is not predictable, or perhaps even reasonable, what happens when that caul is pierced. Aickman's stories have been compared to Walter de la Mare's for "inconclusiveness", for the emotional impact of obscure events. In **"Just a Song at Twilight"**, the most acid of this collection, Lydia and Timo, an exhausted English couple hunting harmony on a Greek island, receive a visit from another exile, an aggressive young woman they do not know. She refuses tea and demands money, then disappears at once, followed at speed and without farewell by Timo. No specific explanation is forthcoming, or even retrievable. As in certain plays of Harold Pinter, banality has invoked nemesis. Lydia has spent most of her inheritance on a remote and doubtful site, and may even have

been swindled; on an uncharacteristic impulse she parts with all the money on her person and the next moment is abandoned by her husband in an empty house. Her deprivation has an inevitable, ritual quality, like an Orphic initiation. It is not that the events Aickman describes are impenetrably unresolved, but that they are distinctly private.

By chance, five of these six stories recount ordeals of young people, obscuring the fact that all Aickman's fiction was that of a man in the last thirty of his sixty-seven years. It is not about the heroic endeavour to master the chaos of life, but as John Clute has demonstrated in a definitive essay about the needs described by Jung in *The Integration of the Personality:* to come to terms with the chaos, and prepare a whole self for death. In **"The Stains"** a civil servant recuperating after the death of his wife begins to notice lichen and fungus sprouting everywhere. He suddenly abandons home, job and dependent elder brother to live in a stone cottage on the moors with a mysterious young woman not altogether human. At the last, the deftly-intensified claustrophobia is transcended in an expressly operatic gesture. Death is a consummation. It is the rest of the blemished world that must go on suffering, mouldering. The extraordinary **"Rosamund's Bower"** (hitherto unpublished) preserves the privacy of Aylwin-Scott's experience through a teasing series of enigmatic emblems and allusions. At the same time it is perfectly clear that, finding the bower and penetrating the maze, the young man is resolved to accept the moment of bliss at its heart, a touch, not even that, at the price of future misery, failure, persecution and debility. Here in the thicket full of mock-Spenserian monitors, Aylwin-Scott's whole psychic life is simultaneously present, and therefore always is, this sweetness cancelling out the vile before and after. The consolation is an illusion, of course, but an illusion that will sustain a life and permit a reconciliation with death.

Others of Aickman's pilgrims fail and remain stuck inside the nightmare, telling their stories over and over. Here especially, in "the dreaded demesne of the heart", sex and death combine, whether the invitation is seized, as in the grotesque **"Mark Ingestre: The Customer's Tale"**, or shunned, as in the sad and powerfully restrained **"Laura"**, whose lonely victim admits: "But you won't possibly understand what I mean. You would have had to be there. One day perhaps you will be."

Colin Greenland, "Invitations of the Intimate Stranger," in The Times Literary Supplement, *No. 4314, December 6, 1985, p. 1407.*

RICHARD GRANT

The Model is a very short and very strange novel—not a ghost story but a ghostly one, shining out of some spectral literary past.

It is the story of a girl named Elena, growing up in an isolated village where her petit-bourgeois family has fallen upon austere times. Her best friend, Tatiana Ivanovna, thinks Elena might be "a changeling: offspring of gypsies, or of the nobility, or of fairies, or of spirits."

Elena considers this seriously. Though she is too pale to be a gypsy, "the other possibilities remained, and there were many more also. Children who were uncertain of their parentage abounded. Elena knew that it was the kind of thing to be expected. No one had told her so. She knew."

These snippets may give some idea of Aickman's artful imposture: the *faux*-folk narrative style, beneath which resides a wry and charming wisdom. *The Model* reads at times like an ingenuous, word-for-word translation: "She had abandoned even that simplest of tasks, the pulling the stalks off cherries which were about to be plunged into the strongest of spirit in order to sustain the family and their friends through the winter, now only a week or two away at the best."

Out of the Old World winter step the von Meyrendorffs, friends of the family, who present Elena with a novel called *Les coryphées de la petite cave.* " 'The theme is somewhat complex for a young girl,' Frau von M. concedes, 'but I take the view that you will not be a young girl always.' "

Indeed she will not. The little book, which tells of a company of young ballerinas, launches Elena into a state of impracticable desire that is her first taste of adolescence. When a grotesque little man presents himself, bearing a box of wooden figurines, she has almost been expecting him. She dresses the dolls in tiny costumes and places them in a miniature opera house, her "model." There is no turning back now; the fantasy has taken material form. Elena's separate worlds begin to interpenetrate: the miniature world of the model, the make-believe but very grown-up world of *Les coryphées,* and the increasingly peculiar world of daily life.

Elena decides to leave home, as a heroine must, to seek her fortune in the wide world. The world turns out, of course, to be a bit wider than she—or the reader—could have anticipated. But Elena faces it pluckily, passing through bizarre encounters (first with a bear who does not care for radishes) and adventures that Tatiana Ivanovna could scarcely imagine. She confronts vast, and often terrifying, possibilities. And she leaves her childhood forever behind.

But this is no wish-fulfilling fairy tale. Just as Aickman's prose cuts deeper than the romantic tradition it evokes, Elena's adventures are unsettlingly sharp-edged: sometimes baffling, sometimes quite funny, they often approximate our own disjointed, future-shocked perceptions. *The Model* owes as much to Kafka as to Hoffmann. Aickman has made the most of that venerable metaphor, "the magic of childhood." But he has painted his magic with the colors scumbled: neither black nor white, but a twilight, 20th-century gray.

> *Richard Grant, "Phantoms of the Opera," in* Book World—The Washington Post, *March 29, 1987, p. 10.*

ROB LATHAM

[*The Model*] is another last novel—only the second, apparently, that Aickman ever penned. This author, who died in 1981, was known chiefly for his many volumes of supernatural tales—"strange stories," as he called them, which indeed they are. Works like **"Ringing the Changes," "The Stains,"** and **"Meeting Mr. Millar"** are absolutely unique in the literature of the supernatural—"ghost" stories which manage to be both palpably allegorical and weirdly elusive, intensely ironic yet deeply felt. Aickman's style is justly famous; no one since James has commanded such a cool, ambiguous voice. There is a completely individual feel to the atmosphere Aickman conjures; effortlessly, he limns a world so seedy, so secularly drab that even the encroachment of supernatural terror can be experienced as a relief. And, despite his penchant for religious allegory (which can tend to be reductive), he has a brilliant eye for the surface quirks and the bottomless depths of character.

The Model, happily, displays all of these strengths; it also marks an increase in vision and imaginative breadth beyond anything Aickman had previously attempted. In the face of its high ambition and startling accomplishment, one can only mourn his loss the more. Unfortunately, it is a very difficult novel to summarize: it can be read as, variously, a quasi-feminist rite of passage, a parable of the fallacies of Romanticism, or an absurdist allegory of the modern world. But, however it is finally interpreted, it shines throughout with Aickman's fiendish wit and dizzying irony.

Set in the Russia of the czars during the waning years of empire, *The Model* is the story of Elena, daughter of a provincial lawyer, whose encounter with a French Romantic novel spurs a series of increasingly wild adventures. Trying to escape the schemes of her parents which would shackle her soul, Elena flees her home to become a ballerina in Smorevsk. . . . The story has a dreamy sort of logic which is entirely convincing—this is the world of Gogol as rendered by Lewis Carroll (or perhaps vice versa). Aickman manages to make even the wildest occurrences seem blandly factual—largely because he remains within the bright focus of Elena's scrupulous, pragmatic mind, but also because of the wealth of brilliant detail with which he meticulously recreates this lost *fin de siecle* world.

"The model" of the title is a toy opera house which Elena builds to compass her fantasies; by the end (when an actual compass appears which "seemed to have become subject to spells of idle spinning"), she has realized the paradoxical truth that life is both simple and unknowable, a straight-ahead journey which is also a return. Though Aickman characteristically secrets his wisdom in devastating irony, the book is nonetheless extremely moving. . . . It is simply a brilliant novel, period. (pp. 31, 48-9)

> *Rob Latham, "History, Mystery," in* Fantasy Review, *Vol. 10, No. 3, April, 1987, pp. 31, 48-9.*

PETER STRAUB

Robert Aickman at his best was this century's most profound writer of what we call horror stories and he, with greater accuracy, preferred to call strange stories. In his work is a vast disparity between the well-mannered tone and the stories' actual emotional content. On the surface of things, if we can extrapolate from the style, diction, and range of allusion in his work, Aickman was a cultivated, sensitive, thoroughly English individual. . . . His chief influences were English, the stories of Walter De La Mare and M. R. James (and probably also the subtle, often indirect supernatural stories of Henry James, England's most assimilated American), and his own influence has been primarily on English writers like Ramsey Campbell and, through Campbell, Clive Barker. . . . In fact, neither Campbell nor Barker is really very much like Aickman. His originality, conscious and instinctive at once, was so entire that although he has provided us with a virtual model of what the "strange story" should be, if anyone tried to write to its specifications, the result would be nothing more than imitative.

Unlike nearly everybody writing supernatural stories now, Aickman rejected the neat, conclusive ending. He was, you might say, Stephen King's opposite. In his work there are no climactic showdowns, in part because his work uses almost none of the conventional imagery of horror. Aickman was sublimely uninterested in monsters, werewolves, worms, rats, bats, and things in bandages. (He did, however, write one great vampire story.) Absent from this list of horror conventions is ghosts, because Aickman *was* interested in ghosts, at least in a way—in the atmosphere a ghost creates, the thrill of unreality which surrounds it. Aickman was a queerly visionary writer, and ghosts, which are both utterly irrational and thoroughly English, would have appealed to him. In this collection a ghost might very well be making telephone calls in **"Your Tiny Hand Is Frozen,"** and a *kind* of ghost, the "old carlie," plays a crucial role in **"The Fetch,"** one of the most explicit and straightforward pieces here. You could stretch a point—stretch it past breaking—and say that **"Never Visit Venice"** concerns an encounter with a ghost. It does not, of course. What attracted Aickman to ghosts was not the notion of dripping revenants but the feeling—composed in part of mystery, fear, stifled eroticism, hopelessness, nostalgia, and the almost violent freedom granted by a suspension of rational rules—which they evoked in him. Ghosts—or the complex of feelings I've just tried to summarize—gave him a degree of artistic freedom granted to only a very few writers.

We are in the age of *Dawn of the Dead* and *Friday the Thirteenth,* and to describe a writer of supernatural stories as cultivated and sensitive is nearly to condemn him. . . . Aickman's general learning gave him a wide referential range: these stories often allude to the worlds of opera, art, and literature, and if you really know nothing at all about Mozart or Wagner or Homer, you will have to pay even more attention than usual while reading some of these stories. Aickman's "cultivation," which to me feels like that of an autodidact, enabled him to draw more kinds of experience, more nuance and shading, into his work; and his sensitivity meant that he felt things very deeply, everyday life as well as great art. Very good horror writers often demonstrate that ordinary life can be horrific and tedious at once for the sensitive person, and one suspects it was so for Aickman. It is a great mistake to read the life of the writing for that of the writer, but these stories leave little doubt that for Aickman's sensibility the contemporary world was a raucous, clanging din growing ever emptier of any real content. He frequently tells us that he abhors man in the mass and the pleasures of the vulgar crowd, what in the wonderfully titled **"Never Visit Venice"** he calls "the world's new littleness." Experience was being flattened out all around him, being rendered coarser, simpler, and more accessible, and this process clearly made Aickman as "sick at heart" as it does his protagonist, Henry Fern.

This response is not merely snobbish. There is too much sadness in it for that; and beneath the educated sadness, too much fear; and beneath the fear, too much respect for the great common human inheritance.

In nearly all of the stories collected here, the world of ordinary experience is as porous and malleable as a dream. **"Growing Boys"** is a deadpan bit of uncharacteristic black humor in which the irrational and grotesque are hauled right into the immediate foreground of the story. (The only other story here as explicit as that, apart from **"The Fetch"** and its family spectre, is **"The Wine-Dark Sea,"** a forthright allegory: as in a myth, man is blindly destructive to the original sacred world of the gods, and even Aickman's typically responsive and insightful lone traveller must be returned to the

noisy, empty world he came from.) In every other story, the immediate result of a finely tuned sensibility finding danger and uncertainty everywhere in ordinary life is to make meaningless the concept of the "ordinary." Aickman's characters find themselves trapped in a series of events unconnected by logic, or which are connected by a nonlinear logic. Very often neither the characters nor the reader can be certain about *exactly* what has happened, yet the story has the satisfying rightness of a poem—a John Ashbery poem. Every detail is echoed or commented upon, nothing is random or wasted. The reader has followed the characters into a world which is remorseless, vast, and inexorable in its operations.

Unconscious forces drive these characters, and Aickman's genius was in finding imaginative ways for the unconscious to manipulate both the narrative events of his tales and the structures in which they occur. Because there are no logical explanations, there can be no resolutions. After the shock of the sheer strangeness fades away, we begin to see how the facts of the stories appear to grow out of the protagonists' fears and desires, and how the illogic and terror surrounding them is their own, far more accurately and disturbingly than in any conventional horror story. **"The Trains"** is a perfect story of this type, and **"The Inner Room"** is even better, one of Aickman's most startling and beautiful demonstrations of the power over us of what we do not quite grasp about ourselves and our lives.

As wonderful as those stories are, **"Into the Wood"** seems to me the masterpiece of this collection. In it all of Aickman's themes come together in an act of self-acceptance which is at once dangerous, enigmatic, in narrative terms wholly justified, and filled with the reverence for the imaginative power demonstrated by Aickman's work in general.

On the narrative surface **"Into the Wood"** is about insomnia. Margaret, the wife of an English road builder, inadvertently comes upon a sanatorium set in a Swedish forest. After she has arranged to stay there for several days, she discovers that the sanatorium, or the Kurhus, is a refuge for those who never sleep: the rest of the world, the "sleepers," cannot tolerate their presence. True insomniacs "have to live with reality twenty-four hours a day," she is told, and their knowledge makes them feared. During the day they rest, aloof even from one another, and at night they walk in the woods around the sanatorium. Margaret's dissatisfaction with the empty social round she must endure as her husband's wife and her uneasiness at finding herself stranded amidst these silent and peculiar people are delineated subtly and economically. Aickman tells us that until her experience at the Kurhus, Margaret would have rejected the idea that she was unhappy, being "insufficiently grown for unhappiness or happiness." Swedish hospitality has exhausted her, but the Kurhus is like the Alice books in its reversal of ordinary rules and customs. Two orders of being are opposed here, and when Margaret enters the woods, she realizes for the first time that her true self, the Margaret of her inner life, requires more spiritual and imaginative freedom than life with her husband provides. . . . She has found within herself a capacity for seeing what is real. That evening a sympathetic Kurhus resident tells her that "only by great sacrifices can we poor human beings reach great truths." Margaret instinctively knows what he means. Some few insomniacs, he says, walk into the great Swedish forest beyond the wood and never return: they have reached their limits and found their deepest truth.

From this point the story moves like a series of tapestries as it enacts the consequences of Margaret's strange encounter with her own being. In a sense, **"Into the Wood"** is an extended metaphor for the separation, even estrangement, between the artist and the conventional world, and the artist's sense of an inner glory and necessity which can be shirked only at the expense of his true relationship to himself; or so I thought when I first read it, and was immediately grateful to have read it. But abstract reflections on "the artist" are seldom satisfactory, and are never as satisfactory, nor as moving, as this story. We could say, far more pertinently, that if stories are ever about anything but the particular ways they are themselves and no other story, **"Into the Wood"** is about being a dedicated, delicately organized man named Robert Aickman; about knowing there is a great wild forest within you; about understanding that you must go into that forest in search of your own limits; and doing so with the knowledge that many other people have felt that a world of unsentimental grandeur lies within and that to deny or ignore it is to choose an uneasy half-life. Aickman's originality was rooted in need—he had to write these stories, and that is why they are so worth reading and rereading. (pp. 7-10)

> *Peter Straub, in an introduction to* The Wine-Dark Sea *by Robert Aickman, Arbor House, 1988, pp. 7-10.*

STEVE RASNIC TEM

Ramsey Campbell called him "the finest living writer of ghost stories." Fritz Leiber referred to him as a "weatherman of the subconscious." And, in the introduction to the short story collection *The Wine-Dark Sea* [see excerpt above], Peter Straub states that "Robert Aickman at his best was this century's most profound writer of what we call 'horror stories' and he, with greater accuracy, preferred to call 'strange stories.'"

With such praise, it is ironic that Aickman, who both as editor and writer influenced many of the current practitioners of the "quiet" school of horror fiction (horror which relies heavily on atmosphere and mood for its effects, as opposed to graphic description), is largely unknown to American readers. (p. 13)

Some of this neglect can perhaps be explained by Aickman's approach. Those who prefer their horror fiction straightforward, populated by the usual werewolves and vampires and walking dead, all wrapped up with a neat and tidy ending, will find little to interest them here. Aickman's strategy is more subtle; his enigmatic, poetic tales often demand, and repay, a second reading.

In ["The Wine-Dark Sea"] a man ventures to an island where the locals will not go, and the three women who live there gradually introduce him to a sacred world predating humanity. Such a straightforward synopsis, however, indicates nothing of the depth of the story—an allegory which requires a close reading in order to understand its various nuances. In "Never Visit Venice" a man finds himself traveling into the landscape of his dreams, but the exact meaning of these dreams remains a compelling mystery both for the narrator and the reader. In "The Next Glade" a woman ponders a number of questions: Did she really love her husband? Does her lover really exist? Her anxiety leads to startling transformations of the surrounding landscape.

The Wine-Dark Sea is one of the best of Aickman's collec-

tions to see print, in part because it amply demonstrates the scope and power of the author. The stories range from that chilling masterpiece **"The Trains"**—in which the author slowly, painstakingly reveals why a woman has waved from a bedroom window to every passing train for twenty years—to **"Growing Boys,"** a rather contemporary piece in which Aickman explores every parent's nightmare with dark-humored exaggeration: the threat of gigantic, animalistic adolescent children who cannot be controlled.

On the surface **"The Fetch"** would seem to be a more traditional piece about a banshee who haunts the members of a family, but Aickman's extended psychological portrait of the narrator becomes a compelling study of the ways in which memory haunts us, traps us, and eventually governs our destinies. **"The Stains"** . . . is virtually a textbook example of how an author can create an atmosphere that shifts from the ordinary to the bizarre with little indication that such a significant transformation is occurring. Its ending encourages a number of possible interpretations. Aickman always seems able to make such ambiguity work for him—obtaining fictional depth where lesser authors achieve only a dissolution of narrative drive.

A transforming landscape figures prominently in most of Aickman's best fiction. Certainly no other contemporary horror writer better understood the connections between the setting of a story and the inner drives and conflicts of its characters. Aickman possessed that rare ability to *show* naturalistic events coaxing and pulling the unconscious out of a character, transforming the world in which that character lives. Thus, Aickman's preference for the term "strange story" over "horror story." He was after something that goes far beyond a simple scare or disruption of sleep. His narratives lead us to question our assumptions about reality itself and show us "strange" landscapes which we soon discover are not so strange after all. They are the landscapes in which we actually live out our lives, which have the most profound influence on our choices and actions. As critic Mike Ashley said, "Aickman's stories . . . are almost always unsettling, not in the visceral sense, but spiritually."

One of the finest stories in this collection, **"Into The Wood,"** introduces us to a woman who has a rather direct encounter with her unconscious. Unhappy with the position and society thrust upon her as her husband's wife, she is inexplicably drawn to a Swedish sanatorium, the Kurhus, that is occupied by true insomniacs, people who *never* sleep, who "have to live with reality twenty-four hours a day." At night they wander the woods which surround the sanatorium, their dirt paths so well-travelled that lush vegetation does not encroach upon them. In the woods she finds a way of being which lies "beyond logic," which will permit her, she feels, to embrace a new, less conventional reality.

In his numerous editorial introductions to the volumes of *The Fontana Book of Great Ghost Stories* anthology, Aickman delineated clearly what he thought the ghost story should be (including an early statement that ghost stories need not actually contain a ghost, their primary trait being that they deal with what is unconscious). Such statements as "the ghost story hints to us that there is a world elsewhere" and that the "ghost story deals with the experience behind experience" help delineate the principle thrust behind what Aickman would later call his "strange" stories.

In stories such as those collected in *The Wine-Dark Sea,*

Robert Aickman eschews the rather specific conventions of ghostly fiction and folklore for a much more ambitious task: offering his readers a glimpse into an entire unconscious world, a world at once more terrible, and more beautiful than our own, and yet alarmingly very much the same. (pp. 13, 18, 22)

> *Steve Rasnic Tem, "A Preference for Strange Sto-ries," in* The Bloomsbury Review, *Vol. 8, No. 5, September-October, 1988, pp. 13, 18, 22.*

Fernando Alegría

1918-

Chilean novelist, poet, critic, editor, short story writer, biographer, and nonfiction writer.

In his fiction, Alegría utilizes striking, often violent imagery to expose the political and social inadequacies of his homeland. Formerly the Cultural Attaché to the Chilean embassy in Washington, D.C. for President Salvador Allende, Alegría frequently expresses in his work his leftist views as well as his opposition to the military junta led by General Augusto Pinochet, which overthrew Allende's socialist government in 1973. While several critics have objected to the polemicism of Alegría's fiction, most have commended his humanistic indictment of repressive governmental policies.

Alegría's works often depict periods of social unrest in Chilean history. His first novel, *Recabarren* (1938), for example, focuses upon the labor strikes of the 1930s, while *Lautaro, joven liberator de Arauco* (1943), portrays the sixteenth-century Araucan Indian leader who revolted against the Spanish conquistadors. In *Caballo de Copas* (1957; *My Horse Gonzalez*), Alegría eschews historical fiction to humorously relate the story of two South American emigrés to the United States who spend their savings on a temperamental racehorse. Alegría returns to social commentary with *Mañana los guerreros* (1964; *Tomorrow the Warriors*), which links the political climate of 1938 Chile to the Nazi presence in Europe. Alegría's subsequent novels include *El paso de los gansos* (1978; *The Chilean Spring*), which draws upon the actual journal entries of photographer Christián Montesino to chronicle the violent months following the assassination of Allende. Returning to Chile from the United States, Montesino joins the underground opposition to Pinochet's regime, but is arrested and executed when his photographs and diaries are exposed. Jeffrey Burke commented that Alegría's "tribute to a modestly heroic photographer becomes a poignant elegy to a nation whose future has been taken from it. That Mr. Alegría accomplishes so much so effectively in so few pages is a remarkable achievement."

In addition to his fiction, Alegría has published several poetry collections, including *10 Pastoral Psalms* (1968), *Instructions for Undressing the Human Race/Instrucciones para desnudar la raza humana* (1969), and *Changing Centuries: Selected Poems* (1984). Although some reviewers objected to Alegría's frequent use of scatological imagery in his poetry, most commended his unconventional examination of political and sexual themes. Alegría is also considered a leading figure in Chilean literary criticism. His works in this genre include *Walt Whitman en Hispanoamèrica* (1954), which examines the influence of the nineteenth-century American poet upon Latin American literature, *Breve historia de la novela hispanoamericana* (1959), a survey of the Latin American novel, and *La Literatura chilena del siglo XX* (1967), which concentrates upon contemporary Chilean literature.

(See also *Contemporary Authors,* Vols. 9-12, rev. ed. and *Contemporary Authors New Revision Series,* Vol. 5.)

BLANCHE WEBER SHAFFER

[The novel *Lautaro*] tells the dramatic tale of the Araucans under their national hero, Lautaro, in their war against the Spanish Conquistadores. Lautaro is captured by the Spanish in sixteenth century Chile and, having gained the confidence of Villagra, their leader, he is trained in Western warfare. Later, as chief of his own people, he uses this training against the invaders. This popular hero, says the author, achieved his first great victory when he was twenty years old, and reached the height of his power at twenty-two. The lovely Indian girl, Guacolda, brings sweetness into Lautaro's stern life. She becomes his wife, and mysteriously disappears after his death. Dramatic battle scenes, daring single combats where the interest centers on Lautaro remind one of the old French epics, the Chansons de Gestes. The fiery addresses of Lautaro and the other leaders are full of Latin eloquence.

The scenes unfold against the background of Chile which is a lovely, but often a dangerous country. One of the most dramatic of the scenes is the superhuman fight of Lautaro and his men against the current of the river. The faith of the Araucans, their superstitions are outlined in beautiful words:

> They worshipped the spirits of the dead, and saw
> in everything, every event, every element of life a

hidden force, a strange power that could influence men and beasts for good or evil. The flight of a bird, the direction taken by a fox were signs foretelling the outcome of a battle. . . . To live this is to live in a strange but stimulating world where the cries of animals foretell death, love or victory; the shadows hide the beloved dead; the sounds of night bring messages from another world. To have such faith is to live fully and be close to the gods.

In a time when Americans, young and old, are trying to understand their neighbors to the south, the story of Lautaro should be a valuable introduction to Chile's history and its literature. It is the record of a glorious past for the young people of today. It is, moreover, an example of the sharing of their literature by the children all over the world. Some years ago in Latin America books for children were chiefly translations from foreign languages, especially English. Today, we in turn receive from South America the literature that is peculiarly its own. Lautaro is one of its epic heroes. (pp. 30-1)

Blanche Weber Shaffer, in a review of "Lautaro," in The Saturday Review of Literature, *Vol. XXVII, No. 46, November 11, 1944, pp. 30-1.*

GLEN L. KOLB

[In *My Horse González*], González is a Chilean racing stallion imported first to New York, then sold by his disappointed owner to a San Francisco stable. This handsome but temperamental animal, capering gracefully before the grandstand with rumba-like gait and prancing powerfully to the starting gate for a fast get-away, is soon pegged by the cynical racing fans as a great fraud who promises much but delivers nothing. He is finally purchased by two Chileans, one a middleaged professional jockey, and the other a disoriented young fellow . . . living in a bawdy boarding house with assorted Latin American leftists, Italian adventurers and Spanish anarchists; and spending his days at the racetrack and his evenings in third-rate night clubs with gamblers, dope addicts, perverts and prostitutes.

Under the expert guidance of the jockey, who understands the horse's "Chilean personality," González wins one race, enriches his owners and then is sold by them because he has "shot his wad" and is no longer useful. Such, in brief, is the story of González.

As a novel this work suffers from serious defects of organization and elaboration. Sixty pages, or nearly one-third of the book, are devoted to introduction or background, before the main theme of the Chilean horse is mentioned; and the author abandons his subject for long periods to recount the details of love affairs, tavern brawls, gambling bouts and dock strikes. If the work were stripped of its extraneous episodes, pointless recollections and tiresome dialogues replete with four-letter obscenities, the narrative of González could, in fact, be reduced to a twenty-five page short story, though not necessarily a successful one.

The effect of pornography and scatology in literature corresponds more or less to that of certain condiments in food: when used sparingly and judiciously they can heighten the flavor and lend zest and interest; if employed to excess, the entire fare is rendered ugly and unpalatable. In the present case, the spice is used indiscriminately and the result is absurd and even grotesque.

The best written passages in the book are descriptions of the city of San Francisco at dawn or dusk, waterfront scenes and the frenzied behavior of crowds at the racetrack. Some of these are very effective, but they often have little or nothing to do with the story and they contrast strangely with the drab vulgarity of the dialogues. In short, the style is extremely uneven and although occasional passages are carefully elaborated, there is every indication that the work as a whole was written in considerable haste and with no particular plan in mind.

Glen L. Kolb, in a review of "My Horse González," in Hispania, *Vol. XLVIII, No. 1, March, 1965, p. 187.*

WILLIS KNAPP JONES

Most ambitious of Alegría's fiction is his new novel of Chile's Generation of '38 [*Mañana los guerreros*], confronting such problems as the Spanish Civil War, the Nazi epoch in Europe and its overtones in Chile, and the Frente Popular. Italicized portions philosophize and link the story line with conditions abroad. The protagonists are Juan Luis, a university student, and Elena, mother of his illegitimate child. Most of the action, developed largely through conversation, is mild, except for the Nazi attack on the Seguro Obrero Building in Santiago, but the emotion is tense and the impact terrific. Its three parts, calendared through the year of 1938, provide unforgettable reading.

Willis Knapp Jones, in a review of "Mañana los guerreros," in Books Abroad, *Vol. 39, No. 3, Summer, 1965, p. 327.*

EDGAR ROBINSON

Fernando Alegría is a great poet. Proof? Look at his metaphor. Aristotle said, and he's right, that the proof of a poet lies in his metaphor; that's where a poet is born, not made.

"#5"

When Fabio runs from the library and Galatea
opens her red kimono and the straps of her
white silk girdle snap and the pubic hairs
open out like a starfish, and Fido on his
knees laps up the soft drops from the spring,
this is called: *A farewell to the wanderer.*

[*10 Pastoral Poems* represents] ten views (they are truly psalms) of love involving three persons, a woman Galatea and two men, Fabio and Fido. At first glance, they may look like pornography, but they are not. They are poetry, joyful and alive, with verve. The distinction? I suppose pornography represents a limited vision, a narrowing of scope, for a specific purpose—to excite the reader. The pornographer, when he sees a *pas de trois* in bed, cannot afford to see them as human beings. Poetry is not limited in this way. It is the same difference that exists between a phantasy and a dream. A phantasy comes at one's bidding, like a lesser spirit, and does its work for the temporary gratification of the ego, whereas dreams come unbidden, and instead of feeding the ego temporarily, they nourish the soul—more precisely, they become the soul.

Alegría is a great poet. (pp. 116-17)

Edgar Robinson, "Nine Kayak Books," in Chicago Review, Vol. 20, No. 1, Summer, 1968, pp. 116-26.

LEWIS WARSH

Each of the twenty-one sections [in *Instructions for Undressing the Human Race*] begins with the word "Undress . . ." followed by the names or titles of various personages, among them: The Bearded Type, The Nun, The Blue Policeman, The Angels and Archangels, The Earth, The Magician, A Spade Cat, and An Astronaut. In sections such as **"Undress The Bureaucrat"**, which ends: "Stuff his ass with pencils freshly sharpened / and use him to write the phrase: / More soldiers, or the word time, if you prefer / the word shit", the poet goes beyond satire and approaches a revolutionary stance, but the basic tone is playful and the poem is entertaining throughout. The idea is a good one and Alegría carries it successfully as far as he can go. (pp. 445-46)

Lewis Warsh, "Out of Sight," in Poetry, Vol. CXV, No. 6, March, 1970, pp. 440-46.

ETHAN FEINSOD

Fernando Alegría's **Instructions for Undressing the Human Race** is not of much use either as poetry or a practical guide. The idea is that one undress people differently according to their character. Consequently, the act of undressing someone is as naked and revealing as the body bared. Mr. Alegría's attitude towards most of the human race is such that he does most of his undressing with a meathook. Nonetheless, he does not even seem to have got the hang of being brutal or shocking. Occasionally he is a bit gentler and then better.

Ethan Feinsod, in a review of "Instructions for Undressing the Human Race," in Chicago Review, Vol. 22, Nos. 2 & 3, January-February, 1971, p. 158.

FERNANDO ALEGRÍA [INTERVIEW WITH CELIA CORREAS DE ZAPATA]

[Correas de Zapata]: Your name is often included in the group of contemporary writers formed by Alejo Carpentier, Juan Rulfo, Gabriel García Márquez, Julio Cortázar, and Jorge Luis Borges. Do you think there are similarities of form and substance justifying this classification, and if so what are they?

[Alegriá]: The authors you mention cover a very broad spectrum. Besides, it would be presumptuous of me to count myself among them. But modesty aside, I would wish to hold in common with Mario Vargas Llosa the painstaking design that precedes his writing of a novel and with Cortázar the desire to demolish that design. I feel for García Márquez the admiration of one who understands and shares his interest in the supernatural phenomena of daily life. This was the theme of my *El Poeta que se Volvió Gusano* [*The Poet Who Became a Worm*], written around 1950. Each of my novels contains a number of saints possessed, who, according to the Bible, are those blessed with the power of levitation. Rulfo is an author who appears to write his stories as Christ wrote his judgments, with a stick in the sand. Of course I would like to be compared to him. . . . The compassion, the tenderness, the secret tension of [Rulfo's] language are the mark of his genius and link him to other Latin American writers whom I acknowledge as comrades: Augusto Roa Bastos and José María

Arguedas, for example. They are presiding over the death and rebirth of a narrative that is being supplemented, through repetition and correction, by many voices, among which I should like to include my own.

The surrealistic overtone that pulls together the isolated episodes in your last book, Amérika, *is a surprise. Roa Bastos calls it a novella, an "allegory of the 'sound and fury' that dominates our life today on a planetary level." Do you agree that* Amérika *is an allegory of the conflicts of our times?*

All reality is surrealistic. The only expression of reality I recognize is not confined to specifics but instead pervades, transfixes, transmutes, and affirms them, ultimately denying and destroying them. . . . I should like it if, etymologically, the word allegory were derived from allege and riant, that is, I allege, you laugh. This would exactly suit my book **Amérika**. Our present conflicts are, of course, contained in **Amérika**. (The book is subtitled *Manifestos on Vietnam* and was written in Berkeley.) But most of the conflicts I refer to have always existed, as for example, the apple in Paradise, the water of St. John the Baptist, the sword of the Archangel Gabriel, the passion and death of Cuzco on the greased pole, the life of mankind in mirrors, and suicide as an act of closing and opening a door. It deals with the dramas of today and of both Testaments, old and new, which are now being lived as a single total happening, rather than rewriting the Bible, which would be not only impossible but in poor taste. (pp. 9-10)

How is your narrative enriched through the décalage of distance characteristic of Cortázar, Carpentier, and Carlos Fuentes, to name just a few?

Remember that the astronauts had to journey to the moon in order to see and understand the earth from a true perspective. The fact is that I *don't live* outside of Chile; I exist elsewhere, but I *live* in Chile. Besides, Chile is everywhere. In my country we protest so much against everything and everybody that we do not see the country itself. . . . Whoever followed the letter of Tolstoy's advice today would not see the universe encompassed in his native village but would only at most discover the extent of his own alienation.

How do you feel the fusion of Chilean, Latin American, and U.S. influences have affected your view of mankind today?

It's very hard to say. I must confess that I have never been infected by the influence of the United States. It may have given me an allergy, but the fact is that I am the one who does the sneezing and not the United States. As far as the "Latin American influence" is concerned, I have my doubts as to whether it exists at all. I'm inclined to think it doesn't. . . . All of us Latin Americans bear a family resemblance to each other, of course. But it's a resemblance to distant relatives we no longer see and whom we meet only in times of crisis or at funerals. We share many things, but we need to identify them gradually, one by one. From this standpoint, that is, of a continuing movement in all our countries, our America has indeed been useful to me. (p. 10)

The theme of violence appears in your book El Poeta que se Volvió Gusano *published in 1956, in the story* "¿A qué Lado de la Cortina?" ["On Which Side of the Curtain?"], *when the Chicanos of today were called "pachucos," though perhaps with a different connotation. Wouldn't you say that you are, without openly taking sides—remember the Revolution of '38 in* Mañana los Guerreros [Tomorrow the Warriors]—*a writer of social protest?*

Violence plays a direct and decisive role in my writing. Sometime I would like to count (I'm not going to, of course) the fights, battles, blows, insults, falls, punches, suicides, renunciations, provocations, and murders that appear in my novels, stories, and poems. Fortunately, almost all of this violence has been inner violence. . . . The pachuco affair was traumatic. I had just arrived from Chile when a shocking racial persecution of Mexicans erupted in Los Angeles, a mixture of xenophobia, fascism, and chauvinistic madness. I went to Los Angeles with the intention of writing an article for one of the Latin American papers. The result was **"?A qué Lado de la Cortina?,"** a story that foreshadowed the aggressive literature of today's Chicanos. . . . The racial riots in Los Angeles were glossed over with a complacency and timidity beneath which the hypocrites of the slums marked time. To have painted this picture in harsh, angry outline is the particular merit of the story you mention. . . .

The sense of humor shown in your books is delightful. Yet you have a dark, apocalyptic, tormented side as well. How do you explain this duality in your literary approach?

Sartre says that art cannot be created with hatred, without love. If we suspend the hatred for at least twelve of the twenty-four hours in the day (either half, waking or sleeping), the other twelve will be spent in living, that is, in laughing with our fellow men. A writer who does not know how to laugh is impotent. . . .

What authors, what books are most important to you right now? In general, what poets, short story writers or novelists have you reread most often?

I find myself reading less and less, perhaps because I have to write more. Unless you read the authors who leave a lasting impression while you are young, it will be too late. Very little is necessary. I read the classics as a child, including many in the Araluce collection, then browsed here and there. . . . Today I read strictly out of love. . . . I won't list them for you because that would be the opposite of what I mean to say: that as Cortázar says, the reader receives a model to assemble and by assembling that model he *creates* his own books. (p. 12)

> *Fernando Alegría, "Talking with Alegría," in an interview with Celia Correas de Zapata in* America, *Vol. 24, No. 8, August, 1972, pp. 9-12.*

VICTOR PERERA

El Paso de los Gansos (*The Goosesteppers*) [is] a journal-novel set in the final days of Allende's government and the first weeks of the military regime. The first part of *The Goosesteppers* is an impressionistic chronicle of Allende's last days, composed in a shifting perspective reminiscent of John Dos Passos's montage technique. The intended effect is an elegy on Allende's personal sacrifice and on the sacrifices of other Chilean martyrs: the poets Victor Jara and Pablo Neruda, the loyal Gen. Carlos Prats. The few glimpses of the "enemy" display them as hate-filled, demented yahoos.

The second, and more affecting half of *The Goosesteppers* is based on the real journal of a 26-year-old Chilean-born Princeton graduate student in philosophy, Cristian Montesino (called Montealegre in the novel), whose marriage and career had fallen apart and who had returned to Chile to pick up the pieces of his life and begin anew. Instead, he met a vio-

lent death at the hands of the military police, who arrested him in the home of his father, a staunch junta-supporter, and executed him for presumed leftist associations.

Christian's view of the terrible events in Chile during and after September 11, 1973, was formed by an introspective, religious sensibility, free of political dogma. The humanistic quality of his journal, as much as the circumstances of his death, make his indictment of the military's actions particularly striking.

"Yesterday, Chile was broken," reads his entry for September 12. "What the military have unleashed they will never be able to put right. They did not know how to do things. Both sides are now pitted in a fratricidal war that will not end in a generation." (p. 151)

> *Victor Perera, "The Coast Is Not Clear: Chileans in Exile," in* The Nation, *New York, Vol. 226, No. 5, February 11, 1978, pp. 149-52.*

JEFFREY BURKE

Christián Montealegre, a 27-year-old photographer, returned to his birthplace in Santiago, Chile, just before the overthrow of Salvador Allende, and was executed two months later for conspiring against the military junta. Working from interviews and Christián's own journal and letters, Fernando Alegría, a Chilean novelist and poet, has written in Christián's voice [*The Chilean Spring*], a fictionalized journal of those last two months.

The narrative is interior monologue, documentary, and at times prose poem. Mr. Alegría frames dozens of brief scenes through the eyes of the photographer: the bread lines and black market, trucks of soldiers blown up, summary executions against the walls of apartment buildings, jets buzzing a church belfry, a soccer stadium converted to a holding pen, a child's unwitting betrayal of his father. The political upheaval is mirrored in Christián's personal life. He stays in Santiago with his father, a smug supporter of the junta, and compares his parents' separation with his own from a wife whose psychotic episodes at one time nearly cost her life and their children's. Rational now, and committed to opposing the junta, she effects a reconciliation so that Christián will join the cause. By doing so he resolves his ambivalence: "Instead of the present events which should be filling my notebook, I'm attracted to the twisted memory of things long past which set the pattern for my reactions today"—at the cost of his life.

Mr. Alegria, who knew Christián personally, was in Chile at the time of the coup, preparing a biography of Allende. His tribute to a modestly heroic photographer becomes a poignant elegy to a nation whose future has been taken from it. That Mr. Alegría accomplishes so much so effectively in so few pages is a remarkable achievement, as are moments in the writing like this sentence:

> I suddenly hear a whisper in the distance, an avalanche, a dull sound, prolonged, subterranean, like a mountain tumbling down, but I can't see anything, and I have the feeling night is tearing itself open in some meadow or in the foothills of the sierra, a broad movement of earth and water, tall trees slapping into deep mud and splattering the sky, all of them crashing into a bottomless pit underneath

the city, so far away and yet at the same time here, under my feet and over my head.

(p. 14)

Jeffrey Burke, "Fiction by Five," in The New York Times Book Review, *May 11, 1980, pp. 14, 36.*

SELDEN RODMAN

This imagined journal [**The Chilean Spring**] by a (real) young photographer-journalist executed by the military shortly after the fall of the Allende government on September 11, 1973 throws no light whatever on Chile's cataclysmic shift from Left to Right. The preface quotes approvingly Allende's misguided assessment of "This grey and bitter moment, when treason is in the ascendant . . ."; it follows that not a clue is offered to explain why the middle class revolted, why the armed forces eventually joined in, and why Allende proved incapable of ruling once he had brought the economy down in ruins.

Selden Rodman, in a review of "The Chilean Spring," in National Review, *New York, Vol. XXXII, October 31, 1980, p. 1344.*

JOHN F. DONAHUE

Very early in this disturbing story [**The Chilean Spring**] . . . one of its narrators pronounces the central problem being explored and the ultimate purpose of the story's having been written: "Exhausted, I try to write you and communicate something of what happened."

To tell what happened requires, it would seem, only an accurate history. But any history, to paraphrase a well-known adage, is but the partial interpretation of a partial record of a partial experience of a past event. In the present instance, the past event is "what happened" during the early days of the Chilean spring of 1973, and Alegría has wisely chosen not to attempt a conventional history. Nor even a historical novel, although the story teems with historically verifiable details.

Several strategies are at work throughout the novel. The first is the presence of multiple narrators, not one reliable in a definitive way. Each is a fragment of perception, though each thinks he—or she—is giving an objective, undiluted view of the events. Not even Cristián Montealegre, the protagonist and sometimes narrator, understands the total action of the story.

A second strategy is the creation of a large cast of vivid characters whose full personal histories are kept tantalizingly out of reach. There is often no visible continuity between a past history and present behavior. This is true for Luz Maria, Cristián's wife, whose bouts of insanity during the early years of their marriage bear no apparent causal relation to her astonishing and courageous involvement at the story's end.

A third strategy is the widescale derangement of time. The story moves in temporal segments, each of which is admirably consistent and familiar in its internal sequence of events. But the segments themselves are out of sequence with respect to each other, and the actors emerge, disappear, and re-emerge in widely separate places and times. The unsettling effect of this dissociation of events is, however, relieved by the introduction of a broad, more conventionally historical back-

drop of Chilean history. All the important pieces of Chile's past are brought in . . . each with its own agenda to follow.

The effect of all this multiplicity is the creation of a cinema-novel in which frames and frame groups are edited into disordered sequences, culminating in Chile's violent breakdown and Cristián's death. Chile and Cristián hold the story together. The action centers on Cristián, the photographer who records the inevitable destruction while himself becoming progressively isolated until he is at last made the victim of a casual murder.

Strategies, however, are not of interest in themselves, unless you are of a Pyrrhic bent of mind. Rather, they serve to focus attention on a particular vision of the truth of "what happened" in Chile during the distressing days of September and October of 1973. The event that "happened" is at a level of truth that supersedes the claims of social institution or class. It has to do with ideas that, today especially, few are very comfortable with: the innocent, powerless victim whose death, usually violent and unnoticed, lets loose energies that ripple through a society, empowering those it touches to break out of the insidious logic of self-interest and self-justification. . . . As Cristián (the name is and is not to be taken literally) says shortly before the end: "There were ruins I had to gather up into images before they became ideas." And as his brother Marcelo says of him after Cristián's death

> I don't think Cristián ever knew he was dying: the fact of death didn't bother him. He knew something was going to come to an end when he came back to Chile. All you have to do is read his letters or his notebook. He died from the inside out, like so many others these days; he dove into the bullets.

The achievement of **The Chilean Spring** is that it shows how such things happen.

John F. Donahue, "That Certain Spring," in Americas, *Vol. 34, No. 2, March-April, 1982, p. 58.*

WOLFGANG A. LUCHTING

[**Caballo de copas**] first came out in 1957 . . . and was soon translated into English—to, as I recall, enthusiastic acclaim. Justifiedly so, for the book is highly entertaining, documents well times gone by and places changed and presents materials not frequent in novels, least of all in Latin American ones: boy meets girl, boy meets horsemen, boy meets horse, boy comes close to losing girl because of horse and horsemen. These withdraw; boy loses horse, keeps girl. And all but the girl are Chileans in California. This permits Alegría to describe a fascinating series of picaresque adventures as experienced by Chilean immigrants in, primarily, San Francisco (about which he offers beautiful passages), in their endeavor to make a go of it in a society so different from Chile's.

The stallion González, brought from Chile by someone who finds his hopes for him as a *campeón* dashed, ends up belonging to the young narrator and some of his friends, racing addicts all, who, however, countrymen of González, find *their* feverish hopes for him fulfilled: he wins one big race and a bundle for his compatriots. For his jockey Hidalgo, this finally means the fare back to Chile; for González, his sale, in the midst of great sadness among the human chauvinists, to serve as a stud, since his owners doubt that he can repeat his feat; for the hero, a return to the university and an only nostalgic love of *equi,* until González dies (because one day he was too much of a Chilean macho at the wrong moment), which is where **Caballo** begins.

Throughout the novel Alegría shows the social sensibility and *conciencia* that were to characterize his later novels and stories. Though he is definitely recognized as a novelist . . . , literary historians, perhaps because of being such, stubbornly apostrophize Alegría with the phrase "better known as a literary critic and historian." **Caballo de copas,** and even more so his subsequent novels and stories, proves that he deserves equal billing as a fiction writer.

> *Wolfgang A. Luchting, in a review of "Caballo de copas," in* World Literature Today, *Vol. 56, No. 3, Summer, 1982, p. 489.*

W. FERGUSON

Fernando Alegría's **Una especie de memoria** provides a passionate history of the author's sentimental, political and literary education in the Chile of the 1930s. The evocation of Santiago during those turbulent years is utterly convincing; syndicalist struggles and government reaction, idealists and cynics, literary anguish and triumph, romantic entanglements, period slang and a truly staggering cast of characters that includes, most notably, the names of Mistral, Recabarren and Neruda. Amorous episodes, presumably autobiographical or nearly so (two sections are called *novelas*), are mingled vertiginously with other enthusiasms (the war for Spain, the Paul Robeson question). "Morir pollo," one of the most affecting parts of this moving book, is about the suicide of Pablo de Rokha's son Carlos . . .

The experiences recounted here must have been so vivid, the reader feels, that only the weight of literature could provide a buffer against the ferocities of memory. Alegría's literary record, both in and out of fiction, is long and distinguished; the fine mix of poetry, nostalgia and criticism in the present volume is an excellent way of taming the past without killing its spirit.

> *W. Ferguson, in a review of "Una especie de memoria," in* World Literature Today, *Vol. 58, No. 4, Autumn, 1984, p. 576.*

M. S. ARRINGTON, JR.

Fernando Alegría, Chilean-born literary critic, novelist, and professor of Latin American literature, reveals his talents as a poet in this bilingual Spanish/English collection of 38 poems [**Changing Centuries: Selected Poems**]. Characterized by a diversity of tone, imagery, and form, the selections include intimately personal lyrics on home and a grandson as well as public, politically committed verse extolling fallen heroes. With gentle modulations, his voice covers a broad spectrum that ranges from the nostalgic to the prophetic. . . . [This volume is an] important collection which will appropriately complement Alegría's **The Chilean Spring.**

> *M. S. Arrington, Jr., in a review of "Changing Centuries: Selected Poems," in* Choice, *Vol. 22, No. 2, October, 1984, p. 273.*

Isabel Allende

1942-

Chilean novelist, journalist, dramatist, and juvenile fiction writer.

In her fiction, Allende often uses a magic realist style that combines elements of realism and fantasy to examine the tumultuous social and political heritage of South America. Frequently drawing upon her own experiences and those of her family, Allende emphasizes the role of personal memory as a testimonial to the violence and repression that characterizes much of Latin American history. While some critics consider her novels derivative or melodramatic, most commend her lushly detailed prose and compelling images, which subtly convey her moralistic and political themes. Alexander Coleman asserted: "[Allende is] the first woman to join what has heretofore been an exclusive male club of Latin American novelists. Not that she is the first contemporary female writer from Latin America . . .—but she is the first woman to approach on the same scale as the others the tormented patriarchal world of traditional Hispanic society."

Allende was born in Lima, Peru, where her father served as a Chilean diplomat. Although Allende's contact with her father ceased following her parents' divorce, she remained close to his family—particularly Salvador Allende, her uncle and godfather, who served as president of Chile from 1970 to 1973. As a child in Santiago, Chile, Allende lived with her maternal grandparents, who would later serve as models for Esteban and Clara Trueba, the patriarch and matriarch of the Trueba family whose history Allende chronicles in her first and best-known novel, *La casa de los espiritus* (1982; *The House of the Spirits*). After spending her adolescence in Bolivia, Europe, and the Middle East with her mother and diplomat stepfather, Allende became a journalist for television and newsreels as well as a writer for a radical feminist magazine. Her life changed abruptly in 1973 when a military coup, lead by General Augusto Pinochet Ugarte, resulted in the assassination of Salvador Allende and the overthrow of his socialist government. While she remained in Chile for several months following the takeover, Allende's efforts to assist the opposition of the new regime ultimately jeopardized her safety and in 1974 she escaped with her family to Caracas, Venezuela.

Allende's first novel, *The House of the Spirits,* began as a letter written in Caracas to her dying grandfather in Chile. Aware of his belief that a person dies only if they are forgotten by the living, Allende recorded her remembrances of her grandfather to reassure him that he would survive in her memory. This correspondence, never sent, evolved into *The House of the Spirits.* Making use of a South American setting that is often identified as Chile, the novel spans six decades to gather the recollections of its three principle characters: grandmother Clara, mother Blanca, and granddaughter Alba. Drawn from journals Clara wrote as a youth, the novel's early chapters abound in magical occurrences closely associated with Rosa the Beautiful, Clara's ethereal, green-haired sister. When Rosa dies, a grieving Clara refuses to speak for nine years but finally breaks her silence to announce that she will marry her sister's fiancé, the tyrannical Esteban Trueba. Primarily focusing upon the years of their turbulent

marriage, the novel relates Esteban's rise to power as an unscrupulous landowner and Clara's growing preoccupation with the spirit world that inhabits their labyrinthine house in the city.

Interspersed throughout *The House of the Spirits* are Esteban's recollections, which reflect his crude, violent nature as well as his fervent familial loyalty. When his daughter, Blanca, becomes pregnant by a young peasant, he forces her into a loveless marriage to another man. However, Esteban develops a close relationship with Blanca's daughter, Alba, despite her socialist views which later conflict with his position as a conservative Senator. Alba's narrative voice emerges toward the novel's end, when a military coup supported by Esteban's political party seizes power. While Esteban's sons are either murdered or exiled by the new regime, Alba's arrest and torture ultimately force the aging senator to acknowledge his role in his nation's downfall. Following Esteban's death, Alba reveals that she composed the entire narrative while confined to her prison cell. Urged by the ghost of Clara to remember, Alba survived her ordeal by mentally drafting a manuscript to help end the political violence in her homeland.

Several reviewers considered *The House of the Spirits* to be closely imitative of Gabriel García Márquez's *One Hundred Years of Solitude,* citing such similarities as its family chronicle structure, magic realist narration, and parallel characters, including Rosa the Beautiful, who greatly resembles García Márquez's Remedios the Beauty. Other critics contended that while Allende does utilize García Márquez's technique of magic realism to chronicle legendary occurrences in the past of the Trueba clan, her own voice emerges in her straightforward, journalistic treatment of realistic events surrounding the military coup. Bruce Allen observed: "Despite its undeniable debt to *One Hundred Years of Solitude,* [*The House of the Spirits*] is an original and important work; along with García Márquez's masterpiece, it's one of the best novels of the postwar period, and a major contribution to our understanding of societies riddled by ceaseless conflict and violent change."

In her next novel, *De amor y de sombra* (1985; *Of Love and Shadows*), Allende eschews the magic realist style of *House of the Spirits* to naturalistically portray the repressive policies of a South American military regime and their effect upon Irene Beltran, a fashion magazine reporter. Assigned with photographer Francisco Leal to investigate the alleged healing powers of Evangelina Ranquileo, a young peasant girl, Irene is involved in an absurd dispute with the military which culminates in the kidnapping of Evangelina by an army officer. Irene's decision to seek the truth concerning Evangelina's disappearance forces the formerly uninvolved journalist to confront the violent political and social realities of her country. Aided by Francisco, with whom she has fallen in love, Irene eventually finds Evangelina's body in a concealed mass grave, and risks her life to reveal her discovery in the national media. Irene and Francisco are then forced to escape into exile. Although several critics faulted *Of Love and Shadows* as overtly polemical, others praised Allende's humanistic approach to its controversial political subject.

Allende's following novel, *Eva Luna* (1988) more closely resembles *The House of the Spirits.* Eva, the narrator of this work, blends fantasy and realism to relate her passage from an illiterate orphan to a successful television scriptwriter. Interspersed throughout this personal chronicle are Eva's exotic sketches of persons integral to her development, including the prostitute who raises her following her mother's death, the Arabic shopkeeper who teaches her to read, and, finally, her lover Ralph Carlé, a survivor of the Nazi concentration camps in Germany who enters the volatile political scene of South America. While some critics regarded *Eva Luna* as melodramatic, others praised Allende's celebration of storytelling and its ability to transcend the banality of everyday existence. Alan Ryan commented that *Eva Luna* "is a remarkable novel, one in which a cascade of stories tumbles out before the reader, stories vivid and passionate and human enough to engage, in their own right, all the reader's attention and sympathy."

(See also *CLC,* Vol. 39 and *Contemporary Authors,* Vol. 125.)

AMBROSE GORDON

The House of the Spirits is not so much a story as many stories, as are all novels in a way, but most of them less so. It is partly, and reflexively, the story of its own inception and creation, beginning in a torture chamber of a modern police state. A young woman, who is the narrator of most of the novel, has been beaten, raped, mutilated, given electric shock, and placed in solitary confinement in a tiny cell called "the dog house," since it is hardly bigger, where she lies in her own excrement and misery, wishing to die. As her mind begins to wander her dead grandmother appears, to remind her that the point is not to die, since that will come anyway, but to survive, which is a miracle, and with the saving suggestion that survival in her case may be accomplished through keeping her mind occupied by writing, in the dark and without paper or pencil, the account of her misery. At first it proves to be almost impossibly difficult; the various characters of her history crowd in and jostle one another for her attention. As she remembers something new she forgets what has just been remembered; but later she develops a key by which she can remember events in order.

The whole comes in her mind eventually to resemble a complicated jigsaw puzzle in which each piece has its own place. "Before putting it all together it seemed to me incomprehensible," she confesses, "but I was sure that if I succeeded in finishing it, a sense would be given to each and the result would be harmonious."

The result *is* harmonious, although how the completed puzzle is to be comprehended remains something of a question. A novel, I think, can be imaginatively rich without necessarily making very clear sense. What comes together in *The House of the Spirits* is not only an often rather jumbled history but also one that is extremely bizarre in detail. Improbability reigns. The point of departure is a young woman with brilliant green hair—naturally that color, not dyed. Although I shouldn't like to go on record that green hair is impossible— if flaming red hair can exist, why not green?—it must be very rare. And if we dream of green eyes as beautiful, and we do, why wouldn't green hair be even more beautiful? The events of the novel are set in motion when a proud and ambitious, but still poor young man, Esteban Trueba, sees Rosa, *la bella,* in the street, follows her home in a trolley, and from that moment determines that she must be his. Through circumstances beyond their control, she never is. Nine years later, however, Esteban, now wealthy, marries her younger sister, Clara, and builds for her a mansion in the city, with formal gardens, colonnades, and marble statuary, *la casa de los espíritus,* more usually referred to simply as "the big house on the corner." It becomes the haunted setting for much of the subsequent action and supplies the novel with its title.

This is, then, the kind of novel in which strange things are going to happen; in which a girl with green hair may suddenly appear (there is more than one); in which one's mother's head may be kept for years in a hatbox in the cellar after her body has been duly interred—for no very good reason. . . . (pp. 531-32)

The House of the Spirits has no hero, but its central character is Esteban Trueba, whom we follow—intermittently, with interruptions for the various spin-off stories—for more than seventy of his ninety years. Since Esteban is the most purposeful character present, he is also the most intelligible. He is destined for defeat by his willfulness and bad disposition. The constants in his life are love and rage. If Esteban represents pure will, Clara, his wife, appears to be all sensibility. She is a more ambiguous and uncertain character.

Clara is the link with the spirit world. Having known the spirits since childhood, she takes them with her to the great house as a kind of dowry. They bring her messages from the time that is yet to be, or messages from the places where lost things lie. . . . Less trivially, the spirits are an extension of her own clear spirit, or what the author seems to regard as Clara's own clear spirit, her rich and loving femininity.

Nevertheless, for the present reader at least, there is also something a bit spooky and offputting about Clara. She is not entirely healthy and in her own fashion is as stubborn as her husband. Since childhood Clara has used her chronic asthma to have her way and she is given to long periods of silence, in one instance nine years. Esteban Trueba, whom she was scarcely forced to marry, is not a man she ever loves and, after they are married, becomes a man from whom she increasingly withdraws into the more congenial company of the spirits.

Everything in *The House of the Spirits* spins around the polar opposition of husband and wife, but it spins rather wildly. In a general way, the blighting effect upon the children, a daughter and twin younger sons, who are the offspring of such a mismatched couple is perfectly predictable, even without the aid of the spirits; yet even with their aid it might prove no easy matter to understand why the particular aberrations of this grotesque, although sympathetic, family had to be. The events of their story, or stories, are intriguing precisely where they arc surprising, seemingly random occurrences, and finally mysterious.

Moreover, it would probably take more than the spirits to establish any clear relation, other than a proclivity to violence, between the family fate of *los Trueba* and the national fate of their—and the author's—beloved country, never named, under the horrors of a military dictatorship of a previously insignificant general, also unnamed, but whose name few of us would have much difficulty in supplying.

Although the author tells us in an autobiographical note that she was born by chance in Lima, in 1942, Isabel Allende remains loyally Chilean. Her two novels were written in Venezuela, where, according to the flyleaf of *De amor y de sombra,* she went with her husband and two children into an exile "imposed by the overthrow of her uncle, President Salvador Allende." She has told also how she took with her into exile a little bag of earth from her garden in which to plant a forget-me-not, and adds: "During these years it has done nothing but grow and grow. Like my homesickness."

The House of the Spirits has likewise done very well; its sales have also grown and grown. (pp. 532-34)

[The novel's] successor, *De amor y de sombra*—less ambitious and also less in the fashionable mode of domesticated magic—is more to my taste, although I doubt that it will make nearly so big a splash. With one major exception things happen in this novel about the way they usually happen, which, when all is said, is strange enough.

The second novel is considerably shorter. It is carefully plotted and, instead of being diffused over seventy years, is focused on the events of one spring where two rather different things are happening concurrently. A young man and young woman are being drawn together in love as the year waxes, days grow warmer, and a forget-me-not begins to blossom, and the same young man and woman fall increasingly under the shadow of terrible events in a police state which, though again never named, is recognizably the Chile of General Pinochet. They are being drawn step by step nearer to exile and away from their strangely shaped and beautiful land (like a long petal, wrote Neruda) and its suffering people, whom they love more deeply as they are themselves uprooted. The events comprise a single unified action composed about equally of love and shadow, *amor y sombra,* or, more accurately, formed of the interplay of love and shadow. It is a more thoughtful book than its predecessor. As readers we are permitted to participate in the action vicariously, but also we are invited to meditate on it and try to reach some understanding.

It is not by chance that the title suggests from the start an essay: Of Love and of Shadow. It seems reasonable then to inquire what is being said in this novel about love and shadow, and about their relation.

Let me come at this matter somewhat indirectly. If one has recently been reading, or rereading, George Orwell's *Nineteen Eighty-Four,* one has learned from Orwell that love cannot survive the oppression of a police state. Such appears, however, not to be Isabel Allende's view at all. *De amor y de sombra* instead seems to be saying that love can survive even in the shadow of Big Brother steadily watching, can survive physical agony and the threat of death, and perhaps also that love needs the shadow to become most fully love. Lovers can meet and love deep in the shadow, can in time escape and live together in hope of return; moreover, they can help to bring about that day. Provided one thing: that they never forget for an instant either their love or the shadow. The unnamed General-President, speaking from his bunker headquarters, remarks to a worried subordinate that the people have short memories. It is the destiny of Allende's lovers to prove him wrong.

The nasty alternative would be to forget as quickly and often as possible, to submit to group amnesia and a frightened cover-up of the truth. Appropriately, the action begins in the Barrio Alto of what is the capital city in an ambiguous setting, the residence of the heroine's mother, which from the outside is a mansion only slightly less palatial than Senator Trueba's "big house on the corner." Inside, there are surprises. Above the ground floor all is elegance and decorum, but the ground floor of the mansion has been converted into a nursing home for the mostly neglected and nearly forgotten grandparents and great-aunts and granduncles of the sort of people who live in this sort of house, the threatened wealthy who choose to overlook and prefer to forget. (pp. 534-35)

By converting the ground floor, Beatriz Alcántara de Beltrán—who is not exactly a widow and not exactly not a widow—can keep up appearances and manage to live almost in the style to which she was accustomed before the disappearance of her aristocratic and, I fear, somewhat rascally husband, the heroine's father. Beatriz remains uncertain whether he is living or dead and equally uncertain whether her husband simply left her or whether he was "disappeared" by the secret police. She finds the latter explanation intolerable, since she has always accepted the military government's official version that no one has disappeared.

Beatriz lives on with her daughter, Irene, in an unstable amalgam of mansion and geriatric center kept well hidden from sight. She is herself of a certain age and is fighting off the inevitable sagging and wrinkles and flab. . . . So far Beatriz's program has worked beautifully in preserving her body but not so well in preserving her less and less flexible mind in its efforts to maintain a distance between the luxurious and protected upstairs and the dismaying world of the lower floor.

By the end of the novel, with the further disappearance of her daughter—the implications of which she is even more reluctant to face—Beatriz has shut herself off from reality almost as completely as have any of the house's pathetic inhabitants. Unwilling to understand, it is as if she were "afloat on a raft with her forgotten and decrepit ancients on an unmoving sea." By that time there is no significant difference between the two levels of her mansion.

Beatriz's daughter, Irene, is at the beginning still partly imprisoned in her mother's world. More than she may have yet come to recognize, she is imprisoned by her professional life as well. Irene is a good, and experienced, journalist committed to presenting the truth; yet she works for a fashion magazine that by its devotion to items of conspicuous display—furs, jewels, the newest fads—is almost professionally blind to poverty and violence under the dictatorship. Irene's own story is the story of how she will free herself from both home and profession with the increasingly loving help of Francisco Leal, a clinical psychologist who has been forced by circumstances to make his living as a fashion photographer. Francisco is a member of the underground and from the start knows at first hand the truth about his country that marble façades and fashion magazines do their best to hide.

Somewhere between truth and the advertisement of whatever is currently in style are human interest stories, which Irene's magazine regards as safe, and it is what begins as no more than a human interest story that sets the events of the novel in motion. . . . [Irene and Francisco] are to investigate a peasant girl who has acquired a reputation as a local saint because of the miraculous cures that she is said to bring about during a trance that she enters into—or perhaps a seizure that she suffers—each day at noon. We have been told that the parish priest regards her condition as pathological. Although most of the peasants believe, the padre is not alone in his skepticism. Some wise ones have hinted that what the fifteen-year-old Evangelina Ranquileo needs is a man, and perhaps, as it is suggested later, the only man she really wants is her brother. Whichever view is right, the wonders go on.

Less uncertain than the exact nature of Evangelina's condition are Isabel Allende's uses for the crucial scene that takes place in the house of the peasant family a few minutes after Irene and Francisco arrive. This scene elicits our special attention. It is the only place in the present novel where the realm of magic, the spirit world, intrudes upon the action. It accomplishes two things. It permits the author to involve her hero and heroine in events from which they can never afterwards extricate themselves; yet the scene does more in composing a symbolic anecdote of much inclusiveness and vividness. It is as though the pressures and repressions of her country were being reflected in this girl. Hidden forces are coming out through Evangelina, which when fully released might even shake a military dictatorship, forces of love and of life but also of sexual craving and violence. *Amor* and *sombra* meet in Evangelina's extraordinary seizure. Irene and Francisco, the journalist and fashion photographer who are as yet scarcely aware of their own love, are there to see it all. It is *not* a human interest story. . . . (pp. 536-37)

In the scene's blending of the uncanny and unexplained with the violently realistic it seems to me to come considerably closer to García Márquez than anything in the often merely capricious behavior of tipping tables and mobile salt cellars of *The House of the Spirits.* Something powerful (but is it something good or bad?) is taking place inside the girl, but also outside her. As the center of action in this novel, Evangelina has become the vortex of forces too long held in check, which seemingly nothing can withstand once they are released, not even the military, who at this juncture arrive unexpectedly to raid the Ranquileos' house. They get a good deal more than they bargain for when their leader, Lt. Juan de Dios Ramírez, tries to remove Evangelina forcibly from the bed and is instead knocked by her onto the floor, picked up by his tunic without the least effort, shaken like a mop, and deposited outside:

> Through the lens [of Francisco's camera, which she snatched from him,] Irene saw Evangelina tow the lieutenant toward the center of the patio. . . . The officer tried to get to his feet, but she administered a few accurate blows to the back of his neck and left him seated there, while giving him several kicks without anger and ignoring the guards who surrounded her, pointing their guns. . . . The girl snatched the machine-gun that Ramírez held clutched to his chest and threw it far away. It fell in the mud where it sank in front of the impassive snout of a pig, who sniffed at it before seeing it disappear swallowed up by the filth.

The symbolic anecdote, which is predominantly hopeful, ends there, while (as they say) the force is still with her. The other function of the strange happenings at the Ranquileos, as I have suggested, is to implicate Irene and Francisco so deeply in defiance of the government that they will be forced into flight and exile. When the trance is over, sadly, the soldiers return and Evangelina is carried off without putting up any resistance—later, as it turns out, to be raped and killed. All that her family knows for sure is that she has disappeared. But that is not quite her end. Evangelina is one of the very few disappeared who reappears. What was buried comes to the surface again with a vengeance, and Irene is the principal agent in bringing that about.

A feeling of identity has been growing between the journalist and this girl from a totally different background, the one still alive and the other now dead. A change has taken place. Irene has become now a determined woman with a quest, to find Evangelina or at least to find her body—which proves to be for her a dangerous and, indeed, very nearly fatal activity. She interviews one of the soldiers. She and Francisco visit the morgue. Other avenues are tried. Eventually a tip leads them to an abandoned mine in the hills—for this novel the heart, if not of darkness, then of shadow. On the mine's being opened, what is revealed is not only Evangelina's body but many others in various stages of decomposition, and when the mine at last gives up its dead, outrage spreads through the country. Irene's activities, however, have not gone unobserved by the alarmed authorities.

As events have brought the journalist and the fashion photographer deeper into danger and involvement—deeper into the shadow—their growing love for one another has emerged from what was before hardly more than a close sympathetic friendship. Their first kiss is exchanged in the shocked aftermath of their visit to the morgue. They make love for the first time, in an abandoned cabin, following the nighttime penetration of the mine, with its horrible stench and more horrible discovery. During the act Francisco, who appears to be an articulate lover, calls out to her (perhaps only in his mind), "Irene honey and shadow." A strange but appropriate yoking. Like Persephone, Irene belongs now to both: *amor* and *sombra* are one.

She must enter the shadow more deeply yet. Once the discoveries in the mine have been made public, the pace of the action picks up, as though everything were being hurried along by the forces that have been released. A few days afterward Irene is gunned down in the street. She is badly wounded but not killed. . . . When she is stronger, although under surveillance, the lovers make their escape from the hospital and from the city, and, following country roads and then a path through the woods, they cross the frontier into freedom and exile. But not into oblivion. Irene and Francisco are able to take little with them, but they take what they most need, their love and their memories of the good and the bad, of everything.

Isabel Allende has emphasized all along the cardinal importance of memory. Memory is the matrix where love and shadow meet. Probably among her characters the person who remembers best—not trivially like Borges's unforgettable and unforgetting Funes, but lovingly—is another peasant girl, Evangelina Flores, almost to the minute the same age as Evangelina Ranquileo and, in a rather complicated way, her foster sister. The girl's father and four brothers were among those who disappeared. Although they have now been dead for five years, when the mine gives up its secret she identifies each. . . . She has the love and the courage to remember. Also, before a military court, and without hesitation, Evangelina identifies Ramírez and each of his men who participated in the detention of her family. Consequently she too must seek refuge abroad.

As the novel closes, Irene and Francisco—perhaps reminiscent of Milton's Adam and Eve wandering through Eden—are left by the author moving "toward the invisible line that divided that immense chain of mountains and volcanoes. They felt themselves small, alone and vulnerable." But Irene is strengthened by a talisman: next to her breast, under her dress, she carries a little bag of earth from her garden, sent to her by a loyal friend, in which she is "to plant a forget-me-not on the other side of the sea."

On the basis of these two novels, what can be said now, more generally, about Isabel Allende as a novelist? I have already tried to suggest certain of what seem to me the strengths and weaknesses of *The House of the Spirits.* Her chief merit I take to be a certain amplitude of imagination, for Isabel Allende is not a petty writer. There is also more, both good and bad, about *De amor y de sombra* than I have yet had an opportunity to discuss.

One of the things that I find particularly admirable is the book's scope. Although the novel is relatively brief and the action focused on the events of only a single spring, a surprisingly large cast of characters makes its appearance, taken from different classes and conditions of life. Not only are we shown the peasant families Ranquileo and Flores and the aristocratic parents of Irene—her disappeared father apparently genuine and her mother on the whole nouveau riche—but the intellectual middle-class parents of Francisco Leal, themselves refugees from Franco's Spain, and Francisco's brother, José, who combines the roles of priest and plumber while working and living among the urban poor. We are shown also the Cardinal, effectively the leader of the resistance, at close range, and the General-President of the Republic from far off, as if in miniature, comically in scattered glimpses. Among the secondary characters there is a sensitive portrait of a fashionable homosexual hairdresser who began his life as the son of a miner and later became secretly a member of the resistance, without any loss of his hairdressing skills. Other well-drawn characters could with equal justice be singled out. Assuming the country, despite its anonymity, to be very like Chile, we feel we have come to know it well by the time we reach the final page.

These characters have not been distributed . . . in a random fashion. Instead, they all stand in some important relation to Irene and Francisco. In particular, we are shown, beside the principal pair of lovers, a wide variety of others into whose love the prevailing shadow has fallen. They include among them the married and the unmarried, the rich, the poor, and in one case the incestuous. Their love stories serve as a background for, and at the same time they intermingle with, the central story.

This bevy of lovers, however, points up what seems to me to be the principal weakness of *De amor y de sombra,* something not detectable in the first novel, a certain softness in the writing which is not everywhere apparent but is disturbing when it appears. When Isabel Allende moves in closely upon the act of love—and she seems to enjoy moving in very closely—she tends to lose her restraint and the prose becomes overcharged, to say the least. (pp. 538-41)

A friend of mine, a good novelist, asked: "Is there something new to be learned, do I *need* to read this book?" The answer, I think, is a qualified "no" for *De amor y de sombra,* as also for *The House of the Spirits.* Unlike certain novels of the [Latin American literary] Boom, *Pedro Páramo, Hopscotch, The Autumn of the Patriarch,* probably others, which enlarge or change our conception of what a novel might be, Isabel Allende has left the novel genre about where she found it. But I am not a novelist and I reflect that novels may also be regarded as weapons. Isabel Allende appears to me to have handled hers with skill to strike a blow for freedom and love against the tyranny that still grips her beautiful country. W. H. Auden once wrote that poems make nothing happen; but novels, less pure, perhaps may. Author and reader alike can live in that hope. (pp. 541-42)

Ambrose Gordon, "Isabel Allende on Love and Shadow," in Contemporary Literature, Vol. 28, No. 4, Winter, 1987, pp. 530-42.

PETER G. EARLE

The story began urgently, if unpretentiously, after a long-distance telephone call from Santiago de Chile to Caracas. Isabel Allende's grandfather, in his ninety-ninth year, was about to die. More precisely, he'd decided his time had come. Despite opposing ideologies, their family relationship had been close; and now, although from the remote region he was about to enter she couldn't expect a reply, she sat down to write him a long letter. Her purpose was to keep him living, in conformity with his own idea of immortality. "My grandfather theorized that death didn't really exist. Oblivion is what exists, and if one can remember those who die—remember them well—they'll always be with him and in some way will live on, at least in spirit.

"Living on" was a persistent tradition in Isabel Allende's family on her mother's side, and her late grandmother—the main model for Clara del Valle, "Clara la clarividente," in *The House of the Spirits*—had been practicing since premature death what Grandfather had always preached in life, with her periodic messages and visitations. The letter to

Grandfather got longer, and longer. A year later (1982) it had grown to five-hundred pages. It was a diary in retrospect, a family chronicle, an autobiography, a political testimony, a group portrait and contemporary history, a series of experiments with magic. In other words, a novel. Allende was a journalist in search of a complementary medium. Aesthetically, she would now participate in the basic ritual of Latin American literature: a celebration of reality. Ethically, she wanted to bear witness to social injustice, political violence, and repression—having been motivated by the betrayal and murder by right-wing conspirators of an uncle on her father's side, President Salvador Allende.

The Latin American celebration of reality in all literary forms encompasses a wide range of motifs. In addition to many overt and covert forms of aggression, one finds oases of lyricism, intense paternal, maternal, filial, marital, and extramarital relationships, bizarre ironies . . . , festivals of the senses, authoritarian and religious constrictions, supernatural events (inherited and shared as well as invented), and ghostly apparitions. . . . García Márquez has testified more than once that virtually all his magical elements are drawn from everyday Colombian or Latin American reality, from characters and happenings that were always verisimilar enough for someone not only to have believed but to have talked about and elaborated on beforehand. Isabel Allende herself recently said that "reality is always richer than anything one can dream."

Richer, and just as turbulent. It invites storytelling and sharpens historical awareness, for history is something that needs constantly to be deciphered through literature— probably its best instrument. . . . [Books] have undeniably been a steadier and more reliable source of disclosure in Latin America than radio, television, or the press. [In **"Writing in Latin America,"** a lecture delivered at the University of the District of Columbia in Washington, D.C.], Isabel Allende has reminded us, not without irony, of the tyrannical Pinochet regime's uncharacteristic leniency toward literature over the last two or three years:

> A poet friend of mine says that since the military doesn't read, it hasn't realized that books can be dangerous. So, in Chile, while they censor press notices of the fall of Marcos and Baby Doc, they still sell in bookstores works like *Missing* or *Labyrinth,* or the books of Antonio Skármeta, Ariel Dorfman, and many others who have written on the tragedy of Chile in recent years.

But of course books *are* dangerous. Even if, in Chile's current economy, one like **The House of the Spirits** sells for the equivalent of a month's salary at the minimum wage, they do get read. They circulate on loan and in photocopies or mimeograph; they're discussed in informal seminars; they help stimulate clandestine opposition and preserve the historical memory.

In what circumstances was the novel under consideration written? In the 1986 lecture quoted above, Allende stressed the importance of the "moment of history the writer is born into," especially in Latin America, a world of great "struggles and defeats, brutality and magic." Increasingly aware of the New World's five-hundred-year tradition of violence, she matured intellectually with her uncle's socialist movement and became a novelist at her reactionary grandfather's death. Thus, her book is the celebration of a momentous social struggle in which those two figures were principals. Only fic-

titious names are used in the story, for places as well as for people, but the implications are obvious: this was to be a composite testimony of many voices (like *One Hundred Years of Solitude,* with which superficial comparisons have often been made), written with a recent exile's sense of urgency, and a family member's intimacy. The political dispersion of the family she tells about is microcosmic, for contemporary Chilean history is also one of dispersion, beginning the day after Salvador Allende's election in 1970 with a complex opposition program that included technical and financial assistance from our Central Intelligence Agency and State Department and accelerating after September 11, 1973, when military forces led by General Pinochet carried out their *coup d'état.*

Soon after Allende's election, Secretary of State Henry Kissinger declared at a National Security Council meeting, "I don't see why we have to stand by and watch a country go communist due to the irresponsibility of its own people." In **The House of the Spirits** President Allende's niece has her principal male character say of the impoverished tenant farmers at Tres Marías, his country estate, "They're like children, they can't handle responsibility." A closer and more impetuous father-figure than the always distant Kissinger, Esteban Trueba was also unwilling to stand by and watch. In his paternalized utopia no one would go hungry, everyone would do his assigned work, and all would learn reading and writing and simple arithmetic—that is, enough to follow simple instructions and read signs, to write brief messages, and to count, *y nada más,* "for fear they would fill their minds with ideas unsuited to their station and condition." (pp. 543-46)

But behind [Esteban's] organizational rigor was an unbridled temperament, and deep sentimental frustrations. His fiancée, Rosa del Valle of memorable beauty, dies in the first chapter, which is narrated—like several other sections of the story— in first person singular by Esteban Trueba himself. Rosa's death is caused by brandy laced with rat poison from a decanter sent as an anonymous "gift" to her father, a prominent member of the Liberal Party. The extraordinary Rosa had bright green hair and the aura of "a distracted angel." Ensconced in the white satin of her coffin, she impressed her grieving fiancé as having been "subtly transformed into the mermaid she had always been in secret." Her autopsy and preparation for viewing are secretly witnessed by her little sister Clara in a semitraumatic state, immediately after which Clara enters a nine-year period of unbroken silence. Her first words will be to announce, in one of the many psychic predictions over her lifetime, that she'll soon be married.

In chapter 2 we are told that not only did Clara, *la clarividente,* foresee her marriage but also the identity of her husband-to-be: Rosa's fiancé [Esteban Trueba], whom she hadn't seen since her sister's funeral and who was fifteen years her senior. Two months later, to be sure, Esteban visits the del Valle residence and immediately formalizes their engagement.

The family was to grow in its strange diversity through three generations, but Clara and Esteban would always constitute its vital, antithetical nucleus. The latter embodies privileged power; the former, humanitarian resistance. History, for Trueba, was paternity and—whenever the situation called for it—aggression. One of his first rituals in organizing Tres Marías as a community was to start populating it, ranging through the wheatfields on horseback in pursuit of the peasant girls, raping and impregnating more than a few. Schopenhauer would have found in him a striking case of "the passage of will into visibility," will—that is—unenlightened by knowledge; impelled, rather, by an atavistic urge for self-assertion. History was procreation, and the father's subsequent attempts to deal with the results of procreation. The most troublesome outcome of his sexual escapades in the environs of Tres Marías was Esteban García, his natural grandson born of an offspring of Pancha García, his first wheatfield victim. After a childhood of deprivation and growing resentment, the grandson has nothing but the grandfather's first name for an inheritance. Since childhood he had wanted to become a policeman. And he became one.

During the ugly reprisals taken by the military government in the aftermath of the President's death (in a series of obvious allusions to the Pinochet regime's repressions starting in September, 1973), García reappears, having risen to the rank of lieutenant colonel in the political police. It is he who presides over the interrogation, confinement, and prolonged torture of his privileged cousin Alba, a university student who has been active in the socialist underground and Esteban Trueba's only recognized grandchild. Alba undergoes her torture partly in trauma, partly in an unconscious state. In the process she's raped an undisclosed number of times, and in the Epilogue we're told that one of the culprits is Colonel García. Third in a lineage of strong-willed women, Alba is the human instrument through which Esteban Trueba is made to pay psychologically for a lifetime of large- and small-scale transgressions. [In a symposium at Haverford College on February 28, 1987, Professor Gabriela Mora in "A Political Reading of Isabel Allende's Novels" contends that in allowing Trueba to die peacefully in his granddaughter's arms, Allende had weakened the moral foundation of her book. In my view the old man still pays a heavy personal price for his myopia and his crimes. But more importantly, the average reader gains from his crude performance throughout the story a better perception of how the authoritarian mentality accommodates criminal methods in its procedures.] That is, instead of retaliating in a direct, physical way against the aged patriarch, Trueba's bastard grandson chooses to punish him through his "legitimate" counterpart: revenge against the privileged by the underprivileged, against the upper-class child of affluence by the peasant-child of want.

The principal antecedent to this reprisal comes in chapter 6. Trueba is then informed by Jean de Satigny, his daughter Blanca's effete and dandified suitor, that Blanca is having nighttime trysts. The secret lover, it turns out, is her childhood playmate at Tres Marías, Pedro Tercero García. . . . About three weeks later [Trueba's illegitimate grandson] Esteban García—then a boy of twelve—presents himself and offers to lead his grandfather to Pedro Tercero's hiding place in the woods. Agreeing to pay a reward, Trueba sets out with a pistol. Surprised in bed, the intended victim is still able to leap out, to dodge the only shot Trueba gets to fire and, a second later, to disarm his assailant by hurling a piece of firewood at him. Whereupon Trueba seizes an ax and swings— and Pedro Tercero, in a reflex-attempt at self-defense, loses three fingers from his right hand. Shock and loss of blood notwithstanding, he rushes from the cabin and escapes in the dark. Adding literal insult to literal injury, Trueba then refuses to pay the boy his promised reward, slaps him, and snarls, "There's no reward for [double-crossers]!"

No reward *then*. But ultimately Esteban García was to obtain one of sorts. Years later, at the very moment Senator Trueba of the Conservative Party was celebrating with champagne the Socialist president's overthrow, "his son Jaime's testicles were being burned with an imported cigarette." After refusing to accept his captors' offer of freedom in return for saying on television that the late president in a drunken state had committed suicide, Jaime is beaten a second time, left with hands and feed bound with barbed wire for two days and nights, then shot together with several other prisoners in a vacant lot. . . . Two weeks later the Senator is told the circumstances of his son's death, but he refuses to believe the eyewitness account. Only when Jaime appears months later as a ghost, "covered with dried blood and rags, dragging streamers of barbed wire across the waxed parquet floors," does he realize that he had heard the truth. It is in this penultimate chapter that he concludes he had been wrong and that, after all, "the best way to overthrow Marxism" had not been found. (pp. 546-49)

The Brazilian critic Antonio Callado remarked in 1974 that contemporary Latin America was "full of new ruins" (e.g., democracy in Uruguay and Chile, the Revolution in Mexico), that Latin Americans have displayed a peculiar resistance to "becoming historical," because they're "always trying to start again" amidst a detritus of infringed constitutions and derelict or disabled governments. The attempted starting-again, we could add, is more often ultraconservative or reactionary than revolutionary, and more motivated by frustration than by hope.

But against this antihistorical resistance, of which the cantankerous Esteban Trueba is a representative figure, another, more imaginative, more perceptive resistance arrays itself. In *The House of the Spirits* Clara, Blanca, and Alba are its persistent mainstays over three generations. Light is freedom and hope, and the luminous names of the three women are clearly symbolic. The dramatic nucleus of the book is the struggle between Trueba and the forces he generates, on the one hand, and the female members of his family, on the other. He is the blind force of history, its collective unconscious, its somatotonic (i.e., aggressive, vigorous, physical) manifestation. They embody historical awareness and intuitive understanding. Trueba is a semicomic version of the "world historical personalities" conceived of by Hegel; never happy, "they attained no calm enjoyment; their whole life was labor and trouble; their whole nature was nothing but their master passion." But unlike the three illustrious examples offered by Hegel—Alexander the Great died young, Julius Caesar was murdered, Napoleon Bonaparte ended up in humbling exile—Esteban Trueba lives through the problems and outrages he helps create. . . . [He] is not permitted to recognize—or forced to acknowledge—the consequences of his acts until he's close to death. His author, it seems, decided to put off his death until he could be made to witness the full historical effect of his own retrogressive ideas and actions, and of his collaboration and conspiracy with like-minded people. Until that time of punitive recognition he is subjected, as are two similarly Dionysian protagonists—García Márquez's Patriarch and [Juan] Rulfo's Pedro Páramo—to recurrent experiences of loneliness and frustration. His estrangement from his family (although he ends his isolation at Tres Marías and joins them in "the big house on the corner") leads him, halfway through the novel, to venture into politics as a Conservative Party candidate for the Senate, "since no one better personified the honest, uncontaminated politician, as he himself declared."

Symbolically in that same chapter, having won election as Senator, he becomes convinced that his body and brain are shrinking and travels to the United States for diagnosis. Symbolically in that chapter his two sons manifest themselves as ideologically incompatible with him and with each other: Jaime is socially and socialistically committed; Nicolás, the childlike seducer, equates the highest good with pleasure. . . . And, symbolically, in that chapter Alba is born (feet first, we're later told), harbinger of a new era.

Clara "la clarividente" died when Esteban was seventy, with twenty-nine years still to go, and when Alba was seven. Did the seven and its multiple of ten portend survival and good fortune for the old man and his granddaughter? Clara, Blanca, and Alba, I've already observed, embody historical awareness and intuitive understanding. Their role throughout the novel is the preservation of moral and social conscience and civic responsibility. Clara departs this life at a relatively young age, but she'll often return as a spirit to the halls and bedrooms of "the big house on the corner," and in chapter 14, to Alba's tomblike prison cell. . . . Clara succeeds in convincing her granddaughter that "the point was not to die, . . . but to survive." Further, she strengthens Alba's will to live by urging her to write. . . . Her reason is that, given the ways in which the *inside* world works (through torture, deceit, abuse, betrayal, and cowardly concealment), no one has a right to ignorance or forgetfulness, and the true heart of literature is neither pleasure nor knowledge, but survival. The paragraph in which Allende describes how Alba tries to reconstruct what has happened to her could easily be adapted to an essay or textbook on the function of memory within the creative process:

> Alba tried to obey her grandmother, but as soon as she began to take notes with her mind, the dog-house [i.e., her undersized, dark prison cell] filled with all the characters of her story, who rushed in, shoved each other out of the way to wrap her in their anecdotes, their vices, and their virtues, trampled on her intention to compose a documentary, and threw her testimony to the floor, pressing, insisting, and egging her on. She took down their words at breakneck pace, despairing because while she was filling a page, the one before it was erased. This activity kept her fully occupied. At first, she constantly lost her train of thought and forgot new facts as fast as she remembered them. The slightest distraction or additional fear or pain caused her story to snarl like a ball of yarn. But she invented a code for recalling things in order, and then she was able to bury herself so deeply in her story that she stopped eating, scratching herself, smelling herself, and complaining, and overcame all her varied agonies.

Of course, after Alba is set free . . . she tells us in the first-person singular Epilogue that her grandfather was the one "who had the idea that we should write this story." He also helped write it, with a memory that was intact "down to the last second of his ninety years." More basic still is the contribution of Grandmother Clara, who had superior psychic powers but a poor memory; but even before becoming deliberately mute at the age of ten she had begun to write copiously in her notebooks about everything that happened in her eccentric family. It is only after finishing the book and then returning to the first page that we can identify with certainty the "I" in the phrase, "never suspecting that fifty years later I would use her notebooks to reclaim the past and overcome terrors of my own." Clara's notebooks—arranged not chronologically but according to the importance of events—are mentioned on the last page in the same context as they were on the first. "Clara wrote them so they would help me now to reclaim the past and overcome terrors of my own."

Clara the Clairvoyant was, then, the creative spirit who at the same time that she bore witness to history was able on occasion to alter it and even to perceive its predetermined elements (for the same reason she frequently foresaw what was going to happen). If observation of what occurs, changing the course of what occurs, and understanding what must occur are the three most important attributes of the narrative writer, then Clara fully and dynamically symbolizes the narrative writer. Although she kept forgetting things—menial everyday details—she forced her memory to work through writing (the Notebooks). Although Esteban Trueba pampered her and regaled her with luxuries including a canopy bed with gauze curtains "that looked like a sailboat on a sea of silken blue water," she had a keen social conscience and on her first stay at Tres Marías immediately sensed the workers' "resentment, fear and distrust" upon which Colonel García as a boy was nurtured. Although with distracted sweetness she "lived in a universe of her own invention," she simultaneously endured the abuses of society and her husband. . . . (pp. 549-52)

Only a writer endowed with a comparably wide range of secret powers is likely to exercise effectively the art of survival in the twentieth century. By the art or literature of survival I mean the ultimate power of testimony through the creative use of memory. That is, creative memory enables testimony to transcend obstacles, ignorance, and repression. It has often been suggested that *The House of the Spirits* coincides too much with the genealogical, magical, and procreative motifs of *One Hundred Years of Solitude,* as well as with the latter work's uses of memory and oblivion. But a succinct commentary by Roger Shattuck [*The Innocent Eye: On Modern Literature and the Arts*] on García Márquez's novel can help us see the difference between it and Allende's work: "the metaphysical picaresque" has become a genre as well as an attitude:

> They're all saying the same thing. It goes on and on. Having assimilated Borges and Robbe-Grillet and God knows who else, Gabriel García Márquez created the masterpiece in the genre. In *One Hundred Years of Solitude* everything begins in reality and ends in fantasy. You can watch it happen. The natural gives birth to the supernatural, the surreal—with no detectable shift in style or tone. Believe or disbelieve the events at your own risk. It's like an unstoppable roller coaster—but we're not supposed to get dizzy! . . .

> Each one of these works of the metaphysical picaresque devises its own particular enactment of *Don Quixote*—but with one major difference: Sancho Panza has been eliminated—gagged or kidnapped or killed outright. Without his voice of sanity and reality, all modes of existence can claim equal status. And they do—*without distinction.* We seem to want that. *One Hundred Years of Solitude* pleases everyone just by the way it keeps overflowing the pot and outdistancing reality. The more a work makes us lose our orientation, our sense of constraints, the more we praise it. The metaphysical picaresque.

"The unstoppable roller coaster," the hurricane, geography that fades into mirage, irretrievable dispersion. In *The House of the Spirits* magic and the flights of fancy are the instrumental privilege of a select few: the "extraordinary women" to whom Isabel Allende dedicates her novel. Amidst the abuse and the madness that surround them, orientation is not lost. When Alba is finally released one night on a garbage-strewn vacant lot, she is granted provisional freedom, a possibility of putting things together again if only in writing. . . . [She] is determined "to break that terrible chain" that hatred has so relentlessly fashioned. She finds her basic hope in Grandmother Clara's insightful Notebooks, and in the pages she herself is engaged in writing. (pp. 553-54)

Peter G. Earle, "Literature as Survival: Allende's 'The House of the Spirits'," in Contemporary Literature, Vol. 28, No. 4, Winter, 1987, pp. 543-54.

MARIA INES LAGOS-POPE

De amor y de sombra, Isabel Allende's second novel, is introduced by the following statement:

> This is the story of a woman and a man who loved each other fully, thus saving themselves from a common existence. I have carried the story in my memory, taking care that time not wear it away and it is only now, in the quiet nights of this place, that I can finally tell it. I will do this for them and for others who entrusted me with their lives saying: take this, write it down so that the wind won't erase it.

Although at first this statement seems trivial, it contains affirmations that need to be highlighted and can serve as a guide for reading the text. First, we notice that the traditional order has been altered, when the author writes that this is the story of "a woman and a man," and not of a man and a woman, which would be the conventional form. Secondly, the writer lets it be seen that, in some way, her text constitutes a transgression, since only now can she tell it. Lastly, her text is a testimony that inscribes the story of a period in her country's history.

As in her earlier novel, *La casa de los espíritus* [*The House of the Spirits*], the external referent for this work of fiction is the recent history of Chile, although this fact is not made explicit through the use of place names or by calling the General by his real name. While *The House of the Spirits* referred to the 1973 *coup d'état* and the months that followed through the story of a family, *De amor y de sombra* alludes to the methods used by the military junta to stay in power. It points out the ways in which the repressive apparatus works and the way in which this machine affects the lives of the people.

Keeping in mind these three aspects, we can relate the novel to two groups of writings. It can be placed with other narratives by women who have also written about the effects of political conflict and revolution or with those narratives that find their roots in the recent history of the Southern Cone nations with their dictatorships, terror and persecution.

In general, and for obvious reasons, this second group of works has been written in exile. . . . [Some] refer to the process that lead to the fall of the democratic government of Salvador Allende. Others describe the climate of terror and the methods used by the military governments to maintain the population in submission and force the opposition into exile. (pp. 207-08)

De amor y de sombra takes as its point of departure the story of the friendship that develops between Irene Beltrán, a young journalist, and Francisco Leal, the son of Spanish refugees, a psychologist by profession. They discover the bodies of missing persons in an abandoned mine.

The emphasis on female characters and the fact that the novel centers on the love between Irene and Francisco ties it to the writings of women authors who have treated the theme of politics from the point of view of a female character. But since the story's perspective is not exclusively female but includes a varied spectrum of characters, we can say that in this novel two different trends converge. We see both the literature of exile and the way in which women writers have approached the theme of politics from a female perspective. The idea of women authors writing about politics is neither recent nor exceptional in the Latin American literary panorama. . . . [The] relationship between literature and the socio-political context, a constant feature in Latin American literature since its origins, is also present in the works of women.

Still, it is necessary to point out that, in general, women view the theme of politics through a very different lens. This can be seen in Isabel Allende's novel as well. . . . [As in previous works by female Latin American authors], the action does not center on political activity. Instead, a political context, left practically without direct description, affects the private life, family life and personal relationships of the protagonists.

It is through the family histories, the impact that the political context has upon the families and the responsibility it has in their disintegration, that the socio-political conflicts are suggested. Although in *De amor y de sombra* reference is made to the important figures of the Church and government, these characters appear on a symbolic level: The Cardinal, the General, the Colonel. Irene becomes politically active and challenges the regime not as a result of ideological understanding but through human contact, because she witnesses the misfortune and misery of her peers and because she sees the brutality used to carry out the repressive policies of the regime. Francisco's situation is very different. He comes from an exiled family of Spanish Republicans in which politics have always been important.

The relevance that the other female characters take on and the solidarity that exists among the women bring out the non-ideological nature of the women's participation in social conflicts. The experiences of characters from a rural environment, Digna Ranquileo and Evangelina Flores, serve to illustrate this point.

Fifteen years earlier, Digna Ranquileo had had a traumatic experience upon facing the irrationality of the authorities in the hospital where her daughter, Evangelina, was born. Immediately after Evangelina's birth they switched her with another baby and, although Digna and the other mother reported the switch, the authorities refused to recognize the mistake and each of the infants grew up with the wrong family. The mother, who had never had much confidence in official organizations, becomes even more skeptical. Evangelina Flores, for her part, when she discovers that among the bodies buried in the mine are those of her brothers and her father, turns into a crusader, who travels the world publicizing the atrocities committed by the authorities.

The profusion of female characters, Digna Ranquileo and her daughter, Evangelina, Evangelina Flores, the elderly actress, Josefina Bianchi, Hilda, Francisco's mother, Rosa, Irene's nanny and Beatriz Alcántara, Irene's mother, and the close relationships among the characters become crucial elements in the development of the fictional world. They bring out the experiences and reactions of the intimate and family setting. It is the strength and bravery of the women, who, in the absence of men, maintain the family and face the authorities, that stand out in this novel. (pp. 208-10)

The absence of the father figure contributes to the telling of the story based on the experiences of the women. For example, Irene's father has abandoned her mother. [Digna's husband] Hipólito Ranquileo works as a clown and is only home during the winter. The Flores brothers and their father are taken prisoner shortly after the *coup* because of their participation in the union and, for this reason, do not participate in the events of the novel. Irene's fiancée, Captain Gustavo Morante, is continually absent, out in the provinces or at the South Pole. (p. 210)

The men are represented by Francisco and his father, Lieutenant Ramírez and Sargent Rivera, and by other secondary characters, such as Captain Morante, Mario the stylist and Francisco's brother, who is a priest. Francisco's father is almost a stereotypical anarchist. Francisco and his brother the priest work for the resistance and help the government's victims. Sargent Rivera is more loyal to his own people than to the police and Mario is a homosexual, also of the opposition, who helps the young lovers in their escape. None of them correspond to the traditional *macho* who supports the methods of the government. (pp. 210-11)

The only hateful male figure is that of Lieutenant Ramírez, who takes revenge on Evangelina, more for pride than for ideological reasons. This is because she had embarassed him by knocking him out in front of his subordinates and the neighbors who had gathered to witness the young girl's seizure.

Among the female characters, the only one who does not rebel against the government's policies is Beatriz Alcántara, who refuses to recognize the intervention of the official powers in her husband's disappearance or in the attempt on her daughter's life. Beatriz Alcántara is a woman who tried to solidify her social position by marrying a man of good status. To her, the most important thing is to feign a happy, blissful existence. She sees her husband's disappearance as a trauma she manages to hide.

Beatriz does not want to see anything negative or anything that does not suit her vision of life and so, she erases it all. In spite of the fact that her house was broken into twice by the police, once after her husband's disappearance and once after the attempt on Irene's life, she wants to believe that everything is a mistake and is completely unrelated to the activities of her husband and daughter. In spite of this, it is difficult to condemn Beatriz, since, on the other hand, she has been abandoned and is a woman of superficial values who is also a victim of the traditional ideology that confines women to the world of the home.

It is evident that in these characterizations we are in the presence of an understanding and reconciliatory spirit, but at the same time this makes the novel lose strength and appear bland and romantic. The creation of a male character like Francisco Leal can be seen as a success in the novel since he is a new type of male hero. He is not the typical *macho,* but quite the contrary, a man who does not impose his views, patient, capable of tenderness and affection, which allows his relationship with Irene to be without hierarchies. On the other hand, the absence of a strong male figure to represent the traditional man who embodies unmistakeably the military regime and who, in fact, does exist historically, lessens the tension of the novel. Let us remember that even Captain Gustavo Morante, upon hearing the story of the Los Riscos mine from Irene's new boyfriend, rejects the Army's methods. This uniformly flattering picture of the male characters sharply disagrees with what historians and sociologists have observed.

In the late 1960's and the early 1970's, in studies done in Chile representing the opinions of both sexes and various social classes, it was found that men considered themselves superior to women and that women also thought themselves to be inferior. Those surveyed felt women should obey their husbands and dedicate themselves to making a home. They believed women were not capable of being in power. In addition, sociologists observed that men's fear of women working was a widespread phenomenon because women might surpass them, deceive them or lose respect for them. (pp. 211-12)

If we keep in mind this obsession for power on the part of men and relate *machismo* to the abuse of power, it becomes artificial to eliminate the other side of the coin in a society that, either tacitly or voluntarily, makes dictatorship possible. (p. 212)

In addition to these nearly ideal male characters, there is the fact that Irene herself has experienced a transformation. From being a generous and compassionate young woman still on the fringes of political activity, she joins the fight against the powers that victimize her people, thus giving the novel an overly romantic tone. Through her work as a journalist, Irene discovers both the oppressive reality in which the poor of her country live and Francisco's friendship, which later turns to love.

Irene's character is attractive since, in spite of having been educated in a pampered and privileged way, she is able to join with others and fight for her ideals. Her tenaciousness and strength are what lead her and Francisco to the abandoned mine and to search out the truth about Evangelina Ranquileo's disappearance. It is also important that this woman is able to act and make decisions about her own life. Irene goes against the wishes of her mother, who thinks that journalism is a profession for the lower classes. She also rejects her fiancée, an Army captain with whom she had been in love since childhood, when she realizes she is in love with Francisco and that both share the same ideals.

Other female characters, such as Digna Ranquileo and Evangelina Flores, demonstrate similar courage in the face of misfortune and even death. As I have suggested, the inversion of the traditional order in the author's foreword when she points out that the novel is the story of a woman and a man, is not accidental. Through her narrative style, Isabel Allende shows how women and their families have suffered the repression of the military junta. What brings this novel close to other novels by women, in which political conflict is presented from the perspective of a female character, is that it does not discuss political ideas or union struggles. Instead, it is through the effect that the dictatorial powers have on the people that the reader is moved to reject the dictatorship. (pp. 212-13)

[*De amor y de sombra*] goes beyond other narratives by contemporary women writers in terms of the active and decided incorporation of the woman in the work force and in the fight against dictatorship. The protagonist, Irene Beltrán, acts on her own convictions. Her relationship with Francisco is without hierarchies or submission; it is open and trusting. But since this novel does not concentrate on the female perspective but rather attempts to present a varied social panorama which portrays different classes and types of people, the emphasis on the absence of a strong male figure is forced and artificial. It is sometimes necessary, however, because of the plot, as in the case of the Flores family whose men perish at the hands of the police.

Although the novel takes place in Chile, where there are murderers and not only victims, these historical details are only suggested. The rest of the population is made up of friendly and mature people who, when they become aware of injustices, do not hesitate to join with the victims of the oppression. Even though this conciliatory tone may be appealing and desirable, to eliminate any trace of malice in such a vast social spectrum and not to show the conflict either on the level of the narrative or of the characters, makes the novel lose interest. It presents a partial and idealized vision of a problematic and highly polarized situation. (p. 213)

> *Maria Ines Lagos-Pope, in a review of "De amor y de sombra [Of Love and Shadow]," in Latin American Literary Review, Vol. XV, No. 29, January-June, 1987, pp. 207-13.*

SARA MAITLAND

I enormously admired Isabel Allende's first novel, *The House of the Spirits,* which seemed to me to take South American 'magic realism' a step further in the direction that I have always felt it could go—to a fictional technique which can carry universal meaning within its own specific location of character and place. This would solve, or move towards solving, a problem in contemporary fiction about how one can address enormous and fairly abstract themes around culture and politics without abandoning the emotional and imaginative territory which is the novel's home base.

So I fell with delighted anticipation on *Of Love and Shadows,* ready and eager to be pleased, and, at first, I was not disappointed. On the contrary, somewhere about the beginning of the second of the three sections I felt that painful jealousy I feel when someone is doing better than I could what I should like to have done myself. Located more strictly in the socially real than *The House of the Spirits,* this second novel has recognisable women and men—journalists, peasants, soldiers, anti-fascist emigrés—with real political positions, thoughts and backgrounds in contemporary settings. But they are still awash with the marvellous; the skin between fantasy and social realism is stretched to its thinnest and most translucent.

Surrounded by magazine deadlines, epileptic mystics, magical senility, decadence and courage, the heroine Irene Beltran moves from bourgeois liberalism to radical commitment through her willing engagement with events and individuals. It is her love for Francisco Leal, a young, radical photographer, which tips the balance, but she is never a stereotypical

camp follower because it is her very capacity to love . . . which is the real source of her radicalisation.

Through the first two sections the novel is almost all it should be: rich without being lush; over-written in the good sense; massive in scale without losing detail. The harsh reality of the Chilean political situation—mass graves, 'disappearances', military interventions leading to chaos, religious confusion, inaccessible leadership—is balanced by the powerful generosity of the land itself; a land not only lovely, but fierce and strange as well. The characters have lives of significance.

And, quite suddenly, the whole thing collapses: the final section of the book is clumsily written, sentimental and pedantic. Irene and Francisco, caught up in events beyond their control, act with exemplary courage and virtue: they exert wit and wisdom to bring to public attention a brutal military mass killing; they are identified and forced to flee their beloved country; with the help of deep, radical networks they escape; they vow on the cold mountain frontier to remember and to return. But it does not work. . . . [I suspect] that the fault is a fault of love: in her dedication to the novel, Allende acknowledges that *Of Love and Shadows* is a true story 'of a woman and a man who loved one another so deeply that they saved themselves from a banal existence'. Her debt to them, and perhaps also her obligation to the resistance movement in Chile to get across the Political Message, seem to weigh down her imagination—as though she has to withdraw her powerful individuality in their humble service. It is a touching and uplifting story—it is indeed the stuff of Girls' Own fiction gone left-wing—but in her subservience to it she has not done the person involved, or herself, or the reader much of a favour.

And yet it is an enormously courageous book; even at the formal level, it pushes out the limits of where such fabulous fictions might go. It creates the hope that it might be possible to write a really great novel bringing together so many passionate themes, such diverse ways of writing.

> *Sara Maitland, "Courage and Convictions," in New Statesman, Vol. 114, No. 2937, July 10, 1987, p. 27.*

GENE H. BELL-VILLADA

Few literary legends can compare to that surrounding *The House of the Spirits,* Isabel Allende's family-chronicle-cum-history of her native Chile. Her very first novel, published when she was in her early 40's, rose to best-sellerdom. Reviewers were indulgent. . . . The troublesome secret was that in prose and format the book was mostly imitation García Márquez.

Happily, Ms. Allende is no longer the novice in *Of Love and Shadows,* a suspenseful thriller. Set in the terrorized Chile of Gen. Augusto Pinochet (himself an occasional character), it tells of the love that grows between Irene Beltrán—feisty, innocent, marginally upper-class and a reporter for a women's magazine—and [photographer] Francisco Leal. . . . Together they cover a variety of beats, but something clicks when they start investigating Evangelina, a 15-year-old peasant girl and fabled miracle worker. During a brutal army search of her family's house, Evangelina, in a trance, single-handedly lifts up a cruel lieutenant and hurls him out the door. . . .

Soon thereafter Evangelina "disappears"; through journalistic tips and footwork the hero and heroine locate the girl's corpse in an abandoned mine shaft, where bodies of dozens of the regime's opponents are also decaying. Francisco takes photos; word spreads; a scandal ensues. Then someone sprays Irene with bullets from a passing car. She survives in the hospital but is obviously marked for Government liquidation. With help from friends she and Francisco assume disguises, quietly flee Santiago and cross the Andes into Argentina, ready to fight the dictatorship from exile. "We will return," they say.

Love and struggle à la *Casablanca*—it's all there. Ms. Allende skillfully evokes both the terrors of daily life under military rule and the subtler forms of resistance in the hidden corners and "shadows" of her title, particularly in the churches or in simple unsung acts of solidarity. At the same time the author ably captures the voices of the regime's apologists— the complex lies and clichés of its proud male foot soldiers and the pat false phrases of its rich lady cheerleaders. A journalist herself, Ms. Allende renders with expert detail such offbeat worlds as the professional routines of a hairdresser, the range of types in a private nursing home or the operations of the Santiago city morgue. While her prose at times verges on soap opera, that is also one of its charms. She can just as deftly depict loving tenderness as convey the high fire of eroticism. And when you've successfully mingled sex and politics with a noble cause, how can you go wrong? . . .

[On] the whole it's a supple piece of work.

Gene H. Bell-Villada, "Eros Makes War," in The New York Times Book Review, *July 12, 1987, p. 23.*

SONIA GERNES

"The ones they take away never come back," the peasant woman says, telling Irene Beltrán of her missing daughter, and it is these missing ones, the political victims, the *desaparecidos* of a Latin American dictatorship, that form the underlying link in [*Of Love and Shadows*], Isabel Allende's tale of lovers who come together in a dangerous and vertiginous search for the truth of these vanishings.

Allende, niece of the slain Chilean president Salvador Allende, never names the country of her fiction, but her novel, based on the actual discovery of a cache of bodies in an abandoned mine, is clearly about her native land: a general in dark glasses rules following a military coup; the stadium of the capital city is used as a political prison; and bodies bearing the marks of torture are stacked up in the city morgue.

These horrors come later in the novel however. It begins slowly, introducing us first to the genteel, upper-class world of Irene. . . . In the slightly comic, slightly surreal mode that characterizes much of the early novel, Allende describes the Will of God Manor, a home for the wealthy, aged, and senile that [Irene's mother] Beatriz unwillingly maintains in the lower floor of her mansion to support herself following her husband's desertion. Allende uses these old people to telegraph immediately Irene's essential character: though flashy and headstrong, she "never missed an opportunity to visit the guests," having "discovered a language that overcame their deafness and faulty memories."

By contrast, the world of Francisco Leal is shabby but intellectually alive. The son of Spanish revolutionary émigrés,

Francisco is a psychologist who turns to photography to make a living after the military coup makes practicing his profession impossible. (pp. 460-61)

Shabbier even than the Leal home is the dirt-floored cottage of Digna Ranquileo, the peasant woman whose daughter Evangelina is attracting pious crowds with her daily noonday "attacks." . . .

Into this scene ride journalist Irene and photographer Francisco, sent by their magazine to cover the story. The miracle begins precisely at noon, and even the arrival of an army truck does not break the mood of comic fantasy for long. When the lieutenant approaches Evangelina, she knocks him to the ground. . . .

Retribution is swift, however. When Irene and Francisco return to the Ranquileo home, they discover that in the night Evangelina has been dragged, barefoot and screaming, into an army truck, and that her brother, a young soldier in Lieutenant Ramiriz's platoon, is also missing. This is the book's turning point. The comic disappears, and for the rest of the tale the reader is drawn into the accelerating pitch of a love affair that is inextricably bound up with a commitment to find out the truth about the missing Ranquileos, whatever the dangers. The search leads them through the morgue, the police station, a mountain hideout, and the ultimate horror of an abandoned mine. This is the trail of the *desaparecidos*.

In her second novel, Allende's storytelling skills are considerable. Her cast of characters is large, ranging from Professor Leal, the aging socialist with a kitchen printing press, to Pradiolo Ranquileo, the young soldier tormented with lust for his foster sister, to the cardinal in his episcopal mansion. Yet each is distinct, unique, a personage who sticks in the mind. Even more skillful is her use of a constantly switching point of view as a means of demonstrating how a military coup could take place and be accepted in a country with a long history of democracy. Beatriz Beltrán negates the unpleasant aspects of the military regime by ignoring them, by absorbing herself in diets and face cream. Pradiolo Ranquileo has been told that the coup saved the nation from Soviet tyranny. . . . (p. 461)

In *Of Love and Shadows,* Isabel Allende is occasionally heavy-handed, driving home points that have already been made, and summarizing where the reader wishes she had dramatized, but these are minor flaws in a novel that takes the risks of combining love story, adventuer story, comic episode, and mortally serious political event. Allende has struck her target with little margin of error. This is one of the most memorable novels this reviewer has read in recent years. (pp. 461-62)

Sonia Gernes, "Lovers & 'Desaparecidos'," in Commonweal, *Vol. CXIV, No. 14, August 14, 1987, pp. 460-62.*

JOHN UPDIKE

[*Of Love and Shadows*] is Isabel Allende's second novel and is smaller, paler, and less magical than her first, *The House of the Spirits,* which transposed into an upper-class, Chilean key the dreamlike sweep of *One Hundred Years of Solitude.* Rather than the Trueba family living through eighty years of history, *Of Love and Shadows* tells of three families—the upper-class though no longer wealthy Beltráns, the middle-class Spanish émigrés the Leals, and the lower-class Ranquileos, whose mother, Digna, runs a farm and whose father, Hipólito, is a circus clown. One of the Ranquileo children, Evangelina . . . , becomes subject, at the age of fifteen, to noontime fits that are taken by some of the superstitious to signify sainthood. Irene Beltrán, a journalist, and Francisco Leal, a photographer, come together on assignment to cover this newsworthy phenomenon and then to investigate Evangelina's abrupt disappearance, and while investigating fall in love and into conflict with their unnamed country's military regime. . . . Evangelina is the only magical character in this somewhat misty but basically realistic novel, and her fits, her curious swap with the Flores infant (also called Evangelina), and her alleged miracles consort uneasily with the book's burden of political protest. So-called "magic realism" I take to be basically a method of nostalgia: the past—personal, familial, and national—weathers into fabulous shapes in memory without surrendering its fundamental truth. Fantasy, for García Márquez and his followers, is a higher level of honesty and directness in the rendering of experiences that have become subjectivized and mythologized. But in rousing the reader to care about a contemporary evil—the thinly disguised Pinochet regime—fantasy intrudes as a softening veil; it allows us to take the protest more lightly. If Evangelina's miracles are merely a manner of speaking, then the cave of corpses that the lovers discover, and the good Cardinal to whom the lovers confide their discovery, and the ordeals and disguises to which they submit, can also be felt as a manner of speaking.

And speaking deteriorates into rhetoric. The diction suffers from primness, of a radical rather than conservative bent. . . . A worker-priest is not merely described but posterized:

> Although José Leal did not claim to be the Cardinal's friend, he knew him through his work in the Vicariate, where often they worked side by side, united in their compassionate desire to bring human solidarity where divine love seemed to be lacking.

This sentence, with its concluding rap on God's knuckles, does help animate the worker-priest movement; but when it comes to a family parting, the mural style smears into lugubrious cliché:

> . . . and their voices and footsteps resounded dully in the desolate air like an ominous omen. . . . Tense, beyond words, they embraced for one last time. Father and son clasped each other for a long moment filled with unspoken promises and guidance. Then Francisco felt his mother in his arms, tiny and fragile, her adored face unseen against his chest, her tears at last overflowing. . . . When they turned the corner, a harsh sob of farewell escaped Francisco's breast, and the tears he had held back during that terrible evening rushed to his eyes. He sank to the threshold, his face buried in his hands, crushed by ineffable sadness.
>
> (pp. 84-5)

Of Love and Shadows comes to life mostly in its corners: Professor Leal's quixotic vow never to wear socks until Franco is deposed, and Irene's fiancé's return from an Antarctic sojourn with "his skin burned almost black from the reverberating snow," and Señora Beltrán's old-age home full of senile dreamers and her young lover who lazes his life away in a far-off beach resort and her incorrigible taste for luxury and her

vain armory of "little bottles of oil for her breasts, collagen for her throat, hormone lotions and creams for her skin, placental extract and mink oil for her hair, capsules of royal jelly and pollen of eternal youth." The senior Leals are unpredictable and vivid in the account of their escape from Fascist Spain and, when a son dies, of their joint descent into and return from an abyss of mourning. The mystery of why military dictatorships are repeatedly allowed to arise is illuminated in a phrase: Irene's soldier fiancé explains to her, "I thought the nation needed a respite from the politicians." (p. 85)

> John Updike, "Resisting the Big Guys," in *The New Yorker*, Vol. LXIII, No. 27, August 24, 1987, pp. 83-6.

DORIS MEYER

Chilean author Isabel Allende's second novel [*De amor y de sombra*] confirms the impression made by *La casa de los espíritus* (1982; *The House of the Spirits*) of her skill as a storyteller. This time, however, instead of an epic portrayal of four generations of women, she has chosen a more limited historical perspective focusing on a transforming experience in the life of one young woman. Still, Allende remains true to the moral imperative behind all her writing, which is to bear witness through literature to a time and place in Latin-American history. . . . Like *La casa de los espíritus, De amor y de sombra* (*Of Love and Shadows*) is a novel set in an unnamed country, which is unmistakably the author's homeland, under the dictatorship of an unnamed general, obviously Augusto Pinochet, in approximately 1978. As much as it is a tale of female self-discovery, it is equally, from beginning to end, a repudiation of military regimes and the mentality that sustains them.

The protagonist Irene Beltrán, a beautiful, vibrant, and sensitive young woman who works as a journalist, could be Allende herself, although the author has said: "Irene Beltrán is the synthesis of three Chilean women, journalists like her who worked at investigating the frightful reality of the dictatorship. Irene's conservative, bourgeois upbringing has sheltered her from the social and political realities of her country, yet she is by nature a free spirit with a humanitarian concern for the poor and the aged. In the course of her work, Irene meets a freelance photographer, Francisco Leal, the son of an exiled Spanish anarchist and his wife. Unknown to Irene, Francisco leads a double life as a clandestine revolutionary. . . .

When they go on assignment together to do a story about a fifteen-year-old peasant girl supposedly possessed of miraculous powers, they unexpectedly find themselves involved in a confrontation with the military police and the subsequent disappearance of the peasant girl, Evangelina. Irene's decision that she must solve the mystery surrounding Evangelina's abduction leads her, accompanied by Francisco, to uncover evidence of atrocities committed by the military. By this time, the intrepid pair of amateur investigators has fallen in love, but their discovery of one another is overshadowed by the *sombra* of violence and death around them. When they reveal what they know—implicating the whole government in mass murders—their lives are in danger and they must flee the country. The supporting characters are as vividly portrayed as the two protagonists: from Irene's egotistical mother, Beatriz, whose main concern is keeping her youthful figure, to Digna Ranquileo, mother of the abducted girl, whose practical, common-sense approach to life does not allow her to believe in her child's miraculous powers. As in *La casa de los espíritus,* the focus in this novel is on women, although men are essential characters who do not fit neat stereotypes. Here again, we see Allende's interest in women's methods of coping with eccentric or errant husbands, and it is the women as keepers of the hearth who exert the strongest influence on their children. Motherhood itself is clearly one of Allende's preferred themes, one which has direct bearing on the subject of this paper.

In an epigraph to the novel, Allende explains that its inspiration came to her from a man and a woman who "confided their lives to me, saying: here, write it, or it will be erased by the wind." Whatever the portion of fiction required to shape their story into literature, the religious tenor of these words invokes Allende's feeling of moral obligation to bear witness to a tyranny and uprooting she knew personally. For fifteen months after the 1973 coup, Allende stayed in Chile working as a journalist and actively supporting the opposition to Pinochet's government. . . . Her decision to leave was motivated by terror rather than politics. . . . After she had moved with her family to Caracas, Allende read documents published by the Catholic press in Chile reporting the existence of a mass grave in Lonquén, fifty kilometers from Santiago. It was this atrocity that formed the background for the story of two lovers caught up in the violence of the dictatorship.

In the novel, Irene Beltrán discovers the truth of the mass murders and must flee for her life. Exile is the final stage of a journey—not only in search of a young woman who has disappeared, but also in search of her own true self. The irony behind the punishment of exile—for Irene, but not for Francisco who accompanies her—is the subject of this paper.

As Roberto González Echevarría has pointed out in his recent book, *The Voice of the Masters,* "a correlation between Latin American writing and exile can all too quickly be established." This is not just because Latin-American writers have been political exiles in this century and in the past, or because they have felt exiled from the cosmopolitan culture of Europe, or even because they, as writers, have been treated as exiles in their own societies. Modern philosophical, psychoanalytic, and linguistic theories all make use of the concept of exile, thus proving its universal function as "one of those founding tropes that literature invokes constantly as part of its own constitution." More powerful still is the theme of exile in mythology, from the wanderings of Odysseus to the banishment of Adam and Eve. The longing for reintegration with the homeland or a return to paradise lost are metaphors for the insufficiency of the human in the face of divine power.

When we consider the relationship between exile and the female condition, then we are not surprised to discover, as much feminist criticism has pointed out, that, since the beginning of patriarchal history (the foundations of Western culture), woman has been, by definition, an exile. . . . Western mythology itself was a patriarchal construct; through its portrayal of woman as the ambivalent projection of man's fears and desires, not as her own independent self, mythology translates the message that woman must respect a "natural order of things" or risk responsibility for human chaos and destruction. This gender-specific mythology, particularly in its Judeo-Christian interpretation, is the foundation upon which a primarily Catholic Latin-American society is built. (pp. 151-54)

Deeply ingrained in the Hispanic psyche is the either/or image of woman as virgin or slut, Mary or Eve; in woman's hands is the power to ennoble or dishonor her male protector. Purity is highest virtue, and, as Rosario Castellanos describes it, "Of course it is a symbol of ignorance. A radical and absolute ignorance of everything that is going on in the world." By placing this moral burden on the female, Latin society virtually exiles her from any corrupting influence, and thus from any possibility of sharing public power. The traditional internalization of the social mythology, on woman's part, has made her an unwitting accomplice in her own displacement. . . . (p. 154)

The women in *De amor y de sombra* are all, in one way or another, exiles from the male-dominated world that controls their destiny. Because of their gender-determined roles as daughters, mothers, wives, or even housemaids, they are relegated to a domestic space where they are oblivious of or powerless against the ruling male authority. Unlike Clara in *La casa de los espíritus,* these female characters do not escape into a world of imagination, practicing what Marjorie Agosín, in another context, has aptly referred to as "an esthetic of silence," which subverts patriarchal authority by creating an inviolate inner space. The women of *De amor y de sombra* are resourceful and often independent, but unquestioning of the world as it is.

An extreme example of this—the woman who is most resistant to facing reality—is Irene Beltrán's mother, Beatriz Alcántara, the most bourgeois of the female characters in the novel. Deserted by Irene's eccentric and philandering father, whose unorthodox business ventures might have angered the military authorities enough to have him "disappeared," Beatriz's dependence on social status makes her incapable of accepting the truth or of sympathizing with other women in a similar plight. . . . In Beatriz's characterization we recognize the most self-indulgent kind of Latin-American female, acculturated to conform to an image of femininity within a given social order and unwilling to acknowledge any threat to that order or her own well-being: "The news in the press was soothing; they were living in a fairyland. Rumors of hungry women and children storming bakeries were completely false." In Beatriz's case, the exile of her womanhood is compounded by the self-exile of her social vanity.

Francisco Leal's mother, Hilda, is a completely different type of woman, totally devoted to her also eccentric husband with whom she fled into exile after Franco's victory in Spain. Accustomed to a life of hard work and deprivation, Hilda finds solace in mothering her three sons and spending her free time in prayer, much to her atheist husband's dismay. Such is her belief in the power of prayer that she joins a group that meets regularly to concentrate their spiritual energy on the destruction of Satan (that is, the General of the Junta) in their midst. . . . When one of her sons commits suicide after being persecuted by the military authorities for his union activities, Hilda turns again to prayer, "accepting the death of her son as one more trial from fate." In a contemporary setting, Hilda's resignation illustrates the persistent tradition of the church as a refuge for the Hispanic-Catholic woman.

Although Hilda's son, Francisco Leal, joins Irene Beltrán in the risky adventure that leads them to proof of the regime's atrocities, his experience as a secret revolutionary prepares him for what they may encounter. It is Irene, sheltered all her life by her sex and her social class, who awakens to the truth of evil around her. As the omniscient narrator makes clear,

Irene's encounter with the shadows of violence and evil is not forced upon her; she seeks it out after her first experience with death. . . . Like the biblical Eve, whose curiosity impels her to eat of the fruit of knowledge, she loses her innocence and is condemned, with Adam, to exile from paradise.

The catalytic incident that leads Irene to her "fall from innocence" is the peasant girl's kidnapping and murder by the police. The young victim, Evangelina Ranquileo, had recently begun to suffer daily convulsions, which neither medicine, religion, nor folk remedies could cure. . . . The narrator informs us that Evangelina is really suffering from a suppressed libido, as she is fatally attracted to her older brother and unable to consummate her desires. Stranger still is the revelation that Evangelina was actually a neighbor's daughter, born in the same hospital at the same time, and exchanged by mistake by the doctors. The two peasant-class mothers recognized the mistake but couldn't convince the self-righteous doctors of their error, so, accustomed to docility, they each took the other's baby home, giving them both the same first name. Later, the military police find out about Evangelina's seizures and see her as a threat to public order. This typically overaggressive reaction, which is farcically portrayed in the novel, sets in motion a series of events that leads to her murder.

In the context of the rest of the novel, the story of the two Evangelinas injects a note of hyperbolic unreality that points to its symbolic value; were it not so tragic, it would be absurd. Here is the ultimate exaggeration of female repression or exile: Evangelina Ranquileo not only must deny her sexuality but also her very identity from birth for the sake of maintaining social order. After her brutal murder, the other Evangelina—a soul sister, one might say—commits her life to combatting the immoral military regime. She realizes that their destinies were exchanged only by a quirk of fate and that "the girl who had disappeared was more than a sister: that girl was she herself; it was her life the other girl was living, and it would be her death that Evangelina Ranquileo died." This realization is mirrored by Irene Beltrán's shedding her own innocence and making up her mind to find Evangelina's murderer. The moral symbolism—a female response to the biblical question "Am I my brother's keeper?"—is central to the novel's meaning.

To bear this out, the narrator tells us about one important incident in Irene's adolescence—an experience that would mark her female psyche from an early age. Again, this episode is symbolically exaggerated in comparison to the realism of the rest of the novel, and we realize that Allende's equation of absurdity with the female condition is critical to the novel's interpretation. One day Irene comes home from school while her parents are away to find the maid Rosa has given birth prematurely without anyone knowing she was even pregnant. When Irene asks Rosa: "Where did that baby come from?" Rosa, trying to maintain the young girl's innocence, responds: "From up there—it fell through the skylight . . . It fell on its head and died. That's why it's covered with blood". Knowing full well where the baby came from but not wanting to offend the beloved servant, Irene accepts the explanation and swears never to tell her parents of the incident. They bury the baby in the garden and plant a forget-me-not on the grave. "From that time on, Rosa and Irene were united by an affectionate complicity, a secret that neither of them mentioned for many years". Here again, as in the case of the poor mothers whose babies are switched in the hospital, two females agree to keep silent and conform to the social order. They adapt and persevere in order to survive, but their adaptation is symbolic of their enslavement.

By making Irene Beltrán's "fall from innocence" the center of her novel, Isabel Allende announces that women must turn silent complicity into outspoken activism. The generation of mothers who shielded their daughters from the truth must give way to a new generation of women who demand the truth and reclaim their share of control over history. Women's condition as exile must end.

It is thus particularly ironic that *De amor y de sombra* concludes with Irene Beltrán's leaving her motherland and going into exile, accompanied by Francisco Leal. Like a latter-day Eve, she is exiled from the garden of "paradise" for having tasted the fruit of knowledge. But that paradise was really a prison for women enslaved by social conditioning; now it has become a hell for male and female alike, its shadows populated by tyrants who rule by intimidation and violence. As in the case of Alba and Miguel in *La casa de los espíritus,* Isabel Allende suggests that it may take the solidarity of women, along with the love of liberated men, to eradicate the serpent of *macho,* militaristic evil and reclaim—in a new gender-equal society—the possibility of paradise. (pp. 154-57)

Doris Meyer, "Exile and the Female Condition in Isabel Allende's 'De amor y de sombra'," in The International Fiction Review, *Vol. 15, No. 2, Summer, 1988, pp. 151-57.*

ROBERT ANTONI

While the first few sentences of *The House of the Spirits* seem to belong to García Márquez and *One Hundred Years of Solitude,* the last few—which, ironically enough, are much the same—belong to Isabel Allende. "Rarely has a new novel from Latin America consciously or unconsciously owed more to its predecessors; equally rare is the original utterance coming out of what is now a collective literary tradition" [stated Alexander Colman in *The New York Times Book Review* (May 12, 1985), see *CLC,* Vol. 39]. That this is Allende's first novel does not excuse the presence of García Márquez (as the critics suggest), though it might explain it, perhaps in terms of a problem facing all post-Boom Latin American novelists, new and other-wise, who wish to follow in the tradition of magical realism: How does one get beyond *One Hundred Years of Solitude,* since all writing in the genre would seem, in the end, a rewriting of this novel? Allende begins with this premise—consciously or unconsciously—and in the rewriting she discovers her own novel, one very different from *One Hundred Years of Solitude. The House of the Spirits* [*La casa de los espíritus*] reads, initially, like a parody of García Márquez's novel, though not a *conscious* sort of parody. . . . Allende does not use García Márquez's language as an expose to destroy it, speaking *through* it in her own language; rather, Allende uses his language as a means to discover her own language, which she *substitutes* for García Márquez's. In other words, we would have trouble isolating a representing discourse which is simultaneously present, and at odds with the represented discourse: there is no obvious wink at the reader. We can, however, contrast an "initial" discourse with a "final" discourse, which *are* at odds with each other. Allende begins speaking in a represented language—a language not her own, but García Márquez's, though perhaps she is not aware of it—and through this language she discovers her own representing language. It is as though Allende "unconsciously" parodies García Márquez early in the novel, then stumbles happily onto her own language—her own story—in the end. But is there unconscious parody . . . , or are we simply speaking here of inattentive writing? Are we simply comparing an established master with a first novelist? (p. 16)

A consideration of the structure of this novel indicates that it is more the result of planning than a happy accident. Allende knew from the onset—at least intuitively—that she was dealing with two stories, two languages, and that one would ultimately replace the other. Let us begin with the first:

> *Barrabás came to us by sea,* the child Clara wrote in her delicate calligraphy. She was already in the habit of writing down important matters, and afterward, when she was mute, she also recorded trivialities, never suspecting that fifty years later I would use her notebooks to reclaim the past and overcome terrors of my own. . . .

This, quite obviously, is the language of magical realism, the language of García Márquez, and we note similarities in tone and technique; there is even a striking resemblance between Allende's first sentences and the well-known first sentence of *One Hundred Years of Solitude:* "Many years later, as he faced the firing squad, Colonel Aureliano Buendía was to remember that distant afternoon when his father took him to discover ice." . . . But there are two conspicuous differences between this sentence and Allende's, which alert us immediately that she is doing something quite different. Most obvious is Allende's first-person reference; instrumental to García Márquez's technique is the use of a God-like, third-person-omniscient narrator, though this narrator is identified in the last pages of the novel as Melquíades, a character of the story. Similarly, Allende informs us in her Epilogue that the unnamed "I" is Alba, as well a character in the story. Melquíades, however, always remains distant. A less obvious difference is Allende's specification, in her first sentences, that the present moment of writing is fifty years after the events; in García Márquez's novel we learn that Melquíades wrote of the Buendías prophetically, one hundred years before the events, thus grounding the story, in the end, in the realm of mythological time. Allende, on the other hand, fixes her novel from the onset in a time which seems more historical than mythical, more *un*spiritual than spiritual.

For the remainder of the first section, Allende narrates from a third-person-omniscient point-of-view, in a voice much like that of García Márquez; the unnamed "I" disappears, and Allende's language is the language of magical realism: synchronic, hyperbolic, crowded with metaphor, oxymoron, synesthesia, personification. This narrative voice is the "feminine" voice in the text. Gérard Genette's term "focalization" may be helpful here in identifying this voice, which is "internal" and "variable," belonging simultaneously to Clara (through her notebooks) and to Clara's granddaughter, Alba, (the unnamed "I" of the second sentence). There is a sense in which this voice belongs also to Blanca, Alba's mother, the third of the novel's heroines. Clearly such information as Blanca's love affair with Pedro Tercero, or her marriage to the Count, could have come to Alba only through Blanca herself; Blanca, like Clara (neither actually speaks in first person), narrates *through* Alba. More precisely, the "focalization" of this "feminine collective" voice shifts in propriety among the three heroines.

Initially however, Clara takes precedence: the first voice in

the story, the voice of magical realism, belongs to the spiritualist. *The House of the Spirits* begins as a family saga—Clara's story—with occasional vague references to politics and history. Language, technique, characters, and events all have correlations in *One Hundred Years of Solitude,* another family saga. A passage from each text illustrates their likeness:

from *One Hundred Years of Solitude:*

> When the gypsies came back, Ursula had turned the whole population of the village against them. But curiosity was greater than fear, for that time the gypsies went about making a deafening noise with all manner of musical instruments while a hawker announced the exhibition of the most fabulous discovery of the Naciancenes. So that everyone went to the tent and by paying one cent they saw a youthful Melquíades, recovered, unwrinkled, with a new and flashing set of teeth. Those who remembered his gums that had been destroyed by scurvy, his flaccid cheeks, and his withered lips trembled with fear at the final proof of the gypsy's supernatural power. The fear turned into panic when Melquíades took out his false teeth, intact—a fleeting instant in which he went back to being the same decrepit man of years past—and put them back again and smiled once more with the full control of his restored youth.
>
> (pp. 17-18)

from *The House of the Spirits:*

> The intrepid traveler was laid to rest in a grandiose funeral. His death made him a hero and his name was on the front page of all the newspapers for several days. The same multitude that had gathered to see him off the day he flew away in his bird paraded past his coffin. The entire family wept as befit the occasion, except for Clara, who continued to watch the sky with the patience of an astronomer. One week after he had been buried, Uncle Marcos, a bright smile playing on his pirate's mustache, appeared in person in the doorway of Nivea and Severo del Valle's house. Thanks to the surreptitious prayers of the women and children, as he himself admitted, he was alive and well and in full possession of his faculties, including his sense of humor. Despite the noble lineage of his aerial maps, the flight had been a failure. He had lost his airplane and had to return on foot, but he had not broken any bones and his adventurous spirit was intact. . . .

The characterization of Tío Marcos quite clearly originates in García Márquez's Melquíades: both characters die and are resurrected (the Melquíades passage above is a foreshadowing of what is to happen in fact); both are adventurers, world travelers, conveyors of great inventions, bearers of magical books; both are alchemists, astronomers, entrepreneurs. They are even similar in appearance: Melquíades with his "untamed" beard and "flashing" smile, Tío Marcos with his "pirate's" mustache and "sharklike" smile. But Tío Marcos is only one of several characters early in the novel modeled after characters in *One Hundred Years of Solitude:* Rosa the Beauty is based on Remedios the Beauty, and, to a lesser extent, Clara on Ursula, Esteban on José Arcadio, Blanca on Amaranta. Allende's narrative technique early in the novel as well comes from *One Hundred Years of Solitude.* Both authors make use of extensive foreshadowing and flashbacks (seen also in the first sentences) to establish verisimilitude and temporal discontinuity. Allende, like García Márquez, speaks in hyperbole, including extravagant documentation, with the naming of "old-world" historical figures. . . . There is [also] a striking similarity in narrative tone; it is a tone which is unemotional, unhesitating, even while speaking of the most improbable events. . . . Finally, Allende's language comes from García Márquez's novel; in addition to the abundant use of figures of speech already noted, the prose style in both novels is characterized by a "simple eloquence," interrupted occasionally by a flourish of convoluted, "antiquated speech": compare García Márquez's "in full control of his restored youth," with Allende's "in full possession of his faculties" and "his adventurous spirit was intact" (two of several formulaic phrases which Allende seems to have taken directly from García Márquez's novel).

The point is not hard-pressed; there is little in Allende's first pages which does not have its correlation in *One Hundred Years of Solitude,* and García Márquez may be felt as a palpable presence well into the novel. Admittedly, there are isolated instances in which Allende seems *consciously* to be parodying García Márquez: for example, Clara's insistence that names should not be repeated in the family because they "created confusion in her notebooks which bore witness to life." . . . In *One Hundred Years of Solitude* García Márquez repeats names and traits to the extent that the characters become almost interchangeable. Such instances of intentional parody are few, however, and García Márquez's novel is not so much destroyed in *The House of the Spirits,* as gradually replaced, as though the literary model were slowly abandoned under the weight of powerful memories.

Yet even in her first chapter, Allende indicates that this displacement will occur, alerting us that she is doing something more than rewriting García Márquez's novel, in Chapter 1—unlike anything which occurs in *One Hundred Years of Solitude*—Allende alternates her third-person-omniscient, magical realist narrations with the shorter, first-person testimonies of Esteban Trueba. His is the second voice in the text, the "masculine" voice, and Trueba is the novel's hyperbolic macho—dictator in his home, patron and rapist on his estate, and bastion of "democracy" in government house. Trueba's narrations are jarring because they interrupt the narrative flow, and disconcerting because his character is disagreeable. Such narrations, however, provide a strong counterpoint with the "feminine" voice; they establish a dialogue. . . . Although Trueba's voice cannot be identified as the political, historical voice early in the novel (such *information* does not come from him entirely), he is at least *representative* of that voice—one well known in Latin America; furthermore, Trueba's voice opposes the magical, "feminine" voice. . . . The historical narrative, however, does *not* belong to Esteban Trueba, though his voice is recognized early in the novel as the "historical" voice: this narrative belongs to Alba, his granddaughter, the political activist.

Perhaps to her benefit, Allende abandons the technique of alternating Trueba's testimonies with the main narration after the first chapter (she comes closest in Chapters 6 and 10, both of which are divisions in the novel); Allende keeps the dialogue alive, however, by giving Trueba occasional sections for the rest of the novel. Nevertheless, the question arises as to why Allende chose to write in Trueba's voice at all. Such a narrative strategy seems risky, if not conspicuously dangerous: by breaking the narrative flow, by providing a contradictory viewpoint, Trueba's narrations work to destroy any

"magic" her omniscient narrations create. An early statement in the novel (coming in the midst of a passage which reads like pirated García Márquez) indicates that this is Allende's objective: "It is a delight for me to read her [Clara's] notebooks from those years, which describe a magic world that no longer exists." . . . In this sentence, like the second sentence of the novel, the unnamed "I" surfaces from the collective-feminine, omniscient viewpoint to transport the reader for the instant to the present moment of writing. It is this "moment" which the book is working toward, the present-tense moment of the Epilogue in which the same "I" states: "At times I feel as if I had lived all this before and that I have already written these very words, but I know it was not I: it was another woman, who kept her notebooks so that one day I could use them. I write, she wrote." . . . Not until the Epilogue is this "I" (with whom the reader may have identified Isabel Allende for most of the novel) named specifically as Alba Trueba, the posited author, though the reader is well aware of this by the last pages. What is also clear is that even though the words of this Epilogue may, in part, belong to Clara—by virtue of owning a share in the collective-feminine voice—they belong almost exclusively to Alba, simply because Clara does not belong to *this* reality: a reality in which "magic" does not exist. Similarly, though the words of the old notebooks may, in part, belong to Alba—by virtue of a shared inheritance—they belong almost exclusively to Clara. *The House of the Spirits* begins in the tradition of magical realism, but as it continues it becomes less and less Clara's (or García Márquez's) book, and more and more Alba's (Allende's) book, until finally there is no longer magic but only realism, and the novel becomes the tragic political history of Chile.

Chapter 1 then reads as a kind of "Prologue", with a confrontation between the polar languages of the novel (masculine and historical, feminine and magical). Significantly, the title of this chapter—"Rosa the Beautiful"—refers to the character who, together with Tío Marcos, is most reminiscent of García Márquez's characters. Rosa dies at the end of this first chapter, leaving behind her only the memory of a "mythological creature;" there is a sense in which Rosa "originates" the Trueba line, in opposition to the final Aureliano who dies in the last pages of *One Hundred Years of Solitude,* "the mythological animal that was to bring the line to an end." . . . Also significant is Tío Marcos' final "disappearance" at the end of Chapter 1, leaving behind him only the chest of "magical" books. Chapter 2, Trueba's chapter, begins the historical narrative of the text. Even though there are political and historical references in the first chapter, such references are not for the most part identifiable, and they are farcical, reading like similar references in García Márquez's novel. . . . (pp. 19-22)

Trueba is the focus of two other chapters in *The House of the Spirits,* Chapters 6 and 10, both of which contain several of his testimonies: these three chapters divide the novel. As has been stated already, the feminine-collective voice belongs primarily to Clara early in the novel, with Alba and Blanca present in an obscure way (again, neither Clara nor Blanca speak in first person). As the book continues, however, there is a gradual shift in the focalization of this voice—from Clara, to Blanca, to Alba—as the book slowly shifts in subject matter—from family saga (fantasy), to love story, to political history. The author conceived an individual narrative for each of her three heroines, and each narrative reflects the way in which, according to Allende, that character attempts to escape the "mediocrity" of her destiny as a Latin American woman: "[Clara] escapes through her contact with the spiritual world, through her charitable work. . . . Blanca, who is a less flamboyant character, has the experience of great love. She lives this experience as if it were a novel and escapes living a humdrum life. Alba, of course, becomes an activist." With Chapter 1 as "Prologue", Trueba's three chapters (2, 6, and 10) then divide the novel into the three narratives of its heroines. . . . (p. 22)

Of course, there is a sense in which all narratives overlap, just as there is a sense in which the feminine voice is a "collective" focalization; a glance at the chapter titles indicates, however, that Allende conceived of her novel with these three divisions, these three epochs. Chapters 3 through 5 consist of Clara's "family saga," the magical realist story, as though it were a continuation of the first chapter without the intervention of Trueba's testimonies. Clara again takes charge of the collective female voice, with the "I" surfacing momentarily toward the beginning of each chapter (as though the unnamed Alba wished in some way to differentiate herself) and with Trueba's "historical" narrative now taken up by the same feminine voice: Trueba narrates only one section among all three chapters. Significantly, in Chapter 5 (the last of Clara's chapters), the earthquake occurs, "[which] signaled such an important change in the life of the Trueba family that from then on they divided all events into before and after that date." . . . Toward the end of the chapter Blanca—who gradually takes charge of the narrative as it shifts toward romance—notices how their lives have changed:

> Blanca noticed that in the course of all these chores not a single ghost appeared from behind the curtains, not a single Rosicrucian arrived on a tip from the sixth sense, nor did any starving poet come running in summoned by necessity. Her mother seemed to have become an ordinary down-to-earth woman.
>
> "You've changed, Mama," Blanca said.
>
> "It's not me who's changed," her mother replied. It's the world." . . .

Trueba again becomes the focus of Chapter 6, and it is at this point in the novel that the "historical" narrative becomes referential: Trueba's mutilation of Pedro Tercero's hand identifies the latter with Victor Jara, the folksinger whose hands were similarly mutilated a few days after Chile's military coup. It is also at this point in the novel that the "magic" begins to disappear, slowly displaced by the "historical" narrative.

Blanca is the focus in Chapters 7 through 9, which tell of her brother's romances, of her own marriage and separation from the Count, of Alba's birth, and of Blanca's clandestine meetings with her lover, Pedro Tercero. The unnamed "I" seldom surfaces from the omniscient viewpoint (as though Alba were no longer as far removed) and the voice becomes more the voice of Alba in the Epilogue. In the last of Blanca's chapters (Chapter 9), two significant events occur: the death of Clara "[which] completely transformed life in the big house on the corner. Gone with her were the spirits and the guests"; . . . and, toward the end of the chapter, Trueba's pledge to send his bastard son to the police academy (he is to become Colonel García, Alba's rapist and torturer in the end of the novel).

Chapter 10, the third of Trueba's chapters, marks a second turning point in the novel. After Chapter 10 the magic dissi-

pates, and *The House of the Spirits* becomes a novel of *historical* realism. Significantly, this chapter is titled "The Epoch of Decline"; it marks the turn toward tragedy in the novel. In addition to Pedro Tercero (Victor Jara), other recognizable figures have been introduced into the text—most conspicuously "the Poet," Pablo Neruda, whose burial is transformed in the novel into a freedom march—but not until the final third of the book do these figures become fully fleshed-out. Not until the final third of the novel do the historical events become identifiable, and not until the magic is gone does the history evoke any real sense of tragedy.

As stated already, however, this historical, political narrative is not the property of Esteban Trueba: it belongs to Alba. In the final third of the novel Trueba's authoritarianism is slowly subdued, and Alba slowly surfaces from the feminine-collective voice to take charge of the novel's historical narrative, as though one voice were gradually consuming the other (Trueba has only two testimonies in the last four chapters). But not only does a "feminine" historical voice emerge in the novel to coincide with the well-known "masculine" historical voice, a "feminine tradition of writing" is instituted to coincide with the "masculine tradition of writing," also firmly grounded in Latin America . . . In *The House of the Spirits* Allende asserts her own feminine tradition, handed down from Clara through her notebooks, and established in Alba's torture chamber, when Clara appears to her suggesting "that she write a testimony that might one day call attention to the terrible secret she was living through, so that the world would know about this horror that was taking place." . . . It is at this point in the story which Alba begins to write the novel which is *The House of the Spirits.* But before Alba is taken away to the torture chamber, a meaningful event occurs in the novel: Colonel García builds a bonfire in the courtyard of the Trueba house which he feeds with all of their personal documents, including a chest of forgotten "magic" books found in the basement. It is from these magic books belonging to Tío Marcos (Márquez?) that both Clara and Alba (Isabel?) have learned to read. In *One Hundred Years of Solitude* it is Melquíades' magical parchments which survive the destructive passage of time. In *The House of the Spirits,* however, it is Clara's magical notebooks which survive, and it is Melquíades' parchments and Tío Marcos' books which Colonel García (García?) destroys.

There is a series of opposing parallel movements which define this novel thematically. Trueba's *machismo* is slowly subdued under the influence of the novel's three heroines, and though it remains "intact" (to borrow an expression from García Márquez via Allende) at the end of the novel, Trueba has won a legitimate claim to humanity. Feminine consciousness evolves over the course of the novel, from Clara who responds to life's atrocities by regressing into silence, to Alba who becomes a political activist. Finally, history replaces magic, tragedy replaces comedy. The same opposing parallel movements occur in the novel structurally, to mirror the thematic movements. Trueba's authoritative discourse is subdued by the internally persuasive discourse of the feminine-collective focalization. Clara's distant, third-person-omniscient voice slowly surfaces, ultimately becoming the first-person, present-tense voice of Alba in the Epilogue. Finally, historical writing replaces magical writing, tragic sentiments replace comic sentiments. All this amounts to a novel which—more consciously than unconsciously—may begin as an attempt to rewrite *One Hundred Years of Solitude,* but which discovers itself as a unique statement. (pp. 23-5)

Robert Antoni, "Parody or Piracy: The Relationship of 'The House of Spirits' to 'One Hundred Years of Solitude'," in Latin American Literary Review, *Vol. XVI, No. 32, July-December, 1988, pp. 16-28.*

ALAN RYAN

> I took a clean white piece of paper—like a sheet freshly ironed for making love—and rolled it into the carriage. Then I felt something odd, like a pleasant tickling in my bones, a breeze blowing through the network of veins beneath my skin. I believed that that page had been waiting for me for more than twenty years, that I had lived only for that instant, and I hoped that from that moment my only task would be to capture the stories floating in the ether, to make them mine. I wrote my name, and immediately the words began to flow, one thing linked to another and another. Characters stepped from the shadows where they had been hidden for years into the light of that Wednesday, each with a face, a voice, passions, and obsessions. I could see an order to the stories stored in my genetic memory since before my birth, and the many others I had been writing for years in my notebooks. I began to remember events that had happened long ago; I recalled the tales my mother told me . . . Little by little, the past was transformed into the present, and the future was also mine; the dead came alive with an illusion of eternity; those who had been separated were reunited, and all that had been lost in oblivion regained precise dimensions.

That is Eva Luna, the narrator of Isabel Allende's third novel [*Eva Luna*], at a climactic moment in her story. For readers given to analyzing the structures of fiction—something another character warns against: "If you start analyzing them, you ruin them"—that scene is technically dazzling, a culmination carefully prepared and anticipated for over 200 pages. For other readers, swept through uncounted pages by Allende's sheer storytelling power, the scene will be merely thrilling.

Eva Luna more closely resembles *The House of the Spirits,* Allende's first novel, filled with a multitude of characters and tales, than her second, *Of Love and Shadows,* a story of dark political intrigue in her native Chile. It is a remarkable novel, one in which a cascade of stories tumbles out before the reader, stories vivid and passionate and human enough to engage, in their own right, all the reader's attention and sympathy.

Allende seems to draw characters and tales from a bottomless well as Eva Luna narrates the story of her life. Some of them are catalogued in the passage quoted above:

> the tales my mother told me when we were living among the Professor's idiots, cancer patients, and mummies; a snakebitten Indian appeared, and a tyrant with hands devoured by leprosy; I rescued an old maid who had been scalped as if by a spinning machine, a dignitary in a purple plush chair, an Arab with a generous heart, and the many other men and women whose lives were in my hands to dispose of at will.

And that last idea—characters "in my hands to dispose of at will"—suggests another dimension of the novel. *Eva Luna,* almost in spite of itself, is about the art of storytelling. (pp. 1-2)

The world and the life that Eva invents—"I describe life as I would like it to be"—is an exciting place, starting from the childhood time when a painting can become a "window on storyland" and radio dramas provoke "a rosary of images." Eva's real world—or, at least, the world she creates for herself—pulses with the same bizarre characters, bright colors, dark melodrama, sharp-edged danger, and sudden twists of fate that fill Latin America's *telenovelas,* those multi-episode television series that tug viewers along by the heartstrings from night to night for months at a time. But Eva's life—her invention—is richer, deeper, faceted and detailed like some fabulous creation of the jeweler's art, and contains constant surprises. . . .

For Eva Luna, everything that happens in life is a conjunction of countless stories already in progress and, at the same time, the starting point for countless others not yet told, not yet lived out. And those stories not yet written can go anywhere, embrace anything. Stories, for her, transform life. When a character tells Eva of the sad death of his sister, Eva invents another story: "All right, she died, but not the way you say. Let's find a happy ending for her." And so it is. . . .

Reading this novel is like asking your favorite storyteller to tell you a story and getting a hundred stories instead of one . . . and then an explanation of how the stories were invented . . . and then hearing the storyteller's life as well.

Does it have a happy ending?

What do you think? (p. 2)

Alan Ryan, "Scheherazade in Chile," in Book World—The Washington Post, *October 9, 1988, pp. 1-2.*

JOHN KRICH

The heroine of this confessional saga [*Eva Luna*] has a "God-given talent for telling stories," yet finds fame and redemption writing the melodramatic potboilers called *telenovelistas.* The trouble with Eva Luna is that this plot seems plausible only as an unwitting confession about the career of its author. Isabel Allende brings to her third novel the same qualities that have won her a popular following: an evident affection for words, compassion for the oppressed and the inarticulate, the daring ambition to draw cross-sections of whole societies and a nearly maternal approach to narrative that bathes characters in a warm, milky light. Here, she has also yielded to her worst tendencies: sentimentality, pat judgments and the need to cram her tale with so many operatic crescendos that one can't help nodding when a voice in the book encourages her, "Keep writing, Eva, I'm curious about how you're going to end such a mishmash."

Our rich (in spirit) little poor girl comes into the world as the outcome of a servant girl's impulse to provide final comfort and sexual sacraments to an Indian dying of snakebite. Despite her origins, Eva Luna's most consistent characteristic is her lack of venom. She accepts her various rough fates with little more than an occasional sigh of, "Enough, enough!" (p. 13)

Latin America is a place that even Latin Americans find unimaginable. This is a muddy historical and spiritual terrain in which the lines have been blurred between things done, things left undone, things that should never have been done and things that still need doing. If that's Isabel Allende's point, then it's been made better before. And while this liberating perspective served to lift the veil from an entire continent, it has now become a stereotype that can only obscure. . . .

Few of the cast of characters emerge as distinctive or entirely believable. Too often, we find Eva Luna's compatriots revealed through generalized attributions rather than their own actions. The dialogue rarely rises above the level of these dying words of Eva's mother: "There is no death, daughter. People die only when we forget them . . . If you can remember me, I will be with you always." A feminist viewpoint is expressed largely through grumblings about how "men had it best," which seems to be forgotten by the next swoon. And if Eva Luna is meant to be some sort of Hispanic Cinderella, then she is one who dwells on the callouses caused by her slipper. What's missing from this portrait of a survivor is the one tool for survival that's evident even to passing observers of the Latin American scene: namely, the street culture's irreverent, insouciant humor, which manages to turn the most bitter moments into sweet triumphs.

Ms. Allende's work glows with the enthusiasm of a relative late-comer to the literary game. Perhaps it's for this same reason that she sometimes revels in a hackneyed phrase as though she were the first writer ever to stumble on it. For instance, on lovers: "Together we entered a private place where time did not exist." On the soldier for the people: "Huberto Naranjo was becoming one more animal in the jungle. . . . The machete and rifle fused to his hands, natural extensions of his arms." . . .

Is this magic realism à la García Márquez or Hollywood magic à la Judith Krantz? We can only marvel at how thin the line becomes between the two, and give Ms. Allende the benefit of the doubt. She is a popularizer who performs a valuable service by making general audiences aware of the rich milieu and timeless fatalism captured by prior practitioners of the new Latin American fiction. In her books, genuine mystical vision is replaced by the incessant consulting of tarot cards; that "smell of rotting guava," which Gabriel García Márquez has called the essence of the tropics, is reduced to a whiff of the jungle and a few sachets.

As for our ultimately unarchetypal Eva, she is spared an expulsion from her intrigue-filled Garden of Eden. We leave her in the arms of "an exceptional love, a love I did not have to invent, only clothe in all its glory so it could endure in memory." Ms. Allende is forced to concede that everything wraps up "exactly as it happens in romantic novels." A bit too exactly. This ending is happy enough to satisfy the most lovelorn readers, a happy ending that has as little to do with the Latin American poor as the rest of *Eva Luna.* (p. 14)

John Krich, "Rich Little Poor Girl," in The New York Times Book Review, *October 23, 1988, pp. 13-14.*

ELEANOR J. BADER

[The title character of *Eva Luna*] is an orphan by her seventh birthday, and her life follows a meandering course—from indentured servitude in homes of the rich and the cruel, to homelessness, to eventual success in the glittery world of TV production. Over the course of approximately three decades,

she has a chance to rub shoulders with leftist revolutionaries and members of the *guardia;* she cavorts with bosses as well as workers, men as well as women.

Hers is a world of survival of the fittest, a world where men, women, and children are encouraged to learn cunning and flaunt no vulnerability. Hardened, all, the book's characters are inured to loss. They are a largely unsympathetic, unlikable lot—cynical, angry, and manipulative. For these reasons, the book falls flat. Despite the dazzling promise of its opening, Allende never makes us care or feel that we are privy to lives that matter. Eva, for example, is careful to a fault, but she exhibits little passion or commitment to anything except storytelling. But storytelling is not done in a vacuum. Who benefits from her tales of fancy? To what end does she weave extensive fantasies and lure listeners hungry for escape? When she helps leftist revolutionaries, it is out of loyalty to old friend Huberto Naranjo, not because she cares a hoot about politics. In fact, her lack of faith in the possibilities of political change is depressing and shocking. . . .

Revenge, she seems to say, is sweet, but change that will rattle the core of the universe is a utopian fantasy, hardly possible in a world run by real-life villains like Pinochet, Bush, and Botha. Where, then, can we turn? *Eva Luna* posits several options. One is the pursuit of individual advancement, getting as much schooling as possible in order to land a lucrative job. The other is reckless sexual abandon. It is tempting to laud Allende's sexual audacity; however, one has no choice but to question a sexual politic that equates incest with fulfillment, a theme repeated more than three times during the course of the novel.

Rolf Carle—a photojournalist weaned on Nazi horrors in his native Austria . . .—is awakened to the joys of the flesh by the lustful indiscretions of two female cousins. Eva learns to appreciate sex after sleeping with Riad Halabi, an Arab businessman who rescued her from homelessness when she was a twelve-year-old street urchin. After five years of maintaining a parent-child facade, the two succumb to desire and a night of passion. In yet another instance, Halabi's wife, Zulema, temporarily shakes off forty years of unhappy domesticity after several encounters with her nephew. Why? Were there no other options?

Unlike Allende's other novels, where the reader becomes enveloped in the lives of the characters, *Eva Luna* is neither compelling nor engrossing. Although it is linguistically well crafted, the plot is confusing and largely unbelievable. We never learn what happens to dozens of key people. In the end Eva sails off into the proverbial sunset with the man of her dreams and nothing else is revealed. It is as if nothing else could possibly matter.

"I try to live my life as I would like it . . . like a novel," says Eva towards the end of the book. Perhaps that is the problem, for a life that reads like dimestore romance is hardly the stuff one expects from Allende.

Eleanor J. Bader, "A Life Like a Dimestore Romance," in Belles Lettres: A Review of Books by Women, *Vol. 4, No. 2, Winter, 1989, p. 5.*

Yehuda Amichai

1924-

German-born Israeli poet, novelist, short story writer, and dramatist.

Internationally known for autobiographical works that delineate the precarious existence of modern Israel, Amichai is generally considered his country's leading poet. He employs perspicuous metaphors and similes to place personal experience into the public spheres of history, religion, and politics. An influential member of modern Israel's first literary generation, Amichai synthesizes the biblical rhythms and imagery of ancient Hebrew with modern Hebraic colloquialisms. Many critics describe Amichai's early work as intensely intellectual and reminiscent of the metaphysical verse of John Donne, George Herbert, and W. H. Auden. In his later poems, Amichai incorporates sensual imagery and colloquial cadences, prompting comparisons to the verse of William Carlos Williams. Edward Hirsch observed: "[Amichai] is like one of Emerson's 'representative men' transferred to Jerusalem and updated for the second half of the 20th century, a prophet who shuns the traditional role and speaks in the guise of an ordinary Jewish citizen concerned with his people and his place."

Amichai first gained the attention of British and American critics with *Amen* (1977) and *Time* (1978), two collections of verse translated by himself and by English poet Ted Hughes. Both volumes address spiritual and political concerns of the Jewish people, and critics lauded Amichai's striking portrayal of love and sorrow. Vernon Young remarked: "A poetry of survival is necessarily a carnal poetry; these poems are about vanity under the sun and the absurd sweetness of that vanity—lust of the blood, hosannas for the young—when faced with the evidence that flesh is temporary." Amichai examines passion and estrangement in *Love Poems* (1981), a collection of new and previously published verse. In this work, he emphasizes the healing capacities of love in a wartorn land. These combat images are informed by Amichai's own experience in four wars: with the Jewish Brigade of the British Army during World War II, in the Israeli War of Independence in 1948, and in the wars against neighboring Arab states in 1956 and 1973. Reviewers often comment that Amichai's past grants authority to his works, which frequently condemn militarism and scrutinize political machinations.

In *Great Tranquillity: Questions and Answers* (1983), Amichai discusses Israel's troubled political history and its paradoxical desert landscape, which is both arid and rich with promise. Several reviewers admired the poem "The Rustle of History's Wings, As They Said Then" as an incisive parable connecting the humiliation of a defeated lover with the devastation of battle. According to Robert Pinsky, the pieces in *Great Tranquillity* "treat the way the reality of a particular, muddled human soul gives meaning to large historical events." "Travels of the Last Benjamin of Tudela" is a sequence of fifty-seven poems in which Amichai analyzes his Jewish identity by comparing his life story with legends of a wandering medieval rabbi. Published separately in book-length form as *Travels* in 1986, this work also appears in *The Selected Poetry of Yehuda Amichai* (1986), a compilation of

verse from ten volumes published over a thirty-year period. With the publication of *Selected Poetry*, Donald Revell remarked: "[The] demonstrated range and faithful, human consistency of [Amichai's] power should secure his place as one of the century's major international poets."

Amichai's prose writings have also earned international acclaim. His novel *Lo me-'akhshav, lo mi-kan* (1963; *Not of This Time, Not of This Place*), generally considered a seminal work of Israeli Holocaust literature, investigates two options for living with the knowledge of Nazi genocide. In a first-person narrative, the German-born Israeli protagonist returns to his ruined birthplace and is consumed with rage over the loss of friends and family. In a parallel third-person narrative, the same man remains in Jerusalem and immerses himself in a love affair, attempting to deny the past by indulging himself in the present. Amichai's short story collection, *The World Is a Room and Other Stories* (1985), expands upon many of his verse themes. While some critics contend that the stories are unstructured and overburdened with poetic diction, many admire Amichai's startling metaphors and sensuous imagery. Dorothy H. Rochmis observed: "[His] stories . . . immerse us in a world of life and death, both real and imagined; it's a world of loving, lost love, lovelessness, of logic, and fate." She added: "His stories immerse us, too, in some of the conflicts of Israeli life and the struggle, in a strife-torn setting, for humanity."

(See also *CLC*, Vols. 9, 22 and *Contemporary Authors*, Vols. 85-88.)

MOSHE RON

For Yehuda Amichai [in his *Love Poems*], to make poetry and love is to seek an antidote to history and a substitute for religion. The ability "to live for a few months / without needing a religion / or a *Weltanschauung*" is the most valuable of love gifts. The temporal limitation here is a mark of moderation, as is the recognition, in another poem, that "Whatever I scream and speak and whisper is / to comfort myself." In contrast there are moments of extravagant hyperbole, as in this early **"Song for Tamar"**:

> Each day of our life together
> Koheleth erases a line from his book.
>
> We are the saving proof in the terrible trial.
> We'll acquit them all.

I admit that this hopeless metaphysical bravado (it makes me think of Donne) is what pleases me most in Amichai's poetry. But I can also appreciate the upside-down wisdom of love when it is not stood on its head. In one of the finest poems in this collection Amichai is looking (in The Prophets' Street, "where there aren't any") for an apartment for a woman who is moving. When he finds one, he'll carry her bed there

> like a cross,
> though it's hard to suppose
> a woman's bed the icon of a new religion.

In these poems, what is called "love" is an experience valued for being nontranscendental, nonpublic, and in a sense even nonmemorable—a liberation from the need to promise in a life where nothing endures anyhow. The poems provide many wistful verbal strategies for dealing with change, preparing for loss, explaining withdrawal. As such they read like a series of exercises in mutability, and when the athlete is well conditioned, a certain glibness can set in. With improved travel opportunities, lovers come and go, trailing behind them ever more diverse cultural exotica. Here the elegy of separation, for me, deteriorates into sentimentality. It is the telescoping of vast geographical, historical, and intellectual distances into the brief, private space of a lover's bed and a few lines (even a single pun) that is Amichai's most vital rhetorical device, both in his best and in his less successful efforts. (p. 39)

Moshe Ron, in a review of "Love Poems," in The New Republic, *Vol. 186, No. 9, March 3, 1982, pp. 39-40.*

GRACE SCHULMAN

Yehuda Amichai has a rare ability for transforming the personal, even private, love situation, with all its joys and agonies, into everybody's experience, making his own time and place general. In [*Love Poems,* a collection] culled from six earlier volumes and translated from the Hebrew by various writers Amichai conveys the largeness of individual passions. He speaks with harshness and insight that are often deflected by irony, understatement and outrageous humor. . . .

Many of the poems are set in Jerusalem, a hard city in which the landscape and the loved one are defined each by the other: "And like the contours of the Judean hills, / we shall never be linked." He writes with urgency of the present moment, often setting it against a background of Biblical places and religious legends, making his juxtaposition of the immediate and the eternal especially witty: a lover exclaims joyfully, "All one hundred and fifty psalms / cry out at once"; another sings, "I stuffed your bed with apples (as it is written in the Song of Songs)." . . .

In his love poems, Amichai speaks of war, at times equating the struggle with tension between a man and a woman, and at other times contrasting war with love's peace. (p. 662)

"You promised me there would be no war," the lover cries in **"Just as It Was."** "And in the unquiet nestled the quiet," a man observes in a poem called **"In My Time, In My Place."** Violence and unrest are never far from the lovers, at least in their memories and fears. In fact, this book is haunting for the poet's skill in writing of fleeting love, and it may well be that in art, unlike life, doomed love has a greater appeal than enduring love. (p. 663)

To love, in Amichai's world, is, sadly, to imagine permanence in a world of change. The theme recalls Shakespeare's mutability: love, rooted in time, is destroyed by time; our vision of permanence is a reaction against the knowledge that we will die. In Amichai's poems, time's shifting sands are more volatile because they are the sands of Israel, and his notion of change involves also the modern tragedy of a nation's instability. So in nearly every poem, there is a heightened, almost visionary, awareness of the external world, a clarity generated by passion. He writes of the present moment, intensified by the transitory quality of human love and made more poignant because of constant reminders of ancient tradition and eternal values.

Another theme that emerges here is the distrust of language for its unfulfilled promise to master our temporal condition. It is a familiar theme in poetry, but especially interesting in the Hebrew of Amichai, who invents an idiom by using the language of industry, commerce and colloquial speech when he writes of love, gaining ironic and even violent effects from their juxtaposition, in the manner of the English metaphysical poets. In addition, his daring images are abundant and exact: "That we were only neighbors in the breeze, / thrown together in an ancient Babylonian khamsin" is outrageous, accurate and evocative of love's transience. The facing text of this unusual edition allows even the reader with a small knowledge of Hebrew to follow the poet's verse with its colloquial flatness and musical effects, and to see the exciting work that is being done by Yehuda Amichai in his language, in his time and in his place. (pp. 663-64)

Grace Schulman, "'In My Time, In My Place',' in The Nation, *New York, Vol. 234, No. 21, May 29, 1982, pp. 662-64.*

GILA RAMRAS-RAUCH

[*Love Poems*] creates a new poetic entity. . . . [It] confirms Amichai's basic metaphoric quality and his characteristic attempt to connect every experience to a wider framework. As always, he fights the liquidity of time with harsh, terse images.

The general impression one has after reading these love poems (covering a period of twenty years) is one of the truncated, fragmented nature of love. The body parts of the beloved are stations in the ever-changing inner and outer landscapes. Amichai moors his experience in a variety of spatial and temporal frameworks, creating an entire reality out of the parts of fragments, thus enlarging his referential sphere rather than probing microscopically into the quintessence of love. The opaque is suggested through simile and metaphor. Amichai's verse usually consists of two stages: a statement, then a simile which shatters or reaffirms the statement—the two being reinforced by the first-person voice that mobilizes them. For example: "Your body is white like sand / in which children never played . . . wisps of your hair as it falls / like smoke from Cain's sacrifice: / I must kill my brother / my brother must kill me."

The simile is usually culled from an apersonal sphere which enlarges the frame of reference—in this case Cain—but also including allusions to other biblical episodes as well as to current streets, places, et cetera. We are therefore faced with an interesting phenomenon regarding the image of the beloved: she is rarely presented in full portraiture, and she never dominates the poem. On the other hand, her very undefined image is framed by devices which serve as the setting for an absent presence, a presence that defies imagistic description but that hovers like an ironic halo over the anonymous beloved. As an example (from the same poem): "All night the mountains keep silent at your side— / at morning, the sand goes out with you, to sea."

Even bold statements of love are studded with spatial, impersonal images: "Once a great love cut my life in two. / The first part goes on twisting / at some other place like a snake cut in two. / . . . And I'm like someone standing in / the Judean desert, looking at a sign: / 'Sea Level.' / He cannot see the sea, but he knows" (**"Once a Great Love"**). The full eroticism of love poetry appears in **"The Achziv Poems"**: "In the afternoon / your one leg was in the east and your second in the west / and I in the middle, leaning on my forelegs, / . . . All night we're together. No / heavy memories, sticky feelings. Just / muscles, tensing and relaxing." Rereading Amichai's love poems gives one the good feeling of reencountering the known in new surroundings and circumstances.

Gila Ramras-Rauch, in a review of "Love Poems," in World Literature Today, *Vol. 56, No. 3, Summer, 1982, p. 566.*

JOSEPH PARISI

Spare, hard-edged, clear, like their arid Middle Eastern settings, these poems [in *Great Tranquillity: Questions and Answers*] speak directly about the nature of the human condition and the harsh realities of history. The burdens of the past are constantly felt, in major and minor ways, as when a Jewish father and an Arab shepherd try to find a child and a kid; in this land, the poet reminds us, such searches can be "the beginning of a new religion." . . . In a battle-scarred land, young people picnic in what were trenches, a newborn child is perceived as "a missile into the coming generation," and tourists gawk at historical sites but do not comprehend, let alone appreciate, the present-day dwellers. In the harsh light, however, the poet also sees the unexpected beauty or humor or irony of this paradoxical land, so ancient but ever new, and the parables he fashions from the concrete details he significantly selects ring with profound authority. In any language, Amichai is a major poet: his beautifully understated style shows, from beginning to end, that the truth unadorned is power enough. (pp. 1441-42)

Joseph Parisi, in a review of "Great Tranquillity: Questions and Answers," in Booklist, *Vol. 79, No. 22, August, 1983, pp. 1441-42.*

ROBERT PINSKY

These new poems [in *Great Tranquillity: Questions and Answers*] by the distinguished Israeli poet Yehuda Amichai have virtues that survive translation—directness of approach linked with a lively and mischievous imagination, and the power of memory balanced by a trenchant sense of what is immediate. . . .

[These] poems have considerable value. They confirm a great mystery of art. First, they treat the way the reality of a particular, muddled human soul gives meaning to large historical events. Conversely and paradoxically, the unique reality of that individual soul shows itself most clearly, in all its haphazard passion, when it reflects mammoth national events, as in the poem, **"The rustle of history's wings, as they said then"**:

> I saw a ceramic plaque on an
>   old house, and I knew
> That this was the name of the
>   son of someone whose girl I
>   took
> Years ago: she left him and
>   came to me
> And the young man was born to
>   another woman
> And didn't know about all this.

This poem, my favorite in the volume, makes this moment become both less heroic in any corny sense, and larger:

> I paid five shillings and changed
>   my ancestral name
>
> From the diaspora to a proud
>   Hebrew name, to match hers.
>
> That whore fled to America,
>   married someone,
> A spice broker, pepper, cinnamon and cardamom,
> And left me with my new name
>   and the war.
>
> "The rustle of history's wings"
>   as they said then,
> Which almost killed me in battle,
> Blew softly over her face.

What I admire about the comedy here is that it heightens, rather than diminishes, the sense of wonder at the poem's center—wonder at the work of chance and history, at survival and memory, and as the closing lines suggest, at the capacity of life to move on:

> And with the terrible wisdom of
>   war they told me to carry

My first-aid bandage right over
    my heart
Over the foolish heart that still
    loved her
And over the wise heart that
    would forget.

The poem delivers with poise its reminder that the terrible context of wars, names, countries and ancestries is also the context in which people make love and split up and compete. It makes the pathos of the ceramic plaque greater through the inconsequential and vital anecdote the plaque inspires.

The charitable irony of that poem is one of several dominant tones in this volume. Another is a sadly-smiling sexual nostalgia that I find horribly self-congratulatory and leering. A poem called **"Air Hostess"** begins:

The air hostess said put out all
    smoking material,
but she didn't specify, cigarette,
    cigar or pipe.
I said to her in my heart: you
    have beautiful love material,
and I didn't specify either.

The benefit of the doubt given to poetry in translation expires here; it seems unlikely, if not impossible, that the lines might be less tedious and complacent in the original.

But there is another tone that sounds in some of the poems in this volume—a rather impressive philosophical distance from the terms of daily life. [**"Great Tranquillity"**], for example, is identical in plot to Whitman's "When I Heard the Learn'd Astronomer." . . .

This big, severe perspective sometimes zooms down effectively to the facts of contemporary Israel. That happens in a poem called **"Relativity."** Musings about what appear to be random impressions—the relative life spans of animals, the way a work of art may have a calming effect even though its subject is violent (a volcano), the change of the color black from associations with mourning to the favored color for bikinis—spiral down to the facts of Sinai as a place to be alone with one's God (the poet does not recommend it).

The poems in *Great Tranquillity: Questions and Answers* show again what cannot and can be taken from poetry in translation. If one does not get unforgettable music, there is the compensating value of a voice saying in a new way one of the primary, implicit utterances of art, "I am here." In the kinds of personal, historical and national observations he provides, Mr. Amichai says that in a way worth hearing.

Robert Pinsky, *"Memory and the Immediate,"* in The New York Times Book Review, *November 13, 1983, p. 27.*

GWYNETH LEWIS

To a young soldier in the title story of poet Yehuda Amichai's most recent collection [*The World Is a Room and Other Stories*], the world seems like "an enormous room, the cities and villages in it, its furniture." The reversal of inside and out conjures up a world where public and private mingle uneasily. Being *inside* a house or a relationship is no longer safe; exposure to the outside brings a paradoxical security—the streets of Jerusalem afford the intimacy of a bedroom. While cities are fragile, the rooms in them are precious shelters from

disaster—until they're blown up, that is. These characters inhabit a world where catastrophe has become quotidian and the domestic terrifying.

In his poem cycle **"Travels of a Latter-Day Benjamin of Tuleda,"** Amichai wrote: "I tried to get out into my times, and to know, but I didn't get further / than the woman's body beside me." In his prose, despite a desire to bear witness to the world, Amichai is seduced by the moment. Moods are more memorable than plots—sensuality takes precedence. Yet most importantly for Amichai, history is not just an intellectual construction; it's as palpable as a human body. In one of the most haunting stories, **"The Battle for the Hill,"** a soldier leaves his wife to go to war: "I stepped outside. I passed a hard wall. I wanted to press myself against the terrible wall of history, like Rashi's mother. I wanted to find myself a niche safe from an intransigent History." Rashi's mother, while carrying the 11th century biblical exegete in her womb, was miraculously saved from being crushed by a cart in a narrow alley, when the walls gave way. Like her, these stories are pushed through the walls of their historical period by the pressure of Amichai's beautiful prose, which glints with hard-edged images, startling metaphors. . . .

For Amichai, history is made up of destiny and time. Time is the orderly chronology of human narratives which destiny can disrupt with its fateful and sometimes miraculous logic: a young soldier observes, "His watch was well-trained; otherwise it would have rebelled, missed the hour. Time is the etiquette of destiny." Since destiny is stronger than time, lovers in another story conduct their affair in reverse—starting with their separation, they move toward ignorance of each other.

Amichai has the remarkable ability to catch absolute time and human time in one sensuous image. Looking at modern Israel he sees not only the day of judgment but also an afterlife: sunbathers shake "the sand from their bodies as if preparing for the resurrection." The luscious, almost desperate sensuality of these stories is, finally, Amichai's response to his "times." The Israeli War of Independence and the Sinai Campaign—History with a capital H—are here, but what's captured most convincingly is the erotica of warfare.

Gwyneth Lewis, *"Realm of the Senses,"* in The Village Voice, *Vol. XXX, No. 27, July 2, 1985, p. 58.*

DOROTHY H. ROCHMIS

The short stories [in *The World Is a Room*] have been written by Israel's leading poet and they are evidence of his magical use of graphic imagery.

The ten stories are prefaced by Elinor Grumet's introduction, in which she notes that they "take the liberty of poems; their structure grows by the juxtaposition of metaphor, their meaning clarifies in the accumulating feeling of imagery." She adds that Amichai conceived of his stories as poems that needed more space to complete themselves. "They are tellings, not tales," she adds.

Frequently, Amichai's poetic bent seems to get in the way of his story and it can become an irritant. On just one page of his story, **"Battle for the Hill"**, he describes taking refuge, near a wall, from a sudden cloudburst. "I stood fixed beneath it like a holy icon in some Christian land." . . . Later on the same page, "The wash was hung out to dry; shirts and pants swayed freed of the body, like our thoughts, which are formed in our bodies but sometimes fly free in the wind."

These are marvelous images, but we seem to be swallowed by them and are given no space for our own minds to soar. For all that, however, his stories (or tellings) immerse us in a world of life and death, both real and imagined; it's a world of loving, lost love, lovelessness, of logic, and fate.

His stories immerse us, too, in some of the conflicts of Israeli life and the struggle, in a strife-torn setting, for humanity.

> *Dorothy H. Rochmis, in a review of "The World Is a Room," in* West Coast Review of Books, *Vol. 11, No. 4, July-August, 1985, pp. 30-1.*

ROBERT ALTER

From his earliest poems, archeology has been a primary source of metaphors for Amichai's perception of the human condition. He sees both the self and history as an elaborate depositing of layers in which nothing is ever entirely buried from sight, in which the earliest strata uncannily obtrude upon the latest. Thus, in his brilliant cycle of poems, **"Jerusalem, 1967,"** the speaker looks out on the Jerusalem landscape:

> Above the houses—houses with houses above them. This is all of history.
> This learning in schools without roof
> and without walls and without chairs and without
>   teachers.
> This learning in the absolute outside.

In an odd way, though Israel is a country obsessed with archeology, Amichai's use of it as a way of conceptualizing history and self is one of the things that have set him apart. "I was raised," he told the Israeli critic Chana Kronfeld in an interview she will include in a forthcoming study of his work, "on two different linear outlooks: the religious and the Marxist." He has in mind, first, his parents' Orthodox home in Wurzburg, Germany, and the schooling they gave him there. His Marxist outlook took form after the family moved to Palestine in 1935 when Amichai was 11 and was fostered by the Socialist youth movement, to which most Jewish adolescents belonged in the Palestine of the 1930's and early 1940's. Against such linearity, he suggests, the notion of archeological stratification has given him a more complex way of conceiving experience in time—and, I would add, a way that is a sober alternative to the messianic optimism of both traditional Judaism and Marxism.

But archeology has another attraction for Amichai, as he goes on to intimate in his interview with Mrs. Kronfeld: "I am drawn to people who are concerned with real things, like archeologists and geologists. That is really pure poetry."

The affinity for real things is, in fact, one of the peculiar strengths of Amichai's poetry and also, I would guess, one of the reasons for its accessibility to so many readers, even when it is formally innovative and utterly surprising in its leaps of metaphor. His Hebrew is often rich in sound-play, wordplay, allusion and other traits of virtuosity that are not readily evident in translation, and his language is a shifting mixture of colloquial and literary. But the poems are anchored in the concreteness of everyday experience through the homey immediacy of their images: a tricycle left out in the rain, kids' chalk drawings, the stub of an old theater ticket

in a coat pocket, rusty plumbing, a refrigerator door. Such objects are used to represent a range of feelings and imaginings all the way from forlornness and love to resurrection and prophetic vision. (pp. 42, 44)

But if Amichai is, in some ways, an irrepressible enthusiast, there is also an element of brooding sadness in the man and his work, sadness about personal loss, aging, mortality, the evanescence of love and the terrible price exacted by one war after another. He has fought in five, beginning as an 18-year-old in the British Army in World War II. When he rose to sudden prominence in Israel with the publication of his first book of verse in 1955, it was partly because he had succeeded better than any of his contemporaries in introducing a new sound into Hebrew poetry, more colloquial, more ironic, more "Anglo-Saxon," as the Israelis say when they mean English-language culture. But his success was also because his articulation of a desperate attempt to cling to the preciousness of private experience, his grasping at love in a landscape of bunkers and barbed wire, spoke so poignantly to the Israeli predicament. In November 1973, a few weeks after the Yom Kippur War, so traumatic for many Israelis, he wrote me: "Again, all of a sudden, my poetry has come back into fashion. Alas for the times when my poetry is in fashion." (pp. 44, 46)

Most readers of Amichai are likely to sense in the poetry an appealing quality of unaffected humanity. How that comes about through the artifice of the poem is a complicated question. I suppose almost all poetry begins with a rejection of certain poetic models and an emulation of others, and such choices were clearly important in the creation of a distinctive Amichai voice. When he began to write at the end of the 1940's, the dominant style in Hebrew verse for more than a generation had been extravagantly literary, sometimes in a histrionic or declamatory fashion, sometimes in a mannered symbolic one. . . .

For Amichai and his contemporaries, who were the first literary generation since ancient times to use Hebrew as a vernacular, there was a compelling need to break sharply with the immediately antecedent poetic tradition. But the new spoken language alone could not be a sufficient guide: literary models were required that could show how an everyday language might be expressively transmuted into verse.

During his service in the British Army, Amichai discovered by chance a Faber & Faber anthology of modern English and American poetry from Gerard Manley Hopkins to Dylan Thomas. It opened a new horizon of poetic possibilities for him: the influence of both Thomas and W. H. Auden is manifest in his early work, and one still sometimes detects a certain Audenesque wryness in his poems. Rilke is another informing presence for him, occasionally in matters of style—he has written vaguely Rilkesque elegies—but perhaps more as a model for using a language of here and now as an instrument to catch the glimmerings of a metaphysical beyond. . . .

Within the Hebrew tradition, Amichai has several times avowed an affinity for two predecessors. Leah Goldberg, a quiet personal voice among the previous generation of Hebrew poets, who favored musical and balladic forms, meant much to him in his early career. . . . Paradoxically, Amichai has also been drawn, from time to time, to the rigorous formal intricacies of medieval Hebrew poetry—he has written some remarkable quatrains, emulating the medieval form—

perhaps because they have helped him realize his program of "saying emotional things dryly." (p. 50)

Amichai's great gift has been his ability to express the concerns of a somberly mature imagination in a style that could seem—sometimes quite deceptively—simplicity itself. Here, for example, is the opening stanza of **"God Has Pity on Kindergarten Children,"** a poem from his first volume of verse that quickly became, for understandable reasons, one of his most anthologized pieces:

> God has pity on kindergarten children.
> He has less pity on school children.
> And on grownups he has no pity at all,
> he leaves them alone,
> and sometimes they must crawl on all fours
> in the burning sand
> to reach the first-aid station
> covered with blood.

The local resonance of these images in an Israel after the costly fighting of 1948-49 hardly needs explaining, but there is also something about the poem, as about many others by Amichai, that makes what is distinctively Israeli in it a deep source of universality. On the surface, these lines are a simple literal statement, proceeding in a geometrically neat series—"saying emotional things dryly"—from the sheltered kindergarten children to the unpitied grownups exposed to the savagery of war. But the poem as a whole requires a double take of figurative rereading as we realize that the initial picture of the bleeding battle casualty crawling for help is also a metaphorical image for all the desperations, public and private, of pitiless adult existence.

Amichai, in fact, often sees a metaphorical equivalence between war and life, each marked by its own terrors, its own necessities for courage and heroic persistence, and it is noteworthy that, on several public occasions, he has characterized poets as "art's combat troops," in contrast to novelists, who enjoy a loftier overview behind the front as "art's generals." The ironic turn of the comparison, it also should be observed, characteristically, turns on Amichai himself, because the poet has written three volumes of fiction. One of them, *Not of This Time, Not of This Place,* a long, formally innovative novel about the split consciousness of a German-born Israeli after the Holocaust, stands as one of the remarkable achievements in Hebrew fiction during the last couple of decades.

For Amichai, there is no contradiction between being a combat soldier and writing poetry as a human being rather than as a poet. This is because we are all engaged in the relentless warfare of living vulnerable lives under the shadow of death, and poetic metaphor is an indispensable weapon in the hand-to-hand struggle with reality. (pp. 50, 54)

His metaphors are typically drawn, as I have indicated, from the sort of everyday scenes and objects that were once outside the pale of poetic decorum. The sorts of connections made through such metaphors are often unexpected, sometimes startling; and, at their best, they provide either a sharper way of seeing reality or a fresh angle of vision for coping with it. Thus, in the middle stanza of **"God Has Pity on Kindergarten Children,"** the speaker, now making the figurative character of his language perfectly explicit, goes on to wonder whether God might not at least have some pity on true lovers, giving them temporary shelter "like a tree over the old man / sleeping on a public bench." This is, of course, a far cry

from the imagery in Psalms of a sheltering God who is a rock or fortress, and the likening of the lovers to a bum on a park bench suggests rootlessness, vulnerability, a pathetic lack of dignity. The vaguely Audenesque simile has the force of a muted prayer, tentative hope for a transient moment of grace. It feels authentic because it is free from poetic pretense and theological illusion.

Amichai is a poet who repeatedly takes chances with his metaphors. Ultimately, I don't think this is a matter of poetic principle but of sensibility. He has a remarkable capacity for childlike playfulness, even when he is dead serious, and reaching for metaphor is his way of making sense of a difficult and often daunting world. Sometimes, he overreaches, but I know of few living poets in whose work metaphor so often seems genuine discovery. At times, the emotional association between the two spheres metaphorically yoked is clear, though the spheres themselves are not ones customarily thought of together. For instance, he links speech and lunch sandwiches in an early poem about his childhood: "Only my mother's words went with me / like a sandwich wrapped in rustling waxpaper."

Perhaps, more typically, the metaphoric connection produces a shock effect: "God's hand is in the world / like my mother's hand in the guts of the slaughtered chicken / on Sabbath eve"; "Your body is white like sand / that children have never played in." . . . Occasionally, the transformational play of metaphor becomes itself the virtual subject of the poem, as in the wittily erotic tour de force, **"The Visit of the Queen of Sheba."** Here is a small specimen of exuberant playfulness from the fourth poem of this eight-poem cycle; the lines describe the Queen's voyage northward up the Red Sea to meet Solomon:

> A solitary bird sang
> in the permanent trill of her blood.
>   Rules fell
> from biology textbooks, clouds were torn like contracts,
> at noon she dreamt about making love naked in the snow,
>   egg yolks dripping
> down her leg, the thrill of yellow beeswax. All the air
> rushed to be breathed inside her. The sailors cried out ·
> in the foreign language of fish.

This sort of carnivalesque proliferation of metaphor is by no means limited to purely playful pieces. It is prominent, for example, in the long autobiographical poem **"Travels of the Last Benjamin of Tudela,"** which concentrates on more brooding existential themes. But metaphor is only a means, however central, for Amichai to get at the immediacy of experience. (pp. 54, 57)

Robert Alter, "Israel's Master Poet," in The New York Times Magazine, *June 8, 1986, pp. 40-57.*

EDWARD HIRSCH

[*The Selected Poetry of Yehuda Amichai*] is a retrospective of [the author's] life's work thus far, the artistic record of his own highly personal 30-year war on forgetfulness and silence. Mr. Amichai is an essentially autobiographical poet with the rare ability to characterize the complex fate of the modern Israeli, the private individual inevitably affected by the public realm of war, politics and religion. In a way, the poet is like one of Emerson's "representative men" transferred to Jerusalem and updated for the second half of the 20th century, a prophet who shuns the traditional role and speaks in the guise of an ordinary Jewish citizen concerned with his people and his place. One of his achievements is to bring to life the individuals behind the blind statistics, to register the human implications of history. Speaking about his own richly felt inner life, he ends up telling the tale of his tribe.

The Selected Poetry brings together work from 10 volumes published between 1955 and 1985. As if to emphasize two Amichais—one early, one later—the translators, Chana Bloch and Stephen Mitchell, have divided the poems into two roughly equal parts. . . . Mr. Amichai is tricky to translate. His work is steeped in the traditional imagery and language of the Old Testament, and his characteristic linguistic strategy is to bring together in wry confrontation ancient biblical Hebrew and the living language of the streets.

In the first part of the book, Stephen Mitchell has taken on the more formal and metaphysical Amichai of the 1950's and 60's, a tender ironist influenced by W. H. Auden (especially in his conjunction of the private and political spheres) and by such poets as John Donne and George Herbert (mainly in his redefinition of the metaphysical conceit). This is the Amichai of such poignant lyrics as **"God Has Pity on Kindergarten Children"** ("on grownups he has no pity at all"), **"Of Three or Four in a Room,"** **"A Pity. We Were Such a Good Invention"** and **"National Thoughts,"** a poem that speaks of a people's struggle to adapt a historical language to harsh contemporary realities. . . . This modern Jacob-like struggle with the angel of Hebrew is one of the central issues of Mr. Amichai's work. It is also a compelling problem for the translator.

In the second section, Chana Bloch translates the mature Amichai of the 70's and 80's, in some ways a sparer and more informal poet whose colloquial free verse rhythms seem modeled, perhaps, on William Carlos Williams and whose profuse imagery and lightning-flash analogies may be compared to Deep Imagism. Mr. Amichai calls the 70's "the decade of fires," and powerful sequences on war such as **"Seven Laments for the War-Dead"** and **"Songs of Zion the Beautiful"** stand at the center of his late work. In these poems Mr. Amichai's sardonic Jewish quarrel with God reaches a fever pitch worthy of the biblical prophets. In one of his darkest war laments he cries out:

> Oh sweet world, soaked like
> bread
> in sweet milk for the terrible
> toothless God.

"We begged / for the knowledge of good and evil," he complains to the Lord in another poem, "and you gave us / all kinds of rules like the rules of soccer."

[Amichai] speaks from experience when he talks of children "growing up half in the ethics of their fathers / and half in the science of war." One of the shocks that gave rise to Mr. Amichai's poetry was the confrontation between the protected world of his childhood (a world of sweet parental love and strict religious observance) and the hard actualities of adult life. As Ms. Bloch suggests in her foreward, he has spent his entire adulthood in the midst of Israel's struggle at first to exist, then to survive. He has not escaped that difficult history, or what he calls "the complicated mess" of Israeli life.

Sometimes the knowledge of war is implicit in his poems, in their background of sadness, terror and loss; but just as often

it is imminent and explicit, violently affecting him. In **"Seven Laments for the War-Dead"** he says everything is written in three languages, "Hebrew, Arabic, and Death," and he asks the heartfelt question, "Is all of this sorrow?" The answer: yes. (pp. 14-15)

At times the ravages of death and destruction almost reduce the poet to silence, as when he confesses: "I have nothing to say about the war, nothing / to add. I'm ashamed." But more often he posits two central consolations: the tender, temporary glories of erotic love (his typical procedure is to use the religious vocabulary of the Psalms to praise his beloved) and the sacred trust of memory. Love is for him a secular salvation, a doomed, momentary stay against the furies of the outside world. So, too, remembering is a terrible and exhausting burden in his poems, but it is also one of his only redemptions. Memory itself becomes a hedge against oblivion.

One of the centerpieces of Mr. Amichai's work is a long autobiographical poem that has never before been translated into English, but that we now have in two versions—in *The Selected Poetry* Mr. Mitchell translates it as **"Travels of the Last Benjamin of Tudela,"** while Ruth Nevo calls [her book-length translation] *Travels.* The poem is a kind of miniature Jewish version of Wordsworth's *Prelude,* charting the growth of a poet's soul from the vantage point of middle age. The poet's playful strategy is to trace the direction of his own life by comparing it with and contrasting it to those of three figures from Jewish history. As an autobiographical narrative, the poem reveals a great deal about Mr. Amichai's personal and religious heritage. It contrasts his "childhood of blessed memory" and his restive adulthood; and it dramatizes his sense of being poised between his father's life and his son's, his struggle to feel worthy and whole, his feelings about his adopted city of Jerusalem, his thoughts about the twin refuges of love and God and his assessment of the way his own life is tied to the fate of Israel. Here, as elsewhere in his work, Mr. Amichai demonstrates that he is a representative man with unusual gifts who in telling his own story also relates the larger story of his people. (p. 15)

Edward Hirsch, "In a Language Torn from Sleep," in The New York Times Book Review, *August 3, 1986, pp. 14-15.*

GABRIEL JOSIPOVICI

Amir Gilboa died in September 1984; Dan Pagis died earlier this summer. Thus the first generation of Israeli poets is starting to enter the annals of history. Both men, like Yehuda Amichai, were born in Europe and Hebrew was not their mother tongue. As with a novelist like Aharon Appelfeld, the fact that they are European Jews first and Israelis second, allied to the fact that the dreadful history of Europe and the Middle East in their lifetimes has forced them continually to ponder their relations to both Judaism and the State of Israel, makes them unique. There will no doubt be good Jewish writers and good Israeli writers in times to come, but perhaps never again this potent combination. . . .

To talk, as people often do in relation to Amichai's poetry, about the speaking voice, is not enough. He has his share of striking opening lines, but the main characteristic of the verse is its apparent effortlessness. But that is the miracle—that it exists at all, without any of the usual props of poetry.

There is a refrain of sorts, of course, as in much of his poetry, but it is really no more than the speaker half-repeating a phrase in order to keep a hold on what he is trying to say. What lends it its surprising authority, I think, is the way the ethical and the aesthetic reinforce each other. Nearly all the poems are in the first person and nearly all of them are in some way autobiographical, yet what the "I" asserts is that it is not a solid entity, that it is made up of others, of parents, of ancestors, of the words of tradition, and that soon it will return to them. It is as though the long journey taken by Eliot from the violent rejection of the self in *Prufrock* to the quiet acceptance of self in *Burnt Norton* was something that Amichai had never needed to go through: what Eliot had to learn so painfully was there, self-evident, from the start. . . .

In a superb poem, sadly not included in [*The Selected Poetry of Yehuda Amichai, Travels,* or *Israeli Poetry: A Contemporary Anthology*], he speaks of the act of writing poetry as being an act of translation, not invention: "Quietly we will transfer words from man to man, / from one tongue to other lips, / and not knowingly, like a father / who transfers the features of his dead father's face to his son / and himself doesn't look like either." The refrain is "we must not get excited", because excitement will get in the way of clarity and honesty, will do harm to the translator's job, which is concerned with truth and accuracy, not emotion or the celebration of individual worth. Yet how much emotion is there in that repeated "we must not get excited"? How much of an injunction is it to himself rather than to others?

For the poet as translator of the world there are words for everything and everything is in need of translation. The only injunction is to be accurate, not to get excited. That is why Amichai has produced so much—nine volumes of poetry, a novel, radio plays—and why some of the poems fall flat and read more like notes. But it is ethically and aesthetically important for him that we realize that speech is a gift and that part of what it means to be human is to be a creature which makes objects to relieve its feelings, objects which are elegy and celebration at the same time. Anything and everything can be a trigger for such artefacts [as in **"Seven Laments for the War-Dead"**]:

I found an old textbook of animals,
Brehm, second volume, birds:
Description, in sweet language, of the lives
of crows, swallows and jays. A lot of mistakes
in Gothic printing, but a lot of love: "Our
feathered friends", "emigrate to warmer
countries", "nest, dotted egg, soft plumage,
the nightingale", "prophets of spring",
The Red-Breasted Robin.

Year of printing 1913, Germany
on the eve of the war which became
the eve of all my wars.

My good friend, who died in my arms and in his blood

in the sands of Ashdod, 1948, in June.

Oh, my friend,
red-breasted.

(Translated by Amichai)

What happens in this poem happens at some distance from the words. The words dramatize for us the speaker leafing through the book, and then the sudden shock of memory. But the words manage both to celebrate the book ("in sweet language") and to make of the sudden memory of his dead friend something more than mere pain, without in any way masking

the pain. How much gets said, about our century, about human beings, how simply and how briefly.

Gabriel Josipovici, "Translating the World," in The Times Literary Supplement, *No. 4359, October 17, 1986, p. 1158.*

C. H. SISSON

The writing of verse is a disease to which too little attention has been paid by the public health authorities. The number of more or less unavoidable cases is small, but the contagion is everywhere. The *Selected Poetry of Yehuda Amichai* shows clearly, even through the medium of translation, that its author is among the small number in whom the disease was, if not congenital, at any rate not to be avoided by any reasonable precautions. From his earliest years he undoubtedly had, as he says,

blood that wanted to get out in many wars
and through many openings,

and one can believe him when he says:

it knocks against my head from the inside
and reaches my heart in angry waves.

Indignation does not itself make verses, though there is Classical authority for saying that it does. . . . Amichai is a complicated character in whose make-up indignation, sometimes violent, is certainly a constituent, but only one of many, which contrast with and qualify one another. He is also a man of what might well be called political commitment, though it is not of a kind which shuts out all but a limited range of impressions. He is resolute only about being what he is. . . .

Amichai's poems are written in Hebrew, and one may regret that [in her "Foreword," Chana] Bloch did not extend a little her extremely interesting remarks on this subject. 'Modern Hebrew,' she says, was 'revived as a spoken language only a hundred years ago.' That sounds like dragging the 19th century screaming into Old Testament times, and must have had a profound effect on the new speakers and their successors, as well as presenting unique problems to the translators. . . . Since modern Hebrew is, Bloch tells us, 'much closer to the Hebrew of the Old Testament than our own language is to 17th-century English', Amichai's allusions are never, apparently, felt to have 'a "literary" air'. . . . The vigour one senses in Amichai's work, through these clearly very competent translations, seems to indicate profound tensions between old words and new meanings. How much of this is a general cultural phenomenon, and how much is due to the individual energies of the poet, it is impossible for the reader without Hebrew to guess.

It appears, however, that the liberal individualism so widely—and on the whole so superficially—spread over the Western world has little place in Amichai's work.

We forget where we came from. Our Jewish
names from the Exile give us away . . .

Circumcision does it to us,
as in the Bible story of Shechem and the sons
                                          of Jacob,

so that we go on hurting all our lives.

What are we doing, coming back here with this
                                          pain?

Our longings were drained together with the
swamps,
the desert blooms for us, and our children are
beautiful.

Even the love poems in this volume carry historical and communal overtones. The religion and the people—in effect the near-desperate politics of Israel—are present even in intimate encounters. Love and war are close together. . . . The shades of ancient vengeance are never very far away. . . . The violence and physicality of much in these poems comes over with the crudity of a newspaper or a television drama. Whether that is the force of the original one cannot know. Certainly the transmutation which the language and rhythm of poetry give to the most recalcitrant subject-matter can rarely be felt here. How could they be? The history of literature shows how slow and partial is the assimilation of the poetry of one language in another—a process extending sometimes over centuries and never entirely finished. The task of producing anything like an equivalent of the selected work of a contemporary poet in another language is strictly impossible. What [translators] Chana Bloch and Stephen Mitchell have done, however, is to give us enough of the content, complex and difficult as it clearly is, to convince us that we know something of the kind of literary phenomenon Yehuda Amichai is, and to leave us with a little more understanding of the real world of Israel. It is a valuable service, the more so since we hear so much from the ineptitude of newsmen and politicians.

C. H. Sisson, "Angry Waves," in London Review of Books, *Vol. 8, No. 22, December 18, 1986, p. 22.*

DONALD REVELL

The most powerful ideas in the arts of our century have been and remain international, and one of the necessary consequences, perhaps even one of the necessary conditions of internationalism, is displacement. It is not surprising, then, that some of the strongest poetry of the twentieth century is the poetry of displacement—voluntary or involuntary, spiritual, historical, or political.

Displacement implies an urgent historical consciousness that gains unique power in being wedded to personal experience and to a critical *self*-consciousness. The poetry of Yehuda Amichai exercises this same power, and with the publication of his *Selected Poetry* (in convincing, beautiful translations), the demonstrated range and faithful, human consistency of his power should secure his place as one of the century's major international poets.

The quality of Amichai's work seems absolutely congruent to that of his life—a life apparently fated to be led along the precipice of history. Born in 1924 into an Orthodox Jewish family in Germany (as precarious a birth as one can imagine), Amichai moved with his parents to Palestine in 1936 and went on to serve in four wars. . . . Thus his personal history is one of various and violent displacements: from cosmopolitan Europe to a circumscribed Middle East, from poet to soldier, from the dream-Israel of the Diaspora to an actual patch of ground to be maintained in the face of external enemies and the difficult, sometimes disheartening business of the real Israel's internal affairs.

Along the way, Amichai exchanged his native German for Hebrew, and in that crucial exchange, his life discovered his work. When he became a Hebrew poet, Amichai did more than adopt the language of his new nation. He also adopted and exalted memory as his muse. Writing Hebrew in itself constitutes an act of historical memory; to write Hebrew poems rooted in a contemporary, international life is to acknowledge the bonds between one person and the history of humanity and of God.

Amichai's precipitous life becomes the vehicle of a widening compassion, an open-ended chronicle of suffering and celebration that retains its intensely personal quality by grace of the poet's unique vision. At the same time, he achieves a sense of the universal by grace of the language (and of the mixed blessings of the mythic and historical significances of that language), which the poet is always conscious of using. Neither a national nor a religious chauvinist, Amichai illuminates the knot of pain and joy at the heart of memory, which is itself the heart of all meaningful experience. . . . Memory is the agony of salvation, the telegram continually delivered to people of feeling and conscience involved with history.

The *Selected Poetry* is an extensive book covering thirty years of the poet's writing life, demonstrating not only his thematic range and commitment, but also the development of his style—from that of a gifted intellectual craftsman to that of a master supple and various enough to embrace the ambiguities of experience whole and without unnecessary metaphorical accommodations. Though the qualities of conscience and sympathy remain constant, Amichai appears to seek and ultimately to find a loosening of style, which, without diminishing his poetic control, opens his work to figures as they occur in life.

In his early poems, Amichai relies heavily on simile and metaphor to translate experience into formal, shaped speech, [as in] **"Poems for a Woman."** . . . The effect is oracular, almost glyphic, and it seems a little out of time. To best serve his vision, Amichai requires a style suited to those oddly particular moments of public and private history in which memory works its difficult, abrupt magic. In his more recent poems, he relies less upon figures of speech than upon the contingent figures of life. The poems recount themselves in quietly fantastic narratives and fragments ideally representative of life lived as Amichai feels it must be—with full consciousness of the self as both intimate lover and Everyman, of history as something that happens both in little rooms and across the face of nations.

Amichai is now writing the poems of a master, poems in which history is revealed as the living allegory of itself and of the complex lives that must endure history even as they create it. The great value of this selection of poems is that it teaches by beautiful example that there is no separating creation from survival.

Donald Revell, "The Heart of Memory & Ferment of Displacement," in The Bloomsbury Review, *Vol. 7, No. 2, March-April, 1987, pp. 6-7.*

GILA RAMRAS-RAUCH

The representative sampling of Yehuda Amichai's verse in *The Selected Poetry* reveals once again the unique voice, idiom, tone, and mood that have continued to fascinate his readers. . . . He is a master of the language games that have yoked the whimsical to the tragic, the mundane to the sublime. Occasionally he creates verbal puzzles out of the *objet trouvé,* combining everyday minutiae and profound speculation—all taking place somewhere between darkness and light.

The speaker in Amichai's verse is Everyman, yet one who presents a unique *parole* by creating and shattering icons. Irony and paradox have made Amichai's poems familiar since his earliest work in the 1950s: characteristically, there will be a mundane generality, followed by a simile that hovers between the vague and the sublime—and then the "I" that binds everything together. Often he will introduce a single image to unify the entire verbal construction, as in **"Yehuda Ha-Levi."** More frequently he will arrange a string of images, their contiguity creating a new pictoriality. Many times a poem of his will begin with a charge, only to ebb and "gain" fatigue. . . .

Amichai's poetry is not clearly associated with politics or political statements. Rather, it is inhabited by the images of Father, Mother, Jerusalem, and other places. Still, a careful reading reveals a deep aversion to war—including the World War I of his father and his own experience in World War II and the 1948 War of Independence—as in **"The Smell of Gasoline Ascends in My Nose"** and **"Seven Laments for the War-Dead,"** among other pieces. The selection in the new volume is well balanced, offering a rich picture of Amichai's work over the years. The translation is uniformly accurate, flowing, and altogether fine.

> *Gila Ramras-Rauch, in a review of "The Selected Poetry of Yehuda Amichai," in* World Literature Today, *Vol. 61, No. 3, Summer, 1987, p. 487.*

PAUL BRESLIN

Amichai, as we meet him [in ***Selected Poetry***], seems a poet well worth knowing. He has, like [English poet Geoffrey] Hill, an ambition to confront the violence of modern history (seen first-hand in his adopted homeland, Israel), but manages to do so without Hill's frigidity and self-importance of manner.

Theme and the architectural plan of a poem survive translation best; metaphorical invention survives more precariously, and auditory imagination is inevitably lost, transmissible only by rough analogues. In Amichai, metaphorical invention seems paramount, that virtue which Aristotle thought the surest mark of genius, the least attainable by craft. Sometimes, in the earliest poems, Amichai's prodigality of metaphor leads him into wretched excess. Encountering, early on, the lines "Your eyes are still warm, like beds / time has slept in," or "All night your empty shoes / screamed alongside your bed," I thought that maybe the translators had accidentally interpolated a sheet from the sophomore poetry workshop. But already in these early pages, one finds wonderfully apt yet surprising figures, often reminiscent of Jewish folktales, as if they were derived from some legend or myth— "My pain is already a grandfather: / it has begotten two generations / of pains that look like it," or "Underneath the world, God lies stretched on his back, / always repairing, always things get out of whack." By the time of his second collection, ***Two Hopes Away,*** Amichai was capable of extraordinary concentration, as in some of the best sections of **"In a Right Angle: A Cycle of Quatrains."** (p. 295)

As Chana Bloch points out in her introduction, "love is at the center of Amichai's world, but he is quick to grant that his mistress's eyes are nothing like the sun, that sex is at once an enticing scent and a sticky business." He also sees a connection between erotic love and the driving force of history, as in **"The Visit of the Queen of Sheba,"** where the queen's visit of state turns into a sexual chessgame with King Solomon. But more typically, he sees love as the one certain good in a world torn by war, mutability, and loss. Not that love is safe from mutability; as Amichai puts it in **"The Elegy on the Lost Child."** . . . To live involves, for Amichai, a continual tension between the imperative to forget and the imperative to remember. He portrays Jerusalem itself as suffering from its memory: "Jerusalem stone is the only stone that can / feel pain. It has a network of nerves." The city

> . . . is built on the vaulted foundations
> of a held-back scream. If there were no reason
> for the scream, the foundations would crumble, the city
>   would collapse;
> if the scream were screamed, Jerusalem would explode
> into the heavens.

The first alternative—to forget the reasons for the scream— would make the city collapse; but to remember too vividly, to allow the scream to escape, would make it explode. (pp. 295-96)

Just before the middle of the book, we begin to encounter the long meditative poems from which I've been quoting—**"The Elegy of the Lost Child," "Jerusalem, 1967," "Travels of the Last Benjamin of Tudela,"** and **"Seven Laments for the War-Dead"**—that show Amichai at his most expansive, ambitious, and public; the last of these, presented only in excerpts, is **"Songs of Zion the Beautiful."** Of these, **"The Elegy of the Lost Child"** seems the most tightly-constructed and best-sustained, **"Travels of the Last Benjamin of Tudela"** the broadest in range, offering a spiritual autobiography of the poet that also attempts to understand what is happening in (and to) Israel. In the last ten years or so, if this selection represents him accurately, Amichai appears to have turned to shorter poems, although in some of these, such as **"When I Was Young, the Whole Country Was Young"** (not an idle narcissistic boast, but a literal truth), **"So I Went Down to the Ancient Harbor,"** or **"1978 Reunion of Palmakh Veterans at Ma'ayan Harod,"** he is still writing public poetry, albeit on a more modest scale. In the best of these poems, one has a sense of wholeness and economy of means often lacking in the earlier work and even in the long pieces of Amichai's midcareer, impressive as those are. Amichai's poems often tend to be loosely-woven and open-ended—one could easily imagine them longer or shorter than they are, had the poet chosen to make them so. That approach to poetic form has its virtues—freedom from affectation and stifling formalism, easy transition from one part of experience to another—but also its drawbacks when it becomes too casual, too complacently sure that the poet's engaging voice and processions of interesting metaphors are sufficient in themselves. (pp. 296-97)

> *Paul Breslin, in a review of "The Selected Poetry of Yehuda Amichai," in* Poetry, *Vol. CL, No. 5, August, 1987, pp. 294-97.*

YEHUDA AMICHAI (INTERVIEW WITH DAVID MONTENEGRO)

Montenegro: *What brought you to write poetry?*

Amichai: I loved to *read* poetry, and it helped me. I really admired a lot of poets in all languages I could read. But after some time I had this need for a kind of do-it-yourself poem, as if I wouldn't completely trust others to write the real poem for me, for my needs.

Poetry helped you. In what way?

Poetry helped me to speak things clearly and to make my life more livable.

Did you feel any conflict between poetry and your experience in the army?

No, because that's exactly what I think about poetry. It's not about "nice" things. Poetry has always been as much or more about sadness than happiness, more about death and disasters and so on.

Actually, poetry is a kind of—should I say—a by-product, but in the highest sense of the word. It's a certain way of documentation—not a willful documentation like a journal or letters to someone that you really write as Rilke did, you know, keeping in mind constantly that this letter would be published—but documentation for my own private needs. I hated to write journals, and I'm not a great letter writer, so I think poetry's a kind of concentrated letter for lazy people—or a journal where you really can concentrate on a few sentences and that's enough. . . .

You said poetry's a by-product, but in the highest sense of the word. Why highest?

I don't know, it might even be lower but more concentrated than life. It's *heavier,* you see, speaking in physical terms.

So it takes on weight, particularly from the harder times in life?

Yes, exactly. . . .

Was Rilke influential for you?

Oh, yes he was. At the beginning, and still up to this present day, I think. But you know how you sometimes like a poet early in your life, and then you get totally disgusted with him and fed up when the time comes. Nowadays there are things in his work that really still hold for me, especially his "Duino Elegies" and his later "Sonnets to Orpheus."

You've lived in Palestine fifty years. You must have seen Hebrew change as it has been revived as a spoken language.

Not so much, no. Hebrew at the time I came was already a spoken language. There were only half a million people, living in small communities, but still it was a language spoken at school and in the streets by everyone. And it has changed, I think, no more than English or German has in fifty years. It just had to take in a lot of words, conceptions from technology and whatnot.

Because of its long religious tradition, does the language feel heavy to you when you use it in a secular way?

No. For me it's natural. I grew up in a very religious household. I had to pray every day and go to synagogue. So the prayers, the language of prayer itself became a kind of natural language for me. Also, I'm *not* religious anymore, but still it's very natural for me. So I use it. I don't try—like sometimes poets do—to "enrich" poetry by getting more *cultural* material or more *ethnic* material into it. It comes very naturally. . . .

But there's no sense of a kind of double exposure in using Hebrew?

There *is,* perhaps, more than in any other language, but I don't know whether it's good or bad. It depends on the use. Because if you make use of it too much it just becomes bad poetry.

And the language of the Bible; do you feel it is something you've had to struggle against or, on the other hand, something you've been able to use?

No, I use it by incorporating it, sometimes in ironical ways and sometimes in admiring ways. I gain mastery over it. It's just I *use* it. I don't reject it.

You've mentioned recently that real things are very important in your poetry. Would you say more about this?

Well, it's actually a need to put something very personal into the poetry—not that you do it deliberately. Everything can be concentrated in, say, a stocking. Or a pair of shoes can become the very center of the whole love affair. And you don't need the whole love affair. You don't need to videotape the whole love affair between two young people which went on for two months, but sometimes it can be concentrated in just a pair of shoes or a book with torn pages or a broken glass or something like this.

I think that out of every experience I've had there always emerge such things, which can be even sentences, phrases I've heard other people saying or people who have been so-called witnesses or innocent bystanders of something that happened to me and who sometimes become more important than the experience itself because they carry the whole witness, the whole image in them without knowing it and without ever *wanting* to do so.

It's like in a court a good judge sometimes says a witness who's very much involved and knows a lot is not as good as someone who was just an innocent bystander and remembers only a few little things for himself that might be much more important because he wasn't involved in what happened. (p. 15)

So precision is important in your poems?

I'm crazy about exactitude. There's nothing more terrible to me than poetry which is all just very beautiful sentences or emotional ones or long, tedious tracts of half-abstract philosophy.

Rhetoric?

No rhetoric can be filled with things. For instance, I think the "Four Quartets" of Eliot until this present day are still to me one of the greatest pieces in literature. It's rhetoric and it's a sermon. It's like a minister preaching. And again I think every poem is kind of a little sermon, which we give the audience of believers, or in most cases we ourselves. But Eliot uses also a lot of real things.

In a way it's amazing those poems work because they use so many abstractions.

Yes, abstractions, and the philosophy is very shallow; it's not a very deep, new thing. That's actually how it should be. Poetry should never be a kind of new way in thinking. It should be very old ways in thinking but newly told. That's the difference between a philosopher and a poet.

Would that mean that the poet has to have the thoughts already in the blood?

Yes, exactly. That's why Sartre never could become a good poet.

Metaphor and simile; what work do they do, what do they satisfy?

Well, I think first of all they're a way out of loneliness. If you use even a very worn-out metaphor or simile—for instance, you are beautiful like a rose—you are not alone. The rose becomes an equal, and it's like stretching a hand out. . . .

So I think metaphor is a reaching out. We are groping for words. We say, "Ah, I'm looking for words. I can't express myself." So we need something, again something *real*. Because if I want to say, "He's such a cruel man," I might say, "His heart is stone," which is also an over-used expression, but you are *groping* for words. You want to keep your head above water, so words become a kind of, I would say, *solid* thing, which you can hold on to in order to make yourself understood. I personally believe that the invention, so to speak, of the metaphor is the greatest human invention, greater than the wheel or the computer.

It allows people to think, to bridge . . .

To bridge. It's also the very source of science, scientific thought. A great inventor has to be a poet, in a way, because he can't see just one way of doing things. He immediately builds bridges to other ways.

Incidentally, I've met quite a lot of very good artists—most in the visual arts—who are very good artists, but not very intelligent. But I've never met a *good* poet who is stupid. I've met poets who are crazy, but never one who is stupid, never, or dull.

So making metaphor is a certain way of thinking which incorporates emotion into intellect. It's actually the ideal, basic, human condition. I still think the poet—not *a* poet, because a poet is nothing, but *the* poet—actually is the quintessence of human culture. (pp. 16-17)

There's a poem by Uri Greenberg, "We Were Not Likened To Dogs Among the Gentiles," which seems striking, because in it simile breaks down. Actually the poetry comes to a halt.

Well, he's referring to the Holocaust. How to say this very simply? I must say that's the limit of human experience. The moment something real happens to you, whether good or bad, you don't *need* poetry. Either you don't need it or it doesn't help you.

You would think, for example, someone who has written about war would find that poetry helps him when he's out there. And it *doesn't*. When you are out there nothing helps you, no words, nothing. Just a few words like mother or God or whatever you use. . . .

Listen, if someone would write a love poem while lying in bed with a woman, well, it should be actually the greatest, but it's not. It's the worst. Poetry only comes after such things. It's not the real thing. In *real* situations you either don't need it or, as I said, it doesn't help you at all. In a way like so many other things in life.

It's movies and fiction which have made people think of the war poet sitting in the trenches with shells falling, and he's writing his great poem. I don't believe it. And if any one does write then, they probably write just journal-like notes or lines which are totally unimportant, which become like a mantra. If you just say, "Oh, God help me! Oh, God help me!" it has nothing to do with prayer.

Poetry starts only after the climax. It's one of the first signs that you have *overcome* something.

You often use a very cool, logical tone in your poetry. At the same time, your poetry's often about the illogical. For example, **"God Has Pity on Kindergarten Children"** *or* **"The Diameter of the Bomb."**

That's exactly my image of the world. Everything looks very logical, but the logical order of things breaks down—not only every now and then, almost every day. (p. 17)

In **Not of This Time, Not of This Place,** *Joel is pursued by memory and pursues it. Why is memory so important, particularly historical memory?*

I don't know why, but it's important. It's part of my life, everyone's life. And again it's a natural thing. Body cells, as we know, have genetic memory. So, in a way, it's the same with us. The DNA remembers how I should look, and how everything should function in me, because I got it genetically from my father. History's a built-in memory which is part of reality. . . .

In **The World Is a Room** *the narrator of all the stories seems to be the same person.*

Those stories are a kind of extended—well, I wouldn't say extended poetry, but in a way they show the background of poetry. Or, if this person had been a poet, these things would have made him write poetry.

How autobiographical is the long poem **"Travels of the Last Benjamin of Tudela"?**

Very much so.

You move from . . .

Yes, but it's not a story from the beginning to the end.

Like your novel, it's musical—with several voices going at the same time.

Yes, exactly. And it's one of the things I wrote in two or three weeks. It's also my longest poem.

In what year was it written?

I can tell you exactly: 1967.

Was there anything in particular that brought that poem about?

No, I think it was a great excitement that was in Jerusalem at that time. And it was also a great break in my personal life. And sometimes it happens that things happening *outside* collide with . . . not collide, but go together with things happening *inside*.

Was the public reference to the Six Day War? Were the public and private upheavals related?

The Six Day War coincided with a personal crisis and a breakthrough in my personal life, in my writing and a relief after the threatening weeks before the war started. (p. 18)

How do you see the poet's relationship to ordinary living?

I believe poets start so low that our high is to do things that so-called normal people do, like having children and working for your life and doing things like every carpenter or doctor or anyone else. So actually my high is to live a normal [laughs], an ordinary life. That's why I enjoy things—children and more, because to me they are high.

That brings to mind John Cheever who at one time had an office where he'd go to write from nine to five, just as if he were working in a bank. In a way, it seems he needed to make himself feel legitimate, since he was so aware of his neighbors commuting to New York every day to work.

Yes, it's a kind of undercover—I don't know—a kind of camouflage.

A mask of normalcy?

But no. *Mask* of normalcy, that's another thing. On the contrary, I want to be like . . . to enjoy things like normal people. For instance, children. A lot of creative people think that children are bad for creative work. I think they may take a lot of time and energy but they are good. And I like to work with them. So, to me it's the highest to be like other people and to enjoy it. Most people living a normal life want to get more excitement, but to me the meat, the very excitement of things . . .

It's like oxygen.

Yes, exactly—oxygen. (pp. 18-19)

In Israel there's been a constant state of siege. Do you think the tension there increases the awareness of the senses?

Oh sure, sure. It still does. Especially for me, because I grew up with that situation, and the kinds of danger change. It used to be Arab dangers, then in World War II it was the danger of the Germans, and so on. Of course this intensifies everything, yes.

It's almost a feverish awareness?

Exactly.

What do you see as the poet's relationship to politics? Do you think the poet should avoid taking an explicitly political stance?

Poets, at least in Israel, cannot allow themselves the luxury of being apolitical.

How has the Arab-Israeli conflict affected you as a writer? As a person?

The Arab-Israeli conflict has affected me indeed. Being a soldier and also feeling the constant threat to my very existence by Arab aggression. (pp. 19-20)

Earlier, you mentioned that you're not religious anymore. Does that still bring up conflicts for you?

No, no, no, no, no. Actually, I'm going on with the discussion I had with my father [laughs]. We loved each other very much, but we had this problem—big problem—so we go on, *I* go on discussing it with him. . . .

When I was a child, like every child, I thought my father was really a god, and when I rebelled against him, he still was God. But then I found out, of couse, he was a human being. I think it's the same with God.

So I'm not *practicing*. Only because being religious is totally meaningless. To believe in some greater power—everyone believes in it. But we don't believe that we can understand everything. Nothing is purposeless. There must be some reason for everything, which we don't understand. Either you become a Rabbi or a scientist or whatever to find out that reason. But practicing religion is a totally different thing.

So your father is still whispering in your ear?

In a way, not whispering. Sometimes really he's *twisting* my ear [laughs].

Your poetry is very sensuous and sensual on the outside and very stark on the inside. To put it another way, you seem to balance between Ecclesiastes *and the* Song of Songs, *swaying more toward the* Song of Songs.

Yes, right. That's actually almost an image to describe being between hedonism and existential despair. I always move between these two states, yes.

But you also wrap the Song of Songs *like a piece of fruit around the knife—reversing your image in* **"Inside the Apple."** *Your poems are palatable. They're easy to swallow but hard to digest.*

Yes. Well, some poets or critics think that the poem should not be understood easily. You know how there's this big discussion. It's always going on. And I don't deny it. But a poem should be what it *is*. Whether it's understood easily or not, it's either a good poem or a lousy poem. So this argument's actually totally meaningless.

God forbid that I compare myself to the Bible or Shakespeare, but they can be understood by very primitive people, and can also be a source for a lot of very intellectual, very psychoanalytical speculation or whatnot. So really I think that every piece of art should first of all have an appeal to many people, and some people hopefully can see suddenly that what seemed so simple is not so simple.

But this discussion is going on and on, and sometimes one type of work is in and one is out. But you should do what you do. That's the best thing—never to ask what's in or what's out. (p. 20)

Yehuda Amichai and David Montenegro, in an interview in The American Poetry Review, *Vol. 16, No. 6, November-December, 1987, pp. 15-20.*

A(rchie) R(andolph) Ammons

1926-

American poet.

A prolific writer, Ammons is widely considered among the most significant contemporary American poets. Often referred to as an Emersonian Transcendentalist, Ammons is praised for his sensitive meditations on humanity's capacity to comprehend the flux of the natural world. Initially characterized as a nature poet in the tradition of Walt Whitman and Robert Frost, Ammons frequently writes in a conversational tone and endows his verse with resonant images of detailed landscapes. While often linked with traditional literary movements, Ammons's poetry is pervaded by a modern skepticism which stems from his refusal to attach universal significance to religious or artistic doctrines. Abstaining from offering any facile resolutions to the tensions in his works, Ammons is concerned with broadening his readers' perceptions of their relationship to the world. Donald H. Reiman observed: "A. R. Ammons has engaged the fundamental metaphysical and psychological issues of twentieth-century man—concerns about the relationships of the individual with the Universe and with his own familial and social roots—and he has shown us a way to triumph without relying on dogmatisms or on mere palliatives."

Ammons was born in Whiteville, North Carolina, and was raised in a rural community of farmers that fostered his appreciation for nature. He began writing poetry while serving in the United States Naval Reserve during World War II, and after the war, he enrolled at Wake Forest College, receiving a bachelor of science degree in 1949. Ammons's first collection of poetry, *Ommateum with Doxology* (1955), conveys a broad range of expression. In his attempt to present a multifaceted view of humanity's relationship with the universe, Ammons vacillates between a scientific and a transcendental perspective. Critics noted that much of *Ommateum with Doxology* is reminiscent of the metaphysical verse of Whitman and Emerson but faulted Ammons's attempt to unite the multiplicity of human existence with an encompassing spiritual truth. Ammons's second volume, *Expressions of Sea Level* (1963), garnered critical praise and established him as an important figure in American literature. In this collection, Ammons's conception of the interdependence between humanity and nature becomes more complex, as he begins to focus on the educative and restorative aspects of the universe. Often using images of sea and wind to represent nature's perpetual motion, Ammons suggests that man is only partially cognizant of external forces. In "Unsaid," one of Ammons's most acclaimed pieces, he acknowledges the limitations of human expression as he asks his readers, "Have you listened for the things I have left out?" In *Corson's Inlet* (1965) and *Northfield Poems* (1966), Ammons continues to examine the complex association between man and nature. Ammons's *Collected Poems, 1951-1971* (1972), which presents selections from several of his early volumes, received the National Book Award in 1973.

In addition to his early collections of short lyric verse, Ammons also published two book-length poems, *Tape for the Turn of the Year* (1965) and *Sphere: The Form of a Motion*

(1974). Noted for its ambitiously innovative structure, *Tape for the Turn of the Year* takes the form of a daily poetic journal and chronicles Ammons's thoughts on the mundacity of everyday life. While some commentators claim that this work is incoherent and indulgent, others praise its rejection of rigid meter and structural constraints. In *Sphere: The Form of a Motion* (1974), Ammons focuses on humanity's futile attempts to impose structure on the environment and to suspend the motion of natural forces. While this work is arranged in 155 numbered sections of four tercets each, Ammons's minimal use of punctuation endows *Sphere* with a fluid style that conveys nature's undaunted motion.

In his later volumes, Ammons has tended toward a less discursive style. In such collections as *A Coast of Trees* (1981), *Worldly Hopes* (1982), *Lake Effect Country* (1983), and *Sumerian Vistas* (1987), he employs short-lined forms to create increasingly philosophical explorations of the natural world. *A Coast of Trees* presents a spiritually oriented view of nature and aligns Ammons's work more closely to the Romantics in its adherence to the primacy of human instinct and emotion. In *Worldly Hopes* and *Lake Effect Country,* Ammons fuses his empirical perceptions with hymn-like tributes to nature. In her review of *Worldly Hopes,* Helen Vendler noted: "Ammons is sure that the number of fluid inner states is infinite, and that the only matrix of possibility ample enough to correspond with the inner world is the massively various outer world. And the only mediating instrument between the liquid currents of mind and the mountains and deserts of matter is language, that elusive joiner of rivers to rock." *Selected Poems, 1951-1986* (1987) gathers Ammons's most accomplished verse from throughout his career.

(See also *CLC*, Vols. 2, 3, 5, 8, 9, 25; *Contemporary Authors*, Vols. 9-12, rev. ed.; *Contemporary Authors New Revision Series*, Vol. 6; and *Dictionary of Literary Biography*, Vol. 5.)

ALFRED CORN

Achieving a style and a subject can be like stranding oneself at the top of a tree. I'm guessing this won't happen to Mr. Ammons, even though the 48 short lyrics of *Lake Effect Country* for the most part present a poet we already know well.

"**I Could Not Be Here at All**" is essentially the same poem as "So I Said I Am Ezra," which stands on the first page of his *Collected Poems, 1951-1971.* "**The Spiral Rag**" and "**Fairly High Assimilation Rag**," with their headlong, wide-angle tercets could easily be outtakes from *Sphere.* A disconcerting corollary to Mr. Ammons's free-form and associationist esthetic is that pieces of poems could easily be moved to other poems, with no one but the author the wiser, much as a rock or a shrub can be transferred from one part of the landscape to another without disturbing the general effect.

Judged independently, however, [*Lake Effect Country*] is thoughtful, inventive and secure in tone. The subjects are philosophical in a vein that will seem more than idle speculation to anyone concerned with the relationship between nature, man and the divine. The poet's arguments rely more on imagery and suggestion than logic and rigor; but of course it is precisely the logical rigor of contemporary philosophy that prevents it from taking up Mr. Ammons's topics at all. In our day, metaphysics has taken refuge in poetry.

Mr. Ammons has few rivals in his capacity to observe natural scenes. Effects of light, wind and water are his special province; and he has the verbal power to cast his observations in lively language, so that we relish the visual and verbal detail both at once. Sometimes he abandons description to talk personally and autobiographically. The transcendental mind proves to be as subject to frustration, pain and self-pity as any other. "**Old Desire**" will join the searching (even wounding) poems "**Easter Morning**" and "**Poverty**" in his previous book, *Worldly Hopes,* to fill out the human portrait of this author. Human, and even suburban, as in this irruption from an Ithaca not like Odysseus':

> society will wind and unwind but we may
> or may not have a nice weekend depending on whether
> or not we have been divorced or have enough booze
> to last through Sunday.

That some of the poems adopt a brusquely dismissive tone is one of the shortcomings of Mr. Ammons's manner we have to shrug off, like his enjambments after "the," his disfiguring "busted's," "thru's," "ongoing" "ongoing's" and "&'s."

Some point about the importance of being roughhewn is being made; and, if it helps him write. . . .

The best (and freshest) poems are the lyrics on religious subjects. While "**Zero and Then Some**" disparages any easy mysticism or a sacrament of praise that is too willed, Mr. Ammons doesn't let this antidevotional mood prevail. In a mere 25 lines, "**Lips Twisted With Thirst**" is grandly apocalyptic, especially at the conclusion. . . . (pp. 8, 15-16)

Even better is "**Singing & Doubling Together**," a poem unlike anything else in Mr. Ammons's work. The interpenetration and reciprocity of the human and the divine have seldom been so tellingly spelled out:

> what but grace
>
> have I to bear in every motion,
> embracing or turning away, staggering or standing still,
> while your settled kingdom sways in distillations of light
> and plunders down into the darkness with me
> and comes nowhere up again but changed into your
> singing nature when I need sing my nature nevermore.
>
> > (p. 16)

> *Alfred Corn, "Dada and the Divine," in* The New York Times Book Review, *September 4, 1983, pp. 8, 15-16.*

JAMES FINN COTTER

A. R. Ammons looks no further than his own backyard to find the . . . undoing and unbeing of existence. . . . [In *Worldly Hopes* and *Lake Effect Country,*] he continues to probe nature for a pattern that will enable him and his readers to relate to what we encounter and what encounters us "out there" in weather, seasons, and things. His image of the sphere is a familiar one, but at the center he reminds us that we discover only emptiness, "nothing / more than a bit of / nothing." The poet comes as close as possible to the point where he will vanish into whatever elemental Will or Way mysteriously works its pattern and purpose through all. "**The Scour**," from *Worldly Hopes,* offers a microcosm of the Ammons vision:

> It was so windy
> last night the snow
> got down nowhere
> except against something.

The poet gives resistance by speaking up: ideally he too should give way to the wind and finally acquire the silence of snow. Like the hermit lark, he may reach a spot so remote that in hiding he will "find deeper / shyness yet: be what you must and will be: / I listen and look to found your like in me." *Lake Effect Country* states the myth even more explicitly, in such poems as "**I Could Not Be Here At All**," "**The Spiral Rag**," "**Debris**," "**We, We Ourselves**," and "**The Only Way Around Is Through**," which begins:

> I've lost my ambition to be somebody:
> what is there to be except
> free of the need to be somebody:

The poet admits that trying to "write free of writing keeps me / writing," so that he may achieve the silence beyond. The infinite, in "**Zero and Then Some**," may be the "least spectacular thing around, the / immediate's most trifling ingredient." The task, then, is to give substance and clarity to what filters through brain and blood, to hold on to permanence in transience, and to trace shape in shapelessness, emptiness in flux. Ammons succeeds in defining what he wants: "sense of place complex / enough to represent reality / and simple enough / to be profoundly clear" ("**Negative Pluses**"). By his "shapely assertion," the poem ceases to be the stranger, the voice of the wind, and becomes our own breath and the beating of our own heart. All true encounters with nature and one another are Self-encounters: "you are as if nothing, and / where you are least knowable I celebrate you most" ("**Singling & Doubling Together**"). It is "your great high otherness" that takes on and gives shape to our seeing and knowing all the way through to our coming encounter with death, "changed into your / singing nature when I need sing my nature nevermore." (pp. 722-23)

James Finn Cotter, in a review of "Worldly Hopes" and "Lake Effect Country," in The Hudson Review, *Vol. XXXVI, No. 4, Winter, 1983-84, pp. 711-23.*

PENELOPE MESIC

There are some people who can't get enough of A. R. Ammons, and then again there are some people who can. To the former, Ammons's fecundity (eighteen books) suggests that of Bach or Balzac; to the latter, that of Edgar Rice Burroughs or Joyce Carol Oates. To the Rice-Oates or granivorous faction, it seems as if life would be sweet if Ammons had instead published nine books with twice as many words to a line. The first poem in [*Lake Effect Country*], "**The Bright Side**," for example, throws a sort of hammerlock of monometer on Ammons's normally free-ish, or unfettered, verse:

> Bliss is the
> trace of
> existence that
> persists in
> the idea of
> nothingness

—an assertion so abstract that, after a second of freakish blankness, perhaps brought on by a surfeit of white space, the poem vanishes utterly from the mind. But those for whom more Ammons is better Ammons would surely point out that "**Yadkin Picnic**," a cheerful exploration of a "terminological landscape," is reminiscent of a Steinberg drawing, a self-mocking but sweet pastoral. "**Lips Twisted with Thirst**" is typical of Ammons at his serious best, very American in its odd quality of seeming to be a fervent exclamation framed for the self and overheard, of possessing a sort of willful peculiarity and, rooted in it, authority. (pp. 303-04)

Penelope Mesic, in a review of "Lake Effect Country," in Poetry, *Vol. CXLIII, No. 5, February, 1984, pp. 303-04.*

GRACE GIBSON

In [*Worldly Hopes* and *Lake Effect Country*,] Ammons continues with increasing strength and eloquence to explore and celebrate the "nothingness and amplitude" of nature, depreciating the human position. Yet he knows the poet's perceiving eye as quintessential, though man may be, in the scale of the universal, inconsequential. In "**I Could Not Be Here at All**," he begins: "Momentous and trivial, I . . ." From nature's motions, often the spiral vortex or whirlwind and the

waterfall, the poet finds "figures visible" to "summon the deep-lying fathers from myself," he writes in the final poem of *Lake Effect Country,* called "**Meeting Place.**"

Although he chooses to leave out nearly every reference to man and his works, this book does include the hurt and the loss in three moving portraits of old, vulnerable people. Ammons knows that abundance, "starved out," may become "abundant space" ("**Making Room**") and in "**Instancing**" he offers to give "quick tips on dining on nothing alone." In "**Limits**" he asks, "since / bent we / break on / time that lets / everything endure / changed / why not take / liberties / and love / what is not?"

Indeed, he explores again and again nothingness, death, and the possibility of immortality. For example, in "**Zero and Then Some**," writing about "what is," he says that "humbly we know too it / bore us and will support us into whatever / rest remains," although "We would not want to persuade ourselves / on eternity with an insistence of our own / . . . nevertheless we would not want to miss a / right praising." In "**Positive Edges**" he speaks of the spirit freeing itself from shapes "the subtraction netting nothing." In "**We, We Ourselves**," nothing holds: "it does—under the / deepest fall the / . . . ultimate / sympathy / . . . turns cupping into/ the levitating explosions, / of meetings, hallelujahs, / upward drafts / after all."

He insists on the limitations of the mind that "figures but even though it wants to do well / never comes up with the source of what it comes up with." In "**Pairing**" he uses short paired lines to say that although "wish is a closer rightness / than reason" when "wish is not to be wished / reason like / a failed mate / roams the woods / of the self / whining for the / lost one."

About his purposes in writing and his qualities as a writer Ammons says that in choosing to write about nature the poet finds "messages sent to / no one, requiring no response" that may nevertheless be / taken / down in strict / observances (like studied regard) / as if to be nearly adequate / messages to no one." He hopes that he "will go through / the period of hunger / for immortality and be stated—" in order to rise from "that death" into "communion with things . . . the wiping out / of borders and prints, stains, ink;" to abide "the / immortality likeliest to last . . . / change's pure arising in constant souls." ("**Written Water**").

Ammons sets down in "**Scribbles**" his paradoxical writing purposes and program, denying all knowledge of truth, embracing perplexity: "To unwrite the writing, unweave, ravel out / the woven, unsay the spoken, and make hard / to perceive the seen and known." The poem "**Negative Pluses**" offers a self portrait [of] "one who . . . feels the / burn of difference, / . . . develops rotundity of preparation / and defense, an undue / awareness of transience; and a sense of place complex / enough to represent reality / and simple enough to be profoundly clear."

It is in *Lake Effect Country* that Ammons' deep, religious impulse becomes most explicit. Consider in "**Localizing**": "God's will (the Way) everybody knows holds / grave assimilations of constancy in change," and "whether we step forward or not, we are forwarded daily to a sparer / dimension, lessened mansion: but surely / there is a Will so high change can't stir / it nor loss nor gain stagger it, spirit / unshadowed and shadowless! but we love it here!"

With the sureness of its spare, coloquial tone, Ammons' language fills the pulpit, matching the profundity of his meaning (or what he calls "my nuzzlings & / whimpers for meaning.") The power of this language provides the levitating force, like the vortex, the "mechanism for taking, changing and / giving out, for holding still while the motion flies!" This language sweeps up closely observed details of backyard and brook along with metaphysical meditations and gives a "standing-motion shape," an "inward-turning whirl" for a meeting of the natural and the metaphysical.

The beautiful, transcendental poem, **"Singing and Doubling Together"** may be read with equal effectiveness as a love poem or as a celebration of man's relationship to what Ammons elsewhere calls "that which is to be praised." This poem, full of tenderness and pain, ranks, in my view with his earlier, much-praised **"Easter Morning"** that appeared in his National Book Critics Circle Award-winning volume, *A Coast of Trees,* in 1981. (pp. 178-79)

The first poem of *Lake Effect Country* speaks of bliss as the "trace of existence that / persists in / the idea of / nothingness—" as "a presence fragile as / the longing look / through / tragedy, the frail whirl / the mind climbs / (the defense / against absolute beginnings / or endings) . . . the light that sets / in the utterly empty eye." In the final poem of the volume, **"Meeting Place,"** Ammons' "gladness in the recognition," shared by many contemporary scientists, that in nature's shapes and motions "instruction is underway . . . an answering is calling" provides an affirmative counterbalance for [an] otherwise tragic view. (p. 180)

Grace Gibson, "Ammons' Last Two Books: In Nature, on Answering Calling," in Pembroke Magazine, No. 16, 1984, pp. 178-80.

KATHERINE DIECKMANN

As A. R. Ammons once wrote, "It's necessary to be quiet in the hands of the marvelous." Good thing he didn't take himself too seriously. In both his 20th book of poems, *Sumerian Vistas,* and the newly expanded edition of *The Selected Poems* (which tags 10 recent texts onto a collection that originally covered 1951-1977), Ammons speaks with force and clarity of the marvelous that is the natural world, and of the way the mind sees itself figured there. To read Ammons is to take a stroll with him—his poems trace the movements of wind, stone, and star, charting labyrinthine patterns of growth and decay. But this is no sappy nature-loving stuff. When Ammons walks a meandering path, science and sex and the laws of gravity, dream and meditation, are as present to him as an intriguing rock formation.

Heir to Whitman and Emerson (not to mention Stevens), with some of Roethke's vegetative passion, Ammons celebrates the differentials to be found in one place: specifically, the dramatic gorges, waterfalls, and rolling hills of Ithaca, New York, where this transplanted North Carolinian has made his home since 1964. The flux of the physical world is more than apparent there—autumn is aggressively bright, winter harsh enough to induce solipsistic reverie—and Ammons has made himself a guardian and interpreter of this changing landscape. In **"The Ridge Farm,"** one of two extended, multisection pieces in *Sumerian Vistas,* Ammons and companions take a wintry walk to a farmhouse on a hill; as they ascend the slope, the poem likewise begins to leave the ground and digress: to contemplate "mutability and muck. . . . the odor of shit is like language"; to offer advice to a young poet ("it is passive / to do the bidding of the voice you have / imagined formed"); and to appraise the accumulation of Ammons's own years of work. Throughout *Sumerian Vistas* one senses a lessened anxiety about the problem of voice, a key preoccupation in *The Selected Poems,* where Ammons's alter ego, Ezra, shouts "So I said I am Ezra / and the wind whipped my throat," struggling to articulate himself against the proverbially burdened poetic past. (The weight of influence is clearly an issue Ammons is familiar with; he's dedicated more than one poem to his friend Harold Bloom.)

Ammons is now a seasoned practitioner, and *Sumerian Vistas* has a sense of both the authority and freedom to play that comes with time. There's plenty of whimsy in the **"Motion's Holdings"** section, a group of short pieces, where the lines tend to be lighter (little of Ammons's passion for long phrases broken by colons), and a poem called **"Postulation"** riffs on the elusiveness of the verb *to be.* His spare style works beautifully in **"Stone Keep"** and **"Power Plays,"** though longer, complex poems allow him to work out images and themes that circulate around each other like the figures of arc and sphere he so often uses, creating the "mishmashes of tinkling circlets" in the closing line of **"The Ridge Farm."**

Throughout *Sumerian Vistas,* Ammons continues to root his vision to a specific place, letting it be an imaginative locus for a moment of exalted contemplation. In **"Cascadilla Falls,"** from *The Selected Poems,* Ammons meditates on the years of activity compressed in a single stone, then drops it in a stream:

> shelterless
> I turned
>
> to the sky and stood still:
> oh
> I do
> not know where I am going
> that I can live my life
> by this single creek.

Life by a single creek, and the variousness of experience available in that one spot, has produced a body of poetry rich in its evocation of the marvelous, and the need to try and articulate it.

Katherine Dieckmann, "Site Lines," in The Village Voice, Vol. XXXII, No. 34, August 25, 1987, p. 52.

ALICE FULTON

Every genius forces us to educate ourselves anew. For those who haven't made the effort yet in regard to A. R. Ammons, the expanded *Selected Poems* offers the best introduction to the glories of his work. From the first, he has been fascinated by duality: the relationships between choice/chance; one/many; microcosm/macrocosm; center/periphery; motion/stasis. His obsession with polarities stems from a wish to break down such oppositions and reveal the underlying unity of forms. In Ammons's mind, art involves motion rather than classical stasis. As a result, his poems are more like kinetic sculptures than well-wrought urns. Nature fascinates because it (unlike art) is constantly in flux. "Honor a going thing, goldfinch, corporation, tree, / morality . . . ," he writes. He delights in fractal forms that fall somewhere between order and chaos, between the Euclidean cracks. Knowledge is that which consigns itself to "approximation, order to the vehicle / of change, and fumbles blind in blunt innocence / toward divine, terrible love." This is a poetry of ideas, yet ideas are important only insofar as they help us live our lives. In human terms, the one/many dichotomy speaks to the need for autonomy versus the need for absorption into the shared experience.

Perhaps Ammons is most famous as nature's scribe and prophet, one in whom river weeds and gulches confide. He is also a seer in the etymological sense of "one who sees." His poems illuminate the marginal: the plants growing on rocks that "people never see / because nothing should grow on rocks. . . ." Like the plants, the self in his poems is a slight presence arguing against or adjusting to its impending abnegation. In fact, the language's intentions are ontological rather than geological. Far from being a cold clinician of the soul, Ammons is keeper of peripheral flames; his stance is one of modesty before the universe and tenderness before humanity. In the magnificent early poem **"Still,"** the speaker sets out to find "the lowly" as "a handy focus and reminder" of his own significance:

> I found a beggar:
> he had stumps for legs: nobody was paying
> him any attention: everybody went on by:
>   I nestled in and found his life:
> there, love shook his body like a devastation:
> I said
>   though I have looked everywhere
>   I can find nothing lowly
>   in the universe. . . .

"Hymn," another important early poem, recalls Whitman in its chanting parallel structure and pantheistic search for a force that exists "past the blackset noctilucent clouds" or with "the microvilli sporangia." Like Whitman, Ammons is fond of cataloging the specimens that comprise the One. Yet the poet of transcendental affirmations is also the poet who asserts "I see no / god in the holly . . ." and who sternly locates the "surrendered self among / unwelcoming forms. . . ."

Formally, this is an experimental poetry. Although the poems are often analogous to prayers or fables, the smaller structural elements are miraculously inventive. Ammons's subjects are reflected in the formation of his lines. Seldom end-stopped, often enjambed with prepositions or articles, they enact the infinite adjustments of balance that comprise equilibrium. The registers of diction within a single stanza can range from oracular to scatological, pastoral to technical. The poems sometimes begin with a thesis ("You cannot come to unity and remain material. . . .") and proceed to argue it out of existence. Ammons's signature colon, the most democratic punctuation, builds equivalence on both sides. Its indeterminate pauses are to his poetry what dashes are to [Emily] Dickinson's.

In fact, Ammons insistently recalls Dickinson. His dazzling turns of abstraction ("parabolas of bliss," the soul as "an area of poise") are hauntingly Dickinsonian, as is his volatile grammar. Both poets favor a compressed, reflexive syntax that requires readers to participate in the process of composition by filling in grammatical deletions. And this process of reconstruction accounts for the interwoven difficulties and pleasures of the poems. The complexity is not there for its own sake, but because the states elucidated are intricate. It

takes a formidable poet to give them voice. Ammons's distinctive vocabulary embraces such Dickinsonian terms as "circumference," "arc," and "difference," in addition to his own lexicon of "sphere," "salience," "periphery," "motion," and so on. And as with Dickinson, you have to read a lot of him in order to say you've read him at all. His canon forms an ongoing, multifarious sequence. In fact, my one complaint about the expanded *Selected Poems* concerns its exclusions. I miss **"Grace Abounding"** and **"Uh, Philosophy"** from the early work. Although the book includes work from three volumes published since 1977, such important and beautiful poems as **"Poverty,"** **"Zero and Then Some,"** and **"Localizing"** are omitted. But I am quibbling. [Throughout *Selected Poems*], one feels the pressure of an inexhaustible intelligence keeping language on the stretch. The resultant poetry opens intoxicating vistas in the heart and mind, coming as it does, "from the self not mine but ours."

In his latest collection, *Sumerian Vistas,* Ammons, like the god Janus, gazes backward to antiquity and forward to mortality, seeking "plateaus of staying and view." One of the book's subjects is inscription: the origins, permanence, and transience of writing. Poetry and epitaphs are seen as efforts to fix time, while nature is read as a script of motion, a text of regeneration. Although the book's title might lead one to expect archaeological finds, Sumeria is invoked as a metaphor of inception. It was there that writing first developed, and antiquity serves as a backdrop for explorations of beginning and closure, of generative cycles.

The first fifty pages are devoted to **"The Ridge Farm,"** a discursive sequence covering a wide aesthetic terrain. A ridge, after all, is a *line* where two upward sloping surfaces meet. The poem investigates the relationship between fluency and form, the paradoxical holding to "the rigid line of the free and easy" within free verse. The ridge (like the poetic line) was there 500 years ago, and it "provides a / measure. . . ." The ridge also stands for the relationship between Self and Other. Those living on the raised land can't see it. What they can see is the non-self of the opposite hillside, an otherness to the east. And since it is an exaltation of landscape, the ridge becomes a metaphor for the divine. Indeed, some of the poem's loveliest lines examine the properties of holiness. The sacred may be recognized by its quality of concern, but it is also "something we could / miss altogether even while it / sustained us throughout." The holy and profane are united, as when "the waste in a woods gives / off the best heat and brightest / illumination." Nature consoles because it has designs without having designs on us. In fact, Ammons goes to nature precisely because it lets him "miss anything personal in / the roar of sunset." In contrast to human cruelty, which frightens since it is "like one's own mercilessness," nature's cruelty is mitigated by its impersonality. Lest all this seem ponderous, I must mention that Ammons has a wicked, self-mocking humor. "I love nature especially if there's / a hospital nearby and macadam or / glass in between," he admits.

Of all our poets, Ammons is perhaps most committed to an aesthetic of inclusion. He is concerned with "how to exclude the central," "how to get out into the looser / peripheries." In his view, "the truth is commodious, abundant: we / must make a room so sufficient it will / include till nothing will be left / over for walls." Given his capacious vision and suspicion of hierarchies, I found myself wondering why "man" appeared generically in the poems. One current limitation of our language is its assignation of otherness or periphery to woman. Although the generic "man" or "he" pretends to encompass everyone, when we read those words, we envision a male. To substitute "woman" for the universal "man," (or create a new inclusive usage) would be to question bedrock assumptions of marginality. "I am . . . maternal as well as paternal," said Whitman. Sympathetic, brilliant, generous—Ammons might, if he chose, prove and define this "main thing," to which Whitman gave a passing nod.

The Sumerians carved their religious poetry on clay tablets. Part Two, **"Tombstones,"** is a meditation upon those tablets we raise against transience. The vista of this long poem is enormous in scope: a human life is compared to a mayfly's and to "a pulse in one of earth's orbits" that "beats once in four hundred thousand years." The motions of wind are contrasted to "the stone's slow swirl" that "keeps the name." "Nothing" is a tangible presence since "grooves of absence" tell the names on tombstones. Perhaps, Ammons suggests, fine things—wind, light—last longest. If love is such a fine evanescence, we dishonor it by trying to name it "on the hard waters of inscription." It follows that blowing dust might be the best memorial, reassuring us "that what is gone is / going on. . . ." In a bold move, the cosmos itself is conceived as "love's memorial:" a vast, complex tombstone. After all, Ammons notes, "ninety percent / of the universe is dead stars, / but look how the light still / plays flumes down / millennial ranges. . . ."

The last sixty-one pages of **Sumerian Vistas** contain many superb poems. **"The Hubbub"** posits mundane actions and Zen-like stillness as respites from "divinity's loftier stations"; **"Telling Moves"** offers insights into aging and our rebellions against the inevitable; **"Recoveries"** illuminates cosmic dissolutions and formations; **"Some Any"** casually persuades us of love and thought's abundance; and the book's final poem, **"Citified,"** opposes the hazards of self isolation to those of community. In **"Autonomy"** and **"Power Plays"** Ammons explores romantic love with sensitivity and wisdom. Here is the latter poem in its entirety:

> I know that splendor's your
> arms, your hands,
> not spools and drifts of stars:
>
> your hair, falling, gives in
> the way desire builds defenseless:
> you soothe my twists; unwinding,
>
> they wind into your calm:
> don't be afraid: deference
> controls me: I can
>
> win or lose you and find
> the bone in your arm
> still too fine to bear.

"The Dwelling," another luminous verse, argues that "the heart's cravings" should flare bright into what is near at hand, earthly. Through Ammons's poems we are consoled into just such celebrations. Reading them, one feels assured " . . . that here the plainnest / majesty gave us what it could." (pp. 360-65)

Alice Fulton, "Main Things," in Poetry, *Vol. CLI, No. 4, January, 1988, pp. 360-77.*

HELEN VENDLER

Ammons believes both that poetry has a public effect and that the effect does not depend on whether poets consciously assume "public responsibility." His wish to draw a distinction between public responsibility (writing with one eye on the topical) and public effect (in the short run, subversion; in the longer run, perhaps, conservation) is only one proof of his careful and anxious intelligence. . . .

[He] is not afraid to represent the human presence as it has actually occurred in the universe: not at the center but at the edge of its galaxy, which itself is one temporary and random point in a very long historical continuum. He not only sees our existence in that light; he *feels* it to be so. At the same time, he respects the way in which consciousness must be a center unto itself, no matter what its position in the universe.

The title of Ammons' new book, **Sumerian Vistas,** emphasizes his long view of human existence. In his youth, he first turned to Sumer (where writing was invented) as a vantage point. At twenty-nine, he published in his first book, **Ommateum,** several lyrics in which he adopted, as a refuge from acute temporal anxiety, the persona of a prophet who had come to ancient Sumer and had perceived the immense distance between besieged life and calm necessity:

> I have grown a marsh dweller
> subject to floods and high winds . . .
>
> rising with a handful of broken shells
> from sifted underwater mud
> I have come to know how high
> the platform is, beyond approach,
> of serenity and blue temple tiles.

The "Sumerian" dweller in catastrophe of that early poem now writes **Sumerian Vistas.** Though Ammons' vistas do not deny age (the grave is mentioned fairly often, and a sequence on inscription is entitled **"Tombstones"**), his tone has not changed: it still has all the spring and backlash and curiosity of his young voice. His titles still show punning casualness (**"Working Out," "Abstinence Makes the Heart Grow Fonder"**) as well as epigrammatic brevity (**"Dominant Margins," "Scaling Desire"**). As usual, his borrowings from scientific diction—**"Information Density," "Negative Symbiosis," "Red Shift"**—are used with high freedom; **"Red Shift,"** for instance, is not about stars but about a winter-pale begonia (and its owner) receiving a new infusion of "bright blood" from the spring sun.

Ammons is a poet of determined factual exactness. In poems as neat as laboratory drawings, he tells the truth about biological life—for example, that everything eats something else in order to live. If a jay stops the song of a cicada, and attacks its eyes as if they were just another set of seeds to crack open for food, that is the nature of existence—a matter for eventoned recognition rather than lament, terror, or indignation. Lament, terror, and indignation nonetheless have their place, as flashes of feeling, in Ammons' poems; but they are components, not determinants, of cognition. (p. 100)

Ammons is so expert in thinking of himself as a corpse, already dissolved into dust and air, that his own dissolution provides an airy poetics of dispersion, reflecting "genetic material's / extravagant loss along the / edging peripheries of accident." The fact of eventual disappearance also suggests an ethics. Given one's end, how should one live? **"Backcasting"** answers this way:

> I can tell by
> the way

gravel will spill
through me some

day it's
all right to
mess around: I can
tell by the way

light will
find me transparent I
can't be gross:
I drift,

slouch about, spoof:
I true the
coming-before
to the consequence.

One can imagine the demands put by Ammons' muse: "Write a poem on dying that will be as light as the dust and transparency you will become. Then deduce from those motes and air a way of living suitable to that ending. From the consequence of eventual dissolution deduce a premise for existence: true the coming-before to the consequence." The deduced premise, for Ammons, is to lessen ponderousness: the poet can mess around, be airy, drift, slouch, spoof. The poem itself must be full of air spaces, loose siftings, casual rhythms, or it will not be the believable messenger of its entropic message.

Ammons was brought up on the Bible (it was the only book in the house, he has said, in his rural North Carolina boyhood), and the earnestness of a Biblical tone has always been part of his repertoire. In the light of that early Biblical impress, his post-Christian (though reverent) position is all the more original. It is still rare to find poetry of serious intellectual premises that can get along without disabling religious or ideological nostalgia. (pp. 100-01)

Ammons' work is post-Christian not only in its marginal positioning of man, and in its acceptance of evolution rather than special creation, but also, in the way it emphasizes the inevitably aspectual nature of perception and cognition. Like his predecessor [Wallace] Stevens, he denies the univocal positing of a single attainable truth (of the sort conventionally proposed by Christian theology). The title of Ammons' first book, **Ommateum,** refers to the compound eye of an insect, and his prose preface to that collection says, "The poems suggest a many-sided view of reality; an adoption of tentative, provisional attitudes, replacing the partial, unified, prejudicial, and rigid."

Tentative and provisional thoughts require discretion and grace in expression. In an interview published in *Pembroke* in 1986 Ammons said:

> To me, the really great poet feels as deeply as anyone these matters, but touches only and controls them lightly with delicate gestures that just merely register they are there. To me, the second- or third-rate poet . . . begins to bushwack and hack and cut and try to create an artificial fury because he thinks that will give him the gestures of great poetry, but it gives him just the opposite.

Readers unaccustomed to discretion in gesture prefer loud noises. For them, poetry is a matter of violent statement. But for Ammons a poem is a "disposition . . . rather than an exposition." He has said, "It may be made out of words but it's no longer saying anything. It's just complete." The poem has found a system of relational completeness in the company of its fellow-poems; both of these are something silent, and they are more complex than statement, though statement is one of the means to them.

Like most of Ammons' other volumes, **Sumerian Vistas** contains long poems as well as short. ("In short poems, I'm on a tightwire, and in long poems, the plain is wide and the direction uncertain," he has said.) Short poems become riddles in which he often deliberately exploits the ambiguous power of words that can serve as several different parts of speech. In the opening of **"Earliest Recollection,"** for instance, the words "thaws," "snow," "clear," "leaves," "touched," "last," "fall," and "gathering" can each act more than one part in the game of syntax: "thaws" could be a verb or a plural noun; "clear" could be a verb or an adjective. We hesitate, placing them, as we read the lines:

> Thaws snow-clear the fields
> and woods, and leaves
> snow's small weight
>
> touched down last fall
> crinkle to the breezes
> and rise gathering dry.

Ammons' suspension of ambiguous parts of speech in an open field mimics the hovering act of perception itself.

Ammons' shorter, poems, like **"Earliest Recollection,"** often recount the vicissitudes of accident or chance, but the longest poem in the new volume, **"The Ridge Farm,"** exemplifies his sense of the sacredness of necessity—that interaction of all universal motions:

> sap, brook, glacier, spirit
> flowing, these are sacred but
> in a more majestic aloofness
> than we can know or reason with.

Ammons acknowledges the deep human wish for the "easy sacredness" of a personal divine providence ("some band or / quality of concern to / recognize us here"), but he calls us to recognize what he sees as a loftier sacredness—"something / high to realize, recalcitrant, / unyielding to makeshift in / its quality." As Ammons, with sternness and accuracy, makes his reports on high impersonal necessity, his country goes on funding television evangelists and papal visits. This standoff would make one despair of the gulf between a poet and his culture were it not that cultures eventually catch up to their poets. **"The Ridge Farm,"** like Ammons' other long poems, offers us a gift we may be reluctant to receive, the privilege of living for a while inside an original and a querying adult intelligence. This intelligence has three chief registers: it notices with joyful precision the Thoreauvian world of natural fact; it spins fine-grained meditations on the mind's ways of being; and it urges an ethics founded on the possibility of cultural illumination and human concern.

It is Ammons' entrancing Southern storytelling voice that carries us along in his narratives of natural fact. Intent, for instance, on watering a dried-up plant in a jar, Ammons picks up a watering can neglected all winter, and the story begins:

> I noticed last fall's leaves in the
> can and though well that will improve
> the juice but I thought it did smell
> funny: I poured water into the jar top
> and most of it, drought-refused, ran over or
> out: so I waited for the soak to take and
> began to think something really

smelled: I poured some more rich brown
juice into the jar and then upended
the can to let the leaves fall out and
out plunked this animal clothed in
leaves so I couldn't tell what he was
except his thick tail looked thicker
than a rat's: mercy: I'd just had
lunch: squooshy ice cream: I nearly
unhad it: I expect the crows will come
and peck it up, up, and away, the way
they do squirrels killed on the
streets: pulling at the long, small
intestines and getting a toehold on
small limbs to tear off the big flesh

the rat was a mole: the arctic air
yesterday afternoon dried him out and
the freeze last night stiffened him much
reduced in size and scent: so
I broke out the shovel, dug up a
spade, dumped in the mole: there let
him rot, the rat: I can see how
something blind could get into my
wateringcan: but with those feet!
I can hear him scratching up the side:
to get in, or out: but also I can hear him
sloshing, the blind water darkened by
night, till nobody came.

There has been nothing like this in American poetry before
Ammons—nothing with this liquidity of folk voice. And this
down-to-earth narration sits at home in Ammons' mind next
to his riddling intellectual speculativeness, which ranges from
creative rummaging ("home is / where the doodle is") to moments of cultural despair:

> culture, hardened to shellac's empty
> usage, defines in definitions
> hoaxdoms of remove from the true life
> which
> is smaller, leaner than a brook, no
> louder, variable as, to the true rain.

Into the hardened hoaxdoms of culture come particles of
human veracity and concern, lighting up one partial space.
Though he rejects religious superstition, Ammons is still the
poet of our Protestant past in his trust in the inner light. That
ethical light is intermittent but, he believes, immortal in its
recurrence:

> a light catches somewhere, finds human
> spirit to burn on, shows its magic's
> glint lines, attracts, grows, rolls
> back space and dark. . . .
>   it dwells:
> it dwells and dwells: slowly the light,
> its veracity unshaken, dies but moves
> to find a place to break out elsewhere:
> this light, tendance, neglect
> is human concern working with
> what is: one thing is hardly better
> or worse than another: the
> split hair of possible betterment makes
> dedication reasonable and heroic:
> the frail butterfly, a slightly
> guided piece of trash, the wind takes
> ten thousand miles.

The strictly limited extent of light and concern is not lost on
Ammons. (pp. 101-04)

By now, Ammons has amassed a lifetime's worth of wayward, experimental, cursive, volatile verse, ranging from the
briefness of **Briefings** (1971) to the long unwinding of **Tape
for the Turn of the Year** (1965)—to name two characteristic
extremes in his practice. His definitive "Collected Poems,"
when it appears, will be one of the influential American books
of this century, notable for its foregoing of dogmatism in a
dogmatic time and for its tender, shrewd, and nonchalant
charting of a way to live responsibly within natural fact, scientific imagination, and ethical discovery. (p. 104)

> *Helen Vendler, "Veracity Unshaken," in* The New
> Yorker, *Vol. LXIII, No. 52, February 15, 1988, pp.*
> *100-04.*

JAMES FINN COTTER

In **"The Ridge Farm"** from his latest collection of poetry, **Sumerian Vistas,** A. R. Ammons describes a conversation with
a poet who gives him a poem with the comment, "this is not
my true voice, only a / line or so." Ammons reflects that this
poet wants "to write by the voice" rather than "to say what
you have to say / and let the voice find itself / assimilated
from the many tones and sources." In his own poetry, Ammons is as concerned about letting this voice speak as he is
about uncovering it in nature and in himself. In wind and
brook we may imagine words of our own making, but nature
says nothing because "it has nothing to say." Knowing and
speaking arise as necessities in us to be engaged in the process
of sun and season, living and dying, motion and rest. The universe around us is dissolving; trees, plants, and people return
to earth. A mole drowned in a watering can or a squirrel hit
by a car provoke the poet to honest descriptions of dissolution
and equally honest reflections. Tombstones carry names chiseled in stone; poems are words on paper. Something endures:

> the wind roars, sweeps, whirls,
> nearly free even in its calms.
> and the wind carries leaves, sand,
> seed, whatever: rain pours,
> puddles, flows: the ground
> yields to this or that pull, break,
> flush: among the swirling
> motions, the stone's slow swirl
> keeps the name
>
>   **"Tombstones"**

In time, the names will "rise out of stone" and disappear.
Like the poet's words they catch the swerve and glint of an
existence before departing, they say what they can, and they
live on in memory. Ammons is a religious poet with a transcendental bent, but with his own stance and creed. In **"The
Dwelling,"** he asserts:

> I would as soon believe
> in paradise as in
> nothing: it is no great
>
> wonder that our spiritual
> energy, purified, returns
> to, is, the eternal
>
> residence: no greater
> wonder than that earth is
> here at all:

The poet has no quarrel with the diety: "here the plainest /
majesty gave us what it could." With a neat twist, he makes
faith itself the veil that separates us from divinity: "belief's
a fine cloth: / a sheen before the eyes." Ammons' vision is one
of gleams and glimpses, motions that curve, spin, and angle.

His most explicitly philosophical poem, with echoes of an Omega point where everything converges and emerges, is titled **"Pots and Pans."** He pins down generalizations and domesticates ideas. His voice is not imitative but adaptive and adoptive. Each poem pursues a new venture into the knowable and sayable. Out of disorder, the poet seeks a pattern: like the catbird that pecks at a stone in a brook, "breaking the reflective surfaces with / mishmashes of tinkling circlets" (**"The Ridge Farm"**). By indirections find directions out.

No poet is fortunate enough to find the voice of every poem. Ammons can be obtuse in avoiding the obvious, so reticent that he risks retiring from his own lines. He wants to describe a scene and disappear into it. His ideal poem is total silence. In his fullest experience, he finds nothing there. What about the reader? May he or she feel left out—even be left out? Ammons appears aware of the problem, but that risk lies in the nature of the venture, the zen of his poetry. He makes even his faults work for him; stumbling at times he makes his way ahead. (pp. 225-26)

James Finn Cotter, "The Voice of Poetry," in The Hudson Review, *Vol. XLI, No. 2, Spring, 1988, pp. 225-32.*

JANE MILLER

If A. R. Ammons is one of our most prolific poets, he is "difficult" and some people don't read him. Although he uses the present tense a lot, it is hard to feel him there. **Sumerian Vistas** is made of two long poems in sections—**"Ridge Farm,"** a fifty-one part description and meditation on place, and **"Tombstones,"** an homage to stone. The last section, **"Motion's Holdings,"** is a group of shorter poems, in which Ammons is generous to and absorbed by nature, somewhat less stiff to human interaction; he is a most impersonal romantic. (p. 10)

Mid-way through **"Ridge Farm,"** he describes the method as if to confirm it, to convince us of it; it is abstract and specific, wholly original like the early Mesopotamians whose Sumerian language has no known relatives, ancient or modern. We get our means of telling time from them, a numerical system on the basis of twelve, our notion of equal justice under the law, and a means by which to measure angles:

> I like, as I have said before,
> maximum implication and
>
> registration of fact and tension before
> integration catches on as to how
>
> it is to work and the point it
> catches on to the finish what a war
>
> between what will and will not be
> captured by design,

This cool, architectonic abstraction and exactness isn't yet vague or hermetic, but it can get that way, choking on its word choice and syntax:

> culture, hardened to shellac's empty
> usage, defines in definitions
> hoaxdoms of remove from the true life
> which
> is smaller, leaner than a brook, no
> louder, variable as, to the true rain:

Poetry is about situations of essence, but here is a blur, a vagueness of abstract nouns, so it is hard to concern ourselves with the discrete or discreet instant. It sounds far away from us, at the periphery of real-time. But let's be careful; quickly on the heels of that, Ammons is microscopically perceptive:

> little showers yesterday evening, quiet
> as rabbits emerging into dusk to feed,
> darkened the macadam except where
>
> overhanging shower-holding trees drew their
> negatives in dry ground:

Ammons does seem precious at times, working the diminutives; the movement through time appears dense, broken, odd, but the sentiment is predictable:

> how
> our forefathers hated woods and sex,
> so much of both to deal with,
> cut down or back: but now the
> coonyus surrounded by taming
> equations of the pill, the sperm
> rage, such a wilderness, shot wild,
> why we can horse deeply in with
> irresponsibility's ease: that's what
> they say: I'm afraid nature's going
> to send the bill: it usually does:
> ferocious tallywhacker

This is description, and though it jags and shifts with the experienced writer's ease from the rhetorical to the figurative, under the syntax is the sentimental intent of the observer—a rendering of the situation, not a transformation.

"Our strong biases for gradual and continuous change force us to view mass extinctions as anomalous and frightening." Stephen Jay Gould is a biologist, but many poets are unable to kill off in themselves the urge to render from the middle ground. This perspective leads to explanation rather than enactment, especially where Ammons intellectualizes:

> we come sponging
> back to the tables of our children
> to be swatted: since this
> is one place,
> going is coming, ending beginning,
> individual shape shed
> like exoskeletons of spiritual flies

Here the simile is absurd and the metaphysics watery. Ammons's quirky diction and syntactical moves often amount to decoration, for when the content is excavated for its meaning, the intent is again sentimental; in this, the weakest section, he can be embarrassing, marmish to the point of mannerism:

> home is
> where the doodle is: today cleared

Later, he is relaxed and intense in the short lyrics that compose **"Tombstones"**:

> nothing though, not stone
> nor light lasts
> like the place I keep
> the love of you in and this
>
> though nothing can write it down
> and nothing keep it:
> nothingness
> last long enough to keep it

This is passionate, but the chopped lines can't transform the easy sentiment. Yet it is captivating to hear the human element sweeten the voice. Ammons need never worry about lapsing into "modernism's adventuresome self-involvement."

Though there's no question of Ammons's intimacy with the natural world and his great ear for the crack of the consonant, Frost's seeming lack of generosity is present, a kind of emotional reduction. Yet when he is not absorbed with technique that literally stalls itself, as in ["**Entranceways**"]

> If not ready to
> go, to be gone
>
> I looked about
> at the heightenings leavetaking
>
> confers,
>
> he can imagine
>
>> things
>> abstracted
>
> useless stricken
> new

At his best, Ammons never makes the reader start over as if he's tripped. Also, a poem really working outside time will never *end* for the reader, despite the reception of meaning. For subject matter is the least important thing; a poem at its best will create a semblance of motion, the swirl of mystery. We will literally be altered by a subliminal comprehension of its gesture, its ability, through fresh language movingly rendered, to ratify "the universality of our desires and our fears as human beings," as David Mamet says.

In Ammons's "**Coming Round**" . . . despite the conventional imagery, the activity of the poem and its syntax, its compound words and romantic sensibility are in the service of a powerful emotional seed. The poem is free of the obtuse wordiness of "**Motion's Holdings**":

>> the branch
> of honeysuckle leaves arcs outward
>
> into its becoming motion but,
> completion's precision done, gives
> over riddling free to other
>
> motions:

or the obvious remarks of "when one loses nothing, one / loses everything"—this isn't redeemed by its line break—or again, "I don't take brooks seriously / but you could say if a brook's dry / it's stopped running or / gravity's off " ("**HairyBelly**"). The overwriting builds in this book, packing time with prepositional phrases: "I still have / next to nothing, heaps of verbal glitterment, / rushes of feeling overrushing feeling" ("**Tertiaries**"); or

> but, on the other hand, to waken
> in an ultimate extremity, death or love,
>
> to a reveille bleaching out the colorful
> penants of beliefc!

("Dominant Margins")

That mixed metaphor and abstract prepositional phrase do not inspire. Yet, where the lyric so impinges on this book that the human condition surfaces, his happenings in nature come alive, take us through experience-in-time while we are suspended during the "time it takes" to read and re-emerge dislocated from our assumptions. If any poet makes a case for

the personal, Ammons is very capable of it. For him it is never an indulgence, it's a respite. (pp. 10-12)

> *Jane Miller, "Working Time," in* The American Poetry Review, *Vol. 17, No. 3, May-June, 1988, pp. 9-21.*

NATHAN A. SCOTT, JR.

It has been a privilege over the past twenty-five years to watch the steadiness with which A. R. Ammons has gradually consolidated his position as one of the major poets of our period—such a privilege, indeed, as one takes the people of an earlier generation to have enjoyed as they watched the progress of a Frost or an Eliot or a Stevens or an Auden. There may be those, however, who feel their present sense of Ammons's distinction to be somewhat remarkable in the light of the various mannerisms and idiosyncrasies wherewith he can so much try the patience of even his most lenient readers. (p. 717)

Though he makes large room in his meditations for "the / violence, grief, guilt, / despair, absurdity" of the world, Ammons seems regularly to be a cheerful, happy poet—one for whom it is not at all out of character at the end of a poem to sign off by saying "toodleoo" (as in "**Cold Didn't Keep the Stuff** "). So it strikes us as a little odd when he permits himself such a querulousness as he expresses when he remarks in Canto 122 of his long poem *Sphere:* "I can't understand my readers: / they complain of my abstractions." But even odder than the uncharacteristic petulance is the unconsciousness it conveys of what is so much a part of his own distinctive signature, for, if there is anything for which his readers must indeed make generous allowance, it is precisely his frequent recourse to a strange kind of rough, windy rhetoric of high (too high) generality that thins out and diminishes the experiential force of his witness—as when, again and again, his tone is that of the following passage from his "**Essay on Poetics**":

>> I am seeking the
> mechanisms physical, physiological, epistemological, electrical,
>
> chemical, esthetic, social, religious by which many, kept
> discrete as many, expresses itself into the
> manageable rafters of salience, lofts to comprehension,
>> breaks
>
> out in hard, highly informed suasions, the "gathering
> in the sky" so to speak, the trove of mind, tested
> experience, the only place there is to stay, where the saints
>
> are known to share accord and wine, and magical humor
>> floats
> upon the ambient sorrow: much is nearly stable there,
> residencies perpetual.

Indeed, so infixed is his bias toward abstractions that on some he confers a recondite kind of tenor and prestige—such terms as "nucleation," "periphery," "curvature," "surround" (used as a noun), "salience," "node," "molecule," "suasion"—and they pop up on page after page, forming a language that simply will not linger in the mind.

Nor does one find particularly engaging his special sort of heartiness—about, say, how nice it is to "eat a pig dinner sometimes and sit / down in a deep chair that rightangles / your unplumping belly out / [and] cuts off the avenues of circulation," so that "boluses of air / form promoting gastric /

distress." And the ribaldry—of which there is a good deal—never seems unforced and is never invigorating, being regularly marked by the grossness of the locker room, as in the following anecdote tacked on at the end of a poem called **"Poetry Is the Smallest"** (in *The Snow Poems*):

> poet friend of mine's
> dick's so short
> he can't pull it long enough
> to pee straight with:
> not to pee on
> anybody by surprise
> sideways, he hunkers
> into the urinal so far
> he looks like, to achieve,
> relief:
> still his fat wife's
> radiant every morning:
> he humps well, probably,
> stringing her out far and
> loose on the frail hook:
> and, too, I notice she
> follows his words
> closely like one who
> knows what a tongue can do.

So, in approaching the massive body of work which Ammons has now produced, captiousness has much to batten on. But our great good fortune is the man's fluency, for, despite all the dross, there are, literally, dozens and dozens of poems whose splendor will make one want to shout, breathlessly. . . . (pp. 718-20)

In its reflections on the relation of the Sublime to the mundane order Ammons's poetry resorts, however, far more frequently to the polarity between the one and the many or between unity and multiplicity than it does to the polarity between the heights and the lowlands of the world; but his mistrust of any sort of mystical angelism is in no way altered by the change in figure. The poem entitled **"Early Morning in Early April"** in his book of 1971, *Briefings,* pictures, for example, a landscape overhung with a rainy mist that has "hung baubles" on the trees, underlacing the maple branches "with glaring beadwork," and the poem says:

> what to make of it:
> what to make of a mist whose characteristic
> is a fine manyness coming dull in a wide
> oneness: what to make of the glass
> erasure, glass: the yew's partly lost.

The unstated assumption is that the diversity, the variety, the multifariousness, belonging to all the concrete particularities with which our world is furnished, offers the human spirit an essential kind of delight and nourishment—whereas the staircase leading to unity takes us (as the poem **"Staking Claim"** says)

> all the way to the final vacant core
> that brings
> things together and turns them away
>
> all the way away
> to stirless bliss!
>
> (pp. 725-26)

Sometimes (as in **"Left,"** the penultimate piece in the *Collected Poems*) the image of the "center" connotes the same range of meaning over which the notion of "unity" presides, as the image of "periphery" replaces that of "multiplicity." And this lexicon of height and unity and center makes a strangely

cryptic language, but one which, for all its enigmaticalness, intends to warn us away from that black mysticism or magical gnosis which seeks some kind of unmediated contact with the Sublime. We are not angels, and, as Ammons often wants in effect to remind us, the path, the narrow and direct path, that we must take into felicity and wisdom is one that leads *through* the immediate, concrete, finite things of this world in which the Sublime is incarnate. As he says in the eighty-sixth canto of his extraordinary long poem **"Hibernaculum,"**

> the sum of everything's nothing: very nice: that
> turns the world back in on itself: such as right
> when you possess everything, you'd give everything
>
> up for a sickle pear: I hope my philosophy will turn
> out all right and turn out to be a philosophy so as
> to free people (any who are trapped, as I have been)
>
> from seeking any image in the absolute or seeking
> any absolute whatsoever.

In short, what we confront is (as Jean Cocteau once phrased it) *le mystère laic,* the "lay mystery" or the secular mystery of transcendence within immanence.

Ammons's profound reverence for this secular mystery is expressed in a vast number of his poems, and it forms one of the principal strands of his work. Here, for example, is the testimony he makes in the opening part of the beautiful poem entitled simply **"Still"**:

> I said I will find what is lowly
>   and put the roots of my identity
>   down there:
>
> each day I'll wake up
> and find the lowly nearby,
>   a handy focus and reminder,
> a ready measure of my significance,
> the voice by which I would be heard,
> the wills, the kinds of selfishness
>   I could
> freely adopt as my own:
>
> but though I have looked everywhere,
>   I can find nothing
>   to give myself to:
>   everything is
>
> magnificent with existence, is in
> surfeit of glory:
> nothing is diminished,
> nothing has been diminished for me.

This devotion of what is "lowly," to the "lovely diminutives" of the world (as Roethke called them—snails and weeds and cockroaches), this sense of "everything" as "in surfeit of glory," as "magnificent with existence"—it is precisely this which attests to Ammons's fidelity to a vision such as Blake's that wants to declare that there is nothing so paltry, so inglorious, as not to be indwelt by holiness and capable of being a means of grace—not even wind-swept grasses and "dry-burnt moss": "nothing is diminished, / nothing has been diminished for me." (pp. 727-28)

Now it is just his great success in **"Tape for the Turn of the Year"** in getting "out of boxes, hard/forms of mind," in breaking "off from *is* to *flowing,"* that makes this poem of more than two hundred pages so exemplary a case of Ammon's art and one of his more impressive accomplishments in the medium of the long poem. (p. 736)

[*Tape for the Turn of the Year*] took the form of a diary, with entries extending from the sixth day of December, 1963, through the tenth day of the following January. And it is a great bucket that catches everything his days bring: the smells of his wife's cooking, what "the checker at/the A & P said," weather forecasts heard on his radio, shopping in Philadelphia at Wanamaker's, the dismantling of the Christmas tree, his attempts at throwing off a bad cold, what he and his wife have for dinner of a certain evening over at "Sompers Point/at Mac's" (fried shrimp for himself and crab for her)—all this being accompanied by such asides as "just went to take a leak" and "(I had/lunch after/'who cannot love')." And he offers frequent interstitial reports on the progress of his writing, as the tape slowly winds down from his typewriter into the wastebasket over the five weeks that this "serious novelty" is being composed. The poem is simply drenched in the reality of the quotidian: its language is that of one who has given himself up to the world and who has no regrets about his surrender. Yet, for all the commitment to "the ordinary universe," Ammons in no way relinquishes here his contemplative vocation, and, as day follows day, he is constantly engaged in a labor of reflection on how all the good things each day brings may "be managed,/received and loved/in their passing." Indeed, in his grateful acceptance of the *claritas*, the radiance, that belongs to the quiddities and haecceities of the world, he puts us in mind of the Williams of *Paterson*, especially when he (in the entry for 23 Dec.) recites his Morning Office:

>   release us from mental
>   prisons into the actual
>   fact, the mere
>   occurrence—the touched,
>   tasted, heard, seen:
>   in the simple event is
>   the scope of life:
>   let's not make up
>   categories to toss ourselves
>   around with:
>   look: it's snowing:
>   without theory
>   & beyond help:
>   I accept:
>   I can react with
>   restlessness & quiet
>   terror, or with
>   fascination &
>   delight: I choose the
>   side of possibility:

In the entry in the *Tape* for 31 Dec. Ammons says: "after this, / this long poem, I hope I / can do short rich hard / lyrics: lines / that can incubate slowly / then fall into / symmetrical tangles." And, indeed, the books that followed—*Northfield Poems* (1966), the *Selected Poems* (1968), *Uplands* (1970), and *Briefings: Poems Small and Easy* (1971)—presented a large and brilliant achievement in this mode: one will think of "**Reflective**," "**One:Many**," "**Saliences**," "**Peak**," "**Sphere**," "**Upland**," "**Periphery**," "**Cascadilla Falls**," "**This Black Rich Country**," "**This Bright Day**," "**He Held Radical Light**," "**Early Morning in Early April**," and a vast number of other poems as exemplifying the kind of mastery that Ammons was regularly demonstrating in his work of the late 60s and early 70s. But already in the *Tape* and in "**Summer Session 1968**" (in *Uplands*) he had shown that, despite his respect for the short, hard lyric, he had the sort of sensibility that liked the chance for expatiation, for the leisurely exploration of a large theme; and this penchant he

submitted to again and again in the mid- and late 70s, for it was during this period that he issued a major series of long poems—the book-length poem, *Sphere: The Form of a Motion* (1974), the cycle of *The Snow Poems* (1977), and those which were collected in the *Selected Longer Poems* of 1980 ("**Pray Without Ceasing**," "**Essay on Poetics**," "**Extremes and Moderations**," "**Hibernaculum**," and, again, "**Summer Session**").

These big poems disclose, of course, the extraordinary *ambitiousness* by which Ammons's career has been driven, and there are those, on the one hand, who have a great enthusiasm for them and those, on the other, who regard them as merely facile and as evidencing no capacity for the kind of systematic "argument" that the long poem needs to sustain. (pp. 736-38)

True, these long poems of Ammons's middle period are, in their prolixity and diffuseness, sometimes flawed, and some of his readers have, therefore, accorded them a very imperfect sympathy. But they are all filled with his special kind of eloquence, and they all belong to what he speaks of in *Sphere* (in the sixteenth canto) as that "anthology [which] is the moving, changing definition of the / imaginative life of the people" of our time.

In his work of recent years, however—in the poems collected in *A Coast of Trees* (1981), *Worldly Hopes* (1982), *Lake Effect Country* (1983), and *Sumerian Vistas* (1987)—he has returned to the short, hard lyric, and the song is simply stunning in its purity and grace. In the "**Essay on Poetics**" at a certain point he playfully turns inside-out and upside-down William Carlos Williams's notion that there are "no ideas but in things," inviting us to consider various alternatives—" 'no things but in ideas,' / 'no ideas but in ideas,' and 'no things but in things.' " Yet in the same poem he avows, very much in the accent of Williams: "I think what I see." And, indeed, in his late work he wants to put aside all "engines of declaration" and to do nothing other than present what he beholds: he wants to "turn / to the cleared particular" and to elicit in us the realization (as he says in the title poem in *A Coast of Trees*) "that whatever it is it is in the Way and / the Way in it, as in us, emptied full."

Nor can one fail to be reminded by the drift of Ammons's testimony in the poems of the 80s of how deeply religious his basic sensibility is. Midway through the "**Essay on Poetics**" he says: "I am just going to take it for granted / that the tree is in the backyard: / it's necessary to be quiet in the hands of the marvelous." And it is in an attitude of such admiring gratitude and veneration that he faces the manifold things of this world—which, as he says in the poem "**Vehicle**," "praise themselves seen in / my praising sight." Moreover, when he suggests that a spruce bough in winter and a running brook and a squirrel bunching branches "praise themselves seen in / my praising sight," he intends to be taken not as merely turning a phrase but as speaking in full seriousness—which is surely made evident in the great poem "**Singing & Doubling Together**" form *Lake Effect Country*:

>   My nature singing in me is your nature singing:
>   you have means to veer down, filter through,
>   and, coming in,
>   harden into vines that break back with leaves,
>   so that when the wind stirs
>   I know you are there and I hear you in leafspeech,
>
>   though of course back into your heightenings I

can never follow: you are there beyond
tracings flesh can take,
and farther away surrounding and informing the systems,
you are as if nothing, and
where you are least knowable I celebrate you most

or here most when near dusk the pheasant squawks and
lofts at a sharp angle to the roost cedar,
I catch in the angle of that ascent,
in the justness of that event your pheasant nature,
and when dusk settles, the bushes creak and
snap in their natures with your creaking

and snapping nature . . .

even you risked all the way into the taking on of shape
and time.

The poem wants to say that the coruscations of glory borne
by leafspeech and pheasant flight and bush-snappings are
nothing other than the blaze of the Sublime that, to be sure,
is "beyond / tracings flesh can take" but that, by virtue of its
immanence within all the things of earth, yet permits them
to *come-to-presence,* finding its tongue in the poet's song
(which becomes *our* song in those moments when we are
most truly human.) In short, the "you" being addressed in
"Singing & Doubling Together" is simply the Wholly Other,
the Incomparable, "the dearest freshness deep down things":
it is none other than Being itself, " 'that / which is to be
praised' " and invested "with / our store of verve." And this
aboriginal reality is addressed as "you," not because Ammons conceives it to be *a* being with personal attributes but
rather, presumably, because he feels it to present itself with
the same sort of graciousness that one encounters in the love
of another person. He chooses not, in other words, to talk
about "God" but, rather, to speak of that which approxi-
mates what Teilhard de Chardin called *le milieu divin.* Or,

we might say that Ammons is a poet of what Stevens in a late
poem, "Of Mere Being," in *Opus Posthumous,* called "mere
Being": we might say that he is a poet of that which, though
not coextensive with all things, yet interpenetrates all things
with the radiance of its diaphanous presence.

Though Harold Bloom's exuberant enthusiasm for Ammons's poetry, in its various expressions over many years, has
no doubt been insufficiently modulated, he was surely right
when, in his book of 1971, *The Ringers in the Tower,* he declared him to be "the central poet" of our generation, for this
indeed is what he is. And he holds such a position in part because his special *pietas* speaks so deeply and so reassuringly
to a malaise by which few reflective people of our period are
untouched. It might be said to be simply an ennui of the
human, a weariness of looking out upon a world that seems
everywhere to be be smudged by ourselves, to have been
shaped by some form of human intentionality—which leads
in turn to a profound yearning to descry some "otherness"
in reality which cannot be made subservient to the engines
of our planning and our manipulation. But it will not suffice,
of course, to find this otherness to be nothing more than the
inert blankness of what Coleridge called "fixities and defi-
nites," for we seek (in Stevens's phrase) "a kind of total grandeur at the end," not a grandeur, as it were, overhead but *in*
"the vulgate of experience," in "the actual landscape with its
actual horns / Of baker and butcher blowing." And it is of
just this that Ammons's poetry offers a presentment. . . .
(pp. 740-42)

Nathan A. Scott, Jr., "The Poetry of Ammons," in
The Southern Review, *Louisiana State University,
Vol. 24, No. 4, Autumn, 1988, pp. 717-43.*

Samuel (Barclay) Beckett

1906-1989

Irish dramatist, novelist, short story writer, scriptwriter, poet, critic, and translator.

The following entry presents criticism on Beckett's play *En attendant Godot* (1953; *Waiting for Godot*). For discussions of Beckett's complete career, see *CLC,* Vols. 1, 2, 3, 4, 6, 10, 11, 14, 18, 29.

The recipient of the Nobel Prize in Literature in 1969, Beckett is probably best known for his tragicomic drama *Waiting for Godot.* An Irish-born author who lives in France and has written primarily in French since 1937, Beckett has consistently expounded a philosophy of negation in works that often center on characters who confront existence without the solace of religious or philosophical absolutes. Regarded as one of the most controversial and seminal works of twentieth-century drama, *Waiting for Godot* is noted for its minimal approach to dramatic form, its powerful imagery, and its concise, fragmented dialogue. Although the play has elicited diverse interpretations, Beckett's portrayal of a world of insignificance and incomprehensibility has lead many critics to identify *Waiting for Godot* with existentialism, a post-World War II intellectual movement based upon the inadequacy of reason to explain human existence, as well as the Theater of the Absurd, a post-World War II trend in drama characterized by experimental techniques and nihilism. Most concur with Eric Bentley's assessment: "[Beckett] has not only been able to define the 'existentialist' point of view more sharply than those who are more famously associated with it, he has also found for its expression a vehicle of a sort that people have been recommending without following their own recommendation."

Whereas most traditional plays begin with some action or event that results in dramatic conflict, *Waiting for Godot* begins with no precipitative movement, only an abstract struggle involving the passage of time. Vladimir and Estragon, two vagrants known to one another by the nicknames Didi and Gogo, wait on a desolate plain by a gnarled tree to keep an appointment with someone called M. Godot. Dressed in the rags and bowler hats common to vaudeville or music-hall comedy, the tramps play games to pass the time and converse on such subjects as Christianity, the monotonous process of waiting, and the possibility of escaping their situation by committing suicide. The pair are generally regarded as opposite components of the dualistic split between body and mind as posited by French seventeenth-century philosopher René Descartes, with Vladimir functioning as intellect and Estragon as the physical half. The tramps soon encounter Pozzo, a determined man who drives his withered and debased slave Lucky forward with a whip. To impress Vladimir and Estragon, Pozzo compels Lucky to deliver an unintelligible but terrifying speech comprised of political, scholarly, and scientific jargon. Unable to silence him, Pozzo and the vagrants attack Lucky, finally quieting him by removing his hat. Pozzo and Lucky depart, and the first act concludes as a messenger informs Vladimir and Estragon that Godot will not arrive today, but probably tomorrow.

While most dramas introduce some twist or alteration in plot in the second act, the latter half of *Waiting for Godot* is essentially a recapitulation of the first. The action seems to take place the following evening, but the twisted tree has sprouted leaves, possibly indicating a change of seasons. The characters seem largely unaware that they are repeating their previous actions, an amnesia that some critics interpret as a reflection of the stagnant process of waiting. Central to *Waiting for Godot* is the irony that each moment the tramps spend waiting for the future brings them a moment closer to death. Like Lear and his Fool in Shakespeare's tragedy *King Lear,* Pozzo and Lucky return in the second act of *Waiting for Godot* transformed by time: Pozzo is blind and Lucky is mute. The play's theme of mortality is summed up in Pozzo's famous lament: "Have you not done tormenting me with your accursed time? . . . One day . . . like any other day he went dumb, one day I went blind, one day we'll go deaf, one day we were born, one day we'll die. . . . They give birth astride a grave, the light gleams an instant, then it's night once more." Vladimir and Estragon are again informed that Godot will not arrive today, but probably tomorrow. The play concludes as it began, with the two tramps waiting for Godot.

Written in the 1940s and published in text form in 1952,

Waiting for Godot garnered fair to mild reviews following its stage debut in Paris in 1953, but gradually gained widespread acceptance and ran for over four hundred performances. Some critics unfavorably compared Beckett's abstract style to that of James Joyce, to whom he had previously served as secretary and literary colleague. While most reviewers objected to Beckett's disregard for such dramaturgical elements as plot, scenery, and dramatic action, others argued that the play's significance derives directly from its opposition to rules of convention. Using a line from *Waiting for Godot* to summarize its general reception—"Nothing happens, nobody comes, nobody goes, it's awful"—French dramatist Jean Anouilh commented: "*Godot* is a masterpiece that will cause despair for men in general and for playwrights in particular. I think that the play's opening night . . . is as important as the opening of Pirandello in Paris in 1923." Despite numerous successful runs in major European cities, including an acclaimed German-language version performed in Berlin, ensuing European productions of *Waiting for Godot* frequently encountered obstacles, including a ban of reviews and advertisements of the play in Spain, where its message was deemed pessimistic, and its threatened cancellation in the Netherlands.

Prior to the first London production of *Waiting for Godot* in 1955, Beckett tightened the play's dialogue in the second act and translated the text into English. Although the drama was dismissed by some British critics as pretentious, most lauded Beckett's ability to challenge and disquiet audiences. Harold Hobson bridged the extremes of critical opinion when he thus characterized the play: "At the worst you will discover a curiosity, a four-leaved clover, a black tulip; at the best something that will securely lodge in a corner of your mind for as long as you live." Inspired by the London production, American producer Michael Myerberg initially presented *Waiting for Godot* in 1956 in Miami, Florida, but the play failed, at least partially due to its misleading billing in area newspapers as "the laugh hit of four continents." Before attempting a second production in New York City, Meyerberg stated in published advertisements in New York's most prominent newspapers: "[*Waiting for Godot*] is a play for the thoughtful and discriminating theatregoer. . . . I respectfully suggest that those who come to the theatre for casual entertainment do not buy a ticket to this attraction." Although some American critics faulted the play's intellectual bias, agreeing with Wolcott Gibb's assessment—"All I can say, in a critical sense, is that I have seldom seen such meagre moonshine stated with such inordinate fuss"—most acknowledged *Waiting for Godot* as an enduring and important contribution to world drama. American dramatists Tennessee Williams and Thornton Wilder endorsed the play, and William Saroyan remarked: "It will make it easier for me and everyone else to write freely in the theater."

Beckett once remarked that the name Godot derives from "godillot," the French word for a military boot, and some commentators suggest that *Waiting for Godot* may arise from Beckett's experience in the French Resistance during World War II, when members spent much time waiting for messages. Eric Bentley has suggested that the name Godot may be a derivative of Godeau, a character whose late arrival is alluded to but never witnessed in *Mercadet; Ou, le faiseur* (1848), a play by nineteenth-century French dramatist Honoré de Balzac. Many reviewers have interpreted *Waiting for Godot* as a religious parable, although Beckett has stated: "If by Godot I had meant God, I would have said God, not

Godot." Those who have viewed the play as Beckett's reaction to his Roman Catholic background posit Vladimir and Estragon as representatives of the fallen state of humanity faithfully awaiting the arrival of an elusive God who promises salvation but never arrives. Some critics have further identified Pozzo as the Pope and Lucky as either a symbol of society's mass allegiance to religion or, because of his terrifying speech, as the cipher of God cut short by human intolerance. Despite their inability to thoroughly explain *Waiting for Godot,* most reviewers agree that the play's religious associations enliven and enrich its sense of fluidity and ambiguity. The twisted tree, for example, can variously symbolize death, the tree of life, the crucifixion, the tree of knowledge of good and evil, and the tree of Judas.

Champions of political interpretations of *Waiting for Godot* have variously endorsed the play as a critique of Franco-German relations, as an allegory of the English domination of the Irish, and as a Marxist work in which Pozzo and Lucky function as paradigms of capitalism and labor. Many identify Pozzo as a power figure and Lucky as institutionalized education personified, his speech functioning as an example of learning driven by power to address humanity's faith in such illusory and limited phenomena as scholarship and science. This view supports the interpretation of *Waiting for Godot* as a work of absurdism or existentialism, in which the play's characters offer futile resistance to malignant forces beyond their control. In this reading, Lucky is construed as the prototypical existential hero who is "lucky" because his actions are determined absolutely by Pozzo and he will never have to confront the futility of action or resistance. Opponents of the absurdist interpretation maintain that *Waiting for Godot* departs from existentialist models, in which life is considered insignificant, to illuminate the meaning of existence in several ways. By suggesting that waiting is an inevitable part of the human condition, Beckett may be said to imply that human connections are both possible and necessary; by presenting a pair of outwardly pessimistic characters who wait faithfully despite the seeming hopelessness of their situation, Beckett refutes critical charges of nihilism; and by presenting an ending in which Godot may yet conceivably arrive, Beckett offers a hopeful vision of humanity's future.

(See also *Contemporary Authors,* Vols. 5-8, rev. ed. and *Dictionary of Literary Biography,* Vols. 13, 15.)

•REVIEWS OF MAJOR PRODUCTIONS•

Paris, 1953

SYLVAIN ZEGEL

[*The essay excerpted below was originally published in French as "Au théâtre de Babylone: 'En attendant Godot' de Samuel Beckett" in La Libération, January 7, 1953.*]

Theater-lovers rarely have the pleasure of discovering a new author worthy of the name; an author who can give his dialogue true poetic force, who can animate his characters so vividly that the audience identifies with them, suffering and laughing with them; who, having meditated, does not amuse himself with mere word-juggling; who deserves comparison with the greatest. When this occurs, it is an event which will be spoken of for a long time, and will be remembered years later. In my opinion, Samuel Beckett's . . . play *Waiting for Godot* . . . will be spoken of for a long time.

Perhaps a few grumblers complained that it is "a play in which nothing happens," because they didn't find the more or less conventional plot used by innumerable authors from Aristophanes and Plautus on; or because, on leaving the theater, they couldn't summarize the play, or explain why they had laughed with embarrassed laughter.

They heard people using everyday words, and they did not feel that by an inexplicable miracle—which is called art—the words suddenly acquired a new value. They saw people being happy and suffering, and they did not understand that they were watching their own lives. But when the curtain fell, and they heard the enthusiasm of the audience, they understood at least this much: Paris had just recognized in Samuel Beckett one of today's best playwrights.

It is hard not to be amazed that this is [Beckett's first major play] . . . , since he has mastered all the exigencies of the stage. Each word acts as the author wishes, touching us or making us laugh. (pp. 11-12)

> *Sylvain Zegel, "At the Théâtre de Babylone: 'Waiting for Godot' by Samuel Beckett," translated by Ruby Cohn, in* Casebook on Waiting for Godot, *edited by Ruby Cohn, Grove Press, Inc., 1967, pp. 11-12.*

JACQUES AUDIBERTI

[*The essay excerpted below was originally published in French as "Au Babylone et au Lancry, deux coups heureux sur le damier du théâtre" in* Arts-Spectacles, *January 16-22, 1953.*]

Prophets without prosody, translators without a word-scale in their heads, all those who believe themselves to be writers because they have written that they are—I invite all of these to listen to Samuel Beckett's *Waiting for Godot* . . . , a perfect work which deserves a triumph.

I won't narrate the play for you; does one narrate a landscape, a face, a pattern, an emotion? One can describe them, or interpret them.

Two tramps wait for Godot on a road, in the company of a tree that is too delicate to be used for hanging oneself. Tired and hungry though they are, they talk continuously. Their sentences are broken. What are they doing? Waiting. For whom? Godot. (p. 13)

Godot doesn't come. At least not this evening. But they are there every evening to wait for him. Nothing comes, except the moon, and a delirious fake blind man in a greatcoat—Pozzo. On a leash, he keeps a domesticated skeleton who knows how to think. To think inexhaustibly, aloud, on command. Nothing comes, except a child who says nothing but that Godot will not come. Probably Godot will never come.

Now then, perhaps Godot has come; it might be Pozzo. Not heartening, if the man in the greatcoat should be God. What! God? Again!

Please note that the author doesn't say so, but he forces us to say it. In "Godot" there is "God." Besides, the waiting men give to this Godot whom they have never seen the white beard and the old age of portraits of the Eternal. But Godot might just as well be a neighboring farmer who could give work to the tramps, and Pozzo might be a raving squire. Symbolism is optional, but applause is obligatory. . . . (p. 14)

> *Jacques Audiberti, "At the Babylone a Fortunate Move on the Theater Checkerboard," translated by Ruby Cohn, in* Casebook on Waiting for Godot, *edited by Ruby Cohn, Grove Press, Inc., 1967, pp. 13-14.*

London, 1955

KENNETH TYNAN

[*The essay excerpted below was originally published in* The Observer, *August 7, 1955.*]

A special virtue attaches to plays which remind the drama of how much it can do without and still exist. By all the known criteria, Samuel Beckett's *Waiting for Godot* is a dramatic vacuum. Pity the critic who seeks a chink in its armour, for it is all chink. It has no plot, no climax, no *dénouement;* no beginning, no middle, and no end. Unavoidably, it has a situation, and it might be accused of having suspense, since it deals with the impatience of two tramps, waiting beneath a tree for a cryptic Mr. Godot to keep his appointment with them; but the situation is never developed, and a glance at the programme shows that Mr. Godot is not going to arrive. *Waiting for Godot* frankly jettisons everything by which we recognise theatre. It arrives at the custom-house, as it were, with no luggage, no passport, and nothing to declare; yet it gets through, as might a pilgrim from Mars. It does this, I believe, by appealing to a definition of drama much more fundamental than any in the books. A play, it asserts and proves, is basically a means of spending two hours in the dark without being bored. (p. 101)

Passing the time in the dark, [Beckett] suggests, is not only what drama is about but also what life is about. Existence depends on those metaphysical Micawbers who will go on waiting, against all rational argument, for something which may one day turn up to explain the purpose of living. Twenty years ago Mr. Odets had us waiting for Lefty, the social messiah; less naïvely, Mr. Beckett bids us wait for Godot, the spiritual signpost. His two tramps pass the time of day just as we, the audience, are passing the time of night. Were we not in the theatre, we should, like them, be clowning and quarreling, aimlessly bickering and aimlessly making up—all, as one of them says, "to give us the impression that we exist."

Mr. Beckett's tramps do not often talk like that. For the most part they converse in the double-talk of vaudeville: one of them has the ragged aplomb of Buster Keaton, while the other is Chaplin at his airiest and fairiest. . . . From time to time other characters intrude. Fat Pozzo, Humpty Dumpty with a whip in his fist, puffs into sight with Lucky, his dumb slave. They are clearly going somewhere in a hurry: perhaps they know where Godot is? But the interview subsides into Lewis-Carrollian inanity. All that emerges is that the master needs the slave as much as the slave needs the master; it gives both a sense of spurious purpose; and one thinks of Laurel and Hardy, the ideal casting in these roles. Commanded to think, Lucky stammers out a ghostly, ghastly, interminable tirade, compounded of cliché and gibberish, whose general tenor is that, in spite of material progress and "all kinds of tennis," man spiritually dwindles. The style hereabouts reminds us forcibly that Mr. Beckett once worked for James Joyce. In the next act Pozzo and Lucky return, this time moving, just as purposefully, in the opposite direction. The tramps decide to stay where they are. A child arrives, presenting Mr. Godot's compliments and regretting that he is unable to meet them today. It is the same message as yesterday; all the same, they wait. (pp. 101-02)

The play sees the human condition in terms of baggy pants and red noses. Hastily labelling their disquiet disgust, many of the first-night audience found it pretentious. But what, exactly, are its pretensions? To state that mankind is waiting for a sign that is late in coming is a platitude which none but an illiterate would interpret as making claims to profundity. What vexed the play's enemies was, I suspect, the opposite: it was not pretentious enough to enable them to deride it. I care little for its enormous success in Europe over the past three years, but much for the way in which it pricked and stimulated my own nervous system. It summoned the music-hall and the parable to present a view of life which banished the sentimentality of the music-hall and the parable's fulsome uplift. It forced me to re-examine the rules which have hitherto governed the drama; and, having done so, to pronounce them not elastic enough. It is validly new, and hence I declare myself, as the Spanish would say, *godotista*. (pp. 102-03)

> Kenneth Tynan, in a review of "Waiting for Godot," in his Curtains: Selections from the Drama Criticism and Related Writings, *Atheneum Publishers, 1961, pp. 101-03.*

HAROLD HOBSON

[*The essay excerpted below was originally published in* The Sunday Times, *London, August 7, 1955.*]

The objections to Mr. Samuel Beckett's play as a theatrical entertainment are many and obvious. Anyone keen-sighted enough to see a church at noonday can perceive what they are. **Waiting for Godot** has nothing at all to seduce the senses. Its drab, bare scene is dominated by a withered tree and a garbage can, and for a large part of the evening this lugubrious setting, which makes the worst of both town and country, is inhabited only by a couple of tramps. . . . (p. 27)

This is not all. In the course of the play, nothing happens. Such dramatic progress as there is, is not toward a climax, but toward a perpetual postponement. Vladimir and Estragon are waiting for Godot, but this gentleman's appearance (*if* he is a gentleman, and not something of another species) is not prepared with any recognizable theatrical tension, for the audience knows well enough from the beginning that Godot will never come. The dialogue is studded with words that have no meaning for normal ears; repeatedly the play announces that it has come to a stop, and will have to start again; never does it reconcile itself with reason.

It is hardly surprising that, English audiences notoriously disliking anything not immediately understandable, certain early lines in the play, such as, "I have had better entertain-

ment elsewhere," were received on the first night with ironical laughter; or that when one of the characters yawned, the yawn was echoed and amplified by a humorist in the stalls. Yet at the end the play was warmly applauded. There were even a few calls for "Author!" But these were rather shame-faced cries, as if those who uttered them doubted whether it were seemly to make too much noise whilst turning their coats.

Strange as the play is, and curious as are its processes or thought, it has a meaning; and this meaning is untrue. To attempt to put this meaning into a paragraph is like trying to catch Leviathan in a butterfly net, but nevertheless the effort must be made. The upshot of **Waiting for Godot** is that the two tramps are always waiting for the future, their ruinous consolation being that there is always tomorrow; they never realize that today is today. In this, says Mr. Beckett, they are like humanity, which dawdles and drivels away its life, postponing action, eschewing enjoyment, waiting only for some far-off, divine event, the millennium, the Day of Judgment.

Mr. Beckett has, of course, got it all wrong. Humanity worries very little over the Day of Judgment. It is far too busy hire-purchasing television sets, popping into three-star restaurants, planting itself vineyards, building helicopters. But he has got it wrong in a tremendous way. And this is what matters. There is no need at all for a dramatist to philosophize rightly: he can leave that to the philosophers. But it is essential that if he philosophizes wrongly, he should do so with swagger. Mr. Beckett has any amount of swagger. A dusty, coarse, irreverent, pessimistic, violent swagger? Possibly. But the genuine thing, the real McCoy.

Vladimir and Estragon have each a kind of universality. They wear their rags with a difference. Vladimir is eternally hopeful; if Godot does not come this evening, then he will certainly arrive tomorrow, or at the very latest the day after. Estragon, much troubled by his boots, is less confident. He thinks the game is not worth playing, and is ready to hang himself. Or so he says. But he does nothing. Like Vladimir, he only talks. They both idly spin away the great top of their life in the vain expectation that some master whip will one day give it eternal vitality. Meanwhile their conversation often has the simplicity, in this case the delusive simplicity, of music-hall cross talk, now and again pierced with a shaft that seems for a second or so to touch the edge of truth's garment. It is bewildering. It is exasperating. It is insidiously exciting.

Then there is Pozzo, the big, brutal bully, and the terrible, white-faced gibbering slave he leads about on the end of a rope. These are exasperating, too, but they have astonishing moments of theatrical effectiveness. The long speech into which the silent Lucky breaks, crammed with the unintelligible, with vain repetitions, with the lumber of ill-assorted learning, the pitiful heritage of the ages, the fruits of civilization squashed down and rotten, is horrifyingly delivered. . . . (pp. 27-9)

Go and see **Waiting for Godot**. At the worst you will discover a curiosity, a four-leaved clover, a black tulip; at the best something that will securely lodge in a corner of your mind for as long as you live. (p. 29)

> Harold Hobson, "Tomorrow," in Casebook on Waiting for Godot, *edited by Ruby Cohn, Grove Press, Inc., 1967, pp. 27-9.*

ANTHONY HARTLEY

[*Waiting for Godot* concerns two tramps who] are sitting by the roadside waiting for a M. Godot to come and employ them. They exchange odds and ends of conversation which are as meaningless and, at times, as gross in their insistence on physical detail as anything to be heard inside an army camp. Godot does not come, but instead there appear Pozzo and Lucky, his servant—the one inhuman in his tyranny, the other in his servility; in the second half of the play this pair are seen again, but now Pozzo has gone blind and Lucky cannot speak at all. Meanwhile the two tramps continue waiting for Godot; they cannot even commit suicide; they have no rope to hang themselves; still Godot does not come.

Superficially, it might appear that this play of metaphysical situation is the product of a deep pessimism. Godot does not come, the one contact the tramps have with the outside world presents them with an example of fearful tyranny (the Pozzo-Lucky relationship serves as a kind of anti-masque to that of themselves) with Godot. . . . Yet, a closer look at the play raises doubts as to whether its meaning is quite so one-sided as that. The ambivalence of the idea of Godot himself is very marked; from one point of view he represents a force which is destroying the two tramps; from another he is their only *raison d'être.* Equally, the Pozzo-Lucky episodes are notable for a certain human sympathy displayed by the tramps in face of Lucky's humiliation and sufferings. The relationship between the tramps themselves (one is the thinking, the other the physical, man) does not exclude communication on some level other than that of the intellect. A frustrated poetry is distilled from the play, a poetry which is a by-product of the human situation. There is always, one feels, a chance that Godot may come.

Mr. Beckett has written a play of great power and skill (the dialogue is masterly), which starts from the undeniable proposition that all men are in the same basic position as regards the universe—*roseau, mais roseau pensant.* Moreover, it is a characteristic of this basic situation that it cannot be altered. No dramatic change takes place throughout **Waiting for Godot** and no change could take place (unless Godot were to come, but that is also impossible within the terms of the situation). What this new school of dramatists is telling us is that all the subjects which have traditionally engaged the attention of practitioners of the art—reversals of fortune, fall of princes, star-crossed lovers, etc.—are superficialities, and that the real subject for the playwright is the basic minimum of human life, something that is not changed one jot by such trifles as jealousy or anger or lust. Of course, the trouble with this theme on the stage is that to hold the interest of the audience a *tour de force* is necessary. If they once realise that strictly nothing is going on, they will be liable to be bored. Hence, a number of dramatists of this school have used violent and striking action to attempt to conceal the want of the genuine article in their plays. It is the singularity of Mr. Beckett to have used means far more consonant with his ultimate aim; that this was possible can be put down to the sheer excellence of his writing.

Anthony Hartley, in a review of "Waiting for Godot," in The Spectator, *Vol. 195, No. 6633, August 12, 1955, p. 222.*

PHILIP HOPE-WALLACE

[*En attendant Godot* features] two tramps, one called Estragon (or Gogo for short) whose name means tarragon and whose boots hurt; the other called Vladimir who is more reflective (are we to see Red propaganda here, perhaps?) Twice during the long wait for Godot, on two successive evenings, a stout gentleman farmer called Pozzo (Italian for a Well) arrives with a dumb idiot servant called Lucky, a fugitive from the Mad Hatter's Tea Party.

At their second appearance, the servant is bear-leading the master who seems to have had a stroke. Twice a rather stupid boy turns up with the disappointing news that after all M. Godot cannot keep the appointment, expecting which has been the only certainty for these two wrecks of humanity sitting on the waste ground by a tree too frail to hang them.

To fill in the time there is desultory conversation, jabberwocky or funny deflating misunderstandings like the cross talk of zanies in a music hall act. Both tramps are dressed as Charlots; perhaps 'Godot' is slang for God? Exasperating though the pointlessness of such an exercise is, it finally distils a pungent sense of the loneliness, insecurity and folly of human life, so long, so short a space and with such dusty answers even for the faithful.

The allegorist, if allegory is intended and not a mere *blague,* is Sam Beckett, once James Joyce's secretary who wrote this 'play' in French, of which language it still bears traces: (e.g. instead of 'Come here boy', we have 'Approach, my child'). Because it is defiantly different and difficult, it has made a name for itself, as is always the way with such things, be they Gertrude Stein's mumblings or the latest fashionable *faux naif* lump of clay.

However people whose judgment is to be respected find the piece as fascinating as a poem: and certainly the . . . audience, in spite of one angry withdrawal on the first night, was not to be caught failing, in Philistine fashion, to see the 'point'. Gales of laughter, which sounded now and again a false note *à la* BBC studio audience, kept the traffic from stalls to stage open.

Not for your aunt, nor the cousins from Cape Town, but for yourself, if you want to be in the movement, this possibly exasperating, possibly 'fascinating' evening may be worth investigation. At any rate, there is at least one London theatre willing to risk an 'Insult to intelligent playgoers.'

Philip Hope-Wallace, in a review of "Waiting for Godot," in Time & Tide, *Vol. 36, No. 33, August 13, 1955, p. 1045.*

THE TIMES LITERARY SUPPLEMENT

No new play on the London stage has had a more unexpected and exciting success in recent years than Mr. Samuel Beckett's **Waiting for Godot.** Audiences and critics have, in this country, immediately apprehended its appeal, but there has been no serious attempt to define its theme. Any discussion about what **Waiting for Godot** "means" soon loses itself in a tangle of cross-purposes. Nor do Mr. Beckett's novels, such as **Molloy** and **Watt,** throw much light on the appeal of the play. In one sense, indeed, they do not share that appeal. In his narrative prose, Mr. Beckett presents the paradoxical picture of a man of very great talent, and possibly even of genius, using all his gifts with enormous skill for the purpose of reducing his readers to a state of tired disgust and exasperated boredom. But *Waiting for Godot* is not, except to the most squeamishly fastidious of playgoers, in the least disgusting. It is anything but boring, it instead extracts from the *idea* of boredom the most genuine pathos and enchanting comedy. Again, the message of Mr. Beckett as a novelist is perhaps a message of blank despair. The message of *Waiting for Godot* is perhaps something nearer a message of religious consolation. Audiences do not leave the theatre, after seeing his play, feeling that life has been deprived of meaning. They feel rather that a new light has been cast on life's meaning, at several deep levels.

What sort of light, however? That is what so far eluded critics of the play as performed. Mr. Beckett is rumoured to have instructed his English producer not, by any manner of means, to tell the actors what the theme of the play was. Yet unless Mr. Beckett whispered his central secret in the producer's ear, the warning was probably unnecessary. The elusiveness of the core has, indeed, led some critics to contend that there is no core; that the whole startling effect of the play on the stage depended on excellent production and acting and on Mr. Beckett's own mastery of the mechanics of stagecraft. . . . theory might be that Mr. Beckett in *Waiting for Godot* dramatizes the notion of emptiness. This, or something like this, was the reaction of the French dramatist Jean Anouilh to the first performance of *En Attendant Godot* in Paris. "Nothing happens. Nobody comes, nobody goes, it's awful! But," M. Anouilh added, "I think the evening at the Babylone is as important as the première of Pirandello, put on in Paris by Pitoeff in 1923." And from what we know of Mr. Beckett's other work, we might assume that to dramatize emptiness, to have his much ado literally about nothing, may have been his conscious intention. Yet, with a play even more than a poem, we have to consider not the author's conscious intention—not what the author, in a conversation, might say he believed about "life"—but the whole complex significance, the valid levels of meaning, of a coherent structure. What *Waiting for Godot* essentially is is a prolonged and sustained metaphor about the nature of human life. It is a metaphor also which makes a particular appeal to the mood of liberal uncertainty which is the prevailing mood of modern Western Europe; and which makes (to judge by the play's failure in Miami) much less appeal to the strenuous and pragmatic temper of the contemporary American mind. It is also a play by an Irishman, by a friend and disciple of James Joyce; a play, therefore, by a man whose imagination (in the sense in which Mr. Eliot used this phrase of Joyce himselfc) is orthodox. In other words, we should consider where Mr. Beckett springs from and what he is reacting against in his roots. Even at his most nihilistic he will come under Mr. Eliot's category of the Christian blasphemer.

The fundamental imagery of *Waiting for Godot* is Christian; for, at the depth of experience into which Mr. Beckett is probing, there is no other source of imagery for him to draw on. His heroes are two tramps, who have come from nowhere in particular and have nowhere in particular to go. Their life is a state of apparently fruitless expectation. They receive messages, through a little boy, from the local landowner, Godot, who is always going to come in person to-morrow, but never does come. Their attitude towards Godot is one partly of hope, partly of fear. The orthodoxy of this symbolism, from a Christian point of view, is obvious. The tramps with their rags and their misery represent the fallen state of man. The squalor of their surroundings, their lack of a "stake in the

world," represents the idea that here in this world we can build no abiding city. The ambiguity of their attitude towards Godot, their mingled hope and fear, the doubtful tone of the boy's messages, represents the state of tension and uncertainty in which the average Christian must live in this world, avoiding presumption, and also avoiding despair. Yet the two tramps, Didi and Gogo, as they call each other, represent something far higher than the other two characters in the play, the masterful and ridiculous Pozzo and his terrifying slave, Lucky. Didi and Gogo stand for the contemplative life. Pozzo and Lucky stand for the life of practical action taken, mistakenly, as an end in itself. Pozzo's blindness and Lucky's dumbness in the second act rub this point in. The so-called practical man, the man of action, has to be set on his feet and put on his way by the contemplative man. He depends . . . on the contemplative man for such moments of insight, of spiritual communication, as occur in his life. The mere and pure man of action, the comic caricature of the Nietzschean superman, Pozzo, is like an actor who does not properly exist without his audience; but his audience are also, in a sense, his judges. Pozzo and Lucky, in fact, have the same sort of function in *Waiting for Godot* as Vanity Fair in *The Pilgrim's Progress.* But they are, as it were, a perambulating Vanity Fair; Didi and Gogo are static pilgrims. It is worth noting, also, that Didi and Gogo are bound to each other by something that it is not absurd to call charity. . . . Pozzo and Lucky are drawn together by hate and fear. Their lot is increasing misery; but if Didi and Gogo are not obviously any better off at the end of the play than they were at the beginning, neither are they obviously any worse off. Their state remains one of expectation.

Waiting for Godot—one might sum up these remarks—is thus a modern morality play, on permanent Christian themes. But, even if the Christian basis of the structure were not obvious, Mr. Beckett is constantly underlining it for us in the incidental symbolism and the dialogue. The first piece of serious dialogue in the play, the first statement, as it were, of a theme, is about the "two thieves, crucified at the same time as our Saviour."

> VLADIMIR: And yet . . . (*pause*) . . . how is it— this is not boring you I hope—how is that of the four evangelists only one speaks of a thief being saved? The four of them were there—or thereabouts, and only one speaks of a thief being saved. (*Pause.*) Come on Gogo, return the ball, can't you, once in a way?
>
> ESTRAGON: (*with exaggerated enthusiasm*). I find this really most extraordinarily interesting.

The discussion goes on to canvas the melancholy possibility that perhaps both thieves were damned. And the effect of the dialogue on the stage is, momentarily, to make us identify the glib Didi and the resentful and inarticulate Gogo with the two thieves, and to see, in each of them, an overmastering concern with the other's salvation. There is also towards the end of the first act a discussion about whether their human affection for each other may have stood in the way of that salvation:

> ESTRAGON: Wait! (*He moves away from Vladimir.*) I wonder if we wouldn't have been better off alone, each one for himself. (*He crosses the stage and sits down on the mound.*) We weren't made for the same road.
> VLADIMIR: (*without anger*). It's not certain.

ESTRAGON: No, nothing is certain.

The tree on the stage, though it is a willow, obviously stands both for the Tree of the Knowledge of Good and Evil (and, when it puts on green leaves, for the Tree of Life) and for the Cross. When Didi and Gogo are frightened in the second act, the best thing they can think of doing is to shelter under its base. But it gives no concealment, and it is perhaps partly from God's wrath that they are hiding; for it is also the Tree of Judas, on which they are recurrently tempted to hang themselves.

Here, in fact, we have the subtle novelty, the differentiating quality, of *Waiting for Godot,* when we compare it with *Everyman* or with *The Pilgrim's Progress.* Didi and Gogo do not complete their pilgrimage nor are we meant to be clear that they will complete it successfully. The angel who appears to them at the end of the first act is an ambiguous angel: the angel who keeps the goats, not the angel who keeps the sheep. And Godot—one remembers that God chastises those whom he loves, while hardening the hearts of impenitent sinners by allowing them a term of apparent impunity—does not beat him but beats his brother who keeps the sheep. . . . Are Didi and Gogo in the end to be among the goats? The boy who appears as a messenger at the end of the second act looks like the same boy, but is not, or at least does not recognize them. He may be, this time, the angel who keeps the sheep. That Godot himself stands for an anthropomorphic image of God is obvious. That is why Vladimir—if he had a blonde or a black beard he might be more reassuringly man or devil—is so alarmed in the second act when he hears that Godot, Ancient of Days, has a white beard. . . .

One main function of Pozzo and Lucky in the play is to present, and to be the occasion of the dismissal of, what might be called "alternative philosophies." Pozzo, in the first act, is a man of power, who eloquently—too consciously eloquently, as he knows—expounds Nietzschean pessimism:

> But—(*hand raised in admonition*)—but—behind this veil of gentleness and peace (*he raises his eyes to the sky, the others imitate him, except Lucky*) night is charging (*vibrantly*) and will burst upon us (*he snaps his fingers*) pop! like that! (*his inspiration leaves him*) just when we least expect it. (*Silence. Gloomy.*) That's how it is on this bitch of an earth. . . .

In the second act, in his far more genuinely desperate state, his pessimistic eloquence is less obviously "theatrical":

> (*Calmer*). They give birth astride of a grave, the light gleams an instant, then it's night once more. (*He jerks the rope.*) On!

There is an echo in the rhythm and idiom of the first sentence, there, of Synge. And since it is the only overtly "poetical" sentence which Mr. Beckett allows himself in this play, and since he is the most calculatingly skilful of writers, one may take it that the echo is meant as a criticism of Pozzo—a criticism of romantic stylized pessimism. If the Nietzschean attitude is dismissed in Pozzo, it is harder to suggest just what is dismissed in Lucky. He is the proletarian, who used to be the peasant. . . . But in Lucky's long speech—the most terrifyingly effective single sustained episode in the play—he stands for a contemporary reality, composite, perhaps, but when presented to us immediately recognizable. He stands for half-baked knowledge, undigested knowledge, the plain man's naive belief in a Goddess called Science, his muddled

appeals to unreal authorities. . . . Lucky's speech is the great bravura piece of writing in the play. Mr. Beckett has never been more brilliantly unreadable; not only Didi, Gogo, and Pozzo but the audience want to scream. What is dismissed in Lucky's speech is perhaps Liberalism, Progress, Popular Education, what Thomas Love Peacock used to call, sardonically, "the March of Mind." The Nietzschean and the Liberal hypotheses being put out of court, the Christian hypothesis is left holding the stage. It is at least a more comprehensive and profound hypothesis, whatever Mr. Beckett may personally think of it; and the total effect of his play, therefore—since most of us, in the ordinary affairs of the world, have more of Pozzo or Lucky in us, than of Didi or Gogo—is not to lower but unexpectedly to raise our idea of our human dignity. Questioning and expectation do give life dignity, even though expectations are never satisfied, and even though the most fundamentally important questions can expect, perhaps, at the most an implicit answer.

"They Also Serve," in The Times Literary Supplement, *No. 2815, February 10, 1956, p. 84.*

KATHARINE M. WILSON

Sir,—It was interesting to see your reviewer's interpretation of *Waiting for Godot* as a Christian allegory [see excerpt dated February 10, 1956]. I should have thought it preached obvious and straightforward existentialism. If this is where waiting for Godot is leading us, then in the words of Estragon, repeated significantly, "Must we wait for Godot?" The Christian interpretation entirely fails to account for Lucky's name. He is the lucky inauthentic man on the existentialist view, since he has got precisely what he wants, the easiest thing in life; he never has to think or decide or worry for himself, merely to obey. Pozzo tells us that Lucky likes to be driven. Moreover, if this were intended as Christian allegory then the progressive deterioration of Lucky into complete inanity, and of Pozzo into absolute blindness, would lack sufficient point. We are told that they deteriorate rapidly. In other words the contemporary situation is urgent. It is not so much that this play presents nothing, which itself is an existentialist conception, but complete inaction; no one does anything to help himself, except Lucky, who to maintain his happy position treads viciously on the toes of his would-be helper. Pozzo, when he falls down, instead of getting up, roars for help. The tramps, although one of them realizes that his friendship with the other is a mistake, and although he wonders whether they ought to wait for Godot, never get beyond unhappy complaint. It can hardly be right to call them contemplatives although they are Christians waiting to be "saved," since they fill in the time of waiting with distractions, with any distraction they happen to think of. . . .

Waiting for Godot exactly fulfils Sartre's definition of an existentialist play as one which sets out to present the contemporary situation in its full horror so that the audience, finding it unendurable, may feel forced to remedy it. He would call your reviewer's attitude a typical instance of the "bad faith" which attributes all our misery to God or fate—as if our human situation were given—in order to evade having to face up to our own responsibility for it. The moral of the play then, as I see it, poses itself in the question, since this is what waiting for Godot is like, must we wait for Godot?

Katharine M. Wilson, in a letter to the editor, in The

Times Literary Supplement, *No. 2818, March 2, 1956, p. 133.*

PHILIP H. BAGBY

Sir,—Surely Mr. Beckett must be chuckling away somewhere in France at the attempts of your reviewer and your correspondents to extract some clear message from the manifold ambiguities of his play [*Waiting for Godot* (see excerpts dated 1956 above)]. Its strength clearly lies in its uncertainties, in the fact that it gives us no final answer, no decisive reason to prefer either hope or despair.

It seems likely that Godot will never come, but it is by no means certain. His messengers (or messenger) may or may not be false prophets. Numerous alternatives are presented: the mutual affection of Vladimir and Estragon, Vladimir's longing for death, Estragon's reliance on Godot's promises, Lucky's dependence on his master and Pozzo's dependence on his slave, waiting and journeying or, if we must find an allegory, Christian consolation and existentialist action by virtue of the absurd. Very likely still other possible courses are offered us in the dense texture of the play, but we are never told whether we should choose one or all or none of these alternatives. One choice seems clearly to be rejected; it is "thinking" or reason as exemplified in Lucky's frightening tirade. Yet, after all, is not Lucky obviously mad?

At the end the playgoer leaves the theatre puzzled, disturbed, forced to worry about the uncertainty of the human situation, but what choice he makes or whether he makes a choice at all is up to him. For my part, I believe that Godot does come—to those who know how to see him. But this answer I find in myself, not in the play. Mr. Beckett asks questions; he gives no answers.

Philip G. Bagby, in a letter to the editor, in The Times Literary Supplement, *No. 2821, March 23, 1956, p. 181.*

WILLIAM EMPSON

Sir,—Mr. Bagby was quite right, I think, to point out the radical ambiguity of *Waiting for Godot* [see excerpt dated March 23, 1956], but not all ambiguity is good. Here it expresses the sentiment: "We cannot believe in Christianity and yet without that everything we do is hopelessly bad." Such an attitude seems to be more frequent in Irish than either English or French writers, perhaps because in Ireland the religious training of children is particularly fierce. A child is brought up to believe that he would be wicked and miserable without God; then he stops believing in God; then he behaves like a dog with its back broken by a car, screaming and thrashing on the public road, so that a passer-by can only wish for it to be put out of its misery. Surely we need not admire this result; the obvious reflection is that it was a very unfairly risky treatment to give to a child.

To be sure, we all ought to feel the mystery of the world, and there is bound to be a kind of literary merit in any play which makes us feel it so strongly; but we need not ourselves feel only exacerbated impotence about the world, and if we did we would be certain to behave badly. . . . In itself this peculiar attitude deserves only a rather disgusted curiosity. But I would hate to suggest a moral censorship against the play; it is so well done that it is an enlarging experience, very differ-

ent for different members of the audience. It would only be dangerous if it was liable to suck a member into the entire background to be presumed for the author, and that it cannot do.

William Empson, in a letter to the editor, in The Times Literary Supplement, *No. 2822, March 30, 1956, p. 195.*

THE TIMES LITERARY SUPPLEMENT

Every now and then some article or review in these pages starts off the kind of correspondence that, if the editorial closure were not at some time arbitrarily applied, might well go on for ever. . . . But a recent article in these pages on Mr. Samuel Beckett's provocative play, *Waiting for Godot* [see excerpt dated February 10, 1956] has, as a provoker of comment, left King Lear's button and what Hopkins really meant by "buckle" standing. The letters that we have published represent a very small proportion of those we have received, and represent, also, only a random sample of the many vividly contrasting attitudes which it is apparently possible for intelligent readers and spectators to take to Mr. Beckett's play.

Two extreme views, not represented in the letters we have published, are worth recording. One is that the play is a hoax on highbrows, and that our reviewer, who found a deep Christian meaning in it, was either Mr. Beckett's ally or his dupe; the other is that the deep meaning of the play was so extremely deep that it was very wrong and presumptuous of our reviewer to attempt its exposition; the meaning was inexpressible, and therefore ought not to have been expressed. Between these extremes, most of the letters we have received have been concerned with the validity of a Christian interpretation of the play. Here again there have been several extreme approaches. Mr. Empson, in his typically lively way [see excerpt dated March 30, 1956], seems to agree that a Christian interpretation is a correct one; adding that this shows what a dangerous thing Christianity can be, especially when, as by the Irish in their youth, it is taken really seriously. He is alarmed lest the liberal agnostic spectator or reader should be "sucked" into Mr. Beckett's vortex. Yet for another correspondent the play, though Christian in its imagery, was not in the least Christian in its theme [see excerpt dated March 2, 1956 by Katharine M. Wilson]. It was rather an atheist-existentialist play, insisting on the impossibility of the individual's shifting his burdens to any pair of shoulders other than his own. . . .

It would have helped greatly if at some stage in this correspondence Mr. Beckett had himself intervened with an authoritative statement of what he was after, but no close student of the play can have expected this to happen. It is a sort of thing that, in fact, rarely does happen. Many a critical argument, for instance, about the sources, the structure, the deeper layers of meaning, and so on, of Mr. T. S. Eliot's poems over the past twenty or thirty years could have been settled, perhaps, by a short letter from the poet to the periodicals in which such discussions took place. But creative artists fight shy of sending such letters; and research students, even, have sometimes a feeling that seeking direct information about a puzzle, from the writer they are puzzling about, is in a way cheating, like looking up the answer at the back of a book. There is a fine piece of vituperation in *Waiting for Godot* in which the culminating insult is the word "Critic!" Though Mr. Beckett has not written to us, it is to be hoped that the variety of the ways in which our readers have taken his work has afforded him an ironical pleasure. A reader who goes back to the text of *Waiting for Godot,* after having followed all the discussion of it in our pages, may be inclined to agree with our reviewer that it is within the framework of certain fundamental traditional Christian attitudes—some of which, like the notion of life as a journey, are common to Christianity and other great religions—that *Waiting for Godot* touches us and makes sense. . . .

[It is probable] that the Christian framework of ideas is not merely moral but cuts down to the metaphysical level. Thus, the Didi-Gogo couple and the Pozzo-Lucky couple can each be seen as standing for two contrasting modes of integration of dual elements in a single personality: Didi standing to Gogo as the soul's intuitions to the body's needs, Pozzo standing to Lucky—Bishop Butler's moral philosophy is relevant here—as the various unselfregarding passions to that rational self-love, that reasonable will, which ought to be their master but which instead they have made their slave.

Agreement on such points leaves, however, our general evaluation of Mr. Beckett's brilliant play still very much an open question. It is hard to judge it purely as a work of literature. It is written with the stage in mind, with beautiful economy; the words on the page, apart from that economy, have hardly a separable literary value. Acting puts flesh on *Waiting for Godot.* It is its structure which compels admiration. Yet the notion of the structure of a dramatic narrative in which, at one level at least, "nothing happens" is a profoundly puzzling one. Discussion of *Waiting for Godot* obviously could go on for ever, and obviously must, alas, at some stage be brought to a stop. Yet there is one final reflection in which perhaps all our correspondents on this topic might concur. We are often told that we are living through a period of literary consolidation, not literary experiment; we hear of "the new conservatism" in poetry as well as in politics. The extraordinary interest which this play has aroused from so many points of view, and at so many levels, suggests that a healthy hunger for novelty is not so dead in us as we may have feared.

"Puzzling about Godot," in The Times Literary Supplement, *No. 2824, April 13, 1956, p. 221.*

New York, 1956

WOLCOTT GIBBS

[*Waiting for Godot* takes place] on a stage barren of everything except a few mortuary slabs of concrete and a single blasted tree. It is the way the world will perhaps look when the bombs have finished with us—as chilly and disconsolate as some landscape on the moon. Into this desolation there presently stray a couple of bums, who also look as if they might be the survivors of some ultimate explosion. They are nicknamed Gogo and Didi, and their conversation is peculiar. They talk mainly about their melancholy lot—they are tired and hungry, their feet hurt, and bands of savage strangers set upon them at night and beat them up. This discourse has a certain graveyard hilarity, having, I suppose, something to do with the idea of infinite misery sustained with no dignity at all but only a kind of lunatic vulgarity. It is also remarkably hard to follow, since few lines are even remotely responsive to those preceding them. The only thing that emerges with reasonable clarity is that they have come to this spot to keep a rendezvous with someone named Godot, a cryptic figure whom they may or may not have met before and who somehow holds the key to their salvation.

They are getting practically nowhere with anything when they are interrupted by the arrival of a powerful and menacingly fashionable man named Pozzo, who is attended by a cowering and horribly emaciated slave with a rope around his neck. The tramps naturally find these newcomers fascinating. . . . It is a very interesting scene, and it ends on a high note when Pozzo, to demonstrate that his debased creature can still think quite nicely, calls on him for a speech and he responds with one beginning:

> Given the existence as uttered forth in the public works of Puncher and Wattmann of a personal God quaquaquaqua with white beard quaquaquaqua outside time without extension who from the heights of divine apathia divine athambia divine aphasia loves us dearly with some exceptions for reasons unknown . . .

This goes on for almost a hundred lines more, and at its conclusion everybody closes in on the orator in an enthusiastic attempt to beat him to death. The remainder of the act is comparatively tranquil. The slave is revived and Pozzo leads him off. Gogo and Didi are embarking on another of their gloomy dialogues when a small boy enters to announce that Godot isn't coming after all. He can be expected without fail, however, the following evening. The partners accept this news with resignation. . . . [The] second act is substantially a duplicate of the first, the only important difference being that this time when Pozzo and his lackey turn up the former is blind, the latter is dumb, and both are visibly close to some common end. (p. 89)

Since the author of *Waiting for Godot,* a follower and former secretary of James Joyce named Samuel Beckett, can hardly have written with no coherent purposes whatever in mind, a secondary and clarifying meaning certainly exists, and it seems to me that the most likely is also the simplest. Gogo and Didi, then, represent the great mass of lost men, and the savior who never comes for them is God. Apparently, in Mr. Beckett's opinion this deity is not only an eternal promise and an eternal betrayal but also an eternal waster of time and imposer of senseless disciplines. . . . Pozzo and his slave, by this same simplification, are just wealth and the artist who has been bought and destroyed by it. Wealth, it seems, is also to be destroyed. Neither of them, in any case, is particularly concerned with Godot, who is an opium reserved exclusively for the masses, as the samplers of my childhood used to say. I have struggled to extract some other and less sophomoric message from Mr. Beckett's play (several of my colleagues have said that the possible interpretations are almost endless), but I'm afraid that this 1934 Model of the Universal Allegory is the best I can do. All I can say, in a critical sense, is that I have seldom seen such meagre moonshine stated with such inordinate fuss. (pp. 89-90)

Bert Lahr, who plays Gogo, has been quoted as saying that he has no idea what the damn play is about. His statement brings up the curious picture of a director, who presumably does understand his script, failing to share this useful knowledge with one of his stars, and it may be unique in the theatre. . . . It is a very sad and confusing situation all around. (p. 90)

Wolcott Gibbs, "Enough Is Enough Is Enough," in
The New Yorker, *Vol. XXXII, No. 11, May 5, 1956,
pp. 89-90.*

NORMAN MAILER

[*The essay excerpted below was originally published in* The Village Voice, *May 7, 1956.*]

It is never particularly pleasant for me to apologize, and in the present circumstances I loathe doing so.

Since I have my pride, I would have preferred to keep my word and not appear again in this newspaper. . . . But I have a duty to my honesty as well, and I did something of which I am ashamed, and so must apologize in the hardest but most meaningful way:—by public advertisement.

I am referring of course to what I wrote about **Waiting for Godot** in my last column. Some of you may remember that I said Beckett's play was a poem to impotence and appealed precisely to those who were most impotent. Since then I have read the play, seen the present Broadway production, read the play again, have thought about it, wrestled with its obscurities (and my conscience), and have had to come up reluctantly with the conviction that I was most unfair to Beckett. Because **Waiting for Godot** is a play about impotence rather than an ode to it, and while its view of life is indeed hopeless, it is an art work, and therefore, I believe, a good. While I still think it is essentially the work of a minor artist because its range of life-experience is narrow if deep, it is all the same, whether major or minor, the work of a man who has conscientiously and with great purity made the uncompromising effort to abstract his view of life into an art work, no matter how unbearable that view of life may be. It is bad enough and sad enough when the critics of any given time attack an artist and fail to understand him, but then this is virtually to be taken for granted. For one artist to attack another, however, and to do it on impulse, is a crime, and for the first time in months I have been walking around with a very clear sense of guilt. (p. 320)

What still distresses me and distresses Beckett as well, I would guess, is that **Godot** has become the latest touchstone in social chi-chi, and people who don't have the faintest idea of what he is talking about, and who as they watch the play, scream and gurgle and expire with a kind of militant exacerbated snobbery, are exactly the majority of people who have promoted **Godot** here. Because not to like **Waiting for Godot** is to suffer damnation—one is no longer chic. (p. 321)

Most of the present admirers of **Godot** are, I believe, snobs, intellectual snobs of undue ambition and impotent imagination, the worst sort of literary type, invariably more interested in being part of some intellectual elite than in the creative act itself. This combination almost always coincides with a sex-hater, for if one is ashamed of sex or is unhappy with sex, then the next best thing is to rise in the social world. But since people with poor sexual range seldom have the energy and the courage to rise imaginatively or defiantly, they obligatorily give themselves to the escalator of the snob which is slow but ultimately sure of some limited social ascension.

And for these reasons I assumed in advance that **Godot** was essentially and deeply anti-sexual, and I was wrong. It has almost no sexual hope within it, but that is its lament, that is Beckett's grief, and the comic tenderness of the story comes from the resignation of that grief. So far as it is a story, it is a sad little story, but told purely.

Two men, two vagabonds, named Vladimir and Estragon (Didi and Gogo), a male and female homosexual, old and exhausted, have come to rest temporarily on a timeless plain, presided over by a withered cross-like tree, marooned in the purgatory of their failing powers. Their memories have become uncertain as vapors, their spirits are broken, they cannot even make love to each other any longer, they can only bicker and weep and nag and sulk and sleep, they are beyond sex, really neither old men nor old women but debilitated children looking for God, looking for the Life-Giver. They are so desperate they even speak wanly of hanging themselves, because this at least will give them one last erection. But they have not the power to commit suicide, they are exhausted and addled by the frustration of their failures to the point where they cannot even commit a despairing action. They can only wait for Godot, and they speculate feebly about his nature, for Godot is a mystery to them, and after all they desire not only sex and rebirth into life, but worldly power as well. They are looking for the potency of the phallus and the testes. Vladimir speaks of the Saviour and the Two Thieves, and how one of the thieves was saved. The implication is that since he and Gogo are withered puff-balls, balls blown passively through life, opportunistic and aimless as small thieves, perhaps one of them and only one may be saved, and he is tempted: perhaps he is the one. Which would be of course at the expense of his life-mate Gogo. So in the religious sense he is not even pure in his despair, but is already tempted into Sin.

Enter Pozzo and Lucky: Pozzo the fat gentleman with the whip and the rope around the neck of Lucky his slave, his wretch, the being at the mercy of his will. Pozzo dominates Lucky, abuses him, commands him about like a cruel brain abusing its own body.

And Vladimir has his opportunity for action, he can rescue Lucky, indeed he protests at the treatment of Lucky. But Vladimir, like Gogo, is seduced by the worldly power of Pozzo, and finally the two vagabonds collaborate in torturing Lucky, or at the very least in aiding Pozzo to beat Lucky into unconsciousness at the end of his single impassioned speech.

Thereafter, the action (what there is of it) descends, and when Pozzo and Lucky reappear, Pozzo is blind and Lucky is dumb—we will hear his wisdom no longer. Their condition is even more debased than Gogo's and Didi's. But for some will remain the echo of Lucky's speech.

It is the one strangled cry of active meaning in the whole play, a desperate retching pellmell of broken thoughts and intuitive lunges into the nature of man, sex, God, and time, it comes from a slave, a wretch, who is closer to the divine than any of the other characters, it is a cry across the abyss from impotence to Apollo (Dionysus is indeed quite beyond the horizon) and Pozzo, Gogo and Didi answer the cry by beating Lucky into unconsciousness. Thereafter, Lucky—the voice, the midwife, to the rebirth of the others—is stricken dumb, for he too suffers from failing powers, he too is overcome by the succession of his defeats and so brought closer to death. Later, much later, at the end of the play, Vladimir talks to the boy who brings the message that Godot will not come that day, and as Vladimir questions him about Godot, the boy says that Godot has a white beard. But Lucky, who has a head of white hair, had begun his speech (which again is the intellectual lock and key of the play) by talking of "a personal God quaquaquaqua with white beard . . ." exactly the speech which the others had destroyed. So Vladimir has a moment of agony: "Christ have mercy on us!" he says to the boy. Through vanity, through cupidity, through indifference, through snobbery itself, Vladimir and Gogo have lost the opportunity to find Godot—they have abused the link which is Lucky. (I must say that I am not altogether unconvinced that Lucky himself may be Godot—it is, at the least, a possibility.) At any rate, Vladimir and Gogo have failed still again, their condition is even more desperate, and so the play ends. "Yes, let's go," says Gogo in the final line, but Beckett follows with the stage direction: "They do not move. Curtain."

It is possible that consciously or unconsciously Beckett is restating the moral and sexual basis of Christianity which was lost with Christ—that one finds life by kissing the feet of the poor, by giving of oneself to the most debased corners of the most degraded. . . . (pp. 321-24)

Yet, there is another and richer possibility. For I believe Beckett is also saying, again consciously or unconsciously, that God's destiny is flesh and blood with ours, and so, far from conceiving of a God who sits in judgment and allows souls, lost souls, to leave purgatory and be reborn again, there is the greater agony of God at the mercy of man's fate, God determined by man's efforts, man who has free will and can no longer exercise it and God therefore in bondage to the result of man's efforts. At the end, Vladimir and Gogo having failed again, there is the hint, the murmur, that God's condition is also worse, and he too has come closer to failure—when Vladimir asks the boy in the closing minutes of the play what Godot does, the boy answers: "He does nothing, Sir." Godot, by implication, lives in the same condition, the same spiritual insomnia, agony, limbo, the same despair of one's fading powers which has hung over the play. (p. 324)

> *Norman Mailer, "A Public Notice on 'Waiting for Godot'," in his* Advertisements for Myself, *G. P. Putnam's Sons, 1959, pp. 320-25.*

ERIC BENTLEY

The minute a statement was released to the press that Beckett's *Waiting for Godot* was not for casual theatregoers but for intellectuals, I could have written Walter Kerr's review for him. And I felt myself being jockeyed into writing a defense of the play as if by its success or failure civilization would stand or fall. Such is criticism.

Or is it? Besides the intellectual anti-intellectualism of a Walter Kerr, two other attitudes, both of them less objectionable, have defined themselves in modern America: one is nonintellectual pro-intellectualism and the other is nonintellectual anti-intellectualism. Both these attitudes were represented in the newspaper reviews of *Waiting for Godot,* and obviously the production benefited as much from the first as it suffered from the second. Both groups of critics found the writing beyond them. The first was prepared to be respectful towards what was not fully understood. The second joined Mr. Kerr in finding something of a scandal in the very existence of difficulty. And there emerged, in his review and theirs, one of the big ideas of the century:

> Thinking is a simple, elementary process. *Godot* is merely a stunt . . .
> —John Chapman, *The Daily News*

> The author was once secretary to that master of obfuscation, James Joyce. Beckett appears to have absorbed some of his employer's ability to make the simple complex . . .
> —Robert Coleman, *The Daily Mirror*

> . . . the rhythms of an artist (Bert Lahr) [the actor who plays Estragon] with an eye to God's own truth. All of them, I think, are the rhythms of musical comedy, or revue, of tanbark entertainment— and they suggest that Mr. Lahr has, all along in his own lowbrow career, been in touch with what goes on in the minds and hearts of the folk out front. I wish that Mr. Beckett were as intimately in touch with the texture of things.
> —Walter Kerr, *Herald Tribune*

The superior insight of genius is unnecessary. All we need, to take upon us the non-mystery of things, is constant communion with the man of non-distinction.

Speaking of obfuscation, what could obfuscate our experience of Beckett's play more than the cloud of conflict between highbrow and lowbrow, highbrow and highbrow, lowbrow and lowbrow? This conflict is, of course, anterior to the play. The play itself presents a problem for our audiences too, and that is the problem of nausea as a playwright's conscious attitude to life.

Though it is permissible to be nauseated by existence, and even to say so, it seems doubtful whether one should expect to be paid for saying so, at any rate by a crowd of people in search of an amusing evening. Yet, since the humor which provides amusement is precisely, as Nietzsche observed, a victory over nausea, it would be hard to stage the victory without at least suggesting the identity and character of the foe. It has taken Krafft-Ebbing and Freud to force a general admission of the importance of nausea even, say, in the work of Swift, where it is most prominent.

American optimism drives American nausea a little more deeply underground: that is the difference between America and Europe. For, if the conscious "thought" of "serious" literature and drama becomes more insistently "positive," a nation's humor, arising from the depths of discomfort, repression and guilt, will become more and more destructive. . . .

Samuel Beckett's point of view seems pretty close to that of Anouilh or Sartre. *Waiting for Godot* is, so to speak, a play that one of them ought to have written. It is the quintessence of "existentialism" in the popular, and most relevant, sense of the term—a philosophy which underscores the incomprehensibility, and therefore the meaninglessness, of the universe. . . . (p. 20)

Like many modern plays, *Waiting for Godot* is undramatic but highly theatrical. Essential to drama, surely, is not merely situation but situation in moment, even in beautifully shaped moment. A *curve* is the most natural symbol for a dramatic action, while, as Aristotle said, beginning, middle, and end are three of its necessary features. Deliberately anti-dramatic, Beckett's play has a shape of a non-dramatic sort; two strips of action are laid side by side like railway tracks. These strips are One Day and the Following Day in the lives of a couple of bums. There cannot be any drama because the author's conclusion is that the two days are the same. That there are also things that change is indicated by a play-within-this-play which also has two parts. The first time that the characters of the inner play come on they are a brutal Master and his pitiful Man; the second time they are both equally pitiful because the Master has gone blind.

What has brought the play before audiences in so many countries—aside from snobberies and phony publicity—is its theatricality. Highbrow writers have been enthusiastic about clowns and vaudeville for decades, but this impresses me as the first time that anything has successfully been done about the matter. Mr. Kerr gave Bert Lahr all the credit for a traditional yet rich characterization, which, however, had been skillfully put together by Mr. Beckett. The author, to recapitulate, has not only been able to define the "existentialist" point of view more sharply than those who are more famously associated with it, he has also found for its expression a vehicle of a sort that people have been recommending without following their own recommendation.

It is, therefore, an important play. Whether it is more important than these two achievements suggest is the question. To me, the play did not come over with the force of revelation nor with that of sheer greatness. Mr. Beckett's voice is interesting, but one does not quite find it individual, because it does not quite seem new. One is surely not exploiting an external fact unfairly in saying that Mr. Beckett is excessively—if quite inevitably—over-influenced by Joyce. If Russian literature is cut from Gogol's *Overcoat,* Irish literature is cut from those coats of many colors, *Ulysses* and *Finnegans Wake.*

I do not think the play is obscure except as any rich piece of writing is obscure. No doubt there are meanings that will disengage themselves in time as one lives with such a work, yet enough is clear from the first not only to arouse interest but to communicate a fine sense of a unified and intelligible image of life. I take it that Beckett belongs to that extensive group of modern writers who have had a religious upbringing, retain religious impulses and longings, but have lost all religious belief. I should differentiate him from, say, Sartre in that he does not write from the standpoint of atheism but, ideologically speaking, from that of skepticism. People who have seen *Godot* are able to suggest this or that solution—Christian, anti-Christian, etc.—precisely because Beckett has left the door open for them to do so. They are wrong only if they intimate that the author himself passed through the door and closed it behind him. Rough words have been spoken about the allegedly excessive symbolism of the play. This is unjust. Beckett's finest achievement is to have made the chief relationships, which are many, so concrete that abstract interpretations are wholly relegated to the theatre lobby. He gives us, not tenets, but alternatives seen as human relationships (between bum and bum, master and man); also as ordinary human attitudes to God, Nature, and Death on the one hand, and, on the other, to the "trivialties," such as clothes, defecation, smells . . . (pp. 20-1)

[I] would have lopped off the last bit of the first act. I would also have been tempted to make cuts at several points where the dialogue stumbles. (The rhythm is very firm for longish stretches but will from time to time just go to pieces.) But reverence towards a script is a good fault, and, on Broadway, an unusual, almost exemplary, one. . . .

A remark—perhaps irrelevant—about the title. "Godot" is the person you are waiting for who, presumably, will set things to rights when he arrives. I assume that Mr. Beckett made up the French word from the English one, God. But, as someone will no doubt inform *The Times Literary Supplement,* there is a once well-known play of Balzac's in which

we spend the whole evening waiting for a character called Godeau, who has still not come on stage when his arrival is announced just before the final curtain falls. (p. 21)

Eric Bentley, "The Talent of Samuel Beckett," in The New Republic, *Vol. 134, No. 20, May 14, 1956, pp. 20-1.*

RICHARD HAYES

The arrival of Mr. Beckett's play [*Waiting for Godot*], preceded by its intimidating vanguard of international opinion, marks a point of intellectual beauty in the season. The Irish Mr. Beckett is an eclectic artist, and for all his abstinent rejection of every investiture of tradition or grace or rhetoric, one may yet read in *Waiting for Godot* other and diverse patterns of the imagination. From Chaplin and the music hall, Beckett has taken the controlling images of the tramps, of shoes that pinch and hats that itch; his language has something of Gertrude Stein's grave intensity, her succinct, hovering implication; the long Joycean farrago—a compost heap of Western thought—spewed forth by the bestial Lucky, wakes with a start of horror out of Finnegan. . . . Yet *Waiting for Godot* is neither a pastiche nor a wealth of fragments: its pattern is drawn with notable purity of draughtsmanship; its poetry is secure. That poetry . . . is one of man's abused smallness and his hope, of the human tenderness which alone succors his outcast state. Surely this is potently felt even by those who have objected to the play's lack of any mastering logic or single meaning. We do ill to ask always for this certain, definable kind of "meaning"; at a point of incandescence, the imagination—particularly the dramatic imagination—works essentially in images, and I take indeed the excellence of *Godot* to reside not in its metaphysical pretensions, but in the grasping power and domination of its images.

I have, however, implied experience and vision: what is the structure of Mr. Beckett's? Here, he brings the metaphysical shudder before the Absurd to its final nullity. "At the end of my work," the dramatist has written, "there is nothing but dust—the nameable." And this attitude of disintegration dictates the various abolitions—of time, of logic—which are a feature of *Waiting for Godot.* Yet as an aesthetic intent, the calculated exploitation of impotence would seem to have its limitations, and what is absent from Mr. Beckett and from his play is any impulse of energy: for all the elegiac intelligence with which *Godot* makes its statement, for all its austere poetry of desolation, the drama has finally no sustaining sense of life. Pirandello made statements of a comparable metaphysical horror, but the area of experience for him always trembles and dilates with possibility; a dreadful stillness is the climate of Mr. Beckett's abyss. That abyss, however, is one over which we have all hovered, and into which the greatest spirits of our time have descended, and the steely, unsolaced courage with which Mr. Beckett confronts its ultimate terrors has a kind of anguished heroism. I would note, too, the curious nobility which colors Mr. Beckett's vision, even at its bleakest; for all the intensity of his shudder before experience, he never succumbs, in *Waiting for Godot,* to the paltry hysteria of what D. H. Lawrence once called doing dirt on life.

Richard Hayes, "The Stage: Nothing," in The Commonweal, *Vol. LXIV, No. 8, May 25, 1956, p. 203.*

BONAMY DOBRÉE

In *Waiting for Godot,* Mr. Samuel Beckett has put a large rampagious cat among the pigeons, the journalistic-critic ones, and perhaps the philosophic theoretic breed. "Mere music-hallery," some of the former judged, entertaining or dreary according to the jadedness of the palate; there was even "blind abuse," and Mr. Terence Rattigan . . . complained of a total lack of humanity in it. Such were reproved by others. . . . (pp. 478-79)

Perhaps the first thing to be said about the play in this context is that it relies on no cultural pattern whatever, not even values, as . . . other plays do. It springs up as the *lusus naturae* defying Mr. Fergusson's generalization; altogether a very queer play, outraging all commonly supported dramatic precepts, falling into no category unless it be that of a Morality Play expressed in contemporary terms. The psychology, naturally, is not so simple as in mediaeval times; we are not so sure of the divisions of virtue and sin, of soul and body. It might be hazarded that the "characters" (if you can call them so) in this play together make up what might be called "humanity" or Everyman, much in the way that the characters in *A Pilgrim's Progress* amount to a total being. Yet the persons are few: two filthy old tramps, a bewildered "successful" man who might be thought to represent Power, accompanied by a slave, and finally a boy. Had it been produced some years ago, critics would have it said, as they did when confronted by Ibsen and Tchekov, "This isn't a play at all." If drama is action this is certainly no play, since nothing whatever happens: it might go on for ever, and does, indeed, go on a few minutes too long. At the end, as at the beginning, the tramps are still waiting for Godot. What is it then? You might at a stretch call it a religious charade; it could certainly be described as a metaphysical one, Existentialist possibly. Farcical, absurd, yes: nevertheless a deadly serious work, the most original and unforeseen the theater can boast of at the moment.

But what is the theme? The human predicament? . . . But in what terms does Beckett conceive this predicament? Perhaps we can get a clue from a little monograph he wrote in 1931 in Paris—where he was secretary to James Joyce—and which is still illuminating, probing, and formative. The passage that follows seems to be, not a summation of part of Proust's thought, but what Beckett himself thinks: at all events it might be taken as a gloss upon this play:—

> The poisonous ingenuity of Time in the science of affliction is not limited to its action on the subject. . . . The individual is the seat of a constant process of decantation, decantation from the vessel containing the fluid of past times. . . . Lazily considered in anticipation and in the haze of our smug will to live, of our pernicious and incurable optimism, it seems exempt from the bitterness of fatality: in store for us, not in store for us.

So what can we make of the main persons who posture before us, the two tramps, Vladimir and Estragon, to each other Didi and Gogo, one of whom, and usually both, occupy the stage the whole time? Derelict creatures, down and out, unwashed, clothed in rags, sleeping when and where they can, finding such nourishment as they may from raw carrots and turnips, they are inseparable, throughout their lives unable to live apart from each other. Then what is the meaning of Gogo departing every night to get beaten up, for no given reason, by people who remain unspecified? We are shown them after every brief separation falling on each others' necks and embracing. Gogo occasionally says that it would have been better if they had never met, and that they ought to part. Didi acquiesces for the moment, but they simply cannot live without each other. Soul and body? Some such implication seems intended. Gogo on the whole would seem to symbolize intuition, Didi intellect: but the ingenuity of the play consists in part of the symbolism never being rigid: the two tramps partake of each others' qualities: and after all, what is soul? what is body? Where does intuition end, and intellect begin? The play seems all the time to pose such questions, to the point indeed of making us wonder what in fact the human predicament is. A "show" such as this should, on the face of it, be heavy and boring, but it is not so in the least; it dances along with a curious gaiety, which might be thought of as a happy nihilism were it not for the shafts of fundamentally serious implication which suddenly strike home.

The opening itself provides an example of this. We first see Gogo painfully maneuvering off one of his scandalous boots, with Didi sympathizing: then, without warning, we are shifted to an utterly different plane by Didi urgently seeking an answer to the question: "Was one of the thieves crucified on either side of Christ saved? If so, why do the Gospels vary in the account? Was he saved?" He passionately wants to know. "Saved from what?" Gogo asks; and when he is told "From Hell," he merely ejaculates "Pah!" and spits. We seem to be given the world that desperately wants to believe, and the world that is utterly indifferent, hardly bothering to be sceptical. And this strange discussion between the two hoboes is set in a rocky, desolately barren landscape, relieved only by one withered tree, which might or might not be a willow, and becomes, vaguely, a symbol of the Cross. All this sharpens our curiosity as to the mysterious Godot for whom the tramps are waiting. He had not come yesterday as promised, but had sent the boy to tell them he would meet them today. He never comes, the first of the two acts concluding with the appearance of the boy bearing a similar message. Didi insists that they should go on waiting; surely he will come, and all their difficulties will vanish, life will be easy, they will, in fact, be "saved." Who then is Godot? Is he a symbol, as has been suggested, of Everyman's secret and eternal hope, or, as Beckett might put it, our pernicious and incurable optimism? But then, at the end, Gogo says "Why wait?", and Didi answers that if they did not, Godot would punish them. All the time the deliberately shadowy, fugitive, and for that all the more stimulating symbolism. One might hazard that Godot is the sort of deity the non-thinking, blundering-through-life man thinks he believes in, Old Nobodaddy who will make everything come right in the end. And while waiting for Godot the tramps talk, quarrel, make it up in a kind of *odi et amo* alternation. . . . They discuss hanging themselves, towards the end going so far as to find a rope, which, of course, breaks. And here again the tree, which in the night between the acts has burst into full-grown leaf, suggests the Cross, more especially as one of them urges taking refuge at its foot.

Maybe the two friends symbolize the personal self, revealed to the self alone, the other characters the outer self, the self that the world is aware of. Part of us is represented by the preposterous bloated figure of Pozzo, vulgar, pitilessly egotistic and power-wielding, complacent yet self-pitying, impervious to the needs and sentiments of others. Something of us may correspond with the miserable creature ironically called Lucky, whom Pozzo drives in harness, addresses as "Slave," loads with burdens till he drops with fatigue, but who still is curiously happy. Do we see something of our dual public selves as we watch Pozzo living through him, since he provides everything on demand—a chair, food, drink, and even thought? One of the most brilliantly amusing of the many amusing passages in the play is when Pozzo orders, "Slave, think!", and Lucky reels off in a reciting voice a delicious rigmarole of contemporary scientifico-philosophic jargon, such as we may read, alas! almost every day, and (let us whisper it to ourselves) sometimes utter. It seems to come off a gramophone disc, of which the needle occasionally slips, so that phrases are repeated, some more than once. Remains only the boy messenger, a kind of not too innocent angel, who when he reappears at the end once more to postpone Godot's appearance, protests complete ignorance of his visit the evening before. Is he, perhaps, the younger generation that forgets the past experience of the race, so that it goes on repeating its disastrous blunders, putting off for ever the salvation of humanity, its Utopia, its Great State, its peaceful Confederation of Nations? Apart from minor symbolisms—at least we suppose they are so without being able to relate them to any system (Lucky biting Gogo in the leg; Gogo's miserable boots being left outside the curtain between the acts, facing us as it were with Van Gogh's painting of just such appalling commentaries on life; Didi's panic when Gogo wants to tell him his dreams;) the play would indeed seem to mirror horribly the eternal *condition humaine*.

It is interesting to try to suggest why this play is attracting London audiences. A fantasy, obviously; yet at the same time shockingly, grimily realistic: Gogo's feet stink, Didi's breath smells. Almost outrageously "unreal" in setting, the thoughts, the issues, the things the characters talk about, are our issues, the things everybody talks about. And, although the play is peopled with symbols, you never feel them to be such. The figures have a vivid actuality, grotesque, ridiculous, touching—we are touched even by the blindness of Pozzo in the second act—at once horrible and compassionating. A symbolic play in terms of realism, if you like, with a musical movement. Could it, one asks amid a multitude of questions, be the forerunner of a type of play that needs no implication of a cultural pattern to make it tell? In technique it combines adherence to the severest neo-classical unities with the freakishness of the music-hall, as when Gogo, Didi, and Lucky turn to prestidigitation with haste. It may be merely a flash in the pan. (pp. 479-82)

> *Bonamy Dobrée, "Drama in England," in The Sewanee Review, Vol. LXIV, No. 3, Summer, 1956, pp. 470-84.*

•REVIEWS OF MAJOR REVIVALS•

MURRAY SCHUMACH

[Now that *Waiting for Godot*] has been repatriated to Europe as part of the United States drama program at the Brussels World's Fair, an international signal has gone out to extol or deride the most controversial play since World War II, of which its author, Samuel Beckett, said: "I didn't choose to write a play. It just happened that way."

Other things that have happened since the play's stormy Paris debut in 1953—called by Jean Anouilh "as important as the première of Pirandello in 1923"—include a ban against any stories of advertising of the show in Spain; near-cancellation in the Netherlands averted by the furious resistance of the cast; successful runs in almost every important city of Europe. And on sophisticated Broadway, where it arrived in 1956, it created one of the most extraordinary phenomena in American show business. For, after the final curtain on many nights, the audience remained and, joined by interested literary figures and laymen, debated the play's meaning and merit. In these debates clergymen were sometimes pitted against each other on whether *Godot* was religious or atheistic. Its continued viability is proved by twenty productions of *Godot* given this year in as many states.

On the surface there is little in this plotless drama to rouse the multitudes. It seems little more than a tale about two derelicts who wait vainly, on a bleak set that features a gnarled tree, for a Mr. Godot to appear and lessen their misery. . . .

Occasionally the pace of *Godot* is changed by comic turns, done by the two derelicts, that range from old-fashioned pratfalls to kicks. The longest speech in the play, a stream-of-consciousness outpouring, is delivered by the slave, who is otherwise mute.

That the force of arguments about *Godot* has not waned appreciably was shown earlier this month at its latest New York revival by the San Francisco Actor's Workshop, which has since taken the play to Brussels. At many of the performances spectators were asked to write comments on *Godot.* At least one-quarter of the 200-odd returns were unfavorable, another third bewildered or undecided, and the rest favorable. . . .

Almost as interesting as the reasons for argument about *Godot* are the lures that bring crowds to see it. Many undoubtedly come because they love the theatre and the play has caused a stir. Others are intellectuals who are curious about a play that is said to have a deeper meaning than that in most dramas. Finally, there are those who are drawn by a sort of egghead snobbery.

Godot has been much easier to blame or praise than to explain. One difficulty for its defenders is that the play's Irish-born author, who created the work in French, has not helped them in the few comments he has made about *Godot.* Thus, when a publisher wrote to him asking for his explanation of the play's symbols, he replied: "As far as I know, there are none. Of course, I am open to correction." And when Sir Ralph Richardson, the British star, asked him if Godot represented God, he replied: "If by Godot I had meant God, I would have said God, not Godot."

Thornton Wilder, leader of the pro-Godotians who scrutinize the play's sixty-one pages with the fiery reverence of cabala students, calls the play "a picture of total nihilism" and a "very admirable work." But, adds Mr. Wilder, . . . "I don't try to work out detailed symbolism. I don't think you're supposed to." Michael Myerberg, who first produced the play in this country, says: "It very much reflects the hopelessness and dead end we've run into. What he's trying to say is: 'All we have is ourselves—each other—and we may as well make the best of it.' "

Bert Lahr, who was in the original Broadway production as Estragon, . . . originally did not know what the play meant. Now he has some unusual interpretations.

"The play," he says,

> is very complex and has many analyses. But mine
> is as good as the rest. The two men are practically
> one—one is the animal side, the other the mental.
> I was the animal. So far as Pozzo and Lucky [mas-
> ter and slave] are concerned, we have to remember
> that Beckett was a disciple of Joyce and that Joyce
> hated England. Beckett meant Pozzo to be En-
> gland, and Lucky to be Ireland.
>
> (p. 36)

Members of the San Francisco troupe have a variety of ideas
about the play. One calls it "a play of despair in which a man
is seeking salvation, frustrated in finding it, and incapable of
coping with waiting." Another says: "This is a fairly modern
state of mind, existential, in which man tries to remove despair and find some strength." A third recalls: "At first I
thought it trite. Then I realized that Beckett is a tremendous
humanitarian. He does not condemn humanity at any time.
He asks mankind to look at itself." A fourth sees Lucky, the
slave, as "the sensitive artist in modern society." (p. 38)

Despite its triumphs in Paris, where it was called *En Attendant Godot,* and London, *Waiting for Godot* had to wait for
production in the United States and very nearly died on the
doorstep. When Myerberg first saw the script, he dismissed
it as impossible to produce. Six months later, in London, he
changed his mind while watching a performance. . . .

With considerable showmanship, he brought it to Broadway,
preceding its opening on April 8, 1956, with an advertisement
in this paper which reads: "This is a play for the thoughtful
and discriminating theatregoer. . . . I respectfully suggest
that those who come to the theatre for casual entertainment
do not buy a ticket to this attraction."

The show extended its run to twice the original four weeks.
Author Beckett, in one of his rare comments, wrote to the
producer: "It is gratifying to learn that the bulk of your audiences was made up of young people. This was also the case
in Paris, London and throughout Germany. I must, after all,
be less dead than I thought." (p. 41)

> *Murray Schumach, "Why They Wait for Godot," in*
> The New York Times Magazine, *September 21,
> 1958, pp. 36, 38, 41.*

RAYMOND WILLIAMS

The [1961] Irish production of Samuel Beckett's *Waiting for
Godot* . . . is very welcome. From the Arts production of
1955 it seemed that performance enhanced and diminished
the play in about equal proportions, but the relation between
text and performance is so variable in modern drama that alternative productions are necessary, as a check. The important differences in the Irish production turn out to be very
useful, especially as the play is now much better known.

Waiting for Godot is a morality, but characteristically of uncertainty rather than of faith. Its basic themes have very simple Christian origins, in two texts which are incorporated into
the dramatic speech and imagery. First, 'hope deferred ma-
keth the heart sick, but when the desire cometh, it is a tree
of life'. Second, 'for they bind heavy burdens and grievous to
be borne, and lay them on men's shoulders, but they themselves will not move them with one of their fingers . . . Ye
fools and blind! for whether is greater, the gift, or the altar

that sanctifieth the gift?' To a medieval moralist, the dramatic
structure would follow from the fact that the opposition of
good and evil could be resolved. To Beckett, evil, though destructive, is strong; while good, though perhaps redeeming,
is weak and broken down. He does not show the triumph of
either, but the deadlock within each and between each. The
form of the action is that of pilgrimage and appointment: neither finally fails, but equally neither can be shown to succeed.

The basic pattern of *Waiting for Godot* is the opposition and
interaction of two contrasted pairs of characters, with a further and comparable opposition within each pair. There is the
direct contrast between the world of Didi and Gogo and that
of Pozzo and Lucky. At one level it is simply that Pozzo and
Lucky are conscious of time and subject to change, while
Didi and Gogo are not:

> VLADIMIR: How they've changed! Those two.
> ESTRAGON: Very likely. They all change. Only we
> can't.

Then there is the contrast between the pairs with regard to
the types of relationship they embody. Pozzo and Lucky are
in a formal world, dominating and being dominated. They
are tied to each other, both ways: the slave is led but the master must hold the rope, which in the second act is the rope
leading the blind. Didi and Gogo—and this is much of the
warmth of the play—are in a different, informal, voluntary
world: loving and resentful, wanting to break away yet still
anxiously returning to each other. For each pair life is a journey, but the cries of Pozzo and Lucky, even at the end, are
'On, on', while Didi and Gogo simply return on themselves,
back to a fixed point. . . .

Beckett has created here a very powerful dramatic imagery,
of a virtually universal kind (this is the main difference, I
think, between *Waiting for Godot* and some of his other
work). The world of the tramps, who were once in the sun
of the Macon country, is a general image of fallen man. The
experience of waiting, of hope deferred, of 'he won't come
this evening but surely tomorrow', is again so general in our
time that its unconscious power is considerable. And the
world of master and slave, as presented, cuts deep into our
general experience: the Pozzo of the first act, the complacent,
sentimental consumer, who has someone else to carry and to
think for him, also has the whip and the rope. The combined
power of these major images makes the play deeply moving
even when only imperfectly understood.

There are further images. There is the fundamental despair
of the tree of life diminished to a bare or almost bare willow,
which the tramps would turn into a cross on which to hang
themselves (the analogy with the two thieves, and with
Christ, is there from the beginning). There is also something
quite different: an interaction between body and spirit which
is very moving, persistently moving, because the body is so
present in the play—its imagery is continually enacted, and
is the source of the very rich deep humour. The emotional
tone of the play is determined by this interaction: the coarse,
unreliable yet often delighted body, across which the claims
of the spirit fall both to inspire and to terrify. This interaction
controls the language, which moves with speed and subtlety
between these dimensions. It is there too, within each pair.
Didi is waiting for Godot, while Gogo is waiting for death;
it is Didi who mainly speaks to the messenger, and who disturbs Gogo's sleep; it is Gogo who wants rest, and Didi who
must restlessly wait. Between Pozzo and Lucky the separa-

tion is more absolute, in their quite different world. It was Lucky who gave Pozzo thought, but the enslaved mind has broken down, into delirium and then dumbness, though it can still terrify the apparently satisfied body, and in the end drags it down into its own collapse. The scheme is quite formal, yet it is also wonderfully alive because the whole texture of the language is woven from the same interaction. . . .

[How far] does Beckett get through? There are two general difficulties. First, the play has become, among some people, a byword for pessimism and decadence: it is a kind of experience they do not want. I can only make my own position clear: that I do not share Beckett's vision but find myself moved by it, as by a grotesque, diminished, but still powerful *Lear*.

The second difficulty is more formidable. Because of its flexibility and subtlety, even its deep ambiguity of tone, it is a play that requires an emotionally educated audience. Yet at the performance I attended, there were many people who seemed to think themselves superior to the tramps. It even seemed, as that unruffled amusement at quaintness went its deadly way, that Pozzo was at last in control—the sentimental consumer at his ease, having bought a writer and players to think and dance for him. It is a good job Lucky can still kick occasionally, and that Didi and Gogo can bear to wait.

> *Raymond Williams, "Hope Deferred," in* New Statesman, *Vol. LXI, No. 1575, May 19, 1961, p. 802.*

IRVING WARDLE

[It] would be excruciating to see *Waiting for Godot* treated as a star vehicle. There is never any danger of this in . . . [the present] production, which devotes itself exclusively to the text. Devotion, even to masterpieces, can go too far; and if there is any objection to this version it is that it exudes rather too much reverence.

The commentaries have done their work. We are never allowed to forget that the piece is a statement on the human condition. Its vaudeville element is held severely in check; every little canter between Didi and Gogo is followed by an appropriate silence for the black chasm to reopen under their feet.

Pozzo's speech on giving birth astride the grave is passionately thundered out; and for the famous passage on the "dead voices" the two tramps sit downstage and deliver their antiphonal exchanges straight out to the house so as to drive home the much-admired lyricism.

Self-conscious as the approach is, *Godot* can take it; and the use of Irish speech is an added protection against freezing the work into a cultural monument. . . .

The production succeeds in forcing you into the situation in which the play's first audiences found themselves: it is not a play about waiting, but one that makes audiences wait. That is an achievement: and I have never seen the two scenes with the boy more poignantly played.

> *Irving Wardle, "Reverence for Beckett Text," in* The Times, *London, January 27, 1971, p. 8.*

JACK RICHARDSON

The heart of *Waiting for Godot* is still beating at a steady, even pace. In the current excellent revival . . . Beckett's tramps are caught on the same bleak terrain as they were fifteen years ago when Bert Lahr gave his classic performance and his producers took newspaper ads calling for, I believe, eighty thousand intellectuals to come to the support of their playwright's debut in New York. Indeed, there is little room for scenic interpretation within the landscape prescribed for *Waiting for Godot.* A desolate plain and a stunted tree. *That is that!* . . . [The] setting for Estragon's and Vladimir's parable of stasis will go through the future unaltered, a dry reminder of as absolute a depreciation of human existence as any artist has had the genius to sustain.

Watching the play performed in 1971, it is hard to believe that its bleak estimate of human teleology and its "absurd"— how long has it been since that word had its vogue—universe could have once been so popular. And by popular, I do not mean that Beckett's world simply suited the taste of a number of important intellectuals and artists of the time. On the contrary, its despairing conclusions almost became a philosophy for the middle class, a sort of solid bourgeois virtue in Europe and a ready-made justification for a generation of more or less cultivated Americans to have little hope for a personal salvation and none at all for a political one. My reaction when I saw *Godot* as a student was something like, "Well, someone has finally found a way to say it." . . .

Well, in the intervening years I hope I've become a bit less callow about *Godot's* meaning. It still, however, seems to me an extraordinary work. Excepting Beckett's own later plays, there is simply nothing like it in our history. Eliot's *Waste Land* at least allowed one to remember a former beauty and purpose inherent in life, but with Beckett, the past, present, and future are all bracketed behind a negation sign, and sighing for the golden age is as out of order as building for either a natural or a supernatural paradise. And this most general conclusion about life is not delivered to us in vague, moral jeremiads, but in a dramatic prose that seems to encompass all the modes of speech in our language. From the play of contradictory hypotheses down to the most gritty, concrete images of human functions, the words swirl about, embracing all the nuances of existence and making them add up to a universal nullity. *Waiting for Godot* is a morality play without capitalized names, a searingly specific deduction from a dark premise about life, which many dramatists have entertained but which none has ever followed to such a precise conclusion.

Gogo and Didi, and even Pozzo and Lucky, the archetypal master and slave, have been given the details of art, and it is these details that infuse *Waiting for Godot* with theatrical life and humor. It may be a bad joke that has been played on man, but it is nevertheless a joke, and there is some laughter to be had from it. As bewildered and tattered as Gogo and Didi are, they still have their full share of questions to ask, hates to be accounted for, hungers to be satisfied, and cruelties to be forgiven. They possess, with human tenacity, existences palpable enough to touch and amuse us even while we are watching ourselves being absorbed into their bleak fate. Gogo and Didi may be futilely waiting for Godot to keep his appointment with them, but their lives are not without incident, and those who dismiss Beckett's representation of life because it does not take into account the complex, delusive ways in which man really passes his time should remember that Gogo and Didi, too, try on hats, philosophize, give and receive affection, and fret over their bodies' inadequacies. In short, in the deepest human sense, they live richly, and it is because, in existential extremis, they worry over the condition of their feet and bladders that we let them stand as our temporary deputies on a barren stage festooned only with a stunted tree.

Temporary because, in the end, we cannot accept the implications of their destiny, with or without Godot. Most of us are really Pozzos, dashing on without any particular purpose, but dashing with an abundance of energy and a necessary sense of self-importance. . . . But we do keep moving: Beckett on to other plays, and I to the end of this short tribute to him. (p. 78)

Jack Richardson, "Shakespeare and Beckett," in
Commentary, *Vol. 51, No. 4, April, 1971, pp. 76-8.*

RONALD HAYMAN

Waiting for Godot was published in Paris during 1952 and staged there in January 1953. The German première, which followed later in the year, was the first of three productions the play had been given at Berlin's Schiller Theater. . . . [The most recent performance is directed by Beckett himself; in] twenty years from now, his German [language] production of *Waiting for Godot* will seem like a major event in European theatrical history, and scholars will be speculating on the basis of very inadequate records about how he did it. . . .

It would have been silly to expect it to be definitive just because he was directing. As he says, the play is above all a game; and with any game the moment-to-moment quality of the experience depends upon the players. If the top of Vladimir's head is lower than Estragon's shoulders, everything—from comic embraces to the balance of power—is going to be affected. In the second of the productions at the Schiller Theater, . . . Estragon's head was lower than Vladimir's shoulders: the same two actors . . . were playing the parts. Directing a new production for the company last year, Beckett took over the disparity but reversed the roles. Both actors still find it difficult to stop themselves from speaking each other's lines, but they are familiar with each other's problems and needs, technical and emotional.

All four actors are highly talented. . . . If they had been invited to work without a director, the result would have been less tasteful—Beckett has impeccable taste—less disciplined and less co-ordinated, but probably not less entertaining and possibly less selfconscious. What the production lacked was the appearance of casualness. Without becoming any more realistic, it could have been made to seem more unrehearsed, and surely it should have. It was very depressing that so many of the more intelligent critics used the word 'choreographed' as if they were paying an important compliment.

As a director Beckett tends to be over-musical. He knows a great deal about theatre but very little about acting, and this makes him tend simultaneously to both extremes—*laissez-faire* and authoritarianism. He has clear notions of the results he wants, but he does not know how to coax them out of the actors' creativity, so he works by pre-fabricating ideas and imposing rhythms which already exist inside his head. . . .

The style of the dialogue has deep roots in the British Music Hall tradition. Probably they are all the deeper for the fact that Beckett wrote the play in French, which must have given him the freedom to develop the manner without feeling he was mimicking it. Although there is no precise equivalent in the tradition of German cabaret, the best German actors are quite capable of picking up the style. . . . But the main source of the energy in *Waiting for Godot* is tension between the profound ontological pessimism and the bright surface of vaudeville foolery, so a great deal depends on articulating the contradiction into a meticulously controlled style, blending vaudeville horseplay and self-consciously literary rhetoric into an appearance of unselfconscious spontaneity. (p. 66)

Two of the most problematic passages are the climaxes of the quartet sequences in both acts. During the only long speech in the play, Lucky's, the other characters are required to react strongly. Pozzo first suffers, then groans, then pulls on the rope. Vladimir and Estragon alternate between listening attentively and protesting. Finally, according to the stage direction, 'all throw themselves on Lucky who struggles and shouts his text'. In the end he is silenced when Vladimir removes the hat which is the *sine qua non* of his thinking. In this production Vladimir and Estragon attacked Lucky with punches that were neither convincingly real nor distinctively stylised, and when he collapsed into silence it was not clear whether we were meant to believe that it was the punches to the stomach or the removal of his hat that had stopped the flow of words.

The equivalent mêlée in the second act occurs when all four characters are on the floor. Pozzo, who is now blind, has fallen over Lucky, who is now dumb, and when Vladimir and Estragon, after many minutes of procrastination, finally try to help them to their feet, they are in turn pulled downwards. This is one of the few places in the text where even a reader is too aware of the seam between metaphysical gloom and music hall knock-about. . . . Realistically Pozzo would have been able to get to his feet unaided, but theatrically it is easier to make him look helpless than to make it look natural that all four of them should stay in a heap. It may be that this problem is insoluble.

Working with human material, Beckett must have had to settle sometimes for more and sometimes for less than he wanted: the actors have obviously contributed not only their personalities but some of the ideas for comedy business. But presumably the set corresponded exactly to what he wanted, though not necessarily to what he had in mind a quarter of century ago when he wrote: 'A country road. A tree. Evening. Estragon is sitting on a low mound.' The low mound has become a rectangular stone, and the tree, which has to stand in for the whole of nature, has become so unnatural that one has more the feeling of being indoors than outdoors, especially when the electric moon appears and climbs rapidly up the back wall. . . . In Beckett's script there is almost nothing that could be removed without loss; the loss of the moon would have been almost a gain. And while it doesn't matter that the tree is too small for us to believe that they are thinking seriously of hanging themselves from it—the thought isn't serious anyway—it does matter that the sense of artefact destroys the indeterminacy and the sense of continuum. Surely it is one of the play's main points that any place is much the same as any other place, while any time is much the same as any other time. The action is circular. We should be able to think that they were waiting for Godot yesterday and will be again tomorrow, and that it makes no difference whether they wait in the same place. . . .

The best of Beckett's directorial innovations was the most democratic: his reduction of Pozzo to the same stature as the other three characters. In all the other productions I've seen, Pozzo had been bigger, bolder, superior. But a master isn't necessarily masterful, and, if he isn't, his domination of Lucky is all the more telling. . . . Beckett has created a challenging precedent for future productions of **Waiting for Godot.**

How scrupulously should a production be modelled on the playwright's intentions? This is a question that needs a fresh answer not only for each author and each play but possibly for each moment of stage action. Intentions which are merely voiced . . . stand less chance of spreading into the play's future than intentions which are expressed in stage directions, but these are not necessarily any more crucial or any more valid. Pre-rehearsal intentions, anyway, are based on partial ignorance. The playwright who works collaboratively with actors is coming incestuously but intimately to grips with his brainchild, and it is a pity that there is no way for Beckett to pass on his new carnal knowledge to future readers, future directors, future actors. (p. 67)

Ronald Hayman, "Beckett's Godot," in The New Review, *Vol. III, No. 26, May, 1976, pp. 66-7.*

STANLEY KAUFFMANN

[*The essay excerpted below was originally published in* The New Republic, *April 23, 1977.*]

Twice in my life I've had the chance to see a masterpiece of drama as directed by its author, and, by coincidence, both plays were in German. The first was *Mother Courage* done in London in 1956 . . . fresh from the hand of the lately deceased Bertolt Brecht. . . . Now I've seen *Waiting for Godot* played in German . . . and directed by Samuel Beckett. Brecht was a professional director: some who knew him say that, as time went on, he became primarily a director who wrote pieces to direct. What's lost sight of about Beckett, who is not a professional like Brecht, is that nonetheless he has done a very considerable amount of directing, of his own plays, since 1966. . . .

This is not only the best production of a Beckett play that I have seen, it is among the best productions of anything I have seen. Many authors cannot, or should not, direct their own plays just as many composers cannot conduct their own scores. But if the author *can* direct, then it's possible—not inevitable—that he will give the work its best imaginable production. I have admired some previous productions of Beckett plays (not of *Godot* particularly), but I've seen nothing quite like this. From the first moment I felt I was being made privy to confidences that had only been hinted at in prior productions, that a texture was being initiated surely and easily. From the first moment I knew I was being given a clear vision of the play, not so much of its center as of its whole. (p. 46)

The predominant quality of the whole performance is . . . one that I haven't seen and hadn't imagined: delicacy. Everything, including the buffoonery and physicality and grossness, seems to be touched lightly, sustained with light fingers. And it all seems to flow, like the best kind of dream: movement flows into movement, speech into pause, pause into speech, movement into stasis and vice versa. The core of the staging procedure is rhythm: everything has been thought of in terms of tempo and fit. Everything has been measured,

but, as in good dance and good singing, the rightness and preciseness of the measuring make the measuring disappear. The flow is seamless.

These tempos are not arbitrary, they grow out of the scene (as well as the scenes on either side of it), out of the moments within the scene. I won't attempt to describe (if I could remember) the color and pace and movement of each scene, I'll note only that the director's aim, through the delicacy and flow, was to keep it all a clown show, two tramps perambulating around a great invisible question mark. Once in a while Beckett underscored the clown-show idea by having them do something together, next to each other, like a chorus line—a move, a turn, a gesture. What a lovely rubric for a play about the fate of Western man.

Theatrically, *Godot* is deceptive. First, it deceives you into thinking that it's easy to perform; then it deceives you into thinking that (again: theatrically speaking) it's a bit tedious. The test of any production is the opening of Act II. The first act has taken us from near-stasis with the two tramps up through an arc that includes a long scene with two newcomers back to the two tramps alone in complete stasis. Then the next act begins in the same barren place (a few leaves added to the gaunt tree) with the same two tramps in the same mood. No matter how much we like the play, at that moment there's a slight apprehension as to whether the actors have sufficient variety to keep us interested for another comparable act. (pp. 47-8)

As many have pointed out, the original French title of the play *En Attendant Godot* translates more literally as *While Waiting for Godot*. We can't fault the translator in this case: it's Beckett himself, of course, who opted for a phrase as easy for the English tongue as the original is for the French. (He didn't do the German translation—it was made by Elmar Tophoven.) But the French title puts more exactly the play's central agon: the passage of time. As Hamlet strives to fulfill his father's mission, as Oedipus strives to help his stricken city, so these two tramps struggle merely to pass the time of their lives. E. M. Cioran once said that the essence of Beckett is not despair but mysticism: as if earthly life were an interruption of a perfect state, an interruption somehow to be endured. Whether that is one's own view or not, this great play certainly puts the enduring of life—the sense of passage through it—under the aspect of eternity. And this delicate, delicately modulated production by the author is a subtle theatrical articulation of these two hours in relation to all of time.

As with lots of good things that come along, I now can hardly believe that this production really happened, although much of it is and will be vivid in my head. The dream on stage is like the realization of something I might have wanted to dream. And I can't see the production again because the company stayed for only seven performances. Still, to commemorate it, here is one small way to certify it and to share it.

There's a better way. Asmus reports that Beckett prepared a *Regiebuch* for this production, a sort of heavily annotated promptbook, and shows a sample. At least one other such *Regiebuch* exists, for Beckett's production of **Happy Days** . . . in 1971. These books should be published: not as law for all future productions but as testaments of how a theater genius saw his work—at least at one point in his life—in the theater. (p. 48)

Stanley Kauffmann, "Productions: 'Waiting for

Godot', " in his Theatre Criticisms, *Performing Arts Journal Publications, 1983, pp. 46-8.*

DENIS DONOGHUE

[The recent New York] production of *Waiting for Godot* is so up-to-the-minute that Estragon, determined to reduce Lucky to silence, screams the supreme insult available in the Age of Bush: "You're a *Liberal.*" . . . Many of those who saw the play . . . may have been seeing it for the first time.

Waiting for Godot is what the published version calls it: a tragicomedy in two acts. Three acts would have forced Beckett to develop further the dramatic situation. He would have to give his layabouts Estragon and Vladimir a formal and therefore a moral destiny. In two acts, no concession to theatrical piety is required. . . .

According to Beckett's fable, two vagrants, Estragon and Vladimir, are waiting for someone called Godot; if he comes, they will be saved, or at least their situation will be transformed. Meanwhile they hang about, passing time which would have passed anyway, though more slowly. . . . Godot doesn't come, but word arrives through a boy that he will certainly come tomorrow. So they wait. Godot doesn't come, but Pozzo and, in the noose of Pozzo's rope, Lucky do come: they are master and slave, voluble in the first act, grounded and blind (Pozzo) and dumb (Lucky) in the second, a consequence eliciting from Estragon and Vladimir not a whit of fellow feeling.

Hugh Kenner once remarked in my hearing that *Waiting for Godot* may have issued from Beckett's wartime experience in the French resistance. Members of the *maquis* spent most of their time hanging about, receiving or failing to receive messages. War may be Hell, but much of it is ennui. The difference between one day and the next is no more dramatic than that between a tree apparently dead and the same tree with a leaf or two on it. The best commentary on *Waiting for Godot* may be those passages in Beckett's [*Proust*] where the themes are time, repetition, habit, "the poisonous ingenuity of time in the science of affliction." In his later plays, especially *Endgame* (1957), *All That Fall* (1957), *Krapp's Last Tape* (1958), and *Happy Days* (1961), Proustian memories of a happy day are allowed to interrupt the otherwise malignant proceedings. In *Waiting for Godot* the play of repartee with no apparent point beyond itself is the only alleviation permitted. As a parody of the heroics sponsored by a one-time Existentialism, the play is ruefully decisive.

The text of *Waiting for Godot* is providing a long headache for the scholars to whom that matter has been entrusted. Whenever Beckett has taken an interest in a particular production of the play, he has tinkered with the references to time and place. . . . In any strict sense, there is no established text of the play. The New York production "uses a text provided by Samuel Beckett in August, 1988, which will be published soon by Faber and Faber." It may turn out that every word delivered . . . is in the new text, though some of them sounded to me like improvised ad-libbing. Certain details from the current published text of 1954 probably can't survive. When Pozzo says, "I've lost my Kapp and Peterson!" the reference must be obscure to anyone who doesn't know that Kapp and Peterson is a distinguished Dublin pipe-making firm. For the play's first several years, such local references as the play had were French: the Eiffel Tower, the Macon country, the Rhone. In the Dublin production, unless my ears deceived me, the Macon country became the Napa Valley, thereby facilitating a bout of rage—"the Crappa Country"—from Estragon. Otherwise, in the Dublin version, there was no indication of the play's setting: the stage was bare, except for a stone and an abstract tree; it could have been anywhere or nowhere. . . .

[In the new] version, the scene is somewhere in the United States—badlands, a bit of desert, a waste patch littered with a few stones, rusty detritus of trucks, hubcaps, a truck tire, bumper, a broken spring, a buffalo skull, a sheep skull. It is theater in the round, befitting a rigmarole in which Estragon and Vladimir, agreeing to go somewhere, do not move. . . .

[This] production is only the third I have seen. I didn't see the original one in Paris. I saw the first London one, and because of . . . [its treatment of] Pozzo I've lived with the conviction that Pozzo is central to the play, and that his being a monster is the means Beckett uses to keep the play terrifying. It is because of Pozzo that one thinks of Kafka's *In the Penal Colony* and *Metamorphosis*. I didn't see the much-praised German version. But in Dublin, and now in New York, the play has been domesticated by taking much of the harm out of Pozzo. I still think he's supposed to be Mussolini. . . . [But the Dublin and the New York productions] make Pozzo almost genial, a good fellow at heart though for the moment a bit rough on Lucky. (p. 30)

[In the present production, it is Pozzo's] pathos, near the end of the play—"They give birth astride of a grave, the light gleams an instant, then it's night once more"—and his final command—"On!"—to Lucky that makes it possible for Vladimir and Estragon, Vladimir more than Estragon, to bring their antics to an end rather than merely call them off. . . . The sense in which words lead us by the nose, or throw a noose around our necks and then shout "On!", has to be acknowledged, but doesn't have to be connived with. Equally, the sense in which words may be selected and joined by a master-craftsman in such a way as to provide spaces in which their participants may somehow, however briefly, live is to be respected. All is not lost.

After the Dublin production, I felt that the domestication of *Waiting for Godot* was now achieved, its power to horrify having been sung away, lullabied into a bourgeois sleep. A society in no mood for apocalypses had triumphed again. After the New York production, which succeeded in being funny in ways for which TV has schooled us, I'm not inclined to make a fuss about the playing down of the metaphysics, the visionary post-World War II talk of *Existenz:* that, too, was a cultural moment, a convention like the Theater of the Absurd it incited. . . . The comedy issues from different social and political conditions; it has more to do with Reagan and Bush than with Sartre and Merleau-Ponty. No matter: the play has not been abused. If it is a mark of the classic, as Frank Kermode maintains, that it is patient of interpretation—it doesn't demand to be received in any one authorized version—this production is valid, in the sense that it allows the audience to enjoy many laughs but not the complacency of thinking that it has had the last one. (pp. 30, 35)

Denis Donoghue, "Play It Again, Sam," in The New York Review of Books, *Vol. XXXV, No. 19, December 8, 1988, pp. 30, 35.*

ROBERT BRUSTEIN

It would be easy enough to satirize . . . [the recent New York] production of *Waiting For Godot.* . . . By casting two comedy superstars as Didi and Gogo [and] by setting the play in what appears to be Death Valley, . . . the director invites charges that he has Hollywoodized an existential masterpiece—carbonated the philosophical heavy water, fizzed up the tragicomic metaphysics. . . .

[Subscribers] are said to be incensed over the shoratage of tickets [to *Waiting for Godot*]. They're not missing a whole lot; the production expunges both the poetry and the pain of the play. . . . [Either the actors have] been encouraged to regard *Godot* as a scenario for improvisation or they've been inspired by the standard *Godot* criticism that the tramps have an affinity with the great clowns of silent films and music hall: Chaplin, Keaton, Laurel and Hardy. . . . But while the leading parts have roots in vaudeville, this is no reason for turning the entire play into stand-up comedy. Beginning with an ominous rumble and a rimshot, the evening realizes only the rimshot. (p. 26)

[The production] has been carefully calibrated, meticulously orchestrated. It is filled with precision, detail, clear choices. It never releases your attention. Yet, somehow, Beckett's European penumbra has been illuminated in all its darkest corners by a sunny American disposition. . . . [The director's] specific behaviorist approach to his material, appropriate enough for American realistic writing, distorts a work that draws its strength from abstraction.

Beckett left his setting for *Waiting For Godot* deliberately unspecified ("A country road. A tree"). This production places us, as I mentioned earlier, in a California desert. I'm told that Beckett himself authorized the change of "Macon" (and "Crackon") country to "Napa" (and "Crapa") country, but it's hard for me to believe that he would have authorized such a radical shift in geography. There may be no vineyards bordering the premises, but there's an ocher-and-tan Western sky beaming over tons of sand. . . . There is, besides, an abundance of identifiable hubcaps, automobile springs, license plates, bones, stones, and Georgia O'Keeffe cattle skulls—so many, in fact, that the amnesia of the tramps regarding whether or not they've visited this area before begins to verge on idiocy. . . . Beckett intended *Godot* to be situated in a generalized purgatory. And regardless what you think of California—even if you agree with Gertrude Stein that "there's no there there"—it still remains a little too site-specific to capture the abstract metaphysics of the play. (pp. 26-7)

Robert Brustein, "Godot in LaLa Land," in The New Republic, Vol. 199, No. 3856, December 12, 1988, pp. 26-8.

•SCHOLARSHIP•

EDWIN KENNEBECK

Waiting for Godot, Beckett's first play, opened in Paris in the winter of 1952, with much success. Now, in a slim, expensive edition, this two-act play becomes the first of Beckett's full-

length works to appear in this country. The translation is by Beckett himself.

Waiting for Godot is an almost textureless "tragicomedy." The language seldom exploits style, metaphor, connotation, though when these do appear they count for a great deal. Unlike Tennessee Williams' *Camino Real,* which also attempted a symbolic commentary on the, or *a,* human condition, but was almost all texture, Beckett's play offers very few "commentaries," only a smattering of wit (though that is mordant and assured), a spare and dis-allusioned vocabulary.

The situation is simple: two old tramps, their lives of action behind them, bored and dismayed to a point where ordinary boredom and dismay might seem thrilling, wait on a bare stretch of road, near a tree, for Godot. Who Godot is nobody knows. He is simply that for which one waits when one has sunk to the bottom, finally touching with heavy feet the very floor of ennui. And not knowing who Godot is is part of the predicament.

This point of standstill is a hideous place. . . . One of the tramps, Estragon, complains about his sore feet, struggles to take his boots off; the other one, Vladimir, removes his bowler, looks inside and finds nothing, puts it on again. They discuss briefly the thief at Christ's side on the Cross who was saved. Then silence falls; it is necessary to find something to talk about—anything—whether or not to commit suicide, whether Godot really said he would come, whether an adequate conversation can be made out of some minor disagreement.

This must be one of the cruelest uses of laughter—Beckett's deliberate *bathètique.* One would not find it in Kafka or Camus or Sartre. In Joyce? At least the comedy in *Finnegans Wake* seems to have some spirit of fun. *Waiting for Godot* isn't fun. The laughter it engenders in a theater must have a strange, embarrassed sound. . . . The play ends where it began. Vladimir and Estragon have spoken about separating, but it is clear that they cannot. They seem to recognize that if there is one evil left for them to experience, it is to be parted from each other. Nothing new has happened to the two tramps, we have merely seen their situation.

It is as if we had looked into a moment of cosmic ennui, despite the low-down tone of the piece. Neither edifying nor purgative, the play nonetheless has an effect; it is appalling and desperate, and not false or pretentious. What an audience could say about it after the final curtain I can't imagine, unless it be something like the respectful word of Jean Anouilh, quoted on the jacket: "Nothing happens, nobody comes, nobody goes, it is *terrible.*"

Edwin Kennebeck, "The Moment of Cosmic Ennui," in The Commonweal, Vol. LXI, No. 13, December 31, 1954, pp. 365-66.

DENIS JOHNSTON

Waiting for Godot is a play by Samuel Beckett, late of Dublin, written originally in French, and now translated back into his native idiom by the author himself, obstructed (so far as the English edition is concerned) by some attentions from Her Majesty's Lord Chamberlain. It is about two tramps who are waiting in no particular place for somebody called Godot. (p. 23)

[In *Waiting For Godot,* Beckett has] provided us with a difficult and allusive text for stage purposes which might, at first glance, be as readily the work of a hoaxer as a play of serious importance. The cult of obscurity sits less comfortably in the theatre than in the realms of poetry, music, and the fine arts, and Beckett, himself, in some of his previous work has occasionally nourished our suspicions. He has shown himself quite ready to write the prevailing gobbledy-gook of the Little Reviews. (p. 24)

So, when we find the Lord Chamberlain coming to grips with the problems of flybuttons, tumescence and urination, we may feel some legitimate doubts as to the artistic integrity that insists on their presence. However, the Lord Chamberlain, as usual, comes out worst in the end by insisting on such inane changes as the alteration of the Russian name, Fartov, to Popov, and by inflicting a certain Mrs. Gozzo with warts, in preference to the clap. A further examination of the cuts and legitimate amendments that have appeared in the text since the publication of the original French version, makes it clear that the author himself has been seriously concerned with the problem of saying what he means. So, if it matters to him, it is presumably worth our while as well.

It is also of some interest to note that in translation, both the American and the English version tend to adopt the vocabulary of the author's native city. *Bavarder* becomes Blathered, and the expression *'Ton Bonhomme'* assumes the familiar lineaments of 'Your Man' *'alors nous serions baisés'* appear as 'Then we'll be banjaxed' (or 'ballocksed' for the benefit of the Americans). . . . Two or three half page cuts from the French version, towards the end of the second part, serve to quicken the climax in English, and show an appreciation of stage tempo for which we can probably thank the Paris production.

All these clues may be unimportant if considered separately, but taken collectively they do indicate a healthy state of affairs—that the play is a living thing, undergoing the changes and modifications that all serious drama must undergo in the course of production, and that the author is fussy about his canon. From which we may assume that it is not a stunt, and may turn out, on more careful examination, to be far from obscure.

Towards the middle of the last scene, at the point where most dramatists may be assumed to be concerned about what they are getting at, we find this passage:

> 'What are we doing here, *that* is the question. And we are blessed in this, that we happen to know the answer. Yes, in this immense confusion one thing alone is clear. We are waiting for Godot to come— or for night to fall. We have kept our appointment, and that's an end to that. We are not saints, but we have kept our appointment. How many people can boast as much?'

How tempting in the light of this straightforward statement of the play's intention, to jump to the facile conclusion that it is also a parable, and that all we have to do is to fill in an agreed set of proper names, and lo, we have the whole thing on a plate. Godot is God; Pozzo—shall we say—is the Pope; and Vladimir—if you like—is the Duke of Windsor. But, fortunately, Mr. Beckett is much too clever to have fashioned anything that can be solved by means of a crib. An allegory is supposed to be like life, but life is like *Waiting for Godot,* as it is like *Alice in Wonderland.* If it could be easily translated it would cease to have general application. If Mr. Beckett

was to admit that Godot is the Almighty, his play would cease to be of such interest to those who do not concur with Happy in his picture of the great quaquaquaqua. Nor should we be led astray by any similarities in names. The play was originally written in French, in which tongue the name of this maker of missed appointments bears no resemblance to Le Bon Dieu.

In short, Mr. Beckett is no simple arithmetician, and is not attempting to say anything so banal as the fact that two and two make four—or even five. His play is algebraic, in that its characters have the quality of X. And what X means, depends not upon him, but upon us. If you feel that the point of this life—the Intangible for which you may be waiting—is God, then indeed you may accept that solution as your X. If, on the other hand, you feel no such thing, then the play can still have a validity in other terms.

Herein lies the great importance of Mr. Beckett keeping his trap shut, so far as explanations are concerned, so leaving us each free to draw his own conclusions, without any rumbles from the horse's mouth. Sam having written a play of universal application, it may well be argued that any exegis from him might turn out to be just as wrong as ours. Authors do not always know the best way in which their plays ought to be produced, and the same paradox may apply with equal force to their efforts to explain their significance.

To me, personally, **Waiting for Godot** has an intelligibility which I understand, but do not fully agree with. The two tramps, Estragon and Vladimir, form one composite character—the Observer—the protesting feet, and the head that searches vainly in its hat for something to say next. 'It is too much for one man' as somebody remarks. Pozzo and his willing and deeply masochistic slave, Lucky, offers a not unrecognisable picture of my fellow men, comfortably chewing chicken bones until struck blind, slavishly enjoying the halter, and treacherously repaying with a hack on the shins any effort to help them. In particular one should note that superb pastiche of the religious and philosophical ideas of the average Western man that is embodied in Lucky's solitary speech, where the prose hesitates at each hurdle and then goes back to try again, like a horse balking at a jump. (pp. 24-6)

Finally we have the little boy—Mr. Godot's messenger—the ill-paid keeper of the goats, who appears from time to time to tell us that Mr. Godot promises faithfully to arrive tomorrow, although unfortunately unable to come tonight. If this is not the message of the Church, it is hard to see what else it can be. (p. 26)

Meanwhile, Mr. Beckett, who is no quietist, is not content simply to stand and wait. Vladimir feels that there is something to be done, even if it is only in helping the blind Pozzo to his feet.

> Let us do something while we have the chance! It is not every day that we are needed. Not indeed that we personally are needed. Others would meet the case equally well, if not better. To all mankind they were addressed, these cries for help still ringing in our ears! But at this place, at this moment of time, all mankind is us, whether we like it or not. Let us make the most of it before it is too late! Let us represent worthily for once the foul brood to which a cruel fate consigned us!

We may not all have experienced so defiant a sense of dedication as our prophet Samuel exhibits here. We are here, he is saying, at life's command. If nothing or nobody turns up to meet us, that at any rate, is not our fault. We have kept our appointment. And in the meantime we can lend a hand, even if nobody wants us personally. It is a challenge to Heaven in a poignant and dignified tone, and in default of its being taken up, the fact that Mr. Beckett feels that some sort of activity is of value for its own sake, shows that there is more in him of Sartre than of St. Simeon Stylites.

But although there is no difficulty in abstracting a meaning from the general impact of the play, there is still plenty left for writers of theses to mull over in the years to come. What is the meaning of the names of the characters—except perhaps Lucky, the only English name in the bunch, and the only apparent misnomer? And why does the little boy address Vladimir on each occasion as 'Mr. Albert,' receiving no correction therein? Why do Estragon's feet always begin to hurt him, just before the arrival of this Messenger? And why is the tree the only living thing that changes for the better? (pp. 26-7)

While these heavy problems remain unsolved, it is still open to you and me to enjoy the play on the stage, because of its humour and its circus quality, thanks to which the London production has been a general success with first-comers. There are rumours that Mr. Beckett does not entirely approve of some of this horseplay at the bottom of his garden. If so, it confirms what I have already suggested about authors and the presentation of their own plays. Great thoughts alone do not catch the attention of the play-going public, and when a dramatist breaks all the rules by having neither incident nor conflict in his first act, and then has the impertinence to give himself a full encore in his second, he need not be surprised if his play remains indefinitely with the Drama Leagues.

But this play, whether so intended or not, has a lot of the pantomime qualities of an Eggheads Harlequinade that makes it a delight from the start. It has Clown and Pantaloon, and Harlequin, and even the rich shopkeeper whose string of sausages is always disappearing. It does not come across as coterie stuff, unless deliberately played for pomposity or facetiousness. Its obscurities are largely superficial, and do not convey the impression that it is a Sphinx trying to conceal the fact that its creator has failed to provide it with any secret. We may not agree with its picture of life, but nobody can validly deny that there is a picture, and an arguable one. (pp. 27-8)

Maybe it is a lamentable fact that the Western world today does nothing but wait, enlivening the tedium, perhaps, with a little ambulance work. But lamentable or not, there is such a basis of truth in the picture that it seems reasonably certain that *Waiting for Godot* is destined to be the Play of the Fifties. In the Twenties and Thirties we were naïve enough not to wait, but to search. And we know what we got. Hence a certain reluctance to investigate nowadays what may be just around the corner. (p. 28)

> Denis Johnston, "Waiting with Beckett," in Irish Writing, No. 34, Spring, 1956, pp. 23-8.

ALAN LEVY

The history of *Waiting for Godot* is as puzzling as the play itself. In America it set off the weirdest chain of events of the 1955-56 season. The Samuel Beckett tragicomedy opened . . . in Miami on January 3, was severely rapped by the critics, and closed, on schedule, on January 14. . . . It seemed certain that Broadway always would be waiting for *Godot*—and not too anxiously. On April 19—with a new cast, new staging, but the identical script—*Waiting for Godot* opened . . . in New York. Many scoffed, but several critics and small, earnest audiences beat the intellectual drums for it. . . .

I saw the play . . . in London last fall. When the second-act curtain rose, at least 20 per cent of the audience had walked out. A few remained behind to heckle the players. Most of those who remained were disturbed, excited or absorbed by this strange, seemingly incomprehensible play. I was fascinated and depressed by *Godot,* and amazed by the audience. Since my return to America I've caught up with many Broadway plays—including, I suspect, a few better ones than *Godot*—and forgotten most of them, but Beckett's play is still as haunting to me as it was that misty night in Piccadilly. (p. 33)

Who or what is the unseen Godot? To some he is death; to others, life; to a few, nothing. To one British critic, Kenneth Tynan, he is a "spiritual signpost." To the director of the Miami production, Godot is the meaning of life. To the man sitting next to me in London, he was beauty. . . . *Time's* reviewer wasn't sure if Godot stands for God or man's unconquerable hope. He wasn't even sure if the play is "a philosophic depth bomb or a theatrical dud." (pp. 33-4)

Both the Paris and London productions of *Waiting for Godot* were flukes, according to Alan Schneider, director of the ill-fated Miami production. Schneider inspected the Paris and London versions and later met Beckett in Paris. "The Paris production," he reported, "was done in a very small theatre and, while it was popular, it didn't set Paris on fire or anything. . . . [*Waiting for Godot*] always required a very special audience and it always had a very special audience in Europe. It was a more sophisticated, more philosophical crowd than what you'd get in Miami or on Broadway." . . .

The London *Godot* treated the script as a tragicomedy, while both American versions—particularly the Miami fiasco—played the same lines for comedy. In London most of the daily critics turned thumbs down on *Godot* when it first appeared. Sunday reviewers like Tynan and Harold Hobson gave it the support it needed, however [see excerpts dated August 7, 1955]. Tynan proudly proclaimed himself a *"godotista"* (italics his) and Hobson championed its "esoteric beauty." . . . [A] B.B.C. critic said "*Godot* is wonderfully, wonderfully successful—tremendously funny."

In Miami, however, critic Jack Anderson of the *Herald* found *Godot* neither funny nor successful. He said he "almost felt sorry for the first-night audience," which was "sandbagged by an allegory." And the correspondent from *Variety* definitely proved no *godotista*. "The import from London," he reported, "is a wearisome two-acter, aimless in plotting, devoid of excitement, an impossible guessing game containing little to keep a theatregoer interested." (p. 34)

I felt like an undertaker when I launched my investigation of the apparent American demise of *Godot* in Miami. Three days after the first production folded, I telephoned Tom Ewell in Greenwich, Connecticut. Ewell . . . was Vladimir during the two weeks in Miami. . . . "I'd rather not talk about it," Ewell said. "I'm terribly upset." He sounded terribly upset. He added: "*Godot* is one of the great plays of our time; it still is. I think it's the most universal play of the last twenty years." Then what went wrong? Ewell wasn't sure. He thought it might have been the choice of Miami as the break-in point. He said he conceived of *Godot's* setting as "the limbo between life and death." Fashionable Miami, during the winter vacation season, is the last place to depict such an existence, Ewell suggested.

Michael Myerberg, the American producer of *Waiting for Godot,* has a reputation in the theatre as an explorer of the unusual. (pp. 34-5)

As soon as I walked into [Myerberg's] office in January, he told me what had gone wrong in Miami. "It was my fault," Myerberg said. "A play of ideas on such a deep intellectual level must be restricted to a small canvas for simplicity's sake." . . . After reading *Godot* forty times and seeing it at least fifteen times, Myerberg feels the play was not properly acted or directed in London. But he admitted that in Miami he went too far in the opposite direction. "I accented the wrong things in trying to illuminate corners of the text that were left in shadow in the London production," he said. . . .

I asked why he had produced the play. "To make money," Myerberg replied. "It made money everywhere else it was produced. It can make money here. And when I do it again, I'm not going to change the script. Every revision we tried proved to be false." I asked him if he thought Broadway would accept a play Miami rejected. He told me the exploitation in Florida had been a mistake that wouldn't be repeated up North. *Godot* was billed in Miami as "the laugh hit of four continents," and audiences came expecting *The Seven Year Itch* and *Harvey*. The next time—and he alone was sure there would be a "next time"—he promised not to aim for popular appeal. He said the audience is part of this play, and its reaction contributes to the theme. "If we have fifty people in the theatre who shouldn't be there, who buy tickets expecting a different kind of play, it can destroy the whole performance," he said. "I intend to do it again as soon as I possibly can, in such a way that the Broadway public will know what it's getting." (p. 35)

In early April, an advertisement appeared in the drama sections of the New York newspapers. It announced that *Godot* was coming to Broadway for a limited engagement. And a signed postscript by Myerberg warned: "I respectfully suggest that those who come to the theatre for casual entertainment do not buy a ticket to this attraction." Bert Lahr had turned down several offers in order to remain available for another chance at Estragon, his first strictly dramatic role. A baffled interviewer asked the veteran comedian what the play is about. "Damned if I know," Lahr confessed.

After months of waiting the New York critics were ready for *Godot*. Some of them liked the play, and most of those who didn't acted hospitable. They left it to the individual reader to decide if *Godot* was his meat or poison. John Chapman of the *Daily News* called it "the most novel theatrical novelty since *The Skin of Our Teeth*." And John McClain conceded in the *Journal-American* that *Godot* is "a fantastically non-conformist evening in the theatre" with "a madness that will make it conversation fodder." But there was also positive thinking about *Godot*. Richard Watts, Jr. of the *Post* used such phrases as "continuously fascinating," "moving," "grotesquely beautiful" and "utterly absorbing." Brooks Atkinson of the *Times* found in Beckett a "strange power . . . to convey the impression of some melancholy truths about the hopeless destiny of the human race." Atkinson concluded:

"Although *Waiting for Godot* is a 'puzzlement,' as the King of Siam would express it, Mr. Beckett is no charlatan. He has strong feelings about the degradation of mankind, and he has given vent to them copiously. *Waiting for Godot* is all feeling. Perhaps that is why it is puzzling and convincing at the same time. Theatregoers can rail at it, but they cannot ignore it. For Mr. Beckett is a valid writer." (pp. 35, 96)

Waiting for Godot has been "adopted" by three Pulitzer Prize playwrights—Tennessee Williams Thornton Wilder and William Saroyan. Williams regards *Godot* as one of the greatest plays of modern times and invested in Myerberg's productions. Wilder saw the play five times in Europe. Saroyan, according to the New York *Times,* all but weeps with emotion when he speaks of *Godot.* "It will make it easier for me and everyone else to write freely in the theatre."

Beckett never expected his play to go as far as it has. His attitude is as cryptic as his play. When director Schneider warned him that the public might not comprehend the play's ideas, he replied: "If they don't understand it, the hell with them." (p. 96)

Alan Levy, "The LONG Wait for Godot," in Theatre Arts, *Vol. XL, No. 8, August, 1956, pp. 33-5, 96.*

HAROLD HOBSON

I began this conversation with Samuel Beckett one summer morning in the bar of the Coupole, [in Paris, France]; . . . and finished it, on a duller, drabber day, in Madame Prunier's in St. James's Street.

"You have lived in France a long time", I said. "Yes", he replied. "But I still have my green Eire passport."

"What we are all arguing about in London," I went on, "is the meaning of *Waiting for Godot.*"

"I take no sides about that," he quickly responded.

"There is," I went on, "the incident of Estragon's boots." The tramp Estragon was always having trouble with his boots. One of them would go on comfortably, and the other would not go on at all. In despair Estragon used to leave the boots in front of the curtain . . . during the interval.

"One of Estragon's feet is blessed, and the other is damned. The boot won't go on the foot that is damned; and it will go on the foot that is not. It is like the two thieves on the cross."

"You were brought up a Protestant?" I enquired.

"Yes. Almost a Quaker. But I soon lost faith. I don't think I ever had it after leaving Trinity."

"And yet the thieves on the cross interest you. Vladimir is troubled to account for one of them being lost and the other saved. How can you be so preoccupied with this when you do not believe in salvation?"

It was at this point that Beckett became eager, excited. His sharp, rugged face leaned over the table. "I am interested in the shape of ideas even if I do not believe them. There is a wonderful sentence in Augustine. I wish I could remember the Latin. It is even finer in Latin than in English. 'Do not despair; one of the thieves was saved. Do not presume; one of the thieves was damned.' That sentence has a wonderful shape. It is the shape that matters."

In all the sentences that Beckett writes it is the shape that matters. His work is founded on an antithesis; he has established in literature the importance of the contradiction, the contradiction that can range from "She loves me, she loves me not" to "Godot will come, Godot will not come." Augustine recalls, immediately he has stated one fact, that the impression it creates will not be a true one unless he immediately recalls another which qualifies it. There is no such thing as simple certainty; at least there is no such thing as simple certainty for Samuel Beckett. (p. 153)

[Upon its debut], audiences at *Waiting for Godot* tormented themselves with the question, what does the play mean? Some people thought that Godot was God; some that Lucky was Godot; some that Pozzo represented Capitalism, and Lucky Labour; some that Estragon and Vladimir were material and spiritual aspects of the same person; whilst one admirer of the play, more ingenious than most, divined that the bully Pozzo was the U.S.S.R., the enslaved Lucky the satellites in eastern Europe, that the two tramps were Great Britain and France, both waiting for Godot, or the United States, to come to their help.

Now, I neither agree nor disagree with these explanations of *Waiting for Godot. . . .* They seem to me merely beside the point. I believe that *Waiting for Godot* has as little or as much meaning as a fugue, or as a sunset, as a rainbow or as a Chippendale chair. There are people who think that a rainbow is God's assurance that there will never be another Flood. I know; I have talked with them. There are others who think it merely an optical phenomenon. The rainbow may be equally beautiful to both classes of people, because its beauty has nothing to do with its meaning, if it has a meaning. Nor has the beauty of *Waiting for Godot* anything to do with its meaning, if it has a meaning. This beauty depends on symmetry, on balance, on shape; on the antithesis between the triumphant Pozzo and the beaten Lucky in the first act, and the reversal of their positions in the second; on the balance between the boy's appearance at the end of the first act and his re-appearance at the end of the second; on the strophe and antistrophe of the speeches of the two tramps; on the musical interplay of words and of silence. The play is not an appeal to reason, nor is it a puzzle. To search for its meaning will reduce to futility the acutest intellect, just as to yield to the exquisite ordering of its ideas, its echoes, and its associations will exalt the humblest spirit. (pp. 154-55)

> Harold Hobson, "Samuel Beckett: Dramatist of the Year," in International Theatre Annual, No. 1, 1956, pp. 153-55.

GÜNTHER ANDERS

[*The essay excerpted below was originally published in German as "Sein ohne Zeit: Zu Beckett's Stück 'En attendant Godot' " in* Neue Schweizer Rundschau, *January, 1954, and revised and republished in the author's study* Die Antiquiertheit des Menschen: Über die Seele im Zeitalter der zweiten industriellen Revolution *(1956).*]

All commentators are agreed on this: that [*Waiting for Godot*] is a *parable*. But although the dispute about the interpretation of the parable rages with the utmost intensity, not one of those who quarrel about who or what Godot is, and who promptly (as though it were the ABC of nihilism) answer this question with "death" or "the meaning of life" or "God," has given the least thought to the mechanism by

which all parables, and hence Beckett's parable too, work. This mechanism we call *"inversion."* What is inversion?

When Aesop or Lafontaine wanted to say: men are like animals—did they show men as animals? No. Instead they reversed—and this is the peculiarly amusing alienation effect of all fables—the two elements of the equation, its subject and its predicate; that is: they stated that animals behave as men. . . . It is this process of substitution which one must have grasped before starting to interpret Beckett's fable. For Beckett too uses it—in an extremely subtle way.

In order to present a fable about a kind of existence, which has lost both form and principle and in which life no longer goes forward, he destroys both the form and the principle so far characteristic of fables: now the *destroyed* fable, the fable which does not go forward, becomes the adequate representation of stagnant life; his meaningless parable about man stands for the parable of meaningless man. True: this fable no longer corresponds to the formal ideal of the classical fable. But as it is a fable about a kind of life that no longer has any point that could be presented in the form of a fable, it is its weakness and its failure itself which becomes its point; if it suffers from lack of cohesion this is so because lack of cohesion is its subject matter; if it renounces relating an action, it does so because the action it relates is life without action; if it defies convention by no longer offering a story, it does so because it describes man eliminated from, and deprived of, history. That the events and fragments of conversation which constitute the play arise without motivation, or simply repeat themselves (in so insidious a manner that those involved do not even notice the fact of repetition), needs to be denied: for this lack of motivation is motivated by the subject matter; and this subject matter is a form of life without a motive principle and without motivation.

Although it is, so to say, a *negative* fable, it nevertheless remains a fable. For despite the fact that no active maxims can be derived from it, the play remains on the level of *abstraction.* While the novels of the last one hundred and fifty years had contented themselves to *narrate* a way of life that had lost its formal principle, this play represents *formlessness as such;* and not only this—its subject matter—is an "abstraction"; also the characters are "abstractions": the play's "heroes," Estragon and Vladimir, are clearly *men in general;* yes, they are *abstract* in the most cruel, literal sense of the word: they are *abs-tracti,* which means: pulled away, set apart. And as they, having been pulled out of the world, no longer have anything to do with it, the world has, for them, become empty. . . . (pp. 140-41)

The two heroes thus are merely alive, but no longer living in a world. And this concept is carried through with such merciless consequence that other attempts at representing a form of life that has lost its world—and contemporary literature, philosophy, and art are by no means poor in such representations—appear cosy in comparison. . . . Where a world no longer exists, there can no longer be a possibility of a *collision with the world,* and therefore the very *possibility of tragedy has been forfeited.* Or to put it more precisely: the tragedy of this kind of existence lies in the fact that it does not even have a chance of tragedy, that it must always, at the same time, in its totality be farce (not, as in the tragedies of our forebears, merely shot through with farce): and that therefore it can only be represented as farce, as *ontological farce, not as comedy.* And that is what Beckett does.

We know from Don Quixote how closely abstraction and farce are connected. But Don Quixote had merely abstracted from the actual condition of *his* world; not from the world as such. Beckett's farce, therefore, is more "radical": for it is not by placing people in a world or situation which they do not want to accept and with which they therefore clash that he produces his farcical effects, but by placing them in a place that is no place at all. This turns them into clowns, for the metaphysical comicality of clowns does, after all, consist in their being unable to distinguish between being and non-being, by falling down non-existing stairs, or by treating real stairs as though they did not exist. But in contrast to such clowns (like Chaplin) who, in order to create ceaseless laughter have to keep themselves ceaselessly busy and who collide with the world almost on principle, Beckett's heroes are *indolent or paralyzed clowns.* For them, it is not just this or that object but the world itself that does not exist, hence they renounce altogether any attempt to concern themselves with it. (pp. 141-42)

Nothing to do any longer. . . . [In the twentieth century], "action" has become more and more questionable; not because the number of unemployed has increased—it has not—but because millions who are in fact still active, increasingly feel that they are *acted upon:* that they are active without themselves deciding on the objective of their action, without even being able to discern the nature of that objective; or because they are aware that their activity is suicidal in its objective. In short: *action has lost so much of its independence that it itself has become a form of passivity, and even where action is deadly strenuous or actually deadly, it has assumed the character of futile action or inaction.* That Estragon and Vladimir, who do absolutely nothing, are representative of millions of people, is undeniable.

But they are so fully representative only because, in spite of their inaction and the pointlessness of their existence, they still want to *go on,* and thus do not belong to the tragic class of those who consider suicide. . . . And it is *not despite* the pointlessness of their life that the Estragons and Vladimirs wish to go on living, but, on the contrary, *just because* their life has become pointless—by which I mean that, ruined by their habit of inaction or of acting without their own initiative, they have lost their will power to decide not to go on, their freedom to end it all. (pp. 142-43)

It is with this kind of life, with man who continues existing because he happens to exist, that Beckett's play deals. But it deals with it in a manner basically different from all previous literary treatments of despair. The proposition which one might attribute to all classical desperado figures (including Faust) might have been expressed as: *"We have no more to expect, therefore we shall not remain."* Estragon and Vladimir, on the other hand, use "inversions" of this formula: *"We remain,"* they seem to be saying, *"therefore we must be waiting for something."* And: *"We are waiting, therefore there must be something we are waiting for."* (p. 143)

To characterize this mode of life in which man continues to wait merely because he happens to *be,* French commentators have used Heidegger's term *"Geworfenheit"* (the fact and state of having been "thrown" into the world). Quite wrongly. For while Heidegger, in using this term, designates the contingency of each individual's being just himself (and demands that each take possession of his contingent being in order to make it the basis of his own "design") the two heroes of Beckett's play do neither, like the millions whom they rep-

resent. They neither recognize their own existence as contingent, nor think of abolishing this contingency, of transforming it into something positive with which they can identify themselves. Their existence is far less heroic than that meant by Heidegger, far more trustful, far more "realistic." They would be as little likely to deprive a chair of its function and attribute to it a mere functionless reality, as to regard themselves in that light. For they are "metaphysicists," that is to say *incapable of doing without the concept of meaning.* Heidegger's term represents an express dethroning of the concept of "meaning of life." Vladimir and Estragon, on the other hand, conclude from the fact of their existence that there must be something for which they are waiting; they are *champions of the doctrine that life must have meaning even in a manifestly meaningless situation.* To say that they represent "nihilists" is, therefore, not only incorrect, but the exact reverse of what Beckett wants to show. As they do not lose hope, are even incapable of losing hope, they are naive, incurably optimistic ideologists. *What Beckett presents is not nihilism, but the inability of man to be a nihilist even in a situation of utter hopelessness.* Part of the compassionate sadness conveyed by the play springs not so much from the hopeless situation as such as from the fact that the two heroes, through their waiting, show that they are not able to cope with this situation, hence that they are *not* nihilists. It is this defect which makes them so incredibly funny. (p. 144)

Although the name "Godot" undoubtedly conceals the English word "God," the play does not deal with Him, but merely with the *concept of God.* No wonder therefore that God's image is left vague: what God does, so we read in the theological passages of the play, is unknown; from hearsay it appears as though he does nothing at all; and the only information conveyed by his daily messenger boy, brother to Kafka's Barnabas, is that, alas, Godot will not be coming today, but certainly tomorrow—and thus Beckett clearly indicates that it is precisely Godot's *non-arrival* which keeps them waiting for him, and their faith in him, alive. (p. 145)

The similarity to Kafka is unmistakable; it is impossible not to be reminded of the "Message of the Dead King." But whether this is a case of direct literary indebtedness does not matter, for both authors are *des enfants du même siècle,* nourished by the same pre-literary source. Whether it is Rilke, or Kafka, or Beckett—*their religious experience springs,* paradoxically, always *from religious frustration, from the fact that they do not experience God, and thus paradoxically from an experience they share with unbelief.* In Rilke this experience springs from the inaccessibility of God (the first Duino elegy); in Kafka from inaccessibility in a search (*The Castle*); in Beckett from inaccessibility in the act of waiting. For all of them the demonstrations of God's existence can be formulated as: *"He does not come, therefore He is."* . . . [Although Beckett] puts the conclusion that the non-arrival of Godot demonstrates his existence into the mouths of his creatures, he not only doesn't share this conviction, but even derides it as absurd. *His play* therefore is certainly *not a religious play; at most it deals with religion.* "At most": for what he presents is ultimately only a faith that believes in itself. And that is no faith.

When we try to find out how such a life, despite its aimlessness, can actually go on, we make a most strange discovery. For although continuing, such a life doesn't *go on,* it becomes a "life without time." By this I mean that what we call "time" springs from man's needs and from his attempts to satisfy them. . . . Now we have seen that in Estragon's and Vladimir's lives, objectives no longer exist. For this reason in the play time does not exist either, life is "treading water," so to speak; and it is for this reason, and quite legitimately, that events and conversations are going in circles. . . . (pp. 145-46)

Beckett carries this concept through with such complete consistency that he presents (which is probably without precedence in the history of drama) a second act which is but a slightly varied version of the first act, thus offering to our startled eyes nothing new or startling. Accustomed as we are to encounter new situations in the course of a play, we are deeply surprised by this lack of surprise, by the fact that the scenes repeat themselves; and we are filled with the horror which we feel in front of people who suffer from *amnesia*. For with one exception, none of the characters is aware of this repetition; and even when reminded of it, they remain incapable of recognizing that their experiences or conversations are merely recapitulations of yesterday's events or talk. Yet presenting the characters as victims of amnesia is absolutely legitimate; for where there is no time, there can be no memory either. And yet time here is not quite as rocklike as so often in Kafka's works. For, as Beckett leaves a rudiment of activity—of what kind this rudiment is we shall see shortly—there still remains a minimum of time. Although a "stream of time" doesn't exist any longer, the "time material" is not petrified yet, it still can somehow be pushed back or aside and thus be turned into something like a "past": instead of a moving stream, time here has become something like a stagnant mush. (p. 146)

The rudimentary activity which can temporarily set this time mush in motion, however, is no longer real "action"; for it has no objective except to make time move which, in "normal" active life, is not the aim of action but its consequence. Although this formula may sound paradoxical, if time still survives here, it owes its survival exclusively to the fact that the activity of "time killing" has not died out yet. . . . [Estragon and Vladimir] resume their "activity" time and again, because this kind of activity keeps time moving, pushes a few inches of time behind them, and brings them a few inches closer to the alleged Godot.

This goes so far—and at this point the play achieves truly heartrending tones—that the two even propose to act out feelings and emotions, that they actually embrace each other, because, after all, emotions, too, are motions and as such might push back the mush of stagnant time. If again and again Vladimir and Estragon wrack their brains what to do next, they are doing so because "it helps to pass the time," or because whatever they do, will, as long as they are doing *something*, reduce the distance which separates them from Godot. The best way to overcome the doldrums is through the activation of their being together, through their ever renewed taking advantage of the chance that it is at least as a *pair* that they have to bear their senseless existence. If they did not cling to each other desperately, if they could not rely on the never ceasing to and fro of their conversation, if they had not their quarrels, if they did not leave each other or reunite—actions which, after all, cannot take place without taking up time—they would actually be lost. That Beckett presents us with a pair is, thus, not only motivated by his technical insight that a play about a *Robinson Crusoe of Expectation* would coagulate and become a mere painting, but also by his wish to show that everyone is the other's pastime;

that company facilitates endurance of the pointlessness of existence, or at least conceals it; that, although not giving an absolute guarantee that time will pass, it helps now and then. (pp. 146-47)

Of course, in "normal life," during the interludes of leisure time, "passing the time" occurs, too. Playing games is an illustration: by simulating activity, we try to make that time pass which otherwise would threaten to stagnate. One could object that we do this only in our leisure time, that, after all, we separate "real life" from "play"; while, in the case of Vladimir and Estragon, it is just the *incessant* attempt to make time pass which is so characteristic, and which reflects the specific misery and absurdity of their life. But is it really legitimate to make this distinction between them and ourselves? Is there really a recognizable boundary line between our "real life" and our "playing"?

I do not think so. The pitiful struggle they are waging to keep up the semblance of action is probably so impressive only because it mirrors our own fate, that of modern mass man. Since, through the mechanization of labor, the worker is deprived of the chance to recognize what he is actually doing, and of seeing the objectives of his work, his working too has become something like a sham activity. . . . For mass-man today has been deprived so completely of his initiative and of his ability to shape his leisure time himself that he now depends upon the ceaselessly running conveyor belt of radio and television to make time pass. (pp. 147-48)

Beckett is wholly realistic when he makes [Estragon and Vladimir] fail in their attempts to play games and when he shows them unable to master their leisure time. They are all the less able to do that because they do not possess yet, as we do, recognized and stereotyped forms of leisure pastimes, neither sport nor Mozart Sonatas, and are, therefore, forced to improvise and invent their games on the spot, to take activities from the vast store of everyday actions and transform them into play in order to pass the time. In those situations in which we, the more fortunate ones, play football and, once we have finished, can start all over again, Estragon plays the *da capo* game "shoe off, shoe on"; and not in order to exhibit himself as a fool, but to exhibit *us* as fools: in order to demonstrate through the device of inversion that our playing of games (the pointlessness of which is already made invisible by its public recognition) has no more meaning than his. The inverted meaning of the scene in which Estragon plays "shoe off, shoe on" reads: "Our playing of games is a shoe off, shoe on, too, a ghostly activity meant only to produce the false appearance of activity." . . . Thus it is not they but we who are the actors in the farce. And this is the triumph of Beckett's inversion.

It is clear that the two must envy the fate of those fellow-men who do not need to keep the "time mush" moving themselves, or who do this as a matter of course, because they don't know of any alternative. These antipodes are Pozzo and Lucky.

Attempts to decipher who they are and what they symbolize have kept the commentators no less busy than the question of the identity of Godot. But all these attempts went in the wrong direction, because the pair itself has a deciphering function. What do I mean?

I mean that the two already *had* existed in the form of concepts, that they already had played a role in speculative philosophy, and that Beckett has now retranslated the two abstractions into concrete figures.

Since the early thirties when Hegel's dialectic and Marx's theory of the class struggle began to interest the younger generation in France, the famous image of the pair *"master and servant"* from Hegel's *Phaenomenologie des Geistes* so deeply engraved itself into the consciousness of those intellectuals born around 1900 that it occupies today the place which the image of *Prometheus* held in the nineteenth century: it has become the *image of man in general.* . . . What is decisive in this new symbol is its *"pluralization"* and its inherent *"antagonism"*: that "Man" is now seen as a *pair of men;* that the individual (who, as a metaphysical self-made man, had fought a Promethean struggle against the Gods) has now been replaced by *men* who fight *each other* for domination. It is *they* who are now regarded as *reality;* for "to be" now means "to dominate" and to struggle for domination; and they alone are seen as the "motor of time." . . . (pp. 148-50)

Now this Hegelian symbol of the motor of history steps onto the stage embodied by the figures Pozzo and Lucky, onto the stage on which, so far, nothing had reigned but "being without time"—if it can be said of such stagnation that it "reigns." It is quite understandable that the entrance of this new pair intrigues the spectator. First for aesthetic reasons: the stagnation which, at the beginning, he had rejected as hardly acceptable, but finally accepted as the "law of the Godot world," is suddenly disturbed by the intrusion of characters who are undeniably active. . . .

But however shy Vladimir and Estragon may feel when first facing the new pair, there is one thing they cannot conceal: that they regard them as enviable. It is evident that, in the eyes of those who are sentenced to "being without time," the champions of time, even the most infernal ones, must appear as privileged beings. Pozzo, the master, is enviable because he has no need to "make time" by himself, or to advance by himself, not to speak of waiting for Godot: for Lucky drags him forward anyway. And Lucky, the servant, is enviable because he not only *can* march on, but actually *must* do so, for Pozzo is behind him and sees to it that he does. And even though they pass the two timeless tramps by without knowing that they have already done so the day before—as "blind history" as it were, which has not yet become aware of its being history—they nevertheless, whether dragged or pushed, are already in motion and therefore, in Estragon's and Vladimir's eyes, fortunate creatures. It is, therefore, quite understandable that they suspect Pozzo (although he has never heard Godot's name and even mispronounces it as a matter of principle) of being Godot himself; for behind Pozzo's whip, they feel, their waiting might find an end. Nor is it a coincidence that Lucky, the beast of burden, is called by that name. For although he has to bear everything and spends his life carrying sacks filled with sand, he is totally freed from all burdens of initiative and if they could stand in his place they would no longer be compelled to wait. . . . (p. 150)

Any attempt to find in this image of man and his world positive or consoling features would, after all we have said, be in vain. And yet, in *one* respect Beckett's play differs from all those nihilistic documents which mirror our age: in its *tone.* The tone of those documents usually is [one of utter seriousness]. . . . The clown however—and that this is a clownish play we have shown—is neither beastly serious nor cynical; but filled with a sadness which, since it reflects the

sadness of all human fate, creates solidarity amongst men and, by doing so, may make this fate a little less unbearable. . . . And although the mere tone of humaneness which springs from this barren soil of meaninglessness may only be a tiny comfort; and although the voice which comforts us does not know why it is comforting and who the Godot is for whom it makes us hope—it shows that warmth means more than meaning; and that it is not the metaphysician who has the last word. (pp. 150-51)

Günther Anders, "Being without Time: On Beckett's Play 'Waiting for Godot'," translated by Martin Esslin, in Samuel Beckett: A Collection of Critical Essays, *edited by Martin Esslin, Prentice-Hall, Inc., 1965, pp. 140-51.*

BAMBER GASCOIGNE

Beckett's *Waiting for Godot* is the most commercially successful 'experimental' play since [Luigi Pirandello's] *Six Characters in Search of an Author.* First produced in Paris in 1952, it has since been translated into eighteen languages and performed all over the world.

Its immediate appeal is due to the fact that, even though nothing much happens, it is intensely theatrical. The endless cross-talk act of the two tramps is always funny and at the same time sad—funny because good cross-talk acts are very funny, and sad because their main reason for talking at all is just to pass away the time, to fill in the void. Under the farcical ripple of the dialogue lies a serious concern. . . .

Serious subject-matter is being presented in music-hall form. The genuine concern of one tramp with the possibility of salvation is constantly broken into by the other with remarks like 'I find this most extraordinarily interesting', and the discussion follows a carefully constructed comic pattern, with Vladimir's logic steadily tightening only to be punctured by Estragon's final 'People are bloody ignorant apes'. This tug between subject-matter and form runs through the whole play. Much of the surface is taken up with farcical satire of conventional social behaviour. . . . But the satire is not mere incidental comedy. As with Eliot, the emphasis on the surface aspects of life has its part in the meaning of the play. At one point fat Pozzo is lying on the ground, unable to get up. Spasmodically he shouts 'Help!'. Vladimir, glad of this chance to be useful for once, says 'Let us not waste our time in idle discourse' and launches into a long speech. This is a typical Beckett scene. The situation itself is farcical and yet has serious implications; and Vladimir's speech, though mock-pompous in tone, contains the real meaning of the play. He says:

> What are we doing here, that is the question. And we are blessed in this, that we happen to know the answer. Yes, in this immense confusion one thing alone is clear. We are waiting for Godot to come—

and later:

> What's certain is that the hours are long, under these conditions, and constrain us to beguile them with proceedings which, how shall I say, which may at first sight seem reasonable until they become a habit. You may say it is to prevent our reason from foundering.

As with Eliot the surface 'proceedings' of life, of which the play is made up, keep mankind's attention off the despair beneath it all. But for Beckett this is a relief (however ironical), because he does not share Eliot's optimistic Christian faith in a redemption beyond the despair.

Waiting for Godot can be, and has been, given many different interpretations. However, having no one meaning is not at all synonymous with having no meaning. Beckett is a very eclectic writer. His play is full of obvious Christian echoes, but it also contains less marked historical and anthropological allusions. Each member of the audience picks up the echoes to which he is most attuned. My own interpretation is that the two tramps are two parts of a person or of a community seen subjectively, with Vladimir representing the more spiritual part and Estragon the more animal; and that Pozzo and Lucky make up a person or a community viewed objectively, Pozzo being the exploiter and the user of ideas, Lucky the exploited and the creator of ideas. In other words we suffer with Estragon and Vladimir, their fears, their hopes, their hatreds and loves; but we view Pozzo and Lucky through their eyes and therefore see in them only the social surface of life. But the question of which precise meaning Beckett had in mind is unimportant. What is important—and this is a factor which is common to nearly all the interpretations—is that these four characters should add up to a picture of humanity at large. This is essential because the play is, above all, about mankind's attempts to fiddle its way through life, setting up a wall of hopes and pretences between itself and despair. The greatest of these hopes—that there is some point to existence, that we are keeping some mysterious appointment on earth and are therefore not random scraps of life—is symbolized by Godot. Critics have asked many questions about the precise nature of Godot, but they are irrelevant questions. The play is not about Godot, but, as its title states, about the waiting for him. It is about life on earth, not hereafter.

Vladimir and Estragon successfully establish themselves as a true lowest common denominator of humanity. Their warmth in the middle of despair is the world's. This, together with its theatricality and the brilliance of its rhythms and language, makes *Waiting for Godot* a great play which will last. Beckett has not since reached such heights. (pp. 184-88)

> Bamber Gascoigne, "The New Playwrights," in his Twentieth-Century Drama, *Hutchinson University Library, 1962, pp. 184-208.*

ERIC BENTLEY

The word *tragi-comedy* can be traced back to ancient Rome but does not seem to have been in general use until the Renaissance. The best definition of it in its earlier forms is, perhaps, Susanne Langer's: "averted tragedy." (p. 316)

Everyone will agree that [*Waiting for Godot*] might, in some broad sense, be called a tragic play, and also that in its procedure from line to line, and section to section, it is comic. There is the big tragedy of man in a disvalued world, an incomprehensible and threatening world, a world either godless or having a God who leaves much to be desired; and there is the little comedy of a couple of bums amusing themselves and us with music-hall patter. *Waiting for Godot* can also, without stretching a point, be called a "comedy with an unhappy ending." Its substructure is the story of two men waiting for a third who will solve their problems. . . . That "Godot" does *not* come is what makes the play a parable of life as seen by modern man.

People talk of Beckett's despair, and how should they not? It is the "modern" despair—despair unrelieved by any last-act *deus ex machina,* a harrowing despair beyond the familiar despairs, further gone into moral paralysis, a despair that needs neither a catastrophe to point it up, nor a climactic speech to sum it up, because it is *there,* insistently, obsessively, monomaniacally. It hangs in the air. You need only walk into a theatre where *Godot* is playing, and the ghastly despondency will cut into you like an icy wind. That people reject Beckett, provided they do not do so flippantly, may be very proper, and a compliment to his power as an artist. . . . In Beckett, the despairing element is so weighty and oppressive it could easily prove dangerous—for anyone who is already in danger.

In danger, that is, of total collapse. We speak of despair as if it were a clear-cut and absolute thing. On Wednesday one felt despair, and on Thursday one did not. In actuality it is a hovering, free-floating thing. . . . Despair is often most active when most hidden. It uses anaesthetics: when one is numb and feels nothing, one may be most under its influence. One can look back on things one has done and say: "I must have been in despair," and there is terror in the thought of having been in such a state of soul and not having known it. (pp. 348-49)

Despair is around all the time but one can never be sure if "this time it is real" because reality is as mysterious, fluid, uncertain, and many-leveled as despair itself. All despairs are real, and it is right, when they happen, to sound the alarm, but there is only one despair that is "really real," ultimate, and a hundred per cent, and that is the despair that precipitates collapse into psychosis, serious physical illness, or suicide. At that stage, a man does not write a poem, novel, or play expressing despair.

He does not write *Waiting for Godot. . . .* Very likely Samuel Beckett sometimes falls into such a state (I speak theoretically, not with personal knowledge) but the existence of his works—several novels, several plays—is proof that he has from time to time fallen out of it. Artistic activity is itself a transcendence of despair, and for unusually despairing artists that is no doubt chiefly what art is: a therapy, a faith. A work of art is organized and rational, a victory of the human in the highest sense of the term: it has dignity. Though it well may be imbued with despair ("He who has never despaired," says Goethe, "has no need to have lived"), and may easily be *about* despair (*Hamlet* opens with a young man wishing he was dead), a work of art is itself a sign that despair is not at the wheel but that a man is.

If Beckett's despair can make the despair of other writers seem "literary," then either he has tapped a deeper despair than theirs or he has expressed an equally deep despair much more vividly. In either case, he got rid of the despair, if only for the time being, *by* expressing it. And so this "more despairing" person is actually a less despairing person than many a miserable fellow who never expressed anything but collapsed into idiocy or suicide.

Of course, the non-despairing element of *Godot* is not to be attributed exclusively to the work's existence as an ordered whole. Even gallows humor is humor: though it springs from despair, and conveys despair, it also springs from joy and conveys joy. Playfulness is playfulness, and in *Godot* Beckett is sometimes playful to the point of being zany and even zestful. There are definite interruptions of the baleful mood, spurts of invaluable frivolity. And all is left in suspense at the conclusion. For this play is tragi-comic in yet another respect: if the conclusion is not the happy one of Godot's arrival, neither is it the unhappiest one imaginable—discovering that Godot does not exist or will never come. He may exist and he may come. A door is open. The suicide tree is not used. (pp. 349-51)

[Yet] the main question remains—on Beckett's tragicomedies and other people's—why is the deadly analysis pushed so very far, why is the relentlessness as relentless as *this,* why is the pessimism so deep, the despair so devastating, what satisfaction can we possibly derive from such dissatisfaction? I find a clue to the answer in the observation often made by middle-brow critics to the effect that we have in work like this of Beckett's a perverse countersentimentality, counteroptimism, counterfaith. The insinuation is that the modernists mechanically invert the philistine, middle-class attitudes. . . . [All] ideals have become suspect, all values thoroughly disvalued. In our time, if the man of letters (read: man of mind and conscience) hears himself uttering the big affirmations he has to ask himself if in seeking his salvation he has not got himself well and truly damned. Now when the affirmations are suspect, negations may be more honorable. In these circumstances, the negative attains the force of the positive.

The last ideal to go is hope, for none of the others can live on unsupported by it. And so in this time of *tabula rasa,* to hope or not to hope, that is the question. We have been swindled so many times that life itself is now most characteristically pictured as the Great Swindle. Comedy, especially modern tragi-comedy, sees life as such, but just as there is despair and despair, so there is belief and belief. One shouts that something terrible is about to happen in the hope that everyone will then stop it from happening. Call this cunning, call it superstition, it is very human. (pp. 351-52)

Eric Bentley, "Tragi-Comedy," in his The Life of the Drama, *Athenæum, 1964, pp. 316-54.*

J. CHIARI

S. Beckett's *Waiting for Godot* is the most original play of the post-war years. Here we are truly in the domain of imagination and poetry. We have . . . characters who are both symbolic and real and a situation which is a metaphor of the human condition. The characters are all mankind, Abel and Cain, rich and poor, exploiter and exploited, dying or living astride their already prepared grave, and waiting like all men, for the revelation of the mystery which is not dead but absconded and keeps their souls and lives in suspense. This is the true metaphysical, Pascalian and Kierkegaardian absurdity and nonsense of life without God or without purpose. . . . [Yet the] anguish of *Godot* is not the anguish of the void but the anguish of absence; it is certainly closer to the anguish of Sartrian freedom which is as much a categorical imperative as if freedom, instead of being purely an immanent value, were also transcendent.

The truth is that it is impossible to posit immanence without some form of transcendence, at least in abeyance. . . . [Religious ideas] endow this play with far-reaching metaphysical reverberations and profound human truth. *Waiting for Godot* bathes in a metaphysical atmosphere which excludes expressionism, abstractions and allegories. Objects like the tree, the hat and the shoes carry symbolic connotations, while even the apparent philosophising of the tramps is fully integrated in the play as a means of exteriorising their feelings and the awareness of their condition. While the words poetry and poems are so lightly bandied about in connection with the modern stage that they are often meaningless, *Waiting for Godot* is a poem and for reasons very different from those generally invoked when the word poetry is used in connection with certain fashionable contemporary dramatists. The first one is that its reality must be experienced as a whole, because the play attempts to mirror the wholeness of life. It is a poem, and it is essentially a symbolist poem, in the direct line of Maeterlinck's drama. The action only progresses in the sense that there are two acts which require a certain amount of sequential time for performance, but there is in fact no dramatic progression or tension. The action is static, confined to waiting for something which is never clearly defined. Waiting is a condition of human kind and those who wait use words as in Maeterlinck's plays, not to construct or defeat arguments, but to keep their anguish at bay and to give meaning and creativeness to silence.

The play is not perfect, the second act lacking, of necessity, the originality of the first; this was very much less noticeable in the English production, which was altogether better than the French, which was too naturalistic. The first act is a masterpiece and the most original piece of dramatic writing of the last twenty years. Beckett has carried to a successful and final conclusion a type of Maeterlinckian drama which cannot be repeated, since he has been able to dramatise in that form the very plight of the human condition. *Endgame, Krapp's Last Tape* and *Embers* are nothing more than continuations, or shreds and left overs from the great theme which he explored in *Waiting for Godot.* . . . Beckett's universal, tragic farce which is connected with the writings of other Irish playwrights like Synge and O'Casey is a mirror of modern life which follows and completes the picture of it presented by *The Waste Land* at the end of the first world war. Time, in Beckett as well as in Eliot, is not sequential time, but time lived; it is the Bergsonian duration. Time, in *Godot,* is meaningless because of the absence of transcendence which confers meaning upon it.

The play takes place during two evenings which seem at one point to be two different seasons, since in the second evening, the tree, by which the action takes place, bears leaves. Although the tree being symbolical of the hanging tree, its bearing of leaves could, of course, be a symbolic sign of the hope which makes it possible for the two tramps to go on waiting. The tree is also the solitary tree of the Noh plays, which Yeats admired and sought to emulate. Life measured by the standards of eternity is *one* day; "one day we are born, one day we die, we live astride a grave". All things are the same since they lack their real meaning which is the reason for which the two tramps are waiting. Didi and Gogo . . . are meaningless, and life is a tale told by an idiot; but all this is due not to inherent absurdity, but to an absence of meaning. The tramps are complex creatures with various levels of meaning which range from the particular to the universal. At one level, they are well-defined, Chaplinesque figures done down by life and carrying clear-cut naturalistic attributes which they share with that category of tramps. At the other level, they are no ordinary tramps; they are, on the contrary, two extremely singular tramps since they stand for something more than their own appearance in that they are the bearers of the most important aspects of the self-consciousness of man. . . . (pp. 68-71)

Their language, loaded with meaning, suggestiveness and ambiguities, is both a poetic and a continuously dramatic language in the sense that it is never used for its own sake, but always in order to develop the dramatic situation in which they find themselves. Their gestures, their clownish tricks, their hunger, fears, quarrels and bad faith are practically all referential and symbolic. . . . The two tramps Vladimir and Estragon are real in the way Alceste of Molière is real; they are recognisable and highly singularised tramps, each one with his own habits, feelings and reactions, and they are also types, representing a whole aspect of human kind. They are real, they eat, sleep, squabble, are slapped and beaten by others, and they suffer and they are in a situation which is that of the human condition. They are waiting for a strange entity called Godot, and they stand for human kind aware of transcendence and waiting for a sign of its presence. We have here no incoherent mixture of fancy and naturalism as in Ionesco; we have, on the contrary, a striking example of the dramatic embodiment of true realism in which every aspect of phenomenal appearance is informed with substance and is symbolic of true reality.

The setting of the play is the earth, practically anywhere; it is sufficiently nondescript to be so, and it fits with the lack of exact biographical details about the two tramps who could belong to any nationality. They don't quite know whence they came, and their social background is of no importance; they neither remember their past clearly nor the exact reasons why they are where they are, and of course, the lack of precision about their social origins only serves to emphasize their true humanity. (pp. 71-2)

They have had ups and downs, but it is obvious that life has been, up till now, worth living. They are neither interchangeable nor are they social types like the characters of social realistic drama; they are two individuals who embody various fundamental aspects of mankind. First, they embody the masculine and the feminine. Vladimir, who is more active, more restless, more intellectualised, is the masculine; Estragon, who is more spontaneous, more childlike, more egotistical, more obstinate, more prone to moods and in need of protection, is the feminine. . . . He threatens to go away and does not, and he is as much tied to Vladimir as some married couples are tied to each other by their respective inability to live apart. The two tramps need each other, have affection for each other, and although their quarrelling is at times comical like all quarreling, they can't part and they have compassion and love for each other. They are two archetypal heroes or characters as much detached from any social historical context as Alceste, Phèdre, or Hamlet. . . . They are a metaphor of the human condition and represent what is unchanging and what transcends the particular and the sociohistorical aspect of human life. They are man in solitude, yet desperately trying to get out of it, and sometimes succeeding, but more often failing in the two most fundamental aspects of human life, which are that man can neither share his sorrows and suffering nor his death. Whatever Godot is, it is obvious that the two tramps, like other men, can only get out of their solitude through God, for togetherness is a religious experience. Here God is in a suspended state of absence and Vladimir and Estragon are in a state of continuous agitation because they cannot face up to the solitude which threatens them. They know the cause of their vain agitation and suffer-

ing, yet they go on, because there is nothing else that they can do. Suicide is too positive an act, and as they have not resolved their contradictions they are not in a position to take such a positive step. . . . Their apathy and natural aptitude to wait are against it, and above all, the hope that Godot might turn up is never entirely given up.

Pozzo and Lucky are society, and they are a world completely alien to that of the two tramps. Pozzo is the master and Lucky is the slave, laden with burdens, tied to him by a rope. The Pozzo-Lucky relationship is the mirror of human degradation and shallowness. Pozzo hides his insignificance and hollowness under a cloak of ritual gestures and ceremonies which are part of the social apparatus of power. In the second act, Pozzo is blind and entirely at the mercy of his slave who now leads him with a rope which has been considerably shortened. At this stage, they encounter again the tramps and they all tumble down in general confusion and try again to get up but without success, as is the case with humankind without God. Pozzo's life is appearance without substance; his life is what he owns, and Lucky is part of it. Lucky is merely an object, a thing, and his life is reduced to mechanical reactions; he not only serves Pozzo, he also has to think for him; he is therefore materially and spiritually Pozzo's slave and has no individual existence. His incoherent speech at his Master's bidding is a brilliant illustration of the subservience and menial position of the intellectual and the artist in a society composed of Pozzos. The final outcome of this type of servitude is delirium and silence.

If the situation of the two tramps is that of the human condition, and therefore something which transcends sociohistorical time, that of Pozzo and Lucky, who are social beings, is entirely subjected to the laws of time. They change from one day to another; Vladimir notes this change and Estragon acknowledges it with the words: "Very likely; they all change, only we can't." The two tramps can't change because time for them has stopped; they are suspended upon the moment of expectancy which represents now and always the very core of the human condition. Pozzo and Lucky, who do not even have a glimmer of the idea of transcendence, are merely part of the contingent world; they represent society at its last gasp, dying of the master-slave relationship. Lucky who, before, could dance, could therefore do something creative, now can only relieve his master's boredom through his intellectual delirium. Soon society will be entirely composed of blind masters and mute slaves. . . . (pp. 72-4)

Whatever happens in **Waiting for Godot** is like the negative of a film; it is something which can only exist if it is developed and brought to light by the positive intervention of the photographer. In the play, action could only be made positive by the appearance of Godot whose absence fills the waiting and negates everything that takes place in this atmosphere of waiting which is a vacuum. Nothing positive could take place in such an atmosphere, since no action could coincide with its purpose which, in this case, does not exist. All the actions are dependent upon waiting for Godot or for God whose absence causes the vacuum of waiting and negates everything, including the tramps' hunger, suffering and fears. Hunger and fear are real enough; they are experienced both physically and mentally, but as they take place in a world from which all meanings have been absolutely sucked out by, and dissolved into, the absence which the tramps are waiting and longing for, these phenomenal happenings, although real, have no meaning. They could only acquire meaning through the appearance of Godot, that is to say through a positive be-lief in God. Without His appearance or, to be precise, without His existence, life, instead of being as it is—bi-polarised be-tween Being and non-being, is merely non-being and mean-inglessness, or if one likes, absurd, although a very definite type of absurdity. It is, in this context, the absurdity of non-being, that is to say something which can have no reality until the emergence of Being. It is only within Being that non-being can be posited, and in this case the absurdity attached to it is not the absurdity of an atheistic, incoherent world, but the absurdity of the subjective judgments of those who, un-able to find a meaning to creation, refuse to accept the un-avoidable margin of irrationality and mystery which neces-sarily pertains to transcendence, and which divides the finite from the infinite.

The absurdity of the atheist is objective absurdity which can only be meaningless and devoid of any hope, since it is looked upon as pure contingence without any informing substance, therefore without any hope of change. It is condemned to be eternally what it is; it is like Sartre's Hell. In it, men will al-ways be what they are, endlessly repeating the same meaning-less, mechanical gestures which are like phantasmic gestures without real existence, or like the limbo world of Nietzsche's eternal cycles. This view of absurdity can be entertained as a dramatic device, or as a kind of intellectual, protective shell, forbidding questioning and metaphysical anxiety, but this very lack of metaphysical anxiety makes it intellectually un-tenable; for, as previously noted, it turns a concept—that of absurdity—into an absolute. There lies the fundamental dif-ference between the concept of the absurd of Ionesco and Co. and that of Beckett, which is also that of Pascal and Kierke-gaard. These two attitudes have nothing in common, except a name. The world of Beckett is only absurd and meaningless because of the absence of Godot. That of Ionesco is just plain incoherent, mechanical and riddled with fantasies and night-mares, and lacking a centre which is the self-awareness of ab-sence. (pp. 75-6)

The world of Beckett is not allegorical but symbolic; it rests not on transcendental nothingness, but on absent transcen-dence, and on an objective embodiment of certain aspects of modern life. Yet, in spite of this objectivity it remains on the whole a subjective, rather static, non-dynamic, practically non-historical world, in the sense that, although his charac-ters are vaguely aware of their past, they live in a negativated present and have no future. The kernel of realism which, transmuted by imagination, is the basis of the greatness of *Godot,* remains a frozen, fixed point in time. It offers a pro-foundly true picture of man, but it is man already partially caught in spreading ice while the earth itself is being slowly covered by it; it is therefore a terrifying picture of man under the looming threat of fossilisation. Lear also has to go through barrenness, icy lands and night, but he is always fully alive, with a past, a present and a finality which give meaning to his death and to that of Cordelia. . . . The Shakespearian world is objective, true to reality as apprehended through imagination, dynamic, coherent and part of a greater whole implying a finality and justice which preclude absurdity. The world of *Waiting for Godot* could not be described in such terms, its reality, instead of being part of a whole, tends on the contrary to be the whole, which is reduced to an image of nihilism and moving despair within the context of absent transcendence.

Godot, of course, is not specifically God, although his vague attributes could fit any powerful master. His behaviour is un-predictable; he treats well the boy who minds the goats, and beats without reason the one who minds the sheep. He could bring joy or tears, and Estragon fears his arrival. . . . The waiting of the two tramps is not the waiting for a definite human being; it is obviously the waiting for something more. Since waiting is their whole life, nothing else matters, except the anxiety to fill the vacuum caused by the absence of Godot, so their waiting inescapably is a parable of the human condi-tion. "We are not saints; but we have kept our appointment. How many people can boast as much?", says Didi; and Gogo significantly answers: "Billions." (pp. 77-8)

Beckett's vision of man is that of a forlorn species in a more or less advanced state of decay and approaching final paralysis. . . . Beckett is a poet and his imagination trans-mutes reality into a super-reality which has a universal mean-ing. His language is always precise and with subtle rhythms which convey a wide range of human attributes. It moves from the apparent incoherence of Lucky to the violent shouts of Pozzo or the puns, clichés and double-meanings of the tramps. It can both communicate and show the incapacity to communicate or the threat of disintegration, and by so doing it shows of course its vitality, while the poet himself shows his artistry and mastery. Beckett's words can act as a screen behind which lurk ignorance and incomprehension, or as a noise to keep at bay the fear of the dark and silence. Above all, they can suggest what logic and reason cannot express, and as such, they are part of a truly symbolist poem in which language is not only a means of describing and making state-ments, but is the very being of the poem. *Waiting for Godot* is an achievement of a high order and the epigoni who try to emulate it without Beckett's poetic insight cannot but fall back on concepts and abstractions which only serve to under-line the high standards and excellence of the original. (p. 80)

J. Chiari, "Drama in France," in his Landmarks of Contemporary Drama, *Herbert Jenkins, 1965, pp. 49-80.*

ERIC BENTLEY

My *New Republic* review of eleven years ago records my first impressions of *Godot* [see excerpt dated May 14, 1956]. "No doubt," I wrote, "there are meanings that will disengage themselves in time, as one lives with such a work." And, in fact, with time I ceased to believe that the play was "undra-matic" and only "theatrical." . . . My early reading of Beck-ett missed out an essential element both dramatic and moral. I might even blame the error, in part, on Beckett himself, in that his English title does not translate the much more apt French one: *En attendant Godot,* which means *"while* wait-ing for Godot." The subject is not that of pure waiting. It is: what happens in certain human beings *while* waiting. Estra-gon and Vladimir do not only wait. In waiting they show, ul-timately, human dignity: they have kept their appointment, even if Godot has not. A lot of comment on Beckett goes wrong in taking for granted a pessimism more absolute than *Godot* embodies, in other words in taking for granted that Godot will not come. This philosophical mistake produces a mistake in dramatic criticism, for to remove the element of uncertainty and suspense is to remove an essential tension— in fact the essential drama.

So much for the insufficiency of my earlier comments on the play. As for its historic destiny, it is summed up in Polish crit-ic Jan Kott's answer to a questioner who asked: "What is the place of Bertolt Brecht in your [i.e., the Polish] theater?" He said: "We do him when we want Fantasy. When we want Realism, we do *Waiting for Godot.*" This remark might also bring to mind the comment of the English poet and critic, A. Alvarez: "The real destructive nihilism acted out in the [extermination] camps was expressed artistically only in works like Beckett's *Endgame* or *Waiting for Godot,* in which the naked unaccommodated man is reduced to the role of helpless, hopeless, impotent comic, who talks and talks and talks in order to postpone for a while the silence of his own desolation." It is the historic destiny of *Waiting for Godot* to represent the "waiting" of the prisoners of Auschwitz and Buchenwald, and also the prisoners behind the walls and barbed wire of Walter Ulbricht, as also the prisoners behind the spiritual walls and barbed wire of totalitarian society generally, as also the prisoners behind the spiritual walls and barbed wire of societies nearer home. I would add to Alvarez's observation that, in this waiting, there is not only an adjustment to desolation, there is a rebuttal to desolation. Even the Auschwitz prisoners hoped, however improbably, to get out: it is not certain that Godot *won't* come. And what Beckett's work ultimately embodies is this hope. Which again might be contained within the definition of what Kott playfully calls Realism. For, whether they should or not, people do continue to hope for Godot's arrival. (pp. 65-6)

Eric Bentley, "The Talent of Samuel Beckett," in Casebook on Waiting for Godot, *edited by Ruby Cohn, Grove Press, Inc., 1967, pp. 59-66.*

MARTIN ESSLIN

[The revised essay excerpted below was originally published in 1961.]

The French translation of [Beckett's novel] *Murphy,* which appeared in 1947, attracted little attention, but when *Molloy* was published in 1951, it created a stir. Beckett's real triumph, however, came when *Waiting for Godot,* which had appeared in book form in 1952, was first produced on 5 January 1953. . . . Roger Blin, always at the forefront of the avant-garde in the French theatre, directed, and himself played the part of Pozzo. And against all expectations, the strange tragic farce, in which nothing happens and which had been scorned as undramatic by a number of managements, became one of the greatest successes of the post-war theatre. . . . seen in the first five years after its original production in Paris by more than a million spectators—a truly astonishing reception for a play so enigmatic, so exasperating, so complex, and so uncompromising in its refusal to conform to any of the accepted ideas of dramatic construction.

This is not the place to trace in detail the strange history of *Waiting for Godot.* Suffice it to say that the play found the approval of accepted dramatists as diverse as Jean Anouilh . . ., Thornton Wilder, Tennessee Williams, and William Saroyan. . . . (pp. 20-1)

When Alan Schneider, who was to direct the first American production of *Waiting for Godot,* asked Beckett who or what was meant by Godot, he received the answer, 'If I knew, I would have said so in the play.'

This is a salutary warning to anyone who approaches Beckett's plays with the intention of discovering *the* key to their understanding, of demonstrating in exact and definite terms *what they mean.* Such an undertaking might perhaps be justi-

fied in tackling the works of an author who had started from a clear-cut philosophical or moral conception, and had then proceeded to translate it into concrete terms of plot and character. But even in such a case the chances are that the final product, if it turned out a genuine work of the creative imagination, would transcend the author's original intentions and present itself as far richer, more complex, and open to a multitude of additional interpretations. For, as Beckett himself has pointed out in his essay on Joyce's *Work in Progress,* the form, structure, and mood of an artistic statement cannot be separated from its meaning, its conceptual content; simply because the work of art as a whole *is* its meaning, *what* is said in it is indissolubly linked with the *manner* in which it is said, and cannot be said in any other way. Libraries have been filled with attempts to reduce the meaning of a play like *Hamlet* to a few short and simple lines, yet the play itself remains the clearest and most concise statement of its meaning and message, precisely because its uncertainties and irreducible ambiguities are an essential element of its total impact.

These considerations apply, in varying degrees, to all works of creative literature, but they apply with particular force to works that are essentially concerned with conveying their author's sense of mystery, bewilderment, and anxiety when confronted with the human condition, and his despair at being unable to find a meaning in existence. In *Waiting for Godot,* the feeling of uncertainty it produces, the ebb and flow of this uncertainty—from the hope of discovering the identity of Godot to its repeated disappointment—are themselves the essence of the play. (pp. 24-5)

Yet it is only natural that plays written in so unusual and baffling a convention should be felt to be in special need of an explanation that, as it were, would uncover their hidden meaning and translate it into everyday language. The source of this fallacy lies in the misconception that somehow these plays must be reducible to the conventions of the 'normal' theatre, with plots that can be summarized in the form of a narrative. If only one could discover some hidden clue, it is felt, these difficult plays could be forced to yield their secret and reveal the plot of the conventional play that is hidden within them. Such attempts are doomed to failure. Beckett's plays lack plot even more completely than other works of the Theatre of the Absurd. Instead of a linear development, they present their author's intuition of the human condition by a method that is essentially polyphonic; they confront their audience with an organized structure of statements and images that interpenetrate each other and that must be apprehended in their totality, rather like the different themes in a symphony, which gain meaning by their simultaneous interaction.

But if we have to be cautious in our approach to Beckett's plays, to avoid the pitfall of trying to provide an oversimplified explanation of their meaning, this does not imply that we cannot subject them to careful scrutiny by isolating sets of images and themes and by attempting to discern their structural groundwork. The results of such an examination should make it easier to follow the author's intention and to see, if not the *answers* to his questions, at least what the *questions* are that he is asking.

Waiting for Godot does not tell a story; it explores a static situation. [As Beckett states within the play], 'Nothing happens, nobody comes, nobody goes, it's awful.' On a country road, by a tree, two old tramps, Vladimir and Estragon, are waiting. That is the opening situation at the beginning of act I. At the end of act I they are informed that Mr Godot, with whom they believe they have an appointment, cannot come, but that he will surely come tomorrow. Act II repeats precisely the same pattern. The same boy arrives and delivers the same message. (pp. 25-6)

[Yet the] sequence of events and the dialogue in each act are different. Each time the two tramps encounter another pair of characters, Pozzo and Lucky, master and slave, under differing circumstances; in each act Vladimir and Estragon attempt suicide and fail, for differing reasons; but these variations merely serve to emphasize the essential sameness of the situation. . . .

Vladimir and Estragon—who call each other Didi and Gogo, although Vladimir is addressed by the boy messenger as Mr Albert, and Estragon, when asked his name, replies without hesitation, Catullus—are clearly derived from the pairs of cross-talk comedians of music halls. Their dialogue has the peculiar repetitive quality of the cross-talk comedians' patter. (p. 26)

As the members of a cross-talk act, Vladimir and Estragon have complementary personalities. Vladimir is the more practical of the two, and Estragon claims to have been a poet. In eating his carrot, Estragon finds that the more he eats of it the less he likes it, while Vladimir reacts the opposite way—he likes things as he gets used to them. Estragon is volatile, Vladimir persistent. Estragon dreams, Vladimir cannot stand hearing about dreams. Vladimir has stinking breath, Estragon has stinking feet. Vladimir remembers past events, Estragon tends to forget them as soon as they have happened. Estragon likes telling funny stories, Vladimir is upset by them. It is mainly Vladimir who voices the hope that Godot will come and that his coming will change their situation, while Estragon remains sceptical throughout and at times even forgets the name of Godot. It is Vladimir who conducts the conversation with the boy who is Godot's messenger and to whom the boy's messages are addressed. Estragon is the weaker of the two; he is beaten up by mysterious strangers every night. Vladimir at times acts as his protector, sings him to sleep with a lullaby, and covers him with his coat. The opposition of their temperaments is the cause of endless bickering between them and often leads to the suggestion that they should part. Yet, being complementary natures, they also are dependent on each other and have to stay together.

Pozzo and Lucky are equally complementary in their natures, but their relationship is on a more primitive level: Pozzo is the sadistic master, Lucky the submissive slave. In the first act, Pozzo is rich, powerful, and certain of himself; he represents worldly man in all his facile and shortsighted optimism and illusory feeling of power and permanence. Lucky not only carries his heavy luggage, and even the whip with which Pozzo beats him, he also dances and thinks for him, or did so in his prime. In fact, Lucky taught Pozzo all the higher values of life: 'beauty, grace, truth of the first water'. Pozzo and Lucky represent the relationship between body and mind, the material and the spiritual sides of man, with the intellect subordinate to the appetites of the body. Now that Lucky's powers are failing, Pozzo complains that they cause him untold suffering. He wants to get rid of Lucky and sell him at the fair. But in the second act, when they appear again, they are still tied together. Pozzo has gone blind, Lucky has become dumb. While Pozzo drives Lucky on a journey without an apparent goal, Vladimir has prevailed upon Estragon to wait for Godot.

A good deal of ingenuity has been expended in trying to establish at least an etymology for Godot's name, which would point to Beckett's conscious or subconscious intention in making him the objective of Vladimir's and Estragon's quest. It has been suggested that Godot is a weakened form of the word 'God', a diminutive formed on the analogy of Pierre-Pierrot, Charles-Charlot, with the added association of the Charlie Chaplin character of the little man, who is called Charlot in France, and whose bowler hat is worn by all four main characters in the play. It has also been noted that the title *En Attendant Godot* seems to contain an allusion to Simone Weil's book *Attente de Dieu,* which would furnish a further indication that Godot stands for God. Yet the name Godot may also be an even more recondite literary allusion. As Eric Bentley has pointed out, [see excerpt dated May 14, 1956], there is a character in a play by Balzac, a character much talked about but never seen, and called Godeau. The play in question is Balzac's comedy *Le Faiseur,* better known as *Mercadet.* Mercadet is a Stock Exchange speculator who is in the habit of attributing his financial difficulties to his former partner Godeau, who, years before, absconded with their joint capital. . . . [The] hope of Godeau's eventual return and the repayment of the embezzled funds is constantly dangled by Mercadet before the eyes of his numerous creditors. . . . The plot of *Mercadet* turns on a last, desperate speculation based on the appearance of a spurious Godeau. But the fraud is discovered. Mercadet seems ruined. At this moment the real Godeau is announced; he has returned from India with a huge fortune. (pp. 27-9)

The parallels are too striking to make it probable that this is a mere coincidence. In Beckett's play, as in Balzac's, the arrival of Godot is the eagerly awaited event that will miraculously save the situation; and Beckett is as fond as Joyce of subtle and recondite literary allusions.

Yet whether Godot is meant to suggest the intervention of a supernatural agency, or whether he stands for a mythical human being whose arrival is expected to change the situation, or both of these possibilities combined, his exact nature is of secondary importance. The subject of the play is not Godot but waiting, the act of waiting as an essential and characteristic aspect of the human condition. Throughout our lives we always wait for something, and Godot simply represents the objective of our waiting—an event, a thing, a person, death. Moreover, it is in the act of waiting that we experience the flow of *time* in its purest, most evident form. If we are active, we tend to forget the passage of time, we *pass* the time, but if we are merely passively waiting, we are confronted with the action of time itself. . . . The flow of time confronts us with the basic problem of being—the problem of the nature of the self, which, being subject to constant change in time, is in constant flux and therefore ever outside our grasp. . . . (pp. 29-30)

Being subject to this process of time flowing through us and changing us in doing so, we are, at no single moment in our lives, identical with ourselves. . . . If Godot is the object of Vladimir's and Estragon's desire, he seems naturally ever beyond their reach. It is significant that the boy who acts as go-between fails to recognize the pair from day to day. The French version explicitly states that the boy who appears in the second act is the same boy as the one in the first act, yet the boy denies that he has ever seen the two tramps before and insists that this is the first time he has acted as Godot's messenger. As the boy leaves, Vladimir tries to impress it upon him: 'You're sure you saw me, eh, you won't come and tell me tomorrow that you never saw me before?' The boy does not reply, and we know that he will again fail to recognize them. Can we ever be sure that the human beings we meet are the same today as they were yesterday? When Pozzo and Lucky first appear, neither Vladimir nor Estragon seems to recognize them; Estragon even takes Pozzo for Godot. But after they have gone, Vladimir comments that they have changed since their last appearance. Estragon insists that he didn't know them. (pp. 30-1)

In the second act, when Pozzo and Lucky reappear, cruelly deformed by the action of time, Vladimir and Estragon again have their doubts whether they are the same people they met on the previous day. Nor does Pozzo remember them: 'I don't remember having met anyone yesterday. But tomorrow I won't remember having met anyone today.'

Waiting is to experience the action of time, which is constant change. And yet, as nothing real ever happens, that change is in itself an illusion. The ceaseless activity of time is self-defeating, purposeless, and therefore null and void. The more things change, the more they are the same. That is the terrible stability of the world. . . . One day is like another, and when we die, we might never have existed. As Pozzo exclaims in his great final outburst:

> Have you not done tormenting me with your ac-
> cursed time? . . . One day, is that not enough for
> you, one day like any other day he went dumb, one
> day I went blind, one day we'll go deaf, one day we
> were born, one day we'll die, the same day, the
> same second. . . . They give birth astride of a
> grave, the light gleams an instant, then it's night
> once more.

And Vladimir, shortly afterwards, agrees: 'Astride of a grave and a difficult birth. Down in the hole, lingeringly, the grave-digger puts on the forceps.'

Still Vladimir and Estragon live in hope: they wait for Godot, whose coming will bring the flow of time to a stop. 'Tonight perhaps we shall sleep in his place, in the warmth, dry, our bellies full, on the straw. It is worth waiting for that, is it not?' This passage, omitted in the English version, clearly suggests the peace, the rest from waiting, the sense of having arrived in a haven, that Godot represents to the two tramps. They are hoping to be saved from the evanescence and instability of the illusion of time, and to find peace and permanence outside it. Then they will no longer be tramps, homeless wanderers, but will have arrived home. (pp. 31-2)

When Beckett is asked about the theme of *Waiting for Godot,* he sometimes refers to a passage in the writings of St Augustine: 'There is a wonderful sentence in Augustine. I wish I could remember the Latin. It is even finer in Latin than in English. "Do not despair: one of the thieves was saved. Do not presume: one of the thieves was damned." ' And Beckett sometimes adds, 'I am interested in the shape of ideas even if I do not believe in them. . . . That sentence has a wonderful shape. It is the shape that matters.'

The theme of the two thieves on the cross, the theme of the uncertainty of the hope of salvation and the fortuitousness of the bestowal of grace, does indeed pervade the whole play. Vladimir states it right at the beginning: 'One of the thieves was saved. . . . It's a reasonable percentage.' Later he enlarges on the subject:

> 'Two thieves. . . . One is supposed to have been
> saved and the other . . . damned. . . . And yet
> how is it that of the four evangelists only one speaks
> of a thief being saved? The four of them were there
> or thereabouts, and only one speaks of a thief being
> saved. . . . Of the other three two don't mention
> any thieves at all and the third says that both of
> them abused him.'

There is a fifty-fifty chance, but as only one out of four witnesses reports it, the odds are considerably reduced. But, as Vladimir points out; it is a curious fact that everybody seems to believe that one witness: 'It is the only version they know.' Estragon, whose attitude has been one of scepticism throughout, merely comments, 'People are bloody ignorant apes.'

It is the shape of the idea that fascinated Beckett. Out of all the malefactors, out of all the millions and millions of criminals that have been executed in the course of history, two, only two, had the chance of receiving absolution in the hour of their death in so uniquely effective a manner. One happened to make a hostile remark; he was damned. One happened to contradict that hostile remark; he was saved. How easily could the roles have been reversed. These, after all, were not well-considered judgements, but chance exclamations uttered at a moment of supreme suffering and stress. As Pozzo says about Lucky, 'Remark that I might easily have been in his shoes and he in mine. If chance had not willed it otherwise. To each one his due.' And then our shoes might fit us one day and not the next: Estragon's boots torment him in the first act; in Act II they fit him miraculously.

Godot himself is unpredictable in bestowing kindness and punishment. The boy who is his messenger minds the goats, and Godot treats him well. But the boy's brother, who minds the sheep, is beaten by Godot. 'And why doesn't he beat you?' asks Vladimir. 'I don't know, sir.' . . . The parallel to Cain and Abel is evident: there too the Lord's grace fell on one rather than on the other without any rational explanation—only that Godot beats the minder of the sheep and cherishes the minder of the goats. Here Godot also acts contrary to the Son of Man at the Last Judgement: 'And he shall set the sheep on his right hand, but the goats on the left.' But if Godot's kindness is bestowed fortuitously, his coming is not a source of pure joy; it can also mean damnation. When Estragon, in the second act, believes Godot to be approaching, his first thought is, 'I'm accursed.' And as Vladimir triumphantly exclaims, 'It's Godot! At last! Let's go and meet him,' Estragon runs away, shouting. 'I'm in hell!'

The fortuitous bestowal of grace, which passes human understanding, divides mankind into those that will be saved and those that will be damned. When, in Act II Pozzo and Lucky return, and the two tramps try to identify them, Estragon calls out, 'Abel! Abel!' Pozzo immediately responds. But when Estragon calls out, 'Cain! Cain!' Pozzo responds again. 'He's all mankind,' concludes Estragon.

There is even a suggestion that Pozzo's activity is concerned with his frantic attempt to draw that fifty-fifty chance of salvation upon himself. In the first act, Pozzo is on his way to sell Lucky 'at the fair'. The French version, however, specifies that it is the *'marché de Saint-Sauveur'*—the Market of the Holy Saviour—to which he is taking Lucky. Is Pozzo trying to sell Lucky to redeem himself? Is he trying to divert the fifty-fifty chance of redemption from Lucky (in whose shoes he might easily have been himself) to Pozzo? He certainly complains that Lucky is causing him great pain, that he is killing him with his mere presence—perhaps because his mere presence reminds Pozzo that it might be Lucky who will be redeemed. When Lucky gives his famous demonstration of his thinking, what is the thin thread of sense that seems to underlie the opening passage of his wild, schizophrenic 'word salad'? Again, it seems to be concerned with the fortuitousness of salvation: 'Given the existence . . . of a personal God . . . outside time without extension who from the heights of divine apathia divine athambia divine aphasia loves us dearly with some exceptions for reasons unknown . . . and suffers . . . with those who for reasons unknown are plunged in torment. . . .' Here again we have the personal God, with his divine apathy, his speechlessness (aphasia), and his lack of the capacity for terror or amazement (athambia), who loves us dearly—with some exceptions, who will be plunged into the torments of hell. In other words, God, who does not communicate with us, cannot feel for us, and condemns us for reasons unknown.

When Pozzo and Lucky reappear the next day, Pozzo blind and Lucky dumb, no more is heard of the fair. Pozzo has failed to sell Lucky; his blindness in thinking that he could thus influence the action of grace has been made evident in concrete physical form.

That *Waiting for Godot* is concerned with the hope of salvation through the workings of grace seems clearly established both from Beckett's own evidence and from the text itself. Does this, however, mean that it is a Christian, or even that it is a religious, play? There have been a number of very ingenious interpretations in this sense. Vladimir's and Estragon's waiting is explained as signifying their steadfast faith and hope, while Vladimir's kindness to his friend, and the two tramps' mutual interdependence, are seen as symbols of Christian charity. But these religious interpretations seem to overlook a number of essential features of the play—its constant stress on the uncertainty of the appointment with Godot, Godot's unreliability and irrationality, and the repeated demonstration of the futility of the hopes pinned on him. The act of waiting for Godot is shown as essentially *absurd*. (pp. 32-5)

There is one feature in the play that leads one to assume there is a better solution to the tramps' predicament, which they themselves both consider preferable to waiting for Godot—that is, suicide. . . . Suicide remains their favourite solution, unattainable owing to their own incompetence and their lack of the practical tools to achieve it. It is precisely their disappointment at their failure to succeed in their attempts at suicide that Vladimir and Estragon rationalize by waiting, or pretending to wait, for Godot. 'I'm curious to hear what he has to offer. Then we'll take it or leave it.' Estragon, far less convinced of Godot's promises than Vladimir, is anxious to reassure himself that they are not tied to Godot. (pp. 35-6)

When, later, Vladimir falls into some sort of complacency about their waiting—'We have kept our appointment . . . we are not saints—but we have kept our appointment. How many people can boast as much?' Estragon immediately punctures it by retorting, 'Billions.' And Vladimir is quite ready to admit that they are waiting only from irrational habit. (p. 36)

In support of the Christian interpretation, it might be argued that Vladimir and Estragon, who are waiting for Godot, are shown as clearly superior to Pozzo and Lucky, who have no appointment, no objective, and are wholly egocentric, wholly wrapped up in their sadomasochistic relationship. Is it not their faith that puts the two tramps on to a higher plane?

It is evident that, in fact, Pozzo is naïvely overconfident and self-centred. 'Do I look like a man that can be made to suffer?' he boasts. Even when he gives a soulful and melancholy description of the sunset and the sudden falling of the night, we know he does not believe the night will ever fall on him—he is merely giving a performance; he is not concerned with the meaning of what he recites, but only with its effect on the audience. Hence he is taken completely unawares when night does fall on him and he goes blind. Likewise Lucky, in accepting Pozzo as his master and in teaching him his ideas, seems to have been naïvely convinced of the power of reason, beauty, and truth. Estragon and Vladimir *are* clearly superior to both Pozzo and Lucky—not because they pin their faith on Godot but because they are less naïve. They do not believe in action, wealth, or reason. They are aware that all we do in this life is as nothing when seen against the senseless action of time, which is in itself an illusion. They are aware that suicide would be the best solution. They are thus superior to Pozzo and Lucky because they are less self-centred and have fewer illusions. (pp. 36-7)

For a brief moment, Vladimir is aware of the full horror of the human condition: 'The air is full of our cries. . . . But habit is a great deadener.' He looks at Estragon, who is asleep, and reflects, 'At me too someone is looking, of me too someone is saying, he is sleeping, he knows nothing, let him sleep on. . . . I can't go on!' The routine of waiting for Godot stands for habit, which prevents us from reaching the painful but fruitful awareness of the full reality of being.

[We] find Beckett's own commentary on this aspect of *Waiting for Godot* in his essay ["**Proust**" (1931)]:

> Habit is the ballast that chains the dog to his vomit. Breathing is habit. Life is habit. Or rather life is a succession of habits, since the individual is a succession of individuals. . . . Habit then is the generic term for the countless treaties concluded between the countless subjects that constitute the individual and their countless correlative objects. The periods of transition that separate consecutive adaptations . . . represent the perilous zones in the life of the individual, dangerous, precarious, painful, mysterious, and fertile, when for a moment the *boredom of living* is replaced by the *suffering of being.*
>
> (pp. 37-8)

Vladimir and Estragon talk incessantly. Why? They hint at it in what is probably the most lyrical, the most perfectly phrased passage of the play:

> VLADIMIR: You are right, we're inexhaustible.
> ESTRAGON: It's so we won't think.
> VLADIMIR: We have that excuse.
> ESTRAGON: It's so we won't hear.
> VLADIMIR: We have our reasons.
> ESTRAGON: All the dead voices.
> VLADIMIR: They make a noise like wings.
> ESTRAGON: Like leaves.
> VLADIMIR: Like sand.
> ESTRAGON: Like leaves.
>   [*Silence.*]
> VLADIMIR: They all speak together.
> ESTRAGON: Each one to itself.
>   [*Silence.*]
> VLADIMIR: Rather they whisper.

ESTRAGON: They rustle.
VLADIMIR: They murmur.
ESTRAGON: They rustle.
[*Silence.*]

(pp. 38-9)

This passage, in which the cross-talk of Irish music-hall comedians is miraculously transmuted into poetry, contains the key to much of Beckett's work. Surely these rustling, murmuring voices of the past . . . are the voices that explore the mysteries of being and the self to the limits of anguish and suffering. Vladimir and Estragon are trying to escape hearing them. The long silence that follows their evocation is broken by Vladimir, *'in anguish'*, with the cry 'Say anything at all!' after which the two relapse into their wait for Godot.

The hope of salvation may be merely an evasion of the suffering and anguish that spring from facing the reality of the human condition. There is here a truly astonishing parallel between the Existentialist philosophy of Jean-Paul Sartre and the creative intuition of Beckett, who has never consciously expressed Existentialist views. If, for Beckett as for Sartre, man has the duty of facing the human condition as a recognition that at the root of our being there is nothingness, liberty, and the need of constantly creating ourselves in a succession of choices, then Godot might well become an image of what Sartre calls 'bad faith'—'The first act of bad faith consists in evading what one cannot evade, in evading what one *is*.'

While these parallels may be illuminating, we must not go too far in trying to identify Beckett's vision with any school of philosophy. It is the peculiar richness of a play like *Waiting for Godot* that it opens vistas on so many different perspectives. It is open to philosophical, religious, and psychological interpretations, yet above all it is a poem on time, evanescence, and the mysteriousness of existence, the paradox of change and stability, necessity and absurdity. (pp. 39-40)

Martin Esslin, "Samuel Beckett: The Search for the Self," in his The Theatre of the Absurd, *revised edition, 1969. Reprint by The Overlook Press, 1973, pp. 11-65.*

BROOKS ATKINSON

In the first act of *Waiting for Godot* Pozzo inquires of Estragon: "What is your name?" "Adam" is Estragon's reply.

That's one clue to the meaning of Samuel Beckett's ironically ambiguous tragicomedy. . . . There are a few other tangential clues. But *Waiting for Godot* is not to be explained. It is a metaphor of life by a gifted dramatist who can make his enigma seem full of ludicrous portents. And if the theatregoer complains that it is futile, Mr. Beckett can make a similar complaint: that the life of human beings on earth is monumentally futile. A civilization that shines with human ideals cannot be imposed on a natural order that imposes death on everything. (p. 241)

In *Waiting for Godot* four strange people are waiting for something that will never happen. They are two vagabonds, Estragon and Vladimir, who are loitering beside a gaunt tree on a lonely country road; a big shot named Pozzo who is driving an overburdened slave at the end of a rope, and a rather shy messenger boy. When the play begins, Estragon is trying to pull off a boot that is too small for him. The first line of the play is his dogma throughout the play: "Nothing to be done." Estragon and Vladimir keep on talking in simple declarative sentences that mark time. They don't know what they are doing. They don't know who Godot is. (p. 244)

Who is Godot? When the play was new, many people assumed that Godot was God. But Mr. Beckett denies that. He says Godot is a common French name that attracted him when he was writing the play. No matter who Godot may be, the play cannot be explained in objective terms. It is part of the empty eternity Mr. Beckett is describing—an interruption of eternal silence.

If it were taken literally, the play would be depressing. For it says that the civilized life we are trying to create with so much energy and idealism is futile. It will be devoured by the death that consumes everything. But Mr. Beckett is not an angry writer. His image of nothing is comic. We laugh, perhaps in self-defense. The dialogue is pithy, the lazy images are droll, and the whole concept is too grotesque to be accepted without a grin of conspiracy. And we may take note of the fact that the play does not include any women. If it did, life might not seem so empty to Estragon and Vladimir, and there might be some continuity to life—a continuity of banality perhaps, but at least something less dismal than the text of this play describes.

When *Waiting for Godot* opened in New York (after the original productions in Paris and London) the producer had the good taste to cast it with personable actors. . . . The production . . . had a surface of straight-faced seriousness like Mr. Beckett's writing. The production had only fifty-nine performances, for the public had a perverse unwillingness to see itself demolished on the stage. It may prove Mr. Beckett's theory that the public behaved in accordance with the last lines of the play:

VLADIMIR. Well? Shall we go?
ESTRAGON. Yes, let's go.

But they do not go. They continue waiting for Godot. (pp. 244-45)

Brooks Atkinson, " 'Waiting for Godot': Samuel Beckett," in The Lively Years: 1920-1973, *by Brooks Atkinson and Albert Hirschfeld, Association Press, 1973, pp. 241-45.*

RONALD HAYMAN

'Nothing to be done' are the first words spoken in *Waiting for Godot,* and the phrase is repeated twice within the first three pages of dialogue. Virtually every previous play had started from the opposite premiss, that there was something to be done, a mystery to be solved, an injustice to be righted, a crime to be punished, an obstacle to be removed, a pair of lovers to be united. Usually, within minutes of curtain-rise, we were presented with an unsatisfactory situation which could not be allowed to continue; in *Waiting for Godot* we are presented with an unsatisfactory situation which cannot be altered. When Estragon says 'Nothing to be done', he is on the point of giving up the struggle to pull his boot off, but Vladimir's answer comically widens the focus:

I'm beginning to come round to that opinion. All my life I've tried to put it from me, saying, Vladimir, be reasonable, you haven't yet tried everything. And I resumed the struggle.

So the premiss for the dramatic action is that action is useless.

But what constitutes dramatic action? The play provides a new answer to this question. As Tom Stoppard has said, *Waiting for Godot* 'redefined the minima of theatrical validity'. And when William Saroyan saw the play, he said: 'It will make it easier for me and everyone else to write clearly in the theatre.' Beckett made it easier by showing how to erect inaction into valid theatrical action. The act of waiting is itself a contradictory combination of doing something and doing nothing, and if you put a pair of characters on stage, with no apparent objective except to wait for someone, the contradiction can come playfully into play. If the characters are aware that there is nothing they can usefully do, this gives them the basis for a theatrical action. (pp. 1-2)

Though it is often said that nothing happens in *Waiting for Godot*—Vivian Mercier's summary of the two acts is 'Nothing happens, twice' [see *CLC*, Vol. 6]—inaction does not entail inactivity. The four characters who wear bowler hats all have a lot of vaudeville-type business with them, and there is some farcical comedy with stinking boots and stinking breath. Vladimir's diseased bladder compels him to rush off-stage and pee in the wings when he laughs. The entrance of Pozzo and Lucky introduces a great many new props—rope, stool, picnic basket, whip, pipe, baggage—which are all used in preventing the conversation from becoming static, and Lucky's monologue (the only long monologue in a script consisting mainly of very short lines) is violently counterpointed by protests from Vladimir and Estragon and groans from Pozzo, who starts pulling on the rope tied around Lucky's waist until all four of them are in a struggling heap on the ground. Lucky still goes on shouting his text until they silence him by putting his hat on. A small act of violence, such as the kick Lucky delivers to Estragon's shin, is comically inflated, and generally there is no shortage of stage movement, as there is, progressively, in Beckett's later plays.

Side by side with this activity, there is a great deal of game-playing that does not involve much movement. 'What shall we do now?' is, in effect, what Vladimir and Estragon are always asking each other, and some of their improvisations are like children's ways of passing time. They play a game of being Pozzo and Lucky, they play at being very polite to each other, at abusing each other, at making it up, and they stagger about on one leg trying to look like trees. The audience is involved most directly when they look out in horror at the auditorium, but it is involved in the game all through, because Beckett is playing with the fact of having actors on a stage playing roles. Instead of working to keep the audience guessing about what's going to happen next, he gives the impression of having written the play without himself knowing how he was going to go on.

Vladimir and Estragon are not *characters* in the conventional sense of the word. There is more contrast between their personalities than there is between Rosencrantz's and Guildenstern's in Tom Stoppard's comparable play about waiting: Vladimir is more tormented, more idealistic and more nostalgic than Estragon, who is more physically involved with the needs of the moment. But there is no firm outline around either character, and only the scantiest biographical data. They are defined not in relation to time, place, or social circumstance, but in relation to eternity and to human longings for a sense of purpose. From Shakespeare to Brecht, dramatists had operated character casually: for Mutter Courage and Galileo, as for Hamlet and Lear, what happens is partly a result of what they are. With different personality traits, we are made to feel, they would have reacted in such a different way

to the same circumstances that they would not have had the same problems. The problem of Vladimir and Estragon is that they are alive. Like everyone and like Everyman, they are trapped between birth and death. What is happening to them does not seem to be consequent either on a specific set of circumstances (situation) or on their behaviour patterns (character). (pp. 2-3)

The audience, then, is deprived of nearly all its normal sources of theatrical pleasure. In a realistic play much depends on recognising something familiar in people, in places and circumstances. Heroic action encourages us to identify with the heroes. We picture ourselves wielding Orestes's sword or Hamlet's rapier. Beckett gives us nothing we can envy or admire: no courage, no gallantry, no glamorous lovers, beautiful costumes, handsome settings or desirable furniture. There is no possibility of tragedy, even when Vladimir and Estragon consider suicide. There is not much theatrical illusion, and very little suspense. It is even difficult to admire the acting. To the average member of the average audience, the actor playing Estragon is less obviously giving a performance than the actor playing Romeo or Jimmy Porter. Admittedly, all these points could be made about two comedians doing a music-hall act. There is no heroism, nothing to admire and not much illusion. So is it by introducing vaudeville comedy into existential drama that Beckett manages to take away so many of our toys without reducing us to tears? Is this the secret of the alternative distraction that *Waiting for Godot* offers?

In the theatre it is easy to make an impact by doing something that has never been done before. In 1896 when Alfred Jarry's *Ubu Roi* was premièred, the opening word 'Merdre' was—despite the extra *r*—enough to provoke fifteen minutes of pandemonium among the audience. Many of the Dadaist performances at the Cabaret Voltaire and many Expressionist dramas were equally defiant of convention, but a play stands no chance of staying in the repertoire unless its negative gestures are accompanied by positive achievement. Beckett has taken a great deal away but also given a great deal. The sheer quantity of argument and critical writing his work has provoked is itself evidence of its power to intrigue, to engage the imagination. *Waiting for Godot's* resonance depends partly on the impression that the central argument is going on inside a single consciousness. (pp. 3-4)

But if everything seems uncertain, it is partly because the form and rhythm of the dialogue disconcertingly resemble the form and rhythm of internal monologue. The components which normally give opacity to drama have been so attenuated that we can see a consciousness arguing with itself. With setting, plot and character almost at the point of vanishing, the reality of the play is defined entirely by its dialogue, and since we are conditioned into the expectation that drama mirrors reality, the appearance of a dramatic argument in a vacuum carries the implication that there is no reality except the reality created by reasoning. Defining scepticism, Hegel wrote: 'The mind becomes perfect thought, annihilating the world in the multiple variety of its determinations, and the negativity of self-consciousness becomes real negativity.' *Waiting for Godot* is, in this sense, the most sceptical play ever written.

In some of Beckett's novels and stories the analytical commentary acts like acid to dissolve the actuality of the events described. In a play there is no space for commentary: the writer's corrosive irony must be absorbed into the self-deflation and self-parody of the characters. One of Beckett's most astonishing successes in *Waiting for Godot* is in making the lightweight banter of Vladimir and Estragon into a powerful solvent. In their suicide attempt, for instance, reality disintegrates. . . . The style of the writing prevents us from taking the possibility of suicide seriously. The experience that the characters might have seemed to be having is de-realised in the process of enactment, as it might be in a music-hall sketch or a Laurel and Hardy film. But this sequence is not merely farcical. Beckett is making a new mixture of slapstick and theatrical poetry. The poetry depends as much on atmosphere as on words, and as much on its references to the human situation in general as on its development of events involving particular people in a particular place. Jacques Vaché, an eccentric who influenced the Surrealists, defined humour as 'a sense of the theatrical and joyless uselessness of everything, once you know'. If *Waiting for Godot* is sad and funny at the same time, part of the reason is that the functioning of the human consciousness is made to seem not only intrinsically theatrical but intrinsically comic.

In what sense, though, does the play imply an annihilation of the world? Is it even possible to imagine an annihilation of the world? Writing a chapter on 'The Idea of Nothing' in his *Evolution créatrice,* Henri Bergson argued that if you close your eyes, block your ears, and suppress all the impressions that have been flooding in, you remain with an impression of yourself and the present state of your body. If you try to imagine the extinction of your consciousness, another consciousness apparently comes into play, 'because the first could disappear only for the second and in the presence of the second'. You can imagine annihilation only by erecting a viewpoint from which to look at it. Vladimir can watch Estragon asleep, and he can ask himself whether he is dreaming, but he cannot watch himself sleeping, which is one reason for needing Estragon, or, better still, Godot, a witness outside space and time. 'At me too someone is looking, of me too someone is saying, he is sleeping, he knows nothing, let him sleep on.' But the conversation Vladimir has with himself or with Estragon proceeds like Hegelian dialectic. For the movement from thesis through antithesis to synthesis Hegel used the word *Aufhebung,* which means both cancellation and preservation. But for him the significance of the ambiguity was determined by a view of history as guided by spirit. Beckett's ambiguity is different, slung between religious images and agnostic assumptions. References to the crucifixion are recurrent in the dialogue of *Waiting for Godot,* and Estragon says that throughout his life he has compared himself to Christ. In *The Imitation of Christ* Thomas à Kempis quotes *Romans* VI 8: 'Learn now to die to the world that thou mayst begin to live with Christ.' The religious imagery in *Waiting for Godot* has the effect of tantalising the men who have no option but to die, gradually, to the world, tormented by the notion of transcendence but without any means of achieving it.

At the same time, the play is jokily a play about the theatrical situation. As in music hall, but as in few previous modern plays, the performers do not pretend that the audience is not there. The faces in the stalls inspire them with comic horror, but the overall effect is to make the spectator an uncomfortable accomplice in the act of waiting. Why are we sitting there? What are we waiting for? The play to be over? It is partly a play about habit, and we are in the habit of going to the theatre. It is hard to imagine that drama could ever be wholly non-representational or non-referential, but Beckett

was taking an important step towards making the play an object in its own right, pointing insistently and amusingly inwards at the fact of its being a play. The possibility of Godot's coming is no more real than the possibility that Vladimir and Estragon will hang themselves. The self-consciously literary cadences and the recurrent dissolution of character into comedian not only undermine our willingness to suspend disbelief but mock us for having started out with it. Beckett is simultaneously demonstrating the hollowness of the theatrical situation and the humiliating similarity between the procedures of consciousness and a dialogue between two clowns. (pp. 5-8)

Ronald Hayman, "Godot and After," in his Theatre and Anti-Theatre: New Movements Since Beckett, *Oxford University Press, 1979, pp. 1-16.*

EDITH KERN

[The] juxtaposition of the farcical and the tragic, the sacred and the profane, is . . . pronounced in Beckett's play *Waiting For Godot,* whose title itself is a bilingual pun on the English word *god* and the French suffix *ot,* which makes laughable whatever it is attached to, such as Pierre (Pierrot), Charles (Charlot), etc. . . . From the very beginning of the play, Didi and Gogo, its protagonists, engage in farcical stage play and conversations that concern the nature of God. They wonder why, at the crucifixion of Christ, only one of the two thieves was saved and why only one of the Evangelists reported this event. In the midst of clowning, they discuss the question whether man is free or, as they put it, whether they are tied to God or Godot. As if in farcical answer to this serious question, the play's master-servant couple, Pozzo and Lucky, appears onstage tied together by a rope, suggesting by contrast that the friends Didi and Gogo need no tangible tie, while leaving unanswered the questions whether belief in God does need concrete evidence, or whether, indeed, God feels himself tied to man.

But it is above all the speech Lucky gives, upon being prompted by his master, that farcically raises the question of God's relationship to man. We hear him grotesquely juxtapose the sacred with the profane and the scatalogical, when his demented mind turns the pattern of reasoned discourse into farce. His stutter seemingly accounts for such words as "acacacademy" and "anthropopopometry," and yet, the seriousness of his concerns becomes apparent when his speech is stripped of its elements of farce and travesty. He then seems to suggest simply that

> given the existence . . . of a personal God . . .
> with white beard . . . outside time . . . who from
> the heights of divine . . . aphasia loves us dearly
> with some exceptions for reasons unknown . . .
> and suffers . . . with those who . . . are plunged
> in torment . . . it is established beyond all
> doubt . . . that man . . . fades away.

This kind of half-serious, half-playful travesty, which abases dogma, naive belief, and theological authority, is also to be found in the fiction of James Joyce. James S. Atherton has shown that Joyce travestied the litany, the liturgy, and even the "Our Father." . . . On another [occasion] it echoes Germanic languages: "Oura Vatars that arred in Himmel" or "Ouhr Former who erred," to mention just a few of the farcical variations.

Our ears are not too well accustomed to this irreverent proximity of the sacred to the profane. But their juxtaposition not only enables modern authors to speak of serious matters playfully. It also represents a revival of an ancient tradition of which Joyce and Beckett—both scholars of medieval French literature—could not but be fully aware. As suggested above, in the Middle Ages, clergymen clearly enjoyed punning of the kind found in *Waiting for Godot,* and Lucky's speech might well be labeled a *sermon joyeux,* a joyous sermon often delivered by laymen in churches during medieval and Renaissance carnivalesque festivities and grotesquely travestying what was normally considered sacred. (pp. 107-09)

> Edith Kern, "Tears and Laughter in Modern Farce," in her The Absolute Comic, Columbia University Press, 1980, pp. 85-116.

RUBY COHN

[In the following essay], I propose to examine avatars of Beckett's most pervasive verbal device, repetition. In his verse and fiction of the 1930s he anchors an order in repetition, but from 1949 to 1976 he seems to erode order through the relentlessness of his repetition, which is one of his ways "to find a form that accommodates the mess." Moreover, verbal repetition can enhance or counterpoint gestural repetition in drama, but my comments concentrate on what Beckett has called the "wordshed" (in his poem **"Cascando"**).

I would have preferred to ponder repetition as discussed by Deleuze, Freud, Frye, or Kierkegaard, but I find them too distant from Beckett's basic verbal practice—the repetition of sound, word, phrase, sentence, or dialogue segment for quite varied effects. (p. 96)

Repetition—whether repetitious or repetitive—occurs early in Beckett's verse and fiction, but he consciously chose that device for his drama. *Éleuthéria* of 1947 does not call attention to its repetitions; *Waiting for Godot* of 1949 does—at several levels. Act II nearly duplicates Act I; characters appear in couples, and one friend often echoes the other; gestures are repetitive—pacing, sitting, waiting, and especially falling; props are repetitive—derbies, high shoes, ropes, swiftly rising moons. Above all, words are repetitive, so that the inattentive actor may miss a cue and omit or repeat a whole scene; the inattentive spectator, lulled by echoes, may miss their deepening force. Beckett means these repetitions to be experienced in the theater, where the audience can neither skip dull pages nor feed a computer for a quick concordance. (p. 97)

A large preponderance of *Godot's* repetitions occur in the form of *simple doublets,* where a word or phrase is heard again immediately or very soon after first mention. Though *Godot's* Boy speaks no simple doublets, the four main characters do. A simple doublet may be a single word:

> VLADIMIR: Relieved and at the same time . . . (*he searches for the word*) appalled. (*With emphasis.*)
> AP-PALLED.
> LUCKY: . . . alas alas . . .

Or a phrase:

> ESTRAGON: What'll we do, what'll we do! . . .

Emphasis is the intention of these repetitions, as abundant as in everyday speech. But emphasis may blend with emotion;

in the quotations, Vladimir is horrified, Lucky grieved, Estragon despairing, and Pozzo threatening. Occasionally, simple doublets seem merely mechanical:

> ESTRAGON: Come come, take a seat I beseech you.
> VLADIMIR: So much the better, so much the better.
>
> (p. 98)

In the simple doublet the speaker repeats his own words. In *the interrupted doublet* another speaker interrupts the original speaker, who then utters his repetition. Early in Act I of *Godot* Estragon repeats after Vladimir's correction:

> ESTRAGON: Looks to me more like a bush.
> VLADIMIR: A shrub.
> ESTRAGON: A bush.

In the verselike sequences of Act II Estragon repeats, "Like leaves" and "They rustle."

In *the distanced doublet* repetition is delayed too long to be readily recognizable in the theater, as in the following example where the repetition is separated by eighty pages in the Grove Press edition:

> ESTRAGON: What is it?   Yes, but what kind?
> VLADIMIR: I don't know. A willow. I don't know.
> A willow.

Despite its many simple doublets, the dominant rhythm of *Waiting for Godot* is set in the duologues of Vladimir and Estragon, a variant of the vaudeville pair of astute and obtuse comedian—a variant because Vladimir is not always astute, nor Estragon obtuse. As in vaudeville, one friend often echoes the other's words, changing the tone, in *echo doublets.* Whereas simple doublets tend to slow stage time, echo doublets usually propel the dialogue forward:

> ESTRAGON: In a ditch.
> VLADIMIR: (*admiringly*). A ditch!
> VLADIMIR: It'd give us an erection.
> ESTRAGON: (*highly excited*). An erection!
>
> (p. 99)

Decidedly less often than doublets, Beckett resorts to *triplets,* whether *simple* or *echo.* A simple triplet may be sarcastic:

> ESTRAGON: That would be too bad, really too bad.
> (*Pause.*) Wouldn't it, Didi, be really too bad?

Toward the end of Act II a triplet enhances Vladimir's doubt about whether Pozzo is Godot: "Not at all!" (*Less sure.*) Not at all! (*Still less sure.*) Not at all!" This triplet attains a climax impossible in a doublet. So, too, in Pozzo's anaphoric triplet: "Let us not then speak ill of our generation . . . (*Pause.*) Let us not speak well of it either. (*Pause.*) Let us not speak of it at all." (p. 100)

The basic building-blocks of dialogue repetition are simple or echo doublets, which can be extended to triplets, quadruplets, and multiplets; larger units tend to break rhythmically into doublets and triplets, as in the exchange about Lucky's dumbness or Pozzo's blindness. At times, however, multiplets pile up into *a pounder,* spoken by a single character. Lucky's speech is the bravura example, pounding several phrases, most notably "I resume" and "alas." Multiplets may be echoed by one or more speakers in *a volley.* An example occurs early in *Godot,* when Vladimir and Estragon volley the words "two thieves," "the Savior," and "saved." A little later, they volley "tied."

After these new terms, it may be a relief to consider a traditional device of verbal repetition, *the refrain.* The only problem is how to define that familiar device. Though refrains are as old as poetry, they have not been explored in drama. The *Princeton Encyclopedia of Poetry and Poetics,* for example, begins its discussion of Refrain. "A line, or lines, or part of a line, repeated at intervals throughout a poem." Problems bristle. Is a single word a valid "part of a line?" How far should "intervals" be spaced? How many repetitions add up to "throughout?" . . . To be applicable to drama, the *Princeton Encyclopedia* definition should be modified to include awareness of an audience: "A meaningful word or words often repeated during the course of a play, so that the audience grows aware of that repetition."

Doublets, triplets, volleys, and pounders account for the large *quantity* of repetitions in **Waiting for Godot,** but the dense qualitative feeling rests on refrains. Six times (two in Act I, four in Act II) we hear:

> ESTRAGON: Let's go.
> VLADIMIR: We can't.
> ESTRAGON: Why not?
> VLADIMIR: We're waiting for Godot.
> ESTRAGON: Ah!

By now this exchange is the best-known refrain in modern drama. Not only do we hear the whole sequence six times, but each phrase of the sequence (including "Ah!") occurs in other word groups, reinforcing our familiarity. Estragon himself utters an abridged version: "Let's go. We can't. Ah!" . . . [Elsewhere in the play, the word "Godot"] rings out as a refrain-word. Vladimir and Estragon twice mention their wait for Godot; each declares "I'm waiting for Godot" or "I waited for Godot." Vladimir's conversations with Godot's Boy contain ten references to Mr. Godot, and Pozzo twice distorts the name. Inscrutable and invisible, Godot is ubiquitous through his refrain-name. (pp. 101-02)

A *polysemic refrain* turns on the friends' question of "what we do." Seven times Estragon asks "What'll we do?" or "What do we do?" His repetitions may be paraphrased as: "What activity can we initiate?" After Estragon casts doubt on the time and place of meeting Godot, Vladimir exclaims, "What'll we do?" meaning: "How can we know the right time and place?" After their discussion of hanging, Vladimir asks anxiously, "What do we do?" Understood though unspoken is "about hanging ourselves." When Estragon next repeats the question, it may be shadowed with the anxieties of Vladimir, who pronounces the last repetition. In Act II he looks at the three men who have fallen to the ground, and he comments, "A diversion comes along and what do we do?" The meaning has shifted to "How do we react?"

My definition of refrain stipulated audience awareness of these periodic repetitions. Less noticeable than interrogatives are repeated negatives. The French concordance counts 513 recurrences of the particle *ne,* usually translated by English "not" or "n't." Though the English disyllable "nothing" is innocuous, it commands attention by virtue of the thirty-odd repetitions in *Godot.* Both Vladimir and Estragon repeat the play's opening line: "Nothing to be done." Vladimir varies it with "Nothing you can do about it," and Estragon with "Nothing we can do about it." Vladimir sustains that sentiment in such phrases as "We've nothing more to do here," "There's nothing we can do," "There's nothing to do." Estragon sees and hears "nothing" and has "nothing" to show. Vladimir insists he has "nothing" to say to his friend. Each

of the friends comments, "It's not certain," but Estragon declares more ambiguously, "Nothing is certain." This can be paraphrased in two ways: "One can be certain of nothing at all" or "The only certainty is nothingness."

"Nothing" is probably noticeable as a refrain, but probably unnoticeable is a comparable refrain repeated by all but Lucky—"I don't know." Vladimir with his half-dozen declarations of ignorance is outdone by Estragon with his dozen. The latter utters a climactic variant: "I don't know why I don't know."

These several refrains—waiting, doing, Godot, nothing—serve as a warp for the measured woof of doublets and triplets. Two adjectives in thematic tension with the waiting refrain are probably unnoticeable as refrain. The words "true" and "happy" often recur, though the play theatricalizes the unattainability of truth and happiness, and it does so in part by reiterating those very words. Vladimir, Estragon, and Pozzo most often mean "Yes" when they say "True." Vladimir is the first to speak the word, agreeing to button his fly, and Estragon speaks it last, agreeing to pull up his trousers. These key "true"s trivialize truth.

In contrast to "true," whose meaning is mechanized, "happy" retains meaning but is unrealizable. Toward the beginning of Act I Estragon recalls a vision of a happy honeymoon. Toward the middle of Act I Pozzo toasts "Happy days" and analyzes his own happiness. Toward the end of the act Estragon cries out: "I'm unhappy." When Estragon is asleep, Vladimir asks whether the Boy is unhappy. The latter doesn't know, and neither does Vladimir. By Act II, however, Vladimir declares that he was happy when alone, then retracts: "Perhaps it's not quite the right word." In Act I Vladimir was "glad" to be back with Estragon again, but by Act II he enacts a happiness he cannot feel. It is an empty exercise, and happiness soon dwindles to a vanishing point. . . . (pp. 103-04)

Other refrain-words are nouns—boot, hat, bone, carrot, turnip, tree, rope, whip, pipe and its synonyms, watch and its parts—concretely present on stage but metaphorically extended through repetition. Less frequent refrains are Savior, thieves, and Christ with their sacramental associations. The number "one" becomes surprisingly significant through repetition as do the several cries for help and the references to beating, though only an alert spectator will recognize them as refrains. The very theme of repetition is repeated in the innocuous word "again," spoken some dozen times by the two friends and Pozzo. Though the word is too common to function as a refrain, Vladimir performs the rare feat of stressing it in a doublet: "There you are again again!"

Waiting for Godot is woven with repetition. Acts and actions repeat; props, lightings, and settings repeat; words repeat—doublets, triplets, multiplets, in a single voice or two voices; less often, three voices, and almost never four. Only the refrain "nothing" sounds in five timbres.

Although Beckett uses the same building-blocks of repetition for all five characters, the emotional effect is quite different. Vladimir and Estragon repeat to fill their endless wait. Pozzo repeats in mechanical commands to Lucky or faltering explanations to the friends, and the cliché comparison of Lucky to a broken record merely emphasizes the mechanical surface of his speech. This variety of repetition is rarely noticed on a first viewing of **Godot,** but Vladimir's round song and Lucky's monologue obstreperously call attention to themselves—differently structured pounders. The Chinese-box song about the doomed dog in the kitchen can be pounded *ad infinitum* about an infinite number of doomed dogs, and we can readily understand its appeal for one of Beckett's temperament.

Unlike the old dog-song, Lucky's monologue is a highly original structure, however it borrows from the vocabulary of logic, theology, medicine, sports, meteorology. These two pounders contrast; the meaning of the dog-song is soon clear, and each repetition is emphasis. Lucky's speech is [incoherent]. . . . (pp. 105-06)

It is entirely reasonable in Lucky's tirade that the most frequent repetition is "for reasons unknown." The phrase embraces Lucky's own learning and the wait for Godot. Lucky's words are flamboyantly repetitive, and they differ from the repetitions of the other characters in being disconnected from stage time, place, props. Lucky is literally as well as colloquially "out of it." Like vaudeville comedians, Vladimir and Estragon quip about immediacies; even Pozzo, for all his rhetoric, discourses on the visible twilight. But Lucky pounds at Western civilization—both repetitive and repetitious. (pp. 106-07)

Verbal repetition serves Beckett as music, meaning, metaphor. The repetitions themselves are very various, and against that background, singular phrases shatter "as one frozen by some shudder of the mind." (p. 139)

Ruby Cohn, in her Just Play: Beckett's Theater, *Princeton University Press, 1980, 313 p.*

NORMAND BERLIN

That suffering brings wisdom is a characteristic of tragedy; the largest wisdom [Shakespeare's] *King Lear* offers is that no one statement about life can hold, that the question mark must persist and confound. The play has many imperatives, but the interrogative remains most potent, as always in tragedy.

In fact, the play can be described as Lear's progress from imperative *to* interrogative, from the firm ground of a palace to an unlocalized chaotic heath, from a sure sense of self to a confrontation with mystery. That is, Lear's movement in the play is toward the most terrifying boundary situation possible, the abyss of himself. (p. 92)

The heath on which Lear roams . . . has no edge. It is absolutely unlocalized, vague, bare, without landmarks, fully exposed to the storm, as "unaccommodated" as those wandering on it. A dark territory, this heath, so dark that it must be considered both a terranean reality and a subterranean reality, a landscape of the demonic, of Dionysus. In fact, this landscape is *all* boundary, where Lear is living at life's edge, forced to look at himself and at the world as he never did before, forced to ask the large questions about man's condition. Life at the edge is unequivocally terrible for Lear—as it is for Oedipus and Antigone and Phaedra and Hamlet—and it is richly complex. (p. 93)

It would not surprise us if King Lear and the Fool met Samuel Beckett's Didi and Gogo on the heath. They do meet Edgar, disguised as the mad Tom o' Bedlam, a confrontation that has given seemingly strong support to Jan Kott's contention that Beckett can be found in Shakespeare. Edgar—an exile in a cruel world, disguised as the lowest of men in the order of nature, naked as the air that surrounds him, dirty as the road he tramps—fits most easily into a picture of the absurd and grotesque. . . . Kott's ideas are provocative but he pushes so hard to find Beckett in Shakespeare that he sometimes forgets Shakespeare. Shakespeare, of course, contains potential Beckettism, just as Shakespeare contains a wide range of attitudes toward human existence. A more revealing, not to mention more logical, pursuit is to find Shakespeare in Beckett. And perhaps (Beckett's favorite word), *perhaps* the most revealing critical pursuit is to investigate the common ground on which both Shakespeare and Beckett meet. The atmosphere of tragedy hangs over that ground.

Certainly, Edgar (as Tom o'Bedlam) and Didi and Gogo belong on the heath, for all three represent the stripped quality of man, unaccommodated man, the thing itself. In *Waiting for Godot,* however, the heath is not the central scene, as it is in *King Lear;* it is the entire scene, the entire play. In fact, it is a scene presented in one act and then presented *again* in a second act. Beckett seems to be indicating there is nothing else. Another way of saying this is that in *Waiting for Godot* Beckett is dramatizing the condition of man, man frozen on the boundary, all heath, stasis. To recognize this point helps us to understand the basic difference in form between a Beckett play and a Shakespeare play—stasis vs. movement, condition vs. action—*and* it also makes more clear the similarity between *Waiting for Godot* and *King Lear* in evoking the feelings associated with tragedy. If we could imagine Lear and the Fool meeting Didi and Gogo in the beginning of *King Lear* and then meeting them *again* in the central heath scene, we would be close to the Pozzo-Lucky meetings with Didi and Gogo in the two acts of *Waiting for Godot.* The confident haughty Pozzo of act 1 becomes the helpless blind man of act 2; his last word "On"—the word of direction, the word for a journey—indicates his "progress" toward death, the tragic progression of Lear. But the frozen condition of Vladimir and Estragon is no less tragic. They are in a boundary situation, and they will remain there. They are exposed and vulnerable, and will remain so. The unanswered questions haunt them too. In short, moving or stationary, acting or waiting, king or tramp, Elizabethan or modern, tied to a macrocosm or merely tied to a friend, man facing mystery points to tragedy.

Admittedly, Beckett calls *Waiting for Godot* a "tragicomedy." Always a troublesome term, shifting its meaning through the ages, the word itself must be confronted. When Plautus first used the term in his prologue to *Amphitryon,* he was alluding to the mingling of gods (who belong to tragedy) and low characters like slaves (who belong in comedy). The Renaissance latched on to this "mingling" as the essence of tragicomedy, an irregular genre which blurred the neat classical distinctions between tragedy and comedy. When such a classicist as Sir Philip Sidney referred to the genre, he did so with contempt. For him, "mingling kings and clowns" produced "mongrel Tragi-comedy." A formal definition was given to the term by John Fletcher in his letter "To the Reader" which prefaced *The Faithful Shepherdess:* "A tragicomedy is not so called in respect of mirth and killing, but in respect it wants deaths, which is enough to make it no tragedy, yet brings some near it, which is enough to make it no comedy. . . ." This definition points to the importance of endings. Classically, a tragedy ends sadly, a comedy happily; a tragedy ends in death, a comedy in marriage. The tragicomedy that Beaumont and Fletcher wrote was "tragi" along the way but ended as "comedy." And with the years this kind of tragicomedy has been cultivated, with the greater emphasis placed on *how* exactly to manipulate a happy ending from seemingly tragic situations, an emphasis clearly recognizable in eighteenth-century sentimental comedy as well as in modern James Bond melodrama. But this is not the tragicomedy that modern dramatists are writing, nor do those modern writers who use the term take any cognizance of Plautus or Sidney or Fletcher. Ionesco, for example, says that in modern times "the comic is tragic, and . . . the tragedy of man is pure derision." He claims that for him there is no "difference" between "the comic and the tragic." Friedrich Dürrenmatt, who labels his *The Visit* a tragicomedy, believes that in our time the tragic comes out of the comic, that comedy, in fact, brings forth the tragic" as a terrifying moment, as an abyss that opens suddenly." His words "terrifying" and "abyss" traditionally belong to tragedy and indicate how difficult it is to state with any sense of exactness what modern tragicomedy is. Perhaps this is as it should be. "Times being what they are," a world without a center, essentially shapeless, must offer blurred terms for the dramatization of that world. Then again, perhaps the incomprehensibility of our modern world is the proper subject of tragedy. Yes, Beckett calls *Waiting for Godot* a "tragicomedy"; yes, the play contains much comedy—vaudeville turns, clever language, pratfalls, Laurel and Hardy routines; yes, laughter is evoked. But let us not forget that for Beckett, as Nell expresses it in *Endgame,* "Nothing is funnier than unhappiness. . . . It is the most comical thing in the world." Both laughter and weeping produce tears. And as we confront a specific term like "tragicomedy," let us acknowledge Beckett's own distrust of language, his belief that words "falsify whatever they approach." My point is simply this: in Beckett the "tragi" and the "comedy" are tied inextricably one to the other, but the "tragi" overwhelms the "comedy," producing the effect we have been describing as tragic. . . . The effect of a reading of *Waiting for Godot,* the effect of a performance of the play, is tragic. The play prods the ultimate questions; it evokes the secret cause; it forces us to face the fact of mystery. Like *King Lear,* which contains much comedy, often of the same kind as *Waiting for Godot,* Beckett's play is a tragedy.

Like Edgar and Lear, Vladimir and Estragon are characters stripped of those robes that hide all. Unlike Edgar and Lear, they have no connection to society, no place in a historical scheme. For this reason they seem purer representations of unaccommodated man, man ground down to his essence, than Shakespeare's characters, who at least have been connected. Vladimir and Estragon possess none of the superfluities; their existence is comprised wholly of man's basic physical and emotional needs. Beckett, like Shakespeare in *King Lear,* relentlessly emphasizes the physical. Estragon struggles to take off his boot. Periodically, he is physically beaten. Vladimir admires him for having found a good ditch to sleep in. Both men discuss the advantages and disadvantages of eating a carrot. Estragon's feet stink; Vladimir's breath stinks. Vladimir has trouble urinating; Estragon enjoys watching him urinate. And so on. We can ask with Lear: "Is man no more than this?" Well, man *is* this—a this we can never forget or neglect—but he is also more. He needs a friend; he needs to pass the time; he has to look forward to something. No matter how reduced man is, he wishes to believe life has some meaning even though there's "nothing to be done," the play's first words which reverberate throughout the play. He wishes to believe there are answers to questions. And questions abound in *Waiting for Godot,* making up one-quarter of the play. Half of these questions remain unan-

swered, and among these are the questions that touch the ultimate uncertainties. Add to this the many qualifications of statements that are not questions ("What is it?" "I don't know. A willow.") and we have a play whose essence is uncertainty, whose mood is relentlessly interrogative.

In the play's beginning, after Gogo's "Nothing to be done"—which specifically refers to his difficulty in pulling off his boot, but becomes a refrain on man's predicament—Didi addresses himself to Gogo: "So there you are again." To which Gogo replies: "Am I?" This is the first question of the play, two little words that point to a big uncertainty. He is there; no question about that since *we* see him. But who *is* he? (A question which belongs in *Oedipus Rex* and *King Lear.*) And is he there *again?* And is he the same "I" that was there before? Or has he changed since then, whenever that was? (pp. 96-9)

Shortly thereafter Vladimir, the more thoughtful of the two, brings up a biblical "fact" that troubles him and sheds an atmosphere of uncertainty over the entire play: "One of the thieves was saved. (Pause) It's a reasonable percentage." At this moment it is a reasonable percentage, but salvation becomes more uncertain, the 50/50 balance more precarious, when he goes on to wonder: "And yet . . . (pause) . . . how is it—this is not boring you I hope—how is it that of the four Evangelists only one speaks of a thief being saved. The four of them were there—or thereabouts—and only one speaks of a thief being saved." Estragon, obviously less troubled by such problems, more willing to accept mystery as mystery, says: "Well? They don't agree and that's all there is to it." Vladimir, unable to dismiss so easily a moment in the life—the death—of Jesus that has such large implications *for him* (will *he* be saved or will Estragon be saved?) repeats the problem: "But all four were there. And only one speaks of a thief being saved. Why believe him rather than the others?" This emphasis on the unreliability of witnesses informs the rest of the play and brilliantly brings into question the status of those witnesses of that very moment on stage—the audience.

Uncertainty hangs over everything that Didi and Gogo have experienced or thought they had experienced or are experiencing. . . . To be frozen at a precise moment in time, unable to *relate* with assurance to a time past, unable to predict with some degree of assurance a time future, is the worst kind of boundary situation. The self needs time as a frame of reference. Without such a frame, the self *must* say "Am I?" to so commonplace an utterance as "So there you are again." Without such a frame, man's experience has no continuity, and the sheer heaviness of the present moment—without a past or a future—could be unbearable. . . . In *Waiting for Godot* the condition of man is waiting, perhaps another way of saying "enduring," and the activity of man is to pass the time while waiting. Nietzsche was correct, of course, in asserting that the man who has a *why* to live will be able to endure any *how.* . . . In Beckett's play, an artifact that has the pressure of our nightmarish history behind it, the how is waiting, the why is the arrival of Godot. Who or what is Godot is the play's most haunting and important question.

Beckett's answer to Alan Schneider's question "Who or what does Godot mean?" has often been quoted: "If I knew, I would have said so in the play." Schneider should not have expected Beckett to answer the kind of question no writer will answer, and in this case a question that has no specific answer. But Beckett's honest indication that an element in his own creation can be as mysterious to him as it is to his audience should not deter that audience from speculating on the meaning of Godot. The play forces the question on us. And the answers have ranged wide and plunged deep. None should be dismissed—including such seemingly limited, because too precise, beliefs that Godot is De Gaulle or a character in a Balzac play—because the solution to the mystery will never be definitely solved. Beckett's word "perhaps" should inform all our speculations on Godot. Nevertheless, some speculations are more acceptable than others because the play itself allows them to exert considerable pressure. We can make the most general statement, as does William York Tindall, and say that Godot is "whatever man waits for," and we can say with Ruby Cohn that Godot is "the promise that is always awaited and not fulfilled." . . . But a play drenched in uncertainty causes such clear statements to serve as beginnings of larger, perhaps darker, interpretations. Of all the interpretations—and the play has received the attention of critics with every kind of interest, from sociological to existential, from Marxist to biographical—those that touch religion hold the greatest interest. Not only because we as human beings seem to need the illusion of God, need to have explanations, need to know the causes of things, but because the play, with its important biblical allusions and echoes, prods us to consider the waiting for Godot as the waiting for God. Beckett may be playing games with us and our needs, but a view of the play that does not recognize the Christian *trap*pings (a word that is operable, perhaps) seems shortsighted.

Jesus' choice of one of the two thieves, as reported in one of the four gospels, has already been discussed as an important ingredient in the play's atmosphere of uncertainty, here the uncertainty of salvation. The tree on stage, the *only* piece of scenery, makes us think of the crosses on which Jesus and the thieves were crucified, as well as the tree of life and death (since the tree sprouts leaves in the second act and the two tramps discuss hanging themselves from the tree), and the tree of knowledge, and the Judas tree. Estragon says that he has always compared himself to Christ, and he claims that his name is Adam. Pozzo is mistaken for Godot, and he responds to the names of both Cain and Abel. The play is laced with references to the crucifixion, since "to every man his little cross." And the Godot who sends messengers has the characteristics of the Old Testament God; he beats one messenger but not the other, for reasons unknown, just as he was pleased with Abel but not with Cain, for reasons unknown. Of course, the name Godot compels us to think of God. Lucky's speech cryptically but forcefully confronts God. The speech takes on great importance because of the character of Lucky—who says nothing else in the entire play, who is literally tied to Pozzo by a rope and by his status as slave to master, who taught Pozzo beauty and truth, who dances a dance called "The Net," a name which pinpoints his condition and man's condition (as we dance our dances within our harnesses), a name which alludes to the Christian trappings of the speech he will proclaim. Because the speech relentlessly goes on for five minutes, it allows us to *experience* the exhaustion of thought. The thought itself—as we unravel bits and pieces and try to string together clauses and *feel* the pressure of key words—makes us realize the truth of Didi's later statement that "what is terrible is to *have* thought." Lucky's thought is terrible. His speech, despite its grammatical incoherence and the confusion of its end caused by Lucky's physical struggle against Didi and Gogo and Pozzo who try to stop his "thinking," does contain disturbingly recognizable thoughts. Lucky places before us and the three listeners on stage "a personal God . . . with white beard," divinely apathetic, lacking

the capacity for amazement, speechless, who "loves us dearly with some exceptions for reasons unknown," and these exceptions will go to Hell. Man, in Lucky's speech, despite strides in science and art and sports, "wastes and pines wastes and pines . . . for reasons unknown." And the earth, "abode of stones,"—"in the great cold the great dark"—is also dying "for reasons unknown." The speech spurtingly approaches its abrupt end with the refrains "on on" and "the skull the skull the skull the skull" and "abode of stones" and "unfinished," a word repeated again and again in the speech and appropriately the last word of the unfinished speech.

That Lucky's "personal God" could be Godot is learned in the play's last minutes when the Boy tells Didi that Godot has a white beard. Didi's "Christ have mercy on us!" reveals his fear that Godot may be the God that Lucky described. That Jesus himself may be Godot—the Jesus who saves one thief, allowing the other to plunge into hell—is a logical speculation in the light of the speech's progress toward death and the image of Golgotha that it hearkens (the great dark, abode of stones, skull). But Lucky's last word is "unfinished," the opposite of Jesus' "finished," the last word he uttered in the sentence "It is finished" as reported in one of the four gospels. Beckett is suggesting, perhaps, that Jesus was more fortunate than modern man; his agony came to an end, a closure, finished. They crucified quicker in those days, according to Estragon. Modern man's agony, his uncertain thoughts about life and especially about death, seem everlasting. Lucky's speech is intolerable to the three characters on stage because his words stress the fact of mortality and the fact of mystery. ("For reasons unknown" is the most repeated phrase in the speech.) Lucky's speech forces them to see themselves on the cross, with the crucifixion an ongoing condition, unfinished. Lucky must be silenced.

The arrival of Godot would change uncertainty to certainty, would provide answers to haunting questions, would finish unfinished thoughts. In this sense he will "save" man from the perennial condition of living a question mark, living at the boundary between question and answer. (pp. 100-04)

Godot is hearkened in **Waiting for Godot** as often as the gods are hearkened in *King Lear,* and in similar ways. And, as in *King Lear,* capriciousness is emphasized (why punish the sheep boy and not the goat boy?) and fortuitousness (Pozzo's "handy-dandy" statement that he could have been in Lucky's shoes and vice versa) and man's essential helplessness and vulnerability. . . . Also emphasized is death, an important ingredient of tragedy and, for some, what Godot represents. Didi and Gogo, situated between question and answer, between apparent meaninglessness and possible meaning, between present and future, are frozen as well on the boundary between life and death. Beckett presents no specific emblem of death—as Shakespeare does in his pictures of Hamlet holding the skull and Lear holding the dead Cordelia—but the play dwells on mortality. Lucky's speech, though unfinished, progressed "on" toward the skull and the stones. References to the death of Jesus dot the play. Didi and Gogo twice contemplate suicide. They talk about the "dead voices" that make noises "like leaves" . . . "like ashes" . . . "like leaves." . . . The play's two most haunting passages dwell on death. Pozzo in act 2, now blind, bewildered, furiously shouts these words to Didi as he leaves the stage:

> Have you not done tormenting me with your accursed time! It's abominable! When! When! One day, is that not enough for you, one day he went

dumb, one day I went blind, one day we'll go deaf, one day we were born, one day we shall die, the same day, the same second, is that not enough for you? (*Calmer.*) They give birth astride of a grave, the light gleams an instant, then it's night once more. . . . On!

The "On!" leads to one place only, the grave, for the night of the play has come to make even darker the night of Pozzo's blindness. Pozzo's words echo in Vladimir's mind when he comes to the clearest realization of his horribly mortal condition: "Astride of a grave and a difficult birth. Down in the hole lingeringly, the grave-digger puts on the forceps. We have time to grow old. The air is full of our cries." The cries belong to tormented man and to newborn babe, leaving grave-womb with the help of gravedigger-doctor, crying at the first moment air is sucked in, and forever after filling the air with cries. (pp. 104-05)

Despite Beckett's insistent use of repetition (which is both a dramatic device and a theme), time in the play is not standing still, although for Didi and Gogo it seems to. It is going "on" to "the last moment," the promised end. The changed condition of Pozzo and Lucky is evidence enough, but more stunning theatrically is the appearance in act 2 of a few leaves on the previously bare tree. Nature, with time, seems to have some possibility of flourishing; in a wasteland even a few leaves are welcome. Man, with time, grows old and dies, but in his condition he is frozen, for there's "nothing to be done." The image of blooming nature vs. petrified man makes death even more insistent and points to an essential difference between comedy and tragedy, the ongoing quality posited by the former, the certainty of an end in the latter. Because the audience is composed of men—"corpses," "not a soul in sight"—interested more in men than in the tree, the human perspective forces us to place this tragicomedy closer to tragedy. Especially interesting and significant in this connection is the "dog" song that Vladimir sings in the beginning of the second act.

> A dog came in the kitchen
> And stole a crust of bread.
> Then cook up with a ladle
> And beat him till he was dead.
>
> Then all the dogs came running
> And dug the dog a tomb—
>
> *He stops, broods, resumes:*
>
> Then all the dogs came running
> And dug the dog a tomb
> And wrote upon the tombstone
> For the eyes of dogs to come:
>
> A dog came in the kitchen
> And stole a crust of bread. . . .

The structure of the song, like that of many "round" songs, seems cyclical and has been considered cyclical by many commentators who believe the song typifies the structure of the play: two acts, one day like the next, waiting for Godot in both, Pozzo and Lucky appear in both, Boy messenger in both, trouble with boots and hats in both, similar games, night falling at the end of both acts, Didi and Gogo say "let's go" but do not move at the end of both acts. The repetitions put enough pressure on the play to make one day seem like the next. But a closer look forces us to realize that time does flow. (Pozzo and Lucky change, boots are switched, a tree acquires leaves.) Certainly, the activity of act 2 is more desper-

ate, more frenzied than in act 1. And death seems more imminent. A closer look at the dog song reveals that the seemingly cyclical pattern progresses to a song-stopping word, "tomb," repeated more than any other word except "dog." Didi's pauses, his repetitions, put great stress on death, and what seemed a circle becomes a line, inevitably drawing toward the last moment, more precisely, the last resting place. Like Lucky's speech—which relentlessly approaches images of death, the finish, although it is unfinished—the dog song approaches an end, death, although it is circular. Unfinished and finished, circular and linear, these paradoxes, centering on death, receiving added force from the atmosphere of uncertainty, from the question mark hovering over the entire play, tilt the seemingly balanced genre, tragicomedy, toward tragedy. And it is only in the context of tragedy that the question "Who or what does Godot mean?" receives its most satisfying answer. With the two tramps in their frozen condition, waiting for that which will give meaning to their lives, which will change uncertainty to certainty, with the two tramps on the boundary between present and future, life and death, Godot is the ultimate mystery, the answer to the question, the cause that will forever remain secret. Clowns in a tragedy, Didi and Gogo represent bewildered modern man facing the fact of mystery. In the most memorable moment of Peter Brook's Beckettian stage production of *King Lear,* when the blind Gloucester sits cross-legged, alone on the bare stage . . . , modern audiences were able to feel the horror of man's vulnerable condition and to feel pride in man's ability to go on in the face of darkness and uncertainty, even when to go on means to sit on the ground and wait. That is the common ground of tragedy shared by Beckett and Shakespeare. (pp. 105-07)

Normand Berlin, "Boundary Situation: 'King Lear' and 'Waiting for Godot'," in his The Secret Cause: A Discussion of Tragedy, *University of Massachusetts Press, 1981, pp. 87-107.*

PER NYKROG

When Samuel Beckett rose to international fame as a playwright following the first performance of **En attendant Godot** in January 1953, it was the disconcerting radicalism of his dramaturgy, and the unsurpassed negativity of his scenarios that struck one's mind. This perception has lingered on in the critical literature on this strangely powerful writer—from the early landmark book [*The Theatre of the Absurd*] by Martin Esslin [see excerpt dated 1969] to the most recent contributions to Beckett studies—and is confirmed and even reinforced by Beckett's later production, in which the search for an ever more reduced stage presence, and an ever more bleak outlook, appear as a natural development of what had been Beckett's hallmark from the outset. Cryptic utterances by the author (on the rare occasions he came out of the seclusion that has been his personal lifestyle) further corroborate this understanding of him—treasured tidbits, such as this early sample (1949), that have fallen into the hungry critics' bowl:

> BECKETT: The situation is that of him who is helpless, cannot act, in the event cannot paint, since he is obliged to paint. The act of him who, helpless, unable to act, acts, in the event paints, since he is obliged to paint.
> DUTHUIT: Why is he obliged to paint?
> BECKETT: I don't know.
> DUTHUIT: Why is he helpless to paint?

BECKETT: Because there is nothing to paint and nothing to paint with.

(pp. 289-90)

[One] may ask, now, more than thirty years after the first performance of *Godot,* when the first shock has subsided and even become absorbed, whether the time has not come to take a fresh look at Beckett's early plays and see if Esslin was right to give his "salutary warning to anyone who approaches Beckett's plays with the intention of discovering *the* key to their understanding, of demonstrating in exact and definite terms *what they mean,*" or to state as a basic fact that **Waiting for Godot** and **Endgame** are "plays drained of character, plot, and meaningful dialogue," a "seemingly impossible tour de force" of doing something with nothing. Over the years a sort of Beckett orthodoxy has developed along these lines. . . . My contention in the following discussion is that, on the contrary, the early plays by Beckett not only deal with something, they have an articulate and identifiable scope. An "intertextual" reading, making use of what seems to be the text behind the text, can help both the identification and the articulation.

It is well known that Beckett is no uncouth savage: indeed, when he started writing his plays, he was an unusually brilliant, cultured and complex academic, carrying a heavy load of the literary and cultural past. In order to reach the state of utter denudation he displays in his later scenarios, he had to rid himself of a rich and complex heritage. (p. 290)

That **Waiting for Godot** (*En attendant Godot,* 1949) carries a certain burden of philosophizing is evident on even a cursory reading: frequent allusions to Christ and to the Passion and an unmistakable preoccupation with salvation are there for all to see on the surface of the dialogue. A religious dimension, however warped, is obvious in the play. It is strongly confirmed by the syllable 'god' in the name of the mysterious offstage character whose presence (or absence) is the key to the entire situation represented. . . .

The clue is so substantial and so promising that it attracted the attention of the interpreter-detectives right away. But though it remains highly significant in itself, it did not seem to lead anywhere; upon investigation, it lost its contour or underwent unexpected and bewildering transformations. When asked about the meaning of the name, Beckett threw one inquirer off the track by saying that it had to do with *godillot,* a military boot, and as early as 1956, another investigator (Eric Bentley) traced the name, and even the title of the play, back to Balzac's comedy *Mercadet, ou le faiseur* (1848), about a wheeler-dealer businessman who is deep in debt because his partner, Godeau, has absconded with the better part of their liquid assets [see excerpt dated May 14, 1956]. (p. 291)

The trail leading to Balzac is good enough—it is extremely improbable that the resemblance is mere coincidence—but it is totally disappointing: there is absolutely no contribution to the understanding of **Godot** to be found in that text. It is, however, instructive in a different connection: it does prove (if that was necessary) that Beckett was not averse to playing the game of the abstruse literary quote. He must have borrowed his title, and the name Godot, from *Mercadet,* and he does not seem to care whether or not the reader or the spectator will grasp the allusion. Who, after all, could be expected to know his *Mercadet* by heart in 1950?

A more fruitful approach, here as in so many other cases,

would be to leave aside for a while the finer points of detail and take a good look at the scenario as a whole. A clue as big as a barn door is easily overlooked, but that does not make it less important.

The stage in **Godot** represents a road. A road is the archetypal metaphor for a movement, a development, a "progress" (pilgrim's or rake's) which takes someone from one place (or state) to others. What is particular about the scenario in **Godot** is that the main characters, Vladimir and Estragon, Didi and Gogo, refuse to make use of the road according to its purpose. They do not move along it; they stay where they are, and where they seem to have been for a long time, totally idle and mortally bored, but stubborn, remaining in spite of all the frustrations and sufferings that make their existence by the roadside so utterly miserable. And why are they blocked there, in the reduced existence that is theirs? They are, obviously, waiting for Godot. (pp. 291-92)

The parable of the virgins, in Matthew 25, is part of the last teaching Christ gave to his disciples before the events of Easter: the following chapter tells of the betrayal by Judas and the Last Supper. The scene is Jerusalem, the occasion a visit the group has made to the Temple. Three evangelists record Jesus' words, but Matthew's account is by far the most detailed. It is a truly terrifying text, one of those that Christians who like their comfort tend to overlook. The theme is the Return of the Son of Man—Doomsday. To the reader who (somewhat incongruously) comes to this immensely important text from the text of **Godot,** with its numerous allusions to the Gospels, a surprising number of details seem to correspond. It is as if **Godot** had been elaborated with the two chapters from Matthew fresh in mind:

There will be "the abomination of desolation." Compare the entire setup in **Godot.**

"For there shall arise false Christs, and false prophets." Compare Pozzo; could he be Godot?

"Now learn a parable of the fig tree; When his branch is yet tender, and putteth forth leaves, ye know that summer is nigh." Compare the leaves that come out on the tree between the two acts of **Godot,** perhaps announcing the Spring.

"Then shall two be in the field; the one shall be taken, and the other left." Compare "it's a reasonable percentage" and the following discussion.

"Watch therefore: for ye know not what hour the Lord doth come." Compare the anguished and obsessional waiting in **Godot.** (p. 293)

In the parable of the talents which follows [the parable of the Virgins], the Lord is seen as "an hard man, reaping where [He has] not sown, and gathering where [He has] not strawed," which matches the total ruthlessness of "Godot" in general (remember that the name also made Beckett think of a *godillot*). This parable leads up to Christ's final fulmination:

> And before him shall be gathered all nations: and he shall separate them one from another, as a shepherd divideth his sheep from the goats: And he shall set the sheep on his right hand, but the goats on the left. . . . And these shall go away to everlasting punishment: but the righteous into life eternal.

Compare the explanation given by the boy in Act I of **Godot** (inverted!): "Mr. Godot" ill-treats the boy who minds the sheep, but not the boy who minds the goats.

The disciples died without seeing these cosmic events, in spite of the explicit promise that Christ had given in the course of His teaching: "Verily I say unto you. This generation shall not pass, till all these things be fulfilled." And many are the moments in history when faithful Bible readers have prepared themselves for the Second Coming—which has never materialized. Didi and Gogo in Beckett's play are less ambitious; all they hope for is to be taken in by a generous host who will feed them and keep them warm. . . . (pp. 293-94)

But alas: Beckett leaves us no doubt that these two simple-minded gamblers will be left there alone for all eternity, holding the bag after a cruel but sustained hoax closely resembling the one perpetrated by means of the Gospels. . . . There is one good that they have sacrificed, however: the use of the road, the movement, the development, the *progress*. It may not be able to take them anywhere, but at least it offers the entertainment value of activity, of choice, and of change.

At least theoretically. For Beckett has taken care of that aspect, too, in his play. In fact, the picture of Didi and Gogo blocked there on the spot occupies only a little more than half of the text; the remainder is dominated by two very different figures, Pozzo the master and Lucky his servant—or rather his slave.

The circumstances under which they appear in the French version of the play are worth observing closely. Gogo, the naïve one, suggests that he and Didi are *tied* to Godot. Didi, the intellectual, more expert at lying to himself and to others, denies this indignantly. At the very moment the word *lié* is first proffered, a faint noise is heard from a distance. A few moments later we learn what it was: the grotesque tandem of Lucky, carrying miscellaneous luggage, and Pozzo, holding him on a long leash and driving him forward with a whip. (pp. 294-95)

Of all the strange brainchildren sprung from Beckett's mind, this couple is the most unforeseeable, the most bizarre. Pozzo is in some ways the more easily understandable, in spite of a number of weird details: he is the "man of property," the master, slave of his role as a master, slave of the rules that circumscribe the admissible behavior of a distinguished person, and, when it comes to it, even the slave of his slave. Lucky is a being so utterly miserable that the existence of Didi and Gogo in their endless waiting seems almost attractive in comparison. When Pozzo and Lucky finally leave, and we are alone again with Didi and Gogo, we feel relief to such an extent that it almost feels good—at least for a short while.

Didi and Gogo are tramps, homeless vagabonds, and their dialogue in the beginning of the play makes us understand that their waiting takes place somehow on the lands dominated or owned by the mysterious, almighty Godot. So we are surprised when we learn from Pozzo that *he* considers himself to be the owner of the entire region: to Pozzo, Godot obviously does not count—he may not even exist. Pozzo knows very well that to Didi and Gogo, Godot is a reality, and he uses that knowledge to keep them from running away from him in disgust. But otherwise Godot is nothing to him—or at most a vague, hypothetical usurper.

Pozzo has artistic pretensions, especially in the direction of resonant literary rhetoric. But much to their surprise Didi and Gogo are informed that, of the two men tied together by the rope, it is Lucky, the dehumanized, beastly pack-carrier, who is the creative, performing artist: "What do you prefer?" Pozzo asks, "Shall we have him dance, or sing, or recite, or think, or—."

Lucky's dancing performance is miserable, but we are told that in the past, "he used to dance the farandole, the fling, the brawl, the jig, the fandango and even the hornpipe." These are mostly folk dances, later adopted by upper-class culture, but it is striking that most of them are known to us primarily as movements in dance suites from the days of Purcell, Handel and Bach. All of a sudden we get a strange impression that Lucky's glorious days as a dancer must have been very long ago indeed.

A similar impression can be extracted, with some difficulty, from the garbled and tattered philosophical discourse with which he entertains the party a moment later. Messy, rambling and confused as it may appear, Lucky's philosophical lecture nevertheless has a rudimentary logical backbone. If one removes the tangle of digressions, repetitions and "footnotes in the text," his reasoning can be pared down to this essential line:

> Given the existence . . . of a personal God . . .
> who from the heights of divine apathia . . . loves
> us dearly . . .
> considering . . . that man [in spite of progress] is
> shrinking and at the same time is growing
> smaller . . .
> And considering . . . that in the plains in the
> mountains by the seas . . . the air is the same
> and . . . the earth . . .

At this point the reasoning becomes totally unclear, contrasting rocks ("the earth abode of stones . . . the stones so blue so calm") and skulls ("alas alas on on the skull the skull the skull the skull"). The beginning has a familiar ring, and so has the end. Lucky starts from something not unlike the premises to Leibniz's problem in the *Theodicy* and ends up stating something that comes very close to Camus's concept of the Absurd. Leibniz raised the problem of the presence of evil in a world created by a God who is almighty, omniscient, and all-good; Camus found that the world is obviously constructed in a way that is incompatible with man's basic demands for truth, justice, and clarity. Leibniz found that what we perceive as evil are the relatively minor side effects of causes that, on the whole, generate more good than evil; Camus stated that the presence of man in the world constitutes a situation of absurdity; Lucky seems to be on the brink of concluding that, considering how man has been reduced lately ("the dead loss per head since the death of Bishop Berkeley being to the tune of one inch four ounce per head . . . round figures stark naked in . . . stockinged feet," "la perte sèche par tête de pipe depuis la mort de Voltaire étant de l'ordre de deux doigts cent grammes par tête de pipe,"), God must have created the world for the rocks, not for human beings.

Again there is a lurking presence in the text of elements pointing to the mid-eighteenth century, confirmed by the two names used to indicate the time of the starting point: Voltaire (*Candide,* 1759) and Berkeley (d. 1753). (pp. 295-97)

What we have in the couple Pozzo and Lucky is a hideous concretization on the stage of the relationship between master and slave. Hegel analyzed that relationship in his *Phenomenology of Mind* (1807), an analysis that was taken up and reinterpreted with enthusiasm by Marx and later [summarized in *The Encyclopedia of Philosophy,* Volume III]:

> The slave is forced to work, whereas the master can enjoy leisure in the knowledge that the slave is reshaping the natural world to provide the products of his labor for the master to consume. Thus, the master's leisure protects him from experience of the negativity of nature, whereas the slave, in struggling with nature's recalcitrance, learns its secrets and puts his mind into it. The master, in consuming, destroys; the slave, in working, creates. But the master's consumption depends on the slave's work and is thus impermanent, whereas the slave's labor passes into things that have a permanent existence. Hegel argued, too, that the slave's work in transforming the natural world is a consequence of his fear of the master, who can kill him. Death is overcome by the works of civilization.

Beckett's setup is a caricature of this, a cruel mockery of Hegel's noble line of thought. The master still contemplates getting rid of his slave, preferably by killing him; but if Lucky was once a creative mind (in the time of Voltaire or Berkeley?), he has since been reduced to the state of a helpless, even mean, beast: a proletarian.

A couple of apparently insignificant details can take us one step further. Pozzo owns a manor; he is obviously a landowner, a country squire. But he seems to prefer roaming aimlessly along the roads with his slave in constant search of company, for left to himself he is not worth much. He has three obsessive occupations, two of which have a familiar look: consulting his watch—"a genuine half-hunter, with deadbeat escapement," i.e., a large, old-fashioned pocket watch—and puffing on his pipe. Substitute the elegant eighteenth-century manner of enjoying tobacco for the more recent way, and the profiles of Jacques the Fatalist and his Master (the two characters, not Diderot's dialogue as such) begin to appear vaguely behind Pozzo and Lucky: " . . . il ne savait que devenir sans sa montre, sans sa tabatière et sans Jacques: c'étaient les trois grandes ressources de sa vie, qui se passait à prendre du tabac, à regarder l'heure qu'il était, à questionner Jacques: et cela dans toutes les combinaisons."

Diderot's couple can be seen as an idyllic manifestation of Hegel's strange theory (with the exception of the servant's fear of being killed by his master). This may not have been Diderot's intention, but his text sustains the comparison: Jacques is obviously far superior to his master in creativity and in insight. Beckett's couple, by contrast, is as far removed from *Jacques* as the waiting for Godot is removed from the experience of a live and authentic religious faith.

What are we to make out of this irruption in an otherwise clear-cut and homogenous scenario? For Pozzo and his slave come on stage as an alien element. In spite of the (uneasy) dialogue between the two couples, they remain strangers to each other: to the two bums waiting for Godot, the tandem is only a half-real phantasm passing by, and to the two travelers, the men standing by the roadside are like a relatively insignificant part of the landscape. They are different worlds, different species.

A brief glance at the history of ideas may suggest a fruitful line of thought. It is a commonplace that the eighteenth century—the Enlightenment—marked the end of the absolute predominance of a transcendental, God-centered understanding of the world. The process had been on its way for a long time (led by those who refused to "wait for Godot," but chose to move along the road of progress), but not until the generations following after Voltaire, Berkeley, and Diderot did the new, liberated Man "kill God," take his world out of the hands of God (the Revolution, Napoleon, etc.). Didi and Gogo in their waiting for Godot quite obviously "represent" the age-old Christian hope and expectation: Pozzo and Lucky, by contrast, "represent" (less obviously) what came out of progressive humanism and Enlightenment.

This almost allegorical reading probably should not be pushed too far down into the details of Beckett's text; it certainly does not explain the words exchanged between the two couples. It is worth mentioning, however, that the differences in the situation between Act I of the play and Act II are very unevenly distributed over the two contrasting couples. For Didi and Gogo the changes are slight: as far as they are concerned there was no pressing need for a second act—we had understood the monotony and the emptiness of their waiting long before the end of Act I. Not so for Pozzo and Lucky: the two acts show them in a process of rapid and radical deterioration. When they come back, Pozzo is blind and Lucky has become dumb, silenced: "He can't even groan."

A trait as important as that has to be significant, and it is not difficult to imagine what its significance could be. In Didi and Gogo, Beckett gives a cruel caricature of the Christian illusion, but it is nowhere near as cruel as the caricature he gives in Pozzo and Lucky of what had once been secular humanism. With time, the hopeful waiting by the roadside has become a pitiable and miserable emptiness; but compared to the other couple, the two bums are quite likeable: at least they are *friends,* side by side, sharing their common lot, supportive of each other. Pozzo and Lucky, by contrast, who do not have an overriding transcendental relationship with which to structure their world, have established a structure within their relationship to each other. Didi and Gogo are *tied* to Godot; Pozzo and Lucky are *tied* to each other, in a relationship which fatally takes the form of domination and subjection—inequality—a "social contract" which is unpleasant and damaging from the outset, and which furthermore leads the partners, locked together in a mutually destructive embrace, down the road to a hideous and totally perverting decline.

Juxtaposed as it is here to the rotting cadaver of what was once progressive humanism, the bleached bones of the long-lost Christian hope come to appear almost attractive. (pp. 297-99)

Per Nykrog, "In the Ruins of the Past: Reading Beckett Intertextually," in Comparative Literature, *Vol. 36, No. 4, Fall, 1984, pp. 289-311.*

JOHN RUSSELL BROWN

[*The essay excerpted below was originally presented as part of a lecture series at the University of Michigan during the academic year 1984-1985 to celebrate Beckett's eightieth birthday.*]

When I read **Waiting for Godot** for the first time, in 1955, I was nonplussed; but, nevertheless, after a couple of years, I began to plan a production of the play. Peter Hall's presentation in London had not encouraged me because its mixture of music hall acts, meaningful statements, and slow-moving narrative had shown me other values than those which had disturbed and silenced me. Nor did the lively discussion that followed that first production do more than widen the context in which I felt insecure because the critics were concerned mostly with the text's obvious and detachable symbols.

After reading only a few pages, I had known that I had been "appalled." This had been suggested by the very first stage direction and the words that follow:

> *Estragon, sitting on a low mound, is trying to take off his boot. He pulls at it with both hands, panting. He gives up, exhausted, tries again. As before. Enter Vladimir.*
> ESTRAGON: (*giving up again*). Nothing to be done.
> VLADIMIR: (*advancing with short, stiff strides, legs wide apart*). I'm beginning to come round to that opinion. All my life I've tried to put it from me, saying, Vladimir, be reasonable, you haven't yet tried everything. And I resumed the struggle. (*He broods, musing on the struggle . . .*)

That was not how characters were introduced in the plays I knew at that time. The interchange of words seemed accidental, and only one of the two speakers seemed to hear the other. And how could the one who listened know what was meant by the one who spoke? Still more strange was the opening stage direction: how long would all this quiet business take to enact? *"Panting"* is not an action established in a brief moment. *"Exhausted"* is not a direction to put into effect easily, and again it takes time. And *why* should the boot fail to move? What obstacle did Estragon encounter, if any? I asked these ordinary, practical questions and became more sure that I had lost my bearings. (pp. 25-6)

[Beckett often makes use of dramatic silence in *Waiting for Godot;* most] alarming or appalling are silences which are followed by words or actions that have little or no continuity from what precedes them: the characters have become nonplussed until something accidental happens—perhaps Estragon's boot comes off—or some new topic for talk rises without apparent connection as if welling up from the subconscious of the character or possibly of the author. After Vladimir's "This is getting alarming," the next words are his: "One of the thieves was saved. (*Pause.*) It's a reasonable percentage. (*Pause.*) Gogo." His mind has moved at a tangent, for reasons unstated: old worries or old consolations have surfaced, claiming the effort of speech, and make play for present consolation by means of attempted communication.

At the end of each act, Vladimir and Estragon seem ready to accept silence and attempt nothing more. They stay stock-still at the end of their dramatic lives without further recourse to speech or movement; their act is finished, played out if not completed. . . . (p. 27)

At one time I was almost sure that Vladimir and Estragon stayed together at the end of each act because they had sensed, in these last moments, that what they needed above all else was each other's company. But I think now that this interpretation sentimentalizes the play. Although actors can relish and communicate the bond that holds the two characters together, the business of making this narrative apparent in performance slows down the action, creating rhythms of behavior that require more time than the rhythms of the spoken text and the patience of audiences will permit. I have sat through a sentimental production of *Waiting for Godot* that lasted well over three and a half hours.

I suspect that both characters have spoken during each act, "in such a place, and in such a world," all that they "can manage, more than they could" and that this is why the play ends. Here I have adapted Beckett's comments about the main characters of *Endgame* to explain those of *Waiting for Godot* because I suspect that the action of both dramas is to draw its characters into a position where no more is possible. If each other's company has helped to bring them this far, their sense of this can take them no further; the end of the play is no occasion to celebrate togetherness, and actors should not be encouraged to take time along the way to respond too hopefully to each other's presence or moments of verbal agreement.

Waiting for Godot is not about the relationship of its characters or the story of their lives, and it does not state any theme or argument. It is rather a presentation of how these characters have been set in motion and speech by their author, on "A country road," with "A tree," at "Evening" on two successive days. Thus, the action of the play is the action of its author's mind at a certain place and time in our present world, given certain dramatis personae as postulates: it is no more, and it seems to be no less.

This dramaturgy holds attention by discrete disciplines, by the economy with which each item of stage reality speaks for itself. In one sense, Anton Chekhov's *The Cherry Orchard* also presents its characters as its author's mind directs, and story and argument are only a small part of its appeal; and it, too, finishes with silence. Bur Firs, the character onstage, together with the visible reality in which he is placed, is not sufficient to bring the play to a close. The audience is forced to think of other realities as well—and the consequences of events for other lives and other times:

> FIRS: [*of Gaev*] Gone off in his light overcoat. (*Sighs anxiously.*) I should have seen to it. . . . Oh, these youngsters. (*Mutters something which cannot be understood.*) My life's gone just as if I'd never lived. . . . (*Lies down.*) I'll lie down a bit. No strength left. Nothing's left. Nothing. Ugh, you—nincompoop! (*Lies motionless.*) *A distant sound is heard, which seems to come from the sky, the sound of a breaking string, slowly dying away, melancholy. It is followed by silence, broken only by the sound of an axe striking a tree far away in the orchard. Curtain.*

The oddity and particularity of Chekhov's language are in contrast to the complete simplicity of Beckett's conclusion to *Waiting for Godot,* where "trousers" is the only word that is not a monosyllable that could be found in a child's reading primer. (pp. 28-30)

In Beckett's plays, action is constantly arrested in silence, and it is brought to a close with unusual simplicity. So the reader or audience is left in possession of little more than what has happened at each moment in the play; no concluding summary or widening vision is provided to put the experience into a further context. At the end there is no more to say or do.

When I read *Waiting for Godot* for the first time, I found this way of writing amazing and unprecedented, and I am still of the same mind. How can Beckett lead us so convincingly to those states of consciousness, to theatrical images which are so complete in their simple elements that they haunt us insistently?

First of all, in this art of the nonplus, I would identify Beckett's ability to stay with chosen elements until each has been tested to the point of destruction. It is no accident that Estragon and Vladimir have talked throughout the play of "going" and have not managed to do so; Pozzo also had known that he "must go" and needed a great deal of encouragement before he could do so. All this earlier drama is echoed in the play's last moment: "Well? Shall we go? . . . Yes, let's go. *They do not move.*" These are characters who have moved cautiously but persistently toward the very end of their tethers. Just before the final curtain falls, they and the audience are brought sharply to a halt as these lines of thought tauten and, giving no more, hold them still and silent. No sound of a breaking string in the air, and no fall of an ax or whip offstage are relevant at that terminus. No "if" is spoken to mitigate the completeness of the moment.

The next feature of this style is its fierce exactness: no detail is unconsidered. Beckett has been observed at rehearsals mouthing the text of **Happy Days** before the actors could speak it although he did not hold a script in his hands. He could prompt more quickly than the stage manager who did hold the book. He knew the placing of a comma, which was unnecessary for making sense, but timed a speech one way rather than another. So exhaustive is his control over language that actors and directors can rely on the change from "Well," to "Well?" at the end of **Godot** with the same assurance that they would give to an exactly placed and fully explicit direction in the text of another dramatist—such as *"He enters" "He shouts"* or *"He falls down."*

Each word is used so precisely that phrases, made of common elements, are rendered uncommonly memorable. Moreover, the placing of each silence provides a moment of comparative rest in which the shape of the preceding talk becomes isolated and its self-sufficiency is recognized—like a completed unit in a musical composition. By means of a sequence of silences, the shape of a whole play begins to become apparent: rhythms are established and recognized, echoes are heard, structures are defined, and the musical form of words are perceived. By the interaction of words and silences and the absence of ordinary reassurances, the minds of an audience move backward and then forward in time and in and out of what is audible and visible. By these means it may come to comprehend and, in some degree, share the author's sense of a play's balance, of that consciousness which depends on going the whole journey and completing the necessary exploration.

Beckett has used silence, I suspect, because it is part of our lives, a necessary element of any individual's attempt to cope with an inner, uncertain self and with the disorder and the (sometimes more frightening) order which lie outside that self. But he had to force silence into the theater. It is not a natural element in those public, noisy, celebratory, holiday theaters, where the "players cannot keep counsel" but must tell all that their author knows in torrents of words and eye-catching exploits. It also seems foreign to those other theaters which delight their audiences with colorful, lively, and unlikely fantasies. But Beckett has shown that silence is also a part of the theater's birthright as it is a part of our lives. He did this by taking infinite pains and by waiting long years for a very small theater to attempt to stage **Godot** for a small audience.

Silence had been used previously only with elaborate supporting devices or only for the most fleeting effects. But Beckett has used both silence and words with such authority that today almost every dramatist follows his lead confidently. (pp. 31-2)

Of course, the increased use of silence in our theater is due in part to the influence of film and television, in which the camera can direct attention without the help of words. But such moments could not have been transferred to the theater so readily had not Beckett and others after him worked precisely and slowly to control silence by the simplest of means. Beckett is like a painter who reduces his palette in order to dwell on the quality of a single color, the play of light on the canvas, and even the apparent difficulty with which the paint is handled. He has refined the attention we bring to all theater representations and to ourselves.

I have spoken so far only of Beckett's use of very simple verbal elements, and before going further, I must correct one impression that this may have given. Words are not for him fixed or finite in sound or effect. He turns them over and over, as they are repeated, so that they become more polished, refined, opaque, varied, or treacherous as the play proceeds. (p. 33)

Beckett's characters breathe an air that is full of cries from former days and different occasions, and these seem to rise into life only to die once more, leaving the speaker stranded with nothing more to say or do. Even when a speaker, like Lucky or Pozzo, consciously attempts to speak with eloquence or passion, the purposes of speech can go awry or be mistaken. Words seem to turn around and achieve either more or less than the speaker intended; the effect is often to stop speech altogether. . . . (pp. 33-4)

Beckett's alarming and invigorating carefulness; his discipline, patience, and precision; and the consciousness we have of his controlling, purposeful command enhance every element of the drama and give to each an importance beyond the ordinary. His plays seem to be full to their brims, full to the limits of the means he uses. Only with such economy can a dramatist search out what happens when no more can be thought honestly or presented coherently.

All this means that the burden placed on actors is more than usually severe, but the contribution that they make is also more than usually crucial for the success of a production. Actors for Beckett's plays must have a technical and imaginative finesse to respond to the finesse of the text: nothing may be slurred or ill-judged; nothing can seem capable of being other than it is. The smallest details of performance have to be attuned to the smallest details of the text, but, more than that, the actors must also go beyond the text in creating living creatures to inhabit and flesh out Beckett's roles. When an actor is able to do this, without contradictions at least and without noticeable effort beyond what the text requires be shown, then an extraordinary event happens because, beyond the text, the embodiment makes its own statement in unprecedented ways. Performance reveals, without fuss or confusion, living concomitants for Beckett's words. In both fleeting and deep-set impressions, the singular beings of the performers become absolutely present as they fulfill selflessly the technical requirements which are as rigorous and demanding as those of any other text that I can call to mind. The outward manifestation of this act of creation may not be large or amazing in itself in much the same way that Beckett's verbal language may seem, before he has put it to his own use, to be ordinary and even commonplace; but when inhabiting these fictions, an actor becomes close to Beckett's mind, and that brings into play the actor's most secret and most individual responses—I think that is why the best actors of Beckett's plays become his friends and associates. (pp. 36-7)

Good actors enjoy Beckett's plays because in them the subtlest modifications of voice, look, posture, breathing, or even pulse rate can become apparent and powerful. It is like discovering a new palette or a new dimension where previously it had seemed that nothing further could be done; and then these new powers are taken to the point where they, too, can achieve no more.

The success with which Beckett has taken theater toward those alarming, probing, delicate, and deeply felt moments of nonplus is evident in the flock of imitators that have pressed forward, as best they may, toward the same destination. For twelve years I was responsible for reading new scripts submitted to the National Theatre in London, and that showed me how pervasive his influence has been, not so much in direct imitation of form and substance—even the youngest or the most struggling playwrights can usually see how difficult *that* example is to follow—but in the handling of incidental exchanges when inner tensions are being established and, still more frequently, at the end of plays. (pp. 37-8)

> *John Russell Brown, "Beckett and the Art of the Nonplus," in* Beckett at 80 / Beckett in Context, *edited by Enoch Brater, Oxford University Press, 1986, pp. 25-45.*

GEOFFREY STRICKLAND

Often when I read Beckett or watch one of his plays or films I feel as if my world were disintegrating; which is, of course, a tribute to his art. To take Beckett seriously can be a shattering experience and salutary if what is shattered in the process are illusions we are better without. But can one take Beckett seriously? For many the answer would appear to be no: fifty years of experiment with avant-garde writing have produced, according to this view, nothing which is not boring, bogus and merely lugubrious. For others it is at the very least paradoxical: that is to say, Beckett may be facetious to the point of nihilism (or vice-versa) but facetiousness or nihilism as witty and eloquent are more easily deplored than forgotten. He disturbs us if only because he leaves us seriously wondering what seriousness is. I think it would be a tribute to Beckett himself, as he enters his eighty-first year, a tribute certainly to the youthfulness of his intelligence, to assume that this more thoughtful view of the matter was one that corresponded to his own. It is a view which remains open to the possibility that what his most dismissive critics are saying could be true, even truer than they themselves realise. Art as original as this runs the risk of utter failure. . . . The questioning view of Beckett is not, however, one with which anyone, whether more or less favourably predisposed towards him, could remain content for very long; for it makes of him not a mystery (and he is, surely, for all his preoccupation with ultimate realities, among the least mysterious of writers) but an enigma. The more disturbing one finds him the more compelling the need to answer the question: should one take him seriously? Seriousness in art is not, we know, the same necessarily as bitterness or misery, even unrelieved misery like that of almost every new piece of writing by Beckett over the past thirty years. Misery, even sincere misery, can be found in art which is merely amateurish. Does enjoyment of the art entail

contemplation of some inescapable truth? And what if those academics are right, who place him among the great classics of our literature? There is little uncontroversial one can say about the writers of the canon but we can usually agree that they give meaning in some way to human destiny, however terrible; whereas the glorious thing about Beckett's art, we are often told, is that it undermines the very means by which meaning is engendered; it shows us the delusive artificiality of all the stories we tell about one another, both false and ostensibly true. . . . If Beckett is in any way a serious artist, his art is, presumably, of the kind of which Eliot speaks in 'Tradition and the Individual Talent', the art which 'modifies' the 'ideal order' formed by the 'early monuments'.

The question is, of course, which work of Beckett's has this power? There is no obvious consensus among his admirers as to which is his *Macbeth* and which his *Titus Andronicus*. . . . The sardonic epigrams and the farcical or terrible moments which have this quality are scattered throughout his entire *oeuvre*, including his best known play **En attendant Godot,** the play that brought him international acclaim. If one wishes to raise the question of Beckett's ultimate seriousness there is perhaps then no better way of beginning than to ask in what sense *Godot* itself, whether it is performed or read in private, comes over to us as the work of a serious artist.

Whatever else we understand by this expression, I think we can assume that it means a work which holds our attention and concentrates it on what could conceivably matter to anyone, whether this is for tragic or comic effect. Anything, of course, might matter to anyone, depending on particular circumstances and needs. How or when one is going to get one's next drop of spirits can matter very much if one happens to find oneself in a certain dependent condition; even the question of how or whether one is going to get one's boot off one's foot. (pp. 13-15)

A play about an ordinary mortal seeing how he could buy or cadge a drink would not be a serious play; a play about an alcoholic to whom it seemed a matter of life or death might well be. . . . A play showing a man trying to get his boot off and realising he was too old and weak to do it on his own might also, in so far as it was about growing old, be serious. At the beginning of *Godot,* the struggle of Estragon with his boot is quite different. It's an effective piece of theatre, i.e. a gift for even the moderately accomplished actor, but it would be naïve to take it tragically. . . . There are critics, none the less, who do find illumination in a literal understanding of the tramp's splendid *phrases*. The novelist Robbe-Grillet, for example, notes approvingly the remarks by Vladimir that there are 'worse things than thinking . . .' [see excerpt dated 1965 in *CLC*, Vol. 10]; though it is a compliment to Beckett's sophistication to assume that the tramps' sententiousness is part of the comedy and, as such, part of the play's overall effect. And it would be preposterous to argue that it's not serious because, to this extent, the play happens to be funny.

One of the main reasons for questioning the seriousness of *En attendant Godot* is the following. As we know (and this is, of course, in no way an objection to it) it is a play without the dénouement that traditionally comes in the third or fifth acts. Significantly, there are only two. It's a play that leaves us asking a great many questions and that drops what might seem like a number of hints as to their answer; especially during the questioning of the little boy who comes on to bring a message from the unseen Godot himself. It has in this respect a certain amount in common with the novel by Robbe-Grillet which inaugurated the age of *le nouveau roman, Les Gommes* which appeared in 1953, the year of the first performance of Godot. Many critics claim that it is a serious play because of the questions it leaves us asking; but I think the objection to this is that these are not questions about the human condition but simply about the meaning of the text. The most obvious question of all is, of course, not who is Godot? The word 'God' can stand for many different things. . . . The crucial unanswered question is what do the tramps themselves believe Godot to be? How does Vladimir, for instance, believe or imagine that Godot has communicated to him the instructions to wait by the tree? Do they see him, as certain believers see God, as the only being who can give meaning to their lives? Is he merely someone who they hope might fill their stomachs and let them sleep on his straw? Are they waiting above all because they have no particular reason for moving on? How much does it matter to them, in other words, whether or not Godot appears? To answer these questions, we would need to know more about Vladimir and Estragon than the text of the play reveals: far more about what it is like to be them. Beckett originally thought of calling the play just *En attendant* and brought in the notion of 'Godot' later. But a play which was just about 'waiting' could obviously not be serious or even interesting. . . . Bringing in 'Godot' makes it a lot less pointless . . . but it still leaves us wondering if it's about anything that matters very much, even to the two main characters.

Yet it is a play, we are often reminded by its critics and any competent director, in which we are acutely aware of the physical presence of the four main characters. The stage directions are both eloquent and precise. The bare décor and the intense lighting throw our attention on to the four oddly-dressed bodies; and at the same time, by depriving us of the means of answering the questions raised by the play, the play brings us back helplessly to the simple fact of their being *there*. (pp. 15-16)

It is doubtful, however, whether this argument can be taken very far either. Obviously, the comic choreography of the play is one of the most remarkable things about it and the sheer physicality not only of the action (if 'action' is the word) but of the dialogue as well: Vladimir's elaborate plans, for instance, of how they might hang themselves in order to achieve erection. However, in so far as this is true, Beckett is working at a disadvantage compared with artists whose performance depends on their own bodily presence, their own barely perceptible movements and the timing of what they do and say. The Vladimir and Estragon we recreate in imagination from the text or that an actor will try to impersonate are mere phantoms unless the actors happen to be actors of genius. . . . (pp. 16-17)

The theory that it is the presence, the sheer *Dasein* of Estragon and Vladimir that the play offers, in the final analysis, has the disadvantage too that the human body is never just a body and the eye of the spectator never a passive recorder like the film in a camera. One of the most obvious things we can say about Vladimir and Estragon is that though they are recognisably tramps, they are tramps such as we have never seen or heard of before; so that if, as spectators, we are fascinated by their physical presence, it is partly, if not entirely, because, in the very act of looking at them, we are asking ourselves what in the world they are.

Perhaps it is in this curiosity which the appearance of Beckett's two lugubrious clowns arouses and which almost everything they say arouses as well that we can find the play's *raison d'être* as well as the reason for its success. It is a play in which all the expectations we bring to the naturalistic theatre or the theatre of ideas are aroused only to be disappointed and yet in which the attention of whole audiences has been held from beginning to end. The means by which suspense is created are numerous and varied, including changes of idiom, register and mood: the build-up, for instance, of indignation and pity in the first of the Pozzo and Lucky interludes leading up to the moment when the play seems about to dissolve into recognisable humanitarian sentiment of the most deplorably reassuring kind; until suddenly, as Estragon goes to wipe away Lucky's tears, he receives his terrible kick on the shins. One's attention is held also by jokes which are unfinished and patent contrivances for filling the time, as well as a few wonderfully inventive gags of the Monty Python variety, such as the prevention of Lucky's voluble 'thinking' by the forcible removal of his hat. The activity of 'thinking', like the state of being 'human' are the subject of some of the best jokes in the play and give it that air of sardonic sophistication which discourages us or which, at least, ought to discourage us from looking within it for philosophical or human significance.

To the extent that it is often a good idea to laugh people *out of being serious, Godot* could perhaps be thought of, paradoxically, as, after all, a serious play and this despite, even because of, the volumes of serious learned commentary it has inspired. But to this extent only. It is, on this view of the play (which is the one I happen myself to find the most convincing), an impressive theatrical diversion, in which one of the main jokes is at the expense of the audience itself. The more knowing members of the audience, when I first saw it in 1956, could be heard laughing when Vladimir observed, after Lucky's and Pozzo's first exit, that their appearance had 'passed the time'; at the tramps' occasional fear that they may having nothing more to say to one another . . . and when the curtain went up for the second act and revealed the bare tree now covered with a few conspicuously artificial leaves. I can only assume that they were laughing at the sheer audacity of the actors and of all those responsible for the evening's entertainment. There must have been, of course, also those who were impressed by what they saw as a religious allegory, a modern Jansenist allegory perhaps in which Godot was not only hidden but conceivably non-existent or mortal and fallible. And those who, like my French companion on this occasion, were intrigued by being caught between both kinds of reaction, rather excitingly unsure. Whatever the reaction, in the kind of theatre represented by Beckett, the audience places itself willingly at the playwrights' and actors' mercy. It allows its emotions to be worked upon freely and its philosophical curiosity aroused. It allows itself to be exploited and hence to gain a common identity as a group. (pp. 17-18)

All theatrical audiences, of course, achieve a conscious collective identity of some kind but the kind of audience which fifty years ago, might have hissed *Godot* off the stage had defined and established its own identity before it went into the theatre, sometimes merely by putting on evening dress. The playwrights and actors were to a far greater extent at the mercy of the audience and compliant to the audience's view of what was decorous and reasonable and the result was naturalistic comedy and drama of a highly conventional kind. The success of *Godot* like the success of the plays of Ionesco and Pinter is an interesting cultural phenomenon in so far as it represents the evolution of the audience into a group finding its identity in the theatre rather than in the world outside. The members of the audience may be drawn mainly or exclusively from what it may still be possible to describe as the bourgeoisie, but it is not any more than the audience at a Rock Festival, collectively a bourgeois audience. A bourgeois audience would have been demanding a farce like the farces of Feydeau or Courteline or else a 'serious' play. (pp. 18-19)

Geoffrey Strickland, "The Seriousness of Samuel Beckett," in The Cambridge Quarterly, *Vol. XV, No. 1, 1986, pp. 13-32.*

Andrei (Georgievich) Bitov

1937-

Russian short story writer, novelist and poet.

In his writing, Bitov combines elements of nineteenth-century Russian Romanticism and twentieth-century post-modernism. Much of his fiction features a character identified by critics as a contemporary Russian Everyman—an alienated, bourgeois, urban individual seeking love, identity, or community. Most commentators laud Bitov's technical skill, particularly his mastery of sophisticated narrative techniques as well as his ability to imbue ordinary objects with deep significance in the manner of Marcel Proust. Karen Rosenberg remarked: "Through his persistent refusal to offer readers an easy out, Andrei Bitov joins the ranks of the best, uncompromising modernists."

Bitov was born in Leningrad during the "terror" of 1936-1937 orchestrated by Joseph Stalin after the assassination of a high-ranking communist official. Primarily a poet in his youth, Bitov began writing short stories under the more lenient administration of Nikita Khrushchev and is most often associated with the "youth prose" group that arose in the Soviet Union in the 1960s. These writers used expressionism and negativity to flout the rule of socialist realism, which demands optimistic, straightforward narratives illustrating the progress of the state toward achieving the socialist ideal. Instead, Bitov's works highlight the guilt, isolation, and pervasive sense of chaos he attributes to his generation because of the brutal sociopolitical atmosphere in the Soviet Union under Stalin. Consequently, although Bitov was allowed to publish his short fiction during the 1960s and 1970s, his novel *Pushkinsii dom* (1978; *Pushkin House*) was repeatedly rejected for official publication because of its "excessive subjectivity. . . . and lack of moral purpose." *Pushkin House* circulated in *samizdat*, the underground system for printing and distributing banned books, until 1988, when it was officially printed by the prestigious Soviet journal *Novy mir.*

Life in Windy Weather (1986), Bitov's first volume in English translation, contains stories selected from two of his earlier collections, *Dni cheloveka* (1976) and *Sem' puteshestvii* (1976). Thematically and stylistically connected, these pieces often feature protagonist Aleksei Monakhov's attempts to end his radical isolation through the discovery of love, stability, identity, or community. In reference to one of the stories in this collection, Robert A. Maguire observed: "The adolescent of 'The Idler' speaks for all of Mr. Bitov's heroes when he complains that everyone 'has a lonely and merciless path. . . . One-person plus one-person—equals two one-persons.' "

The title *Pushkin House* refers to the Leningrad museum dedicated to the seminal nineteenth-century Russian poet Aleksander Pushkin, where a crucial segment of the story is set. The title also refers to the body of famous Russian literature, often referred to as "the house that Pushkin built," much of which is alluded to throughout the narrative. The book begins with the death of Bitov's protagonist, Lyova Odoevtsev, in a duel, then recounts his progression from childhood to

this apparent death. Near the conclusion of the novel, however, the initial pages are repeated, and Lyova is miraculously revived in time to meet the author. *Pushkin House* has been compared to Laurence Sterne's irreverent eighteenth-century novel *Tristram Shandy* for its unusual narrative structure which encompasses broad shifts in style, extensive digressions, plot reversals, essays in literary criticism, and frequent authorial intrusions. John Updike commented: "Bitov contrives a microcosmic hyperactivity of phrase, sentence, and image which is, even through the hazy scrim of translation, engagingly vital."

ROBERT A. MAGUIRE

It was seeing Fellini's movie *La Strada* that helped Andrei Bitov decide to chuck the detested career of geologist for that of writer. He says in an autobiographical note at the beginning of [*Life in Windy Weather*], "For the first time I was witness to the possibility of the contemporary expression of contemporary reality." Like many other Soviet prose writers who started out in the 1960's, Mr. Bitov avoided such topics as World War II, social heroics, political corruption and labor camps, exploring instead the mundanities of daily life. A Leningrader, born in 1937, he has produced one novel, *Pushkin House* . . . and several volumes of stories. Now we have the first collection of his work ever published in English, well translated by various hands. It reveals a writer of impressive power, subtlety and originality.

Though brought together from various sources and different times, the stories in *Life in Windy Weather* are connected thematically and stylistically, and read like chapters of a single novel. Each is narrated by or through a central character in a different stage of life, from childhood to middle age. That character is male (with one exception), a city dweller (mostly Leningrad), a successful professional (technologist, writer or bureaucrat), with a family and a circle of friends (including mistresses) and perks that set him squarely in the Soviet privileged class, though not in the elite. As an adolescent, he is "overcome by the feeling of being at loose ends, of alienation and uselessness" (**"The Idler"**). What he says he wants has presumably been instilled by the Soviet system: to be "like everyone else." Because he is not, he sometimes craves punishment: "I have no right to walk among people and pretend I am like them. They should isolate me or something. Put me in prison . . . ?" These feelings carry into adulthood, and are emblematized in the surname the narrator often bears: Monakhov (monk). What makes this hero especially interesting in the Soviet context, though not unique among writers of Mr. Bitov's generation, is his growing awareness that he cannot look to others for definition but is finally responsible for himself.

Far from being plotless, as some critics have complained, the stories are structured around quests: for an unattainable woman (**"The Door"**), for family stability (**"The Forest"**), or for the secret of an old man's life (**"The Soldier"**). These quests are either furthered or, more often, thwarted by various encounters. Along the way, the hero's mind is flooded with images from the outside world—with sensations, emotions, thoughts and even "thoughts about thought" that teem within him. As an intellectual, he expects his experiences to make sense and provide guides to action. But the conventional boundaries of time and space, the ordinary acts of judgment, even the ability to make simple choices, elude him. What really matters is the process itself of experiencing the workaday world in all its detail.

Few Russian writers since Tolstoy and Chekhov have registered commonplace emotions and sensations with such fine tuning. (Perhaps this is why Mr. Bitov's treatment of love is more compelling than anything that I have read in Soviet literature to date.) And we have to look back to Yuri Olesha and Nabokov for comparably sensitive evocations of the texture and feel of ordinary objects. As a result, we almost always believe in the palpability and reality of these worlds, even when the characters do not.

The adolescent of **"The Idler"** speaks for all of Mr. Bitov's heroes when he complains that everyone "has a lonely and merciless path. . . . One-person plus one-person—equals two one-persons." Being Russians, these bewildered men wish to believe that the world possesses a unity, despite all evidence to the contrary. Only rarely is this belief confirmed here. For instance, in **"Infantiev,"** the best of the stories, a solidly placed official who has treated his wife with indifference, even contempt, finds that he misses her painfully once she is dead. At the cemetery he happens upon a woman (coincidence being rampant in this writer's work) who had been in a similar marriage situation. When words fail them, they discover intuitively that their absent spouses still create an overpowering sense of presence in which they can both share.

Like generations of Russian writers, Mr. Bitov frequently locates the possibility of communion in the world of childhood. In [**"Life in Windy Weather"**], the hero is himself a writer who feels estranged from the world and cannot work. Suddenly and inexplicably he acquires the capacity to view his surroundings through the eyes of his infant son, and grasps that everything is filled "with meaning and life." This truth is embodied in the simplest of objects—a train, a cow, a meadow—and is ultimately communicated to all present through a humble piece of fluff, like dandelion fluff. . . .

It may well be, as Priscilla Meyer states in her useful introductory essay, that the "real hero" of these stories is "literature," but only if we take that to mean Mr. Bitov's ability, so brilliantly realized on nearly every page, to reveal the extraordinary in the ordinary. This collection provides splendid testimony to his achievement.

> Robert A. Maguire, "One Plus One Equals Two Ones," in The New York Times Book Review, September 14, 1986, p. 33.

KAREN ROSENBERG

It would be condescending to call Andrei Bitov the greatest living Soviet writer. But it might also be true. The categories of Soviet literature fail to describe him adequately: although he emerged from the "Young Prose" movement of the 1960s, his writing is less self-consciously trendy and less cloyingly moralistic than most literary products of that school. In fact, Bitov's subtlety sets him apart. [*Life in Windy Weather*] is not as striking as his novel *Pushkin House,* now being translated into English. One fears that his stories, like Chekhov's, may be overlooked by readers hooked on gross effects.

Part of this author's discretion may derive from the fact that the hero of many of his stories, Alexei Monakhov, is a man of small emotions. As alienated as any Western, urban anti-hero, he vaguely wanders from skirt to skirt, uncommitted even to the search for love. Romance is a feeling from youth he occasionally recalls—and Bitov brilliantly conveys the way childhood slowly decays in each adult.

The Soviet housing shortage has produced overcrowded conditions but not a sense of community, in Bitov's prose. Monakhov's long waits for lovers in frigid stairwells and his awkward moments with them in packed apartments gain humor through constant repetition. In **"The Garden," "The Third Story," "The Forest,"** and **"The Taste"**—all part of *The Lover, a Novel with Ellipses,* and so placed consecutively in this volume—the middle-aged Monakhov is frustrated by missed opportunities. Gradually it also becomes clear that the prized goal of privacy will provide no satisfaction to a man who, sometime or other, misplaced his ability to feel, and can't even remember when. Bitov implies that constructing more buildings won't solve the problems of Soviet society. It's not hard to see why this author has displeased orthodox materialists in the Soviet Union. Franz Kafka—the archenemy of Stalinists and neo-Stalinists in the Soviet camp—is present in Bitov's repeated image of an estranged man, and is even named in the story entitled **"Notes from the Corner."** . . .

A screenwriter, [Bitov] carries images from film into his prose fiction: forgotten memories are called frames lost; recognition is described as the playback in reverse of a filmed sequence. Yet neither film, nor poetry, nor nature are romanticized by Bitov as the sure site of the beauty and authenticity that his characters lack. Through his persistent refusal to offer readers an easy out, Andrei Bitov joins the ranks of the best, uncompromising modernists.

Karen Rosenberg, in a review of "Life in Windy Weather," in Wilson Library Bulletin, *Vol. 61, No. 2, October, 1986, p. 69.*

CHARLES ROUGLE

It is gratifying to note that Andrej Bitov, who was immediately acclaimed one of the most promising Soviet "Young Prose" writers of the early 1960s, is now also receiving due recognition from translators. [*Life in Windy Weather,* edited by Priscilla Meyer,] includes **"Infantiev"** and **"Life in Windy Weather,"** the only two stories available in English thus far, and adds eleven more short works from the period 1960-80.

Bitov calls several of his longer works "novels," but perhaps "novel with ellipses," the subtitle of the third section (*The Lover*) of Meyer's collection, more accurately describes his favorite compositional structure, which consists in a series of autonomous or semi-autonomous works linked together more by theme and narrative modality than by plot in the conventional sense. This inherent tendency in all of Bitov's prose is sensitively observed in the selection and arrangement of the stories in *Life in Windy Weather,* and it imparts to the volume a cohesion that allows it to be read as a single work.

Its development from story to story reinforced by similarities of setting (Leningrad or its environs) and characters (the autobiographical Aleksej Monaxov and his family), Bitov's central theme is consciousness—the inner workings of the process by which the individual attains growing awareness of self, external reality, and the obscure but vital truths that give existence deeper intelligibility and meaning. The hypersensitivity and feeling of isolation from his fellows that are established as salient features of Monaxov as a child in **"The Leg"** are developed further in his portrait as an adolescent in **"The Idler,"** where his first attempts to define himself lead to expressions of alienation and morbid self-deprecation that inevitably and despite Bitov's own disclaimers recall Dostoevskij. Partly, perhaps, to shield himself from the findings of this sort of probing, Monaxov develops an unconscious ability to suppress painful thoughts and emotions. In **"Penelope,"** his shabby treatment of a girl obviously in distress demonstrates this mechanism at work. Only when it is too late to repair the damage he has done does he gain any insight into his behavior. Infantiev, the middle-aged, well-established title-character of the next story, completes a similar odyssey. . . .

[In **"Life in Windy Weather"**], the problems of identity, awareness, and emotional maturation adumbrated in the earlier stories acquire new depth and complexity in a portrait of Monaxov—now a writer—that at the same time eloquently formulates Bitov's view of art. Depicted through an intricately interwoven tapestry of images, themes, and motifs . . . , Monaxov at last succeeds in overcoming the flaws in his consciousness through a recapturing of the naive, childlike astonishment that Bitov defines as the essence of creative inspiration.

It is not far from this romantic view of art as a rediscovery of the wellsprings of being to the notion that the creative quest is basically religious in nature, and in the next work (**"Notes from the Corner"**) insight into the interpenetration of the aesthetic and religious dimensions emerges as a major theme. Realizing as he reflects upon the experience described in **"Life in Windy Weather"** that he has thus far been futilely laboring to attain a view *of* himself, Monaxov now is able to achieve a view *into* himself, and there within finds the God he thought he had lost.

The stories in *The Lover* (**"The Door," "The Garden," "The Third Story," "The Forest," "The Taste"**) backtrack chronologically and thematically to earlier phases in Monaxov's development, to the now familiar quests for love, identity, and stability. Read in the light of the two central pieces, however, they do not seem repetitive, but rather tend to round off the whole with a new wealth of subtle psychological and philosophical observations.

Although there are spots that do not quite do justice to the suppleness and versatility of Bitov's style, all of the translations are quite readable and many are very good indeed. This is as it should be, for it will help ensure Bitov the broader readership he deserves. (pp. 450-51)

Charles Rougle, in a review of "Life in Windy Weather," in Slavic and East-European Journal, *Vol. 31, No. 3, Fall, 1987, pp. 450-51.*

JOHN BAYLEY

[Bitov's novel *Pushkin House* is a very different affair from Leonid Borodin's novel *Partings*]. Originally trained as a geologist he became a dropout in the Sixties, wrote a lot of poems, turned to prose, and had some success in Russia with his story collections, *Days of Man* [*Dni cheloveka*] and *Seven Journeys* [*Sem' puteshestvii*]. A selection of them called *Life in Windy Weather* was published in America by Ardis [in 1986]. Well translated as is Borodin's novel, *Pushkin House* nonetheless runs into difficulties in English that *Partings* does not, for its fantasy and humor, both of which are a little too determined, depend on an idiom and a linguistic vitality that have no ready Western equivalent. Its modishness is more than recognizable; it can be placed among the current kinds of clever novels concerned with the nonexistence of the hero and the convertibility of the text. But its individual spirit is harder for a Western reader to get hold of, enclosed as it is in a game of perpetual allusiveness to scenes, lines, and contexts in the Russian classics. There are excellent individual scenes, like the vodka binge of the "hero" Lyova and his friends; and they are punctuated by the appearance of the author to explain why things have turned out this way, in view of the convention he is using and its relation to a story by Pushkin or Krylov, or a film acted and directed by Bondarchuk.

Bitov has been called a Soviet Nabokov, but his novel is actually more like the kind of exercise in evasion and replication fashionable for some time now in the West, and represented by Julian Barnes's *Flaubert's Parrot* and Peter Ackroyd's *Hawksmoor*. The metaphysical premise of such novels is that both history and literature are an overlapping sequence of interpretations, an accumulation of imitative metaphor that in former days passed itself off as reality. The author and the "hero" comment on each other's lack of existence: Bitov's

"Prologue, or A Chapter Written After the Rest" is entitled "What Is to Be Done?," the title of Chernyshevsky's novel of 1863; "a flat wind the colour of an aeroplane" is flying over the city, revealing a body, perhaps that of Pushkin lying in the snow after the duel, a pistol close to his hand; the statue of Peter on his horse; the legendary cruiser of the revolution, the *Aurora*, lying at anchor in the Neva. The northern capital has always seemed to Russian writers a city of dreams and visions, most graphically exploited in Andrei Bely's novel of 1913, *Petersburg*. There is thus a traditional familiarity in Bitov's phantasmagoric method, with the modern theory of fictional discourse added on.

Bitov's politics seem to follow logically from his aesthetics. By exploiting the present-day cliché that a novel can only be constructed from other novels he also implies that revolution is impossible, because radicals and innovators are tied to the past as helplessly as poets and artists. The Marxist ambition to change history rather than to understand it is technically impossible, for the same reason that no novelist can write a new novel. Bitov's "hero," Lyova, works in Pushkin House, the museum of the poet in Leningrad, and he reincarnates a couple of the archetypes the poet created—the "superfluous man," like Yevgeny Onegin, and the downtrodden "little man," like Pushkin's other Yevgeny, the hero of *The Bronze Horseman,* who, following the flood that drowns his fiancée, goes mad after presuming to threaten the great Czar on his bronze horse, and imagines the statue is galloping after him. Lermontov took up the idea of the "superfluous man" in *A Hero of Our Time,* as did Turgenev in *Fathers and Sons;* while Gogol and Dostoevsky developed in their novels and stories the type of the persecuted "little man." Each of the sections of Bitov's book is called after the title of one of these Russian classics, and one of them invokes no fewer than five famous fictional duels.

In an afterword the translator remarks that after a peek inside the book the staff of a college bookstore shelved *Pushkin House* under criticism instead of fiction. And yet it is not, she says, just "an academic tour of literary history,"

> or even a sentimental odyssey through the living literature in quest of meaning in present-day Soviet life. It is a double of life itself, in a country where the national literature has always been a focus of the struggle between state and individual. To read this book is to experience the wild paradoxes lived by a contemporary Soviet intellectual.

She feels that all readers who have responded to Joyce and Nabokov will understand the method and feel the same. That is probably true, and Bitov's novel is certainly entertaining and instructive as an image of contemporary literary consciousness, presented in a Russian setting. But as so often happens when a good writer gets the bit between his teeth, episodes and characters career away from the method, as Peter's bronze steed gallops its granite plinth in Pushkin's poem, creating a life and fantasy of their own. (pp. 9-10)

> *John Bayley, "Riding the Bronze Horse," in* The New York Review of Books, *Vol. XXXIV, No. 16, October 22, 1987, pp. 9-10.*

DAVID REMNICK

During each of the three Russian waves of emigration, departing writers endured the sound of officials wishing them

ill, claiming it would be impossible to create Russian literature on foreign soil. Just look at the precedents. Gogol, in voluntary European exile, suffered the deprivations of living and writing apart from his comic sources and wrote a feeble conclusion to *Dead Souls.*

And yet the success stories of exile, bittersweet as they are, prove that the all-embracing sentimental connections between "home" and literature are hooey. Joseph Brodsky was only 32 when he was hounded out of the Soviet Union, and he has written his best work in the un-Slavic plains of Ann Arbor and Greenwich Village. Tyranny could not steal his language. His Nobel Prize honored not only Brodsky, but the whole of émigré literature; it honored the idea that many writers, among them Vasily Aksyonov, Vladimir Voinovich and Yuz Aleshkovsky, could prove the imagination a portable thing.

So great is the success of exile literature that one is left wondering: Are there any writers of the first rank left in the Soviet Union?

The publication in English of Andrei Bitov's extraordinary novel *Pushkin House* not only answers the question in the affirmative, it brings to American attention a work of prose that stands with the best of modernist fiction. Published [in the United States in 1978] in Russian by Ardis, *Pushkin House* has long been ignored in the Soviet Union. Occasionally part of the novel appeared in sanctioned journals as an article or short, but so far *Pushkin House* is a classic only to the privileged few. Finally, the editor of *Novy Mir* has announced plans to publish the novel.

Part of the bravery and triumph of *Pushkin House* is its language and formal daring. Bitov's sentences whirl and glide on the page. He is a sensational digressor. *Pushkin House* must terrify the censors as much for its technical innovations—which mock the dreariness of so many Sons of Sholokov—as for the subjects it embraces.

Pushkin House is a literary institute in Leningrad, where the hero is a philologist. The title also refers to Russian literature itself, the House That Pushkin Built. In the life of Lyova Odoestev, the novels and epics and lyrics of Russian literature are as palpable as schools and parents and purges. Books are given their proper place as powerful agents of change and sources of love in *Pushkin House.* The novel is, like its precursor, Nabokov's *The Gift,* a self-conscious confrontation with books. Bitov's novel is full of references to Pushkin, Lermontov and the rest of the pantheon.

But *Pushkin House* does not have that quality of coolness present in many Western modern fictions, and the reader lacking an intimate knowledge of Russian literature will still find satisfaction in Bitov's story and descriptive power. Bitov has an immense talent for focusing at length and with great emotional power on the telling moment or touch, and in this way he is a kind of Soviet Proust. Here he is, early in the novel, describing a confrontation between father and son. It all comes through in a handshake:

> Lyova remembered forever Father's long handclasp on the threshold of that study, unchanged from his childhood, as always half dark, as always it made him want to speak in a whisper . . . For a long time Father clasped Lyova's narrow cool hand in his own hot, dry ones and said things; Lyova, aloofly observing the movement of his lips, no longer even heard. Father was blocking the desk

lamp, his flyaway hair shone and seemed to stir in an invisible draft, and as Lyova studied this martyr halo he suddenly compared Father to a dandelion. And because the tremor of Father's handclasp was transmitted to him, he also thought that a dandelion will fly apart if you blow on it. For a third time Lyova fixed his father in memory . . . this time forever. . . .

To sense one's aging father as a fragile dandelion, as a shadow, but without sentimentality, shows a mastery of language and emotion. The book is filled with passages in which the introduction of a few physical details or a scrap of memory bring to the narrator's mind a range of emotions and ideas.

This is an intellectual novel in the best sense. Lyova's decisions and thoughts are emblematic of the decisions and thoughts faced by Soviet intellectuals now in maturity.

In writing about the Soviet intellectual, Bitov does not stop at straightforward narrative. His authorial voice is constantly standing back from the story and reconsidering, playing with alternatives. Bitov's hero becomes the hero in a dozen works of the past, a Dostoevskian "little man," a "superfluous man" out of Turgenyev and Pushkin. He is everyman and every character without becoming a two-dimensional emblem. As with Andrei Bely's *Petersburg,* even the city of Leningrad is a living mind, a roadmap of memories and allusions. There is an element of play to that, but not one of frivolity. One man's alternatives and a society's own choices are at the core of Bitov's essential criticism of modern Soviet life and culture.

When he is finally published entirely in the Soviet Union, Bitov will become an extraordinarily important figure in Russian literature. The readers of the Soviet Union need *Pushkin House* every bit as much as *Doctor Zhivago.* Andrei Bitov's novel is as rich in description and experience as Pasternak's, and it is a superior artistic achievement.

> David Remnick, *"The Russian Writer Who Stayed Home,"* in Book World—The Washington Post, *November 29, 1987, p. 5.*

FRANK KERMODE

Andrei Bitov is not, on first inspection, a dangerously political writer, but he has had trouble getting published in the Soviet Union; and by the time you've digested [*Pushkin House*] you will understand why.

Born in Leningrad in 1937, Mr. Bitov studied at the Mining Institute there, but he was expelled for spending too much time writing poetry. He worked as a stevedore, served in the army, returned to the Institute and started writing prose. In 1963 he became a full-time writer of stories, most of which were published in Russia. The best of them were published in translation as *Life in Windy Weather.* One of them kept growing and turned into a novel, *Pushkin House,* which was finished in 1972 and published in Russian, though not in Russia, in 1978. A brief autobiographical note he wrote in 1974 informs us that Mr. Bitov has or had in hand a "quasi-English" novel called *The Teacher of Symmetry,* and a theoretical dissertation on fiction. No information about these works seems to be available.

Pushkin House, a novel full of fiery intelligence, is, it must be said, a work of formidable complexity, and readers should be warned that first time round they are in for a rough ride. But if they are, at the outset, admirers of the amazing range and power of the classic Russian novels (which this book constantly invokes), they should strap themselves in and set forth. The very title has multiple significance: Pushkin House is the name of the literary institute in which the hero works; it is also Russian literature as a whole ("the house that Pushkin built"); and it is this book itself, which houses not only Pushkin, though he is its household god, but also Gogol, Lermontov, Dostoyevsky, Turgenev, Tolstoy and Chernyshevsky. Susan Brownsberger, the learned and resourceful translator, seems to think Nabokov is a principal model for *Pushkin House,* but it strikes me that the author this work most vividly recalls when at its eloquent and weird best is Dostoyevsky. Anyway, it is crammed with allusions to all these writers, expertly annotated by Ms. Brownsberger.

A larger problem is the presence in the text of all manner of bizarre metaphors (on the first page, "a flat wind the color of an airplane") and other manifestations of a style so idiomatic, so intense, so florid and finally so playful, that the translator says it is difficult even in Russian. One feels for her as, sitting back from her scrupulous and evidently successful labors, she still laments her inevitable failure to reproduce all the wordplay and sound patterning of the original.

Another problem, and perhaps the toughest, arises from the lucid liberties Mr. Bitov takes with his story, which is so contorted and self-subverting that any summary account of it is bound to be misleading. The story—or rather the book—begins with the death of the hero, Lyova Odoevtsev, in a drunken duel. This is followed by an account of his childhood, boyhood and youth, curiously parallel to those of the author. They were both born in 1937, during the Stalinist purges; read Pushkin zealously in 1949, a time of renewed terror; finished high school in 1953, the year of Stalin's death. Both spent their time mainly in Leningrad, a city that figures richly in the book. Lyova's "fatal" drinking bout and duel occurs on the night of Nov. 7, 1967, the 50th anniversary of the Revolution, which happened before their time but still dominates their lives and gives them an oddly second-hand and flattened character.

But *Pushkin House* is much more than a complaint about the dullness of contemporary Russian life. It is also a treatise on fiction, and Mr. Bitov incorporates quantities of theoretical speculation in the text of his novel. He seems obsessed with the idea that novelists can do exactly as they please. For example, they can recount a series of events, and then, if they so wish, point out that the matter could have been treated in an entirely different manner; they may then go on to do so, offering what the novel calls "variants" that may very well contradict or falsify the original version.

If Mr. Bitov chooses—and he does choose—he can bring his hero Lyova back to life after his death by pistol shot. Not dead at all, he wakes up with a hangover (like everybody else in Leningrad on Nov. 8) and surveys the frightful destruction wrought by himself and his drunken companions in the Institute, the scene of their drunken party. Windows are broken, Pushkin's death mask is smashed to pieces. Lyova is now said, with an implausibility frankly acknowledged, to have collected workmen and repaired all the damage before his colleagues return to work on Nov. 9. They notice nothing. (The death mask wasn't after all unique; there are dozens in the basement.) How did he manage this on a public holiday?

Well, the truth is the author did the cleaning and repairing with his pen.

Fooling around with the conventional idea of the novel is a practice as old as the novel itself, the original master being Laurence Sterne. That the same person can die twice, or walk down a pier and yet remain on the ferry, are commonplaces of the French New Novel. "Essayism"—interlarding essays on anything and everything—was a habit of Robert Musil. So there is nothing very new about Mr. Bitov's method, which some readers may even find a bit old-fashioned. Some may even suspect that he isn't in any ordinary sense a novelist at all, but a short-story writer, here festooning his work with all these essays and allusions.

We first meet Lyova as a child with an unsatisfactory father, an interesting alcoholic uncle and a scholar-grandfather, returned from Siberian exile and capable of immense outlandish tirades on the tedium, the lack of interest, in modern Soviet life. The old man regrets the prerevolutionary past in which "the meaning and possibility of man survived—at the cost of mere social inequality." Nowadays nobody engages with *life,* and everybody is much like everybody else. Even protesters against the regime are *Soviet* protesters. "Your boldness and your freedom," he tells the younger intellectuals, "are measured out to you as if by ration cards."

As if to confirm these insights, Lyova leads a rather vague and superfluous existence. He doesn't actually betray a friend, but conveniently happens not to be around when the friend is arrested. His relationships with women (very well portrayed—comic, sad and true) are full of willed self-delusion and lack emotional force. He is in thrall to a somewhat demonic proletarian called Mitishatyev, a crafty, envious fellow and an obsessed anti-Semite. Mitishatyev knows just how to get under Lyova's skin, and after a drunken argument he smashes the death mask and provokes the duel fought with Pushkin's pistols.

Mr. Bitov is at his best, I think, in this climactic scene, the like of which it might be hard to find outside Dostoyevsky. Of course the duel is very literary, alluding to many famous duels in the Russian classics (that is, in Pushkin's house, where *this* duel is taking place). But the power comes from Mitishatyev's mad, fervid rhetoric. . . .

At the point where Mitishatyev "kills" Lyova, the opening pages of the book are repeated verbatim, as if the story had come full circle: here again is the gray, hung over Leningrad morning, the wind colored like an airplane. But this isn't the end (Bitov speculates a lot about ends) and the book has 50 pages more to go. They include a slightly embarrassed confrontation between the author and his hero.

It may be just as well that Mr. Bitov's subsequent project was for two books, one for a story and one for the theory. Here they are served simultaneously. However, the whole book, story and theory alike, is an effort to put some distance between a true perception of life and the "ready-made" substitutes of modern existence—"ready-made behavior, ready-made explanations, ready-made ideals." Lyova has "learned to explain everything very competently and logically before thinking." Nothing much of interest happens to him except when he has had a lot of vodka. He is a victim of the pseudo-bourgeois oppressiveness of Soviet society. In this book a stultified middle class is given its hearing, as the poor got theirs in Dostoyevsky's *Humble Folk.*

And this, of course, is why Mr. Bitov is not exactly a favorite of the party. How, he asks, except in books, can one get through to a life deeper than the forms of contemporary Russian society—the vodka, the parades, the petty affairs, the dull compliance of even the educated with things as they are? The Revolution somehow ties them to the past. It happened long before their time, but it shapes the conditions under which they live. And perhaps only art, a modern art, can break through into a condition more like truth, more like freedom.

Mr. Bitov's book, then, is, for all its fooling and all its recondite allusions, an attempt on that truth and a call for that freedom. In Russia it was condemned for "excessive subjectivity. . . and a lack of moral purpose." Here the book can be published, and all these condemnations transformed into praise. But we should remember that the Russians take books much more seriously than we do, which is why, having read them carefully, they condemn so many.

Frank Kermode, "Lyova's Death Was Temporary," in The New York Times Book Review, *January 3, 1988, p. 10.*

ELAINE KENDALL

Though Andrei Bitov's previous books were not only published but widely acclaimed in the Soviet Union, **Pushkin House,** his most ambitious work, has circulated only in *samizdat*—bootleg copies passed by hand from one reader to another. Structurally similar to those Russian dolls that open to reveal ever smaller dolls inside, this novel shelters several sub-themes within its capacious outer shell.

Rejected by the Soviet distributors ostensibly because its intense subjectivity apparently exceeded the rigid bounds of Socialist Realism, **Pushkin House** exposes and satirizes the shortcomings of the political system. While "excessive subjectivity" is now often overlooked, a harder line is taken with material as overtly critical of the regime as this. Bitov has not only ridiculed "the system"—fair game for virtually any Russian writer—but the entire literary tradition of his culture. Despite the improvements brought about since *glasnost,* there are obviously still restraints upon the writer's autonomy and limits to the tolerance of the literary authorities.

By making his protagonist a philologist laboring in Pushkin House, the official shrine to the Russian literary tradition, Bitov is able to review and examine the celebrated monuments of his country's literature. Heavily larded with tags from Dostoevsky, Tolstoy, Lermontov, Chernyshevsky and Turgenev, in addition to the venerated Pushkin himself, the text also includes references to painters, film makers, critics and various academics who have influenced the Soviet aesthetic in one way or another. Some of these references are respectful, even admiring; many are not.

While a number of the allusions will be comfortably familiar, others may elude all but specialists in Russian history and culture. Fortunately, the translator has supplied notes at the back of the book identifying both the obvious and the obscure. These help, but even the most dedicated readers may find the process of checking footnotes an unexpected obstacle to their enjoyment of a work presented as a novel. (pp. 1, 6)

As the novel proceeds, we realize we're reading a recapitulation of the last half-century of Russian history; the style shifts continually between the techniques of the more avant-garde contemporary Western writers and the traditional practitioners of the Russian novel with its distinctive mannerisms. Adding to the difficulties are the frequent glides from dream to actuality; the leaps in and out of Lyova's subconscious mind, but most taxing of all, the various versions of events perceived from differing points of view. Burdened with the obligation to be a Russian version of Everyman, Lyova is too busy reflecting history and interpreting its effect upon him and his family to spend much time engaging our sympathies or attention. He's a symbol, and his most intimate connections are with the state.

While Lyova has parents (including a father who betrays his own father in order to gain the old scientist's university chair), an appealingly eccentric Uncle Dickens (so-called because of his admiration for the English writer) and an assortment of friends and lovers, all the experiences of Lyova's life remain oddly impersonal. Archetypical of his generation, imprisoned in his role of the beleaguered Russian intellectual, the hero becomes merely the unwitting object of social forces beyond his control. Subsidiary characters seem to exist only to illustrate facets of contemporary life that cannot be contained within Lyova's own broad but still particular frame of reference. Accustomed to—and perhaps spoiled by—our own direct way of dealing with conflicts between the individual and the state in nonfiction, American readers may grow impatient with the elaborate subterfuges employed here. Sensitive issues cannot be confronted head on; the regime must be analyzed within the framework of fantasy. . . .

Bitov provides frequent author's asides to the reader; erudite, often humorous commentaries upon the narrative proper. From time to time, he seems to be warning us not to take all of this too seriously, but the asides often have precisely the opposite effect. "The title of this novel is stolen, too. Why, that's an institute, not a title for a novel! With nameplates for the departments: The Bronze Horseman. A Hero of Our Time. Fathers and Sons. What Is to Be Done? And so on, through the school curriculum. A tour of a museum novel. The nameplates guide, the epigraphs remind. . . ."

And so they do, but the result is in fact exactly what Bitov deplores; "a museum novel." **Pushkin House** is a scholarly, inventive, elaborate *jeu d'esprit,* but a game that will be fun only for those with Bitov's home court advantage. (p. 6)

> *Elaine Kendall, "Defacing the Monuments of Russian Literature," in* Los Angeles Times Book Review, *January 24, 1988, pp. 1, 6.*

EDWARD J. BROWN

[In his early narratives collected in **Life in Windy Weather**], Bitov wrote of the psychological experiences of a character at a moment of intense inner agitation, which is usually occasioned not by weighty events either public or private but by deeply felt, though minor, personal crises. Bitov's descriptions of the mind's approach to ordinary notions of cause and effect is often startling, producing images that remind us of Andrei Bely, Nabokov and Yuri Olesha. Like Nabokov, a chance visual surprise is generalized (mistakenly, but effectively): "Have you ever noticed how all animals run a little sideways?" Or consider some red motorcycles described as "grazing" at the side of the road. These examples of linguistically realized naïve apprehension are from **"A Country**

Place," a subjective account of a writer's drift and uncertainty when the white pages on his study table, intended to receive his fictions, remain white. Curiously anticipating the structure of **Pushkin House,** this account of a writer's experience is accompanied by some **"Notes From a Corner,"** in which the author illuminates the process of turning life into fiction. Some critics have complained that Bitov writes only about himself; he of course agrees, asking, "What else is there to write about?"

The main action of **Pushkin House** occurs, speaking metaphorically, in a place of that name—the many-chambered mansion of Russian literature founded, so to speak, by Alexander Sergeyevich Pushkin early in the nineteenth century. The real Pushkin House, which serves as the vehicle of the metaphor, is a former mansion now a literary research institute on the Makarov Embankment of the Neva River. The hero, whose name is Lyova, is a literary scholar who works at the institute and whose mind is a resonance chamber that produces constant echoes of bright verbal moments in Russian literature, not only from Pushkin but from Tyutchev, Lermontov, Blok, Esenin, Tolstoy, Dostoyevsky and many others, most of them identified here by the editor/translator in a useful set of footnotes intended for readers unfamiliar with this literature. One must admit that a lot of the book's poetic delight will be lost on such readers, although the editor has done what could be done, and there is much else to enjoy. In its literary allusiveness, the novel bears some resemblance to Nabokov's *The Gift* and of course to Bely's *Petersburg* and Joyce's *Ulysses.* It thus feeds on and develops an old and well-established literary tradition, the writing of a self-reflexive prose, bearing a sweet surfeit of already formed symbolic language.

Lyova is provided with a surname, Odoevtsev, that suggests descent from a noble Russian family and ties him firmly to the Russian past. His father, also a scholar, has fatally compromised his own honor and any claim to Lyova's respect by cowardly adjustments to official ideology. For Lyova there are really no excuses for this conduct, certainly not phrases such as, "You have to remember how things were. . . . It's hard to explain it all." But Lyova has Uncle Dickens and he has his grandfather, both of whom have been in trouble with the regime and are recently "back from somewhere." They are models of intentional maladjustment to Soviet society. The final answer of either to questions about contemporary life is likely to be the excremental expletive, which covers almost any situation that might arise. What distinguishes both relatives is their individualism, their absolute rejection of the stereotypes provided by Soviet culture, both the "evil" stereotypes of Stalin, and the "good" ones applied to his former victims, such as "rehabilitation," "undeserved punishment," "admission of errors" and the like. It's all shit! says grandfather, whose long alcoholic monologue provides us with a magnificent portrait of a mind incapable of compromise. Such a mind must reject the popular stereotype according to which he had suffered "undeservedly." Grandfather insists he was guilty; he did try to undermine the regime, and he'd suffered *deservedly* and proudly.

The structure of relationships worked out here is a variant on the fathers and sons theme, and Turgenev's novel is frequently invoked. Lyova rejects his proximate father in favor of more remote fathers and uncles, not only his grandfather and Uncle Dickens but also ultimately Pushkin, in whose "house" he works. The kinship structure is itself a metaphor of literary succession in the Russian formalist analysis, according to which important writers of the present reject their immediate predecessors (the fathers) in favor of "grandfathers" or "uncles." The writing of Bitov and some of his contemporaries may be taken as an illustration of that historical model; they rejected the socialist realist style of the 1930s, 1940s and 1950s in favor of a return to Bely and the symbolists, and the readoption of a distant uncle, Nabokov.

The novel is interspersed with discussions of other ways it might have been written or its characters developed; there are also other reflexive asides, such as apologies for the appearance of a character out of proper chronological order. . . . *Pushkin House* frequently calls to mind Sterne's *Tristram Shandy,* in which the narrator is often in a state of mock paralysis, lasting for a page or two, over a fictional character's conventional indifference to the real dimensions of time and space. But Bitov's work also calls to mind a Russian "novel in verse" that owed much to the Shandyian model, Pushkin's *Eugene Onegin,* where subversions of narrative convention abound and are frequently commented on by the author.

At a critical point in his narrative Bitov tells us what it is all "about." "And if you asked us at this moment what the whole novel is about, we would not, at the moment, feel bewildered, but would confidently reply: 'Disorientation.' " At that point he seems to have in mind the agonizing suspense of a human being, and of the writer who undertakes to describe him, in an uncertain area where obvious biographical or historical facts do not account for either feelings or behavior, but where other and unprovable facts dominate the story. The author's disorientation seems to mimic that of his characters. He can't finally decide between versions and variants of his fiction. The peculiar power and teasing sense of the novel lies, I think, in that precarious balance of the narrator, who is none other than the Soviet writer Bitov, Andrei Georgievich, inventing and testing himself as he goes along. And Bitov gropes conscientiously among the facts of life and literature, using the best evidence he can find. (pp. 346-47)

Edward J. Brown, "Rehabilitating Bitov," in The Nation, *New York, Vol. 246, No. 10, March 12, 1988, pp. 346-47.*

JOHN FREEDMAN

Andrei Bitov's work belongs to one of the richest lines of the Russian literary heritage. A current resident of Moscow, Bitov grew up in Leningrad, where he was informed by the rich and fantastic tradition that emerged in that murky, "most intentional of cities" through the works of Pushkin, Gogol, Dostoevsky, and Bely. His short stories (dating from 1960) have often referred to, or used, common Petersburg themes or symbols, but only in *Pushkin House* do these themes and symbols receive their full expression. . . .

Pushkin House is set in the 1960s in Leningrad, where its young hero, Lev Odoevtsev, is an employee at Pushkin House, the archives of Russian literature, and its main problem revolves around Lev's search for a national, historical, and personal identity. That search occurs on several levels from the abstract (cultural memory) to the concrete (family history), although the lines between these concepts are never so clearly drawn. Notions of the Russian literary tradition permeate these pages not only in the echoes of well-known titles, images and themes from Russia's literary past, but also

because Lev's fundamental ideas about himself and the world are so dependent on them. Lev's writings about Pushkin, Lermontov, and Tyutchev—not unlike the real-life case of Andrei Sinyavsky/Abram Tertz, whose fictive essays *Strolling with Pushkin* and *In Gogol's Shadow* scandalized the Russian literary establishment in the 1970s—are less literary criticism than they are an attempt to recapture cultural myths from the stagnation of official literary canon.

A seemingly more tangible link to Lev's identity is provided by his cultured, mysterious grandfather (whose mystery derives primarily from a long absence spent in the prison camps). Lev creates an image of his grandfather as a dashing, honorable, kindly man who serves for him as a kind of role model, but when they finally meet, Lev is disappointed to find him entirely unlike what he had imagined. However, the fictional image has so influenced his sense of self that he must recognize that the fictional grandfather is for him at least as real as the real one. Bitov's narrator explores degrees of fiction and reality by offering numerous versions of characters and events in the novel, though no one version can be accepted as a real picture of experience. Rather, the possibilities that exist in the gaps between the different versions offer the best approximation of a picture of Lev's identity in the context of his present and his past.

The narrator's literary self-consciousness reaches its apogee at novel end when the author himself visits his hero. Hoping to learn more about his own work, the curious author seeks access to several of Lev's literary articles. But his god-like ego is offended when—like an exhausted actor backstage after a performance—Lev barely tolerates the intrusion. The author's continuing search for the essence of his own creation—like Lev's search for an identity—is reminiscent of the reader's odyssey in Italo Calvino's *If on a Winter's Night a Traveller.* However, it also differs in that the search in *Pushkin House* is not so neatly completed. Despite the author's control over his characters' individual traits and experiences, he is helpless before the sum of their literary parts. The telling of Lev Odoevtsev's story acquires a life of its own that refuses to submit to a neat summing up, and in fact, refuses to end. No less than life itself, the novel cannot be finished, but only abandoned while still in process.

But if, as the narrator writes, "reality had no room for the novel," the novel provides the best possible vehicle for attempting to achieve at least a partial understanding of reality. Time and again through digressions, reversals, clarifications, mock literary criticism, and footnotes, the author seeks to embrace the experience and identity of his hero Lev Odoevtsev. The paradox is that while each new detail complicates, and occasionally obscures, our specific understanding of what has happened, our understanding of Lev's identity is deepened.

Unlike a novel such as [Anatoli Rybakov's] *Children of the Arbat,* whose limits and aspirations are strictly defined by a specific historical and political reality, *Pushkin House* enlists literature's power to exceed the limits of history, of time, and of reality, thus providing us with a broader and deeper understanding of them all. In doing so, Bitov succeeds in telling us something about his characters, about his culture, and about our world. *Pushkin House* . . . , is a masterwork of modern literature that in time will stand alongside Andrei Bely's *Petersburg* and Mikhail Bulgakov's *Master and Margarita* as one of the pinnacles of twentieth-century Russian fiction.

John Freedman, "Searching in the Archives," in The American Book Review, Vol. 10, No. 1, March-April, 1988, p. 14.

SALLY LAIRD

At first sight, **Pushkin House** is a cross between a Russian-style whodunnit (or who-is-guilty) and an academic treatise. On page four, the hero appears to be dead, face down among scattered papers in a deserted museum with an ominous Pushkinian wind blowing in through the broken window. A glance at the list of contents, however, reassures us that he isn't dead at all but will still be alive in 1999, when—graced by then with the title of Academician—he'll add a commentary on **Pushkin House** to its already formidable array of authorial notes and appendices. The commentary will start on page 373, which docs not, of course, exist in this edition. . . .

Like Nabokov's *Gift*, Bitov's novel is a tribute to "the house that Pushkin built": the title refers not just to the literary institute in Leningrad where Bitov sends his hero, Lyova Odoevtsev, to work, but metaphorically to the whole of Russian literature. It's also, however, an act of vandalism on that house, or on the museum that has been made of it. It's an attempt at once to rescue literature from the museum, and life from quotation marks. The "literariness" of the novel is not just a game, but reflects the real (or unreal) experience of the modern Russian *intelligent*.

Bitov is too ironic, and too self-knowing, to romanticize his act of liberation. . . . The equality that Bitov establishes between author, characters and readers is that of shared experience and time. Lyova Odoevtsev is Bitov's exact contemporary, born, like him, in Leningrad in 1937, and the novel which tells his story is explicitly addressed to their generation: to the children of the war and the terror who grew up in the "thaw". Bitov shares their bewilderment and guilt, and his dilemma as a writer is also theirs: how, as he wrote in 1973, "to evaluate the present, tied as it is to an undigested past?" Yet in posing that problem—the central problem of all his work—Bitov simultaneously suggests its solution. Behind his irony and agnosticism there's a residue of romantic—almost religious—faith: faith in the self, the expression of which, in literature, is style. It is this faith which invests Bitov's "post-modernism" with an air of celebration, and it's Bitov's concept of literature as "the total surprise of information about a man", rather than his reliance on "the coauthorship of time and environment", that gives this novel its compelling intimacy. Bitov's work can be seen in this light to have a single hero, to be a kind of Proustian enterprise for which **Pushkin House** provides the manifesto.

With Proustian exactness, Bitov tells the history of his generation through his hero's inner story—Lyova's changing relationships with his family and with his friend/enemy Mitishatyev, his love (or need) for the three women in his life. Bitov's descriptions have a kind of tender ruthlessness; they are at once shocking and plausible. . . . Lyova's tortured relationships form the ostensible plot of the novel; but a secondary plot is mapped out through Bitov's analysis of his characters' personal and literary styles. . . . Lyova's grandfather and Uncle Dickens, his neighbour, are each discussed as writers, and Lyova's own essay on Pushkin, Tyutchev and Lermontov is analysed at length: Bitov commends it for its "subjectivity" and draws our attention to Lyova's particular triumphs, to the way, for example, that he "names the word

'duel' and rides it, long and beautifully, from sentence to sentence, stitching them together like the bobbin in a sewing machine".

Here, and in his self-mocking commentaries on the progress of his own work, Bitov is alerting us to the tasks he has set himself. He tells us that the hardest things to describe are "the world of the child, the world of the drunk, and the world of the false or talentless man"—then proceeds to give a virtuoso performance in the genre: a large part of the novel takes place in an alcoholic haze. The world of the drunk represents, of course, a heightened version of the unreal world in which Bitov's characters live all the time. But it also mimics the painful, hilarious, perilous state of the writer himself, hovering on the brink of both brilliance and silliness, snatching moments of insight between long passages of darkness, trying to keep track of time as it shifts, stands still, or races out of control.

Despite his protestations to the contrary, Bitov can be as dictatorial as any Realist when he chooses (witness the fate of poor Albina, Lyova's rejected girlfriend, rescued from oblivion at the end of the novel merely so that she can wash the floor). But he does offer a new freedom to his readers: in reminding us of how literature works, how it is made, he reminds us also of how it is to be enjoyed . . . .

Happily, this funny, exuberant, brave novel has now been serialized in *Novy Mir* and is due to appear in book form in the coming year. Happily, too, it has been served by a translation which, apart from a few hiccups at the beginning, captures much of the vigour and style of the original.

Sally Laird, "The Total Surprise of Information About a Man," in The Times Literary Supplement, No. 4451, July 22-28, 1988, p. 801.

JOHN UPDIKE

Glasnost, like the sun breaking through, brings shadows. More, clearly, is to be permitted in the Soviet Union, but how much more? *Doctor Zhivago* can now be published, as being not sufficiently injurious to the health of the Revolution, and so can a smattering of formerly scorned émigrés such as Joseph Brodsky and Vladimir Nabokov. . . . (p. 108)

Two ambitious novels by Soviet citizens have been recently translated into English and published here, after suffering misadventures on the way to their local printer's. **Pushkin House,** by Andrei Bitov was written in the mid-seventies, circulated in samizdat, was published in Russian by Ardis Publishers, in Michigan, in 1978, and last year achieved publication in the Soviet Union. *Children of the Arbat,* by Anatoli Rybakov was suppressed for twenty years before, in "one of the most daring steps of *glasnost*" (to quote the words of Yevgeny Yevtushenko on the back of the jacket), it was published in the U.S.S.R., "where public libraries have a readers' waiting list for it in the thousands." The jacket of **Pushkin House,** too, bears an encomium: Vassily Aksyonov writes, "Although **Pushkin House** has not been published in the Soviet Union as of yet, this novel has stood up for ten years as a firm part of the contemporary Russian artistic and intellectual environment. Andrei Bitov belongs to the St. Petersburg-Leningrad School of Prose with its ambitions to inherit the perfection of the Silver Age." On the other hand, Yevtushenko tells us, "*Children of the Arbat* is written in the tradition of the Russian social novel of the nineteenth century. It is a geological cross section of *terra incognita* revealing all the layers of society of the early 1930s in Moscow." The symmetry of the blurbists is striking: Yevtushenko is the most internationally conspicuous of those now middle-aged writers who blossomed during Khrushchev's brief cultural thaw twenty-five years ago, and have since elected to tough it out as Soviet artists; Aksyonov, his former confrere and almost exact contemporary, is the best-known child of the thaw to immigrate to the United States, and now resides, jogs, and gives interviews in Washington, D.C. Their respective endorsements suggest that Rybakov's novel is that of an insider ("One of Russia's most successful writers," the back flap tells us) working close to the edge, and Bitov's that of an outsider (though five books of his short stories were published in Moscow between 1963 and 1972) who would rather not think about the edge. Suddenly allowed, last year, to appear at a Washington conference on literature, Bitov—a tall, rather stately man with thinning hair and a drooping, graying mustache—said of the new climate under Gorbachev, "Personally, I am tired of all the changes taking place because I no longer have time to sleep. . . . Change, even for the better, causes discomfort."

Pushkin House is a brilliant, restless, impudent novel, reminiscent of *The Gift* in that it refracts a sensitive young man's moral and aesthetic progress through a prism of allusions to earlier Russian literature, and of Andrei Bely's *Peterburg* in that it makes the city now called Leningrad a vivid and symbolically freighted presence and swathes a few hectic domestic events in a giddy whirl of metaphorically packed language. All three of these novels feel to the American reader as if they were losing a lot in translation. The Silver Age mentioned by Aksyonov has no precise equivalent in English prose; its peculiar shades of purple and playfulness and its close alliance with symbolist poetry suggest distinctly minor writers like Ronald Firbank and Edgar Saltus, while there is nothing minor, in Russian, about Bely and Nabokov. Perhaps Nabokov's English-language novels *Pale Fire* and *Ada,* and the more philosophically expansive Saul Bellow works, like *Henderson the Rain King* and *Humboldt's Gift,* better suggest the controlled explosions, the high-energy conflux of poetic language and way-out thought, that the great Russian tradition threw off before Lenin and Stalin shut it down. Pushkin House is a literary institute and museum in Leningrad, and in a broader sense the house of which Pushkin laid the cornerstone—classic Russian literature. Epigraphs from and allusions to this literature (attentively footnoted by the translator) abound in Bitov's text, whose three sections bear titles taken from four masterpieces: *Fathers and Sons* (Turgenev), *A Hero of Our Time* (Lermontov), and "The Humble Horseman" (combining Pushkin's *The Bronze Horseman* and Dostoyevski's *Humble Folk,* a combination rerigged in the epilogue as "Bronze Folk"). There is also some pointed, mischievous parallelism with Chernyshevsky's seminal radical novel, *What Is to Be Done?* It would no doubt help us to have read all these works, as even the mildly educated Russian reader has, but perhaps we can get the idea anyway—the idea, that is, of the superfluous man, the gentleman who floats above the depths of Russian society, and whose existence is especially problematical for literature, since in his superfluity he is nevertheless the principal bearer of culture.

Aristocrats in the dashing old style of Pushkin's Onegin and Lermontov's Pechorin no longer exist, but Soviet society has evolved new élites, and Bitov's hero, Lyova Odoevtsev, belongs to the professorial élite and is also a member, through his ancestors, of the nobility. Though Lyova's sensibility, monstrously coupled with the talkative author's, occupies the entire foreground of this novel, he is not terribly easy to picture, or to love. His face is not described until near the end, and then with cunning indeterminacy:

> His facial features were devoid of individuality; although his face was unique in its way and fitted no usual type, still—how should I put it?—even though one of a kind, it was typical and did not wholly belong to itself. An expert might have described these features as regular and large, almost 'strong,' but there was something so hopeless and weak in the sudden down-ward rush of this sculpted mouth and steep chin that it betrayed, within the Slav, the Aryan with his irresolute courage and secret characterlessness.

Vague as he is, Lyova serves as the focus of three extensive, jumbled episodes: the return from exile and scholarly rehabilitation of his grandfather, the oscillating amorous life he splits among three young women, and the disastrous three days he spends as lone caretaker at Pushkin House while the rest of Leningrad is celebrating the fiftieth anniversary of the October Revolution. The first and last episodes include long scenes of drunkenness, wonderfully rendered in its colorful, fluctuating fog and torrents of mock-profound discourse; "Vodka is the plot's myrrh-bearer," we are told at one point. In the plot, things happen and then unhappen; a lively character called Uncle Dickens dies, and is revived at a moment when his assistance would be convenient. Alternative plot possibilities are freely discussed, and sometimes several are pursued. The over-all movement is that of a "sluggish dream" lurchingly flowing toward a meaningless denouement: "And here at last is the sum, peak, crescendo-mescendo, apogee, climax, denouement—what else?—the NOTHING; here at last is that critical NOTHING, idol, symbol: a small, smooth, darkly glossy little thing, prolate, fits in the palm of your hands . . . ! now you see it; now you don't!" The novel not only is difficult but feels to be *about* difficulty. In the U.S.S.R., into which Lyova is born in 1937, at the height of Stalin's purges, and in which he is glimpsed some thirty years later, concluding on the banks of the Neva that his life "exists only through error," nothing is easy or obvious. Family life is difficult, career choices, career politics, love life; what's more, writing a novel, in this post-Pushkin, post-Stalin, post-modernist world, is difficult, a procedure so tricky and tortuous that the difficulty (I confess) spreads even to writing a review of it.

Within the large and unappetizing inertia of this vodka- and doubt-propelled plot, this "always postponed story," Bitov contrives a microcosmic hyperactivity of phrase, sentence, and image which is, even through the hazy scrim of translation, engagingly vital. Dip in anywhere; small surprises keep crystallizing. "He kept looking at the watch on Karenina's arm. The watch impressed him: golden and tiny on her wide puffy wrist, it had drowned in the folds and lay there smiling." "The swollen Leningrad ceiling hung like a heavy, veined belly. Not rain, not snow—a sort of torn sky-flesh was coming down now, and it plastered the wayfarer in an instant, smothering him like the hateful and nauseating mask of a faint." The sketch of Lyova's family is surprisingly prickly:

> Since the chapter is titled "Father," we should mention this: it seemed to Lyovushka that he did not love his father. . . . Father didn't even seem

capable of tousling Lyova's hair correctly—Lyova would cringe—or taking him on his lap—he always caused his Lyovushka some sort of physical discomfort—Lyovushka would tense up and then be embarrassed by his own embarrassment.

And yet when Lyova at last meets his grandfather, a linguistics scholar who was imprisoned for thirty years and should by all liberal and sentimental logic be sympathetic, the old man is repulsive, with an elastic face that seems to be of two halves, and a number of eerie mannerisms. . . . Lyova initially has trouble distinguishing his grandfather from the old man's former labor-camp commandant, Koptelov, who has become, in a grotesque bit of *perestroika,* a crony. Where Lyova expects familial warmth, a young poet, Rudik, has usurped a favorite's place. As vodka flows, Lyova is roughly teased and mercilessly harangued by his grandfather, who rails against "this affront of rehabilitation. They're not afraid of me anymore: I'm slag. They threw me out into retirement—I've served my time as a prisoner and I'm no good for anything else. That's how capitalist countries treat workers in the textbooks." At last, Lyova is dismissed into the bitterly cold "failed space" of outer Leningrad, where his sensations mimic the pace of the novel: "He was oddly aware of time flowing through him. It was uneven and seemingly fitful: it dragged, stretched out, thinned like a droplet, forming a little neck—and suddenly broke."

A real writer's wheels are spinning, and a fine mind is trying to follow truth's rapid changes of direction. "Were they [Lyova's acquaintances] this many at the very beginning, I wonder, and did I, as author, fuse them into one Faina, one Mitishatyev, one . . . in order to give at least some kind of focus to Lyova's blurred life? Because the people who affect us are one thing, and their effect on us is quite another; very often the one has no relation to the other, because their effect on us is already ourselves." The women in Lyova's triangular romantic life pop free of his obsessive concern with his own feelings—worthy of a Philip Roth hero's—only for moments of feverish vision: "Now at last Lyova saw that Albina was beautiful, her lofty neck . . . that she might be desired and loved, though again, for some reason, not now, but by the remote Lyova who so generously had not loved her, by that Lyova, not this one still sitting beside her, still not leaving, and almost loving her." Thus we learn that Albina, the unloved, has a long neck. Bitov's authorial hesitations and apologies have a comic vivacity, often:

> In concluding our coverage of this gathering, we must confess that we've been somewhat carried away, somewhat too literal about our task, too ready to rise to the bait. This is all vaudeville, and not worth the trouble. Now it's too late. We have trampled this stretch of prose—the grass will no longer grow on it. We shouldn't have lost our temper.

As in one of Nabokov's layered fictions, the hero begins to realize he inhabits a work of fiction, and is allowed to exult in "the cracks in the scenery (wind blowing in) . . . the general negligence, the hack melodrama, of a dream." A work so energetically, intelligently self-deconstructive as *Pushkin House* must, of course, make literary commissars uneasy, while Communism's cardboard house shudders and rattles around them. But renewal emerges from disintegration, and Bitov's loving demolition of the grand Russian tradition forms a new installment in that tradition. (pp. 108-110, 112)

John Updike, "Doubt and Difficulty in Leningrad and Moscow," in The New Yorker, *Vol. LXIV, No. 30, September 12, 1988, pp. 108-10, 112-14.*

T. J. BINYON

It would be difficult to find more of a contrast [to Anatoli Rybakov's novel *Children of the Arbat*] than Andrei Bitov's **Pushkin House,** originally published in Russian in 1978, probably the most interesting work to come out of Soviet literature since the Twenties. It is pleasingly coincidental that its appearance in English should coincide with the first appearance in the Soviet Union of Nabokov's works, for it is, both in tone and manner, undeniably Nabokovian. Where Rybakov deals with a group, Bitov probes an individual; where Rybakov employs a wide, panoramic sweep and introduces historical characters, Bitov concentrates his action and deals only with creatures of the imagination; where Rybakov is historically precise, Bitov is carefully vague; but, most of all, where Rybakov is stubbornly and conventionally naturalistic, Bitov is playfully and modernistically experimental. Yet in the end both can be seen to be confronting the same problems.

The title **Pushkin House** refers, not only to the Leningrad literary institute in which the hero, Lyova Odoevtsev, works (this, of course, is not the famous Pushkin House, the Pushkinskii dom, attached to the Academy of Sciences, but another with the same name), but also to the house of Russian literature, which, in the sense that all Russian writers have emerged from Pushkin, can truly be said to be his. The novel opens on the day after the annual holiday commemorating the October revolution. On the floor of the exhibition hall of the institute, among the wreckage of the exhibition itself—including Pushkin's death mask, broken into several pieces—lies the lifeless body of Lyova Odoevtsev, whose history Bitov then relates. Born at the height of the Stalinist terror in 1937, and so a coeval of the author, Odoevtsev finished school in 1953, the year of Stalin's death, and dies, it is hinted, in 1967, on the 50th anniversary of the Revolution: killed in a duel, after a heroic drinking spree, by one of Pushkin's pistols in the hands of Mitishatyev, his best friend and worst enemy. But then the author relents, resurrects his hero the following morning with a terrible hangover, and even, with a stroke or two of the pen, aids him to repair the damage done to the museum.

Though the novel purports to be mainly, indeed exclusively, about Odoevtsev, and particularly about his relationship with three women—Lyubasha, Faina and Albina—it is in fact as much about Russian literature. It is stuffed full of literary references . . . while the centrepiece of the book is a critical essay by Odoevtsev on Pushkin, Lermontov and Tyutchev, a brilliant *tour de force,* which manages to be both a viable and illuminating work of criticism, a rumination on the history of Russia, and a commentary on the mode of thought of Odoevtsev and his generation.

Yet above and beyond this—and it is here that Bitov's aim coincides with that of Rybakov—the novel is concerned with the problem of coming to terms with the past, a past of arbitrary imprisonment, of terror, of labour camps—and evaluating its significance for the future. Odoevtsev, like [Rybakov's protagonist] Pankratov, is personally involved: his grandfather, a famous scholar, was denounced by his father and sent to Siberia; now, freed and rehabilitated, the old man returns to Leningrad; Odoevtsev visits him, suffering, in a brilliantly written scene, agonies of embarrassment, not so much from the emotional problems as from the social difficulties posed by the situation.

Paradoxically, though Rybakov's open, crowded and public narrative promises a general assessment of the impact of Stalinism on his generation, in the end the impression is intensely private and personal: *Children of the Arbat* is in some senses an attempt at self-therapy, a means for the author of exorcising and coming to terms with the experiences of imprisonment and exile. The introverted, introspective narrative of ***Pushkin House,*** on the other hand, with its intense concentration on the imperceptible movements of the individual psyche, turns out to provide—if metaphorically—that generalised public statement which would have been expected from the other novel. (p. 6)

T. J. Binyon, "Sasha, Stalin and the Gorbachovsh-china," in London Review of Books, *Vol. 10, No. 16, September 15, 1988, pp. 6-7.*

Vincent (Thomas) Buckley

1925-1988

Australian poet, critic, essayist, and editor.

Buckley writes metaphysical verse in which he expounds upon his Roman Catholic beliefs and often explores Christianity in historical terms. Buckley's spirituality is also evident in poems exploring political and social issues of his native Australia in language critics find both forceful and elusive. Reviewers maintain that his strongest verse concentrates on such basic human concerns as grief, love, death, and the importance of family. P. K. Elkin observed: "[Buckley's] poems are the reflections of a devout and studious person. They are cool and deliberate, without crudities, and unmistakably sincere."

Buckley acknowledges that his first collection of verse, *The World's Flesh* (1954), is strongly influenced by the poetry of Hart Crane and Francis Webb. While delineating spiritual thoughts, this volume also discusses familial bonds and the unspoiled Australian landscape of the poet's childhood. *Masters in Israel: Poems* (1961) also emphasizes Christian theology in pieces focusing upon youth and family, and life's prosaic moments are explored in such poignant poems as "Reading to My Sick Daughter." With the publication of *Arcady and Other Places* (1966), Buckley emerged with a less rhetorical, more unified style. Ironic and passionate, the volume was praised for Buckley's balanced intensity of political concerns with more intrinsic, pensive themes. The often anthologized "Eleven Political Poems," for example, examines ardent commitments in an ideologically divided society, while the critically acclaimed "Stroke" contemplates the ambiguous nature of love and sorrow as it addresses the illness and death of Buckley's father.

The title work of *Golden Builders and Other Poems* (1978), Buckley's next collection, is a sequence of twenty-seven poems which correlate the cosmopolitan city of Melbourne to Australia's pastoral, romantic past. *Late Winter Child* and *The Pattern* were published simultaneously in 1979. Commended for its lyricism, *Late Winter Child* is a recollection of Buckley's second marriage at mid-life and his reactions to the birth of his daughter. *The Pattern* explores the Irish heritage common to many Australians. Two collections of essays, *Cutting Green Hay* (1983) and *Memory Ireland* (1986), also focus upon Buckley's quest to acquire more knowledge of his Irish lineage.

Buckley's literary criticism shares many of the thematic concerns of his verse. His first critical study, the highly regarded *Essays in Poetry: Mainly Australian* (1957), attempts to establish literary standards for modern Australian poets. *Poetry and Morality* (1959) discusses moral implications in the works of Matthew Arnold, T. S. Eliot, and F. R. Leavis, and *Poetry and the Sacred* (1968) examines the theological discourses of such authors as William Blake, Herman Melville, and William Butler Yeats.

(See also *Contemporary Authors,* Vol. 101.)

P. K. ELKIN

Vincent Buckley's poems [in *Masters in Israel*] are the reflections of a devout and studious person. They are cool and deliberate, without crudities, and unmistakably sincere. Some deal with more or less ordinary situations, a father reading to a sick child, a man in a bar listening to the talk of some Anzacs who are drinking near him, or the tutor of a late class feeling in an obscure way that he is letting his students down.

Other poems, such as **"To the Blessed Virgin"** and **"Song for Resurrection Day"**, as their titles declare, are religious in purpose, and most of the remainder, even though they might not be expressly religious in aim, are imbued with spiritual feeling. **"In Time of the Hungarian Martyrdom"** deals with the Mindszenty affair. It treats it not politically but for its illumination of the nature of the (Catholic) Church and of the sacred duty of the Christian to suffer for the cause of humanity.

All the poetry in the volume, as already indicated, is contemplative in character. It shows no outward excitement, and it is never loose. Certainly it cracks no jokes. It is serious intellectual verse straining towards generalisations. "Nothing except in things": William Carlos Williams' dictum would not serve as a motto for Mr. Buckley, who uses things merely as an index to passages of reflection. **"Borrowing of Trees"**, for example, which contains an unusual amount of sensuous detail, culminates nevertheless in an intellectual phrase. After telling us of the moods he has been in the habit of associating with trees all his life, he sums up:

> I was born
> Under this usury of trees: Their noise
> A lent wisdom of guardians talking together

Similarly, in **"The Wedge-Tailed Eagle"**, though there is a sky and it is grey and there are apparently gums and scrub about, the eagle is presented hardly at all for its own sake—for its beauty and power of flight, for example—but as Ixion, a "hard careerist" or "tribune of some revolution", a symbol of cruelty and isolation and distraught impotence.

As is to be expected with verse of this kind, it is at times indefinite, as well as unexciting at the surface level. Diction and imagery tend to remain formal. A chestnut tree is "straining", rain "gathering", a world "pregnant", and his sick daughter's face "pursed" and her will, inevitably, "febrile", all in the first couple of stanzas of **"Reading to my Sick Daughter"**. "Often I stood with *them*" (italics mine), we are told at the beginning of ***"Sinn Fein: 1957"***, but we are never given any idea of what "they" are like, though we are expected to feel their reality all through the poem. Possibly this lack of definition, and the static nature of Mr. Buckley's reflections, are what make a number of the poems, in **Masters in Israel** unsatisfying. The reader hears a clear measured voice, yet sees, hears and feels nothing in particular: he is conscious of a literary blur. This is literature, he may say to himself, poetry no doubt, but life seems to have been left behind. (pp. 54-5)

> *P. K. Elkin, "Poems from Literature and from Life," in* Southerly, *Vol. 22, No. 1, 1962, pp. 53-5.*

THOMAS W. SHAPCOTT

As a collection [***Arcady and Other Places***] reflects the ruthless honesty of Buckley's search for a true and poetically valid modern voice, it is a big step away from his previous volumes of verse, **The World's Flesh** and **Masters in Israel**. One of Buckley's **"Eleven Political Poems"** [(**"Return of a Popular Statesman"**) is included in *Australian Poetry, 1966*, edited by David Campbell,] where its poised and ironic assessment still reads as convincingly as it did when the set was originally published in *Prospect* in 1962. These Political Poems of Buckley, as a matter of fact, seem to form a sort of watershed, not only in his own work, but in the general movement of Australian poetry. In his own corpus, they represent a deliberate and decisive re-appraisal of his technique and poetic aims, obviously in the light of criticisms made against **Masters in Israel** . . . They are, therefore, an indication of absolute poetic dedication and humility, not at all of any fashionable volte-face or eclecticism. As far as the general development of Australian verse is concerned, Buckley's **"Eleven Political Poems"**, in one strike, . . . proclaimed openly the re-entry of political subject-matter into our poetic consciousness.

The other poems in Buckley's collection show how, after the re-thinking of poetic techniques and attitudes in the Political Poems, Buckley has learned to apply his solutions and discoveries to his basically reflective and thoughtful nature, notably in the intensely moving personal poems (such as **"Parents"**), which cumulate in the long sequence **"Stroke"**. Some

of the religious poems show closer traces of earlier habits of writing, but the poem **"Shining Earth: A Summer Without Evil"** moves to an ending which is one of those harrowing and human outstretchings we all would seek to come to in poetry:

> . . .Poverty treated behind wire,
> The heart pitted like a peach-kernel
> Outgrowing its fruit, the bones fired,
> Mankind ridden like an animal,
> And all his loves devoured in their prime.
> Although the Host still fills my throat
> I strain towards the air like a blind man,
> Sending out fears, phrases,
> Like flames across dead grass.

> *Thomas W. Shapcott, "Alive, Alive-O," in* Australian Book Review, *Vol. 6, Nos. 2 & 3, December, 1966 & January, 1967, p. 33.*

S. E. LEE

The theme of passionate commitment in an ideologically divided world is explored in Vincent Buckley's eleven political poems [in ***Arcady and Other Places***]:

> The ache of violence is not for him.
> Other men may faint under the waves
> Of blood, or history, or self. He swims
> A canting backstroke near to shore.

> Only the ebb-tide makes him flap and sweat.
> His great ambition: not to be swept out
> From the soft uplifting swell to where the net
> The bones break in the living roar.

> **("Neutralist")**

So much for Yeats's observation that it's "the best" who lack all conviction! Mr. Buckley however, really takes off the gloves in his eight brief **"Margins"** and in longer poems like the **"Puritan Poet Reel"**, though it appears that the poet and his folk are hurt by the return salvoes that this kind of verbal sparring inevitably invites. . . . I believe that Mr Buckley writes his best poetry when he deserts the intellectual square ring to explore sensitively and with compelling honesty and integrity such things as the ambivalent nature of grief and love in the long opening poem **"Stroke"**, and shorter lyrics like **"Two Funerals"** or **"Burning the Effects"**. It is noticeable incidentally that many of the poems written since *Eight by Eight* (in 1963) show a preoccupation with death and social decay. Also, Mr. Buckley obviously writes slowly and revises painstakingly—as examination of the poems reprinted from *Eight by Eight* shows. There's a lesson here for the younger exuberant writers: inconspicuous mastering of technique does not come easily. (p. 61)

> *S. E. Lee, "Poetic Fisticuffs," in* Southerly, *Vol. 27, No. 1, 1967, pp. 60-71.*

VINCENT BUCKLEY [INTERVIEW WITH HENRY ROSENBLOOM]

[Rosenbloom]: *Are you worried, or have you worried, either before you became a recognized poet, or since, that your response to things and people isn't acute enough, or doesn't live up to the standards which you think people expect of you, or of a poet?*

[Buckley]: Well, the question is a bit obscure to me, but I'd answer it by saying that, first, when I think of my state of mind while actually writing, I'm not really conscious of anybody's expectations at all; I think that's the honest and full answer to that part of it. So far as the rest of it's concerned, I am conscious that my poetry doesn't seem to—many people have said this—doesn't seem to present the full range of interests I actually do have. This is related to what I said before about what had been taken as a split between two kinds of attention. For example, there aren't many jokes in my poetry; and it seems to me that one of the best ways one has of living in the world is just to make jokes about it, quite a lot of the time—and the more gratuitous the jokes the better. Well, there's not much of this in my poetry.

I wasn't thinking specifically, or only, of your poetry; but generally, as you walk around the world and you're confronted with a situation, do you ever have a self-consciousness about the way you should be responding, and the disparity between that and the way you are responding?

Oh yes, very much. . . .The thing is that at certain times in one's life one has to choose what amounts to a self-preservative tactic: that is, there seems to be some almost biological urge to say, 'Beyond this point I can't at the moment commit myself to . . .whatever it is. I will have to spend some time in recollection, regathering forces, and so on.'

Well, during those periods, of course, one's conscious all the time of tasks undone, or tasks done badly; and in particular—I'm quite sure you're right about this—one's conscious of a failure in oneself to respond to what seem to be clear . . .not so much demands, as clear invitations, almost, to share in other people's lives. And of course like most people I'm always sharing their lives at an unsatisfactory level, or unresponsive level. And this is bound to affect poetry. Though on the other hand if one goes around the world responding like mad to every bloody thing there's no poetry at all; or, surprisingly enough, you get fake poetry. You get poetry which is in a simplistic way just an extension of a response which is so habitual that it's become a stock one.

And I would like to distinguish between honesty and sincerity. It seems to me that the cult of sincerity, which is what we've got in lots of places now, is rather an unfortunate one, because it's as though people feel that they've got a responsibility to be spontaneous. Now, I think there's not enough joy in life, and that joy is the most elevated of the spontaneous emotions. There's not enough joy, but there's a kind of gritted-teeth gaiety, which is the direct product of the cult of sincerity. It seems to me that a man is being honest when he recognizes what's phony in himself, whether he can control it or not.

In your poetry, do you think that you say what you mean?

That calls for a dialectical reaction, doesn't it? I suppose the clever thing to say would be that it's more important to mean what you say than to say what you mean. But I don't really think that . . . well, two things: I don't really think that anybody says exactly what he means; and secondly, I'm sure those people are right who've said many, many times that, in a sense, you don't know exactly what you mean to say until you say it.

Do you consciously feel a disparity between your waking, walking self, and the self that expresses itself in your poetry?

I'll say yes to that. It's not a question I've ever asked myself,

and it's rather odd that I haven't asked myself—as a matter of fact until you asked me it never occurred to me that this could be a question. But now you ask me I think the answer would be yes; but I'd have to think fairly hard and at some length before I knew exactly what I meant by that. (pp. 319-21)

What kind of validity does poetry have, since you don't respond in iambic pentameters, your responses don't rhyme, you don't perceive experience in stanzas, and you probably don't discern metaphoric possibilities at the instant of perception?

'Validity' is not a word I'm very fond of; I've never found a use for it in talking about poetry. It seems to me that successful poems testify to the 'validity' of the process which has led to them, in such a way that their own validity can never then be questioned. In what you say there's an unintentional depreciation of human growth. That is, as Lawrence points out, one doesn't want any work of art to be the product of a static personality; a personality rested at a certain point. What you're asking is, can a poem be sincere if the personality which goes into its ending is different from the personality which goes into its genesis? I don't think the concept of 'sincerity' has got much to do with the whole business.

I'd approach the matter by using the word 'memory'. That is, I think that remembering what you might describe as *'the experience'*—although I prefer not to talk in these ways—remembering it can actually enhance it; not by changing it to make it more agreeable to one's present self, but by revealing possibilities in it that weren't perceived at the time. Now, if this is deemed to be insincere in some way, then I would say: so much for sincerity.

I don't *really* care what I was like twelve months ago, except in terms of what I'm like now, and I don't *really* care what I'm like now, except in terms of what I'm going to be like. In other words, one has to focus on the whole business of the process, the life-process, the process of growth. And by *fixing* the issue in, as it were, a separate instance, you are in fact depreciating this quality of growth, and depreciating memory. (pp. 321-22)

How much do you think poetry can achieve? How closely can it approximate to the texture of experience?

There are two things to be said about this, and they may sound contradictory. There's the old twentieth century business of the experience not being there, really, until the poem is written. I agree that a poem is not a business of trying to reproduce, or record, or reshape experience, in the plural, but is a matter of trying to give a rhythmic shape to a whole life-experience, whose relevance presents itself in this or that mode at this or that moment.

I may seem to be saying that poetry is an autonomous activity, and that it doesn't have much to do with life-experience at all. In fact I'm saying this; I wouldn't want to say anything like that. The autonomy of a poem has been far too stressed in the criticism of this century. But I do think it has to be said that it's not 'experiences' that one's trying to do something with, but a whole life-experience presenting itself in different modes.

And the second thing is that poetry can approach very closely, very closely indeed, to the actual texture of one's life. It can present it in an enhanced fashion, and can enhance *it*. I think it's the highest humanist act. That is, it's the act which can most show people what it means to be human. Now, by what means it does this . . . well, that's a long story, and it differs from poet to poet, anyway. But whether you deal with it in terms of rhythm, or in terms of metaphor, or in whatever terms you deal with it, it's a humanity-making act; more so than the novel, because the novel is in part some kind of mirror. I don't think poetry is anything like a mirror.

Men just learn through poetry, if they approach it in a sustained and loving way. They learn what it's like to be a fully alive, rhythmically breathing being, who is conscious in ways that no other being is conscious. It seems to me that all this is just built into poetry, and the very shape of the poem is a kind of guarantee, or witness to this. If you began from scratch and asked what one kind of thing a man could do which would in its own inner structures show the meaning of being a man, you might well come up with the notion of poetry. (p. 323)

What dissatisfies you most [in your own poetry]?

I could point to a number of things that dissatisfy me a lot—critics have discovered them anyway, so I may as well mention them. One is the prevalence of a kind of personal poetic jargon, or what has been called a 'repertoire'. Another is the falling into too glib a lyric line—and so on. But what dissatisfies me most is underneath all these things. And that is a failure to carry on and complete, on the page, or as it were *out there,* something which I'm conscious of in myself as a potentially complete rhythmic movement. In other words, what dissatisfies me most about my own poetry is the number of times poems are quite simply not complete so that there's something almost factitious about the way they get finally shaped.

What are you trying to achieve as a poet?

I'd revert to the business about rhythmic shape. It seems to me that all the greatest poetry has a quality of utterance; a quality of revelation of what's in the psyche; a quality of revelation of what's in the world that the psyche confronts: a quality of the thing made, the thing shaped. And it seems to me that it's by a stress on rhythm, that is, on complex rhythm, that these seemingly separate features of the enterprise get brought together. So that, if I had to say in a couple of words what I regarded myself as doing, it would be that I'd like to create, or bring about, or bring out, rhythmic shapes which are both true to the world as it actually is, and true also to what I take to be an enduring aspiration of men: that is, to the paradisal possibilities of life.

That is, if you can get realism, and the paradisal aspiration, into a poem, or into a body of poems, then you're going to do it largely through rhythmic shaping, and that's what I'd like to do. For example, I'd like to—if I knew Hebrew—I'd like to translate the *Song of Solomon;* except that the competition there is pretty stiff.

And to what do you want your poetry to bear witness?

To the sense that there are powers and principles in life which are of overwhelming importance, and which work or are displayed most fully in a relationship with other people and/or the world of art. And the recognition of these powers and principles is what we call religion, and so I want my poetry to bear witness to the possibilities in life which I'd call religious.

Have you always tried for this?

My earlier poetry tended to limit the operation of these powers and principles to more standard situations: death, Christian symbols, etc. The later poetry has become a great deal less denominational; I think it's become more religious. There is a certain phoniness in the denominational stance.

I also once thought you could speak more directly to others than I do now; or, that speaking fully means being heard fully. The effect can be seen in the **"Stroke"** sequence, the **"Song for Thomas Nashe,"** and **"Places,"** which give an idea of what I'm up to. It's made me keener on realizing the world as a presence, not just a repository of things to be sacked, or sucked, or fiddled with.

Finally, how important is your poetry to you?

I can answer straight away that poetry is the most important thing in life for me. How important is *my* poetry, to me? I'd have to divide this question into two parts, and say that I would find life impossible without writing poetry, and without thinking poetry, and without feeling poetic possibilities in things that happen, pretty well all the time. But if it were a question of how important to me is the poetry that I've written, I wouldn't know how to answer that because I'm conscious of having written only a fraction of the poetry that, as it were, I've experienced. And in fact I'm not very happy with the great majority of the poems I've written.

But I'm sure there are all sorts of subtleties that I could introduce into this question, which I'm a bit diffident about doing because I'm afraid of giving a false impression, you see. For example, if you say to me, 'Well, yes, you say that poetry, that writing, thinking, feeling poetry, is the most important thing in life, why then don't you write more?'—if you say that to me I wouldn't know how to answer it. I could, of course, plead circumstances—which would be a partial answer. If I thought more about it, however, I'd be forced to say that the hope of actually getting a great deal of what I consider most important revealed in poetry is a very difficult one to hold on to. One's conscious so often of missed opportunities, mistakes, failures, and so on that although one knows one can do the job in a sense, the hope of getting a world shaped in poetry is a pretty desperate one. And I would think this was one reason why I didn't write more.

As I said before, there's too much poetry written, and each of us has, in the past, written too much poetry. It might have been absolutely essential for one to have written too much poetry in order to keep going at all, but I think one did. And I'd sooner write rather more than I do, and rather less than I used to. (pp. 324-25)

Vincent Buckley and Henry Rosenbloom, in an interview in Meanjin, *Vol. XXVIII, No. 118, September, 1969, pp. 317-25.*

A. K. THOMSON

Behind Vincent Buckley's poetry and criticism is an outlook which in his sense is authentic, coherent, and realistic, based on perennial metaphysical and religious principles. The particular outlook is not one which obtains universal assent, and indeed makes many uneasy. He treats Christianity as history not as myth. He is guilty of the sin of particularity. This without doubt interferes with the reception of his work, but Buckley is a considerable poet and, since understanding comes before criticism, this essay attempts some understanding of his poetry.

He takes the title of his first book, *The World's Flesh,* from the poem **"Eucharist"** in the same volume:

> Flesh of the world, my heart's wild flesh, who come
> Burning the hands that may not touch, and eyes
> That lift up their preparedness like a room
> Which only you may enter, give me now
> The body's quiet, the high candid strength
> To bear some iron cross upon the brow,
> And wisdom, for the world in all its length.

The very title illustrates one of the difficulties inherent in Buckley's treatment of diction. 'Flesh' in this context is the Body of Christ which sustains and nourishes the world. His use of diction and imagery in this first volume was one of the main reasons critics found his work obscure. (p. 293)

Some of the poems in *The World's Flesh* are overtly religious and with too palpable a design. **"The Death of St. Catherine of Siena"**, the saint turned politician, and **"Tarsisius"**, the boy martyr, are not completely successful, but they contain competent writing. Whether one thinks of the martyr or the small boy, the following is beautifully written. The imagery is in the tradition and raises meanings in widening circles, the syntax moves at ease within the limits of the verse, and the sense is clear:

> Our times are withered, and we cannot think
> Of love ablaze in gardens, or of the green
> Rose-tree, plant of Jericho—or think
> Of martyred souls, and of the lonely
> Sacrifice ascending like a breath
> Into the hands of God: but think only
> Of the small boy stretched in death.

"The Flight Into Egypt" is an eloquent poem in which effective and individual use is made of traditional imagery. It is interesting because it is a companion piece to [T. S.] Eliot's "Journey of the Magi" and because, in part, it illustrates how complex Buckley's writing can be, and how the complexity is justified by the largeness of the effect obtained within the compass of a few words.

> Yet she who burns with a midsummer fire
> Is closed like a green branch upon her fear,
> Feeling a greater menace, knowing at last
> That Egypt leads to a high room
> Of light, in which the intimate speech of doom,
> Black as a smoking torch, shall pass him round:

The high room is the room in which the Passover, the Flight from Egypt, was celebrated by Christ and his disciples at the Last Supper, the origin of Mass, and where the pending betrayal was foretold. The handling and the culmination of the imagery is superb.

[Poetry] to Buckley is a vocation: it celebrates that which is sacred in his life. It is a seeing of ultimate meanings, not a surrender to immediate experiences, whether serious, emotional, or even intellectual. His poem **"Country Town"** is remarkable for its insight and should be contrasted with Slessor's "Country Towns". The intention in the two poems is quite different. Slessor's is a brilliant description of surface impressions: Buckley's attempts to get beneath the surface. His poem renders admirably the harshness and brashness of the country town and he does this by using among other things a simile derived from whisky.

> The town settles, dawdling into her streets
> Like whisky against dark wood, the ancient grain
> That limits and matures; but still, harsh on the tongue,
> (As though a rawness touched our very bones),
> Swirls in some vague, fierce recollection:
> And we are its vaguer, fiercer connoisseurs.

Buckley in his **"Image of Man is Australian Poetry"** takes the usual line that the poet had first of all to feel at home in his environment before he could write unselfconsciously about it. This is true up to a point, but it doesn't take into account the writer of talent. Good writers have a literary independence because they have an individual outlook which is never dependent entirely on the books they have read, and most poets write poetry because they have read poetry. Good poets are also as a general rule well educated, using the word in a wide sense. The minor poet's inspiration is entirely literary and what he writes is wholly derivative; the writer with talent has an inspiration partly literary, but because of his skill with words he transcends his exemplars to reach an individual style, which must include the seeing of the environment in an individual way. Buckley has rendered admirably the working class Irish in poetry, and in this he has extended the Australian sensibility. His religious poems, too, using the terms in a wide sense, are a new departure in Australian poetry. (pp. 295-96)

In this first volume are to be found the subjects that continue to form the material of Buckley's later poems. He is intensely interested in his family, immediate and remote. His immediate family he sees as a sacred unit and it is in keeping that his poem to his daughter should be a prayer, that it should be concerned with her salvation, and that it should lament the decadence of uncertainty of our times. The poem shows Buckley's certainty with syntax, the ease with which clause fits into clause to join in a stanza whose dignity fits its subject. It uses the traditional and dignified images—'flower', 'apple,' 'ice'—images invested with the poet's originality and individuality.

> May she not seek the heaven of an hour,
> Nor the parched heaven of unbelief—that bind
> Our thoughts under the root of death's great flower;
> Nor need the oblique elegy of the wind
> To straighten or define a life
> Filled with its splendid form, and brief
> As a poised apple quivering on its bough.
> Pride earns no autumn strength, but withering ice
> That burns through flesh, till all we see or know
> Is virtue matched with its particular vice.

Buckley is interested in the larger family, the society of which he and his family form a part, and the physical environment in which that society lives and by which in part it is formed. The ideals and beliefs which animate that society and which influence its shape are of the greatest importance to him because these determine its health, and the happiness and security of its individual members. He deplores both vitalism and nationalism. Vitalism he defines 'very crudely as the view which considers the primitive forces of life, amoral and irresistible, more important than the pattern of moral and aesthetic discrimination by which the adult being lives', and he argues that it would substitute the reign of impulse and sensation for that of any kind of realism—whether sensuous, natural, intellectual, or social. (pp. 296-97)

Buckley's second volume of poetry, *Masters in Israel* (1961) appeared seven years after publication of *The World's Flesh.* There are important differences in the two books. The diction of *Masters in Israel* is more direct, more individual, and contains much less rhetoric. The subjects treated are much the same but the scope is widened. The religious poems have become more catholic and less Catholic. Buckley has become more of a poet and less of a spokesman. A close consideration of the differences in the two books reinforces the impression that he is the best critic of his own work.

The title of the book occurs in the Gospel of St. John, but the immediate source of the title appears to be a poem by James McAuley, "An Art of Poetry", dedicated to Vincent Buckley. McAuley writes:

> Since all our keys are lost or broken,
> Shall it be thought absurd
> If for an art of words I turn
> Discreetly to the Word?
> Drawn inward by his love, we trace
> Art to its secret springs:
> What, are we *masters in Israel*
> And do not know these things? [Italics added]

Buckley places a very high value on poetry and it is consistent that some of his poems should deal with poetry. In his essay **"Poetry and the New Christians"** he writes of Vernon Watkins:

> This is not the poetry of a man who is overcome by dread or sloth; it is the poetry of a man who says: 'God can fill both my soul and my body with life that is the fruit of love. Yet man is sick and suffering from the world; let me go to him through my poetry, for poetry is the only means I have'.

The first poem in *Masters in Israel,* **"Late Tutorial"**, is about poetry and it arises out of a familiar situation involving Buckley as a university teacher. Whether the essay was written before the poem or after is not important. What is important is that he either paraphrased part of the poem in his essay, or he had the poem in mind when he was writing the essay:

> O man is sick and suffering from the world,
> And I must go to him, my poetry
> Lighting his image as a ring of fire,
> The terrible and only means I have;

"Reading to My Sick Daughter" is another poem about poetry, set in the familiar setting of home. A third poem dealing with the writing of poetry is **"Before Pentecost"**. Buckley has written poems dealing with poetry in his rôle of teacher, of father, and of believer. (pp. 298-99)

His best poem about poetry, **"Impromptu for Francis Webb"**, is addressed to a friend. It deals with much more than poetry, of course. It is concerned with that sickness of the mind which results in total withdrawal from the world and, too often, total immersion in an abyss of misery, when

> The soul speaks in its harsh natural language,
> And the world shrinks to an involuted shell
>
> Carrying your passion as rumour or complaint
> Into the ear of death.

It touches on those who have a vision of paradise:

> We cannot cease
> Visioning an age without barrier or taint,
> The resurrected body in its peace
>
> Walking its heaven;

It also gives the world its place in effective under-statement:

> This is our world, this is our only world,
> Which lives, and breathes, and will be glorified;
> Displaying, as a woman, naked but not wild,
> The silvering shadows of her rounded side.
>
> Has any man, poet or fool or saint,
> In leaving her not started and cried out
> Till his very bones re-echoed the complaint:
> 'No, I'll not leave . . . not leave . . .'And broken his heart?

The most immediately appealing of the familiar poems is **"Father and Son"**. The poet has chosen to write it, for the most part, in octosyllabic couplets, and shows some of the mastery of this form that we usually associate with Yeats. There is the semi-humorous reference to the self, 'Two small, self-wounding, fearful men.' The poem never degenerates into sentimentality because the poet exercises strict control of tone and, more important, perfect tact. Also, and this is rare in Australian poetry—and indeed in any poetry—he is entirely successful in his handling of conversation, which reveals character, within the poem. The poem catches, too, a nicety, the gap of years, of circumstance and of nature that makes it difficult for father and son to meet; and the desperateness of the son's endeavours to meet the father. In order to see just how much Buckley has added to Australian poetry with poems of this kind, in approach, in the handling of metre and language, and in sensibility, this poem should be compared with, say, Judith Wright's "The Garden". (p. 302)

Arcady and Other Places represents a considerable advance on *Masters in Israel.* A valid general criticism of *Masters in Israel* was that in many instances the poems suffered from a lack of direction. The poems in his third volume are more direct, although this is in part due to the subject matter, and to the tone. The subjects are familiar: his family, religion, politics, poetry—aspects of

> the impulse to establish the sense of man's life and his human relationships as being connected with, or, better, bonded with forces in the universe, which have their correlations in his own psychic life and so in at least some of his chief relationships, but which cannot be accounted for in *terms of* his psychic life, are in some sense superior to him, in some sense govern him, or manifest to him in terms of power and presence, and in some sense require of him adoration, worship, and celebration.

This is part of a general definition of religious poetry, and in this wide sense everything that Buckley writes is religious. He goes on to say that religious poetry 'may or may not involve the further concepts of a communal salvation, and an eternal life lived either in personal or communal terms'. In his poetry all these concepts are present and persistent, but the poetry moves steadily away from a specialized use of them, that is from a use special to any one church, and towards a more generalized approach. Both specialized and general aspects are present in *Arcady and Other Places,* but while knowledge of a special use may enrich a poem, it is not, strictly speaking, necessary for understanding.

The titles of Buckley's volumes of poetry are always significant. The phrases 'The World's Flesh' and 'Masters in Israel' indicate clearly enough the tenor of the poems that comprise the two collections. 'Arcady and Other Places' is an ironical phrase, almost savagely so. The poems have been arranged carefully in a deliberate order and cover a wide range, which is necessary to give the irony full play. The workmanship is consistently high.

So far as physical environment is concerned Buckley gives the impression of moving within a relatively small compass, despite the fact that his poems may be set in Melbourne, Dublin, Prague, or Cambridge. This seems to be because the experiences which made him what he is took place within small confines: it may be because there are certain experiences to which he constantly returns as the years and events throw additional light on them. It is interesting to see how he writes of these experiences as his skill increases. Trees, for example, mean a great deal to Buckley, and we have to be clear about the two ways, not necessarily exclusive, in which he uses them. He is intensely aware of the religious symbolism of trees but he is equally aware of their actual presence in his own life. They were part of the intimate surroundings of his childhood, and it is this, in the first place, that makes their use so vivid in his verse. They are symbols but they are also actual trees. . . . In **"Willow and Fig and Stone"**, in *Masters in Israel,* he uses the fig and the vine as symbols and the poem also contains detailed descriptions of a fig tree.

A summation of what trees mean to him is contained in **"Borrowing of Trees"**:

I was born under a continual
Movement of trees.

In **"Parents"** *(Arcady and Other Places)* trees are used with great certainty and economy:

I stare
At the rust encroaching on the walnut branches
Or the pile of litter where the biggest pine tree
Used to stand, before my absence killed it.
Their door has a vine over it.

And here the vine transcends the actual vine to become a symbol which, because of the skill with which it is used and placed, is also personal and unique:

I nod, but the names, perils, dates mean nothing,
And where that's true, the deepest bonds are lost.
How will the vine bear this year? . . .

Buckley moves from using trees—and other objects—too consciously and cautiously as symbols in a religious drama, to using them unselfconsciously and naturally as part of his own background, as part of his own drama, and in the process they become more effective symbols. This is one of the notable advances from *The World's Flesh* to *Arcady and Other Places.*

The first poem in *Arcady and Other Places* is **"Stroke"**, a sequence of seven poems made intensely personal by its subject, the suffering and death of a father, and by its intensity of vision in which the paraphernalia of suffering is sharply focused by use of the right word and the right rhythm. (pp. 303-05)

With **"Stroke"** should be read **"Parents"** and **"Burning the Effects"**. These two poems are written in the familiar style Buckley handles so well, but with the addition of an economy of words difficult to achieve, and extremely effective. In this and in other ways they are better than poems of the same kind in *Masters in Israel.* This would also apply to the poem to his daughter, **"For Brigid"**, and to **"Market Day"**, in which he takes another clear-eyed look at the Irish:

A settled people whose good eye
Is closed to all but lechery,
Who spare neither the great nor young,
Who hate what the body understands,
Whose food is grass, whose wealth is dung.

Buckley's **"Eleven Political Poems"** remind us that he is a Latin scholar, and indeed one section of the same book contains distinguished translations from Catullus. The political poems are satires in the Roman fashion; that is, they are epigrams, and have much in common with **"Margins"**. They are witty, neat, and pointed, and they deal with types and not with individuals. As Swift observed, 'Satire is a sort of glass wherein beholders do generally discover everybody's face but their own; which is the chief reason for that kind reception it meets with in the world and that so very few are offended with it'. The poems are addressed rather to the practical understanding than to the imagination, and they have their roots in social and political circumstances of the time. (pp. 305-06)

Buckley's chief quarrel with totalitarian systems is that they deny man on the metaphysical level. He holds that salvation based on material prosperity leads men ultimately to turn from life, or as he puts it in **"Revolutionary Situations"**, men

Sense at heart our longing is the thirst
To blend our marrow-bones in the damp ground.

This leads to the situation he describes in the last poem but one in the book, **"Grace at World's End"**. This is, of course, too simple a statement of Buckley's stand, and he himself stated it better as far back as 1955:

The material universe is not seen in its fullness, it
is not even seen truly, if it is seen as the object of
human greed . . . the great heresy from which
Christianity shrinks is not the love of the material,
but the lack of spiritual realism with regard to it.

Whether this diagnosis is correct or not, few would deny that the malaise of our time is caused by a deepening realization of the divorce between the abstractions we live by, whether Christian or Utopian, and the realities of our existence.

Buckley also states that 'the material universe is harmful only if it is seen as the object of self-gratifying human desire, and not as a pattern of signs signifying God's presence in the world'. Many of his religious poems are concerned with this seeing of a pattern of signs. **"Places"** is a good example of this. The three places in the poem, described most vividly, are places in which he became aware of the presence. (p. 306)

"Death in January" is important for its Australian background, for its content, for its originality and independence of outlook, for its scope, for the extent to which it depends on tone, and for its sustained irony. The poem opens with a brilliant description of the sea, that 'striding coolness, that paradise entering all paradises'.

It is fitting that the last poem in the book should be **"Lament for the Makers"**, one worthy to stand beside Dunbar's poem of the same name, which Buckley says 'shows a dialectic of defeat and victory'.

Arcady and Other Places contains thirty poems if the Catullus translations are disregarded. They cover an amazing range of subject and emotion. They display a wide scholarship and offer evidence of a talent flexible enough to profit from a knowledge of what has been written before and how it has been written. They show a mastery of style that ranges from the deeply moving through the intimate and familiar to the ironical. They possess a surely handled rhythm that reinforces sense and mood. They reveal a rounded philosophy which everyone will not accept, but which is consistent with itself. They display a talent which has clearly moved away from the confines of the narrowly Australian to take a place in English letters. *Arcady and Other Places* is one of the most important collections of poems to appear in Australia. (pp. 307-08)

A. K. Thomson, *"The Poetry of Vincent Buckley: An Essay in Interpretation,"* in Meanjin, *Vol. XXVIII, No. 118, September, 1969, pp. 293-308.*

ALAN GOULD

The title sequence of *Golden Builders* is a meditation in twenty-seven parts set in Melbourne, in which a speaker, moving about the nightmarish inner city of towering scaffold and deafening jackhammers, agonizes over redemption. The objects of his compassion are various individuals who intrude on his life, haunted, estranged figures similar to the shades of Dante's *Inferno*. Indeed we are privy in these deliberations to a hell-on-earth, and the evidence for this is presented in frequent passages of rhetorical force, whether it be the opening lines:

> The hammers of iron glow down Faraday.
> Lygon and Drummond shift under their resonance.
> Saws and hammers drawn across the bending air
> shuttling like a bow; the saw trembles
> the hammers are molten, they flow with quick light
> striking; the flush spreads and deepens on the stone.
> The drills call the streets together
> stretching hall to lecture-room to hospital;

or the visit of a girl to an abortionist:

> The abortionist
> has the skill of an engineer
> his eyes brood like a pilot's. His hand is steady
> as he lifts it away from her sweating legs.
> So she imagines that something cried
> weakly at the furnace door
> wrapped in trash paper;

or the picture of the speaker's dying father:

> weeping with one side of his grey mouth.

Beside the Dante derivation, there is a closer ancestor to these poems, namely Eliot's *Waste Land*. In vision, technique, and occasionally in the voice itself, Buckley parallels Eliot. The literary echo is useful, anchoring the poem to similar works in the past and establishing a blood-tie with authors of a particular religious disposition. It is also the first clue to an absence of imaginative assurance in this sequence and elsewhere in the book, for on those occasions where the echo becomes simply a mannerism, the projection of this poet's landscape becomes a pallid imitation of the original. (pp. 71-2)

In other sections of the book my irritation stemmed, not from gratuitous allusion, but from sensitive stammer. I mean by this that whereas visual and tactile sense impressions are rendered with excruciating vividness, they exist in the poems as a form of debris, refusing to bond into an understanding of the matter in hand. As if proving that it will function with micro-nicety, the poet is flexing his sensory equipment, but

this sensibility serves to make poems that are impotent in directing a reader's attention on to a public, or at least a shared world, involuting it instead upon his sensitivity. There is a suspicious smell of narcissism in this operation. Consider how the searing sensual information in the following

> the ice brittles in your nostrils
> the small cuts open
> on your hands——the cigarette
> tears at your lip,

serves this rather limp conclusion,

> Edmonton——they had you listed
> as humid continental——but I found
> winds like ropes falling,
> walkable snow

I suggest that a preoccupation with sensibility per se in poetry, meaning the emphasis on the communication of sensation, is a morbid one, for it is wont to supplant the expression of forceful *ideas* with the instinct for unimportant details. It also has the effect of debilitating the imaginative force with which material is recreated into lines of poetry, replacing a fidelity in the rendition of entireties with an anxiety in rendering parts. There are signs that the interest in sensibility per se is waning in Australian poetry, and any restoration of a balance between idea and sensation, detail and entirety, is a move from infirmity to health. The danger of course is that the schools, in their next solution to the question "what does a poem do?", will proceed to another, and different, imbalance. (pp. 72-3)

Alan Gould, *"Unfolding versus Unloading,"* in Poetry Australia, *No. 64, October, 1977, pp. 68-73.*

CHRIS WALLACE-CRABBE

Vincent Buckley has a compound, and complex, reputation in Australian letters. It is not only that he exists as both poet and critic: many people do that. It is also that he has moved across a great deal of territory in the past twenty-five years or so, that he is a most difficult figure to pin down and label. His poetry produces an effect at once forceful and evasive.

As critic he first made his name with the pieces that were collected in *Essays in Poetry: Mainly Australian* (1957). Lively and idiosyncratic, rhetorical and colloquial, these essays pressed towards establishing a canon of twentieth-century Australian poets, a canon which still exerts wide authority. In a graver critical study, *Poetry and Morality* (1959), he turned his gaze upon Arnold, Eliot and Leavis, three workers in that moral-evaluative tradition which has long appealed to Buckley's fellow-Melbournians. His third substantial book of criticism, *Poetry and the Sacred* (1968), yokes together opening chapters on the concept of the sacred in literature and a bunch of single studies of writers whose work displays the glow of the numinous, exemplars as different as Wyatt, Blake, Melville and Yeats, the last-names being a recurrent visitor to his imagination.

There is no doubt that Buckley's cultural reputation has been further clouded, or further illuminated, by his different kinds of political commitment, distinctively Irish-Australian and, within a broadly social-democratic frame of reference, responding subjectively to successive public crises over the years since the Second World War.

Buckley's early verse, as gathered in *The World's Flesh* (1954), was an odd kettle of fish. Aspects of its lofty swaying eloquence sounded quite archaic ("O dead kin of my heart!"): almost as though they had descended to him through Christopher Brennan's version of the Celtic twilight. At the same time there was a taste for strong brews of language, for mixed diction which had affinities with Ransom, with Hart Crane and with Buckley's tormented contemporary, the late Francis Webb. In this and in the next book, *Masters in Israel* (1961), the poetry could be full of the strong physical apprehensions of a country childhood . . .or it could be high and aloof, or ravishingly obscure.

It was with *Arcady and Other Places* (1966) that the different kinds of poetic impulse began to cohere into a compelling style, a manner that truly delivered the goods. Whether in the extended reverie on familial pain and loss, **"Stroke"**, or in the plumcake-rich evocations of nature in **"Places"**, the poetry there showed that it had earned its authority.

Now Buckley's latest collection, *Golden Builders and Other Poems,* takes over the reins and goes on from where *Arcady* left off, especially in the title-poem, which makes up about half the book in pages, and a great deal more in achievement. In fact the **"Golden Builders"** sequence has won its reputation already: it is almost with a sense of surprise, or of *déjà vu,* that one finds it taking its place between covers for the first time.

It is a poem in twenty-seven sections—a topographical meditation, but dramatic for all that—upon the city of Melbourne as city, as home, as repository of the *mémoire involontaire* from which vivid pulsations rise to agitate the poet, and as a bustling, temporal copy of Blake's visionary Golgonooza. But the core of the achievement lies in the fact that Buckley has devised a kind of poetry here which can modulate from sonorous tetrameter quatrains to long, prophetic lines and to hemistichs or gapped lines of a Poundian kind. The grander gestures, the shifts of tone, grow out of the absolute sureness with which he recreates known details of a city, its inner-urban areas in particular: whether it be in terms of the wide, throbbing streets names after nineteenth-century English lords, or the queer glories of industrial pollution. . . .

Alongside the pictures, alongside the religious yearnings, **"Golden Builders"** is also an autobiographical poem: autobiography, that is, constructed mosaically, spatially, without chronology or causal sequence. What it creates is something like Freud's city of memory, "a mental entity . . . in which nothing once created has perished, and all the earlier stages of development had survived alongside the latest". Friends, loved ones, acquaintances, trees, swathes of townscape, all are set down in vivid juxtaposition by the poet, "the Montale watcher-figure", himself shaped by it all. All other poems in the book tend to be dwarfed by this. The comic reflection, **"Give me time and I'll tell you"**, and **"Christmas Cold"** are perhaps the best of them, along with a wry, bounding prose poem called **"Brought up to be Timid"**.

Many smaller lyrics give us the poet's peculiar ability in feeling images with his body: a sort of inward synaesthesia by which modulations of light, heat or moisture are felt with an almost neurotic intensity. In their tendency to Amygism (or Slessorism, it might be said) some of these minor pieces call to mind Empson's complaint that "most poetry today is in the Imagist tradition, and it simply isn't the fashion in poetry today to understand things". Towards this uncertain category might also fall the energetic poems about racehorses; but then, horseracing is intrinsic to the Australian Irishry.

Whatever one feels about such less demanding modes of impressionism, the presence of **"Golden Builders"** and half a dozen other fine poems makes this collection a substantial one, a frequently passionate exploration of the interplay between inherited Romantic traditions and one's own regional asphalt.

> *Chris Wallace-Crabbe, "Meditations upon Melbourne," in* The Times Literary Supplement, *No. 3975, June 9, 1978, p. 643.*

THOMAS F. MERRILL

Buckley has been compared to Robert Lowell, probably because he tends to anchor his verse to intimate, personal experience. On this account he deserves classification, along with Lowell, as a "confessional poet." . . . *Late-Winter Child* serves as convincing supporting evidence for such a judgment. It is a poetic sequence which documents the poet's second marriage, his middle-aged emotional reactions to the birth of his daughter, and, throughout, his responses as a lover to the alienating presence in his beloved's womb. *Late-Winter Child* is clearly a romantic enterprise, although one can discern in its lyric mesh Buckley's contempt for what he calls "vitalism," the view which "considers the primitive forces of life, amoral and irresistible, more important than the pattern of moral and aesthetic discriminations by which the adult human being lives." A mature, humanist rigor, for example, attends this mood which stoically braces against the sheer buffetings of time against the lovers' relationship:

> It was so tempting to construct
> an angry, taut 'I', spinning out
> lifetimes of poems. My passivity saved me.
> Your touch (was) the heat that upheld me.
>
> Believing nothing, I could hope
> to see, not a god, but a child,
> a place:—sunrise:—a whistle:—bird on stem:
> a low sky, downy with rednesses.

What makes *Late-Winter Child* more appealing to me than *The Pattern* is its willingness to remain content with particulars and avoid the insistent pressures of the "angry, taut 'I'" which, more often than not, generates over-adornment and rhetorical excess in Buckley's other efforts. These poems are generally quiet renderings which trust the inherent powers of "sunrises," "whistles," and "birds" to produce their own effects. Typically a lyric in *Late-Winter Child* will report a series of objects, responses to objects and perceptions simply drawn, and then effect a closure with a brief reflective summation such as, "restlessness of the new home," "I shiver with the pleasure / of earliness," or this telling, objective juxtaposition closing a subtle account of two lovers suffering a contretemps: "a warp / runs double / in the grain of this table."

The poems of *The Pattern* do not enjoy the simplicity and cohesion that naturally comes from a clear narrative development and, despite their obvious determination to fix their philosophical generalizations to local instances and place, they are deeply subjective, privately obscure and irritatingly self-conscious. Buckley has drawn criticism in his previous work for an uneasy accommodation of lyricism and rhetoric, and I think in many of these poems we find art seriously meddling with the natural sincerity of the verse. The "devices" overtly intrude, and they intrude, one comes to see, with mechanical predictability. Each and every reported object must generate its simile, each act must spawn its referential parallel. Metaphor competes with fact so relentlessly that the reader soon learns to trust neither. Clouds are "rank as animals," a hand is "solemn as a clock," the sun whitens like "disc of paper." Were these similes which integrated the elements of the poem there would be little to object in them, but more often than not they are discrete, self-contained events which perform as distracting redherrings leading us *away from* the business of the poem rather than into it. If only the verse would relax and resist the compulsion for elaborate artifice. Instead we are too aware of a self-conscious straining for profundity which in many cases seems unearned by the facts.

The accumulation of rhetorical activity in **The Pattern** finally leaves the impression that a sort of translating operation is going on: prose being methodically converted to poetry through a conscious process. The natural expected verb, for example, is rejected in favor of a perversely unanticipated one. A metaphoric qualification sends an otherwise concise and striking aperçu careening in an unexpected direction which confuses rather than clarifies. There is something unefficiently baroque about such images as "The cloud dilates like an eye," "Your eyes with the curtains / folded over them," or "A weasel-head / of darkness comes behind him, / and the coarse water flows to / one cloud electric on the shore." Invariably, our attention becomes fixed not to reality but to that which is *referential* to reality. Artifice does not so much imitate life as overwhelm it. There is so much that is potentially moving and interesting in these poems which have so much to say about the ways in which the Irish experience is continuous from land to land, as the book jacket announces, and from age to age, that one can't help resenting the murkiness that attends them. It is a murkiness not the consequence of a genuine mystery being addressed but one artificially induced by conscious art. (pp. 123-25)

In **"Ceol-Beag for James McAuley,"** there is a characterization of the relationship of Buckley and his friend and fellow Australian which reads:

> For years we'd argued; *or,* I listened, laughing,
> to the baroque inventions of your scorn.
> Style was your art; pain, art; philosophy
> an art like politics; and politics
> an art, too, like drawing hair from stone.

"Baroque invention" might accurately sum up Buckley's verse at its worse, but if one can patiently wait for the invention to wear itself down and for the poetry to take its rightful place, he will discover that Buckley's "scorn," his "pain," his "philosophy" and even his "politics" will prove rewardingly insightful. As with his friend McAuley, style is Buckley's art too, but in **The Pattern,** an art too zealously pursued. (pp. 125-26)

> *Thomas F. Merrill, in a review of "The Pattern," and Late-Winter Child," in* The Journal of Irish Literature, *Vol. IX, No. 3, September, 1980, pp. 122-26.*

GARY CATALANO

I have the impression that Vincent Buckley has finally escaped the dominance of his will and is now writing the poems

that come naturally to him, not those he believes he should. So much the better. Yet his current work still poses a problem for the reader.

Although nearly all of the poems in his two new volumes, [*Late Winter Child* and *The Pattern*] are written in a relaxed verse paragraph, in his handling of the form Buckley hardly catches the run of ordinary speech. Given the peculiar gravity of his tone I don't see how he could do this with any success, yet the somewhat ponderous movement of his lines can have the effect of making his work seem unduly solemn and portentous. The effect is an unfortunate one, for Buckley's poetry has a great deal to offer. His range of perception is certainly unique, and each poem puts you in touch with a person clinging fiercely to an innate vulnerability. The outer world indeed abuts the skin.

Perhaps the main thing which makes his perceptions unique is their firm tactile quality. Rather like an infant, Buckley apprehends the world by reaching out and dragging it to him. Although the following passage is neither as weighty nor as sticky as much of his poetry can get, it indicates something of what I mean:

> The only smell
> came from their clothes, where fireside
> smoke had been absorbed like sweat.
> Lake-flat land that held the hoofbeats
> of the Rakes of Mallow. The bog-cotton
> shuddered in the breeze, touching
> a scum of anemone-like small flowers.
> Glass glittered, strips of cloth wagged
> by the curing well. I made
> their rounds, I touched each smooth and whitened
> stone, hearing the tree-trunks settle
> in the peat, fathoms down.
>
> **("At Millstreet")**

It is true that some lines could do with a bit more fine-tuning (if 'smooth and whitened' were given a line of their own then the act of touching would be physically rendered, not just noted), yet the lengths to which Buckley has gone in order to register that complex web of sensations are indeed deserving of respect. We have an inveterate tendency merely to look at the world, a detachment which can all too easily issue in contempt and self-hatred:

> Now the hired cars bring us, full of effusion, to
> look, half-idly, at this still-soft body-scar from
> which we were leeched off so long ago. We wanted
> something to be proud of.
>
> **("Gaeltacht")**

The 'we' here are the Australian Irish returning to Munster and there gazing on a country both foreign and distressingly familiar.

Although a number of poems in **The Pattern** poignantly explore and document this return, it seems to me that right at the heart of Buckley's poetry origins (or at least defined, documented ones) are of no consequence. Does he not say as much in the following passage from the above-quoted poem?

> the origin is not
> one place but ten thousand:
> not a particular but a general
> fish web of fathers: something so ordinary
> you sit half-suffused with fear
> in front of it.

I may be guilty of mistaking the drift entirely, yet what he seems to be implying is, crudely put, that one's being is a country in itself. The search begins and ends there. While a particular landscape may help one to see place in human terms (he is always referring to the groin of the land, its cleft, abyss or vortex), the final search is always back to that 'closed soft place, with its must / of dark orderings, and dried rot'. As with Seamus Heaney, the 'dark' is almost entirely benevolent.

If Buckley can be said to have a vision, then it is simply one of the world's essential wholeness. Whether the immediate subject be a group of blind children whose pale heads are 'like a worm's', potatoes rolling like 'thrashing fish / out of the furrow', stone houses which bear 'stretch marks' or, indeed, 'a scum of anemone-like small flowers', every perception serves to re-awaken your lapsed belief that the whole of creation fits together as one unified thing. I cannot recall him actually stating such a belief anywhere in *The Pattern,* yet it can be felt on any one of its pages.

I am less enthusiastic about *Late Winter Child,* a sequence of 29 poems which celebrates the birth of a daughter. On the whole I do feel Buckley has managed the delicate task of exploring the subject at the same time as he respects its grave and private nature, yet it's often at the cost of a hypersensitivity which strikes me as mannered. I began my review of his two books by observing that he has finally escaped his will, yet in these poems one too frequently confronts a tremulous voice which Buckley, one feels, can slip into **at will.** It is most evident in the fifteenth poem in the sequence, with its quite baffling notations of heat, water, lightning and shivering light. (pp. 355-57)

> *Gary Catalano, "Stroking it Open: A Poetry Chronicle," in* Meanjin, *Vol. 39, No. 3, October, 1980, pp. 351-63.*

HERBERT LOMAS

[Vincent Buckley]—Australia-based, in spite of extended visits to his ancestral Ireland—still has, it seems, unsevered tap-roots in historical Europe. . . .

The Pattern is the inheritance of history: not something left behind but re-experienced in every generation as guilt and consequences, the 'common burden' we go on suffering: 'I'm terrified of the Ireland inside me,' says his James McAuley.

Perhaps it's also archetypal, 'in the night-patterns'. Definitions Buckley takes from the dictionary are: matrix, mould, example, precedent, and artistic design. At points the Pattern seems to approach the Logos, or divine pattern, of Herakleitos and Eliot. The Irish meaning of 'pattern' is a 'patron saint's day' and its festivities; and this derives from a connection between 'patron' and 'pattern'. The stone circles, like music, seem to suggest a vertical cosmic connection, as well as a horizontal.

> And further out, on the peninsula, the stones in their intricate circle seem almost to decorate the sun that pleasures them.
>
> (p. 130)

Buckley's a poet of pieties. He accepts his place among the accused of history, as well as the accusers. It's a useful irony that **"Dick Donnelly"**—an aborigine, 'the last member of his tribe, a man weathered as coal whose language no-one in the whole world shared'—had been given an Irish name. Buckley

doesn't doubt . . . the wisdom of being born. At birth, [in *Late Winter Child*] the unborn is the only one who doesn't ask 'How can we stand this?'; his travail is like the journey of a Bangla Deshi exile: 'We will fight our way home'. Yet

> I can see by the way you rally
> your own body into the world
> out there, between her legs,
> you will fight your way home;
> and I will at last
> touch you with full hands.

His hands are already full, with responsibilities, but they are to be fulfilled by the birth.

Buckley's language is not always interesting. . . . [Yet he] produces images of impact:

> Outside, on the earth hard as stone,
> the sparrow's embryo was smooth
> as a section of intestine.

The success here is a rather exceptional linguistic one: the surgical 'section of intestine' has a prosaic pungency that contrasts with 'hard as stone'. He rarely gets as far afield or as near to cliché as this. Often the words and their order are those of plain prose, yet the observation is fine-edged:

> The only smell
> came from their clothes, where fireside
> smoke had been absorbed like sweat.
>
> hearing the tree-trunks settle
> in the peat, fathoms down.
>
> and all the time
> I can feel your spirit
> emptying itself of your body. . . .

But there is sometimes a blandness about his vocabulary, and it's as if this shortage of words makes him strain them to create an equivalent to those subtle effects he observes.

> the intent colour
> that flows towards your eyes
> under the room's pressure.

I almost get the impression here, but not quite, and I suspect it's the fault of the formula, not me.

This is cavilling. The work is studded with clarities:

> the thunder comes in
> clean as a cat.
>
> Mouth and womb open together,
> the eye, too, seeking birth.
> Sometimes, I can hardly breathe
> for the smell of pregnancy: a tiny
> bud-creature altering the hormones
> so that I smell the change in your limbs,
> in your hair-parting
> a second lust.

Even in the poems that are not about the birth of his child, there's often a kind of sensual softness to which Buckley is always reaching, as if to a supernatural mother's flesh. He writes in a poetry of haiku-like images, Chinese or Japanese in its observation of striking isolated phenomena, at once irrelevant and relevant to the cosmos. (pp. 130-32)

> *Herbert Lomas, "Taproots," in* London Magazine, *n. s. Vol. 20, Nos. 8 & 9, November-December, 1980, pp. 126-32.*

GEORGINA BITCON

Vincent Buckley's poems in *Late Winter Child* are remarkable for the self-effacement of the poet:

> It was so tempting to construct
> an angry, taut 'I', spinning out
> lifetimes of poems. My passivity saved me.

The poems themselves focus on the pregnancy of Buckley's wife and his reactions to the subsequent birth of their daughter. In a recent issue of *Australian Literary Supplement,* David Malouf noted how even the best Australian poets have resisted major stylistic changes. Buckley does, however, appear to be trying to make a change to a clearer, more lyrical simplicity, right for the subject-matter, but I feel that the poems, although perfectly competent, are sadly rather more flat than lyrically simple. There are individual poems of the sequence of course, where this simplicity is perfected. . . . But in other poems the writing slips into flatness, and lines that are skillfully written seem nonetheless to lack imagination. This happens with poem XVI, whose second stanza begins promisingly enough:

> Deep smell of solstice flower
> they gave out, durable and blue
> a whole summer of bunched sprigs
> ready to burn.

In a poem that intricately relates the growing embryo and the mysterious, almost threatening quality of this unknown life-force, the poet moves towards his discovery that the lavender has gone, but the lines themselves let the poem down rather badly: "but this year, when I looked, / they'd cut the banks of lavender." The lines certainly dispel all the half-connections that the poem has been hinting at between the "new darkfound life" and the flowers redolent with their stored heat, but they do it in a disappointing way.

Part of the difficulty with the poems as a whole is that there is not enough tonal variety. The large and complex range of emotional states described by the poems is not accompanied by significant tone differentiation. One tends to tire of the careful gentleness and intellectual quality of poem after poem. Even at the moment of the child's birth, there is a sense of emotion being recollected pragmatically in tranquillity, and the poem has no sense of the powerful immediacy of childbirth, even though, like so many of the other poems, it is a fine piece of writing. . . . (pp. 474-75)

There is a similar problem of distance in *The Pattern,* a book of considerably more depth and complexity than *Late Winter Child. The Pattern* is an exploration of Buckley's own Irishness, an attempt to understand what this heritage means to him. This is particularly interesting because a Celtic background is part of the experience of so many Australians, but only Les Murray and now Buckley have set out to find what it means to have inherited this background. However, despite what appears to be a search of a very personal nature, a search for his own Gaeltacht as it were, *The Pattern* doesn't actually conjure up a very personal note on the whole. It is more an evocation of the Irish landscape and representative personalities of both past and present. It is an evocation of some strength, however. The poems show that peculiarly Australian trait of intense awareness of the landscape: there are abounding images of light and dampness, and the physical environment impinges constantly upon actions and reactions, states of mind. The poet is very much the outsider, the stranger, building all he experiences into a pattern in the hope of discovering his own place within it:

> Through the rain-shellacked glass
> you keep looking for some way
> into it, letting your mind bulb around one
> image or another: Damp paddocksfull
> of white refuse burning
> near Milltown: At Dingle, among papier mache
> cowboy hats, the butcher stooping
>
> into his car's trunk for the carcasses:
> Errigal the cone of buckled waste, its evening
> light spitting at your eyes
> like boiling metal: and at
> Meenlaragh the young girls flirting
> disdainfully with old men.

> ("Gaeltacht")

In the [**"The Pattern"**], the poet speaks of his intention to "go to" and "come back from" this "slow starved pattern" of Irishness in his own and other lives, his intention to follow the pattern "with inflamed nerves". Unfortunately, his nerves seem to be inflamed throughout the book, which means that alongside some stunning images ("All day, / travelling in the chipped moon-landscape, / your eyes were / heavy as milk."—**"Spanish Point"**) there is much that is simply overdone:

> Mollusc, membrane. Who
> has put the sea under this stone,
> drove down with hanging fingers to the
> seabed's flat cavernlands where mussels.
> whelks lay with their mouths
> together, their pulp
> flowing with invisible metal links.
> letting the water steep them
> in their dead colour
> Ireland as usual

> ("Membrane of Air")

This straining for effect also extends itself to the notion of the "pattern" that the poet wants to discover. It is the *desire* to discover it that is perhaps the stumbling block, for it does not appear to evolve naturally out of the sequence of the poems but is rather more a schema that has been forced on to them externally. By suggesting the search for the pattern in the first poem, the poet allows a kind of predictability to operate in the subsequent poems. There is a predictability in the attitudes he strikes, attitudes that are not discovered in the course of writing, and the push towards a preconceived goal produces images that are often too ardent, too easily come by. . . . The sheer complexity of some poems (such as **"Blind School"**) also makes it difficult to see where they fit into the poet's scheme of things. As with *Late Winter Child,* there is no greatly varied sense of rhythm: the poet makes very little use of it to enforce a point, and occasionally, through a lack of rhythm, poems become quite pedestrian:

> Her hand on her face
> pushing invisible strands
> becomes solemn as a clock
> as she wills herself
> lifted up in her own sunset.

> ("Fine Western Land; Cloud-Light")

Despite this, *The Pattern* contains much that is beautifully written and the reader is always aware of Buckley's obvious technical skill. Perhaps the irony is however, that despite Buckley's final claim that nothing separates him from the pattern but "a membrane of air", there is a possibly unwanted but nonetheless distinct elegiac note that runs through the book which suggests that, on the contrary, there is an irrevocable distance between the poet and his pattern, a suggestion that he is still "looking for some way into it". (pp. 476-77)

Georgina Bitcon, in a review of "Late Winter Child," and "The Pattern," in Southerly, *Vol. 41 No. 4, December, 1981, pp. 469-77.*

(Charles) Bruce Chatwin

1940-1989

English travel writer, novelist, essayist, and journalist.

Chatwin's semiautobiographical works combine cultural investigations with philosophic pursuits to depict strikingly different worlds. From South America to West Africa to central Australia, Chatwin's narratives limn obscure and dramatic landscapes where his physical journeys become metaphysical quests. Concerned with the origins of human nature, Chatwin explores "primitive" societies, relating his observations in spare prose punctuated with erudite allusions. Chatwin's fascination with nomadic cultures is reflected in works that argue against the pessimism, ethnocentricity, and materialism of modern Western civilization.

According to Chatwin, his enchantment with nomadism began with a medical prescription. As the youngest man ever appointed director of modern art at the prestigious auctioning firm of Sotheby & Co., twenty-five year-old Chatwin used his self-taught art expertise to acquire his own antiquities collection. When Chatwin temporarily lost his vision, his physician diagnosed his illness as a psychosomatic condition caused by scrutinizing pictures too closely and concluded that he would be cured by searching out long horizons. Upon regaining his sight, Chatwin travelled to the African Sahara, where he first encountered nomadic societies.

After brief ventures in archaeology and journalism, Chatwin began writing what he called "a letter from the end of the world." The resulting text, *In Patagonia* (1977), was praised by many critics as an imaginative rejuvenation of the travel genre. David Rieff commented that this highly personal account of a journey through South America's southern tip "quite simply revived travel writing from the genteel, philistine slumber in which the genre had reposed since the great days of Lawrence, Waugh and Robert Byron." In this work, which won the 1978 Hawthornden Prize and the 1979 E. M. Forster Award of the American Academy of Arts and Letters, Chatwin enhanced factual encounters with elements of fiction to delineate a desolate land scattered with misfits, refugees, and bandits. Chatwin portrays Patagonia as a cultural mosaic of Araucanian Indians, Welsh sheep farmers, and Jewish merchants colored with the legends of Ferdinand Magellan, Charles Darwin, and Butch Cassidy. Many critics agreed with Alistair Reid, who lauded Chatwin's ability to take the reader on an "armchair journey" to a fabled land.

The exotic kingdom of Dahomey is the setting for *The Viceroy of Ouidah* (1980), which was originally intended as a biography of a nineteenth-century Brazilian slave trader. Travelling in the West African country of Dahomey (later known as the People's Republic of Benin) to research the life of Francisco Felix de Souza, Chatwin was arrested as a mercenary and threatened with execution. He later formed his notes into a tightly compressed novel that fictionally presents a factual paradox: the flamboyantly brutal Christian slave-trader whose African descendants worship him as a demigod. While some reviewers objected to the book's explicit accounts of savagery in the slave trade, many lauded Chatwin's powerful images. *The Viceroy of Ouidah* was adapted for film by di-

rector Werner Herzog. Chatwin then challenged classifications of him as a travel writer with *On the Black Hill* (1982), a conventional novel about identical twins who spend eighty years on a remote Welsh farm. Important events in the story are confined to the family homestead; the peculiarities and limited perspectives of that existence emerge through a series of compact, keenly observed episodes. John Updike stated, "[Chatwin's] studied style—with something in it of Hemingway's chiselled bleakness, and something of Lawrence's inspired swiftness—touches on the epic."

Chatwin shifted locale once again for his fourth book, *The Songlines* (1987), which earned substantial critical praise in both Great Britain and the United States. A semifictional account of Chatwin's inquiry into Australian aboriginal culture, this largely plotless narrative becomes a medium for the author's meditations on the future of civilization. "Part adventure-story, part novel-of-ideas, part satire on the follies of 'progress,' part spiritual autobiography, part passionate plea for a return to simplicity of being and behavior," wrote Andrew Harvey, *The Songlines* is a chaotic mix of "anecdote and speculation and description, fascinating, moving, infuriating, incoherent, all at once." The novel's protagonist, a British writer named Bruce Chatwin, accompanies a railroad advisor as he surveys the aboriginals' sacred footpaths—the "songlines" of aboriginal ancestors who walked the land in a "dreamtime" singing every rock, cave, and ant-hill into existence. Into this explication, Chatwin introduces excerpts from the "moleskin notebooks," which contain his observations on other nomadic cultures and erudite references to works by Søren Kirkegaard, Konrad Lorenz, Buddha, and Herodotus. These allusive notebooks become Chatwin's vehicle for transforming an adventure narrative into a philosophical treatise on the natural state of humanity. While some critics objected to Chatwin's disjointed construction, and others denounced his characterization of aboriginals as stereotypical, many praised Chatwin's innovative cultural analysis and entertaining style.

Chatwin's last work of fiction, *Utz* (1989), examines the nature of materialism from a different perspective. The novel centers on Kaspar Utz, a Czech aristocrat who amassed a priceless collection of Meissen figurines during World War II and the Soviet occupation of Prague. When Utz dies, the treasures he had promised to the communist regime disappear. The narrator, a British writer who had briefly met the collector seven years earlier, tries to recover the porcelain and to reveal Utz's past in a city of furtive intellectuals. Critics agreed that Chatwin evinces his art expertise in this study of a life usurped by possessions. Christopher Driver remarked that this compressed, detailed novella proves Chatwin "a master of the miniature as of the Great Divide."

During the final year of a debilitating illness, Chatwin compiled *What Am I Doing Here,* a collection of essays published posthumously in 1989. This volume of new and previously published pieces includes accounts of Chatwin's arrest in Benin, his tour of India with then-Prime Minister Indira Gandhi, and his appraisal of a Chinese corporate geomancer. Reviewers commented that together, the essays form an illuminating, entertaining self-portrait. Diane Ackerman commented: "What brings [the essays] alive is [Chatwin's] special talent for noticing life's strange, riveting details. He was a born Autolycus, a snapper-up of unconsidered trifles. What comes through in his last book is a life miscellaneous and on the move, traveled on foot, but never pedestrian."

(See also *CLC* Vol. 28 and *Contemporary Authors* Vols. 85-88, 127.)

THOMAS KENEALLY

I feel I saw a little of the origins of this extraordinary book [*The Songlines*]. One hot March day in 1984 I said goodbye to Bruce Chatwin in the lobby of an Adelaide motel as he was checking out to go to Alice Springs in central Australia to pursue a life-long obsession with nomads and the mystery of nomadism. . . .

He wished to inquire into the Aboriginal 'Dreaming-tracks' or 'Songlines' which cross Australia, often running from the Indian Ocean coast to the beaches of South Australia. Each ancient hero sang himself out of nothingness and into both an animal and human form, and then progressed across the landscape *singing* it into existence. 'One should perhaps,' says Chatwin, 'visualise the Songlines as a spaghetti of Iliads and Odysseys, writhing this way and that, in which "every episode" was readable in terms of geology.' As Chatwin says,

even today men of the Pintubi tribe 'sing up the country' as they travel along one of these ancient Songlines where every boulder, hill and spring represents a particular ancient but eternally present feat.

Chatwin's mediator with the Pintubi people was a Russian Australian called Arkady, son of a Cossack, whose work was to negotiate between railroad engineers and traditional Aboriginal owners of land. . . .

Through Arkady and through other Caucasians who work on the edges of the great Songline mysteries, Chatwin meets an extraordinary succession of Pintubi elders. Some of the white Australian auxiliaries to the Aboriginal cause give him a hard time. 'And what makes you think you can show up from Merrie Old England and clean up on sacred knowledge?' one asks. Chatwin sees their insecurity as the reflection of all the insecurity of sedentary man in the face of the great nomadic puzzle.

Chatwin considers the question of whether man is better and happier as a nomad and the question of whether God abominates the settled. He suspects, as Pascal did, that 'All man's troubles stem from a single cause, his inability to sit quietly in a room.' But then he goes on to ask whether our nomadic past is rooted in an Original Sin of murder and cannibalism, or an Original Triumph of humankind over the Beast?

It is not surprising that a writer of such a compassionate and sanguine temperament should plump for the side of Original Triumph: perhaps over a long-vanished species of panther called *Dinofelis*. It is beyond most readers' competence to comment on how definitive any of this is meant to be scientifically, but it makes an exciting tale.

Chatwin's earlier novel, **On the Black Hill,** delighted by pleasant stealth, through a succession of apparently inconsequential incidents. There is that same quality here, a circling—through pub conversations, shopping mall encounters in Alice, backyard barbecues, long drives westwards, and prosaic questions of Arkady the Cossack's attachment to a girl called Marion—towards the centre of the mystery. . . .

This brave and robust book may not cohere as well as some of Chatwin's other work does. The—at first—apparently random excerpts from his notebooks on his travels amongst African and other nomads, and his conversations with anthropologists and philosophers, known and unknown, do not always seem to fit well onto the Australian sections of the book. The faint sentimentality of Arkady's marriage sits poorly with the great dignity of the three old men who end the book, lying on hospital bedsteads in a clearing, having come there to die close to their *tjuringa* store.

It happens that the *tjuringa* is a wooden or stone plaque which represents a man's external soul. The greatest tragedy is for a human to lose his *tjuringa,* but these three ancients were in secure possession. 'They knew where they were going,' writes Chatwin, 'smiling at death in the shade of a ghost gum.' The sentence is characteristic of Chatwin's casual power. [*The Songlines*] is a remarkable and satisfying book.

Thomas Keneally, "Going for a Songline," in The Observer, *June 28, 1987, p. 23.*

JANE DORRELL

The first sentence [of *The Songlines*] sets the scene brilliantly: 'In Alice Springs—a grid of scorching streets where men in long white socks were forever getting in and out of Land Cruisers—I met a Russian who was mapping the sacred sites of the Aboriginals'.

Bruce Chatwin went to Australia to study Aboriginal culture at first hand. With the Russian, Arkady, as his knowledgeable guide he travelled through the Northern Territory meeting the inhabitants and hearing the legends of their history. *The Songlines* is his account of this expedition.

The Aboriginals believe that long ago, in the 'dreamtime', their ancestors walked the length and breadth of the land singing each feature of the landscape into existence. The tracks they made are the songlines; the songs they sang have been handed down through the ages, each tribe having its own which, like birdsong, marks the boundary of its territory. . . . It is not hard to see why there are problems when the white man approaches with plans for land development. The surveyor is not going to be too sympathetic when his is told that his projected railway line cannot follow the route he has chosen because it would cross a sacred, though invisible, songline.

But Chatwin, as we know from his previous books, is fascinated by what he calls 'the question of questions: the nature of human restlessness'. This is not a novel about the struggle of the Aboriginal in modern society; there are no scenes of confrontation between Black and White, there is no plot and no dénouement. Rather it is a novel of ideas. He weaves a narrative from these themes. From the Aboriginal myths and legends, from his reflections on man's nomadic and aggressive nature which he illustrates with long extracts from writers as diverse as Ardrey, Rimbaud, Ibn Batuta and Lorenz, and finally from descriptions of the life and customs of the outback which are often hilarious and which bring one happily back to earth after a long passage of ethnophilosophy. We hear of Chief Tabagee who committed the cardinal sin of singing his ancestor's sacred song to men from another tribe. Since then he has been known as Chief Cheekybugger Tabagee. (p. 21)

Literature plays an unexpectedly important part in the outback. A local storekeeper keeps his customers waiting while he finishes the account of the Duchesse de Guermante's dinner party—Proust having priority over sales—and an ancient Aboriginal lawman has a copy of *Thus Spake Zarathustra* among his bedside books. It won't be long before he adds *The Songlines* to the pile for it will surely be as much enjoyed by those immediately involved as by armchair travellers on the other side of the world.

Chatwin has done for the Northern Territory what he did ten years ago for Patagonia. He has written an absorbing book on a disappearing world, a world in which it is said that 'by spending his whole life walking and singing his Ancestor's songline a man eventually becomes the track, the ancestor and the song'. (p. 22)

Jane Dorrell, "The Ancestor and the Song," in Books, *London, No. 4, July, 1987, pp. 21-2.*

ROGER CLARKE

[The review excerpted below was slightly revised from its original form by the critic.]

Bruce Chatwin's tipple is displacement. His fascination with the nomadic has brought him into contact with an extraordinary assortment of rootless individuals far from their own countries, far from their own time, rather like the hippies of India who tell you that Kennedy is dead. Mixed in with most of his novels is a pronounced autobiographical streak, he's conscious of himself as both writer and traveller. . . . Like Byron, Chatwin is haunted by colourful and restless forebears, and the knowledge that many uncles died in all parts of the world seems to catch him in a genetic imperative.

Chatwin shares affinities with Conrad, particularly with *Heart of Darkness*. Francis Coppola's personal addendum to this novel's sullied humanity involved Marlon Brando heaving with sweat over decaying volumes of T. S. Eliot and Jesse Weston in the black heart of the Vietnam jungle. [In *The Songlines*] Bruce Chatwin follows a similar line with Spinoza-reading policemen in the Australian Outback, with an Aborigine who ponders Nietzsche and another desert-dweller who declaims Marx before meals (he later suffers an intestinal blockage). Is Chatwin a latterday Kurtz, throwing in a worldly career, seeking the extreme places of the world in which to ruminate?

Chatwin's theory is as follows: that the restlessness of man is simply a vestigial urge to migrate. He acknowledges the apparent 'happiness' of nomadic tribes—how, interestingly, it is often the women who keep the tribe nomadic while their husbands grumble about maisonettes. Often the status of the nomad is lower than the most menial land-tiller (witness the general disgust at the Stonehenge caravan, and the gypsies in general). Gypsies, in common with Aboriginals, refer to all settlers as 'meat'. It's the same word the Aborigines use for their social security cheques. Chatwin quotes Koestler to the effect that man is fundamentally insane—is this the result of a city-dwelling civilisation? . . .

It seems Chatwin has fallen in an old trap—he is instinctively drawn to the spiritual, yet somehow shys away with a lot of anthropological musings on fossils and the sabre toothed, great beast, who preyed on man's early ancestors. It is crammed with quotations from the most esoteric sources, and is clearly the result of many years' deliberation. Chatwin once tried to write a book on nomads and failed—this then is its shattered remains. Chatwin just doesn't seem up to the magnificence of the questions he poses, and occasional chapters retreat into a shell-shocked and quivering palsy of learning—pages and pages of quotes, albeit very illuminating ones. The whole story achieves a glazed, unsatisfying tone. He sees rituals, hears about Dreamtime, witnesses the exploitation of the Aborigines. But he never makes a connection.

However, it is still streets ahead of the average conceit that gets 'novelised' these days, and Chatwin has given himself a tough brief. Often his prose is of great beauty, and I like the way he always gives himself good lines.

Roger Clarke, "Walkabout," in The Listener, *Vol. 118, No. 3019, July 9, 1987, p. 29.*

WALTER GOODMAN

In the mythology of Australia's aboriginals, Bruce Chatwin

tells us at the outset of his ruminative journey deep into their continent and their dreams. "Songlines" are "a labyrinth of invisible pathways which meander all over Australia." . . .

It's a lovely notion, and in this rich book [*The Songlines*], Mr. Chatwin, a British writer and traveling man who feels linked to migratory peoples, dreams up scruffy little towns of the Australian desert that sit atop age-old deposits of myth. It's a trip into anthropology, religion and philosophy, as well as into the edgy coexistence of the whites and aboriginals in his imagined outback. For want of a word, he calls the result a novel, but that's misleading. Think of it rather as a travel book of a special, speculative sort. . . .

Mr. Chatwin's descriptions of the rough country and its inhabitants are pithy: "Bruce had quarter-to-three feet, red hair, flabby buttocks and oval jowls. His arms were tattooed with mermaids." Wherever he and [and his guide] Arkady go, they find fellow intellectuals, such as Red, the police chief in a place called Popanji who lifts weights and reads the *Ethics* of Spinoza. Or Rolf, a storekeeper and sometime novelist in Cullen, who favors espresso coffee and Gauloise cigarettes and subscribes to the *Nouvelle Revue Française* and *The New York Review of Books*.

The more convincing characters, however, are neither well read nor of delicate sensibility; some see the aboriginals as nuisances, a species that needs to be subdued or eliminated. Without making a cause out of it, Mr. Chatwin contrasts the existence to which the country's native peoples have been reduced and the natural rhythms of nomadic life. But moved though he is by their myths, he does not paint today's aboriginals in Rousseauesque colors. The strongest episode in his book is a harrowing account of a couple of them using a car to run down a kangaroo. Their regard for human life, he makes plain, does not extend to the lives of other animals.

The book's narrative, not as sturdy as the land cruisers that everybody seems to drive, breaks down altogether as the author is stranded in Cullen. . . . Mr. Chatwin takes up the notebooks he has kept on his travels from Swartkrans in the Transvaal to Shahrak in Afghanistan to Steiermark in Austria, where he talked with Konrad Lorenz, whose views on mankind's aggressiveness make sense to him. He connects his encounters around the globe (not excepting Berkeley, Calif., and Miami) with his readings of everybody from Kierkegaard to Rimbaud to Herodotus. His theories are summed up by a pensée of Pascal. "Our nature lies in movement, complete calm is death."

It is Mr. Chatwin's conjecture that man has been designed by Natural Selection "for a career of seasonal journeys *on foot* through a blistering land of thornscrub or desert." He goes on in typically bracing prose: "If this were so; if the desert were 'home'; if our instincts were forged in the desert; to survive the rigors of the desert—then it is easier to understand why greener pastures pall on us; why possessions exhaust us, and why Pascal's imaginary man found his comfortable lodgings a prison."

You don't have to accompany Mr. Chatwin all the way in his view of man as a perpetual nomad to be stirred by the idea of the Songlines. Toward the end of his journey, his anthropology opens into realms of enchantment:

> I have a vision of the Songlines stretching across
> the continents and ages; that wherever men have
> trodden they have left a trail of song (of which we

may, now and then, catch an echo); and that these trails must reach back, in time and space, to an isolated pocket in the African savannah, where the First Man opening his mouth in defiance of the terrors that surrounded him, shouted the opening stanza of the World Song. "*I AM!*"

> *Walter Goodman, in a review of "The Songlines,"*
> *in* The New York Times, *July 29, 1987, p C20.*

EDWARD HOAGLAND

[Bruce Chatwin] is best known for his stunning, acrobatic-minded travel book, *In Patagonia.* He has also published *The Viceroy of Ouidah,* a lusciously exotic novel set in Brazil and Dahomey during slaving days, and *On the Black Hill,* a fine, idiosyncratic novel about twin bachelor brothers in Wales, told with fairytale colors and compression. More recently, [for *The Songlines*], he went from England to Alice Springs, in "the dry heart of Australia," in search of what such pilgrims often go abroad after: a Golden Age, a new time frame, a calmer self and yet the piquancy of aboriginal motivations and exile desperation. A travel writer's success depends a good deal upon the vagaries of happenstance—whom he falls in with, or fails to meet, what salient events he chances to see, what side trips are being made by other people who may allow him to tag along—as well as how he holds up under usage and whether he can control his swings of mood.

Chatwin was fortunate enough to win the trust of a young Russo-Australian named Arkady Volchok, warm in spirit, fearless, competent, whose improvised job in this raw desert region of the down-under continent was to tease out of the elders of various aboriginal tribes the locations of their "Songlines"—the landmarks of mishaps and better adventures, the marriages and burials of the numerous separate 1000-mile mythic wanderings of their clan ancestors, like Emu, Honey-ant, Honeysuckle, Native Cat, Big Kangaroo, Budgerigar, Black Cockatoo, Monitor Lizard, Spider, Snake, Bandicoot Man and Porcupine, as told down through the generations by means of intricate, memorized chants that had sung "the world into existence" and finally wrapped the whole world in a web of song—so these sacred places won't be obliterated by a railroad line.

Chatwin is a spontaneous-sounding chronicler, very brief in his chapters, off-hand in conveying meticulously gathered information, a master of description: Home for an aborigine named Joshua "lay on the highest point of the saddle between Mount Cullen and Mount Liebler. It consisted of a gutted stationwagon which Joshua had rolled on to its roof so he could lie under the bonnet, in the shade. The cab was wrapped in a black plastic sheet. A bundle of hunting spears poked out from one window." . . . Chatwin's method is to write down whatever occurs. If a white man he is visiting sneezes into one hand and dries it surreptitiously under his chair, he puts that in. If four aborigines go hunting for kangaroos in a truck and chase and ram into a nursing mother three times before killing her with a tire iron, and then abandon the meat, he records that too. (pp. 1-2)

[The] magnificent theme of songs drawn from the Dreamtime and rehearsed and kept fresh in the mind by walkabouts—a "prodigious sense of orientation" in a 1000-mile world which is to be maintained intact—is given eloquent treatment here, together with an affectionately pungent portrait of the decay and ennui afflicting the bushmen's society since their conquest by the whites. The whites in these deserts are mostly fractured souls, bombastic, intransigent, anxious runaways devising a momentary agenda for themselves, although the women do tend to hold up better than the men. Perhaps Chatwin's favorite person is a hermit priest who lives in a hut by the Timor Sea—Father Terrence, "with reddish hair, what was left of it, and not too many flaky brown teeth. He wrapped the teeth in a hesitant smile. He would soon have to go to Broome, he said, to have the doctor freeze off his skin cancers." Religion is often a centerpiece in Chatwin's writing, and they walk the beach happily.

Despite its virtues, however, [*The Songlines*] seems a bit off-stride, overly shaky and lonesome in tone sometimes (a shakiness he never acknowledges or makes interesting), and it has been fattened with recollections and excerpts from diaries that he had kept during several sojourns in the Sahara a decade before for a book about nomads, the manuscript of which he says he ultimately burned. He is too sure a craftsman to let these numerous selections become a bore; but Australia's aborigines really do not appear to have as much in common with the Nemadi of Mauritania, the Quashgai of Iran, the Beja of the Sudan's Red Sea Hills, and other untrammeled peoples he has met in Kabul, Timbuktu, Cameroon, Niger, China, Peru and Brazil, as he wishes to claim. Passionately believing that all mankind has songlines circumnavigating the globe, Chatwin takes pains to lay out his ideas about the origins of man as a nomad in dry country threatened by toothed animals—one particular genus of tiger, *Dinofelis*, he suggests, was specifically adapted to prey upon us. But he has said earlier that in Australia the fauna were relatively inoffensive, and in other respects, too, he has grafted one unfinished book onto a different one, hoping that the seams will fit. They don't entirely, but it's all charming and impeccably stylish, and rises unexpectedly to a jubilant ending. (p. 2)

> Edward Hoagland, "*Walkabout on the Wild Side,*" in Book World—The Washington Post, *August 2, 1987, pp. 1-2.*

ANDREW HARVEY

Nearly every writer of my generation in England has wanted, at some point, to be Bruce Chatwin; wanted, like him, to talk of Fez and Firdausi, Nigeria and Nuristan, with equal authority; wanted to be talked about, as he is, with raucous envy; wanted, above all, to have written his books—*In Patagonia,* that perfect and most famous of recent travel books, but also *The Viceroy of Ouidah* a baleful, mock-historical fantasy of a Brazilian slave trader in 19th-century Africa, and *On the Black Hill,* his first novel, set in Wales, a brooding pastoral tale full of tender grandeur.

No writer has meant as much to my generation. From Mr. Chatwin, we learned to dare to be obsessive, irregular, learned, exotic; learned to burn our school ties and Wellingtons and despise Little Englanderism; learned to mock and avoid a literary establishment that loves to reward poems to goldfish and novels about the tepid lusts of women librarians. From Mr. Chatwin, we learned that most undemocratic, un-Anglo-Saxon of lessons—never to repeat ourselves; each of his books has been a different delight, a different feast of style and form. For us, he has stood for what contemporary England and its nannies of left and right seem dedicated to stifling; inner wildness; the true dandy's fierce and exacting ele-

gance; the old Elizabethan sense that the world and its wonders are the writer's province. In Margaret Thatcher's ropy aviary of provincial jays, squabbling finches and "worthy" sparrows, Bruce Chatwin has been our bird of paradise, solitary and unpredictable in his apparitions, grand and electric in his markings.

The Songlines, his new book, is his bravest work yet, the one in which we come closest to penetrating his mind and heart. (p. 1)

It engages the full range of the author's passions: his obsession with travel; his love of nomads and the nomadic way of life; his horror at the vulgarity and exploitativeness of the modern world; his hunger to understand man's origins and essential nature and so find some source of hope for the future. Part adventure-story, part novel-of-ideas, part satire on the follies of "progress," part spiritual autobiography, part passionate plea for a return to simplicity of being and behavior, *The Songlines* is a seething gallimaufry of a book, a great Burtonian galimatias of anecdote and speculation and description, fascinating, moving, infuriating, incoherent, all at once. If *The Songlines,* judged by the highest standards, fails, it fails in the kind of dashing, vulnerable way that commands our admiration. No one will put it down unmoved, however rickety they may in the end find its form and conclusions.

The central failure of *The Songlines* lies, mysteriously, in an area that has hitherto been one of Mr. Chatwin's chief strengths—the evocation of landscape. The Australian bush and desert fail to come alive in this book, fail to permeate it with majestic presence as they should if the work is to do what it wants to do—celebrate the aborigines' adoration of their earth and the resource of mind it breeds. Australia, it seems, is a very hard subject; there is something imperial, aloof and unfamiliar in its landscape that resists all but the most intensely poetic of writers like D. H. Lawrence or Patrick White, that demands a dazzled abandon and not the meticulous spare watchfulness that Mr. Chatwin commands so well. (pp. 1, 27)

Was Mr. Chatwin afraid of trying to emulate these two predecessors (who wouldn't be?). Did he feel threatened by the power of the Australian land and realize he would have to shatter the crystalline technique that has served him so handsomely elsewhere if he were to rise to its challenge? Of course he can write beautifully: "A pair of rainbows hung across the valley between the two mountains. The cliffs of the escarpment, which had been a dry red, were now purplish-black and striped, like a zebra, with vertical chutes of white water." To write beautifully, however, of *this* landscape is not enough; something wilder is required, especially if you are trying, as Mr. Chatwin is, to depict the aborigines' ecstatic relationship with their land. There is a reticence in the prose that comes to seem not tact but fear, an all-too "modern" desire to keep the assessing, watching self intact and untransformed. For all his artfulness, Mr. Chatwin never conveys Australia and why the aborigines continue to "sing it into being" with such love.

The aborigines also remain an oddly shadowy presence in the book. They are shown fighting in bars; lying dead-drunk in ditches; haggling for good prices for their "native" paintings; hunting kangaroo. But we are never taken into the heart of their rituals or imagination, as Werner Herzog did with such dignity in his 1984 film *Where the Green Ants Dream* and as D. H. Lawrence did with the Mexican Indians in *The White Peacock.* The "Abos" are talked about endlessly; the Aborigine Problem is presented from a variety of sharp angles; but the people themselves wander like ghosts through the book, largely voiceless extras in a play supposedly dedicated to them, statues on which ideas are draped, not beings vibrant in their own right.

Distance between a modern sensibility and an ancient one is inevitable, but Mr. Chatwin should have done more to explore this distance, or worry about it in ways that would have made it richer and more poignant for the reader. We begin to feel, perhaps uncharitably, that the ideas the Songlines arouse matter more to Mr. Chatwin than the people who sing them. The "Moleskin notebooks"—excerpts from which counterpoint his exploration of Australia and which deal largely with his travels in Africa—show the author celebratory of the Arab nomads he meets, delighted by their elegance and hospitality; the aborigines seem to evoke no such admiration in him. They are difficult to imagine as the musical Homers he wants us to believe they are.

It is equally hard to imagine the Songlines themselves. We are given clear *discussions* of them; the author quotes pertinently from the philosophers Vico and Heidegger, the poet Rilke and others about the relationships between singing, land, being and walking. Yet he has not given us any aboriginal poetry itself or described even one of the languages it is written in at any length. To do so would have been risky and difficult; such poetry tends to be repetitious, as well as incomprehensible outside its ritual context; the attempt to transcribe the sounds of an aboriginal language might have degenerated into academic parody. Mr. Chatwin should, however, have found *some* way to make the songs accessible to us. They are described, hinted at, elliptically eulogized, but like Godot they never appear. Without their being present in the book we never really believe in them and so do not completely care about the subtle, marvelous vision they are said to enshrine.

The most controversial part of **The Songlines** will undoubtedly be the long meditation on the origin of man that it contains. This is an old fascination of Mr. Chatwin's, as lovers of **In Patagonia** will remember. From a mass of different kinds of material—anecdotes about the Nemadi, descriptions of meetings with Konrad Lorenz, witty destructions of the Johannesburg anatomist Raymond Dart's blood-soaked theories about man's early behavior patterns (popularized by the writer Robert Ardrey in his book *African Genesis*)—a Chatwinian theory of origins slowly emerges. Man came from the desert; his first way of life was migratory; paleontological evidence suggests that man's initial aggressive forays were not against other men but against menacing predators (chief predator, according to Mr. Chatwin's favored source, was the false saber-tooth, genus *Dinofelis*).

From this theory of origins, Mr. Chatwin sweeps on to draw conclusions about man's nature and the future of civilization. We will survive, he is telling us, if we return to the truths of the desert, and to our nomadic nature, with its essential unaggressiveness and reverence for the world: true freedom is the freedom of the soul from things, the nomad's irreverent and generous happiness of spirit; this freedom is not a fantasy of travelers or romantic poets or "primitivist" anthropologists but a reality rooted in man's earliest experience of the earth still alight and shining in the lives of those nomadic people who have not been "civilized." (p. 27)

At a time when so many writers indulge in what Auden used to call "apocalyptics," Mr. Chatwin's belief in human sanity,

his sense of some fundamental calm splendor in human nature are moving and refreshing. You can, however, admire his vision (even want to share it) without quite believing it or consenting to the way in which it is presented. The main difficulty in taking it seriously is the author's unsubtle insistence on polarizing everything. Either we are for the Aggression Boys' theory of human origins, or we are against it; either we are ground between the molars of the State or we rush out into the wastes and set up our tents; either we believe man is innately evil or we see he is a singer, essentially wise and in harmony with the world. The truth, as the great religions rather darkly remind us, seems to lie in neither the "optimistic" nor the "pessimistic" vision of man but in a spiritual realism starker and more exacting than either. . . .

When placed against contemporary jeremiads, Mr. Chatwin's vision seems exhilarating; when seen against some of the texts he quotes—the Buddhist sutras, Lao Tzu, Kierkegaard, Dostoyevsky—it seems naïve, unhistorical in the broadest sense, and inadequate in its understanding of horror and evil. The complexities of our contemporary choice seem to defeat most modern writers, and on this evidence Mr. Chatwin is no exception. He has put on the robes of a prophet, but lacks the prophet's almost insanely sharp and intense vision. Mr. Chatwin is not a visionary, which he would need to be to make this part of his book as convincing as it is interesting. He lacks the poetry, the agony, the personal religious wisdom. I suspect that, with his native nomadic shrewdness, he knows this—which is why the burden of his philosophizing is carried by quotations from others and not by explorations of his own experience.

Whatever we feel or think about what he has said in **The Songlines,** there can surely be no doubt about the often superb way he says it. He remains one of our clearest, most vibrant writers. Who else could have written of the Beja tribe, "They anointed each other's hair with scented goats' cheese and then teased it out with corkscrew curls, making a buttery parasol, which instead of a turban, prevented their brains going soft"; of the lifestyle of the Governor of Walata, Mauretania, "at meal-times, a pink fingered lutanist would serenade us through the couscous while the Governor reconstructed, with my prompting, a street map of the Quartier Latin"; of his childhood in wartime England, "All the frenzied agitation of the times communicated itself to me; the hiss of steam on a fogbound station; the double clu-unk of carriage doors closing; the drone of aircraft, the searchlights, the sirens; the sound of a mouth-organ along a platform of sleeping soldiers"?

The Songlines is full of such exact and shining things, full too of incidental reflections—on Jahweh, Tower of Babel, the Perenty lizard, the habits of villagers in Nuristan, the quirks of Australopithecus—that no one else could have expressed with such verve and dazzle. Bruce Chatwin is "Le Chatwin" still, England's toughest and most alert exotic; not the sage he may have wanted to be, perhaps, but still a writer no one who cares for literature can afford not to read. (p. 29)

Andrew Harvey, "Footprints of the Ancestors," in The New York Times Book Review, *August 2, 1987, pp. 1, 27, 29.*

JENNIFER HOWARD

As long as there has been an England there have been Englishmen who felt compelled to leave it, abandoning the busy streets and turning wheels of home for the greener pastures of the unknown. Shakespeare, not a traveler himself, put his finger on it when he spoke of England as "this little world . . . bound in with the triumphant sea." That feeling of being *bound in*—spiritually, intellectually, and physically—united Plantagenet crusaders, Tudor privateers, and Victorian imperialists; all left England thinking that they could do better elsewhere, that they would be richer, holier, or freer people if they explored the world's reaches.

But what role is left to twentieth-century adventurers now that the motives of past wanderlust have lost their respectability? With *The Songlines,* Bruce Chatwin, the latest in the long line of Britons abroad, comes up with an answer: philosopher.

Had he been born in the last century, Chatwin might have hired himself out to the Royal Geographic Society to explore the vastnesses of Africa, hoping, as Alan Moorehead wrote of the Victorians, to see what "benefits civilization could confer on the benighted blacks." Born in 1940, however, Chatwin travels instead as a reverse sort of missionary, hoping to gather the benefits that the "benighted blacks" can confer on civilization. . . .

Chatwin's enthusiasm for the exotic goes back to his childhood. In the early pages of *The Songlines,* he recounts days spent with his Aunt Ruth in Stratford, reading poems from "an anthology of verse especially chosen for travellers, called *The Open Road.*" From Aunt Ruth he learned that their surname had been corrupted from "Chettewynde," which in Anglo-Saxon means "the winding path." In Chatwin's mind "the suggestion took root . . . that poetry, my own name, and the road were, all three, mysteriously connected." Later, having quit his job as an expert on modern painting, he journeyed to the Sudan where his guide, a nomad named Mahmoud, triggered a fascination for nomads. "The Pharaohs had vanished," Chatwin writes. "Mahmoud and his people had lasted. I felt I had to know the secret of their timeless and irreverent vitality. . . . The more I read, the more convinced I became that nomads had been the crankhandle of history, if for no other reason than that the great monotheisms had, all of them, surfaced from the pastoral milieu. . . ." And with that statement Chatwin trades in a traveler's pack for the intellectual baggage of a theorist. (p. 44)

[*The Songlines*] begins encouragingly enough as an autobiographical account of Chatwin's foray into the "pastoral milieu" and what he found there, its setting Central Australia, its main characters the nomadic Aborigines of the area. What drew Chatwin down under were tales of "the labyrinth of invisible pathways which meander all over Australia and are known to Europeans as 'Dreaming Tracks' or 'Songlines'; to the Aboriginals as the 'Footprints of the Ancestors' or the 'Way of the Law.' " (pp. 44-5)

Intrigued by the idea of the Songlines, Chatwin travels to Australia to track them himself. To serve as his guide to Central Australia he locates another peripatetic, a "tireless bushwalker" by the name of Arkady. The son of Russian émigrés, Arkady lives in the Center, with no possessions other than a harpsichord and his favorite books. Once a teacher among the Aborigines, he knows them intimately; so intimately that he has been hired by a railway company to survey the Songlines and to advise the railway how to lay track in order not to disturb any Dreamings.

To do this, he must travel around the bush with the Aborigines on whose land the tracks will run. Chatwin tags along with him, and the first part of the book is more or less what one expects from a travelogue: anecdotes of the whites and their settlements, snapshots of life among the Aborigines, conversations recorded along the way. Chatwin delights in caricaturing the whites in Alice Springs ("a grid of scorching streets where men in long white socks were forever getting in and out of Land Cruisers") and the other large towns he passes through. Most of the white Australians come across as boors and racists, as in the following exchange between Arkady and a policeman in a bar in Glen Armond:

> "So why do you bother with them?" The policeman jerked his thumb at the Aboriginals.
>
> "Because I like them."
>
> "And *I* like them," he said. "I *like* them! I like to do what's right by them. But they're different."
>
> "In what way different?"
>
> The policeman moistened his lips again, and sucked the air between his teeth.
>
> "Made differently," he said at last. "They've got different urinary tracks to the white man. Different waterworks! That's why they can't hold their booze!"
>
> "How do you know?"
>
> "It's been proved," said the policeman. "Scientifically."

The policeman concludes that what holds for "waterworks" also holds for brain power. Arkady, however, argues that by white standards many Aborigines, with their ability to memorize, would rank as "linguistic geniuses." The other whites who work closely with the "Abos"—those who teach them, broker their paintings to white tourists, run stores and clinics among them—seem to agree. But their good feelings toward Abos, as pictured by Chatwin, are curiously paternal, the feelings that a master of hounds might have for his pack: respect alloyed with amused condescension.

Drunk on the white man's liquor, haggling with American tourists over artwork, the Abos appear in *The Songlines* to be drunkards, connivers, or naive innocents: stick figures, hardly human, not the blissful songsters of Chatwin's promises. He makes it difficult to imagine anything other than elusive, fuzzy-haired figures with some strange affinity for song, intriguing but never revealed.

Nor does the land itself emerge from the shadows of the book. Chatwin hints at the "incandescent sky," the scrubby brush and ragged outcrops that make up the Central Australian landscape. But never does he indicate what quality it is that so enthralls the Aborigines. Only rarely does it become the entity that the natives constantly sing into being. This is a pity, considering Chatwin's considerable stylistic talents. Occasionally a satisfying description comes along: " . . . the country changed from the yellow-flowering scrub to a rolling, open parkland of bleached grass and rounded eucalyptus trees—blue-green, the colour of olives with their leaves turning white in the wind; and if you soft-focused your eyes, you'd think you were in the lit-up Provençal landscape of Van Gogh's *Cornfield near Arles.*" Too often, though, the style shuffles lazily off into sentences such as "It was a bright, moonlit night."

In fact, this first part of *The Songlines* serves as little more than a warm-up for the second: a compendium of quotes, anecdotes, and thoughts assembled over the years and recorded by the author in a series of moleskin notebooks (bought specially in a Parisian *papeterie*). The quotes provide documentation for the Chatwinian theory that the nomad is the quintessential man, or, as Dostoevsky wrote, that man is a "wanderer in the scorching and barren wilderness of this world." Or, more pleasantly, that we are born to wander.

It's not an unappealing idea, especially for anyone ever forced to work in a windowless office, and Chatwin's assemblage of quotations makes it even more palatable. . . . Interestingly enough, his anecdotes about the Arab nomads he has met are crisper and far more sincere than those about the Aborigines. But though he tells good stories, he relies too much on other writers to lay out the bones of the argument without himself providing any connecting tissue.

From nomadism it is for Chatwin an easy journey backward to the origin of man. Discussing our break from the apes, he turns his attention to a number of conflicting anthropological opinions on the subject. One school, led by Raymond Dart, holds that man descends from bloodthirsty ancestors who delighted in bashing each other over the head. Dart and his followers interpret the seemingly violent fossil record of man's emergence (smashed skulls, etc.) as evidence of our innate barbarity. To Chatwin's great relief, however, another anthropologist named Robert Brain rescues man's reputation by reinterpreting the evidence and concluding that the seeming violence, which Dart attributed to the Beast Within, was in fact caused by a Beast Without, a prehistoric cat species named *Dinofelis*. This cat may have been our specific predator; Chatwin calls him "the Prince of Darkness in all his sinister magnificence." By developing superior cranial power, man evolved out of reach of the claws of *Dinofelis,* but "perhaps it had to be a Pyrrhic victory: has not the whole of history been a search for false monsters? A nostalgia for the Beast we have lost? For the Gentleman who bowed out gracefully—and left us with the weapon in our hand?" In Chatwin's mind, the whole Locke vs. Hobbes, nomad vs. the state debate springs from these two views of human nature: man as killer or man as prey.

And how does this all relate to the Songlines? Man, says Chatwin, defying the Beast, "opening his mouth in defiance of the terrors that surrounded him, shouted the opening stanza of the World Song, 'I AM!' " The Songlines are but a continuation of that first song. Chatwin feels that nomads remain closer to that first, enviable group of men, men who banded together not to save them from themselves but from the nasty things lurking just outside the circle of firelight.

Plausible, perhaps; interesting, certainly. And it is good to read a book founded on an enduring faith in human nature. But it would be nice to put down *The Songlines* feeling as though it had offered a vicarious walk among the Australian nomads. Instead Chatwin gives us Aborigines with all the depth of paper cutouts and a half-grown theory of human nature. *The Songlines* begins a journey into nomadism that loses itself in intriguing but aleatoric philosophizing. (pp. 45-6)

Jennifer Howard, in a review of, "The Songlines,"

in The American Spectator, Vol. 20, No. 11, November, 1987, pp. 44-6.

DAVID RIEFF

The Songlines is not just a book drunk on the idea of nomadism and the nomadic life, it is a book that all but asserts that nomadism is the only sane life people may live. "*Solvitur ambulando,*" Chatwin notes in *The Songlines,* "it is solved by walking"; and later, "I felt the Songlines were not necessarily an Australian phenomenon, but universal; that they were the means by which man marked out his territory, and so organized his social life. All other successive systems were variants—or perversions—of the original." The greatest perversion of all, Chatwin suggests over and over, is the sedentary life: that is the life of most people on the earth.

Small wonder that Chatwin's Australia is the alternately sublime and brutish country of the Central Australian Outback, rather than the cluttered coastal regions of that continent where cities and suburbs sprawl and expand, and in which the overwhelming majority of Australians, whether they are the descendants of transported convicts or newly arrived Vietnamese refugees, make their homes and lives. It is not that the reader wants Chatwin to describe Sydney or Melbourne, anymore than it would be reasonable to expect Naipaul to write an irenic travel book about the Caribbean. Rather, what discomfits is that Chatwin seems to feel that only those who lead nomadic lives can be decent people. Everyone else is presented as a monster, a fraud, or a boob.

Chatwin's hero, Arkady Volchok, is the noble white nomad, *sans peur et sans reproche. The Songlines* begins with Chatwin meeting him, and largely sets the ground for all that follows:

> Nothing in Arkady's temperament predisposed him to live in the hugger-mugger of Anglo-Saxon suburbia or take a conventional job. He had a flattish face and a gentle smile, and he moved through the bright Australian spaces with the ease of his footloose forbears.
>
> His hair was thick and straight, the color of straw. His lips had cracked in the heat. He did not have the drawn-in lips of so many white Australians in the Outback; nor did he swallow his words. He rolled his r's in a very Russian way. Only when you came up close did you realize how big his bones were.
>
> (p. 37)
>
> He was a tireless bushwalker. He thought nothing of setting out, with a water-flask and a few bites of food, for a hundred-mile walk across the Ranges. Then he would come home, out of the heat and light, and draw the curtains, and play the music of Buxtehude and Bach on the harpsichord. Their orderly progression, he said, conformed to the contours of the Central Australian landscape.

The passage is breathtaking. Few writers can incarnate a place with such effortless economy; and one feels that Volchok . . . is a character as real as any in literature. And yet there is something terribly wrong, even unworthy, about what Chatwin is up to. His hero is a man who has abandoned his daughter in favor of hundred-mile bush walks (with only a few bites of food—if he carried a full pack he would no longer be a hero), on the face of things scarcely a noble exchange.

And while Volchok's possessions are few and his life is ascetic, he has perfect possessions (books and musical instruments) and perfect taste. Imagine for a moment that Volchok liked to return after his hike, crack open a beer, and watch a game show. No, it's Buxtehude or bust.

As one reads *The Songlines,* one feels increasingly queasy about the adamantine aestheticization that Chatwin uses as a yardstick for judging people and phenomena. The beautiful, the elegant, and the ascetic are good; the fat, the indelicate, and the sedentary are bad. In the end Chatwin's extraordinary achievement as a storyteller seems tainted by assumptions that would better have been left to people like Leni Riefenstahl.

As the book unfolds, there is no letup in this aestheticizing. We meet a few other white nomads, associates of Arkady's in the Aboriginal rights movement, who are subtle, and therefore OK. We also meet hermits such as the Marxist Hanlon, who denounces Chatwin, in a brilliant section, as a snobby Pom, yet weeps when Arkady and Chatwin get up to leave. There is also Rolf Niehart, who runs a general store in the tiny settlement of Cullen while living in a caravan bursting with books in a half dozen languages and copies of the *Nouvelle Revue Française* and the *New York Review of Books.* (Surely only Chatwin could find such a person.) What unites these people, and Chatwin describes them with a marvelous combination of tough-minded accuracy and affection, is their originality, their contempt for authority (synonymous, in *The Songlines,* with the whites intent on cheating the Aboriginals or, worse, destroying their Songlines), their unwillingness to live in the sordid closeness of the sedentary world.

The core of *The Songlines,* of course, is Chatwin's own encounter with the Aboriginals. Apparently he had intended to write a book that would have been a general theory of nomadism, and to that end traveled for many years. Perhaps it was for the best that *The Songlines* turned out to be a story of Chatwin's travels in a specific nomadic world, only buttressed, in "the moleskin notebooks," with the shards of that larger, abandoned project; for Chatwin is at his best when he is specific, evocative, and untheoretical. In contrast to his rather dubious theories about the origins of human aggression, the narrative of the journey to the Outback is beautiful, simple, and refreshingly tentative. (pp. 37-8)

As Chatwin construes it, Australia became for the Aboriginal clans one vast musical score, a thick grid of Songlines; to travel was a journey along these various songs. . . . But since, as Chatwin observes, "there was hardly a rock or creek in the country that could not or had not been sung," the real work is the well-nigh impossible task of reconciling two opposing understandings of place: the white view of a nature that is both mute and malleable, and the Aboriginal view of the singing land in which the right life is the "walk-about," abutting, as it does, at least in Chatwin's conception of it, in the "right" death. As he notes, beautifully, at the very end of the book:

> In Aboriginal Australia, there are specific rules for "going back" or, rather, for singing your way to where you belong: to your "conception site," to the place where your *tjuringa* is stored. Only then can you become—or re-become—the Ancestor. The concept is quite similar to Heraclitus's mysterious dictum, "Mortals and immortals, alive in their death, dead in each other's life."

It is when Chatwin reveals that the real subject of *The Songlines* is this "right way" to die that his book begins to soar. One can object to Chatwin's remorseless aestheticizing, and quarrel with his theories about nomadism and the origins of aggression, but only a foolish or arrogant reader could fail to recognize the beauty and seriousness of what Chatwin set out to do. *The Songlines* is, finally, a book about learning to die, and, in so doing, learning to live.

The last entry in the last chapter is Chatwin's *gai savoir* at its most relentless and its most magnificent. Arkady, his new wife, Marian, and Chatwin come upon three dying Aboriginal men:

> They were almost skeletons. Their beards and hair had gone. One was strong enough to lift an arm, another to say something. When they heard who Limpy was, all three smiled, spontaneously, the same toothless grin.
>
> Arkady folded his arms, and watched.
>
> "Aren't they wonderful?" Marian whispered, putting her hand in mine and giving it a squeeze.
>
> Yes. They were all right. They knew when they were going, smiling at death in the shade of a ghost-gum.

Chatwin is able to incarnate in his effortless, spare prose both the agony of death and the jubilation of being. Finally *The Songlines* is a book of consolation dressed up in a novel's clothing. If it fails to achieve everything its author intended, and even at times rightly gives offense, it is still one of the few recent books that seems to matter, and that people a hundred years on might read with pleasure, exasperation, and instruction. (pp. 38-9)

> *David Rieff, "The Wanderer's Wisdom," in* The New Republic, *Vol. 197, No. 22, November 30, 1987, pp. 36-9.*

ADAM MARS-JONES

As befits the creatures of a traveller and travel-writer—a wanderer who depends on the relative fixity of his audience for the value placed on his wanderings—the people in Bruce Chatwin's novels make a wide variety of accomodations with place, from the all but vegetable twins of *On the Black Hill* to the nomads of *The Songlines.* The eponymous hero of Chatwin's new novella, *Utz,* a collector of Meissen porcelain resident in Prague, represents perhaps his most sophisticated attempt to reconcile a strong sense of place with a countervailing conviction of displacement, and a temperamental restlessness.

After the Second World War Utz has a chance to leave Czechoslovakia: his doctor prescribes taking the cure at Vichy—despite the profusion of spas on offer domestically. Utz will have to leave behind his porcelain, but when he takes stock of his options in Vichy he thinks not of his Meissen but of his loyal, and now lonely, housekeeper Marta. . . .

Utz's life, being a series of private losses and renunciations, is not the obvious stuff of narrative. Chatwin lends it texture by intermittently using a narrator, but one who has no characteristics to distinguish him from the author. The passages written directly from Utz's point of view are full of interior glimpses, but the narrator admits late on in the novella to having fabricated them, often against the grain of what he knows of Utz's life. The narrator, whose acquaintance with Utz is revealed rather surprisingly—also late in the book—to have amounted to a total of nine and a quarter hours, has no choice but to invent what he hasn't witnessed. Even as a witness, though, he isn't altogether reliable, disclaiming knowledge of the relevant languages but passing on conversations verbatim just the same.

More beguiling than this rather awkward narrative structure are Chatwin's style and sensibility. Like his hero, Chatwin is a collector, but not of anything as tangible as porcelain. He is a connoisseur of experience, an aesthete even when he is dealing with politics or history. Sometimes this makes him less than completely convincing, as when he has Utz, on the day the Gestapo take him for questioning, unable to focus on "the abstractions of death and deportation", and thinking only of a particular plate of *haricots verts,* eaten at a restaurant by a white road in Provence.

Bruce Chatwin's fiction is always a pleasure to read, packed with richness, allusion and lore, discursive even within the narrow confines of a novella like *Utz.* If he has a weakness it is that the insistent detail can seem in some way self-advertising, drawing attention not to the things seen but to the quality of the eye seeing them. If there is a spiritual side to Utz's connoisseurship, after all, there is a materialist side to Chatwin's, and his sentences can seem like shelves for items of beauty, for fragments of history and culture that have developed beyond mere footnotes but seem somewhat inert as the ingredients of fiction. *Utz,* though, for all its slightness, contains much that Bruce Chatwin's admirers will enjoy, even if Utz's final renunciation of precious things in favour of a precious person—as fondly imagined by the narrator—seems sentimental, after the book's more troubled meditations on the demanding consolation to be found in the perfection of objects.

Adam Mars-Jones, "Taking the Cure," in The Times Literary Supplement, No. 4460, September 23-29, 1988, p. 1041.

JOHN LANCHESTER

The albatross which features in 'The Ancient Mariner' isn't really an albatross—that's to say it isn't the albatross you first think of, the Great Wandering Albatross. It's either the Sooty Albatross or the Black-Browed Albatross (both of which are much smaller and easier to hang round your neck if you feel guilty about having killed one). Butch Cassidy did not die in a gunfight in Bolivia in 1909, as portrayed in *Butch Cassidy and the Sundance Kid:* in 1925 he turned up at the family home in Circleville, Utah and ate blueberry pie. Hitler was a vegetarian.

Admirers of Bruce Chatwin's writings will recognise these facts, which are gleaned from his books and reflect one of their pleasures. He has a talent for the offbeat and the out-of-the-way, a kind of archaeological talent for the excavation of interesting data. *In Patagonia,* Chatwin's first book, was built out of that kind of data—built out of facts and encounters and stories. It is a kind of cubist travel book, to which the reader comes expecting the familiar exoticism of travel writing and instead finds a bleaker and more melancholy foreignness, which constantly feeds back into English literary and cultural history: Coleridge's albatross; the influence of Wed-

dell's *Voyage towards the South Pole* on Poe and on Darwin; the fact that Caliban 'has a good claim to Patagonian ancestry'. Chatwin's prose is pared-down, effective and syntactically uncomplicated: it concedes nothing to the standard-issue 'colourfulness' of the genre's attempts at evocation. (My favourite sentence from *In Patagonia:* 'The beach was grey and littered with dead penguins.')

One of the most haunting stories in the book is that of the Tierra del Fuegian boy kidnapped by Captain Robert Fitzroy, Chief Officer of HMS *Beagle,* in 1830. The boy was given a name by the crew—Jemmy Button—and taken to London, where he 'saw a stone lion on the steps of Northumberland House, and settled down to a boarding-school at Walthamstow'. On the *Beagle*'s return voyage to Tierra del Fuego Jemmy Button was accompanied by Darwin, who was appalled by the Fuegians; he 'confessed he could hardly make himself believe they were "fellow creatures and inhabitants of the same world"'. Meeting them 'helped trigger off the theory that Man had evolved from an ape-like species.' In November 1869 Jemmy led a mob of Fuegians who attacked an Anglican congregation at Wulaia. The eight white worshippers were clubbed and stoned to death. In the belief-system of Jemmy's tribe, 'the outside world was Hell and its people no better than beasts. Perhaps, that November, Jemmy Button mistook the missionaries as envoys of the Power of Darkness. Perhaps, when he later showed remorse, he remembered that pink men also were human.' Bald summary makes the moral of the story—which resides in the close similarity of Darwin's belief and Jemmy's—much more obvious than it is in Chatwin's telling. There is a Flaubertian quality to Chatwin's recountings; nowhere does he editorialise or draw conclusions. 'Jemmy lived into the 1870s to see a proper mission established at Ushuaia and see the first of his people die of epidemics.'

It would have been easy for *In Patagonia* to have been less than the sum of its parts. When I'd finished the book I found that I couldn't square my memory of what was in it—lots of lively local detail, lots of good stories—with my memory of its effect, which was deeper and more complicated. *The Songlines,* Chatwin's fourth book, made clearer what had given *In Patagonia* its coherence and odd, unsettling aftertaste. The narrator of *The Songlines,* a novel about the tracks of song which mark out Aboriginal routes across Australia, is 'a Pom by the name of Bruce'. . . . Writing about travel and distant places often gains its force from the mixture of motives on the part of the traveller, the blend of self-extinction and self-discovery which is brought on by immersion in alien surroundings. Like the people in his books, the people whose stories he has travelled to tell, Chatwin is a wanderer and an obsessive: it's this which sets up the resonance between the upper-middle-class Englishman and the Patagonians, Australians and nomads whose company he keeps. If he wasn't the narrator of his books he could easily be one of the people the narrator meets. Consider the way he began his travels:

> When I was in my twenties . . . I had a job as an 'expert' on modern painting with a well-known firm of art auctioneers. We had sale-rooms in London and New York. I was one of the bright boys. People said I had a great career, if only I would play my cards right. One morning, I woke up blind.
>
> During the course of the day, the sight returned to the left eye, but the right one stayed sluggish and

clouded. The eye specialist who examined me said there was nothing wrong organically, and diagnosed the nature of the trouble.

'You've been looking too closely at pictures,' he said. 'Why don't you swap them for some long horizons?'

'Why not?' I said.

'Where would you like to go?'

'Africa.'

In the Sudan Chatwin met his first nomads, and became fascinated by people 'whose journeys, unlike my own, had neither beginning nor end'. He left his job and spent the next ten years or so trying to write a big book about nomads—the book which was eventually to become *The Songlines.*

This life-story has an unlikely quality to it, the kind of unlikeliness which occurs in real life but which tends to get left out of fiction, where it would seem a bit too . . . well, too unlikely. (As Walter Nash has recently remarked in these pages, fiction will always prefer a plausible impossibility to an implausible possibility.) Chatwin is committed to the anomalous and the improbable, and though his writing blends fact and fiction ('I once made the experiment of counting up the lies in the book I wrote about Patagonia. It wasn't, in fact, too bad'), the fiction is present less for its own sake than as a way of organising and shaping the factual material. Chatwin's second book, *The Viceroy of Ouidah,* extends and explores this technique. The two books he wrote after *In Patagonia* could not be more different from it, or from each other: *The Viceroy of Ouidah* tells the life-story of a low-caste 19th-century Brazilian who enriched himself as a slave trader and befriended the King of Dahomey in the process; *On the Black Hill* tells the life-story of a pair of identical twins in a Radnorshire farmhouse. Both books have a basis in fact, though the second has the label 'novel' attached to it; both books reflect Chatwin's interest in the anomalous and the one-off.

In *The Viceroy of Ouidah,* it's as if the exoticism Chatwin repressed to such effect in *In Patagonia* all at once erupts. Francisco Manuelo da Silva's life embraced sensual extremes—'the taste of armadillo meat roasted in clay; the shock of aguardiente on the tongue'—and much spectacular violence, from the time his father was found hanging from a tree, choked to death on his own hat cords in a freak riding accident, to the time when he himself goes to see the King of Dahomey. 'At one village there were heads on poles: at another, women pointed up a tree to where a crucified man croaked for water in a library of sleeping fruit bats.' Chatwin, as already mentioned, is something of a Flaubertian: *The Viceroy of Ouidah* is his *Salammbo,* objective and detached in the midst of the lurid cruelty it chronicles. At no point in the book is there any comment on the morality of the slave trade, though the hypocrisy of some of slavery's respectable beneficiaries is effectively exposed.

On the Black Hill is about one of nature's anomalies. Identical twins Benjamin and Lewis Jones spend their whole lives in the farmhouse on the Welsh border in which they were born in 1900. Apart from Benjamin's military service in World War One—which he spends being treated sadistically in Hereford barracks—neither twin ever goes anywhere. ('It's always irritated me to be called a travel writer. So I decided to write something about people who never went out.') The story conveys very well the texture of ordinary rural life—

Hardy and Lawrence were mentioned by reviewers—and there is more humour in *On the Black Hill* than in the book which preceded it: the Radnorshire people prefer the Old Testament to the New 'because in the Old Testament there were many more stories about sheep-farming'. But *On the Black Hill* and *The Viceroy of Ouidah* are alike in that they both sustain a close and vivid focus on a particular set of historical circumstances. Neither book opens out suggestively in the manner of *In Patagonia* or *The Songlines,* which causes some people to like them more, and some less, than Chatwin's other two books. (The effect of adopting a Flaubertian 'cinematic' technique is perhaps apparent in the fact that both books have been made into successful films.) For myself, I like *On the Black Hill* very much, while not thinking that it is where Chatwin's originality is best demonstrated, and I like *The Viceroy of Ouidah* too—but then, I'm a fan of *Salammbo,* which certainly isn't everyone's cup of aguardiente.

The reader who is starting to get wise to Chatwin, and particularly to the way each book of his seems to set out to contradict the expectations aroused by its immediate precursor, could construct an idea of Chatwin's new novel by reversing the postulates of his last one, *The Songlines.* That book discussed Aboriginal creation myths, which 'tell of the legendary totemic beings who had wandered over the continent in the Dreamtime, singing out the name of everything that crossed their path—birds, animals, plants, rocks, waterholes—and so singing the world into existence'. . . . *The Songlines* takes off from these facts into hypothesis about the metaphysics of walking and of song [and] the inherently nomadic nature of humanity. . . . Chatwin has an unfashionable and very refreshing confidence in the innate goodness of man: an early encounter with nomads had led him 'to reject out of hand all arguments for the nastiness of human nature'. It's this confidence which fuels his interest in noble-savage figures, and which propels him into his wonderfully batty speculations about Man v. Dinofelis. This optimism contributes heavily to the 18th-century flavour of *The Songlines:* it's a book Diderot would have enjoyed hugely. Extrapolating negatively, then, we can guess that Chatwin's new novel [*Utz*] is unsprawling and unmetaphysical, un-18th-century in tone and in technique, set in the Old World and with a central theme which has something to do with not being a nomad.

And so it proves. The Utz of the novel's title is a fanatical collector of Meissen porcelain whose tiny flat, overlooking the Jewish Cemetery in Prague, contains over a thousand high-quality pieces; another two hundred-odd are in a Swiss bank vault. Utz is seen from many different perspectives during the book, which is written in Chatwin's leanest and most pared-down manner. At one point we are told that Utz is impotent, at another that in fact he is a tremendous Don Juan, specialising in opera stars; at one point apparently given over to aestheticism (' "Wars, pogroms and revolutions," he used to say, "offer excellent opportunities for the collector" '), it turns out that he has risked his life hiding Jews from the Nazis, and given the Nazis information about the whereabouts of sought-after objects for Goering's collection: 'What, after all, was the value of a Titian or Tiepolo if one human life could be saved?' The multiplicity of viewpoints, and the conflicting evidence, generate an uncertainty which is added to by a narrator who is not identified by name, and who may well be Chatwin himself. Although he isn't quite the full-blooded Unreliable Narrator beloved of Post-Modernism, he comes close: 'Did he have a moustache? I forget. Add a moustache, subtract a moustache . . .' . . .

Utz is, in terms of Chatwin's work, a hybrid. It has a close focus on one person's life, but at the same time it opens up questions and throws off ideas with cheerful abandon. You are provoked to wonder about collecting and about the consequences of a life-choice like Utz's, and you are also regaled with a lot of theories and a lot of facts about porcelain. . . . The novel gives the reader the sense that Chatwin, like his narrator, is a little bit puzzled by Utz, a little unsure quite how to sum him up. It's as if, to the primordial opposition of Abel and Cain, nomad and settler, of which Chatwin has written so often, a new category has been added: the collector.

Utz has had opportunities to defect to the West, but hasn't liked what he has seen of it—he takes an annual holiday in Vichy, which would put anyone off—and prefers to stay in Prague, with his porcelain. He is one of a class of Czech intellectuals who 'inflict a final insult on the state, by pretending that it does not exist.' Prague is a city where the man who clips your tram ticket is a scholar of the Elizabethan stage, and the street sweeper has written 'a philosophical commentary on the Anaximander fragment'. Czech intellectuals everywhere pursue their interests outwith the state: the fact is familiar, but the light which *Utz* casts on it is not. This is not a rehashing of the Cold War account of life in the East. The version of Prague life recounted in *Utz* is roughhewn, plausible and funny. (p. 10)

Prague life is built up out of this kind of incongruity, which highlights the oddness of the human beings who populate the city, or populate Chatwin's version of it. When the narrator first meets Utz, they and Dr Orlik go to lunch at the Restaurant Pstruth 'Trout'. Unfortunately the only trout on the premises have been requisitioned by four fat party members, and eels, the second choice, are also off. The only fish available is carp—and on the English-language section of the menu, the 'a' and 'r' of 'carp' have been transposed. The narrator explains the mistake to his companions: the fastidious Utz is embarrassed, while Orlik thinks it is the funniest thing he has ever heard. ' "And to begin?" asked the waiter. "Nothing," said Orlik. "Only the crap!" ' (p. 11)

John Lanchester, "A Pom By the Name of Bruce," in London Review of Books, *Vol. 10, No. 17, September 29, 1988, pp. 10-1.*

JOHN KRIZANC

With *Utz,* Bruce Chatwin has succeeded in writing the first epic novella. In a mere 154 pages (padded with large type and wide margins), Chatwin almost casually manages to convey the psychopathology of the compulsive collector, recount the legend of the Golem, write a history of Czechoslovakia in this century, explain the technique of bringing an operatic diva to orgasm and paint an indelible portrait of a city. . . .

Like K., the anti-hero of Kafka's The Trial, Chatwin's Kaspar Utz is a nondescript and almost faceless man. Chatwin so skilfully places himself as a character in his own book that I want to believe it is a work of biography, not fiction. Chatwin's only encounter with Utz was in the summer of 1967, while he was in Prague to write an article about the passion of Emperor Rudolf II for collecting exotica.

Utz is an aging Jewish aristocrat and esthete who collects porcelain. . . . The Emperor Augustus once commented that "the craving for porcelain is like a craving for oranges," but just as Chatwin's description makes a reader hungry, Utz reminds us that his porcelain collection "has ruined my life." . . .

As Utz's collection grows, events in the real world recede into the background. For him, "this world of little figures was the real world. And that, compared to them, the Gestapo, the secret police and other hooligans were creatures of tinsel. And the events of this sombre century—the bombardments, the blitzkriegs, putsches and purges—were, as far as he was concerned, so many 'noises off.' "

Without his collection, Utz would not have a life worth recalling. It is the realization of this fact, the insight that everything Utz has done has been to maintain his collection, which has imprisoned him, so that finally he tries to make a break from it.

At a spa in Vichy, he comments at every turn that he is "certainly not enjoying this," and reluctantly concludes that "luxury is only luxurious under adverse conditions." For in spite of his money in Switzerland, the true source of his luxury is the peasant maid Marta and her knowledge of the black market. But when he decides to return to Prague for love of Marta, he fears the porcelain ladies will "re-exert the power of snobbery" and push her back into the kitchen.

Unlike Rabbi Loew, who was actually able to bring his clay golem to life, Utz's figurines live only on a metaphysical plane, but even there they must inexorably die. After asking if images crave their own destruction, Chatwin answers this question as an author by revealing new information on the life of Utz and the fate of his collection. This final arabesque truly makes *Utz* a work worth rereading—and collecting.

John Krizanc, "The Pathology of the Compulsive Collector," in The Globe and Mail, *Toronto, December 24, 1988.*

FRED SHAFER

What Chatwin wants to create in *Utz,* it seems, is a more compact, tightly organized variation on his nonfiction books. By setting his narrator to deciphering the personality and life of a fairly nondescript character, Chatwin attempts to develop a story line free of digressions or other unnecessary moves—as if the book were a finely polished miniature that had been crafted to test the author's powers of structuring a plot around a single effect.

The narrator hopes that he will find an answer to the enigma of Utz in the glazed and enameled animals, the rococo lovers and harlequins and the ornate table settings that crowd the man's shelves. . . . [Chatwin] gives his narrator the ability to see the porcelains in rich and careful detail. As he admires this collection, the narrator recalls the power exerted by Meissen figures on their original patron, the Duke of Saxony, who was weakened politically by the cost of his "porcelain mania." Awed, the narrator ponders the mystical beliefs of the alchemists who developed the formula for the porcelain while looking for "the substance of immortality."

Only when he starts to project himself into Utz' thoughts and feelings does the narrator reach insights that he can trust. Long sequences of the story are rendered through the other man's point of view. One passage shows Utz, on his first trip to the spa at Vichy, foregoing a plan to defect from Czechoslovakia. To the narrator, Utz's motives for returning to Prague seem entirely human and understandable. And when Utz finally remarks of his collection. "Of course, it has ruined my life," the narrator discovers that he feels empathy for the man.

Those interior sequences work so well that it is a surprise to find them dropped as the plot approaches a conclusion. Utz dies in 1974, and the final issue is whether or not the state has received the porcelains, and if not, what has happened to them. After conducting his own search, the narrator offers a series of speculations—which are based on surprising, previously withheld facts about Utz, as well as on new developments in his own life that seem implausible when presented in brief summary.

While *Utz* puts on display much that is good about Chatwin's work—his ability to get characters performing in dialogue, his fine control over physical details, his graceful voice and wit—it seems unfortunate that the novel has to end as it does. Perhaps Utz has outgrown the narrative, becoming a character too complex for a short novel. More likely, the weaknesses arise because Chatwin holds so tightly to his scheme, allowing no room for the imaginative speculation that, earlier in the book, brought involvement with Utz.

Shapely and elusive, the final scene of *Utz* suggests that Chatwin prefers the indirect path to his subject after all. By that time, however, we're more concerned with whether all of the questions introduced in the book have been resolved. And we still aren't sure whether the title character is a person to be taken seriously or just a curious, enameled figure who has been put back on the shelf before we could fully assess him.

> Fred Shafer, "A Finely Crafted Miniature from Novelist Bruce Chatwin," in Chicago Tribune— Books, January 8, 1989, p. 6.

ROBERT STONE

Bruce Chatwin's new novel, *Utz,* begins with a funeral in one of Prague's old Baroque churches. Readers of other Chatwin works will understand what I mean when I say that it is a scene only this author could create, alive with shrewd observation, pathos and absurdist humor. Its sense of place is dead-on and its component prose lapidary. It introduces us to the world of the decedent, one Kaspar Joachim Utz.

The late Utz was a Sudeten German of the poetry nobility, partly Jewish by background. Sensitive and cultivated, he embodied the spirit of ultracivilized *Mitteleuropa*. Both intellectual and aristocrat, Utz was condemned to witness the 20th century and thus the utter moral failure of those cultural values to which he was so exquisitely attuned. Irony became his very blood. A half-caste to the Gestapo, a German and a baron to the Czechoslovak Communist police, Kaspar Utz was born to be pursued by every fury in history's black box. But if he was a born victim he was equally a born survivor.

We are told:

> Politically, Utz was neutral. There was a timid side to his character that would tolerate any ideology providing it left him in peace. There was a stubborn side that refused to be bullied. He detested violence, yet welcomed the cataclysms that flung fresh works

of art onto the market. "Wars, pogroms and revolutions," he used to say, "offer excellent opportunities for the collector."

> The Stock Market Crash had been one such opportunity. Kristallnacht was another. In the same week he hastened to Berlin to buy porcelains, in U.S. dollars, from Jewish connoisseurs who wished to emigrate. At the end of the War he would offer a similar service to aristocrats fleeing from the Soviet Army.

In life, Utz survives the Nazi occupation of Prague by brandishing his father's German World War I decoration—and by collaborating with Goering's rip-off squad in its hunt for valuable objets d'art. After the Communist coup, he ingratiates himself with the new regime. All the same he is not a complete immoralist. His activities during the war enable him to hide Jewish friends and colleagues successfully.

> "What, after all, was the value of a Titian or a Tiepolo if one human life could be saved?"

It has to be said that this humanistic reflection, attributed to Utz early in the narrative, ends up seeming somewhat out of character.

Many things are going on in this short novel, which represents Bruce Chatwin at his most erudite and evocative. The narrator is a nameless scholar who encounters Utz in Prague. . . . Utz's great passion—his redeeming passion for purposes of characterization—is a mania for Meissen china figurines. He owns a priceless collection, which he figuratively and precariously carries amid the disasters of war, clinging to it like a Beckett character to his bicycle. The metaphorical china is pregnant with resonance, distantly evoking a host of themes, *Mitteleuropean* and otherwise—Dresden and its destruction, the Golem of Rabbi Loew, Frankenstein, puppetry, civilization's fragility. *Utz* provides its readers with a rich and rewarding meditation.

The world of Bruce Chatwin's writing—as exemplified in the roving observations of his travel books *In Patagonia* and *The Songlines* and his novels *The Viceroy of Ouidah* and *On the Black Hill*—is a stern, unforgiving place; the worst crime there is obviousness, followed in order of gravity by complaining and scrupulosity. In *Utz* also, so high and dry is the spiritual landscape that any display of principle (other than artistic) is a mark of vulgarity, and good intentions are equivalent to philistinism. . . .

Hard as he is on the conventional-minded, Bruce Chatwin dearly loves obsessives, and he forgives the lordly Utz much for his perversely ascetic egotism and transcendent lust for porcelain. Much fine prose and elegant shadow-play go into the main character's creation, but not every reader will be persuaded to invest the sympathy required to make Utz's final act of autonomy resound. In reacting to the intense estheticism and multiple ambiguities of which *Utz* is composed, a reader may have difficulty making up his mind about its eponymous un-hero. Is Utz finally (and ironically, of course) a champion of spiritual freedom in the mode of traditional Czechoslovak indirection? Or is he just a sentimental inflation of that proverbial central European smoothie who gets in the revolving door behind you but gets out first? *Utz* is a work in which first-rate style and observation contend with questionable substance.

> Robert Stone, "The Connoisseur as Survivor," in

The New York Times Book Review, *January 15, 1989, p. 3.*

MICHAEL DIRDA

[Bruce Chatwin] left readers only five books, but each is an off-beat masterpiece. To the despair of librarians, and the pleasure of everyone else, Chatwin blithely mixed fact with fiction and never published the same kind of book twice. Restless with the restrictions of genre, he was always lighting out for new territory. (p. 1)

[*Utz*] plays off the ambiguity between fact and fiction. On a journey through contemporary Czechoslovakia, a young art expert is told to look up a private collector of Meissen porcelain. He does so, visits the old man's apartment where his porcelain "dwarfs" are displayed, and sometime later starts to reconstruct this crotchety character's history. Neatly, Chatwin modulates into and out of Utz's point of view, describing the birth of his collecting urge, his subterfuges to preserve his figurines during the Second World War, his vain effort to escape Cold War Prague, the final disposition of his property.

Along the way, Chatwin offers homage to much of East European literature: His autobiographical frame recalls that of a Turgenev "sportsman's sketch," and Gogolian humor marks a restaurant scene where Utz and his friend Dr. Orlik argue about trout. The spirit of Chekhov hovers over a sad visit to a health spa, while the relationship between Utz and his housekeeper Marta mirrors, in miniature, that of the book collector and his servant in Elias Canetti's *Auto-da-Fé*. Even closer to home, there are echoes of Kafka and allusions to the Jewish monster of Prague, The Golem, immortalized in the novel of Gustav Meyrink.

All of this is enlivened by Chatwin's lucid, deceptively simple style. It is hard to convey in brief quotation the mix of *gravitas* and humor that makes Chatwin's prose so commanding. Absolutely clear, employing declarative sentences and very brief paragraphs, it is a prose that relies on quiet turns of rhythm and exact word choice to achieve a stately music. . . .

At the heart of this deceptively intricate novella lies the passion for collecting. Chatwin, the former art auctioneer and small-time antiquities smuggler, understandingly evokes the pleasures of investing one's life in objects, and through them, of forgetting personality, history, politics. . . .

There are splendid scenes here of collector and dealer haggling, of bored visitors forced to feign interest in an obsession they do not share, of the heart-bounding delight in simply looking at one's treasures on display. And yet, ultimately, Chatwin reproaches this unnatural passion for things—"the changeless mirror in which we watch ourselves disintegrate." A solitary vice, collecting deflects love from the human, away from its proper focus. In the tale's ambiguous climax, Chatwin comes to believe that Utz himself finally had to choose between flesh and porcelain.

Despite its brevity, *Utz* wonderfully depicts that sad, romantic city of Prague, the ham-handedness of East European politics, a small gallery of deftly drawn characters. Chatwin's deepening portrait of Utz is cunningly achieved—the tentative first meeting, the uncertain memory of whether the collector sported a mustache or not—and he turns the character

this way and that, adding and changing a detail here, letting everything about him remain a little shadowy and open-ended.

But there is nothing shadowy or uncertain about Chatwin's book: It is a triumph. (p. 5)

Michael Dirda, "Bruce Chatwin and the Collector of Prague," in Book World—The Washington Post, *January 22, 1989, pp. 1, 5.*

GABRIELE ANNAN

[*Utz*] is a mine field of clues, false, ambiguous, some possibly real. Nothing is what it seems: even the stuffed bear in a Prague restaurant turns out to be not a brown bear from the Carpathians, but a grizzly shot in the Yukon. So *Utz* needs to be read with circumspection—a good idea anyway, because Chatwin's prose can slip down too quickly to be appreciated as it should be. It's a kind of throwaway Mandarin, compensating by its simplicity for the profusion of baroque facts collected for one's instruction, amusement, and very likely some more secret purpose as well.

Utz is about collecting, and is also itself a collection of esoteric data. "Collecting," Baron Thyssen said the other day, "is an activity that is not quite normal, there are no logical reasons why you do it. They can come later." Utz himself pronounces collecting to be a sin—a form of idolatry. In form, *Utz* is a mystery, the puzzle being not whodunit, but why did he do it. There is a classic narrator-sleuth who has no characteristics that would not fit Chatwin himself: he is laconic, funny, a cool mimic (the Anglo-Czech conversations are a big syntactic joke), and idiosyncratically encyclopedic. The opening is classic too; the story begins with the funeral of the chief character, attended by the narrator. It takes place in a Prague church in 1974. The narrator has not seen Utz since their one and only meeting seven years before. In 1967 he was visiting Prague to do research for an article on "the Emperor Rudolf II's passion for collecting exotica: a passion which, in his later years, was his only cure for depression. I intended the article to be part of a larger work on the psychology—or psychopathology—of the compulsive collector." Quite a lot of clues there.

Kasper Joachim Utz is the owner of an incredibly rich collection of Meissen porcelain. . . . [He] is a scion of the minor—minimal—Saxon nobility. Before the war the family had a house in Dresden, estates in the Sudetenland, and wealth acquired through Utz's grandmother, a Jewish heiress. It was in her nineteenth-century chateau at Czeske Krizove in Bohemia that the child Utz fell in love with a Meissen harlequin and his lifelong passion began. Passion or disease? King Augustus the Strong of Saxony, who founded the Meissen factory, spoke of his obsession with porcelain as *die Porzellankrankheit*—the porcelain disease. It ruined his finances.

Utz has no financial worries. A Central European vicar of Bray with a Swiss bank account, he is fond of proclaiming that "wars, pogroms and revolutions . . . offer excellent opportunities to the collector." He collaborated with Goering's art squad, swapping his knowledge of the whereabouts of hidden works of art for the safety of his Jewish friends. He is German when Hitler is in the ascendant, Czech when the Allies march into Central Europe, and Jewish when being Jewish is an advantage under the Gottwald regime.

After the war he did a deal with the government: his collection was officially numbered and photographed, and understood to be the property of the state after his death. Meanwhile he was allowed to keep it. There were over one thousand pieces, so he needed a room to keep them in, but a two-room apartment was more than the authorities would allow a bachelor to occupy. So in 1952 he solved the problem by a *mariage blanc* to his housekeeper Marta. After the civil ceremony she moved in and slept on the livingroom floor among the china cabinets. . . .

Apropos of flirtations: early on in the novella the narrator mentions Utz's ludicrously small prick; he also presents him as being in love with his Meissen Columbine. For these and other reasons one is misled into assuming that Utz has no sex life. Then suddenly the narrator discovers a string of operatic mistresses and decides that Utz must have had a seductive mustache after all. All along, he proposes alternative versions of his story. It is unsafe to march too confidently in any direction he may point to.

Shortly after the narrator's visit to Prague, Utz is rebuffed by a prospective lay and "forced to revise his image of himself as the eternal lover" (Harlequin in the Meissen collection). He turns to Marta. She exacts a church wedding, and goes to the altar with the Utz wedding veil on her head and "minor sweatstains under the arm-pits." How could the narrator know about those? There are a lot of occult things going on.

Marta, for instance, enters the story just before the war as an orphan goose girl in love with a gander. Utz sees her being hounded by the villagers at Czeske Krizove, rescues her, and takes her on as his maid. When the narrator first sees her thirty years later she is "cradling"—the verb must be significant—a swan-shaped porcelain dish belonging to King Augustus's famous swan service. Ganders can turn into princes, goose girls into princesses, and swans can be Zeus in disguise. Everything vibrates with mythical overtones, and Prague is an eerie city. It was here that the sixteenth-century Rabbi Loew formed the monster Golem out of clay to be his servant: as God formed Adam and Kändler—the famous Meissen sculptor—formed his porcelain pieces. And before Kändler there was Böttger, the "inventor" of European porcelain, who was really an alchemist—as the collector Emperor Rudolf had been a century before him. Utz tells the narrator about Rabbi Loew as they sit on a bench in the old Jewish cemetery where the rabbi lies buried. Utz's apartment overlooks the cemetery.

A lot of arcane and esoteric matter has seeped in through the window, and into Chatwin's novella too. By a miracle of which the rabbi might have been proud he manages to fit into his 150 pages an account of the cabbalists; the history of porcelain from ancient China to the factory founded at Capo di Monte by Augustus the Strong's daughter when she became Queen of Naples; the etymology of the word "porcelain"; disquisitions on alchemy, the commedia dell'arte, and Winckelmann's views on the rococo; and the information that Prague is *the* place for terrorists to have their facial surgery done. He also manages to get in digs against Czech professional exiles with their "anti-Communist rhetoric . . . as deadly as its Communist counterpart," and against Western "dissident-watchers" "who, instead of watching animals in an East African game-park, had come to spy on that other endangered species, the East European intellectual."

It may or may not be significant that it is an East European

intellectual who leads the narrator to a possible solution of the central mystery. The central mystery is this: Utz has a mild stroke in 1973. Afterward, the authorities force him to sign an agreement (until then there had been only an understanding) that his collection will belong to the Prague museum; they also force him to import his Swiss collection into Czechoslovakia. In 1974, Utz dies of a second stroke. The narrator, as we know, attends the funeral (an extremely comical occasion). After the funeral Marta retires to her native village, and the collection is nowhere to be found: the cabinets are empty. The curators wring their hands. What has happened? . . .

The narrator concludes that Utz came to regret his life of subterfuge and trickery, and to recognize the faithful Marta as his true "eternal Columbine." From their second wedding onward, "they passed their days in passionate adoration of each other, resenting anything that might come between them. And the porcelains were bits of old crockery that simply had to go."

An unlikely tale for the reader to believe. Still, the narrator believes it and goes to seek out Marta in her village. At her gate he is met by "a snow-white gander" followed by an old peasant who says: "Ja! Ich bin die Baronin von Utz." A baroness is not quite a princess, but still. . . . Believe what you like. It's part of the pleasurable unease of being involved in a highly sophisticated, highly civilized *jeu d'esprit* whose rules are not divulged, and may not exist.

        Gabriele Annan, "Rules of the Game," in The New
        York Review of Books, *Vol. XXXVI, No. 1,* February
        2, 1989, p. 6.

PAUL DRIVER

The title of Bruce Chatwin's posthumous book [*What Am I Doing Here*] has no question-mark attached, and if it seems to confess to a bewilderment made all the more poignant by the illness which overtook the still young author it also begs to be adjusted into a statement and an answer. These stories, profiles and travel essays are a wonderful testimony to what Chatwin was doing here: he was fulfilling a unique vocation to look, to listen, to learn, and to share discoveries.

His curiosity was limitless, and he was governed by little else. If he had his obsessions, he was free from ideology and prejudice. He had the will to pursue his perceptions through world-literature and to the ends of the earth. He created a style of writing which is the luminous envelope of pure curiosity. On the evidence of this volume he never undertook a journalistic assignment which would not significantly enlarge his own and his reader's picture of the world. With his quiet voice he compels rapt attention to the most esoteric of subjects. He enables his reader, quite simply, to see more of this planet. He was one of the great geographers of our day.

To speak of journalistic assignments, however, is slightly misleading. Although eight of the 35 items collected here were written for the *Sunday Times* (for which Chatwin worked from 1972-75), and most of the others originally appeared in magazines or journals, the author points out that with one exception (a record of Mrs Gandhi's election campaign) the pieces were 'my ideas'. One hardly needed to be told this: the ideas are far too good; and one is lost in admiration for Chatwin's ability to put himself on the journalistic market and yet remain wholly himself in each periodical. One wouldn't know, without consulting the book's bibliographical note, whether an article had been written for *Granta,* the *New York Review of Books* or *House & Garden.* Only the *History Today* contribution on **"Nomad Invasions"**—Chatwin's central obsession, which led him to his most famous book, *The Songlines*—betrays a hint of conciliatory—in this case, academic—tone.

Chatwin himself selected and arranged the material in the volume; it was presumably his final task. Throughout his illness he went on writing, and the result is a number of short pieces published here for the first time. The book begins with a 600-word 'story' called **"Assunta"**. The word 'story', according to the author's Introduction, 'is intended to alert the reader to the fact that, however closely the narrative may fit the facts, the fictional process has been at work'. . . . It is—like **"Assunta"**, which follows—a mimicking and affectionate evocation of his nurse, to whom unlikely things had happened.

Among the other new things in the book are a touching mini-memoir of his father, and four glintingly well-wrought, highly condensed **"Tales of the Art World"**. The piece about the South African-born composer Kevin Volans, whose Fourth String Quartet was inspired by *The Songlines* and who is, for Chatwin, 'one of the more inventive composers since Stravinsky', only appeared in the *New York Review of Books* after *What Am I Doing Here* had gone to press.

In his last year Chatwin also managed to produce a hilarious description of the filming of his novel *The Viceroy of Ouidah* by Werner Herzog in Ghana (a real king, Nana of Elmina, took the role of Ghezo, King of Dahomey: 'Nana, like most kings, was obviously longing to play in a movie'). He also wrote a learned, colourful reminiscence of a visit in 1973 to the Moscow home of Konstantin Melnikov, the visionary architect, long ago anathematised by the Soviet State.

Two earlier pieces constitute a little section on Russia, the first a portrait of George Costakis, 'the leading private art collector in the Soviet Union', which further reflects Chatwin's intense interest (one of so many passions) in the Leftist art movement of the post-Revolutionary 1920s. A section on China contains an idyllic account of the eccentric career of the Austro-American botanist Joseph F. Rock.

"The Chinese Geomancer", placed not in the China section but under the heading **"Strange Encounters"** (and, though written in 1985, apparently not published before now), is vintage Chatwin—a gloss, not without its wry humour, on *The Songlines.* It describes a meeting with a Mr Lung, 'a modest practitioner of the venerable Chinese art of geomancy, or *feng-shui',* who was called in by the Hongkong and Shanghai Bank to give assurances that the site of its prestigious new headquarters—a 47-storey construction by Norman Foster—lay happy with respect to those underground currents of positive energy known to the Chinese as 'dragon-lines'. **"Maria Reiche: The Riddle of the Pampa"** is also prophetic of *The Songlines;* while the evocation of Donald Evans and his private miniature world of stamp-design draws Chatwin a step closer to his novel about the inhabitant of a world of porcelain treasures, *Utz.*

My favourite item is, I think, the pen-portrait of the painter Howard Hodgkin. No one writes better about his friends than Chatwin, and the tone of this piece is a marvellously sympathetic blend of the intimate and the objective.

> When walking down a street, he lets his arms swing loose and gives the impression of butting into a whirlwind.

The justness of this observation I, and perhaps other frequenters of the British Museum (near where Hodgkin lives and works), can verify.

Such a sentence typifies the meticulous elegance of Chatwin's prose, into which so much hard work must surely have gone while leaving so little trace. (pp. 24-5)

> *Paul Driver, "Curiouser and Curiouser," in* The Listener, *Vol. 121, No. 3113, May 11, 1989, pp. 24-5.*

SALMAN RUSHDIE

What Am I Doing Here (could the fastidious Chatwin really have agreed to the omission of the question mark?) is what we have left. His last book, a 'personal selection' of essays, portraits, meditations, travel writing and other unclassifiable Chatwinian forms of prose, was put together during his final, terrible year of wasting away, and it is inevitably a little patchy in places; but one of its chief delights is that it contains so many of its author's best anecdotes, his choicest performances.

Here is Bruce's 'snake story', as told to him by Assunta, the cleaning lady from Palermo, and her monologue is really Bruce 'doing' Assunta, all waving arms and flashing eyes, a figure not from life but from a comic opera. Here is Bruce's encounter with the footprints of the Yeti, and his visit to a Mansonesque hippy family in Boston. His campier performances are here, too: a delicious snatch of Diana Vreeland, and my own favourite Chatwin story, the one about his meeting with Noël Coward, who told him: 'I have very much enjoyed meeting you, but unfortunately, we will never meet again, because very shortly I will be dead. *But* if you'll take one parting word of advice, "Never let anything artistic stand in your way." '

There are, it should be said, many more substantial pleasures to be had from this collection. Bruce Chatwin was often at his best when furthest afield, and *What Am I Doing Here* contains some superb pieces from, for instance, Russia—an unforgettable Nadezhda Mandelstam, carelessly stuffing her errant breasts back into her blouse; a concise, brilliant account of the decline of the Leftist Movement in post-revolutionary Russian art, and of its excavation and preservation by the collector George Costakis; and a trip down the Volga that is a classic of 'travel writing'. Bruce was planning a large-scale Russian novel when he died; he might have proved to be a kind of Nabokov-in-reverse. We'll never know.

Africa, in which that 'desert mutation' *homo sapiens,* the nomad, the walker, first evolved, is the setting for some equally fine pieces: the account of the coup Chatwin stumbled into in Benin while researching *The Viceroy of Ouidah,* and the very different (comic rather than scary) account of how Werner Herzog and Klaus Kinski set about filming *Viceroy* (retitled *Cobra Verde*) some years later, in Ghana. In this latter essay, Bruce has untypically, and kindly, censored himself, omitting the no doubt libellous accounts of sexual shenanigans on location, and also his less-than-complimentary view of the finished film, both of which were included with relish in the oral version of the tale.

Bruce's politics could be, to put it politely, a little innocent. He could bang on about how things were really getting a lot better in South Africa, and he could fail to understand why Nadine Gordimer was irritated by his insistence on referring to Namibia as 'South West Africa'. But he could also get things magnificently right, and the essay in this collection entitled **"The Very Sad Story of Salah Bourguine",** which uses an inter-racial murder in Marseilles as a way of opening up the unsavoury subject of French colonialism in North Africa, is one of the most vivid things ever written on this difficult topic.

Bruce was much attracted (and attractive) to formidable ladies of a certain age, and this volume offers us quite a gallery of them: the aforesaid Nadezhda Mandelstam and Diana Vreeland, but also Madeleine Vionnet, 'the Architect of Couture', who designed her clothes on a doll because she didn't dare tell her father the extent of her business (he worried, as a result, that she might be retarded), and Maria Reiche, spending her life trying to decode the mystery of the lines and patterns on the Peruvian pampa. And the piece on Mrs Gandhi is as wonderful in writing as it was when he told it aloud. 'How that woman wants to be PM!' Mrs G says of Mrs Thatcher. 'I felt like telling her "If you want to be PM that badly, you'll never make it." ' Which just goes to show that even Mother Indira could be wrong.

What Am I Doing Here is, as the blurb suggests, a sort of autobiography, but it is an autobiography of the mind. In this book, as in life, Bruce Chatwin is secretive about the workings of his heart. I wish it were not so, for he was a man of great heart and deep feeling, but he rarely let it into his prose. Exceptions here are the moving vignette of his father; and an elegy for the Afghanistan known to Robert Byron, and trampled by Russian troops, that will read, to Bruce Chatwin's many admirers, like a lament for what we have lost through his untimely death:

> We will not sleep in the nomad tent, or scale the Minaret of Jam. And we shall lose the tastes—the hot, coarse, bitter bread; the green tea flavoured with cardamoms . . . Nor shall we get back the smell of the beanfields. . . . or the whiff of a snow leopard at 14,000 feet.

Salman Rushdie, "Before the Voice We Lost Fell Silent," in The Observer, *May 14, 1989, p. 48.*

PHILIP HOWARD

[*What Am I Doing Here*] is a selection (made by [Chatwin] himselfc) of 35 of his favourite pieces written over 20 years, and published in various places, some of them obscure. They range the globe from China to Peru, and exhibit the genres from the search for the Abominable Snowman to the discovery that Mrs Gandhi, although a catastrophic politician, was simply the little girl who wanted to be Joan of Arc. Some of them are slight, and some are coded messages for friends. The erudition is formidable. When Chatwin says he was rereading Gide's *Nourritures terrestres* when pulling into Dassa-Zoumbé station, or remembering Turgenev while sailing down the Volga with a package tour of Stalingrad veterans, you'd better believe him. Some of the higher journalism, like the long piece about the Algerians in Marseilles and maybe the Mrs Gandhi notes, when he almost fell in love with her while following her around on her comeback, saw things in a new way before anybody else. . . .

This sprightly selection is full of mind-boggling flashes of information. Did you know that the Huns bought, sold, slept, ate, drank, gave judgement, even defecated without dismounting?

He was a great traveller and a fine stylist, a good companion, an original nomad, and clearly a nice man. His work will last.

Philip Howard, "Have Pen, Must Travel," in The Times, *London, May 25, 1989.*

John Crowley

1942-

American novelist and scriptwriter.

Acknowledged as one of the leading authors of science fiction and fantasy to emerge during the 1970s, Crowley is praised for incorporating standard themes from these genres with various literary modes, including magic realism and modernism. Writing in a lyrical style, Crowley uses experimental writing techniques replete with symbolism, allegory, and allusion to address such universal concerns as humanity's quest for knowledge and enlightenment and the interplay between past, present, and future. Although each of Crowley's works are dissimilar in theme and form, his recent novels generally rely less on conventions of science fiction and more upon the forms of fantasy and romance.

While Crowley's early novels are often based upon science fiction premises, most are set on planets similar to Earth and eschew such standard elements of the genre as time travel and extraterrestrial characters. In his first novel, *The Deep* (1975), Crowley uses multiple viewpoints to portray a society of primitives who engage in intricate feudal conflicts on a large disc controlled by the Leviathan, an entity symbolic of the primordial forces of creation. His second novel, *Beasts* (1976), is set on a war-ravaged planet where wildlife has largely become extinct apart from a few species that genetically combine humans and animals. In this work, Crowley illustrates his contention that "beasts are not less than men, . . . but as complete; as feeling, as capable of overmastering sorrow, hurt, rage, love." *Beasts* draws from fables of the Middle Ages in which animal characters played prominent roles to describe the efforts of human and hybrid species to defeat an authoritarian government that seeks to eradicate wildlife for the benefit of human beings.

Crowley's next novel, *Engine Summer* (1979), garnered an American Book Award nomination as well as critical acclaim for its deft language and critique of contemporary American culture. Set in a depopulated and disintegrating future America, this work describes the quest of a member of an isolated Californian tribal community to achieve sainthood and discover lost truths through the spoken word. Crowley ironically portrays America as a paradise inhabited by ecologically-conscious oral cultures whose way of life is ultimately revealed to be as impermanent as that of the American Indians they have forgotten. John Clute called *Engine Summer* "[Crowley's] finest novel to date, and in the dark close warmth of its imprisoning integrity one of the best novels yet to come out of the [science fiction] genre." *Little, Big; or, The Fairies' Parliament* (1981), for which Crowley received a World Fantasy Award, was described by Douglas Barbour as a "marvelous example of late modernist writing." This work combines romance, fairy tale, and fantasy to describe the transformation of twentieth-century Earth into a mythic, pre-Edenic world populated by gnomes, fairies, and sibyls. Making complex use of allegory and abstract symbolism, *Little, Big* chronicles five generations of the Drinkwater family from the years 1890 to 2000. This novel is largely set on a labyrinthine estate in upstate New York that is constructed to house an orrery, or clockwork model of the universe. Although related from several points of view, the novel primarily describes a romance that leads to the birth of a child named Auberon. Traveling to an unnamed city similar to New York, Auberon experiences an unhappy love affair with a Puerto Rican girl, nicknamed Titania, prior to writing a soap opera about his family history that becomes a prototype of the book itself.

Tom Easton characterized Crowley's next novel, *Aegypt* (1987), as "a metanovel, about history, about the nature of fiction, even about itself." This book blends fantasy, satire, and philosophical romance in the magic realist tradition of Italo Calvino and John Barth to explore the hopes of Pierce Moffet, a specialist in Renaissance history. Moffet seeks to write a book titled *Aegypt*, about the meaning of the world, that would draw from Egypt's reputation as a source of magic and inspiration. Pierce's quest for enlightenment leads him to Rosie Mucho, a woman who helps him discover an unfinished manuscript that is essentially the novel he sought to compose. While some critics faulted *Aegypt* as tedious and inconclusive, most praised Crowley's synthesis of diverse themes and genres as ambitious and imaginative. In addition to his novels, Crowley is also the author of scripts for several documentary films, including *No Place to Hide* and *America Lost and Found*.

(See also *Contemporary Authors,* Vols. 61-64 and *Dictionary of Literary Biography Yearbook: 1982.*)

GERALD JONAS

[Science] fiction has evolved into a useful vehicle for writers who feel the need to reinterpret archetypal materials in the light of modern experience. A recent novel that exemplifies this kind of science fiction is *Beasts* by John Crowley. Crowley's inspiration seems to have been the "beast-epics" of the Middle Ages, which in turn go back to Aesop's fables for their themes. In the medieval tales, wily Reynard the fox was a principal character, along with Nobel the lion and Ysengrim the wolf. A fox and a lion figure prominently in *Beasts* with the role of the wolf being reserved for human protagonists.

The story is set in a future America that has seen the breakup of the central government after a long civil war and the partition of the continent into vaguely defined "autonomies." Crowley leaves no doubt that a new Dark Age has begun, but most of his characters see nothing "dark" about it, since the end of the central government has also put an end to the "mindless" destruction of the environment. Little by little, the land and the beasts are making a comeback—but this is not simply a return to some pre-industrial Eden. In the last days of the United States, genetic engineers created a new kind of beast—a cross between a lion and a man, called a leo. Painter, the leader of the leos, has all the majesty of a self-sufficient animal, with the intelligence of a human being (he can talk, reason, use a gun). . . .

The basic metaphor of *Beasts* is, appropriately enough, the hunt, although it is not always clear who is hunting whom. Some humans see the leos as a threat to the revival of the old order; these are the minions of USE, the Union for Social Engineering, which Crowley likens to a latter-day Society of Jesus in its "militant, dedicated, selfless" struggle to restore the power of the "old Federal government." (A more obvious comparison might be to the corporate incarnation of evil known as N.I.C.E. in C. S. Lewis's *That Hideous Strength.*) But there are other humans who see the advent of the leos as signaling a new dispensation for all living creatures.

In describing the fundamental conflict between those who would live in harmony with nature and those who would try to master it, Crowley displays a prodigious inventiveness. The point of view keeps shifting from one person to another, and from human beings to various beasts and half-beasts, but Crowley's control never slips, and his writing from inside the mind of a falcon or a leo or a dog recalls the breathtaking passage in *That Hideous Strength* when Lewis enters the mind of a bear.

Pulp magazine editors once advised writers to keep the reader's attention by introducing at least one new character per chapter. Crowley goes this formula one better by introducing a fresh concept in each chapter. One particularly effective invention: a pacifist and vegetarian commune, housed in a huge glass skyscraper, that exercises stewardship over a vast domain of wilderness. The reactions of the rather simpleminded nature lovers to the truly wild nature of the leos and the feral viciousness of the USE agents provides a dramatic focus to

a memorable tale that ends too soon, leaving this reader at least eagerly awaiting a sequel.

Gerald Jonas, in a review of "Beasts," in The New York Times Book Review, *November 21, 1976, p. 67.*

GERALD JONAS

For an example of the risks that must be taken to bring off a science-fictional apocalypse, the reader can turn to [*The Deep*] by John Crowley. Several columns ago I praised Crowley's hardcover novel, *Beasts,* which was published last year. *The Deep,* his first novel, is not as tightly structured as the new book, and its basic plot is hardly fresh: A feudal society on some earth-like planet is disturbed by a newly arrived outsider, who knows that he has a vital mission to perform if only he can remember what it is. Yet despite the air of familiarity, nothing in this situation is quite what it seems, and events move unexpectedly toward a confrontation with [primordial forces]. . . . Paraphrase is useless to convey the intensity of Crowley's prose; anyone interested in the risk-taking side of modern science fiction will want to experience it firsthand. (pp. 42-3)

Gerald Jonas, in a review of "The Deep," in The New York Times Book Review, *March 27, 1977, pp. 42-3.*

SONYA DORMAN

On your next trip to your local library, look for *Beasts,* by John Crowley. Crowley is a strong, skillful writer who uses his wilderness lore and knowledge of birds, such as Canada geese and peregrine falcons, to point out healthy future possibilities for a ravaged planet.

Against a background of political machinations between shaky and contentious autonomies on the North American continent, he tells a story of man, and man's experiment with a hybrid species. There are leos, man-lions, in the wilderness, but the experiment is considered a failure by USE, the Union for Social Engineering. This powerful government agency wants the planet back for man only, and hunts the leos down.

Combating USE, each in his own way, there's Loren, the falconer, tutor of an assassinated politician's son and daughter; Meric, who leaves his Soleri-type of home, peaceloving and vegetarian, to go out into the world of forests and leos; Caddie, the indentured servant girl who is illegally sold to Painter, King of the Beasts. She lives with him and his pride, loving him, adapting to the pride's ways. . . . And there is Reynard, man-fox, the trickster, government emissary, double agent and traitor to both sides, court jester and counselor to Painter.

Crowley manages to make the hybrid species absolutely convincing. He writes of the leos with sensuous beauty and of the humans with compassion. Toward the end, Loren the falconer and lover of unspoiled land, meets Painter, the man-lion. Well met, they accept each other, and each in his own way learns to accept himself.

This is the kind of science fiction that is passionately concerned with man and this planet; with the limited concepts of too many of our species; with the greed of a few that leads to endless waves of starving refugees. Crowley takes his characters through all kinds of devastation to suggested hope, implied peace. Perhaps the ending has one promise too many; perhaps you'll be glad that it does. (pp. 169-70)

Sonya Dorman, "Man and Beast," in Analog Science Fiction/Science Fact, *Vol. XCVII, No. 6, June, 1977, pp. 169-72.*

DAVID A. TRUESDALE

[*Beasts*] is a curious book, an enigmatic book, a book I feel contained all the elements of a truly good book, but somehow most certainly failed. At bottom line it tries to deal with the persecution and alienation of half-animal mutants called the leos in a future time when a corrupt government unlike—in terms of structure and name—ours of today attempts to rule a society that has warred with itself and is in a fragmented and relatively anarchistic state.

Through advances in modern genetic engineering we have developed the ability to create a half-human, half-leonine species of "human" which is capable of interbreeding with homo sapiens. They are few, and are castigated by the common people as well as the Union for Social Engineering. . . . They are very close to total extinction.

Crowley sets his stage adequately enough, for near the close of the book our sympathies must of necessity be with the starving, misunderstood, maligned and murdered leos—but then the book ends with the half-fox mutant Reynard reappearing miraculously (he has had the foresight to clone himself), and plotting with a group of underground leo sympathizers, their aim to begin a 'new age' of life and understanding for all Beasts everywhere, the final hope given us in the final line of the book. All that is well and good. But . . .

. . . Henry Kuttner did all this for us *years* ago, and in *so* much more successful fashion, with his perceptive, sensitive, touching tales of the Baldies, those telepathic mutants who were also outcast and feared for their dangerous differentness from mankind as a whole. Kuttner knew what he wanted to say of alienation and living amongst those who would hate and kill if you let your differentness be indiscriminately exposed, and he said it. He got right to the point and *showed* us, made us *feel* what it is like to be a second-class citizen because one is better. He didn't take up nearly an entire novel with average characterization, average intrigue and by-play before getting down to the nub of things, and herein lies the major fault with *Beasts.* It is a very shallow imitation of Kuttner's Baldies—in concept—and just managed to *end* somewhere close to where Kuttner *started.*

If I were you I'd pass this one by.

David A. Truesdale, in a review of "Beasts," in Science Fiction Review, *Vol. 7, No. 5, November-December, 1978, p. 27.*

MICHAEL BISHOP

John Crowley's *Engine Summer* presents a depopulated, far-future America where crumbling interstates and brontosaurian shopping malls testify to both the might and the folly of their makers. Rush that Speaks, a member of the isolated Little Belaire community of truthful speakers, sets out from his forest home to "find all our things that are lost, and bring them back." Like all meaningful quests, this one has a psy-

chological dimension, which Crowley illuminates with uncommon sensitivity and grace.

Nowadays sf and fantasy quests are as numerous and annoying as gnats on an August lake shore. Amid this swirl of formulaic mediocrity *Engine Summer* is a strikingly original and involving book.

To accommodate the lovely idea that Rush that Speaks is recording his hagiography on pieces of eight-sided glass, Crowley calls the subsections of his novel "facets" and its four major divisions "crystals." Because Rush wishes to become a "saint"—that is, to live a "transparent life" worthy of many retellings—the structural strategy of *Engine Summer* is made to reflect (pun altogether appropriate) its thematic content. Indeed, Crowley's ending suggests a circular storytelling pattern that is simultaneously rejuvenating and imprisoning for Rush that Speaks, and we are both moved and horrified by his predicament. Its author's third novel, *Engine Summer* is as rare and welcome as those brief out-of-season respites so gently and humorously evoked by its title.

Michael Bishop, "In Dark Corners of the Universe," in Book World—The Washington Post, *March 23, 1980, p. 6.*

JOHN CLUTE

[*Engine Summer* is Crowley's] finest novel to date, and in the dark close warmth of its imprisoning integrity one of the best novels yet to come out of the sf genre. The integrity of *Engine Summer* begins and ends with the title. At first glance a slightly irritating play on Indian summer, by novel's end it has become not only the meaning of the book but—complexly—the book itself, for ultimately we come to see that the very text of the book—the first-person narrative of its protagonist, Rush that Speaks—is precisely an engine summer.

Like *Beasts,* to which it is a kind of thematic sequel, *Engine Summer* is set in a post-holocaust America, though in this case so long after the event that pre-collapse humans are referred to as angels (but without approbation), and Indians have been so long forgotten that the glorious days of early autumn, during which much of the story takes place, are referred to as engine summer. Set in the midst of the long diffuse tedious terrifying collapse of technological Faustian man, *Beasts* is damagingly plotted around the kind of technophilic revanchist conspiracies that make up the narrative substance of far too many American sf novels about our Balkanized future after the roads fail. The America of *Engine Summer,* in contrast, seems to be a kind of paradise inhabited by a series of ecologically modest oral cultures deeply attuned to the natural world; there seems to be no alienation.

Born into the Palm cord of Little Belaire commune, Rush that Speaks grows up obsessed with the notion, entirely proper to his culture, of becoming a saint. In Little Belaire terms, a saint is an individual man or woman whose life is a tale of such transparency that others can hear the truth of the world through its telling. . . . In Little Belaire, an oral community the telling of whose dead saints' lives comprises the very warp and woof of all history and meaning, words are deeply important, and "truthful speaking" lies at the heart of those strings of narrative (or cords) that maintain social comity, for how else can the lives of the saints be seen through? As are all members of his particular cord, Rush that Speaks is an intensely dedicated truthful speaker, but for him to radiate that saintly transparency through which others can hear themselves be human, he must lead an exemplary life. He grows up longing to. *Engine Summer is* that longing. Is it exemplary?

After the girl he loves disappears one spring with the clan of roaming traders called Dr Boots' List, Rush eventually follows her into the outside world, which seems almost as pastoral as Little Belaire itself. He hibernates with Blink, a saint of no fixed cord; he treks southwards, coming across the List's home base, where he finds his love strangely transformed, impassive, translucent, seemingly unconscious of the passage of time, for when she receives once a year, as do all members of the List, a "letter" from Dr Boots, the world begins afresh for her. He manages to receive a letter of his own; it turns out to an epiphany; a strange glowing ball from the time of the angels briefly possesses him, infusing him for a moment with his love's translucently inhuman acceptance of the unchanging garden of the world. But he is troubled in his heart. A letter from Dr Boots is more like a lobotomy than an infusion of sainthood. He has lost her.

So he has to leave. After further adventures, he discovers an angel-crafted silver hand, which the tales of the saints have always significantly linked with a glowing ball, one of several. Almost immediately, his dreams of angel cities in the sky are confirmed when a genuine angel, alerted by his discovery of the lost hand, parachutes down to him through the air, and the novel begins to close in on the deep pathos of its underlying premise. The angel, by name Mongolfier, explains to Rush that the hand is a device for the control of the glowing balls, which are themselves angel devices for the imprinting and subsequent replaying of entire personalities. Before humans had been recorded, however, experiments had been thought necessary, and the ball that had struck Dr Boots' List into timelessness, for instance, contained the personality of a cat named Boots. But now Mongolfier has an offer to make, that of immortality. The floating angel city desperately needs an exemplary human personality to remind its inhabitants of their original nature as the centuries pass. Mongolfier offers to imprint Rush that Speaks into a permanent glowing transparency. Though the human Rush that Speaks will himself live on, an aging mortal on a quest for sainthood, he will also have been transformed into a sentient playback in the heavens, and will remain in the heavens forever.

Engine Summer is of course that sentient record's longing tale; the frame of the book is a conversation between "Rush that Speaks" and a deeply moved listener, a conversation taking place 600 years after the events "he" relives, events which comprise his immediate life and memories and goals, even though he has all unknowingly repeated them 300 times. No matter how often told, however, this life and the words of its retelling remain paradigmatic. They are nothing but truth. They can be seen through. "Rush that Speaks" has become a radiance—a saint—through which generations of angels learn the meaning of themselves.

But for reasons the novel makes complexly and amply clear, the warm pastoral garden of a world so described is not an engine summer merely because, after all, a kind of engine is doing the job of re-creation; it is an engine summer because the world so lovingly described is precisely a contrivance of autumn, a dying Arcadia, for the cultures that make up this idyllic America are scattered and dwindling, and human fertility is only precariously maintained through limited sup-

plies of an angel powder; and winter is nigh. 600 years on, *Engine Summer* is only a text. And that is its ultimate truth. Typically of Crowley, the final revelation of truth turns out to be a demonstration of control. As in all his work, peace and solace are no more than cat's-cradles in the fingers of a huge closing hand.

Rarely in sf (or elsewhere) will form and message cohabit as powerfully as they do in *Engine Summer*. . . . (pp. 48-50)

John Clute, in a review of "Engine Summer," in The Magazine of Fantasy and Science Fiction, *Vol. 58, No. 4, April, 1980, pp. 48-50.*

STEVE LEWIS

Crowley has and [in *Engine Summer*] he demonstrates, a superbly fine sense of language. In no way is this book for those who dote on *Star Wars* space opera only. In no way is this a book that grabs you with the first line or the first paragraph and refuses to let go.

That is, not in the sense that that favorite cliche of hack reviewers usually implies. There is a plot, a slow, serpentine one that twists back around upon itself until suddenly, with perhaps the second reading of the final chapter, all is at last made crystal clear.

With sparkling and glittering revelations of exultant triumph, one might say, if one were so inclined. I won't. It would be a lie, an exaggeration. The revelations, the triumphs are both inner ones. The future is still murky and uncertain.

Rush That Speaks (that's his name) lives in a post-holocaust world. . . . [He] has learned the art of truthful speaking and has already ventured into the outside world with the ambitious intent of becoming a saint.

It is doubtful that he knows it, but by the time that his story has concluded, that is what he has become. Telling more is impossible without a mere repeating of the story and I can't improve upon it. Nor in fact is all the story explained or explainable and if you'll allow me a purely personal reaction, I admire Crowley all the more for it. (pp. 48-9)

Steve Lewis, in a review of "Engine Summer," in Science Fiction Review, *Vol. 10, No. 2, Summer, 1981, pp. 48-9.*

JOHN CLUTE

John Crowley's ambitious fourth novel, *Little, Big,* easily defeats any attempt to compress its dazzling intricate riches into a brief summary.

At the heart of the largesse of the book does lie a Tale, all the same. It is the story from 1890 to 2000 of the extended Bramble/Drinkwater family, who live at Edgewood in Washington Irving country north of New York, and who are secure in the knowledge that, by living their lives as fully as possible, they are taking part in—are in fact the actual substance of—an enormously long and terribly important Tale whose resolution, as the novel begins, is nigh. The world will change utterly.

It is about 1975. After courting Daily Alice Drinkwater for two years, Smoky Bramble now obeys her command to come to Edgewood, where they will be married. From New York he treks northward into something like but not exactly heaven. Lying at the center of five villages seemingly inhabited mostly by extensions of the family, Edgewood is a huge oak-shaded five-sided dwelling constructed to hold an orrery—a clockwork model of the universe—at its heart, and intimations of the Renaissance Art of Memory (along with the Tarot) in its innumerable rooms and complex interlocking facades and duskily serene grounds; but most important of all, Edgewood is that secret place in the Wild Wood where mortal lands intersect with the domain of Faerie, where Little becomes Big, if you step inwards.

Here Smoky will spend the rest of his contented busy life as America declines, the only resident of Edgewood not related by blood to everyone else there, and though we will learn a great deal about the once and future Bramble/Drinkwaters in the 538 pages of the novel, he will remain our mortal center of consciousness. The orrery is broken; he will spend much of his life trying to repair it, finding at last that, properly attuned to the heavens, *it* powers the house, not vice versa. There will be numerous children needing education; he will teach them, often using as text his father-in-law's newspaper fables about the Wild Wood and Old Mother West-wind and the Green Meadow and the talking animals who live there, in a world of imagination halfway through the portal to Faerie. Though children's author Thornton W. Burgess is not mentioned by name, Crowley clearly intends a homage to him in these passages; the effect is strangely moving.

And Smoky will help Daily Alice raise their four children, three of whom are the Fates or Moirai reborn . . . The fourth child, Auberon, goes to the wilderness of New York, where he stays with relatives, falls desperately in love with Sylvie (a Puerto Rican nicknamed Titania in childhood) and is eventually hired to script the popular TV soap opera, *A World Elsewhere,* which he gradually transforms into another version of the tale of his family, transfixing what's left of America after the reborn Barbarossa has brought winter to its heart and then himself gone back to sleep for another thousand years.

But I am just hinting at the riches of this dense, marvelous, magic-realist family chronicle about the end of time and the new world to come when Daily Alice finally takes on Mrs. Underhill's mantle and becomes the breathing spirit of Nature animate. Crowley's style has a calm unremitting clarity, and though the text is chock-a-block with parodies and echoes of writers from Lewis Carroll to T.H. White, the ultimate effect is of an uncluttered mature steadiness of vision, with hardly a wrong note, though Barbarossa never quite convinces. Crowley's only substantial problem seems to be how to end the book while continuing the Tale, whose underlying promise is that there is no ending.

His solution has panache.

Never having quite managed to believe in what lay about him like a dance, Smoky dies of his angina, after a good life. Metamorphosis transfigures everyone else; they become the new world; who can tell the dancer from the dance? But before becoming king of the fairies, and plunging once again into eternal sexual imbroglios with his loving Titania, Auberon must terminate *A World Elsewhere,* just as *Little, Big* must be terminated. After sending off the last pages, which he can't remember writing, "he thought, laughing, of that schoolboy device he had once used, that last line that every schoolboy had once used to complete some wild self-indulgent fantasy otherwise uncompletable: *then he woke up.*"

He awakens. He closes the book, which is fiction. He enters the Tale.

John Clute, "On the Edge of the Other World," in Book World—The Washington Post, *October 4, 1981, p. 5.*

DOUGLAS BARBOUR

Little, Big, Crowley's fourth published novel, is a fantasy, a story of fairy connections in the new world, and like his previous novels, it defies conventional genre expectations.

Little, Big is on one level one of those familiar family epics, tracing the adventures of at least three generations of the Drinkwater family as they live in, leave, and return to the rambling family mansion built by John Drinkwater for Violet Bramble at the turn of the century. Violet is the daughter of an English clergyman who has a "theory" about fairies based on his understanding of of her encounters with them. This theory [states] that as you pass into the "smaller" realms of Faërie which can be found inside our universe they turn out to be, in fact, "larger," so that when you finally reach the smallest and most inaccessible one you will find yourself in a world of infinite size and wonder. . . . John Drinkwater's house, on the edge of a new world fairywood, is his attempt to give the theory form architecturally: it is a mélange of many possible houses all intersecting crazily so that even family members who have lived there all their lives sometimes get lost in its seemingly endless interiors.

Sometime in the 1960s, Smoky Barnstable, a slightly anonymous young dreamer from the big city, meets Daily Alice of the Drinkwater family. They fall in love, and her passion for him gives him substance. Following the orders of a strange pack of Tarot-like cards handed down from Violet to Aunt Cloud, he sets out to walk to Edgewood and marry Daily Alice. They have children: three girls who seem, like their mother, to have intercourse with Faërie, and Auberon, who eventually returns to the city—now decaying and dangerous—toward the end of the century.

But all the many characters of *Little, Big* have their parts to play in "The Tale," which has been narrating itself for millenia, whether they believe it (like Daily Alice and Aunt Cloud) or do not (like Smoky and Auberon). And Crowley invokes mythic and literary analogues at every turn to make this one story somehow represent the whole history of humanity's encounters with Faërie. At the same time, he tells a warm story of love and domesticity, growing up and growing old, in a large family. One of the finest qualities of *Little, Big* is its generous and humane treatment of its characters. Each has his or her specific speech patterns and modes of behavior; while behind these lies the rolling, richly idiomatic style of the narrative, capable of switching easily from the discourse of Victorian romanticism to that of mythic game-playing to that of urban drug argot.

As a mixture of magic realism and traditional fantasy, *Little, Big* is a successful, richly populated novel; but it is also something more complex and more interesting. In his earlier books, especially the visionary *Engine Summer,* Crowley has proven that he comprehends both modern science fiction and the fiction of high modernism. In its ornate metaphorical and fictional structure, *Little, Big* is a marvelous example of late modernist writing. Taking the basic idea of smaller worlds within our world which are really larger when you enter them, the narrative discovers a variety of analogues in its fictional world to substantiate the theory: the house, the cards, a special memory method, a collection of photographs, a soap opera Auberon writes based on what he's learned of "The Tale," the mind itself, and, finally, surrounding all, this novel, every section of which contains the whole story in small and reveals more of the suggestive background against which it is told.

It is the combination of pure storytelling—the history of the Drinkwater family throughout the twentieth century—and metaphorical structure—how the novel invites us into Faërie even as it—almost science fictionally—explains it—that lifts *Little, Big* above most recent genre fantasies. Unconcerned with writing just another conventional fantasy, Crowley has successfully expanded the usual boundaries of the genre. If the conclusion does not quite live up to the various interlocked stories preceding it, perhaps that's beyond any writer, and the disappointment one feels is slight, for the journey through the intertwined lives that make up this huge novel has been so entertaining and moving. *Little, Big* is, as Le Guin says, "a splendid madness, or a delightful sanity, or both." It is one of those rare books readers will want to read again and again. (pp. 19-20)

Douglas Barbour, in a review of "Little, Big," in Science Fiction & Fantasy Book Review, *No. 1, January-February, 1982, pp. 19-20.*

ALAN BOLD

This ostentatiously inventive saga [*Little, Big*] is not designed for the common reader. It is, rather, made to measure for those already addicted to fantasy literature and ready, willing and able to stick with a book whose formidable length is given over to allegory, abstraction, supernaturalism and symbolism. John Crowley drops names and references into the narrative as clues to the attentive reader who can then place the novel in a suitably impressive context. . . .

From the first page to the last Crowley takes the reader into his confidence. The book is not meant to be read as a transcription of reality, for it is "Make-believe . . . it's a Tale. And Tales work out." The working out of the archetypal Tale allows Crowley to indulge himself to the extent of eschewing conventional fictional logic, making his characters much larger than life and seemingly able to transcend time and space even as the Tale unfolds in the present century. This, in fact, is something of a Transcendental Tale, set in a rural retreat in New England and delighting in the contrast between a pastoral paradise and an infernal city. . . .

Crowley's earthly paradise is constructed by the founding father of the Tale. John Drinkwater, an eccentric architect whose follies are worth millions of dollars, builds a particularly whimsical folly called Edgewood. This house, to be fit for the Tale, takes a shape that can incorporate theosophical doctrine; above all it reflects the belief that "the other world is composed of a series of concentric rings, which as one penetrates deeper into the other world, grow larger. The further in you go, the bigger it gets." This occult theory of relativity explains the title of the book. . . .

How far the reader will believe in this story depends on his tolerance for book-lore and literary showmanship: Crowley has an allusive and occasionally flashy style. Every person is a personification; every conflict involves a moral principle.

Describing a work attributed to John Drinkwater, Crowley provides his own aesthetic ideal:

> pages and pages studded with capitalized abstractions . . . marginal glosses every page or so, and epigraphs, chapter headings, and all the paraphernalia that makes a text into an object, logical, articulated, unreadable.

Actually his own text is extremely readable, though there are times when the prose becomes as decorative as a Pre-Raphaelite picture. . . .

Although Crowley is seeking to convey an impression of timeless innocence, it is possible to date his vision. Paradise is defined as "A world elsewhere" and there are telling details of this alternative world. It thrives on permissive sex, psychedelic brilliance and the odd hallucinatory experience; it counterpoints gentle gurus with presidential baddies; and it advocates a return to nature. This is nothing less than a full-blown celebration of 1960s hippieness. Flower children cavort like fairies and the hippies are as loveable as hobbits. Crowley has a fundamental belief in the poetic purity of that time, and has transformed an era into a rich period piece in prose.

Alan Bold, "Heads and Their Tales," in The Times Literary Supplement, *No. 4130, May 28, 1982, p. 593.*

ROZ KAVENEY

Too often critics have taken as the sole and crucial matter of fantasy the preoccupations of Tolkien, the quest for a remedy to the world's pain that will not destroy innocence with the temptations of power. . . . After all, the grail is only worth seeking if you can believe in a god who put it there to help those who help themselves, in an Avalon to which burnt-out heroes can retire with dignity. There is another great Matter for fantasy, one of more obvious resonance for the creative artist—the reconciliation of faerie and humanity, of the passion, power and wit of a world of sensuality, magic and danger with the requirements of kind and ordinary life. That is an important part of the work of Angela Carter, the subject of Hope Mirrlee's neglected *Lud-in-the-Mist* and, in particular, of John Crowley's extraordinary and excellent *Little, Big.*

Crowley is a writer of surpassing, almost overweening, intelligence and cleverness. Some writers set the tone of their works with the first sentence—Crowley tends to start the ball of multiple meanings going with his very titles. His last novel was *Engine Summer* (1980), whose title plays with, and alludes to, the mood of elegy, the portrait of a post-technological decay in which engines are as much a memory as Indians and the hero's apotheosis as a perpetually recorded memory of growth, maturity, and joy. Nor is *Little, Big* different; in its title the comma is as important as the words whose relationship it multiply defines. *Little, Big* is a formula cognate with Hermes Trismegistus's "As above, so below". The comma can also imply a simple listing—Little *and* Big; given the frequency with which Dr. Johnson occurs in the chapter epigraphs this can be taken as a self-mocking reference to the lexicographer's remark à propos of Swift that once you had thought of the little men and the big men the rest was easy. *Little, Big* has a subtitle, "The Fairies' Parliament"—which taken in conjunction with chapter epigraphs from the Persian poem "Parliament of Birds" drops to the alert and the informed a hint of the novel's resolution; it has six books—each with a title—26 chapters—each with an epigraph—and just over 200 sections—each with a title. It is not necessary for enjoyment or understanding of this novel to sit down and draw out the meaning of each of these, or of the relationships between them in numerological terms which I have an awful suspicion exist—Crowley is not Joyce, demanding a lifetime's study. In their complexity and multiplications of meaning they add to that tinge of pleasure that warms the reader from a level below that at which you can at all times be conscious of what is going on.

And what is going on? Well, among other things a richly peopled novel of the generations of a clan. At the beginning of this century, successful beaux arts architect John Drinkwater marries the pregnant British theosophist Violet and takes her to Edgewood in upper New York State. Around the middle of the century, the amiably vague Smoky Barnable marries their great-grand-daughter Daily Alice, has an inconclusive affair with her sister Sophie and settles uneasily into the routine of a family and community where he loves and is loved but is forever a stranger. At the century's end, his son Auberon returns to the City—superstitiously unnamed but obviously New York—to seek his fortune amid its crumbling buildings and economy; he loves and loses the Puerto Rican Sylvie, becomes a drunken vagrant and then a successful writer of television soap opera. And amid all this we are regaled with the inquiries and machinations of the clairvoyant Ariel Hawksquill, the rise to power of the demagogue Russell Eigenblick, known as the Lecturer, and the education of Sophie's child Lilac, whom the fairies stole. Every detail of this complex narrative has its relevance to the whole; every detail is planned or rapidly improvised around by the folk of faerie, who whisk continually half-seen round the corners of the plot and whose intrigues turn out to be as complex, ambiguous, and intricate as those of the author.

In Crowley's novel, magic stands for what is done in the story but also for what the author is doing in the book. Magic is something that happens as you blink your eye or turn your back; Smoky lives among his wife's family for years, knows that they think they talk to fairies and never believes a word of it—but when as a young man he proofread telephone directories, he assumed to be misprints places like the Seventh Saint Bar and the Church of All Streets which become important parts of his son's city life: where magic is concerned common sense is not to be relied upon. Magic is a sudden switch of perspective or blurring of image: it is impossible to say at what precise moment we realize that the Grandfather Trout in whom young Alice confides is literally her transformed grandfather, the promiscuous August, punished for double-dealing but principally used by the fairies for their selfish convenience. . . . Magic is a sudden intrusion of the outlandish into the every day—the giant mirror that falls and guarantees ill fortune on Auberon's first day in New York, the fake changeling Lilac that eats live coals and explodes amid fireworks. Magic is a coming to knowledge: Hawksquill's clairvoyance is no trumpery affair of mirrors and crystal balls but a search through filed and structured memories for knowledge one may not know one has but which may be found if the mind is laid out for searching. . . . Magic is a telling of tales; the animal stories of Alice's father the doctor, the soap operas of Auberon, are full of truths for a world that cares to hear, full of the knowledge of "Brother North-Wind's secret", that after winter comes summer and after summer, winter.

Part of Crowley's subject is America. It is in the spring of America's century that Drinkwater brings his bride to Edgewood; at its high summer that Smoky walks there one June to his bride; it is in autumn storms that Auberon suffers loss and degradation in a City that has become the most dangerous of forests. . . . Drinkwater decorated the rising City; as it falls, Auberon learns through an alcoholic haze the secret paths and hidden places that his ancestor and his colleagues almost unknowingly provided.

The tale is full of people, clearly visualized and likeable; it is without villains, though those who like Hawksquill and August abuse power have to pay a price. Crowley manages seemingly effortlessly to portray a variety of good people from the vague Smoky to the ardent and bitter Auberon and the earlier gentler Auberon, Violet's son by Hawksquill's grandfather, who wastes his life wistfully cataloguing photographs in the hope he can unambiguously prove the existence of faerie. . . . Crowley perpetually shifts tone to capture the mental and moral atmosphere each character breathes, talks and perceives through—so many of them share early memories and basic assumptions that this is not as difficult as it might seem. He is sparing with the presence of the fairies . . . but when he lets us see them full face, theirs is no hollow mask of sweetness but a powerful sinister lovely presence. There are other presences floating in the book—Lewis Carroll and Dr. Johnson for example; the novel deals with the extravagant and wild but does so with witty logic and with a sense of moral balanced reason. (pp. 16-17)

Crowley's subject is one which might have succumbed to feyness and looniness; if his prose at times risks a too knowingly meaty rhetoric it is to restrict naïveté to the passages where it is called for. The prose has a supple tough-minded energy, a luxuriance of conceit that renders the book full of lines and passages that have the air of being quotations from some famous book one has not read. All his characters are dreamers who wander through miracle almost without noticing—they are continually surprised when pain hurts and Crowley's eloquence makes us share the sudden surge of their joy or regret. He manages in prose images of love as compelling as most in poetry—for Auberon in his days of requited love "Happiness was a season; and in that season Sylvie was the weather. Everyone within him talked about it, among themselves, but no one could do anything about it, they could only wait till it changed". . . .

This is a novel full of wit and terror, of passionate creativity and energetic discipline, of young and of eternal love. It sets out to justify the wonderful and the hardworking everyday, and succeeds by never pretending that all pain can be mitigated, that all tragedies can be glossed over; there are gods who must die that other gods may mourn them. Crowley's fairies are artists, concerned for their own interests and for what is elegant and beautiful; they are not kind or just, though their actions often seem so. Crowley balances losses and gains; like the hero of *Engine Summer,* Drinkwater's descendants are transmuted into immortality—"Stories last longer; but only by becoming only stories." Hawksquill gains power by a proper ordering of her mind; Auberon overcomes grief by organizing his memories of love; Crowley avoids easy answers by a preparedness to show the good faith of strenuous thought and effort, by hard sayings—he reconciles the fantastic and the mundane by ordering them in a vigorous, upsetting and consoling fable. (p. 17)

Roz Kaveney, "Wit and Terror," in Books and Bookmen, *No. 321, June, 1982, pp. 16-17.*

MICHAEL DIRDA

Little, Big, John Crowley's tale of an American family's long involvement with the realm of faerie, embraced everything from the Tarot to television, from Thornton W. Burgess' animal fables to poignant love stories. Confirming, and surpassing, the artistry of his earlier novels—*The Deep, Beasts,* and *Engine Summer*—that superb book established its author as a master of lyrical fantasy, equal in ambition and accomplishment to Ursula Le Guin and Russell Hoban.

If lyrical fantasy sounds rather schmaltzy, another term for Crowley's kind of book might be philosophical romance. His new novel *Aegypt,* for instance, manages to intertwine the stories of a disaffected college teacher and a confused divorcée with an inquiry into the nature of history and man's place in the universe. Crowley himself calls it a "fantasia" on themes suggested by Frances A. Yates and other scholars of the Renaissance occult. This means that its pages explore such undeniably bizarre questions as

> why the voices wailed that Pan was dead . . . why Moses had horns, and why the Israelites worshipped a golden calf; why Jesus was a fish, and why a man with a water-jug on his shoulder directed the Apostles—the Twelve—to an upper room.

For many readers this will consequently be a strange, even recondite book, though an immensely readable one: Crowley's prose remains bright and beautiful, absolutely assured, no matter how teasing his purpose. Fans of, say, Italo Calvino, the intellectual comedies of Thomas Love Peacock, or (especially) the Gnostic fantasies of David Lindsay and Harold Bloom, will immediately recognize a kindred spirit.

In essence, *Aegypt* traces several different story lines that gradually converge, indeed become manifestations of a single pattern of conceptual breakthrough. In one, Pierce Moffett, a specialist in Renaissance history, starts a journey toward enlightenment when a revered teacher asks him the question: "Why do people think that Gypsies can tell fortunes?" The answer, he discovers, is that Gypsies were thought to be from a land shrouded in mystery, one ruled over by priest-mages who could command angels and elixirs, whose legendary prophet Hermes Trismegistus may have surpassed Moses in power: Egypt. But not the muddy Egypt of ordinary history, rather the *Raiders-of-the-Lost-Ark,* Erich-von-Daniken realm of legend and popular belief: Aegypt.

Pierce—his name, by the way, deliberately echoes that of Perceval, the Grail-seeking knight—travels further on his mystical quest after his own involvement with a Gypsy, a beauty never called by her true name: "When he first met her she was masked and naked, and he was being paid by her mother to caress her." Eventually, this enchantress leads him into cocaine, high-living and sexual mysteries; it is partly as an escape from the heartache she brings him that Pierce flees the city to find himself and to write his "unhistory" of Aegypt.

In the pastoral setting of the Berkshirelike Faraway Hills, Pierce discovers a former pupil named Spofford who has inherited some land and literally set himself up as a shepherd. . . . Spofford, we learn, loves the elusive Rosie Mucho, the book's other major character, who passes her days in a kind of spiritual listlessness, reading historical romances and waiting for a divorce. Around Rosie circle various symbol-laden figures. These include Beau Brachman, a small-town guru of immense charm, who just may be able to ascend up through the celestial spheres toward God. . . . And "Boney" Rasmussen, Rosie's uncle, old as time itself, head of the mysterious Rasmussen Foundation, and once a good friend of the historical novelist Fellowes Kraft.

Both Pierce and Rosie find Kraft's novels strangely disturbing, and Crowley reproduces large portions of several, each set in the swashbuckling Renaissance of Thomas B. Costain and Samuel Shellabarger. These apparent fictions—but are they, in fact, fiction?—loosely interconnect: In one book young Will Shakespeare visits the celebrated magus Dr. John Dee; in another Dee meets up with the medium Talbot, a scryer who can look into magical showstones and converse with angels. Still another traces the life of thinker Giordano Bruno, sometimes called the first modern man, the discoverer of infinity (burned in 1600 as a heretic). That last "novel"—developing several ideas from *Little, Big*—breaks off just when Bruno and Dee are about to meet, after which—we are told by an angel—"nothing . . . will ever be the same." Not by accident, this is the same phrase Pierce uses to describe the excitement and sense of new possibility of the 1960s, the new Age of Aquarius. . . . This sounds pretty hokey, but Crowley makes it high intellectual adventure . . . In *Aegypt*'s climax various disparate elements grow together toward a kind of alchemical marriage: Bruno makes the conceptual breakthrough that will destroy the medieval mindset; Rosie's divorce comes through just as she suffers an emotional death of the heart; and Pierce concludes—whether rightly or no—that mages, illuminati and Freemasons "have not had power in history, but the *notion* that secret societies have had power in history *has* had power in history." Above all, each character is primed for a new life, one less burdened by the loneliness and sense of spiritual incompleteness that otherwise marks all the book's principals.

Aegypt is clearly a novel where thought speaks louder than action, where people, places and events are at once actual and allegorical. Early on, Rosie's rearview mirror falls off her car and she "can't see behind me. Can't see where I've been." Spofford throws a party that resonates with images of Saturnalia and Shakespearean comedy (this key section might well be called "the confusions of a night"). (p. 5)

Crowley wants readers to appreciate his foreshadowings, echoes, bits of odd lore, multiple voices—in the evolution of complex pattern is his art. But, it must be added, some of his planted hints never quite flower here: Did Fellowes Kraft discover the Grail during an expedition to the Giant Mountains? Are the Faraway Hills invested with an occult power similar to that of ancient Glastonbury? Why do certain women of the Faraways share a peculiar detachment about sex, a kind of erotic indifference? Is the text we are reading the edited, polished version of a manuscript found among Kraft's papers? Could there be more than one "History of the World"? In all cases, the answer would seem to be yes, but the reader needs to know more.

Despite a satisfying close, *Aegypt* is clearly then only the first movement in a quartet. Its sections—*Vita, Lucrum, Fratres*—are names drawn from the first three of the 12 astrological houses. Crowley's publisher gives no indication that three more books will follow, but we have obviously been prepared to find out more about these characters, especially Rosie's husband Mike, his mysterious girlfriend Rose and the "science" of Climacterics. For all *Aegypt's* undeniable grandeur and achievement it seems that this book, like one of Fellowes Kraft's, should end with the words "The Beginning." (p. 7)

Michael Dirda, "A Secret History of the World," in Book World—The Washington Post, *April 19, 1987, pp. 5, 7.*

JOHN CLUTE

Beginning *Aegypt* is not half the battle; it is very nearly the whole war. John Crowley's fifth book is much less a novel than a series of portals. Full of beginnings, plot spirals that return us to beginnings, and sudden vistas that signal a new myth of the universe, it does in fact literally begin several times with an author's note that becomes part of the text, a "Prologue in Heaven" after Goethe's *Faust*, a "Prologue on Earth" to balance the first prologue, and more than one chapter of initiation. And each beginning—each portal—remains open. Nothing is resolved. The last pages of *Aegypt* close on nothing.

It is a dizzying experience, achieved with unerring security of technique, in a prose of serene and smiling *gravitas*. Mr. Crowley's history as a published writer . . . has not been of the sort to generate a wide reputation, and it will be of great interest to learn if he can reach a welcoming public with this daunting anomaly of a book, this gaping gateway that leaves us staring into a deeply strange world.

Just what this book is or will become—and the text makes it clear that three further volumes are planned—may be almost impossible to say. In conventional generic terms, the first volume is neither fish nor fowl, neither fantasy nor conventional novel, while at the same time it adroitly mixes both modes together. On the surface, *Aegypt* seems to be no more than the story of a young historian, Pierce Moffett, who loses both tenure and his lover and apparently by accident finds himself in upstate New York, where he begins to find a pattern of preternatural coincidences and meanings. In this rural setting, he begins to discover that the magical tales he read as a child are true and hint at a new understanding of the universe, in which he himself may be intimately involved. (p. 9)

At the center of the book's vision is the figure of the Renaissance occult philosopher Giordano Bruno, whose heliocentrism points to the figure of Hermes Trismegistus, a mythical sage of pre-Christian Egypt, to whom the Renaissance mistakenly attributed a number of Greek Gnostic writings. Though it might seem impossibly intricate to the unlearned eye, Hermes' universe as Bruno interpreted it was a single living entity which, in all humility and love, could be *understood*. In his Theater of the World—an advanced version of the elaborate imaginary structures used to file facts for future recall in the medieval arts of memory—Bruno intended to create a neoplatonic representation of the entire universe itself. It was a universe in which nothing (as Fellowes Kraft and Pierce Moffett long to believe) was meaningless.

Pierce Moffett's name reflects his nature, for he is both penetrant and woolly, rather like *Aegypt* itself. From childhood he has longed to inhabit a world he could recognize as being intended, pregnant with meaning, animate; and this longing, this sense of *desiderium*, informs his every moment. As an adult and a historian, he searches for a version of the world that might *account* for the nature of things, but in vain. Vic-

tim and master of a poignant yearning heterosexuality, he falls uncontrollably in love with several women, each time with a view to seeing the universe entire. Signs and portents of some imminent transformation multiply around him—or perhaps he breeds them, perhaps Pierce Moffett is a visitor to our sphere who will bring the world alive, as it essentially has always been.

The Manhattan Pierce inhabits for much of his life, like the Manhattan of *Little, Big,* of Jerome Charyn's numerous urban fables and of Mark Helprin's *Winter's Tale,* is very much a storied isle, drenched in significance, in the story of itself, as in a fount. It is not merely a city. It is the City, and one only leaves the City if one is in search of the Golden Age. When Pierce finally leaves Manhattan it is to write a book about the meaning of the world, which he hopes to call *Aegypt;* and by this time in the story it is not surprising that in Blackbury Jambs, his new hometown somewhere upstate, he finds a world far more drenched with implication than the slightly anodyne pastoral it first seems to represent. (pp. 9, 11)

The portrait of Pierce Moffett, gangling, vulnerable, sharp and sheepish, is lovingly comprehensive (he is a kind of portmanteau version of Smoky Barnable and Auberon, the two main characters of *Little, Big*). The inhabitants of Blackbury Jambs sing through their lives with the innocence of children, for that is their pastoral destiny; but at intervals they seem human, too. The narrative itself, which spirals through time and space rather like a maze that Pierce must penetrate, startles the reader again and again with the eloquent rightness of the web of coincidences that structure it. And in moments of sudden realization, when Pierce sees for the first time something he had always inwardly known, the universe of *Aegypt* seems to talk itself awake. But what this artful (and sometimes arch) opening of portals will amount to, we can only guess.

At times most movingly, at other times rather doggedly, *Aegypt* embodies the sense that it is itself meant ultimately to be read as a Theater of the World. (p. 11)

John Clute, "This Way to the Meaning of the Cosmos," in The New York Times Book Review, *May 3, 1987, pp. 9, 11.*

TOM EASTON

[*Aegypt*] is a remarkable . . . what? Well, it is certainly a book. It isn't SF. It is—maybe—fantasy. Is it a novel? In a sense. But in a more important sense, it is a metanovel, about history, about the nature of fiction, even about itself in at least two ways—Pierce Moffett, historian with visions of how the world is not as it always was, begins to write a book predicated on the idea that the Aegypt of mystic knowledge was as real as the Egypt of the hieroglyphs, and as he coins phrases for its beginning we recognize the beginning of *Aegypt*. Later, he finds the last, incomplete manuscript of historical novelist Fellowes Kraft, whose books enlightened his own youth and consume at least one more of Crowley's characters, and that manuscript, built on the same premise, is also *Aegypt*. (p. 181)

Have I lost you? I'm not surprised. Though *Aegypt* may seem to belong on the same shelf as Wilson's Illuminatus trilogies, it is a far more serious work. It also struck me as a very slow read, unexciting, deliberately confusing and obfuscatory, and my perception may even be an accurate sense of the book. On the other hand—let me be honest—I read it during Christmas week, a time rich with distractions . . . and while I was quitting smoking, an activity not precisely conducive to concentration. I was therefore not reading the book under the best possible conditions. *But*—the best possible books do have a way of conquering the worst possible conditions, and this one didn't do that.

Or did it? I stayed with it, after all, and Crowley's creation lingers yet in my mind. His tale is slow, then, but powerful. We meet Pierce as he buses from New York City to an outland school for a job interview. This bus breaks down near the town of Blackbury Jambs. He meets old friend and student—now a shepherd, of all things—Spofford, and then a Rose. He reflects on his past—a childhood of strange books which first gave him the dream of Aegypt, a high-flying girlfriend, coke deals, debt, trouble with his school. We learn of a Kraft-reading, husband-leaving Rose, upon whom Spofford has designs, and if we think the two Roses are the same, well, Crowley has so set his trap.

Pierce learns that the job for which he is supposed to interview does not in fact exist; the computer has been pulling his leg. He returns home to rearrange his life, to take refuge in his dream of Aegypt, eventually to build the dream into a book proposal, and then to return to Blackbury Jambs, there to learn more of Kraft and Aegypt and his own personal destiny. Along the way, Crowley feeds us lengthy excerpts from Kraft's novels. This ploy slows the tale more than anything else, but the excerpts—oddly intersecting lives of Dr. Dee, Will Shakespeare, and Giordano Bruno—do illuminate the difference between our world and that of Aegypt and inform us more of Crowley's metafictional concerns.

I expect *Aegypt* will draw raves from all quarters. It will deserve them, too, for Crowley writes most excellently, with extreme gifts of sensibility and description and characterization. But *Aegypt* may be the least finished book of the year. That is, people will buy it. They will recognize its quality and the interestingness of what Crowley has to say and the way he chooses to say it. But they will turn aside to other books and movies and parties of less intellectual interest and more excitement, and *Aegypt* will languish.

I said that *Aegypt* is about itself. I should add that Crowley puts in it a remark that says much the same thing as that last paragraph of mine: Great stuff, but who'll read it? (p. 182)

Tom Easton, in a review of "Aegypt," in Analog Science Fiction/Science Fact, *Vol. CVII, No. 8, August, 1987, pp. 181-82.*

JOHN PEAKE

From *The Deep* to *Little, Big,* John Crowley's novels have grown steadily in size. But there has been no accompanying increase in flab. Rather, the greater the length, the greater the richness of the language, the depth of perception and the sense of solidity, reality and wonder. This new book continues that exponential growth. It is as sizeable as *Little, Big,* and the first volume in a projected sequence of four; and it makes even its predecessor seem shallow by comparison.

Crowley is an artificer: the structures he creates, the object of paper and ink he finally produces, are all as vital to *AEgypt* as the story he has to tell. He makes no secret of the fictionality of this work. It opens with an author's note, which is later reproduced by the main character as the author's note to his own book, and the breakdown of the distinction between the real and the fictional is part of what *AEgypt* is about. . . .

History lecturer Pierce Moffett stops off in the Faraway Mountains on his way to an interview for a new job, and never completes the journey. What he finds in the town of Blackbury Jambs provides him with a retreat, and the inspiration for a new book. This book is about AEgypt, a country of the imagination which may be congruent with the real Egypt, and which has been, throughout history, a source of magic and inspiration. His book, which he is only starting work on by the end of this volume, is about creativity and the historical imagination, and it shares more than a few features with Crowley's *AEgypt.*

One of Moffett's inspirations for the book is the historical novelist Fellowes Kraft, former resident of Blackbury Jambs, whose books themselves form a considerable part of the content of *AEgypt.* Thus we meet Giordano Bruno whose advanced ideas set him at odds with the sixteenth-century Vatican; and we see Doctor Dee and a young William Shakespeare discovering angels in a scrying glass.

All this would be rich enough for most novels, but it barely gives a glimpse of what is to be found here. In Crowley's universe everything interacts with everything else. The families in Blackbury Jambs with whom Moffett comes into contact all have their parts to play; as do the child-minder whose meditations take him out into the depths of space; Rosie and her child, getting over a divorce, whose family possessions include the papers of Fellowes Kraft; and above all the astrological system that seems, in some way, to subsume the rest.

I don't know whether this system is a recognized one or has simply been invented by Crowley; in the long run it doesn't really matter. The twelve houses each have their own attribute, and the main part of this novel is divided into three, each chapter bearing the name of one of these zodiacal houses. "Vita", life, "Lucrum", possessions, and "Fratres", family and friends, are the first three signs of this zodiac; and it is possible to see that each chapter reflects, obliquely, the attribute of the house it is named for. It seems likely that the full significance of this, as of so much else in the book, will only come clear when the full zodiac of twelve houses and four novels is laid before us.

This may suggest that *AEgypt* is a dense, slow, difficult book, and in a sense it is. But its own vivid reality is an absorbing one, and it leaves the reader impatient for the second volume.

John Peake, "Putting the House in Order," in The Times Literary Supplement, *No. 4416, November 20-26, 1987, p. 1274.*

T(homas) S(tearns) Eliot

1888-1965

American-born English poet, critic, essayist, dramatist, and editor.

The following entry presents criticism on Eliot's poem *The Waste Land* (1922). For discussions of Eliot's complete career, see *CLC*, Vols. 1, 2, 3, 6, 9, 10, 13, 15, 24, 34, 41, 55.

Considered among the most innovative, influential, and controversial poems of the twentieth century, *The Waste Land* challenged conventional definitions of poetry upon its publication in 1922 and helped occasion the shifting of values that inaugurated the Modernist period in literature. Composed of numerous mythic allusions, varying voices, settings, and tones, colloquial, lyrical, and fragmented language, and quotations from works by other writers, *The Waste Land* develops a series of abruptly changing formats in which disillusionment, spiritual ennui, and casual sexuality are projected as representative elements of a post-World War I European sensibility. The disjointed form of the poem accentuates bold metaphors and symbols that are often juxtaposed with deadpan irony, confronting readers with disparate and ambiguous images and narrative events. Among many factors, the work's seemingly chaotic structure and Eliot's inclusion of notes to elucidate and cite his various references have engendered charges of purposeful obscurity and contributed to the notoriety of *The Waste Land*. Acknowledging its complexity, Hugh Kenner contended that the poem's imposing structure and erudite references invite active and imaginative readings: "*The Waste Land* is suffused with a functional obscurity, sibylline fragments so disposed as to yield the utmost in connotative power, embracing the fragmented present and reaching back to that 'vanished mind of which our mind is a continuum.'"

Critics frequently address *The Waste Land* as a depiction of social turmoil in Europe following the devastation of World War I, as a reflection of personal emotions, and as a spiritual quest pertaining to Christian and Buddhist tenets. Much attention focuses on the poem's allusions to fertility rituals discussed in *The Golden Bough*, by Sir James G. Frazer, and *From Ritual to Romance*, by Jessie L. Weston. Weston's book, which draws upon Frazer's anthropological investigations of the myths and rites of numerous peoples, explores the influence of various pre-Christian cults on legends surrounding the quest for the Holy Grail. The title of Eliot's poem was suggested by a motif explored in Weston's book. In most Grail legends, a sacred vessel is sheltered in the Waste Land, a drought-plagued realm presided over by a liege named the Fisher King. The sterility of the land is connected with the Fisher King, who has been rendered impotent as a result of either a wound, an illness, or a sexual transgression. Regenerating forces and salvation will be attained when a questing knight passes various tests and achieves the Grail. In the modern setting of *The Waste Land*, Eliot intimates that casual sexuality, decadence, and despoilation of nature have created a spiritually and physically barren world. These themes are illuminated through social criticism and satire of modern life and are enhanced with phrases drawn from great works of literature, opera, and spirituality. In addition, some critics trace Eliot's personal difficulties in their interpretations of the poem, noting that he wrote *The Waste Land* while suffering from disillusionment and nervous exhaustion.

In its original form, *The Waste Land* comprised a series of narrative poems and was significantly longer than the final version of 433 lines. During its composition, Eliot turned to his friend, poet and scholar Ezra Pound, for suggestions on how to make the work more effective. Pound made numerous editorial contributions that significantly altered the form of the piece. He helped Eliot shape several poems into one, suggested the removal of some extended passages, condensed others, and commented freely upon word choice and phrasings. Pound referred to himself as a *sage homme* (male midwife) in the creative process of this poem, and his editorial contributions are generally considered invaluable. The original drafts of the *The Waste Land*, replete with Pound's notes and his correspondences with Eliot, were rediscovered more than forty-five years after the poem's initial appearance and are reproduced in *The Waste Land: A Facsimile and Transcript of the Original Drafts, Including the Annotations of Ezra Pound* (1971). Peter Ackroyd commented: "Pound had an extraordinarily good ear, and he located in the transcripts of *The Waste Land* the underlying rhythm of the poem—the music of which Eliot was so distrustful and which he surrounded with more deliberate and dramatic kinds of writing. Pound heard the music and cut away what was for him the extraneous material which was attached to it." The poem's original title, *He Do the Police in Different Voices,* taken from an utterance by a character in Charles Dickens's novel *Our Mutual Friend,* reflects Eliot's desire and ability to blend mimicry, parody, allusions, and modern idioms through a succession of narratives. Critics have speculated on whether the voices in *The Waste Land* represent different characters or are filtered through a single consciousness—most often identified as Tiresias, the seer from classical literature who appears in the poem. Calvin Bedient isolated this question as one of the central concerns confronting readers of *The Waste Land:* "Is it 'Eliot' who speaks the work (or speaks in it)? Or a polyphony of equal voices? Or Tiresias? Or a nameless narrator-protagonist? Or still some other possibility?"

The Waste Land is composed of five sections. In "The Burial of the Dead," the first section, the famous opening—"April is the cruellest month"—reflects a sensibility that contends against the regenerating forces of spring. This passage is often contrasted with Geoffrey Chaucer's celebration of spring in the Prologue to *The Canterbury Tales,* and critics also note the influence of Frazer's and Weston's discussions of vegetation deities who died in winter and were resurrected in the spring. The brusque, fragmented structure of *The Waste Land* is evidenced in this section. A voice that projects a preference for listlessness is interrupted by a conversation in German that underscores the sense of Europe's disconnectedness and ethnological confusion after World War I. This aside is followed by a childhood reminiscence, and the passage concludes with a sense of ennui. A prophetic voice then utters such oracles as "for you know only a heap of broken images" and "I will show you fear in a handful of dust." Brief quotations from the tragic love story in Richard Wagner's opera *Tristan und Isolde* frame a passage in which a man is awestruck by the beauty of a young woman and experiences an intensity that leaves him silent and sightless. The setting switches abruptly to a tarot reading which foretells the appearance of several characters later in the poem. The scene then shifts to a bleak depiction of modern London, where a mass of people trudge to work in the early morning, and the section ends as a speaker cries out a disorienting greeting to a long-lost acquaintance.

The second portion of *The Waste Land,* "A Game of Chess," spans several eras and social classes but is unified by common themes of despair, decadence, and failure in relationships and sexuality. This section begins with an opulent detailing of a boudoir containing aphrodisiacs and baroque objects and is followed by a scene in which a bored couple fail to communicate, emphasizing a motif of silence and futility. A brief passage revealing lack of purpose among the idle rich is juxtaposed with a scene in a bar between two lower-class women who discuss sex in cockney dialect. In another example of stifled regeneration, one of these women has recently endured an abortion. Critics note that this section of the poem contains many images of unnatural sexuality. In the third section of *The Waste Land,* "The Fire Sermon," the title of which is taken from a teaching by Buddha concerning desire, Eliot comments upon lust and lovelessness. He introduces the hermaphrodite prophet Tiresias, and a note advises the reader that both sexes merge in this individual, who serves as the most important personage in the poem. "What Tiresias *sees,* in fact, is the substance of the poem," according to the note. Tiresias foretells a seduction scene between a swaggering

clerk and an indifferent typist, which Eliot satirically renders in rhymed iambic pentameter. "The Fire Sermon" concludes with a quote from St. Augustine's *Confessions.* The placement of this quote purposefully collocates Christian and Buddhist ascetics. The brief fourth section—"Death by Water"—contains references to a drowned sailor first mentioned in the tarot reading in "A Game of Chess."

The Waste Land concludes with a section entitled "What the Thunder Said." After developing further images of sterility, death, and fear in an arid mountain setting reverberating with thunder, the poem connects modern London with a series of historical cities that fell into ruin and decay. Similar to a task undertaken by the hero in Grail legends, a quester reaches an empty chapel, whereupon a gust of wind brings rain to the parched land. Thunder mimics the sounds of three words of wisdom from a Upanishad: datta (give), dayadhvam (sympathise), and damyata (control). Although critics disagree as to whether this section is pessimistic or optimistic, they generally regard these three words as Eliot's prescription for escaping the modern waste land. A series of fragments drawn from such disparate sources as Dante's *Purgatorio,* Thomas Kyd's *Spanish Tragedy,* and a nursery rhyme ("London bridge is falling down") follow in rapid succession. The poem concludes with the words "Shantih Shantih Shantih"—a formal ending to a Upanishad that can be translated as "The peace which passeth understanding."

Many critics scorned *The Waste Land* upon its publication. Poet Amy Lowell is quoted as having said, "I think [the poem] is a piece of tripe," and several commentators voiced suspicions that the poem was a hoax perpetrated by Eliot and his influential literary friends. Detractors generally faulted *The Waste Land* for obscurity, lack of unity, and its despairing tone, claiming the poem projects a defeatist attitude and a fashionable malaise that appealed to cynical young intellectuals. Nevertheless, the poem was championed by many reviewers and soon became a source of scholarly exegeses. The most enthusiastic supporters of *The Waste Land* have likened its appearance to that of *Lyrical Ballads* (1796), a collection of poems by William Wordsworth and Samuel Taylor Coleridge that contained verse radically different from conventional poetry of the time. Just as *Lyrical Ballads* spurred the Romantic movement that supplanted neoclassicism as a dominant literary mode, so too, critics have argued, *The Waste Land* helped replace Edwardian and Victorian sensibilities with Modernist literary values. E. M. Forster's assertion that the poem captured the disillusionment of a generation has been echoed by numerous literary historians, even though Eliot himself refuted this view. Some critics have compared the form of *The Waste Land* to a musical composition, noting Eliot's use of such techniques as recurring themes, rhythms, dissonance, and counterpoint, while others have likened its development to the creation of a collage or mosaic. Scholars have traced the ambiguities, allusions, and symbols within the poem, drawing upon Eliot's critical writings and personal sentiments to explicate pattern and meaning. Among other approaches, *The Waste Land* has been interpreted in terms of Christian doctrines, Buddhist beliefs, mythic structures, and anthropological studies.

Most later critics, partly as a response to the voluminous scholarship generated by *The Waste Land,* stress the importance of the reader's initial responses to the poem. These commentators note that ambiguities and sundry implications lend the work a vitality that may offer new interpretations for succeeding generations of readers. Some critics argue that the poem's nondiscursive form suggests that it should not be explained as a statement of beliefs. Frank Kermode summarized this view: "[*The Waste Land*] resists an imposed order; it is part of its greatness, and the greatness of its epoch, that it can do so."

(See also *Contemporary Authors*, Vols. 5-8, rev. ed., Vols. 25-28, rev. ed. [obituary]; *Dictionary of Literary Biography*, Vols. 7, 10, 45, 63; and *Dictionary of Literary Biography Yearbook: 1988*.)

EDMUND WILSON, JR.

Mr T. S. Eliot's first meagre volume [*Poems*] was dropped into the waters of contemporary verse without stirring more than a few ripples. But when two or three years had passed, it was found to stain the whole sea. Or, to change the metaphor a little, it became evident that Mr Eliot had fished a murex up. His productions, which had originally been received as a sort of glorified *vers de société,* turned out to be unforgettable poems, which everyone was trying to rewrite. There might not be very much of him, but what there was had come somehow to seem precious and now the publication of his long poem, **The Waste Land,** confirms the opinion which we had begun gradually to cherish, that Mr Eliot, with all his limitations, is one of our only authentic poets. For this new poem—which presents itself as so far his most considerable claim to eminence—not only recapitulates all his earlier and already familiar motifs, but it sounds for the first time in all their intensity, untempered by irony or disguise, the hunger for beauty and the anguish at living which lie at the bottom of all his work.

Perhaps the best point of departure for a discussion of **The Waste Land** is an explanation of its title. Mr Eliot asserts that he derived this title, as well as the plan of the poem "and much of the incidental symbolism," from a book by Miss Jessie L. Weston called *From Ritual to Romance.* The Waste Land, it appears, is one of the many mysterious elements which have made of the Holy Grail legend a perennial puzzle of folk-lore; it is a desolate and sterile country, ruled over by an impotent king, in which not only have the crops ceased to grow and the animals to reproduce their kind, but the very human inhabitants have become unable to bear children. The renewal of the Waste Land and the healing of the "Fisher King's" wound depend somehow upon the success of the Knight who has come to find the Holy Grail.

Miss Weston, who has spent her whole life in the study of the Arthurian legends, has at last propounded a new solution for the problems presented by this strange tale. Stimulated by Frazer's *Golden Bough*—of which this extraordinarily interesting book is a sort of offshoot—she has attempted to explain the Fisher King as a primitive vegetable god—one of those creatures who, like Attis and Adonis, is identified with Nature herself and in the temporary loss of whose virility the drouth or inclemency of the season is symbolized; and whose mock burial is a sort of earnest of his coming to life again. Such a cult, Miss Weston contends, became attached to the popular Persian religion of Mithraism and was brought north to Gaul and Britain by the Roman legionaries. When Christianity finally prevailed, Attis was driven underground and survived only as a secret cult, like the Venus of the Venusberg. The Grail legend, according to Miss Weston, had its origin in such a cult; the Lance and Grail are the sexual symbols appropriate to a fertility rite and the eerie adventure of the Chapel Perilous is the description of an initiation.

Now Mr Eliot uses the Waste Land as the concrete image of a spiritual drouth. His poem takes place half in the real world—the world of contemporary London, and half in a haunted wilderness—the Waste Land of the mediaeval legend; but the Waste Land is only the hero's arid soul and the intolerable world about him. The water which he longs for in the twilit desert is to quench the thirst which torments him in the London dusk.—And he exists not only upon these two planes, but as if throughout the whole of human history. Miss Weston's interpretation of the Grail legend lent itself with peculiar aptness to Mr Eliot's extraordinarily complex mind (which always finds itself looking out upon the present with the prouder eyes of the past and which loves to make its oracles as deep as the experience of the race itself by piling up stratum upon stratum of reference, as the Italian painters used to paint over one another); because she took pains to trace the Buried God not only to Attis and Adonis, but further back to the recently revealed Tammuz of the Sumerian-Babylonian civilization and to the god invited to loosen the waters in the abysmally ancient Vedic Hymns. So Mr Eliot hears in his own parched cry the voices of all the thirsty men of the past. . . .

In the centre of his poem he places the weary figure of the blind immortal prophet Tiresias, who, having been woman as well as man, has exhausted all human experience and, having "sat by Thebes below the wall and walked among the lowest of the dead," knows exactly what will happen in the London flat between the typist and the house-agent's clerk; and at its beginning the almost identical figure of the Cumaean Sibyl mentioned in Petronius, who—gifted also with extreme longevity and preserved as a sort of living mummy—when asked by little boys what she wanted, replied only "I want to die." Not only is life sterile and futile, but men have tasted its sterility and futility a thousand times before. T. S. Eliot, walking the desert of London, feels profoundly that the desert has always been there. Like Tiresias, he has sat below the wall of Thebes; like Buddha, he has seen the world as an arid conflagration; like the Sibyl, he has known everything and known everything vain.

Yet something else, too, reaches him from the past: as he wanders among the vulgarities which surround him, his soul is haunted by heroic strains of an unfading music. Sometimes it turns suddenly and shockingly into the jazz of the music-halls, sometimes it breaks in the middle of a bar and leaves its hearer with dry ears again, but still it sounds like the divine rumour of some high destiny from which he has fallen, like indestructible pride in the citizenship of some world which he never can reach. In a London boudoir, where the air is stifling with a dust of futility, he hears, as he approaches his hostess, an echo of Anthony and Cleopatra and of Aeneas coming to the house of Dido—and a painted panel above the mantel gives his mind a moment's swift release by reminding him of Milton's Paradise and of the nightingale that sang there.—Yet though it is most often things from books which refresh him, he has also a slight spring of memory. He remembers someone who came to him with wet hair and with hyacinths in her arms, and before her he was stricken sense-less and dumb—"looking into the heart of light, the silence." There were rain and flowers growing then. Nothing ever grows during the action of the poem and no rain ever falls. The thunder of the final vision is "dry sterile thunder without rain." But as Gerontion in his dry rented house thinks wist-fully of the young men who fought in the rain, as Prufrock longs to ride green waves and linger in the chambers of the sea, as Mr Apollinax is imagined drawing strength from the deep sea-caves of coral islands, so in this new poem Mr Eliot identifies water with all freedom and illumination of the soul. He drinks the rain that once fell on his youth as—to use an analogy in Mr Eliot's own manner—Dante drank at the river of Eunoë that the old joys he had known might be remem-bered. But—to note also the tragic discrepancy, as Mr Eliot always does—the draught, so far from renewing his soul and leaving him pure to rise to the stars, is only a drop absorbed in the desert; to think of it is to register its death. The memory is the dead god whom—as Hyacinth—he buries at the begin-ning of the poem and which—unlike his ancient prototype—is never to come to life again. Hereafter, fertility will fail; we shall see women deliberately making themselves sterile; we shall find that love has lost its life-giving power and can bring nothing but an asceticism of disgust. He is travelling in a country cracked by drouth in which he can only dream fever-ishly of drowning or of hearing the song of the hermit-thrush which has at least the music of water. The only reappearance of the god is as a phantom which walks beside him, the deliri-ous hallucination of a man who is dying of thirst. In the end the dry-rotted world is crumbling about him—his own soul is falling apart. There is nothing left to prop it up but some dry stoic Sanskrit maxims and the broken sighs from the past, of singers exiled or oppressed. Like de Nerval, he is disinher-ited; like the poet of the Pervigilium Veneris, he is dumb; like Arnaut Daniel in Purgatory, he begs the world to raise a prayer for his torment, as he disappears in the fire. (pp. 611-14)

It is true [Eliot's] poems seem the products of a constricted emotional experience and that he appears to have drawn rather heavily on books for the heat he could not derive from life. There is a certain grudging margin, to be sure, about all that Mr Eliot writes—as if he were compensating himself for his limitations by a peevish assumption of superiority. But it is the very acuteness of his suffering from this starvation which gives such poignancy to his art. And, as I say, Mr Eliot is a poet—that is, he feels intensely and with distinction and speaks naturally in beautiful verse—so that, no matter within what walls he lives, he belongs to the divine company. His verse is sometimes much too scrappy—he does not dwell long enough upon one idea to give it its proportionate value before passing on to the next—but these drops, though they be wrung from flint, are none the less authentic crystals. They are broken and sometimes infinitely tiny, but they are worth all the rhinestones on the market. I doubt whether there is a single other poem of equal length by a contemporary Amer-ican which displays so high and so varied a mastery of En-glish verse. The poem is—in spite of its lack of structural unity—simply one triumph after another—from the white April light of the opening and the sweet wistfulness of the nightingale passage—one of the only successful pieces of con-temporary blank verse—to the shabby sadness of the Thames Maidens, the cruel irony of Tiresias' vision, and the dry grim stony style of the descriptions of the Waste Land itself.

That is why Mr Eliot's trivialities are more valuable than other people's epics—why Mr Eliot's detestation of Sweeney is more precious than Mr Sandburg's sympathy for him, and Mr Prufrock's tea-table tragedy more important than all the passions of the New Adam—sincere and carefully expressed as these latter emotions indubitably are. That is also why, for all its complicated correspondences and its recondite refer-ences and quotations, *The Waste Land* is intelligible at first reading. It is not necessary to know anything about the Grail Legend or any but the most obvious of Mr Eliot's allusions to feel the force of the intense emotion which the poem is in-tended to convey—as one cannot do, for example, with the extremely ill-focussed Eight Cantos of his imitator Mr Ezra Pound, who presents only a bewildering mosaic with no cen-tral emotion to provide a key. In Eliot the very images and the sound of the words—even when we do not know precisely why he has chosen them—are charged with a strange poi-gnancy which seems to bring us into the heart of the singer. And sometimes we feel that he is speaking not only for a per-sonal distress, but for the starvation of a whole civilization—for people grinding at barren office-routine in the cells of gi-gantic cities, drying up their souls in eternal toil whose prod-ucts never bring them profit, where their pleasures are so vul-gar and so feeble that they are almost sadder than their pains. It is our whole world of strained nerves and shattered institu-tions, in which "some infinitely gentle, infinitely suffering thing" is somehow being done to death—in which the maiden Philomel "by the barbarous king so rudely forced" can no longer even fill the desert "with inviolable voice." It is the world in which the pursuit of grace and beauty is something which is felt to be obsolete—the reflections which reach us from the past cannot illumine so dingy a scene; that heroic prelude has ironic echoes among the streets and the drawing-rooms where we live. Yet the race of the poets—though grown rarer—is not yet quite dead: there is at least one who, as Mr Pound says, has brought a new personal rhythm into the language and who has lent even to the words of his great predecessors a new music and a new meaning. (pp. 615-16)

Edmund Wilson, Jr., "The Poetry of Drouth," in The Dial, *Chicago, Vol. 73, December, 1922, pp. 611-16.*

LOUIS UNTERMEYER

The Dial's award to Mr. T. S. Eliot and the subsequent book-publication of his *The Waste Land* have occasioned a display of some of the most enthusiastically naive superlatives that have ever issued from publicly sophisticated iconoclasts. A group, in attempting to do for Mr. Eliot what *Ulysses* did for Mr. Joyce, has, through its emphatic reiterations, driven more than one reader to a study rather than a celebration of the qualities that characterize Mr. Eliot's work and endear him to the younger cerebralists. These qualities, apparent even in his earlier verses, are an elaborate irony, a twitching disillusion, a persistent though muffled hyperæsthesia. In **"The Love-Song of J. Alfred Prufrock"** and the extraordi-narily sensitized **"Portrait of a Lady,"** Mr. Eliot fused these qualities in a flexible music, in the shifting nuances of a speech that wavered dexterously between poetic colour and casual conversation. In the greater part of *Poems,* however, Mr. Eliot employed a harder and more crackling tone of voice; he delighted in virtuosity for its own sake, in epigram-matic velleities, in an incongruously mordant and disillu-sioned *vers de société.*

In **The Waste Land,** Mr. Eliot has attempted to combine

these two contradictory idioms with a new complexity. The result—although, as I am aware, this conclusion is completely at variance with the judgment of its frenetic admirers—is a pompous parade of erudition, a lengthy extension of the earlier disillusion, a kaleidoscopic movement in which the bright-coloured pieces fail to atone for the absence of an integrated design. As an echo of contemporary despair, as a picture of dissolution, of the breaking-down of the very structures on which life has modelled itself, *The Waste Land* has a definite authenticity. But an artist is, by the very nature of creation, pledged to give form to formlessness; even the process of disintegration must be held within a pattern. This pattern is distorted and broken by Mr. Eliot's jumble of narratives, nursery-rhymes, criticism, jazz-rhythms, Dictionary of Favourite Phrases and a few lyrical moments. Possibly the disruption of our ideals may be reproduced through such a *mélange,* but it is doubtful whether it is crystallized or even clarified by a series of severed narratives—tales from which the connecting tissue has been carefully cut—and familiar quotations with their necks twisted, all imbedded in that formless plasma which Mr. Ezra Pound likes to call a Sordello-form. Some of the intrusions are more irritating than incomprehensible. . . .

It is difficult to understand the presence of such cheap tricks in what Mr. Burton Rascoe has publicly informed us is "the finest poem of this generation." The mingling of wilful obscurity and weak vaudeville compels us to believe that the pleasure which many admirers derive from *The Waste Land* is the same sort of gratification attained through having solved a puzzle, a form of self-congratulation. The absence of any verbal acrobatics from Mr. Eliot's prose, a prose that represents not the slightest departure from a sort of intensive academicism, makes one suspect that, were it not for the Laforgue mechanism, Mr. Eliot's poetic variations on the theme of a super-refined futility would be increasingly thin and incredibly second rate.

As an analyst of desiccated sensations, as a recorder of the nostalgia of this age, Mr. Eliot has created something whose value is, at least, documentary. Yet, granting even its occasional felicities, *The Waste Land* is a misleading document. The world distrusts the illusions which the last few years have destroyed. One grants this latter-day truism. But it is groping among new ones: the power of the unconscious, an astringent scepticism, a mystical renaissance—these are some of the current illusions to which the Western World is turning for assurance of their, and its, reality. Man may be desperately insecure, but he has not yet lost the greatest of his emotional needs, the need to believe in something—even in his disbelief. For an ideal-demanding race, there is always one more God—and Mr. Eliot is not his prophet.

Louis Untermeyer, "Disillusion as Dogma," in The Freeman, *New York, Vol. VI, No. 149, January 17, 1923, p. 453.*

CONRAD AIKEN

Mr. T. S. Eliot is one of the most individual of contemporary poets, and at the same time, anomalously, one of the most "traditional." By individual I mean that he can be, and often is (distressingly, to some) aware in his own way; as when he observes of a woman (in **"Rhapsody on a Windy Night"**) that the door "opens on her like a grin" and that the corner of her eye "Twists like a crooked pin." Everywhere, in the very small body of his work, is similar evidence of a delicate sensibility, somewhat shrinking, somewhat injured, and always sharply itself. But also, with this capacity or necessity for being aware in his own way, Mr. Eliot has a haunting, a tyrannous awareness that there have been many other awarenesses before; and that the extent of his own awareness, and perhaps even the nature of it, is a consequence of these. He is, more than most poets, conscious of his roots. . . . [In] *The Waste Land,* Mr. Eliot's sense of the literary past has become so overmastering as almost to constitute the motive of the work. It is as if, in conjunction with the Mr. Pound of the *Cantos,* he wanted to make a "literature of literature"—a poetry not more actuated by life itself than by poetry; as if he had concluded that the characteristic awareness of a poet of the 20th century must inevitably, or ideally, be a very complex and very literary awareness able to speak only, or best, in terms of the literary past, the terms which had moulded its tongue. This involves a kind of idolatry of literature with which it is a little difficult to sympathize. In positing, as it seems to, that there is nothing left for literature to do but become a kind of parasitic growth on literature, a sort of mistletoe, it involves, I think, a definite astigmatism—a distortion. But the theory is interesting if only because it has colored an important and brilliant piece of work.

The Waste Land is unquestionably important, unquestionably brilliant. It is important partly because its 433 lines summarize Mr. Eliot, for the moment, and demonstrate that he is an even better poet than most had thought; and partly because it embodies the theory just touched upon, the theory of the "allusive" method in poetry. *The Waste Land* is, indeed, a poem of allusion all compact. It purports to be symbolical; most of its symbols are drawn from literature or legend; and Mr. Eliot has thought it necessary to supply, in notes, a list of the many quotations, references, and translations with which it bristles. He observes candidly that the poem presents "difficulties," and requires "elucidation." This serves to raise at once, the question whether these difficulties, in which perhaps Mr. Eliot takes a little pride, are so much the result of complexity, a fine elaborateness, as of confusion. The poem has been compared, by one reviewer, to a "full-rigged ship built in a bottle," the suggestion being that it is a perfect piece of construction. But *is* it a perfect piece of construction? Is the complex material mastered, and made coherent? Or, if the poem is not successful in that way, in what way *is* it successful? Has it the formal and intellectual complex unity of a microscopic *Divine Comedy;* or is its unity—supposing it to have one—of another sort?

If we leave aside for the moment all other considerations, and read the poem solely with the intention of understanding, with the aid of the notes, the symbolism; of making out what it is that is symbolized, and how these symbolized feelings are brought into relation with each other and with the other matters in the poem; I think we must, with reservations, and with no invidiousness, conclude that the poem is not, in any formal sense, coherent. We cannot feel that all the symbolisms belong quite inevitably where they have been put; that the order of the parts is an inevitable order; that there is anything more than a rudimentary progress from one theme to another; nor that the relation between the more symbolic parts and the less is always as definite as it should be. What we feel is that Mr. Eliot has not wholly annealed the allusive matter, has left it unabsorbed, lodged in gleaming fragments amid material alien to it. Again, there is a distinct weakness consequent on the use of allusions which may have both intellectual and emotional value for Mr. Eliot, but (even with the notes) none for us. The "Waste Land," of the Grail Legend, might be a good symbol, if it were something with which we were sufficiently familiar. But it can never, even when explained, be a good symbol, simply because it has no immediate associations for us. It might, of course, be a good *theme*. In that case it would be *given* us. But Mr. Eliot uses it for purposes of overtone; he refers to it; and as overtone it quite clearly fails. He gives us, superbly, a waste land—not *the* Waste Land. Why, then, refer to the latter at all—if he is not, in the poem, really going to use it? Hyacinth fails in the same way. So does the Fisher King. So does the Hanged Man, which Mr. Eliot tells us he associates with Frazer's Hanged God—we take his word for it. But if the precise association is worth anything, it is worth *putting into the poem;* otherwise there can be no purpose in mentioning it. Why, again, Datta, Dayadhvam, Damyata? Or Shantih? Do they not say a good deal less for us than "Give: sympathize: control" or "Peace"? Of course; but Mr. Eliot replies that he wants them not merely to mean those particular things, but also to mean them in a particular way—that is, to be remembered in connection with a Upanishad. Unfortunately, we have none of us this memory, nor can he give it to us; and in the upshot he gives us only a series of agreeable sounds which might as well have been nonsense. What we get at, and I think it is important, is that in none of these particular cases does the reference, the allusion, justify itself intrinsically, make itself felt. When we are aware of these references at all (sometimes they are unidentifiable) we are aware of them simply as something unintelligible but suggestive. When they have been explained, we are aware of the material referred to, the fact, (for instance, a vegetation ceremony,) as something useless for our enjoyment or understanding of the poem, something distinctly "dragged in," and only, perhaps, of interest as having suggested a pleasantly ambiguous line. For unless an allusion is made to live identifiably, to flower, where transplanted, it is otiose. We admit the beauty of the implicational or allusive method; but the key to an implication should be in the implication itself, not outside of it. We admit the value of esoteric pattern: but the pattern should itself disclose its secret, should not be dependent on a cypher. Mr. Eliot assumes for his allusions, and for the fact that they actually allude to something, an importance which the allusions themselves do not, as expressed, aesthetically command, nor, as explained, logically command; which is pretentious. He is a little pretentious, too, in his "plan,"—"qui pourtant n'existe pas." If it is a plan, then its principle is oddly akin to planlessness. Here and there, in the wilderness, a broken finger-post.

I enumerate these objections not, I must emphasize, in derogation of the poem, but to dispel, if possible, an illusion as to its nature. It is perhaps important to note that Mr. Eliot, with his comment on the "plan," and several critics, with their admiration of the poem's woven complexity, minister to the idea that *The Waste Land* is, precisely, a kind of epic in a walnut shell: elaborate, ordered, unfolded with a logic at every joint discernible; but it is also important to note that this idea is false. With or without the notes the poem belongs rather to that symbolical order in which one may justly say that the "meaning" is not explicitly, or exactly, worked out. Mr. Eliot's net is wide, its meshes are small; and he catches a good deal more—thank heaven—than he pretends to. If space permitted one could pick out many lines and passages and parodies and quotations which do not demonstrably, in any "logical" sense, carry forward the theme, passages which unjustifiably, but happily, "expand" beyond its purpose. Thus the poem has an emotional value far clearer and richer than its arbitrary and rather unworkable logical value. (pp. 294-95)

[The] poem must be taken,—most invitingly offers itself,—as a brilliant and kaleidoscopic confusion; as a series of sharp, discrete, slightly related perceptions and feelings, dramatically and lyrically presented, and violently juxtaposed, (for effect of dissonance) so as to give us an impression of an intensely modern, intensely literary consciousness which perceives itself to be not a unit but a chance correlation or conglomerate of mutually discolorative fragments. . . . If we perceive the poem in this light, as a series of brilliant, brief, unrelated or dimly related pictures by which a consciousness empties itself of its characteristic contents, then we also perceive that, anomalously, though the dropping out of any one picture would not in the least affect the logic or "meaning" of the whole, it would seriously detract from the value of the portrait. The "plan" of the poem would not greatly suffer, one makes bold to assert, by the elimination of "April is the cruelest month," or Phlebas, or the Thames daughters, or Sosostris or "You gave me hyacinths" or "A woman drew her long black hair out tight"; nor would it matter if it did. These things are not important parts of an important or careful intellectual pattern; but they are important parts of an important emotional ensemble. The relations between Tiresias (who is said to unify the poem, in a sense, as spectator) and the Waste Land, or Mr. Eugenides, or Hyacinth, or any other fragment, is a dim and tonal one, not exact. It will not bear analysis, it is not always operating, nor can one with assurance, at any given point, say how much it is operating. In this sense *The Waste Land* is a series of separate poems or passages, not perhaps all written at one time or with one aim, to which a spurious but happy sequence has been given. This spurious sequence has a value—it creates the necessary superficial formal unity; but it need not be stressed, as the Notes stress it. . . .

We reach thus the conclusion that the poem succeeds—as it brilliantly does—by virtue of its incoherence, not of its plan; by virtue of its ambiguities, not of its explanations. Its incoherence is a virtue because its 'donnée' is incoherence. Its rich, vivid, crowded use of implication is a virtue, as implication is *always* a virtue;—it shimmers, it suggests, it gives the desired strangeness. But when, as often, Mr. Eliot uses an implication beautifully—conveys by means of a picture-symbol or action-symbol a feeling—we do not require to be told that he had in mind a passage in the Encyclopedia, or the color of his nursery wall; the information is disquieting, has a sour air of pedantry. We "accept" the poem as we would accept a powerful, melancholy tone-poem. We do not want to be told what occurs; nor is it more than mildly amusing to know what passages are, in the Straussian manner, echoes or parodies. We cannot believe that every syllable has an algebraic inevitability, nor would we wish it so. We could dispense with the French, Italian, Latin and Hindu phrases—they are irritating. But when our reservations have all been made, we accept *The Waste Land* as one of the most moving and original poems of our time. It captures us. And we sigh, with a dubious eye on the "notes" and "plan," our bewilderment that after so fine a performance Mr. Eliot should have thought it an occasion for calling "Tullia's ape a marmosyte." Tullia's ape is good enough. (p. 295)

Conrad Aiken, "An Anatomy of Melancholy," in The New Republic, *Vol. XXXIII, No. 427, February 7, 1923, pp. 294-95.*

HERBERT S. GORMAN

The Waste Land has become a battle-field. Across its arid stretches sally the cohorts of critics, waving their swords and, most of the time, shouting so loudly that one is unable to understand what they are saying. There is a maximum of noise and a minimum of sense. No poem since the advent of the *Spoon River Anthology* has aroused so much infuriated discussion, and no book, not even James Joyce's *Ulysses*, has been approached more blindly. Its adherents see nothing but its virtues; its detractors see nothing but its faults. Somewhere between these two camps *The Waste Land* really lies.

Mrs. Mary M. Colum [in *The Literary Review*, January 6, 1923] dismisses T. S. Eliot as an assimilative writer. Louis Untermeyer [see excerpt above] attacks the poem because of its many quotations and its incoherence. Christopher Morley appears to think that it is a hoax. Mrs. Elinor Wylie [in *The Literary Review*, January 20, 1923], uncritical but impassioned, writes a noble defense of *The Waste Land* that is almost a poem in itself. Edmund Wilson, Jr. [see excerpt above], a little lacking in humor, offers a grave defense that would lift *The Waste Land* to the plane of the few great poems of modern times. Gilbert Seldes [in the *Nation*, December 6, 1922], rather unable to cope with imaginative literature, also defends it. Burton S. Rascoe [in the *New York Tribune*, November 11, 1922] chatters amusingly about it, but presents no coherent criticism. Keith Preston picks out the soda-water line for ridicule, apparently arriving at the naive conclusion that Eliot meant pop. One wonders if Mr. Preston is a bachelor. Edward Anthony thinks that the expanse from which the trees were hewn which went to make the paper for Mr. Eliot's poem should be called "The Waste Land." Conrad Aiken [see excerpt above], offered a wise and reasonable judgment which recognized the virtues of the poem and at the same time did not blink at the faults. And so it goes. Ferocious blows are dealt by tin swords upon tin armor, and the audience on the sidelines sits and snickers agreeably.

From the whirl of dust a few intelligent comments come. The best of the attacking party appears to be Mr. Louis Untermeyer. The best of the defenders are Conrad Aiken, Elinor Wylie and Edmund Wilson, Jr. The accusation of hoax is unsupported by any evidence, and one must arrive at the conclusion that the wish is father to the thought in this case. It is not so much life as an old accepted idealism broken to bits beneath the hard piles of Time that T. S. Eliot observes through tragically ironic eyes. It is possible that he has progressed since the composition of *The Waste Land*, and that that poem may be regarded as an aspect of a cruelly sophisticated nature. But that does not lessen the importance of the poem for those readers in whom it struck (or rather smashed) an emotional chord.

The laborious subterfuges that have carried Man forward into the arid stretches of modern civilization have failed. That is what Mr. Eliot states in *The Waste Land*. We have come to a dry desolation, and there is nothing here but hard rock and the faint mirages of a freshness that actually existed once, but which has now dwindled into the haunting fragments of broken memories. And because the present wreckage may be pictured only through shattered recapitulations of the past things that once made Life green and fruitful, we find the poet employing an allusive method of composition in *The Waste Land*, driving new connotations home through the employment of the old beauties that starred literature, repeating lines and fragments of lines, phrases and words (but always adjusting them to a new significance), giving, as it were, the reverse of the shield, the mocking hollowness of those ancient and inspired thoughts repeated among these hard calcined rocks of our petty practicalities and hypocrisies.

There are two ways of approaching *The Waste Land.* One is to place the eye of the mind very close to the pages and observe only the incoherent parts as they follow one another in a more or less unconnected manner. The same might be done with canvases of Whistler and Claude Monet, speculating on the various daubs of paint, and so, viewing the parts instead of the whole, see nothing but the strokes of the palette-knife and the hair-marks of the brushes. This has been a favorite critical attitude from time immemorial. The second method of approach is to stand back a bit and permit these sections to fall into an ensemble. It is readily granted that some of these sections do not accept their places in the general scheme of the poem with any degree of acquiescence, and this is the fault of the poet. But the general outline is there for those who care to see it; the mood is a unified one; the total impression is one of singular compactness; one affirmation is driven home by varying strokes. It is one of the provinces of poetry to awaken a sad nostalgia, and this *The Waste Land* does.

The vexed question of the liberal use of many quotations arises. Well, why not? If these flash-backs to other works of literature come to the reader with a new significance, why may they not be used? Dvořák and Strauss both employed snatches from other musical compositions in their work, yet the integrity of their performances was not appreciably diminished thereby. Indeed, this entire question of using tags from other poets has been hoisted into a significance that it does not merit. Any well-read person is aware of most of them, and *The Waste Land* has assuredly been written for well-read persons. It will never be a poem of general popularity, any more than any type of cerebral poetry will be accepted by the general mass of readers. In a final analysis, is it necessary to know the source of these quotations? Do they not fit into *The Waste Land* as the author intended? And was his intention not to fling up at the reader the broken ejaculations, the pitiful salvage of an intellectual consciousness that has reached the arid places and can exist only on the shattered fragments of an idealism that has perished? "These fragments I have shored against my ruins." We may not believe it, but surely T. S. Eliot may make his poem as personal an expression as he desires, and we must accept his attitude in all sincerity, searching only for poetry and not for a propaganda that will walk hand in hand with our own ideas of modern life. The motif of *The Waste Land* is stated in the four opening lines:

> April is the cruelest month, breeding
> Lilacs out of the dead land, mixing
> Memory and desire, stirring
> Dull roots with spring rain.

And so memory and desire are mixed in the opening section, broken flashes-back at childhood, when "summer surprized us, coming over the Starnbergersee." But these things are gone now. (pp. 46, 48)

Following the introduction of the motif of *The Waste Land*, the mood shifts to more scattered memories of past times. There is a "hyacinth girl," there are even snatches from *Tristan und Isolde*. The idea of the Tarot cards is pictured, and after this the poet observes in a wistful and beautiful snatch of poetry the City about him, a sadly ironic contemplation:

> Unreal City,
> Under the brown fog of a winter dawn,
> A crowd flowed over London Bridge, so many,
> I had not thought death had undone so many. . . .

There are twisted quotations in the last part of this section, but do they not come naturally enough? Is it not possible to conceive of an educated man breaking out into ironic paraphrases of great lines when stirred mightily by either triumph or despair?

Broken scenes follow, snatches of conversation apparently irrelevant, bits of ragtime, but a hard passionate despair may be sensed through them all. Contrast is cleverly employed. There is the sophisticated woman talking with immense futility in her elaborate room, to be immediately followed by the coarse conversation from the pub outside, these last speeches frequently broken into by the anxious bartender with his "Hurry up, please, it's time," meaning that he must close up shop. "The Fire Sermon," emphasizing the crude descent from the high old idealism, is followed by the long speech of Tiresias, the blind seer, half-man and half-woman. Here is the heart of the poem, for all men and all women meet in this symbolical figure, and what he sees through his blind eyes is the very meat of the poem. And what he sees is the heartbreaking degradation of that clean, fiery-white passion, known of old time, to the automatic lusts and commonplaces of these modern times. Then, further emphasizing this dark disillusionment, follow the songs of the three Thames maidens, the first of them Queen Elizabeth, the others calloused modern types. The episode of the drowned Phœnician Sailor, sonorous with vague thunders, completes the full presentation of the Waste Land. (p. 48)

The poem grows more feverish, as tho a parched man were thrusting hard words from him. Sounds of lamentation are in the air; the City that is all cities cracks and bursts in the violet light.

> A woman drew her long black hair out tight
> And fiddled whisper music on those strings;
> And bats with baby faces in the violet light
> Whistled, and beat their wings
> And crawled head downward down a blackened wall;
> And upside down in air were towers
> Tolling reminiscent bells, that kept the hours
> And voices singing out of empty cisterns and exhausted
> wells.

Are not these tragic implications plain enough? Is it possible for one to read and not be stirred by the hard, dry, gasping emotion that would seem almost to strangle the poet as he tears it from him? Yet, in spite of these passages, T. S. Eliot has been dubbed a mere epigrammatist and *The Waste Land* a hoax.

To the grumbling thunder of phrases from the Upanishads the poem ends. Datta, Dayadhvam, Damyata—Give, Sympathize, Control. Each word is followed by an explanatory paragraph. It is in a welter of quotations that the poem ends, but for me the most important lines in the conclusion are:

> I sat upon the shore
> Fishing, with the arid plain behind me.
> Shall I at least set my lands in order?

Such a hurried résumé can give but a sketchy idea of *The Waste Land* and its construction. The unity that knits it together is one of mood, and altho the lines shift from tragedy to irony, from lyric utterance to a bitterly light juggling of conceits and parodies, that one mood remains unshaken. It is disillusionment, a disillusionment induced, perhaps, by a hurried reading of life, but none the less authentic. The cerebral qualities of the poem can hardly be doubted. Each picture is, perhaps, a picture first evolved in the brain and only secondarily in the heart; they become a conscious compilation. But, strangely enough, taken all together they form an overwhelming emotional mood, a mood that may not be set down on paper in intellectual terms. One may easily isolate a passage and call it chaff from a spinning mind, just as one may isolate a bit of colored glass in a kaleidoscope and note that it is nothing more than glass. But the ensemble becomes a thing of magic.

We may not believe that modern life is a waste land, any more than our fathers believed in James Thomson's "The City of Dreadful Night." But we must allow the poet his own personality, accept his premises for the sake of the art involved, and judge the achievement from within itself. If T. S. Eliot considers the world about him to have reached the dried rivercourses of drouth, it should be the endeavor of the critic to ascertain whether or not he has achieved poetry in his visualization of it. And *The Waste Land* seems to me to be decidedly cut from the cloth of authentic poetry, but that cloth has been cut with a difference. There is much left unsaid as there is said, but it appears to be suggested by many implications. There are overtones to *The Waste Land* which remain with the reader after he has put the book down.

What really matters is whether or not *The Waste Land* itself arouses a troubled, twisted ecstasy in the reader, a regret that is like a sob in the throat beneath its glittering surface of ironic nuances. The fact that it would seem to do so in not a small number of undeniably intelligent minds may not be proof of its authenticity as a poem, but it is a proof of something, and perhaps that larger group of admittedly intelligent minds which seem to find nothing in the poem will tell us what it is. For my own part, *The Waste Land* is an unusual poem, for it shook me violently. (pp. 48, 64)

Herbert S. Gorman, "The Waste Land of the Younger Generation," in The Literary Digest International Book Review, *Vol. I, No. 5, April, 1923, pp. 46, 48, 64.*

THE TIMES LITERARY SUPPLEMENT

The poetic personality of Mr. Eliot is extremely sophisticated. His emotions hardly ever reach us without traversing a zig-zag of allusion. In the course of his four hundred lines [in *The Waste Land*] he quotes from a score of authors and in three foreign languages, though his artistry has reached that point at which it knows the wisdom of sometimes concealing itself. There is in general in his work a disinclination to awake in us a direct emotional response. It is only, the reader feels, out of regard for some one else that he has been induced to mount the platform at all. From there he conducts a magic-lantern show; but being too reserved to expose in public the impressions stamped on his own soul by the journey through the Waste Land, he employs the slides made by others, indicating with a touch the difference between his reaction and theirs. So the familiar stanza of Goldsmith becomes

When lovely woman stoops to folly and
Paces about her room again, alone,
She smoothes her hair with automatic hand,
And puts a record on the gramophone.

To help us to elucidate the poem Mr. Eliot has provided some notes which will be of more interest to the pedantic than the poetic critic. Certainly they warn us to be prepared to recognize some references to vegetation ceremonies. This is the cultural or middle layer, which, whilst it helps us to perceive the underlying emotion, is of no poetic value in itself. We desire to touch the inspiration itself, and if the apparatus of reserve is too strongly constructed, it will defeat the poet's end. The theme is announced frankly enough in the title, *The Waste Land;* and in the concluding confession,

These fragments I have shored against my ruins,

we receive a direct communication which throws light on much which had preceded it. From the opening part, "The Burial of the Dead," to the final one we seem to see a world, or a mind, in disaster and mocking its despair. We are aware of the toppling of aspirations, the swift disintegration of accepted stability, the crash of an ideal. Set at a distance by a poetic method which is reticence itself, we can only judge of the strength of the emotion by the visible violence of the reaction. Here is Mr. Eliot, a dandy of the choicest phrase, permitting himself blatancies like "the young man carbuncular." Here is a poet capable of a style more refined than that of any of his generation parodying without taste or skill—and of this the example from Goldsmith is not the most astonishing. Here is a writer to whom originality is almost an inspiration borrowing the greater number of his best lines, creating hardly any himself. It seems to us as if the *The Waste Land* exists in the greater part in the state of notes. This quotation is a particularly obvious instance:—

London Bridge is falling down falling down
                                falling down
Poi s' ascosc nel foco chi gli affina
Quando fiam ceu chelidon—O swallow swallow
Le Prince d'Aquitaine à la tour abolie.

The method has a number of theoretical justifications. Mr. Eliot has himself employed it discreetly with delicious effect. It suits well the disillusioned smile which he had in common with Laforgue; but we do sometimes wish to hear the poet's full voice. Perhaps if the reader were sufficiently sophisticated he would find these echoes suggestive hints, as rich in significance as the sonorous amplifications of the romantic poets. None the less, we do not derive from this poem as a whole the satisfaction we ask from poetry. Numerous passages are finely written; there is an amusing monologue in the vernacular, and the fifth part is nearly wholly admirable. The section beginning

What is that sound high in the air . . .

has a nervous strength which perfectly suits the theme; but he declines to a mere notation, the result of an indolence of the imagination.

Mr. Eliot, always evasive of the grand manner, has reached a stage at which he can no longer refuse to recognize the limitations of his medium; he is sometimes walking very near the limits of coherency. But it is the finest horses which have the most tender mouths, and some unsympathetic tug has sent Mr. Eliot's gift awry. When he recovers control we shall ex-

pect his poetry to have gained in variety and strength from this ambitious experiment.

> *"A Fragmentary Poem," in* The Times Literary
> Supplement, *No. 1131, September 20, 1923, p. 616.*

F. L. LUCAS

Readers of *The Waste Land* are referred at the outset, if they wish to understand the poem or even its title, to a work on the ritual origins of the legends of the Holy Grail by Miss J. L. Weston, a disciple of Frazer, and to the *Golden Bough* itself. Those who conscientiously plunge into the two hundred pages of the former interesting, though credulous, work, will learn that the basis of the Grail story is the restoration of the virility of a Fisher King (who is an incarnation, like so many others in Frazer, of the Life-spirit), and thereby of the fertility of a Waste Land, the Lance and the Grail itself being phallic symbols. While maintaining due caution and remembering how

Diodorus Siculus
Made himself ridiculous,
By thinking thimbles
Were phallic symbols,

one may admit that Miss Weston makes a very good case. With that, however, neither she nor Mr. Eliot can rest content, and they must needs discover an esoteric meaning under the rags of superstitious Adam. Miss Weston is clearly a theosophist, and Mr. Eliot's poem might be a theosophical tract. The sick king and the waste land symbolise, we gather, the sick soul and the desolation of this material life.

But even when thus instructed and with a feeling of virtuous research the reader returns to the attack, the difficulties are but begun. To attempt here an interpretation, even an intelligible summary of the poem, is to risk making oneself ridiculous; but those who lack the common modern gift of judging poetry without knowing what it means, must risk that. (p. 116)

[Interpreting *The Waste Land*] is very difficult; as Dr. Johnson said under similar circumstances, "I would it were impossible." But the gist of the poem is apparently a wild revolt from the abomination of desolation which is human life, combined with a belief in salvation by the usual catchwords of renunciation—this salvation being also the esoteric significance of the savage fertility-rituals found in the *Golden Bough,* a watering, as it were, of the desert of the suffering soul.

About the philosophy of the poem, if such it be, it would be vain to argue; but it is hard not to regret the way in which modern writers of real creative power abandon themselves to the fond illusion that they have philosophic gifts and a weighty message to deliver to the world, as well. In all periods creative artists have been apt to think they could think, though in all periods they have been frequently harebrained and sometimes mad; just as great rulers and warriors have cared only to be flattered for the way they fiddled or their flatulent tragedies. But now, in particular, we have the spectacle of Mr. Lawrence, Miss May Sinclair, and Mr. Eliot, all sacrificing their artistic powers on the altar of some fantastic Mumbo-Jumbo, all trying to get children on mandrake roots instead of bearing their natural offspring.

Perhaps this unhappy composition should have been left to sink itself: but it is not easy to dismiss in three lines what is being written about as a new masterpiece. For at present it is particularly easy to win the applause of the *blasé* and the young, of the coteries and the eccentricities. The Victorian "Spasmodics" likewise had their day. But a poem that has to be explained in notes is not unlike a picture with "This is a dog" inscribed beneath. Not, indeed, that Mr. Eliot's notes succeed in explaining anything, being as muddled as incomplete. What is the use of explaining "laquearia" by quoting two lines of Latin containing the word, which will convey nothing to those who do not know that language, and nothing new to those who do? What is the use of giving a quotation from Ovid which begins in the middle of a sentence, without either subject or verb, and fails to add even the reference? And when one person hails another on London Bridge as having been with him "at Mylae," how is the non-classical reader to guess that this is the name of a Punic sea-fight in which as Phœnician sailor, presumably, the speaker had taken part? The main function of the notes is, indeed, to give the references to the innumerable authors whose lines the poet embodies, like a mediæval writer making a life of Christ out of lines of Virgil. But the borrowed jewels he has set in its head do not make Mr. Eliot's toad the more prepossessing.

In brief, in *The Waste Land* Mr. Eliot has shown that he can at moments write real blank verse; but that is all. For the rest he has quoted a great deal, he has parodied and imitated. But the parodies are cheap and the imitations inferior. Among so many other sources Mr. Eliot may have thought, as he wrote, of Rossetti's "Card-Dealer," of "Childe Harold to the Dark Tower Came," of the "Vision of Sin" with its same question:

> To which an answer peal'd from that high land,
> But in a tongue no man could understand.

But the trouble is that for the reader who thinks of them the comparison is crushing. *The Waste Land* adds nothing to a literature which contains things like these. (pp. 116, 118)

> *F. L. Lucas, in a review of "The Waste Land," in*
> New Statesman, *Vol. XXII, No. 551, November 3,*
> *1923, pp. 116, 118.*

I. A. RICHARDS

[*The essay excerpted below was originally published in 1925 in the critic's collection,* Principles of Literary Criticism.]

We too readily forget that, unless something is very wrong with our civilisation, we should be producing three equal poets at least for every poet of high rank in our great-great-grandfathers' day. Something must indeed be wrong; and since Mr Eliot is one of the very few poets that current conditions have not overcome, the difficulties which he has faced, and the cognate difficulties which his readers encounter, repay study.

Mr Eliot's poetry has occasioned an unusual amount of irritated or enthusiastic bewilderment. The bewilderment has several sources. The most formidable is the unobtrusiveness, in some cases the absence, of any coherent intellectual thread upon which the items of the poem are strung. A reader of **"Gerontion,"** or of **"Preludes,"** or of *The Waste Land,* may, if he will, after repeated readings, introduce such a thread. Another reader after much effort may fail to contrive one. But in either case energy will have been misapplied. For the items are united by the accord, contrast, and interaction of their emotional effects, not by an intellectual scheme that

analysis must work out. The value lies in the unified response which this interaction creates in the right reader. The only intellectual activity required takes place in the realisation of the separate items. We can, of course, make a 'rationalisation' of the whole experience, as we can of any experience. If we do, we are adding something which does not belong to the poem. Such a logical scheme is, at best, a scaffolding that vanishes when the poem is constructed. But we have so built into our nervous systems a demand for intellectual coherence, even in poetry, that we find a difficulty in doing without it.

This point may be misunderstood, for the charge most usually brought against Mr. Eliot's poetry is that it is over-intellectualised. One reason for this is his use of allusion. . . .

Allusion in Mr Eliot's hands is a technical device for compression. *The Waste Land* is the equivalent in content to an epic. Without this device twelve books would have been needed. But these allusions and the notes in which some of them are elucidated have made many a petulant reader turn down his thumb at once. Such a reader has not begun to understand what it is all about.

This objection is connected with another, that of obscurity. To quote a recent pronouncement upon *The Waste Land* from Mr Middleton Murry: 'The reader is compelled, in the mere effort to understand, to adopt an attitude of intellectual suspicion, which makes impossible the communication of feeling. The work offends against the most elementary canon of good writing: that the immediate effect should be unambiguous.' Consider first this 'canon'. What would happen, if we pressed it, to Shakespeare's greatest sonnets or to *Hamlet*? The truth is that very much of the best poetry is necessarily ambiguous in its immediate effect. Even the most careful and responsive reader must reread and do hard work before the poem forms itself clearly and unambiguously in his mind. An original poem, as much as a new branch of mathematics, compels the mind which receives it to grow, and this takes time. Anyone who upon reflection asserts the contrary for his own case must be either a demigod or dishonest; probably Mr Murry was in haste. His remarks show that he has failed in his attempt to read the poem, and they reveal, in part, the reason for his failure—namely, his own overintellectual approach. To read it successfully he would have to discontinue his present self-mystifications.

The critical question in all cases is whether the poem is worth the trouble it entails. For *The Waste Land* this is considerable. There is Miss Weston's *From Ritual to Romance* to read, and its 'astral' trimmings to be discarded—they have nothing to do with Mr Eliot's poem. There is Canto xxvi of the *Purgatorio* to be studied—the relevance of the close of that canto to the whole of Mr Eliot's work must be insisted upon. It illuminates his persistent concern with sex, the problem of our generation, as religion was the problem of the last. There is the central position of Tiresias in the poem to be puzzled out—the cryptic form of the note which Mr Eliot writes on this point is just a little tiresome. It is a way of underlining the fact that the poem is concerned with many aspects of the one fact of sex, a hint that is perhaps neither indispensable nor entirely successful.

When all this has been done by the reader, when the materials with which the words are to clothe themselves have been collected, the poem still remains to be read. And it is easy to fail in this undertaking. An 'attitude of intellectual suspicion' must certainly be abandoned. But this is not difficult to those who still know how to give their feelings precedence to their thoughts, who can accept and unify an experience without trying to catch it in an intellectual net or to squeeze out a doctrine. One form of this attempt must be mentioned. Some, misled no doubt by its origin in a Mystery, have endeavoured to give the poem a symbolical reading. But its symbols are not mystical, but emotional. They stand, that is, not for ineffable objects, but for normal human experience. The poem, in fact, is radically naturalistic; only its compression makes it appear otherwise. And in this it probably comes nearer to the original Mystery which it perpetuates than transcendentalism does.

It it were desired to label in three words the most characteristic feature of Mr Eliot's technique, this might be done by calling his poetry a 'music of ideas'. The ideas are of all kinds: abstract and concrete, general and particular; and, like the musician's phrases, they are arranged, not that they may tell us something, but that their effects in us may combine into a coherent whole of feeling and attitude and produce a peculiar liberation of the will. They are there to be responded to, not to be pondered or worked out. This is, of course, a method used intermittently in very much poetry, and only an accentuation and isolation of one of its normal resources. The peculiarity of Mr Eliot's later, more puzzling, work is his deliberate and almost exclusive employment of it. (pp. 51-4)

Only those unfortunate persons who are incapable of reading poetry can resist Mr Eliot's rhythms. The poem as a whole may elude us while every fragment, as a fragment, comes victoriously home. It is difficult to believe that this is Mr Eliot's fault rather than his reader's, because a parallel case of a poet who so constantly achieves the hardest part of his task and yet fails in the easier is not to be found. It is much more likely that we have been trying to put the fragments together on a wrong principle.

Another doubt has been expressed. Mr Eliot repeats himself in two ways. The nightingale, Cleopatra's barge, the rats, and the smoky candle-end, recur and recur. Is this a sign of a poverty of inspiration? A more plausible explanation is that this repetition is in part a consequence of the technique above described, and in part something which many writers who are not accused of poverty also show. Shelley, with his rivers, towers, and stars, Conrad, Hardy, Walt Whitman, and Dostoevski spring to mind. When a writer has found a theme or image which fixes a point of relative stability in the drift of experience, it is not to be expected that he will avoid it. Such themes are a means of orientation. And it is quite true that the central process in all Mr Eliot's best poems is the same: the conjunction of feelings which, though superficially opposed—as squalor, for example, is opposed to grandeur—yet tend as they develop to change places and even to unite. If they do not develop far enough the intention of the poet is missed. Mr Eliot is neither sighing after vanished glories nor holding contemporary experience up to scorn.

Both bitterness and desolation are superficial aspects of his poetry. There are those who think that he merely takes his readers into the Waste Land and leaves them there, that in his last poem he confesses his impotence to release the healing waters. The reply is that some readers find in his poetry not only a clearer, fuller realisation of their plight, the plight of a whole generation, than they find elsewhere, but also through the very energies set free in that realisation a return of the saving passion. (pp. 54-5)

I. A. Richards, "Comments and Reactions," in T. S. Eliot: 'The Waste Land', a Casebook, *edited by C. B. Cox and Arnold P. Hinchliffe, Macmillan and Co. Ltd., 1968, pp. 51-5.*

F. R. LEAVIS

[*The essay excerpted below originally appeared in the first edition of* New Bearings in English Poetry (*1932*) *by Leavis.*]

The title [of ***The Waste Land***], we know, comes from Miss J. L. Weston's book, *From Ritual to Romance,* the theme of which is anthropological: the Waste Land there has a significance in terms of Fertility Ritual. What is the significance of the modern Waste Land? The answer may be read in what appears as the rich disorganization of the poem. The seeming disjointedness is intimately related to the erudition that has annoyed so many readers and to the wealthy of literary borrowings and allusions. These characteristics reflect the present state of civilization. The traditions and cultures have mingled, and the historical imagination makes the past contemporary; no one tradition can digest so great a variety of materials, and the result is a break-down of forms and the irrevocable loss of that sense of absoluteness which seems necessary to a robust culture. (pp. 90-1)

In considering our present plight we have also to take account of the incessant rapid change that characterizes the Machine Age. The result is breach of continuity and the uprooting of life. This last metaphor has a peculiar aptness, for what we are witnessing to-day is the final uprooting of the immemorial ways of life, of life rooted in the soil. (p. 91)

The remoteness of the civilization celebrated in ***The Waste Land*** from the natural rhythms is brought out, in ironical contrast, by the anthropological theme. Vegetation cults, fertility ritual, with their sympathetic magic, represent a harmony of human culture with the natural environment, and express an extreme sense of the unity of life. In the modern Waste Land

> April is the cruellest month, breeding
> Lilacs out of the dead land,

but bringing no quickening to the human spirit. Sex here is sterile, breeding not life and fulfilment but disgust, accidia and unanswerable questions. It is not easy to-day to accept the perpetuation and multiplication of life as ultimate ends.

But the anthropological background has positive functions. It plays an obvious part in evoking that particular sense of the unity of life which is essential to the poem. It helps to establish the level of experience at which the poem works, the mode of consciousness to which it belongs. In ***The Waste Land*** the development of impersonality that **"Gerontion"** shows in comparison with **"Prufrock"** reaches an extreme limit: it would be difficult to imagine a completer transcendence of the individual self, a completer projection of awareness. . . . There are ways in which it is possible to be too conscious, and to be so is, as a result of the break-up of forms and the loss of axioms noted above, one of the troubles of the present age (if the abstraction may be permitted, consciousness being in any case a minority affair). We recognize in modern literature the accompanying sense of futility.

The part that science in general has played in the process of disintegration is matter of commonplace: anthropology is, in the present context, a peculiarly significant expression of the scientific spirit. To the anthropological eye beliefs, religions and moralities are human habits—in their odd variety too human. Where the anthropological outlook prevails, sanctions wither. In a contemporary consciousness there is inevitably a great deal of the anthropological, and the background of *The Waste Land* is thus seen to have a further significance.

To be, then, too much conscious and conscious of too much—that is the plight:

> After such knowledge, what forgiveness?

At this point Mr Eliot's note on Tiresias deserves attention:

> Tiresias, although a mere spectator and not indeed a 'character,' is yet the most important personage in the poem, uniting all the rest. Just as the one-eyed merchant, seller of currants, melts into the Phoenician Sailor, and the latter is not wholly distinct from Ferdinand Prince of Naples, so all the women are one woman, and the two sexes meet in Tiresias. What Tiresias *sees*, in fact, is the substance of the poem.

If Mr Eliot's readers have a right to a grievance, is it that he has not given this note more salience; for it provides the clue to *The Waste Land.* It indicates plainly enough what the poem is: an effort to focus an inclusive human consciousness. The effort, in ways suggested above, is characteristic of the age; and in an age of psycho-analysis, an age that has produced the last section of *Ulysses*, Tiresias—'venus huic erat utraque nota'—presents himself as the appropriate impersonation. A cultivated modern is (or feels himself to be) intimately aware of the experience of the opposite sex.

Such an undertaking offers a difficult problem of organization, a distinguishing character of the mode of consciousness that promotes it being a lack of organizing principle, the absence of any inherent direction. A poem that is to contain all myths cannot construct itself upon one. It is here that *From Ritual to Romance* comes in. It provides a background of reference that makes possible something in the nature of a musical organization. Let us start by considering the use of the Tarot pack. Introduced in the first section, suggesting, as it does, destiny, chance and the eternal mysteries, it at once intimates the scope of the poem, the mode of its contemplation of life. It informs us as to the nature of the characters: we know that they are such as could not have relations with one another in any narrative scheme, and could not be brought together on any stage, no matter what liberties were taken with the Unities. The immediate function of the passage introducing the pack, moreover, is to evoke, in contrast with what has preceded, cosmopolitan 'high life,' and the charlatanism that battens upon it:

> Madame Sosostris, famous clairvoyante,
> Had a bad cold, nevertheless
> Is known to be the wisest woman in Europe,
> With a wicked pack of cards.

Mr Eliot can achieve the banality appropriate here, and achieve at the same time, when he wants it, a deep undertone, a resonance, as it were, of fate:

> . . . and this card,
>
> Which is blank, is something he carries on his back,
> Which I am forbidden to see. I do not find
> The Hanged Man. Fear death by water.
> I see crowds of people, walking round in a ring.

The peculiar menacing undertone of this associates it with a passage in the fifth section:

> Who is the third who walks always beside you?
> When I count, there are only you and I together
> But when I look ahead up the white road
> There is always another one walking beside you
> Gliding wrapt in a brown mantle, hooded
> I do not know whether a man or a woman
> —But who is that on the other side of you?

The association establishes itself without any help from Mr Eliot's note; it is there in any case, as any fit reader of poetry can report; but the note [to line 46] helps us to recognize its significance. . . . (pp. 92-7)

The Tarot pack, Miss Weston has established, has affiliations with fertility ritual, and so lends itself peculiarly to Mr Eliot's purpose: the instance before us illustrates admirably how he has used its possibilities. The hooded figure in the passage just quoted is Jesus. Perhaps our being able to say so depends rather too much upon Mr Eliot's note; but the effect of the passage does not depend so much upon the note as might appear. For Christ has figured already in the opening of the section (see "What the Thunder Said"). . . . The reference is unmistakable. Yet it is not only Christ; it is also the Hanged God and all the sacrificed gods: with the 'thunder of spring' 'Adonis, Attis, Osiris' and all the others of *The Golden Bough* come in. And the 'agony in stony places' is not merely the Agony in the Garden; it is also the agony of the Waste Land, introduced in the first section. . . .

> What are the roots that clutch, what branches
>   grow
> Out of this stony rubbish? Son of man,
> You cannot say, or guess, for you know only
> A heap of broken images, where the sun beats,
> And the dead tree gives no shelter, the cricket
>   no relief,
> And the dry stone no sound of water.

In "What the Thunder Said" the drouth becomes (among other things) a thirst for the waters of faith and healing, and the specifically religious enters into the orchestration of the poem. But the thunder is 'dry sterile thunder without rain'; there is no resurrection or renewal; and after the opening passage the verse loses all buoyancy, and takes on a dragging, persistent movement as of hopeless exhaustion. . . . —the imagined sound of water coming in as a torment. There is a suggestion of fever here, a sultry ominousness—

> There is not even solitude in the mountains

—and it is this which provides the transition to the passage about the hooded figure quoted above. The ominous tone of this last passage associates it, as we have seen, with the reference (ll. 55-56) to the Hanged Man in the Tarot passage of "The Burial of the Dead." So Christ becomes the Hanged Man, the Vegetation God; and at the same time the journey through the Waste Land along 'the sandy road' becomes the Journey to Emmaus. Mr Eliot gives us a note on the 'third who walks always beside you'. . . . (pp. 97-9)

This might be taken to be, from our point of view, merely an interesting irrelevance, and it certainly is not necessary. But it nevertheless serves to intimate the degree of generality that Mr Eliot intends to accompany his concrete precision: he is both definite and vague at once. 'Just as the one-eyed merchant, seller of currants, melts into the Phoenician Sailor, and the latter is not wholly distinct from Ferdinand Prince of Naples'—so one experience is not wholly distinct from another experience of the same general order; and just as all experiences 'meet in Tiresias,' so a multitude of experiences meet in each passage of the poem. Thus the passage immediately in question has still further associations. That same hallucinatory quality which relates it to what goes before recalls also the neurasthenic episode in "A Game of Chess" (the second section):

"What is that noise?"

   The wind under the door.

"What is that noise now? . . ."

All this illustrates the method of the poem, and the concentration, the depth of orchestration that Mr Eliot achieves; the way in which the themes move in and out of one another and the predominance shifts from level to level. The transition from this passage is again by way of the general ominousness, which passes into hallucinated vision and then into nightmare:

—But who is that on the other side of you?

What is that sound high in the air
Murmur of maternal lamentation
Who are those hooded hordes swarming
Over endless plains, stumbling in cracked earth
Ringed by the flat horizon only
What is the city over the mountains
Cracks and reforms and bursts in the violet air
Falling towers
Jerusalem Athens Alexandria
Vienna London
Unreal.

The focus of attention shifts here to the outer disintegration in its large, obvious aspects, and the references to Russia and to post-war Europe in general are plain. The link between the hooded figure of the road to Emmaus and the 'hooded hordes swarming' is not much more than verbal (though appropriate to a fevered consciousness), but this phrase has an essential association with a line (56) in the passage that introduces the Tarot pack:

I see crowds of people, walking round in a ring.

These 'hooded hordes,' 'ringed by the flat horizon only,' are not merely Russians, suggestively related to the barbarian invaders of civilization; they are also humanity walking endlessly round in a ring, a further illustration of the eternal futility. 'Unreal' picks up the 'Unreal city' of "The Burial of the Dead" (l.60), where 'Saint Mary Woolnoth kept the hours,' and the unreality gets further development in the nightmare passage that follows:

And upside down in air were towers
Tolling reminiscent bells, that kept the hours
And voices singing out of empty cisterns and
  exhausted wells.

Then, with a transitional reference (which will be commented on later) to the theme of the Chapel Perilous, the focus shifts inwards again. 'Datta,' 'dayadhvam,' and 'damyata,' the admonitions of the thunder, are explained in a note, and in this case, at any rate, the reliance upon the note justifies itself. We need only be told once that they mean 'give, sympathize, control,' and the context preserves the meaning. The Sanscrit lends an appropriate portentousness, intimating that this is the sum of wisdom according to a great tradition, and that

what we have here is a radical scrutiny into the profit of life. The irony, too, is radical:

Datta: what have we given?
My friend, blood shaking my heart
The awful daring of a moment's surrender
Which an age of prudence can never retract
By this, and this only, we have existed

—it is an equivocal comment. And for comment on 'sympathize' we have a reminder of the irremediable isolation of the individual. After all the agony of sympathetic transcendence, it is to the individual, the focus of consciousness, that we return:

Shall I at least set my lands in order?

The answer comes in the bundle of fragments that ends the poem, and, in a sense, sums it up.

Not that the *poem* lacks organization and unity. The frequent judgments that it does betray a wrong approach. The author of *The Lyric Impulse in the Poetry of T. S. Eliot,* for instance, speaks of 'a definitely willed attempt to weld various fine fragments into a metaphysical whole.' But the unity of **The Waste Land** is no more 'metaphysical' than it is narrative or dramatic, and to try to elucidate it metaphysically reveals complete misunderstanding. The unity the poem aims at is that of an inclusive consciousness: the organization it achieves as a work of art is of the kind that has been illustrated, an organization that may, by analogy, be called musical. It exhibits no progression:

I sat upon the shore

Fishing, with the arid plain behind me

—the thunder brings no rain to revive the Waste Land, and the poem ends where it began.

At this point the criticism has to be met that, while all this may be so, the poem in any case exists, and can exist, only for an extremely limited public equipped with special knowledge. The criticism must be admitted. But that the public for it is limited is one of the symptoms of the state of culture that produced the poem. Works expressing the finest consciousness of the age in which the word 'high-brow' has become current are almost inevitably such as to appeal only to a tiny minority. It is still more serious that this minority should be more and more cut off from the world around it—should, indeed, be aware of a hostile and overwhelming environment. This amounts to an admission that there must be something limited about the kind of artistic achievement possible in our time: even Shakespeare in such conditions could hardly have been the 'universal' genius. And **The Waste Land,** clearly, is not of the order of *The Divine Comedy* or of *Lear.* The important admission, then, is not that **The Waste Land** can be appreciated only by a very small minority (how large in any age has the minority been that has really comprehended the masterpieces?), but that this limitation carries with it limitations in self-sufficiency.

These limitations, however, are easily over-stressed. Most of the 'special knowledge,' dependence upon which is urged against **The Waste Land,** can fairly be held to be common to the public that would in any case read modern poetry. The poem does, indeed, to some extent lean frankly upon *From Ritual to Romance.* And sometimes it depends upon external support in ways that can hardly be justified. Let us take, for instance, the end of the third section, "The Fire Sermon":

la la

To Carthage then I came

Burning, burning, burning, burning
O Lord Thou pluckest me out
O Lord Thou pluckest

burning

It is plain from Mr Eliot's note on this passage—'The collocation of these two representatives of eastern and western asceticism, as the culmination of this part of the poem, is not an
accident'—that he intends St Augustine and the Buddha to
be actively present here. But whereas one cursory reading of
From Ritual to Romance does all (practically) that is assigned
as function to that book, no amount of reading of the *Confessions* or *Buddhism in Translation* will give these few words
power to evoke the kind of presence of 'eastern and western
asceticism' that seems necessary to the poem: they remain,
these words, mere pointers to something outside. We can
only conclude that Mr Eliot here has not done as much as he
supposes. And so with the passage in "What the Thunder
Said" bringing in the theme of the Chapel Perilous: it leaves
too much to Miss Weston; repeated recourse to *From Ritual
to Romance* will not invest it with the virtue it would assume.
The irony, too, of the

Shantih   shantih   shantih

that ends the poem is largely ineffective, for Mr Eliot's note
that ' "The Peace which passeth understanding" is a feeble
translation of the content of this word' can impart to the
word only a feeble ghost of that content for the Western reader.

Yet the weaknesses of this kind are not nearly as frequent or
as damaging as critics of **The Waste Land** seem commonly
to suppose. It is a self-subsistent poem, and should be obviously such. The allusions, references and quotations usually
carry their own power with them as well as being justified in
the appeal they make to special knowledge. 'Unreal City' (l.
60), to take an extreme instance from one end of the scale,
owes nothing to Baudelaire (whatever Mr Eliot may have
owed); the note is merely interesting—though, of course, it
is probable that a reader unacquainted with Baudelaire will
be otherwise unqualified. The reference to Dante that follows—

A crowd flowed over London Bridge, so many,
I had not thought death had undone so many

—has an independent force, but much is lost to the reader
who does not catch the implied comparison between London
and Dante's Hell. Yet the requisite knowledge of Dante is a
fair demand. The knowledge of *Antony and Cleopatra* assumed in the opening of "A Game of Chess," or of *The Tempest* in various places elsewhere, no one will boggle at. The
main references in **The Waste Land** come within the classes
represented by these to Dante and Shakespeare; while of the
many others most of the essential carry enough of their power
with them. By means of such references and quotations Mr
Eliot attains a compression, otherwise unattainable, that is
essential to his aim; a compression approaching simultaneity—the co-presence in the mind of a number of different ori-
entations, fundamental attitudes, orders of experience.

This compression and the methods it entails do make the
poem difficult reading at first, and a full response comes only
with familiarity. Yet the complete rout so often reported, or

inadvertently revealed—as, for instance, by the critic who assumes that **The Waste Land** is meant to be a 'metaphyscial
whole'—can be accounted for only by a wrong approach, an
approach with inappropriate expectations. For the general
nature and method of the poem should be obvious at first
reading. Yet so commonly does the obvious seem to be missed
that perhaps a little more elucidation (this time of the opening section) will not be found offensively superfluous. What
follows is a brief analysis of "The Burial of the Dead," the
avowed intention being to point out the obvious themes and
transitions: anything like a full analysis would occupy many
times the space.

The first seven lines introduce the vegetation theme, associating it with the stirring of 'memory and desire.' The transition
is simple: 'April,' 'spring,' 'winter,'—then

Summer surprised us, coming over the Starnbergersee
With a shower of rain . . .

We seem to be going straight forward, but (as the change of
movement intimates) we have modulated into another plane.
We are now given a particular 'memory,' and a representative
one. It introduces the cosmopolitan note, a note of empty sophistication:

In the mountains, there you feel free.
I read, much of the night, and go south in the
    winter.   [Cf. 'Winter kept us warm']

The next transition is a contrast and a comment, bringing this
last passage into relation with the first. April may stir dull
roots with spring rain, but

What are the roots that clutch, what branches grow
Out of this stony rubbish?

And there follows an evocation of the Waste Land, with references to *Ezekiel* and *Ecclesiastes,* confirming the tone that
intimates that this is an agony of the soul ('Son of man' relates
with the Hanged Man and the Hanged God: with him 'who
was living' and 'is now dead' at the opening of "What the
Thunder Said"). The 'fear'—

I will show you fear in a handful of dust

—recurs, in different modes, in the neurasthenic passage of
"A Game of Chess," and in the episode of the hooded figure
in "What the Thunder Said." The fear is partly the fear of
death, but still more a nameless, ultimate fear, a horror of the
completely negative.

Then comes the verse from *Tristan und Isolde,* offering a positive in contrast—the romantic absolute, love. The 'hyacinth
girl,' we may say, represents 'memory and desire' (the hyacinth, directly evocative like the lilacs bred out of the Waste
Land, was also one of the flowers associated with the slain
vegetation god), and the 'nothing' of the Waste Land changes
into the ecstasy of passion—a contrast, and something
more. . . . In the Waste Land one is neither living nor dead.
Moreover, the neurasthenic passage referred to above recalls
these lines unmistakably, giving them a sinister modulation:

'Speak to me.   Why do you never speak.   Speak.
'What are you thinking of ? What thinking?
    What?
'I never know what you are thinking.   Think.'

(pp. 99-110)

The further line from *Tristan und Isolde* ends the passage of
romantic love with romantic desolation. Madame Sosostris,

famous clairvoyante, follows; she brings in the demi-monde, so offering a further contrast—

> Here is Belladonna, the Lady of the Rocks,
> The lady of situations

—and introduces the Tarot pack. This passage has already received some comment, and it invites a great deal more. The 'lady of situations,' to make an obvious point, appears in the "Game of Chess." The admonition, 'Fear death by water,' gets its response in the fourth section, "Death by Water": death is inevitable, and the life-giving water thirsted for (and the water out of which all life comes) cannot save. (p. 110)

With the 'Unreal City' the background of urban—of 'megalopolitan'—civilization becomes explicit. The allusion to Dante has already been remarked upon, and so has the way in which Saint Mary Woolnoth is echoed by the 'reminiscent bells' of "What the Thunder Said." The portentousness of the 'dead sound on the final stroke of nine' serves as a transition, and the unreality of the City turns into the intense but meaningless horror, the absurd inconsequence, of a nightmare:

> There I saw one I knew, and stopped him, crying:
>   'Stetson!
> 'You who were with me in the ships at Mylae!
> 'That corpse you planted last year in your garden,
> 'Has it begun to sprout? Will it bloom this
>   year? . . .'

These last two lines pick up again the opening theme. The corpse acquires a kind of nightmare association with the slain god of *The Golden Bough,* and is at the same time a buried memory. Then, after a reference to Webster (Webster's sepulchral horrors are robust), "The Burial of the Dead" ends with the line in which Baudelaire, having developed the themes of

> La sottise, l'erreur, le péché, la lésine

and finally *L'Ennui,* suddenly turns upon the reader to remind him that he is something more.

The way in which *The Waste Land* is organized, then, should be obvious even without the aid of notes. And the poet's mastery should be as apparent in the organization as in the parts (where it has been freely acclaimed). The touch with which he manages his difficult transitions, his delicate collocations, is exquisitely sure. His tone, in all its subtle variations, exhibits a perfect control. If there is any instance where this last judgment must be qualified, it is perhaps here (from the first passage of "The Fire Sermon"):

> Sweet Thames, run softly till I end my song,
> Sweet Thames, run softly, for I speak not loud or
>   long.
> But at my back in a cold blast I hear
> The rattle of the bones, and chuckle spread from
>   ear to ear.

These last two lines seem to have too much of the caricature quality of **"Prufrock"** to be in keeping—for a certain keeping is necessary (and Mr Eliot commonly maintains it) even in contrasts. But even if the comment is just, the occasion for it is a very rare exception.

The Waste Land, then, whatever its difficulty, is, or should be, obviously a poem. It is a self-subsistent poem. Indeed, though it would lose if the notes could be suppressed and forgotten, yet the more important criticism might be said to be, not that it depends upon them too much, but rather that without them, and without the support of *From Ritual to Ro-*

mance, it would not lose more. It has, that is, certain limitations in any case; limitations inherent in the conditions that produced it. Comprehensiveness, in the very nature of the undertaking, must be in some sense at the cost of structure: absence of direction, of organizing principle, in life could hardly be made to subserve the highest kind of organization in art.

But when all qualifications have been urged, *The Waste Land* remains a great positive achievement, and one of the first importance for English poetry. In it a mind fully alive in the age compels a poetic triumph out of the peculiar difficulties facing a poet in the age. And in solving his own problem as a poet Mr Eliot did more than solve the problem for himself. Even if *The Waste Land* had been, as used to be said, a 'dead end' for him, it would still have been a new start for English poetry.

But, of course, to judge it a 'dead end' was shallow. It was to ignore the implications of the effort that alone could have availed to express formlessness itself as form. So complete and vigorous a statement of the Waste Land could hardly (to risk being both crude and impertinent) forecast an exhausted, hopeless sojourn there. As for the nature of the effort, the intimacy with Dante that the poem betrays has its significance. There is no great distance in time and no gulf of any kind between the poet of *The Waste Land* and the critic who associates himself later with 'a tendency—discernible even in art—toward a higher and clearer conception of Reason, and a more severe and serene control of the emotions by Reason'; and who writes of Proust 'as a point of demarcation between a generation for whom the dissolution of value had in itself a positive value, and the generation which is beginning to turn its attention to an athleticism, a *training,* of the soul as severe and ascetic as the training of the body of a runner.' (pp. 111-14)

F. R. Leavis, "T. S. Eliot," in his New Bearings in English Poetry: A Study of the Contemporary Situation, *1932. Reprint by AMS Press, Inc., 1978, pp. 75-132.*

HERBERT E. PALMER

The Waste Land has had more influence on the verse of the last half dozen years than any other long poem of note. At any rate we are repeatedly told so. . . . Young enthusiasts have written about the poem as a "landmark." One of them went so far as to say "that by the literary historian of 2030 *The Waste Land* will be regarded in much the same light as Wordsworth's and Coleridge's *Lyrical Ballads* are to-day, as marking the end of one literary epoch and the beginning of a new one." While in the same prominent weekly a reviewer of *Ash Wednesday* wrote, "suddenly—*The Waste Land,* and it may be said with small exaggeration that English poetry of the first half of the twentieth century *began.*"

But surely Mr. Eliot never intended *The Waste Land* to be taken quite so seriously, at least not quite so constructively, especially as it exhibits too many of the features of a hoax. At any rate hoax and earnest are strangely, hypnotically and bafflingly blended. It is as if Mr. Eliot were saying, "Take this you fox-terriers; it's all you are worth. Here's a bone for a dog." If *The Waste Land* means anything to me in relation to 2030 it is that *The Waste Land* will be truly a waste land, unknown and unhonoured, leering out of the darkness at all other English poetry, which will be equally unknown and unhonoured. For surely, only in that way can *The Waste Land* mark "the end of one literary epoch and the beginning of a new one"—the Age of the Supremacy of Prose, particularly of Prose which shall combine expression of excessive Realism and Machine-made Thought with the skeleton incompleteness and nebulous aura of Intuition. The serious way in which this sardonic jest and frightfully clever literary medley has been received and treated is proof enough to me that the dessication and disintegration of Poetry are beginning. *The Waste Land* has a certain bony virility and hypnotic strangeness of suggestion (otherwise, of course, it couldn't have continued); so that the transmitted sound of some of it may bring stiffening into the work of a few other poets,—often, it is to be feared, to their disadvantage. Beyond that it has no importance except as a gesture of mockery and disillusion, and contempt for the reader and critic; no value except as a warning of what may overtake literature, and particularly poetry; no value except as the banner of present-day War weariness and spiritual barrenness—one might almost say mental and moral degeneracy. It is in this last characteristic of decadence, that it is, of all our literature, the completest condensed expression of the feelings, thoughts, attitudes, activities and tendencies of the Present Age. High praise, and yet most damning praise. And as the rhythm of Modern Life is so mixed and jarred and full of dissonances and artificial derivations you do, of course, find the expression of all this in the rhythms and movements and quotations and kaleidoscope patterns of *The Waste Land*—which is suggestive of gramophone renewals, wireless adjustings, machinery buzzings, fog-horn explosions, cinema clackings, motor-traffic, underground traffic, street ramblings, the tarred road, comic opera, jazz, typewriter clickings, and sandwich-paper rustlings. The poem is a waste land in its *methods,* in the way it says and does things, even more than in what it actually pretends to say—which is, perhaps, that Western Civilization is coming to an end . . . . Though personally I would rather drive a pony and trap up Mount Vesuvius (as I have so often done) than emulate T. S. Eliot by driving a motor car in Hell.

Mr. T. S. Eliot, though an American, is a man of wide reading, a notable critic (if somewhat eccentric and overestimated critic) and *at his best* a poet in a cellar and an original prose writer. Considering all this, for many long months I took the poem quite seriously. But certain defects in it were a little too apparent. Either everything a man had learnt at school and the university was utterly wrong or Mr. Eliot was a stammering pretentious man of genius lacking the rudiments of solid education. In course of time the microscope revealed nearly everything that could be revealed. This is what I brought together on the tablecloth: (*a*) Bad grammar of both sense and syntax; (*b*) Absurd punctuation—which very often amounted to no punctuation at all; (*c*) Things upside down; (*d*) Disconnected thought, disconnected landscapes of thought, feeling, and ocular scenery; (*e*) The life of a man asleep, particularly of one suffering from a nightmare, rather than the life of one actively conscious; (*f*) An enormous number of tags, phrases, sentences and echoes from other poets (though Mr. Eliot has confessed to most of these in supplementary notes); (*g*) The use of wrong epithets; (*h*) The queerest crudities of construction; (*i*) In at least two instances violent coarseness of content—almost equal to the most revolting pages in *All Quiet on the Western Front;* and even in a sense much worse as they are unpoetically sordid, unrelieved by the Aristotelean "pity and terror"; (*j*) An unpoetically assertive, if not pretentious, use of French and Ger-

man; (*k*) Too many borrowed backgrounds, more than in all Milton's works put together. (pp. 11-13)

Disconnection, crudity, insufficient punctuation, plagiarism—they are all so apparent! What at first is not quite so apparent is the false and muddled grammar of sense and syntax in such a passage as:

> Musing upon the king my brother's wreck
> And on the king my father's death before him.

Or in the even more elusive "can see at the violet hour. . . . food in tins," a marvellous creation of baffling hotch-potch.

A glaring example of mispunctuation is the full stop instead of a comma after "him," because, of course, the man was musing upon the "white bodies" as well as the other things. A not very apparent (though actual enough) instance of a wrong epithet is the use of "low" before "dry garret" because, of course, although a garret is never lofty, it is at the top of a house and is in no sense a cellar, which the words "bones" and "cast in" seem to imply. This use of wrong epithet is nothing like so prominent or frequent as the other anarchies, but it occurs several times, nevertheless. In the first part of the section entitled "A Game of Chess" a passage more consistent and Elizabethan in form than the introductory part of the poem would lead us to expect, we get:

> Glowed on the marble, where the glass
> Held up by standards wrought with fruited vines
> From which a golden Cupidon peeped out. . . . .

Just as we are beginning to admire the first twenty-eight lines we discover that they are full of confusion, that very little is clear to the senses, and that "fruited vines" ought to be "metal vines" or "mahogany vines" or something like that, since the vines are manifestly devoid of natural life. While towards the end of the poem an extraordinary, but not too apparent instance of an inversion, or thing upside-down, occurs in:

> We think of the key, each in his prison
> Thinking of the key, each confirms a prison.

For surely it is the prison that confirms the key, and not the key the prison. Keys lock and unlock other doors besides prison doors.

Most of *The Waste Land* cannot be understood, because *it was never meant to be understood,*—except in patches (two or three of them, certainly, of some length). A man does not understand his lonely night of bad dreams, his disconnected bedroom panorama of sensations, mental pictures, broken, twisted images floating down into a tunnel of nightmare horror and dread. T. S. Eliot has thrown all literary discipline and discretion to the winds, and while he has actually created something (created the Disintegration of Creation) the midnight hour of one who has lost touch with God, or the delirious afternoon of one who is parting from his reason, he has blotched and stifled Victorian and Georgian poetry to an extent that is very disturbing. Had Mr. Eliot labelled his poem, "A Nightmare," or "My Neighbour's Inceptions of Lunacy," or "A Tale told by an Idiot. . . . signifying Nothing," or "A Despairing Night of Sleeping Unrest" the poem might have been accepted at its true value. But his methods and intentions were not at all clear, and so a certain section of the literary world has only too willingly allowed itself to be hoaxed. Just because the poem was impossible to understand, it was believed by many admirers to be intensely intellectual and imaginative. How Mr. Eliot must have laughed! And yet it is equally probable that he has been more worried about it than amused—which certain sentences in *Ash Wednesday* seem to proclaim.

But it would be untrue to intimate that *The Waste Land* contains no poetry whatever. Indeed, it contains three or four astonishing passages, as witness the following (characteristically insufficiently punctuated, and ungrammatical or grammatically obscure, in the last line [where "And voices singing" surely should be "And there were voices singing"]):

> A woman drew her long black hair out tight
> And fiddled whisper music on those strings
> And bats with baby faces in the violet light
> Whistled, and beat their wings
> And crawled head downward down a blackened
> wall
> And upside down in air were towers
> Tolling reminiscent bells, that kept the hours
> And voices singing out of empty cisterns and ex-
> hausted wells.

But through that flare of sombre beauty (almost reminiscent of Dante) Mr. Eliot makes a gesture by which he seems to have intended giving himself away; as also in the following passage, near the end of the poem:

> *Datta:* What have we given?
> My friend, blood shaking my heart
> The awful daring of a moment's surrender
> Which an age of prudence can never retract. . . . .

As also in the final passage of the first section of the poem, though chiefly in its last line (quoted from Baudelaire):

> You! hypocrite lecteur! mon semblable,—mon frère!

As also in several other passages. But those readers who were not blind, for some reason or other (perhaps because of their shackling sophistication) seem to have made up their minds not to give the show away. Mr. Eliot insults his reader by calling him a hypocrite, but all the time advancing behind the shield of quotation, thinks to put a bandage round the wound by associating the poor fellow with himself. "The awful daring of a moment's surrender"—probably in committing this strange medley to print. The ordinary reader who is prominently a fool won't be able to see, and the intellectual reader who is prominently a hypocrite, or something equally unpleasant, will put his tongue in his cheek, or keep silence. While, of course, mixed up from those two are the sheep who are out for any profit they can get. So perhaps "the awful daring" was no real daring after all. Is it not evident, Mr. Eliot seems to say, that the light and courage of the human mind have long since been routed and put out! All that is left is a *Waste Land.* Yes, in a way, Mr. Eliot is and has been well justified, and deserves, at least, a crown of thorns. He has spoken in his strange ironic idiom and definitely revealed something. But how difficult to praise at all, or to entirely damn. For he is one of the least desirable and yet most necessary activities in creation—*a practical satirist.* And like so many practical satirists he refuses to be a good English schoolboy and "own up." (pp. 13-18)

And finally a word upon metre. *The Waste Land* has been excessively praised for its original rhythms,—and some critics seem to think that it was written to teach poets Technique. But there is nothing metrically new in *The Waste Land* save by what appears to be due to miraculous accident or too-arduous intent. It has nothing like the metrical seduction and originality of Mr. Eliot's early poem **"The Love Song of J. Alfred Prufrock."** There is nothing in it more fresh and original than we find in the prosodical innovations of W. B. Yeats, Robert Bridges, H. D., Humbert Wolfe, J. Redwood Anderson, J. C. Squire, Walter de la Mare, or Edith Sitwell (vide *Gold Coast Customs*) or even of Austin Clarke, or Sherard Vines, or Robert Graves, or Robert Nichols, or Thomas Moult, or John Masefield (vide *Lollington Downs*). Its framework, for the most part, is a mixture of quite customary free verse, rhymed verse, and blank verse, with a few simple variations thrown in, some of them bald prose, and others the *rhymed* prose and free-verse feats of Ford Madox Hueffer (vide, for instance, that fine poem *Antwerp*). Equally good free verse (if not better) has also been written by Richard Aldington, Richard Church, F. S. Flint, D. H. Lawrence, John Gould Fletcher, and Ezra Pound (all of whom, save Richard Church, were publishing books of verse before the War). Equally good prose-verse was written immediately after the war by Susan Miles (she has a very gripping and individual medium of expression). While of the blank verse there is nothing in *The Waste Land* to equal the best passages of the Elizabethans, or for that matter those of Gordon Bottomley, or Lascelles Abercrombie, or Sturge Moore, or Lawrence Binyon, or W. B. Yeats, or Edward Thompson (all of whom were going strong before the War) or Edmund Blunden, or Miss Sackville West, or J. Redwood Anderson, or Austin Clarke, or John Drinkwater, or Richard Church, or Conrad Aiken, or R. L. Mégroz (vide *Ruth*) since the War.

In the way of interwoven free verse and blank verse nothing better during the last ten years has been written than Robert Trevelyan's "Moses and the Shepherd," a poem of fine content as well as fine technical accomplishment.

Yes, *The Waste Land* more than any other Eliot poem has been monstrously overpraised; for it is no more than the waggling grinning skeleton of a great poem, something that T. S. Eliot was spiritually and mentally unable to clothe with flesh and raiment, something which unable to complete or revise, to link with links and vitalise with sinews, he made the subject of an act of sabotage, a Creation of Disintegration. The other explanation is that he cut it down from a much longer poem, telescoping or dovetailing or jamming into one another the isolated fragments of what he chose to rescue, with a glittering eye all the time on the baffling and the ridiculous; again an act of sabotage, a Creation of Disintegration. Surely that is it; he has sabotted his own poem; for that is all this perverse moon-stricken generation is worth. (pp. 18-19)

> Herbert E. Palmer, "The Hoax and Earnest of 'The
> Waste Land'," in The Dublin Magazine, *n.s. Vol.*
> *VIII, No. 2, April-June, 1933, pp. 11-19.*

CLEANTH BROOKS

In view of the state of criticism with regard to [*The Waste Land*], it is best for us to approach it frankly on the basis of its theme. I prefer, however, not to raise just here the question of how important it is for the reader to have an explicit intellectual account of the various symbols and a logical account of their relationships. It may well be that such rationalization is no more than a scaffolding to be got out of the way before we contemplate the poem itself as poem. But many readers (including myself) find the erection of such a scaffolding valuable—if not absolutely necessary—and if some readers will be tempted to lay more stress upon the scaffolding than they should, there are perhaps still more readers who, without the help of such a scaffolding, will be prevented from getting at the poem at all.

The basic symbol used, that of the waste land, is taken of course, from Miss Jessie Weston's *From Ritual to Romance*. In the legends which she treats the ⟨ ⟩ the land has been blighted by a curse. The crops do not ⟨ ⟩w and the animals cannot reproduce. The plight of the la⟨ ⟩ is summed up by, and connected with, the plight of the ⟨ ⟩d of the land, the Fisher King, who has been rendered impotent by maiming or sickness. The curse can be removed only by the appearance of a knight who will ask the meanings of the various symbols which are displayed to him in the castle. The shift in meaning from physical to spiritual sterility is easily made, and was, as a matter of fact, made in certain of the legends. As Eliot has pointed out, a knowledge of this symbolism is essential for an understanding of the poem.

Of hardly less importance to the reader, however, is a knowledge of Eliot's basic method. **The Waste Land** is built on a major contrast—a device which is a favorite of Eliot's and is to be found in many of his poems, particularly his later poems. The contrast is between two kinds of life and two kinds of death. Life devoid of meaning is death; sacrifice, even the sacrificial death, may be life-giving, an awakening to life. The poem occupies itself to a great extent with this paradox, and with a number of variations upon it.

Eliot has stated the matter quite explicitly himself in one of his essays. In his **"Baudelaire"** he says:

> One aphorism which has been especially noticed is the following: *la volupté unique et suprême de l'amour gît dans la certitude de faire le mal*. This means, I think, that Baudelaire has perceived that what distinguishes the relations of man and woman from the copulation of beasts is the knowledge of Good and Evil (of *moral* Good and Evil which are not natural Good and Bad or puritan Right and Wrong). Having an imperfect, vague romantic conception of Good, he was at least able to understand that the sexual act as evil is more dignified, less boring, than as the natural, 'life-giving,' cheery automatism of the modern world. . . . So far as we are human, what we do must be either evil or good; so far as we do evil or good, we are human; and it is better, in a paradoxical way, to do evil than to do nothing: at least, *we exist* [italics mine].

The last statement is highly important for an understanding of **The Waste Land.** The fact that men have lost the knowledge of good and evil, keeps them from being alive, and is the justification for viewing the modern waste land as a realm in which the inhabitants do not even exist.

This theme is stated in the quotation which prefaces the poem. The Sybil says: "I wish to die." Her statement has several possible interpretations. For one thing, she is saying what the people who inhabit the waste land are saying. But she may also be saying what the speaker of "The Journey of the Magi" says: " . . . this Birth was / Hard and bitter agony for us, like Death, our death / . . . I should be glad of another death."

The first section of "The Burial of the Dead" develops the theme of the attractiveness of death, or of the difficulty in rousing oneself from the death in life in which the people of the waste land live. Men are afraid to live in reality. April, the month of rebirth, is not the most joyful season but the cruelest. Winter at least kept us warm in forgetful snow. . . . Men dislike to be roused from their death-in-life.

The first part of "The Burial of the Dead" introduces this theme through a sort of reverie on the part of the protagonist—a reverie in which speculation on life glides off into memory of an actual conversation in the Hofgarten and back into speculation again. The function of the conversation is to establish the class and character of the protagonist. The reverie is resumed with line 19.

> What are the roots that clutch, what branches grow
> Out of this stony rubbish?

The protagonist answers for himself:

> Son of man,

> You cannot say, or guess, for you know only
> A heap of broken images, where the sun beats,
> And the dead tree gives no shelter, the cricket no relief,
> And the dry stone no sound of water.

In this passage there are references to Ezekiel and to Ecclesiastes, and these references indicate what it is that men no longer know: The passage referred to in Ezekiel 2, pictures a world thoroughly secularized:

> 1. And he said unto me, Son of man, stand upon thy feet, and I will speak unto thee.
> 2. And the spirit entered into me when he spake unto me, and set me upon my feet, that I heard him that spake unto me.
> 3. And he said unto me, Son of man, I send thee to the children of Israel, to a rebellious nation that hath rebelled against me: they and their fathers have transgressed against me, even unto this very day.

Other passages from Ezekiel are relevant to the poem, Chapter 37 in particular, which describes Ezekiel's waste land, where the prophet, in his vision of the valley of dry bones, contemplates the "burial of the dead" and is asked: "Son of man, can these bones live? And I answered, O Lord God, thou knowest. 4. Again he said unto me, Prophesy over these bones, and say unto them, O ye dry bones, hear the word of the Lord."

One of Ezekiel's prophecies was that Jerusalem would be conquered and the people led away into the Babylonian captivity. That captivity is alluded to in Section III of **The Waste Land,** line 182, where the Thames becomes the "waters of Leman."

The passage from Ecclesiastes 12, alluded to in Eliot's notes, describes the same sort of waste land. . . . (pp. 136-40)

The next section of "The Burial of the Dead" which begins with the scrap of song quoted from Wagner (perhaps another item in the reverie of the protagonist), states the opposite half of the paradox which underlies the poem: namely, that life at its highest moments of meaning and intensity resembles death. The song from Act I of Wagner's *Tristan und Isolde*, "Frisch weht der Wind," is sung in the opera by a young sailor aboard the ship which is bringing Isolde to Cornwall. The *"Irisch kind"* of the song does not properly apply to Isolde at all. The song is merely one of happy and naïve love. It brings to mind of the protagonist an experience of love—the vision of the hyacinth girl as she came back from the hyacinth garden. The poet says

> my eyes failed, I was neither
>
> Living nor dead, and I knew nothing,
> Looking into the heart of light, the silence.

The line which immediately follows this passage, *"Oed' und leer das Meer,"* seems at first to be simply an extension of the last figure: that is, "Empty and wide the sea [of silence]." But the line, as a matter of fact, makes an ironic contrast; for the line, as it occurs in Act III of the opera, is the reply of the watcher who reports to the wounded Tristan that Isolde's ship is nowhere in sight; the sea is empty. And, though the *"Irisch kind"* of the first quotation is not Isolde, the reader familiar with the opera will apply it to Isolde when he comes to the line *"Oed' und leer das Meer."* For the question in the song is in essence Tristan's question in Act III: "My Irish child, where dwellest thou?" The two quotations from the opera which frame the ecstasy-of-love passage thus take on a new meaning in the altered context. In the first, love is happy; the boat rushes on with a fair wind behind it. In the second, love is absent; the sea is wide and empty. And the last quotation reminds us that even love cannot exist in the waste land.

The next passage, that in which Madame Sosostris figures, calls for further reference to Miss Weston's book. As Miss Weston has shown, the Tarot cards were originally used to determine the event of highest importance to the people, the rising of the waters. Madame Sosostris has fallen a long way from the high function of her predecessors. She is engaged merely in vulgar fortune-telling—is merely one item in a generally vulgar civilization. But the symbols of the Tarot pack are still unchanged. The various characters are still inscribed on the cards, and she is reading in reality (though she does not know it) the fortune of the protagonist. She finds that his card is that of the drowned Phoenician Sailor, and so she warns him against death by water, not realizing any more than do the other inhabitants of the modern waste land that the way into life may be by death itself. The drowned Phoenician Sailor is a type of the fertility god whose image was thrown into the sea annually as a symbol of the death of summer. As for the other figures in the pack: Belladonna, the Lady of the Rocks, is woman in the waste land. The man with three staves, Eliot says he associates rather arbitrarily with the Fisher King. The term "arbitrarily" indicates that we are not to attempt to find a logical connection here. . . . The figure is that of a scarecrow, fit symbol of the man who possesses no reality, and fit type of the Fisher King, the maimed, impotent king who ruled over the waste land of the legend. The man with three staves in the deck of cards may thus have appealed to the poet as an appropriate figure to which to assign the function of the Fisher King, although the process of identification was too difficult to expect the reader to follow and although knowledge of the process was not necessary to an understanding of the poem.)

The Hanged Man, who represents the hanged god of Frazer (including the Christ), Eliot states in a note, is associated with the hooded figure who appears in "What the Thunder Said." That he is hooded accounts for Madame Sosostris' inability to see him; or rather, here again the palaver of the modern fortune-teller is turned to new and important account by the poet's shifting the reference into a new and serious context. The Wheel and the one-eyed merchant will be discussed later.

After the Madame Sosostris passage, Eliot proceeds to complicate his symbols for the sterility and unreality of the mod-

ern waste land by associating it with Baudelaire's *"fourmillante cité"* and with Dante's Limbo. (pp. 141-43)

The references to Dante are most important. The line, "I had not thought death had undone so many," is taken from the Third Canto of the *Inferno;* the line, "Sighs, short and infrequent, were exhaled" from the Fourth Canto. (p. 143)

The Dante and Baudelaire references, then, come to the same thing as the allusion to the waste land of the medieval legends; and these various allusions, drawn from widely differing sources, enrich the comment on the modern city so that it becomes "unreal" on a number of levels: as seen through "the brown fog of a winter dawn"; as the medieval waste land and Dante's Limbo and Baudelaire's Paris are unreal.

The reference to Stetson stresses again the connection between the modern London of the poem and Dante's hell. After the statement, "I could never have believed death had undone so many," follow the words, "After I had distinguished some among them, I saw and knew the shade of him who made, through cowardice, the great refusal." The protagonist, like Dante, sees among the inhabitants of the contemporary waste land one whom he recognizes. (The name "Stetson" I take to have no ulterior significance. It is merely an ordinary name such as might be borne by the friend one might see in a crowd in a great city.) Mylae, as Mr. Matthiessen has pointed out [in *The Achievement of T. S. Eliot*], is the name of a battle between the Romans and the Carthaginians in the Punic War. The Punic War was a trade war—might be considered a rather close parallel to [World War I]. At any rate, it is plain that Eliot in having the protagonist address the friend in a London street as one who was with him in the Punic War rather than as one who was with him in the World War is making the point that all the wars are one war; all experience, one experience. (pp. 144-45)

I am not sure that Leavis [see excerpt above] and Matthiessen are correct in inferring that the line, "That corpse you planted last year in your garden," refers to the attempt to b[...] memory. But whether or not this is true, the line certainly refers also to the buried god of the old fertility rites. It also [...] to be linked with the earlier passage—"What are the roots that clutch, what branches grow," etc. This allusion to the buried god will account for the ironical, almost taunting tone of the passage. The burial of the dead is now a sterile planting—without hope. But the advice to "keep the Dog far hence," in spite of the tone, is, I believe, well taken and serious. The passage in Webster goes as follows

> But keep the wolf far thence, that's foe to men,
> For with his nails he'll dig them up again.

Why does Eliot turn the wolf into a dog? And why does he reverse the point of importance from the animal's normal hostility to men to its friendliness? If, as some critics have suggested, he is merely interested in making a reference to Webster's darkest play, why alter the line? I am inclined to take the Dog (the capital letter is Eliot's) as Humanitarianism and the related philosophies which, in their concern for man, extirpate the supernatural—dig up the corpse of the buried god and thus prevent the rebirth of life. For the general idea, see Eliot's essay, **"The Humanism of Irving Babbitt."**

The last line of "The Burial of the Dead"—"You! hypocrite lecteur!—mon semblable,—mon frère!" the quotation from Baudelaire, completes the universalization of Stetson begun by the reference to Mylae. Stetson is every man including the reader and Mr. Eliot himself.

If "The Burial of the Dead" gives the general abstract statement of the situation, the second part of *The Waste Land,* "A Game of Chess," gives a more concrete illustration. The easiest contrast in this section—and one which may easily blind the casual reader to a continued emphasis on the contrast between the two kinds of life, or the two kinds of death, already commented on—is the contrast between life in a rich and magnificent setting, and life in the low and vulgar setting of a London pub. But both scenes, however antithetical they may appear superficially, are scenes taken from the contemporary waste land. In both of them life has lost its meaning.

I am particularly indebted to Mr. Allen Tate's comment on the first part of this section. To quote from him, "The woman . . . is, I believe, the symbol of man at the present time. He is surrounded by the grandeurs of the past, but he does not participate in them; they don't sustain him." And to quote from another section of his commentary: "The rich experience of the great tradition depicted in the room receives a violent shock in contrast with a game that symbolizes the inhuman abstraction of the modern mind." Life has no meaning; history has no meaning; there is no answer to the question: "What shall we ever do?" The only thing that has meaning is the abstract game which they are to play, a game in which the meaning is assigned and arbitrary, meaning by convention only—in short, a game of chess.

This interpretation will account in part for the pointed reference to Cleopatra in the first lines of the section. But there is, I believe, a further reason for the poet's having compared the lady to Cleopatra. The queen in Shakespeare's drama— "Age cannot wither her, nor custom stale / Her infinite variety"—is perhaps the extreme exponent of love for love's sake, the feminine member of the pair of lovers who threw away an empire for love. But the infinite variety of the life of the woman in "A Game of Chess" *has* been staled. There is indeed no variety at all, and love simply does not exist. The function of the sudden change in the description of the carvings and paintings in the room from the heroic and magnificent to "and other withered stumps of time" is obvious. But the reference to Philomela is particularly important, for Philomela, it seems to me, is one of the major symbols of the poem.

Miss Weston points out (in *The Quest of the Holy Grail*) that a section of one of the Grail manuscripts, which is apparently intended to be a gloss on the Grail story, tells how the court of the rich Fisher King was withdrawn from the knowledge of men when certain of the maidens who frequented the shrine were raped and had their golden cups taken from them. The course on the land follows from this act. Miss Weston conjectures that this may be a statement, in the form of a parable, of the violation of the older mysteries which were probably once celebrated openly, but were later forced underground. Whether or not Mr. Eliot noticed this passage or intends a reference, the violation of a woman makes a very good symbol of the process of secularization. . . . The portrayal of "the change of Philomel, by the barbarous king" is a fitting commentary on the scene which it ornaments. The waste land of the legend came in this way; the modern waste land has come in this way. (pp. 145-48)

The Philomela passage has another importance, however. If it is a commentary on how the waste land became waste, it

also repeats the theme of the death which is the door to life, the theme of the dying god. The raped woman becomes transformed through suffering into the nightingale; through the violation comes the "inviolable voice." The thesis that suffering is action, and that out of suffering comes poetry is a favorite one of Eliot's. For example, "Shakespeare, too, was occupied with the struggle—which alone constitutes life for a poet—to transmute his personal and private agonies into something rich and strange, something universal and impersonal." Consider also his statement with reference to Baudelaire: "Indeed, in his way of suffering is already a kind of presence of the supernatural and of the superhuman. He rejects always the purely natural and the purely human; in other words, he is neither 'naturalist' nor 'humanist.' " The theme of the life which is death is stated specifically in the conversation between the man and the woman. She asks the question, "Are you alive, or not?" Compare the Dante references in "The Burial of the Dead." (She also asks, "Is there nothing in your head?" He is one of the Hollow Men—"Headpiece filled with straw.") These people, as people living in the waste land, know nothing, see nothing, do not even live.

But the protagonist, after this reflection that in the waste land of modern life even death is sterile—"I think we are in rats' alley / Where the dead men lost their bones"—remembers a death that was transformed into something rich and strange, the death described in the song from *The Tempest*—"Those are pearls that were his eyes."

The reference to this section of *The Tempest* is, like the Philomela reference, one of Eliot's major symbols. A general comment on it is therefore appropriate here, for we are to meet with it twice more in later sections of the poem. The song, one remembers, was sung by Ariel in luring Ferdinand, Prince of Naples, on to meet Miranda, and thus to find love, and through this love, to effect the regeneration and deliverance of all the people on the island. . . . The allusion is an extremely interesting example of the device of Eliot's already commented upon, that of taking an item from one context and shifting it into another in which it assumes a new and powerful meaning. The description of a death which is a portal into a realm of the rich and strange—a death which becomes a sort of birth—assumes in the mind of the protagonist an association with that of the drowned god whose effigy was thrown into the water as a symbol of the death of the fruitful powers of nature but which was taken out of the water as a symbol of the revivified god. (See *From Ritual to Romance.*) The passage therefore represents the perfect antithesis to the passage in "The Burial of the Dead": "That corpse you planted last year in your garden," etc. It also, as we have already pointed out, finds its antithesis in the sterile and unfruitful death "in rats' alley" just commented upon. (We shall find that this contrast between the death in rats' alley and the death in *The Tempest* is made again in "The Fire Sermon.")

We have yet to treat the relation of the title of the second section, "A Game of Chess," to Middleton's play, *Women Beware Women,* from which the game of chess is taken. In the play, the game is used as a device to keep the widow occupied while her daughter-in-law is being seduced. The seduction amounts almost to a rape, and in a *double entendre,* the rape is actually described in terms of the game. We have one more connection with the Philomela symbol, therefore. The abstract game is being used in the contemporary waste land, as in the play, to cover up a rape and is a description of the rape itself.

In the latter part of "A Game of Chess" we are given a picture of spiritual emptiness, but this time, at the other end of the social scale, as reflected in the talk between two cockney women in a London pub. (It is perhaps unnecessary to comment on the relation of their talk about abortion to the theme of sterility and the waste land.) (pp. 148-50)

"The Fire Sermon" makes much use of several of the symbols already developed. The fire is the sterile burning of lust, and the section is a sermon, although a sermon by example only. This section of the poem also contains some of the most easily apprehended uses of literary allusion. The poem opens on a vision of the modern river. In Spenser's "Prothalamion" the scene described is also a river scene at London, and it is dominated by nymphs and their paramours, and the nymphs are preparing for a wedding. The contrast between Spenser's scene and its twentieth century equivalent is jarring. The paramours are now "the loitering heirs of city directors," and, as for the nuptials of Spenser's Elizabethan maidens, in the stanzas which follow we learn a great deal about those. At the end of the section the speech of the third of the Thames-nymphs summarizes the whole matter for us.

The waters of the Thames are also associated with those of Leman—the poet in the contemporary waste land is in a sort of Babylonian Captivity.

The castle of the Fisher King was always located on the banks of a river or on the sea shore. The title "Fisher King," Miss Weston shows, originates from the use of the fish as a fertility or life symbol. This meaning, however, was often forgotten, and so his title in many of the later Grail romances is accounted for by describing the king as fishing. Eliot uses the reference to fishing for reverse effect. The reference to fishing is part of the realistic detail of the scene—"While I was fishing in the dull canal." But to the reader who knows the Weston references, the reference is to that of the Fisher King of the Grail legends. The protagonist is the maimed and impotent king of the legends.

Eliot proceeds now to tie the waste-land symbol to that of *The Tempest,* by quoting one of the lines spoken by Ferdinand, Prince of Naples, which occurs just before Ariel's song, "Full Fathom Five," is heard. But he alters *The Tempest* passage somewhat, writing not, "Weeping again the king my father's wreck," but

> Musing upon the king my brother's wreck
> And on the king my father's death before him.

It is possible that the alteration has been made to bring the account taken from *The Tempest* into accord with the situation in the Percival stories. In Wolfram von Eschenbach's *Parzival,* for instance, Trevrezent, the hermit, is the brother of the Fisher King, Anfortas. He tells Parzival, "His name all men know as Anfortas, and I weep for him evermore." Their father, Frimutel, is dead.

The protagonist in the poem, then, imagines himself not only in the situation of Ferdinand in *The Tempest* but also in that of one of the characters in the Grail legend; and the wreck, to be applied literally in the first instance, applies metaphorically in the second.

After the lines from *The Tempest,* appears again the image of a sterile death from which no life comes, the bones, "rattled by the rat's foot only, year to year." (The collocation of this figure with the vision of the death by water in Ariel's song has already been commented on. The lines quoted from *The Tempest* come just before the song.)

The allusion to Marvell's "To His Coy Mistress" is of course one of the easiest allusions in the poem. Instead of "Time's winged chariot" the poet hears "the sound of horns and motors" of contemporary London. But the passage has been further complicated. The reference has been combined with an allusion to Day's "Parliament of Bees." "Time's winged chariot" of Marvell has not only been changed to the modern automobile; Day's "sound of horns and hunting" has changed to the horns of the motors. And Actaeon will not be brought face to face with Diana, goddess of chastity; Sweeny, type of the vulgar bourgeois, is to be brought to Mrs. Porter, hardly a type of chastity. The reference in the ballad to the feet "washed in soda water" reminds the poet ironically of another sort of foot-washing, the sound of the children singing in the dome heard at the ceremony of the foot-washing which precedes the restoration of the wounded Anfortas (the Fisher King) by Parzival and the taking away of the curse from the waste land. The quotation thus completes the allusion to the Fisher King commenced in line 189—"While I was fishing in the dull canal."

The pure song of the children also reminds the poet of the song of the nightingale which we have heard in "The Game of Chess." The recapitulation of symbols is continued with a repetition of "Unreal city" and with the reference to the one-eyed merchant.

Mr. Eugenides, the Smyrna merchant, is the one-eyed merchant mentioned by Madame Sosostris. (pp. 151-53)

The Syrian merchants, we learn from Miss Weston's book, were, along with slaves and soldiers, the principal carriers of the mysteries which lie at the core of the Grail legends. But in the modern world we find both the representatives of the Tarot divining and the mystery cults in decay. What he carries on his back and what the fortune-teller is forbidden to see is evidently the knowledge of the mysteries (although Mr. Eugenides himself is hardly likely to be more aware of it than Madame Sosostris is aware of the importance of her function). Mr. Eugenides, in terms of his former function, ought to be inviting the protagonist into the esoteric cult which holds the secret of life, but on the realistic surface of the poem, in his invitation to "a weekend at the Metropole" he is really inviting him to a homosexual debauch. The homosexuality is "secret" and now a "cult" but a very different cult from that which Mr. Eugenides ought to represent. The end of the new cult is not life but, ironically, sterility.

In the modern waste land, however, even the relation between man and woman is also sterile. The incident between the typist and the carbuncular young man is a picture of "love" so exclusively and practically pursued that it is not love at all. The tragic chorus to the scene is Tiresias, into whom perhaps Mr. Eugenides may be said to modulate, Tiresias, the historical "expert" on the relation between the sexes.

The fact that Tiresias is made the commentator serves a further irony. In *Oedipus Rex,* it is Tiresias who recognizes that the curse which has come upon the Theban land has been caused by the sinful sexual relationship of Oedipus and Jocasta. But Oedipus' sin has been committed in ignorance, and knowledge of it brings horror and remorse. The essential horror of the act which Tiresias witnesses in the poem is that it is not regarded as a sin at all—is perfectly casual, is merely the copulation of beasts.

The reminiscence of the lines from Goldsmith's song in the description of the young woman's actions after the departure of her lover, gives concretely and ironically the utter breakdown of traditional standards.

It is the music of her gramophone which the protagonist hears "creep by" him "on the waters." Far from the music which Ferdinand heard bringing him to Miranda and love, it is, one is tempted to think, the music of "O O O O that Shakespeherian Rag."

But the protagonist says that he can *sometimes* hear "the pleasant whining of a mandoline." Significantly enough, it is the music of the fishmen (the fish again as a life symbol) and it comes from beside a church (though—if this is not to rely too much on Eliot's note—the church has been marked for destruction). Life on Lower Thames Street, if not on the Strand, still has meaning as it cannot have meaning for either the typist or the rich woman of "A Game of Chess."

The song of the Thames-daughters brings us back to the opening section of "The Fire Sermon" again, and once more we have to do with the river and the river-nymphs. Indeed, the typist incident is framed by the two river-nymph scenes.

The connection of the river-nymphs with the Rhine-daughters of Wagner's *Götterdämerung* is easily made. In the passage in Wagner's opera (to which Eliot refers in his note), the opening of Act III, the Rhine-daughters bewail the loss of the beauty of the Rhine occasioned by the theft of the gold, and then beg Siegfried to give them back the Ring made from this gold, finally threatening him with death if he does not give it up. Like the Thames-daughters they too have been violated; and like the maidens mentioned in the Grail legend, the violation has brought a curse on gods and men. The first of the songs depicts the modern river, soiled with oil and tar. (Compare also with the description of the river in the first part of "The Fire Sermon.") The second song depicts the Elizabethan river, also evoked in the first part of "The Fire Sermon." (Leicester and Elizabeth ride upon it in a barge of state. Incidentally, Spenser's "Prothalamion" from which quotation is made in the first part of "The Fire Sermon" mentions Leicester as having formerly lived in the house which forms the setting of the poem.) (pp. 153-55)

The third Thames-daughter's song depicts another sordid "love" affair, and unites the themes of the first two songs. It begins "Trams and *dusty* trees." With it we are definitely in the waste land again. Pia, whose words she echoes in saying "Highbury bore me. Richmond and Kew / Undid me" was in Purgatory and had hope. The woman speaking here has no hope—she too is in the Inferno: "I can connect / Nothing with nothing." (p. 156)

The songs of the three Thames-daughters, as a matter of fact, epitomize this whole section of the poem. With reference to the quotations from St. Augustine and Buddha at the end of "The Fire Sermon" Eliot states that "the collocation of these two representatives of eastern and western asceticism, as the culmination of this part of the poem, is not an accident."

It is certainly not an accident. The moral of all the incidents which we have been witnessing is that there must be an asceticism—something to check the drive of desire. The wisdom of the East and the West comes to the same thing on this point. Moreover, the imagery which both St. Augustine and Buddha use for lust is fire. What we have witnessed in the various scenes of "The Fire Sermon" is the sterile burning of lust. Modern man, freed from all restraints, in his cultivation of experience for experience's sake burns, but not with a "hard and gemlike flame." One ought not to pound the point home in this fashion, but to see that the imagery of this section of the poem furnishes illustrations leading up to the Fire Sermon is the necessary requirement for feeling the force of the brief allusions here at the end to Buddha and St. Augustine.

Whatever the specific meaning of the symbols, the general function of the section, "Death by Water," is readily apparent. The section forms a contrast with "The Fire Sermon" which precedes it—a contrast between the symbolism of fire and that of water. Also readily apparent is its force as a symbol of surrender and relief through surrender.

Some specific connections can be made, however. The drowned Phoenician Sailor recalls the drowned god of the fertility cults. (pp. 157-58)

Moreover, the Phoenician Sailor is a merchant. . . . The vision of the drowned sailor gives a statement of the message which the Syrian merchants originally brought to Britain and which the Smyrna merchant, unconsciously and by ironical negatives, has brought. One of Eliot's notes states that the "merchant . . . melts into the Phoenician Sailor, and the latter is not wholly distinct from Ferdinand Prince of Naples." The death by water would seem to be equated with the death described in Ariel's song in *The Tempest*. There is a definite difference in the tone of the description of this death—"A current under sea / Picked his bones in whispers," as compared with the "other" death—"bones cast in a little low dry garret, / Rattled by the rat's foot only, year to year."

Further than this it would not be safe to go, but one may point out that whirling (the whirlpool here, the Wheel of Madame Sosostris' palaver) is one of Eliot's symbols frequently used in other poems (**Ash Wednesday, "Gerontion," Murder in the Cathedral,** and **"Burnt Norton"**) to denote the temporal world. . . . At least, with a kind of hindsight, one may suggest that "Death by Water" gives an instance of the conquest of death and time, the "perpetual recurrence of determined seasons," the "world of spring and autumn, birth and dying" through death itself.

The reference to the "torchlight red on sweaty faces" and to the "frosty silence in the gardens" obviously associates Christ in Gethsemane with the other hanged gods. The god has now died, and in referring to this, the basic theme finds another strong restatement:

> He who was living is now dead
> We who were living are now dying
> With a little patience

The poet does not say "We who *are* living." It is "We who *were* living." It is the death-in-life of Dante's Limbo. Life in the full sense has been lost.

The passage on the sterility of the waste land and the lack of water provides for the introduction later of two highly important passages:

> There is not even silence in the mountains
> But dry sterile thunder without rain—

lines which look forward to the introduction later of "what the thunder said" when the thunder, no longer sterile, but bringing rain, speaks.

The second of these passages is, "There is not even solitude in the mountains," which looks forward to the reference to the Journey to Emmaus theme a few lines later: "Who is the third who walks always beside you?" The god has returned, has risen, but the travelers cannot tell whether it is really he, or mere illusion induced by their delirium.

The parallelism between the "hooded figure" who "walks always beside you," and the "hooded hordes" is another instance of the sort of parallelism that is really a contrast. In the first case, the figure is indistinct because spiritual; in the second, the hooded hordes are indistinct because completely *unspiritual*—they are the people of the waste land—

> Shape without form, shade without colour,
> Paralysed force, gesture without motion—

to take two lines from **"The Hollow Men,"** where the people of the waste land once more appear. Or to take another line from the same poem, perhaps their hoods are the "deliberate disguises" which the Hollow Men, the people of the waste land, wear.

Eliot, as his notes tell us, has particularly connected the description here with the "decay of eastern Europe." The hordes represent, then, the general waste land of the modern world with a special application to the breakup of Eastern Europe, the region with which the fertility cults were especially connected and in which today the traditional values are thoroughly discredited. The cities, Jerusalem, Athens, Alexandria, Vienna, like the London of the first section of the poem are "unreal," and for the same reason.

The passage which immediately follows develops the unreality into nightmare, but it is a nightmare vision which is something more than an extension of the passage beginning, "What is the city over the mountains"—in it appear other figures from earlier in the poem: the lady of "A Game of Chess," who, surrounded by the glory of history and art, sees no meaning in either and threatens to rush out into the street "With my hair down, so," has here let down her hair and fiddles "whisper music on those strings." One remembers in "A Game of Chess" that it was the woman's hair that spoke. . . . The hair has been immemorially a symbol of fertility, and Miss Weston and Frazer mention sacrifices of hair in order to aid the fertility god. (pp. 158-61)

The "violet light" also deserves comment. In "The Fire Sermon" it is twice mentioned as the "violet hour," and there it has little more than a physical meaning. It is a description of the hour of twilight. Here it indicates the twilight of the civilization, but it is perhaps something more. Violet is one of the liturgical colors of the Church. It symbolizes repentance and it is the color of baptism. The visit to the Perilous Chapel, according to Miss Weston, was an initiation—that is, a baptism. In the nightmare vision, the bats wear baby faces.

The horror built up in this passage is a proper preparation for the passage on the Perilous Chapel which follows it. The journey has not been merely an agonized walk in the desert, though it is that; nor is it merely the journey after the god has died and hope has been lost; it is also the journey to the Perilous Chapel of the Grail story. In Miss Weston's account, the Chapel was part of the ritual, and was filled with horrors to test the candidate's courage. In some stories the perilous cemetery is also mentioned. Eliot has used both: "Over the tum-

bled graves, about the chapel." In many of the Grail stories the Chapel was haunted by demons.

The cock in the folk-lore of many people is regarded as the bird whose voice chases away the powers of evil. It is significant that it is after his crow that the flash of lightning comes and the "damp gust / Bringing rain." It is just possible that the cock has a connection also with *The Tempest* symbols. The first song which Ariel sings to Ferdinand as he sits "Weeping again the king my father's wreck" ends

> The strain of strutting chanticleer,
> Cry, cock-a-doodle-doo.

The next stanza is the "Full Fathom Five" song which Eliot has used as a vision of life gained through death. If this relation holds, here we have an extreme instance of an allusion, in itself innocent, forced into serious meaning through transference to a new context.

As Miss Weston has shown, the fertility cults go back to a very early period and are recorded in Sanscrit legends. Eliot has been continually, in the poem, linking up the Christian doctrine with the beliefs of as many peoples as he can. Here he goes back to the very beginnings of Aryan culture, and tells the rest of the story of the rain's coming, not in terms of the setting already developed but in its earliest form. The passage is thus a perfect parallel in method to the passage in "The Burial of the Dead":

> You who were with me in the ships *at Mylae!*
> That corpse you planted *last year* in your garden . . .

The use of Sanscrit in what the thunder says is thus accounted for. In addition, there is of course a more obvious reason for casting what the thunder said into Sanscrit here: onomatopoeia.

The comments on the three statements of the thunder imply an acceptance of them. The protagonist answers the first question, "What have we given?" with the statement:

> The awful daring of a moment's surrender
> Which an age of prudence can never retract
> By this, and this only, we have existed.

Here the larger meaning is stated in terms which imply the sexual meaning. Man cannot be absolutely self-regarding. Even the propagation of the race—even mere "existence"— calls for such a surrender. Living calls for—see the passage already quoted from Eliot's essay on Baudelaire—belief in something more than "life."

The comment on *dayadhvam* (sympathize) is obviously connected with the foregoing passage. The surrender to something outside the self is an attempt (whether on the sexual level or some other) to transcend one's essential isolation. (pp. 161-63)

The third statement made by the thunder, *damyata* (control), follows the condition necessary for control, sympathy. The figure of the boat catches up the figure of control already given in "Death by Water"—"O you who turn the wheel and look to windward"—and from "The Burial of the Dead" the figure of happy love in which the ship rushes on with a fair wind behind it: *"Frisch weht der Wind . . ."*

I cannot accept Mr. Leavis' interpretation of the passage, "I sat upon the shore / Fishing, with the arid plain behind me," as meaning that the poem "exhibits no progression." The comment upon what the thunder says would indicate, if other passages did not, that the poem does "not end where it began." It is true that the protagonist does not witness a revival of the waste land; but there are two important relationships involved in his case: a personal one as well as a general one. If secularization has destroyed, or is likely to destroy, modern civilization, the protagonist still has a private obligation to fulfill. Even if the civilization is breaking up—"London Bridge is falling down falling down falling down"—there remains the personal obligation: "Shall I at least set my lands in order?" (pp. 163-64)

The bundle of quotations with which the poem ends has a very definite relation to the general theme of the poem and to several of the major symbols used in the poem. Before Arnaut leaps back into the refining fire of Purgatory with joy he says: "I am Arnaut who weep and go singing; contrite I see my past folly, and joyful I see before me the day I hope for. Now I pray you by that virtue which guides you to the summit of the stair, at times be mindful of my pain." This theme is carried forward by the quotation from *Pervigilium Veneris:* "When shall I be like the swallow." The allusion is also connected with the Philomela symbol. (Eliot's note on the passage indicates this clearly.) The sister of Philomela was changed into a swallow as Philomela was changed into a nightingale. The protagonist is asking therefore when shall the spring, the time of love, return, but also when will he be reborn out of his sufferings, and—with the special meaning which the symbol takes on from the preceding Dante quotation and from the earlier contexts already discussed—he is asking what is asked at the end of one of the minor poems: "When will Time flow away."(p. 164)

The ruined tower is perhaps also the Perilous Chapel, "only the wind's home," and it is also the whole tradition in decay. The protagonist resolves to claim his tradition and rehabilitate it.

The quotation from *The Spanish Tragedy*—"Why then Ile fit you. Hieronymo's mad againe"—is perhaps the most puzzling of all these quotations. It means, I believe, this: The protagonist's acceptance of what is in reality the deepest truth will seem to the present world mere madness. ("And still she cried . . . 'Jug Jug' to dirty ears.") Hieronymo in the play, like Hamlet, was "mad" for a purpose. The protagonist is conscious of the interpretation which will be placed on the words which follow—words which will seem to many apparently meaningless babble, but which contain the oldest and most permanent truth of the race:

> Datta. Dayadhvam. Damyata.

Quotation of the whole context from which the line is taken confirms this interpretation. Hieronymo, asked to write a play for the court's entertainment, replies:

> Why then, I'll fit you; say no more.
> When I was young, I gave my mind
> And plied myself to fruitless poetry;
> Which though it profit the professor naught,
> Yet it is passing pleasing to the world.

He sees that the play will give him the opportunity he has been seeking to avenge his son's murder. Like Hieronymo, the protagonist in the poem has found his theme; what he is about to perform is not "fruitless."

After this repetition of what the thunder said comes the benediction:

> Shantih   Shantih   Shantih

The foregoing account of *The Waste Land* is, of course, not to be substituted for the poem itself. Moreover, it certainly is not to be considered as representing *the method by which the poem was composed.* Much which the prose expositor must represent as though it had been consciously contrived obviously was arrived at unconsciously and concretely.

The account given above is a statement merely of the "prose meaning," and bears the same relation to the poem as does the "prose meaning" of any other poem. But one need not perhaps apologize for setting forth such a statement explicitly, for *The Waste Land* has been almost consistently misinterpreted since its first publication. (pp. 164-66)

> *Cleanth Brooks, " 'The Waste Land': Critique of the Myth," in his* Modern Poetry and the Tradition, *The University of North Carolina Press, 1939, pp. 136-72.*

DELMORE SCHWARTZ

A culture hero is one who brings new arts and skills to mankind. Prometheus was a culture hero and the inventors of the radio may also be said to be culture heroes, although this is hardly to be confounded with the culture made available by the radio.

The inventors of the radio made possible a new range of experience. This is true of certain authors; for example, it is true of Wordsworth in regard to nature, and Proust in regard to time. It is not true of Shakespeare, but by contrast it is true of Surrey and the early Elizabethan playwrights who invented blank verse. Thus the most important authors are not always culture heroes, and thus no rank, stature, or scope is of necessity implicit in speaking of the author as a culture hero.

When we speak of nature and of a new range of experience, we may think of a mountain range: some may make the vehicles by means of which a mountain is climbed, some may climb the mountain, and some may apprehend the new view of the surrounding countryside which becomes possible from the heights of the mountain. T. S. Eliot is a culture hero in each of these three ways. This becomes clear when we study the relationship of his work to the possible experiences of modern life. The term, possible, should be kept in mind, for many human beings obviously disregard and turn their backs upon much of modern life, although modern life does not in the least cease to circumscribe and penetrate their existence.

The reader of T. S. Eliot by turning the dials of his radio can hear the capitals of the world, London, Vienna, Athens, Alexandria, Jerusalem. What he hears will be news of the agony of war. Both the agony and the width of this experience are vivid examples of how the poetry of T. S. Eliot has a direct relationship to modern life. The width and the height and the depth of modern life are exhibited in his poetry; the agony and the horror of modern life are represented as inevitable to any human being who does not wish to deceive himself with systematic lies. Thus it is truly significant that E. M. Forster, in writing of Eliot, should recall August 1914 and the beginning of the First World War; it is just as significant that he should speak of first reading Eliot's poems in Alexandria, Egypt, during that war, and that he should conclude by saying that Eliot was one who had looked into the abyss and refused henceforward to deny or forget the fact. (pp. 199-200)

Philip Rahv has shown how the heroine of Henry James is best understood as the heiress of all the ages. So, in a further sense, the true protagonist of Eliot's poems is the heir of all the ages. He is the descendant of the essential characters of James in that he is the American who visits Europe with a Baedeker in his hand, just like Isabel Archer. But the further sense in which he is the heir of all the ages is illustrated when Eliot describes the seduction of a typist in a London flat from the point of view of Tiresias, a character in a play by Sophocles. To suppose that this is the mere exhibition of learning or reading is a banal misunderstanding. The important point is that the presence of Tiresias illuminates the seduction of the typist just as much as a description of her room. Hence Eliot writes in his notes to *The Waste Land* that "what Tiresias *sees* is the substance of the poem." The illumination of the ages is available at any moment, and when the typist's indifference and boredom in the act of love must be represented, it is possible for Eliot to invoke and paraphrase a lyric from a play by Oliver Goldsmith. Literary allusion has become not merely a Miltonic reference to Greek gods and Old Testament geography, not merely the citation of parallels, but a powerful and inevitable habit of mind, a habit which issues in judgment and the representation of different levels of experience, past and present.

James supposed that his theme was the international theme: would it not be more precise to speak of it as the transatlantic theme? This effort at a greater exactness defines what is involved in Eliot's work. Henry James was concerned with the American in Europe. Eliot cannot help but be concerned with the whole world and all history. Tiresias sees the nature of love in all times and all places and when Sweeney outwits a scheming whore, the fate of Agamemnon becomes relevant. So too, in the same way exactly, Eliot must recognize and use a correspondence between St. Augustine and Buddha in speaking of sensuality. And thus, as he writes again in his notes to *The Waste Land,* "The collocation of these two representatives of eastern and western asceticism as the culmination of this part of the poem is not an accident." And it is not an accident that the international hero should have come from St. Louis, Missouri, or at any rate from America. Only an American with a mind and sensibility which is cosmopolitan and expatriated could have seen Europe as it is seen in *The Waste Land.*

A literary work may be important in many ways, but surely one of the ways in which it is important is in its relationship to some important human interest or need, or in its relationship to some new aspect of human existence. Eliot's work is important in relationship to the fact that experience has become international. We have become an international people, and hence an international hero is possible. Just as the war is international, so the true causes of many of the things in our lives are world-wide, and we are able to understand the character of our lives only when we are aware of all history, of the philosophy of history, of primitive peoples and the Russian Revolution, of ancient Egypt and the unconscious mind. Thus again it is no accident that in *The Waste Land* use is made of *The Golden Bough,* and a book on the quest of the Grail; and the way in which images and associations appear in the poem illustrates a new view of consciousness, the depths of consciousness and the unconscious mind.

The protagonist of *The Waste Land* stands on the banks of the Thames and quotes the Upanishads, and this very quotation, the command to "give, sympathize, and control," makes possible a comprehensive insight into the difficulty of his life in the present. But this emphasis upon one poem of Eliot's may be misleading. What is true of much of his poetry is also true of his criticism. When the critic writes of tradition and the individual talent, when he declares the necessity for the author of a consciousness of the past as far back as Homer, when he brings the reader back to Dante, the Elizabethans and Andrew Marvell, he is also speaking as the heir of all the ages.

The emphasis on a consciousness of literature may also be misleading, for nowhere better than in Eliot can we see the difference between being merely literary and making the knowledge of literature an element in vision, that is to say, an essential part of the process of seeing anything and everything. Thus, to cite the advent of Tiresias again, the literary character of his appearance is matched by the unliterary actuality by means of which he refers to himself as being "like a taxi throbbing waiting." In one way, the subject of *The Waste Land* is the sensibility of the protagonist, a sensibility which is literary, philosophical, cosmopolitan and expatriated. But this sensibility is concerned not with itself as such, but with the common things of modern life, with two such important aspects of existence as religious belief and making love. To summon to mind such profound witnesses as Freud and D. H. Lawrence is to remember how often, in modern life, love has been the worst sickness of human beings. (pp. 200-02)

In *The Waste Land,* the theme of love as a failure is again uppermost. Two lovers return from a garden after a moment of love, and the woman is overcome by despair or pathological despondency. A lady, perhaps the same woman who has returned from the garden in despair, becomes hysterical in her boudoir because her lover or her husband has nothing to say to her and cannot give her life any meaning or interest: "What shall I do now?" she says, "what shall I ever do?" The neurasthenic lady is succeeded in the poem by cockney women who gossip about another cockney woman who has been made ill by contraceptive pills taken to avoid the consequences of love; which is to say that the sickness of love has struck down every class in society: "What you get married for, if you don't want children?" And then we witness the seduction of the typist; and then other aspects of the sickness of love appear when, on the Thames bank, three girls ruined by love rehearse the sins of the young men with whom they have been having affairs. In the last part of the poem, the impossibility of love, the gulf between one human being and another, is the answer to the command to give, that is to say, to give oneself or surrender oneself to another human being in the act of making love. (pp. 202-03)

Difficulty in love is inseparable from the deracination and the alienation from which the international man suffers. When the traditional beliefs, sanctions and bonds of the community and of the family decay or disappear in the distance like a receding harbor, then love ceases to be an act which is in relation to the life of the community, and in immediate relation to the family and other human beings. Love becomes purely personal. It is isolated from the past and the future, and since it is isolated from all other relationships, since it is no longer celebrated, evaluated and given a status by the community, love does become merely copulation. The protagonist of "Gerontion" uses one of the most significant phrases in Eliot's work when he speaks of himself as living in a *rented* house; which is to say, not in the house where his forbears lived. He lives in a rented house, he is unable to make love, and he knows that history has many cunning, deceptive, and empty corridors. The nature of the house, of love and of history are interdependent aspects of modern life.

When we compare Eliot's poetry to the poetry of Valèry, Yeats and Rilke, Eliot's direct and comprehensive concern with the essential nature of modern life gains an external definition. Yeats writes of Leda and he writes of the nature of history; Valèry writes of Narcissus and the serpent in the Garden of Eden; Rilke is inspired by great works of art, by Christ's mother and by Orpheus. Yet in each of these authors the subject is transformed into a timeless essence. The heritage of Western culture is available to these authors and they use it many beautiful ways; but the fate of Western culture and the historical sense as such does not become an important part of their poetry. And then if we compare Eliot with Auden and with Pound, a further definition becomes clear. In his early work, Auden is inspired by an international crisis in a social and political sense; in his new work, he writes as a teacher and preacher and secular theologian. In neither period is all history and all culture a necessary part of the subject or the sensibility which is dealing with the subject. With Pound, we come closer to Eliot and the closeness sharpens the difference. Pound is an American in Europe too, and Pound, not Eliot, was the first to grasp the historical and international dimension of experience, as we can see in an early effort of his to explain the method of the *Cantos* and the internal structure of each *Canto:* "All times are contemporaneous," he wrote, and in the *Cantos,* he attempts to deal with all history as if it were part of the present. But he fails; he remains for the most part an American in Europe, and the *Cantos* are never more than a book of souvenirs of a tour of the world and a tour of culture.

To be international is to be a citizen of the world and thus a citizen of no particular city. The world as such is not a community and it has no constitution or government: it is the turning world in which the human being, surrounded by the consequences of all times and all places, must live his life as a human being and not as the citizen of any nation. Hence, to be the heir of all the ages is to inherit nothing but a consciousness of how all heirlooms are rooted in the past. Dominated by the historical consciousness, the international hero finds that all beliefs affect the holding of any belief (he cannot think of Christianity without remembering Adonis); he finds that many languages affect each use of speech (*The Waste Land* concludes with a passage in four languages).

When nationalism attempts to renew itself, it can do so only through the throes of war. And when nationalism in America attempts to become articulate, when a poet like Carl Sandburg writes that "The past is a bucket of ashes," or when Henry Ford makes the purely American remark that "History is the bunk," we have only to remember such a pilgrimage as that of Ford in the Peace Ship in which he attempted to bring the First World War to an end in order to see that anyone can say whatever he likes: no matter what anyone says, existence has become international for everyone.

Eliot's political and religious affirmations are at another extreme, and they do not resemble Ford's quixotic pilgrimage except as illustrating the starting-point of the modern American, and his inevitable journey to Europe. What should be made explicit here is that only one who has known fully the deracination and alienation inherent in modern life can be moved to make so extreme an effort at returning to the tradi-

tional community as Eliot makes in attaching himself to Anglo-Catholicism and Royalism. Coming back may well be the same thing as going away; or at any rate, the effort to return home may exhibit the same predicament and the same topography as the fact of departure. Only by going to Europe, by crossing the Atlantic and living thousands of miles from home, does the international hero conceive of the complex nature of going home.

Modern life may be compared to a foreign country in which a foreign language is spoken. Eliot is the international hero because he has made the journey to the foreign country and described the nature of the new life in the foreign country. Since the future is bound to be international, if it is anything at all, we are all the bankrupt heirs of the ages, and the moments of the crisis expressed in Eliot's work are a prophecy of the crisis of our own future in regard to love, religious belief, good and evil, the good life and the nature of the just society. *The Waste Land* will soon be as good as new. (pp. 204-06)

Delmore Schwartz, "T. S. Eliot as the International Hero," in Partisan Review, *Vol. XII, No. 2, Spring, 1945, pp. 199-206.*

HUGH KENNER

The Waste Land was drafted during a rest cure at Margate ("I can connect / Nothing with nothing") and Lausanne ("In this decayed hole among the mountains") during the autumn of 1921 by a convalescent preoccupied partly with the ruin of post-war Europe, partly with his own health and the conditions of his servitude to a bank in London, partly with a hardly exorable apprehension that two thousand years of European continuity had for the first time run dry. It had for epigraph a phrase from Conrad's *Heart of Darkness* ("The horror! The horror!"); embedded in the text were a glimpse, borrowed from Conrad's opening page, of the red sails of barges drifting in the Thames Estuary, and a contrasting reference to "the heart of light." "Nothing is easier," Conrad had written, ". . . than to evoke the great spirit of the past upon the lower reaches of the Thames."

In Paris that winter, Ezra Pound has recalled, *"The Waste Land* was placed before me as a series of poems. I advised him what to leave out." Eliot, from about the same distance of time, recalls showing Pound "a sprawling chaotic poem . . . which left his hands, reduced to about half its size, in the form in which it appears in print." (pp. 145-46)

[*The Waste Land*] was conceived as a somewhat loose medley, as the relief of more diffuse impulses than those to which its present compacted form corresponds. (pp. 147-48)

[The] first quality of *The Waste Land* to catch a newcomer's attention, its self-sufficient juxtaposition without copulae of themes and passages in a dense mosaic, had at first a novelty which troubled even the author. It was a quality arrived at by Pound's cutting; it didn't trouble Pound, who had already begun work on *The Cantos*. But Eliot, preoccupied as always with the seventeenth-century drama and no doubt tacitly encouraged by the example of Browning, naturally conceived a long poem as somebody's spoken or unspoken monologue, its shifts of direction and transition from theme to theme psychologically justified by the workings of the speaker's brain. **"Prufrock"** and **"Gerontion"** elucidate not only a phase of civilization but a perceiving—for the purpose of the poem, a presiding—consciousness. For anyone who has undergone immersion in the delicate phenomenology of Francis Herbert Bradley, in fact, it is meaningless to conceive of a presentation that cannot be resolved into an experienced content and a "finite center" which experiences. The perceiver is describable only as the zone of consciousness where that which he perceives can coexist; but the perceived, conversely, can't be accorded independent status; it is, precisely, all that can coexist in this particular zone of consciousness. In a loose sequence of poems these considerations need give no trouble; the pervading zone of consciousness is that of the author: as we intuit Herrick in *Hesperides,* or Herbert in *The Temple.* But a five-parted work of 434 lines entitled *The Waste Land,* with sudden wrenching juxtapositions, thematic links between section and section, fragments quoted from several languages with no one present to whose mind they can occur: this dense textural unity, as queer as *Le Sacre du Printemps,* must have seemed to Eliot a little factitious until he had gotten used to the poem in its final form; which, as everyone who has encountered it knows, must take some time. So we discover him endeavoring to square the artistic fact with his pervasive intuition of fitness by the note on Tiresias, which offers to supply the poem with a nameable point of view:

> Tiresias, although a mere spectator and not indeed a "character," is yet the most important personage in the poem, uniting all the rest. Just as the one-eyed merchant, seller of currants, melts into the Phoenician Sailor, and the latter is not wholly distinct from Ferdinand Prince of Naples, so all the women are one woman, and the two sexes meet in Tiresias. What Tiresias *sees,* in fact, is the substance of the poem.

If we take this note as an afterthought, a token placation, say, of the ghost of Bradley, rather than as elucidative of the assumption under which the writing was originally done, our approach to *The Waste Land* will be facilitated. In fact we shall do well to discard the notes as much as possible; they have bedevilled discussion for decades.

The writing of the notes was a last complication in the fractious history of the poem's composition; it is doubtful whether any other acknowledged masterpiece has been so heavily marked, with the author's consent, by forces outside his control. The notes got added to *The Waste Land* as a consequence of the technological fact that books are printed in multiples of thirty-two pages. (pp. 148-50)

"A Game of Chess" is a convenient place to start our investigations. Chess is played with Queens and Pawns: the set of pieces mimics a social hierarchy, running from "The Chair she sat in, like a burnished throne," to "Goonight Bill. Goonight Lou. Goonight May. Goonight." It is a silent unnerving warfare

> ("Speak to me. Why do you never speak. Speak.
> "What are you thinking of? What thinking? What?
> "I never know what you are thinking. Think.")

in which everything hinges on the welfare of the King, the weakest piece on the board, and in this section of the poem invisible (though a "barbarous king" once forced Philomel.) Our attention is focused on the Queen.

> The Chair she sat in, like a burnished throne,
> Glowed on the marble, where the glass
> Held up by standards wrought with fruited vines
> From which a golden Cupidon peeped out

> (Another hid his eyes behind his wing)
> Doubled the flames of sevenbranched candelabra
> Reflecting light upon the table as
> The glitter of her jewels rose to meet it,
> From satin cases poured in rich profusion. . . .

This isn't a Miltonic sentence, brilliantly contorted; it lacks nerve, forgetting after ten words its confident opening ("The Chair she sat in") to dissipate itself among glowing and smouldering sensations, like a progression of Wagner's. . . . The woman at the dressing-table in *The Waste Land,* implied but never named or attended to, is not like Belinda [in Alexander Pope's *The Rape of the Lock*] the moral center of an innocent dislocation of values, but simply the implied sensibility in which these multifarious effects dissolve and find congruence. All things deny nature; the fruited vines are carved, the Cupidons golden, the light not of the sun, the perfumes synthetic, the candelabra (seven-branched, as for an altar) devoted to no rite, the very color of the fire-light perverted by sodium and copper salts. The dolphin is carved, and swims in a "sad light," not, like Antony's delights, "showing his back above the element he lives in."

No will to exploit new sensations is present; the will has long ago died; this opulent ambience is neither chosen nor questioned. The "sylvan scene" is not Eden nor a window but a painting, and a painting of an unnatural event:

> The change of Philomel, by the barbarous king
> So rudely forced; yet there the nightingale
> Filled all the desert with inviolable voice
> And still she cried, and still the world pursues,
> "Jug Jug" to dirty ears.

Her voice alone, like the voice that modulates the thick fluid of this sentence, is "inviolable"; like Tiresias in Thebes, she is prevented from identifying the criminal whom only she can name. John Lyly wrote down her song more than two centuries before Keats (who wasn't interested in what she was saying):

> What bird so sings yet so dos wayle?
> O 'Tis the ravished Nightingale.
> Jug, Jug, Jug, tereu, shee cryes,
> And still her woes at Midnight rise.
> Brave prick song! . . .

Lyly, not being committed to the idea that the bird was pouring forth its soul abroad, noted that it stuck to its script ("prick song") and himself attempted a transcription. Lyly of course is perfectly aware of what she is trying to say: "tereu" comes very close to "Tereus." It remained for the nineteenth century to dissolve her plight into a symbol of diffuse *Angst,* indeed to impute "ecstasy" amid human desolation, "here, where men sit and hear each other groan"; and for the twentieth century to hang up a painting of the event on a dressing-room wall, as pungent sauce to appetites jaded with the narrative clarity of mythologies, but responsive to the visceral thrill and the pressures of "significant form." The picture, a "withered stump of time," hangs there, one item in a collection that manages to be not edifying but sinister. . . . [In] this room the European past, effects and *objets d'art* gathered from many centuries, has suffered a sea-change, into something rich and strange, and stifling. Sensibility here is the very inhibition of life; and activity is reduced to the manic capering of "that Shakespeherian Rag," the past imposing no austerity, existing simply to be used.

> "What shall we do tomorrow?

> "What shall we ever do?"
>   The hot water at ten.
> And if it rains, a closed car at four.
> And we shall play a game of chess,
> Pressing lidless eyes and waiting for a knock upon
>   the door.

If we move from the queens to the pawns, we find low life no more free or natural, equally obsessed with the denial of nature, artificial teeth, chemically procured abortions, the speaker and her interlocutor battening fascinated at second-hand on the life of Lil and her Albert, Lil and Albert interested only in spurious ideal images of one another . . . this point is made implicitly by a device carried over from *Whispers of Immortality,* the juxtaposition without comment or copula of two levels of sensibility: the world of one who reads Webster with the world of one who knows Grishkin, the world of the inquiring wind and the sense drowned in odors with the world of ivory teeth and hot gammon. In Lil and Albert's milieu there is fertility, in the milieu where golden Cupidons peep out there is not; but Lil and Albert's breeding betokens not a harmony of wills but only Albert's improvident refusal to leave Lil alone. The chemist with commercial impartiality supplies one woman with "strange synthetic perfumes" and the other with "them pills I took, to bring it off," aphrodisiacs and abortifacients; he is the tutelary deity, uniting the offices of Cupid and Hymen, of a world which is under a universal curse.

From this vantage-point we can survey the methods of the first section, which opens with a denial of Chaucer:

> Whan that Aprille with his shoures soote
> The droughte of March hath perced to the roote
> And bathed every veyne in swich licour
> Of which vertu engendred is the flour. . . .
> Thanne longen folk to goon on pilgrimages. . . .

In the twentieth-century version we have a prayer-book heading, "The Burial of the Dead," with its implied ceremonial of dust thrown and of souls reborn; and the poem begins,

> April is the cruellest month, breeding
> Lilacs out of the dead land, mixing
> Memory and desire, stirring
> Dull roots with spring rain.

No "vertu" is engendered amid this apprehensive reaching forward of participles, and instead of pilgrimages we have European tours:

>   we stopped in the colonnade,
> And went on in sunlight, into the Hofgarten,
> And drank coffee, and talked for an hour.

Up out of the incantation breaks a woman's voice, giving tongue to the ethnological confusions of the new Europe, the subservience of *patria* to the whim of statesmen, the interplay of immutable fact and national pride:

> Bin gar keine Russin, stamm' aus Litauen, echt deutsch.

—a mixing of memory and desire. Another voice evokes the vanished Austro-Hungarian Empire, the inbred malaise of Mayerling, regressive thrills, objectless travels:

> And when we were children, staying at the archduke's,
> My cousin's, he took me out on a sled,
> And I was frightened. He said, Marie,
> Marie, hold on tight. And down we went.
> In the mountains, there you feel free.

I read, much of the night, and go south in the winter.

"In the mountains, there you feel free." We have only to delete "there" to observe the collapse of more than a rhythm: to observe how the line's exact mimicry of a fatigue which supposes it has reached some ultimate perception can telescope spiritual bankruptcy, deracinated ardor, and an illusion of liberty which is no more than impatience with human society and relief at a temporary change. It was a restless, pointless world that collapsed during the war, agitated out of habit but tired beyond coherence, on the move to avoid itself. The memories in lines 8 to 18 seem spacious and precious now; then, the events punctuated a terrible continuum of boredom.

The plight of the Sibyl in the epigraph rhymes with that of Marie; the terrible thing is to be compelled to stay alive. "For I with these my own eyes have seen the Cumaean Sibyl hanging in a jar; and when the boys said, 'What do you want, Sibyl?' she answered, 'I want to die.' The sentence is in a macaronic Latin, posterior to the best age, pungently sauced with Greek; Cato would have contemplated with unblinking severity Petronius' readers' jazz-age craving for the cosmopolitan. The Sibyl in her better days answered questions by flinging from her cave handfuls of leaves bearing letters which the postulant was required to arrange in a suitable order; the wind commonly blew half of them away. Like Tiresias, like Philomel, like the modern poet, she divulged forbidden knowledge only in riddles, fitfully. (Tiresias wouldn't answer Oedipus at all; and he put off Odysseus with a puzzle about an oar mistaken for a winnowing-fan.) *The Waste Land* is suffused with a functional obscurity, sibylline fragments so disposed as to yield the utmost in connotative power, embracing the fragmented present and reaching back to "that vanished mind of which our mind is a continuation." As for the Sibyl's present exhaustion, she had foolishly asked Apollo for as many years as the grains of sand in her hand; which is one layer in the multi-layered line, "I will show you fear in a handful of dust." She is the prophetic power, no longer consulted by heroes but tormented by curious boys, still answering because she must; she is Madame Sosostris, consulted by dear Mrs. Equitone and harried by police ("One must be so careful these days"); she is the image of the late phase of Roman civilization, now vanished; she is also "the mind of Europe," a mind more important than one's own private mind, a mind which changes but abandons nothing en route, not superannuating either Shakespeare, or Homer, or the rock drawing of the Magdalenian draughtsmen; but now very nearly exhausted by the effort to stay interested in its own contents.

Which brings us to the "heap of broken images": not only desert ruins of some past from which life was withdrawn with the failure of the water supply, like the Roman cities in North Africa, or Augustine's Carthage, but also the manner in which Shakespeare, Homer, and the drawings of Michelangelo, Raphael, and the Magdalenian draughtsmen coexist in the contemporary cultivated consciousness: fragments, familiar quotations: *poluphloisboio thalasse,* to be or not to be, undo this button, one touch of nature, etc., God creating the Sun and Moon, those are pearls that were his eyes. For one man who knows *The Tempest* intimately there are a thousand who can identify the lines about the cloud-capp'd towers; painting is a miscellany of reproductions, literature a potpourri of quotations, history a chaos of theories and postures (Nelson's telescope, Washington crossing the Delaware, government of, for and by the people, the Colosseum, the guillotine). A desert wind has blown half the leaves away; disuse and vandals have broken the monuments—

> What are the roots that clutch, what branches grow
> Out of this stony rubbish? Son of man,
> You cannot say, or guess, for you know only
> A heap of broken images, where the sun beats,
> And the dead tree gives no shelter, the cricket no relief,
> And the dry stone no sound of water. . . .

Cities are built out of the ruins of previous cities, as *The Waste Land* is built out of the remains of older poems. But at this stage no building is yet in question; the "Son of man" (a portentously generalizing phrase) is moving tirelessly eastward, when the speaker accosts him with a sinister "Come in under the shadow of this red rock," and offers to show him not merely horror and desolation but something older and deeper: fear.

Hence the hyacinth girl, who speaks with urgent hurt simplicity, like the mad Ophelia:

> "You gave me hyacinths first a year ago;
> They called me the hyacinth girl."

They are childlike words, self-pitying, spoken perhaps in memory, perhaps by a ghost, perhaps by a wistful woman now out of her mind. The response exposes many contradictory layers of feeling:

> —Yet when we came back, late, from the Hyacinth garden,
> Your arms full, and your hair wet, I could not
> Speak, and my eyes failed, I was neither
> Living nor dead, and I knew nothing,
> Looking into the heart of light, the silence.

The context is erotic, the language that of mystical experience: plainly a tainted mysticism. "The Hyacinth garden" sounds queerly like a lost cult's sacred grove, and her arms were no doubt full of flowers; what rite was there enacted or evaded we can have no means of knowing.

But another level of meaning is less ambiguous: perhaps in fantasy, the girl has been drowned. Five pages later "A Game of Chess" ends with Ophelia's words before her death; Ophelia gathered flowers before she tumbled into the stream, then lay and chanted snatches of old tunes—

> Frisch weht der Wind
> Der Heimat zu . . .

while her clothes and hair spread out on the waters. "The Burial of the Dead" ends with a sinister dialogue about a corpse in the garden—

> Has it begun to sprout? Will it bloom this year?
> Or has the sudden frost disturbed its bed?

—two Englishmen discussing their tulips, with a note of the terrible intimacy with which murderers imagine themselves being taunted. The traditional British murderer—unlike his American counterpart, who in a vast land instinctively puts distance between himself and the corpse—prefers to keep it near at hand; in the garden, or behind the wainscotting, or

> bones cast in a little low dry garret,
> Rattled by the rat's foot only, year to year.

"The Fire Sermon" opens with despairing fingers clutching and sinking into a wet bank; it closes with Thames-daughters singing from beneath the oily waves. The drowned Phlebas

in Section IV varies this theme; and at the close of the poem the response to the last challenge of the thunder alludes to something that happened in a boat:

> your heart would have responded
> Gaily, when invited, beating obedient
> To controlling hands

—but what in fact did happen we are not told; perhaps nothing, or perhaps the hands assumed another sort of control.

In *The Waste Land* as in *The Family Reunion,* the guilt of the protagonist seems coupled with his perhaps imagined responsibility for the fate of a perhaps ideally drowned woman. . . . It must give this man an unusual turn when Madame Sosostris spreads her pack and selects a card as close to his secret as the Tarot symbolism can come:

> Here, said she,
> Is your card, the drowned Phoenician Sailor,
> (Those are pearls that were his eyes. Look!)—

and again:

> this card,
> Which is blank, is something he carries on his back,
> Which I am forbidden to see.

(In what posture did they come back, late, from the Hyacinth Garden, her hair wet, before the planting of the corpse?) It is not clear whether he is comforted to learn that the clairvoyante does not find the Hanged Man.

Hence, then, his inability to speak, his failed eyes, his stunned movement, neither living nor dead and knowing nothing. . . . (pp. 152-63)

At the end of "The Burial of the Dead" it is the speaker's acquaintance Stetson who has planted a corpse in his garden and awaits its fantastic blooming "out of the dead land": whether a hyacinth bulb or a dead mistress there is, in this phantasmagoric cosmos, no knowing. . . . (p. 164)

Part Two, "A Game of Chess" revolves around perverted nature, denied or murdered offspring; Part Three, "The Fire Sermon," the most explicit of the five sections, surveys with grave denunciatory candor a world of automatic lust, in which those barriers between person and person which so troubled Prufrock are dissolved by the suppression of the person and the transposition of all human needs and desires to a plane of genital gratification. . . . The "tent," now broken would have been composed of the overarching trees that transformed a reach of the river into a tunnel of love; the phrase beckons to mind the broken maidenhead; and a line later the gone harmonious order, by a half-realizable metamorphosis, struggles exhausted an instant against drowning. "The nymphs are departed" both because summer is past, and because the world of Spenser's *Prothalamion* (when nymphs scattered flowers on the water) is gone, if it ever existed except as an ideal fancy of Spenser's. . . . From the "brown land," amorists have fled indoors, but the river is not restored to a sixteenth-century purity because the debris of which it is now freed was not a sixteenth-century strewing of petals but a discarding of twentieth-century impedimenta. The nymphs who have this year departed are not the same nymphs who departed in autumns known to Spenser; their friends are "the loitering heirs of city directors," who, unwilling to assume responsibility for any untoward pregnancies,

Departed, have left no addresses.

Spring will return and bring Sweeney to Mrs. Porter; Mrs. Porter, introduced by the sound of horns and caressed by the moonlight while she laves her feet, is a latter-day Diana bathing; her daughter perhaps, or any of the vanished nymphs, a latter-day Philomel

(So rudely forc'd.
Tereu.)

Next Mr. Eugenides proposes what appears to be a pederastic assignation; and next the typist expects a visitor to her flat.

The typist passage is the great *tour de force* of the poem; its gentle lyric melancholy, its repeatedly disrupted rhythms, the automatism of its cadences, in alternate lines aspiring and falling nervelessly—

The time is now propitious, as he guesses,
The meal is ended, she is bored and tired,
Endeavours to engage her in caresses
Which still are unreproved, if undesired.

—constitute Eliot's most perfect liaison between the self-sustaining gesture of the verse and the presented fact. Some twenty-five lines in flawlessly traditional iambic pentameter, alternately rhymed, sustain with their cadenced gravity a moral context in which the dreary business is played out; the texture is lyric rather than dramatic because there is neither doing nor suffering here but rather the mutual compliance of a ritual scene. The section initiates its flow with a sure and perfect line composed according to the best eighteenth-century models:

At the violet hour, when the eyes and back

which, if the last word were, for instance, "heart," we might suppose to be by a precursor of Wordsworth's. But the harsh sound and incongruous specification of "back" shift us instead to a plane of prosodic disintegration:

when the eyes and back

Turn upward from the desk, when the human engine waits
Like a taxi throbbing waiting,

The upturned eyes and back—nothing else, no face, no torso—recall a Picasso distortion; the "human engine" throws pathos down into mechanism. In the next line the speaker for the first time in the poem identifies himself as Tiresias:

I Tiresias, though blind, throbbing between two lives,
Old man with wrinkled female breasts, can see . . .

There are three principal stories about Tiresias, all of them relevant. In *Oedipus Rex,* sitting "by Thebes below the wall" he knew why, and as a consequence of what violent death and what illicit amour, the pestilence had fallen on the unreal city, but declined to tell. In the *Odyssey* he "walked among the lowest of the dead" and evaded predicting Odysseus' death by water; the encounter was somehow necessary to Odysseus' homecoming, and Odysseus was somehow satisfied with it, and did get home, for a while. In the *Metamorphoses* he underwent a change of sex for watching the coupling of snakes: presumably the occasion on which he "fore-suffered" what is tonight "enacted on this same divan or bed." He is often the prophet who knows but withholds his knowledge, just as Hieronymo, who is mentioned at the close of the poem, knew how the tree he had planted in his garden

came to bear his dead son, but was compelled to withhold that knowledge until he could write a play which, like **The Waste Land,** employs several languages and a framework of allusions impenetrable to anyone but the "hypocrite lecteur." It is an inescapable shared guilt that makes us so intimate with the contents of this strange deathly poem; it is also, in an age that has eaten of the tree of the knowledge of psychology and anthropology ("After such knowledge, what forgiveness?"), an inescapable morbid sympathy with everyone else, very destructive to the coherent personality, that (like Tiresias' years as a woman) enables us to join with him in "foresuffering all." These sciences afford us an *illusion* of understanding other people, on which we build sympathies that in an ideal era would have gone out with a less pathological generosity, and that are as likely as not projections of our self-pity and self-absorption, vices for which Freud and Frazer afford dangerous nourishment. Tiresias is he who has lost the sense of other people as inviolably other, and who is capable neither of pity nor terror but only of a fascination, spuriously related to compassion, which is merely the twentieth century's special mutation of indifference. Tiresias can see

At the violet hour, the evening hour that strives
Homeward, and brings the sailor home from sea,
The typist home at teatime, clears her breakfast, lights
Her stove, and lays out food in tins.

Syntax, like his sensibility and her routine, undergoes total collapse. A fine throbbing line intervenes:

Out of the window perilously spread

and bathos does not wholly overtopple the completing Alexandrine:

Her drying combinations touched by the sun's last rays.

"Combinations" sounds a little finer than the thing it denotes; so does "divan":

On the divan are piled (at night her bed)
Stockings, slippers, camisoles and stays.

Some transfiguring word touches with glory line after line:

He, the young man carbuncular, arrives,

If he existed, and if he read those words, how must he have marvelled at the alchemical power of language over his inflamed skin! As their weary ritual commences, the diction alters; it moves to a plane of Johnsonian dignity without losing touch with them; they are never "formulated, sprawling on a pin."

"Endeavours to engage her in caresses" is out of touch with the small house-agent's clerk's speech, but it is such a sentence as he might *write*; Eliot has noted elsewhere how "an artisan who can talk the English language beautifully while about his work or in a public bar, may compose a letter painfully written in a dead language bearing some resemblance to a newspaper leader and decorated with words like 'maelstrom' and 'pandemonium.' " So it is with the diction of this passage: it reflects the words with which the participants might clothe, during recollection in tranquillity, their own notion of what they have been about, presuming them capable of such self-analysis; and it maintains simultaneously Tiresias' fastidious impersonality. The rhymes come with a weary inevitability that parodies the formal elegance of Gray; and the episode modulates at its close into a key to which Goldsmith can be transposed:

> When lovely woman stoops to folly and
> Paces about her room again, alone,
> She smoothes her hair with automatic hand,
> And puts a record on the gramophone.

With her music and her lures "perilously spread" she is a London siren; the next line, "This music crept by me upon the waters," if it is lifted from the *Tempest,* might as well be adapted from the twelfth book of the *Odyssey.*

After the Siren, the violated Thames-daughters, borrowed from Wagner, the "universal artist" whom the French Symbolists delighted to honor. The opulent Wagnerian pathos, with its harmonic rather than linear development and its trick of entrancing the attention with *leitmotifs,* is never unrelated to the methods of **The Waste Land.** (pp. 164-70)

Wagner, more than Frazer or Miss Weston, presides over the introduction into **The Waste Land** of the Grail motif. In Wagner's opera, the Sangreal quest is embedded in an opulent and depraved religiosity, as in Tennyson's *Holy Grail* the cup, "rose-red, with beatings in it, as if alive, till all the white walls of my cell were dyed with rosy colours leaping on the wall," never succeeds in being more than the reward of a refined and sublimated erotic impulse. Again Eliot notes of Baudelaire that "in much romantic poetry the sadness is due to the exploitation of the fact that no human relations are adequate to human desires, but also to the disbelief in any further object for human desires than that which, being human, fails to satisfy them." The Grail was in mid-nineteenth-century art an attempt to postulate such an object; and the quest for that vision unites the poetry of baffled sadness to "the poetry of flight," a genre which Eliot distinguishes in quoting Baudelaire's "Quand partons-nous vers le bonheur?" and characterizes as "a dim recognition of the direction of beatitude."

So in Part V of **The Waste Land** the journey eastward among the red rocks and heaps of broken images is fused with the journey to Emmaus ("He who was living is now dead. We who were living are now dying") and the approach to the Chapel Perilous.

The quester arrived at the Chapel Perilous had only to ask the meaning of the things that were shown him. Until he has asked their meaning, they have none; after he has asked, the king's wound is healed and the waters commence again to flow. So in a civilization reduced to "a heap of broken images" all that is requisite is sufficient curiosity; the man who asks what one or another of these fragments means—seeking, for instance, "a first-hand opinion about Shakespeare"—may be the agent of regeneration. The past exists in fragments precisely because nobody cares what it meant; it will unite itself and come alive in the mind of anyone who succeeds in caring, who is unwilling that Shakespeare shall remain the name attached only to a few tags everyone half-remembers, in a world where "we know too much, and are convinced of too little."

Eliot develops the nightmare journey with consummate skill, and then maneuvres the reader into the position of the quester, presented with a terminal heap of fragments which it is his business to enquire about. The protagonist in the poem perhaps does not enquire; they are fragments he has shored against his ruins. Or perhaps he does enquire; he has at least begun to put them to use, and the "arid plain" is at length behind him.

The journey is prepared for by two images of asceticism: the brand plucked from the burning, and the annihilation of Phlebas the Phoenician. "The Fire Sermon," which opens by Thames water, closes with a burning, a burning that images the restless lusts of the nymphs, the heirs of city directors, Mr. Eugenides, the typist and the young man carbuncular, the Thames-daughters. They are unaware that they burn. "I made no comment. What should I resent?" They burn nevertheless, as the protagonist cannot help noticing when he shifts his attention from commercial London to commercial Carthage (which stood on the North African shore, and is now utterly destroyed). There human sacrifices were dropped into the furnaces of Moloch, in a frantic gesture of appeasement. There Augustine burned with sensual fires: "a cauldron of unholy loves sang all about mine ears"; and he cried, "O Lord, Thou pluckest me out." The Buddhist ascetic on the other hand does not ask to be plucked out; he simply turns away from the senses because (as the Buddhist Fire Sermon states) they are each of them on fire. As for Phlebas the Phoenician, a trader sailing perhaps to Britain, his asceticism is enforced: "A current under sea picked his bones in whispers," he forgets the benisons of sense, "the cry of gulls and the deep sea swell" as well as "the profit and loss," and he spirals down, like Dante's Ulysses, through circling memories of his age and youth, "as Another chose." (An account of a shipwreck, imitated from the Ulysses episode in Dante, was one of the long sections deleted from the original **Waste Land.**) Ulysses in hell was encased in a tongue of flame, death by water having in one instance secured not the baptismal renunciation of the Old Adam, but an eternity of fire. Were there some simple negative formula for dealing with the senses, suicide would be the sure way to regeneration.

Part V opens, then, in Gethsemane, carries us rapidly to Golgotha, and then leaves us to pursue a nightmare journey in a world now apparently deprived of meaning.

> Here is no water but only rock
> Rock and no water and the sandy road
> The road winding above among the mountains
> Which are mountains of rock without water
> If there were water we should stop and drink. . . .

The whirling, obsessive reduplication of single words carries the travellers through a desert, through the phases of hallucination in which they number phantom companions, and closes with a synoptic vision of the destruction of Jerusalem ("Murmur of maternal lamentation" obviously recalling "daughters of Jerusalem, weep not for me, but for yourselves and your children") which becomes *sub specie aeternitatis* the destruction by fire of civilization after civilization

> Jerusalem Athens Alexandria
> Vienna London
> Unreal

The woman at the dressing-table recurs:

> A woman drew her long black hair out tight
> And fiddled whisper music on those strings;

her "golden Cupidons" are transmogrified:

> And bats with baby faces in the violet light
> Whistled, and beat their wings
> And crawled head downward down a blackened wall

and where towers hang "upside down in air" stability is imaged by a deserted chapel among the mountains, another place from which the life has gone but in which the meaning is latent, awaiting only a pilgrim's advent. The cock crows as it did when Peter wept tears of penitence; as in *Hamlet,* it disperses the night-spirits.

> Then a damp gust
> Bringing rain.

There the activity of the protagonist ends. Some forty remaining lines in the past tense recapitulate the poem in terms of the oldest wisdom accessible to the West. The thunder's DA is one of those primordial Indo-European roots that recur in the *Oxford Dictionary,* a random leaf of the Sibyl's to which a thousand derivative words, now automatic currency, were in their origins so many explicit glosses. If the race's most permanent wisdom is its oldest, then DA, the voice of the thunder and of the Hindu sages, is the cosmic voice not yet dissociated into echoes. It underlies the Latin infinitive "dare," and all its Romance derivatives; by a sound-change, the Germanic "geben," the English "give." It is the root of "datta," "dayadhvam," "damyata": give, sympathize, control: three sorts of giving. To sympathize is to give oneself; to control is to give governance. . . . The first surrender was our parents' sexual consent; and when we are born again it is by a new surrender, inconceivable to the essentially satiric sensibility with which a Gerontion contemplates

> . . . De Bailhache, Fresca, Mrs. Cammel, whirled
> Beyond the circuit of the shuddering Bear,

and requiring a radical modification of even a Tiresias' negative compassion.

> The awful daring of a moment's surrender . . .
> Which is not to be found in our obituaries
> Or in memories draped by the beneficent spider
> Or under seals broken by the lean solicitor
> In our empty rooms.

The lean solicitor, like the enquiring worm, breaks seals that in lifetime were held prissily inviolate; the will he is about to read registers not things given but things abandoned. The thunder is telling us what Tiresias did not dare tell Oedipus, the reason for the universal curse: "What have we given?" As for "Dayadhvam," "sympathize":

> DA
> *Dayadhvam:* I have heard the key
> Turn in the door once and turn once only
> We think of the key, each in his prison
> Thinking of the key, each confirms a prison

—a prison of inviolate honor, self-sufficiency, like that in which Coriolanus locked himself away. Coriolanus' city was also under a curse, in which he participated. . . . After his banishment he goes out "like to a lonely dragon," and plots the destruction of Rome. His final threat is to stand

> As if a man were author of himself
> And knew no other kin.

He is an energetic and purposeful Prufrock, concerned with the figure he cuts and readily humiliated; Prufrock's radical fault is not his lack of energy and purpose. Coriolanus is finally shattered like a statue; and if

> Only at nightfall, aethereal rumours
> Revive for a moment a broken Coriolanus,

it may be only as the Hollow Men in Death's dream kingdom hear voices "in the wind's singing," and discern sunlight on a broken column. Do the rumors at nightfall restore him to momentary life, or restore his memory to the minds of other self-sufficient unsympathizing men?

> DA
> *Damyata:* The boat responded
> Gaily, to the hand expert with sail and oar
> The sea was calm, your heart would have responded
> Gaily, when invited, beating obedient
> To controlling hands

Unlike the rider, who may dominate his horse, the sailor survives and moves by cooperation with a nature that cannot be forced; and this directing, sensitive hand, feeling on the sheet the pulsation of the wind and on the rudder the momentary thrust of waves, becomes the imagined instrument of a comparably sensitive human relationship. If dominance compels response, control invites it; and the response comes "gaily." But—"would have": the right relationship was never attempted.

> I sat upon the shore
>
> Fishing, with the arid plain behind me

The journey eastward across the desert is finished; though the king's lands are waste, he has arrived at the sea.

> Shall I at least set my lands in order?

Isaiah bade King Hezekiah set his lands in order because he was destined not to live; but Candide resolved to cultivate his own garden as a way of living. We cannot set the whole world in order; we can rectify ourselves. And we are destined to die, but such order as lies in our power is nevertheless desirable.

> London Bridge is falling down falling down falling down
> *Poi s'ascose nel foco che gli affina*
> *Quando fiam uti chelidon*—O swallow swallow
> *Le Prince d'Aquitaine à la tour abolie*
> These fragments I have shored against my ruins

An English nursery rhyme, a line of Dante's, a scrap of the late Latin *Pervigilium Veneris,* a phrase of Tennyson's ("O swallow, swallow, could I but follow") linked to the fate of Philomel, an image from a pioneer nineteenth-century French visionary who hanged himself on a freezing January morning: "a heap of broken images," and a fragmentary conspectus of the mind of Europe. Like the Knight in the Chapel Perilous, we are to ask what these relics mean; and the answers will lead us into far recesses of tradition.

The history of London Bridge (which was disintegrating in the eighteenth century, and which had symbolized, with its impractical houses, a communal life now sacrificed to abstract transportation—

> A crowd flowed over London Bridge, so many,
> I had not thought death had undone so many.

is linked by the nursery rhyme with feudal rituals ("gold and silver, my fair lady") and festivals older still. Dante's line focuses the tradition of Christian asceticism, in which "burning" is voluntarily undergone. . . . As for the Prince of Aquitaine with the ruined tower, he is one of the numerous *personae* Gerard de Nerval assumes in *El Desdichado:* "Suis-je Amour ou Phébus, Lusignan ou Biron?" as the speaker of *The Waste Land* is Tiresias, the Phoenician Sailor, and Ferdinand Prince of Naples. He has lingered in the chambers of the sea . . . and like Orpheus he has called up his love from the shades. . . . So *The Waste Land* contains Augustine's cries and the song of the Thames-daughters; but de Nerval, the pioneer Symbolist, is inclosed in a mood, in a poetic state, surrounded by his own symbols ("Je suis le ténébreux,—le veuf,—l'inconsolé"), offering to a remembered order, where the vine and the rose were one, only the supplication of a dead man's hand, "Dans la nuit du tombeau," where "ma seule étoile est morte": under the twinkle of a fading star. It is some such state as his, these images suggest, that is to be explored in *The Hollow Men;* he inhabits death's dream kingdom. The mind of Europe, some time in the nineteenth century, entered an uneasy phase of sheer dream.

> These fragments I have shored against my ruins
> Why then Ile fit you. Hieronymo's mad againe.

Here Eliot provides us with a final image for all that he has done: his poem is like Hieronymo's revenge-play. Hieronymo's enemies—the public for the poet in our time—commission an entertainment:

> It pleased you,
> At the entertainment of the ambassador,
> To grace the king so much as with a show.
> Now, were your study so well furnished,
> As for the passing of the first night's sport
> To entertain my father with the like
> Or any such-like pleasing motion,
> Assure yourself, it would content them well.
> HIER: Is this all?
> BAL.:   Ay, this is all.
> HIER: Why then, I'll fit you. Say no more.
> When I was young, I gave my mind
> And plied myself to fruitless poetry;
> Which though it profit the professor naught,
> Yet is it passing pleasing to the world.

It profits the professor naught, like Philomel's gift of song; and pleases those who have no notion of what it has cost, or what it will ultimately cost them. Hieronymo goes on to specify:

> Each one of us
> Must act his part in unknown languages,
> That it may breed the more variety:
> As you, my lord, in Latin, I in Greek,
> You in Italian, and for because I know
> That Bellimperia hath practised the French,
> In courtly French shall all her phrases be.

Each of these languages occurs in *The Waste Land;* all but Greek, in the list of shored fragments. Balthasar responds, like a critic in *The New Statesman,*

> But this will be a mere confusion,
> And hardly shall we all be understood.

Hieronymo, however, is master of his method:

> It must be so: for the conclusion
> Shall prove the invention and all was good.

Hieronymo's madness, in the context provided by Eliot, is that of the Platonic bard. If we are to take the last two lines of *The Waste Land* as the substance of what the bard in his sibylline trance has to say, then the old man's macaronic tragedy appears transmuted into the thunder's three injunctions, Give, Sympathize, Control, and a triple "Peace," "repeated as here," says the note, "a formal ending to an Upanishad." (pp. 170-81)

Hugh Kenner, in his The Invisible Poet: T. S. Eliot, *McDowell, Obolensky, 1959, 346 p.*

DAVID CRAIG

[The essay excerpted below was originally published in Critical Quarterly, *Autumn 1960.]*

T. S. Eliot's *The Waste Land* is one of the outstanding cases in modern times of a work which projects an almost defeatist personal depression in the guise of a full, impersonal picture of society. Lawrence's *Women in Love* is a much more substantial case of the same thing, but the response it demands is much less easy. Both, however, in my experience, encourage in readers, especially young students, a sort of superior cynicism which flatters the educated man by letting him feel that he is left as the sole bearer of a fine culture which the new mass-barbarians have spurned and spoiled. Eliot has characteristically slid out of responsibility in the matter by means of his remark that *The Waste Land* pleased people because of 'their own illusion of being disillusioned'. But, I suggest, the essential (and very original) method of his poem and the peculiar sense of life which it mediates are such that they invite that very response—and get it from the most considerable critics as well as from young cynics. (p. 200)

The technique of *The Waste Land* is very various; it gives the impression (compared with, say, Pound's *Cantos*) of rich, or intensely-felt, resources both of literature and of life direct. But one method stands out: that way of running on, with no marked break and therefore with a deadpan ironical effect, from one area of experience, one place or time or speech or social class, to another. Section II, "A Game of Chess," throws shifting lights on the woman protagonist by changes of style. At first Cleopatra is present, but a Cleopatra who lives in an indoor, lifelessly ornate setting. . . . (p. 201)

There is . . . in mid-section, a change of social class, from wealthy life ('The hot water at ten. / And if it rains, a closed car at four') to ordinary ('When Lil's husband got demobbed, I said . . .'). But life is fruitless here too, and the poet's aloof revulsion is conveyed by similar means. The working-class women in the pub talk about false teeth, abortions, promiscuous sexual rivalry between the wives of Great War soldiers, in a lingo which sprawls over any kind of formal elegance of metre or rhyme; and the poet does not intrude on the common speech until the closing line:

> Goonight Bill. Goonight Lou. Goonight May.
>   Goonight
> Ta ta. Goonight. Goonight.
> Good night, ladies, good night, sweet ladies, good
>   night,
>   good night.

'Sweet ladies'—the irony is, to say the least, obvious. As well as the effect of 'sweet' there is the reminiscence of the innocently hearty student song (this seems more relevant than Ophelia's mad snatch in *Hamlet*). The effect is identical with what he does by incorporating Goldsmith's ditty from *The Vicar of Wakefield* at the end of the typist's dreary seduction in "The Fire Sermon":

> 'Well now that's done: and I'm glad it's over.'
> When lovely woman stoops to folly and
> Paces about her room again, alone . . .

This technique, which is typical of the transitions of tone and of the collocation of two cultures which occur throughout the poem, seems to me unsatisfactory in two ways. The irony is no finer than ordinary sarcasm—the simple juxtaposing of messy reality and flattering description (as in a common phrase like 'You're a pretty sight'). The pub women and the typist have been made so utterly sour and unlovely that the poet's innuendo, being unnecessary, does no more than hint at his own superior qualities. Secondly, using earlier literature to embody the better way of life which is the poet's ideal depends on a view of the past which is not made good in the poem (it hardly could be) and which the reader may well not share—unless he is pessimistic. Consider some further instances. The Thames as it is now is given at the beginning of "The Fire Sermon". . . . [The life evoked] is unpleasant—but so is the poet's attitude, notably the pointed but prudishly or suggestively tacit hint at contraceptives. At the same time, for us to respond as the poet means, we have to accept his glamourising view of Spenser's London, Elizabethan England with its pure rivers and stately ways. The same suggestion occurs in the lyrical passage which is meant to parallel the Rhinemaidens' song from *Götterdämmerung*. Modern:

> The river sweats
> Oil and tar
> The barges drift
> With the turning tide . . .
> The barges wash
> Drifting logs
> Down Greenwich reach
> Past the Isle of Dogs.

Renaissance:

> Elizabeth and Leicester
> Beating oars
> The stern was formed
> A gilded shell
> Red and gold
> The brisk swell
> Rippled both shores . . .

The poet's meaning is clear: modern civilisation does nothing but spoil what was once gracious, lovely, ceremonious, and natural.

Here it must be said that the poet's comparative view of old and modern culture is not quite one-sided. As Hugh Kenner suggests, it may not be implied that Spenser's nymph-world 'ever existed except as an ideal fancy of Spenser's', and as Cleanth Brooks suggests, the Elizabeth passage has 'a sort of double function': historically, Elizabeth flirted so wantonly with Leicester, in the presence of the Spanish bishop de Quadra, that Cecil at last suggested that as there was a bishop on the spot they might as well be married there and then (Froude's *Elizabeth,* quoted in Eliot's note). As Brooks says, the passage 'reinforces the general contrast between Elizabethan magnificence and modern sordidness: in the Elizabethan age love for love's sake has some meaning and therefore some magnificence. But the passage gives something of an opposed effect too: the same sterile love, emptiness of love, obtained in this period too: Elizabeth and the typist are alike as well as different.' In the whole poem, however, it is certainly old magnificence which is given the advantage, and it is as well to say straight out that this is an absurdly partial outlook on culture—groundlessly idealising about the old and warped in its revulsion from the modern. If magnificence is desired, modern life can supply it well enough, whether the show of Royalty or big-business ostentation. And if one thinks of the filth, poverty, superstition, and brutal knock-about life invariable in town or country four centuries ago, one realises how fatuous it is to make flat contrasts between then and now. History, reality, are being manipulated to fit an escapist

kind of prejudice, however detached the writer may feel himself to be.

As one would expect, the cultural warp has as strong an equivalent in the poet's way of presenting personal experience. Consider the attitudes implied in the seduction of the typist. In this most cunningly-managed episode, one is induced to feel, by means of the fastidiously detached diction and movement, that a scene part commonplace, part debased, is altogether unpleasant. . . . The unfeeling grossness of the experience is held off at the fingertips by the analytic, unphysical diction—'Endeavours to engage her in caresses'—and by the movement, whose even run is not interrupted by the violence of what is 'going on'. The neat assimilation of such life to a formal verse paragraph recalls Augustan modes. But if one thinks of the sexual passage concerning the 'Imperial Whore' in Dryden's translation of Juvenal's sixth Satire, or even the one concerning the unfeeling Chloe in Pope's *Moral Essay* 'Of the Characters of Women', one realises that the Augustans did not stand off from the physical with anything like Eliot's distaste. Eliot's style is carefully impersonal; it enumerates with fastidious care the sordid details:

> On the divan are piled (at night her bed)
> Stocking, slippers, camisoles, and stays.

But here one has doubts. This is given as a typically comfortless modern apartment, suggesting a life which lacks the right pace, the right sociableness, the right instinctive decency for it to merit the name of civilisation. (Were Elizabethan houses and habits any better?) But the touch in the second line feels uncertain: is the heavily careful art with which the line is built up not too contrived for the rather ordinary modern habit it is meant to satirise? When we come to 'carbuncular'—an adjective which, placed after the noun and resounding in its slow movement and almost ornamental air, is deliberately out of key with the commonplace life around it—I think we begin to feel that Eliot's conscious literariness is working, whatever his intention, more to hold at arm's length something which he personally shudders at than to convey a poised criticism of behaviour. There is a shudder in 'carbuncular'; it is disdainful, but the dislike is disproportionately strong for its object; queasy emotions of the writer's seem to be at work. The snobbery is of a piece with this. 'He is a nobody—a mere clerk, and clerk to a *small* house agent at that. What right has *he* to look assured?' That is the suggestion; and we are also left wondering what warrant the poet has for uniting himself with some class finer, it seems than the provincial bourgeoisie. . . .

One may agree or not that modern civilisation has its own kind of health; one may agree or not that the petty bourgeoisie are a decent class. But one must surely take exception to a method which seeks its effects through an irony which is no more than smart sarcasm. It is amazing that Dr Leavis should speak of 'delicate collocations', when the contrasts are regularly so facile in their selection of old grandeur and modern squalor.

To put the matter in terms which refer directly to life: if, as Brooks says, 'the same sterile love, emptiness of love, obtained in this period too', then why does the criticism work so consistently against contemporary civilisation? And when Dr Leavis says, 'Sex here is sterile', does he really mean that love between men and women has deteriorated as a whole? (One remembers similar extraordinary duggestions about intercourse now and formerly in *Lady Chatterley's Lover.*). . .

I think we may take it that the comparison of cultures to the advantage of the older is either impossible, pointless, or else feasible only by specific fields and not overall. The question remains why critics have surrendered so gratefully to an almost nastily despairing view of the civilisation we live in. This occurs in Leavis's *New Bearings* and Edmund Wilson's *Axel's Castle*. It is seen at its most irresponsible in Hugh Kenner's glib explication of the pub scene: 'If we move from the queens to the pawns, we find low life no more free or natural, equally obsessed with the denial of nature, artificial teeth, chemically procured abortions, the speaker and her interlocutor battening fascinated at second-hand on the life of Lil and her Albert, Lil and Albert interested only in spurious ideal images of one another.' 'Battening fascinated at second-hand' means no more than 'listening with interest to the tale of someone else's experiences': Mr Kenner's condemnation comes from the general atmosphere of moral depression which the poem generates rather than from anything established by the dramatic speech of that scene—here the critic's sourness outdoes the poet's. And the reference to false teeth, lumped with abortions, as though false teeth were not simply an admirable achievement of medical science in giving comfort where nature has broken down, is a glaring case of that blind dislike of science which nowadays has become an intellectual's disease. It is primitivist; and it thoughtlessly ignores the experience involved. (pp. 202-08)

The Waste Land . . . seems to me to work essentially against life, for the range of opinions it mobilises, that come welling up in response to it, are all negative. In the final section Eliot uses the philosophy of F. H. Bradley. The lines

> I have heard the key
>
> Turn in the door once and turn once only
> We think of the key, each in his prison
> Thinking of the key, each confirms a prison . . .

he himself glosses from Bradley's *Appearance and Reality:*

> My external sensations are no less private to myself than are my thought or my feelings. In either case my experience falls within my own circle, a circle closed on the outside; and, with all its elements alike, every sphere is opaque to the others which surround it . . . In brief, regarded as an existence which appears in a soul, the whole world for each is peculiar and private to that soul.

This thought of Bradley's has led on to that barren line of philosophy which includes John Wisdom's *Other Minds*. To say what must suffice here: if our sensations, thoughts, and feelings are perfectly private and the sphere of each person's life 'opaque', how is it that speech and literature themselves are intelligible—and intelligible so fully and intimately that to reach understanding with a person or appreciate a piece of writing can seem to take us inside another existence? That the question of whether one mind can get through to another should even have arisen seems to me a perversion of thought. (Historically, it is perhaps a cast from the anti-co-operative state of existence brought about by entrepreneur capitalism. It seems similar to the helplessly solipsistic 'denial of objective truth' which Lenin refutes in *Materialism and Empirio-Criticism*. In each case the individual ego relies less and less on anything outside itself.)

The obscurity of *The Waste Land* is significant likewise, for though the trained reader no longer jibs at it, it is certainly impossible that it should ever become popular reading as did

earlier important literature (Burns, Byron, George Eliot, D. H. Lawrence). Dr Leavis writes on the issue of 'minority culture' which this raises: 'that the public for it is limited is one of the symptoms of the state of culture which produced the poem. Works expressing the finest consciousness of the age in which the word "high-brow" has become current are almost inevitably such as to appeal only to a tiny minority.' The argument that follows is dubious at a number of points. In the first place, Lawrence expressed many sides of the 'finest consciousness of the age' and he has been read in cheap editions by the million (as has Gorky in the Soviet Union and James T. Farrell in the United States). The usual obstinately pessimistic reply is that 'They only read Lawrence for the sex, or the love story'. But this is only reaching for another stick to beat the times, for is it not good that a major writer should have devoted himself to the universal subject of love and sex? Dr Leavis goes on to say that the idea that the poem's obscurity is symptomatic of our cultural condition 'amounts to an admission that there must be something limited about the kind of artistic achievement possible in our time'. But if this were so, how account for the work of Lawrence and of the many other considerable novelists of our time? Finally his question 'how large in any age has the minority been that has really comprehended the masterpieces?' contains an equivocation—'really'. If one sets the highest standard, of course 'real' (that is, full) comprehension is attained by few; but if the numbers of even the *total* public reached are small, as has happened with *The Waste Land*, then there is indeed a significant difference between its meaningfulness and appeal for readers and that which the major novelists have regularly achieved (George Eliot, Hardy, Lawrence, Tolstoy, Gorky, Farrell). *The Waste Land*, in short, is *not* the representative work of the present age, and to make it so implies that pessimistic view of the present age which I have already challenged.

What has been made of *The Waste Land* illustrates two more issues important in our times. It is significant that Dr Leavis should meet the charge that the poem is a 'dead end', literarily and morally. When he says, 'So complete and vigorous a statement of the Waste Land could hardly . . . forecast an exhausted and hopeless sojourn there', he implies a proper distinction between Eliot's quality of art and that of Pound's *Cantos* or Joyce's *Ulysses*—both recognisably from the same line of art distorted by the break-up of cultural forms. *The Waste Land*, it is true, does not cut life into bits and juggle them into patterns interesting only for their intricacy, or meaningful only to their manipulator. At the same time there turns out to be little that Dr Leavis can plead convincingly when he has to say what way beyond the Waste Land Eliot found. He quotes some bracing sermons from the *Criterion*: 'a tendency—discernible even in art—towards a higher and clearer conception of Reason, and a more severe and serene control of the emotions by Reason', and 'the generation which is beginning to turn its attention to an athleticism, a *training*, of the soul as severe and ascetic as the training of the body of a runner'. The vague 'dedication' of this recalls the loftiness with no definite direction which characterised the more serious of the *fin de siècle* writers, notably Yeats, when they were being Hellenic or religiose. Its abstractness, its lack of reference to any social facts, suggests Eliot's inveterate drift away from anything progressive in society with which he might have co-operated in a practical way. (pp. 210-13)

David Craig, "The Defeatism of 'The Waste

Land', " *in* T. S. Eliot: 'The Waste Land', a Case-book, *edited by C. B. Cox and Arnold P. Hinchliffe, Macmillan and Co. Ltd., 1968, pp. 200-15.*

KARL SHAPIRO

[The essay excerpted below originally appeared in Shapiro's In Defense of Ignorance *(1960).]*

The Waste Land is the most important poem of the twentieth century, that is, the one that has caused the most discussion and is said by critics to be the culmination of the modern "mythic" style. . . . That it is lacking in unity is obvious (assuming, as I do, that unity is a literary virtue). Any part of **The Waste Land** can be switched with any other part without changing the sense of the poem. Aside from the so-called "mythic" form, which is worthless and not even true—for Eliot misread James Joyce's *Ulysses* when he saw it as a parallel to Homer—the underlying unity of the poem is tonal and dramatic, exactly as a Victorian narrative poem would be. Eliot tries to conceal this indispensable literary method by mixing languages, breaking off dramatic passages, and by dividing the poem into sections with titles. But what really keeps the poem moving is its rhetoric, its switches from description to exclamation to interrogation to expletive, sometimes very beautifully, as in the passages beginning "Unreal City." The straight descriptive passages are weak: "A Game of Chess" is one of the dullest and most meretricious of Eliot's writings, indicating his own dissatisfaction with that kind of verse. The dialogue, on the other hand, is generally good. The best moments of all are the image passages, where the images are set in dramatic tonalities: "What the Thunder Said" is the finest of these. The very worst passages are those which are merely quotes; even Eliot's most abject admirers can find no justification of the last lines of the poem, with its half-dozen languages and more than half a dozen quotations in a space of about ten lines.

The Waste Land, because of its great critical reputation, not because of any inherent worth it might have, is one of the curiosities of English literature. Its critical success was, I dare say, carefully planned and executed, and it was not beyond the realm of possibility that the poem was originally a hoax, as some of the first readers insisted. But hoax or not, it was very shortly made the sacred cow of modern poetry and the object of more pious literary nonsense than any modern work save the *Cantos* of Pound. The proof of the failure of the "form" of this poem is that no one has ever been able to proceed from it, including Eliot himself. It is, in fact, not a form at all but a negative version of form. It is interesting to notice that in the conventional stanzas of the quatrain poems Eliot is more personally violent and ugly about his own beliefs; in his unconventional style the voice of the poet all but disappears and is replaced by characters from his reading. (pp. 21-2)

Karl Shapiro, "T. S. Eliot: The Death of Literary Judgment," in his The Poetry Wreck, Selected Essays: 1950-1970, *Random House, 1975, pp. 3-28.*

FRANK KERMODE

[The essay excerpted below originally appeared in The Sewanee Review, *1965-1966.]*

Eliot ridiculed the critics who found in **The Waste Land** an image of the age's despair, but he might equally have rejected the more recent Christian interpretations. The poem resists an imposed order; it is a part of its greatness, and the greatness of its epoch, that it can do so. 'To find, Not to impose,' as Wallace Stevens said with a desperate wisdom, 'It is possible, possible, possible.' We must hope so.

No one has better stated the chief characteristics of that epoch than the late R. P. Blackmur in a little book of lectures, *Anni Mirabiles 1921-1925;* though it contains some of the best of his later work, it seems to be not much read. We live, wrote Blackmur, in the first age that has been 'fully self-conscious of its fictions'—in a way, Nietzsche has sunk in at last; and in these conditions we are more than ever dependent on what he calls, perhaps not quite satisfactorily, 'bourgeois humanism'—'the residue of reason in relation to the madness of the senses.' Without it we cannot have 'creation in honesty,' only 'assertion in desperation.' But in its operation this residual humanism can only deny the validity of our frames of reference and make 'an irregular metaphysic for the control of man's irrational powers.' So this kind art is a new kind of creation, harsh, medicinal, remaking reality 'in rivalry with our own wishes,' denying us the consolations of predictable form but showing us the forces of our world, which we may have to control by other means. And the great works in this new and necessary manner were the product of the 'wonderful years'—in English, two notable examples are *Ulysses* and **The Waste Land.**

The function of such a work, one has to see, is what Simone Weil called *decreation;* Stevens, whose profound contribution to the subject nobody seems to have noticed, picked the word out of *La Pesanteur et la Grâce.* Simone Weil explains the difference from destruction: decreation is not a change from the created to nothingness, but from the created to the uncreated. 'Modern reality,' commented Stevens, 'is a reality of decreation, in which our revelations are not the revelations of belief '; though he adds that he can say this 'without in any way asserting that they are the sole sources.'

This seems to me a useful instrument for the discrimination of modernisms. The form in which Simone Weil expresses it is rather obscure, though she is quite clear that 'destruction' is 'a blameworthy substitute for decreation.' The latter depends upon an act of renunciation, considered as a creative act like that of God. 'God could create only by hiding himself. Otherwise there would be nothing but himself.' She means that decreation, for men, implies the deliberate repudiation (not simply the destruction) of the naturally human and so naturally false 'set' of the world: 'we participate in the creation of the world by decreating ourselves.' Now the poets of the *anni mirabiles* also desired to create a world by decreating the self in suffering; to purge what, in being merely natural and human, was also false. It is a point often made, though in different language, by Eliot. This is what Stevens called clearing the world of 'its stiff and stubborn, man-locked set.' In another way it is what attracted Hulme and Eliot to Worringer, who related societies purged of the messily human to a radical abstract art.

Decreation, as practised by poets, has its disadvantages. . . . But we can see that when Eliot pushed his objective correlative out into the neutral air—'seeming a beast disgorged, unlike, / Warmed by a desperate milk'—he expected it, liberated from his own fictions, to be caught up in the fictions of others, those explanations we find for all the creations. In the world Blackmur is writing about, the elements of a true poem are precisely such nuclei, disgorged, unlike, purged of the suffering self; they become that around which a possible new world may accrete.

It would be too much to say that no one now practises this poetry of decreation; but much English poetry of these days is neither decreative nor destructive, expressing a modest selfishness which escapes both the purgative effort and the blame. America has, I think, its destructive poetry, which tends to be a poetry of manifesto; and in Lowell it seems to have a decreative poet. One way to tell them is by a certain ambiguity in your own response. *The Waste Land,* and also *Hugh Selwyn Mauberley,* can strike you in certain moments as emperors without clothes; discrete poems cobbled into a sequence which is always inviting the censure of pretentiousness. It is with your own proper fictive covering that you hide their nakedness and make them wise. Perhaps there is in *Life Studies* an ambivalence of the same sort. Certainly to have Eliot's great poem in one's life involves an irrevocable but repeated act of love. This is not called for by merely schismatic poetry, the poetry of destruction.

This is why our most lively sense of what it means to be alive in poetry continues to stem from the 'modern' of forty years ago. Deeply conditioned by the original experience of decreation, we may find it hard to understand that without it poetry had no future we can now seriously conceive of. It is true that the exhortations which accompanied Eliot's nuclear achievement are of only secondary interest. What survives is a habit of mind that looks for analysis, analysis by controlled unreason. This habit can be vulgarised: analysis of the most severe kind degenerates into chatter about breakdown and dissociation. *The Waste Land* has been used thus, as a myth of decadence, a facile evasion. Eliot is in his capacity as thinker partly to blame for this. Arnold complained that Carlyle 'led us out into the wilderness and left us there.' So did Eliot, despite his conviction that he knew the way; even before the 'conversion' he had a vision of a future dominated by Bradley, Frazer, and Henry James. We need not complain, so long as the response to the wilderness is authentic; but often it is a comfortable unfelt acceptance of tragedy. *The Waste Land* is in one light an imperial epic; but such comforts as it can offer are not compatible with any illusions, past, present, or future.

This is not the way the poem is usually read nowadays; but most people who know about poetry will still admit that it is a very difficult poem, though it invites glib or simplified interpretation. As I said, one can think of it as a mere arbitrary sequence upon which we have been persuaded to impose an order. But the true order, I think, is there to be found, unique, unrepeated, resistant to synthesis. The *Four Quartets* seem by comparison isolated in their eminence, tragic, often crystalline in the presentation of the temporal agony, but personal; and closer sometimes to commentary than to the thing itself. When the *Quartets* speak of a pattern of timeless moments, of the point of intersection, they speak *about* that pattern and that point; the true image of them is *The Waste Land.* There the dreams cross, the dreams in which begin responsibilities. (pp. 74-7)

> *Frank Kermode, "A Babylonish Dialect," in his* Continuities, *Random House, 1968, pp. 67-77.*

ROBERT W. FRENCH

[*The Waste Land: A Facsimile and Transcript of the Original Drafts, Including the Annotations of Ezra Pound,* edited by Valerie Eliot,] is invaluable, not only for the mass of new material it offers but also for the introduction, designed to give the reader some sense of the circumstances surrounding the composition and publication of *The Waste Land.* As much as possible, [Valerie Eliot] has allowed Eliot to tell the story in his own words, through letters. The introduction shows that an edition of Eliot's letters, should we ever see it, will be of extraordinary interest, for the excerpts in this volume depict clearly the strains, tensions and anxieties under which Eliot was laboring during these difficult years. He was overworked and exhausted, his finances were precarious, and there were constant problems of health, his wife's even more than his own. . . . It may be that Eliot's achievement is even more remarkable than we had hitherto suspected.

The Waste Land manuscript contains, in addition to the lines that became the poem we know, several hundred lines once considered for inclusion in the poem and several hundred more lines of miscellaneous poems. The manuscript is, of course, the one that was presented to Ezra Pound for his annotations in 1922, was sent to John Quinn later in the same year, and was long assumed to have been lost until in 1968 it was revealed to be in the New York Public Library. Of Pound's role, Eliot has written: "It was in 1922 that I placed before him in Paris the manuscript of a sprawling, chaotic poem called *The Waste Land* which left his hands, reduced to about half its size, in the form in which it appears in print. I should like to think," Eliot added, "that the manuscript, with the suppressed passages, had disappeared irrecoverably; yet on the other hand, I should wish the blue penciling on it to be preserved as irrefutable evidence of Pound's critical genius." The manuscript is fascinating reading, and will not soon be exhausted. The facsimile of the manuscript appears on the left-hand page and the transcript on the right, with Pound's annotations in red. (pp. 470-71)

The evidence of the manuscript points to at least two basic conclusions. It has been suggested in the past that if we had the original text, the poem might be more coherent, the transitions clearer and the structure more sharply defined. Not true; if the complete manuscript had been printed in 1922, the same kinds of questions would still have been asked and the poem would still have been called incoherent. If anything, the complete manuscript creates more problems than the published text, if only because it is longer and offers more parts to be accounted for. When Eliot himself was asked in 1959 if the excisions changed "the intellectual structure" of the poem, he answered, "No, I think it was just as structureless, only in a more futile way, in the longer version."

The second conclusion has to do with Pound's role. Sometimes Eliot took his advice and sometimes he did not; but of course we do not know, apart from a few scattered remarks preserved by Eliot, exactly what Pound may have *said* to him in Paris during their discussion of the poem. Pound's notations sometimes point to definite revisions, sometimes not; but when his meaning is clear, he is generally sound and right. As a critic, in short, Pound looks very good. He is especially helpful in pushing Eliot toward conciseness and precision. For example, in a draft of the typist episode Eliot wrote: "Across her brain one half-formed thought may pass." Pound growled, "make up yr. mind you Tiresias if you know know damn well or else you dont." Tiresias made up his mind; in the published text the line reads, "Her brain allows one half-formed thought to pass."

Three major sections were deleted from *The Waste Land,* but none of them would make the poem any better than it is; Eliot was right to leave them out (and of course the final decision was his, whatever suggestions Pound may have made). It was Eliot, apparently, not Pound, who canceled the original opening of the poem, a fifty-four line section in which the speaker recalls a night on the town ("First we had a couple of feelers down at Tom's place"). It is a relaxed and colloquial piece of writing, but compared to the verse of the pub scene—that other bit of low life—the verse is slack and lacks tension; it would have made a slow opening to the poem.

The second major deletion was an eighty-seven-line imitation of Pope, intended as the opening of Section III, "The Fire Sermon." Pound scratched a line through the entire poem, and he was absolutely right. As Eliot has recalled, Pound told him that "Pope has done this so well that you cannot do it better; and if you mean this as a burlesque, you had better suppress it, for you cannot parody Pope unless you can write better than Pope—and you can't." The verse is patterned after *The Rape of the Lock* and one cannot read far in it without thinking of how good Pope's poem is. For Belinda, Eliot offers us Fresca (who, though deleted from *The Waste Land,* remains to make her bid for immortality in the closing lines of *Gerontion*), but something is missing. Compared, say, to the complex harmonies of the opening lines of "A Game of Chess," where *The Rape of the Lock* hovers lightly in the background, the Fresca section is trivial and not even very clever; certainly there is nothing in its bland couplets of the distinctive tones that Eliot has given to modern poetry. Reading the manuscript, we feel both shock and relief when we make the sharp transition from Fresca to:

> A rat crept softly through the vegetation
> Dragging its slimy belly on the bank . . .

By these lines and those that follow (187-202 of the published text), Pound has written just what he should have: "O.K." and "Stet" on the typescript; and on the carbon, one word, "Echt."

The most interesting of the major deletions is the third, the original opening of Section IV, "Death by Water." This is an eighty-three-line poem inspired by Ulysses' narrative in the *Inferno,* Canto XXVI, and to a lesser extent by Tennyson's *Ulysses;* it tells of voyage and shipwreck off the New England coast, and it includes the "Phlebas the Phoenician" lines at the end as a sort of coda. Pound didn't like the poem; without comment he canceled lines and whole sections of it. (Disappointed, Eliot wrote him from London to ask if Phlebas should also be deleted, but Pound insisted that Phlebas was an integral part of the poem and should be retained.) The poem opens with three quatrains extolling the effect of the sea on the sailor, who "Retains, even ashore, in public bars or streets, / Something inhuman, clean and dignified." This is an intrusive bit of moralizing and deserves to be cut, but the narrative itself moves with admirable directness to a conclusion in Dantean wordplay:

> And if Another knows, I know I know not,
> Who only know that there is no more noise now.

Pound may have thought the passage too derivative, and probably he was right to urge its omission, for Phlebas alone is sufficient to carry the theme. Still, it is good that the poem has been preserved.

So we have it now, the long-lost manuscript, and like *The*

Waste Land itself, it is simply unavoidable; there it is, large in the foreground, and there is no way around it. Nor should there be. If I may speak from personal experience, I have found in teaching Eliot to undergraduates that he is increasingly regarded as a kindred soul; it may be that he is about to become a contemporary poet again. (pp. 471-72)

Robert W. French, "The Invisible Poet," in The Nation, *New York, Vol. 213, No. 15, November 8, 1971, pp. 470-72.*

HUGH KENNER

[*The Waste Land: A Facsimile and Transcript of the Original Drafts* is the lost] manuscript with the legendary Pound revisions. . . . Three years ago, divulging its whereabouts, the New York Public Library allowed the distinguished bibliographer Donald Gallup some 20 hours to make notes for a descriptive article. Next the public was allowed to gawk at the sheets under glass, while guards hassled anyone spotted with a notebook. Now scholarship has been spared years of unseemly squabbling by the fact that the poet's widow and literary executor, a woman of decision and scholarly talent, has undertaken to prepare a facsimile edition herself.

No one should want to carp about it. Valerie Eliot has worked with skill and devotion: let one anecdote illustrate. About 25 lines into "A Game of Chess" Pound scribbled marginal words which Mr. Gallup in his hurried session with the papers transcribed "Too perrty." To Mrs. Eliot that double *r* looked like an *n*. "Penty"? Pentametric? She hied her to Venice and consulted the ancient oracle. "I have never in my life used the word 'perrty.'" Nevertheless a pen was placed in the maestro's hand; nevertheless he was persuaded to write "penty" and also "perrty"; next these inditings were compared with the ms., and when we find "penty" in the type-facsimile facing the photo-facsimile, we may be sure the reading was not lightly arrived at. (p. 25)

Elsewhere Eliot undertook revisions after Pound had marked the unsatisfactoriness. Often whole pages went out. And once we can watch a virtual collaboration, as the two of them wrest majestic eloquence from the passage that began "At the violet hour . . ." and then meandered its way through 17 quatrains, 68 lines that are now 41.

"Verse not interesting enough as verse to warrant so much of it," says the marginal injunction. There was so much of it—so many weak lines—because quatrains were being filled out:

> I Tiresias, old man with wrinkled dugs
> Perceived the scene, and foretold the rest,
> Knowing the manner of these crawling bugs,
> I too awaited the expected guest.

Pound marked the third of these lines "too easy"; it went out, and we have, miraculously, not a wounded quatrain but a rhyme's augmented intensity. Out, too, went many weak lines meant to characterize "the young man carbuncular" (a salvaged phrase). Out went the typist's window-seat ("?not in that lodging house?"). Eliot restitched the remnants, and with many lines deleted and some conflated, the rhymes of dismembered quatrains burst like starshells. The admirable off-rhyme of one couplet—

> Bestows one final patronizing kiss
> And gropes his way, finding the stairs unlit

—survives from a draft in which these were no couplet at all but the *a* and *b* lines of a rhyme *abab.* And though we can now detect the ceremonies of such sonnets as Romeo and Juliet exchanged at their first meeting, these ghost sonnets were evidently quite unpremeditated, perhaps even unnoticed.

That is part of the fascination of *The Waste Land,* that the sheer authority of its verse makes relevant much that the author need not have been thinking of. And whether Eliot achieved that verse unaided (as in Part V, of which the pencil holograph, in substantially its final form, seems the work of one sitting), or whether the firm cadence was shaped by his friend out of protoplasmic tumtum, or whether the two of them hacked at a draft together, the verse as it finally went to the printer is seamless, as though there existed an impersonal style: as though they had been two 18th-century poets, for whom collaboration would not have been strange in the least.

In that age, well before the poetic of spontaneous overflow, the criteria for strong verse were everywhere sure, and another man's invention might supplement your own. Dr. Johnson revised Goldsmith's *Traveller* and *Deserted Village,* and actually wrote the concluding passages of both. Writers living and dead furnished lines for *The Dunciad,* much as many dead writers supplied details of *The Waste Land* (and both poems were eventually published with notes). So little were pith and elegance any man's property, that Pope translating the *Iliad* accumulated and adapted whatever good bits he could glean from former translations. Eliot in his long poem had aspired toward verse as impersonally assimilative as Pope's or Johnson's, which explains the fact that Pound could help him perfect it without their two personalities variegating the result. With the benefit of the parts that were cut out, we can see that one of the models for his poem was the 18th-century urban moral satire.

The name of Johnson may remind us of two titles that would have been appropriate for *The Waste Land.* Eliot might have called it *The Vanity of Human Wishes,* which is the lesson the Fire Sermon teaches. Still better, he might have called it *London: A Poem.* London is everywhere its focus.

> London, the swarming life you kill ·
> and breed,
> Huddled between the concrete and
> the sky,
> Responsive to the momentary need,
> Vibrates unconscious to its formal
> destiny . . .

—so commences a transitional passage which Pound first tinkered at and then deleted. Though ill-written, it alerts us to the Augustan tradition of the poet-moralist gazing through the city's prism at moral decay. That tradition sponsored a long section about drunken playboys which Pope might have conceived though he would have written it differently, and underwrote two fascinating Eliot pages that commence "The inhabitants of Hampstead have silk hats," and certainly shaped a pastiche of *The Rape of the Lock* in which Eliot tried to write as Pope would have written:

> Admonished by the sun's inclining
> ray,
> And swift approaches of the thiev-
> ish day,
> The white-armed Fresca blinks, and
> yawns, and gapes,
> Aroused from dreams of love and

pleasant rapes . . .

And against this weight of satiric particularity, of implicit measured denunciation, Eliot had poised a different order of 18th-century pastiche, rhymed trifles, an Exequy, and Elegy.

None of these survived, nor for that matter did the draft's least Augustan passage survive, a shipwreck narrative of which "Phlebas the Phoenician" is now the sole trace. What survived was what Eliot after all wrote best, stuff rooted in the Post-Impressionist tradition, not the Augustan, transposing into luminous riddles his private agonies. Yet as Racine's Alexandrine underlay the authority Baudelaire and Mallarmé could command, so the Augustan pentameter steadied Eliot's diction when he was writing scenes Pope could never have tackled, concerning the woman who said her nerves were bad.

For central to the poem's impulse lay his disastrous first marriage. . . . Vivien—it is tempting to call her Eliot's Zelda—was much of the time out of her mind, and yet she had a gift of brilliant mimicry (a few lines in the draft are in her hand). She drove Eliot nearly out of *his* mind, in ways we may guess at from the "bad nerves" interchange, which sounds transcribed from the life. (Pound's marginal comment was "Photography"; it is unsettling to read Vivien's comment also: "WONDERFUL.") (pp. 25-6)

"Most women have no characters at all," wrote Pope, meaning no fixed idiosyncratic scheme of passions. She metamorphosed before Eliot's eyes like a globule of quicksilver, glistening, deadly. Imitating from Pope and Johnson the moralist's persona, he struggled to fix in verse such an urban world as might contain her.

He handled the Augustan rhetorical machinery badly, and most of what he did with it was scrapped. The Augustan steadiness abided, to precipitate verse so impersonally strong, though with deeply personal origins, another man could help improve it. And the century was granted its most influential poem, achieved by an indirection and at a cost there was no means of estimating till now. (p. 26)

Hugh Kenner, "Where the Penty Went," in The New Republic, *Vol. 165, No. 20, November 13, 1971, pp. 25-6.*

RICHARD ELLMANN

Lloyd's most famous bank clerk revalued the poetic currency forty-nine years ago. As Joyce said, *The Waste Land* ended the idea of poetry for ladies. Whether admired or detested, it became, like *Lyrical Ballads* in 1798, a traffic signal. Hart Crane's letters, for instance, testify to his prompt recognition that from that time forward his work must be to outflank Eliot's poem. Today footnotes do their worst to transform innovations into inevitabilities. After a thousand explanations, *The Waste Land* is no longer a puzzle poem, except for the puzzle of choosing among the various solutions. To be penetrable is not, however, to be predictable. The sweep and strangeness with which Eliot delineated despair resist temptations to patronize Old Possum as old hat. Particular discontinuities continue to surprise even if the idea of discontinuous form—which Eliot himself was to forsake—is now almost as familiar as its sober counterpart. The compound of regular verse and vers libre still wears some of the effrontery with which in 1922 it flouted both schools. The poem retains the air of a splendid feat.

Eliot himself was inclined to pooh-pooh its grandeur. His chiseled comment, which F. O. Matthiessen quotes, disclaimed any intention of expressing "the disillusionment of a generation," and said that he did not like the word "generation" or have a plan to endorse anyone's "illusion of disillusion." To Theodore Spencer he remarked in humbler mood,

> Various critics have done me the honor to interpret the poem in terms of criticism of the contemporary world, have considered it, indeed, as an important bit of social criticism. To me it was only the relief of a personal and wholly insignificant grouse against life. It is just a piece of rhythmical grumbling.

This statement is prominently displayed by Mrs. Valerie Eliot in her superb decipherment and elucidation of *The Waste Land* manuscript. If it is more than an expression of her husband's genuine modesty, it appears to imply that he considered his own poem, as he considered *Hamlet,* an inadequate projection of its author's tangled emotions, a Potemkin village rather than a proper objective correlative. Yet no one will wish away the entire civilizations and cities, wars, hordes of people, religions of East and West, and exhibits from many literatures in many languages which lined the Thames in Eliot's ode to dejection. And even if London was only his state of mind at the time, the picture he paints of it is convincing.

His remark to Spencer, made after a lapse of years, perhaps catches up another regret, that the poem emphasized his disgust at the expense of much else in his nature. It identified him with a sustained severity of tone, with pulpited (though brief) citations of Biblical and Sophoclean anguish, so that he became an Ezekiel or at least a Tiresias. (In the original version John the Divine made a Christian third among the prophets.) While Eliot did not wish to be considered merely a satirist in his earlier verse, he did not welcome either the public assumption that his poetic mantle had become a hair shirt.

In its early version *The Waste Land* was woven out of more kinds of material and was therefore less grave and less organized. The first two sections had an over-all title (each had its own title as well), "He Do the Police in Different Voices," a quotation from *Our Mutual Friend.* Dickens has the widow Higden say of her adopted child, "Sloppy is a beautiful reader of a newspaper. He do the Police in different voices." Among the many voices in the first version, Eliot placed at the very beginning a long, conversational passage describing an evening on the town, starting at "Tom's place" (a rather arch use of his own name), moving on to a brothel, and concluding with a bathetic sunrise. . . . This vapid prologue Eliot decided, apparently on his own, to expunge, and went straight into the now familiar beginning of the poem.

Other voices were expunged by Eliot's friend Ezra Pound, who called himself the *"sage homme"* (male midwife) of the poem. For example, there was an extended, unsuccessful imitation of *The Rape of the Lock* at the beginning of "The Fire Sermon." . . . The episode of the typist was originally much longer and more laborious. . . . (p. 10)

Pound persuaded Eliot also to omit a number of poems which were for a time intended to be placed between the poem's sections, then at the end of it. One was a renewed thrust at poor Bleistein, drowned now but still haplessly Jewish and luxurious under water. . . . Pound urged that this and several other mortuary poems did not add anything either to *The Waste Land* or to Eliot's previous work. He had already written "the longest poem in the English langwidge. Don't try to bust all records by prolonging it three pages further." As a result of this resmithying by *il miglior fabbro,* the poem gained immensely in concentration. Yet Eliot, feeling too solemnized by it, thought of prefixing some humorous doggerel by Pound about its composition. Later, in a more resolute effort to escape the limits set by *The Waste Land,* he wrote "Fragment of Agon," and eventually, "somewhere the other side of despair," turned to drama.

Eliot's remark to Spencer calls *The Waste Land* a personal poem. His critical theory was that the artist should seek impersonality, but this was probably intended as not so much a nostrum as an antidote, a means to direct emotion rather than let it spill. His letters indicate that he regarded his poems as consequent upon his experiences. When a woman in Dublin remarked that Yeats had never really felt anything, Eliot asked in consternation, "How can you say that?" *The Waste Land* compiled many of the nightmarish feelings he had suffered during the seven years from 1914 to 1921, that is, from his coming to England until his temporary collapse.

Thanks to the letters quoted in Mrs. Valerie Eliot's Introduction, and to various biographical leaks, the incidents of these years begin to take shape. (pp. 10, 12)

The personal life out of which came Eliot's personal poem now began to be lived in earnest. Vivienne Eliot suffered obscurely from nerves, her health was subject to frequent collapses, she complained of neuralgia, of insomnia. Ezra Pound, who knew her well, was worried that the passage in *The Waste Land,*

> My nerves are bad to-night. Yes, bad. Stay with me.
> Speak to me. Why do you never speak? Speak.
> What are you thinking of? What thinking? What?
> I never know what you are thinking. Think.

might be too photographic. But Vivienne Eliot, who offered her own comments on her husband's verse (and volunteered two excellent lines for the lowlife dialogue in "A Game of Chess"), marked the same passage as "Wonderful." She relished the presentation of her symptoms in broken meter. She was less keen, however, on another line from this section,

> The ivory men make company between us,

and got her husband to remove it. Presumably its implications were too close to the quick of their marital difficulties. Years afterward Eliot made a fair copy of *The Waste Land* in his own handwriting, and reinserted the line from memory. (It should now be added to the final text.) But he had implied his feelings six months after his marriage when he wrote in a letter to Conrad Aiken, "I have lived through material for a score of long poems in the last six months."

Russell commented less sympathetically about the Eliots later, "I was fond of them both, and endeavoured to help them in their troubles until I discovered that their troubles were what they enjoyed." Eliot was capable of estimating the situation shrewdly himself. In his poem **"The Death of Saint Narcissus,"** which *Poetry* was to publish in 1917 and then, probably at his request, failed to do, he wrote of his introspective saint, "his flesh was in love with the burning arrows. . . . As he embraced them his white skin surrendered itself to the redness of blood, and satisfied him."

For Eliot, however, the search for suffering was not contemptible. He was remorseful about his own real or imagined feelings, he was self-sacrificing about hers, he thought that remorse and sacrifice, not to mention affection, had value. In the Grail legends which underlie *The Waste Land,* the Fisher King suffers a Dolorous Stroke which maims him sexually. In Eliot's case the Dolorous Stroke had been marriage. He was helped thereby to the poem's initial clash of images, "April is the cruellest month," as well as to hollow echoes of Spenser's *Prothalamion* ("Sweet Thames, run softly till I end my song"). From the barren winter of his academic labors Eliot had been roused to the barren springtime of his nerve-wracked marriage. His life spread into paradox.

Other events of these years seem reflected in the poem. The war, though scarcely mentioned, exerts pressure. In places the poem may be a covert memorial to Henry Ware Eliot, the unforgiving father of the ill-adventured son. Henry Eliot died in January, 1919, and Eliot's first explicit statement of his intention to write a long poem comes in letters written later in the year. The references to a father's death probably derive as much from this actual death as from *The Tempest,* to which Eliot's notes evasively refer. As for the drowning of the young sailor, whether he is Ferdinand or a Phoenician, the war furnished Eliot with many examples, such as Jean Verdenal, a friend from his Sorbonne days, who was killed in the Dardanelles. But it may be as well an extrapolation of Eliot's feeling that he was now fatherless as well as rudderless.

The fact that the principal speaker appears in a new guise in the last section, with its imagery of possible resurrection, suggests that the drowning is to be taken symbolically rather than literally, as the end of youth. Eliot was addicted to the portrayal of characters who had missed their chances, become old before they had really been young. So the drowned sailor, like the buried corpse, may be construed as the young Eliot, buried in or about *"l'an trentiesme de son eage,"* like the young Pound in the first part of *Hugh Selwyn Mauberley.*

It has been thought that Eliot wrote *The Waste Land* in Switzerland while recovering from a breakdown. But much of it was written earlier, some in 1914 and some, if Conrad Aiken is to be believed, even before. A letter to Quinn indicates that much of it was on paper in May, 1921. The breakdown or, rather, the rest cure did give Eliot enough time to fit the pieces together and add what was necessary. (p. 14)

The manuscript had its own history. In gratitude to John Quinn, the New York lawyer and patron of the arts, Eliot presented it to him. Quinn died in 1924, and most of his possessions were sold at auction; some, however, including the manuscript, were inherited by his sister. When the sister died, her daughter put many of Quinn's papers in storage. But in the early 1950s she searched among them and found the manuscript, which she then sold to the Berg Collection of the New York Public Library. The then curator enjoyed exercising seignorial rights over the collection, and kept secret the whereabouts of the manuscript. After his death its existence was divulged, and Valerie Eliot was persuaded to do this knowledgeable edition.

She did so the more readily, perhaps, because her husband had always hoped that the manuscript would turn up as evidence of Pound's critical genius. It is a classic document. No one will deny that it is weaker throughout than the final ver-

sion. Pound comes off very well indeed; his importance is comparable to that of Louis Bouilhet in the history of the composition of *Madame Bovary.* Yeats, who also sought and received Pound's help, described it to Lady Gregory, "To talk over a poem with him is like getting you to put a sentence into dialect. All becomes clear and natural." Pound could not be intimidated by pomposity, even Baudelairean pomposity:

> London, the swarming life you kill and breed,
> Huddled between the concrete and the sky;
> Responsive to the momentary need,
> Vibrates unconscious to its formal destiny.

Next to this he wrote "B-ll-S." (His comments appear in red ink on the printed transcription which is furnished along with photographs of the manuscript.) Pound was equally peremptory about a passage which Eliot seems to have cherished, perhaps because of childhood experiences in sailing. It was the depiction at the beginning of "Death by Water" of a long voyage, a modernizing and Americanizing of Ulysses' final voyage as given by Dante:

> Kingfisher weather, with a light fair breeze,
> Full canvas, and the eight sails drawing well.
> We beat around the cape and laid our course
> From the Dry Salvages to the eastern banks.
> A porpoise snored upon the phosphorescent swell,
> A triton rang the final warning bell
> Astern, and the sea rolled, asleep.

From these lines Pound was willing to spare only

> with a light fair breeze
> We beat around the cape from the Dry Salvages.
> A porpoise snored on the swell.

All the rest was seamanship and literature. It became clear that the whole passage might as well go, and Eliot asked humbly if he should delete Phlebas as well. But Pound was as eager to preserve the good as to expunge the bad: he insisted that Phlebas stay because of the earlier references to the drowned Phoenician sailor. With equal taste, he made almost no change in the last section of the poem, which Eliot always considered to be the best, perhaps because it led into his subsequent verse.

Eliot did not bow to all his friend's revisions. Pound feared the references to London might sound like Blake, and objected specifically to the lines,

> To where Saint Mary Woolnoth kept the time,
> With a dead sound on the final stroke of nine.

Eliot wisely retained them, only changing "time" to "hours." Next to the passage,

> You gave me hyacinths first a year ago;
> They called me the hyacinth girl,

Pound marked "Marianne," and evidently feared—though Mrs. Eliot's note indicates that he has forgotten—that the use of quotation marks would seem an imitation of Marianne Moore. But Eliot, for whom the moment in the hyacinth garden had obsessional force—it was based in part on an incident in his own life—made no change.

Essentially Pound could do for Eliot what Eliot could not do for himself. There was some reciprocity, because when the first three *Cantos* appeared in 1917, Eliot offered criticism which resulted in their being completely altered. It seems, from the revised versions, that he objected to the elaborate windup, and urged a more direct confrontation of the reader and the material. A similar theory is at work in Pound's changes in *The Waste Land.* Chiefly by excision, he enabled Eliot to tighten his form. Perhaps partially in reaction, he studied out means of loosening his own in the *Cantos.* (pp. 15-16)

Richard Ellmann, "The First Waste Land—I," in The New York Review of Books, Vol. XVII, No. 8, November 18, 1971, pp. 10, 12, 14-16.

BERNARD BERGONZI

In 1956 Eliot wrote, apropos of John Livingston Lowes' *Road to Xanadu,* "poetic originality is largely an original way of assembling the most disparate and unlikely material to make a new whole." "Assembling" is not a word one usually applies to writing poetry, but it is very relevant to Eliot's own methods. . . . Eliot's basic method of composition was more traditionally Romantic than is often realised, with a frank reliance on unconscious sources of inspiration to produce brief poetic passages, or perhaps just single lines, of great isolated intensity. The next, and equally arduous, stage in the assembling of a whole poem was akin to the methods of an artist in mosaic or collage. Fragments or phrases not suitable for one poem would be carefully kept, sometimes for years, until they could be used in another. It is this aspect of Eliot's art that is most fascinatingly revealed in the long-lost manuscripts of *The Waste Land,* a poem whose most crucial line is certainly *"These fragments I have shored against my ruins."*

For a long time readers have wistfully assumed that if only those legendary manuscripts would turn up then the worst difficulties might be resolved, since Eliot's *ur*-version must have been more lucid and coherent than the final product of Ezra Pound's ruthless editing. That notion, at least, is now dispelled. The first draft of *The Waste Land,* brought back by Eliot from his rest-cure at Lausanne in the autumn of 1921, was, as he once deprecatingly told an interviewer, "just as structureless, only in a more futile way." The original manuscript consisted of several extended sections—in blank verse, quatrains and heroic couplets—plus a number of shorter fragments, that Eliot hoped could be somehow "worked in." If Eliot's original design had a unity it was of a very loose kind, for the work that he brought back for Lausanne was essentially a set of separate poems; even after *The Waste Land* was published in 1922 reviewers tended to refer to it as "poems" rather than "a poem." Mrs Eliot's admirable edition shows clearly the streamlining effect of the editorial cuts, by no means all of which were made by Pound, as Eliot modestly implied. It was a pencil stroke in Eliot's own hand that excised the original opening, a low-pressure chatty passage about Boston low-life, thereby ensuring that the first line was "April is the cruellest month" rather than "First we had a couple of feelers down at Tom's place." Most of the material that was cut out, whether by Eliot himself, or by Pound, deserved to go. But I think Eliot was mistaken when he removed, at Pound's suggestion, the original epigraph from Conrad's *Heart of Darkness:*

Did he live his life again in every detail of desire, temptation, and surrender during that supreme moment of complete knowledge? He cried out in a whisper at some image, at some vision—he cried out twice, a cry that was no more than a breath— "The horror! the horror!"

If *The Waste Land* had been prefaced with this quotation it might have been evident from the beginning that the poem is, at bottom, and anguished reliving of subjective experience, and not the "impersonal" meditation on cultural decline that so many commentators—whether sympathetic or unsympathetic—have assumed it to be. Conrad's lines point to the real subject of the poem; the word "surrender" had a peculiar significance for Eliot, and Conrad's use of it seems to be echoed later in *The Waste Land,* in "The awful daring of a moment's surrender" (and perhaps in **"Tradition and the Individual Talent"**, where Eliot says of the poet, "what happens is a continual surrender of himself as he is at the moment to something which is more valuable").

There is one other place where Pound's excisions may have been misdirected. Part IV, "Death by Water", was originally much longer. After a very inferior set of opening quatrains, the verse develops into a mostly well-written account of a disastrous voyage by a New England fishing vessel, with deliberate echoes of Tennyson's and Dante's Ulysses. There are striking anticipations of the Quartets of twenty years later. . . . Some cutting, particularly of the sailor's talk, was probably required, but it is a pity that the whole section had to go; the parallel between the New England fishermen and Phlebas the Phoenician was effective, and the Phlebas passage by itself (an adaptation from the closing lines of one of Eliot's French poems of 1918, **"Dans le Restaurant"**) stands rather too abruptly. Eliot, in fact, wanted to delete that too, when the first part of "Death by Water" went, but Pound dissuaded him. Characteristically, though, Eliot hung on to a couple of phrases from the deleted lines, which later turned up in **"The Dry Salvages"** and **"Marina."**

On the other hand, Pound's editing greatly improved "The Fire Sermon." This section originally opened with a long set of Popean couplets, which were adroit enough in their way, but which only reiterated points made more tersely elsewhere about the emptiness of fashionable life. As an exercise in the smart neo-classicising of the twenties—there are musical parallels in Stravinsky or Prokofiev—they have a certain curiosity value, but it wasn't really Eliot's kind of thing. Nor, for that matter, were the quatrain poems, like **"Sweeney Erect"**, that he wrote between 1917 and 1919, largely as a result of reading Gautier under Pound's influence. In the first draft of "The Fire Sermon" the account by Tiresias of the seduction of a bored typist by the "young man carbuncular" was told in a long sequence of such quatrains. Pound's cuts boldly ignored the rhyme scheme, so that the lines ended up as the section of continuous and irregularly rhyming verse that appeared in the published version. One of the minor puzzles in that version is the peculiar syntax of the lines,

the evening hour that strives

Homeward, and brings the sailor home from sea,
The typist home at teatime, clears her breakfast, lights
Her stove, and lays out food in tins.

It now looks as if this elision was the result of inadequate suturing after the editorial cuts. The manuscript read

The typist home at teatime, who begins
To clear away her broken breakfast, lights
Her stove, and lays out squalid food in tins. . . .

Pound's marginal comment on these lines was "verse not interesting enough as verse to warrant so much of it." Certainly the taut and rapid final version is a vast improvement on the laboured quatrains. At first there was a good deal more about the young man, whom Eliot seems to have regarded with immense distaste but with a certain novelistic interest, describing him as a layabout who frequents the Café Royal, and a crude but confident womaniser. If some readers find these lines deplorably snobbish and anti-life, one can only say that the original version was far more so; the young man's departure might have read like this, were it not for a cautious comment by Pound:

> —Bestows one final patronising kiss,
> And gropes his way, finding the stairs unlit;
> And at the corner where the stable is,
> Delays only to urinate, and spit.

Eliot was much closer to his central concerns in some fragmentary and unused lines about London, seen, as elsewhere in *The Waste Land,* as a Baudelairean inferno. A line, cancelled by Eliot himself, which read "London, your people is bound upon the wheel," reflects one of the central configurations of his imagination: "I see crowds of people, walking round in a ring" and "Here we go round the prickly pear."

The most interesting material lies not so much in the cancellations as in the early fragments, in some cases written several years before the 1921 draft, from which Eliot extracted lines or images for use in *The Waste Land.* "The Death of Saint Narcissus" is one such which provided the source for "Come in under the shadow of this red rock." Perhaps the most powerful lines in *The Waste Land* are those beginning "A woman drew her long black hair out tight," and in this edition there is a draft of them which Mrs. Eliot suggests, on the evidence of handwriting, may have been written in 1914, or even before. In another manuscript of the same early date, we find a version of the opening lines of "What the Thunder Said", astonishingly combined with a Laforguean conclusion in the manner of Eliot's first poetic exercises written at Harvard in 1909:

> After the ending of this inspiration
> And the torches and the faces and the shouting
> The world seemed futile—like a Sunday outing.

Such pivotal lines look both forward and back, emphasising the imaginative unity of Eliot's work. So, too, does a seemingly later fragment called "The Death of the Duchess." I found this exciting, because it provided the missing link between two passages of Eliot's verse which have always struck me by their resemblances, although quite separate in time: the edgily dramatic speech of the two neurotic women in **"Portrait of a Lady"** (1910) and "A Game of Chess" in *The Waste Land* (1921). "The Death of the Duchess" takes its point of departure from *The Duchess of Malfi,* in the scene where the Duchess is surprised in her bed-chamber by her evil brother Ferdinand. This draft by Eliot contains most of the lines later incorporated into the middle section of "A Game of Chess", while being an unmistakable attempt to recapture, perhaps even imitate, the manner of **"Prufrock"** and **"Portrait of a Lady."** There is a similar nervous but intense sexuality:

> With her back turned, her arms were bare
> Fixed for a question, her hands behind her hair
> And the firelight shining where the muscle drew.

At one place Pound has scribbled in the margin, "cadence reproduction from Prufrock or Portrait of a Lady."

When the *Waste Land* manuscripts were first discovered I feared that they might disintegrate the poem as we have always known it. But Mrs Eliot's edition reassuringly makes this look unlikely: *The Waste Land,* in its final version, is so obviously superior to the drafts—apart from the special case of "Death by Water"—that they are not likely to affect our reading of it. What they can provide is the traditional Romantic pleasure of seeing how a great poet's mind works. (pp. 80-2)

Bernard Bergonzi, "Maps of the Waste Land," in Encounter, *Vol. XXXVIII, No. 4, April, 1972, pp. 80-3.*

GEORGE STEINER

Whether we will or not, the simple fact of time plays decisive tricks on our judgments of art and literature. When they were producing their major work, in the years 1910 to 1940, Ezra Pound, T. S. Eliot, and James Joyce impressed their audience as iconoclasts, as demolition experts bent on blowing up traditional literary and linguistic forms in the name of esoteric modernism. They were the radicals, sacking the Victorian citadel from outside, coming from Idaho, Missouri, and Ireland to display their wild wares in London and Paris. Today, this picture looks all wrong. What seems to us obvious in the genius of "Personae" and the *Cantos,* in *The Waste Land* and Eliot's essays, in *Ulysses* is the overwhelming force of tradition, the explicit recourse to a body of epic and lyric poetry that goes back to Homer and Catullus. Pound's travelogue through history and civilization, Eliot's constant reference to Aeschylus, Dante, the Elizabethans, and Baudelaire, Joyce's variations on the themes of Homer now appear to us like the very opposite of iconoclasm. They are deliberate acts of conservation, of inventory. They are a nostalgic, obsessed voyage through the museum of high culture just before closing time, or—in Eliot's own famous phrase—"fragments shored" against the impending ruin of classical and European values. Seen in this way, the marginal origins of Pound, Eliot, and Joyce, their upbringing on the frontier of the declining cultural imperium, make beautiful sense: only a man from Idaho or St. Louis would bring such indefatigable zest, such "tourist-passion" to the job of discovering and cataloguing the old splendors of Latin and Christian Europe. The Baedeker guidebooks to which Eliot referred scathingly in his poetry were, in fact, his own, diligently disguised, yet visible almost to the end, under his remarkable powers of social assimilation. It is now clear that the great masters of the first half of the twentieth century—Picasso, Stravinsky, Pound, Eliot, and Joyce—were the last classicists. Their works are crammed with quotations from, allusions to, pastiches and parodies of the best art, music, and literature of the previous two thousand years. They were not destroyers but custodians of tradition. This is exactly why so much of Picasso's painting, of Stravinsky's music, of the *Cantos* and *The Waste Land* is collage, the cunning juxtaposition and kaleidoscoping of bits and pieces from the masters of the past: Velázquez, Ingres, Mozart, Vergil, Donne. Collage is another way of saying "anthology."

A great part of what is most characteristic in the "modernist" movement now looks like inspired anthologizing and editing. The famous string of allusions in the last twenty-six lines of *The Waste Land*—to Webster's *White Devil,* the *Inferno,* the *Purgatorio,* the *Pervigilium Veneris,* Nerval, Thomas Kyd's *Spanish Tragedy,* and the Upanishads—strikes one nowadays as the manifesto of all archivists and graduate students, a final race through the stacks before the illiterates and the book burners take over. This view, obviously, is in its way as distorted as was that of the contemporary public, which regarded Eliot's verse and Joyce's prose as the last word in avant-garde extravagance and subversion. Pound's "Mauberley," Eliot's **"Love Song of J. Alfred Prufrock,"** *Ulysses* clearly *were* revolutionary acts that knocked feeling into new shapes, that rearranged the inner landscape just as explosively as did *The Rite of Spring* or Picasso's *Demoiselles d'Avignon.* The question is, how did they do it? What was radical and new about works so explicitly grounded in classical myths and the poetry and fiction of the past? Can there be a kind of iconoclastic academicism, a strategy that keeps tradition vital by often violent appropriation and distortion? This, in fact, was what happened. A good deal of what is alive of Homer and the epic manner for us today belongs to Joyce. To the degree that they are a "present past"—certainly in the Anglo-American context—Dante, the Jacobean dramatists, and the French Symbolists come to us via Eliot's readings and citations. But just because these readings have themselves taken on a certain classic authority, we find it hard to reimagine what was modern—indeed, shocking—in the techniques of **"Gerontion"** or *The Waste Land.* They have themselves become a part of that long legacy of echo that has controlled Western literature from the Romans to at least the nineteen-forties. This dilemma of ambiguous distance is especially acute with regard to Eliot, now seven years gone. A sudden dip of reputation, a bit of limbo, usually ensues immediately after the death of a great writer. Shaw and Gide are in such a limbo now. But the case of Eliot is more complicated. His influence as a critic remains formidable in the academic world; much of the current syllabus in the study of English literature is the direct product of his essays and pronouncements, a good many of them occasional and opaque. A number of his poems are probably all that the high-school student and layman will ever be forced to meet of modern, "difficult" verse. Yet at other levels they are curiously inert (and all but one of the plays, *Murder in the Cathedral,* are dead). If Eliot's poetic influence is ubiquitous, it is also hard to pin down. Is there today an important poet besides Robert Lowell who is really continuing in Eliot's vein? Pound's actual role in shaping modern literature, in enforcing the values of style that we have until very recently felt to be right, seems more important than that of Eliot, more disinterested and comprehensive. There are now moments in which Yeats looks a greater poet than Eliot—*not* the more influential, not the more critically significant, but simply the writer of more poems absolutely of the first rank. And the taut marvel of Yeats' late, experimental plays still waits for general discovery. If anything, those Victorian and *fin-de-siècle* tastes that Eliot sought to demolish but that both Yeats and Pound partly incorporated in their own modernism are coming back into the light. There are aspects of the early Eliot, and even of *Four Quartets,* that now appear to us more dated than Tennyson and certainly less urgent than the best poems of Hardy. Time is an odd mirror.

Such uncertainties have added particular excitement to the publication of a facsimile and transcript of the original drafts of *The Waste Land.* (pp. 134, 137)

Mrs. Eliot's edition of *The Waste Land* is a model of scholarly tact and presentation. It includes a photographic facsimile of the original material . . . a well-annotated transcript, an exact reprint of the first edition, by Boni & Liveright in New York in 1922, and an introduction setting the poem in its biographical context. By the use of different colors and fronts, Mrs. Eliot allows the reader to distinguish between the poet's own cancellations and revisions, the marginalia of Ezra Pound, and the important comments and objections from the hand of Eliot's first wife, Vivien. The resulting mosaic is so fascinating, and gives so unusual a look into the workshop of a great writer, that the student of poetry and of psychology will want to live patiently with this extraordinary text, much of whose importance lies in minute details.

Some general points can nevertheless be made. Under Pound's criticism, Eliot reduced his original draft by more than half. . . . [The] fact that *The Waste Land* ends as we know it seems due directly to Pound's stringency. In addition to his large-scale editorial interventions, there are very many local touches, corrections of metre, excisions of a line or of a word, queries as to exact meaning and intention. Pound's bite is characteristic and creative. "Across her brain one half-formed thought may pass," said Eliot of the lady who "turns and looks a moment in the glass." Pound circles and strikes out "may," commenting, "make up yr. mind you Tiresias if you know know damn well or else you dont." As we run down the margin of the page in the typescript that begins "The typist home at teatime" we find almost every facet of Pound's critical genius. He objects to "inversions not warranted by any real exigence of metre," he throws out a phrase on "crawling bugs" as "too easy," he damns the use of "perhaps" where decisiveness is called for, he quotes Verlaine to show up the weakness of a rhyme. Frequently Pound's contribution is a minute but vital alteration: "Under the brown fog of your winter dawn," in the great London passage, becomes "Under the brown fog of a winter noon"—an example of particular interest because it was Pound's dissatisfaction with the pronoun that led to the improvement of the whole line. Responding to the marginal note "Too tum-pum at a stretch," Eliot excised a single adjective from line 2 of the "A Game of Chess" section and gave the opening its now familiar tautness.

Yet the more one studies these drafts, the more difficult it is to arrive at a clear view of Pound's responsibility in the final product. On the one hand, he is indeed "the better craftsman" of Eliot's famous tribute. His ear for rhythm is surer, his demand for absolute tightness is emphatic and grounded in precisely the feeling for dramatic proportion that Eliot so often lacked. The heavy cuts Pound makes, giving *The Waste Land* the subtle unbalance, the close meshing via sudden leaps that we now know, suggest that he understood the poem better than did Eliot. Or, more precisely, that he understood a certain poem—the one we have. The drafts show us another possible poem—much looser, more personal, more local. But this is probably an oversimplification. A number of major excisions, among them a remarkable passage,

> Highbury bore me. Highbury's children
> Played under green trees and in the dusty Park,

were made by Eliot himself. These may have come as a direct result of conversation with Pound. We simply don't know. In other crucial instances, Eliot accepts Pound's criticism but recasts the text entirely in his own way, and finds a powerful improvement where Pound had only called for adjustment. In short, Pound's role seems to have been in the strictest sense maieutic: he elicited from Eliot excellences that were latent in Eliot himself—in himself alone and in his vision of the poem. Pound has never claimed more. And it may well be that Eliot's deep sense of indebtedness to Pound in regard to *The Waste Land* lay less in the improvement of the poem—

though Pound *was* a reader and objector of genius—than in the fact that Pound found even the first draft so prodigiously exciting and inspired ("About enough, Eliot's poem, to make the rest of us shut up shop," he wrote to Quinn a month after he had seen the text). Confidence was what Eliot, at that moment in his life, desperately needed.

It is the private misery behind the public poem that emerges most clearly from Valerie Eliot's preface, reticent as it is. She chooses as motto to her edition a remark by Eliot disclaiming any social import for *The Waste Land:* "To me it was only the relief of a personal and wholly insignificant grouse against life; it is just a piece of rhythmical grumbling." That "grouse" had, nevertheless, brought the poet to the edge of suicide. Though Mrs. Eliot quotes generously from her husband's letters, she also leaves a great deal in twilight. It is clear that the period from 1917 to 1922 was, for the young Eliot, one of almost constant nervous and financial strain. His health was at several points on the verge of complete collapse. Much of *The Waste Land* appears to have been written at a sanatorium in Lausanne, and the poem can be understood, in some part at least, as a therapeutic act, the working out of a "logic in disorder" without which Eliot's mental and physical stability might have broken down utterly. Valerie Eliot and the literary establishment have taken violent exception to the speculations about the master's private life that have been revived by this edition of *The Waste Land* and by the wholly unauthorized *T. S. Eliot: A Memoir,* by Robert Sencourt. As it happens, the late Mr. Sencourt's attempt at biography offends less through its indiscretion and inaccuracies than through the sickening snobbery and vulgar adulation of its tone. But whatever one's respect for the rights of privacy, the position is more complicated than Valerie Eliot was at first prepared to allow. (She is now, one understands, inclining to the view that Eliot's own wishes will have to be overruled, and that a serious biography is inevitable.)

Eliot's first marriage, to Vivien Haigh-Wood, had been problematic almost from the very beginning (June, 1915). This lively, gifted young Englishwoman seems to have suffered from recurrent bouts of mental disequilibrium. Soon a good part of Eliot's life became nightmarish, and it was rendered bearable only by frequent separations, made definitive in 1933, during his stay at Harvard. But if there was grave illness on Vivien's side, there seems to have been mental and or physical ailment on Eliot's side as well. Eliot himself wrote of "aboulie and emotional derangement which has been a lifelong affliction." Just what was wrong?

One inquires not in a spirit of prying impertinence but because our full understanding of *The Waste Land,* and of the special pilgrimage that took Eliot to Anglo-Catholicism and the *Four Quartets,* does in significant degree depend on the answer. Nothing is more tragic and, in the valid, necessary sense, indiscreet than the publication by Valerie Eliot of the marginal interjections that Vivien pencilled across early pages of the poem, among them the tart rejoinder "If you don't like it you can get on with it" to the line "Others can pick and choose if you can't," and the stark "What you get married for if you don't want to have children," near the close of "A Game of Chess" (originally entitled "In the Cage," for reasons less literary, it seems to me, than those indicated by the distinguished editor). Early readers of the poem, as well as such critics as I. A. Richards and Randall Jarrell, have pointed to a pervasive fear and even loathing of sexuality. These come out savagely in the cancelled heroic

couplets. The world view of *The Waste Land* is dark, and often nauseated, in a very special way. It differs sharply from the public, zestful gloom of Pound's "Mauberley" and the final, life-enhancing "Yes" of *Ulysses.* The cold fog, the vision of hollowness stem immediately from the worn nerves of the poet, exactly as Eliot says in his later, ironically dismissive judgment. Indeed, the sexual ambiguity or "erotic absence" of the poem makes for much of its haunting strength. We know and do not know just what it is telling us—about men and women, about Gentile and Jew, about the need to go beyond sex toward love.

The poem thus remains as difficult as is the place of Eliot's work as a whole between tradition and modernism. By producing a text that tells so much and yet leaves so much unsaid, Valerie Eliot has enriched not only our experience of T. S. Eliot but our experience of poetry as such. This does not happen very often. (pp. 138-42)

> George Steiner, "The Cruellest Months," in The New Yorker, *Vol. XLVIII, No. 9, April 22, 1972, pp. 134, 137-42.*

CALVIN BEDIENT

Two issues have continued to remain unresolved in the growing yet often largely repetitious commentary on T. S. Eliot's 1922 masterpiece—the quintessential poem of Anglo-American modernism—*The Waste Land.* One is that of the emotional, intellectual, and cultural disposition of the poem, its stance (if a simplifying figure may be used) toward history, modernity, erotic love, women, the metaphysical. Is it a poem, as many have thought, of despair? Or a poem, as others have believed, of heroically attained salvation? Or, as still others have suggested, of something peculiarly in-between, something baulked? This bewildering range of response—a result, in part, of the tricky reserve, the justifiably profound reticence, of Eliot's poem—characterizes the other major critical issue as well: that of the existence or nonexistence of a single protagonist; of the nature or purpose of the apparent medley of voices. Is it "Eliot" who speaks the work (or speaks in it)? Or a polyphony of equal voices? Or Tiresias? Or a nameless narrator-protagonist? Or still some other possibility?

The two issues are linked in that, until the second is really taken out of the storehouse to which it is usually confined and thoroughly aired, examined front and back, the first must remain subject to a chance accumulation of impressions taken from the poem, not to mention to the accidents of assumptions (that faith and modernism do not mix; that Eliot was not yet a supernaturalist; that Eliot was already the caretaker of the "European mind," and so on). If it can be argued in detail, in the closest listening to the text, that there is a single presiding consciousness in the poem, that of a poet-protagonist who is "dramatizing" (for want of a more exact word) the history of his own religious awakening, then the metaphysics of the poem (for the poem and the poet-protagonist would then be one), its relation to the past, to contemporaneity, to "the silence," to the possibility of salvation, indeed its very nature as a poetic performance and structure, could perhaps be determined with more exactness than has been demonstrated before.

As [the title of my book, *He Do the Police in Different Voices*] suggests, I argue for the view that all the voices in the poem are the performances of a single protagonist—not Tiresias but a nameless stand-in for Eliot himself—performances, indeed, of a distinctly theatrical kind, as I believe that Eliot's working title for the poem, which mine echoes, pointedly indicates. To ask why the protagonist must be theatrical starts up a complex of topics: pre-Oedipal mimesis and uncertainty; Oedipal phobias; historical hyperconsciousness, hence heteroglossia and heteromodality; and a metaphysical critique of identity, consciousness, language, and voice. . . . The gist of the matter, as I see it, is this: in the protagonist, both a psychoanalytical and a historical straying (the first the situation, perhaps, of every man, the second of every representative of Western "culture") come to crisis over against, and finally begin to find redemption in, an experience and cultivation of a metaphysical reality: a One transpsychic, transhistorical, and thus literally beyond words, though it may be the ultimate happiness of words to die into it.

I should perhaps add that my admiration for the genius of the poem has little to do with its metaphysics—stirring as metaphysics usually is to the imagination—though a good deal to do with an openness of temperament that perhaps accounts equally for its mimetic brilliance (the "doing" of the voices) and the protagonist's sympathy with aethereal rumors. I cannot believe, however, that the frequent resistance displayed toward this aspect of the work does justice to its metaphysical daring. This philosophically severe poem itself indicates how it should be read. That Eliot did not more directly state until later his supernaturalist and superhumanist allegiances should not, I think, prevent us from perceiving and granting the radical metaphysics of *The Waste Land.*

His earlier poems are in fact more of a piece with his later work than is perhaps generally acknowledged. Certainly his conversion to Anglicanism in 1927 did not mark a sudden dividing point, with nihilism on the youthful side and religious belief on the other. On the contrary, his Anglicanism was even a retrenchment from the metaphysical absolutism to which everything in *The Waste Land* refers (mostly, of course, by an acutely suffered or unwittingly abject banishment from it). In fact, the heroes of Eliot's two earlier masterpieces, **"The Love Song of J. Alfred Prufrock"** (1911) and **"Gerontion"** (1919), anticipate precisely the struggle both against and *of* faith in the protagonist of *The Waste Land.* In this regard, the three heroes form a progression. The "overwhelming question" that Prufrock cannot bring himself to face is a puritanical absolutism that, having already seeped into him, has destroyed his relations with women: he is more a man of faith than he knows, but, all the same, of a miserable reluctant faith, so that he can be decisive neither for the sensual nor for the unseen. Gerontion marks an advance in that, though more cynical than Prufrock—an Eliot prematurely aged by the Great War, by the ashes of history raining on his hair—he is also more agonizingly restive, desperate to rationalize his failure to have lived by a faith that he was nonetheless unable to deny: "I that was near your heart," he says, addressing (it must be) "Christ the tiger," "was removed therefrom / To lose beauty in terror, terror in inquisition." The protagonist of *The Waste Land* differs from his predecessors simply in *acting* on his faith—none too soon, and having to overcome a winter slumber of inertia and unwillingness before doing it, but doing it—*doing* a voice of conversion, and then a voice of (allegorical) highest pilgrimage.

Allegory is not a mode usually associated with modernism. Yet, as a mode always to be equated with estrangement from the sensory world and with a quest for purity, a mode almost openly artificial, confessing at the outset the arbitrary nature of representations, it is exactly suited to a representation of a conversion from this world—from history—to the eternal silence. Of all literary forms, it is the least an offense to this last, the most of an accommodation.

Throughout the poem, Eliot's "allegorical style" displays an intelligent economy of language that moves to check—by its chastity, its formal arrangements—the forsaken babble of historical discourse. In *The Waste Land,* poetry is mustered against both overweening literary style and spates of narcissistic speech, even as both are richly, if ironically, represented. (Indeed, all style is here potentially ironized as pose or mask.) The mercurial theatricality of the protagonist performs the illusion of "being someone," indeed many, in a void in which identity is a fiction. But what might at least approach purity is the right performance, a properly chastened one. In any case, the eternal silence cannot be conceived except in relation to temporal language, which, though always based in abjection, can counter it through original disciplines of form. By 1921, allegory had come round again to freshness, and, in any case, the severe splintering of literary form (that further, pricking discipline) was in vogue.

So, again, [my] reading of the poem places emphasis on the self-conscious if abysmal theatricality of a protagonist who, at first hardly aware of it himself, is bent, however ambivalently, on transcending the theater of consciousness altogether. It posits and traces a change within a poet-protagonist whose lugubrious and all-too-lyrical awareness of abjection is, after an initial surprise assault by the Divine, gradually lifted by more gentle intuitions of the inconceivable (because utterly pure) Absolute: a protagonist not ineradicably steeped in nihilism, after all, but, instead—openly likening himself to devious Hieronymo in Thomas Kyd's *The Spanish Tragedy*—cunningly conscious of the need to get round the hostile skepticism of the age by disguising an extremism of faith with an apparent extremism of ironic disorder. (pp. ix-xi)

Calvin Bedient, in his He Do the Police in Different Voices: 'The Waste Land' and Its Protagonist, *The University of Chicago Press, 1986, 225 p.*

JOHN XIROS COOPER

The Waste Land is a poem that does not merely reflect the breakdown of an historical, social, and cultural order battered by the onslaught of violent forces operating under the name of modernity. For Eliot the disaster that characterized modernity was not an overturning, but the unavoidable, and ironic, culmination of that very order so lovingly celebrated in Victoria's last decade on the throne. Unlike the older generation, who saw in events like the Great War the passing of a golden age, Eliot saw only that the golden age was itself a heap of absurd sociopolitical axioms and perverse misreadings of the cultural past that had proved in the last instance to be made of the meanest alloy. The poem's enactment of the contemporary social scene in "The Burial of the Dead," "A Game of Chess," and "The Fire Sermon" exhibits the "negative liberal society" in which such events and people are typical. Eliot's choice of these events and people—Madame Sosostris, the cast of characters in "A Game of Chess," and the typist—as *representative* of a particular society is susceptible, of course, to a political analysis, which is to say, their representativeness is not self-evident, though they are presented as if it is. The "one bold stare" of the house-agent's clerk, put back in the bourgeois context where staring is one of the major lapses in manners, does not hold up the mirror to a simple gesture, but illuminates the underlying conditions that make a mere clerk's swagger possible. What is exposed is the "fact" that clerks in general no longer know their place. What we are to make of this fact is pointedly signaled by the disgust that the specifics of the rendering provoke and the social distance generated by the Tiresian foresufferance.

If the poem spoke the idiom of the positive moralist, then we might be justified in calling this procedure satiric. All we can really say under the circumstances is that these parts of the poem, and they have been previously identified, carry a satiric force. However, the authority they draw on, which gives weight to such a force, does not take the form of a known or an achieved civil and personal code. The authority on which *The Waste Land* rests is quite different and this difference accounts, I believe, for the revolutionary impact it made on its first readers.

As its social critique was aimed negatively at the liberal ethos which Eliot felt had culminated in the War and its disorderly aftermath, *The Waste Land* could not visibly adopt some pre-liberal code of values. In the same way, the poem could not propose a postliberal, historicist or materialist ethic without an historicizing epistemology. The poem's authority rested instead on other bases that provided, not a system of ideas as the primary form of legitimation, but a new lyric synthesis as a kind of experiential authenticity in a world in which the sacred cosmologies, on the one hand, had fallen prey to astrologers and charlatans, while, on the other, the cosmology of everyday life, i.e. the financial system (the "City" in the poem), had fallen into the soiled hands of racially indeterminate and shady importers of currants and the like, among them, of course, the pushing Jews of the plunderbund. In the case of Madame Sosostris in the third section of "The Burial of the Dead," we have one of Eliot's more obsessive themes and character-types. Later, in **"The Dry Salvages,"** he would make more explicit the text that is only implied in the Madame Sosostris section of *The Waste Land.* There he would demolish, or so he thought, the liberal faith in pluralism by caustically enumerating a rich harvest of possibly virile, but irredeemably false faiths, which are balanced, and then outweighed, by what he calls in that poem "an occupation for the saint." (pp. 85-6)

But what kind of authority does the poem claim by grounding its placing judgments on what I [call] a new lyric synthesis? The poem does not choose to contest on rational grounds the world view implied in its own metonyms, its choices of "representative" events and character-types. That terrain, progressively in the bourgeois era, falls to positivist, materialist, and instrumental conceptions of human reason, all of which Eliot found inimical to the Thomist conception he came to adopt (Nott, *Emperor's Clothes*). He closes off debate in that direction by choosing to submerge rational argument in a metonymic procedure that both advances the Concrete in all its supposed unanswerable obviousness while stealing a march on the General through the assumed representativeness of concrete metonyms. The poem attempts to penetrate below the level of rationalist consciousness, where the conceptual currencies of the liberal ethos have no formative and directive power. Below that level lay the real story about human nature, which "liberal thought" perversely worked to obscure, by obscuring the intersection of the human and the

divine at the deepest levels of consciousness. That stratum did not respond to the small-scale and portable logics of Enlightenment scientism, but to the special "rationality" of mythic thought. Its "logic" and narrative forms furnish the idiom of subrationalist, conscious life. To repeat: if not on the conventional rationalist basis, where does Eliot locate the authority of *The Waste Land,* an authority that can save the poem from mere eccentric sputter and give it a more commanding aspect? I think it was important for Eliot himself to feel the poem's command, and not simply to make it convincing to sceptical readers; Lyndall Gordon's biography makes this inner need for strength in his own convictions a central theme in Eliot's early life. But to answer our question: the authority the poem claims has two dimensions.

The first is based on the aesthetics of French *symbolisme* and its extension into the Wagnerian music-drama. Indeed the theoretical affinities of Baudelaire et al. and Wagner, which Eliot obviously intuited in the making of *The Waste Land,* can be seen now as nothing short of brilliant. Only in our own time are these important aesthetic and cultural connections being seriously explored. From *symbolisme* Eliot adopted the notion of the epistemological self-sufficiency of aesthetic consciousness, its independence from rationalist instrumentality, and thus its more efficacious contact with experience, and at the deeper levels, contact with the divine through its earthly language in myth. From his French and German forebears, Eliot formulated a new discourse of experience which in the 1920s was still very much the voice of the contemporary avant-garde in Britain and, in that sense, it was a voice on the margins, without institutional authority. But here the ironic, even sneering, dismissal of the liberal stewardship of culture and society reverses the semiotics of authority-claims by giving to the voice on the margins an authority the institutional voices can no longer assume since the world they are meant to sustain has finally been seen through in all those concrete ways the poem mercilessly enacts. *The Waste Land* is quite clear on that point. We are meant to see in "The Fire Sermon," for example, the "loitering heirs of City directors" weakly giving way to the hated *métèques,* so that the City, one of the "holy" places of mercantilism, has fallen to profane hands. The biting humor in this is inescapable.

From *symbolisme* and the Wagnerian music-drama Eliot synthesized a new lyric voice that brought to his poetry an experiential intensity and candor that gained authority from the quality of its perceptions and, ironically, from its social marginality, that is, its isolation in a contaminated environment. It appealed to his own generation by the vivid contrast this lyric voice set up with the unraveled remnants of Victorian "high seriousness," a tone the Edwardian sons and grandsons still thought worth adopting. But such a tone was already a dead letter by 1895, the year of Wilde's *The Importance of Being Earnest.* In Baudelaire, Verlaine, Rimbaud, Laforgue, Wagner a new kind of seriousness shapes the voice, and it is this voice, capable of wider and more delicate effects of irony and temperament, that informs the second section of "The Burial of the Dead," the first and most of the second sections of "The Fire Sermon," "Death by Water," and "What the Thunder Said."

This new lyric consciousness, marked by the extended tonal range that more accurately captures the experience and ironies of life at the end of an era, was designed to provoke those whose ear for the voice in poetry rested with the reigning Swinburnianism. Here the collocation of *The Sacred*

Wood and *The Waste Land* becomes particularly important. In addition to hearing this new lyricism as one more mutation in the development of the lyric voice in English poetry, we must hear in it, not just a new music, but a claim to authority operative in a particular social climate. In all the spiky relationships this voice, and what it is saying, sets up with the immediate common intuitive life of the liberal bourgeoisie, we hear singing the tone of a *then* unsurpassable authenticity.

The second dimension of the authority on which *The Waste Land* rests involves the new discourse on myth that comes from the revolutionary advances in anthropology in Eliot's time associated with the names of Emile Durkheim, Marcel Mauss, and the Cambridge School led by Sir James Frazer and Jane Harrison. We know that Eliot was well acquainted with these developments at least as early as 1913-14. The importance of these new ideas involved rethinking the study of ancient and primitive societies. The impact of these renovations was swift and profound and corresponds, though much less publicly, to the impact of *On the Origin of Species* on the educated public of midcentury Victorian life. Modernist interest in primitive forms of art (Picasso, Lawrence, and many others), and, therefore, the idioms and structures of thought and feeling in primitive cultures, makes sense in several ways. Clearly the artistic practices of primitive peoples are interesting technically to other artists of any era. Interest in the affective world or the collective mentality of a primitive society is another question altogether. That interest, neutral, perhaps, in scholarship, becomes very easy to formulate as a critique of practices and structures in the present that one wants to represent as distortions and caricatures of some original state of nature from which modernity has catastrophically departed. Eliot's interest in the mythic thought of primitive cultures, beginning at Harvard, perhaps in the spirit of scientific inquiry, takes a different form in the argument of *The Waste Land.* There it functions pointedly as a negative critique of the liberal account of the origins of society in the institutions of contract, abstract political and civil rights, and mechanistic psychology.

The anthropologists rescued the major cultural production of primitive societies—myth—from the view that saw these ancient narratives either as the quaint decorative brio of simple folk, or if they were Greek, the narrative mirrors of heroic society. Instead myth, and not just the myths of the Greeks, was reconceived as the narrative thematics of prerationalist cosmologies that provided an account of the relationship between the human and the divine. Myth was also interpreted psychologically, and Nietzsche is crucial in this development, as making visible the deeper strata of the mind. If the concept is the notional idiom of reason, myth is the language of unconscious life. What Eliot intuited from this new understanding was that myth provided a totalizing structure that could make sense, equally, of the state of a whole culture and of the whole structure of an individual mind. In this intuition he found the idiom of an elaborated, universalizing code which was not entirely the product of rationalist thought. In addition, this totalizing structure preserved the sacred dimension of life by seeing it inextricably entwined with the profane. For the expression of this intuition in the context of an environment with a heavy stake in the elaborated codes of a rationalist and materialist world view which had subordinated the sacred to the profane, Eliot adapted for his own use the poetics of juxtaposition.

The textual discontinuity of *The Waste Land* has usually been read as the technical advance of a new aesthetic. The poetics of juxtaposition are often taken as providing the enabling rationale for the accomplishment of new aesthetic effects based on shock and surprise. And this view is easy enough to adopt when the poem is read in the narrow context of a purely literary history of mutated lyric forms. However, when the context is widened and the poem read as a motivated operation on an already always existing structure of significations, this technical advance is itself significant as a critique of settled forms of coherence. Discontinuity, from this perspective, is a symbolic form of "blasting and bombardiering." In the design of the whole poem, especially in its use of contemporary anthropology, the broken textual surface must be read as the sign of the eruptive power of subrational forces reasserting, seismically, the elemental totalities at the origins of culture and mind. The poem's finale is an orgy of social and elemental violence. The "Falling towers," lightning and thunder, unveil what Eliot, at that time, took to be the base where individual mind and culture are united in the redemptive ethical imperatives spoken by the thunder. What the poem attempts here, by ascribing these ethical principles to the voice of nature and by drawing on the epistemological autonomy posited by *symbolisme,* is the construction of an elaborated code in which an authoritative universalizing vision can be achieved using a "notional" (mythic) idiom uncontaminated by Enlightenment forms of rationalism.

Powerful as it is in the affective and tonal program of the poem, functioning as the conclusion to the poem's "argument," this closural construction is, at best, precarious when seen beyond the shaping force of the immediate social and cultural context. This construction, achieved rhetorically, in fact is neither acceptable anthropology, nor sound theology, nor incontestable history, but draws on all these areas in order to make the necessary point in a particular affective climate. The extent to which the poem still carries unsurpassable imaginative power indicates the extent to which our own time has not broken entirely with the common intuitive life that the poem addressed 60 years ago.

Eliot himself abandoned his creation as soon as it was formulated, migrating to a Christian orthodoxy in the Anglican church. This movement to an institutionally established authority displaced the special kinds of authority claimed for the perceptiveness and argument in *The Waste Land.* The same perceptions and the same argument were, in the mid-1920s, lodged in a social institution; the critique of "negative liberal society" continued without interruption, but no longer from the margins. The lyric voice, alloyed on the margins, was not abandoned however; it was adapted to the new situation within an historical institution and within the discursive and notional modes that institutional affiliation provided.

From this new social position Eliot's critique of the liberal orthodixies of thought and feeling continued. The attack, as before, remains focused on the liberal-romantic account of experience. Important as immediate personal experience seems to be in *The Waste Land,* enacted in the lyric intensity of the metaphoric voice, it cannot be taken as final or absolute. The sharp focus on experience in *The Waste Land* is primarily strategic in the service of the dispersal of the liberal-romantic hegemony of thought and feeling. Eliot is more sensitive to the way men and women *talk* about experience, than to experience itself. The brilliantly achieved collocation of lyric consciousness, myth, and Indo-Christian scripturality embosomed by a sacramentalized nature, a synthesis that would have served lesser artists for a lifetime, was soon itself dispersed in Eliot's announcement of his final theme, the one that he would carry forward for the rest of his life.

The escape from his own brilliant creation coincides in fact with Eliot's own changing social position in England. By the late 1920s, he had closed socially on what he felt was the center of English life in its most important and guiding social faction. His earlier ambiguous position in an established and stratified society, a hierarchy in which he had no inherited privilege and thus no access to a voice "natural" to any one of its discriminated ranks, led him, as we have seen, to construct one. This new lyrical voice gave his middle-class audience a vision of the reality that embraced them, from a place (on the margins) that was not implicated in the psychoethical impotence of the reigning order. But this composite voice was ultimately like Blake's, as Eliot described it in *The Sacred Wood,* adrift without an anchor in a "framework of accepted and traditional ideas," a voice "with a capacity for considerable understanding of human nature, with a remarkable and original sense of language and the music of language, and a gift of hallucinated vision", but without the historical nourishment of an institutionalized and cosmological tradition. Blake required respect for "impersonal reason . . . common sense . . . the objectivity of science". But the reason, common sense, and science that Eliot recommends here were not the orders of rationality that *The Waste Land* assaults. Eliot was not against reason, common sense, and science; he was simply against the way these were used in the liberal ethos. With the publication of *For Lancelot Andrewes* (1928) and

"**Ash Wednesday**" (1930) Eliot moved decisively towards gaining the institutional authority he believed Dante to have had.

The name of Dante brings to a focus a final, philosophical point. One of the many revolutionary intellectual impulses of Enlightenment thought was the progressive alloying of reason and freedom as constituting the two elements of a single human essence informing each and every individual. The consequences of this identification have been profound in every area of human life. But for Eliot this union of reason and freedom in the individual represented the crucial seed of discord in modernity, planted at the beginning of the bourgeois era. *The Waste Land* presents the consequences of what seemed to him a misguided faith. From *The Waste Land* on, he more explicitly moved to reestablish the notion that reason is intrinsic to, that it inheres fundamentally to, historical institutions, not to the atomic individual, and that an apostolic and historical Church embodies to the profoundest degree Reason as such, or at least a Reason that carries a nonhuman, divine authority. From this perspective, the individual, as conceived in Christian doctrine as limited and fallen, approaches Reason the closer he is to its sacred source and, in that way, and in that way alone, can guarantee his freedom. Having come to this position, acknowledged in practice in 1927 by his acceptance of the Anglican confession, Eliot began to point his poetry in a different direction. (pp. 87-92)

John Xiros Cooper, in his T. S. Eliot and the Politics of Voice: The Argument of 'The Waste Land', *UMI Research Press, 1987, 121 p.*

Percival L. Everett
1957?-

American novelist and short story writer.

Everett earned critical respect for his first and best known novel, *Suder* (1983). In this work, Everett charts the tribulations of Craig Suder, a black third baseman for the Seattle Mariners who dreams of playing the saxophone like his idol Charlie Parker and flying without mechanical assistance. When his adulterous wife and troubled son aggravate him during a humiliating batting slump, Suder leaves his family and his teammates to embark on a trip through the American Northwest. During this picaresque journey, Suder encounters cocaine smugglers, befriends a nine-year-old runaway girl and an obese Oriental homosexual, and adopts an elephant named Renoir. Carolyn See deemed *Suder* "a mad work of comic genius, combining symbols and myths from ancients and moderns, white culture and black, juxtaposing heartbreak with farce to make up a narrative that has never, never been told before." While some reviewers objected to the novel's frantic pace and ambitious scale, most commended Everett's imaginative plot and chimerical ending.

Everett's other novels develop in a more concise and serious manner. *Walk Me to the Distance* (1985) details a Vietnam veteran's search for acceptance and fulfillment, and *Cutting Lisa* (1986) centers on a retired obstetrician who discovers his pregnant daughter-in-law's infidelity. Everett has also written a collection of short stories, *The Weather and Women Treat Me Fair* (1987).

N SEE

the epigraphs to novels—especially first novels— little more than that the author is well read, the right person. But the two in front of *Suder* glow in the dark, kindle a flame Percival Everett coaxes carefully into sustained and glittering incandescence. "Our swords are ready," the first epigraph, from *Agamemnon,* reads. "We can die." And the second, eminently sensible answer to that gloomy statement, both from Nietzsche and Everett: "But why perceive such painful matters? Assuming one does not have to."

Percival, you sport! Do you know how transcendentally al it is for an American novelist to think that way, particularly a serious novelist, a male novelist, and—wow!—a black novelist?

When one thinks of black novelists in this country, one has to think of, *must* think of, Richard Wright, the grinding ironies and sadness of *Native Son* and the rest of those bleak visions. Or one thinks of James Baldwin—the resignation and bitter loss that went into *Sonny's Blues,* that drug and jazz classic, or the blind eroticism that covered over a world of loss, injustice and, again, an overwhelming sense of the sadness of life. We live in a bitter time, those novelists said, and the lot of the black man may be the saddest of all.

And all that is true. And the horror extends now to the black man's oppressor, driving freeways in what Baldwin once called their "pseudo-elegant heaps of tin"; extinction in front of us, boredom and anomie right with us: "Our swords are ready. We can die." So what?, Percival Everett says. We can live, too. Maybe we can fly out of the situation.

With all due fear of hexing a novelist on his first time out, of making it impossible for him to write a second one that measures up to the first attempt, I must suggest Percival Everett has created here a mad work of comic genius, combining symbols and myths from ancients and moderns, white culture and black, juxtaposing heartbreak with farce to make up a narrative that has never, never been told before. I mean, who has ever, in this world, intuited first that one of the nicest things about being a baseball player is to hit a fly ball (especially when it turns into a home run), that, second, they called the great black musician-hero Charlie Parker "Bird" for a reason—not just that his fingers flew, or his musicianship was dazzling, but that by the "blowing of a line on an old set of changes" he could take the steady and predictable chords of "Cherokee" and make them into the unimaginably celestial "Koko"—a whole new ball game, so to speak. Without changing injustice or horror or tedium, Bird could fly out of the situation.

Now, wait! Given all that, who could meld baseball and jazz with the most wistful male myth of all—the Icarus myth— remembering that Daedalus really did do it. He flew. It's a measure of our sadness that we remember Icarus falling and not Daedalus flying. (p. 1)

At first it doesn't look as if Suder, a young black baseball player, is going anywhere. He's been in such an awful slump; his son is afraid to go to school; his teammates fall silent around him; the trainer is so sure it's a leg problem that Suder—through sheer funk—finds himself beginning to limp. And things are terrible at home. Suder's going through a little slump there, too, and his wife, Thelma—the kind of wife who sends her husband to the store to buy Kotex for her— ostentatiously releases her sexual tensions on a stationary bicycle.

Life grows so bad that they give Suder a surprise party on his 33rd birthday. The good news is Suder doesn't get crucified like that other 33-year-old; the bad news is that his presents are an electric razor, a Water Pik and a stuffed dead dog his manager picked up off the road.

That's about the time Suder starts listening to *Ornithology*. Sure, people still listen to Charlie Parker, but with Suder it's a little out of hand. He takes his record and a portable record player with him everywhere, to bars and restaurants, to the ball park. He gets to be a damn nuisance with that record. Then he goes out and buys a saxophone, and you know what it's like to be around a person who's constantly tootling on a sax. Thelma comes home with a big smile on her face and doesn't ride the stationary bicycle any more. Suder takes his record, his record player and his horn, and runs away.

Before we discover what's going to happen next, we find out—we have to—some of the things that put Suder in the position he's in now, a gifted man, benched by the relentless exigencies of his own life. A series of flashbacks takes us to the rural South: a young Suder raised by a sad and understanding dad; a mom driven so mad by the injustice of her life that she wears winter coats in the depths of summer and tries to transcend her world by running around the perimeters of the town. Suder's brother sees which way the wind blows in this awful world and grows up to be a dentist who effectively ends all communication by jamming his fingers in his brother's mouth. (pp. 1, 8)

But there's an alternative to madness, and in the hideous domestic world where Suder's mother routinely threatens to castrate him to keep him from masturbating, there's another house guest besides that demented dentist. Bud Powell, who played with Bird in the celebrated recording session when "Cherokee" was turned into "Koko," is seen here as just a mellow family friend about to drown in his own problems, but still able to tell the young and very depressed Suder, "Jazz is one step beyond one giant step. . . . Charlie Parker is dead now, but not really."

Back in the grinding present, Suder strives (or relaxes) to take the step beyond the giant-step. He has some adventurous charades and dope deals; an obese Chinese homosexual falls madly in love with him; he rescues the most charming elephant in the history of all literature; and he manages to pull a little white girl out of a bad situation. He flees, and hides— and finally flies, a life redeemed in one exquisite burst of sunshine and sky and feathers. (p. 8)

Carolyn See, in a review of "Suder," in Los Angeles Times Book Review, *July 31, 1983, pp. 1, 8.*

PAUL GRAY

The hero of [*Suder*] is a black third baseman with the Seattle Mariners named Craig Suder. Given the salaries and perks enjoyed by contemporary athletes, Suder's position on and off the field would seem to be enviable. Unfortunately, he has a few problems, including a batting average of .198: "Things are bad. I can't make love to my wife, I can't run bases, and I couldn't get a hit if they was pitching me basketballs underhanded. And my kid hates me. To top it off, I got a bum leg that don't hurt." Manager Lou Tyler is solicitous, if gruff: "Now, about that slump of yours. You know, it wasn't but a few years ago that you blacks was allowed in this league. The way you been playing lately, they might kick you all out." . . .

Suder's predicament seems the stuff of sure-fire fiction, an unusual and interesting character struggling with mysterious demons. But after deftly establishing this premise, Rookie Author Percival L. Everett . . . darts off in another direction entirely. Suder simply walks out on his wife, his team, Seattle. He buys a saxophone and tries to learn to play it like Charlie Parker. He hitches up with an older acquaintance who takes him on a boat ride across Puget Sound. The purpose of the trip turns out to be cocaine smuggling, and Suder manages to push his host overboard and sail off with all the loot. Then he wins an elephant at a carnival and names it Renoir.

People who think pachyderms are intrinsically funny will find the rest of *Suder* sidesplitting. Renoir certainly provokes his share of double takes. The man robbed by Suder tracks him to a cabin in Oregon, where he notices the large pet: "What's that?" Suder's reply: "That's an elephant." And then there is the joke about Suder's manager, an amateur taxidermist, who shows up unexpectedly and tries to kill Renoir with a chain saw: "I can't wait to stuff this sucker." By now, Suder has acquired other eccentricities. His cabin mate is a nine-year-old girl named Jincy, a runaway from an abusing mother. She comments: "This is weird. I'm in a strange barn, shoveling hay for an elephant that belongs to a nigger." Meanwhile, Suder has decided to build a pair of wings and fly over a nearby body of water called Ezra Pond.

It is impossible to tell just how bananas Suder is supposed to be going; he is the only spokesman for his misadventures and he says he feels better and better. But along the way, Everett's novel develops a severe case of enforced sit-com wackiness. Jokes wag the tale; characters seem willing to do anything for a laugh track.

Paul Gray, "Laugh Track," in Time, New York, *Vol. 122, August 22, 1983, p. 70.*

ALICE HOFFMAN

Percival L. Everett's *Suder* is about a black third baseman for the Seattle Mariners who may be experiencing the worst slump in history. . . . When the Mariners' manager (an amateur taxidermist who seems more interested in collecting the bodies of animals killed along the highway than in baseball) suggests a vacation, Suder takes off on a quest for freedom and—literally—human flight.

Carrying a beloved Charlie Parker record, he finds himself on the run from his wife, his ball club and, later, a gun-toting smuggler. On his way to a hideout in the Cascade Mountains, Suder collects an elephant named Renoir, a 9-year-old runaway and an overweight Chinese homosexual. If all this seems a bit much, it is. The humor is exaggerated and slapstick. Mr. Everett intends to show us madness as a crazy quilt, and he gives us the story of a life filled with chance events, some laughable, others tragic.

The narrative alternates between past and present, and it's the story of Suder's early life that is most touching. In these sections of the novel, the characters are absurd yet human: Dr. McCoy, a racist dentist who prays for a steady hand before drilling; Martin, Suder's sex-crazed brother; Bud Powell, the famous jazz pianist, who makes an appearance and teaches Suder how to take a risk; and Suder's mother, a madwoman who loves her son a little too well. Here we see Mr. Everett's real talents as a storyteller. He knows the terrors of childhood, and his warm humor can be charming. This is Suder on the day of his grandmother's funeral:

> As I looked around I thought of Pernell Watkins, the funeral director. He was tall, slender, and light-skinned. . . . In the office I saw a picture of the original Watkins, a dark-skinned guy. However, as I looked at the pictures of the descendants of the original Watkins I saw that each Watkins was lighter in color than the previous one. I figured dealing with death had that effect.

If *Suder* does not always succeed, it's because the author is trying to do too much. The final sections are particularly unsatisfying. There's something a little too sweet in this novel, and its frantic pace obscures Mr. Everett's strengths. (p. 26)

> *Alice Hoffman, "Slumps and Tailspins," in The New York Times Book Review, October 2, 1983, pp. 9, 26.*

PAUL STUEWE

[In *Suder*], a slumping major-league baseball player on the run from his marriage and team-mates meets up with an elephant, a precocious nine year old, and a baker's dozen of assorted weirdos. Unfortunately, the author's prose is as unbearable as his imagination is exhilarating, and many nice touches of plot and character are flattened by the book's distressingly mundane language. Basically, what's here is a promising outline and a pretty dreadful novel, with a lot of subcontracting work yet to be completed in the fleshing-out and livening-up departments.

> *Paul Stuewe, "Late-Night Thoughts . . . Tracking Time . . . History for Flick Fanatics," in Quill and Quire, Vol. 50, No. 1, January, 1984, p. 33.*

PUBLISHERS WEEKLY

Each Vietnam vet adjusted in his own way upon returning from the jungle. [In *Walk Me to the Distance*], David Larson's chance landing in Slut's Hole, Wyo., affords him relative solitude, and provides him distance from other vets, from a sister and the too-familiar heat in his native Georgia; soon, he also finds people to care about. . . . From the women he meets in town, to the people who stop at the highway rest area he tends and to the local men who join him in the posse

the night [the widow] Sixbury's son disappears, David's life is swept mainly by chance, until he and Sixbury adopt a Vietnamese girl in whose defense he is eventually obliged to kill another man. Though at times the sparseness of his prose leaves readers to infer more than they should about the causes of the vet's "ill-defined alienation," Everett (*Suder*) manages to tell a great deal about one man's moral dilemma and his cluttered path to repatriation. The note of hope on which this moving story ends, though tentative, is fully deserved.

> *A review of "Walk Me to the Distance," in Publishers Weekly, Vol 226, No. 25, December 21, 1984, p. 81.*

WENDY SMITH

When David Larson returns from Vietnam [in *Walk Me to the Distance*], he is alone. His parents have died in a car crash; his sister and her hippie husband want nothing to do with a former soldier. Aimlessly driving west from his native Georgia, he stops in a small Wyoming town simply because his car breaks down there. The beauty of the landscape and tough friendliness of the people attract him, so he gets a job and stays on as a boarder with Sixbury, an elderly widow with a retarded son to support. David tentatively begins to put down roots in the town, which seems to him a refuge from the confusion of post-Vietnam America, but modern life's complications manifest themselves even in rural Wyoming. His relationships with the various women who enter his life are tense and problematic; a 7-year-old Vietnamese girl is abandoned in the rest station where he works; he is caught up in an act of old-fashioned frontier justice that has contemporary implications and consequences. The novel ends on a note of chastened hope. . . . Unfortunately, the reader may well have wearied of David's problems long before he resolves them. The comic inventiveness praised by critics in Mr. Everett's first novel, *Suder,* is virtually absent here, replaced by a terseness that verges on blankness. Presumably intended to reflect the spirit of the West, the book's laconic prose fails to create any resonance of theme or character. There are a few nicely observed scenes of alienation and dislocation, but in general *Walk Me to the Distance* doesn't travel very far beneath the surface.

> *Wendy Smith, in a review of "Walk Me to the Distance," in The New York Times Book Review, March 24, 1985, p. 24.*

ROSELLEN BROWN

Percival Everett's *Walk Me to the Distance,* a graceful and more old-fashioned novel . . . in construction and in its refusal to be cynical, lures an emotionally distant Vietnam veteran into an accidentally created family where he finds an affection and engagement he can use to shore up his ruins. Yet Everett, who is black, does not choose to make race so much as a tacit subject, whereas ten years ago it would have been central. (The title character of his first novel, *Suder,* was a black baseball player.) This is surely not to dictate that every black writer must be continuously preoccupied by racial problems, but it does seem symptomatic of a moment when many young writers have stepped back from difficult confrontations of self and society. (p. 8)

> *Rosellen Brown, "The Emperor's New Fiction," in*

Boston Review, *Vol. XI, No. 4, August, 1986, pp. 7-8.*

KIRKUS REVIEWS

[In *Cutting Lisa*], John Livesey, 66, a widower and recently retired obstetrician, travels from Virginia to the Oregon coast—where he'll spend the summer with son Elgin (a history professor), pregnant daughter-in-law Lisa, and eight-year-old granddaughter Kathy. And most of this very short novel simply follows John through the summer as he enjoys Kathy's sweet company and forms some bittersweet new attachments . . . ; he also finds renewed vigor and pride in an affair with a beautiful young woman—until disillusionment arrives (in clichéd melodrama manner).

Meanwhile, however, John is becoming increasingly disturbed about Lisa—who's an oddly unenthusiastic mother-to-be. Soon, in fact, he realizes that Lisa is having a secret affair (with Elgin's best pal!), that the baby isn't Elgin's, that his son and granddaughter's future happiness is in jeopardy. So, in the novel's stagy and unconvincing fade-out, John (who has toyed with the idea of killing Lisa's lover) instead prepares to perform a kitchen-table abortion, taking forceful personal responsibility for his family's well-being.

Everett (*Suder, Walk Me to the Distance*) fails to invest John's final act here with thematic heft—despite a portentous prologue in which John is appalled/impressed by a Virginia man's willful decision to deliver his wife's baby at home (complete with do-it-yourself Caesarean). The moral issues involved remain murky; the domestic doings—though flecked with laconic charm and lean narrative force—verge on soap opera. And the ultimate effect is thin, alternately bland and shrill, as if two or three short-story ideas have been uneasily intertwined.

A review of "Cutting Lisa," in Kirkus Reviews, *Vol. LIV, No. 17, September 1, 1986, p. 1309.*

JANE K. LARKIN

[In *Cutting Lisa*], John Livesey, a recently widowed physician, visits his son's family at their beach house on the Oregon coast for what promises to be a relaxing vacation. Events don't go according to plan, however, and the summer becomes a time that tests John's deepest convictions about his duty to family and friends. His son's marriage is foundering; Lisa, his daughter-in-law, is pregnant, but no one is happy about it. . . . He eventually discovers the truth about Lisa's pregnancy and must decide whether or not to intervene. [Everett's] brief but unusually moving novel offers a sensitive view of family dynamics.

Jane K. Larkin, in a review of "Cutting Lisa," in Booklist, *Vol. 83, No. 3, October 1, 1986, p. 188.*

Maggie Gee

1948-

English novelist.

In her novels, Gee examines the intricacies of human relationships as well as contemporary social and political issues. Frequently ominous in tone, her works usually center upon solipsistic characters who must acknowledge their own moral failures and those of society when confronted by such events as suicide, murder, and nuclear war. While critics are occasionally daunted by the graphic imagery in her narratives, most have praised Gee's witty, unconventional style, which often features abrupt shifts in time and perspective. Lorna Sage observed: "[Gee's originality] consists in a kind of ghoulish candour. Her texts are—like primitives, or children's paintings—less representations than fetishes, fragments of superstitious magic."

In her first novel, *Dying, in Other Words* (1981), Gee uses a stream-of-consciousness narrative style to examine the life and apparent suicide of Moira Penny, an aspiring writer. With narration shifting between Moira's friends, who include a homosexual lecturer, a mysterious recluse, and a sadistic hoodlum, *Dying, in Other Words* recounts their various descents into despair and violence following her death. These testimonies precede Moira's unfinished papers, which consist of explicit, surrealistic descriptions of a future nuclear apocalypse that situate the narrators' individual acts of brutality against a greater social immorality. In *The Burning Book* (1983), Gee more directly addresses the subject of nuclear annihilation. Punctuated throughout by images of the Hiroshima and Nagasaki bombings, this elliptical narrative randomly relates the intertwined histories of three British families as the present generation progresses toward nuclear war. Unwilling to acknowledge their imminent destruction, the modern protagonists continue to pursue trivial ambitions and rivalries until they perish in the final conflagration. Several critics objected to the novel's moralistic tone, but most considered *The Burning Book* a soberly convincing anti-war statement and praised Gee's inventive juxtaposition of the mundane and the apocalyptic to illustrate humanity's moral irresponsibility in the nuclear age.

In her next novel, *Light Years* (1985), Gee eschews the sinister subject matter of her previous works to comically portray a self-involved couple who separate after nearly two decades of marriage. Linking the evolution of their relationship to images of the natural world, this novel moves from the couple's initial quarrel over the death of their rare pet monkey to their chance reunion a year later at the small mammal house of the local zoo. While some critics faulted the work as sentimental, most praised Gee's insightful characterizations and innovative approach to traditional domestic themes. Gee's next work, *Grace* (1988), is based upon the alleged involvement of the British intelligence community in the murder of English anti-nuclear activist Hilda Murrell in 1984. In the novel, a psychotic killer hired by the government stalks the title character, an octogenarian pacifist, and her pregnant niece, Paula, an author working on a manuscript about Murrell's death. Although Paula's escape from her assassin at the novel's end symbolizes hope for Great Britain's future, Gee chiefly por-

trays the country as a land despoiled by governmental corruption and nuclear waste. Peter Reading commented: "*Grace* is more than just another addition to the compulsive, nail-biting canon; it is a sustained valediction, an elegy for a moribund society, nation, empire and species."

STODDARD MARTIN

The setting of Maggie Gee's novel [*Dying, in Other Words*] is a "damp dull" house in a crescent in suburban Oxford. The house is inhabited by a nonagenarian Frenchwoman, Clothilde, who is studying to be an artist; a twenty-five year old redhead, Moira, who sunbathes on the balcony between bouts of typing rhapsodic prose; a redundant clerk, Frank, who claims to be writing a book on "Jokes"; [and] a fastidious and handsome but (alas for Moira) homosexual lecturer, Jean-Claude. . . . Moira, self-confessed alter ego of the author, plummets to her death from the balcony. The death appears to be suicide but in the end we discover there's more to it than that. Meanwhile, all Moira's intimates begin to disintegrate. Besides the others in the house, these include: John

X, a political ideologue from London; Felicity, John's lady, who teaches retarded children; and Macbeth, a punk hoodlum who once took Moira's virginity but in fact prefers homosexual rape.

The novel provides several ironic tableaux of the sexual revolution of the 1970s. John leaves Felicity for Moira, even though Moira is dead. Felicity, distraught and booze-sodden, opens a present John intended for Moira while alive: it is a statuette of the Virgin Mary that on closer inspection reveals itself to be a dildo. Felicity is shocked. The gift seems to belie John's old assertion that "sex isn't important" and to confirm that the "other woman" will always triumph. Felicity's distress deepens. Senselessly drunk now, she drowns her overweight (she thinks) pink body in the bath.

There are many such mishaps. Jean-Claude expires at the hand of Macbeth, who is avenging his own homosexual rape at thirteen. All Jean-Claude himself ever wanted was a cosy marriage with Moira; but Moira rejected him, saying that their relationship had "too much flattery, too many cushions, and no sense of violence". Violence is what they get as a result. Macbeth, the violator, survives by "going on the run, like a wolf". Clothilde, clutching the idea that Frank is pining for her, is the only other survivor; but old age relentlessly stalks her.

The book ends with fifty pages of aphorisms, poetry and prose envisioning the end of the world. "This is not a realistic novel", Maggie Gee has warned in one of many preliminary notes; "this is not quite a novel". The author, we are told by the jacket, has a Ph.D. in "Self-consciousness in the 20th Century Novel". She has written an extremely self-conscious novel herself; it is inundated with interior monologue and sinks under an endless flow of present participial clauses, many of them inexplicably rhymed. Some of the surrealistic scenery is vivid, but the thickets surrounding are impenetrable. Some of the characters are more appealing than the solipsistic presentation of them lulls one into assuming—they deserve the relief of dialogue. With revision this book might have made a sharp, telling statement on its period. As it stands, it is as damp as that house in the crescent; as melancholy as the fade of some over-long rock-song echoing from lost marijuana days.

> *Stoddard Martin, "Violent Bodies," in* The Times Literary Supplement, *No. 4085, July 17, 1981, p. 820.*

ANGELA HUTH

Maggie Gee, in her first novel **Dying, In Other Words,** has sensibly stuck to the old favourite of gloom and decay in all around she sees, and made a brave job of it. It is not her fault that her publishers allow David Lodge to hail it as 'experimental' on the cover, and proclaim in the blurb it 'challenges all the assumptions of the traditional novel.' It does no such thing, although it starts on a bad note with the message 'How not to read this novel'. The writing is often pretentious—'Light which grows damp and dull on the dull damp reds of the damp dull North Oxford houses'—and the characters are made of black sequins rather than flesh and blood. Moira Penny, the heroine, is found splattered on the pavement, fallen from a window. Why? This danse macabre of a book pirouettes through the acquaintances in her life, through whom we learn little of Moira or the answer to her death.

All through the story is the underlying dread that Moira's 'papers' are going to be reproduced—which they are, in the end, and turn out to be as disappointing as when an actor representing an artist shows his painting on the stage. But for all that, when she is not trying too hard, there is an admirable coruscation about Miss Gee's writing: she is good on glitter (frost, black ice, steel, cold milk bottles), accurately savage on physical appearance—'the milkman's eyes had been pressed open on too many icy mornings, were resentful and raw as strips of anchovy.' I look forward to Miss Gee's next book, when perhaps her M. Litt. on surrealism has faded a little and she will subject us to less cleverness.

> *Angela Huth, "Marriage Matters," in* The Listener, *Vol. 106, No. 2721, August 6, 1981, p. 120.*

JOHN MELLORS

Dying, in other words is notable not for the events it describes, nor for the ideas it projects, but for the jewel-bright images scattered through its pages. For the most part, these are images of sex and death. A girl on a beach, under the pier, has 'underwear smelling of cheap lemon perfume and seaweed'. Felicity opens a parcel and finds a plastic dildo, which on one side is a Virgin Mary, 'long robes and halo and demure blue veil'. Felicity gets drunk and sets fire to herself, 'waking from deep dead sleep . . . a wild girl shining with sweat and coronaed by clear orange flame'.

Gee looks after her minor characters, treating them with affection even when scrutinizing them closely. Clara is always powdering herself with a huge, white, satin-backed, swansdown puff: 'like all courageous attempts of the un-beautiful at beauty, sad'. Clara drowns herself in her bath. Indeed, if the book has a message it is that life is a series of steps towards death: living is 'dying, in other words'. However, the content is subordinate to the style in this 'not quite a novel'. Incongruities are a speciality. Fifteen-year-old Pet has her first sex with leather-jacketed Macbeth, on the bare boards of the floor. When she gets home she finds chewing-gum stuck to her buttock, 'which she took to be the dried glory of Macbeth's sperm'. . . . [There are also] small, shapely *objets trouvés* here and there for the reader to pick up. Frank is making a joke-book. He's been working at it for years—'all the best things were slow, like thinking, and love, and history'. In this, her first novel (because that is what it is, whatever she says about it), Maggie Gee shows how well she can write. What she has still to prove is that she can write a good book. (pp. 89-90)

> *John Mellors, "Beware of the Dog," in* London Magazine, *n.s. Vol. 21, No. 8, November, 1981, pp. 88-90.*

LORNA SAGE

[Ms Gee's originality] consists in a kind of ghoulish candour. Her texts are—like primitives, or children's paintings—less representations than fetishes, fragments of superstitious magic. Thus **The Burning Book** incarnates a crude pun: nuclear family/nuclear holocaust. It is an everyday story of married folk rudely interrupted by apocalyptic noises off (shrill whispers in italics, bouts of shouting capitals) that gradually crowd out the language in which life goes on.

You get a most disturbing sense of the characters as a threatened species. They are clumsy mammals burrowing in the nooks and crannies of this violent century like thieves of time, grabbing their last moments unawares. Uncles may have died in wars, and a grandfather may have gone missing, but the Ship family—Henry, Lorna and three children—live 'like everyone else' in a cosy intrigue in the present, preoccupied with money troubles, middle age, adultery, sibling rivalry and what have you. It's through their nightmares and phobias that the outer dark seeps in: in Lorna's childhood revulsion against eating meat, Henry's drunken violence, and their younger son's racism. These horrors Ms Gee digs away at until her people are wrinkled out of their shells, and skinned. . . .

The effect is of a furious, didactic cartoon, not unlike Steadman or Scarfe. Bloated meat-eaters belonging to the Empire Party tower over the scene; bodies are squelchy bombs, bags of guts; scattered, spindly plant-like people stand greenly for life. Ms Gee spells out her world-picture in deliberate doggerel: '(All of us live in a novel, and none of us do the writing. Off stage there are grim old men, planning to cut the lighting.)' However, partly because, after all, her medium *is* words, it's at such moments that the drawbacks of her strategy are clearest. There is a sadly predictable hiatus between the graphic images of *The Burning Book* and the paranoid vagueness of the accusations it levels against faceless 'authors' of our fate.

> Lorna Sage, "Nuclear Noises," in The Observer, September 18, 1983, p. 30.

LINDA TAYLOR

How should novels end? Heroines and heroes who could once look forward to domestic bliss have found themselves dying or becoming worldly-wise or learning to live with life's horrid ambivalences. [In *The Burning Book*], Maggie Gee has another (indeed, final) solution—she kills off all her characters in a nuclear holocaust. The Third World War is no respecter of persons or place, and wherever people have got to . . . they are speedily (or slowly) annihilated by flames or radiation or both.

There but for the grace of God . . . For Maggie Gee's novel is an antiwar argument, a lesson to us all that if we don't watch out for the signs, if we don't do something to avert The End, we'll all be roasted in our beds. Better to burn books and characters than the world, and after the blank black final pages, in which Lorna and Henry and Rose and Frank and Angela and John go up in smoke, Gee allows us an epilogue of "hope": "Walking again from the book you look out of the window at stillness. The sunlight on the pavement lying pale and still as peace." . . .

The Burning Book is cathartic—its people, like those in our nightmares, are folk we almost know, do know. We can identify with them; we can vicariously experience their pain. As in her first novel *Dying, in Other Words,* they are a curious assembly of misfits—Wolverhampton sub-gentility moved to London. The families (Cleavers, Lambs, Thrupps and Ships) span a century. Ostrich-like small shopkeepers, they fear the world and hide from its realities—they don't, won't believe IT will happen. It's their sensibility rather than their class that is important—the fact that they refuse to look beyond petty ambitions for money and marriage and happiness. For Maggie Gee's characters are not the rounded, psychological-

novel variety, they are cardboard cut-outs, symbols of attitudes . . . dreaming innocents in a world of unacknowledged savagery. Meanwhile, the mess and rottenness lie around like the packets of ancient black liver lying under the ice-cream in Henry's freezer. "Nothing", thinks Lorna, when her friend, Maisie, takes her to the farmyard, "was like the pictures . . . The fields weren't smooth and green. . . . The chickens weren't playing in the farmyard . . . There weren't any horses *at all.*" It is a "dream" that "had gone wrong." Dreams, while seemingly innocent, are dangerous, and in an attempt to make us face up to the horror or die, Maggie Gee peppers her text with reconstructions of Hiroshima and Nagasaki. . . .

The rhythmic sentences repeatedly end on the down-beat. Maggie Gee's writing, with its constant references to the hidden ugliness of life, presages doom. It is a relief when the bombs, which we know are coming, have come and gone, when we can awake from the fiction and begin again. *The Burning Book* is an odd kind of novel but a marvellously cogent anti-war statement.

> Linda Taylor, "Or We Shall Die," in The Times Literary Supplement, No. 4199, September 23, 1983, p. 1011.

MARION GLASTONBURY

[In *The Burning Book*], the well turned phrase and the well chosen word put a brave face on ominous prospects. . . . [Gee's] homely account of successive private lives is interrupted by the screams of contemporary massacres, 'noises offc' from China and Japan. Snapshots of four generations in a typical English album are blurred by 'smoke drifting across from the future'. Uncle George gets killed in the Second World War and is mourned together with the fallen whose names are recorded on earlier war memorials, while the nameless 'hibakusha' implore us to recognise them, the forgotten victims of nuclear weapons.

The days of the Ship family are also numbered. From the first, we know how old Lorna and her daughter will be when the 'final violence' strikes. Angela has already realised that pensions are now a joke. Short of a miracle, no one will ever again complete life's natural span.

This reluctant prophecy and the spirited peroration that gives the lie to it—'words against death'—will, I suspect, win commendations more earnest than enthusiastic. For all its political fervour and structural ingenuity, *The Burning Book* is regrettably easy to put down. The Ships are a glum lot who plod rancorously through their respective destinies, the women no sooner ripe than shrivelling, and the men forever carving the Sunday joint: a dripping roast that is wincingly described as if it were a holocaust in its own right. (p. 26)

> Marion Glastonbury, "Last Judgments," in New Statesman, Vol. 106, No. 2742, October 7, 1983, p. 26-7.

RONALD DE FEO

Maggie Gee is among those young British novelists who strive to refresh the form. For her doctoral dissertation Miss Gee wrote a study of Virginia Woolf, Vladimir Nabokov and Samuel Beckett, and, not surprisingly, their diverse spirits and concerns are evident in her fiction—Woolf's domestic claustrophobia and despair, Nabokov's playfulness, Beckett's gloom. Her first novel, ***Dying, In Other Words*** . . . was cast as a mystery story about the death of an enigmatic young Oxford woman. But its fragmented, elliptical structure, its constantly shifting points of view and its detailed explorations of a variety of sensibilities demonstrate that it is a pseudo-mystery with a distinctly literary focus.

Miss Gee's second novel, ***The Burning Book,*** is less slippery and indirect, but it too proceeds in a fractured, restless manner as it traces several generations of a middle-class English family living under the threat of a nuclear holocaust. It is an apocalyptic novel that transcends its own thematic limitations. At its best, it is a wonderfully inventive saga of dreams and disillusionment in which the bombing of Hiroshima and Nagasaki is sporadically recalled and doomsday is foreshadowed.

As in her previous novel, Miss Gee works with a fairly large cast of characters. She is initially concerned with a shopkeeper, Henry Ship, his wife Lorna and their children Angela, George and Guy, but she soon broadens her scope to include Henry and Lorna's parents and *their* parents. Moving freely back and forth in time, from one generation to another, from one consciousness to another, she creates a world populated by unfulfilled, lonely souls for whom genuine happiness always seem just beyond reach. . . .

The more Miss Gee illuminates her characters—always with marvelously unpredictable details and observations—the more self-centered and isolated they appear. They seem victims of their own impossibly high expectations. For instance, when as a young girl Lorna visits a farm, she is deeply disappointed by how little it conforms to her dreams. . . . Lorna's failure to confront the world beyond her own small, safe, self-contained realm, is a trait that is also seen in other of Miss Gee's characters. Only Angela, who as a schoolgirl is terribly shaken to learn that the world can blow itself up and who later joins the antinuclear movement, seems strongly aware that "history" is "blackening the sky" and that death is in the air.

Although Miss Gee's critical view of her characters' noninvolvement and the horrors they will face as a result of it is certainly valid and well taken, her repeated reminders sometimes seem too arbitrarily imposed. Such messages might well be dropped into almost any story featuring self-involved people. Their inclusion here appears particularly heavy-handed because the text they interrupt is otherwise so unpretentious, imaginative and fresh.

Nonetheless, the novel's tragic ending is suggestively, almost poetically conveyed, and it is terribly affecting. The story concludes on a hopeful note partly because we the readers are capable of producing a different ending. In this regard as well as in its ceaseless invention and finely measured prose, Miss Gee's somber, sobering book burns bright.

Ronald De Feo, "Paying for Their Expectations," in The New York Times Book Review, *October 14, 1984, p. 28.*

MICHAEL WOOD

[In Gee's novel ***Light Years***], Harold and Lottie, a married couple, 45 and 35 years old, have a brawling row, and Harold leaves. They are thoroughly miserable on their own, even when they are pretending they are not. They have sad, self-deceiving affairs with others, and they stay apart, through pride and confusion and a little bad luck, for a whole year. The book follows them diligently, month by month, notes their dipping and swerving moods, the changing weather, the foliage, the migrations of birds and the conjunctions of the stars. Harold and Lottie finally fall into each other's arms at the zoo, animals doomed after all to happiness. (p. 17)

Lottie is very rich—when she feels depressed she fills her house with £500 worth of spring flowers from Harrods. 'If something was lost, she would simply get another.' Harold is a would-be writer, not writing. They don't have much in common, and have agreed to differ on, among other things, America, the Bomb, feminism, religion, bedtime and dope. Harold is the feminist. What they do have in common, they painfully, stupidly discover, is their terrible lack of each other. . . . The immediate cause of Lottie and Harold's quarrel was a Golden Lion tamarin, a rare new-world monkey which Lottie bought as a pet. The poor creature cringes in its fancy cage, gets sick, and dies within days, to everyone's guilty dismay. Harold's sorrow over the animal is lessened by his gloating at the thought of how ashamed Lottie will be, and *this* thought in turn makes him ashamed. 'We're a horrible species.' We imprison and humiliate other species; torture each other.

Animals loom large in the novel. They share the planet with us . . . . [But] Lottie's fondness for animals doesn't stop her going to the zoo in furs. Animals and plants and stars remind us of our shabbiness and unreality. 'Neither people nor their pain seemed real. Most of the world, after all, wasn't human. What about bears and plankton? What about cacti, and stars?' We have a precarious, unlikely tenure on our territory. 'Very weird to think of humans and elephants chancing to live on the same planet.'

But stars and space loom even larger than animals, are scattered everywhere in the text, like treasures of spectacular fact. . . . [Harold sees the universe] as a body of knowledge to shut away terror, a twist on Pascal. It doesn't help him much, though, only adds to his sense of smallness and bewilderment, his feeling that the world he can reach is wretched and 'Harold-sized'. Maggie Gee herself, however, uses astronomy and earth history as formal and thematic markers; refrains and signs; time flies, time stretches, how late we are. The device can be sentimental at times, a dive into the pathetic fallacy: 'But the silvery water refused to mourn.' The water can't mourn, or refuse to. Most of the world isn't human. There are other sentimentalities too, a cosmic or biological maundering: 'Love slips away in the beat of a heart.' At other times the device triggers metaphors of loneliness, as I've suggested. But mainly, and most beautifully, it works like a bit of Flaubertian cross-cutting or distancing. It stakes out discrepancy, sometimes so total as to produce the sense of a gag rather than pathos. 'After this, events began to move very fast, or rather the speed with which they moved became apparent, for all the time they were going very fast, as the Earth spun on its axis at a thousand miles an hour . . .' It's a long way across the galaxy, but it's a long way between people, when they meet by chance in Paris, for example, and can't bring themselves to talk to each other, or test their mutual apparitions. And the final effect of this is not loneliness but an odd sense of order, or orbit—as if distance were not something to be travelled, but something that dies in time. Harold and Lottie are close in their separation, thinking the same thoughts.

Maggie Gee has a quick curiosity about her characters and their habitats, and a willingness to accept them. Lottie is reprehensible in all kinds of ways, thoughtless, bitchy, arrogant, spoiled, ignorant, but we like her all the same—partly because we see how her quiet, decent, 16-year-old son likes her and needs her and gets on with her. Harold is attractive to Lottie, but otherwise a well-intentioned creep, too self-absorbed to command our entire interest. What about me? is his constant cry, and he can't use his self-pity to understand others. Lottie's adamant, wrong-headed refusal of the very idea of self-pity is much more appealing. I wonder if Harold is meant to be quite so unsympathetic. Probably not.

There are moments when Gee's invention flags. I could do without the cleaning lady who thinks in tautological saws ('Money is money,' 'A home's a home,' 'An employer is an employer'), and there are preachy touches too: 'Actually it seems that only humans spoil a fertile planet with war.' But generally the writing is crisp, attentive to surfaces, affectionate and encyclopedic in its chronicling of human and other change. It is writing that manifestly enjoys what it does. It jumps about in time, in tone, rustles up sharp similes like a conjuror producing unheard of rabbits. 'Light runs faster than love or writing,' Gee says in an overwrought last sentence. I wonder. You can't read light, and this is very fast writing, which misses little on its rounds. (pp. 17-18)

Michael Wood, "Theory with a Wife," in London Review of Books, *Vol. 7, No. 17, October 3, 1985, pp. 17-18.*

ROZ KAVENEY

There are things it is hard to make new, emotional situations which have become clichés by being common parts of human life; moments of parting, recrimination and forgiveness, for example. To adopt an experimental approach to the novel is obviously appropriate when what is described is that which ordinary fiction finds difficult; the triumph of Maggie Gee's *Light Years* is that in it she applies a battery of fictional techniques similar to those in her more overtly radical earlier novels to precisely those subjects which more conventional novelists find easy, too easy. . . . *Light Years* is distinguishable from [conventional fiction] in few details of its plot, yet its moral atmosphere, its sheer feel are so out of the common run as to make it hard to remember that we have been here before.

Gee has made play before with the distancing effect which results from linking her main narrative to a stream of imagery that is entirely unrelated to it at any explicit level. In *The Burning Book,* this consisted of the rumours of war and memories of Hiroshima always at the ear of the family saga's narrator; here it is the silence of infinite space and the inhospitableness of even those fragments of solidity, the planets of the Solar System, that act as counterpoint to her narrative of separation. Occasionally this drifts into something more conventional, almost an example of the pathetic fallacy, but is infused with a parodic tone by being too close and obvious a link, as when Harold's claustrophobia on a cross-Channel ferry is juxtaposed with the "lethal yellow hothouse" of

Venus. The discoveries of astronomy do eventually come to be an explicit metaphor; the minor parodic flirtations with the idea of their doing so prevent our making the connection too soon. The opposition of human microcosm and the stars is hardly original; what is new is the way in which the implicit metaphors are so fully present without swamping the narrative and the way interest in this counterpoint is sustained.

One factor in this is that while mankind in general, and Harold and Lottie, the estranged couple, in particular, are shown against a backdrop of stars, they are also shown surrounded by animals, a warmer aspect of the natural world, vulnerable, as the stars are not, to the consequences of human failing. The original quarrel focuses on a tamarin monkey which Lottie buys illegally as a present, and which dies of neglect as a result of their separation; it is when she and Harold independently make amends to its shade and visit the Small Mammal House in the Regents Park Zoo that they fall back into each other's arms. Lottie learns much, it is implied but never stated, from her observation of the sterile bondings of the zoo's gorillas. Harold sustains himself through his exile from her with readings from Victorian books of natural wonders. Again, a parodic tone creeps in and makes it possible for us to take this almost Victorian theme of the healing power of observation of the natural world seriously, by telling us we do not have to. Part of Gee's innovativeness is this offer to the reader of an illusory free will. In the end, what we are offered is a rhetorical freedom only; we will comply with the author's intentions if we are to enjoy the book as the artefact it is, and do so more willingly for the subversive seeming offer.

Unlike her gloomy earlier two novels, this one is gently comic. Lottie is rich and spoiled; Harold principled, lazy and feckless; neither of them is allowed to get away with much. Almost because the author is quite hard on them, we appreciate all the more the positive qualities and moments of triumph that she does allow them. It is because she is subject to so many minor indignities, because the narrator so often ticks her off, that we are so delighted when Lottie takes a piece of effective direct action, retrieving at gun-point from a messy Somerstown flat the jewels stolen from her by her son's punk friend Smeggy. There are false notes to some of the humour; Lottie's attempt to forget Harold in bed takes the form of a tedious, sexually expert Franco-Swiss businessman, who is a little too ludicrously dreadful to be quite true; Harold gets off lightly with a shop assistant, with whom he has a somewhat pedagogic love affair that is allowed to be touching and warm as well as comically disastrous. At times, Maggie Gee's personal and political disapproval of women like Lottie contaminates the narrator's purely artistic, cultivated, comic disdain for her, raising, not entirely to the novel's advantage, the ultimately irrelevant question of whether we should be as glad as in the event we are about the eventual reconciliation, the couple playing piggyback in the snow.

Apart from the sardonicism and the occassional discordant sourness, this is a genial, peopled book; Harold and Lottie's lives take place in a human world as well as the worlds of the stars and beasts. Gee has a particular gift for making vividly present characters who may only be glimpsed by the principals, but who teach them lessons; the two elderly lesbian gentlewomen who counsel Harold in a Bournemouth guest house, for example, have an important function, but are memorable walk-ons too. Foregrounded figures like Lottie's son Davey, or Harold's lover April, are socially and emotionally credible, have moments of dominating our sympathies, yet are kept on a tight leash, never stray from their job of supporting and supplementing the objects of our real attention.

This is so fine a novel because so completely a planned and crafted one, even when its events seem most contingent or haphazard, when its tones and concepts clash. This craft, and the book's posed philosophical view, pile up all of human possibility and perception as a barrier against the cold and the dark; the tamarin died of isolation and neglect and the middle-aged Harold and Lottie find they cannot afford to be apart. Maggie Gee's experimentalism is one which, also, refuses to be merely clever and cold.

> Roz Kaveney, "Against the Cold and the Dark," in The Times Literary Supplement, *No. 4305, October 4, 1985, p. 1097.*

MAUREEN FREELY

Maggie Gee is an atomic age missionary: she writes not to entertain but to alarm and instruct. She doesn't think we learned enough from Chernobyl, and in [*Grace*], her fourth novel, she sets out to fill in the gaps.

She wants us to know that the danger of radiation is always with us. She frightens us with statistics of nuclear waste. She also wants to remind us that the people who monitor the industry are themselves monitored by MI5. Most of all, she wants us to remember Hilda Murrell, and ask ourselves what her brutal and unsolved murder tells us about England.

To this end, she has invented Paula, a 37-year-old writer and avid anti-nuclear campaigner who is working on a novel about Hilda Murrell, and Grace, an 85-year-old pacifist who is Paula's aunt and Hilda Murrell's *Doppelgänger*. Both Grace and Paula spend most of their waking hours worrying about England, and though they do not meet until the end of the book their thoughts run along parallel lines. . . .

Maggie Gee saves her own poison for Bruno, the private investigator under contract to MI5 who lives next door to Paula's Mothercare man-friend, Arthur. He is an inspired paranoid fantasy: a right-wing patriot and fitness freak who worships nuclear power and hates all things organic. . . . Although he also hates children, old ladies, left-wing loonies, and anyone who looks weak, poor, or untidy, 'he loves the human race. To be human meant being top of the heap. Humans had brains. Humans . . . didn't walk around showing hairy parts.'

It will come as no surprise that Bruno, who likes to walk around in wigs and women's clothing, is a disaster waiting to happen to Grace, Paula and Mr Mothercare. That is the main problem with this book: there are no surprises. With her emphatic, repetitive, and passionately angry style, Maggie Gee does create an ominous mood, but her symbols are so potent they almost glow in the dark. . . .

As the book progresses there is a greater and greater gap between the characters and the things they are meant to stand for. This is particularly true of Paula, whose unexpected pregnancy is supposed to be a much-needed ray of hope for the future.

I admire Maggie Gee for the sincerity and scope of her intentions. In so far as the novel is a warning, it works. But there's

a womb-centred complacency to the resolution: the world is not going to be saved by women becoming accidentally pregnant. The difficult question (and the one I wish she had asked) is not how to give birth to a child in the shadow of Chernobyl, but how to protect that child once it's here—and what to teach it.

> Maureen Freely, "Atomic Gooseflesh," in The Observer, *September 25, 1988, p. 43.*

PAUL OLDFIELD

[The] fall-out from nuclear development—irrational fears, disbelief in any future, escalating state secrecy— . . . resounds through Maggie Gee's *Grace.* Yet we learn most, not from this novel's deeply concerned characters (who even serve as pegs for quotes from anti-nuclear non-fiction), but from the unattractive Bruno. This would-be undercover agent, who spies on neighbours he misguidedly takes for nuclear saboteurs, incarnates male technocracy as "the rape of nature". He can only suppress his fear of victimisation, his night terrors, and his unstable sexual identity (by night he becomes the transvestite vamp Brunnhilde) by a pathological Michael Ryan/James Bond masculinity. He assaults uncleanness, weakness, feminity wherever it confronts him. So he's aligned with the city, clean technologies, the secret service's cold war.

It's a perceptive look at the construction of masculinity, but Bruno becomes a dumping place for everything Maggie Gee wants to criticise. None of her other characters need accept any guilt for "the bomb inside" at all.

Gee and her sixties left-overs, Paula and Arthur, can only see technology as an abuse. "Nature" is their creed. Unlike Bruno, they laugh when toddler Sally defecates in the garden. Soil and blood and shit are the right stuff, apparently. Maybe they've displaced their taboos onto the nuclear "wastes" travelling past their house. Whatever is natural is *celebrated:* even the October hurricane is gleefully described as an overdue lesson for computer-bound technicians.

This is the problem with *Grace.* Gee's writing can be marvellously illuminated when her characters suddenly feel the intensity of "the here, the now". But too often everything, like the hurricane or the crumbling hotels that keep reminding us of Britain's decline, is creakily emblematic. And new "hopes" are grafted in almost as heavy-handedly as the fourth-hand apocalyptic rhetoric.

Paula's illness turns out not to be Chernobyl-induced cancer but morning sickness: it's her baby that will usher in a new dawn at the end. Her lover Arthur is described as a *mother* all along, a fleshy, child-minding cook and house-husband. In fact, the litmus test applied by the novel is always the characters' attitude to children. If they're unhappy with them, they're either deficient, like the elderly Grace, or they're monsters, like Bruno.

Grace, who'd refused to have children, is forcibly redeemed when she's inundated by the blood of a stranger whom she assists in labour. It even becomes a surrogate birth-giving for her. Bruno, too, is oddly co-opted into this birth at some deep level: it's his semen stains, left on Grace's clothes after he breaks into her hotel room and masturbates, that stir up her memories of her long-dead lover's wish for children. It's almost as if the spilled seed *has* had an issue, after all. And, somehow, the world is going to be saved by these miraculous pregnancies. *Grace* is a *doctrinaire* humanist-holist tract that doesn't so much await the birth of a new Messiah as fetishise the fact of birth, its closeness to "nature, in itself." Today, though, we're saturated with such messages ("you must be caring, sane, convivial, ecological . . .") from all sides anyway. It's hardly a bold step to disseminate them in fiction.

Paul Oldfield, "The Bomb Inside," in New Statesman & Society, *Vol. 116, No. 3000, September 30, 1988, p. 42.*

PETER READING

At one, very compelling, level, Maggie Gee's distinguished new novel [*Grace*] reads like a thriller. Seedy, schizophrenic, transvestite, paranoid and vicious private detective Bruno Janes is casually recruited by the Special Branch to assemble evidence of the unpatriotic "subversive activities" of Paula Timms and her endearing aunt, the eponymous, sprightly eighty-five-year-old Grace Stirling. For the two women have exhibited tendencies likely to irritate the security services—feminism, pacifism, open opposition to the nuclear power game. Paula is a "train-spotter", recording the incidence of locomotives trundling through heavily-populated areas of London with their burden of lethal radioactive spent rods from reactors for reprocessing in Cumbria, and "she's written plays on related themes"; Grace, a pacifist since 1916, went round the world in the 1950s with Dora Russell's Peace Caravan and has a friend in Czechoslovakia whom she sometimes telephones. Paula lives in London, Grace in Sussex. Bruno bugs Paula's phone and hounds Grace with increasingly murderous intent through a narrative of brilliantly modulated and suspenseful impetus, from her holiday hotel at the seaside resort of her childhood, back to her home where a tense and sanguinary débâcle is enacted.

But *Grace* is more than just another addition to the compulsive, nail-biting canon; it is a sustained valediction, an elegy for a moribund society, nation, empire and species. The exemplary Grace's harassment and decline is, of course, also grace's (and for Stirling one could read sterling). Gee, in addition, introduces Faith, the innocent, practical, determined, pregnant chambermaid; Arthur, the big, good, protective, Arthurian lover of Paula; and a couple of shabby, crumbling hotels called Empire and Albion. Yet one is never troubled by any heavy-handed Bunyanese. Indeed, allegory is employed in a subtle, uncontrived manner. . . .

Similarly, the repeatedly expressed significance, for Grace, of the lighthouse, which she first saw in her infancy, is symbolically presented, but in a way which just manages to avoid portentousness:

> Grace thought of the light pouring over the water, the regular turning of the mighty beam. It could only reach out a certain space; it could only touch the edge of the void, but it would hold the human world together, it would bring the human ships safe home. . . .

In two memorable passages, forming the lyrically powerful crescendo of the book (four remarkable pages which could almost be scanned as galloping, loose anapaestic tetrameters), this lighthouse assists Grace at the birth of Faith's child, when a hurricane hits the shaky Empire Hotel and causes power failure.

Faith, grace, light and chivalrous decency, however, are unable to hold together against the crazy entropy and filth of our contemporary realm. The Hilda Murrell case, the subject of Paula's unwritten novel, is introduced to shadow unobtrusively the course of Grace's adventures. . . . Despite a temporary victory over the personification of rottenness, when batty, bestial Bruno is zapped at the last moment, we know there will be increasing numbers like him, for such appalling childhoods as his (intimated here with a surprising, delicate compassion) are common enough for the malady to be perpetuated. . . . And although love is affectingly treated—Grace's tenderness for her dead artist lover, Arthur's affection for his daughter of a previous relationship, as well as his and Paula's love for each other and their own nascent child—it remains an emotion which is powerless to transcend, can only console. Though the couple plans a new start away from the city, an earlier image of post-Chernobyl dead reindeer piled in a ruck in the tundra lingers. Meanwhile the trains with their sinister finned flasks rumble ominously on and on through a benighted London where the trash amasses, the loonies and alcos proliferate and the resident strumpet of the defunct Albion opines, "If you ask me, this country is fucked. It's not just me love. It's the whole country."

Peter Reading, "Compulsively Moribund," in The Times Literary Supplement, *No. 4461, September 30-October 6, 1988, p. 1068.*

ANITA BROOKNER

Maggie Gee's excellent novel [*Grace*] treads a sure path between love and fear, taking as its starting point sinister and secret happenings in contemporary England—the silent movement of nuclear waste through London at night and the assassination of Hilda Murrell, no explanation of which has ever been available. It raises an authentic frisson, which is only dissipated by the charm of its main character, 85-year-old Grace, who was once loved·by a major painter and who is now tracked by an alarming contract killer. . . .

Cleverly, the author discharges all her information in the first few pages. In the 1950s Grace went round the world with Dora Russell's Peace Caravan. She has a friend in Czechoslovakia whom she occasionally telephones. She has a niece; Paula, who watches the nuclear trains go by from her window in Kensal Rise. Paula is also trying to write a book about Hilda Murrell. Between watching the trains carrying spent fuel rods and working on her book Paula feels exceedingly ill and wonders about the effects of radiation from the Chernobyl fall-out. Neither Paula nor Grace are breaking the law but odd things happen to their telephones. In fact they are under surveillance by Bruno, who lives next door to Paula and whom one of several government agencies (they are named and we are given a choice) have selected to do their work for them. Those in charge do not know, or if they know they do not care, that Bruno is a psychopath. . . .

Having dispensed this information Maggie Gee then concentrates on Grace, who closes down her bookshop in Sussex and chooses to go for a week's holiday to Southbourne, a cross between Bournemouth and Eastbourne, promising herself a treat, a trip to the lighthouse. (This is the only detail I found obtrusive). Grace, recognisably an English spinster of the Hilda Murrell variety, has not had an entirely arid emotional life. She was the mistress of Ralph Dunne, whose child she refused to have. . . .

Now her only love is her niece Paula, although she dislikes Paula's lover, shaggy Arthur. She wonders, in Southbourne why Paula fails to keep her appointment to visit her for the day, why the visit is put off so many times. In fact Paula is pregnant, Arthur has disappeared, and a storm . . . is brewing. All this, apart from the storm, Bruno knows through his phone taps.

He is out to kill the old lady. The novel is concerned with this, with Paula's pregnancy, which is material to the story, with Bruno's appalling preparations, and with Grace's innocent days at Southbourne. If Grace is the heroine then Southbourne is the place of safety, although the cracks are beginning to show even here. . . . But London is infinitely worse. The trains pass silently at night, and the owner of the Albion Hotel, where Arthur works as manager, thinks of turning the place over to the DHSS and charging it the earth for the privilege of housing the homeless. The skill with which Maggie Gee gets Grace, Paula, and Arthur out of their respective fixes is considerable. The story ends not only happily but hopefully: a baby is born and there is another on the way.

This is only incidentally a polemical novel, although serious considerations lie behind it. Sources such as Judith Cook's *Who Killed Hilda Murrell?* and Rosalie Bertell's *No Immediate Danger: Prognosis for a Radioactive Earth* are acknowledged but are so internalised that the novel reads like a thriller, with Bruno's stalking of Grace as its major theme. Even minor strands are drafted seamlessly into the narrative, which is extremely steady, refusing to make capital out of its sensational material. It would be disquieting (it *is* disquieting) if the reader did not trust Grace so absolutely. At the end one wonders whether matters did not in fact arrange themselves in this way. Who *did* kill Hilda Murrell?

It is an exciting book and an excitingly written one. . . . The affirmative ending comes as an enormous relief and only then does one notice that the tension has been effortlessly maintained. I read it twice, and it was even better the second time.

Anita Brookner, "A Storm is Brewing," in The Spectator, *Vol. 261, No. 8363, October 22, 1988, p. 35.*

Richard Greenberg

1959?-

American dramatist and screenwriter.

A writer whose works often satirize upper-middle class East Coast society, Greenberg is best known for his drama *Eastern Standard* (1988). The play begins in a trendy New York eatery where four young urban professionals meet for clever conversation and romantic intrigue. When a homeless woman enters the restaurant and demands Perrier water, she challenges the wealthy four to reassess their ethics. Infused with both guilt and good intentions, they invite the woman and a struggling actress/waitress to join them at an elegant beach house. Their beach holiday sours when one character describes her involvement in a Wall Street scandal and another reveals that he has contracted AIDS. Ultimately, the four friends' simple-minded solution to homelessness fails miserably. While some critics deemed *Eastern Standard* contrived, others compared it to Philip Barry's high-society comedies and lauded Greenberg's originality and wit. Greenberg's characters, according to Frank Rich, are "people who got fat from the ethos of the 1980s but may finally begin to examine the connection between their own behavior and the sick city left in the wake of the spree."

Among Greenberg's other full-length dramas, *The Bloodletters* (1984), is a comedy about a Jewish boy whose iradicable body odor renders him friendless. *Life Under Water* (1985) is a one-act play that many critics considered a consistently funny and telling portrait of a group of upper-middle class Long Islanders. *The Vanishing Act* (1986), another one-act comedy, centers upon an emotionally distressed suburban family. Of Greenberg's earlier plays, *The Maderati* (1987) garnered the most attention. An absurd satire of poseurs and self-promoters in New York's artistic community, this work was commended for its sharp humor and pointed observations.

In addition to his original work for the stage, Greenberg adapted the stories and letters of Franz Kafka for *The Hunger Artist* (1987), a multi-media theatrical work about the Czech author. Greenberg also wrote two teleplays and adapted Laurie Colwin's "An Old-Fashioned Story" for public television in 1989.

FRANK RICH

No one ever claimed it was all fun growing up middle-class Jewish on Long Island, but Corky Sutter has it harder than most. Corky, the awkward teen-age protagonist of Richard Greenberg's ***The Bloodletters*** is not merely the victim of his oppressive, widowed mother and an overactive, if unfulfilled, sexual imagination. He also suffers from an incurable disease that leaves its victims with a single, but devastating, infirmity—a disgusting stench redolent of "an old bathroom."

So what's a fellow to do? According to Mr. Greenberg . . . , Corky spends most of his time playing checkers, scrubbing down with industrial soaps and masturbating. His only friend is a one-time high-school football hero, Defe, whose own medical history (an aneurysm) has left him with the crucial attribute essential for fraternizing with Corky: a corroded olfactory nerve. Corky's mom pays Defe $100 a week to serve as her son's companion, with the rest of her money apparently budgeted for air fresheners. The Sutters' Levittown living room . . . is a warehouse of such products—of the spray, disk and wick varieties, in a rainbow of scents.

The Bloodletters, which takes "La Vie en Rose" as its informal, ironic theme song, does not, in any sense, come up all roses. Mr. Greenberg, the program tells us, is still a student at the Yale School of Drama, and his comedy can be immature. Jokes, particulary of the Jewish-mother genre, are pushed too far (even Michael Korda is dragged into one of them); after intermission, the humor is crushed under a heavy load of terminal despair. But the play is so daffily conceived that one must admire its promising author's antic spin of mind even when he is straining too hard. . . .

Corky may indeed be the most ordinary character on stage. His older brother, Reid, is an academic who has recently suffered a crackup and is now devoting his enforced sabbatical to researching the medical and spiritual uses of leeches.

Reid's emasculating gentile wife, Annie, is busy philandering, even as her husband lusts after an old pal, Callie van der Vlis. Callie, a homosexual and once a poet, woke up one morning and found himself "incapable of metaphor." He now has a successful career as a "food stylist"—a calling that requires him to "make fruit look attractive for television commercials" and that allows him to meet "many interesting and attractive people."

Much of the play's plot, which occurs over one long "terrible weekend," involves the eternal search for romance—or, if not love, sex. There are two overlapping all-male triangles; heterosexuality is primarily represented by Jake Abrams, a vulgar record-company entrepreneur who has been pursuing Corky's mom ever since they sat shiva together for Corky's late dad. Yet, no matter who ends up sleeping with whom, Corky will always be odd man out. A genuine untouchable, he feels that he is "stuck in a piece of soundproof glass," forever doomed to find life's promised pleasures just out of reach.

Worse, Corky doesn't know who he is. His sole identity is as "a conversation piece." Intelligent, kind and sexually ambivalent, he may, as his mother says, possess "a beautiful soul, like the Elephant Man." But he may also be, as his sister-in-law claims, a complete nonentity whose only distinction is his "comical stigma." In truth, Corky isn't all that different from any other nice Jewish boy trying to find a pathway from post-adolescence into young adulthood: His disease is but an allegorical exaggeration of the angst that afflicts the young heroes of so much contemporary Jewish-American fiction in the Philip Roth mold.

It's disappointing that Mr. Greenberg ultimately loses his original, neo-Kafkaesque vision of his familiar material to conclude with standard cries of self-martyrdom and a literal realization of the play's title conceit. . . .

Neither a whiner nor a freak, [Corky is] just a sweet, normal boy whose cosmic body-odor problem is every American high-school kid's worst nightmare come true.

Frank Rich, " 'The Bloodletters,' a Comedy," in The New York Times, December 7, 1984, p. C3.

FRANK RICH

The Ensemble Studio Theater, always a bustling home for new and established voices in the American theater, has now reached its annual fever pitch. "Marathon '85"—the E.S.T.'s eighth yearly festival of one-act plays—has gotten under way. . . . [Even] the minor offerings—one of them by David Mamet—seem like petty inconveniences once we've seen the two gems that conclude the evening.

Actually, the final play on the bill—*Life Under Water* by Richard Greenberg—is no mere gem. It is a full-bodied 45-minute work that marks the arrival of a young playwright with a big future. Mr. Greenberg made his debut at the E.S.T. last fall with *The Bloodletters,* a promising family comedy that at times suggested a blend of Philip Roth and Albert Innaurato. There's a little of Roth in *Life Under Water,* too—and more than a little John Cheever—but it is Mr. Greenberg's own arresting sensibility that informs every pungent line and bristling scene.

The setting is the present-day Hamptons, where two sunbath-

ing college-age girls [Amy-Beth and Amy-Joy] just want to have fun. That fun arrives in the form of an attractive, self-dramatizingly sensitive preppie [Kip], who is in flight from the summer home he shares with his overbearing, divorced mother. While this premise might lead to a bittersweet saga of teen-age romance, the author is after much more than that. *Life Under Water* dramatizes three different love affairs spanning two generations. In the end, it yields a lacerating portrait of a contemporary upper middle-class that is as bored, self-indulgent and emotionally reckless as the Long Island idlers of Scott Fitzgerald's day.

Mr. Greenberg holds out some hope for his characters at the final curtain, but not before we have watched them casually smash [Amy-Beth], the most psychologically fragile of the vacationers, as if she were a helpless crab washed up on the beach. Disturbing as *Life Under Water* can be, it is also consistently funny. The author knows both the Jewish and Wasp folkways of his milieu, but, instead of merely recording the familiar manners, he transforms them into slightly surreal, thematically rooted comic conceits.

Frank Rich, "One-Act Plays: 'Marathon '85,' " in The New York Times, May 16, 1985, p. C23.

MEL GUSSOW

The ephemera of fashion are an amusing running motif in Evening B of the Ensemble Studio Theater's Marathon '86. Although none of the four plays are as fully realized as Horton Foote's *Blind Date* in Evening A, they are more evenly balanced. Each has something to offer—an attitude, an idea or an intriguing situation. . . .

Richard Greenberg's *Vanishing Act* is the longest and by far the most ambitious of the four plays—and also the most elusive. As the author of *Bloodletters* and *Life Under Water,* Mr. Greenberg is one of the Ensemble Studio Theater's developing talents.

This time his intention is to write a post-Absurdist comedy about a normally insane American family. Almost all of the characters are idlers and dabblers in the noonday sun—a grandfather who feigns decrepitude, a mother whose home crafts include architecture, and offspring who are in various stages of attempted suicide and continuing inertia.

The strangest things occur with no motivational accountability, but ever on its own dreamlike terms, the play is disjointed. However, as led by the director, [the actors] and others animate the Goreyesque tale.

Mel Gussow, "Ensemble Studio's Marathon," in The New York Times, May 21, 1986, p. C23.

FRANK RICH

"The glitterati were as thick as porterhouse steaks," says Rena deButts, a contemporary hostess with the mostest, on the morning after throwing a party for all the rising young novelists, artists and photographers in Manhattan. According to *The Maderati,* Richard Greenberg's new comedy about Rena and her soigné crowd, the glitterati are actually thicker than porterhouse steaks and a great deal tougher besides. Mr. Greenberg's characters are the sort who produce just enough "art" by day to garner one of the longer captions in *Vanity Fair,* then spend each night on the prowl for ever more publicity and "shiftless moneyed friends." They're esthetes who pretentiously bemoan "this terrible sickness of being alive" even while happily pursuing "a life of hollowness and shellac."

Mr. Greenberg is a young and witty writer whose best previous plays . . . offered devastating insights into the mad folkways practiced in middle-class Levittown (*The Bloodletters*) and the toney Hamptons (*Life Under Water*). *The Maderati* . . . doesn't quite do for Manhattan what its predecessors did for Long Island. Working in a hermetically sealed, absurdist manner that recalls his least fruitful previous venture (*Vanishing Act*), the playwright can't always compete with journalistic accounts of the real-life scene inhabited by the likes of Tama Janowitz and Julian Schnabel. Pitted against the more materialistic rites of post-modernism, the comic arsenal of absurdism seems almost genteel.

The Maderati is at its funniest when it is vicious. As Mr. Greenberg . . . [whips] us in and out of several terminally hip apartments on a particularly frantic Sunday, we meet some supremely unappealing characters, each equipped with a Perelmanesque name and at least one wickedly satirical costume. Keene Esterhazy is a writer so bored that he tends to doze off while searching, invariably in vain, for the mot juste that might complete his latest second-hand simile or metaphor. The Brooklyn-bred, clandestinely homosexual publisher Martin Royale speaks with a pompous English accent, while the Method actor and notorious rake Danton Young mutters as inaudibly in the boudoir as he apparently does in the theater. . . . A feminist who loves men literally to death, [Danton's lover Cuddles Molotov] is so humorless that her choice of a weight-reduction regimen is "the diet of worms."

What brings this crowd together is a rumor concerning the accidental killing—or possible suicide—of a poet named Charlotte Ebbinger. Charlotte is very depressed but in fact very much alive. It's Mr. Greenberg's point that in an arts aristocracy based on self-promotion rather than merit, people who ignored the poet in life will immediately exploit the privileged knowledge of her presumed death for social cachet. . . .

Although the spread of a malicious rumor has promise as a farcical premise, Mr. Greenberg never develops its possible permutations or those of his characters' interlocking love triangles. As has been true of his previous plays with the exception of *Life Under Water,* this one is structurally slack. The saner characters painstakingly introduced at the outset, Rena and her stolid novelist husband Chuck deflate quickly, providing merely perfunctory plot facilitation rather than the intended thematic counterpoint to their nuttier friends. In mid-Act II, *The Maderati* comes to a complete standstill as the speeches get longer and the author searches frantically for narrative and philosophical sums larger than his play's disjointed individual parts.

Prior to that point, Mr. Greenberg reveals his keen ear in a number of shapely comic lines, especially when catching his characters in strained stabs at phrasemaking ("the crème de la thoughtful") or fatuous pronouncements ("I'm so tired of hearing the pieties of my generation—we need new pieties") or stalled aperçus ("I deplore the uncertainty of a ringing phone"). But without other dramatic propulsion—and with proficient rather than inspired performances in most of the key roles—the scattering of sharp jokes, diluted by the many more numerous mild ones, can't sustain an evening. "Nobody

ever finishes anything these days," is Rena deButts's damning final verdict on Manhattan's fast literary set. While Mr. Greenberg is far more gifted than the dilettante writers he lampoons, *The Maderati,* true to current glitterati fashion, is an inflated sketch, not a finished play.

Frank Rich, " 'The Maderati' by Richard Greenberg," in The New York Times, *February 20, 1987, p. C3.*

JOHN SIMON

It is bad for the title of a play to be an unpunning pun: Richard Greenberg's *The Maderati* derives from "literati" the way "glitterati" does, but without rhyme or felicity. The opening scene features Rena (getting out of bed) and Chuck (not getting out) de Butts—both of them writers—the morning after a party they have given for their literary and other more or less artsy friends, none of whom they can really stand. There is wit, visual comedy, and an air of promise. The bickering, while Rena tries on a variety of unlikely outfits with which to confront existence, has a crazy veracity to it: "Our lives are blighted with sterility; just once I would like the breakdown *du jour* to be mine." It seems that Charlotte Ebbinger, a suicidal poetess—having incurred such party disasters as facing the publisher who jeeringly rejected her verse, then being mistaken for a chair and sat on by said publisher—has gone to the hospital for a routine morning checkup of her mental health and has been promptly locked up as insane. Rena is off to spring her, and Chuck is to alert the rest of their circle.

We meet the gang of mostly viperish or supine friends who have one thing in common: near-total self-absorption. . . . Everyone is at cross purposes with everyone, injudicious attractions and well-founded revulsions proliferate, with everybody pursuing or trying to escape from somebody, if only from himself.

But unlike in a solid farce, the situations do not build, the characters' weirdness does not reach new heights, the talk far outweighs the sight gags, and so elaborate a routine as putting up mourning crêpe in the apartment of someone who hasn't died yields no comic payoff. Moreover, in a good farce, absurdist or not (and this one cannot quite decide which it is), the goofiest personages elicit some kind of guilty sympathy from us. Not so here, where drolly conceived characters quickly pall. There are quite a few funny lines ("Things must be called by their rightful names!" "Yes, or by others"; "Charlotte, think of us together, married, poets—like the Brownings, only untalented"), but they strain too hard and are sometimes out of character. The ending is clumsy and pointless. (pp. 111-12)

The cast play cartoons in a suitably cartoonish way, . . . but all are finally stranded as the humor, taking off on tangents of its own, leaves them behind. (p. 112)

John Simon, "Name That Lyric," in New York Magazine, *Vol. 20, No. 9, March 2, 1987, pp. 111-12.*

EDITH OLIVER

[*The Maderati*] deserves a salute of some kind. Its subject is the garish behavior of the literary and artistic set in this city right now, and its style is appropriately absurdist. . . .

The play itself takes a while to get launched (or else my resistance to it took a while to collapse, since I have small patience generally for absurdist comedy), but it gets better and better as one scene follows another. Most of the characters have at least a toe in the arts. Poor Charlotte has written a book (at the party, we are told, she was sat on by the publisher who rejected it, who then complained about the springs in the sofa); Chuck has been working on a novel; Dewy is a photographer; her husband, Ritt, is a stockbroker, afflicted with sudden epiphanies, which are ignored by all; there is a poet, in love with Charlotte, whose muse abruptly switches off when he badly needs her, and who tends to fall suddenly asleep. There is an actor, the embodiment of Method mannerisms, who is an object of desire among several of the ladies and an object of highhearted ridicule by the dramatist. We first see him asleep on a bed, with his current girlfriend, one Cuddles Molotov, poised above him knife in hand. . . . [She] is the sexpot of many a Saul Steinberg drawing, and no prettier or funnier sexpot ever existed.

The Maderati is young and sharp and frisky, and though little construction is allowed to interfere with the flow of jokes and ideas from Mr. Greenberg's teeming brain I didn't miss it.

Edith Oliver, "Merry Chaos," in The New Yorker, *Vol. LXIII, No. 2, March 2, 1987, p. 76.*

FRANK RICH

[In *Eastern Standard*] Richard Greenberg captures the romantic sophistication of the most sublime comedies ever made in this country: those produced by Hollywood from the middle of the Depression until the waning days of World War II.

Mr. Greenberg's characters have youth, brains, money and classy professions. Their last names—Wheeler, Paley, Kidde—are redolent of Philip Barry's Park Avenue, their fresh good looks and bubbly voices recall Katharine Hepburn and Henry Fonda. And like Carole Lombard, the heiress who adopts a tramp in *My Man Godfrey,* or Joel McCrea, the Hollywood director who goes underground as a hobo in *Sullivan's Travels,* they are driven by conscience to see how the other half lives. The bright young things of *Eastern Standard* invite a bag lady to stay with them in the Hamptons.

If Mr. Greenberg's only achievement were to re-create the joy of screwball comedies, from their elegant structure to their endlessly quotable dialogue, *Eastern Standard* would be merely dazzling good fun. But what gives this play its unexpected weight and subversive punch is its author's ability to fold the traumas of his own time into vintage comedy without sacrificing the integrity of either his troubling content or his effervescent theatrical form. *Eastern Standard* opens with its characters meeting cute in a Manhattan restaurant, it ends with them toasting their future happiness on a Long Island beach. Yet in between, both Mr. Greenberg's people and his audience have been rocked by the plight of a city in the midst of "a nervous breakdown." It's a city where developers rob the poor of their homes and the entire citizenry of its sunlight. It's a city where people constantly wake up with hot sweats—whether they are guilty perpetrators of financial corruption or innocent victims of AIDS.

When we first meet the four incipient lovers of *Eastern Standard* at a restaurant serving such dishes as grouper tortellini, they are too selfish and complacent to worry much about all that. Drew, is a downtown painter whose épater le bourgeois pose and haughty verbal "reflex of belittlement" are at hypocritical odds with his decadent existence. His best friend from Dartmouth days, Stephen, is an architect just awakening to his own complicity in Manhattan's urban blight. At the neighboring table are Phoebe, a Wall Street investment counselor caught up in an insider trading scandal, and her brother, Peter, a television producer who spends "days at a time defending nearly invisible principles" while pounding socially conscious scripts into fluff at CBS.

Since Drew and Peter are both gay, and Stephen and Phoebe are not, it's only minutes before the college chums and brother and sister can mix and match in a way Preston Sturges never could have imagined in *The Palm Beach Story.* In his ingenious first act, Mr. Greenberg achieves the couplings with three overlapping scenes, Alan Ayckbourn-style, that replay the same action from the varying perspectives of different tables in the restaurant. Even then, a disturbing counterpoint accompanies the heavy-breathing flirtations. As the sexual repartee reaches its crescendo, so do the disquieting obscenities of an unseen woman trying to storm the barricades of Upper East Side trendiness.

That woman is the homeless May, a casualty of welfare bureaucracy who just wants "to sit like everyone else and drink some Perrier water." When her wish comes true in screwball fashion at Stephen's beach home after intermission, Mr. Greenberg manages to uphold the escapist tone of his classic Hollywood models while refusing to permit his characters to escape. Act II of *Eastern Standard* . . . retains the champagne-informed dizziness of the poolside wedding eve in *The Philadelphia Story.* Freed from inhibition as if by magic, the characters switch partners, quit their jobs and vow to be reborn. But May isn't a cuddly homeless doll; she refuses to disappear in "the wonderful solvent of a politically correct project." When the pretty lovers of *Eastern Standard* finally sober up, it is not merely because they've figured out whom they really love but because they at last see their true roles, hardly attractive ones, in the urban nightmare they've tried to flee. . . .

Eastern Standard goes by so blithely that not until after it's over can one dip beneath the play's brilliant surface to explore its depths. Mr. Greenberg, a 30-year-old writer whose previous work includes a one-act play of great promise (*Life Under Water*) as well as the arch full-length *Maderati* is maturing at an accelerating rate. *Eastern Standard* itself has been enriched considerably since its May premiere at the Seattle Repertory Theater.

As always, this playwright is a fount of epigrammatic lines and bright jokes. Julian Schnabel (among others) is described as being on "the cutting edge of the passé," and one offstage mother is deemed so conservative that "there's not a revolution in history that would have failed to execute her." The laughs never depart from a human foundation. Here is that uncommon writer who can make heterosexual and homosexual romances equally credible and erotic. The play's close sibling relationship is also gripping, and so, most impressively, is the college-spawned fraternity between Drew and Stephen. Whether engaging in juvenile locker-room humor or propping each other up in tearful sorrow, these two friends achieve a fluent intimacy that, in my experience, has never previously been alloted to male stage characters of opposite sexual preference. . . .

[Peter, Drew's love interest,] is touching as the producer determined to resist self-pity despite having AIDS. "No one ever looked at me without thinking I'd live forever," he says, and, indeed, he looks like a Bruce Weber model in an advertisement for Ralph Lauren beachwear. Later, when [Peter] breaks the tranquillity of the pose and its setting by crying out a simple, terrifying line—"I'm sick!"—the effect is devastating. As his rage tears through the Hamptons landscape, it seems to lower the curtain on a Bloomingdale's diorama of a decade in which easy money and easy pleasure were unlimited for the privileged few.

Just the same, and perhaps to the distress of ideologues, the author refuses to condemn outright his once-charmed and always charming characters. Mr. Greenberg has no better utopian schemes for conquering social inequities than they do. Like Drew, who is a middle-class artist because "no other class is open to me," Mr. Greenberg must write about what he knows: people who got fat from the ethos of the 1980's but may finally begin to examine the connection between their own behavior and the sick city left in the wake of the spree.

True to form, *Eastern Standard* holds out hope for its people and their post-crash society much as Hollywood's Depression comedies did. It will be up to history to determine whether Mr. Greenberg's faith in the fundamental decency of his characters is as justified as Frank Capra's was. But that's our problem, not the author's. For anyone who has been waiting for a play that tells what it is like to be more or less middle-class, more or less young and more or less well-intentioned in a frightening city at this moment in this time zone, *Eastern Standard* at long last is it.

> Frank Rich, "Comedy with a Subversive Punch," in
> The New York Times, October 28, 1988, p. C3.

EDITH OLIVER

Last winter, Richard Greenberg's *The Maderati,* a merry satiric comedy about the outlandish behavior of the literary and artistic set in this city right now, was one of the happiest surprises of the season. His comedy *Eastern Standard,* . . . is a sad surprise. A trendy piece if ever there was one, the play ticks off AIDS, the homeless, homosexual and heterosexual love, ugly buildings that are blotting out the New York sunlight, and so on. The dialogue has a kind of forced sprightliness that is very trying, and the characters, of sawdust, make tedious company for two and a quarter hours. . . . There are many indications, amid the clinkers, that Mr. Greenberg is in the right profession. The play is a fake, but the playwright is not.

> Edith Oliver, "At the Crown," in The New Yorker,
> Vol. LXIV, No. 39, November 14, 1988, p. 121.

MERVYN ROTHSTEIN

[*The following excerpt was taken from an interview with Greenberg.*]

O.K., Richard Greenberg, let's get to the point right away. Your new play, *Eastern Standard* is a comedy, a romantic and screwball comedy, but also a serious comedy, about a bunch of yuppies who invite a bag lady to a house in the Hamptons. There's a homosexual yuppie who has AIDS, another homosexual yuppie who falls in love with him, and a couple of heterosexual yuppies who are trying to work out a relationship.

Frank Rich, in *The New York Times* praised your play highly [see excerpt above]. . . . But some other critics panned it, calling it and its characters glib and superficial. You, a self-acknowledged yuppie, have been termed a defender of your breed.

So what do you have to say for yourself, Mr. Greenberg?

"The play came from a careful and prolonged scrutiny in the past few years of who I am and who my friends were and how we operated in the world," the 30-year-old Mr. Greenberg says, sitting at a table in the theater's lobby, a few feet from the Hamptons beach house in which his characters spend the summer. "I looked at the images of us, the people of my generation, people like me, from a similar class and educational background, and mostly what I've seen have been cartoonish satires that make us out to be these predators, these greedy blind omnivores, leaving despair and destruction in their wake."

"When I considered who I knew and how I lived, I realized that these images were insufficient," he says. "I looked at us and I saw that there was a lot of self-absorption, yes, and a lot of foolishness, but at the same time there was, in most of us, a basic generosity and, I thought, an innate goodness—but an innate goodness that operated within a very narrow circumference. It seemed to be ordered by domestic and career issues.

"But they lived—we lived—in a very small world, and suddenly the outer world, what we would call the real world, which we somehow expected to be immune from, started to crowd us, to become overwhelming. We're in such a chaotic and pressured and divisive and unsettled time. And there is no way to ignore it without being utterly disgusting, without being deliberately and irresponsibly insular. There just isn't a way."

"The play started on a hunch," he says. "It started from a sense of things in transit. Lately I've been making contact again with all my friends, and it's as if there's some kind of strange scent in the air. Everyone I know is going through these major upheavals, transforming themselves and enlarging their perspectives." . . . (p. C17)

"I suppose in important ways I was awfully sheltered," he says. "I grew up on Long Island, in East Meadow, in a highly middle-class environment"—he lives in Chelsea now. "I went to wonderfully sheltered schools. It always felt as if everything could be brought down to an intellection. And that's really stupid."

"I went to all these schools," he says—he is an alumnus of Princeton, attended graduate school at Harvard for a year, then went to the Yale School of Drama. "There's something about entering those environments and flourishing in them, where the tasks set out for you are ones you're able to perform wonderfully well. You're living in a world where intelligence is the thing that's rewarded, and a certain charm is rewarded, and once you've mastered those things you function admirably.

"And I think that what happens then is that you enter the real world thinking that you have the tools to face any task.

And for a few years you can, because it's about establishing yourself.

"But then suddenly you find yourself coming up against things that are complex and mysterious. You come upon irreconcilable truths, you get to the place where the keenest intellect won't go—real life in all its complexity, moral issues, traumas, a bigger world, the fact that we're not in a cocoon, we're not operating just between our houses and our workplaces."

That's what happens to the characters in *Eastern Standard,* he says. "They possess language. They're very fluent. In any given situation, they'll have an attitude, there'll be a point of view and they'll be able to express it forcefully. And I think in a way the journey of the play is from our glibness to an appreciation of greater complexity and our own insufficiency. And then the play attempts to track the distance between a good intention and a useful act."

"It's not an issues play," he says. "It's not about AIDS. It's about what love can be in a time of AIDS. It's not about homelessness. It's about privileged people waking up to the responsibility they have toward the disenfranchised." (pp. C17, C22)

Mervyn Rothstein, "In Defense of Yuppies, Their Basic Decency and New Perplexity," in The New York Times, *November 15, 1988, pp. C17, C22.*

ROBERT BRUSTEIN

[*Eastern Standard*] is destined to be a movable commercial success; indeed, success seems to be its animating purpose. The play abuts on two major afflictions of the day—AIDS and homelessness. But *Eastern Standard* bears about the same natural relationship to disease and poverty as silicone does to mammary tissue.

The play is actually a romantic comedy, in the Philip Barry manner, about two couples who cannot express their love for each other until they overcome an obstacle. For the heterosexual couple, the obstacle is a former lover habituated to suicide attempts; for the homosexual couple, it is the disease that one of them has secretly contracted. These problems emerge after a good deal of witty stage chat over cocktails and Perrier, first at a fashionable cocktail lounge and later on the deck of a summer home in Long Island. Making an unlikely appearance at both these venues is a garrulous female derelict with nowhere else to go.

How she gets to the Hamptons—indeed how all the characters, including the cocktail lounge waitress, eventually end up there for the summer—is one of the many artificial twists of plot that make this play seem so contrived. But the most contrived thing about *Eastern Standard* is the way it manages to wrinkle its brow over serious issues while using them chiefly as pretexts for resolving romantic relationships. This stunt is engineered partly by softening the afflictions of the characters—the wisecracking derelict has a heart of gold, the infected gay is a cheerful hunk with no trace of his disease—and partly by providing them with trendy professions. Stephen is an architect ("Talent becomes a nightmare when you hate what you're doing with it"). Phoebe is on Wall Street ("I loved crossing my legs in a swivel chair"). Drew is a painter, Peter a TV scriptwriter, Ellen an actress doubling as a waitress, May a bag lady. . . . Of all these enameled figures, only

Drew will develop any reality, mainly because he's a prize bitch. The rest seem to exist in order to satirize the patronization of the poor, to tidy up the plot, to exercise the author's wit, and (no doubt unconsciously) to demonstrate the profound superficiality of young urban professionals. (pp. 33-4)

Eastern Standard concludes with loving embraces and a toast after May has departed with all their possessions and the playwright has skated over every modern affliction except muscular dystrophy. As for the production . . . it meets the play appropriately on its glib and facile terms. (p. 34)

Robert Brustein, "Robert Brustein on Theater: Yuppies, Past and Present," in The New Republic, *Vol. 199, No. 21, November 21, 1988, pp. 32-4.*

THOMAS M. DISCH

Richard Greenberg, the 30-year-old author of *Eastern Standard,* . . . aspires to tell a story that can be understood as a scale model for our time and kind, but he represents a very different milieu. In an interview in *The New York Times* Greenberg speaks of growing up on Long Island in "a highly middle-class environment" [see Rothstein's excerpt above], and *Eastern Standard* has been characterized by both those who applaud and who denigrate it as a salute to yuppiedom. In calling himself middle-class, Greenberg employs a common evasion, for unless "upper-class" is to refer only to Rockefellers and royalty, then the society Greenberg springs from and sings of is surely upper class; lower-upper, if one wants to niggle.

Greenberg writes quick, punchy dialogue in the manner of a latter-day Philip Barry, and like a with-it hostess in the society he depicts he admits the discreeter sort of gays into his list of dramatis personae and even allows them to provide half the romantic interest. (The price to be paid, as you might guess, is that one of the lovers has AIDS.) His play has ruffled some feathers, however, because of its unsentimental, not to say cruel treatment of its two lower-class characters, a waitress and a bag lady, whom the architect hero has misguidedly invited to his Hamptons summer home along with three of the right sort. . . . The bag lady avenges her threatened eviction by running off with everyone's valuables, and the waitress shows her true colors by trying to vamp her host when her stockbroker rival has absented herself to see a former lover. The playwright's not-quite-unstated message is that the lower orders, through no fault of their own, are not to be trusted; that it is probably safer nowadays to do without servants altogether (the bag lady has been a cook) and either do one's own cooking or eat out (Act I takes place in a posh restaurant). Greenberg's view of class relations seems an accurate reflection of the new social ethos in which liberalism has become the L-word (though the plot is not so different from that of *Ways and Means,* Noel Coward's one-act comedy of 1935. *Plus ça change*). But Greenberg expresses his illiberal views with vigor and wit, and surely that must count in his favor as a dramatist.

Thomas M. Disch, in a review of, "Eastern Standard," in The Nation, New York, *Vol. 247, No. 18, December 12, 1988, p. 663.*

JOHN SIMON

It's possible for yuppies to have problems, I daresay, and it's okay to write plays about them, though a glut may be imminent. It's permissible to make the principals of **Eastern Standard** liberal do-gooders, who also have their problems. And it is nice to have a playwright deal simultaneously with a heterosexual and a homosexual love affair and, though clearly more interested in the latter, be eminently fair to the former. There is concern here for many (too many) of the troubling issues of the eighties, and there is a tart intelligence at work observing them. The only thing missing is a play.

Richard Greenberg is so with-it, so cool, so consistently witty in exactly the same way for several characters, and writing so detachedly from so many directions, that there is no point of view, no gutsiness, no passion. . . .

Ellen allows the author to make jokes about actors; May permits him to be at once scabrous and concerned about the homeless; Stephen enables him to mock postmodern architecture; Peter lets him make fun of television's hypocrisy while also waxing serious about AIDS; Drew, the raisonneur, empowers him to be perceptive, epigrammatic, charming, mildly self-critical, and to take swipes at postmodern painting. As you may gather, this is like trying to cram an athlete's foot into a baby's sock. Worse, issues such as AIDS and the homeless are too serious to be dealt with in sentimental pieties alternating with sly humor, neither of them an adequate mode and each giving the other the lie. Which brings me back to Greenberg's facile idea-mongering that neither wit nor up-to-date smartness can mold into a continuous action. The courage to take a position—any position—would help, but it might also offend someone and so prove uncommercial. Yet spinelessness, too, may offend—especially with the all-round-happy ending the play hastily settles for without suitable preparation. . . .

Given the state of Broadway, we should be grateful for this much; but let us not be too liberal with our gratitude. (p. 79)

John Simon, "Long Island Longueurs," in New York *Magazine, Vol. 22, No. 3, January 16, 1989, pp. 79-80.*

Josephine Humphreys
1945-

American novelist.

In her novels, Humphreys utilizes dry humor and poetic language to explore the disintegration of seemingly idyllic suburban families. Set in her native South Carolina, Humphreys's works feature the transformed "New South" of shopping malls and highrise buildings. She employs sharp wit and unusual metaphors to examine the dynamics of contemporary personal, sexual, and racial relationships. The accomplished style, strong characterization, and immediate theme of *Dreams of Sleep* (1984) earned Humphreys the Ernest Hemingway Foundation Award for first fiction.

Dreams of Sleep explores the impermanence of love and what Humphreys perceives as the emotional barrenness of marriage. This novel centers on Alice, a bored and unfulfilled housewife, who learns that her husband has been unfaithful. The family's babysitter, Iris Moon, an eccentric seventeen-year-old, jolts Alice out of her passivity and rescues the marriage from unnecessary dissolution. Critics praised Humphreys for her perceptive depiction of the loneliness and alienation of a failing marriage. Humphreys's next novel, *Rich in Love* (1987), also features an idiosyncratic and precocious teenager. When Lucille Odom's family nearly disintegrates due to her mother's sudden abandonment, Lucille quits school in order to care for her retired father. She asks her older sister, Rae, to return home without realizing that she has her own marital problems. Lucille soon discovers her inability to direct the lives of others, or even her own. Acknowledging her shortcomings, she learns about the nature of love and attains maturity. Although some reviewers deemed Humphreys more adept at portraying familial discord than domestic harmony, her humor, sympathetic characterization, and poetic imagery won widespread praise. Michael Malone remarked: "In finding words, joining them into sentences, crafting sentences into paragraphs, [Humphreys] shows an often exquisite judgment, a tone of almost perfect pitch and rhythm, a feel for metaphor and image that is always sure and sometimes stunning."

(See also *CLC*, Vol. 34 and *Contemporary Authors*, Vol. 121.)

FRED CHAPPELL

A wistful, bright adolescent might look out upon the adult world and decide it is a place where total war has been declared upon good sense. So Lucille Odom, the heroine of *Rich in Love*, Josephine Humphreys's engaging second novel, concludes—and with good reason. Her parents have been married for 27 years when her mother, Helen, walks out, leaving only a brief note of graceless farewell. Later, when her mother telephones, Lucille asks, "Well, is this something feminist? Or is it something real?"

The humor and subdued pathos in her question point toward the salient qualities of the whole novel, which is set in

Charleston, S. C. In an unstable world, family relationships have become tenuous and ambiguous, and the process of achieving adulthood ever more dangerous. But *Rich in Love* does not traffic in a lot of smug folk sociology. In even the healthiest personalities the desire for order and security is at odds with a thirst for novelty and adventure. Lucille, who is a good girl in the best implications of that phrase, recognizes these contradictions in herself. "People like me are sometimes hanging onto their so-called goodness by a thread. I didn't know how I was going to turn out." . . .

Lucille's stunningly beautiful sister Rae returns to Charleston from Washington, pregnant with a child she does not want and in the company of a husband she wants even less; her girlfriend, Rhody, has taken to wearing strange disguises while wandering about town in search of material for her book, which is to be "a book that reveals the truth." After these complications, the plot involves itself even more thoroughly with each of its elements in predictable but honest ways.

This fairly complex but easily comprehensible story proceeds, in fact, by a series of self-revelations. As each of the characters understands something fresh about himself, he acts upon this knowledge and begins to change—so that new relationships with the other characters must necessarily develop. "I got her pregnant on purpose," Billy tells Lucille. He is the bridegroom besotted with her sister Rae. "It was the only way I could get her to even consider marrying me." Having admitted to this knowledge for the first time, he is now able to part with Rae if he must. When Lucille's ambivalent relationship with her own friend, Wayne Frobiness, becomes clear to her, she understands that they too must part.

Ms. Humphreys has written a novel in which self-knowledge is not only an end in itself but also a motivation for future acts. There is something winningly cheerful in this view of behavior, and her portrayal of it links *Rich in Love* with two other recent novels by young Southern women, Candace Flynt's *Mother Love* and Marianne Gingher's *Bobby Rex's Greatest Hit*. All three of these books are marked by a willingness on the part of the authors to allow their characters to master their lives and to accept the inevitable responsibilities. If these authors point toward a trend, it will surely be a refreshing one after a decade of flabby hysteria in novels about domestic life.

Even if *Rich in Love* did not possess its strong characters, entrancing story line and vigorous outlook, it would still be interesting because its author is a dazzling stylist. It is customary for adolescents in books—and in our experience too—to complain that no one understands them. But this is how Lucille Odom puts it:

> I had heard about a new theory that knowledge is shared within a species regardless of space and time, so when one rat learns a new maze, other rats have an easier time with it, even if they are in a different lab. This sounds like baloney at first, but when you think about it—why not? Many things happen invisibly and mysteriously. Creatures have links with their own kind. I knew what love was without the aid of empirical evidence, and furthermore, I believed that I did have it. It was in me. It had been accumulating silently over the years like equity in a house. I was rich in love, even though no one could see it.

Hard to resist a young girl who talks, who thinks, like that.

> *Fred Chappell, "Good Girls Can Turn Out Well,"* in The New York Times Book Review, *September 13, 1987, p. 9.*

MICHAEL MALONE

Josephine Humphreys has written only two novels, both of them modest and accessible in their design, modest and domestic in their subject matter—primarily the personal relations of husbands and wives, parents and children. She is neither a grand old-style storyteller nor a modernist littérateur, and her tone is as far from minimalist fashions as her setting is from SoHo. Her characters are not particularly remarkable individuals; her plots are quiet and simple. She is a Southern writer, in that she lives and works in her native Charleston, the setting of her books, but the Southern Gothic never pushes far into her vision. There are no Popeyes or Misfits, no sisters who shoot their husbands, no rapists devoured by tigers. Southernness is integral to the personalities of her characters, yet never the focus of their lives, and (at least by the standards of Southern literary tradition) those lives are for the most part fairly uneventful. . . . (p. 388)

It is not the stories per se that engage us, but Humphreys's ability to convey the ways in which her people inhabit their stories. Through words she gives us people's responses to their own lives; that is to say, Humphreys is someone, in Henry James's phrase, on whom nothing is lost—at least, nothing at which she has chosen to look. Within the compact borders of her landscape, she knows where and how and what to see. In a housewife at the sink, watching her daughters in the yard, she sees women's "careless ease with dishes, ceaseless care with children." . . . In finding words, joining them into sentences, crafting sentences into paragraphs, she shows an often exquisite judgment, a tone of almost perfect pitch and rhythm, a feel for metaphor and image that is always sure and sometimes stunning. That is what we mean by "really writing," and I suspect that is what Reynolds Price (who taught her, and in whose lineage her style belongs) meant when he praised the "wise beauty" of *Dreams of Sleep.*

In fact, that first novel in some ways succeeds less as a narrative than as a beautifully written tone poem, a subtle counterpoint of moods—the sad, somnolent drift of a dissolving marriage set against the sharp pain of love and growth. Like its Charleston setting, there is a quiet, pale shimmer to its central characters. The doctor, Will, in his "too cool and soft" office, who (particularly under the influence of "poetry and bourbon and honor") sees sadness everywhere, and slow decay, and who "has to keep reminding himself that he's alive." His wife, Alice, once a mathematician, now a housewife, who does not feel at home in her house, and for whom the world outside the house has become a foreign "toy town" busy at the endless "shifting of goods and wastes." The teenage baby sitter, Iris Moon, who for all her clear, resilient, competent youth, has had to struggle to come back from hospitalized despair after a breakdown, when she felt "I can't carry myself another step into this life." For all three, life has been a dream of sleep, in which, as an elderly black woman laments, "Everything goes into thin air. You can't hold it." The book ends with the rich promise of reunion for the couple, new life for the young woman, but we must take it on faith that those promises will prove true.

I've summarized *Dreams of Sleep* because the situation of *Rich in Love* is a variation on its plot. But here the unhappy housewife runs away at the beginning, not the close of the book, and she does not turn around and come back. Here the teen-age girl who wants to hold the world together is not hired help but the younger daughter of that affluent middle-aged couple. Lucille Odom is, however, very like the earlier Iris Moon in her courage, kindness and will—even in sharing a threadlike scar on her upper lip. So it isn't surprising to hear that the germ for *Rich in Love* was Humphreys's fondness for Iris Moon, and her impulse to do more with such a character. Nor is it surprising that her decision to let Lucille narrate *Rich in Love* felt at first a little suffocating after the technical freedom provided by the omniscient narrator of her first novel. Ordinarily one would expect the coming of age theme of *Rich in Love,* with its first-person female voice, to precede the more technically complicated *Dreams of Sleep.* But in execution, *Rich in Love* is in no way inferior to its predecessor. Less of a lyric poem, it is in fact, in its construction of scenes, in the trueness of its dialogue, a better novel.

Humphreys has said that she is "more interested in the words" than the story, has sought the "story as a vehicle for words." In *Rich in Love* she has not only found a story, she has given it an immensely likable storyteller. As the book begins, Lucille informs us that due to sudden family calamity (her mother has run off, her sister has come home "accidentally" married and discontentedly pregnant), her own life has become "for a short while the kind of life that can be told as a story—that is, one in which events appear to have meaning." Now, that's a writer talking, and a little of it goes a long way. When Lucille adds that she's had a premonition of something happening ("I sensed that I was on a verge. A large block of time was due to crack open in front of me"), when she tells us that she's worried that her bereft father will "blow his mental fuses" by suddenly turning to philosophy books for consolation, after a life of an annual Louis L'Amour or *Cujo* ("For an amateur, [tackling the nature of good and evil] is more than the mental system can handle"), that's a character talking, one whose story we're happy to sit back and hear. Far from being suffocating, Lucille Odom is a gust of clean, bright air. Most refreshing of all, she has a wry wit, and fine comic timing—talents it would have been impossible to predict from the comparatively humorless *Dreams of Sleep.*

At 17, Lucille thinks of herself as an introspective, observant young woman with a fondness for solitude, vigilance, Latin etymologies and taking charge. . . . When her mother (who likes to discuss nuclear waste and Indian health care, who still wears peasant blouses and carries macramé purses) leaves all the "creeping clutter" of her married life behind with a matter-of-fact note to her husband ("To make a long story short, it is time for me to start a second life"), Lucille is so sure that the note's "hard as a hatchet-chop" tone will hurt her "innocent," "romantic" father, "a man with a breakable heart," that she rewrites it to make it more emotional: "Please do not blame yourself, Warren, my love." The result is that Pop assumes Mom's been abducted: the tone's all wrong, like "someone forced her to write" it. Throughout the novel, Lucille is going to try to "fix" things like the note, with the same organizational energy with which she takes over the household cooking. A bit of a purist (she doesn't smoke, drink or fool around; she's tried sex with her boyfriend, but can take it or leave it), her "fixing" will show her to be something of a moral bully: she threatens her mother with the police if she doesn't come home; when she finds her father in bed with a new girlfriend, she responds, "Did they think they could carry on like that under my roof?"

Like almost all teen-agers, Lucille complains of being misunderstood, inarticulate ("what came out when I spoke was only a hacked-up version of the thoughts that lay graceful and complete in my brain"), lonely and "not normal." She locates a major source of her sense of separateness, as well as her empathy with other outsiders, in the fact that she was born with a split upper lip (surgically corrected so that no one but her even notices it). But, like Austen's Emma—another young woman who's taken charge of her father's life—Lucille makes serious mistakes because she assumes she knows much more than she really does, both about herself and about others. All her childhood, she's been in love with the virtuous, tough, "steady comfort" of her parents' love; assumed, first, that they were immune to divorce; assumed, second, that her father would never recover from her mother's "abdication." Both assumptions prove wrong.

The progress of *Rich in Love* is the progress of all its characters—most believably, Lucille—in learning to give up the shelter of old assumptions. In this painful process, Lucille falls in love with the man who "recognizes" her, who sees how rich in love she is: "You love more things than anyone I've ever run into." *Rich in Love* is most vibrant when it expresses that capacity in its narrator. Lucille is intensely attuned to the world, so aware, so quickened in her heart, that things glitter, sometimes more than she can bear. . . .[She] seems to see *into* things, with a sort of intrasensory perception that she calls "invision." She sees and loves the book of the world, the warm concrete of sidewalks, old junk furniture, "the myrtle hummocks brown in the lavender sage," the smell and color of a shopping bag, a firefly "fooled into . . . eternally unrequited love" for a star. Her hope for her sister's baby daughter is that she will be someone on whom nothing is lost: "What I want her to know is the strength and fragility of things, the love and the luck hidden together in the world." It's a wonderful, if not always happy, gift to possess, and a gift the gods of writing have most assuredly given Lucille's creator. (pp. 388-89)

Michael Malone, "Rich in Words," in The Nation, New York, Vol. 245, No. 11, October 10, 1987, pp. 388-89).

DOROTHY WICKENDEN

The dispirited husband in Josephine Humphreys's first novel, *Dreams of Sleep,* returns home one evening to comfortable household sounds and is stricken with panic. "A house with a woman and children in it at dusk is frightening to the man who draws near and hears the muffled voices, those dishes being washed. The pure domestic horror of it rings down his spine." In *Rich in Love* Humphreys writes again about the domestic horror and seductive tyranny of family love.

Humphreys's subjects are seemingly enviable, smoothly functioning nuclear families that have been slowly corroding from within. She seizes upon them just when the machinery breaks down. Unlike *Dreams of Sleep,* however, a contemporary drama about the trials of a husband and wife struggling with a failing marriage, *Rich in Love* is an old-fashioned coming-of-age novel. Its central character as well as its plot and theme are staples of American fiction: the narrator, a shrewd, square, warmhearted 17-year-old, moves at first hesitantly, and then decisively, from her parents' moral orbit into her own. The novel could easily have slipped into the trite and saccharine, but once again Humphreys reveals an extraordinary ability to explore inner lives with subtlety, originality, and deadpan humor. *Rich in Love* avoids banality by ironically exploiting the catalog of clichés about unhappy families.

Lucille Odom perceives home as a place of refuge and comfort. (She likes to play Scrabble, collects modern gadgets and worthless antiques, and openly admits to her old-maid tendencies.) "The American family needed to hold itself more closely, I thought. Like mine. We were a hermit family. We had each other and we had our house, and nothing could touch us." But one afternoon she discovers her mother's VW van pulled off the driveway in front of the house, the door thrown open, and groceries melting on the front seat. The farewell note to Lucille's father, "hard as a hatchet-chop," waits inside.

Not long afterward her self-possessed older sister, Rae, returns from Washington, D.C., five months pregnant and just married, and proceeds to have a nervous breakdown. Her father, even while yearning for the return of his wayward wife, takes up with a cheery hair stylist named Vera Oxendine. And Lucille herself, to her astonishment, falls in love with her new brother-in-law, Billy McQueen. The novel follows her for the next six months as she attempts to entertain her father and sister, track down her mother, and revise her own stuffy ideas about love, sex, and marriage.

At the beginning of the family crackup, Lucille sees herself as the sole voice of sanity, the brisk yet deeply concerned caretaker of her irresponsible elders. "Do not think I didn't know what love was. . . . It had been accumulating silently over the years like equity in a house. I was rich in love, even though no one could see it." Her evaluations of the others are a mixture of exasperation and tenderness. She observes her father's initial misery with alarm:

> When I left he was still stretched out on his side, looking at the window. It is disconcerting to see a man lying on his side, which is somehow a very feminine position. An odalisque. His arms and back had a slack look, as if all the muscles in them had been cut. . . . Uh-oh, I thought: Can a man become effeminate as the result of the loss of his wife?

And, reluctantly warming to Billy as she conspires with him to rouse Rae from her "stewing in the craziness of pregnancy," she worries about his vocation as a history teacher: "It made my stomach sink. My teachers had always been morose because of their jobs. One reason I got straight A's in school was that I wanted to make these people happier. They were tired and hungry for love; and what's more, their cars broke down constantly." (pp. 45-6)

These people are shaped with seeming spontaneity, through their own honest responses to life's haphazard course. Lucille's sudden reappraisal of her lifelong tie to her father and her recent friendship with Billy are artfully conveyed in a few brief scenes. Her discovery of love's unpredictable demands, which appears almost offhand, is perfectly in keeping with her pragmatic and probing approach to new experience.

Taking her father his coffee one morning, she is startled to hear him whistling in the shower, and even more startled when she finds Vera Oxendine in his bed. "I could have made a scene and demanded to know what was going on here, did they think they could carry on like that under my roof; but I didn't have the energy for it." By the time she ends up in Billy's bed, she has developed a savoir faire that she can't begin to muster. She coolly recognizes that this is a single encounter between a tender man who is desperate to recapture his wife and a girl who is intent upon experiencing sexual passion and physical comfort. . . .

Humphreys is less successful when she ventures outside the boundaries of domestic discord. As in *Dreams of Sleep,* she sets the novel around her hometown of Charleston, South Carolina, and to broaden her picture of contemporary alienation, she tries to mingle the lives of black and white. The two races represent "two human worlds of identical misery and passion," as the wife puts it in *Dreams of Sleep,* "but occupying opposite quadrants. . . . In a way, equal but separate." In *Rich in Love* Humphreys creates a black family whose eccentricities are meant to mirror those of the Odoms. The ties between the two families are purportedly deep yet mysterious. . . .

There are scattered references to Rae's close friendship with her classmate Rhody Poole, and to Rae's earlier incarnation as a singer in a black band; and the Pooles become accomplices in the flight of Lucille's mother. Yet in the end the family has no more than a totemic significance, uttering the stray

prophecy and guiding the befuddled white clan toward a more honest existence. In one of the novel's few contrived scenes, Lucille runs into Rhody Poole and receives some wise instructions about how to handle Rae, her mother, and herself. "A new day was dawning on me," Lucille reflects with uncharacteristic ponderousness, "now that Rhody had given me answers to questions that had long held a cloud over my head."

And Humphreys herself is occasionally heavy-handed. She is more adept at conveying people in turmoil than she is at rendering their recovery. Her satiric vision gives way at the end to a mannered sentimentality and a tendency to succumb to pat psychology. *Dreams of Sleep* concludes with a reverie about the possibilities of regeneration and the "reweaving" of "hopes and dreams." . . .

Humphreys could have dispensed with these homilies and ended the novel far more effectively with another scene. Late one night Lucille looks out her bedroom window and sees her father—to whom she has denied the car keys—sitting "tall, almost noble, riding his Snapper lawn mower into the dark of the oaks along Bennett Street," speeding toward the house of Vera Oxendine. That gesture of paternal defiance says all that needed to be said about the erratic ways of family love. (p. 46)

Dorothy Wickenden, "What Lucille Knew," in The New Republic, *Vol. 197, No. 16, October 19, 1987, pp. 45-6.*

JOYCE JOHNSON

A good novel exists in its own time, makes its own self-contained world. For the writer of serious fiction, the topicality that strains toward trendiness is therefore a risky proposition. Taken too often to the K-mart, the reader may awaken from the fictional dream, may look around with a cold eye and ask rudely: Is that the way things really are? We do not question the human truth of Tolstoy's "Happy families are all alike, but an unhappy family is unhappy in its own way." But we lose some of our trust in what is being related to us when we come upon a sentence like "All around me I saw the American family blowing apart, as described in *Psychology Today,*" an assertion made by Lucille Odom, the 17-year-old narrator of *Rich in Love.* The reference is so current that the statement seems curiously passé. "Hey, wait a minute," we think. "When was that *Psychology Today* article published?"

Like *Dreams of Sleep,* Josephine Humphreys' second novel, *Rich in Love,* is set in the New South in a landscape rapidly losing its character and history to bulldozers and shopping malls. In this very real setting, she has placed the Odoms, her fragmenting American family, giving us not realism but a kind of fairy tale. Peopled with almost obligatorily eccentric characters, *Rich in Love* is winning and touching at times, but the spell Humphreys attempts to cast over the reader is undermined throughout by forced relevance, forced "wisdom." . . .

Lucille Odom is special, we learn very early on, set apart, like some heroine of romantic fiction. She was born with a harelip; all that remains of it by her 17th year is a tiny white scar, though that scar looms large within her consciousness. She was Helen's unwanted second child; in fact she has learned that her life was saved by the inefficiency of the suction method, which aborted her twin but left Lucille inside her mother undetected and relatively intact. The missing twin is another thing that makes Lucille feel odd, incomplete. What she has been blessed with is a surplus of intelligence and intuition—almost more intelligence and intuition than this novel can bear.

It's not just that Lucille is one of those kids who's a precocious reader (everything from Virgil to *Psychology Today*) even though she's dropped out of high school to take care of her grief-stricken 60-year-old father. It's that Josephine Humphreys has made her so incredibly all-knowing. Lucille Odom knows more about life than a 45-year-old woman, despite her youth and staid middle-class upbringing in a Charleston suburb. Unfortunately, no one is more aware of this than Lucille herself. "I see lots of things no one else sees," she rather smugly tells her would-be boyfriend, Wayne.

Sometimes she is authentically prescient, and her narrator's voice is right on the mark: "I was regarded as an abstainer in every respect, a good girl. But I felt the pang now and then. People like me are sometimes hanging onto their so-called goodness by a thread." (p. 4)

Other times, however, the reader feels assaulted by Lucille's deep perceptions—always presented in the most authoritative cadences, never with a touch of self-irony. Lucille looks at her father and thinks: "The sorrow of a big man is worse than that of a small man, rocks him deeper, lasts a longer time." This has the ring of an eternal verity, but is it really necessarily true of big men? And who is really addressing the reader at such moments—the character or the author, having her own say, indulging herself with yet another graceful sentence?

Although immersed in her own sorrows, Lucille constantly reminds us that the American family is not the only thing blowing apart. She worries earnestly and vocally down a checklist of current issues: the Greenhouse Effect, the nuclear submarines in the harbor, the urbanization of the environment. The novel is so relentlessly up-to-date that Billy McQueen reveals to Lucille that he has deliberately impregnated Rae by punching holes in a series of condoms.

Of course, Lucille has her sexual awakening—only halfway with Wayne, then much more thoroughly with her dangerously depressed sister's husband. They make love on Halloween as Rae gives birth upstairs into a toilet. "Tragedy, well-known for its convoluted methods, reunited the family."

When we last see Lucille, she is holding baby Phoebe on her lap and being profound one more time: "What I want her to know is the strength and fragility of things, the love and the luck hidden together in the world. How to say so is hard. We ride farther and farther to get a view; we forget more and more what ought to be remembered. But she is like me, and she will know."

And what do we learn from all this? Motherhood triumphs over all ambivalence? Nothing can replace the nuclear family but a less closely linked family of fragments in separate households? Once " 'Family' meant people in a house together. But that was in a language so far back that all its words are gone, a language we can only imagine." Somehow Humphreys intends this to be optimistic though hardheaded wisdom for our troubled times, but in the context in which it is presented it is only an expression of the New Sentimentality. (pp. 4-5)

Joyce Johnson, "Southern Living and Loving," in Book World—The Washington Post, *November 8, 1987, pp. 4-5.*

CARLA SEAQUIST

Depleted by minimalism? Freaked for our future by the literary Brat Pack? Yearning for another feisty female voice?

Meet Lucille Odom, 17, narrator of Josephine Humphreys's second novel, **Rich in Love,** and direct descendant of Eudora Welty's narrator in "Why I Live at the P.O." A maximalist, Lucille is filled not with anomie but with love—for Charleston, her house, even shifting the car from reverse to first, "a moment of grace between backward and forward." Romantic love has yet to hit, but "Do not think I didn't know what love was . . . . It had been accumulating silently over the years like equity in a house. I was rich in love." Not the usual shrugging adolescent then, whom Lucille herself cannot abide: "People my age were murder."

But never mind peers, what compels Lucille is the universe. Setting her apart is a "hardly noticeable" harelip (though "Does 'hardly noticeable' mean 'noticeable' or 'not noticeable'?"), but setting her above is a finely tuned vigilance: "Let the world do its worst, Lucille Odom was ready." For its part the world is doing just that. A Latinist, she cites the battle of Herculaneum; surveying history, she sees "men in packs making messes"; monitoring Charleston's naval base, she watches submarines sneak out "like Mafia Cadillacs." Clearly, something dire is afoot—a prospect paralyzing most "heroes" of contemporary fiction but animating Lucille: "Beauty-doubled and tripled around me. The place was doomed." Biking past the mall she sees shopping as "an indicator of human trust in the future," exclaiming, "Look at them swarming into the Garden Centre, coming out with flats of two-toned petunias and soaker-hoses!" . . .

Vigilant though she is, Lucille is blindsided by the sudden exit of her mother, Helen, the act mobilizing the novel's story. Reviewing the past, Lucille fails to connect the dots: her newly retired father trailing Helen as she vacuums; her own expectations of Helen as chauffeur/laundress; Helen's discontent with bequeathing rather than using a lore ranging from Walt Whitman to Supreme Court decisions to Indian health care. Thus, when Helen calls in, Lucille's first question to her is, "Well, is this something feminist. . . . or is it something real?" Understanding is within Lucille's reach, though. "Probably every woman has a singing self," she thinks. . . .

Meanwhile, what can Lucille do, "stupid, seventeen, powerless," but rewrite Helen's farewell note for more feeling, cook for her father, and provide commentary? Pop, a fey mix of demolitions expert and innocent, lies in bed like "an odalisque," fending off despair with pre-Helen memories, taking up finally (to Lucille's chagrin) with Vera Oxendine, the barbershop's stylist. And sister Rae, leaving a Washington job to fix things at home, shows up married, pregnant, and depressed—no help at all. . . .

Out of this chaos Humphreys presents a sympathetic male: new brother-in-law Billy, a historian. At first a threat, he is soon Lucille's tutor: "Not only did I pass with all A's, but I found myself walking around with an overview." But even better, in a priceless scene, he connects with her: "You come across strong as Fort Sumter . . . but then half of your sentences start out with 'I love.' You have a lot of love in you."

Well! Lucille is in love ("That was *the* me. I had been recognized"), but *that* cannot be expressed to Billy, so sometime-boyfriend Wayne, next on the dock, is the surprised beneficiary. Initially secret love suffices ("No wear-and-tear"), but soon enough she is stifling "inappropriate" remarks that would reveal everything, like " 'Don't wear that shirt,' " comments one makes "only to a loved one."

Inappropriate, yes, but not for bean-spilling. With experience Lucille may ditch the notion that love manipulates, along with the one that marriage confines. Certainly, she has given the subject due thought. Now to focus on the other half of Freud's love-and-work formula for happiness. Because, *attenzione:* Given her "excess," Lucille will either find the cure for AIDS or become the crank in Accounting. And, crucially, she must address something else: her literal formative experience. Lucille survived her mother's misfired abortion; her legacy is a lost twin and the harelip. This, coupled with her mother's beauty, is emotional dynamite that the novel, while noting "that searching nozzle," only skims.

But no matter, Humphreys has created what a reviving Pop Odom went looking for: a "permanent" book. The Odoms are real, not Southern gothics, the humor is on-point, not hit-and-run. The story surges. And there is the splendid Lucille, who *lives* and, unlike the fictional representatives of the prevailing slackjaw chic, *cares.*

Carla Seaquist, "Someone Who Cares," in Belles Lettres: A Review of Books by Women, Vol. 3, No. 5, May-June, 1988, p. 5.

EILEEN BATTERSBY

As the most recent of a long line of writers from the South to be published in Britain, South Carolinan Josephine Humphreys combines the reflective tone of Richard Ford with several qualities of her own: an instinctive understanding of human nature, a rare feel for metaphor, and a superb ear for the cadences of Southern dialect. Her first novel, *Dreams of Sleep,* won the Hemingway Prize, and now appears in paperback. Her second novel is *Rich in Love.*

Its focus is the Odom household. Life here may have been uneventful—even predictable—but at least it was constant. That is, until Mother, after 27 years of marriage, returns from a trip to the supermarket and decides to leave everything behind her, even down to the ice cream melting on the car seat. This leaves Pop, 'a man with a breakable heart', wondering what he did wrong. Why did this wonderful woman marry him in the first place? . . .

Rich in Love is not a domestic tragedy but a study of mayhem. Set in South Carolina, the novel's strength lies in its calm narrative voice which subtly captures the rhythms of Southern speech without resorting to exaggeration. Lucille is alert and philosophical, but she is also scared of the dark. She admits to being self-conscious about a small facial irregularity and aware that she is the surviving twin of an abortion—she has enough reasons for not seeing herself as a 'normal teenage girl'.

Much of what is happening goes on inside Lucille's head, and her response to the physical world is well served through Humphreys' often lushly sensuous language. Sharpness is maintained through the comic episodes: Rhody (Rae's lifelong black pal) doing human research while heavily disguised on a city bus tour; or the image of Pop—stripped of his licence for speeding—setting off on his Snapper lawn mower to visit his loyal lady friend.

Intuitive and sympathetic, this is an unusually well-balanced novel. Humphreys has placed her characters at the mercy of a South Carolina summer, and the relentless sun keeps everyone locked into a deadening lethargy. It's the control, psychological insight and humanity which makes *Rich in Love* far more than just another very good novel.

Less panoramic in small-town scope is the earlier novel, *Dreams of Sleep.* Here Humphreys demonstrates her rare intuitiveness by taking a look at the drama which gradually unfolds when love 'rots'. . . .

Inertia is the central theme, with the author exploring in her ever deliberate, purposeful way how relationships fall apart 'not in sudden collapse, but by slow fragmentation'. With both Alice and Will wandering in contrasting states of suspended animation, it takes the arrival (and quickly all-encompassing influence) of a young home help to bring about a reconciliation.

As with *Rich in Love,* Humphreys' message is about hope in the face of disintegration. Through her understatement, restrained descriptive prose and an apparent belief in the individual's ability to walk to the very edge before stepping back towards a more acceptable, if not completely ideal, reality, she has crafted fiction of much warmth, intelligence and low-key realism.

Eileen Battersby, "Walking to the Very Edge," in The Listener, Vol. 120, No. 3080, September 15, 1988, p. 31.

Danilo Kiš

1935-1989

Yugoslavian novelist, short story writer, dramatist, translator, and essayist.

Kiš gained international attention for his novel *Basta, pepeo* (1965; *Garden, Ashes*) and his volume of short stories *Grobnica za Borisa Davidovica* (1976; *A Tomb for Boris Davidovich*), both of which focus upon the persecution of European Jews during World War II. In his fiction, Kiš often explores the complex nature of authoritarian ideologies and their detrimental effect on individuals. He frequently blurs the distinction between fact and fiction by interweaving real historical figures and invented characters and juxtaposing neutral, journalistic narration with lyrical passages. His work has been termed "documentary" fiction or, as Kiš called it, "faction." Branko Gorjup described this style: "Rooted in cool intelligence and drawn towards objectivity, the writer of documentary fiction delights in arranging all of the 'borrowed' fragments—regardless of whether they are documents, *quasi* documents, or imaginative literature treated as documents—into an integrated and uniquely personal mode of expression."

A member of the generation of Serbian writers who came to artistic maturity in the early 1960s, Kiš benefitted from the intellectual freedom that followed the demise of Soviet leader Joseph Stalin's regime. Kiš eschews literal depictions of historical or social events to focus instead on the thoughts and personal experiences of people who sense disparity between their own observations and the state's version of reality. The largely autobiographical *Garden, Ashes*, Kiš's first book translated into English, recounts a Jewish family's misfortunes in Yugoslavia during World War II. Narrated by a young boy, this novel centers on his eccentric father and the combination of horror and fascination he evokes in the child before the father is killed in the Holocaust. *Peščanik* (1972; *Hourglass*) is Kiš's first work to feature his documentary approach to fiction. The text of this novel consists of a fragmented, nonlinear series of letters, diaries, and citations from official registers. Employing a cold, distant voice, Kiš depicts a Jewish family tyrannized by the Nazi government. Edmund White deemed *Hourglass* "the most convincing account we have of the Jewish experience in World War II."

A Tomb for Boris Davidovich, which has been frequently compared to Arthur Koestler's *Darkness at Noon* and George Orwell's *1984*, consists of seven interconnected stories about anti-Semitism and the purges conducted by Stalin. Written as a series of fake biographies in a clinical, ironic tone, six of these tales portray militant communist Jews destroyed by the very system they had advocated. One piece, "Psi i knjige" ("Dogs and Books"), depicts the death of a Jew during the Inquisition, illustrating the cyclical nature of history. In the short story collection *Enciklopedia mrtvih* (1983; *The Encyclopedia of the Dead*), Kiš mixes authentic historical documents with falsifications and includes elements of fantasy to distort ordinary perceptions of reality. The title story, for example, consists mainly of a woman's dream in which she visits an archive where the lives of all unremarkable dead people are thoroughly documented. Through an excerpt in this massive "Encyclopedia of the Dead," the protagonist learns

about her father's life, which assumes an appearance of existential significance through the book's rendering of all events as equally meaningful. This story exemplifies what Josef Škvorecky identified as the volume's foremost theme: "the uniqueness, and therefore the equal importance, of every human being." Kiš also wrote several dramas and fictional works.

(See also *Contemporary Authors,* Vols. 109, 118, and 129 [obituary].)

MURLIN CROUCHER

Originally written in 1965 when Kiš was thirty years old, this autobiographical novel [*Garden, Ashes*] of his childhood demonstrates his rich yet youthful and slightly hyperbolic style. . . .

In *Garden, Ashes* the events of the author's childhood are brought out in a loosely connected chronological sequence of half-explained adventures. The initial lack of omniscient narration forces the reader to encounter the happenings as would a child; that is, events are perceived and described without rational understanding. Bits and snatches of memories remain intact, but the cause and effect relationships appear to have been forgotten or never understood by the narrator. As the book develops and the child turns adolescent, his life is described with greater clarity and understanding.

Eventually the author focuses his narration on his enigmatic and half-crazed father, a man with an eloquent tongue and a fanciful mind who frequently abandoned family, sobriety and reason. Kiš has deftly portrayed a man who strikes the reader as being simultaneously repulsive, inspiring and pathetic, a drunkard who has taken poetic flight from the injustices of his harsh environment. Kiš ingeniously declines to give any final moral judgment of either his father or himself and is obviously allowing each reader his own interpretations. . . .

It is impossible to separate fact from fiction in this depiction of what must have been a childhood spent in the midst of financial impoverishment in Yugoslavia just prior to and during World War II. But the specific events mentioned in the book do not really delineate a concrete environment within a historical setting, for it is Kiš's subjective and poetic interpretations of these events with which he expresses the meaning of his youth. Some of the depictions may tend to border on the cliché . . . , yet they accumulate with power and give the reader emotional photographs of Kiš's memories.

The English translation reads well and demonstrates Kiš's reflective, if somewhat uncontrolled style. Despite the clever language, the memorable scenes and the narrator's occasional confessional openness, the novel on the whole seems to lack an overall message or higher purpose. Whether this is a result of the genre or the writer remains to be seen in his subsequent works.

Murlin Croucher, in a review of "Garden, Ashes," in World Literature Today, *Vol. 51, No. 1, Winter, 1977, p. 127.*

MATEJA MATEJIC

[*A Tomb for Boris Davidovich*] contains seven stories closely united by one central theme: persecution and execution of human beings in the name of ideals and ideologies. Gruesome details of the torture and execution of individual victims under the terror of Stalinism and the Inquistion are masterfully presented in these stories. Jews are the principal characters and identified victims in six of the seven stories; the Jew in the seventh story, A. A. Darmalatov, dies a natural death and, also a victim of the terror, is actually guilty of silence and of compromising his literary talent in order to survive. In five stories the five principal characters are victims of Stalin's terror. A parallel of that terror with the terror of the Inquisition is drawn by inclusion of the story **"Psi i knjige"** (**"Dogs and Books"**), in which a massacre of Jews takes place in 1330 in Italy. It is relatively easy to understand the author's idea behind the inclusion of this story in the book: it suggests that the names of ideologies and/or religions may change, but their oppressive power is identical in all times and places.

A Tomb for Boris Davidovič is an angry book, yet its anger is wrapped in a nonchalant, seemingly detached manner of narration. It is an attack on terror and oppression, on the type

of power which, in the name of ideological and religious principles, commits atrocities. There are no emotional outbursts and no pathos. On the contrary: the style is characterized by the frequent use of irony and litotes and may be regarded as unsuitable for telling such stories of horror. Yet it is this very style that makes the book unforgettable and far more effective in describing human suffering than is the tearful style of sentimentalism.

Mateja Matejic, in a review of "Grobnica za Borisa Davidovica," in World Literature Today. *Vol. 51, No. 2, Summer, 1977, p. 468.*

LUDMILLA THORNE

Although small and unassuming, this novel [*A Tomb for Boris Davidovich*] about the Russian Revolution bursts with a cavalcade of characters, some historical, others fictitious. They are of different nationalities and backgrounds, but all are fired by a zeal that places no limits on their actions. Eventually, they are reduced by fate to mere playthings in a monstrous game of history.

Miksha, a Czech revolutionary who can flay a live skunk or rip out the entrails of a Polish colleague with equal ease (on the mere suspicion of treachery), dies of pellagra in a Soviet prison. Gould Verschoyle of Dublin, the exterminating angel who proclaims *"viva la República"* in Catalonia, ends his revolutionary sojourn in the Karaganda labor camp, where he is murdered.

Dr. Karl Taube, a pharmacist's son born in Hungary, spends four years in Vienna. Disillusioned by that city's "slow progress of revolutionary ferment," he leaves for Berlin and finally ends up in Moscow as a member of the Comintern. A year later, he is arrested and spends the next 17 years in Soviet labor camps. He is released, only to be killed by Kostik, the Georgian king of thieves, a fellow Gulag survivor.

A. L. Chelyustnikov, the editor of the Ukrainian newspaper *New Dawn,* dispels a visiting French mayor's suspicions about the persecution of religion in the Soviet Union by masquerading as a priest and conducting a service at the Cathedral of Saint Sophia. (In 1934, writes Kis, "it was easier to meet a reindeer than a priest in Kiev.") Under Chelyustnikov's personal supervision, too, 120 prisoners from a nearby labor camp carry out a quick restoration of the church, and the slogan "Religion is the Opiate of the People" is promptly replaced with the more metaphysical sign, "Long Live the Sun, Down with the Night." Yet even achievements as extraordinary as these do not save Chelyustnikov from prison.

But the character most central to this miniature novel is Boris Davidovich Malamud—"the Bolshevik Hamlet"—a mixture of Lenin, Mazurin and Bukharin, who would go down in history under the name of B.D. Novsky. His story serves as a vivid example of the author's major theme—that the Revolution devours its most devoted children.

A few years before the Bolshevik upheaval, Novsky is a young engineer, a perfect dandy much sought after in the elegant salons of St. Petersburg. He is, however, also an anarchist, who participates in "expropriations" (armed robberies), transports explosives and arms to Russia and is the mastermind behind spectacular assassinations that shock his cultured friends. Assisted by Zinaida Maysner—"the muse of the Revolution"—a sexy version of Krupskaya, Novsky escapes to Paris via Constantinople and moves on to Berlin, where he becomes a collaborator on two Social Democratic papers. The first sparks of the Revolution catch him in Basel and are quick to bring him home. He becomes an agitator among the soldiers and is instrumental in cutting Lieutenant General Anton Denikin's rear guard.

In 1919, Novsky marries Zinaida aboard the torpedo boat *Spartacus,* anchored in Kronstadt harbor. By that time he is already an important political commissar of the new regime. His career continues to ascend until 1930, when it abruptly falls, like a red comet. Arrested, he confronts a bizarre spate of accusations, including spying for Britain and sabotaging the economy. Thus begins the liquidation of Novsky, a process well known to the world from the real-life cases of Lev Kamenev, Grigory L. Pyatakov, Karl Radek, et al.

Kis' handling of the purge ritual, starting with interrogator Fedukin's endless efforts to persuade Novsky of his "moral obligation to make a false confession," is classical in its power and lyricism. (Besides being an accomplished Yugoslav novelist, Kis is also a poet.) The interplay between the prisoner's internal line of defense ("I've reached my mature years—why spoil my biography?") and Fedukin's full use of his victim's egocentricity, is fascinating to observe. Finally, Fedukin finds the key to Novsky's downfall—"each day of his life would be paid for with the life of another man." Novsky signs a purely fictitious 10-page confession, diligently composed by the two men like a college term paper.

But he is not executed for his crimes. Longing for death, he is instead exiled, only to be rearrested in that terrible winter of 1937. He wanders through the camps like an apparition; unable to escape, he commits suicide by leaping into a cauldron of molten iron. The revolutionary fire has turned into a wisp of smoke. (pp. 15-16)

A Tomb for Boris Davidovich bears traces of Orwell's *1984* and Koestler's *Darkness at Noon,* but it has its own special flair, particularly since it comes to us from someone who is there, *on the other side.* (p. 16)

> *Ludmilla Thorne, "Victims of Revolution," in* The New Leader, *Vol. LXI, No. 25, December 18, 1978, pp. 15-16.*

IVAN SANDERS

[In *A Tomb for Boris Davidovich*], Kiš presents a series of terse biographies, and remarks that his revolutionaries' stories "would have to be told in Romanian, Hungarian, Ukrainian, or Yiddish; or, rather, in a mixture of all these languages." The peculiarities of the East-Central European locale, as well as quirks in the history of modern Communism are behind Kiš's bizarre narratives, although in assuming the role of an historian culling relevant biographical data from fragmentary and often highly questionable sources, he pretends to be as precise as his heroes. The facts, however, are too horrible, and imagination is a balm. Kiš finds that he cannot "forgo the pleasure of narration, which allows the author the deceptive idea that he is creating the world and thereby, as they say, changing it."

Like most East European writers providing insights into their region's recent history, Danilo Kiš is mindful of the interconnectedness of past and present. In one of his tales a Ukrainian activist, A. L. Chelyustnikov, is given the task of staging a mass in Kiev's famed Cathedral of Saint Sophia for a visiting French dignitary. The year is 1934, the great church has been used for years as a brewery; but in a matter of hours it is temporarily restored to its original function by prisoners summoned from a nearby jail. Borrowing props and a make-up man from the local theater, Chelyustnikov himself becomes a priest for the day, and celebrates mass for the mayor of Lyons and a group of grim-faced party functionaries who were also ordered to participate in the masquerade. The naive Frenchman listens for a while to Chelyustnikov's mumblings, then leaves, convinced that there is freedom of worship in Communist Russia after all. Rather than reflecting on the nature of Stalinist evils, Danilo Kiš offers a history of the cathedral, and of Holy Kiev, "mother of Russian cities," reminding us pointedly that after Russia became Christian, "the brutality of the believers in the true faith . . . was not less barbaric than pagan brutality, and the fanaticism of the believers in the tyranny of one god was still more fierce and efficient."

The title story ["**A Tomb for Boris Davidovich**"] also has far-reaching implications. Its hero, Boris Davidovich, is the prototypical radical: brilliant, volatile, obsessed, "a strange mixture of amorality, cynicism, and spontaneous enthusiasm . . . a cross between a professor and a bandit." He serves the revolution and the young Soviet state in various capacities, under different aliases, until his inevitable arrest during one of Stalin's purges. His interrogator has a difficult time breaking his will, for Boris Davidovich is a hardened nihilist by now, offering "nothing for nothing." In a way the torturer welcomes this challenge. He has a young prisoner shot before Davidovich's eyes every day that he remains silent—a diabolical reminder that integrity has no place in a prison cell. Our revolutionary is unmoved at first, but then realizes ruefully that he is not above conventional morality, and winds up signing the confession. (p. 38)

A Tomb for Boris Davidovich may be viewed as a political novel. . . . Yet what the author demonstrates most compellingly in these narratives is that his revolutionaries and political activists are animated by passions and prejudices that are far more deep-rooted than their political convictions. (pp. 38-9)

> *Ivan Sanders, in a review of "A Tomb for Boris Davidovich," in* The New Republic, *Vol. 180, No. 1, January 6, 1979, pp. 38-9.*

JOSEPH BRODSKY

When, after great difficulties, [*A Tomb for Boris Davidovich*] was first published in 1976, in Zagreb, Yugoslavia, it was immediately assaulted in the press by the conservative "Stalinist" elements at the top echelon of the Yugoslav literary hierarchy. The war cry emanating from the top was picked up at the bottom by Serbo-Croatian nationalists, who are traditionally pro-Russian and traditionally anti-Semitic, for the bulk of Danilo Kiš's characters are Jews, as is the author himself. Yugoslavia is a small country, and the politics in a small country are always big, literary politics especially. Due to this proportion, an attack against a writer becomes extremely focused. It was focused sharply enough to send Danilo Kiš into "nervous shock."

There are several topics an author may deal with which can jeopardize his well-being, and history is one of them. Depending on its proximity to the present, history provides a writer with background, content, cast of characters, and sometimes, as in the case of Kiš, with the writer's actual context. The very fact of describing historical events is regarded by history as an attempt to demote it into the past and is resisted vehemently. An historical novel becomes therefore a vehicle of time, an instrument that purports to outline the boundaries between past and present by means of estrangement from its subject. A narrative reduces history to a story and creates, by being conducted from a certain "outside," a new time category, heretofore unknown.

Apart from the general "cause-and-effect" principle, history claims the present through its most viable extension: through ideology. Having failed to triumph at the moment of its emergence, an ideology rapidly develops what one may call a utopian complex and gravitates to timelessness. Correspondingly, a portrayal of ideology or of its carriers is considered by the latter as an attempt to pin it down, to compromise its purity, and to rob it of its future.

In the case of *A Tomb for Boris Davidovich*, history's claim on the present may seem all the more valid because the epoch with which this book deals isn't really so ancient. Its author, a Yugoslav writer, Danilo Kiš, describes events that took place in the first half of this century and their impact on the lives of his seven characters. For all seven the impact turned out to be the same: deadly. (pp. ix-x)

From the outside the storm over *A Tomb for Boris Davidovich* seems all the more peculiar because this book has literally nothing to do with Yugoslavia and its internal situation. None of its characters are Yugoslav: They are Poles, Russians, Rumanians, Irish, Hungarians; most of them are of Jewish origin. None of them ever set foot in Yugoslavia. Basically, *A Tomb for Boris Davidovich* is an abbreviated fictionalized account of the self-destruction of that berserk Trojan horse called Comintern. The only thing that its passengers—the heroes of Danilo Kiš's novel—have in common with this small country is the ideology that this country professes today and in the name of which they were murdered yesterday. Apparently, that was enough to infuriate the faithful.

So in the absence of familiar turf and being unable to argue over the book's substance (for fear of calling too much public attention to it), those faithful, led by the then chairman of the Yugoslav Union of Writers, went on assaulting this book on literary grounds and accused its author of plagiarism. The list of allegedly plagiarized authors was impressive and included Aleksandr Solzhenitsyn, James Joyce, Nadezhda Mandelstam, Jorge Luis Borges, the Medvedev brothers, and others.

For one thing, an author capable of aping writers so diverse within the space of a 135-page novel deserves every kind of commendation. Also, unsound as it is, this list reveals something important about the accusers themselves: their between-the-chairs nonaligned cultural stance, a kind of missing-link position between East and West. However, precisely because of their provincialism, with its weakness for generalization and for treating all remote objects as concepts or symbols, this list deserves more than simple mockery.

It is understandable, for instance, why they mention Joyce: One of Kiš's characters is Irish, and even for a Yugoslav party official, Joyce today is a synonym for Ireland as well as for Western culture's decadence. The presence of Borges is of a less obvious nature and is intended to compromise the book stylistically by trying to reduce the vignette technique that Kiš employs in his cautionary tales to a mannerism borrowed from a remarkable Argentinian, but this is utter nonsense. Kiš is a great stylist, and the fabric of his writing has more in common with Franz Kafka or Bruno Schulz or with the writers of the French *roman nouveau* than with anyone in the Third World. Besides, to attack Danilo Kiš's prose in *A Tomb for Boris Davidovich* is a kind of delayed reaction: If anything, his writing here is a lot more sparse than in his *Garden, Ashes,* a veritable gem of lyrical prose, the best book produced on the Continent in the post-war period. The more pertinent names on that list, in other words, are the Russian ones, yet again for reasons that have nothing to do with the book's texture and all to do with its core.

At first glance *A Tomb for Boris Davidovich* may indeed seem like a spin-off from *The First Circle, The Gulag Archipelago* (as yet unpublished in Yugoslavia), Nadezhda Mandelstam's *Hope against Hope,* and the Medvedev brothers' various writings. The point is that the bulk of the novel has to do with the fate of several people who perished during the Great Terror of the late 1930s. For an account of that the sources are unfortunately mostly Russian. With sixty million dead in the civil war, collectivization, the Great Terror, and things in between, Russia in this century has produced enough history to keep the literati all over the world busy for several generations. The aforesaid authors already belong to the second generation. The first was Arthur Koestler's, and several chapters of the Kiš book bear a general resemblance to *Darkness at Noon,* although surpassing it in both horrifying detail and narrative skill.

The process of transforming Russian history of this period into the new mythology of our civilization is well under way in *A Tomb for Boris Davidovich.* What simplifies its author's task is that apart from being chronologically modern, this history also displays signs of a considerable modernism, manifested by the distinct surrealism of its metamorphoses and the utterly antiheroic nature of its archetypes. Due to the numbers involved, it is safe to say that there was hardly ever an epoch in human history when fear and duplicity were so pervasive and voluminous.

Although it is arguable that this history has delivered a new religion (as so many claim), it inflicted upon the human race and human psyche a destruction of a mythological scope, and on these grounds alone this history qualifies for a new creed. Sooner or later, every upheaval ends up in a work of fiction. The most disturbing thing about this particular book, however, is the unbearable and, because of that, paradoxically appropriate excellence of Kiš's prose, which provides his moribund metamorphoses with additional beauty.

By virtue of his place and time alone, Danilo Kiš is able to avoid the faults of urgency which considerably marred the works of his listed and unlisted predecessors. Unlike them, he can afford to treat tragedy as a genre, and his art is more devastating than statistics. Kiš writes in an extremely condensed and therefore highly allusive fashion. Since he deals in biographies, the last bastions of realism, each of his vignettes sounds like a miniaturized Bildungsroman accomplished by a movie-like montage of shrewdly chosen details that allude both to the actual and to the literary experiences of his reader. (pp. xi-xiv)

With his emphasis on imagery and detail, combined with ironic detachment, Danilo Kiš's obviously poetic prose puts his horrid subject matter into the most adequate perspective by alerting the reader to this prose's own intelligence. Thus, the reader's ethical evaluation of the phenomena described ceases to be merely a matter of his distraught sentiment and comes out as a judgment made by his profoundly offended supreme human faculties. It is not that the thought is felt but, rather, that the feeling is thought.

Unlike prose, poetry doesn't so much express an emotion as absorb it linguistically. In this sense, Kiš's writing is essentially a poetic type of operation, and the vignettes of which the chapters of his book consist could be read and appreciated separately as short poems. Some passages could be simply memorized. What prevents one from regarding this book as a prose poem, however, is neither its subject matter (which is still out of reach no matter how avant-garde as poetry) nor its typically prosaic coherence; it is mostly Danilo Kiš's own undercutting technique, to which he resorts when a vignette approaches real sublimity. All the same, *A Tomb for Boris Davidovich* is built like a long dramatic poem crowned with that really monstrous, terrifying "rhyme" of cabalistic coincidence in **"Dogs and Books,"** which achieves what the best poetry usually achieves: the metaphysical impact of the last lines that gape, along with their reader's mind, into pure *chronos*—which is presumably a formula for equating art to human reality.

The standard perception of tragedy, as distinct from a regular existence, is that it is a violation of time. In the case of *A Tomb for Boris Davidovich,* whose superb prose nearly overshadows the story itself, tragedy almost gets redefined as an occasion for time's high eloquence. A hero—or, more precisely, a victim—suddenly emerges from the reticence of ordinary life as a spokesman of time's arbitrary opposition to human presence in it. Since the usual incongruity between living matter and the matter of time (normally manifested by death) can be elucidated only by the latter, the description of the tools time employs for such an undertaking (historical events, ideologies, etc.) requires an appropriately lucid condensation of the language. It is a fairly disquieting thought that in Danilo Kiš we have a writer whose skills are adequate to those of time itself.

Perhaps the only service a real tragedy renders in leaving its survivors as speechless as its victims is that of furthering its commentators' language. The least that can be said about *A Tomb for Boris Davidovich* is that it achieves aesthetic comprehension where ethics fail. Of course, the mastery of language can hardly pass for a safeguard in our enterprising century; but at least it creates a possibility of response, without which people are bound to remain slaves of their experience. By having written this book, Danilo Kiš simply suggests that literature is the only available tool for the cognition of phenomena whose size otherwise numbs your senses and eludes human grasp. (pp. xv-xvii)

> *Joseph Brodsky, in an introduction to* A Tomb for Boris Davidovich *by Danilo Kiš, translated by Duška Mikić-Mitchell, Penguin Books, 1980, pp. ix-xvii.*

NORBERT CZARNY

If Kiš's novels are not directly autobiographical, we nonetheless find there the sign of lived experience, the intensity of yesterday which is told without any nostalgia (unlike Joseph Roth's works). Here the troubled centuries belong to the past: the Empire is dead and with it all the protections that it gave

have disappeared. The frontiers are moving, the political situations are unstable, the social status of men and women is permanently and insidiously threatened.

At the beginning of **Garden, Ashes,** Kiš's first novel . . . , there is a description of the first three experiences which mark the narrator's childhood. First of all, he becomes conscious of the reality of death—it might be his mother's death and his own death. This awareness is linked with the anguish of sleeping. Thus the child tries to find himself falling asleep:

> Sometimes I woke up ten times in a row, with the last effort of my consciousness, the supreme force of will of the one who was going to outwit death someday. My sleep game was practice from the grand struggle with death.

The pleasure of travelling that his father gave him helps the child to get away from his fear. Names of towns, "had poisoned [him] with longing." Travelling is seen as a "peaceful feast."

> At such moments I did not fear sleep, I even felt that the exciting speed with which my body was hurtling through space and time was liberating me from death, that this speed and movement represented a triumph over death and over time.

To destroy the limits of time and space in order to free oneself from death and go beyond the frontiers that men impose on themselves, these are the ambitions of the narrator's father, of this Eduard Sam that we find again under his own initials in Kiš's third novel **Hourglass,** writing his timetable of road, sea, rail and air transport.

> It was a holy, apocryphal Bible in which the mystery of the genesis was repeated but in which all the divine injustices and the powerlessness of men were corrected. In the five books, the long distances which split the worlds, so cruelly increased by God's will and original sin, were brought back to a human dimension. My father with Prometheus's and a demiurge's blind anger did not accept the distance between earth and heaven.

Behind the somehow ironic bombast of this passage, the narrator defines a certain form of literature. Like the timetable, the novel gives an account of what is real up to the tiniest detail which reveals the whole. In face of the dissolving power of time, it works as a resistance. The means he uses are as diverse as those things he has to account for. Kiš takes up the polyphonic form found in Broch's *The Sleepwalkers.* His novels combine a classical narration, an essay, a biography, the summary of an interrogation; they play on different levels. Kiš parodies, quotes, enumerates. For him listing is as much a poetic exercise as a mnemonic process. It is a way of inscribing forever by accumulating names and things. It shows a will to define a whole, not letting anything escape.

The narrator of *A Tomb for Boris Davidovich* resembles an archivist. He tells the lives of revolutionary militants, victims of Stalinist purges during the 30's, as if he were simply digging up documents. Actually it is, as the title suggests, seven versions of the same story. Taube, a Hungarian doctor, Gould-Verschoyle, an Irish Republican, and Boris Davidovich (Novsky) an 'Old Bolshevik' Revolutionary, are one and the same person, also reflecting Baruch David Neumann, a Jewish victim of the Inquisition in Pamiers in 1337. All of them are sincere and devoted militants and they are struck in the same way by the Stalinist Inquisition.

The novel is a variation on the themes of victim and torturer, of traitor and hero. It is also, more simply, an expansion of the real. Danilo Kiš does not invent much. The lives he tells are those of people met by Karlo Stajner whose book *7000 Days in Siberia* is a powerful testament of a communist militant's life in the Goulag between 1936 and 1956.

Danilo Kiš links together the episodes, using cross-references or echoes. Those imaginary lives which have 'only the misfortune to be real,' could be recorded in some Encyclopedia Sovietica, if such a work decided to name and rehabilitate the millions of victims of the Purges. Nothing is more effective than stylization of an encyclopedia to bring reality to light. The process of writing at the boundary of reality and imagination allows Kiš to reveal the basis of a still unknown "History." By subtly playing on auto-censorship—the author eludes or partly conceals certain episodes—he thus denounces the more real effects of censorship in the totalitarian countries.

Nothing is more precise and concrete than a police interrogation. All trace of feeling is absent from such an investigation. Above all the purpose is to define one truth or "the truth," to find a coherent time table, to set up a fixed relationship between men. This is the process used by the writer-narrator of *Hourglass.* E.S., the hero of the novel, is questioned by the police. What he tells and the hypotheses drawn from that are recorded in chapters called 'Investigation.' The writer does not know more than the policeman who questions or the reader. Whole portions of the reality are missing, whereas apparently insignificant details emerge throughout.

At the beginning of the novel, we are shown a mere anecdote, conflicts within a family that E.S. sums up at the end of the book in a letter:

> . . . You see to it that I have something to write about: my dear cousins and nephews generously give me the theme of a bourgeois horror story to which I could give the following titles: "Parade in a Harem" or "Easter Feasts in a Jewish Residence" or "Hourglass" (everything flows, dear sister).

The letter is authentic. It was sent by Danilo Kiš's father in 1942. But the letter is as Gombrowitz would say a 'scrap'—a point of origin. It is a microcosm: individual history works like a distorting mirror of "History."

Yet the novel does not depart from a kind of cold and distant tone even when it describes persecutions. Kiš's meticulous and precise writing resembles Robbe-Grillet's, for instance in Kiš's description of the slaughter of the Jews of Novi-Sad in 1942.

The story which is told by Danilo Kiš in *Hourglass* is the story of the persecution of the Jews, particularly of his family, during the last world war. This century's violence is also to be found in *A Tomb for Boris Davidovich* and *Garden, Ashes.* It is certainly what sets Kiš apart from some aspects of the *nouveau roman* to which he is in other respects very close. We are shown the same refusal of psychologism, of realist illusion and of characters with a well-ordered civil status. There is the same concern for form and for visual objectivity. But the school of "reality" is not the school of "vision" and Kiš wants specifically to speak of the real life of which no one can speak except direct witnesses.

The anti-semitic violence appears when E.S. and his friend Gavanski list their friends who have been murdered and when he describes the brain of a Jewish doctor, beaten to death, lying on the ground. In another part, the narrator shows E.S., a hard worker, subjected to the violence of his 'guards.'

Like in some of Kafka's works, such as *The Penal Colony,* there is no concession to the pathetic; Kiš refuses to use such rhetorical processes to describe the conditions of the Jews. The word 'Jew' itself is seldom used and we must wait fifty pages to learn in a symbolic scene, that E.S. is a Jew. (pp. 280-83)

The fragmented or refracted vision that Kiš gives us of the conditions of the Jews under Naziism skillfully amplifies each single detail, producing the enigmatic form of the book. Reading it is similar (as is a police investigation) to a search for clues, whose final organization and interrelationship renew our vision of the event.

Just as the condition of the Jews is not described in *Hourglass* with the rhetoric often used in martyrologies, the heroes shown in *A Tomb for Boris Davidovich* do not appear as victims to be pitied, but almost as mute symbols of a constantly possible story. Following the example of Boris Davidovich, sent to Siberia but often thought to be seen on Red Square, they are intemporal and this is their ultimate trickery. A kind of sleep protects them from death, forgetting and nostalgia.

The father who is absent, desired and magnified as the Emperor Franz Joseph by Joseph Roth, omnipresent, hated and destroyed by Kafka, wonderful and celebrated in the poetic prose of Bruno Schulz, is one of the major obsessions of Middle European literature. The image of the father is also present in Danilo Kiš's works, and this characteristic links him to the Middle European tradition. The father is not only the person who gives a name and protects, he also is the person who invents, creates, and gives a form and a meaning to the world.

Kiš's *Garden, Ashes* is the story of a childhood, an ode to the father, who is a kind of Prometheus or Modern Don Quixote. As Schulz writes of his father, he is "the hopeless fighter for the poetic cause" before the Philistines of this frontier province, which is as lifeless as Schulz's Drohobycz.

Writer, prophet, wandering Jew, magician, swindler, inventor, spending his life in a café, Eduard Sam intoxicates himself and others with words. He lives at the boundaries of his country and on the boundaries between animality and humanity. He invades the story more and more, contaminates it, becomes the plot of the novel:

> Quite unexpectedly and unpredictably this account is becoming increasingly the story of my father, the story of the gifted Eduard Sam. His absence, his somnambulism, his messianism, all concepts removed from any earthly—or if you will, narrative—context, this subject is as frail as dreams and notable above all for his primordial negative traits: his story becomes a densely woven, heavy fabric, a material of entirely unknown specific weight.

The mythical dimension goes beyond the real dimension, the father becomes human destiny.

> My role as a victim which I have been playing with greater or lesser success all my life—we all act out our lives, our own destinies, after all—that role, as I said, is gradually coming to an end. You must remember this once and for all, young fellow, you

can't play the role of a victim all your life without becoming one in the end. There is nothing I can do about it now. I'll have to do my best to complete that role with dignity right up to the very end. The forgiveness you will give me will be my redemption.

Thus the clown becomes the hero, the body according to Gombrowitz, the 'parody of a body.' The world comedy is acted by a body who reveals himself only by remaining pure appearance.

The modernity of the Middle European novel, which is represented by Danilo Kiš among other writers, may reside in this subtle movement between reality and its simulation, in the lucid and cunning game with History which 'like a sow devours her farrow.' (pp. 283-84)

> Norbert Czarny, "Imaginary-Real Lives: On Danilo Kiš," translated by Catherine Vincent, in Cross Currents, *University of Michigan, No. 4, 1984, pp. 279-84.*

CELIA HAWKESWORTH

[*Garden, Ashes*] is at once an intellectual and a lyrical work. The autobiographical account of a childhood, it is set in a Jewish family in war-time Yugoslavia. This context of war and persecution is unobtrusive, simply one aspect of the world into which the child is growing, glimpsed in fragments and only intermittently understood. There is no clear chronological framework, but rather a kaleidoscope of isolated incidents evoking a world full of unexplained forces. The particular flavour of the work stems from the combination of such partial and emotionally charged glimpses of the world by the sophisticated mature imagination.

Garden, Ashes avoids the pitfalls of sentimentality and egotism because it is not dominated by the child through whose eyes it is seen. The main protagonist is in fact the father, and the child's vision of him becomes a remarkable, subtle appreciation of a complex, unstable character. Portrayed as a mysterious, almost magical being, he is at best irresponsible, obsessed with a need to "follow his star", given to drunken sprees lasting for several days. Increasingly, these fits are of real madness, necessitating regular spells in an institution, hinted at, again, throught the child's imperfect understanding. There is a grandeur about the nature of Eduard Scham's madness, however, which arouses the awed admiration of the child and the sympathy of the reader. Employed as a railway official, but at heart an intellectual, Scham has compiled two volumes of railway timetables. His projected third volume, however, is expanded to include world-wide train, boat and air travel, thereby linking the whole world in one coherent scheme. The timetable then becomes the framework for a vast volume which draws together all branches of human endeavour. The dominant presence of this magnificent clown with his magic hat and stick gives the book a distinct and potent charm, and expands its implications from the narrowly personal to universal ideas about the futile but noble fate of the intellectual in general and the fate of the Jew in particular.

> Celia Hawkesworth, "Childhood Kaleidoscope," in The Times Literary Supplement, *No. 4269, January 25, 1985, p. 86.*

JAMES LASDUN

Garden, Ashes purports to be the story of its author's childhood in Yugoslavia during World War II. The approach is poetic rather than novelistic; a series of lyrical evocations of moods, people and events, refracted through a child's mind, and flowing in and out of each other in a blurred, dreamlike fashion.

I use the word "purports", not because there is any reason to doubt the authenticity of the material, but because the sensibility with which Kiš endows Andi (the name he uses for his young self) is too studiedly that of a tremulous, hypersensitive young writer-to-be for it ever to ring quite true. A too-visible layer of *post factum* artifice lies over his archetypal childhood fears and desires—particularly his recurrent fear of his own, and his mother's, mortality.

Recollection of the genesis of this fear (the death of an uncle) begins with a more or less believable picture—"I stood petrified, thinking that one day I too would die. At the same time I was horror-stricken that my mother would also die"—upon which Kiš proceeds to impose an improbably precise piece of synaesthesia ("All of this came rushing upon me in a flash of a peculiar violet color") that at once plunges us into the realm of fanciful apostrophe, which realm the book seldom leaves. (p. 50)

What suffers most from this apostrophising tendency is the character of Eduard, Andi's father. Eduard appears to have been an extraordinary man: compulsive traveller, polymath, "pantheistic genius", drunk, obsessive compiler of an annotated, scholarly timetable for world-wide travel, concentration camp survivor . . . in short, a rich subject for his son to explore. But to my mind, Eduard never quite emerges into visibility through the clouds of determinedly oblique description with which Kiš surrounds him, and he remains a lost opportunity; one of many in a book that promises the visionary illuminations one associates with the great novels of childhood, but which seldom delivers anything more than glimpses. (pp. 50-1)

> James Lasdun, "The Great or the Good?" in Encounter, *Vol. LXV, No. 2, July-August, 1985, pp. 47-51.*

EDMUND WHITE

This essay will focus on three books in which Danilo Kiš has recounted events from the same period of his life, but which differ extraordinarily in their method, their tone, and even their content.

The first volume of the Kiš trilogy, called *Rani Jadi* in Serbo-Croatian and *Chagrins précoces* in the beautiful French translation by Pascale Delpech . . . is a book ostensibly for adolescent readers—or, as the subtitle puts it after a line from Max Jacob, "pour les enfants et les raffinés."

The essential narrative, which will emerge more clearly in the later two volumes, is splintered here, refracted, reflected. The horror of the situation (wartorn Yugoslavia in 1942 under Fascist rule) and the anguish of the child's parents (the mother a Christian, the father a Jew already enlisted in crushing forced labor and soon to be sent off to Auschwitz) are uniquely glimpsed from a boy's point of view. For instance, on the very first page, we read a lyrical description of chestnuts in autumn. We learn: "Certain chestnuts contained twins; but it's still possible to tell them apart, for one wears a mark on its forehead, like a horse. So its mother will always be able to pick it out—by the star on his forehead."

This innocent-appearing "star" becomes more ominous when we learn in the later *Hourglass* that Edouard Sam, the father, was forced to wear the yellow Star of David. And in an interview Mr. Kiš has remarked that although he was the baptized son of an Orthodox Christian mother, she had been obliged to sew a yellow star for him, a stigma that was held in readiness for him should the racial laws in Yugoslavia change.

Similarly, the boy's Jewish heritage, which the mother understandably attempts to conceal, emerges in another tale, **"The Game."** The Jewish father spies on his son through a keyhole as the child plays. Although the gentile mother has felt her "Little Blond Boy" will be above suspicion, the boy, unprompted and unconscious, amuses himself by impersonating his Jewish grandfather, "Max the Wanderer," Max Ahasvérus, the feather merchant. The child bows before a reproduction of the *Mona Lisa* and addresses her, "Madame, wouldn't you like some pure white swan's down?" His gestures and carriage, even his wheedling voice, reproduce those of the old man—whom he's never seen or even heard of. The anxiety this mimicry awakens in his mother (and the perverse pride in the father) are mostly left to the reader to infer. It's a cruel story, made harsher by the title.

If these short tales (some no longer than a page) are subtle, their subtlety is that of phenomenology—the presentation of sensuous experiences with a minimum of interpretation and a maximum of incomprehension, the celebrated "defamiliarization" of the Russian Formalists, that strategy whereby the quotidian is observed as though it were miraculous, and whereby the dross of habit is transformed into the gold of the first encounter. Kiš is never at home in the world, and his uneasy purchase makes him alert to metaphor and detail—the metaphor that hears unexpected chords struck off disparate objects, like one of those Jamaican bands that sounds a steel drum with a half-filled milk bottle; and the keen, bizarre detail that dips dusty things into lucent liquid. (pp. 364-65)

In the foreground of these stories are animals—the boy's dog Dingo, the cow Mandarine which Andi, our hero, loses, the cavalrymen's mounts which founder from hunger. Psychologists tell us that children often identify with pets since they see that animals and children occupy the lowest status in the household—and that parental attitudes toward animals give a clear reading of their true attitudes toward children. In one three-paragraph story, **"Pears,"** a neighbor woman makes a quite explicit connection between the child and the dog:

> "Just look,"said Mrs. Molnar, the child's new employer, "the Sam boy is sorting the pears, God forgive me, like a dog, by smell. We should take him out hunting. That's just what we're missing, good dogs."

If animals are in the foreground, what hovers in the background, retained only as a faint afterimage, is the boy's father. In **"Autumn Meadow,"** which starts out to read like Joyce's "Araby" about the confrontation of a child with the magical world of the circus and adult sexuality, the direction suddenly veers off with the father's entrance: "Suddenly in the west out of the tall grass loomed my father, his cane raised high." The father discovers, trampled into the mud, a leaf torn from a German cookbook and left behind by someone in the circus—a recipe for sorrel sauce. The father has

a sorrel recipe of his own that calls for nothing but water, salt, and "some spices anyone could find but whose names he jealously conceals." With the ferrule of his cane he stabs at the offending German recipe and its vile call for crème fraîche—a petty act of vengeance reminiscent of his use elsewhere of Hitler's newspaper photos for toilet paper.

The very next tale, **"The Fiancés,"** is a story of first love written in the third person (since "after so many years Andreas Sam is perhaps no longer me"). It ends with a vision of the father in the distance, a force of nature or a change in the weather:

> When he opened his eyes he saw his father, immense, cane in hand, wearing his black hat with the sturdy brim, lingering behind the cart, standing out distinct against the purple horizon.

The father ("the man who came from far away") is seen full-face only in the story **"Pages from a Velvet Photograph Album,"** from which paradoxically he has already vanished. In this text the young writer fully discovers the duty of literature to serve as necrology. When his aunt announces that the father "no longer exists" (i.e., has been arrested), the boy persists in believing in his father's immortality. The boy is certain that when the soldiers separate the fit men from the women, the children, and the ill, his father will be cast into the group rejects ("for at the same time he was a major invalid and a hysterical woman eternally swollen with a false pregnancy like an enormous tumor, and he was also a child, the big baby of his period and tribe").

As the boy, his mother and sister board a train, they take with them a suitcase that, like a funeral urn, contains "the ashes and sad remains of my father: his photographs and papers," especially two of his letters, to which the boy gives the Villon-like names "Le Grand et le Petit Testament." The so-called "Grand Testament," a litany of woes and a jeremiad of accusations, will supply the artistic center and the last pages of *Hourglass.*

For the child, his sole heritage consists of these papers, the family's eiderdown quilts and a few books, among them his father's unpublished travel guide, *l'Indicateur yougoslave et international des lignes d'autobus, de train, de bateau et d'avion*—a volume, the narrator avows, "which would undergo its reaffirmation and astonishing metamorphosis, its Assumption, in one of my books."

In this very first volume of the trilogy, Kiš has already established his themes (loss, memory and fear) and begun to cast a mythic glow over the figure of the father with his bowler, his cane, his peripatetic habits—this combination of the Little Tramp, the Wandering Jew, and Don Quixote. *Garden, Ashes* will magnify this radiance and turn the father into a classical deity, all stormy petulance and fabulous gab. *Hourglass,* in turn, will dismantle the legend, discovering the suffering, fragile, *historic* man under the myth. In the first of the three books, the father appears as a sliver of the moon glimpsed by day; in the second as a fully bloody harvest moon; in the last as a pale, leprous moon consumed by clouds.

From one volume to the next, there is an alternation and several kinds of progression. First, the books address readers of different ages—adolescence, early adulthood, and maturity. The three texts are geared to those different audiences in content and style, since *Chagrins précoces,* as the title suggests, is about early losses (of love, home, innocence, a father), whereas *Garden, Ashes* (a title that is also made up of a pair of opposites) concerns both the noon of life and the evening of regret. Finally, *Hourglass* is a reckoning, the clear-eyed measure of things an old man makes, a demystification. If *Chagrins précoces* is composed of short lyrical fragments, *Garden, Ashes* is a continuous myth, carried along by the tone of romantic elegy. By contrast, *Hourglass* is a dry *procès-verbal,* an inquest; poetic license has been traded in for a prosaic order for arrest. One could even say that the three books trace a sentimental education, or rather graph out the stages passed through before one can contemplate horror. These stages move from childish incomprehension to a self-protecting exaggeration and end with a painfully concrete, objective catalogue.

In *Garden, Ashes . . .* the father is shown as having courted his misfortunes. If he is a victim, he has willfully, perversely elected to play that role; we are told "he is artfully hiding behind one of his numerous masks." The conventions of theater and religion, Christian and pagan, are elicited precisely because the reader is assumed not to believe in them. The father is a lyrical clown and a Pharoah. If the father is the master of make-believe, he can undo his doom as easily as he originally conjured it into being. The adjectives applied to the father and his stage properties (even his cigarettes are "ubiquitous and immortal") as well as the nouns that describe his essence ("his absence, his somnambulism, his messianism") emphasize his mysterious invulnerability. Even before he is shipped off to the concentration camp, he is already invulnerable, since he is already an invincible legend, a Christ before the Crucifixion: "All the stories stamped with earthly signs and framed within a specific historical context take on secondary significance, like historical facts bound up in a destiny that no longer concerns us: we shall record them without haste, when we can."

His suffering, like Christ's, is something he has chosen, and like Christ he can predict his own Passion: "My role as a victim, which I have been plotting with greater or lesser success all my life—we all act out our lives, our own destinies, after all—that role, as I said, is coming to an end." This is *defensive voluntarism,* we might say, a sort of prophylaxis against catastrophe. Psychoanalysis is familiar with the phenomenon—indeed, psychoanalysis *is* the phenomenon, since the patient is encouraged to attribute his misfortunes to an affliction of the will rather than to the slings and arrows of outrageous fortune.

Similarly, the helplessness of the son, although dramatized by his twin fears of sleep and death, is disguised by the tone of the entire book, so allusive to both Proust and Nabokov, those chroniclers of the sheltered bourgeois childhood. In an echo of Nabokov's "First Love," Kiš writes: "I had become intoxicated by the music of travel, sounded by the train wheels and inscribed by swallows and migrating fowl in closely bunched trios on the telephone-wire notation system, in ad-lib performances and improvisations in between three-quarter pauses interrupted—suddenly and noisily—by the great organs of bridges." The Proustian fear of sleep is reenacted, as is the Proustian education of the youthful narrator through sensual exploration and amorous disappointment.

The function of these borrowings and assimilations (for Kiš is as quick as T.S. Eliot to expose his influences and sources) is in the service of wish-fulfillment. The narrator develops problems (the neurotic fear of sleep as an emblem of death) in order to ward off real fears (the father's inevitable death in a concentration camp). These imaginary problems are both proleptic and apotropaic, for they delay or avert more painful recognitions.

Of all Kiš's books, *Garden, Ashes* is the favorite of most readers. Everyone feels affection for (sometimes affectionate exasperation over) the father, that combination of Meistersinger, mage, god, bum, and Old Testament prophet. He is the seer intoxicated with glory and alcohol, the epic wanderer, the man who is a "bankrupt in love and stockholder in sentiment." It is the father who "would have been able to befuddle death with his eloquence, with his philosophy, with his theories." He is the Wandering Jew, the Ahasuerus after whom *his* father was named. He is a pantheistic hermit and a wandering philosopher, a Zoroastrian—whatever is a mythic embodiment of the forces of nature.

The book, moreover, is filled with a tender, magical regard for detail that most writers would envy. Everything glistens under the "golden dust of time." The diction takes pleasure in its own versatility; we read about a dog and "these trembling paws that open and close like a thorny blossom." At points the style swells and resonates with the *vox humana* of a great organ. As the boy works his way through his small school Bible, he reexperiences all the epochs of man and imagines Noah's ark as "that great laboratory of life . . . sailing away, full of human and animal sperm, of specimens of all species classified and labeled with Latin inscriptions as in a pharmacy, with a fresh crop of onions and potatoes, with apples sorted in wooden crates as in a fruit market, with oranges and lemons that conceal within themselves a grain of light and eternity, with birds in cages that will soon enrich the air with the tiny seedlings of their chirping and will ennoble the wasted emptiness of the sky with their skillful flights." This, surely, is a passage that in its religious intensity surpasses anything in modern literature with the possible exception of some pages written by Bruno Schulz, whose fiction is the most evident model for *Garden, Ashes.*

F.W. Dupee once observed that in *Pale Fire* Nabokov made a "team" of the poet and novelist in himself. Similarly, Kiš in *Garden, Ashes* captures in prose all the poetry of wish-fulfillment. He wishes his father had been a free agent who had chosen his destiny rather than passively suffered his fate. The mythic mode itself aspires toward a world in which character defines action, in which deeds are decisive and in which everything can be read as a portent or as a consequence (the mythology of causation). Even when the actions themselves are gloomy (the boy's fears, the father's death), the overall *stimmung* enjoys the freedom of a dream, since here intentions produce results and the only tragedies are self-inflicted.

Myths move from the specific to the general. In a classical Greek myth the fable ends in the explanation of the origin of plants (the reed, the narcissus) or of a phenomenon (the echo) or of various customs or rites. In each case a metamorphosis transforms the individual into a whole species. This proliferation in *Garden, Ashes* is comforting, since it makes private suffering into universal pain.

Hourglass is an entirely different enterprise. . . . Nothing, in fact, could be a better demonstration than a comparison of the two books of the power of presentation to change subject matter—of physiology to modify anatomy. The fable, the setting, and even many of the incidents remain the same, but the spirit of *Hourglass* is as dry and accurate and pitiless as a legal investigation. The experimental technique that *Hourglass* invents is realism.

The title itself refers partly to the sense of time running out and partly to that familiar perceptual trick in which the figure-ground relationship reverses, first to produce a white hourglass against a black background, then to resolve into identical black profiles facing one another across a white background.

Who are the facing twins? Psychologically they are the son who writes the trilogy and the father who is the principal character, two interchangeable faces contemplating one another across a void of time (that white "noise of time" Kiš so often mentions. (pp. 366-71)

Esthetically the facing profiles represent the principle of symmetry that governs this elegantly structured book. In particular, the symmetry is one of a miniature but repeating figure *"en abîme."* (pp. 371-72)

Equally well-ordered are the divisions of the book into repeating units of several sorts: "travel pictures," which recount actions objectively observed in the third person; "instruction," a series of questions and answers in which someone is reporting on Edouard Sam; "hearing of the witness," questions and answers in which the responses are given by Edouard Sam; and "notes from a madman," which are selected jottings from Sam's own notebooks. Finally, the book ends with a letter from Edouard to his sister Olga, a long reproachful document written after that disagreeable Easter of 1942. This letter is also the table of contents, in the sense that everything that precedes it, the bulk of the book, is nothing but Danilo Kiš's imagined recreation of the circumstances that led up to that letter (the letter is a real document).

What is important to notice is that every word in *Hourglass* is something that has been *written* by someone or other. In *Garden, Ashes* the narrator speaks as a voice through a cloud from the timeless, placeless vantage of memory. This unspecified situation of the narrator is a common but always potent mystification that contributes to the illusion of narrative freedom. In *Hourglass,* by contrast, the text is a series of discontinuous documents. Why they are cited and by whom is at first no easier to determine than what they refer to, but at least the factuality, the written, impartial nature of these documents, is incontrovertible, and they are all written by people (Fascist interrogators or Sam himself) whom we can easily locate in a time and place virtually coterminous with the actions they describe. Indeed, the rhetorical device of the document, the miniaturization *en abîme,* the compression of narrative time, the tone of cold objectivity—these are all *nouveau roman* strategies Kiš has adopted as one might take up any device of advanced fiction.

Incidentally, as one reads on one begins to structure a hypothesis that the behind-the-scenes narrator of the entire novel may be the son of Edouard Sam, a boy who has now become an adult and is reading his father's letter. While Edouard's son muses over the letter during the course of one long night, he rehearses imaginatively the scenes the letter conjures up. At first such fictions are vague, jumbled, inexpert, but as dawn approaches the occasions become sharper, clearer. This transition from partial vision to fearful clarity is the same trajectory the entire trilogy describes.

Victor Schlovsky once observed that the character of Don Quixote, far from having inspired the book Cervantes wrote,

is in fact almost a technical afterthought, a solution to the purely formal problems of juxtaposing literary genres. This argument used to strike me as more fanciful and suggestive than true, but my skepticism was due to a lack of counterexample. What other character could Cervantes (or Pierre Menard) have invented?

Now I take the theory more seriously, since Kiš has provided an answer to the question. Whereas the father in *Garden, Ashes* must be a demigod—elemental, free, eccentric (he *must* be eccentric in order to explain how a free being can become a victim), the father in *Hourglass* is quite simply the victim, a more or less ordinary man crushed by tyranny. A demigod is consonant with a mythic novel, a victim with an objective novel composed largely of documents.

But to consider *Hourglass* as a mere piece of virtuoso writing would be impertinent, absurd. Ravishing and ingratiating as *Garden, Ashes* is, *Hourglass* is a greater work of art because it is truer. Whereas the Freudian notion of wish-fulfillment might explain our heady pleasure in *Garden, Ashes,* our more sober but lasting satisfaction in *Hourglass* derives from a set of feelings Freud explained with the later theory of the repetition complex: we recreate traumas in all their painful detail—through art, dreams, or play—in order to feel a retrospective mastery over events that originally crushed us. A Yugoslav Jew forced to wear a yellow star and to perform chain-gang labor (though he is past fifty and in bad health) is not a deity but a victim. He does not choose the role of victim; other people have imposed it on him.

Readers are wily in ducking out from encounters with pain. Holocaust literature (embracing Holocaust documents, films, television programs) is by now, alas, so familiar that the reader or viewer has become expert in substituting solemnity for suffering. To give this ax a new cutting edge, it must be ground on a new stone. Kiš has found the artistically (and politically) potent approach—that of the oppressor. For page after page an interrogator asks precise, exhaustive questions about the subject's slightest activities and affiliations. When the subject faints from weariness, he is forced to go on. (pp. 372-74)

In *Garden, Ashes* the father is given to Lear-like rages against his relatives. These rages now have become the victim's effort to find someone, something he can oppose, combat, force to submit to his will, if even for a second. His love of litigation is no longer Jovian ire but rather a half-mad, wholly human vaccine against the legal processes about to destroy him.

The mythic style of *Garden, Ashes* suppresses the specificity of locale and time in order to emphasize the universal applicability of the tale. The only details that are lingered over are those luminous with fond memory, Proustian keys to recollection. In *Hourglass,* however, we learn everything, absolutely everything, and in the most painful specificity. (p. 375)

In this discussion I've touched on only one aspect of this complex novel, which embraces so many other themes and techniques, a whole panoply of feelings (sensuality, familial *schadenfreude,* love, and primarily fear) and literary devices (including gargantuan inventories, as when the effects of drink are listed, and dazzling syncopes, as when the sound of a moving train is imitated in a passage about travel). All that I've wanted to underscore here, however, is the way in which the movement in the trilogy from sketch to myth to document parallels an intensification in authorial vision and reader response. No wonder *Hourglass* is the most convincing account we have of the Jewish experience in World War II. (p. 376)

Edmund White, "Danilo Kiš: The Obligations of Form," in Southwest Review, Vol. 71, No. 3, Summer, 1986, pp. 363-77.

JOHN J. LAKICH

All the stories [in *Encyclopédie des morts*] are well written and contain elements of the fantastic and the imaginary, of irony and erudition. Several stories have as a point of departure Gnostic, literary, and other writings.

As is the case with many collections, the literary value of the stories in *Encyclopédie* is uneven. The most original and striking are the first three, all of which deal, on various levels, with the theme of revolt. In **"Simon le Mage"** we meet with the metaphysical revolt: man against gods and his human condition, and his perseverance. **"Honneurs funèbres"** presents a spontaneous but vague revolt of the have-nots—longshoremen and sailors—not against higher classes but against those classes' customs and values. Through it, the have-nots show their ability to outdo the bourgeoisie in one of the latter's old customs: burial with honors. The person honored, a prostitute, is barely remembered: she serves as a speck around which the accumulated bitterness is crystallized. **"L'encyclopédie des morts,"** a subtle and superbly written story with an element of the mysterious, is in appearance the biography of an ordinary man who dies from cancer. However, he unconsciously transforms the root of his illness into art forms.

The other stories do not match the skill and inventiveness demonstrated by the first three. Style and the narrative approach are repetitive to the point of revealing a formula for writing. . . . Still, taken as a whole, the collection merits attention.

John J. Lakich, in a review of "Encyclopédie des morts," in World Literature Today, Vol. 60, No. 3, Summer, 1986, p. 491.

BRANKO GORJUP

Throughout his writing career, Kiš has questioned the role of the muse as the source of inspiration. He has rejected the concept that invention determines the level of originality, and his fiction has inclined towards the documentary method of writing. Rooted in cool intelligence and drawn towards objectivity, the writer of documentary fiction delights in arranging all of the "borrowed" fragments—regardless of whether they are documents, *quasi* documents, or imaginative literature treated as documents—into an integrated and uniquely personal mode of expression. Kiš's work, especially *A Tomb for Boris Davidovich* and *Enciklopedija mrtvih (The Encyclopedia of the Dead)*, has been described as "documentary" fiction, or "faction," a term that Kiš has himself used when referring to the prose he has produced in the past decade. (p. 387)

In his early work, Kiš employed a number of features of realism. His stories were dominated by either a central consciousness or the subject's psyche whose role was to mediate between the author and the reader. Whether the story assumed the third-person point of view of an outside narrator or that of the first person, told by one of the characters from within the story, the function of either source of narrative was ultimately identified with that of a screen upon which the author projected both his vision of the world and his perception of reality.

Central to this type of narrative technique are the created psychological portraits of the characters involved in the internal cosmology of the work but who, in effect, reflect the external world of the writer's memories, dreams, and nightmares, or his experiences of the time and space in which he lives. In such a relationship between author and reader, it is expected that the reader should rely almost entirely on the narrator's system of values, or on his ego, as a sufficient guarantor of truth. When, for example, one reads *Garden, Ashes,* it appears as if the narrator is asking the reader: "Have you experienced this? If not, I will tell you all about it." The reader is then presented with the story of a man who revisits the place of his childhood and early adolescence in search of his father, a protean figure who escapes definition.

In the quest for the father, Kiš investigated the narrator's inner life, the destinies of Eduard Scham, the protagonist of **"The Family Cycle,"** and of his family on the eve of the Second World War. Through the narrator's memory, Kiš reconstructed Scham's bizarre life and his mysterious disappearance, both faciliated by his formidable learning, his challenging non-conformism, and his Jewishness. *Garden, Ashes* was Kiš's reconstruction of the world he knows best, a world of his childhood and adolescence which he wished the reader to perceive as believable.

In a published interview, Kiš pointed out that in his early work he left it "up to the reader to believe" his words. His intention was to "try to deceive the reader" through the manipulation of the language so as to convey "doubts" and "trepidations" associated with a child's growing pains and early sorrows. The success of this "deception" depended upon the effect of "recognition" on the part of the reader. The magic use of words, the reliance on "Valery's *charmes,*" according to Kiš, were the only literary means "to win over" the reader in order to convince him that what he is reading is not "a mere invention of an idle person, but rather a specific truth and experience."

The notion of "deception" through the use of language to enchant the reader into accepting the illusion of a created reality as reality places Kiš outside the mainstream realists who sought to reproduce reality as closely as possible. In order to render the subject's world real, they, unlike Kiš, relied on an accurate and detailed transcription of that world. With *Peščanik (The Hourglass)*, however, the last novel from "The Family Cycle," Kiš's method of convincing or "deceiving" the reader about the "truthfulness" of the written text began a process of transformation. The illusion of reality previously conjured up by the magic power of words was replaced in *The Hourglass* by a reality created on the basis of "documents," letters, diaries, and citations from official registers. Although most of these "documents" were apocryphal, they were intended to instil a sense of authority and authenticity into the text. In addition, a more detached and objective third-person voice replaced the intimate, confessional, first-person one, thus further minimizing the subjective quality of the novel.

With the publication of *The Hourglass,* Kiš exploded conventional narrative technique, such as the chronological unfolding of plot through time, and left in its place a loose structure composed of fragments. Dispersed through the novel but held together by four headings—"Scenes from a Journey," "Notes of a Madman," "The Method of Inquiry," and "Questioning of a Witness"—these fragments presented four different stories "derived" from diverse sources. With such a multiple viewing, Kiš reduced the function of the narrator to the bare minimum and, in turn, reinforced an "objectified" presentation of Eduard Scham's character. While the participation of the narrator was reduced, that of the reader was increased because he was expected to fill in the empty spaces and make the necessary corrections.

The vast amount of "documentary" material that Kiš used to prop up Scham's character might appear incidental to Scham's existence, but as one critic has suggested, this material was necessary because it revealed Scham's essence. The importance that Kiš attributes to "insignificant" material, such as the biographical fragments that ordinary people usually leave to the oblivion of time, is best illustrated in a passage from "Scenes from a Journey":

> . . . perhaps this small fragment from the family history, this short chronicle, carries as much weight as those biographies which, when they appear after many years, or even millennia, become testimonies of their time—and here it is not important who their authors were—just as with the fragments from the manuscripts found in the Dead Sea or in numerous temples or on the walls of prisons.

This scene describes Scham's realization of the importance of his personal notes which contain a brief history of his family. Scham becomes aware of the importance of all written material, particularly of all the anonymous fragments of texts scattered around the world, out of which, for the most part, human history has been woven.

The use of fragments as a structural principle was also reflected on the level of metaphor. Scham's immensely complex personality, bursting out of four separate textual segments, suggested the protagonist's psychological disintegration. As the segments revealed, there were at least four different Schams with four separate personalities. Formed on the basis of apocryphal documentation, each unique Scham was determined by the author's technique of spotlighting one predominant feature in the protagonist's psychological make-up. This was accomplished through the selection and manipulation of the appropriate "documentation." The ultimate effect of putting together all the segments was not the creation of a fully developed character but rather of an unfinished portrait, suggesting the impossibility of completion as well as the many-sided nature of reality.

Although in *The Hourglass* Kiš entirely abandoned realism, his use of the documentary method was only tentative. The documentary material in this transitional work, for example, the letter at the end of the novel, the journal, the transcription of the police interrogation, and the various citations of fines, court summonses, and newspaper articles, was false. Kiš invented these "documents" for the purpose of objectifying the text by creating an "authentic" cold and neutral tone, devoid of dramatic intensity and psychological intent. With the publication of *A Tomb for Boris Davidovich,* Kiš expanded the scope of the documentary to include the actual literary and para-literary sources in the structure of the novel.

In *A Tomb for Boris Davidovich,* which consists of seven chapters united by the theme of "one common history," Kiš's fiction makes use of documentary material in two distinct ways. First, most of the plots in the work are derived or borrowed from already-existing sources of varied literary significance, some easily recognizable—for example, those extracted from Roy Medvedev and Karl Steiner—while others are more obscure. Second, Kiš employs the technique of textual transposition, whereby entire sections or series of fragments, often in their unaltered state, are taken from other texts and freely integrated into the fabric of his work.

In terms of poetic sensibility, Kiš, who once stated that the history of fiction can be divided into the pre- and post- Borghes periods, belongs to the latter, at least since the publication of *A Tomb for Boris Davidovich.* With Borghes, Kiš shares an attitude to fiction according to which the source of the material used for the new composition is not important in itself. Instead, what is essential is the manner in which the borrowed material is shaped. In this type of writing the structural fragments are not selected for their aesthetic or moral values, but rather for their power to evoke the works from which they were extracted. The ultimate success of the textual transposition is the ability of the new text to emanate fresh meaning that is independent of the sources from which the fragments have been taken.

Kiš's departure from Borghes is significant especially in view of his original application of the documentary method in *A Tomb for Boris Davidovich.* Unlike Borghes, Kiš formulates his plots from historically and politically relevant material. While Borghes's fiction heavily extends its references to life's extraordinary manifestations, involving metaphysical elements, that of Kiš gravitates towards more ordinary phenomena, defined by temporal references. As shown in *A Tomb for Boris Davidovich,* Kiš takes over from fiction those historical elements which, like Stalinism, are still remembered by contemporaries.

By treating the literature of others as documents and by consulting history for specific temporal references, Kiš's fiction, exemplified by *A Tomb for Boris Davidovich,* assumes the quality of truthfulness, credibility, and, above all, authenticity. The illusion of an accurate reality, convincing to the reader, is achieved through the author's intimate knowledge of the period in which his work is set. This knowledge, according to Kiš, this accurate understanding of the period's cultural sensibility, psychological and philosophical perceptions, and precise topography, may be gained from numerous literary and non-literary sources. By presenting a collective response to one of the period's unique features—for example, to Stalinism, at the time of Stalin—Kiš's use of "documents" imparted to *A Tomb for Boris Davidovich* the necessary tone of authoritative objectivity.

Derived from different sources, the stories presented by the seven chapters in *A Tomb for Boris Davidovich* are thematically in agreement; they reveal the irony of the tragic lives of those who fell victim to the very political system they had helped to create. As a counterpoint to the time of Stalin, Kiš moves one story into fourteenth-century southern France, at the time of intense Jewish pogroms, in order to indicate temporal and spatial analogies and emphasize the cyclical nature of history.

The tendency of the documentary method to present the subject objectively checks the author's temptation to diagnose the subject's character arbitrarily; it prevents him from turning the subject into his own projection. In his cool anatomizing of the diabolic nature of Stalinism in *A Tomb for Boris Davidovich,* Kiš refrained from pointing an accusing finger at a particular nation or race. Nor did he question the meaning or the validity of the ideal in which "sacrificed" revolutionaries fervently believed until the very end. Instead, as in the title story, based on the life of Boris Davidovich Lenski, Kiš portrayed the moral integrity and psychological endurance of an individual who, despite torture, refused to confess to the accusations fabricated against him by his former co-revolutionaries.

In *The Encyclopedia of the Dead,* . . . Kiš pursued the application of the documentary method; however, he reinforced its prosaic character to such an extent as to reveal the "crazy" patchwork of bizarre facts operating on the level of ordinary experience. The illusion of reality which in *A Tomb for Boris Davidovich* the documentary method so successfully objectified is in *The Encyclopedia of the Dead* inverted, echoing Kiš's dictum that "nothing is more fantastic than reality." The effect of the documentary in *The Encyclopedia of the Dead,* as one critic has noted, was to give ordinary reality the appearance of the fantastic. Another source of the fantastic within the framework of ordinary experience is created through Kiš's choice of characters. Since *A Tomb for Boris Davidovich,* his fiction has explored the crooked alleys and dark corners of reality experienced by individuals who belong, in most cases, to the margins of general history and have been lost in the anonymous grave of the vast multitudes of common people.

The title story "The Encyclopedia of the Dead" illustrates the process by which Kiš inverts a given reality. The prosaic, the outer framework of the story, reveals the fantastic, which it contains, when the narrator informs the reader that more than half the story already told is simply a dream of the main character. In the dream, part of the story of a female protagonist is described during a visit to unusual archives in which the lives of all dead people, except the famous, whose lives have been documented elsewhere, are preserved in every single detail. In an excerpt from the vast encyclopedia of the dead which, in fact, constitutes the core of the story, the life of the protagonist's father is disclosed. The tone of the passage is encyclopedic, detached, monotonous, yet meticulous. The narrative approach also follows the technique used by the encyclopedists, that of summarizing long sections from the life of a person and of reducing all events from that subject's life to the same level of significance. The documentary method, in this case, based on the apocryphal encyclopedia, imparts to the biography of the father the illusion of existential seriousness. As one critic has pointed out, Kiš's concept here is "that every human being has the right to a place in the eternity of the document."

Although the illusion of the documentary is shattered for a moment when the father's story is revealed as the dream of the protagonist, it is restored when the reader discovers that the description of the cause of the father's death, disclosed in the dream, coincides with the actual cause of death.

The distortion of ordinary reality through the injection of fantastic elements, such as mysticism, magic, and the occult, is explored further in other stories from *The Encyclopedia of the Dead.* Whether these elements derive from the Bible or from folk tales and legends, when incorporated into Kiš's writings, they reflect the "dignity of the document." Kiš's urge to explore all types of "reality" is fundamental to his notion of fiction. As indicated in this study, Kiš's fiction has evolved from a manner of writing in which the illusion of a created reality is achieved by more conventional means—the reliance on the magic power of words to instil credibility in a work of fiction—to a method that aspires to assure fictive authenticity through the application of documents—real, apocryphal, or fantastic. (pp. 388-94)

Branko Gorjup, "Danilo Kiš: From 'Enchantment' to 'Documentation'," in Canadian Slavonic Papers, Vol. XXIX, No. 4, December, 1987, pp. 387-94.

BRENDAN LEMON

The Encyclopedia of the Dead may not completely remedy the neglect . . . . [Kiš's work thus far has received]. . . . "The Story of the Master and the Disciple," about an intellectual engagement between a reputable scholar and his inquisitive student, and "The Mirror of the Unknown," about a young girl's crime-solving clairvoyance, return to Kiš's central setting: the vanishing world of Eastern European Jews. ""To Die for One's Country Is Glorious" describes the death throes of a condemned Hungarian nobleman, Esterházy, and traverses, in a manner reminiscent of [Robert] Musil and [Joseph Roth], the teetering fortunes of early modern Mitteleuropa. Like Zita, the last Hapsburg consort, who, since her husband Charles's death in 1922, has worn only black and who even today insists that her family hold court in her presence, Kis remembers the Empire.

Some of *Encyclopedia's* stories chart new directions. Kis can be as ecumenical of place as the dead Hamburg prostitute he commemorates in the volume's second entry, "Last Respects." . . . Through Kis's active fancy glide Samarian heretics ("Simon Magus"), Ephesian oneirists ("The Legend of the Sleepers") and a lovestruck Parisian correspondent of a great man ("Red Stamps With Lenin's Picture"). A Kis chronology can be postwar or imperial, biblical or contemporary, as precise as a stopwatch or as indeterminate as a dream.

The title story ["Encyclopedia of the Dead"], in fact, is a dream (in every way). A middle-aged Yugoslavian woman awakes in sweat from a nightmare, which she immediately records. In her reverie, she visits Sweden at the invitation of a theater institute. After a performance of Strindberg's *Ghost Sonata,* her official guide takes her to the Royal Library, the building housing a Borgesian compilation of biographical knowledge, the *Encyclopedia of the Dead.* It's a multivolume work that is both comprehensive and idiosyncratic. "What makes the *Encyclopedia* unique (apart from its being the only existing copy) is the way it depicts human relationships, encounters, landscapes—the multitude of details that make up a human life. . . . It records everything. Everything." It's a fact-checker's dream.

The *Encyclopedia's* entries are more than mere facts. Kis too readily suspects pure knowledge to settle for a dreary biographical catalogue of an undistinguished man, especially when he can throw in dark, discomfiting tidbits about the work's compilers. For the *Encyclopedia* is also more than a copious outpouring of information; it's the work of a religious organization whose program stresses an "egalitarian vision" of the dead, a vision inspired by biblical precept and intended to grant all God's creatures a place in eternity. In industry if not in theology, the project is more or less Mormon. Kis makes the connection to the Utah sect's vast, subterranean archive in his postscript, a guide to sources which should have been cut from a chapter to a few footnotes judiciously placed within the text. The postscript is a sorry surprise for readers accustomed to Kis's usually luminous conclusions. The document at the end of *Hourglass* (an actual letter written by Kis's father which Kis had lost and then found after the war) stitches together the patchy narrative pieces that came before it. Similarly, the moralistic coda to **"The Short Biography of A.A. Darmolatov"** (the last installment of *Boris Davidovich*) sharpens the story of the daft, elephantiasis-swollen poet preceding it: "To write one must have more than big balls."

Kis is full of such daring in **"The Book of Kings and Fools,"** *Encyclopedia's* longest section. Concocted as an essay about the anti-Semitic classic *Protocols of the Elders of Zion*, **"Kings"** became a story when Kis "realized that in the domain of research . . . [about the document] there was no further progress to be made." And so, as Borges would say, he omitted some details, added others. The fixes are few, however, aside from the document's name: Kis calls it "The Conspiracy." **"Kings and Fools"** cleaves to *Protocols'* familiars: The document is published in Russia early in this century as part of a work compiled by Sergei Nilus, a czarist functionary; translated and disseminated throughout Europe; and exposed as spurious in a 1921 London *Times* article by Philip Graves, who spots similarities between "The Conspiracy" and *A Dialogue in Hell Between Montesquieu and Machiavelli*, an 1864 satire written by the Frenchman Maurice Joly. Kis retains *The Protocols'* connection to the Russian secret police—the fictional link is Capt. Arkady Belogortsev. Belogortsev is an émigré holed up in Constantinople in 1921. Down on his luck, he sells his books; one of them is an edition of Joly's *Dialogue*. The buyer, "X," is indifferent to the library's contents, but by chance he picks up a sparsely stamped volume: the Joly. "X" notices the similarity between it and "The Conspiracy," and he tips off Graves.

That "X" ignores an entire library (of Tolstoy, Thackeray and Gogol, among others) and settles upon the *Dialogue* illustrates one of Kis's preferred themes: "Books in quantity are not dangerous; a single book is." Taken too literally, or sacralized, the single book hardens into dogma and is used to justify curbs on imaginative freedom. (pp. 313-14)

"The Book of Kings and Fools" does more than retouch the tale of *The Protocols*. It preserves a realistic account within a work of fantasy, like a clean bullet encased in flabby flesh. The account is nothing less than an abbreviated history of modern anti-Semitism. . . . [There] is little playing for pathos, no great hue and *Geschrei*—nothing to betray the fact that Kis's own father died at Auschwitz in 1944. Kis's use of documentary techniques and his heightened sense of mid-century historical reality recall the German writer and filmmaker Alexander Kluge, but Kis's affective abilities are nonpareil. He is a master of indirectly rendered emotion. And with each book his artistry becomes more restrained, more assured.

Yet as a purveyor of ideas Kis remains in conflict with himself. This may reflect his divergent personal history (his mother was Christian, and for safety's sake he was baptized in 1939), a naturally unsettled temperament or the situation he shares with all those, that is, who fancy themselves part ethically concerned rabbi, part pleasure-seeking dandy. Like other such centaurs (Leonardo Sciascia, Alberto Savinio), Kis never quite reconciles the two roles. And he doesn't want

to: He's too busy practicing the art of irresolution. An eloquent partisan of artistic freedom, he can stand on either side of a cultural divide, without seeming melancholy or neutral. . . .

The Encyclopedia of the Dead is the sediment of a lifetime of reading, of what Kis has remembered. The book's feats are Funesian, which is appropriate: This is one of the finest fantastic collections since Borges's *Ficciones*. (p. 314)

Brendan Lemon, "Dead Heads," in The Nation, New York, Vol. 248, No. 9, March 6, 1989, pp. 313-14.

JOSEF ŠKVORECKÝ

[*The Encyclopedia of the Dead*] is a very beautiful *Necronomicon*, a book of dead names, of forgotten names now made unforgettable by an extraordinary writer. . . . It is no wonder. Kiš is a Jew who grew up in Yugoslavia, in one of the bloodiest parts of Europe during the killing years of Nazism; and that domain of death did not really end with the passing of the Nazi era, but continued, diminished, throughout the years of the "more equal among the equals," the decades of pompous cults and anonymous tragedies.

A shadow of death darkens this book, but it is a beautiful shadow and a luminescent darkness. Let me illustrate what I mean by a lengthy quotation from **"Simon Magus,"** the opening story, a fresh reworking of a traditional Gnostic legend:

> And now let me collect my strength and my thoughts and focus with everything I have on the horror of our earthly existence, on the imperfection of the world, on the myriad lives torn asunder, on the beasts that devour one another, on the snake that bites a stag as it grazes in the shade, on the wolves that slaughter sheep, on the mantises that consume their males, on the bees that die once they sting, on the mothers who labor to bring us into the world, on the blind kittens children toss into rivers, on the terror of the fish in the whale's entrails and the terror of the beaching whale, on the sadness of an elephant dying of old age, on the butterfly's fleeting joy, on the deceptive beauty of the flower, on the fleeting illusion of a lover's embrace, on the horror of spilt seed, on the impotence of the aging tiger, on the rotting of teeth in the mouth, on the myriad dead leaves lining the forest floor, on the fear of the fledgling when its mother pushes it out of the nest, on the infernal torture of the worm baking in the sun as if roasting in living fire, on the anguish of a lovers' parting, on the horror known by lepers, on the hideous metamorphoses of women's breasts, on wounds, on the pain of the blind . . .

The Encyclopedia of the Dead abounds in such passages. They can be labeled, surely, "lyrical prose," but that tells very little about their magic, and about the history of how this particular kind of prose came about in the raw and epic genre of fiction, which once relied almost exclusively on strong plots and often grotesquely mimetic characters. (p. 36)

But Danilo Kiš's crime, of which he was accused in his native Yugoslavia, was not lyricism, was not that he imported poetry into the robust genre to the point where, as Joseph Brodsky observed, the chapters of his first book, *A Tomb for Boris Davidovich,* could be "read and appreciated separately as individual poems." The crime of which Kiš was accused was, rather, plagiarism. . . .

Kiš certainly did not plagiarize. If we give his ferocious detractors the benefit of a doubt, and concede to them that they were moved by the uncontrollable anger that truth tends to arouse in those who, for dark reasons, are hysterically sensitive to it, then their criticism was based on a misunderstanding. There has never been a good writer who did not derive his inspiration from two sources, his life experience and the work of those who wrote before him. Naturals exploiting only what happened to them personally may be amusing, but they are extremely rare. And men of the library may be able to produce fictions that are, by all objective measurements, technically perfect, but they are stillborn imitations. Good fiction is always a marriage of *Dichtung* and *Wahrheit,* of poetry and truth; and the *Dichtung* may be someone else's, not only one's own. (p. 37)

Kiš once wrote that the history of fiction can be divided into pre-Borges and post-Borges. His novel under fire, ***A Tomb for Boris Davidovich,*** marks the beginning of his own post-Borges period, which has culminated in ***The Encyclopedia of the Dead.*** The earlier fictions of this amazing writer were more or less in the sophisticated, mimetic tradition of realism. There was magic, to be sure, that attempted to "deceive" the reader into a "recognition" of reality as Kiš had lived it, but the work remained traditional realism nevertheless. With ***Boris Davidovich,*** Kiš entered definitively into the poetics of "documentary fiction" or, as he sometimes calls it, "faction." Its object is still reality; but reality sifted not just through experience, but also through secondary sources that, because they already contain the vision of somebody else, are once or several times removed from raw reality, and therefore imbued by imagination. Kiš's subject, in other words, is the mystery of others as a scenic route by which to approach the spectacle of human life.

Borgesians such as Kiš (and Poe) use two kinds of secondary sources: genuine documents and apocrypha, facts and "invented" facts, without indicating to the reader which is which. Sometimes this is because, when basing their "faction" on real events of history—such as the story of the *Protocols of the Elders of Zion,* which Kiš uses in his breathtaking reconstruction titled **"The Book of Kings and Fools"** in ***The Encyclopedia of the Dead***—some crucial documents are simply missing, and so they make them up. At other times—and here the difference between fiction and "faction" escapes me—*all* the documents are fabricated, as in Kiš's delightful satire on literary overinterpretation, **"Red Stamps with Lenin's Picture."**

Among the several recurrent themes of Kiš's lovely text, perhaps the most prominent is the uniqueness, and therefore the equal importance, of every human being. The narrator of **"Last Respects"** has the following to say about a woman buried by sailors in a Hamburg cemetery: "She was unique, inimitable; she *was* a harbor whore." The uniqueness of the individual is a thought of which many would approve in theory. I have the impression, though, that it is held in bloody earnest, and most truly felt, only by those who are the surviving part of man-made holocausts, of the deadly experiments of modern social engineering.

The theme finds its most moving and politically eloquent expression in [**"The Encyclopedia of the Dead"**], where the female narrator on a visit to Sweden finds an incredible encyclopedia of all men and women who ever lived, from which only the "famous" are excluded:

> . . . this is what I consider the compilers' central message—nothing in the history of mankind is ever repeated, things that at first glance seem the same are scarcely even similar; each individual is a star unto himself, everything happens always and never, all things repeat themselves ad infinitum yet are unique. That is why the authors of the majestic monument to diversity that is *The Encyclopedia of the Dead* stress the particular; that is why every human being is sacred to them.

Let me conclude with another quotation. It condenses a great deal of this remarkable book: the reverence for ordinary men, the Serbian original's evocative close-up of common life, the quality of the translation:

> . . . names of teachers and friends, the boy's "finest years" against a backdrop of changing seasons, rain splashing off a happy face, swims in the river, a toboggan speeding down a snow-swept hill, trout fishing, and then—or, if possible, simultaneously—soldiers returning from the battlefields of Europe, a canteen in the boy's hands, a shattered gas mask abandoned on an embankment. And names, life stories. The widower Marki meeting his future wife Sofija Rebrača, a native of Komogovina, the wedding celebration, the toasts, the village horse race, pennants and ribbons flapping, the exchange-of-rings ceremony, singing and kolo-dancing outside the church doors, the boy dressed up in a white shirt, a sprig of rosemary in his lapel.

This book brimming with death is brimming with life. (pp. 37-8)

Josef Škvorecky, "Light in Darkness," in The New Republic, *Vol. 200, No. 15, April 10, 1989, pp. 36-8.*

ANGELA CARTER

The scrupulously intelligent and thought-provoking stories in ***The Encyclopedia of the Dead*** are fiction, but also, in an important way, *about* fiction. Implicit in the book is the question that all fiction raises by its very existence: what is real and what is not—and *how can we tell the difference?* In a story called **"The Legend of the Sleepers,"** Danilo Kis, a Yugoslav writer living in Paris, puts it this way: "Oh, who can divide dream from reality, day from night, night from dawn, memory from illusion?"

The question is clearly rhetorical, and Mr. Kis's apparatus of postscript and notes gives shape, purpose and an edgy, more documentary dimension to his storytelling, Mr. Kis himself tells us that the stories are all about death—the one truly inescapable reality.. . . .

Truth is always stranger than fiction, because the human imagination is finite while the world is not, and Mr. Kis seems to be ambivalent about making things up from scratch.

Indeed, he almost seems to apologize for the story **"Red Stamps With Lenin's Picture,"** because it is "pure fiction," about a literary love affair. He quotes Nabokov sympathetically: "I never could understand what was the good of thinking up books or penning things that had not really happened in some way or other." Not for Mr. Kis art for art's sake, but for truth's sake, perhaps.

Everywhere in these stories the correspondence among what is real, what might be real, and the mediation of the written word between these conditions, reverberates on many levels. In the superb **"Book of Kings and Fools,"** Mr. Kis investigates the morality of the written word itself.

In this story, the central character is itself a book, titled "The Conspiracy, or The Roots of the Disintegration of European Society." We are told that the existence of the book was first hinted at as a rumor in an article in a St. Petersburg newspaper in 1906, the time of the Jewish pogroms. This rumor concerned a document "demonstrating the existence of a worldwide conspiracy against Christianity, the Tsar and the status quo."

No sooner is it rumored than the book appears, incorporated into a hysterical text by a fanatically mystic Orthodox priest.

"The Conspiracy," as the book is called, offers universal explanations, always popular. In Germany, it seeds the mind of "a then unknown (as yet unknown) amateur painter." It makes a deep impression on "an anonymous Georgian seminary student who was *yet to be heard from.*" Soon it finds it way into the delirious paranoia of human practice. It is the obscene triumph of the anti-book—a forged text designed to destroy.

Mr. Kis scrupulously instructs us as to the nature of the reality constructed by the book's most zealous readers—the reality of the death camps, a reality beyond the power of the human mind easily to imagine.

In his essential postscript, Mr. Kis tells us that his intention was "to summarize the true and fantastic—'unbelievably fantastic'—story of how *The Protocols of the Elders of Zion* came into existence." The story began as an essay, but in researching the obscure history of that anti-Semitic forgery whose construction is one of the greatest of all crimes against humanity, there came a point where Mr. Kis "started imagining the events as they *might have happened.*" Then he moved into fiction; the fable is no less powerful than fact.

Books don't really have lives of their own. They are only as important as the ideas inside them. The book, as we know it, took shape with the invention of the printing press in the 15th century; it was the tool of the dissemination of humanism but can, just as easily, spread the antithesis of humanism. "In point of fact," says Danilo Kis, "sacred books, and the canonized works of master thinkers, are like a snake's venom: they are a source of morality and iniquity, grace and transgression." He is wise, grave, clever and complex. His is a book on the side of the angels.

Angela Carter, *"Rumors Come Too Often True," in* The New York Times Book Review. *April 23, 1989, p. 14.*

MICHAEL HOFMANN

The nine stories that make up *The Encyclopedia of the Dead* are set at the juncture of violence, scholarship and the after-

life. The prevailing tone is one of dutiful, dependable academic narration, and even when the stories are told by a persona, there is a whiff of erudition and privileged access to them, as in the title story, [**"The Encyclopedia of the Dead"**] where the narrator "went to Sweden at the invitation of the Institute for Theatre Research", or in **"Red Stamps with Lenin's Picture"**, which is in the form of a letter addressed to a scholar by the lover of a dead poet. Somewhere in Kiš's scheme, the hallucination of death meets the hallucination of scholarship: the two deaths of Simon Magus are described ("according to another version . . ."); a daughter reads the book of her father's life in *The Encyclopedia of the Dead;* a mysterious premonition is accepted by "the celebrated Kardec, an undisputed authority on the subject and a man known to have allied himself with the powers of darkness". The scholarly is forever encountering and accommodating the inexplicable, the wicked and the batty.

Perhaps it all sounds wonderful, it probably does. But if it isn't, then it's because these stories are not so much chronicles of deaths foretold, as deaths twice-told—and that isn't referring only to poor Simon Magus. . . . There is a . . . staleness and coarseness about most of the stories, as cursory looks at their beginnings and endings—including trick-endings—will confirm. At one point Kiš describes his style as "an unlikely amalgam of encyclopaedic conciseness and biblical eloquence". His stories have bold outlines and—without being naturalistic—a good deal of background. Too often, though, the former are predictable, and the latter scratchy. In stories that have the form of parables, the detail is often both redundant and unconvincing. One simply doesn't believe schoolgirls who can't tell whether their new desks are an inch or two higher than their old ones or not, but who appreciate that "the bed was larger, the sheets starched, the eiderdown soft and warm". There is something inadequate and theoretical about these sketched-in backgrounds, and they do nothing to contradict one's impression that this is all *déjà lu.*

And so, in fact, it is. In a "Postscript", Kiš supplies nine pages of notes, in which he speaks of the "obvious ironic and parodic undercurrent" of the collection. To what end, he doesn't say. Even so, this "Postscript"—and surely this kind of thing is the *bête noire* of publishers of translated fiction—is the clearest and most dramatic part of the book. It shows the stories for mere screens to ward off the reader, while behind them the author is getting up to all kinds of interesting things with source and analogous material, with Stalin, Tito, Diderot, the SS and the Mormons. Aptly, this "Postscript" is printed in the same Poe-ishly horripilating italics as the dénouements of some of the stories: surely this is where their real drama resides. One should praise Kiš for his curiosity and his learning, but his stories themselves have few amenities.

Michael Hofmann, *"A Meeting of Hallucinations," in* The Times Literary Supplement, *No. 4500, June 30-July 6, 1989, p. 713.*

Peter Klappert

1942-

American poet.

Klappert experiments in a wide range of poetic styles and modes. The appearance of puns, lists, and unusual rhymic and metrical schemes, as well as innovative auditory and visual juxtapositions of words confirm Klappert's fascination with language. He has asserted: "Words are not simply a means: they are in themselves—in their heft, feel, plunge, resonance, shape, aerodynamics—part of the end." Klappert often works in a baroque, heavily allusive style, frequently characterized by dark humor and surreal imagery, but he also writes austere, elegiac verses that contrast effectively with his more stylistically complex work.

Klappert's first collection, *Lugging Vegetables to Nantucket,* received the Yale Series of Younger Poets Award in 1970 and was published the following year to glowing reviews. Stanley Kunitz, who judged the prize, wrote: "Peter Klappert is such a recklessly clever poet that one's first inclination is to mistrust his seriousness. His wit, his sophistication, his delight in wordplay are constituent elements of his craft." "The Babysitters," the volume's central piece, is a sequence of poems in the form of an internal monologue that satirizes pompous academics gathered at a literary cocktail party. Aborted, partially scratched out, unsent letters to Elsie, the speaker's former lover, appear intermittently in each section of the poem, illustrating the speaker's distractedness and giving the poem its interrupted, seemingly chaotic structure. Although several critics expressed doubts regarding the suitability of Klappert's juxtaposition of academic satire and emotional pathos, most were impressed by his verbal skill and adventurous formal experimentation. "Pieces of the One and a Half Legged Man," also in this collection, exemplifies Klappert's belief that isolation and entrapment are fundamental elements of the human condition. Offering a surreal vision of the modern ego as a "Jesus Christ Remnant" living in a zoo and cruelly tortured by visitors, this poem is considered one of the darkest in this collection. Poems in the title section of this volume were noted for their engaging simplicity and directness.

In his next collection, *Circular Stairs, Distress in the Mirrors* (1975), Klappert utilizes surreal imagery to envision the Jungian concept of the double, or the shadow self. Critics singled out "The Trapper," "Chapter 30," and "Lucifer Praying" as particularly evocative portrayals of this phenomenon. Also in the Jungian tradition, "The Prisoner," "Cerebral Cortex," and "The Lord's Chameleons" critique Western civilization's excessive emphasis on rationality.

Throughout the 1970s, Klappert worked on a series of poems inspired by Dr. Matthew O'Connor, a character in Djuna Barnes's acclaimed novel, *Nightwood* (1936), which is set in Paris between the World Wars. These pieces are collected in *The Idiot Princess of the Last Dynasty* (1984; two sections of which appeared in 1977 as *Non Sequitur O'Connor*), an extended series of monologues by Doc Dan Mahoney. An inebriated yet disquietingly perceptive commentator, Mahoney is an Irish ex-Catholic from San Francisco, a homosexual,

and an abortionist. As such he is a quintessential outcast and eccentric—the extreme of a character-type found throughout Klappert's work. Such poems as "The Babysitters" and "Pieces of the One and a Half Legged Man" from *Lugging Vegetables to Nantucket,* "Chapter 30" and "Lucifer Praying" from *Circular Stairs, Distress in the Mirrors,* and "Saint Daniel the Paranoiac," "Does Daniel Believe in Order?," and "The Subjects of Discontent" from *The Idiot Princess of the Last Dynasty* express concern for those alienated from society and demonstrate the ill-effects of enforced conformity. Mahoney's commentary begins with the political situation in Paris in late 1939 and expands to include pertinent moral issues, including collaboration and resistance, simultaneously providing a persuasive commentary on middle class ethics and priorities. *The Idiot Princess of the Last Dynasty,* in the words of J. P. White, "may well become as essential to the poetry of the last years of this century as Eliot's *Waste Land* was to the poetry written before World War II."

(See also *Contemporary Authors,* Vols. 33-36, rev. ed., and *Dictionary of Literary Biography,* Vol. 5.)

STANLEY KUNITZ

Peter Klappert is such a recklessly clever poet that one's first inclination is to mistrust his seriousness. His wit, his sophistication, his delight in word-play are constituent elements of his craft. Among some five hundred manuscripts submitted to the 1970 [Yale Series of Younger Poets] competition, *Lugging Vegetables to Nantucket* is the only one, to the best of my recollection, that made me laugh, and perhaps in a sorry world that is as good a reason as any for being partial to it. Who else could have rewarded me with the little joke of the lady anthropologist, otherwise known as the dean of menopause: "But I have lost touch with the Touchwas"? I do not mean to suggest that this is a light-hearted poet. If one fails to catch the joke, one might as well shudder.

The gift for nonsense is one of the signs of the poetic character. Some of Peter Klappert's simplest inventions have the auditory smack of a child's counting-rhyme:

> Up in my attic I've got a bazooka
> That used to belong to Joe Palooka.

When Klappert takes aim at the human comedy, his "bazooka" transforms itself into a more complicated instrument of social satire, as in **"The Babysitters,"** the central poem of [*Lugging Vegetables to Nantucket*]:

> When I wriggled my big toe in under
> Her dichotomous athletic ass, she took off
> Ostrogoth's shoe and stroked his sole.
> When I ran my right hand under her jersey
> And tweaked her left breast, she ran her left hand
> Up his leg as far as the crotch. Loyal
> Faithfully watched.

In its offhand polymorphous way the passage exemplifies Klappert's impertinent assurance as a writer—some might call it his "nerve"—and his cool, almost allegorical, vivacity. An examination of **"The Babysitters"** may help to reveal the disciplines he works with and certain of his characteristic poetic strategies. (pp. xi-xii)

The action occurs in the mind of the protagonist at a literary party, where the main preoccupation of the guests is with one-upmanship and sexual conquest. (The analogy, in a larger context, would be a concern for power and self-interest rather than for truth or beauty.) The different "voices" of the poem represent aspects of the speaker's personality. Sometimes he asserts his presence as a detached observer, sometimes as a resentful participant, sometimes as a self-pitying introspective sensitive plant; sometimes he lapses into free-association, and sometimes, as in his letters to Elsie, he attempts (generally without success) to be honest. The poem opens formally, with everything, it would seem, under reasonable control. As the situation gets out of hand, we experience a gradual process of disintegration, with both language and sentiment running down.

The seven sections of [**"The Babysitters"**], I am advised by the author, take their titles from "the Lasswell Formula," by which any communication is divided into seven elements: (1) who, (2) says what, (3) to whom, (4) under what circumstances, (5) by what means, (6) with what purpose, and (7) with what effect. The poem ends with the knowledge of the loss of Elsie and with an effort to live with that knowledge. Having failed to establish communication with others, the protagonist faces the necessity of reconciling himself to himself, of finding his place in the scheme of things.

Here as elsewhere one of the implications of Klappert's work, never directly stated, is that he must mediate between his sense of a poetic vocation and his other role as bemused guest at the festival of life, the higher nonsense of a dissolving universe. He must pass beyond the flippancy that permits him, or one of his voices, to say, "We are all caught up in a masquerade, / It's in moments like these that poets get made"; and he must search within himself for the grain of authentic feeling: "Elsie, I am so angry, and so lonely, and sorry about everything."

Another key work in the collection is the opening poem, **"Pieces of the One and a Half Legged Man,"** a nightmarish vision, as powerful as it is outrageous, of the mutilated self, "Jesus Christ Remnant," sitting in the center of the world's zoo, suffering obscene indignities at the hands of others, vainly appealing for succor to the malign authority of The Court of Divine Justice, before which he must plead "filthy or not filthy." (pp. xii-xiii)

"Pieces of the One and a Half Legged Man" is more than simply ironic or satiric. It is one of the cruelest poems I know, a cleverly brutal phantasmagoria, swarming with images of the grotesque and ugly, and creating out of them a kind of triumph, a bravura spectacle of human entrapment. If there is an easy way out, the speaker's naked voice at the last does not pretend to have found it:

> I can betray you
>
> with no resolution; this is the metropolis
> and you are in danger here, but where will you go?

Peter Klappert's speech is natural and colloquial, though steeped in his literary information and sometimes deliberately salted with echoes, as in the Eliotish rhythms of the first movement of **"The Babysitters."** The search for a form is part of his poetic process, and when it suits his purpose he lets the process show or simulates its effect—for instance, in the canceled portions of his letters to Elsie. On the other hand, his poems are full of prosodic secrets. **"Rowayton at 4 P.M."** is based on the principle of alternating nine- and seven-syllable lines. **"A Man I Knew"** is essentially syllabic, but it conceals an internal, irregularly spaced Petrarchan rhyme scheme (strong, guest, request, belong, wrong, invest, rest, long, fence, table, block, sense, fable, locks). He is so confident of his ear and of his technical virtuosity that he does not hesitate to ring repeated changes on a rhyme or to build a towering pyramid of redundancies. In the breakdown phase of **"The Babysitters"** he alternates between semidoggerel and gross invective, of which he proves himself a master. When the burden of his voice is elegiac, he is capable of a broad, deep-channeled music that reaches back in time to a great tradition. I quote from his moving lines **"In Memory of H. F.":**

> Summer upon summer the Sound
> fell upon the mouthing river,
> striped bass and bluefish wandered
> among the rocks, weed creatures scavenged
> in the breakwater wash. Broad summers
> we have known the land would shift;
> we could not catch the momentary trembles
> but saw, on morning walks, sand fill
> our footprints, and found new boulders
> in the sea below the bluff. We know
> of sea, that it breaks the whole world down,
> or builds it, in some other sea.

Peter Klappert has made an elegant and bold beginning. Few poets of his age—or you may multiply his age—can equal him in his command of craft. He has a wicked eye, a nimble mind, audacity, and zest. Nothing fools him long, even his own postures. As he has written, "*Camera* is a childhood game, almost as fun as *Doctor.*"

Despite his taste for extravagances, he has too much existential awareness and too highly developed a critical faculty ever to settle for an ornamental art. "Melville," he observes, "knew the cost / of falling off the portico / into a design of hanging vines."

For a young man he has already disburdened himself of much of the gear and baggage of his adolescence, those guilts and hangups that make so many poets hobble for a lifetime. He is strong enough to contemplate the ultimate absurdity of being alive, and free enough to keep on searching for ancestors and meanings. At twenty-nine Klappert has already made a brilliant voyage and caught a vision of those hills on the islands where "men are raising broccoli, grapes, bayberries, beach plums, and lighting their lamps with whale oil." I wish for him that he will continue lugging vegetables to Nantucket. (pp. xiii-xv)

> *Stanley Kunitz, in a foreword to* Lugging Vegetables to Nantucket, *by Peter Klappert, Yale University Press, 1971, pp. xi-xv.*

MARIE BORROFF

Two first volumes, Peter Klappert's *Lugging Vegetables to Nantucket* and Stephen Dobyns' *Concurring Beasts,* seem to reflect in contrasting ways the strains and disillusionments of recent years, one antic and flippant, the other tortured and obscure. Klappert . . . cavorts about on a kind of poetic jungle gym, demonstrating facility in many modes while committing himself to none. He is great at bad jokes and bad rhymes, and can pull off a neat exercise in malarkey:

> The seven-toed Dodo is not so extinct
> as you thinkd. It is commonly found
> floating on grey weather in uncertain
> backwaters, where it is, nevertheless,
> due to the origin of speciousness,
> survival of the fittedest,
> and its resemblance to a bruised
> and somewhat deflated beach-ball.

He conjures up a surrealistic nightmare ("I forced the pheasants' eyes until / they burst in the hot solarium. / What was left, later, was spaghetti / stuck in a pan"); he indulges himself in undergraduate humor (**"Instructions from the Dean of Menopause"**), then turns to and writes a solid pastoral (**"The Locust Trees"**) or a finely-tuned elegy (**"In Memory of H. F."**). He mixes modes, slices one poem into another, resorts to prose: in **"The Babysitters,"** successive versions of a love letter to "Elsie" (unfortunate name), crossed-out lines and all, appear from time to time during a Mad Hatter's literary cocktail party spiked with allusions to T. S. Eliot. In other poems the ghost of Stevens looms large, notably **"On a Beach in Southern Connecticut"**:

> Gradually the monotony of his rhythms
> overwhelmed him, like the repetition of small waves
> on a beach in southern Connecticut.
> This had been good, a good; but moderation
> in excess, even the moderate luxury

of a rocky coast, became, finally,
one lesson in the same, old discipline:
excess leading to wisdom, and what good is wisdom?

Again, the somewhat deflated beach-ball. Here, disillusionment of half-past four, following a prolonged exercise in abstraction, gives way to a catalogue of solid hors d'oeuvres,

> Gin and bitters: crackers, triscuit, sea biscuit:
> gouda, port salut, cheddar: braunschweiger:
> anchovies or smoked mussels: and then dinner.

But the abstract and the concrete do not really encounter and affect each other here, as in Stevens; the poet's heart does not seem to be in either of them. Klappert speaks in many voices, but gives us no sense of a presiding consciousness, with roots and real concerns. His book ends, symbolically perhaps, with the poet at sea, invoking another hopefully redemptive catalogue of concrete specifics:

> The crowded smoke lifts
>
> —LAND HO!
>
> On the hills of these islands
> men are raising broccoli, grapes, bayberries, beach plums,
> and lighting their lamps with whale oil.

One wishes him a happy landfall, and a staked-out claim on solid ground. (pp. 83-4)

> *Marie Borroff, in a review of, "Lugging Vegetables to Nantucket," in* The Yale Review, *Vol. LXII, No. 1, Autumn, 1972, pp. 83-4.*

JILL BAUMGAERTNER

The new poets are restless independents, difficult as a group to place into any particular school of poetry. Although these four poets share few common techniques and concerns, they do typify trends and tangents and seem together to define our age. Plath is a blooded confessionalist; Berryman, an elated lyricist; Merrill, a dramatic impressionist; and Klappert, an intellectual mind-whipper. (p. 16)

Of this quartet [Klappert's] poetic world is probably the most remote. One does not merely browse through *Lugging Vegetables to Nantucket;* one must consciously plunk himself into Klappert's settings and grip the characters and images until meaning and order are wrestled from them. One critic has said that it is enough to "experience" these poems; one need not understand them. That is the lazy way out. Get rid of the fireplace and wine and turn on some examining lights. What you will find here is strong stuff.

"The Babysitters" is a collection of seven poems which must be read together. The frenzy builds until the end of the fifth poem **"By What Means"** where in a spectacular, explosive, 140-word invective, the narrator releases a volley of metaphors which, in case of emergency, one is tempted to memorize for some very creative name-calling. "Elsie" seems to be the reason for it all and **"The Babysitters"** is a rough record of the narrator's attempt to free himself from her influence and to redefine himself apart from her. It is a wild, sometimes incomprehensible, thought-word-action process, but it does offer a challenge to any puzzle-lover not easily shocked.

Reading Peter Klappert is sometimes like witnessing the birth of a poem. Because much of his space is devoted to word-play, many of his poems *become* only in their last few lines. His use of puns, rhymes, and repetitions at times proves that cleverness is not necessarily genius, as in **"For the Poet Who Said Poets Are Struck By Lightning Only Two or Three Times."**

> . . . and the impression
> I get on occasions when
> I am struck by the sidewalk
> is something I will not talk
> about. How pedestrian
> can you get. (Though each upset
> makes me considerably more
> concrete than I was before.)

There may be a truth here, but one sees only cunningness. However, this love of words and what they can do to other words and ideas is what poetry is all about, and Peter Klappert can play very delightfully, as in **"Pieces of the One and a Half Legged Man,"** where in a surrealistic stream of poetry, one word sets it all off.

> . . . what kind of fantasy
> life is that remnant? *trinity divinity unity*
> *infinity yes*
> *yes, but cut 'em into bacon strips I'd say.*
>
> Catechism
> remnant repeat after me: this man is a
> state of mind
> this man is a state of mind (repeat after
> me after me)
> *Ears!* Catechism remnant repeat after Me:
> trinity is a delta
> in the stream of traffic, trinity is a play-
> ground for scholars,
> trinity is a pretty ring in the orchestrated
> chaos.

On the basis of **"Pieces . . .,"** a five part poem, one is tempted to conclude that if Listerine sells, so should Klappert. Its cruelty hurts ("They love / their Little Boy, and / he has been a Great Bargain to them"). It requires deliberate work to understand it; but its message is probably very good for you.

[The section] "Lugging Vegetables to Nantucket" is a varied collection of easier poems—self-contained, and, for the most part, tight, disciplined studies. These prove that Peter Klappert *can* be simple and direct and this approach produces some very effective poems. A few lines and images are especially striking, as in **"No Turtles"** where there are "no turtles blooming in the turtle trees" or **"The Invention of the Telephone"** or **"Iowa"** or **"The Drawer"** or **"Instructions from the Dean of Menopause."** **"Mail at Your New Address"** suggests in an original way the misunderstandings, mysteries, worries, fears, and cautions of a remote parent. . . .

Of these four poets, Berryman is the stethoscope through which a life beat is heard. Merrill provides the gentle, probing fingers, but both Klappert and Plath seem to touch nerves with a fine steel instrument. Together, the four reflect our health and illness. Maybe reading them will provide a cathartic cure. (p. 17)

> *Jill Baumgaertner, "Four Poets: Blood Type New,"*
> *in* The Cresset, *Vol. 36, No. 6, April, 1973, pp. 16-*
> *19.*

MATHEW WINSTON

I have known some of Peter Klappert's poems for a long time; it is good to meet them again in *Lugging Vegetables to Nantucket* and to find that poems which have become familiar continue to be fresh and vital. What pleases me most about this collection is not merely the finesse of the individual poems, but also their diversity, variety of tones and poetic forms, and multiplicity of perspectives.

The book begins with **"Pieces of the One and a Half Legged Man,"** a cruelly satiric indictment of modern man which still maintains sympathy for the pathetic remnant man has become. . . . The effect of the poem is threatening. Yet in the midst of images of the mechanical, the dismembered and the grotesque, one finds humor and the beauty of language played with in a meaningful way: "trinity is a delta / in the stream of traffic, trinity is a playground for scholars, / trinity is a pretty ring in the orchestrated chaos, trinity."

The long poem that follows, **"The Babysitters,"** is set at a literary cocktail party where there is much talk of poetry and much maneuvering for the gratification of assorted egos and libidos. The speaker participates, remembers, and, above all, observes and listens. . . . The party is seen from a satiric distance, but the normative assurance of satire is undercut by the speaker's distrust of his own detachment, by his suspicion that he may be only "the ethologist with small binoculars." Despite his apparent detachment, he is desperately trying to remember and write and rewrite "the only love poem I've ever written," a letter, in prose, to a former lover named Elsie. As fragments of party chatter intercept his thoughts, the speaker tries to cope with and by his own mixture of languages: narrative and scenic description, scientific analysis, outrageous punning, Chaucerian quotation, bawdified nursery rhymes and scabrous invective. Finally he is reduced to a simple statement of honest emotion, "Elsie, I am so angry, and so lonely, and sorry about everything."

In the poems that follow, Klappert often depicts the vulnerable individual responding to the force of love in all its forms—desire and friendship, hurt and bitterness, gratitude and compassion—and to its counterforce, the protective impulse of the man who "thinks he wants not to want / When he wants not to suffer."

> Gradually the monotony of his rhythms
> overwhelmed him, like the repetition of small
> waves
> on a beach in southern Connecticut.
> This had been good, a good; but moderation
> in excess, even the moderate luxury
> of a rocky coast, became, finally,
> one lesson in the same, old discipline:
> excess leading to wisdom, and what good is wis-
> dom?

At other times Klappert reveals himself as a very witty and funny poet, a man who titles a piece **"Instructions from the Dean of Menopause"** and who rhymes "quackery" with "daiquiri." He is particularly adept at turning his wickedly ironic pen to social interactions.

> She fingers a figurine. Then they ascend
> to another level and she returns
> a damaged child. Or he dies
>
> of immaturity and collapses
> into a pile of sleep.

He handles form with the same mastery he shows over language, concealing a Petrarchan sonnet within an unrhymed poem or writing a variant sestina to express a laconic New

England or Midwestern voice. Perhaps the excellence of his craft shows most clearly in the sound and image, thought and feeling of his elegy **"In Memory of H.F."**

> Summer upon summer the Sound
> fell upon the mouthing river,
> striped bass and bluefish wandered
> among the rocks, weed creatures scavenged
> in the breakwater wash. Broad summers
> we have known the land would shift;
> we could not catch the momentary trembles
> but saw, on morning walks, sand fill
> our footprints, and found new boulders
> in the sea below the bluff. We know
> of sea, that it breaks the whole world down,
> or builds it, in some other sea.

I think that these lines, alone, are worth the price of the book. (pp. 74-6)

> *Mathew Winston, in a review of "Lugging Vegetables to Nantucket," in* The Greenfield Review, *Vol. 3, No. 3, 1974, pp. 74-6.*

HALE CHATFIELD

Circular Stairs, Distress in the Mirrors gives us a good, full look at Peter Klappert's way of working. He is careful; he is not prolific; the poems are short and precise; there are only twenty of them. But all of that is to speak superficially of the poet and the poems—to say, merely, that Peter Klappert is one of those poets who work slowly and with great care, and are not given to barbaric yawping.

The poems are diverse, and that is the chief reason why this book shows Klappert so well: it shows him in a great variety of attitudes, moods, and modes. As was evident in *Lugging Vegetables to Nantucket,* one of those modes is Surrealism; but here it works even better, because the theme of the book (that of the double) gives the dream symbols a context—such as dream symbols naturally have in the dream itself: a *preoccupation,* if you will. Thus **"The Trapper"** is not just a strangely compelling poem hinting at an identity between cosmos and self, but a very specific near-nightmare about being the hunter of oneself, one's own prey.

The book is witty, with the kind of wit that truly hurts. That is a great deal more than being wry—more effective and undoubtedly more costly. **"Closing in New Haven"** is a poem that does not so much laugh through tears as it makes wisecracks while bleeding. It ends:

>   Critics
> have called the action
> "better than vaudeville" "almost melodrama"
> but claim the plot still lacks
> a denouement: for two and a half hours, no one
> gives birth, dies, falls in love, or is cured
>   of blindness.

What in love poems (because we tend to believe in the "I" or "we" of love poems readily and literally) seems brave attains a keen empathy in poems about the loves of other people. In **"Your Impending Divorce,"** the poet makes three attempts (in three stanzas) at making sense of tragedy in stoical, existential reminders about the nature of things—and abruptly gives it over in a truncated final stanza:

> He was not Theseus, you were not Ariadne, I am
>   not Catullus.

Another of Peter Klappert's gifts is his ability to sketch scenes which a weaker poet might be tempted to saturate with unnecessary color. Two such poems are **"Gun, White Castle"** (which is, stunningly, as black and white as the title suggests) and **"Boy Walking Back to Find His Father's Cattle"** (which is brown, green, and red: precisely the colors of war in Laos). The latter poem, because it has an action, a tendency to chronology, might have taken the shape of a ballad; we are grateful that it refuses to become anything so insistent, but is content to be shaped, spare, and restrained—thus assuring us that the poet trusts not only his own impulses and responses, but ours as well.

Still another virtue in Peter Klappert's poetry is its often impeccably accurate imagery, as in this pair of lines from **"Nora's Journal"**:

> When she begins to speak the words
> come one by one, like barnacles opening.

Finally, we are captured by the poignancy of poems like **"Lucifer Praying"** and made glad of any such captivity by such superb poems as **"Chapter 30,"** which I regard as the best poem in the book, probably because it is a compendium of the book's artistic virtues. (pp. 38-9)

> *Hale Chatfield, in a review of "Circular Stairs, Distress in the Mirrors," in* Hiram Poetry Review, *No. 22, Fall-Winter, 1977, pp. 38-9.*

GARY Q. ARPIN

Peter Klappert's first volume, *Lugging Vegetables to Nantucket,* published in 1971, was justly praised for its satiric bite and verbal facility. The language of the poems in that volume was often extraordinary, and Klappert's interest in language was clearly intense. "Words," he wrote a year after *Lugging Vegetables* appeared, "are not simply a means: they are in themselves—in their heft, feel, plunge, resonance, shape, aerodynamics—part of the end." With this respect for language goes a sensitivity to its abuse: words carelessly used or allowed to dwindle into conventional utterances can be harmful. Stale, insincere poetic language is not simply dull, it is dangerous, serving to alienate people from their experience and from each other. This is the point of much of the satire in *Lugging Vegetables*—it is central to **"Poem for L. C."** and **"The Babysitters,"** for example—although reviewers did not note it. In such poems, Klappert criticized a poetry removed from life and at the same time attempted to create "an unbroken language" which would not falsify our experiences and relationships. Much of what appeared to reviewers of that volume as self-indulgence was a healthy mistrust on Klappert's part of his own talent—a refusal to fall into a conventionalized Stevensian diction, and thereby a conventionalized Stevensian world-view, in the way that Robert Lowell, for example, fell into a conventionalized Tate-like diction in his early work.

A recurrent theme in *Lugging Vegetables,* related to this concern for language, is human estrangement. Figures are often trapped in themselves—estranged from each other, from the landscape and from God. Characters live alone, like **"A Man I Knew,"** who isolates himself both physically and intellectually, or they remain physically close but emotionally and spiritually separated, like the figures in **"The Babysitters."**

These concerns—the intense interest in language and the depiction of varieties of estrangement—are of great importance in Klappert's most recent work as well, much of which is even more impressive than the poems in *Lugging Vegetables.* In *Circular Stairs, Distress in the Mirrors*—a collection of short poems—and *Non Sequitur O'Connor*—parts of a long poem—Klappert manages a richness of language while maintaining a sincerity of tone and idea at some distance from the conventional. *Lugging Vegetables* marked Klappert's emergence as a promising young writer; these volumes make it clear that he is one of the most important poets working today.

In Klappert's work, to be fully human—aware of one's own potentialities for good and evil, capable of real relationships with other people and at home in one's environment—is an intensely difficult task. Klappert's characters, failing to achieve one or more of these qualities, become, like **"A Man I Knew,"** trapped in and alienated from themselves—as that marvelous phrase "distress in the mirrors" indicates. Imprisoned characters, incapable of communication or love, abound in *Circular Stairs.* The trap is often created, implicitly or explicitly, by an imbalance between the rational and irrational. In **"The Prisoner,"** for example, which is a dramatic monologue spoken by an unfinished marble sketch by Michaelangelo, the trapped figure is weighed down by thought:

> my feet will not move for all this
> thinking   The inert mass of it
> weighs on my shoulders   an unopened
> box or a pod
> heavy with morbid seed that drags
> the whole plant forward

In **"Cerebral Cortex"** (the rational, thinking part of the brain), an artist makes a model of his non-rational self, his "enemy," and becomes obsessed with this figure that he comes both to love and hate. The narrator is ultimately ruined as an artist—he chases the image of his alter ego through the streets, "pursuing his poses through the sonorous alleys," while his work suffers:

> Such work as I accomplish
> is interesting only at the margins.
> In the center is another
> broken monologue, words wasted upon
> something ideal and anonymous

(pp. 134-35)

One of the most impressive poems in *Circular Stairs* is **"Chapter 30,"** from which the title of the volume comes. **"Chapter 30"** is a three-stanza prose poem which answers, in elliptical fashion, the question stated in its first line: *"What took you so long?"* The answer is provided in part by surreal descriptions of wartime experiences:

> Explosions at dawn and at evening.
> Questions at headquarters, Mme. La Chaise and
>   the tea
> ritual. Circular stairs, distress in the mirrors, the
>   zeroes,
> the ampersands, tunnel vision.

Related to this violent landscape, and perhaps causing it, is a philosophical problem. The beginning and the end of the poem present a kind of capsule critique of the history of Western thought. After the initial question, the poem begins: "Sanity. Rational philosophy. Walking upright." The poem ends:

> But

finally, and really, the loss of a landscape, the loss of a motive, the night nurse, the graveyard shift. Rational. Philosophy.

This is a haunting, mysterious and frightening poem. The accompaniment of "Sanity" and "Rational Philosophy" is "the loss of a landscape," of a fitting relationship to our world. This estrangement from the landscape is evident in other poems as well. Lucifer, in **"Lucifer Praying,"** for example, perceives a world reminiscent in its richness of [Wallace] Stevens' "Sunday Morning," but it remains a world from which he is, by his nature, alienated: "Father / in Heaven we / are not happy here."

"The Lord's Chameleons" is a sestina on this theme, a formally brilliant poem which in its exotic setting and lush imagery again recalls Stevens, but which, unlike the work of Stevens, emphasizes the failure of the imagination in the face of an overwhelming natural vision. The chameleons, arguing from "an arc of color" about the nature of the true Chameleon they desire to imitate, suddenly have a vision of what godhead, "a three-horned sullen head in thunder color." When that lordly Rhinoceros Chameleon disappears (perhaps eaten by a snake), the chameleons are bereft and see "no color / now in the monotony of leaves." As a result,

> The poor chameleons, stuck in all these tongues,
> started to forget their splendid vision
> of themselves, grown mythical with color.
> And so their vision turned a darker color
> and their tongues grew tired of imitation
> and they were left to hug what was, and eat the air.

In other poems, the landscape is wrenched away from some figures. In **"Nora's Journal"** (a *Nightwood* poem written before Klappert decided to concentrate on the figure of Doctor O'Connor), when Robin deserts Nora for Jenny Petherbridge, "She takes the landscape with her when she leaves." Violence—on a large scale this time, in Laos—accomplishes a similar kind of estrangement in **"Boy Walking Back to Find His Father's Cattle."**

The sense of being "left"—left behind, deserted—and being forced to "hug what (is)," with only language to rely on, is also strong in *Non Sequitur O'Connor.* This volume consists of two sections from a long poem in progress, tentatively entitled *The Idiot Princess of the Last Dynasty: The Apocryphal Monologues of Doctor Matthew O'Connor.* O'Connor is the strange and haunting character from Djuna Barnes' *Nightwood,* and it is his voice and his image that give that novel much of its power. These two aspects of O'Connor—his voice and his image—are the reasons for Klappert's interest in him. The voice of O'Connor—earthy, vituperative, anguished, rich in metaphor—allows Klappert all the linguistic freedom he needs. Indeed, the voice of Klappert's O'Connor is just as powerful, as captivating and as convincing as the voice of Barnes' O'Connor. It is difficult to show this by quoting just a few lines, but take these for evidence. Describing an old woman ("Dead of a whimsical lung / poor toad") who used to wash in the holy water fonts of the church (as O'Connor himself did in the novel), O'Connor says:

> A drop of holy water to quench the brow,
> a scrub behind the ears, two splashes, one
> under each arm, and some people feel
> fresh as a fleur-de-lys. Well for all that
> and the laundry she hung out in confession,
> Madame Dumont-Dupont still smelled like one sock
> missed the hamper.

Talking to Jenny Petherbridge:

> Jenny,
> if you were a priest at the Elevation
> you could turn wine into good grape jelly.

Klappert pictures O'Connor in Paris between September 1939 and June 1940, several years after the period covered in *Nightwood,* literally "left" by the other characters. The novel, he says, was "Famous for the way it finished, everyone off, / but left some of us out in the world / to answer Dustbin's questions." ("Dustbin" seems to be a composite figure representing O'Connor's audience and world.) O'Connor is a spoiled priest of sorts, both confessing and hearing "the confessions in the Dustbin," absolving much (but not all), because "when you've heard the confessions a carcass makes / you can absolve a flatulent cheese." He recalls scenes from his earlier life as recounted in Barnes' novel—especially the long discussion with Nora (if "discussion" is the word for it) in "Watchman, What of the Night"—but he uses these occasions to explore a multitude of themes: metaphysics, violence, the hazards of love and the depths of human activity and thought which are associated with the night, "the aqueous solution / where, stalkers all, we shed vestigial skins / and act whom we most fear."

In two parts, **"Matthew in the Marshes (I)"** and **"Matthew in the Marshes (II),"** Klappert imagines O'Connor meeting, in 1939, Jenny Petherbridge, who is implicitly associated with the Germans—both simply moved in and took what they wanted, both seem avatars of the chaos to come, which O'Connor must, as long as he is able, withstand. Jenny he does not absolve. "Go to Hell," he tells her, "You can be forgiven for what you are / but what you are won't forgive itself."

It is difficult to describe the power of Klappert's extraordinary portrait of O'Connor in these sections of the poem. It is important to note, however, that Klappert is not writing pastiche here, nor is he engaging in a sophisticated exercise in literary criticism. Although he occasionally quotes Barnes, weaving bits of her material into his fabric, and although he comments frequently on the novel (indeed, *some* knowledge of the novel is necessary for an appreciation of the poem), Klappert is creating a parallel O'Connor, not an imitation one. Using O'Connor's tongue, his "*little* trowel," Klappert is doing his own digging. One precedent here is John Berryman's *Homage to Mistress Bradstreet,* in which Berryman creates as Anne Bradstreet out of her own words, historical fact and his imagination. It is of course difficult to make a judgement from just two parts of a long poem, but while reading **Non Sequitur O'Connor** I was reminded of Robert Fitzgerald's comments on *Mistress Bradstreet:* "He bided his time and made the poem of his generation." **The Idiot Princess of the Last Dynasty** may well turn out to be the poem of Klappert's generation. (pp. 136-39)

Gary Q. Arpin, "Loss of Landscape," in The Greenfield Review, *Vol. 7, Nos. 3 & 4, Spring-Summer, 1979, pp. 134-39.*

SVEN BIRKERTS

Poets write at length, in sequence and otherwise, for any number of reasons: to do justice to the scale of a subject (Pound's vision of history), to achieve expressive effects denied to the shorter lyric (Eliot's explorations of musical recurrence in *Four Quartets*), for larger cognitive reach (Olson's archeologies in *The Maximus Poems*), or to encompass material that is in itself sequential (Lowell's and Berryman's graphing of successive states of the psyche in time; Merrill's tracing of his Ouija board experiences). Doubtless they have other motivations, too, that derive from the particular demands of expression. But as I survey the pile of recently published book-length works before me—most of them by younger poets—I have to wonder whether there might not be other factors involved as well. In almost no case did the artistic ends warrant the length. Either the talent would not stretch to support the conception, or else the conception was a cobbled-together pretext for something else. So my reasoning went. And that something else? I confess that I thought first of the A-word and the E-word. If anything disfigures the natural life of poetry in our times it's Ambition and Egotism.

I don't believe that most of these young poets are writing large sequences because they have great themes, important cognitive designs, or zeal for new expression. No, more likely they are trying to declare their importance to the world in terms that the world understands. Marginal to the life of our culture, isolated from spheres of power, these poets cynically declare—*contra* Mies van der Rohe—that more is more. This is both understandable and excusable—psychologically. Unfortunately, even as permissive a mode as the sequence must argue its necessity. The reader will tolerate more slackness and discursiveness than he would in a shorter lyric, but he expects to be rewarded in some commensurately large way for his tolerance. I would like to examine in this light three sequences by highly-touted younger poets—Michael Blumenthal's *Laps,* Alfred Corn's *Notes from a Child of Paradise* (which is, strictly speaking, a narrative), and Peter Klappert's **The Idiot Princess of the Last Dynasty**. The hazards of foliation are evident in each; only **The Idiot Princess** could be said to surmount them. (p. 80)

Peter Klappert's **The Idiot Princess of the Last Dynasty** is the eccentric guest at this table. Indeed, it is so unlikely a work that it requires some preliminary explanation. In Klappert's own words:

> These are the imaginary monologues of "Doc' Dan Mahoney," speaking in Paris in 1939 and 1940. Daniel Mahoney has had at least three previous incarnations: as the vulgar and queeny title character in Robert McAlmon's story "Miss Knight," as "Dr. Matthew O'Connor (Family Physician to the Ryders)" in Djuna Barnes' first novel, *Ryder,* and as the more arch, flamboyant, and declaratory "Dr. Matthew-Mighty-grain-of-salt-Dante O'Connor" in Miss Barnes' celebrated *Nightwood.*

There are conflicting stories about the flesh-and-blood Mahoney, but from a composite of recollections emerges the image of a brilliant, dissolute homosexual-savant, a habitué of low-life Parisian dives during the period between World War I and the German occupation. The link between Klappert's Mahoney and Djuna Barnes's Dr. O'Connor will be obvious to anyone who has read *Nightwood.* Because of this—so the story goes—**The Idiot Princess** could not be published so long as Miss Barnes was alive; the fine points of the case are unknown to me. At any rate, Djuna Barnes has died, and Dan Mahoney's monologues are now out. They constitute the strangest poetic sequence in recent years.

The Idiot Princess is, at first—and second, and third—sight, a maniacal assemblage. The sections are linked insofar as they are all monologues spoken by Mahoney (in varying stages of intoxication), but there are few filaments of narrative; auditors and settings shift according to the principle of the kaleidoscope. What's more, the contents of Mahoney's mutterings and jeremiads are often personal, local, or have direct, unexplained reference to historical and political situations that few readers will know. (I prepared by reading *Nightwood* and Herbert Lottman's *The Left Bank,* a fascinating documentary history of the period in question, but a majority of these references escaped me nonetheless.) The monologues, writes Klappert in his preface, "assume an audience in a café which is familiar with French history and with political events between 1919 and 1940. . . . But even that audience would miss some of Mahoney's references. Such is his manner, such the angularity of his mind, the pace of his conversation."

Here is something taken quite at random from one of the early monologues:

> The King of the Belgians
> journeyed all the way to Paris
> to hear a man with an aspirating anus
> toot out airs. And Le Pétomane could snuff a dip
> at half a meter—not the last Pierrot
> to "pay no author's royalties."
>   Indeed, why *not*
> a few lies of Paradise?
> *Because these are the only lies that are never believed.*
> Saint Artemius.
>   Saint Febronia! In Byzantium
> the battles are not fought in the arena,
> they are fought among the lookers-on.
>   This?
> I call this number
>   *Caught on the Teeth of Time,* or *Life
> Torn Full Circle.*
>   Ammonia.
>
> Spikenard, ginger, siphium—and pepper. And goodnight.

Many people will not know who, or what, Le Pétomane is, what "snuffing a dip" is—is it done differently at a meter's distance?—or identify Saints Artemius and Febronia. And why would the latter merit an exclamation?

Still, there is something thrilling about the very opacity of the passage—we heed the rhythmic glide, the witty way in which the sibillance of line 3 is cut (so to speak) by "toot," the sudden shift from near-absurdity to the frank declaration of the italicized line. Rabelais and Villon stand in the wings. I would argue, further, that the absence of clear sense unsheathes the sound-values—and that this is Klappert's intent. For the early sections are far more obscure in this way than the later ones. It's as if the poet wanted us to limber the tympana, to listen to the work first as a modern chamber piece and only later to grasp it as a lament.

We begin, then, by accepting certain terms: that the speaker is a drunk with an over-furnished mind and that not everything that he says will be clear to us; that what intelligibility there is will be more serial than sequential in its expressions; that words will be used as much for their sounds as for their designatory value. In exchange, we soon realize, we will be treated to a Stravinskian whirl of rhythm and tone. We are the more delighted when we start coming upon passages knit by sense. . . . (pp. 89-91)

Mahoney's monologues draw us in increasingly as we read. We get accustomed to his drunkard's transitions, the sudden jumps from trivial observation to impassioned apostrophe, as well as to his posturings; he is, by turns, sorrowful, catty, perverse, outraged, penitent. . . . We catch on, too, to the premise of the book—that this anomalous individual, drunk or no, feels in his soul the tremors from the future. He is very close at points to being the Old Testament Daniel that Klappert evokes in the later sections: he sees the outlines of catastrophe, not just in Hitler, but in the smug anti-Semitism of the French, in the faces of young fascist thugs roaming the streets of the city. He senses all about him the eroding of the will to resist; he can anticipate the double-dealer and the collaborationist. The squalor and wretchedness of the alleys and *boîtes* are for Mahoney the outward emblem of a morally bankrupt civilization. Once we grasp this, the sequential sense of the monologues comes to matter much less than the emotional import of his words. His outpourings come from every part of the soul's register: (pp. 91-2)

No quilt of snipped bits can give an accurate sense of the modulations of Mahoney's despair. The effects are cumulative and orchestral. Consonantal vituperations are set against vowel-heavy lamentations; vulgar argot bleeds together with unaffected tenderness. Mahoney is a French-speaking American Irishman, and Klappert has taken full advantage of the linguistic possibilities. James Joyce (*Finnegans Wake* was published in 1939) is never out of earshot.

[*The Idiot Princess of the Last Dynasty*] is, finally, a drunkard's fever-dream. Mahoney's ruined synapses fire as they will. He brings the glass to his lips to steady himself. Everything in the world connects; everything, therefore, is doomed. This drinker drinks because he cannot bear the world. He cannot bear the world because it is unbearable. *In vino veritas.* Klappert insists that Mahoney is as much a visionary as he is a toper. To his last section he appends an epigraph from the Old Testament *Book of Daniel:* "And he said, Go thy way, Daniel." Clearly it is in his prophetic capacity that he sees the coming of apocalypse.

For all of its strangeness—because of it!—*The Idiot Princess* succeeds. Klappert has taken on a most daring and difficult conceit in order to hurl new tonal possibilities our way. English-language poetry has been so dispirited in recent years, dividing its estate between the ever-more-aerated constructins of the formalists and the solipsistic exhalations of the free-verse opposition. Klappert has vaulted right over the controversy—his eccentricity renders the terms of the debate irrelevant to his book. I expect that *The Idiot Princess* will have a liberating effect on younger poets. It points the way back to an adventurous use of sound and proves that there *are* new possibilities of arrangement. The opacities may be troublesome, but they may also, as I suggested, open the way to a purer hearing. Not the least of Klappert's accomplishments is to have stripped some of the soil away from the rich Gallic seam of our language. If the poet's job is to invigorate the speech of the tribe, then here is a poet who is earning his keep. (p. 94)

Sven Birkerts, "Three Times before Drowning: Modern Sequences," in Parnassus: Poetry in Review, Vol. 12, No. 1, 1984, pp. 78-94.

J. D. McCLATCHY

It is easier to milk a bat than to predict what may attract a poet. Some inexplicable blend of temperament, style, compulsion and accident will lead one to Eden, another to a gnarled apple tree in the backyard, a third to his pocket calculator. "We all have to choose," T. S. Eliot reminded us, "whatever subject-matter allows us the most powerful and most secret release; and that is a personal affair."

It has been Peter Klappert's affair—or, since it has persisted for over a decade, his obsession—to concoct dramatic monologues in the voice of Dr. Matthew-Mighty-grain-of-salt-Dante-O'Connor, the central character of Djuna Barnes's 1936 novel, *Nightwood*. They have been turning up for years in magazines. He has now brought these poems together in [*The Idiot Princess of the Last Dynasty*]—a single long poem, in fact, given its shape and momentum and force by the voice of its speaker, who purportedly sits in a Paris cafe, cadging drinks and dispensing stories to the clientele during the "phony war" of 1939-40. This is the character who talked, Eliot said, "to drown the still small wailing and whining of humanity, to make more supportable its shame and less ignoble its misery."

Mr. Klappert has changed his character's name, as if in some dressing room between appearances first in the magazines and now in this book. Now—or I should say, again—he is called Dr. Daniel Mahoney, the actual figure on whom Barnes based her "valuable liar," whose fabrications were "the framework of a forgotten but imposing plan; some condition of life of which he was the sole surviving retainer." Mahoney-O'Connor is the quintessential outsider: a resident alien, a lapsed believer, an unlicensed doctor, a homosexual, a drunk, a wit and a truth-teller. He has survived because he has been excluded, and because excluded, saved:

> Better the ceremony of self-wastage
> and a maniac conversation, than going to bed
> night after night crushing garlic
> between your teeth—or shoving your hulk
> through the mist of your own mildew on the dawn.
> Better, he says, a curable case of guilt
> than these recurring palpitations of regret
> —and that other smell, "the oiled breath
> of spiritual paraffin," the lifelong
> petit point of one who's posing always at the mirror
> for a portrait by Madame Tussaud.

We are asked to read the poem as a history of the rise and fall of the Third Republic. It is too narrow and askew for that, but there is a good deal of history in it. The poem is a feat of research and pastiche. Mahoney vividly remembers the trenches ("the gluey pits") of World War I, the general strike of 1934, the resistible rise of Hitler and of the far-right in France (Charles Maurras, Pierre Drieu de la Rochelle, and the like). While others collaborate or flee, Mahoney stays and watches his city:

> Now we've taken
> the colored light from Sainte-Chapelle,
> removed the gentle anomalies from the zoos, gassed
> all snakes, shot the brown bears and leopards.
> We have drafted inedible horses, branded
> others for slaughter, identified and numbered the aliens,
> photographed Julien-le-Pauvre
> for posterity, encased Napoleon's arc
> in wooden boxes, packed-up
> all the unnecessary paintings in the Louvre
> and polished the bones of vanished aristocrats.

There are some telling swipes at the French character—at its anti-Semitism, for instance:

> the honor, you mean, of lexicographers, who joined
> almost as a body
> The Philosophes of the Fatherland, quipping,
>   "Dreyfus,
> the only innocent Jew" and
> "I'm not an anti-Semite but
> I would not object to your becoming one."

And there is a gamy digest of low-life characters and lingo and gags from the Paris of the 1930's. There are facts, yes—facts of newsreel history and facts of language—but they are not marshalled. Perhaps they could not have been, put into the mouth of such a character. Mahoney in his cups, and Mr. Klappert at his typewriter, are given to the same garrulous self-indulgence. Whole sections could have been shuffled or deleted without loss. But something more nagged my reading of this book. There was a festering grandeur to Miss Barnes's O'Connor, for whom life was "the permission to know death." His eloquent depravity was "time easing itself of endurance." But Mr. Klappert too often settles, literally, for the one-liner, and has written what he calls, in a Joycean pun, a "roaratorio." He has taken the Tiresias from *Nightwood* and made him merely into the Bearded Lady.

But I am sure there are readers who will be as enthralled by the voice of Mahoney as Mr. Klappert has been, and who will love the poem beyond the point where criticism can make a difference. There is much to admire here—amplitude, virtuosity, the funny and wrenching bits, the portrait of a witness and survivor. But there is a great deal of blarney besides, and a lack of purpose in the last quarter. The book is unlikely to win a large audience, but it may deserve a cult. That is to say, instead of being a masterpiece, [*The Idiot Princess Of the Last Dynasty*] is a formidable curiosity. (pp. 54, 56)

> *J. D. McClatchy, "Cafe Chat and Body Language,"*
> *in* The New York Times Book Review, *December*
> *2, 1984, pp. 54, 56.*

SARAH WHITE

In *The Idiot Princess of the Last Dynasty,* Peter Klappert evokes Daniel Mahoney, Irish-American expatriate, abortionist, and raconteur, a figure in Paris Left Bank life from World War I until the German occupation. As Klappert explains in a note, the "Doctor" has inspired several fictions, including Matthew O'Connor in Djuna Barnes's *Nightwood*. *The Idiot Princess*'s fiction is that someone "somehow" overheard and transcribed Mahoney's voice, conversing with itself and a small cast of walk-ons, in a bar during the winter preceding France's defeat. I'm not sure whether this is the longest dramatic monologue in the world, but I know it is extensive, intricate, and moving. Its mirror visions of self and other, language and life, poetry and history, raise innumerable questions. Like other intimacies, the relation between Persona Mahoney and Poet Klappert tends to resist logical explanation while inviting curious speculation. How *did* Klappert and Mahoney get together and work together to spawn an Idiot Princess?

Klappert, the 1971 Yale Younger Poet, was praised by Stanley Kunitz for having "disburdened himself of much of the gear and baggage of adolescence, those guilts and hangups that make so many poets hobble for a lifetime" [see excerpt above]. Kunitz admired the author of *Lugging Vegetables to Nantucket* for being "strong enough to contemplate the ultimate absurdity of existence." This is a tall order for a thoroughly schooled, tasteful, well-connected writer who'd shucked off so many adolescent symptoms. Indeed, Klappert-Poet, in *Circular Stairs, Distress in the Mirrors* (1975), and *52 Pick-Up* (1984), did seem to grow ever more tense, terse, and wittily hermetic in his expression. Klappert-Mahoney, by contrast, is expansive and garrulous, allowing himself limitless vulgarity. This is a persona loaded to the gills with "gear and baggage," "guilts and hangups": petulance, self-dislike, misogyny, drunkenness, exhibitionism, to name a few. Could it be that some of these loosen the tongue?

The backstairs butcher of women in trouble explains himself as: ". . . a good Catholic, too, / if a canceled ticket from the womb / is the conservation of innocence." Mahoney the butcher furnishes Klappert with occasions to indulge an old fascination with the psycho-sexuality of body parts, human and animal, dead and alive. In **"The Flower-Cart and the Butcher,"** a meat-market anecdote prompts Mahoney's lurid descriptions of carcasses hung on hooks. Then two old widows "stuffed into their coats / like flour in two patched sacks" call up bad memories: the 1871 Siege of Paris, when city-dwellers were reduced to killing pets and zoo animals for food, and the Great War, when so many humans were made into meat ("You remember your father / who ate spaniel under the siege, your husband / who was dismembered in '17"). Mahoney is sickened by the women, by most women, but turned on by their imagery and by the surrounding *boucherie* scenes. He spots, and lusts after, a boy meatpacker, who eludes him. The Doctor diverts his frustration by taunting the women with other sadistic tales of '71 atrocities, and by running off with a "flayed squirrel." . . . The mongrel Irish lilt and franglais, the confessions of a Catholic in spectacular lapse, the stifled pederast's itch, none of this would have attracted me to Mahoney the person; but in Mahoney the persona I find much lyricism as Klappert tracks him through a vale of tears. Studying and voicing the history of Mahoney's vale has been another source of creative zing to Klappert.

"The Last Dynasty" is an image of the "transvestite obstetrician's" times. He has experienced nearly the whole decline of the Third Republic, from "La Belle Epoque," which gave us the Dreyfus case and the Pétomane (or fart-singer), through the '30s, whose complacency and illusory prosperity groomed France for Defeat and Collaboration. "The Idiot Princess," I think, incarnates the briefer period during which Mahoney is said to perform these poems, a period of blindness, frenzy, and perverse glamour. The months from September 1939 to June 1940, the so-called Phony War, were borrowed time: the "Butcher of Bohemia" had struck in Poland and the Low Countries but not yet in France.

Given Klappert's interest in this historical moment, he couldn't have picked a better voice than Dan Mahoney's. Like his Biblical forebear, Daniel has a prophetic gift and sees horrors on the horizon: "O jerum! jerum! jerum! / O quae mutatio rerum! / How things will change!" Because this gift fills his head with awful visions, he needs another talent, drunkenness, to stave off paralysis and mute despair. "Il faut être toujours ivre!" said Baudelaire, and *he* didn't know the half of it!

Daniel's great talents as a *vox clamante* create the one problem of the Mahoney-Klappert collaboration. To me, an occasionally sober unbeliever, prophecies, swear words, and besotted confessions can fall to the ground in a clatter. Though at times I am hearing prodigious poetry, at times I am just being harangued, and I resist. But, rereading, I become more willing to hear Daniel out. I like his descriptions of the good stuff, things that are bound to be banned in a country like Pétain's defeated France: anything "close to the skin, / against the grain, under the rose, / secret, intimate, contrary, private, or free."

I like Mahoney when he speaks his loves as well as his disgusts. I like him when he dies, *listening,* for a change, to Harry his Heavenly Father, another good Catholic who takes His turn confessing to this Prodigal Son. I will not quote His words, and spoil the final poem for future readers. But, in it, Klappert-Poet disarms a load of indignant wrath in Klappert-Mahoney; then, even an unbeliever has an odd sense of redemption.

Sarah White, "Confessions of a Meat-Eater," in The Village Voice, *Vol. XXX, No. 4, January 22, 1985, p. 45.*

VERNON SHETLEY

The Idiot Princess of the Last Dynasty consists, Peter Klappert informs us in a prefatory note, of "the imaginary monologues of 'Doc' Dan Mahoney speaking in Paris in 1939 and 1940." . . . Klappert does not attempt, quite, to recreate Barnes's character; his Mahoney interests himself rather less in metaphysics and more in politics than Barnes's Dr. O'Connor, and his staccato prosody contrasts sharply with the broad rhythms of Barnes's prose. While Barnes's character tended to leave circumstances behind in his forays through the dark night of the soul, Klappert anchors his within his milieu, though that milieu is conceived on a grandiose scale as the twilight of Western civilization.

Most long poems of the twentieth century have been sequences, of more or less tenuous unity. *The Idiot Princess* is no exception, being very much an aggregation welded together only by the voice of its speaker. In this it bears more than a passing resemblance to Pound's *Cantos,* and like that work it presents (deluges?) the reader with rambling ruminations from a mind long on information and short on organization. . . . Like Pound, Klappert relishes the odd anecdotes and details in the margins of history, and it would take more erudition than is at my command to determine which of his stories are authentic, which apocryphal, and which mere *blague.* Klappert bars no holds in his attempt to make the sequence one continual crescendo or tour de force; but the danger of chaos always hovers over the endeavor, and Klappert lets it land on more than one occasion. That danger is compounded by his treatment of the units of the sequence. Few of the monologues round themselves off to whole, separate poems in their own right, yet the narrative and thematic continuities between them remain tenuous, and in the absence of any clear principle of organization, the *longeurs* natural in any work of this length become hard to take.

Klappert can summon considerable power, especially in those passages where Mahoney recalls his experience of trench warfare in the First World War:

> But in that convulsion,
> the noise of history manufactured
> regardless of expense, I was ecstatic
> to be lost among the rest. I never fought
> for myself (indeed, *I* never fought at all),
> but always for the inevitable

dead gassed and blinded—for the beautiful
Alsatian eyes in the recruiting posters.
Everything was part of me, one flank my arm
another my left leg, my eyes crawling
somewhere up ahead, my fingers digging in
my tongue commanding "On Brave Boys! On!"
even as my bowels bleat retreat.

But *The Idiot Princess* never delivers on its promise of containing or representing history. Klappert's notion of history seems to come down, in most cases, to a one-liner or a string of names. "Unreal City," one murmurs as Klappert reels off the following: "Barcelona Oslo Helsinki Addis Ababa Berchtesgaden." When he would evoke the age, he resorts to a list of period furniture: "Cubism, surreality, psychoanalysis, / short skirts, arrested flappers, *Ulysses* / and Gauguin's cane." Klappert deserves the highest praise for attempting to do something genuinely different from his peers; in that way *The Idiot Princess* is experimental in the best sense. Yet one finds beneath its deliberate obscurities and eccentricities at best only a new slant, rather than a new vision, on the world. It will more likely be remembered for the peculiarity of its premise and for a few brilliant passages than for its exploration of new imaginative terrain. (pp. 47-8)

Vernon Shetley, in a review of "The Idiot Princess of the Last Dynasty," in Poetry, *Vol. CXLVI, No. 1, April, 1985, pp. 47-8.*

EDMUND WHITE

The essence of modernism in poetry and painting is collage, or as Pound put it, "radical juxtaposition without copula." Collage is the principle by which Pound himself assorted his bright particulars, a phrase from Jefferson beside a character crucial to Confucian ethics. *Ulysses* is an extended collage, *The Wasteland* a compressed one, and even *The Sound and the Fury,* which confounds past and present, is a psychological collage.

In recent American poetry, modernist collage has been set aside in favor of other strategies. James Merrill's epic *The Changing Light at Sandover* is a masque in which each member of a large cast of characters speaks in distinctive tones. John Ashbery, deploying a quite different set of structures, has created a new and peculiar voice out of the demotic and hieratic registers of contemporary speech, an unstable compound held together by elaborate syntax. Merrill, in other words, separates out his various competing voices, whereas Ashbery fuses them all into a strange hybrid diction. The poems of each of these masters compose divergent voices, vocabularies, or structures, but they all eschew the abrupt disjunctions of collage.

Peter Klappert can be inserted into this discussion only at an odd angle. In *Lugging Vegetables to Nantucket,* his first book (published in the prestigious Yale Series of Younger Poets), he used a complex *mise en page* to orchestrate several voices in the long, stunning poem **"The Babysitters."** Typographically and on the level of diction, he distinguished several voices and wove them in and out with remarkable skill.

Now, in [*The Idiot Princess of the Last Dynasty*], he has chosen a single speaker and assigned him the memory of a replete but dying culture. The speaker is holding court in a Paris café from September 1939 to June 1940. His astonishing range of reference alludes to the Bible, the Dreyfus Affair, World War I, church history, Rilke, Versailles, German children's books, popular nostrums of the period, Byzantium, Nazi propaganda, and more. . . .

The speaker is Daniel Mahoney, a real, historic American Irishman from San Francisco who came to France during the Great War and stayed on, supporting himself as a shady doctor and amusing himself with Left Bank lowlife. He appeared in many of the memoirs of the period, but most fully and memorably as "Dr. Matthew-Mighty-grain-of-salt-Dante O'Connor" in Djuna Barnes's *Nightwood.* There he figures as a compassionate if disreputable seer, a great Blarney stone tapped for streams of eloquence, someone who attempts to comfort Nora for the loss of her lover Robin by discoursing on the nature of the night. . . .

The Idiot Princess is a poetic homage to a queer prose work, one of the few famous American novels written between the wars that provided an alternative to realism. Moreover, the original text was already close to poetry in its exactitude of language, in the sense that every word was *travaillé.* (p. 50)

Klappert's Mahoney revives the modernist collage technique but presses all the tesserae into a mosaic designed with great dramatic force and urgency. Mahoney is aware that the imminent Nazi invasion will level what is good in traditional French society as well as expose its hypocrisy, its inherent xenophobia and virulent anti-Semitism (which had already surfaced earlier in the Dreyfus Affair). Indeed, one section of the book, "La Belle Époque," deals with precisely this ultra-right-wing tradition in French politics.

Mahoney, however, is not just a political consciousness. He is also a homosexual, a bounder, a sub-Catholic, a mocker, a sentimentalist, a wit, and a sing-for-his-supper stand-up comedian. He can speak with the moving hurdy-gurdy naïveté of François Villon, as in the prayer **"Minimal Mahoney, in His Cups"** ("I am weary of the sun's loud voice, / which sears even the timid mosses / in their hermitage / and draws the color from old boards").

At times the pure, hard, elegiac diction of Pound can be overheard (". . . the air / standing silent on marble tables"). Best of all, perhaps, is the blarney. Like Yeats's Mrs. Mary Moore, Mahoney "puts a skin" on everything he says. Mahoney's "Nobody feels good these days. / It's the mortality that does it" could only be said with a Dublin accent, which is equally true of this invocation:

> Sweet Merciful
> Father of the cricket
> in the pond, of the field mouse warm in
>   the hinge of the snake
> and the thrush against the wind-screen. . . .

To die is to be "measured for wooden pyjamas." One short lyric ends with an injunction right out of *Malone:* "If innocent / beat until conscious." Safe sex is "a gooseberry lay," and a death in the trenches occurs "when all his two fine eyes exploded" (the poetry is all in the "all"). Equally Irish is the blasphemy: "Paul-Antoine / (who has the face of a Christ with the clap)." In the manner of Beckett, every jingle, no matter how Irish, can equally easily be expressed in French:

> "If 'ifs' and 'buts' were pots and pans
> There'd be no need for tinker's hands"
> *—avec des "si" et des "mais"*
> *on mettrait Paris dans une bouteille!*

Dr. Mahoney, "physician / in attendance on the night," is also a tearoom cruiser, a part-time drag *artiste,* and the humor of the eternal queen blazes forth with hellfire fulgurations in a set piece called **"Another Merry Widow."** Mahoney calls a rival queen "a pavement tragedy" who "had on a paralytic fit / (or was it a dirndl?) in two tints / that swore at each other. . . ." Dr. Mahoney (I almost wrote "Dr. Benway," for one old abortionist recalls the other) swears:

> "Lucy," I said,
> "you can go to la Place de la Bastille
> and hold up your head
>   by its hair
> and tell them *Justice is done!* "

A moment later this camp humor is derailed by a feathery touch of dread:

> and the unexpected pounces
> with both its knuckles brassed. . . .

Klappert has written a dirge for a dying era, and he has composed it in the very language of that culture. Among other things, *The Idiot Princess of the Last Dynasty* is a consummate piece of ventriloquism. Only Thomas Pynchon in *Gravity's Rainbow* has reproduced with the same authenticity the European slang, politics, popular entertainment, brand names, hopes, and anxieties of this World War II epoch. That Klappert was only three years old when the war ended merely serves to heighten the miraculous nature of his recuperation of this vanished world. Not only has his ambition been vast but his achievement has also been distinguished. *The Idiot Princess* is a final and original expression of the very modernism the war brought to an end. (pp. 50-1)

> Edmund White, "The Poet as Ventriloquist," in The New Republic, *Vol. 193, No. 18, October 28, 1985, pp. 50-1.*

NIGEL HINSHELWOOD

Klappert's challenging recent book, *The Idiot Princess of the Last Dynasty,* contains nearly 200 pages worth of dramatic monologue in which colloquial speech is mixed with literary information and general history pertaining to the years between the wars. And so Klappert's work creates a curious effect in which the reader, while feeling that he should know the history to "get" the poetry, can imagine that he is listening to an amiable bar patron, tight but not inebriated, allusive but not obscure, excitable but not incoherent, whose story is really quite graspable in all its essential details for those willing to stick with it and hear him out. Whereas in his earlier work this effect surfaces through a variety of approaches, in *The Idiot Princess of the Last Dynasty* it comes to the forefront as a central concern; his subject is history and the tensions between history lived and history spoken (as well as heard).

With so much poetry being written for the printed page, it is significant to note that Klappert's poetry must be read aloud to be fully appreciated, for the effect described above to begin to work its way into our understanding of his poetry. For this reason Klappert's 60 minute cassette tape, *Internal Foreigner,* is an important addition to Watershed Tapes' collection of contemporary poetry. It is impossible to read his poems and not wonder how they should be spoken, and how, in particular, he would speak them. Klappert establishes an unhurried, even-handed tone from which any variation is eas-

ily registered. This allows him to deliver satire with great force, as in **"The Court of Divine Justice,"** the morbidly powerful poem from [*Lugging Vegetables to Nantucket*] which opens the tape. There is a nearly permanent note of sadness as an undercurrent in Klappert's voice, dominant in a few poems such as **"In Memory of H. F.,"** one of the most musical efforts (and one of his finest—his reading of the final line, "it is quiet as the sun rises above the Sound," manages to be both perfectly appropriate and perfectly unexpected). Other highlights from the early (up to 1975) work include **"The Drawer"** (in which Klappert's delivery of the line "What is it you need?" constitutes one of the moments of sharpest feeling offered here) and **"Boy Walking Back to Find His Father's Cattle,"** in which the menace of war and the exigencies of everyday life are mingled as a young boy wanders through the jungle in southeast Asia on his timeless mission.

The real potentials of Klappert's voice are not realized, however, until he begins to read from his latest book, *The Idiot Princess of the Last Dynasty.* Taking up all but a small bit of the second half-hour of the tape, his readings from this book manage to combine the effects of a bullshitter just bullshitting (the historical premise of the poem) with more level-headed postures of a poet reading a poem with certain rhetorical and musical aims in mind. The format, dramatic monologue, allows him a much greater freedom of expression, and the general liveliness of his voice throws his flatter deliveries into sharper relief, often with hilarious results, as in the lines "When you've heard the confessions a carcass makes / you can absolve a flatulent cheese," and "I don't know that I would survive / in a permanent state of orgasm." . . . [*The Idiot Princess*] is surely a book to be heard as well as read; the infusion of history and historical anecdote, bewildering at times when read from the page, takes on a new life in the mouth of the raconteur, through the rough energy of his harangue. The little taste this tape affords creates the hunger for a full rendition.

> Nigel Hinshelwood, in a review of "Internal Foreigner," in Washington Review, *Vol. XI, No. 5, February-March, 1986, p. 28.*

J. P. WHITE

Throughout our tortured and transitional century, there have been a number of poets whose work bears witness to the social and political realities of our time. From Yeats to Eliot, from Neruda to Milosz, from Rich to Forché, all these poets have explored the tragic lyric as a means of ennobling the suffering of those who are victimized or estranged. But there has been a conspicuous shortage of satirical poets whose work recognizes the absurdity of individual destiny in the presence of the terrible abstractions of history.

For those poets who have assumed the obligations of witnessing, their work is an ongoing testimony that 20th century life is an inescapable tragedy punctuated with small moments of joy. For Peter Klappert, life is a no-win comedy hyphenated by tragedy, and his new book, *The Idiot Princess of the Last Dynasty* is perhaps the most challenging and disturbing book of poetry yet written in America from the stronghold of a satirical, absurdist vision. For that reason alone, it may well become as essential to the poetry of the last years of this century as Eliot's *Waste Land* was to the poetry written before World War II. Why such praise for Klappert? Because seldom has a poet in any age raised his ambition so high as to arraign an entire century for its unacknowledged crimes, as well as create a language that is as densely textured and polymorphic as his times. And perhaps no other poet has provided such trenchant criticism of the discreet charms of the bourgeoisie—charms that shifted from silent compliance to inertia to repression, and finally to a self-accepting death march.

What is the vehicle for Klappert's arraignment? None other than the personality and political acumen of one Doc Daniel Mahoney, an historical character who enjoyed an earlier incarnation in the celebrated novel, *Nightwood,* by Djuna Barnes. Holding court in a Left Bank café on the eve of the Nazi occupation of Paris, Mahoney addresses the café's habitués in a series of independent but related dramatic monologues. As readers, we enjoy and suffer (oh, how we suffer) the effect of the audience on trial. We are told in Klappert's prose introduction that Mahoney is an Irish Catholic abortionist who came to Paris after his stint in the first World War, and that now he is speaking between September 1939 and June 1940—during the time of the so-called "Phony War".

The order of the previous adjectives describing Mahoney is important to an understanding of this complex and argumentative book that will thread all its images through the personality of its speaker. As an Irish Catholic, he is a born raconteur as well as a penitent well-versed in dueling with God. As a flamboyant homosexual given to campy mannerisms, he is clearly held in contempt in the eyes of the church. And as an abortionist, he stands outside the law at the threshold of life and death, between church doctrine and individual choice. Excommunicated in both flesh and spirit, Mahoney acts as both judge and penitent. As such he has one 24-hour compulsion: to peel away the layers of sexual, spiritual and political hypocrisy that cloak the good intentions of a society whose preoccupation is the denial of evil. After all, even in 1939, most of the French leaders still believed that the ridiculous "Maginot Line" erected along the French-German border would completely protect French citizens from the Nazi blitzkrieg. (pp. 16-17)

Standing like the Magus figure in the Tarot deck—with one hand raised to heaven like a lightning rod and the other hand cast down to hell—Mahoney draws his oracular voice from both worlds. His intimacy with the dark side of human nature (what Jung called the "projection of the shadow") gives him special insight into the imminent ethical collapse and the ultimate cruelty people are capable of. Like his historical contemporary, Freud, Mahoney gives testament that "only the wounded physician can heal". Only he who has entered the underworld of his own "shadow" can possibly attain a brief moment of apotheosis and offer that insight to others. The poet H. D. said of her analysis with Freud that, "He is midwife to the soul," and even though Mahoney is by trade an abortionist, his obsessed personality functions more like that of a midwife in search of a new soul within his audience.

And like Eliot's "Prufrock," Klappert's Mahoney will shift in tone from the baroque to the vernacular, from the acerbic to the tender, in a constant testing of the reader's sensibility, and in richly musical and thick-textured diction that's been all but absent from American poetry for the last 40 years. This ailing outcast in the limelight of a debacle begins his self-made Resistance with an admission of defeat:

> The more I chew this stuff
> the bigger it gets.

>   I thought Men think
> with their heads and suffer from claustrophobia:
> I will think with my tongue, I will
> find my truth in the elaboration of lies,
> I will dig through with this little trowel
> to the land of sweet meats where my mother hums
> and waits by the four rivers
> to bathe me in primary light.
>   And would you know
> where my tongue led me? Into
> Cholera, Dysentery,
> Typhus. Oh, I've traveled
> like the Guinea worm—the Fiery Serpent
> of the Bible if you didn't know it—and grown
> three feet and miserable in a human form.

(from **"Mahoney the Bad Traveler"**)

During the course of this absurdist epic that runs some 200 pages, one at times loses the densely allusive texture of Mahoney's monologues for he is a speaker encumbered with too great a knowledge of history. We do not know what he knows, and so we cannot imaginatively reclaim all the implications of his references. His barrage of names, facts, and places becomes an elaborate texture, a kind of background music against which more accessible melodies are played. However, there are much more serious tracking problems because the book does not always provide a clear typographical matrix for Mahoney's voice.

Mahoney *is* always the speaker in these monologues and yet, at times, the indentations do not allow us to score the text. The book appears to be organized like this: Mahoney's own voice is always flush left on the page, and when he is quoting someone else, the line is indented by five spaces. When he is quoting himself in a dialogue, the line is moved still further in. As you can see, any single page in this book presents a formidable challenge for we must constantly separate and connect the cross-weaving of Mahoney's own obsessive voice.

The problem is that this organizational structure is not consistent throughout and therein lies the confusion. An added note by Klappert explaining his formal concerns would have been useful, and at times, essential. Of course, readers of this book are certain to complain that the indentations and many of the references are obscure, but a thoughtful reading of the "Idiot Princess" will serve as its own guide through most of the poems.

If we sometimes lose Mahoney in the labyrinth of his own knowledge, we find him again in the originality of this caustic wit and irony. Wit (originally meaning knowledge) came in the late Middle Ages to signify the intellect, the seat of consciousness, and Mahoney is a tireless speaker cursed with a well-spring of swift associations, paradoxes, puns, and a wide array of sophisticated verbal manipulations that both press forward and retreat, banter and cajole. When this kind of wit stands alone on its own self-aggrandizing turf, it becomes merely incestuous sport. But when it's combined with a political judgement in the voice of Mahoney, then that wit becomes a "little trowel" digging not only to the sources of Mahoney's earthly allegiances, but also a tool to combat the connivance between public lies and private wishes that nothing is wrong with the world at large.

When Mahoney tells a joke, you can almost bet that the punchline will turn serious, even nightmarish and cruel. (pp. 17-19)

Like a rebellious Kierkegaard, Mahoney shines with the gift of "mastered irony," i.e. he can momentarily suspend his own pain to assess the lives and delusions of others. Since he has plumbed the riddles of his own defeated psyche and become like the "Fiery Serpent of the Bible," he can enter the riddles of world without flinching. This ironic position is Mahoney's central technique to communicate an embattled vision of the world overcome by sordidness and self-deception. Far from being either a dogmatist or a nihilist, Mahoney, like Kierkegaard, remains both committed to his vision that life and death are jockeying for position, as well as absurdly detached from the outcome. It is this paradox he lives with supreme skill, cunning and anger. He knows what he knows in order to survive, but he cannot act beyond the projection of his own voice. He is the quintessential modern absurdist hero, caught in the crossfire of his own observations, a man of action who advocates action, but who takes no action himself.

As the book progresses and the public language around him becomes increasingly more blurred and removed from reality, Mahoney also becomes increasingly more unforgiving toward the sophisticated forms of self-deception that prevail. Of course, he has caustic remarks to make towards just about everyone (including himself) but to the prosperous middle-class who appear to be made only more giddy with the impending war, he reserves the most unrelenting blasphemy. . . . Mahoney has no patience with the acquiescence of the French people, who by their very silence agree to empower the right-wing extremists who would have France enter the war on the side of the enemy. The daily little choices about behavior (that truly define a political self) have been supplanted by a collective, societal need to preserve the appearance that the country is well-defended. With a persistent refusal to examine the inner life that might very well be at war with circumstance, the French become permanently disenfranchised from their anger as well as from their power to assess insane propositions no matter how sensibly they are presented. For those who deny the war, even as it is happening, Mahoney has this to offer:

> To the sea of fools
> led the path of the children
> and none who took part were spared the failure.
>
> —They lacked an amphibious doctrine
> and were immobilized by general mud.

(from "Laughter in the Peroration")

Mahoney's contempt for a citizenry's willingness to fight in battle long after the resistance should have begun continues in the blistering poem, **"Doc Mahoney and the Laughter of War"**:

> The boys went West
> and are athletic in the grave.
> Though perhaps even now beyond the Meuse
> the remains of Nietzsche's beast, blondness
> and emptiness, is down on its knees
> in an alley, praying to a swagger stick.
> If their seed is so good
>   why don't they make a strudel of it?

In one of the most remarkable poems in this book of painful monologues, **"Does Daniel Believe in Order?,"** Mahoney tackles head on the advocates of "Moral Education," as the instigators of the deep roots of conformity and ultimately of fascism itself, which originated not in Germany but in France during the Dreyfus Affair of the 1890's. It's been said that the

20th century is a race between education and catastrophe, and here Mahoney presents his cogent arguments against the prevailing education, one that works at all costs to be "at war . . . with Three Vices: Indocility, Independence and Contradiction." The alleged morality of this education that denies questions, explorations, detours and endless curiosity turns into a moral vacuum that enables the child to follow orders later on as a docile adult. The implications of this education of "Perpetual Concession" in the hands of a demonic tyrant—the repressed one within ourselves—gives Mahoney a moment of gallows' glee . . .:

> Ach zo! Herr Hitler alzo only vantz
> to keep hiz equilibrium, his zenz ov Ordnung,
> so he refrains from alcolhol tobacco
> sex and meat
> and beats up Jews

Mahoney knows that France wants to feed on bland and evasive propaganda about the nature of the war for then its positive self-image can remain intact, but still he feels compelled to address this blithe indifference. In the prophetic poem, **"The New U,"** which has as much to say about our present reality as it does about 1939 France, Mahoney turns his anger toward those who have followed the voice of patriarchal reassurance that nothing is wrong, dangerous or unfriendly. Even though defeat is near at hand, the utopian ideal of order replaces any clash with reality:

>   What do you dream
> in your country under the ice?
>
>   *No. Let me tell you.*
> Odds against dying a natural death
> (if you are a codfish) are one hundred
> thousand to one, and the cocoon
> is the home of only the worm.

One might think that such dark, mocking discourse would turn sour, but Klappert's Mahoney rewards us with his compassion and his begrudging affection in much the same way that Henry Miller, André Gide and Albert Camus often bolster—not with a promise of eternity but with an undeniable tenderness for the earth and its doomed creatures. Such a moment comes when Mahoney speaks to the romantic poet, Estienne, who would know joy even if he "must compose in a dead language." Mahoney is not entirely forgiving of Estienne's blind spots, his lyric excursions which lead him away from the facts, but he does acknowledge the small light one man can be for the other as Estienne faces mortality:

>   Light,
> the only light comes from each man
> rubbing against the darkness,
> though a soft and a sulphurous match
> that man might be.
>   I'm not clear what I
> can do about God.
> Try not to hurt Him, I think, stay alive,
> I think, in His rare and expensive sunlight."

(from "Estienne Redivivus")

In some of the most compassionate writing of the book called **"The Subjects of Discontent,"** Mahoney questions repeatedly what will happen to the less fortunate citizens, the ones who have no means of protection, nothing to barter for safety, nothing to compromise, no strength to battle the swift invasion of rhetoric that claims to protect them:

—What will they do, what will they
think to do, when the last wrinkled toe
of stuffed intestine has gone from the cobbler's win-
    dow
and the last Parisian act of valor has been called
"strong butter on dry beans," when everything
has been used, nothing used as intended,
when the tins have all been scoured of their mutton,
when cages in the zoo gape and clang open
like ruined ancient stadiums at midnight
and the growling voice in the stomach haunts a
    country.

As the book traces the fall of France, the personal conces-
sions and defections occur with an all too frightening familiarity. When the French Vichy government is in place (and
it's clear that French militarists were in collaboration with
Germany all along), the middle class do what they have always done: they cover their tracks and try not to make waves
or many just escape to the South. As we learn in the dazzling
section, **"Sero Medicina,"** the psychic medicine is prepared
too late when the illness has grown strong by long delay.
There is a casual self-acceptance of moral failure that smacks
of bravado:

We have robbed the graves of the past to outfit
ourselves in plausible alibis.

The middle class makes all the right moves to protect itself
from danger to the point where even an overt endorsement
of the enemy is condoned. Here, Mahoney is quick to set himself apart, not in moral superiority, but in the observation of
how his psyche moves away from the reassuring illusions of
safety: "My happiness is not a hope there are no enemies."

After his biting observations on censorship, compulsory reading, applause, the heightened demonic powers of the frightened middle class, and the almost universal temptation to
pray for deliverance, Mahoney starts the long trek back to
God, his final duel. Like his historical contemporaries,
Camus and Sartre, Mahoney believes that if God exists, he
is only another being to wrestle with, and throughout this
book some of the most blistering wit is directed towards
God's alleged omnipotence. Late in the book, Mahoney offers
this slice of defensive assault:

                        I may or may not
know more than the priest who spoke on Sunday,
but I do not correct the Magnificat, I do not
frank souls to kingdom come, I do not
piss more than I drink,
            and I do not give pap with a hatchet.

Before his final wrestling match, Mahoney stops to chat with
Satan, whom he regards as one more ally of the good-
intentioned middle class. Because the middle class is convinced of its judgments long before all the information is collected, their epistemology ultimately becomes the opposite of
what it claims to be, i.e., righteous and pure. The children of
God have now become warriors for Satan. Mahoney makes
fair use of traditional snake imagery to dramatize his conviction that

Evil, my dear,
is the willful ignorance of a Narcissus
having its way with the world.

Terrified of his separateness from the world, the narcissist—
with his origins in infantile self-centeredness—seeks to deny
that separation not just by adapting himself to the political

expectations of others, but also by killing that which denies
him the ability to sustain the illusion of oneness. . . . (pp.
20-5)

As the Nazi persecution of Jews, Protestants, free-masons,
and internal foreigners takes hold (internal foreigners are
people like Mahoney who cannot prove their French-
Catholic descent), Mahoney hits the high-gear of his sardonic
wit:

The Ministry of Fashion, of course,
needed your clothes for their moths,
so now you are examined by the Shirt Police:
We've a serious shortage of hangars.
Are you using those collarbones?

(from **"Saint Daniel the Paranoiac"**)

It becomes quite clear that some of the habitués of the café
where Mahoney has served as both judge and penitent will
not survive. But Mahoney will survive for he knows how to
keep one step ahead of the law (whether it be run by the Nazis
or not) and he will not flee Paris. He will live, despite impossible odds, to have his final say with God, who by the end of
the book is called, simply, Harry—a being whose attention
span has been reduced to reading comics and the sports
pages, and who remains frequently "under sedation." Despite
what he has witnessed, Mahoney rallies for an outrageous
pun:

Oh for Christ's sweet Sake.
                        Ghosts are perfectly
acceptable to me, some of my best
friends have become ghosts, but would you
really want your little girl
to marry one?

In this last poem, **"Low Sunday,"** Mahoney plays different
parts of his own personality as well as recalls an earlier conversation with God. In places it sounds like a dialogue, but,
as from the beginning, Mahoney's voice is the only one. In
a recollection, God asks Mahoney's forgiveness (as though
only Mahoney's journey downward into sordidness were
keeping him alive), and the Irishman shouts back that he's
heard enough babble about tempered humility and forgiveness. But God—who has been lambasted and skewered for
some 200 pages—gets the best last lines in Mahoney's memory:

Go, mon bon zigue
tell me again what it smells like. View for me
life through the sockets of a skull.
You may hear jackass bray on your left,
and it may be answered by a jackass on your right.
Do not take that for an omen.

For all his excoriating Irish blarney, Mahoney's victory at the
end of *The Idiot Princess of the Last Dynasty* may appear
to be a small one. He has made no compromises in finding
the *mot juste* to describe his psychic journey, and he has not
altered his voice to appease present political company. Like
Ionesco's hero at the end of *Rhinoceros,* he has not capitulat-
ed to the political, spiritual and sexual designs of his historical realities. And God's reward for this resistance is simply
this: the chance to continue. He is alone, as he began, detached and involved—a comic who finds tragedy everywhere.

The Idiot Princess of the Last Dynasty is a difficult, demanding and highly ambitious tale about a journey into the darker
side of human nature. And for all its wit and punning, it real-

ly is not a very funny book. God knows we need more joy in 20th century writing, but Klappert has only been able to find it, obliquely, by first making the journey down through the "moil of Europe". Klappert's embattled vision—one that affirms the autonomous individual at his or her hard-headed, questioning best—has never been more sorely needed than now. For though we may not have the threat of Nazi Germany looming in the distance, we have far more potentially devastating political horrors to counterpoint and equally despicable crimes and collaborations in Southeast Asia that have yet to be accounted for.

In the absence of a desire to cross-examine political anxiety when it occurs, we easily attribute evil to something we know nothing about—National Socialism, fascism, communism—but *The Idiot Princess of the Last Dynasty* suggests that we need not look beyond ourselves for the seeds of evil. For they have been growing inside our unconscious—in ignorance, cowardice and self-deception—for generations, and those seeds can be made to bloom at any moment in the hands of a belligerent Officialdom that sells "nothing wrong" propaganda.

Klappert's book—and it is a great one in a sea of tame fishes—dramatically reveals how a denial of evil eventually leads to ethical collapse and to evil itself, fully embodied in ourselves. For that reason alone, Klappert's Mahoney—though he be a wildly perverse and ailing imp—is one of the more decent and astonishing characters in American poetry you are ever likely to meet. (pp. 25-7)

J. P. White, "An Outcast in the Limelight of a Debacle: The Absurdist Vision of Peter Klappert," in The Greenfield Review, *Vol. 14, Nos. 3 & 4, Summer-Fall, 1987, pp. 16-27.*

John Krizanc

1956-

Canadian dramatist.

Krizanc has established a reputation as an inventive dramatist based upon his plays *Tamara* (1981) and *Prague* (1984). *Tamara* enjoyed extended runs in such unconventional theatrical venues as an abandoned house in Toronto, a mansion in Hamilton, Ontario, an American Legion hall in Los Angeles, and an armory in New York City. The sets on these sites were designed to represent several rooms and floors of an elaborate Italian villa during the mid-1920s, where a famed poet and his guests are involved in sexual, political, and criminal intrigues. *Tamara* attracted substantial publicity for its unusual staging. A limited number of theater patrons are admitted to the productions and are expected to stroll about the sets to follow the play's action. Because scenes involving various characters are acted simultaneously on different sets, playgoers are invited to compare notes and share information during lavish buffets at intermission and following the play's conclusion.

Tamara is based on actual events involving such personages as Italian poet Gabriele D'Annunzio, a World War I hero who accepted bribes for not opposing Benito Mussolini's rise to power, and Polish painter Tamara de Lempicka, whom D'Annunzio attempts to seduce. The play comments upon politics, particularly fascism, the role of artists, and, as one character states, the conflict between "love and duty." Concerning his unorthodox approach in *Tamara*, Krizanc stated: "I thought the best way to write a critique of Fascism was to give people more democratic freedom than they've ever had in the theatre."

Prague, which won the Governor General's Literary Award for drama, was described by Urjo Kareda as a political play, a thriller, a backstage drama, and a wise-cracking slapstick comedy. Set in Czechoslovakia in 1983, *Prague* concerns members of the Bread and Dreams Theatre Company, a small theatrical group involved in dissident activities. When the company's state-approved dramatist completes a play celebrating the 1968 Soviet invasion of their country, the director decides to revise the work to denounce oppressive government forces. Keith Garebian observed: "[*Prague*] is a wry, bitter satire of a society in which the counterfeit, the deceitful, and the manipulative hold political power, and where characters play roles-within-roles. The theatrical metaphor serves to expose this dynamic and to captivate an audience with admirably balanced tensions."

MARK CZARNECKI

Tamara is a delight, an exotic confection which could easily have been just a gimmick but instead provides a unique theatrical experience. The play takes place in a renovated Victorian mansion; in an ingenious expansion of *Upstairs, Downstairs* the 10 characters, from the chauffeur to master Gabriele D'Annunzio, the Italian poet and patriot who remained shamefully silent during Mussolini's regime, reproduce two days of their lives in the rooms and hallways of the mansion. The audience (limited for logistical reasons to a maximum of 50) can follow whichever characters they choose. At intermission, when the cast has "gone to bed," the audience, assembled in the kitchen for a "midnight" pastry snack, is encouraged to compare notes and knit together the various strands of the plot.

A docudrama with operatic flourishes, *Tamara's* historical basis is the visit of Tamara de Lempicka, a glamorous Polish futurist artist, to D'Annunzio's mansion in order to paint his portrait, but the poet is more interested in reclining than sitting. Meanwhile, revolution boils up from the servants' quarter, threatening to engulf D'Annunzio in a rebellion against Il Duce. John Krizanc's overly long script . . . is more libretto than play. . . . (pp. 66-7)

With its $20 ticket and restricted audience, the work is elitist in the extreme, recalling the chamber works enacted before kings and courtiers. But it is more than that, since it reexamines basic theatrical principles which echo the experiments of the Living Theatre in the '60s. Where Living Theatre generally failed to break down performer-audience barriers by recruiting the audience into the production, *Tamara* succeeds by allowing viewers to create their own play and see it too. Audiences are voyeurs by definition, so why not let them fully indulge this vicarious pleasure? Sitting by chance alone, while inches away Tamara and Gabriele court and spark, the spectator slowly realizes that one more permutation of the alchemy by which life is transformed into art has reached a logical and enlightening conclusion. (p. 77)

Mark Czarnecki, *"Do-It-Yourself Blackshirts,"* in Maclean's Magazine, *Vol. 94, No. 22, June 1, 1981, pp. 66-7.*

SALEM ALATON

One evening during a characteristically unpredictable performance of *Tamara,* a local bag lady wandered into historic Strachan House and led two patrons to an upstairs room where she proceeded to tell them she was the Queen. Not only did the theatre-goers find nothing unusual about the occurrence, but they continued to look on smilingly as Richard Rose, the play's director attempted to halt the unsolicited soliloquy; they thought he was part of the show, too. . . .

The action takes place in 20 rooms—any number of them all at once. Members of the audience, limited to 50 people, follow the character of their choice, scampering up and down stairways, through halls, into narrow bedrooms, eavesdropping outside doorways, hovering inches away from seductions or beatings, and even bolting out the front door at the sound of squealing tires or gunshots. Recreating the 1927 household of Gabriele d'Annunzio, poet laureate of Fascist Italy and a decadent prisoner of his own mansion, the show is rife with intriguing subtexts that compel spectators to make some worrisome split-second decisions as to which theme they wish to pursue; characters keep hurriedly diverging and regrouping. When [a character] leaped out the main floor window, one of the avid onlookers, not missing a stride, leaped right after him.

The active response of the audience has had its share of dramaturgical hazards for the performers. [During] a scene in which the maid must quickly tidy a room in which a gun is hidden, [the actress] had to fend off offers to help with making the bed. [Dante] sustains a mock beating from Finzi the Fascist agent during the course of the show, and on one occasion he was given some solicitous aid from a doctor in the audience. One hot evening during a crowded dining room scene, writer John Krizanc recalls, "a lady fainted, just dropped to the floor." So one performer simply remarked . . . , "Pick that lady up, Dante." . . .

At intermission, the buzzing of the crowd rarely strays to ponderings on the weather or the economy: "Finzi thinks Mario the chauffeur is a Communist spy. Has d'Annunzio seduced Tamara yet?" Answer: "No, but I saw Aelis the housekeeper making overtures to Carlotta!"

Not all the spectators have bought a ticket, however. Strachan House faces Bellwoods Park and is flanked on the west side by Crawford Street; *Tamara* has found itself drawing attention from the neighbors. For example, says author Krizanc, "The other night I was listening from upstairs, and a window opens (on one of the Crawford homes) and this guy starts (yelling) 'The Party no longer needs you!' It turns out he knows all the lines for the end of the play." Rose remarked on a juvenile cheering section outside that gives advice to the beleaguered Aldo Finzi: "We have kids who gather in the park and shout, 'Run, Aldo, run!' Somebody was saying we have the potential for a *Rocky Horror Picture Show* cult." . . .

[It] is interesting to note that at one early point, Casa Loma was discussed as the site for *Tamara;* "It's booked for the next two years, though," says Krizanc with a tinge of regret.

Salem Alaton, *"Tamara Plays to a Full House in All 20 Rooms,"* in The Globe and Mail, *Toronto, June 20, 1981, p. E1.*

JOHN KRIZANC

One day in the summer of 1980 I got drunk. I'd just taken the first draft of a new play over to my director's house for an assessment and, as he read it, I began drinking. By page three, *he* began drinking.

Richard Rose has been my best friend since we met as high-school students in Sudbury, Ontario. His encouragement brought me to the theatre and he directed my first two plays; his intelligence guides me; I rely on his judgment.

"This is shit," he said. Directors are not known for their tact.

I felt like putting down my pen and going back to the Toronto bookstore where I worked (as I still do) when not writing plays. I poured another drink and reflected that at twenty-four I might be washed up.

Richard suggested I put my script in a drawer for a while and instead write another play for the Toronto Theatre Festival, then a year away. "What about doing something with the D'Annunzio story?"

We'd come across the story in a book about the modern Polish painter Tamara de Lempicka. So little is known about her life that the publisher had to use the journals of Gabriele D'Annunzio's housekeeper to serve as a text. The journals record what took place during one week in 1927 when the beautiful young Tamara arrived to paint the portrait of D'Annunzio, the Italian poet and First World War hero. It was a tale of failed seduction, but also potentially a story about art and politics. D'Annunzio could have stopped Benito Mussolini's rise to power, yet he did nothing. He allowed himself to be bought off, to be kept in opulent splendour, in drugs and women, in exchange for his silence.

"We'd never get the money to do it," I said. "We couldn't even afford the sets. D'Annunzio lived like a king in a castle."

"Casa Loma!" said Richard. He was talking about the mock castle in midtown Toronto which bankrupted the man who built it seventy years ago.

"They wouldn't let us in. Besides, it's too big."

"Every room is a set! Imagine! If you write a scene set in a kitchen, we'll use the kitchen. A real kitchen!"

A couple of months later I'd worked out an outline, and Richard and I toured Casa Loma. I told him about the characters and plots I'd been dreaming about. "I'm not sure how it happened, but I've got at least ten plays in my head."

Richard stared up at the castle. "Let's do them all. All ten plays, all happening at the same time in different rooms of the castle."

"Not ten plays, just one. Imagine that every character is the star of his or her own play. The other nine characters are the supporting cast. I'll weave them all together and the audience can make their own play by choosing the character they follow. Let them follow whomever they want, as long as they follow someone."

It would be an entirely different kind of play. We'd treat the audience in a new way—send them scurrying through the rooms of the castle in pursuit of the actors.

By the end of the afternoon we'd come up with a set of rules and by the end of March, 1981, I had almost finished a first draft. There was only one problem: we had no castle. Casa Loma had said no. The only other suitable place was Strachan House in Trinity Bellwoods Park. When we found out the house was run by the City of Toronto property department, we hurried off to see the property commissioner. Without much interest he promised to read our proposal. As we stood by the elevators, a curious senior employee asked us to step into his office. Richard told him about the project. He told us all about the property department. When we left, we knew how to approach city hall. Richard went to an alderman and I went to the mayor's office. On Saturday we enlisted the support of several prominent businessmen and federal politicians. On Monday we got the house.

The toilets at Strachan House were broken. The actors read in the dark because there was no power. After an eight-hour rehearsal, they would stay to paint walls, lay tile, or cook dinner. This zeal soon spread to friends, even strangers in the park. Everyone wanted to help: a grade-eight class spent an afternoon gathering up garbage, a carpenter volunteered labour in exchange for tickets.

Coordinating all this was our designer, Dorian Clark. With only $2,000 to create D'Annunzio's villa she had to borrow beds, tables, a grand piano, my entire library. A year later, Dorian won an award for set design and *The Toronto Star* asked why—after all, the house was already there.

Tamara opened quietly on May 8, 1981, as part of the Toronto Theatre Festival. When critics from *Maclean's* and *The Globe and Mail* stayed behind to talk, Richard told me we had a hit. In spite of good notices, however, we ran at only sixty per cent attendance for the first weeks. We would soon have to close.

The person who saved *Tamara* was Gina Mallet, then the theatre critic for *The Toronto Star*. A week after the play opened, she wrote a piece which carried the headline "It's full house for festival hit called *Tamara*." It was more a profile of Richard and myself than a review, but the public saw it as an endorsement and the phones began to ring. Gina Mallet had not yet seen the play; when she did come, about a month later, she walked out. (She claims she returned later and saw the whole show, but neither Richard nor I can remember that visit.)

If you have a cast of ten and can accommodate only fifty people per show, it's impossible to make money. Not only did I get no royalty, I cleaned the toilets every night. As we appeared to become more successful, though, it became increasingly difficult to get favours. Suddenly we had to pay rent for the car and the piano; everyone wanted a share of the nonexistent wealth. By the end of July we had a $10,000 overdraft, covered by Richard's father; we calculated that if we could run until October we might pay it back. Then the phone rang.

"This is Moses Znaimer. I met you briefly last week. Can you come over tonight to talk, here at CITYTV? Eleven o'clock?"

Moses is an entrepreneur, a Canadian version of a Hollywood mogul. He runs a television station (and lately has started a cable network, MuchMusic). He occasionally backs movies and other ventures.

About three weeks after our meeting we signed a contract with Znaimer. It wasn't a perfect deal but we went for it because it would get us out of our overdraft, it was the only way we could keep the show open, and we liked Znaimer. (pp. 34-6)

Six months after opening in Toronto, *Tamara* was forced to close. The Anglican Church and the city had agreed to turn Strachan House into a men's residence. And in the last months the quality of the performances had deteriorated drastically. The sense of family which created the show had disappeared. People were frustrated; they wondered why they were not deluged by requests to act in other plays if this show was such a hit. But somehow that feeling disappeared when we transferred to Dundurn Castle in Hamilton. The last shows there were our best. The closing night party was quiet; we were all tired, and afterward there was crying in the parking lot. Everyone hugged. Someone said: "I can't believe that tomorrow I'll wake up and there'll be no *Tamara*."

For me, though, it didn't end. Znaimer kept saying we'd be opening in Los Angeles in six months. Three years passed. Znaimer hired location scouts, but they were unable to find a suitable house for the play. One day, as he was driving along Highland Avenue, Znaimer became intrigued by the architecture of an American Legion building. Once inside, he knew he had found our location. Down in the bar he found several vets and began his pitch: "Let me tell you a story." A few months later I was heading south, to L.A.

I'd told Richard I wanted a stretch limo to pick me up at the airport. At the baggage claim area I spotted a man holding a sign with my name on it. It was the stage manager, Sam Burgess. He had a rusted-out Honda. (p. 36)

When *Tamara* played in Toronto, it ran three-and-a-half hours. Znaimer insisted that I cut it to two-and-a-half. In Los Angeles most of the major cuts were made on the freeway. One day we spent three hours in traffic and cut thirty minutes. Whenever Richard had to think about something, he'd grab me and say: "C'mon, let's go find some traffic." (p. 37)

A clause in our lease with the Legion prohibited scenes that were "obscene or un-American." One scene worried Richard. Early in act two, the Fascist captain, Finzi, interrogates the suspicious-looking new chauffeur, Mario:

> Finzi: "Are you now, or have you ever been, a member of the Communist Party?"
>
> Mario: "No."
>
> Finzi: "I ask again: are you a Communist?"
>
> Mario: "No."
>
> Finzi: "Have you ever known a Communist?"
>
> Mario: "No."
>
> Finzi: "Three times you answer no."

When that scene was first rehearsed, the temperature in the

room seemed to drop twenty degrees. Everyone got goose bumps. The actor playing Mario broke character and asked, "Can you feel it?"

We could. Thirty years ago, the building had housed the hearings concerning the Hollywood Ten. Those words have become synonymous with McCarthyism and I had put them in the play to draw the parallel between McCarthyism and fascism. Every house has its ghosts. In this case the ghosts didn't haunt our production: the legionnaires, though they had script approval, may never have actually read the 300-page script. (pp. 37-8)

In Toronto there hadn't been much anxiety. We were a small show and we would have been happy to run three weeks. In L.A. careers and money were on the line. We had to be a hit, and we didn't even have an ending. During the preview two nights before opening, halfway through the first act, Richard grabbed me and dragged me into the parking lot. "John, I've got it. I've got the new ending!" . . .

When I flunked grade nine, my mother didn't say anything, just left a note on my pillow: "There's no failure if you've done your best." At the time it seemed pretty hokey. But standing in a Los Angeles parking lot, waiting to see what the critics would make of *Tamara,* I thought—for the first time in my life—I've done my best.

As it turned out, the reviewers also thought it was good: most of the reviews were enthusiastic, some of them wildly so. Four months later *Tamara* was still running to ninety per cent houses and yet—because of the necessarily limited audience and the large costs—remained financially shaky. And I was back in Toronto, working in the bookstore. (p. 38)

> *John Krizanc, "Innocents Abroad," in* Saturday Night, *Vol. 99, No. 11, November, 1984, pp. 34-8.*

MATTHEW FRASER

Prague, the latest play by John Krizanc, who wrote the highly popular *Tamara,* is about the strained relationship between art and the state in a Communist-bloc country. It's a subject that—although not entirely irrelevant in Tory Ontario, where the Government censors art with some frequency—doesn't exactly press on the consciences of people in the West.

However, the issue is never irrelevant, and in *Prague* . . . Krizanc has succeeded in articulating the question of art viv-a-vis the state in a way that hits very close to home. Mixing clownish humor and harsh realism, *Prague* is a dazzling piece of comic absurdity. . . .

The first scene is a marvellous piece of staging. Like something out of Fellini, four clowns laugh and grin in big happy caricatures. The stage is littered with beachballs, a drum, a striped umbrella, a cake—all in a colorful dadaist tableau. There is laughter and applause, but one clown is pointing a machine gun at the others, while another holds a bazooka. The weapons jab discordantly, and portentously, into the candy-cane fantasy.

That opening scene, which flashes like an absurd image, foreshadows the central problem in the play: how to insert true reality into state-sanctioned art that will only permit its own false reality. That reality—socialist realism—has been enforced so effectively that the greatest Czech writer, Kafka, is

virtually unknown in his native country because his reality was too honest.

The acting company, headed by Vladmir, is rehearsing a new play called Magnificat, which is a disguised piece of subversion. A tale about foreign invaders who behead a noble, right-minded duke, it's an allegory for the Soviet takeover of Czechoslovakia in 1968, when the popular Alexander Dubcek was replaced by a leader considered more co-operative.

Magnificat—the play-within-a-play—is supposed to be a tragicomedy, a romantic epic with a heroic, populist ending. *Prague,* however, is a comic-tragedy. In the end, the state prevails, and art becomes state art.

The hypocrisy of the state doesn't escape Krizanc's sharp sense of irony, though. The three state representatives—Kura, a dandy playwright in cream suit, Zuzanna, who wears lipstick and jeans, and Major Zrak, who likes Frank Sinatra—are the only characters who look and act Western. . . .

Although intellectually cluttered at points, *Prague* is compelling. . . . As for the question of art and the state, the clown predictably has the final word: "Exile—that's what they mean by 'the truth must out.' "

> *Matthew Fraser, "Prague's Comedy Dazzling," in* The Globe and Mail, *Toronto, November 21, 1984, p. M12.*

MARIANNE ACKERMAN

Marshall McLuhan's remark that Canada is a great place from which to observe the world clearly is magnificently borne out by *Prague*. . . . Next to the synthetic propaganda of, say, Mikhail Baryshnikov's current film *White Nights,* John Krizanc's play about the moral complexities of life under communism is a marvel of complexity and balance. . . .

Set in present-day Czechoslovakia, *Prague* is about the turmoil caused when the artistic director of a state-controlled theatre tries to stage a thinly disguised attack on the regime. Vladimir Rozek's motives are strictly private: he's seeking atonement for having publicly renounced his dissident father to save his theatre company and career.

But his father's recent death has shattered Rozek's survival instinct; He proceeds knowing *Magnificat* will endanger the entire troupe, including his pregnant wife, and force into exile the official author, a party hack whose politically correct plays Rozek has ghostwritten for pay.

Very funny and highly theatrical, *Prague*'s dense plot has been clarified by rewrites of Act 1 since the 1984 Toronto premiere. But clarity's gain is tension's loss. Not until the second half does exposition fully give way to the momentum of events, building to a moving revelation of Rozek's personal anguish.

After a slow start, [the] cast does a fine job juggling humor and pathos, recovering the grace of pacing in time to render the last rehearsal of *Magnificat* a wonderful absurdity. . . . [Rozek's] eventual outburst is an utterly convincing exposé of survival's emotional price.

It's difficult to imagine anything like Krizanc's string of smart oneliners on a Czech stage, yet director Richard Rose has managed to evoke a sense of fatigue among the players which fits their context. You can laugh through *Prague* and still sense the utter impossibility of these lives, feel how thoroughly the human spirit is ground down by the arbitrary menace of totalitarian rule.

Marianne Ackerman, *"Prague at the Centaur: A Fine and Complex Evening of Theatre,"* in The Gazette, *Montreal, January 11, 1986, p. D9.*

URJO KAREDA

John Krizanc's *Prague* began its life on paper as *Magnificat,* a six-hour medieval epic about the development of the heavy plough. I can clearly remember John coming into my office carrying an awesome bundle of some three hundred foolscap sheets covered with his impetuous handwriting. But as the script was barely legible, John sat down and attempted to outline the narrative of his play. Nearly two hours later the list of characters numbered more than twenty. We stopped. It was agreed that I would wait for the first full *typed* draft. The next time that John dropped in, the massive medieval play had been twisted into an even larger structure; the epic needed a context: it was now a play-within-a-play performed by members of a contemporary Prague theatre company. Under the insistence of John's growing interest in the dynamics within the theatre company and their wary relationship with the government, the medieval portion of the play kept dwindling. In *Prague,* the *Magnificat* is a vignette glimpsed in the middle of a chaotic rehearsal. It is an emblem of the historical issues that had first animated John's intellect and imagination. (p. 10)

Prague is a political play: a thriller ("Where *did* that counterfeit money come from?"); a backstage drama ("Will the opening night go as scheduled?"); and a wisecracking slapstick comedy (Lenka as eastern Europe's *Born Yesterday* naif).

There isn't a thing in the rather surprising populist modes he chooses for *Prague* that is in any way a betrayal of the deeper themes and tensions he wishes to explore. A thriller opens up the ritual questions of crime, motive and punishment which, when located in the complexities of survival in post-1978 Czechoslovakia, are closer to Kafka than Christie. The theatrical setting reinforces the problem of choosing the right role, in an existential sense, again in the context of a society in which being miscast affects not only the next job but, indeed, effects survival. And in this atmosphere of desperate ironies and generous falsehoods, what better tools exist than the wisecrack of the comprehending sensibility, or the slapstick of the intellect?

Because of the bravura of Krizanc's theatricality (sustained by his collaborators in direction and design) and the high gloss of his verbal invention, too little attention has been given, I feel, to the seriousness and depth of human observation. John Krizanc writes movingly about loyalty and friendship in *Prague.* He has said that he believes that everything people do is motivated by private desires. That is as complex an issue for the artist as it is for the politician (his great concerns in both his major plays). Yet within the dangerous traps of ambition and panic and desperation and conservatism, all so acutely charted in the play, Krizanc still discovers a margin of feeling in the relationship between Honza and the Rozeks, father and son, a shadow of unexpected gallantry in Lenka, a residue of displaced hope in the marriage of Vladi-

mir and Helena, and an affection for the weakness of a Kura, a Zrak, a Jancocova. The long journey from the heavy plough ends in small indelible gestures of defiance, of generosity, or self-forgiveness. The origins of *Prague* were epic; its new form is something much more intimate, but its intellectual curiosity and emotional understanding make *Magnificat* look puny. (pp. 10-11)

Urjo Kareda, *in an introduction to* Prague: A Play in Two Acts *by John Krizanc, Playwrights Canada Press, 1987, pp. 10-11.*

JOHN GILBERT

[*Prague*] plays much better than it reads. And this is exactly as it should be. Unlike so many plays by young playwrights, which overstate their purpose, *Prague* in the text retains its mysteries and ambiguities, reserving its final clarity for the compelling images that only performance can conjure up. Not surprisingly, then, the play resists summary, although the bare bones are clear enough.

Prague 1983. The members of a small theatre company, *Bread and Dreams,* grapple with the problems, both personal and public, that beset artists in the oppressive climate of Czechoslovakia since the Russian invasion of '68. Will they be able to perform a play containing a critical allegory of the invasion for a group of visiting Russians? The play written by Stefan Kura, the womanizing, flashy "official" playwright, has been given a new ending by Vladimir, the company's director. Will Lenka, company actress, get a letter to a potential marriage prospect in the West, to enable her to leave the country? Will counterfeit U.S. dollars be traced back to Kura or eventually to Vladimir's father by the police investigator, Major Zrak? . . .

For all its trappings of a thriller, *Prague* explores profounder themes. Dazzling theatricality fills in the gaps left by the text and dialogue. the final moment of the play bursts like an epiphany on the audience illuminating in one striking effect the manifold meanings of the play. Vladimir's redemption is postponed, and [a] debate about truth suddenly crystallizes.

Prague is a political play, and its meaning reaches beyond Prague and Czechoslovakia in 1983. This could be post-Vietnam America or any political society where the "ending" is in danger of being rewritten. Truth, in a society where the counterfeit is the order of the day, where official versions prevail, is always in jeopardy.

All this is supported by Krizanc's wonderful sense of the theatrical. He exploits the constant shifting back and forth between illusion and reality, through the theatrical metaphor of the play-within-the-play, exposing roles within roles. Honza, the clown, the man of many masks, proves by feats of sleight of hand that the truth can literally be made to disappear.

Krizanc's first major play, *Tamara,* attracted a cult following. *Prague* goes a long way to confirming his talent and the fascination he holds for his audience. I for one await his next with eager anticipation.

John Gilbert, *"To Tell the Truth,"* in Books in Canada, *Vol. 16, No. 2, March, 1987, p. 17.*

KEITH GAREBIAN

Prague is a play-within-a-play. The Bread and Dreams Theatre Company, under the omnipresent threat of censorship and punishment, is to stage a political allegory that enlarges its members' concerns about truth, freedom, loyalties, and friendship in post-1968 Czechoslovakia.

The play—originally a safe piece written by the company's "official" playwright—is cunningly altered by the director, who wishes to strike back at the state and redeem himself for having betrayed his own father, a political dissident. The major question, of course, is whether the play will be halted, the actors arrested, and lives irreparably harmed.

Prague opens as an abbreviated clown show, in which concealment and illusion are themes expressed with comic economy. But we soon see that these themes are a prologue to an almost Kafka-esque drama of espionage and deception, in which desperate ironies rub against one another with profound consequences.

John Krizanc never flounders. His characters are acutely rendered, with their theatricality sharpening rather than blunting the political impact. The comedy is a wry, bitter satire of a society in which the counterfeit, the deceitful, and the manipulative hold political power, and where characters play roles-within-roles. The theatrical metaphor serves to expose this dynamic and to captivate an audience with admirably balanced tensions.

Keith Garebian, in a review of "Prague," in Quill and Quire, *Vol. 53, No. 6, June, 1987, p. 31.*

MEL GUSSOW

As a play, *Tamara* exists on three levels—upstairs, downstairs and in Gabriele d'Annunzio's chamber. . . . [It] is an entertaining party game and murder mystery theme park. Whatever it is—and *Tamara* is self-defining—it is unlike any other show currently in New York. It is a shot of adrenalin for sedentary theatergoers who are accustomed to sitting in the dark and watching actors do all the work.

For almost three hours, *Tamara* keeps us on our feet and on the alert—looking, thinking (trying to piece together the devious plot) and rushing from room to room. Ostensibly, this environmental escapade deals with d'Annunzio—poet, playwright, politician and legendary lover—and with Tamara de Lempicka, the Polish artist who has come to d'Annunzio's villa to paint his portrait. But around them swirls a story filled with intrigue and good-natured decadence.

Events occur in a dozen rooms, on several staircases and in various passageways of the armory, part of which has been redesigned for the occasion. Scenes are performed simultaneously, which means that theatergoers choose what they think they want to see. One can follow a single character or proceed tag-style from character to character. Periodically, plots collide. Return visits to the play are encouraged, but it is possible to comprehend *Tamara* in one standing, especially if one communicates with other theatergoers. The show demands an openness on the part of the audience.

The nimble actors run from floor to floor with the audience in hot pursuit. One of the rules of the game is that when a door is closed, we do not attempt to open it. Think of that as no dead end; around the corner, something else is happening. A would-be prima ballerina is feverishly dancing, a pretty maid is hiding a revolver in the chauffeur's basement bedroom, d'Annunzio is chasing Tamara, who appears to be the only woman in his villa who has not yet succumbed to his charm. . . .

Tamara is labeled "a living movie," but it is a movie in which each theatergoer does the editing without ever seeing the rushes. Eyewitness accounts differ. As a guide to prospective theatergoers, it should be said that neither d'Annunzio nor Tamara is really the principal character. That role may well belong to Mario, the mysterious chauffeur. The play might more appropriately be called "Mario," but then some people might confuse it with a more recent political cliffhanger ("Waiting for Mario" in Doonesbury).

Mario is far more than a chauffeur, and he is the fastest runner in the villa. He and his fellow performers have all mastered the art of high intensity acting. This is in keeping with the dialogue, which is often thunderstruck, as in [Mario's] exclamatory, "No one is innocent in Italia!" . . .

As for d'Annunzio, his mind always seems to be on romantic conquest, although occasionally his appetite wanders. Stopping by the kitchen, I overheard him demand, "Aelis, get me some zucchini." The line could be regarded as foreshadowing. Shortly thereafter, the action stops and the audience has a buffet supper in d'Annunzio's elegant dining room. Food and champagne are included in the price of admission (from $85 for matinees to $135 Saturday evening)—and there is no stinting in quality.

The audience is almost as much a show as the play itself, as couples try hard to follow separate tracks of the story and, to their surprise, find themselves in the same boudoir or ballroom. Sometimes theatergoers talk back to the actors and, at intermission, the actors willingly respond in kind.

The play is intended as a commentary on the rise of Fascism in Italy in the 1920's and, in the chauffeur's words, on the conflict between "love and duty." There are references to politics and also to art of the period, but *Tamara* is not to be taken too seriously. It is basically a clever diverting whodunit. . . .

The show ends precipitately with a gunshot, leaving several plot strands untied—enough for *Tamara Two.* Again, the audience gathers to compare notes. *Tamara* is, and will be, a stimulating conversation piece.

Mel Gussow, in a review of "Tamara," in The New York Times, *December 3, 1987, p. C24.*

CLIVE BARNES

When is a play not a play? When it's *Tamara.* . . .

[*Tamara*] it is seemingly aimed at gourmandizing voyeurs with a gourmet taste in fast food washed down with very decent champagne, who can take an undemanding satisfaction from quick peeks.

You also have to be prepared to pass out a certain amount of cash. (p. 87)

Also, while you are enjoying your excellent buffet meal during the evening's half-hour "intermezzo," or your creme brulee, served after the performance with coffee and strawberries, you can have the dramatic/political frisson of realizing that only two floors up in this very same Armory, are being housed some of New York's homeless.

What an interesting juxtaposition! Only in New York, my friends.

The show starts as soon as you enter. You are crowded in the cheery lobby and line up to get your "passport." Then you have to get this stamped by a severe blackshirt guard who tells you that if you get caught without this document "you will be deported."

I wonder if deportees get their 135 bucks back. Never mind, only the homeless have to worry about such sordid details.

Now the fun starts in earnest—you are offered a "Tamara" cocktail, said to be potent, or the first glass of genuinely "unlimited" Perrier Jouet (non-vintage) champagne.

For me the most surprising thing about *Tamara* in retrospect, is how ingenious and intellectually valid its basic concept is. It doesn't work, but it's a lovely concept. (pp. 87-8)

In life an exit from one scene is always an entrance to another. *Tamara* tries to focus all at once on all the happenings in the house on this January day in 1927.

The house contains 10 people (apart from the audience and, of course, the homeless upstairs) and you can either follow one character and find out what happens to him or her, you can stay in one room and wait for things to happen, or you can flitter and flutter like a starstruck moth.

The story is obviously complex—and you can only spy and eavesdrop on certain parts of it. It is a jigsaw puzzle—and you may be seeing one significant part in the basement kitchen only to be missing another in the master's bedroom.

And who is the master? This is the Italian poet, patriot and bedroom bandit Gabriele d'Annunzio, at this point 63 years old with most of his loves past, his vaunted military occupation of Fiume seen as an act of empty bravado, his poetry already losing popularity, who is now being dangerously turned into a decorative puppet for Mussolini's Fascists.

This is 1927—two months earlier Mussolini had suppressed all opposition. Italy is becoming an armed camp. Should D'Annunzio escape to England and oppose the dictatorship he helped inspire?

A painter, Tamara de Lempicka, has come to the villa to paint the cocaine-sniffing poet. (In the best line I heard all evening her tardy arrival was lamented as "Will Tamara never come?" something that, set to music, could have come from *Annie*.)

The performances are perfectly adequate, but the melodramatic script (by John Krizanc) is perfectly irritating.

Richard Rose's direction solves its logistic problems—all these multifarious actions through 10 rooms must be dovetailed together—but cannot prevent the evening from exuding the same air of triviality inherent in charades.

Things a little like this—the James Joyce Liquid Memorial Theater and Irene Maria Fornes' *Madame Fefu*—have been done before, and more significantly.

But if you like charades, creme brulee and perfectly decent nonvintage champagne, and have nowhere to go on Saturday night but $135 to go with, this, old bud, might be for you.

Personally I'd rather spend 50 bucks on a Broadway show and have $85 left over for subway tokens. But for others it could be Tamara, and Tamara and Tamara. And all D'Annunzio's yesterdays. (p. 88)

Clive Barnes, "Champagne & Charades," in New York Post, *December 3, 1987.*

JOHN SIMON

Tamara takes place simultaneously on three floors and in various rooms and crannies of the Park Avenue Armory, transformed into Il Vittoriale, Gabriele d'Annunzio's palatial villa. The aging literary and military lion, kept under house arrest by his friend the Duce, awaits a professional visit from Tamara de Lempicka, the Polish Art Deco painter and aristocratic refugee from the Bolsheviks. It is January 10, 1927; D'Annunzio, the lover of many famous women, wants to add another scalp to his proto-Fascist belt; Tamara merely needs another portrait commission, and hates Fascism, Communism, and—by now, men equally. As the Canadian author, John Krizanc, has imagined it, the guests and staff of the villa are all dallying with one another or with Gabriele while spying on him or trying to enlist him in their causes.

The spectators are, as it were, visitors to a D'Annunzio theme park and harangued, hectored, or herded by Dante Fenzo, the valet; Aldo Finzi, a Jewish Fascist guard; or Aelis Mazoyer, Gabriele's lesbian confidante and social secretary. Split into three groups, we follow one or another of these guides, often at breakneck speed, as—upstairs, downstairs, and in the basement—*Tamara* and *Tamara* and more *Tamara* creeps at no petty pace. A spectator can keep up at best with one third, not necessarily the most important, and not enough to piece together the whole story. For this purpose, there is a catered dinner during intermission and a kaffeeklatsch after the show, where, consulting one another or a uniformed official (the premises crawl with waiters, waitresses, and sundry *ufficiali* who, on the strength of a couple of mispronounced Italian words, pretend to exude authenticity), we can fill in the gaps.

The idea for such a roving spectacle originated with Luca Ronconi's production of *Orlando Furioso*, where, however, anyone could pre-acquaint himself with the plot of Ariosto's epic; here one feels puzzled and frustrated as heard-of murders and suicides, rapes and lesbian seductions, take place in *other* rooms. Almost every speech is gimcrack rhetoric, every second line is a specious quasi-epigram; yet, at *Tamara's* prices, one wants it all. I, for example, hardly got anything of the fake chauffeur, said by many to be the true protagonist. And I got far too much of the aspiring ballerina . . . who wants D'Annunzio to recommend her to Diaghilev. And too much anti-Semitism way before it became a serious problem.

Language often makes no more sense than chronology: We are to believe that a French and an Italian speaker cannot understand each other—though the way languages are mauled here, that might just be the case. . . . Had I paid megabucks for *Tamara,* I might have felt otherwise; as it is, helped by pleasant drinks and food, as well as useful exercise up and down the stairs, I took it all with a benevolent, though not quite beatific, smile. (p. 46)

John Simon, "Methods of Madness," in New York Magazine, *Vol. 21, No. 1, January 4, 1988, pp. 45-6.*

JOHN KRIZANC [INTERVIEW WITH ANN JANSEN]

[Ann Jansen]: **Tamara** is a giant puzzle, with the audience putting together the pieces. Does puzzling it out distract from the intent of the play?

[Krizanc]: To some extent it does. To me the play's about that puzzle. I thought the best way to write a critique of Fascism was to give people more democratic freedom than they've ever had in the theatre. In this pluralistic society people of many different political and religious beliefs are trying to function together. For the audience, the intermezzo is important because it's about freedom of information, which you don't have in a Fascist state. In this theatrical democracy we set up, strangers have to make the play work by sharing information. **Tamara** is the only play I've been to where people actually talk about the play. But on the other hand, **Tamara** is destroyed by the sum of its parts, because the subtleties of the play, its implications, are overwhelmed by the experience. When Richard Rose and I conceived the play, it was never our intention that it should be about running around the house and drinking champagne. It grew out of a political concept, and the idea that one of the problems with theatre is that you're subjected to the particular politics of the authors or directors. As a small-l liberal, while I respect the intentions of that writing, I often find that I withdraw from the overstated politics. I like a theatre that is informative, but not one that is overtly aggressive.

Your work is often described as political theatre. Do you agree with that label?

I don't see myself as a political person. I think I tell morality stories. I try to be as compassionate as I can towards my characters; I try to humanize the bad guys. To me, **Prague** is not a Cold War play. I'd say this to the actors in **Tamara** all the time too. Shove all this political stuff under the rug. These characters live it: they've had these conversations a thousand times. They're just interested in surviving.

*Why did you choose politically charged situations for both **Tamara** and **Prague**?*

I was interested in my responses to them. D'Annunzio could have stopped Mussolini's rise to power, but he allowed himself to be bought, to be kept in women and cocaine. He had a live-in architect, a live-in string quartet and he spent his days designing his house. He lost his moral centre; to me, it's very tragic. **Tamara** is a cautionary tale.

Where does this moral questioning come from?

It probably comes from being a Catholic. We've killed off God but we still have all this guilt, and all these questions. We have to build our own theology again based on a sense of humanity.

You grew up in a politically aware household. Can you describe your political past?

My family's very political. We didn't eat dinner until my father finished reading Hansard. My father was a real Pearsonian Liberal and my brother was an NDP-er. They had tremendous fights. But I was always against politics. I hate people who are politically correct. I think it would be nice if the world was like that—if we could always know what side we should be on. I like moral activism. What I hate is people who let the truth become subservient to political ideology. I think it has to be a personal truth.

You've been quoted as saying, "Everything I've written is fundamentally about the struggle, the very hard struggle, to maintain the liberal views I was brought up with."

Yes. So much of being a small-l liberal is the ability to compromise. So often we're left standing still in the middle of the road not knowing which way to go because we're busy weighing the alternatives and trying to give each a fair shake. And we end up getting run over by a truck. The left and right have always intrigued me. My father's from Yugoslavia. His brother was a Communist, and denounced him, so he had to flee the country. Now his brother's retired, and they're finally reconciled, after 40 years of not seeing each other. When I write, I say, "Well, here's a problem. How do I feel about it? I don't know exactly how I feel about it, what about this side, what about that side?" I try to look at the issues from as many different perspectives as I can. And I think that's a very Canadian way to perceive the world. Compromise is essential to the Canadian character and is one of the Canadian virtues.

But you're also writing about the people who do take stands, however wrong-headed.

My interest is in exploring the personal reasons behind public actions. The frustration is that the material of drama is heroism. We're looking for modern ethics, wondering why we can't have tragedy any more, why everything is reduced to melodrama. But it's impossible to believe in heroes now. If you believe in a black-and-white Luke Skywalker approach to dramaturgy, you're not going to have a good time at any of my plays. I just don't see the world that way. In **Prague** I started out with bleeding-heart liberal intentions to write about some noble dissident, so I could live vicariously through somebody who takes a stand. It was also a response to **Tamara,** where D'Annunzio sells himself out to Fascism. I was intrigued by Vaclav Havel and Pavel Kahout and the other Czech writers who were standing up against Communist totalitarianism. I really admire those writers; I read everything in English on Czechoslovakia—hundreds of books. I went to Czechoslovakia; I was saddened because the dissident movement had been so successfully crushed. But I also have to question the consequences of those actions, of the stands that were taken. For example, Pavel Landovsky, who signed the Charter of 77, is now in Vienna and he's been told not to return. But as a result of that action, his first wife lost her job, the son from that marriage was kept out of the university, and the daughter was not allowed to graduate. Her apartment isn't heated, so she has a hacking cough and goes around like Camille. You think, so he's a better man for this because signing the Charter was the right thing to do. But what is the human cost? How many people have to fall in order for there to be goodness? (pp. 34, 36)

Ann Jansen, in an interview with John Krizanc, in Books in Canada, Vol. 17, No. 2, March, 1988, pp. 34, 36.

VIVIANA COMENSOLI

[In **Prague**], Krizanc explores the relation between politics, identity, and art in a totalitarian state. The year is 1983 and the setting is a stage where the Bread and Dreams Theatre Company of Prague is rehearsing *Magnificat*, a disguised allegory of the 1968 Soviet invasion of Czechoslovakia. By staging the subversive play for an audience which is to include Russian dignitaries, the author and artistic director Vladimir Rozek is prepared to sacrifice the company and his craft in order to atone for his betrayal of his dissident father. Prior to his father's death, Vladimir's strategy of survival was to compromise all principles for the sake of art: "If I hadn't renounced my father we wouldn't have a company, it's as simple as that." Vladimir's struggle foregrounds the play's central question, namely whether it is the artist's ethical imperative to be the conscience of society. It is to Krizanc's credit that the play never resorts to facile answers. Although Vladimir is a sympathetic character, his transformation from a writer of politically correct plays to a bold defender of the principles of the defunct Charter 77, the "non-political" group of playwrights, intellectuals, and workers to which his father belonged, occurs too late to be politically effective, and his script is never performed as he intended.

A more predictable line of action exposes the contradictions at the heart of totalitarian rule. Krizanc's harshest indictment is against the pseudo-aesthetics of "socialist realism," which extols mimes and clowns while maligning artists such as Franz Kafka for their lack of "optimism." However, Krizanc carefully balances the political theme with broad humour and compassion for all of his characters. Major Zrak, the aging police investigator for whom "culture is a great impediment" and foreign values counterfeit, listens to Frank Sinatra and seeks the autographs of party hacks. The Major, however, suffers from obvious melancholia and his maxims are as hollow as his eyes. Lenka, a clown in the troupe who plots to immigrate to the West, once worked in an illegal burlesque club whose status has been pending since one of the party secretaries caught crabs there. Lenka is the play's most spirited character, her brazen earthiness and passionate nature underscoring the insipidness of the world around her.

Krizanc has carefully balanced the inextricable link between role, script, and audience with the larger political and ethical contexts of playmaking.

> Viviana Comensoli, in a review of "Prague," in Canadian Literature, No. 118, Autumn, 1988, p. 136.

VACLAV TABORSKY

The prehistory of **Prague,** which won the 1987 Governor General's award for drama, is something of a theatrical joke by now. John Krizanc was writing a play "Magnificat" which grew to about 300 pages or six hours long. Both the writer and his director and friend Richard Rose realized it was unrealistic to proceed. Reading a book about Vaclav Havel and the Charter 77 at the time, Krizanc got an idea how to save at least part of the original project. Havel always wanted to write about people determined to improve the human condition, whatever the costs. Krizanc decided to write a play about a theatre company rehearsing that medieval play, that oversized "Magnificat." He believed he could reduce the original work to one historical act out of a three-act contemporary play. In the end, in **Prague** Krizanc used only several lines from "Magnificat."

Prague follows the fate of several people from "Bread and Dreams," a small theatre company in Czechoslovakia. They are staging escapist clown shows while rehearsing a serious historical play. The drama becomes a metaphor, a symbol of contemporary problems. The actors have to fight with state censorship, with their colleagues' opportunism, with misdirected ambitions which could jeopardize the company's existence. Their main goal is to survive. The actors have different recipes for survival: they drink, sleep around, want to escape to the West. Some collaborate with the authorities, some find recourse in creative work which will never be published.

Permanent stress conditions all the characters. Their struggle for survival means that people have several layers of resistance: subtle ways of defying the system, of escaping the system, and of a pretended compliance with the system. In an interview with me, John Krizanc said, "In Czechoslovakia everybody pretends he is acting in the best interest of everybody else, in the best interest of society. There is a lot of such false pretense."

In the second act we find out that **Prague** is also a play about wavering between principles and compromises. How much does an artist have to give up to express his beliefs; how much is he willing to sacrifice? The real moral question of the drama is focused on loyalty. Krizanc admits, "There are two problems in the play. One is survival. The other one has something to do with the form of the play. In a way, **Prague** is a medieval morality play. It deals with moral problems, not only from the Czech perspective, but also from the perspective of the contemporary world. It is about betrayal, and the consequences of such a betrayal."

Krizanc has researched his play thoroughly. The idea of capturing the problems of a small theatre company was based on the writer's visit to several small theatrical groups during his five weeks in Czechoslovakia. Many other details were based on observations from everyday life. Josef Rozek's death describes exactly the way Josef Patocka, a prominent Czech historian, and one of the leading members of the dissident movement Charter 77, died.

How important are the problems of **Prague** to our North American reality? Why should we care? Krizanc answers this question simply: "**Tamara** was about art in a fascist country, whereas **Prague** is about a theatre company in a communist country. Both plays are about relationship between artists and society."

Prague captures the struggle of everyday existence. True, our theatre companies, writers and other creative artists do not have to submit their work to state censors for approval (unless they get into trouble because of the infamous bill on pornography). Yet they are forced to fight for the public's approval and support with every new play or book. Fight for existence in our country takes a social, not a political form.

The company members in **Prague** are not what they seem to be at first sight. They are complex and controversial. The viewers have to balance the actors' character features: positive and negative, moral and immoral. Vladimir Rozek is an example. He is a party member, a conformist. Apart from that, he is also an unashamed opportunist, having renounced his dissident father. In the second act we find out, to our surprise, that he is the true author of Stefan Kura's popular plays. Vladimir gets hundreds of US dollars for his ghost writing. He passes the hard currency on to the father he had betrayed to alleviate his father's difficult material situation and also to alleviate his own guilt. (p. 85)

Krizanc has created many complex and controversial characters in his play: Vladimir Rozek, Stefan Kura (the successful communist writer), Zuzana from the Ministry of Culture, or

Honza, "part-time clown and full-time drunk" who comments on the events in the style of Czech passive resistance, in the way of Hasek's famous fictional hero. Jaroslav Hasek, the author of "Good Soldier Schweick," would be pleased by *Prague.*

Krizanc succeeds in capturing the plight of artists in a country where all media are controlled by the government. The actors from the "Bread and Dreams" company represent a true-to-life mixture of idealism, frustration and black humour. Most of them are loyal to their real friends; they are determined to keep the company going. (pp. 85-6)

> *Vaclav Taborsky, in a review of "Prague," in* Canadian Theatre Review, *No. 56, Fall, 1988, pp. 85-6.*

Robert (Paul) Kroetsch

1927-

Canadian novelist, poet, critic, editor, and travel writer.

Kroetsch is considered one of Canada's foremost practitioners and theoreticians of postmodern literature. Like many experimental writers, Kroetsch subverts such literary conventions as plot and character development and writes in a playful, ironic, and self-reflexive style. Central to Kroetsch's fiction is the importance of place and its impact on the psyche. Tensions resulting from his childhood in rural Alberta and his teaching experiences at American universities are reflected in the diversity of narrative voices Kroetsch employs, ranging from vernacular to erudite. Kroetsch often bases his novels on myths while exploring such themes as exile, loss, gender roles, and selfhood. Laurence Ricou commented: "Kroetsch discovers a symbolic richness in an empty vastness which has so often defied the imagination. But further, Kroetsch articulates new comprehension of the prairie landscape, both embracing the destructive nullity of his environment and defying it by a comic ebullience which celebrates man and life."

Kroetsch's childhood in rural Alberta, where most of his work is set, informs both his fiction and poetry. His family's penchant for storytelling imbued Kroetsch with a deep appreciation for oral narrative, which often emerges in his writing in the form of tall tales and ribald humor. After graduating from the University of Alberta in 1948, Kroetsch worked for six years in the Canadian North. His initial jobs on riverboats on the Mackenzie River led to the conception of his first and most conventional novel, *But We Are Exiles* (1965). In this work, which is based on the myth of Narcissus, Peter Guy navigates a boat up the Mackenzie River in search of the corpse of Michael Hornyak, his boss, ex-friend, and sexual rival, who has died aboard ship in an explosion that was possibly Guy's fault. When Hornyak's body is eventually put on a cast-off barge, Guy decides to join it. Kroetsch suggests that Hornyak and Guy represent the two faces of Narcissistic self-obsession and that Hornyak, Guy's *doppelgänger,* lures Guy to his death.

Kroetsch's next three novels, *The Words of My Roaring* (1966), *The Studhorse Man* (1969), and *Gone Indian* (1973), comprise what he calls the *Out West* triptych. In these works, Kroetsch explores the myths surrounding the Canadian prairie while also incorporating Greek and Roman mythic structures and recording momentous social changes from the 1930s to the 1970s. *The Words of My Roaring* chronicles political upheavals in Depression-era Alberta. This novel centers on a charismatic undertaker who wins a seat in the Legislative Assembly by promising to bring rain to drought-stricken farmers. In *The Studhorse Man,* which won the Governor General's Award, Kroetsch reworks *The Odyssey.* Narrated by Demeter Proudfoot, a madman sitting in an insane asylum bathtub, this novel takes the form of a biography of Hazard Lepage, the last "studhorse man." Lepage is seeking the ideal mare to mate with his prize stallion, Poseidon, the last of a breed nearing extinction because of increasing mechanization in rural Alberta. As the book progresses, the narrator inserts his own experiences into the story with increasing

frequency until the two tales merge. The novel ends ironically: Lepage impregnates his fiancée just before he is trampled to death by Poseidon, and the horse is used to help produce a birth control ingredient. Many critics interpreted *The Studhorse Man* as a parable about the termination of the lifestyle that created the cowboy myth of the American West. *Gone Indian,* the final volume of the *Out West* triptych, deals with several themes common to Kroetsch's work: differences between spoken and written language, distinctions between Canadians and North Americans, and contrasts between repressive forms of civilization and primitive types of existence. In this novel, an English professor urges a student suffering from writer's block and sexual impotence to leave his New York college and apply for a post at the University of Alberta. The student discovers the benefits of the northern wilderness and conquers his problems by transforming himself into his idol, Grey Owl, an Englishman who adopted an Indian lifestyle.

Kroetsch's next novel, *Badlands* (1975), revolves around a 1916 paleontological expedition in Alberta led by William Dawe, who is obsessed with finding large dinosaur fossils in hopes of achieving renown in the science world. Much of this book consists of his daughter Anna's commentary upon the sparse field notes Dawe left behind. Anna and an old Indian woman recreate her father's expedition fifty years after the event, revealing the absurdity of the project and male ambitions in general. In *What the Crow Said* (1978), Kroetsch utilizes a magic realist style to explore gender differences in Big Indian, Alberta. *Alibi* (1983), cited by critics as Kroetsch's most self-conscious novel, reiterates his interest in the quest myth and the rejuvenating power of water. William Dorfendorf, who procures objects for a mysterious oilman and collector, is sent on a worldwide search for the "perfect spa." Through his quest, Dorfendorf comes to understand the fundamental dichotomy of body and soul, sex and death, and art and life.

Several themes in Kroetsch's fiction recur throughout his poetry. In his early verse, collected in *The Stone Hammer Poems: 1960-1975* (1975), Kroetsch depicts prairie life in an imagistic, unaffected manner. Much of his subsequent poetry displays an irreverence toward language in order to expand its limits. Since 1975, Kroetsch has been composing an extended long poem-in-progress entitled *Field Notes*. A collage of memories, anecdotes, documents, and tall tales reflecting his preoccupation with the difficulties of literary expression, persona, and the burden of traditional poetic forms, *Field Notes* has been published in partial form in the volumes *The Ledger* (1975), *Seed Catalogue* (1977), *The Sad Phoenician* (1979), and *Advice to My Friends* (1985). As in his fiction, Kroetsch's poetry strives to, in his words, "demystify the written word." Some critics place *Field Notes* in the tradition of such epic poems as Ezra Pound's *Cantos,* William Carlos Williams's *Paterson,* and Charles Olson's *The Maximus Poems.*

Kroetsch is also a highly regarded literary critic. His critical essays evidence his interest in phenomenology, structuralism, deconstructionism, and linguistics, particularly as the latter relates to the ideas of Ferdinand de Sausurre. He also cofounded and served as editor for *Boundary 2,* a journal devoted to postmodern literature.

(See also *CLC,* Vols. 5, 23; *Contemporary Authors,* Vols. 17-20, rev. ed.; *Contemporary Authors New Revision Series,* Vol. 8; and *Dictionary of Literary Biography,* Vol. 53.)

PETER THOMAS

Kroetsch's novels and poems disclose the parody of Narcissus behind the Orphic mask and in the interplay of these symbolisms the poetics of silence is inescapable and central. In his poetry, furthermore, Kroetsch addresses fundamental problems of language and selfhood. These problems are given complex and sometimes diffuse expression in the novels, though any strict division of genre could be, in this context, misleading.

By way of introduction, some summary of perhaps familiar material is necessary. The Orphic and Narcissistic motifs are distinguished most radically at their points of seeming analogy. Both make a "dark descent" but that of Narcissus is, by definition, sterile and without issue or return. Not only is the embrace superficial, selfc's image not its "ground," but the function of language to "connect" with the "other" is disdained. Narcissus' silence is thus expressly a repudiation of

otherness. There is no reconstituted self. He chooses silence, descends, and is silenced.

While the Orphic is capable of immense sophistication—indeed, contains an imperative for such—some of its most persistent and available features can be stated quickly. The dark descent is metamorphic, there is a return and a newly made self incorporates loss with an agonized and guilty awareness of the other. The Orphic is despairing: language becomes impotent and contains no adequate expression for the human realization of love and death. Silence is also the inability to express private grief in public song. The Orphic must contain lyric, elegaic, and potentially tragic perceptions, yet is cursed by irony, since to speak is to find "voice," to affirm being, at the very same time and by the same action as to lose and fail. Words must falsify and disguise as much as they reveal or discover. To find tongue is also a losing. At the limits of experience "the rest is silence" for even the most eloquent of speakers. By withholding language, Orpheus can be seen as retreating into the self which will not "connect." He, thus, seemingly appears closer to Narcissus.

In *Badlands,* when William Dawe writes in his field-notes/journal, "I have come to the end of words," the echo of *Hamlet* is surely intentional, and with it the kinds of resonating questions concerning language and selfhood posed by the play. Dawe's fieldnotes are consistently Narcissistic, an attempt to provide an historical record of devotion to scientific aims which is really Dawe's "heroic" self-projection. The language of the notes vacillates between the cryptic and the poetic as Dawe struggles to maintain his fictive self, necessarily exclusive, against the claims of human relationship and love. The death of Tune, probably his severest test, brings forth only the pinched and grudging *"Tune. Dead,"* and the fact that Tune is himself an Orphic figure (the musician rescued from a coal-mine), at least potentially, makes this death-notice pointedly expressive. For Dawe first attempted to make a "son" out of Tune, by accommodating the latter to his own obsessive search for dinosaur bones—the same obsession which causes Tune's death. Narcissus must eradicate any trace of the Orphic in himself and Dawe's acknowledgement of Tune's death is about as far from the elegaic as language can go. It is, therefore, entirely appropriate, a way-station to silence.

Kroetsch has claimed that "silence is a terrible temptation to Canadians. Young Canadian writers I meet are terribly tempted just to embrace silence. . . . Canadians have this terrible fear that they'll look in the mirror and nobody's there." The embrace, the mirror, even the "terror" (too easily dismissed as an interview-tic) expose Kroetschian compulsions present from his first novel, *But We Are Exiles,* where the Narcissus motif is expressed in the epigraph. It provides the main structural narrative symbolism, in the relations of Peter Guy/Mike Hornyak, two faces of self-love embracing at the conclusion, and their Echo, Kettle Fraser. Like Dawe's Narcissistic refusal to assay the language of loss or love, Guy's consciousness (the narrative point of view) is reflected in prose sparse to the point of anonymity, a kind of hoarding of innerness, a fear of the vulnerability of "voice."

Characteristically—for he continues to work with dual, paired, or antithetical strategies—Kroetsch shifted from the language of concealment and evasion to the pseudo-confessional Johnnie Backstrom, in *The Words of My Roaring,* a quintessential talking-man who moves, in the course of the novel, from one tone to another, always tempted by hyperbole. Backstrom is not much good at loving either, though Kroetsch works hard at redeeming him through his energy and yearning for "the old chaos." In his relations with his wife and Helen Murdoch, Backstrom combines Hornyak's apparent fire with Guy's final icy untouchability, his yielding only to himself. In moments of self-scrutiny, however, Backstrom begins to allow, like Dawe later, the possibility of a language of loss and intimacy, only to fall back into the self-centered and unconnected "roaring" of the title.

In *The Words of My Roaring,* the lyric and tragic potentiality is resisted by the first stirrings of Kroetsch's thanaturgical comedy. Backstrom is the first of Kroetsch's bullshitters (excluding the vestigial Hornyak)—a role which he invests with more than usual importance. In one major scene, where Backstrom witnesses the death of a rodeo clown, he approaches the meaning of the Orphic silence only to withdraw into the Narcissism of compulsive speech, the song of himself.

He reads the symbolism himself. "The body mangled and ripped by those gouging horns, the innocent figure mutilated, rolled and trampled in the stinking dust. The spirit struck into frantic despair; I saw it all right." Some identity is implied when we are told that the clown is about Backstrom's height. But this figure of innocence and despair also symbolizes the failure of language before death. "He kept trying to say something to me, a perfect stranger, but he couldn't make it. He tried to raise a hand and point but couldn't and I wanted to point for him but didn't know where." The unspeakable wisdom of the endgame, our last failure of connection; against this, Backstrom's speech to the crowd is ironic. "Vote for the clown" introduces all the force of his new-found biblical eloquence, a flood of language seeming to compensate for the clown's own lapse into silence. Backstrom thus becomes a paradoxical clown of death, the undertaker who returns from his vision of despair and wordlessness, the impossibility of connection, to an absurd roaring which substitutes for terror and which is language not as communication/connection, but as self-display.

It may be, as George Steiner has written, that "Whenever it reaches out toward the limits of expressive form, literature comes to the shore of silence." When Kroetsch employed the device of a tale told by an idiot, in *The Studhorse Man,* he not only invoked "unreliability" but also the justification of fictive elaboration. After Backstrom's desperate roaring, came Demeter Proudfoot's rigmarole. As his career developed, Kroetsch became more committed to the *zeitgeist,* at least insofar as it could be described as "Post-Modern," and his co-editorship of *Boundary 2* (devoted to the definition of that term) must be taken seriously. Louis K. MacKendrick has made a useful summary of the growing terminology of Post-Modernism. "The literature of exhaustion," "metafiction," "fabulation," "irrealism," "surfiction," "the architechtonic novel" are all ways of describing

> fiction whose subject is fiction in the making, the creative process in action. It is often manifested in parodic forms and an indulgence in private fantasy which threatens to become precious. But in its sophisticated examples this species of reflexive writing sports with and flaunts the mechanics of the imagination and the devices of expression. . . . Its motives still reverence the light-bearers, Apollo and Prometheus, but its patron is the self-regarding, Echo-haunted Narcissus.

This is well-stated. It also begs questions—primarily, whether "exhaustion," implying a loss of faith in traditional imaginative forms and the stability of structures of language as such, can ever be anything, despite its busy knowingness and cannibalistic verbal dances, but a declaration of despair. A good example of "exhaustion," though presented comically, comes when Jeremy Sadness tries to describe his union with Bea Sunderman in *Gone Indian:*

> To speak would be to boast. And I was speechless. Perhaps I roared. I am not certain now. I did not moan. To say that we were joined, Bea and I, would be, once again, to underline the failure of language. We were welded in the smithy of our mutual desire. Fused in the bellowed flame. Tongued and hammered. . . . No no no no no no. I have ransacked my twenty-five years of education for a suitable metaphor. I have done a quick review of logic, called upon the paradigms of literature and history. I have put to test the whole theory of a liberal education.
>
> Nothing.

This is close, dangerously close, to one of Kroetsch's main narrative strategies. Centred in the sexual act and its metaphorical possibilities, his novels ring the changes upon traditional narrative forms by parodies of quest archetypes, alternating points of view and familiar character types, before confronting the unknown and unutterable in an "open" ending. All those clever words to draw back a curtain on the void? Yet to say this is unfair to Kroetsch's serious questioning of how to speak. The author, unlike his persona, flees and returns.

Nevertheless, this suspicion of faithlessness before the act of utterance itself, however comic its expression, is the Post-Modern version of the Orphic agony. Kroetsch is too critically aware not to recognize that his ingenuity and virtuosity with parodic forms and the structural pun can lead to Narcissistic faking of that agony. The writer's skill so easily becomes his image, the book his mirror, the terror shut-out. In this sense, the satire upon "print" or "Gutenberg" men in Kroetsch's novels is part of an attempt to free voice from the suppressed tyranny of the book as a structure. Roderick W. Harvey observes that both Demeter Proudfoot and Jeremy Sadness "are Gutenberg men who are trapped, respectively, by print and tapes," and this entrapment is even plainer in the case of Liebhaber, in Kroetsch's most recent novel, *What the Crow Said,* a printer who shuffles type-face in grotesque efforts to form words. His name is as Orphic as they come. But love can be reduced to a twitchy helplessness before language.

What the Crow Said is the least compromising novel Kroetsch has written, in terms of this meeting with silence. Only a brief and selective account can serve here, though the absolute question of who speaks and by what authority, implicit in the title, does beg some analysis. Metaphorically, the Dawe of *Badlands* who reaches silence before his death is punningly resurrected in the talking crow of Kroetsch's next novel (*dawecrow*), whose speech, for all the ominous weight of its death symbolism, consists of banal, jokey obscenities. This traditional harbinger of death is denied all elegiac or tragic overtones. Not only this, but the crow is peculiarly irritating to Liebhaber, the putative "hero," a caricatured semblance of faithful devotion whose doom is a happy ending. In their exchanges, Love and Death speak to each other like cartoon mouse and cat. While it would be unproductive to summarize the "plot" of a novel which is clearly part of the war against plot (to adopt the title of one of Jeremy's abortive theses), its intention is to unmake notions of narrative "development" and "motivation," by employing a series of fabulous happenings in and near the Prairie town of Big Indian, some crypto-mythical, some merely fantastic, all having their sanction in the oral story-teller's freedom from temporal and spatial determinisms. In short, what the crow says is almost all bull-shit.

In the opening scene, Vera Lang is impregnated by a swarm of bees. Later, she gives birth to a miraculous child, a boy, only to fling him to a pack of wolves as she makes her escape by sled. But Vera's Boy reappears as a wolf-boy and succeeds in learning only a substantially unintelligible form of human speech. This set of events has one meaning plainer than others. The wondrous birth, strange and sacred, with all its associations of honeyed earth and golden flight, speaks gibberish. But the case of Tiddy Lang (Vera's mother) and her son is even plainer, in these terms. John Gustav is perfectly beautiful, smiling radiantly all the time, and is "eternally young." He also refuses to speak a word. The silence of this Narcissus is broken only by the crow, which arrives soon after his birth, and "sometimes spoke on behalf of JG." A carrion spokesman for supreme self-love—yet JG's silence is not perhaps his most emphatic expression of contempt for "connection" with the other. Everywhere he goes, boy and man, he fills his pants. An infantile *reductio ad excretum* of the human predicament, to smile benignly, in shit and silence, on the world.

Since *What the Crow Said* includes a War Between Earth and Sky, the relations of fundament and firmament are clearly in mind. The novel is a parody of metaphysics in its cosmic religious and existential dramas, seen respectively in the inane speculations of Father Basil and in Vera's orgasmic experience, a Kroetschian pun on bee-ing and bee-coming. JG's reduction of language to fundament is further reiterated late in the novel by the death of Joe Lightning who falls into a cesspit after trying to fly. Flight, aspiration, and even the Fortunate Fall are reduced to crap—this is a powerful nihilistic strain, admittedly drawn from a complex novel.

Kroetsch's fondness for antithesis—Eden and Apocalypse, male and female, flight and descent, only to begin the list—leads him to extreme statements of extreme situations. In *Badlands,* the symbolism of the two women, Anna Yellowbird and Anna Dawe, is firmly dualistic. Both may be versions of the *anima,* as Connie Harvey has suggested, but the relations of the surnames exposes the Orphic/Narcissistic problem sharply. Both women are necessary. Yet the songbird (canary) and the croaker (crow), expressing the spring/winter duality, have different implications for language. (pp. 33-9)

> *Peter Thomas, "Robert Kroetsch and Silence," in*
> Essays on Canadian Writing, *Nos. 18-19, Summer-*
> *Fall, 1980, pp. 33-53.*

DAVID MACFARLANE

Alibi concerns itself with the exploits, mainly sexual, of William Dorfen (known as Dorf to his friends), a globe-trotting procurer of unusual objects for Jack Deemer, a millionaire Calgary oilman and collector. For mysterious reasons, Deemer instructs Dorfen to "find me a spa," and for even more obscure reasons, Deemer's mistress, Julie Magnuson, seduces Dorfen in the Banff hot springs and tells him that if he does find a spa, she will have to kill him. Orgasms, scalding showers, an avalanche, more orgasms, water cures and mud baths ensue as clues to a central puzzle. The plot, not to be outdone by the thickening symbols, steadily congeals in its passage from Banff to Bath, in England, Wales, Portugal and Greece. In the Aegean Sea an octopus seizes Dorfen's private parts, and he muses, "Is not life itself our own vexed adhesion to what we do not comprehend?" By that time, the reader begins to suspect that Kroetsch is not so much interested in weaving a story as in preparing a syllabus of essay topics for undergraduate students of Canadian literature.

Alibi is about bathing, healing, curing, purifying, cleansing, drinking, sweating, ejaculating and vomiting. Lest anyone forget his grand theme of liquids, Kroetsch dispenses with almost everything else between the two covers. Its pages are sodden with imagery, but the characters are faceless and uninteresting; their adventures are neither vivid enough to be plausible nor outrageous enough to be fantastic.

Apparently, Kroetsch intended the straight stuff of both his "meaning" and his more poetic passages—some of which are admirably, even beautifully written—to be mixed with the soda pop of his comic flourishes. *Alibi's* chapters have titles such as *A Visitor Arrives And Dorf Is, To Say The Least, Discombobulated.* The quasi-surrealistic, quasi-picaresque rambunctiousness of the novel could only have been intended to add up to what some critics invariably call "a high-spirited entertainment." In fact, that intention is so obvious, self-conscious and finally irritating that Kroetsch's humor is, to say the least, as flat as day-old ginger ale.

> *David Macfarlane, "Outpourings of a Leaky Imagination," in* Maclean's Magazine, *Vol. 96, No. 35,*
> *August 29, 1983, p. 51.*

ALBERTO MANGUEL

One of the few basic plots available to a writer of fiction is that of the quest. The purpose of the quest may be hidden even to the writer (in fact, the obscurity of the goal may be, as in Kafka, the purpose of the story); the obstacles encountered along the way become the story itself. Robert Kroetsch's past fiction explores a number of such quests. We understand that in the beginning something has been lost, and that the characters set out in search of that something. Whether they achieve their goal or not is no longer important: essential to the novel is the quest itself. (p. 20)

In *Badlands* and *The Studhorse Man* Kroetsch's Aegean is the province of Alberta. [*Alibi*] is also a quest, but unlike the others it is not limited to one part of the world. In *Alibi* the traveller has suddenly widened his horizons: Alberta yes, but also England, Portugal, and above all Greece, where the Ulysses theme is brought back to its source. It also serves as contrast: Alberta (vast, wintery, or green) set against Greece (small, summery, and dry). This time the quest is borrowed: it is not the hero's own, even though it does become his own in the end. We guess at the plot: Kroetsch seems to be saying that whatever we look for, in the end we find only ourselves. We are the answer, no matter what the question might be.

Alibi is told through the voice of Billy Billy Dorfendorf (Dorf for short), a man in his 40s whose wife has been unfaithful and who is now employed by an invisible millionaire called Deemer to scour the world for all kinds of things that take the millionaire's fancy. Names have a special significance in Kroetsch's work. "Dorfendorf" repeats the German word for "village" (Kroetsch was brought up in a bilingual household), and the idea of travelling "from village to village" is imbedded in Dorf's name. Deemer (Old English for "judge") is a modern superpower, infernally rich, with spies in every country. He is that faceless, voiceless god (Dorf speaks only to his secretary) who spins his servant's destiny. We can guess that, like Chesterton's Sunday in *The Man Who Was Thursday,* perhaps the finest example of a modern quest, Deemer becomes anything his servant dreads or wishes, a divinity fashioned by man's prayers, an ogre bred by man's own nightmares. The novel's title is of course Latin for "elsewhere"—the exile's home, and also his excuse.

The novel begins when Deemer sends Dorf on one of his wild quests: this time in search of a spa. . . .

The first spa Dorf discovers is in the Rockies, and he decides to visit it accompanied by a lady friend, Karen Strike, a filmmaker. As soon as they arrive (barely five pages into the book) Dorf, in the spa's steaming pool, meets a beautiful floating head: her name is Julie Magnuson, and Dorf makes love to her in the hot, vaporous waters. When Julie unexpectedly blurts out "I'll kill you," Dorf begins to suspect that his life may be in danger. (pp. 20-1)

Next day Dorf persuades Karen to leave him on his own in the spa (he hopes to see Julie again) and to come back a few days later with a change of his clothes. In a laundromat he comes across his third woman, Estuary, and Dorf's pilgrimage begins. First Bath, in England (on the plane Dorf meets his elder sister Sylvia), then Portugal where, as if by chance, he sees Julie again, this time accompanied by a dwarf, a Portuguese doctor called Manuel de Medeiros. Dorf, Julie, and the small doctor form a curiously shaped love-triangle until Julie is killed in a car accident seemingly intended for Dorf. Dorf leaves for Greece, Karen comes to join him, and Dorf's two teenage daughters (in his former wife's custody) drop in to visit. In Greece he takes to mud-bathing, which he believes will cure him of all his ailments (whatever they may be), and while wallowing achieves the best orgasm of his life in the capable hands of a group of Greek women.

At last Dorf returns to Calgary, and somewhere near Banff he finds the perfect spa. Mysteriously, all the characters meet, including a spectral Deemer and the ghostly voice of the dead Julie. Why? How? The novel ends with a few pages from Dorf's journal (a gift from Karen) in which a few more facts, mainly dealing with ornithological matters, are given. The final note seems to read "to be continued," but that is no excuse: the book as it stands should make sense in itself. Perhaps Kroetsch is saying that after a long quest for a spa, Dorf has discovered that whatever we seek for (like Maeterlinck's blue bird) lies at home.

Two important variations occur in *Alibi's* Odyssean plot (I might add that in one of Dorf's adventures he meets a character who, like Ulysses, calls himself Nobody). The first is a variation on the fountain of eternal youth theme: spas, health, youth, water, sex, and the passage of time are traditionally linked. Karen points out that Deemer may be looking for just such a fountain, and in drinking the waters from many spas Dorf is more or less consciously (we infer) looking for the miraculous one that will cure all evil. The very notion of its existence gives hope to the quest; simply believing that a miracle may be encountered tinges life with a sense of the miraculous.

Dorf, who has found so many strange things for Deemer (Sicilian dominoes, a collection of teeth, the skeletons of every kind of sea-creature in the world including a mermaid, a showcase of rare eggs) does not question Deemer's demands: he acts on the assumption that if it can be requested it can be found, and furthers this belief by supposing that if it can be looked for it must exist. (p. 21)

The second variation, whether deliberate or not, is a parody of the James Bond films, and this unsuccessful parodic style is, I believe, at the root of *Alibi's* failure as a novel. *Don Quixote* is, among many other things, a parody of novels of chivalry, and as such it works because books such as *Amadis* or *Tirant lo Blanc* did not set out to outdo themselves, to become their own caricatures. The James Bond films, on the other hand, *intend* to appear larger than life (and twice as real); they are, so to speak, their own parody; it is impossible to carry the joke one step further. Even though Kroetsch may not have used the James Bond theme intentionally, all the elements that stereotype the genre are there: the adventurous unattached man, the beautiful, willing (but deadly) women, the acrobatic love-making, the invisible M-like boss, the money-is-no-object attitude, the five-cities-in-three-days setting.

Alibi can be defined as a parodic quest in which neither the language, nor the characters nor the story itself, is convincing. (pp. 21-2)

Kroetsch's *Alibi* fails in that the language, the characters, the visible plot, are not up to the quality the *intended* story requires, the story one dimly sees behind the dregs of the story presented. Given the rest of Kroetsch's work, one cannot but suspect the existence of a better idea behind *Alibi.* Here and there along the 239 pages are intimations of immortality, as when Dorf reflects on Calgary's cemetery, and his thoughts lead on to other "great cities of the New World", and Calgary itself sees the fate of the "great Mayan places . . . as sun-scarred and ambitious and intent as this one" (every one of these three adjectives is perfectly chosen and necessary), or as when Dorf meets Nobody in the cavern. Unfortunately, these are just glimmers that heighten the general sensation of fogginess. (p. 22)

Alberto Manguel, "No Excuses," in Books in Canada, *Vol. 12, No. 8, October, 1983, pp. 20-2.*

DAVID CLARK

[Like most of Robert Kroetsch's other fiction], *Alibi,* is episodic, shaped by the movement of its main character through beds, bars, and other badlands. After receiving enigmatic orders from his wealthy employer, William William Dorfen sets out on a quest for the "perfect spa" which takes him to England, Wales, Portugal, and Greece—far from the prairie environment Kroetsch's work usually occupies. Along the way he and we learn all about something called "hydrotherapy, the wonderful tradition of treating disease with that most cleansing of all the elements, water itself." The diseases plaguing all "the bruised and hurting people" who visit these spas are, however, a metaphor for a more profound soul-sickness that afflicts the novel's central characters, if in different ways.

The novel's title is the key, for it describes a condition of mental displacement in which one lives "somewhere else," a doubled life just as Dorfen's Christian name is doubled. "We all live by our alibis," one of his lovers points out, meaning that we suffer from a restlessness that thwarts our ability to act on our own desire and create ourselves. (pp. 74-5)

A turning point comes when, with Kroetsch's love of conjoining the bizarre and the profound, a sticky encounter with a friendly octopus moves Dorf to a sense of his own troubled life. "Is not life itself," he wonders, "our own vexed adhesion to what we do not comprehend?" Acceptance of the limits of making sense is the first step enabling him to revalue the sense that can be made. Through a series of symbolic woundings, meetings with ambiguously threatening women, and immersions in the healing waters of various spas, Dorf begins the process of making "peace" with himself.

To be human, Kroetsch's novel suggests, is never to achieve the unself-conscious stupidity that Dorf envies in the octopus; it is to live life along the pulses, with all the peril that implies, inventing and reinventing the world as Dorf does when he writes the journal that makes up *Alibi.* In the winter darkness of a hotel room Dorf is asked to speak his mind. "I want to be loved" is all he says, in a phrase whose simple pathos seems for the moment uncharacteristically impervious to Kroetsch's parodic knife. Intimacy is the cure for alibi; the act of writing represents, as it does for the narrators of several of Kroetsch's earlier novels, a closing of a psychic wound, an intimacy with the self won through the assertion of the imagination. . . .

Notwithstanding the irony of the chapter titles, Dorf is quite able to sink his own ship. Too often he falls back on clichés to describe his insights. Nudism, eating large quantities of feta cheese, and sex under water are all associated by Dorf with what he calls being "natural" or "in touch with the world." When, at the novel's end, he retreats to a lonely cabin in the Rockies to do things like assessing the aesthetics of his morning stool, it appears as if one pathology has replaced another. If we are to take this triteness at face value, then Kroetsch has gone too far. But more likely, considering Kroetsch's interest in undercutting literary conventions, we are expected to see through such simple-minded Rousseauism, and come away from the novel sensing both the limitations and victories of its narrator. Dorf's water peace is dangerously close to infantilism, and his search for it leads him in the end to a regressive state of prenatal isolation.

What is interesting is that Kroetsch has sabotaged his narrator but not his narrator's discoveries. In the process he gives us a beautifully written story of strange tensions and suggestive ambiguities, as befits a diagnosis of the disease called man. (p. 75)

David Clark, "Water on the Brain," in Saturday Night, *November, 1983, pp. 74-5.*

LINDA HUTCHEON

That a novel entitled *Alibi* should begin in the following way is perhaps not surprising: "Most men, I suppose, are secretly pleased to learn their wives have taken lovers; I am able now to confess I was." The "confession" that follows, however, is anything but a conventional spy or detective story alibi. Yes, the trappings are there: the lone hero; the dangerous sexy women; even the first-person narrative based on journal notes and the intrusion of a third person in the often sarcastic chapter headings. . . . But the subtle doubling of voicing that occurs through the ironic tension between heading and

chapter is the formal analogue of the entire structure of a novel whose hero, named after two grandfathers with the same name, is Billy Billy Dorfen (or, in full, William William Dorfendorf). His two daughters, he has named Jinn and Jan (suggesting Ying and Yang, as well as *Jules et Jim*). Dorf is a man with two lives and two lovers; things happen to him in twos, even attempts on his life. . . . (pp. 76-7)

His first life, as a husband, father, and museum curator ends when he points a gun at his wife's lover and realizes he could pull the trigger. In his second life, he rejects all human ties that cannot be dealt with "in financial terms": he organizes his time around the whims of a reclusive Alberta oil millionaire, Jack Deemer, a man bent on collecting anything there is to be collected. . . . As the novel progresses, the collector becomes a discoverer figure, like Columbus, and a conqueror, like Philip II. Or rather, it is the collector's agent that makes these roles possible: "The collection itself only confirms the discontinuity of this scattered world; it's my talk that puts it together," according to Dorf. The ambivalence of *Alibi's* collecting is what marks it as different from that of Fowles in *The Collector* where to collect is to kill. Here, collecting is still lethal, but it is also an attack on randomness; it is a way of coping with time past, "a calling up of ghosts from a million ancestral pasts"; it is a means of "acting out reality." In all these functions, collecting becomes, for Dorf, a metaphoric surrogate for writing. Karen, the woman who gives Dorf his journal as a gift, realizes: "You invent yourself, each time you sit down to make an entry." When ordered to investigate and buy a collection of skeletons, Dorf makes the connection for us: "I couldn't leave the city to go to whatever Turkish port was home to that treasure. Just as I couldn't write in my journal."

Dorf's two lives are separated by his realization that he is capable of killing someone. The presence of death looms over this novel, a paradoxical novel that, on one level, is a bawdy and amusing romp. Yet, the deliberate echo of Joyce's "The Dead" ("I drove through the falling snow. Snow was general on the eastern slope of the Rockies") signals to the reader that this story will also be one about loving, living, and dying. As in the poetry of Yeats and Eliot, ambivalence is the key to interpreting the dominant imagery of earth and water: both are sources of life and death—mystically and in specific plot terms in the novel itself. The story revolves around Dorf's search for a perfect spa for Deemer. From the bowels of the earth (the source of his oil money), Deemer appears to seek some fountain of youth in healing waters. In the first spa he visits, Dorf meets Julie, Deemer's dangerous lady, who offers him both spa-style (underwater) sex and a simultaneous threat of death, should he find that perfect spa. Julie, in particular, but woman, in general, partakes of the same ambivalence as water and earth: she is both womb and tomb, the goddess of abundance and life (Dorf's sister is an egg producer in Alberta) and the vengeful deity of death, who (presumably) is ultimately trapped in her own machinations. To enter the earth's caves in search of healing waters is linked to being buried under an avalanche of frozen, considerably less healthy water, and it is Julie who leads Dorf to both. Sex and death are another of Kroetsch's doubles in this novel.

The underlying duality, however, is a basic and familiar one—that of body and soul: "We dwell in the body, nowadays. With the world gone hank-end and haywire too, we live in the selfc's body. As if to cure the body's pain is to be cured. We are all St. Augustines in this broken world; saints not of the soul but of the body, of the bloodstream and back." Hence the search for the curing waters that leads Dorf from Alberta to Bath to Portugal and finally to Greece. Throughout, the doubling proliferates. Meeting Julie again at a spa in Portugal, Dorf becomes involved in a bizarre sex triangle with Julie and a dwarf doctor, Manuel de Medeiros. (pp. 77-8)

The imagery involving sex and woman in the novel is always doubled or ambivalent, even when related to the source of life. To Dorf "omphalos" may be a "mountain word," but it is clearly also another of those ubiquitous "holes in the ground" of the mother/earth that brings forth both healing and death. All of these metaphors culminate in the "smelly woman" in Greece and her mud cave. We are prepared for the centrality and universality of this scene by parallels drawn with the earlier parts of the novel (more doubling, if you prefer): to Dorf, Greece is reminiscent of the prairies at home; Philippi, near the mud cave, was also an important mining centre. Lining up with the other men to enter the cave, Dorf has his vision of Everyman: "We were a road-construction gang, ten threshing crews from the dirty thirties. We were the people who miss every bus on a wet and muddy street with a lot of traffic passing. We were a soup line. We were the ragtag survivors of Napoleon's visit to Moscow." Then he adds: "We were the bearers of human ache." Realizing "what work and disease and age will do for the human body," Dorf enters and discovers that conjunction of water and earth: mud. One figure in the mud draws "an opening," or female genitalia on his head: "As if he'd figured a way to escape the world. Or enter it." This figure turns out to be the "smelly woman"—that is, an hermaphrodite. In accepting all the dualities and ambivalences that constitute life, Dorf can begin to construct himself, literally, out of mud. He breaks the rules of the spa: he exits naked but "decently coated in mud," is reborn as part of nature, and then re-enters the cave to plunge into the mud—this time during the women's hour. This very overt return to the womb results in another of Dorf's sexual experiences fraught with symbolic value, but this time the mud and the women offer love and life, not death.

The final "resolution" of the ambivalences of the novel is not here, however. At Julie's coffin, Dorf finds a message about what will be Deemer's perfect spa and its name is not insignificant: Deadman Spring. Here Dorf works out his salvation. In a parodic inversion of Ulysses and the Cyclops, Dorf gives a nameless, one-eyed man one of his names (Billy), and his cure and curing both begin. Dorf must be led from his initial vision of life—"blood, semen, sweat, shit, hair, fingernails, toenails, piss, pus. The infinite dribble of excrement that is life. Why go on? For the mixed pleasure of an orgasm?"—to an acceptance of the body and its desires as natural and good. And what comes to be associated with the same qualities is the act of writing: Dorf tends his journal "as a gardener tends his sprouts and his blossoms." Desire exists in word and deed: "To be intimate. To intimate." He tries to explain to Julie that to touch is to talk: "Intimacy is, finally, an intimacy of telling." Hence, the journal; hence, the novel.

At Deadman Spring, Dorf waits for Deemer (whom he has never met or spoken to), a Godot figure earlier described as "unapproachable," a "conundrum," "a mystery." Heralded by Karen Strike and her documentary cameras ("Deemer sent me."), is he too a doubled figure, a punning *re*-Deemer? He arrives, enters the cave in a blinding light (Karen's cam-

era lighting) as a "walking skeleton." In the equally blinding darkness that follows, the cave becomes the cosmic "final black hole" in which touching takes on its full scope of meaning. (pp. 78-9)

Retreating afterwards to a cabin on a cliff in the woods, Dorf composes the narrative we have read. Instead of constructing a mud man, this time he makes a word man. But the last pages are pure journal and as such provide no neat, satisfying ordering or resolving; in short, no fictionalizing. The doubled or twice written story ends with a memory of Julie's death as Dorf is "violated," a memory and a metaphor: her car plunging over the cliff "like a period, on a blank page." To leave one's mark on the landscape or on the page is to court death, as Kroetsch explored in **What the Crow Said.** Writing fixes and kills, but like collecting, it can also offer a means to new life through art. Alone in nature, writing, Dorf can accept ambivalence, most succinctly symbolized by the salmon "spawning and dying" in the creeks. His interest in the young osprey learning how to fly is countered by his being accidentally responsible for another death. The doubled cry of the osprey ("*Gwan-Gwan*") that ends the novel reasserts life in the face of death. Plummeting to the ground on their first and perhaps fateful attempt to fly, the young birds find their wings and soar, tearing at last, in Dorf's words, "the sadness from my heart."

These final words of the novel suggest some resolution, but it is one that must come from acceptance of ambivalence. Quests in modern literature do not always lead to one answer, be they in Eliot's *Wasteland* or in Kroetsch's *Alibi.* There are always excuses; there are always elsewheres. The final great collectors, the final artists, are universals that defy single meaning: "Death, like love, is a great arranger. This collector, too, has a corrosive sense of style." The final duality we are left with is the novelist's eternal obsession: that of art and life. (pp. 79-80)

Linda Hutcheon, "Double Vision," in Canadian Literature, *n. 102, Autumn, 1984, pp. 76-80.*

ROBERT LECKER

In **Labyrinths of Voice,** a book-length interview conducted with Robert Kroetsch by Shirley Neuman and Robert Wilson, Kroetsch remarks that "falling out of cosmologies is at least an illusion of freedom, of becoming a fragment again, of opening up possibilities." In one way or another this statement can be applied to all of Kroetsch's novels, which increasingly equate the discovery of "freedom" with the denial of any cosmology that binds story to inherited narrative models and conventions. But if "falling out of cosmologies" provides only "an illusion of freedom," the question remains: how can *true* freedom be found? The story-teller confronted with this question faces a double bind, for the very act of telling consigns him to a temporal cosmology. However "experimentally" conveyed, story is communicated through language, pattern, and forms that imply a shared and rooted understanding of how narrative works. Based on identifiable codes, words, and names, story is founded in recognition and is by nature historical, dependent for its meaning on something previously known. To be involved in story is to be involved in temporality, and temporality, in human terms, implies death. If Kroetsch's novels are increasingly concerned with defying temporal structures through anti-story (a concern linked to his postmodern stance), it is because they are pro-life, pro-movement, pro-freedom. To the question: how can true freedom be found? the paradoxical answer is this: true freedom means *not* telling the story.

One way of explaining this paradox is to see it as the product of Kroetsch's emphasis on an ongoing dialectic between binary forces. Both sides of any equation must be maintained for their sliding centre to survive. But this explanation really skirts the issue: Kroetsch cannot authentically embrace the freedom offered by anti-story because to do so would require that he *not* write, that *he* provide us with the blank page he forces his characters to seek. The double bind plagues Kroetsch; indeed, the narrative strategies he employs in successive novels suggest that he has persistently tried to balance story and anti-story, not so much because the balance affirms a dialectic, or even a postmodern stance, but because it is the only way he can distance himself from the kind of writing which implicitly questions the writing act that defines him. In *But We Are Exiles* (1965) Peter Guy moves toward anti-story by fleeing his Ontario-based father, yet he cannot abandon his past; in *The Words of my Roaring* (1966) Johnie Backstrom escapes writing by ostensibly defining himself as Voice, but the story is nevertheless produced by his narration; in *The Studhorse Man* (1969) Demeter Proudfoot approaches anti-story as he begins to approximate the silent Hazard Lepage, yet he maintains a distaste for his metamorphosis; and in *Gone Indian* (1973) Mark Madham goes so far as to articulate a theory of anti-story as he traces Jeremy's flight from concluded speech, but he is repelled by the theory and seeks to evade it at every turn. None of Kroetsch's characters has truly embodied the drive to anti-story that Kroetsch both evokes and evades. What stops them?

The most obvious answer is that Kroetsch wants to keep writing. The product of this desire is guilt (why do I insist on creating story while I stake my reputation on anti-story?). His means of coping with this guilt is to foist it on the narrative, so that the text must paradoxically resolve the double bind that he, the writer, cannot. This is why the narrative impulses behind Kroetsch's novels are increasingly guilt-driven. In the early novels, Kroetsch is uneasy with the contradiction between his "longing for influence" and his "insistence upon discontinuity," but he is prepared to let the characters in the story carry this uneasiness. The doubled characters in *Exiles* invent no elaborate schemes to avoid Kroetsch's dis-ease; they live it out. But Johnnie Backstrom's character demonstrates dis-ease becoming guilt: he questions the value of his own voice and the narrative strategies he pursues. In *The Studhorse Man* the guilt is subject-matter: Demeter writes about the gap separating his pursuit of story with his recognition of the anti-story embodied in Hazard Lepage. And in *Gone Indian* the guilt is expressed even more potently through confession: Madham exorcises the tale that possesses Jeremy (and by implication, Kroetsch). But even this narrative tactic is not enough to grant the anti-story Kroetsch claims to pursue. In fact, rather than work toward the silence it recommends, *Gone Indian* reveals, through Madham's intense confession, further barriers that Kroetsch will struggle with in his doubled attempt to defy and dwell on closure.

Of these barriers, one of the most formidable is Woman. Woman not only represents for Kroetsch "the female claim in time," but also the notion of completed story, of home, closure, endings, entrapment. As Peter Thomas says:

> The female *mythos* is associated by Kroetsch with place, fixity, moral and social realism—in the sense

of narrative form, with containment and closure. The male is drawn to dispossession, chaos, open territory, fictions always larger than the self's capacities.

If Kroetsch is to escape story, he must also escape the notion of Woman that his novels propose. Perhaps when *that* barrier is broken "true freedom" will be closer still. But Woman, like the closure She represents, cannot be escaped, just as story itself cannot be evaded. The notion of "true freedom" must therefore be modified. True freedom means more than not telling the story; it also involves escaping "the female claim in time" that is synonymous with story. Yet Kroetsch *cannot* abandon story or Woman, for without story/Woman the dialectic he uses to evade the double bind defining (and defeating) him would immediately collapse. The difficulty, then, becomes one of writing a story which is not a story, and of retaining Woman while denying her "claim in time." The problem seems complex and labyrinthine, but its presence provides concrete evidence of the multiplying tactics Kroetsch uses to escape his own rich failure to create two-sided structures which defy their own two-sidedness. In *Badlands,* the tactics Kroetsch uses to convey this failure create an intricate web of narrative evasions. The book unites Kroetsch's drive to anti-story with his repudiation of the female claim in time through a complex narrative structure that is highly, and appropriately, ironic.

[*Badlands*] focuses on two central figures, William Dawe and his daughter Anna. As the "Chronology" indicates, William Dawe's expedition in search of dinosaur skeletons entered the Alberta badlands via the Red Deer River in 1916. In Anna's rendering, the voyage itself assumes the form of a quest for what is apparently the past, the hidden, the submerged, the dead. But as a *river* voyage which *descends* into *unknown territory* through stratified *layers* of rock back to *source,* the *journey* takes on a host of metaphorical connotations: it is a symbolic *Homeric* voyage, a descent into the *underworld,* another *heart of darkness* excursion into *hidden realms of consciousness,* a plunge into the *grave,* the *dig,* the *site,* into *chaos, legend, trace, text.* The packed, bone-filled landscape is fertile. Perhaps *too* fertile, as my emphases are meant to suggest.

Wait. Let the chronology take its course. In 1916, released from his voyage, returned to the world, Dawe brings back the skeleton of a dinosaur he has unearthed. Ten years later, Anna is conceived during one of Dawe's annual fall pilgrimages "to his wife's bed." She is born the next year, when her father is again absent, "collecting dinosaur skeletons." Dawe visits Anna when she is fifteen; her curiosity about him is aroused. But it is not until 1972, ten years after her father's drowning that Anna, at the age of forty-five, accompanies Anna Yellowbird, "an Old Indian Woman" who was mistress to Dawe and his crew, on a voyage back to the Alberta badlands her father explored. Together, these two women travel, with "two cases of Gordon's gin and a cardboard box half-full" of Dawe's field notes, on a second voyage in search of the "true Dawe," "the true past," "the true text" that obsesses Anna in her attempt to define her own identity.

The conventional approach to the novel sees Anna freed at the end as she hurls away her father's notes and redefines her individual, and female, identity. As Connie Harvey writes: "Anna comes to understand and accept her father as an individual and a male." Her commentaries on her father's voyage provide "the record of her self-discovery and the creation of a new perception." But can we so readily accept that "through her recreation of Dawe's journey, Anna comes to know herself as an individual"? Or is the opposite the case: in a huge ironic inversion, Anna finds that she is "free" to be what Kroetsch has always claimed Woman to be free for—story?

Anna seems to have escaped from history, from the female stereotype confining all of Kroetsch's women, but what she escapes into is precisely that time consciousness she tries to evade through her narrative quest. It is left to *Anna* to recreate her father's story, and her own. It is left to *Anna* to establish time, place, and incident. It is left to *Anna* to "house" the text. When she wonders "*Why it was left to me to mediate the story I don't know,*" we *do*: Kroetsch has aligned the concept of anti-story with the male quest by allowing a woman the power of narration. Before *Badlands,* the "double bind" conundrum seemed inescapable so long as Kroetsch insisted on pursuing story through a male narrator who was increasingly uncomfortable with the role. Now that story is transferred to Woman, Man is free to live in the silence of anti-story. This is why none of the male characters in *Badlands* ever speaks, except through Anna's imagining, why what Dawe "writes" is "undecipherable," and why we learn, finally, that Dawe had "come to the end of words" right from the start. So while the quest for time, history, and recovery of the past appears to be male oriented, it only appears that way because the orientation is directed by a female narrator who knows no other way. Conversely, while the quest for personal freedom, liberation from the past, and invention appears to be female oriented, it only appears that way because it is *undirected* by those male characters who know *no* way.

Since irony implies inversion, one way of testing this argument is to reverse the novel and begin it at its end, for the end *is* its beginning. At the end of *Badlands,* we learn that Anna Yellowbird flings her photographs to the sky. Her gesture mocks the suspended grizzly bear who seems to represent the triviality of male sexuality and being. Then Anna Dawe "*took out the field book [she] had carried like a curse for ten years*" and "*threw it into the lake.*" Then both Annas "*walked all the way out*" of Dawe's landscape, "*and [they] did not once look back, not once, ever.*" This is the most ironic statement in the book, and also its greatest lie—one that should alert us to the beginning of a grand inversion process. For no sooner has Anna announced that "*we did not once look back*" than she proceeds to look back on a story which brings her to the point at which she tells us she did not look back. The story, we realize, is not created in process; it is *recollected,* and apparently built on Anna's imaginative reconstruction of Dawe's notes, contrived excerpts of which we see throughout the text. But if Anna never looked back ("*not once, ever*"), if she drowned the notes, why is it that they appear with such insistence to form the imaginative core of her story? The truth is that she has *only* looked back, that she has *not* thrown away the notes, that she wants to provide an ending appropriate to her intent, but an ending she cannot live. At the end of the novel she is left in a vicious narrative circle, forever creating the story she will never be able to forget.

If the end of the novel comments on its beginning, its beginning might qualify its end. And that "end" consigns Anna to be namer, story-teller, historian, finalizer. This is why she begins by naming herself ("*I am Anna Dawe*") and then by telling us that her subject will be both father and history—the two forces that Kroetsch's male questers persistently reject. Her historical ambition is explicitly tied to narrative intent,

for Anna will build her story on those field notes that she claims to have discovered before the story is begun, the same field notes that meant little to those men "*who held the words themselves in contempt.*" Anna recognizes this contempt, but she misses the narrative point: the field notes are fragments representing an anti-story virtually realized, and even *that* realization is held in contempt by the men, yet she continues to believe that the notes have value because her task is to piece together fragments, to make story. So while Anna is disputing the traditional role of Woman (and by extension casting herself in the role of one who will reject the stereotype), she is in fact reinforcing the stereotype by playing it out. She complains that "*women are not supposed to have stories. We are supposed to sit at home, Penelopes to their wars and their sex. As my mother did. As I was doing.*" These words, which are spoken after Anna finds her final "freedom," suggest that she is continually forced to live a lie: by "mediating" the story she wins the freedom to create a narrative that increasingly details her enslavement to it. She bears Kroetsch's guilt, tries to work through it, fails, and founds a text that masks her failure with precisely the narrative strategies that Kroetsch, through Anna, destroys. For it is Anna who casts Dawe's story in archetypal terms. It is Anna who provides the book with its symbolic overkill. It is Anna who must see Dawe's voyage as a quest. It is Anna who wants detail, time, place, verisimilitude: "Anna's commentary is 'realistic': hers is the voice of verisimilitude, of temporal consistency, seeking to disallow the comic energy of the tall tale her father inhabits." Her father: Dawe: Kroetsch.

To read through the italicized portions of the text comprising her first-person narrative is to be struck by the degree to which Anna accepts the stereotype she claims to have repudiated, often to the extent that her commentaries read as conscious self-parodies of her narrative intent. How much faith can we place in the sound and the fury of a woman who buys her gin "*by the case*" and who, in what is ostensibly a half-drunken state, "*imagined to [herself] a past, an ancestor, a legend, a vision, a fate*"? The "imagined" list contains all the "right" things to be invented by a woman seeking self-definition through historical inquiry. But it contains so many "right" things that they ultimately contradict each other: Anna imagines a past, which is then mythologized into legend, which is then converted through metaphoric association into a vision—but of what? The list becomes progressively more expansive in terms of metaphoric possibility, until the sudden deflation offered by the final word: "fate." Regardless of her imaginative powers, Anna's transformation, her "vision," will lead to the end—the "fate" Anna cannot escape. Her dream of endless artifice is inspired by books and booze. Anna knows this, as her contrived list of imaginings suggests. She is living in a dream world. And the dream convinces her that "*there is nothing else*" but the past, even while she destroys the evidence left by her father who "*went out and looked for that past,*" even while she tells us that she "*did not once look back, not once, ever.*" Anna is split: she wants the past, she walks away from the past; she wants a future, she thrives in history; she wants to find herself, she labours at disguising herself. We can't take her seriously. So when she tells us that the boat she has placed these men on resembled "a badly managed stage," we sense that she is the one who is managing it badly, forcing the stage, the boat (the book), to zigzag between every narrative possibility she is aware of (and none of which she will have).

These possibilities, we learn, are often inspired by Anna's voracious reading. Influenced by a host of narrative strategies, she is confused about the theoretical stances she should evoke at various points in the story, unsure about how to employ the manipulative tricks the teller can bring to the tale. Through her, Kroetsch parodies his own sense of the writer as manipulator working from an arsenal stocked with narrative clichés and using "every trick in the book" to achieve his ends. (pp. 160-66)

Once we have learned to "read" Anna, her narrative tricks become more and more obvious. To get the "true" story we have to follow her ironic casting and invert everything she says. So when she claims that the men of Dawe's expedition "were trying to tell each other" a *"western yarn,"* we must read: the men told each other nothing, but from that void Anna would contrive a "western yarn." Indeed, Anna contrives several yarns as she turns *Badlands* into a mythical descent, an archetypal quest, an abstracted collage, a photographic essay, a film script, a metaphoric dig, a fabled hunt, a vision, a legend, a confession, a novel. All this turning suggests that she is over-stuffed with story, with vague ideas about the nature of narrative. She considers it strange that *"action and voice . . . should have so little connection,"* then wonders if there is any connection at all *"between the occurrence and the most exact telling."* This woman, who is *"determined to set straight the record,"* is also determined to prove that there *is* no record to set straight, for *"there are no truths, only correspondences."* Thus Anna provides us with her primer definition of metaphor, one that she attempts to employ by creating a confused babble of equivalencies signifying nothing. At the end of the book, as at its beginning, she still insists that *"we live in time, we women."* No wonder Anna's narrative is circular and self-reflexive: she spends her time talking to herself.

If we cannot trust this teller, we certainly cannot trust her tale. But we *can* see how Anna tries to manipulate the story to numerous, uncertain ends. There are two parts to Anna's narrative. The first, which I have considered, is presented in the first person. The second, which provides an account of the Dawe expedition in 1916, is presented in a self-conscious, third-person voice that oscillates between omniscience and reportorial overkill. Ostensibly, it is this narrative which Anna produces, or rather imagines, from the fragmented field notes left by her late father. Confronted by his cool, rational, scientific language, and his deliberate omission of all emotional detail, Anna is forced to invest Dawe's story with Meaning, not because it has Meaning, but because by giving it Meaning Anna will ostensibly give significance to her own personal quest. The completion of the story—a narrative act—is paralleled by Anna's sought-after completion—a psychological act. But here, as in Anna's first-person account, we must ask what Anna actually finds at the end of her narrative quest. What does the record she produces—which we know as *Badlands*—reveal about her own personality, about her own narrative assumptions?

It is a mistake to see Anna's record of the Dawe voyage as a reflection of her growing self-discovery through quest. It is a mistake to claim that she discovers herself by discovering her father, or even by inventing him. It is a mistake to argue that "through her recreation of Dawe's journey Anna comes to know herself as an individual." Rather, Anna's account of the Dawe expedition becomes a sustained parody of the quest motif, and a sustained mocking of the figure who believes that she can find *her* form by giving form. Yet she gives that form

with a vengeance: the book not only reads like a sustained parody of Faulkner; it is also full of symbols and archetypes that are consciously overworked. A landscape layered with bones (death made present, origins preserved); the Red Deer canyon (layered with time, with consciousness, with "levels" of narrative meaning); a boat as raft (ladened with Huck Finn, explorers, Marlows, Homers, Childe Rolands, questers, jesters, fools). And all of these layers, strata, are ostensibly "held" together by an uncertain voice that does not know whether it is imitating Faulkner or Robert Kroetsch, that does not know whether it wants to speak in run-ons or in staccato prose, that is so confused it only manages to convey its astonished attempt to bring together such a wealth of contrived and contradictory narrative levels. Is this Kroetsch's confusion, or Anna's?

Ann Mandel suggests that "the tone is that of a writer who, without the protection of a persona for most of the novel, does not trust the marks of identity or style he recognizes as his own, yet does not want to abandon or go beyond the tensions imposed by traditional forms. Such a writer necessarily chooses parody." It is clear that Kroetsch's use of parody in *Badlands* does express his own uneasiness with the unmasking process implied by his own choice of persona and narrative stance. But at the same time, this parody is applied to a narrator that Kroetsch has quite consciously cast as a woman. The parody played out, then, is about what happens to story when it is put in the hands of someone convinced s/he must live by it (as Anna lives; as Kroetsch must live). Anna complains that women are never given stories. Fine. Now she will be given all she demands—full narrative control—and Kroetsch will be free to blame the result on her, even to write badly, in full knowledge that we will pronounce the book a parody—and call Kroetsch brilliant for conceiving it as such. . . . Now Anna can be left to cope with what Kroetsch has never coped with: the tension between tradition and invention, the conflict between mimetic and expressive literary modes. And while Anna is struggling (as Kroetsch does) to give form to formlessness, Kroetsch will contemplate those heroes he truly envies: not Anna, who falls prey to story in the worst way, but Dawe, who lives out a magnificent anti-story, defying language at every turn. Dawe, whom we can describe as trickster, shaman, pathfinder, borderman, bone priest. This man Dawe was enslaved, we are told, to history, control, origins, permanency. Yet after all the labels, all the obsessions, *we know nothing about him.* The reports are all contradictory, and besides, they are all synthesized by Anna, the unreliable narrator *par excellence.* Ultimately Dawe is nothing but what others have projected him to be, what others would make him become in order to affirm their own self-centred notions of identity and purpose. But Dawe, by virtue of being named so often, remains powerfully un-named and free. In contrast, Anna remains enslaved to doing all that men once did: now she is the namer, the shaper, the historian, the digger.

Is this freedom? No. She is constrained to live in the time frame she might have escaped had she not demanded story. Now she will discover that true freedom is to be without story. But she has given away her chance by following, as she does, the clichéd equivalence between finding story and finding self. This is not "freedom and re-birth"; it is incarceration and death in a storied realm that by its very nature cannot escape closure. Anna's narrative comprises a predictable response to this trap: caged in a labyrinth of time, she runs back and forth between narrative possibilities, unwilling to choose any possibility because choice implies the closure she is supposed to be transcending. Realizing her predicament, she pretends that it is intentional, that she has chosen the labyrinth as a means of freedom. Over the pain, she tries to laugh, and to show the silent people outside (the reader, Dawe, Kroetsch) that it is really all intentional, that she can smile at her folly, that she knows what she is doing: parody. So when we read Anna's record of Dawe's expedition, we should look not for Dawe (he is absent), not for his notes (they have been thrown away), but for the uncertain voice of the narrator who tries to "make us believe" that Dawe exists, that the notes can be deciphered, that there *is* a story to tell and a person who can be redeemed through the telling. (pp. 167-70)

I have already suggested that Anna's narrative constitutes a parody of traditional narrative forms, and that the tendency toward parody is deliberately provoked by Kroetsch. If we accept this argument (and Ann Mandel's accurate description of the novel's parodic elements suggests that it cannot be ignored), then we must also be prepared to accept that Anna, an authorial surrogate and agent for Kroetsch, is entirely conscious of the parodic undertones and strategies inherent in "the work," her story. And if she is conscious of employing these tactics that invite us to label her voice naive, self-indulgent, excessive, contrived, then we must ask what end this parodic self-consciousness is directed toward. The answer, I think, is that Anna's story, like Dawe's, is never really written at all. The *end* of her parodic self-consciousness is to demonstrate her *imagined* creation of a story which she *knows* will never work. In this context, Anna becomes the agent, and most powerfully the voice, of the tall-tale tradition that Kroetsch himself is beginning to pursue—a tradition that defies tradition by using forms that contradict each other, and by envisioning an "end" that is a "non-end" in terms of its paratactic impulses. Anna is not writing; she is telling tall tales. And the imaginative, free-flowing basis of her telling is indicated from the start, when she tells us that she will imagine—create—reality: "*imagined to myself a past, an ancestor, a legend, a vision, a fate.*" This emphasis on the imaginative aspects of Anna's narrative creation suggests that she may be seen as a kind of oral poet who is trying to bypass what Kroetsch calls "the danger of the heirloom model for inherited stories" which "suggests a fixed thing" and a "fixed text." Anna may, like Kroetsch, be seen as one who supports the bypass and is "tempted by oral models where the story in the act of retelling is always responsive to individuals, to the place, to invention." The connection between Anna's imaginative impulses and her oral response to the story she has "inherited" are implicit in Kroetsch's statement, and confirmed by the book, which can actually be seen as an intentional pastiche contrived by a voice that likes to hear itself talk to no end.

I am suggesting that through Anna we find the way out of the problem that haunts Kroetsch: how to find "the truth" while recognizing that "the truth" is always false. The writer who becomes the oral poet is freed from the conundrum: everything is possible when spoken by one whose aim is to embellish, backtrack, invite interjection, refuse closure. Anna does all of these things while simultaneously rejecting written narrative. By throwing away her father's notes, she discards precisely the "heirloom model" which would compel her to record, rather than to imagine. In abandoning "the record," with its scientific associations, Anna also rejects the notion of mimesis that obsesses Kroetsch (one should not forget that mimetic realism, like Dawe's putative notes, finds its basis in

the notion of scientific observation of phenomena). By extension, she acts out an expressive code: the speaker will project, create, illuminate experience. Speaker and world will be one. Since the entire narrative which comprises *Badlands* is imagined by Anna, she gives the lie to any sense of "reality" as something solid and fixed. She breaks down received meaning. She casts away the notes. From this perspective, the Anna who assumes the role of oral poet is also a trickster who defies the rational frame, impregnating the novel with voice.

But how are we to explain the presence of a trickster who shows up in female guise? One explanation is that by allowing Anna (the fool) to fool with the story, Kroetsch has simply extended the inversion process which characterizes the text from the start. But another way to read the trickster figure here is to see in her fooling the greatest sign of her true freedom, which involves nothing less than her liberation from story. Some critics have argued that if *Badlands* contains a trickster figure, it is Web. As Peter Thomas says: "Web is a thoroughly comic shaman, initiated in ignorance, unaware of the meaning of what he has done, the clownish mask that Dawe, who does understand, albeit reluctantly, will not wear. He is the parody of Dawe's quest, its antic reproof." Thomas amasses considerable evidence to show that Web does assume the role of comic shaman, and trickster. But it can also be argued that the very words Thomas applies to Web may also be applied to Anna: she acts out her contrived ignorance, she has no knowledge of her ultimate ends, she assumes Dawe's mask, she effects a parody of Dawe's quest, and, by doing all of these things, she provides by way of *Badlands* her "antic reproof." This may be why Anna tells us, right from the start, that "*Web was the man I imagined most often,*" the same Web, we recall, who insisted that "*there is no such thing as a past,*" the same Web whose greatest moment comes when he assumes the role of oral story-teller mimicking the metaphors of creation and apocalypse. Beginnings and endings.

But if Anna is a trickster, she will do more than imagine Web until she can assume his role; she will imagine *every* character until she can assume *every* role, thus providing us with an ultimate parody of "characterization" and "identity." It is in this context that Anna's observations about how "*every man*" is "*symbolic of another*" may be understood anew. As the female trickster, she has the power to assume and transcend all roles. She will be more than Web the tale-teller.

She will be McBride who, Thomas says, "accepts the self-in-time, the 'double hook' of 'the home place,' rejecting the fictive self of story ('yarn')." Like McBride, Anna argues for her identity in time and for "*the willingness to be the agent of orderly existence.*" By reconstructing Dawe's voyage she attempts to order her existence and to find a home place so that she can apply to herself the words used to describe McBride: "*Home was a word he understood, and heroes cannot afford that understanding. Which meant that he must become the fool among those fools.*" Here, Anna recognizes in McBride her own role as trickster, the fool among fools who understands her need for home, but repudiates it at every turn.

She will be Grizzly, who becomes "a taciturn witness to the absurdity of Dawe's quest." Anna tells us that Grizzly "*recovered his loss, not by fighting back, but by submitting—with an irony so blatant that even my father had difficulty pretending he missed it.*" Anna's story, the recovery of *her* loss, is gained by submitting to the tale with precisely those blatant forms of irony characteristic of her trickster role. But Grizzly's irony—Anna's—has a narrative intent as well: it directs us to the figure of the mediator who will balance between stories, embracing all and none. This may be why Connie Harvey describes Grizzly as "a man of balance" and as "male and female at once." Anna's parallel position as a balancer who unites male and female types is again suggested at the opening, where she tells us that her task was to *"mediate the story,"* and by the final vision of the grizzly bear, who, caught between sky and earth, provides the two Annas not so much with freedom as with evidence of the fact that "the male/female contention is never resolved in Kroetsch's work—by definition it is eternal and implicit—so that, while Anna Dawe may be understood to be cured of her neurotic fixation upon her father by this 'vision' of impotent maleness, the dual narrative of the novel remains." Grizzly: she who dupes others and is always duped herself.

Anna will be Sinnott, "presenting history as a series of 'stills' caught, by definition, at the expense of protean reality" and thriving "on precisely that need for perpetuated *personal* history exemplified in Dawe." The segments comprising Anna's mediated story are narrative stills that serve the same purpose as Sinnott's photographs: they freeze time and confirm the illusion of historical closure that Anna ostensibly seeks. The titles of Anna's chapters, like those attached to Sinnott's photos, "illustrate the two contradictory tendencies displayed throughout Kroetsch's writing—to fable the image or claim an unadorned formal realism." They affirm the historical act and simultaneously reject it, for as Anna allows Sinnott to realize: "Everything is vanishing."

Including Dawe. If the narrative doubles back on itself in a parody of self-reflexiveness, it is because Anna *is* Dawe. A:D. But Dawe has vanished, erased himself from word, world, and page, just as Anna, who "reads" him as we read her, erases herself through an imaginative telling that dislocates traditional notions of identity, reality, writing, reading—and exegesis itself. Dawe's "fake" field notes become Anna's "faked" book. And she, the faker become father become Woman affirms the fool's stance, mimicking her imaginary, magical, maniacal dream of a man whose silence betrays her, betrays him. Anna *Kilbourne* Dawe. At the end, she assumes her father's position: lost (found), absent (present), uncreated (created), killed (born), she dreams herself into being and comes, as Dawe came, "to the end of words." It is through this silence, rather than through any conventional notion of freedom, that Anna's story starts. And where will it *end*? No one knows. What, after all, is an ending? (pp. 182-86)

Robert Lecker, *"Freed from Story: Narrative Tactics in 'Badlands',"* in Essays on Canadian Writing, No. 30, Winter, 1984-85, pp. 160-86.

LESLEY CHOYCE

[At first, *Advice to My Friends*] seemed like lukewarm bath water. There was something obtuse and limiting about the first section of the book, which appeared to be a selection of private poems addressed to such people as Eli Mandel, Fred Wah, Michael Ondaatje, Doug Jones, and others. Was this what Canadian poets are supposed to do once they turn 50? Do they just write poems to each other and let outsiders eavesdrop? Since I didn't drink beer with any of these people, as Kroetsch apparently did, I felt somehow cheated, left out and dissatisfied. It was like listening in on only one side of a telephone conversation.

But sections titled **"Mile Zero," "Delphi Commentary,"** and **"The Frankfurt Hauptbahnhof"** illustrated a wonderful sense of line-play and experiment in form. Much of the work was presented to appear as work-in-progress, with arrows and inserts and such. . . . I studied these possibilities for a while, but found many of the poems to be little more than stylistic diversions.

For such a personal book, the content simply wasn't intimate enough. The experiment welcomed the reader to participate, but it was a little too much like growing a beard just to prove that you could do it. Further in the book, I discovered the lines, "We write books/to avoid writing books," and wondered if that's what this one was all about.

Nonetheless, . . . I found myself moving beyond these lyrical badlands and into the heartland of the book—the sections titled **"Letters to Salonika"** and **"Postcards from China."** Now I was convinced that I was eavesdropping on worthwhile stuff. The first concerns a record of time spent by the poet while his lover was away in Greece. There's loneliness, loss, and sadness here, but Kroetsch is able to rise above it because he can turn it into impassioned poetry.

"Letters to Salonika" is written as a diary of sorts, and the poems are rather prose-like but rarely prosaic. . . .

Earlier he has insisted, "The world is ending, but/the world does not end." This is a believable statement if he can hold onto the passion and avoid boring sections about drinking beer with other poets and going to all those damn restaurants.

"Postcards from China" concerns Kroetsch's adventures as part of a Canadian literary invasion of China. These prose poems remind me of Gary Snyder and they truly savour the discoveries to be had inside a mysterious country. The poet is awake, alive, and breathing life into everything. That's all a poet ever should do, and Kroetsch, when he's up for it, can do it well.

Lesley Choyce, *"From Bath to Verse,"* in Books in Canada, Vol. 15, No. 1, January-February, 1986, pp. 30-1.

PAUL HJARTARSON

Advice to My Friends consists of eight sequences of poems: five of them have previously appeared in print; the remaining three, **"Advice to My Friends,"** and the two remarkable sequences, **"Sounding My Name"** and **"The Poet's Mother"** are published here for the first time. Together they constitute the second volume in Kroetsch's continuing poem, *Field Notes,* and establish that work as one of the most important poems published in Canada in many years.

"We go into the unknown, even the unknown," the speaker in **"The Frankfurt *Hauptbahnhof"*** declares, "with expectations." Readers of *Field Notes* will find many of their expectations met in this second volume. Certainly the speaker of the poems is familiar; he is that lonely, self-conscious, slightly bemused, often sad, frequently amusing figure encountered in the earlier poems. From **"Delphi: commentary":**

Meggie was taking pictures. Laura and I stood behind the omphalos and Meggie took a picture. Meggie and I stood behind the omphalos and Laura took a picture.

How does one   Frazer: *Even in his*

pose for a picture taken at the belly button of the earth? What smile is not a smile of embarrassment? of self-satisfaction? of hybris? What angle of the arm does not betray a certain inappropriate possessiveness?

best days he [Apollo] did not always rise to verse, and in Plutarch's time the god appears to have given up the attempt in despair and to have generally confined himself to plain, if not lucid, prose.

Here, as in so many of the earlier poems, the situation is commonplace; the poet as tourist, smiles self-consciously for the camera, caught in the discourse of the obligatory photos. . . . The language, too, is commonplace, sometimes taking on the colour and energy of colloquial speech, sometimes taking flight, but more often than not, quietly insisting, like the speaker himself, on its own prosaic qualities. (p. 135)

The seeming simplicity of the poetry is belied at the level of discourse: one column speaks to another, one poem to another, one text to the next. In **"Mile Zero"** the original version of the poem becomes the intertext of the new work; in **"Delphi: Commentary"** the contemporary poet's account of his tour of Delphi is juxtaposed with passages from Pausanias' *Descriptions of Greece,* a second-century A.D. guidebook:

> *From this point the high road to Delphi grows steeper and more difficult to a man on foot. Many and diverse are the tales told about Delphi, and still more about the oracle of Apollo.* (Pausanias. His scattered Greece under Roman rule.)
> It is always that way, the poem, the abandoned poem, in which the hero, seeking the answer to the impossible question, seeking the impossible question, takes to the road. Hero. Eros. The evasion that is the meeting. The impossible road.

And we follow (so the story goes). We find ourselves entranced in the play of texts, find ourselves in the relations of the texts.

In *The Postmodern Condition* Jean-François Lyotard defines postmodern simply as an "incredulity toward meta-narratives." In the postmodern world there are no master narratives; we have, finally, not one narrative but many. Kroetsch characteristically finds his own formulation closer to home, in a passage from Ken Dryden's *The Game* which serves as an epigraph for the new **"Mile Zero"**:

> . . . hockey is a *transition game*: offence to defence, defence to offence, one team to another. Hundreds of tiny fragments of action, some leading somewhere, most going nowhere. Only one thing is clear. Grand designs don't work.

This passage could easily serve as an epigraph not just to **"Mile Zero"** but to the seventeen sequences that, to date, make up Kroetsch's continuing poem, for in *Field Notes* poetry *is* a transition game, writer to reader, reader to writer, "hundreds of tiny fragments of action, some leading somewhere, most going nowhere." The evasion that is the meeting.

"(Insert here a passage on / nature— / *try:*"). From **"The Frankfurt *Haupbahnhof*,"** written in response to bp Nichol's question about notation in *Field Notes*:

> Notation in *Field Notes,* Barry, is the reader in the text. The narrator, always, fears his/her own tyranny. The notation, in the poem occasions the dialogic response that is the reader's articulation of his/her own presence (the ecstatic now of recognition? the longer, if not always enduring, experience of transformational vision?)
>
> "Silence, please."
>
> Bugles.
>
> > the gone stranger
> > the mysterious text
> > the necessary
> > transfer.

The necessary transfer. Kroetsch's poetry insists on that transfer, insists on the evasion that is the meeting.

As these brief excerpts suggest, *Advice to My Friends* is, among other things, a meditation on the transition game that is poetry; it is, above all, an exploration of "the other" conceived and addressed in discourse. The need for and creation of the other in discourse is made readily apparent in the opening poem of the **"Advice to My Friends"** sequence, titled "for a poet who has stopped writing":

> if we could just catch a hold of it,
> catch aholt, some kind of line,
> if the sun was a tennis ball or something
> but it ain't, the impossible thing is the sun
> if words rhymed, even we could catch a holt
> (a bush) and start the stacking, words
> lined up, I mean, like, in the old days
> wood behind the kitchen stove
>
> but you take now your piecemeal sonnet
> wow, certain of these here poets,
> these chokermen can't even count to
> fourteen
> and as for Petrarch, well, I mean
>
> I've been to bed with some dandy and also skilled
> ladies, sure, but would I a ballyhoo start
> for the keen (and gossipy) public?
> I'd be sued or whatever, maybe killed
>
> but (now and then) you've got to tell *some*body
> and a reader has I guess, in spite of all, ears.

The poet as chokerman. What he catches aholt of here, gets a line on, are the ears of the other, the other conceived *as* ears, as *some*body. (pp. 136-37)

The most remarkable poems in *Advice to My Friends* are the two closing sequences, **"Sounding My Name"** and **"The Poet's Mother,"** toward which the volume as a whole seems to move. Both focus on the figure of the poet's mother. In *Labyrinths of Voice* Kroetsch acknowledged some years ago that he had kept the mother figures very silent at the centre of his writing, partly because the death of his mother caused him such pain, and added:

> . . . it's funny how I kept that silent and one of the things that I can see happening, in the next few years as I go on writing, is a kind of enunciation.

But I can feel even my long poem, *Field Notes*
drawing toward that.

In the last two sequences we have that enunciation, poems
that bespeak an almost unbearable pain, poems written with
the guard down, with the arms wide open:

> In the fall of snow
> I hear my mother.
> I know she is there.
> In the weight of the snow
> I hear her silence.
>
> I count white stones
> in October moonlight.
>
> I break dry bread
> with a flock of gulls.
> I tear sheep's wool
> from barbed wire fences.
>
> The visible,
> the visible—
>
> where are you?

Advice to My Friends is a collection of poems written for and
about the other, about the self's need for and discovery of
that other. (pp. 137-38)

> Paul Hjartarson, *"Discourse of the Other,"* in Cana-
> dian Literature, *No. 115, Winter, 1987, pp. 135-38.*

MARGARET E. TURNER

If Robert Kroetsch and his writing have become a "cottage
industry" in western Canada, it is for good reason. Kroetsch
recreates his *place* every time he writes; this is a profoundly
interesting activity to the people who live in that place. In a
sense, he accomplishes again and again what Sheila Watson
did when she made the Cariboo "real" in *The Double Hook.*
The difference, of course, is that Watson has been determined
to maintain a distance from her work, while Kroetsch has demanded recognition of the complex relationship between
himself and his texts. One reason for that difference may be
simply a function of personality. The more interesting reason
has to do with Kroetsch's self-conscious and public exploration of the writing process. Kroetsch does not allow that the
processes involved with literature—the writing of poetry and
fiction, or the acts of criticism or reading—are closed. If writing reinvents the world, reading reinvents the text. His poetry, fiction, and criticism function as commentary and extension of each other: he demonstrates his theories of culture and
literature by reference to his own texts. In Kroetsch's own
words, all are part of the story: "It's the story, its treatment,
the narrative itself, that's the model, not an outside
conception. . . . I think criticism is really a version of story,
you see; I think we are telling the story to each other of how
we get at story."

Kroetsch demands recognition of the self-reflexive nature of
his work early in his writing career: in fact in his fourth novel,
Gone Indian, published in 1973. Although it is a major novel,
there has been very little critical attention paid to *Gone Indian,* much more attention has been given to the other two novels of the Out West triptych, and to the novels and collections
of poetry since *Gone Indian.* The point remains, however,
that Kroetsch highlights issues and ideas in *Gone Indian* that
have preoccupied him in his subsequent work: play with tra-

ditional imaginative forms, and with the stability of the structures of language, interrogation of the nature of author, of fiction, of place. *Gone Indian* maps the territory that Kroetsch
has travelled since the early seventies.

Discussion of Kroetsch's work involves a discussion of place.
The particular place of his writing is western Canada, often
Alberta. The *idea* of place is not so simply defined. E. D.
Blodgett argues that the frontiers of English-speaking western Canada were drawn in linear patterns of railroad, survey
lines, and sections that enforced a geographic and psychological closure even as they opened the West. He extends this
contradiction to include a further contradiction between the
geometric design of place and the genres of English-Canadian
fiction of the West. In a sense the linear design does apply to
Kroetsch's *Gone Indian*: Jeremy states his horror of "the inevitable circle" just before he vanishes, and his movement
throughout the novel is not cyclic. The point, however, is
made explicit that linearity does *not* require closure. It is precisely this contradiction between the perception of place and
the manner in which place is presented in literature that
Kroetsch addresses in *Gone Indian.* Jeremy wants to carry
his quest further and he can: he is *not* trapped, either in the
northwest or in reality. Because Kroetsch deliberately makes
the place more real in language than in fact, Jeremy can
transfigure himself *out* of it into what can be seen as an extension of the tall tale world he has encountered from his arrival:
Jeremy goes Indian, and disappears. For Kroetsch, and for
Jeremy, then, [according to Blodgett], "to go west [is] to enter
the mind's geometry, a long journey, one might say, of self-
reflection, of finding one's self lost."

Kroetsch's texts raise the question of place, an important
question in Canadian writing. In a very real sense, Canada
itself does not exist until it is written. Until that happens,
until Kroetsch and Watson and others write the new world
into existence, we remain mired in a middle passage—caught
in the movement from the old world of Europe, the source
of Canadian colonists in the eighteenth and nineteenth centuries, to a secure and authentic existence in the new world. The
middle passage is figured in absence, of both public and social
structures of organization, and private and individual structures of belonging and identity. It is also figured in silence:
silence is the logical and necessary condition in the middle
passage, the pendulum swing between somewhere and nowhere, between old and new worlds. As the pendulum
pauses—for a moment, forever—personal and cultural identity, history, memory, language do not exist. The middle passage raises questions about the nature of place, *this* place, and
the nature and possibility of human being in it. To move from
Canada as nowhere to Canada as somewhere involves finding
a language, and using it to describe—to name—place.

Kroetsch's work is positioned at this point of the middle passage. For Kroetsch Canada, and especially the Canadian
West, is nothing if not an idea; to use Henry Kreisel's words,
it is a state of mind. Much of Kroetsch's writing comes out
of that idea: he is convinced that we can—*must*—make a new
literature out of the new experience, new land, new place, and
new language. As he says of himself and of naming: "Naming
a new world has intrigued me . . . it's been a primary concern, that sense of a misnamed world or an unnamed world
that had to be named." He begins by un-naming and un-
inventing, and reinvents place, as he makes language the site
of his writing.

Kroetsch's awareness of the significance, possibilities, and limits of literary and social construction is developed in the dialogue that occurs within and between his literary texts and his critical writing, a dialogue which often bears on the nature of writing in this country. The distinction between forms is frequently blurred: in *Gone Indian,* as elsewhere, fiction is the subject of his fiction. Kroetsch uses the idea of the critical act as a way to write fiction: *Gone Indian* is a novel made out of Madham's commentary on Jeremy's taped text. Kroetsch denies the convention that the novel is not a fiction by engaging the reader in the fiction-making process. The fiction becomes *fiction,* and at the same time becomes more *real* than fiction. As Kroetsch has it, we create the world by naming it: the translation into fiction makes our identity and experience real. Robert Lecker [see essay above] argues that the border is a key to Kroetsch's work: it is the point at which opposites unite and undergo a metamorphosis, and is always in the process of transformation as it defies the static structures of a fixed world. In *Gone Indian* Kroetsch signals his interest in the border between security and diffusion of personality; in ontological terms between existence and annihilation; in language between creating and uncreating words and worlds.

We see Kroetsch, with Jeremy, inventing the Canadian northwest in the writing of *Gone Indian.* The novel is an exercise in the creation of self and place, a point that Kroetsch makes explicit. one of Jeremy's unfinished doctoral dissertations begins with "Christopher Columbus, not knowing that he had not come to the Indies, named the inhabitants of that new world—. Like Columbus, on his trip to Canada Jeremy does not *really* know where he has landed but soon finds out that the strangeness and possibility of the place equal, if not surpass, his expectations. His transformations, from graduate student to Grey Owl, from weakling and victim to the Winter King, and from impotent human to buffalo bull are aspects of his invention of what becomes *his* northwest.

Jeremy defines himself in his tape recordings and the notebooks he has ready for another attempt at his dissertation. In a similar manner Madham creates himself in his letters to Jill Sunderman and his purportedly scholarly comments on Jeremy's work. Madham's definition in words may well be more significant than Jeremy's, although Jeremy seems to be the main character: everything we see and hear of him, however, is filtered through Madham's eyes and words. Madham's is the controlling consciousness of the novel, and he is clearly not reliable in the traditional sense. Of course this is part of Kroetsch's design: through Madham's slanted telling of the novel we come to question not only *his* assumptions and beliefs but our own perceptions, as well as the place and experience we thought we knew and understood. Madham's narration is also the source of irony and humour in the novel: "*It is my own opinion that everything he [Jeremy] says can be taken at face value. He was as surprised as are we by the course of events, failing to understand, as he did, the nature of freedom.*" Of course nothing that Madham *says* Jeremy says can be taken at face value, nor can Madham's comments about himself; we learn later that it is Jeremy, not Madham, who understands the nature of freedom.

Jeremy is preoccupied with the necessity of his own self-creation in language: after nine years as a graduate student in the English Department of an American university, his unwritten dissertation threatens to ruin his life—as it has his sexual performance. He has many failed attempts at the dissertation to his credit:

"Going Down With Orpheus." Eighteen months and four hundred pages. Abandoned. "The Artist as Clown and Pornographer." Nine months of reading and three hundred index cards. Sold to an M.A. candidate for twenty dollars. "The Columbus Quest: The Dream, the Journey, the Surprise." Eighteen weeks. I couldn't get past the first sentence.

Unable to write he carries a tape recorder so that, in Madham's words, "he might commit to tape the meditations and insights that would help him complete his dissertation." He finally sets out on his own Columbus quest in imitation of his childhood hero, Archie Belaney. The ostensible reason for his trip west is a job interview which Madham has arranged for him "at that last university in the last city on the far, last edge of our civilization"—the University of Alberta. However, at the airport he answers the Customs officer's "Purpose of trip?" with "I want to be Grey Owl. . . . I want to become—." Only in Grey Owl's country—Canada—can his dream of transformation come true:

"Sadness," old Madham says to me one day, "there's only one problem in this world that you take seriously."

"Right," I said.

"No," he said. "I mean yes. Why did Archie Belaney become Grey Owl?"

"How," I said. I raised my right hand, the palm facing the good professor's beaming face. Why he was sweating I do not know.

"The story of a man," I agreed, "who died into a new life."

"He faked the death."

"But he woke up free nevertheless."

"Be serious."

"One false move, Professor, and instead of addressing you, I'll be you. That's serious."

That is, of course, exactly what happens: the twist in the novel is that it is *Madham's* quest that Jeremy lives out. All the discussion of identity comes from Madham, who controls the content of the book by presenting his edited transcriptions of Jeremy's tapes: "Of course I have had to select from the tapes, in spite of Jeremy's instructions to the contrary: the mere onslaught of detail merely overwhelms." Of course he also controls and disrupts chronological time in his presentation. Jeremy becomes real as Madham tells his story—and Madham does too. At the beginning of the novel he sums up Jeremy's motivations for the reader:

Jeremy believed that his whole life was shaped and governed by some deep American need to seek out the frontier. A child of Manhattan, born and bred, he dreamed always a far interior that he might in the flesh inhabit. He dreamed northwest, that is undeniable. Only let me assert: it was I who sent him there.

Madham is preoccupied with the transformation of identity because *he* has died into a new life. His words about Jeremy apply equally to himself: "The possibility of transformation, I must recognize, played no little part in Jeremy's abiding fantasy of fulfilment. It gave him, in the face of all his inadequacies, the illusion of hope." Madham's hope is that he can go home again, and through Jeremy he does.

The random naming of Jeremy after Jeremy Bentham is no less bizarre than Madham's assigning of his own new name: Kroetsch seems to be saying that all identity is accidental, relative, random, and changeable. Curiously Jeremy is trapped into living out "the accident of his name: that one portion of identity which is at once so totally invented and so totally real"—his mother tells him that his absent father "wanted [him] to grow up . . . to be a professor." Like Madham's, Jeremy's status is figured according to academic standards. He has yet, however, to complete his degree and become a success in Madham's terms: "Professor Madham, you did this. You sent me out here. You, with your goddamned go-get-a-job syndrome, publish, head a committee. Become a dean and die." He has spent his years of graduate school being guilty about the academic work he is not doing, which results in his inability to perform sexually:

> Guilt. Old-fashioned guilt. Every time I lie down
> I feel guilty because I'm not up and studying. Work
> on your new dissertation, Sadness. Review for the
> final oral. Retake that German exam. Write that
> paper that's four years overdue. I'M TOTALLY
> GUILTY.

His rebellion against his eastern life is also figured in academic standards. On his trip west he begins by reacting against Madham and the university: "*Instead of doing as I instructed, he [Jeremy] used the recorder to insult everything the university must stand for.*" Naturally enough, he addresses his tapes to his thesis supervisor. After missing his job interview twice he gradually surrenders himself to the principles of the new order, which results in his discarding the tape recorder and disappearing. His problem of guilt is solved in the process: he and Bea Sunderman become lovers and disappear together.

After trying to live up to his namesake, and then to his supervisor, Jeremy tries to become his own hero. Like Madham, Jeremy eventually invents his new name and makes it and his new identity *real.* Like the reborn Grove, Jeremy is the quintessential Kroetsch hero. He and Grove create a past while their real journey is into a future of possibility. Like Grove, Jeremy is not acting out the quest for identity as the given authentic self, but the belief that the chosen fiction is the fullest and most free imaginative act. Kroetsch says of Grove that "as his reality, so to speak, comes into doubt, he comes more and more to represent our own predicament." We might say the same of Jeremy.

Madham attributes one thing to Jeremy which is corroborated by Jeremy himself: his need to seek out the wilderness. Jeremy substitutes the border for the frontier, and performs the liberating but risky act of crossing it. . . . What Jeremy sees as wilderness is Binghamton, the centre of cultivation and civilization that Madham fled to from the northern prairie. Jeremy's and Madham's imaginations *make* Binghamton signify whatever it does for each of them: in Lecker's border metaphor, it would constitute a border between prairie wilderness and Manhattan civilization. As Kroetsch points out repeatedly, truth is not absolute: "A lie, I thought to myself. A downright lie. What has happened to truth?" Kroetsch would say that nothing has happened to truth, but much has happened to our *idea* of it, and whether or not we even believe that it exists. Much of *Gone Indian* illustrates that, especially in the new world, truth, reality, and individual existence are not fixed and are not what we may have thought them to be. (pp. 57-62)

Kroetsch holds that we create our place, and our selves, in language. The place, the past has no meaning until it is dealt with—accounted for, if you will—in the writer's ledger. Occasionally the account balances: often it does not. And often the results seem to be inconclusive. Such is the case with *Gone Indian.* Jeremy remains in motion: endings be damned indeed. Kroetsch believes that the absence of certainties is not a disadvantage or a falsehood: the absence of limit is the presence of possibility. As Madham says, getting into a corner on the prairie is not easy. (p. 70)

> Margaret E. Turner, "Endings Be Damned: Robert Kroetsch's 'Gone Indian'," in Canadian Literature, No. 119, Winter, 1988, pp. 57-71.

MANINA JONES

[Given our experience with his] beguiling body of prose fiction, it would surely be an understatement to say that we approach the title of Kroetsch's recent work, *Excerpts from the Real World: a prose poem in ten parts,* with a certain degree of scepticism. The real world is surely something that has never been very closely associated with Kroetsch's fiction. His writing, however, is *always* associating itself with the "real world" by invading and undermining the discourses that constitute that world, discourses we think of as "true" or "natural" or "real."

Excerpts from the Real World is certainly no exception to this (mis)rule. It is, for example, a "prose poem." Any dictionary of literary terms will tell us that prose poetry is a form of prose that makes extensive use of the figurative language and imagery characteristic of poetry. If we uphold such a definition with relation to *Excerpts from the Real World,* however, the term "prose poem" begins to sound redundant. This work violates the generic boundaries its subtitle implies, boundaries that seem to distinguish between poetry—writing that works by tropes and figures, and prose—writing that is, presumably, somehow transparently referential. In doing so, it also transgresses the boundary that distinguishes between the "literary" work and the "critical" discourse that comments on it.

Excerpts from the Real World is self-consciously cryptic, bizarre, and often opaque. Written in the form of a dated journal, it confronts us with such puzzling entries as this:

14/4/85

> Here in the Highlands the budded trees, obscenely
> mauve, ache to blossom. How do man and woman,
> in these blocky houses, speak against such arrays
> of stone? Thinking of you, I forgot to pack a sweat-
> er. Tell your new lover to wear glass pyjamas when
> he sets out from Winnipeg to transport bull semen
> around the world.

One might tend, on first reading, to respond to such a passage with, "If this is the 'real' world, then it is a strange one indeed!" But is it? There is something strangely *familiar* about the language of the preceding passage. There is nothing out of the ordinary about its syntax or vocabulary. It is the way familiar language has been arranged, the ways we are forced to read it that makes it strange.

Kroetsch's poem is surrealistic in its use of a sort of dream logic, its strategy of placing ordinary words, phrases, and images in incongruous juxtaposition so that the reader feels called upon to "interpret" them as metaphorical (that is, to read them as poetry) in order to make any sense of them at all. A section of one entry takes us through this process: "Blue apricots are rare. Perhaps the apricots are plums." We have no conventional referent for "blue apricots," but we can provisionally explain the unfamiliar conjunction of adjective and noun as a metaphor for "plums." As readers we are being made aware of the process of interpretation that goes into *any* act of reading, indeed any act of perception *as* an act of reading. *Excerpts from the Real World* leads us down the garden path of conventional realism by using familiar situations, places, and dates, but that garden path is consistently exposed as a textual rug, and pulled out from under our naïve reading practices. For example:

17/7/85

The hawk on the telephone pole, folding its wings like an angel at rest, is planning a gopher's visit to the blue sky. The grasshoppers hit our windshield like hail. You raise your head from my lap, asking what the sound is. This is called writing a landscape poem.

Perhaps the best counsel for the confused reader is inscribed in the poem itself: "Relax, and you'll kitsch yourself laughing." This is playful language that calls attention to its own pretentiousness, to the fact that by attempting to treat it strictly and simplistically as "referential" we are taking it too seriously.

Or not nearly seriously enough, for it is language that *creates* what we call the "real." Without attempting a comprehensive interpretation of the passage quoted earlier (the poem precludes such interpretations), one can not help but notice that it is "bull semen" that is being transported around the "real" world. Could it be that blatant fictions (bull) are being dis-*semin*ated here? Is there a world market for prairie bullshit? And why is it important to wear glass pyjamas? So we can witness the "dissemination process?" *Excerpts from the Real World* may in many respects be opaque, but it reveals its own processes of signification in a way that "real" realist texts never do.

Kroetsch's work takes the conventionally "referential" prose forms of the autobiographical journal, travel diary, and love letter and turns them inside out. They refer, we must conclude, not outward to an external pre-textual reality, but to the "reality" constructed by texts themselves, the fictions they make real. (pp. 120-21)

While the conventional speaker in a journal seems to act as a "medium" between world and word, as a sort of messenger, in this case it becomes clear that the medium *is* the message, that we can make no easy distinction either between the spoken and what it speaks, or between the speaking speaker and the spoken speaker. "His" enunciation in the poem is equivalent to a birth, an "entry"—as both an ingress and an item in the journal—into the world of the poem: "I liked the telegram, the one you sent me announcing my birth." In *Excerpts from the Real World,* it becomes increasingly obvious that the speaking "I" is a creation of discourse, and is dependent on discourse. Each time the pronoun is enunciated its context changes. It is, therefore, never self-identical, and we can hardly expect a coherent speaking "voice" for the poem. (p. 121)

"I" is always defined in relation to an other, to a "you," which is, in one sense, a souvenir, the trace of the absent "I," seen from the outside, after the fact: "Like the ashtray I bought in Edinburgh (the castle, the castle), *you* remind me of where *I* once was" (my emphasis). *Excerpts from the Real World* deals with the traditional subject matter of the love letter, the relationship between an "I" and a "you," but the "you" of the poem is as indeterminate as its "I." How, for example, can either be established as a stable entity in such an ironic formulation as this: " 'But most of all I luv you cuz yr you.' If you see what I mean"? "You" may be both lover and alienated self as in Rimbaud's *"je est un autre"* or the *autre* of the formulations of Lacanian psychoanalysis: *"L'autre.* The author. I'm not myself today. The other is a tramp. Confloozied." The other is a tramp, perhaps, because it is unstable, like a vagabond. It has no firmly established conventional signified; its meaning varies according to context, and is therefore "unfaithful" to any particular referent: it refers "promiscuously," like a "floozie," a "tramp."

In another excerpt, the "speaker" asks his lover, "When will you leave your retailer of bull semen, there on the outskirts of Brandon, and buy a ticket to the Equator." The alternative presented is, perhaps, "dissemination" as defined by contemporary literary critics like Jacques Derrida, a dispersal of meaning over the web of signifiers that constitutes a text, producing "a non-finite number of semantic effects," as opposed to a one-way trip from word to meaning that somehow "equates" one with the other. The very possibility of "getting the message accross" in the latter fashion is being questioned at every turn in *Excerpts from the Real World.* (p. 122)

Like "I" and "you," "here" and "there" signify only in context, so that we must, as one entry says, "Let place do the signing for us." Place, therefore, in *Excerpts from the Real World,* may be defined as discursive space. The travelogue, rather than being a narrative of travel, becomes a record of its own changing meaning, its "travelling *logos,"* and the journal "entry" can therefore no longer function simply as a "passage" to or from its author's meaning or pre-textual events. The poem's first line, "I want to explain why I didn't answer the door," is supplemented by the information that "Doors, in a manner of speaking, are descriptive. Otherwise we wouldn't be here now." The journal entries ("doors," in a manner of speaking) are both entrances and exits. Appropriate to a travelogue, they are places where meaning is "just passing through."

The reader of *Excerpts from the Real World* comes along for the ride. She is drawn into a "relationship" with the text, since in any reading situation its "you" may allude to her: "The affair I never mention, the one that turns out to be with you, was occasioned by an ice storm that toppled power lines and brought angels crashing into the frozen fields." Any reading of such a passage necessarily sounds reductive, but a possibility exists that the "affair" never mentioned is one between reader and text, an implicit relationship that takes place intertextually, rather than along the simplistic "power lines" of author and reader. In such a situation, "transcendental" meaning (the angels?) comes toppling down into the fields (of the play of signification?). One thinks of such complex intertextual relationships as those that occur in another passage: "Peter Eastingwood quotes John Cowper Powys to me. 'I like a chaotic strung-along *multi-verse*'." The "real world" is not a monolithic *uni*verse "out there." It exists within the polysemic world of the poem as "multi-verse."

"A chaotic, strung-along *multi-verse*" is a good way of describing the "real world" of **Excerpts from the Real World,** multiple both in meaning and form (the poem's numerous "excerpts"), and "verse" in its strategic *turn* of "realistic" discourse back on its own "poetic" or rhetorical status. **Excerpts from the Real World,** then, is a per/versely realist work. It exploits what Jerome Klinkowitz calls "the ultimate realism of words on the page and signs at play." (pp. 122-23)

Manina Jones, "Roses Are Read," in Canadian Literature, *No. 119, Winter, 1988, pp. 119-23.*

(Georges-) André Malraux

1901-1976

French novelist, autobiographer, nonfiction writer, and critic.

Well known as a novelist, art critic, political revolutionary, and statesman, Malraux is a prominent figure in the development of twentieth-century thought. He is considered by many a prototype of such existentialist writers as Jean-Paul Sartre and Albert Camus for both the diversity of his career and the nature of his philosophical viewpoints. In his works, Malraux portrays human existence—what he termed "la condition humaine"—as a tragic state characterized by alienation and absurdity resulting from Western civilization's loss of faith in God. Nevertheless, Malraux offers the concepts of "fraternité virile," or brotherhood, and metamorphosis as means of escaping this predicament. His fiction is distinguished by frequent incidents of violence and rapidly paced plots that are governed by the force of ideas rather than events. W. M. Frohock remarked: "Malraux is a writer whose ideas are as important as his emotions. His novels are a product of both intellect *and* sensibility and, even more, of a need to establish an equilibrium between intellect and sensibility with respect to what Philip Rahv calls 'the political problem'."

Malraux was born in the Montmartre district of Paris and raised in a nearby suburb. An avid reader, he turned his love of books into employment as a broker for a rare-book dealer, and he later edited a series of luxury editions of classical literary works. During the early 1920s, Malraux contributed literary criticism to avant-garde magazines and enhanced his appreciation of art by touring the museums and galleries of Paris. His first works of fiction, *Lunes en papier* (1921), illustrated by Cubist painter Fernand Léger, and *Royaume farfelu* (1928), demonstrate the influence of Surrealism and constitute Malraux's only experimentation with fantasy literature. In 1921, Malraux met and married Clara Goldschmidt, the daughter of a wealthy Franco-German family, who shared his love of art, literature, and film. Their archaeological expedition to French Indochina in 1923 proved a turning point in Malraux's life and work. While attempting to appropriate an invaluable sculpture from the ruins of a Khmer temple in Cambodia, Malraux was arrested and imprisoned by colonial authorities. This experience inspired Malraux to found *L'Indochine,* one of the region's first anti-colonial newspapers. After the paper's closing in 1926, Malraux continued to protest colonialism in numerous articles and essays. His first major work of fiction, *La tentation de l'Occident* (1926; *The Temptation of the West*), was illuminated in part by these Asian adventures and explores Eastern and Western conceptions of existence. An epistolary novel, this work focuses on the theme of modern Western civilization's obsession with the individual, an issue that Malraux addressed throughout his career.

In 1925, while working for *L'Indochine,* Malraux reported on the nationalist uprisings in China, events that provided the basis for *Les conquérants* (1928; *The Conquerors*), his first full-length novel. Relayed through brief scenes that emphasize the chaos of revolution, this work marks the first appearance of Malraux's "new man," an individual aware of the ab-

surdity of existence who combines, in Malraux's words, "a talent for action, culture and lucidity." The plot unfolds over a conflict between Garine, a character who embodies this "new man" ideal, and Borodine, a Russian communist bureaucrat, in their efforts to mobilize the Chinese against their colonial oppressors. Critics favorably remarked on the cinematic nature of Malraux's storytelling, in which he juxtaposes imagery and individual scenes as a primary method of narration. *La voie royale* (1930; *The Royal Way*) is based on Malraux's experiences during his search for archaeological treasure in the jungles of Southeast Asia. This novel illuminates Malraux's belief, later associated with Existentialism, that death is not only a physical state, but also a metaphysical circumstance characterized by ignorance of the human condition and an unthinking acceptance of bourgeois values. Unlike existentialist protagonists who agonize over the possibility of meaningful action, however, Malraux's characters are impelled to act by their awareness of the abyss. The disciple/mentor relationship between the two main characters is an early example of male-bonding that Malraux eventually highlights in his fiction as a source of transcendent value.

Malraux's third and most highly acclaimed novel, *La condition humaine* (1933; *Man's Fate;* published in Great Britain as *Storm in Shanghai;* republished in Great Britain as *Man's*

Estate), won the Prix Goncourt, France's most prestigious literary award. In this work, Malraux returns to the settings and events of the Chinese revolution featured in *The Conquerors* to dramatize humanity's unmitigated solitude and the impossibility of finding permanent meaning. As with both *The Conquerors* and *The Royal Way*, critics consider the pervasive atmosphere of violence in *Man's Fate* less significant than Malraux's exploration of the beliefs that govern the lives of his characters. Unlike his previous novels, however, *Man's Fate* presents the possibility of vanquishing death through human dignity. Recent critical inquiry has focused on this novel's female characters and the psychology of Tchen, a terrorist whose severe isolation convinces him that absolute value lies only in acts of violence.

With the rise of fascism in Europe during the 1930s, Malraux's political stance became explicitly communist. He viewed communism as a more powerful opposition to fascism than capitalism because it avoided capitalism's preoccupation with the self, an obsession Malraux had decried as early as *The Temptation of the West*. Critics interpret Malraux's next two novels, *Le temps du mépris* (1935; *Days of Wrath*; published in Great Britain as *Days of Contempt*) and *L'espoir* (1937; *Man's Hope*; published in Great Britain as *Days of Hope*) as fundamentally propagandistic. *Days of Wrath*, an early literary exposé of Nazi atrocities, affirms the values of collectivism over individualism and demonstrates that "brotherhood" can furnish humanity with transcendant meaning. In 1936, along with many other leftist writers and artists, Malraux became involved in the Spanish Civil War—first as a delegate from an international anti-fascist group, then as a procurer of arms and aircraft for the Spanish Republican army, and finally as the leader of an international air squadron. *Man's Hope* utilizes these experiences to illustrate Malraux's belief in the power of fraternity and to demonstrate his opposition to war.

Malraux enlisted in the French tank corps in 1939 at the outbreak of World War II. In 1940 he was captured by the Germans, but five months later escaped to the French free zone, where, before joining the Resistance in 1942, he wrote his last novel, *Les noyers de l'Altenburg* (1943; *The Walnut Trees of Altenburg*). Through the memories of a prisoner of the Nazis, this work investigates humanity's attempts to deny its impermanence. *The Walnut Trees of Altenburg* offers reconciliation with a hostile universe through imagery associated with permanence and stability. After World War II, Malraux twice served in the government of President Charles De Gaulle. In 1969, he retired from civil service and devoted himself to writing and revising his multi-volume autobiography.

Since Malraux's death in 1976, much critical attention has centered on his autobiographical works. The well-received first volume, *Antimémoires* (1967; *Anti-Memoirs*) subverts the usual autobiographical narrative that emphasizes the continuity of the self by questioning the validity of individual self-perception. The subsequent volumes, *Les chênes qu'on abat . . .* (1971; *Felled Oaks*; published in Great Britain as *Fallen Oaks*), *Lazare* (1974; *Lazarus*), and *Hôtes de passage* (1975), were revised and published together with *La tête d'obsidienne* (1974; *Picasso's Mask*) as *La corde et les souris* (1976). Critics have observed that by combining personal reminiscences and meditations on art, philosophy, and politics with scenes from his novels, Malraux's autobiography redefines the boundary between fiction and nonfiction, just as he sought within those forms to clarify the meaning and pur-

pose of existence itself. Shortly before Malraux's death, the substantially revised *Anti-Memoirs* and *La corde et les souris* were published in two volumes under the collective title *Le miroir des limbes* (1976). Recent commentary on this work utilizes post-structuralist critical theories to explore the significance of Malraux's amalgamation of fact and fiction.

In addition to his novels and volumes of autobiography, Malraux wrote several works on aesthetics and art history. Partially a continuation of his interrogation of the human condition, these studies examine art as anti-destiny, a means of denying the absurdity of existence. Malraux also faults European museums for separating works of art from their original, usually sacred, function. His extensive investigation of the history and purpose of art begins in the three-volume series entitled *Psychologie de l'art,* (1947-1949; *The Psychology of Art*), which was revised and published as *Les voix du silence* (1951; *The Voices of Silence*).

(See also *CLC,* Vols. 1, 4, 9, 13, 15; *Contemporary Authors,* Vols. 21-22; Vols. 69-72 [obituary]; *Contemporary Authors Permanent Series,* Vol. 2; and *Dictionary of Literary Biography,* Vol. 72.)

W. M. FROHOCK

Malraux's techniques depart radically from those common in France. His themes are universal: human suffering, human solitude, humiliation and human dignity, the constant imminence and irrevocability of death, the inanity of life. His heroes are rarely French: Perken, Kyo, Kassner, Garine, Manuel, and Vincent Berger are either people of indefinite origins, or of mixed blood, or foreigners. And the values Malraux deals in are perhaps less remote from [Americans] than from the French. Action and violence are not radical departures for us, at least in literature. (p. viii)

Malraux is a writer whose ideas are as important as his emotions. His novels are a product of both intellect *and* sensibility and, even more, of a need to establish an equilibrium between intellect and sensibility with respect to what Philip Rahv [in his *Image and Idea*] calls "the political problem." For the central, crucial experience of Americans and Europeans alike has been the familiar political choice between passivity and revolution, and Malraux's name is high on the list of writers who moved away from democratic capitalism in the 'twenties and 'thirties, only to move back again when events culminating in the Non-Aggression Pact of 1939 revealed that the brave new world was not so perfect either. His novels had their first and greatest success as the work of the most distinguished of French fellow travelers. They are nourished by the imperious need he felt to clarify his experience by transposing it into art; their special excellence lies in his ability to feel the relations between politics and the characteristic ideas, preoccupations, apprehensions, and anxieties that torture our time. This excellence is one that our American novelists, however fine otherwise, do not have. (pp. viii-ix)

The logic of the stories—of situation and circumstance and inevitable outcome—invariably leads in one direction, to one conclusion, and the conclusion is invariably unpalatable. *La Tentation de l'occident* (which happens not to be a novel but which contains an implicit story) demonstrates the inanity of

Occidental life; *The Conquerors* demonstrates the absurdity of *all* life, East or West; *The Royal Way* presents the final ignominy of death; *Man's Fate* illustrates our inability to rise above the human predicament and our inability this side of death to achieve a fitting dignity. And so on, with the exception of *Days of Wrath,* through the whole Malraux canon. Malraux does not reject these conclusions—how could he?—but he turns their logic, juxtaposing to them some picture, figure, image, or poetic symbol which affirms, oracularly, the opposite of what the rational discourse affirms. Thus in *Man's Fate* the manner of Katow's death makes the reader forget how thoroughly both he and Katow are subject to human bondage. The technique here is the technique of [Malraux's] art books: it consists of omitting links—of not setting down, for example, a reason why Katow's behavior as he goes out to be burned in the locomotive is at all relevant to what we have seen, for several hundred pages, to be man's fate. But in the art books we call this incoherence a defect and in the novels we call it an artistic technique. His craft is a craft of ellipsis. (p. x)

I have tried to avoid removing Malraux's ideas from their context, and have preferred to let his techniques of ellipsis and juxtaposition lead me to an interpretation which has at least the merit of taking a man who has spent his life writing books to be above all a literary artist. In turn, this means treating the political aspects of his books as if politics were merely a very engrossing literary theme, or as if it were a sort of context which permits the outlines of human destiny to appear in all sharpness. This is not to deny the importance of politics in the novels, but to define it. We all subscribe, and Malraux more firmly than most, to the belief that the political problem is the crucial problem of our lives. The importance of politics in the novels is precisely that the crucial nature of the political problem makes their poetry possible. (p. xii)

The real importance of [Malraux's] first writings is less literary than psychological. They represent the kind of art against which he will shortly rebel. The result of the rebellion will be the tone of high seriousness which will mark everything he writes after his return to Europe from Indochina. Already in 1925, the structure of *La Tentation de l'occident* constitutes an implicit rejection of the form of imagination that takes the world apart and then reassembles the parts according to its pleasure: a Prologue written in the manner, tone, and color of *Royaume farfelu* precedes a text written in a style which aims at the opposite extreme. (p. 26)

[In] the essay called **"D'une jeunesse européenne,"** Malraux will make the reasons for the change in styles explicit and clear, for when he rejects the idealist, subjective aesthetics of artists like Kandinsky, he also rejects the aesthetics of his own explorations of the private world of the imagination. (pp. 27-8)

La Tentation de l'occident consists of sixty-five hermetic pages, made up of sixteen letters supposed to be exchanged between two young men, alert, educated to the brink of erudition, particularly well versed in art, and dedicated to the search for quintessences. The author of five of the letters is the young European traveling in the Orient, "A. D." The rest are written by "Ling W.-Y.," a young Chinese traveling in Europe.

The more Ling moves about Europe, the more he is convinced that European culture rests upon a base of confusions. Europeans seem unable to distinguish being from acting, or order from civilization. Gradually he comes to the point of saying that the European's notion of reality is itself confused and self-contradictory. And at last what he has seen brings him to use a phrase which re-echoes through the remainder of the book: *in the depths of European man, where it dominates the great moments of his life, there resides an essential absurdity.* The italics are in Malraux's text.

"A. D." replies that he agrees that Western man is the creature of the Absurd and takes over the rest of the book to enumerate additional reasons for thinking so and to explore the possible consequences. (p. 28)

[To] a man like "A. D." not only God is dead, but, going beyond Nietzschean formula, Man is dead also. At least, one of his manifestations, the European, has succumbed. He has managed to destroy his accustomed mode of consciousness of himself. His ideals and his idols have deserted him. In an empty world, under an empty heaven, he stands alone and for his loneliness there is no palliative. Recent readers of *The Psychology of Art* cannot fail to recognize in this a first statement of the central thesis of the *Psychology* (and of *Les Voix du silence*), to wit, that Europeans must forge a new and adequate idea of man.

But in 1925 Malraux is framing only the negative premise, that the old idea of man has fallen apart, and this is as far as his thought goes at the moment. His first two novels are based upon the same negative conviction. *The Conquerors* and *The Royal Way* will exploit at length this awareness of the meaninglessness of life and thus do much to turn the abstraction of the Absurd into one of the most essential bases of the common metaphysic of our time. They will, however, go further than does *La Tentation.* For the man confronted by the Absurd in *La Tentation* is Western man; the dilemma is the dilemma of the Occidental. The East is in danger only to the extent that it may be contaminated by the West. Malraux has not yet reached the tragic assumption that life is absurd for all men everywhere. Even in the first two novels, the heroes who are most completely aware that they are powerless against the Absurd are Europeans, scions of the middle class who, like "A. D.," have forsaken class and country. But the degree of completeness will be greater, because, when they meet their destiny through their discovery of the Absurd, they do so less because they are Europeans than because they are men.

To the attentive reader, this midway position in the development of Malraux's attitude seems entirely appropriate to the moment when the book was written. The dedication to Clara Malraux, and the fact of the book's having been finished in 1925, authorize the suspicion that *La Tentation de l'occident* represents the state of his feelings as they were at the end of the first Indochina enterprise. The tone of the letters is primarily one of repudiation, and what he is repudiating is Europe. His adventure had contained everything necessary to make him aware of the differences between Europe and Asia and—ending so perilously close to a colonial jail—had been such as to make him acutely aware of certain kinds of absurdity. The book as a whole thus stands as a further announcement of the rupture. (pp. 29-30)

His book announces a rupture, but not a program. Malraux is so frequently represented both by friends and adversaries to be the great apostle of action that his skepticism about the value of action in *La Tentation* is a real surprise. To Ling the European cult of action is one of the more trying incomprehensibles with which he has to cope. To "A. D." the value set upon action is the source of Western man's conflict between dream and reality; it contains that promise of a final outburst of destruction which threatens to be his bloody destiny. Most of the European's metaphysical discomfort rises from his yearning to act. The author of *La Tentation* knows already how certain his future man-of-action heroes are of being defeated. The certainty will not prevent Malraux himself from seeking an adventurous life or from writing stories which attach value to action. But he already realizes that his hero's plight is one from which he can be rescued only by an act of poetry—the creating of a poetic situation which somehow turns defeat into victory. (pp. 30-1)

Two years later, in the essay, **"D'une jeunesse européenne,"** Malraux foregoes the poetry. The central figure is again the abstract Western man who, Malraux says, wants to rid himself of the burden of his civilization as he once wanted to be rid of the burden of God. The notion of reality which his civilization has given him no longer suits the European's taste, and he no longer has the Christian assurance of the unity, permanence, and responsibility of humanity. Thus, Malraux says, he has to attain a new notion of man. Meanwhile he is full of anxiety, loneliness, and a Nietzschean *inquiétude* regarding himself. Nietzsche's work, for Malraux, merely expresses a despair and violence which already existed.

The great obstacle in the way of "creating a new reality"— the expression is synonymous with attaining a new notion of man—is the modern ego. The notion of God has been replaced by the great new passion of individualism. And individualism places men in unhappy straits. There is nothing on which to found a new conception of man except the consciousness each man has of himself. And here we totter, he says, on the brink of the Absurd, for there is no way for a man to know himself. The instruments we use in judging others cannot be brought to bear. Even our memory is conditioned, and what we remember of our own acts is private, and dependent on all the forces which condition our memory. There is no way of examining our past lives which does not employ subjective and thus completely undependable means. (pp. 31-2)

By this reasoning, Malraux concludes that to carry the search for one's ego to the ultimate extreme, accepting (as one must) one's own vision of the world as the valid vision, is to give in to the Absurd. Our civilization has no spiritual goal upon which individuals may establish common ground. Our thought and our sensibility are at odds. We are uncomfortable in our individualism; the burden is heavy and our hearts are no longer in carrying it. The best reflection of ourselves is the resultant anxiety.

A man who knows his thought to be only a system of allegories knows, Malraux says, that he cannot comprehend himself. In addition, the young men of Europe, those who have come to maturity in the years since the war, realize that certain ideas alone have the power of defending men against the gradual, constant wear of time. They are thus uneasily searching for the Idea which will preserve them from their own individualism and at the same time hold them permanent amid the flux of the years. Malraux does not allege that they have found the idea. He does not mention communism.

The reader, following Malraux's already somewhat oracular utterances—written in declarative sentences which state, without qualification and with scant regard for the relations between them, ideas which are presented as aspects of universal truth—is ready at any moment to find Malraux proposing that European youth take the road to Moscow. . . . But actually the essay leads up to the proposal and stops short of it. And unless one is prepared to read into the text more than the words say, the essay must be taken as a negative document. It simply refuses to accept the conditions of European civilization. Like *La Tentation de l'occident,* the essay is at once a diagnosis of what is wrong with Europe and a rejection. And like "A. D.," Malraux has closed a door behind him. (pp. 32-3)

The immediate effect of Malraux's experience in Asia seems to have been both to make Malraux ask these "basic questions" and to answer them in a tone of discouragement. His first novels are dark with the apprehension of death and sad with the vanity of life, and haunted by the inevitable, tragic defeat of man's attempts to impart real meaning to what he does. They contain hardly a hint that in some way life may acquire meaning through the fraternity of revolutionary action and sacrifice. This suggestion will come in 1933, in *Man's Fate.*

In 1927 he appears to have been in the predicament of a young and able composer whose head teems with more materials than he can use in a single piece of music. Not only do *La Tentation* and the **"Jeunesse"** essay contain in germ what will go into the first novels; they also adumbrate the themes of all the later works. What remained to be done was to establish the relationships between the themes and to find the people to incarnate them.

The man who lives in calm distress, aware of the conflicts between his acts and his inner life, will be Garine, the hero of *The Conquerors.* The one who is wiling, as "A. D." puts it in his last letter, to risk death in the name of hatred alone, will be Hong, the terrorist in the same novel. Out of "A. D.'s" somewhat Dostoevskian remark, "the taker of a life . . . may discover that he is penetrated either by his crime *or* by the new universe which his crime forces upon him," will come the figure of Tchen at the beginning of *Man's Fate,* murdering a man in a hotel bedroom and then discovering that his act has admitted him to a new, private, and very lonely world. And it will turn up again, most significantly, in connection with the hero of *Les Noyers de l'Altenburg.* Perken, in *The Royal Way,* will be a victim of the eroticism which puts the protagonist of the sexual drama in the intolerable position of having to experience both his own sensations and those of his partners. (This is the same situation which makes Ling first suspect the absurdity of European life; it is later seen in **"D'une jeunesse"** as an inevitable product of European individualism.) Ferral, in *Man's Fate,* will suffer the same torment. The great conflict between acting and being, which so impresses Ling, will underlie Garine's decision to join the Communists in *The Conquerors,* will be dramatized by the gradual rise to power of the Communists and the death of Hernandez in *Man's Hope,* and will have a decisive influence on Vincent Berger's career in *Les Noyers.* The great question, whether it is possible for man to be considered a permanent, continuously identical entity, is a central theme of both *Les Noyers* and the books on art. The fear of growing old, and of discovering that time itself has decided one's destiny, will be another source of Perken's anguish.

Such are the themes, already stated and soon to be made flesh. Certain additional ones are present by implication. We have heard nothing so far of human dignity, for which Kyo is willing to die in **Man's Fate,** or of virile fraternity, the experience of which is vouchsafed to heroes like Kyo's friend Katow, and to Kassner in **Days of Wrath.** But these themes are really responses to earlier questions. Human dignity is an opposite of the Absurd, since it supposes the discovery of meaning in life, and virile fraternity is the counterpart to man's feeling of estrangement. (pp. 34-5)

Other writers of the late 1920's had also convicted the world of its desolate vanity. Hemingway, for example, had done it in *The Sun Also Rises,* and had taken a title straight from Ecclesiastes for a book that has been said to speak for a whole generation, and doubtless does. But Malraux's first novels will begin with the affirmation with which Hemingway's stops: he grants the world's inanity, just as he grants the political and cultural bankruptcy of bourgeois civilization. In the natural logic of his emotional response to the world about him, Hemingway will come directly to his position expressed in *Death in the Afternoon,* "let those who want to save the world." The logic of Malraux's emotions will not be quite so simple. The Absurd will haunt and frustrate the heroes of his first two novels, but at the same time—by a reasoning which refuses to submit to the constraints of a syllogism—awareness of the Absurd never appears to him a valid justification for withdrawing from the world. It still leaves the door open to political action. Man's position is absurd, but his position is clearly the work of his civilization. Change his civilization and it is possible that the menace of the Absurd will become less real. (p. 36)

[Malraux] conceived **The Conquerors** as political by its setting and action, tragic by its tone, and metaphysical by its implications. Since revolutionary events move fast, he had to find a form and a style that would keep up with their fundamental rhythm and preserve the feeling essential in all his novels up to **Man's Hope,** that history will not wait for an individual to settle his destiny at leisure. (p. 37)

The narrative itself is entrusted throughout to the same first-person narrator. He is unnamed and his personality is kept intentionally unobtrusive; though he is a participant, his acts are always the carrying out of orders and are not significant. He has known Garine a long time, and the latter has put him to doing some vague sort of liaison work for the Communists, but his one real function is to be the Jamesian "central intelligence."

His record is virtually a diary. Action is noted in the present tense and as though at the narrator's first moment of leisure, as soon as possible after it has taken place, *and without his knowing what will happen next.* The device adds greatly to the effect of immediacy and to the reader's feeling of being present at the action. The account starts *in medias res* and with a rush. (This is not a novel where events grow out of contacts between characters; the events would happen anyway even if these characters did not exist.) Radio bulletins alternate with fragmentary explanations and bits of conversation. Each notation bears a date (from June 15 to August 18, 1925) and often an hour. As the story hurries along the reader is always kept aware of time, not the time which wears men away and in this sense works upon and changes characters, but the time which sets a limit in which a man must do what he has to do. The characters rarely relax, sleep fitfully, hardly eat, and are always under dramatic tension.

The style of the diary is impressionistic, in places telegraphic,

and rarely in need of the grammatically complete sentence. (p. 38)

Malraux sees his scenes much better than he hears them; in places the dialogue may be too smooth to be true, and too elliptical for the characters to have understood each other, but his eye is as true as Hemingway's, and his study of gesture so complete that at times he can get on without dialogue. The scene where finally the captured terrorist Hong is brought before [Garine] is handled without a spoken word. (p. 39)

Malraux sees the scene with the precision of a good movie lens, and to what extent his eye is cinematographic becomes clear in the pages directly following the confrontation with Hong, when Garine and the narrator go to see the mutilated bodies of their murdered friends. They are in a shed where a Chinese sits at the door, kicking away a dog that persistently tries to get in. The dog leaps and dodges, and keeps coming back. Garine and the narrator approach. The Chinese leans his head against the wall, eye half-closed, pushes the door open for them. The large, dirt-floored room has dust piled in the corners. In spite of the blue shades the light is too strong and blinds them. The narrator drops his eyes, raises them again, and sees the corpses *standing up,* not laid out but leaned against the wall. Garine tells the guard to get covers. The guard has to be told three times before he can understand; Garine lifts a fist, then tells him that he will get ten *taels* for bringing covers within half an hour. The narrator's muscles relax when he hears spoken words, but tighten again as he sees that the mouth of a dead friend has been mutilated, widened with a razor. He squeezes his arms against his sides and leans against the wall. A fly lights on his forehead and he does not drive it away. . . .

Recent criticism says much about this kind of immediacy of sensation. The visual detail and the narrator's visible reaction to the detail are passed on to the reader for interpretation: no need to tell the reader what the fly's remaining on the narrator's forehead means. And because the reader interprets he participates. He is as close to the action as he can be, and seems to live it rather than contemplate it. In other words, aesthetic distance has been cut to a minimum.

The effect is one of compelling authenticity. Malraux seems quite aware of what he is doing, and even introduces a gratuitous but particularly striking and immediate image on occasion to re-enforce the reader's feeling of being present. (p. 40)

The sharpness of Malraux's visual imagination is of course a vast advantage. When he is ready to write **Man's Hope** ten years later, he will return to the device of telling his story in brief, sharply cut episodes like these and make the most use possible of the visual effects. But the Spanish War novel is a complicated one, and much of its meaning is conveyed through juxtaposition of scenes that vary greatly in tone, color, and emotional mood, whereas the story of **The Conquerors** is simple and rectilinear, a matter of aligning the scenes one after the other in the order of the chronology of narration—from the passage of the ship up the South Asia coast to the moment when Garine realizes that his strength is exhausted and he must leave Canton while he still can, in public victory but in private defeat.

Technically, so far as telling a story is concerned, **The Conquerors** was a success. The sharp-focused point of view, the skillfully maintained pace, the extremely immediate imagery, are achievements which Malraux has never bettered.

But Malraux's technique is one that makes the presentation of character inordinately difficult. Personal relations such as the traditional novel exploits can hardly exist here. The only event that could be alleged to develop out of a personal relationship—Garine's refusal to let Hong be tortured—can be attributed more accurately to his understanding a human case very like his own. Otherwise the important relationship for each character is his political role, and his connection with the other characters is professional.

The characters are primarily types, defined by their attitudes toward life and politics. Borodin is the man who has submerged his individuality in the Revolution. Hong is the Terrorist. Nicolaïeff is the Torturer. Tcheng-dai is the Moral Force. Rebecci is the Anarchist who has talked away his energy. The fact that they are also men emerges very slowly, even in the case of Garine. (p. 41)

Originally Malraux had written a ten-page scene in which Garine discusses Borodin at length with the narrator. Borodin here sounds much less the typical functionary than he does in the finished book. The propagandist, we learn, is in the Revolution because he enjoys the activity; he wants the Revolution to go on and on. Success is not the object. He lives for his role. The doctrine not only has to be spread, but it must be spread *by him*. This Borodin is far and away more interesting than the one in the finished novel, and there is no doubt, after these ten pages, that Malraux was deeply interested in Borodin as one kind of human being. There is also no doubt that the passage had to be suppressed. These were ten pages in which, because of the requirements of point of view, nothing could happen—and a ten-page stretch with no action is awkwardly long, given the rhythm of the narrative. Coming so late in the action, long after the exposition was finished, this scene would have broken the stride of the story. Technically speaking, Malraux had no choice. The passage was published separately a year after the novel.

And so, two years later, when he is ready to try a second novel, he discards a relatively successful technique. *The Royal Way* will have rapid pace, but attain it by other means; we will not see narration in short scenes again until *Man's Hope*. The impressionistic style will be greatly chastened. He will abandon the political setting and eliminate all the interesting but minor characters, who, in *The Conquerors*, threaten to become major. And yet in spite of all this, he will be telling the same fundamental story and orchestrating the same fundamental theme. (p. 46)

Clearly *The Royal Way* is a less successful novel than *The Conquerors*. In eliminating the minor characters and the minor themes, Malraux had also eliminated no little of the primary stuff of which any novel is built, the texture and the feel of life. In taking his story out of the political setting he has sacrificed much of the interest by which, in the twentieth century, a political novel naturally and quite legitimately benefits. Perken is not only a less imposing hero than Garine because the shifting point of view in *The Royal Way* blurs the picture of him, but also because his situation in life is nearer that of the nineteenth-century outposts-of-empire man than to man in our own time or to Man in general. Garine, on the other hand, is potentially either a picture of ourselves or of Man as we know him.

And even more clearly than in *The Conquerors*, we see that Malraux's troubles are related to the size of the job he has set himself. At bottom, part of *The Royal Way* is an adventure

not greatly different from *The Heart of Darkness*. . . . But the difference between Malraux's story and Conrad's is not merely that Malraux's people have two objects in view instead of one and that his story continues after the finding of the jungle-rotted white man. Conrad's aim is to tell a story most effectively whereas Malraux's is to load a story with oblique comment and accreted significances. In *The Conquerors* Malraux had succeeded better with the actual task of narration and like Conrad left the accretion of meanings more to chance. In the second, concern for the meanings interferes with the exercise of the novelist's art. The result is incoherence. (pp. 55-6)

In addition to displaying heroes whose lineaments are extremely similar, who have the same feeling of rupture from the world that produced them, who are equally aware of the invincible power of the Absurd, and who live through fundamentally similar experiences, [*The Conquerors* and *The Royal Way*] also present the peculiarities which will gradually become the hallmarks of a Malraux novel: the atmosphere of violence, the scene in which the hero affirms his intention to maintain his hero's status, and the noble picture in which Malraux seems himself to affirm what the logic of the narrative denies.

Malraux has never written a book in which violence has not been an element of man's fate. His novels need it so that whatever acts the hero is forced to perform will have the necessary quality of decisiveness: what he does must be irremediable. For most of his protagonists a life of violence is the only satisfactory one. Violence provides them a field where action is possible despite their feeling of rupture and separation from their fellows. Both Garine and Perken resort to an act of violence as a symbol of their refusal to accept their ultimate destinies. (p. 56)

These acts of violence are closely associated with the technique of ellipsis which is a permanent aspect of Malraux's writing. They form a part of the corrective picture in which he juxtaposes to the evidence of man's weakness the poetic proof of his tragic stature. Perken's story is an illustration of man's defeat by the Absurd, but he is not defeated until after he has stalked across the empty commons of the native village toward his potential murderers and until he has killed the two natives. Garine comes out of his fever in the hospital to tell his friend that he refuses to allow the absurdity of life to make him live absurdly, and proves his point later by shooting the well-poisoner. In both cases the scenes are charged with emotion. But as of 1930 Malraux has not begun to capitalize upon the dramatic possibilities offered. In both early novels the scenes which contradict the logic of events are not situated for maximum dramatic effect. In *Man's Fate* and *Man's Hope* the corresponding scenes will be placed at the last high point of the action. But nevertheless the characteristic juxtaposition, although not yet fully exploited, is already present. (p. 57)

[Politically], *Man's Fate* is a very ambiguous book. Official Communist critics have been right, from their point of view, in approaching it warily; for them it is tainted by an individualism such as Trotsky had already denounced in *The Conquerors*, and this individualism is one which no few readers, including the brilliant and non-Communist Sartre, have felt to be extremely middle class. To be sure, since in the end Kyo and Katow enjoy a human dignity and a feeling of fraternity which is denied to the other characters, revolution appears to be at least an instrumental good. But beyond this? Kyo and

Katow may not be identifiable with the "Conqueror" type, like Garine (who would like to find in revolution a Good-in-itself); but they are no more imaginable as "curés de la révolution," the custodians of progress who take over when the fighting has finished; their place in the classless society of the Marxist future is hard to see. And much of the pathos of the book emerges from the inevitable conflict between the legitimate interests of the individual and those of the grand revolutionary enterprise. (p. 82)

Certain of Malraux's characteristic themes are compulsive drives that determine conduct. Human dignity does not belong among these, even though its opposite, humiliation, certainly does. Dignity is a moral value. It does not drive men to die; when they die for it they die by choice. In a purely negative way a concern for it underlay the conduct of Hong in *The Conquerors*: his hatred was directed at those who respect themselves and he could not imagine such people respecting themselves without scorning someone else. But he was less intent on relieving the burden of social injustice than on exterminating those who profit by it or even those who simply do not object to it. (p. 86)

Kyo and Katow are obviously something new among Malraux's heroes. Neither is a case of exacerbated individualism seeking in action (revolutionary or other) the relief of a private anguish. Kyo is protected from some forms of anguish by his sense of the heroic. He is subject like other men to the feeling of solitude . . . but his loneliness has been largely relieved by his love for his wife. What anguish Katow may have known belongs apparently to the past. As we see him in the novel, except at the end, where, after all, he has every right to feel for a moment that he has been abandoned, he seems even less concerned than Kyo about escapes. These certainly do not figure among his present motives. And possibly this is why, until the book comes to its climax, Kyo and Katow attract the reader's attention less than do Tchen, Ferral, and Clappique; they are both reasonably well adapted to the lives they have chosen and thoroughly devoted to the revolution. Consequently they are less picturesque as psychological cases.

Kyo's devotion to human dignity is what liberates him, in the last moments of his life, both from the feeling of solitude and from the "metallic realm" of the Absurd. Lying there in the school hall among all these men who are about to die, he realizes that his death, as much as his life, has meaning. (pp. 86-7)

This picture is what turns defeat into tragic victory and in a sense orients and orders all the values in the book. The destiny of the man whom the International has abandoned is so much more brilliant than the destinies of those who survive the insurrection that the political import of the novel pales before the more broadly human import. Revolution now seems to be not the subject but the setting in which the qualities and defects, the strengths and weaknesses of human character stand clearly out.

Just before the deaths of the heroes we watched Clappique sneak aboard the steamer in disguise. Shortly after, we move to Paris and see Ferral sit frustrate while a group of candy-chewing financiers decide whether or not they will let him go on being a great man. Then we pick up old Gisors, waiting in Kobe for death to end meaningless suffering. From their destinies we know the power of the Absurd. But at the same time we have also seen Katow go out to die, and we know that there inheres in man's fate, in spite of all the possibilities of defeat, the possibility of the power and glory of being a man. (p. 89)

[The] theme of the Absurd, however dear it may have been to Malraux in the past, has to be absent from *Days of Wrath* for the story to make sense. For the one reading which accounts for all the materials and techniques is this one: a man is thrown into a predicament from which, if he must depend upon his own strength alone, he can extricate himself only through death or insanity; he struggles against insanity and realizes that he has failed; he accepts the alternative, but before he can kill himself he receives help from an unknown comrade; then another unknown elects to lay down his own life in the hero's place, and still a third is willing to run horrible risk to fly him out of danger. In its strict unity, *Days of Wrath* is limited not merely to one fable and one hero, but to the orchestration of one theme, and this theme is not the Absurd but Virile Fraternity. Never, not even in the horror of solitary confinement, is Kassner completely alone. He experiences in all its plenitude the feeling of communion which Kyo and Katow know only at the end of their lives and at the briefest of moments.

Within the data of the story, the opposite of Virile Fraternity is less human loneliness than human indignity. Thus, the feeling of communion is a reward for a victory over humiliation. It is no small victory. *Days of Wrath* is, as a matter of fact, the only one of Malraux's fictions in which the hero comes out the winner and the only one in which Malraux is not forced to contradict the logic of the outcome of events by the juxtaposition of the corrective picture. For the moment the familiar note of interrogation is absent: there is no questioning the values to which Kassner is consecrated. They also are assumed to be essential data.

Kassner's victory is no less a tragic one. He has escaped the present danger, but it is clear at the end of the story that he will remain in Prague only long enough to assume a new identity and then return to the hazardous fight against the Nazis, and that he will go on fighting until at last he is caught and killed. "Even your next departure . . ." his wife says to him brokenly. She means to add, "I can accept even that." The modern reader, intently concerned with Kassner's present safety, suddenly realizes with a shock that he has been somewhat like a spectator at the *Oedipus* who innocently hopes that this time nothing unpleasant will happen and that for once things will go well with Thebes.

It is as if Malraux had attempted to bring together once and for all, within the form of fiction, all the elements of tragedy. All the stripping down, all the concentration of focus upon a single figure, the subordination of all else to the plight of the human being, the unremitting tension, these all work to the same end. Characters and spectators are never permitted to relax. Here is a man fighting against the evil that wants to beat him down; and next a man beaten about by Nature; and finally the same man searching for the woman; and when the tension is at last relieved the story is finished. The Preface leaves no doubt that this search for a narrative form which can accommodate a tragic mood was intentional. If *Days of Wrath* attracts less attention from his critics than do the other novels, the reason is doubtless that Malraux made good his intention.

Whether result was worth the effort is another question. One does not finish the story with the satisfaction one feels at the end of *Man's Fate,* the feeling of complete fulfillment that comes at the end of the successful tragedy. Possibly admiration for a technical success is as much as one can be expected to feel. More likely, one's very awareness of the technical success itself supplants the appropriate tragic emotion. But in any case, Malraux had now exhausted the possibilities of the tragic novel. After the great effort of concentration that *Days of Wrath* is, there was no going further in that direction.

In *Days of Wrath* he had a novel that perhaps conformed with his notions about the proper way to make propaganda. He did not, apparently, have one that realized his aspirations regarding propagandistic fiction. Two years later, *Man's Hope* would differ, except that it would keep the essential theme of fraternity and the intention to make propaganda, in every possible way. This time, however, the intention of the literary artist would conflict directly with the intention of the propagandist. (pp. 103-04)

The subject [of *Man's Hope*] makes certain major differences from the earlier novels obligatory. All Malraux's novels use a historical event for their background, but in the others concern for the destinies of certain individuals is dominant: here, most of the time, the event dominates the private destinies. The figure of the hero, the lone tragic figure looming over the whole book, disappears, and as a result of the disappearance Malraux has to renounce using many of his habitual devices. The workings of one individual *Angst* or another are no longer appropriate as motives of action, and in the whole book there is only one *Angst*-ridden figure whose fate is determined by his *Angst*—Hernandez. (pp. 121-22)

There is little need in *Man's Hope* to intensify the action and to concentrate it by the familiar foreshortening of time, or try to sweep the reader along in the illusion that the destiny of the characters will not wait. The characters have time to eat and sleep and do so abundantly; and they talk. *Man's Hope* is full of verbose people, and their conversation is frequently tangential to the concerns of the novel as narrative rather than styled to advance the progress of the book. The pace of events is the historical pace of the early months of the war, and where the narrative leaps across gaps of time, as it does occasionally, there is no implication that the events omitted are insignificant. Rather, the implication is merely that there are enough significant events in the book without adding to the number. (p. 122)

The great advantage of the narrative technique that Malraux adopts, and which in essence consists of conveying the detail of war in the brief, narrative-unit scenes and of grouping them so that the manner of grouping implies a commentary, is precisely that it meets the multiple problems presented by the subject. The individual scenes permit the play of the visual imagination which is perhaps his most valuable gift, and with their great, keen immediacy of sensation handle the feel of actual participation. Grouping them takes care of the panoramic view and at the same time permits revealing the significance of what has happened. Quite probably the feeling of greater "density" or of richer "texture," which critics find in this book as compared with the others, rises from this. (pp. 123-24)

In *Days of Wrath,* virile fraternity was already the opposite value both of human solitude and human indignity; in *Man's Hope* it is even more clearly the opposite of indignity or humiliation. The wounded Barca explains that he has been fighting because he does not like other men to disdain him. And the instinct of the besiegers of the Alcazar is to give

razor blades and cigarettes to the defenders just to show that they are not the kind of men the besiegers can scorn. . . .

The opposite of humiliation is probably too vague an emotion for Malraux to be able to give it a single, satisfactory name. Certainly he feels it to be an escape from scorn, but he feels it also to be the "harsh, fraternal exaltation" that supports the courage of the dynamiters as they move forward against the Fascist tanks. It comforts Siry and Kogan as they wait in the mud for the Moors to charge and whistle to each other like a pair of birds because they have no common language for a Bulgar and a Frenchman to talk in. It has its apotheosis in the descent from the mountain. (p. 124)

The marked similarity of subject matter, technique, and even of moods between *Les Noyers* and the Descent from the Mountain sequence [in *Man's Hope*] compels attention to the change which has taken place in Malraux's basic attitudes somewhere along the way. In the books before these one hardly sees the common man. The heroes of *Man's Fate* do not come from the working class. Only one character in *The Conquerors* represents the people for whose good the Revolution is supposed to function: Hong. Elsewhere Malraux's eye is on men whose backgrounds are like his own; the heroic pictures are pictures of bourgeois intellectuals. But the figures of the peasants on the mountain, of the mutinous German infantrymen, and (later in *Les Noyers*) of the men in the tank, all come from the anonymous mass. Malraux seems to have a certain impatience with intellectuals. If Vincent Berger enjoys a kind of privilege and is exempt from Malraux's scorn, the other participants in the colloquy are certainly disparaged. (p. 135)

The four men in the tank, pounding forward through the night toward the enemy, are as different from each other as men of the same century can be: Prade, the gap-toothed peasant who drives; Bonneau, the frightful little bluffer of a thug from the slums who runs the motors; Leonard, the nondescript radio operator; Berger, the intellectual. The chapter starts with enough observation of the ways and characters of the first three to identify them with the changelessly human types who, in the preceding part, were to go over and follow up the gas attack. Then the tank crashes down into a trap. They wait through an eternity for the German shells to come. There are no differences between them now. They are merely men, and man is "the only animal who knows that he will die." The shells do not come. They discover that a wall of the pit has crumbled and they get the tank out. And in the freshness of the next morning (as the book ends), young Berger realizes that he has discovered "a simple, sacred secret." Here again, the secret is what the intellectuals of the Altenburg did not know. (p. 136)

Berger's knowledge is intuition and poetry, and Malraux's art remains an art of juxtaposition and ellipsis: verification can come only from the cumulation of further insights of the same poetic order.

Thus *Les Noyers* is a reaffirmation of the significance and relevance of Malraux's old, fundamental themes. (p. 137)

W. M. Frohock, *in his* André Malraux and the Tragic Imagination, *Stanford University Press, 1952, 175 p.*

ROCH SMITH

Le Miroir des limbes was published in a Pléiade edition shortly before André Malraux's death in 1976. Each portion had appeared earlier as a separate book, beginning with *Antimémoires* in 1967, which, in revised form, now makes up Part I of *Le Miroir des limbes.* Part II, entitled *La Corde et les souris,* includes the final versions of such previously published works as *Hôtes de passage* (1975), *Les Chênes qu'on abat . . .* (1971), *La Tête d'obsidienne* (1974), and *Lazare* (1974).

In view of such a publishing history, and in light of the novel organization of a work which short-circuits time and space— as it moves freely from 1965 to 1934 and back again, or from Léopold Senghor to a Paris clairvoyant—we may sympathize with a reviewer who described the then unfinished *Miroir des limbes* as "this shifting and labyrinthine ensemble." Yet, despite apparent vagaries, *Le Miroir des limbes,* admittedly a complex work, becomes somewhat less enigmatic when one is able to recognize its ultimate unity. For not only does Malraux consciously project a unified work from the outset, but he makes revisions to the original, separately published texts largely having the effect of linking the various sections more closely. The fact that the author ignores the original order of publication and ends the book with the revised text of *Lazare* also suggests that Malraux conceived of the finished work as a unit. (p. 147)

Through a retrospective look at his fiction and his lived experiences—encompassing great men, great dreams, and great events, all of which must pass—Malraux confronts, in a final and particularly personal way, the questions that death poses to the significance of the world. In a sense, the unity of *Le Miroir* is but a reflection of the fundamental unity that Françoise Dorenlot perceived in Malraux's overall work. Yet *Le Miroir* stands apart because of its nostalgic lyricism, a quality rather aptly identified by Jean-Michel Maulpoix in a recent "Hommage à André Malraux," when he stated, "Le romancier redevient poète, quand au héros se substitute l'héritier." For reasons I hope to make clear, this transition from hero to heir betrays a shift from a deep-rooted Promethean attitude to a vision that seems increasingly Orphic.

The notion of a Promethean Malraux, whose heroes rebel against their fate in a context of human fraternity, is so widely accepted that it hardly requires additional comment here. Rather, it is the opposite view, of an Orphic Malraux, that may seem surprising, especially in light of the fact that Malraux recalls many heroic and fraternal scenes of rebellion in *Le Miroir.* To be understood, such a view requires a more precise definition of the word "Orphic."

In a consideration of the Orphic element in Malraux's *Miroir des limbes,* Elizabeth Sewell's sensitive analysis of the Orphic voice and Walter A. Strauss's more recent, perceptive examination of the Orphic theme in modern literature are particularly enlightening. Both begin by outlining the three stages of the story of Orpheus, namely: Orpheus who brings harmony through song, descent into Hades in search of Eurydice, return from the underworld and final dismemberment. In Sewell's view, the Orphic tradition is one in which poetic thinking is a marriage between mind and nature, so that the myth emphasizes harmony. She further observes that the Orphic song, whose potency is demonstrated in each of the three stages of the myth, represents the harmonizing power of the poetic voice. Finally, one of Sewell's most original percep-

tions is that of the self-reflective quality of the Orphic myth. Because Orpheus is himself a poet, "mythology," as she points out, "is considering, in the person of the poet, the power and the fate of poetry . . . In the Orpheus story, myth is looking at itself. This is the reflection of myth in its own mirror."

Strauss goes beyond Sewell's analysis in taking into account, as he explains it, "the impact of . . . nihilism upon this mythological material. In particular, he stresses the importance of metamorphosis in the modern Orpheus myth, which is "located in a context of change." He also recognizes the Orphic power of song, particularly as it transcends ultimate dismemberment. But it is when considering the implications of the Orphic myth as "le mythe de l'évasion," to use Eva Kushner's phrase, that Strauss's analysis is especially trenchant. For he sees in what he calls the "refusal" of Orpheus, the antithesis of Promethean rebellion. As Strauss explains,

> Orpheus does not rebel; he refuses to accept the world as it is . . . . Prometheanism aims for an outer transformation of society; it proposes to ameliorate man's lot by external action. Orphism proposes to transmute the inner man by a confrontation with himself. . . .

Yet it is not André the individual, but Malraux the artist and combatant that the author confronts in his *Miroir des limbes.* . . . From the outset, as he turns his poetic word-mirror toward the enigmatic music of life, like Sewell's Orpheus, Malraux creates a myth reflecting myth. Thus, his account of his official trips as Gaullist minister, or his description of conversations as De Gaulle's confidant at Colombey are reflections, in both senses of the word, on "le mythe Malraux," rather than mere recollections of the past. Like Clappique, that apparent misfit from *La Condition humaine,* Malraux is somewhat "mythomane." In fact, he may well be offering a subtle hint that myth reflects myth in his last work when, in Part I, he has Clappique recount the story of *La Voie royale,* a novel that appeared three years before *La Condition humaine.* At the very least, this passage is emblematic of the self-reflective quality of *Le Miroir des limbes.* Indeed, Malraux ostensibly repeats portions of several of his novels in *Le Miroir.* Yet he is not so much recasting the story of earlier novels as consulting these novels as myths, which he, like Clappique, has created.

Similarly, a lyrical Malraux reflects upon the myth of other combatants and other artists, such as Alexander the Great and Picasso. Like the Clappique episode in Part I, Malraux's account of the legend of Alexander in Part II seems emblematic of the self-reflective property of *Le Miroir des limbes.* For Malraux's myth of Alexander the Great—which might be summarized as the intense, exuberant Western hero conquering the all-encompassing East and being surreptitiously transformed by his experience—has much of Malraux's own story about it. In the case of Picasso, Malraux presents a painter whose art subsumes metamorphosis and is in turn subsumed by it. (pp. 148-49)

Metamorphosis is central to Malraux's view of art. While it may be tempting to see in this more evidence of an Orphic outlook, we must remember that metamorphosis in art is the very process that permits man to rebel against the fate imposed by an indifferent universe. As such, it is fundamental to Malraux's idea of art as anti-destiny, which is essentially a Promethean stance. In Malraux's art theory, art is not in harmony with life but with itself. . . . (pp. 149-50)

In *Le Miroir des limbes,* however, Malraux expands the concept of metamorphosis to include human life in general. Indeed, the title of Part II was once to have been *Métamorphoses.* And, while he clearly does not discard the idea of metamorphosis in art, Malraux now seems to see metamorphosis as basic to contemporary man for whom everything is constantly changing. . . . To the extent that metamorphosis is the very feature of the Orphic myth which, in Strauss's view, can best account for modern nihilism, Malraux's enlargement of this concept beyond its historical role in art to that of the fundamental human reality of our time further suggests a particularly Orphic cast to *Le Miroir des limbes.* (p. 150)

Thus, as the process of metamorphosis becomes even more central to Malraux's vision of the world in *Le Miroir des limbes,* it also becomes more problematic, for it can jeopardize those very values that have emanated from his life and work. By returning to elements of his fiction, his art theory, or his life which gave rise to these values, Malraux is not simply reasserting former beliefs. Rather, in examining his own myth within the context of metamorphosis, and in the twilight of his life, Malraux confronts the possibility of nothingness and meaninglessness more directly than even before. Strauss has pointed out that "the Orphic poet seeks to regenerate himself particularly by means of the voyage downward, with its attendant self-recognition through remembrance and its mandatory self-transformation, followed by return to the world that will become the ground of a vaster metamorphosis". Clearly, the various elements of the Orphic theme, such as self-reflection, metamorphosis, as well as descent and return are interwoven. Having considered the first two, we now turn to the question of descent and return in *Le Miroir des limbes.*

As Strauss suggests, memory can be a form of descent downward. And since *Le Miroir des limbes* is a consideration of the fateful questions posed by death, Malraux's descent through memory strikes a particularly Orphic chord. In Part I, or *Antimémoires,* the author considers the question of death as he returns to the myth of Malraux the art explorer, the Resistance fighter, the orientalist, the tank corpsman, and the government minister. But the one experience of hell he has not had, is that of torture. . . . For this, he must rely on survivors of concentration camps, who surprise him by their petty bickering over the kind of memorial to erect in honor of Resistance leader Jean Moulin. Malraux surmises that these "déportés" were able to return to life only by trying to forget. . . . Interestingly enough, the discussion of suffering and death in the camps, at the end of Part I, reminds Malraux of Lazarus, to whom he will return more fully at the end of Part II. The Lazarus story shares with that of Orpheus the descent and return stage, but with some essential differences: the descent of Lazarus into the realm of death involves suffering and loss of consciousness, and, unlike Orpheus, Lazarus presumably does not remember his experience. . . . Thus the legend of Lazarus is an especially appropriate representation of descent into a particular kind of limbo. Its hallmark is not mere danger or even the threat of death, as in the case of Orpheus, but the most atrocious suffering and the experience of oblivion.

Throughout *Le Miroir des limbes,* Malraux makes several references to his famous episodes of "return to the earth." He recalls such passages, for example, when recounting his aerial search for the ruins of the city of Sheba, or when transposing, from the closing pages of *Les Noyers de l'Altenburg,* the story of Colonel Berger's narrow escape from death during a tank battle. . . .

Through his descent into his own myth, which includes earlier descent and return experiences, Malraux initially encounters a most menacing limbo: time and the impermanence of human civilizations.

It is, of course, in the last section of *Le Miroir,* previously published as *Lazare,* that we find the other form of limbo. Here, a hospitalized Malraux, like a modern-day Lazarus, struggles with unconsciousness and coma. Unconcerned with the threat to his individual identity, Malraux transforms his encounter with this personal hell into the broadly human question of the meaning of life in the face of suffering and annihilation. Yet he responds to both modes of limbo, when he recalls *Les Noyers de l'Altenburg* and the famous episode of the gas attack at Bolgako. In the spontaneous reaction of the horrified German soldiers who carry their Russian enemies to safety, the author is especially struck by a kind of primeval fraternity stemming from the basic life instinct. Malraux sees a timeless, fundamentally human quality in the soldiers' awareness of suffering existence. Passions and doctrines, these "hôtes de passage," go by, but not the struggle inherent in life. Metamorphosis may well be particularly human, as civilizations die and their works are transformed, but there remains an unchanging instinct for life whose human and fraternal quality stems from an awareness of a shared struggle for existence. . . . Returning from his last descent into limbo, Malraux's profound discovery is that the meaning of life is not to be found in an interrogation of death, as religions and he himself have done. . . . Comparing this last epiphany to earlier ones, he insists, once again, on life, in harmony with the cosmos, as the source of revelation in those former return experiences. . . . Troubled by his sense of a broadened metamorphosis, which, unlike the metamorphosis of art, threatens to reduce and even destroy man's efforts, Malraux is able to discover a bond between a life instinct, conscious of its suffering, and his long-standing value of human fraternity. On the one hand, he specifically associates this "fraternité sauvage" ["primitive fraternity"] with "le défi de Prométhée" ["the defiance of Prometheus"]. Conversely, in view of the evidence that death reveals nothing, it is not rebellion but a timeless, fundamental human existence in accord with the cosmos, as in Hugo's "Booz endormi," that prevails. Such a view of man in harmony with the universe plainly suggests the Orphic.

We are left, therefore, with the realization that *Le Miroir des limbes* does not fully transcend the antithesis of the Promethean and Orphic themes. Rather, as we examine the ambivalent mythical substrate of *Le Miroir,* it is the relationship of one mode to the other that reveals what is most original in Malraux's vision.

This mythical ambivalence betrays a profound yearning for harmony in Malraux's work, despite his repeated emphasis on the separation of man and nature. Early visions of harmony, such as that of Perken, who glimpsed an accord between his ebbing life and the ongoing life of nature at the end of *La Voie royale,* or that of Manuel who discovered song and life in the closing paragraphs of *L'Espoir,* occurred in novels which otherwise insisted on the existential duality of man and the world. Within *Le Miroir des limbes,* Malraux first accentuates duality, then harmony in the return experiences. Indeed, there is much to suggest that his epiphanic conclusion to *Le Miroir des limbes*—with its perception that life, and not death, can be the only source of revelation—was meant as a final reconciliation of opposing forces in his work. Some of these tensions, such as permanence versus instability, knowledge versus faith, and human freedom versus cosmic certainty carry special stress in *Le Miroir des limbes,* as if to render even more dramatic the ultimate resolution of opposites through reconciliation between man and the cosmos. The tables have been turned, as the ironic grimace of death is replaced by the reconciled smile of a man who has returned from the realm of darkness and is now able to view the unmasked face of death with supreme irony. . . . (pp. 151-54)

It is doubtful that the fundamental antithesis between the Promethean outlook and the Orphic attitude can be overcome, except by choosing one view over the other. But it would be difficult to contend that Malraux attempts to resolve the dilemma in this way, for he emphasizes the Promethean qualities of his myth throughout *Le Miroir.* It would seem more appropriate, therefore, to speak of an Orphic *temptation* in *Le Miroir des limbes.* By turning inward, by descending into his own myth, Malraux endeavors to make that myth endure, to transcend, through the power of his creative voice, the threat of disintegration faced by that myth. The myth itself is essentially Promethean; it is the legend of the hero. The effort to reflect it and thereby project it beyond death and annihilation, beyond a threatening metamorphosis, is manifestly Orphic; it is the labor of the heir. (p. 154)

Roch Smith, "Malraux's 'Miroir des limbes' and the Orphic Temptation," in Symposium, *Vol. XXXII, No. 2, Summer, 1978, pp. 147-55.*

SUSAN RUBIN SULEIMAN

> Re-vision—the act of looking
> back, of seeing with fresh eyes, of
> entering an old text from a new
> critical direction.
>   Adrienne Rich

The thought that it might be time to take another look at Malraux's novels first occurred to me a few years ago, while I was reading the passionate, angry pages that Annie Leclerc devoted to him in *Parole de femme.* "L'emphatique Malraux," she calls him—the repetitive proponent of conventional values, and first and foremost of the value of the hero: ["The hero; it's me-me-me, for as long as possible. *My* mark, *my* takeover, *my* possession for eternity"]. Grandiose and ridiculous, ever the posturing male, Malraux's hero deserves all the scorn that a woman's word can heap on him.

Leclerc exaggerates, of course; hers is not a critique but an attack, not a reading but a caricature. She bases her indictment on a few well-known quotations from *La Voie royale,* makes no distinction between Malraux and his character Perken, ignores the other novels, does away with ambiguities and contradictions. Malraux doesn't interest her; she merely uses him to make a point, then passes on.

And yet, her few acerb words prompted me to think once again, in a way I had not thought before, about Malraux's novels and their contemporary significance. . . . Malraux was, for me, a familiar and admired writer, exemplary in his concern for questions of the broadest human significance. Although the 1930s had receded into history, and Malraux himself had undergone a metamorphosis (perhaps more than one) since those impassioned days, his novels remained for me, like those of Sartre, Camus, and a few others, representa-

tive of a kind of fiction—serious, urgent, eloquent—which I regarded with what might be called historical nostalgia: they were not repeatable today, but they were definitely worth saving.

Now along came Annie Leclerc, telling me that he is not worth saving—not by, or for, women, in any case. And that made me pause. . . . Might I find, after so many years, that when Malraux speaks of the problematic glory of man's fate, he is not speaking to me? Might I discover, in his novels, what Judith Fetterley sees in the whole expanse of American fiction by male writers: "In such fictions the female reader is co-opted into participation in an experience from which she is explicitly excluded; she is asked to identify with a selfhood that defines itself in opposition to her; she is required to identify against herself "?

Clearly, a re-reading—or, rather, a re-vision as Adrienne Rich defines it: rereading from a new critical perspective—was in order. A feminist perspective? Yes, to the extent that the whole enterprise was provoked by my reading of contemporary feminist writers and critics, and that its underlying question could not have been formulated outside a feminist problematic. At the same time, I was, and am, extremely wary of the temptation that besets any critic with a strong ideological allegiance: to transform commentary into polemics, and to start a critical investigation from foregone conclusions. I therefore decided to proceed as gingerly, and with as much "verifiability," as possible: rather than attacking head-on the question of Malraux's heroes, about whom in any case a great deal has been written, I would look instead at Malraux's . . . heroines? No, his women. Who are they? Where are they? What do they do? Who speaks to them, to whom do they speak? And what difference does it make?

My first observation brought with it a shock of discovery: in Malraux's six novels, with their total cast of hundreds of characters, only five women are named. Of these, two have only a first name and are evoked fleetingly: Perken, in *La Voie royale,* talks to Claude Vannec about the woman he once lived with, whose name was Sarah; Vincent Berger, in *Les Noyers de l'Altenburg,* had a servant named Jeanne. That leaves three women who have full names and who appear as more than mere evocations: May Gisors, Valérie Serge, Anna Kassner. (pp. 124-26)

[There] are a great many dead or absent wives in these novels, very few who are *there.* I would contend that their absence is not explicable only by the fact that Malraux wrote chiefly about war and revolution, two activities in which the presence of women is rare. That would certainly not account for the considerable number of dead wives and mothers, or for the apparently nonexistent ones, like Vincent Berger's wife (young Berger's mother) in *Les Noyers de l'Altenburg,* who is never mentioned. Whereas the father-son (or its variant, grandfather-grandson) relation is privileged in almost every novel—Claude and his grandfather in *La Voie royale,* Kyo and Gisors in *La Condition humaine,* Jaime Alvear and his father in *L'Espoir,* the three generations of Bergers in *Les Noyers,* not to mention the large number of "spiritual father-spiritual son" relations ranging from Rebecci-Hong or Gisors-Tchen to Ximenez-Manuel—Malraux's heroes seem to have experienced no affective ties at all to their mothers. The absence of women in their emotional lives is, thus, attributable to more than the mere circumstantial *données* of the fictions.

Of the unnamed women who are present in the novels, it may be accurate to say that they are not so much figures [as Roland Barthes defines the term in his *S/Z*] as *figurantes:* they are "extras" on a stage where men are the objects of destiny. The chief characteristic of a *figurant* is silence. Malraux's men are inveterate talkers, but they rarely address a word to a woman. Talking to a woman would, of course, be difficult, because there are so few of them around. But there is something else at stake here, too, a kind of fundamental incompatibility between what a man has to say and what a woman can understand or cares about. ("To have a man's heart and not to notice that one is explaining that to a woman who doesn't give a damn is quite normal"), says Garine. (pp. 128-29)

Quite a lot has been written about the eroticism of Malraux's "adventurer" or terrorist heroes: Garine, Perken, Ferral, Tchen. Eroticism is, as the eroticists themselves explain it, first of all a need to dominate the other, to use the other as a means of gaining possession of one's self. Thus Ferral: . . . ("He derived his pleasure from putting himself in the place of the other, that was clear; of the other, compelled: compelled by him. In reality he never went to bed with anyone but himself, but he could do this only if he were not alone"). The woman in such a situation is obviously there to be negated, and she must be silent. It is true, as Lucien Goldmann and others have noted, that Malraux—or, if one prefers, the implied author of *La Condition humaine*—does not endorse eroticism as a positive value; it is clear in the novel that Ferral's drive to dominate women is merely the sexual side of a more general drive to impose his will on others, just as Perken's eroticism was the sexual counterpart of his desire to "leave a scar on the map." Significantly, in both instances the adventurer's project ends in failure.

The adventurer's scorn of women, his refusal to talk to them or allow them to speak—in other words, to consider them as fully human beings—is, thus, not attributable to the author of *La Condition humaine;* indeed, one can cite Valérie's letter to Ferral, in which she proclaims her refusal to be "only a body," as proof to the contrary. What seems to me more significant, however, is that even Malraux's revolutionaries, the men of goodwill like Kyo, Katow, Hemmelrich, Kassner, Garcia, or Manuel, find it extremely difficult to communicate with women. Leaving Kyo and Kassner aside for the moment, since theirs are the most fully developed relations with women (I discuss them in the next section), let us look at a few others.

Garcia and Guernico, walking on the street during the bombardment of Madrid, are stopped by a woman who tugs at Guernico's sleeve and asks whether he thinks she should leave the city. . . . Concentrating on the exchange between the woman and the two men, we note the following: she asks Guernico a question, to which he does not reply, turning instead to Garcia to explain who she is. The woman rephrases her question, and this time Garcia replies curtly that her husband is surely right (in asking her to leave). She responds by talking about her feelings, allowing her voice to trail off at the end of the sentence. Garcia's attention turns to the sound of the accordion in the background; then he thinks *to himself* that "They're all alike, these women," and that she might end up causing her husband's death. He does not tell her his thoughts, however; he clearly is scornful of her "typically feminine" ("they're all alike") lack of good sense, and, indeed, he does not address a word to her again. Guernico's question to her elicits a reply that shows courage (she is not

afraid to die), but that also reinforces the impression that she is vacillating (note all the points of suspension), and that she lacks good sense: since she is pregnant, the answer to her own question should be evident. Garcia is no longer interested, however, and he doesn't even hear Guernico's rejoinder. After the woman disappears into the shadows, the two men resume their conversation, which is long and philosophical.

This is a minor incident in a lengthy novel, but it is not insignificant. It is one of the very rare scenes in *L'Espoir* where a woman speaks, or, what is even rarer, where a woman speaks to express her feelings. True, Garcia's indifference may not be due only to the fact that she is a woman—she is, after all, a total stranger, and he has many things on his mind—but there is no mistaking the scornful tone of the phrase "Toutes les mêmes," which explicitly marks her sexual difference. What is even more important, this difference represents, in his eyes, a potential threat of death for her husband: women can be dangerous; in any case, they hamper the serious activities of men.

In *La Condition humaine,* besides Kyo there are two other revolutionaries who either are or have been married: Hemmelrich and Katow. Hemmelrich lives with a Chinese woman and has a child by her; the child is seriously ill. After a first attempt to bomb Chang-Kai Shek's car, Tchen and his two friends seek shelter in Hemmelrich's store. He refuses to let them stay, fearing that if the police find them there with their bombs, they will kill the woman and the child. After the three leave, Hemmelrich goes upstairs to the bedroom where the sick child is, hating himself meanwhile for having let down his comrades. . . . He thinks, with increasing fury and frustration, about the misery of his life, present and past. The only thing that keeps him from going out and joining the terrorists is the thought that his wife and child depend on him. A little later, Katow arrives, and Hemmelrich confides his sense of guilt and also his anger to him; his wretched life is somehow summed up by his wife, in whom he sees a poor humiliated creature like himself. . . . Katow, who for reasons of his own understands only too well how Hemmelrich is feeling, tries to reassure him:

> " . . . If you believe in nothing, *especially* because you believe in nothing, you're forced to believe in the virtues of the heart when you come across them, no doubt about it. And that's what you're doing. If it hadn't been for the woman and the kid you would have gone, I know you would. Well then?"

> "And as we live only for those virtues of the heart, they gobble you up. Well, if you've always got to be eaten it might as well be them . . ."

It is not clear whether the "elles" in Hemmelrich's reply refers to "qualités cardiaques" or to women like his wife—devoted, alien, and mute—who are the immediate subject of the conversation. But it hardly matters, since the "qualités cardiaques" belong to those women. Hemmelrich is saying that he is tied down by his wife (or, rather, that he is "eaten up," and the choice of that image is not insignificant), that he accepts his situation but is not happy about it. Katow, in the meantime, thinks but does not dare to say out loud: . . . ("Death will free you"). Hemmelrich is in fact "freed" shortly afterward, when the woman and the child are killed by a grenade attack on the store. (pp. 129-33)

Katow will find his apotheosis in the gesture of self-sacrifice which links him to the two men for whom he gives up his cyanide pill and consents to be burned alive. For him as for Hemmelrich, it is the revolution that provides dignity and genuine communion with others—and those others are men, generically opposed to the "vague idiote" [his wife] with whom he once spent his days. This opposition is, curiously, echoed and reinforced by one of Kassner's internal monologues while he is in the Nazi prison. Remembering his martyred comrades in China, Russia, and Germany, Kassner exclaims: . . . ("You, my companions, it is what exists between us that I call love").

Katow and Hemmelrich both choose (if that is the right word) women who are below them socially and intellectually, and whose death signifies liberation and the possibility of self-fulfillment for the revolutionary hero. Their humiliated companions bear at least some resemblance to the wordless prostitutes over whom Garine, Perken, and Ferral assert their manhood. Although the revolutionary is not an eroticist, his relations with women are not altogether different from those of the adventurer. As an older "Clappique" told Malraux in a conversation in Singapore (reported in the **Antimémoires**), the first characteristic of the adventurer is that he is unmarried. Unhampered by a woman, free to act—that seems also to be the ideal state toward which the revolutionary hero tends.

When the narrator of **Les Conquérants** first meets Nicolaieff, he makes a remark that I find extremely illuminating in this context: . . . ("The fat man speaks French with a very slight accent. His tone of voice—despite his clipped answers, you'd think he was speaking to a woman, or was about to add 'My dear fellow'—, his calm face, the unctuousness of his manner, make one think of an ex-priest"). What not only is implied here, but is taken for granted, is that when men speak to women, they do not speak as they do among themselves. The "unctuous" intonation of a man speaking to a woman is enough to feminize him, make him appear less masculine (an "ex-priest"). Not speaking to women, or speaking to them in a "special" way, these are but two aspects of a single phenomenon: the fundamental scorn that Malraux's heroes feel toward women, and their deep-seated fear of them.

Not for nothing was Malraux a brilliant writer, however. If on some level he and all his heroes shared in . . . ("the fundamental misogyny of almost all men"), he seems to have had the necessary lucidity to realize it, and—like his creature Kyo—to be ashamed of it. We can read his treatment of Valérie Serge, May Gisors, and Anna Kassner as a compensatory gesture, a way of righting the balance, as it were. At the same time, their stories—or rather, their episodes, for they ultimately play a small part in the two novels in which they appear—repeat, in different modes, the dominant theme of separation, of an inalterable and unbridgeable difference between the sexes; they also repeat, rather unexpectedly, the valorization of the masculine that we have already encountered elsewhere.

Valérie's is the mode of irony. In this woman, in whom Ferral senses . . . ("a pride akin to his own"), the eroticist adventurer meets an adversary to his own measure. Valérie is beautiful, rich, articulate—a woman who earns her own way and speaks her mind. During a conversation in his bedroom, shortly before they make love, Ferral tells her that a woman must of necessity give herself, and a man must of necessity possess her; to which she replies: . . . ("Hasn't it occurred to you, dear, that women never give themselves (or hardly

ever) and that men possess nothing? . . . Listen, I'm going to say something very wicked—but don't you think it's the story all over again of the cork which considered itself so much more important than the bottle?"). By insisting on leaving the light on while they make love, so that he can watch her face as she reaches orgasm, Ferral seeks to assert the superiority of the "cork" over the "bottle." Valérie then retaliates with the famous scene of the canaries, in which Ferral plays the role of *dindon de la farce* while she plays that of director; whereupon Ferral does her one better and transforms her hotel room into an enchanted forest full of tropical birds: . . . ("Through hatred he would have offered Valérie his handsomest gift"). But the aim of the gift is clear: . . . ("It was necessary above all that, if Valérie told the story of the cages—she would not fail to do so—he would only have to tell the end in order to escape ridicule").

It is in this context of a somewhat bitter drawing-room comedy, where what matters above all is the protagonists' image in the *salons,* that Ferral—and the reader of **La Condition humaine**—reads Valérie's letter: . . .

> You know a good many things, dear, but you will probably die without its ever having occurred to you that a woman is *also* a human being. I have always met (perhaps I shall never meet any who are different, but so much the worse—you can't know how thoroughly I mean 'so much the worse') men who have credited me with a certain amount of charm, who have gone to touching lengths to set off my follies, but who have never failed to go straight to their men-friends whenever it was a question of something really human (except of course to be consoled).

Valérie, in her mocking way, seems to be pointing her finger here not only at Ferral, but at all of Malraux's heroes; wasn't it a hero, after all, who said that to keep one's mind on "serious things," the best thing is to "sleep with [women] and forget about it"? Isn't it true that not a single one of Malraux's heroes—not an adventurer, not a revolutionary, not Gisors the philosopher, not Alvear the art historian, not even Kyo or Kassner—ever talks to a woman about any of the "truly human things" that preoccupy them all so persistently, and about which they talk to each other with such urgency and eloquence?

At the same time, it is worth noting that by humiliating Ferral, Valérie adopts a quasi-masculine stance: she will certainly not "convert" him to her point of view, she merely asserts her own power in a struggle where both self-respect and public image are at stake. Her gesture is a declaration of war, with all the aggressiveness that such declarations imply. If we admire her, as we are surely meant to do, it is because she is a woman with "masculine" pride and self-assertiveness. For that very reason, however, it seems clear that she can never have any but an adversary relationship with men.

May and Anna are quite different; they are the only two women in Malraux's novels who have what might be called an egalitarian love relationship with a man. Goldmann devotes some lyrical pages to his celebration of the love between Kyo and May; theirs is, in his words, "one of the purest and most beautiful love stories to have been described in the important works of the twentieth century." According to Goldmann, the love that Kyo and Kassner feel for their wives is the counterpart to their feeling of authentic revolutionary community with their fellow men. The love between man and woman, in other words, is the private aspect of the more generalized love that unites men in "la fraternité virile." This is an attractive interpretation, one that allows Goldmann to explain why adventurers (for example) are not able to love women; what it fails to take account of are the very precarious nature of the love relationship as it is actually experienced by the two men in question (we never know exactly what the emotions of the women are, since Malraux maintains a strict internal focalization on the men when they are together), and the possibly problematic rather than integrative relation that exists, in Malraux's novels, between heterosexual love and "virile fraternity."

The love between Kyo and May is placed at the outset under the sign of ambiguity—of at least two ambiguities, in fact. First, there is the ambiguity of May's appearance: . . . ("Her blue leather coat, of an almost military cut, accentuated what was virile in her gait and even in her face. . . . Her very high forehead as well had something masculine about it, but since she had stopped speaking she was becoming more feminine"). When May speaks, she appears to Kyo like a man (here we find a familiar paradigm—to be fully feminine, the woman must be silent); at the same time, it is her sensual mouth, with its full lips, that most clearly marks her as a woman.

The other ambiguity is more complex: it has to do with Kyo's sense of closeness to her and at the same time with his feeling of total separation from her. The alternation of these two feelings defines Kyo's relationship to May (and hers to him? We cannot be sure), which may be one reason why Gisors, after Kyo's death, thinks of their love as an "amour intellectuel et ravagé."

Kyo's greatest feeling of alienation from May comes, understandably enough, after she tells him that she has finally slept with one of her colleagues at the hospital where she is a doctor. Although their marriage is not based on sexual exclusiveness and although he knows that her act had no more than passing significance for her, he cannot help feeling angry and jealous. What is more important in our context, however, is his discovery, after her "confession," that May had begun to recede from him way before—that it was not her infidelity, but time and habit, which would eventually separate her from him. The passage in which this realization hits Kyo must be quoted almost in full in order for its impact to be felt . . . :

> He continued nevertheless to look at her, to discover that she could make him suffer. For months, whether he looked at her or not, *he had ceased to see her;* certain expressions, at times. . . . Their love, so often hurt, uniting them like a sick child, the common meaning of their life and their death, the carnal understanding between them, *nothing of all that existed before the fatality which discolors the forms with which our eyes are saturated.* "Do I love her less than I think I do?" he thought. "No. Even at this moment he was sure that if she were to die he would no longer serve his cause with hope, but with despair, as though he himself were dead. *Nothing, however, prevailed against the discoloration of that face* buried in the depth of their common life as in mist, as in the earth. He remembered a friend who had had to watch the disintegration of the mind of the woman he loved, paralyzed for months; *it seemed to him that he was watching May die thus, watching the form of his happiness absurdly disappear like a cloud absorbed by the gray sky. As*

though she had died twice—from the effect of time, and from what she was telling him. (my emphasis)

Kyo's alienation from May, in other words, is not the temporary alienation of a husband who is angry at his wife; it is a much more deeply anchored thing, against which even his love for her is no protection. And it is a thing that *kills* her—not once, but twice. May is also, in a sense, a "dead wife." Finally, as if this weren't enough, Kyo realizes that something else separates her from him: not anger or hatred, not jealousy, not even the destructive power of time, but a feeling without a name that suddenly transforms her into something incomprehensible: . . . ("This body was being invested with the poignant mystery of a familiar person suddenly transformed—the mystery one feels before a mute, blind, or mad being. *And she was a woman. Not a kind of man. Something else . . .* She was getting away from him completely") [critic's emphasis].

The fundamental alienation between men and women is here orchestrated in a tragic mode. Kyo's reaction, when he realizes his separation from May, is to want to clasp her to him: . . . ("To lie with her, to find refuge in her body against this frenzy in which he was losing her entirely; they did not have to know each other when they were using all their strength to clasp their arms around their bodies"). Sexual union would be a way of escaping from the awareness of a more irremediable separateness. This union is prevented, however, for at that point the bell rings and Clappique enters; Kyo then goes out, and it is only later, while walking with Katow, that he is able to rediscover (or perhaps to reason himself into believing?) his sense of closeness to May: . . . ("Since his mother had died, May was the only being for whom he was not Kyo Gisors, but the most intimate complicity").

The same alternation between alienation and communion (where, paradoxically, May's presence provokes the former, her absence the latter) occurs in the only other scene that Kyo shares with May, shortly before he is arrested and killed. His refusal to allow her to go with him to the meeting is in one sense a revenge for her earlier infidelity, and they both understand it as such; at the same time, it is an attempt on his part to protect her. After she finally lets him leave, he realizes that their kind of closeness does not allow for either revenge or protectiveness, and he returns to get her: . . . ("Before opening the door, he stopped, overwhelmed by the brotherhood of death, discovering how insignificant the flesh appeared next to this communion, in spite of its urgent appeal. He understood now that the willingness to lead the being one loves into death itself is perhaps the complete expression of love, that which cannot be surpassed").

Paradoxically, the love Kyo feels for May can find its ultimate expression only in death. Could their love story be a revolutionary version of *Tristan et Iseult?* That might explain why Lucien Goldmann found it so powerful and pure; but as readers of Denis de Rougemont know, the source of Tristan's love is narcissism . . .

It seems to me significant that Kyo's final, "fraternal," communion with May is explicitly contrasted, by Kyo himself, with the "dérisoire" quality of merely carnal love. One critic has remarked that Kyo's and May's marriage is a fraternal, rather than a conjugal, union. I think it more exact to say that Kyo's heterosexual desire (which is mentioned in both of the scenes he has with May) is constantly deflected or sublimated toward a "higher goal," this higher goal being that of the homophilic (even if not homosexual in the usual sense) communion of revolutionary *brother*hood: *la fraternité virile.*

The same sublimation, I would argue, occurs in the Kassner-Anna marriage in **Le Temps du mépris.** The revolutionary activist Kassner, after being imprisoned by the Nazis and thought dead by his wife, returns home, to her and their child. The couple's reunion is extremely awkward. . . . Kassner realizes how much she has suffered in his absence, and how much she will continue to suffer (for his return is temporary, and he will have to leave again to be killed sooner or later), but that very realization separates him from her. . . . As they talk and as she has a chance to express her sadness even while affirming that she accepts the life she has chosen, he begins to feel closer to her. They caress each other gently as they talk; then, Kassner has a sudden "epiphany" as he thinks about the meaning of his life and of his approaching death—he must go out with Anna, walk with her in the street. The novel ends as he is waiting for her near the door.

Here, as in **La Condition humaine,** the revolutionary hero, already marked by death, subordinates the heterosexual drive (if that is still the right word—Kassner, unlike Kyo, doesn't seem to feel any physical *desire* for his wife) to a more mystical communion with his fellow men. Although he apparently includes Anna in this communion, it is striking how often in this novel we encounter what James Greenlee has called the "redundantly masculine" expression of *fraternité virile*. At the demonstration where he goes to look for Anna, Kassner hears an old woman tell the crowd about the imprisonment of her son; he sees a number of women in the crowd whom he mistakes for Anna. Yet, when at the end of the episode he must sum up for himself the meaning of this experience . . . , his way of expressing it is characteristically unisex: . . . ("No human speech went so deeply as cruelty. But *virile fraternity* could cope with it, could follow cruelty to the very depths of blood, to the forbidden places of the heart where torture and death are lurking") [critic's emphasis]. Earlier, in his prison, Kassner had already stated (in a sentence I quoted earlier) that genuine love was what existed between him and his (male) comrades. After he is released, he looks at the pilot who is flying him to safety and feels a strong bond with him: . . . ("Their common action joined the two men like an old and *firm* friendship") [critic's emphasis].

After this, and despite Kassner's love for his wife, there seems little doubt that the word *homme* and its derivatives (e.g., *humain*) are to be understood, in this novel (perhaps in all of Malraux's novels?), in a gender-specific sense. What this means as far as women—even beloved women—are concerned is, of course, problematic. At one point during the demonstration, Kassner looks at the crowd and finds in it an expression of . . . ("the passions and the truths which are given only to men gathered together"). In his mind, the exaltation of his communion with "les hommes assemblés" becomes joined with his "femme invisible," who is hidden from him by the crowd. But it is significant that the process is later repeated in reverse, when Kassner's reunion with Anna expands to become joined with the crowds of the street: individual—specifically, sexual—union with the beloved woman is rejected, or at least deferred, in favor of "les hommes assemblés." It is almost as if, in order to participate in Kassner's love, Anna had to become a man.

May, in her appearance and actions, was already *à demi-virile;* Valérie, in whom Ferral recognizes a pride similar to his own, chooses the male arena of contest and one-upsmanship in which to assert herself. Without wishing to indulge in paradox, one might well advance the proposition that the only women *characters* in Malraux's fictional universe—the only women deserving of a name and of either hateful or loving recognition by men—are men in disguise.

The foregoing raises a number of questions, and first of all this one: what difference does it make? What is the usefulness of rereadings such as the one I have been practicing, given that they only confirm what might seem by now to be an all-too-familiar fact: the literature of adventure and heroism, whether in the past or in our own time, has been overwhelmingly male—written by men, about men, for men, embodying male fantasies and founded on the most enduring male fantasy of all: the fantasy of a world without women. Is there really a point in demonstrating, as if no one had noticed (even if they didn't talk about it) that Malraux's novels are exclusively "masculine" fictions? Yes, there is. It is one thing to notice something and leave it unexpressed, or cover it up like a guilty secret; it is quite another to examine it and attempt to state its significance. The fact that (to my knowledge, at least) none of the hundreds of articles, books, special issues of journals and commemorative pieces devoted to Malraux since his death—not to mention the thousands that appeared while he was still alive—has seriously questioned, or sought to explore the implications of, the status of women in his works is indicative of a certain critical blindness. (pp. 134-42)

The usefulness, indeed the necessity, of such shake-ups for and by women readers and critics has been emphasized by recent works of feminist criticism. Judith Fetterley has called on women to become "resisting readers" in order to counteract a tradition in which, "as readers and teachers and scholars, women are taught to think as men, to identify with a male point of view, and to accept as normal and legitimate a male system of values, one of whose central principles is misogyny." (pp. 142-43)

Rather than denouncing Malraux, or any antifeminine writer, as the enemy (which Fetterley tends to do), we can analyze him as a symptom; and today that kind of analysis is as urgent, as important, for men as it is for women. What is it, in our culture and history—some would even claim in our biology—that has obliged men to prove their masculinity always and only through the repeated affirmation that they are "not female?" Why is misogyny a transcultural and transhistorical phenomenon, apparently as universal as the incest taboo? Is the need to negate woman—which is always, in the last instance, the need to negate one's mother—a permanent feature of male psychology? Questions such as these, which are prompted by, but go far beyond, the rereading of writers like Malraux, are being raised today increasingly not only by women or feminists or students of literature, but also by anthropologists, sociologists, psychologists, and cultural historians, male and female, who seek to understand our past and the direction of our future. If it is true, as Walter J. Ong (who is not a feminist) recently wrote in the conclusion of an important and thought-provoking book that "The entire history of consciousness can be plotted in relation to the always ongoing male-female dialectic," then it behooves all of us to attend to that dialectic. What is at stake is not only our words, but our world. (pp. 143-44)

Susan Rubin Suleiman, "Malraux's Women: A Revision," in Gender and Reading: Essays on Readers, Texts, and Contexts, *edited by Elizabeth A. Flynn and Patrocinio P. Schweickart, The John Hopkins University Press, 1986, pp. 124-46.*

ROBERT W. GREENE

Two apparently unrelated but in fact convergent concerns lie at the heart of *La Condition humaine:* the difficulties inherent in verbal communication and the plight of women. The first of these concerns has often been remarked upon, if only in passing, by Malraux scholars, and was even acknowledged by the writer himself [in his *Les voix du silence*]. The second, however, has so far attracted very little critical attention. Moreover, to date, the crucial matter of the link between the two concerns has gone entirely unnoticed. But the relative reticence of critics regarding the feminist implications of Malraux's fictional masterpiece, and their silence regarding the relationship of these implications to the problematizing of speech in *La Condition humaine,* can perhaps be understood in light of the novel's focus on "amour viril," the strong sense of bonding that characterizes the friendship of its male protagonists. For the Hemingwayesque, "men's club" ambience of much of the text and the adroit use of elliptical narrative techniques reminiscent of film (particularly in passages devoted to the depiction of violent action), with the attendant illusion of unmediated vision that such techniques foster, no doubt distract readers from the novel's reflective dimension, from its probings into (for example) the feminine condition and the limits of language—in short, from the moral and intellectual explorations that occur within or alongside the gripping adventure story. (pp. 161-62)

Among the more important issues examined in Malraux's novel is the question of woman's place in a male-oriented world. The writer's interest in this subject dates from virtually the beginning of his career. It is broached on several occasions in his first book, *La Tentation de l'occident* (1926), and it is a basic constituent of two relatively early essays, one on *Lady Chatterley's Lover* (1932) and the other on *Les Liaisons dangereuses* (1939). But without doubt the highwater mark in his exploration of the status of women may be found in *La Condition humaine* (1933), where the matter so dominates the text that the standard English translation of its title—*Man's Fate*—seems finally quite ironic, if not altogether inappropriate.

The two main female characters in *La Condition humaine,* May and Valérie, are the principal means by which the novelist dramatizes "woman's fate." In a pioneering article published nearly three decades ago and entitled, fittingly enough, "Woman's Fate," Micheline Herz states:

> May represents Malraux's attempt at describing a woman liberated from the "feminine" myth, liberated also from the European bourgeois tradition that curtails the development of a full personality. . . . May as a character is an adventure in a virgin field. She represents the ideal of the times to come, a brand of woman which does not quite exist yet, at least on a large scale.
>
> Malraux, before Simone de Beauvoir, is perhaps the first writer to attempt such a portrayal.

As for Valérie, who is in some ways even more emancipated than May, she breaks off her relationship with Ferral by writing him a farewell letter that is a veritable feminist manifesto in miniature.

But feminist themes in *La Condition humaine* go beyond these striking portraits of liberated women. Observations about woman's lot are both more numerous and more pointed here than anywhere else in Malraux's fiction. Kyo, for example, reflects on "la misogynie fondamentale de presque tous les hommes" ["the fundamental misogyny of nearly all men"], (surely one of the earliest occurrences of the term "misogynie" in French fiction). (pp. 163-64)

Beneath the surface of explicit textual reference to the plight of women, feminism plays an even more pervasive role in the novel. Thematic conflicts involving solitude and solidarity, dignity and humiliation, lucidity and intoxication, which constitute the core of *La Condition humaine,* achieve a kind of resolution in its final pages through the invocation of two antithetical models of womanhood. Utterly alone, humiliated by grief to the point of paralysis, fallen back into his opium habit, the widower Gisors, father of the now dead Kyo, in conversing with his daughter-in-law for the last time, realizes that he has little taste for women like May, "pour les femmes à demi viriles" ["for mannish women"]. . . . Fondly remembering his docile, subservient wife, he daydreams for a moment of a geishalike child-woman, a soothing embodiment of ritualized obsequiousness. Gisors's patriarchal fantasy, however, clashes with his actual interlocutor, May, a real, grieving, but vibrant adult woman who accepts the past's pain while resolutely facing a future she is determined to help shape. At the novel's close, Gisor's reverie and May's reality thus stand opposed to each other, leaving readers with, among other things, the sense that in any genuinely broad-based attempt to overthrow injustice and oppression, the most oppressed, hence most emblematic, heroic figures must inevitably be women. (p. 164)

May has suffered the loss of a beloved husband, and Gisors, that of an adored son, but only she will continue the good fight elsewhere, far from China. Moments before her brief terminal (and terminating) avowal, she learns that her father-in-law has opted to remain in Japan as a professor of art history, a calling ideally suited to his erudition, articulateness, and intellectual turn of mind. Gazing out the window while listening to Gisors wax eloquent about his anguish, May suddenly makes a simple, wordless gesture that speaks volumes to Gisors, that tells him exactly why she, for her part, must carry on the struggle for justice and human dignity. . . . The capacity of verbal expression to provide a nexus of understanding between individuals is in fact an issue as central to *La Condition humaine* as the plight of women, and both themes merge in the novel's culminating confrontation between its still fluent but now defeated patriarchal figure and its laconic but stalwart woman warrior (Kyo, it will be recalled, thinks of May as his "chère guerrière" ["dear warrior"]). In this perspective, the novel's concluding pages cast a retrospective light across the entire text and, in doing so, illuminate aspects of it that have been somewhat scanted by scholars and critics.

Not a work of self-conscious fiction, *La Condition humaine* never flaunts its artifice as discourse, its status as verbal construct. On the thematic level, however, a certain calling attention to language occurs throughout the novel. Some of this metalinguistic material no doubt works in concert with the periodic indications of date and time to create an aura of documentary authenticity for both the "historic" events chronicled and the exotic setting. After all, what better way to show that we are in turbulent, intrigue-riddled Shanghai in 1927 than to register the various languages used by the novel's characters, and even the various accents and dialects in which the languages are spoken? And what does it matter if the amount of detail included concerning language, accent, and verbal tics and idiosyncracies seems finally excessive, quantitatively greater than would be required just to fix the novel's locale and to establish separate identities for its polyphony of voices? Indeed, none of this would matter were it not for the fact that the perceived surplus of information here, especially when added to the other metalinguistic data present in the text, has a particular, cumulative effect on the novel. In order to specify this impact, let us consider some of the ways in which speech acts per se are brought to the foreground in *La Condition humaine.*

The first conversation (if it can be called that) in the novel takes place in a hotel elevator. Tchen, a terrorist, has just killed an arms merchant staying at the hotel so as to secure papers that will enable the insurrectionists in Shanghai to steal a desperately needed shipment of guns. Trying to flee the scene of the crime as quickly and unobtrusively as possible, he finds himself in the hotel elevator being addressed by a complete stranger. . . . [In the brief exchange, an] opening gambit in English—with, interestingly enough, phallocratically complicitous, sexually exploitative overtones—is rebuffed in a conclusive remark uttered in a North-Chinese dialect. By a kind of reverse iconicity, Tchen's response enacts precisely what it says, inasmuch as the Burmese (or Siamese) drunk, it may be assumed, neither speaks nor understands the Pekinese in which Tchen has couched his terse declaration of linguistic incompetence. Of particular interest to the present discussion is the fact that the novel's dual preoccupation with the plight of women and the problematics of verbal communication is effectively adumbrated in this initiatory, sexist, emphatically foreclosed conversation.

From this point forward in the narrative, frequent allusion to the material and conventional nature of speech makes the problematics of verbal communication increasingly palpable. These reminders usually take such direct form as the phonetic transcription of accents or of idiosyncratic habits of speech. Tchen, for example, pronounces the word "non" as if it were written "nong." . . . [Malraux's] concise summary of Tchen's manner of speaking French serves at least two distinct purposes. It helps, first of all, to individualize the fictional character in question. But it also underscores the fraternal bonds that link Tchen with Kyo and, in doing so, reinforces the simulacrum of a father-son relationship that exists between Gisors and Tchen, the biological parent-child bond between Gisors and Kyo being mirrored in the spiritual one between Gisors and Tchen. The latter relationship contributes significantly to the novel's themes (and is reprised, in a minor key, in Tchen's relationship with the missionary Smithson) in that it ratifies Gisors in his role as the novel's wise patriarch. We have already seen that Gisors serves in just this capacity as one of the novel's basic polar figures, his antipode being his other "child," his daughter-in-law May, one of whose main functions, ironically, is to call into question the whole value system implicit in the notion of patriarchy. (pp. 164-67)

[Katow] operates in Russian, French, English, and Chinese, depending on the requirements of the situation. Ironically, however, Katow alone harbors doubts about the capacity of ordinary language to insure communication at life's most critical moments. . . . [Early] in the narrative, well before

his arrest, he had sought to comfort the Belgian shopkeeper Hemmelrich, who was overwhelmed by feelings of rage toward his family and guilt toward Tchen because he had refused, out of fear of compromising the security of his abjectly dutiful wife and sickly child, to allow the terrorist to take refuge in his record shop. Katow seeks to convince the Belgian that he has done right to think first of protecting those most dependent upon and devoted to him. As in a parable from the Gospels, Katow tells a story from which he hopes Hemmelrich can draw the strength to accept his moral choice without bitterness. Katow's anecdote, clearly about himself, concerns a couple, a totally devoted woman and a man who reacts sadistically to the woman's constancy. According to Katow, if the woman can somehow transcend the man's verbal abuse, he (and the relationship) will be changed, remade. . . . The episode draws to a close with no clear indication of the possible effect on Hemmelrich of Katow's words or mere presence.

At the same time, however, the conversation between the two men lays bare Katow's deep distrust of language, his apparent belief that words must be bypassed by those who would make contact with, and be guided by, "qualities of the heart." The conversation also implies a valorization of conflicted but genuinely connected couples like Hemmelrich and his wife, Katow and his, and in their way, Kyo and May (Kyo struggling to comprehend his anger and confusion when May tells him of a casual infidelity with a medical colleague), as opposed to such empty pairings as Ferral and Valérie and, on another level, Gisors and his deceased wife. . . . This view of the couple, redemptive and (first impressions to the contrary notwithstanding) fundamentally egalitarian, perhaps reflects the same ethos that informs the poetry of Paul Eluard and André Breton in the late 1920s and early 1930s. Whether influenced by Surrealism or not, however, Malraux's conception of the couple in *La Condition humaine* validates only those males who, like Katow and Kyo, and possibly Hemmelrich, are ready to work through the concrete, sometimes contradictory conditions of human love beyond the bounds of discourse.

The art and antique dealer Clappique, Katow's moral opposite in this respect, has no interest whatever in communicating with another human being, perhaps least of all with women. The quintessence of logorrhea, of self-inflating tale-spinning and fraudulent declamation, his nonstop mythifying cuts him off irrevocably from those around him. He completely lacks Katow's dialogic orientation, a desire for meaningful exchange with others. And yet, somewhat paradoxically, it is precisely because of his prolixity, in combination with his failure as a communicator, that Clappique deserves our attention.

In his classic study of Malraux, W. M. Frohock argues that "in writing the novel, Malraux became so fascinated with his Clappique that the latter threatened to run away with the story." The entirely persuasive evidence that Frohock adduces in support of his contention is of less interest in the present circumstances than the looming fact of Clappique's flamboyant presence in the novel. No other figure in *La Condition humaine,* for example, foregrounds speech as steadily and systematically as Clappique. His seemingly possessed way of talking is attention-getting in the extreme, but there are also numerous explicit references in the text to his "mythomanie," his compulsion to invent the most outlandish tall stories. In addition, his pet phrase "pas un mot," ["not a word"] which he liberally sprinkles throughout his monologues, giving them a tone of mock conspiracy, on the literal level suggests a categorical rejection of ordinary language. Clappique's use of this phrase points directly to what he may embody for Malraux, the living denial of words as a universally reliable means of communication.

An episode in part 4 of the novel would seem to identify Clappique with just such a symbolic function. He has gone to Gisors's home in order to warn Kyo that, because of his suspected involvement in the robbery of the gun shipment, he may soon be arrested. Since Kyo has not yet returned home, Clappique joins in the conversation between Gisors and his brother-in-law Kama, a Japanese painter there in the company of two of his disciples. In preliminary small talk, Clappique compliments Gisors on a newly acquired cactus plant. From the Chinese inscription on the plant's support stake, Clappique learns that it is a gift from Tchen. Though he reads Chinese, however, Clappique does not know Japanese; hence he must rely on Gisors or on one of Kama's followers to translate the painter's replies to his queries. The subjects taken up in the ensuing conversation are among the most fundamental: art, love, language, death. (pp. 168-70)

Because of the increasingly metaphysical, if not to say mystical, tenor of Kama's remarks; because of Clappique's surprising attentiveness to them (mythomaniacs, after all, usually listen only to themselves); and because of the retarding effect of formal translation, the conversation seems to enjoy a special status and to serve a special purpose in the novel. Played out as if in slow motion, it pits the character who is at once the most talkative and the least communicative (Clappique) against the one who is the most sensitive to the need for communication, solidarity, and even communion with others (Kama).

The shocking extent of Clappique's detachment from his fellow humans, however, comes fully to the fore at a later point in the narrative. He has just betrayed Kyo by not warning him of an impending police roundup of Communist leaders. Seeking oblivion from the pangs of guilt unleashed by his treacherous inaction, Clappique plunges headlong into a conversation with a prostitute whose sexual services he is about to purchase. In a complete fabrication, a stream of verbiage wholly disconnected from reality and truth, he casts himself in the sordidly glamorous part of a former gangster who is about to commit suicide. This time, the cozy, unreal world he has created with his words is a conscious, deliberate piece of fiction, including, especially perhaps . . . the specious solidarity he has temporarily forged with the duped prostitute. With this tissue of lies, Clappique has made, more outrageously than ever before, an utter mockery of the value of connectedness that is articulated by Kama and embodied by Katow (along with Kyo and May), and that functions as a kind of moral compass for the entire novel.

The essential connection in *La Condition humaine* exists or occurs between the "communicating vessels" of the loving couple. The man-woman relationship is thus primary, despite the novel's stress on male friendship. In fact, the former act of bonding allows the latter to come into being and, beyond that, allows human solidarity on a broader scale to develop. Kyo and Katow (and even Hemmelrich) can reach out to each other and, eventually, to the oppressed masses around them precisely because at some point they ceased to look upon the women in their lives as objects and as instances of an eternally foreign Other. The love that Kyo and May share, for example—intersubjective, virtually interpenetrating—

precludes even the possibility of such alien otherness. At a critical juncture in the story—when Kyo has told May of his decision to go alone to an emergency meeting of Shanghai's Communist cadre, an act he suspects may be his last as a free man—May, trying to persuade her husband to let her accompany him on this dangerous outing, asks simply, and rhetorically, "Suis-je 'un autre,' Kyo?" ["Am I 'Other'?"]. Later, after Kyo's death, May retrieves his body. . . . Where does she stop and Kyo begin, she could once wonder. But now the flesh of her flesh has been torn from her forever. Death has sundered the couple and in the process reasserted solitary suffering as May's fate. What lingers in the mind, however, is the couple's solidarity in life, their total, unconditional acceptance of each other, their common refusal to view alterity as something menacing, and the meliorative impact of that expansive refusal on their conduct as socially responsible beings.

Even the admirable Katow is spiritually enhanced by his contact (albeit at a remove) with such connectedness, as is suggested in the novel's climactic pages, those devoted, first, to Kyo's and, then, to Katow's death. Having decided to commit suicide rather than permit himself to be executed, Kyo performs a secular ritual of recollection to ready himself for the moment of truth. In the course of his meditation, he draws special strength from thoughts of May. . . . Then, at the very instant of his passing, he hears and feels Katow, sprawled beside him among the other prisoners condemned to death. . . . In context, this terminal act of touching—replicated moments later when Katow hands his suicide pill over to young Souen and his companion—resembles a mythic last rite, the transference of moral force at death. It is as if through this concrete, gestural affirmation of connectedness Katow were taking on his fallen comrade's fortitude, adding it to his own, and thence rising to a level of bravery he had hitherto not known, a plane of action and solidarity where he could choose to give away his cyanide capsule—and not just once, but twice—and face up to the horror of execution by fire. For Katow's extraordinary generosity in this situation appears to result directly from his absorbing the dying Kyo's spiritual strength. Kyo, for his part, seems to have found the courage to cleave to his choice of suicide by reflecting upon the solitude-canceling love he had found earlier with May. Thus do both courageous deaths trace back to the values of connectedness and communication that inform the relationship between May and Kyo, with May assuming the role of ultimate enabler or catalyst in this scheme.

But if May occupies a dramatically (and socially) privileged position in the novel, she is no less a woman for all that, no less subject to the scorn, invisibility, and humiliation reserved for her sex generally in *La Condition humaine.* Accordingly, the sober, balanced argument she makes for talking seriously about improving the legal situation of abused wives in China falls on deaf ears, even in the case of Kyo. We have already noted the mistrust and antipathy with which she is viewed by Gisors, who dismisses her in his mind as one of those mannish women he cannot abide. Nevertheless, against the background in the novel of the limitations imposed on women as a class, the circumstances of May's life seem almost idyllic.

A number of passages scattered throughout the text reveal these limitations in all their power to belittle women, to reduce them, in one way or another, to the role of the threatening and/or contemptible Other. (pp. 171-73)

Misogyny in its harshest form issues, not surprisingly, from

Ferral. If Gisors's intoxication is opium, Tchen's terrorism, and Clappique's mythmaking, Ferral's is control over others, especially women. A connoisseur of erotic art, in sexual relations he is essentially a voyeur; he prefers watching to touching, a not insignificant predilection in light of the novel's valorization of connectedness. Above all, his will must prevail over his partner's. As a consequence, the shadow of exploitation and contempt falls across all of his encounters with women.

But in Valérie, who is a prosperous dress designer, Ferral has met his match, and his nemesis. Successful in business, hence economically independent, emancipated in all of her attitudes, a disabused pragmatist in the conduct of her love life, she has what is for Ferral the unsettling knack of talking as if she had just stepped out of *Les Liaisons dangereuses*. With a smile, she can drop the most jaded comment into the middle of an intimate conversation with her lover. Furthermore, her sense of moral autonomy is easily as strong as Ferral's. If she loses one battle of wills with him, she wins the war between the sexes in which they are engaged. To avenge her humiliation by Ferral when, against her manifest wishes and efforts to the contrary, he kept switching the lights back on during their love-making so as to watch the transformation of her features during orgasm, Valérie arranges a stunning scenario of retaliation in which she wounds Ferral in his pride far more deeply than she was shamed by his fit of domination over her. The "coup de grâce" in her elaborate settling of accounts is a witty, disdainful farewell letter. . . . (pp. 174-75)

The debonair, casually insulting tone of Valérie's letter makes its pithy message all the more vibrant. She is clearly preaching to Ferral while at the same time letting him know that she knows that he is beyond the reach of her words. Her arch, superior tone also lets him know that she is not in the least interested in persuading him of anything. She argues her case (on behalf of women's liberation) brilliantly but, like a legal dandy, does not deign to show any concern for the possible effect of her brief on her adversary. Her letter has, therefore, something gratuitous about it. Patently indigestible to its addressee, it also goes against the grain of the smooth narratorial *style indirect libre* that dominates the novel as a whole. A verbal jewel, it sits there on the page unassimilable to its textual surroundings.

And yet, both structurally and stylistically, Valérie's letter-manifesto . . . is entirely justified within the novel, and not only in thematic terms where its usefulness and perhaps even its necessity are obvious, for in its polished style it recalls Clappique's lush inventions. Both characters treat discourse as something to be fashioned with care and brio, but Valérie's moves in a direction diametrically opposed to Clappique's, toward reality and truth. On the other hand, by his speech, whether paraphrased or directly reported, Clappique sensitizes us to the phenomenon of empty or dissembling rhetorical flourish, thereby preparing us for the genuine article, for truth-bearing eloquence, when we encounter it. Paradoxically, his tall tales lend Valérie's epistle a degree of conviction and appropriateness it might otherwise not possess. In the perspective of the whole novel, Clappique's baroque deceptions call out to and almost call for Valérie's elegant argument.

The presence of Valérie's letter in the narrative is further justified by its immediate context. Though an eminently persuasive document, it does not, as we have noted, attempt to convince its recipient of its validity. So presented, it hangs suspended in a rhetorical void. But analogous circumstances obtain whenever May speaks of the same subject, the plight of women. Both female characters make statements on behalf of their sex that are met with silence at best on the part of the novel's male characters. The rhetorical situation of Valérie's letter makes that silence explicit and active, if not altogether deafening. It is thus by a fitting ironic twist that Ferral's greatest humiliation, prefigured in the whole episode involving Valérie's letter, should take the form of the repeated silences with which his pleas for financial support are greeted by bankers and government officials on his return to Paris near the novel's close.

Essentially, the plot of **La Condition humaine** follows the unfolding events of the Shanghai uprising; yet the narrative's propulsive energy derives not from any chronicle but rather from certain recurrent, interlocking antitheses, and from our awakened and then sustained desire to reach a resolution, an end, to these conflicts. The most fundamental of these, doubtless, is the ongoing dialectic between dignity and humiliation, a conflict that motivates characters as diverse as Kyo, König, and Ferral. At one point Kyo goes so far as to define the notions in terms of each other, as each other's opposites. Significantly, if Kyo (along with May and Katow) is committed to introducing a measure of dignity into the lives of the most oppressed members of Chinese society by lifting the burden of injustice and humiliation from their shoulders, Ferral and König, by contrast, are concerned only with their own sense of humiliation and lost dignity. Thus once again we see the novel's major figures dividing into antinomous groups of altruists and egoists.

What the egoists have in common is a heterophobic, androcentric view of the world. For them, self must always take precedence over other, as must male over female, and the abstract will always win out over the concrete, as will death over life, fantasy over reality, book knowledge over the wisdom gained from living, and essentially narcissistic cogitation over a continuing dialogue between logic and experience. Tchen typifies these biases. His university-acquired Marxism fuels his thoroughly private addiction to terrorism, in dramatic opposition to the hunger for social justice that has animated his friend Souen ever since the latter witnessed his father's torture and subsequent murder by political thugs. . . . In order to convey to Gisors his scorn for men who have not yet killed, Tchen derisively refers to them as "puceaux," or male virgins, a term that inevitably recalls—and in its context here disparages—the more frequently seen and traditionally honorific feminine form of the word "pucelles"; thus does Tchen manage once again to denigrate women. He is an isolate and a fantast unconnected to his fellow combatants and, for want of memory, to the anchor of his past life. (pp. 175-78)

Thematically, as we have seen, language is foregrounded and its reliability questioned virtually throughout the novel. On the other hand, definitions and glosses of all sorts abound, even turning up in footnotes. Mythomania, intoxication, intelligence, eroticism, the human condition, for example, are all discussed and explained at length. Terms still quite new to fiction, like "geisha" and "sadique" and "paranoïque," are used with ease and aptness. Dialects and accents are identified and commented upon (and with even greater frequency than the instances cited above might indicate). Taken together, the novel's manifold metalinguistic allusions at first give the impression that the verbal tools necessary for uncovering its secrets are, so to speak, handed to us on a silver platter. In fact, however, *La Condition humaine* resists facile penetration via the terms, definitions, explanations, and commentaries it offers us so freely. Words alone, abstracted from their socio-historical contexts and circumstances, can only deceive—or so Malraux's text seems to be signaling to us from somewhere beneath its surface. For the novel's great users of speech are also its blatant abusers of speech—the glib explainers (Gisors), manipulators (Ferral), rationalizers (König), liars (Clappique), and nihilists (Tchen)—all of whom are possessed by their bloodless utterances rather than the other way around.

Communist homily and propaganda are directly associated with such lifeless, mechanized palaver in part 3 of the novel. Kyo and Tchen have gone to the city of Han-Kéou to convince Vologuine, a high Party functionary, that it would be suicidal for the Shanghai insurgents to obey the Party's latest directive and surrender their weapons to Chiang Kai-shek. In the name of the long-range good of the Revolution, Vologuine turns down their manifestly valid request to have the directive rescinded. He does so at considerable length and with great patience. . . . Following their fruitless meeting with Communist officialdom, Kyo and Tchen stand disconsolately for a moment on the sidewalk outside Vologuine's offices. Suddenly Tchen invites his friend to listen. . . . In the steady vibration of the earth beneath his feet, Kyo understands that his life, as well as that of Tchen and their comrades back in Shanghai, is even now being sacrificed to "ces machines à fabriquer la vérité," the thundering maw of the Party's printing presses, grotesque echo of Vologuine's labored but cool assertions.

May, for her part, explicitly rejects talk spun out of speakers in self-encasing cocoons. She contrasts (it will be recalled) the chilling anecdote of a young bride's failed suicide and her mother's dismaying regret . . . with feminist addresses that are detached from life as it is actually lived beyond the reach of formal speeches, fine distinctions, and flowery disquisition. In May, evidently, a devotion to feminist principle (and to political liberation generally) does not exclude a basic diffidence with regard to language, including that of feminist discourse.

At the same time, however, inarticulateness hardly characterizes her verbal style, not even at the novel's close. Although Gisors would have much preferred a daughter-in-law who embodied the rhyming dictum "sage comme une image," May's quasi-muteness by the conclusion of the narrative in no way signifies that she has at last reconciled herself to decorous, self-effacing silence as her preordained lot. On the contrary, in the end she represents, more starkly than ever before, the inexorable rise of someone who will finally be heard, of that traditionally most censored Other, that ideal and yet real alternate subjectivity, the self-liberated woman. Ultimately in this perspective, the title of Herz's schematic but heuristic study, translated back into French, perhaps best epitomizes the novel, at least metonymically. For, so the text amply demonstrates, humanity's at once wretched and noble destiny attains its most compelling if also its most occulted form in woman's fate. What better way, then, to read *La Condition humaine* than as a palimpsest, with the last word of its title written over a blanked-out "féminine"? (pp. 178-80)

Robert W. Greene, "Women and Words in 'La condition humaine'," in Modern Language Quarterly, *Vol. 46, No. 2, June, 1985, pp. 161-80.*

ROBERT ELBAZ

In *Antimémoires,* André Malraux offers us a new conception of the autobiographic text, a conception indicative of a discursive shift which will take time to come to its maturation. For in *Antimémoires* Malraux transgresses the basic tenets of the autobiographical tradition: he postulates a redefinition of selfhood which negates the concepts of truth and veracity by abolishing the distinction between reality and fiction, and which promotes the fictional dimension of the self. Malraux's autobiographical venture can be understood only if it is inscribed within the complete text of his fiction; its coherence depends upon our rejection of the differentiation between fiction and non-fiction. For every text, be it autobiographic or not (if we accept for the moment the existing classification), constitutes a narrative—a story, and the meaning of this narrative lies between story and history. Meaning is the metaphorisation of history by the story. Malraux's self as presented in *Antimémoires* as well as in his fiction arises in the relationship—that irreducible bond—between story and history. Malraux's autobiography takes meaning in contributing to the production of a socially oriented literature: with the rejection of psychologisation and the promotion of a language of action, Malraux places himself and his protagonists within historical transcendence. Subjectivity as a self-contained entity disappears to make room for a socio-historical consciousness in its ongoing search for historically determined roles and their fulfilment.

Antimémoires is looked upon by the critical literature as a collection of essays duplicating in various ways Malraux's fictional works. It is nowhere referred to as an autobiography mainly because it satisfies none of the existing definitions of the genre. But if our point of departure is the ideological presuppositions of the genre as it evolves at the moment, then the demystification of the genre can lead to a new conception of autobiography and concurrently to a new conception of selfhood. Indeed, our purpose is to indicate in what way Malraux produces a text which makes room for a new literary form that we may term 'antimemoirs' as well as a departure from the ideologies of the 'centre'.

How does one read Malraux's *Antimémoires?* The reader of autobiographies is baffled by the chaos of this text for chronology does not seem to be a guiding factor in its organisation. Clearly, it is not a story of a life, although here and there we encounter fragments of biographical data; nor is it a transcription of historical data since there is no obedience to historical fact. It cannot be a pure work of fiction: many characters in the book are real people. One is tempted to define these 'memoirs' as a random accumulation of unrelated pieces, but we know that Malraux has achieved a considerable degree of cohesion in his fiction. A careful scrutiny of the text leaves us with the conviction that this chaos is intentional, that it is conditional to the meaning of the text. Indeed Malraux seems to be postulating that autobiography, the story of the self, is a combination of a number of disorders. The confusion, however, is only apparent; in fact the text advances a new and coherent view of the self, the world and the relationship between them. Malraux's text suggests that self is not and cannot be defined, and therefore no narrative can encompass it; it constitutes an ongoing process of redefinition dependent upon the transcendental-historical phenomena which shape it. And autobiography, the story of the self, will therefore have to be the story of the phenomena which continually give birth to that self. (pp. 119-20)

As an autobiography, *Antimémoires* in no way satisfies the reader in search of biographical curiosities. But this is a new education in reading; Malraux refuses us his biographical data because he wants us to look for something other than his self, and also because those facts, if they do exist, are inscribed within a narrative, a fictional discourse calling for interpretation. Interesting in this connection is Malraux's own lack of corroboration or negation of critics' and biographers' accounts of his own deeds, for the simple reason that André Malraux, the individual, is also a fictional creation, one protagonist among many others in fictional narratives. What is Malraux's purpose behind a seemingly random recollection of fictional chapters from his novels? In what way do these chapters constitute his autobiography? For there is no doubt that he wants us to take these accounts as the story—or stories, for there is always more than one story to a life—of his life.

The reader's concern ought to be for the intentionality behind Malraux's repetitive process. Malraux is not short of words; he could very well have written 'new' texts. He certainly cannot be said to be promoting his novels; if that were the case, they would have been kept whole, not fragmented and collected into a hybrid unit. Repetition here is an ideological configuration, the purpose of which is the creation of an equation between fiction and non-fiction. Malraux is suggesting through this process that his fiction is his autobiography and his autobiography is his fiction. *Le Miroir des limbes* is not a remembrance of things past as lived by an individual but a remembrance of created fictional worlds which coincide with the story of the remembering—creating consciousness. The emphasis is not on linear memory but on creative imagination, intentionality and action.

Antimémoires is written in 1965 when Malraux, on his doctor's advice, undertakes a world tour. This journey brings back to memory other trips to the same places: Egypt, India, China. The voyage backwards, that is, the telling of the trips of 1923, 1929, 1934 and 1958, constitutes a description of historical events that changed the face of the world and the Third World in particular. One should note, however, that these expeditions to India, Egypt, and China are not only trips to the immediate past; they are also voyages into the cultural and artistic heritage of these nations, dating back millenniums (in contrast to the relatively short span of Western Christian culture which, in Malraux's view, has met a dead end).

Apart from the parallel trips (to Ceylon in 1923, to the holy cities of northern India in 1929, the political mission of 1958 on behalf of De Gaulle to strengthen relations with India, and to the French colonies of Guadaloupe, Haiti, and Martinique to promote a French cultural commonwealth following their independence), there is another journey to the scenes of the Second World War, its destruction and atrocities filtered through the fictional accounts of the battles of the French Maquis and the real account of concentration camp survivors.

If *Antimémoires* constitutes the narration of major historical events that have shaped the twentieth century, it is also the story of certain personalities who have shaped these events. Again, it is not the story of the lives of these personalities but the story of the relationships between these men and the events they helped shape. Attention to physical traits is minimal—in contrast to Rousseau, for example. It is not mere chance that three major dialogues are central to the book:

they constitute one of the many centres of the book. De Gaulle, Nehru, Gandhi, Mao tse-Tung and Senghor, among others, are real characters but not in the Balzacian sense of the term; they are central to the extent that they have an impact on the destiny of the world in fulfilling a role presented to them by history. These characters in themselves are of no interest to Malraux; we are not exposed to anecdotes that might shed light on their personalities; they are answers to situations. They meet their respective vocations—the call of destiny.

The reader must try to understand in what sense Malraux's life story is the story of Mao, De Gaulle and Nehru. In what sense it is also the story of the Sphinx and the pyramids of Egypt, the story of Madura, Ellora, Benares—the holy cities of India, the story of the Lascaux caves, the story of Nazi survivors, and so on. One cannot ask the question of Malraux's presence in the *Antimémoires* for he is everywhere and nowhere. Everywhere because dispersed and spread over all the phenomena he relates and describes, and nowhere because the entity André (Malraux) is non-existent. It is replaced at best by fictional characters or performers: the Minister of Culture undertaking the clean-up of Paris and the restoration of museums, the tank commander showing solidarity with his crew, the archaeologist and thief of art works, the Maquis commander.

Of crucial importance is this last role of the Maquis commander. Malraux wrote about Colonel Berger before he lived the life of Colonel Berger, the Maquis commander whose name used to be André Malraux. Malraux lives the life of Colonel Berger first in fiction and then, in 1944, in real life when he assumes the command of the Alsace-Lorraine Brigade. Fiction foretells life but it is not forced upon life (à la Rousseau). Fiction in (with) Malraux comes before life, prior to the immediate, in the consciousness of a relationship to the world. Fiction is the explanation of reality because it is a relationship to that reality, a mediation of it, and *Antimémoires* is the spreading out of an infinity of complex relationships. *Antimémoires* is pure juxtaposition and simultaneity. The present shapes the past; the trip of 1965 filters all other phenomena and translates them. (pp. 121-23)

The *Antimémoires* constitutes a negation of memoirs; it counters unity with dispersion. But dispersion does not mean chaos; it means mainly the replacement of a particular conception of unity by another conception of unity. In Rousseau, for example, unity means particularity and uniqueness, separateness; in Malraux, it means being one with the world, being in relationship to the world. The preoccupations of this text transcend the immediate; the *Antimémoires,* by extension, reach to the infinite in all directions of time and space, since every relationship multiplies into a variety of relationships. The book, of course, contains a limited number of relationships; it is finite in its 600 pages, but it postulates an infinity of relationships and transcendence. Malraux seems to want to include the history and prehistory of all civilisations and the relationships among them.

The trip to India, for example, is not told from A to Z: in opposition to the Rousseauist model, it does not follow a linear sequence. The second and third sections of the book deal with the various trips to India but criss-crossing these trips are major events that occur in other parts of the world. . . . [In *"The Antimémoirs* of André Malraux," Germaine Brée wrote]:

A multilayered time-space network, a multilayered itinerary, a multiplicity of narrative voices, the universe of the *Antimémoires* is, from a literary point of view, a whirling prism of color, form, sound, in which legend and reality, fiction and fact, past and present, memory and dream, mingle and fuse.

Times and places interrelate, criss-cross and interpenetrate one another, the only guiding factor being the power of relationship or association—the workings of a living consciousness and not an artificial ordering of events. Malraux's imprisonment by the Nazis is relived in terms of Ghandi's imprisonment and his statement about the relationship between imprisonment and freedom. The tank anecdote follows a segment on the meaning of death in India in opposition to the meaninglessness of life as a result of the war. Following the tank anecdote Malraux tries to imagine an Indian counterpart to Pradé, Bonneau and Leonard, the members of his tank crew . . . The purpose of this text is not to portray the divisibility or separateness of the event but its comprehensiveness. . . . The ruins of Mareb, which Malraux discovers on his search for the kingdom of Saba, relate to the ruins of Nuremberg after the war; the flames in the Nuremberg stadium evoke the flames on the altars of ancient Persia; the funerary room in the pyramid recalls Hitler's underground quarters in Nuremberg: the 'same' staircase seems to be leading to both; the veins formed by water on the earth as seen from a plane recall the disappearing lines on the hand of Malraux's dead mother. What strikes us . . . is the complexity of the material world that Malraux tries to impart to the reader, and the way a consciousness experiences such a complexity.

The simultaneity and juxtaposition of events prevails throughout Malraux's writings, demonstrating that an individual life does not exist in a vacuum and does not order the world around its centre; rather, the individual is enmeshed in historical contingency. The complexity of phenomena and the irreducible multiplicity of dimensions come through forcefully in a passage from *Hôtes de passage* in which Malraux dialogues with Senghor on the revival of Negro-African culture, its music and dance, as well as the recent revival of the Third World with its anxieties over Western hegemony. . . . No analysis of this passage can exhaust it; it resists any kind of closure. The suspension periods Malraux inserts between the lines point to the text's irreducible openness. We would venture to say that the lines are inserted between the suspension periods, that suspension encompasses the text. For suspension means the endlessness of the historical process, only an infinitesimal part of which a text can cover. Suspension throughout Malraux's text—be it suspension periods, the elliptical language of action, the absence of narration and characterisation—is omission, not a given omission but pure omission. It is not the elliptical omission we encounter in the detective novel, for example, that can be filled to restore the completeness of the text: it is not the omission the writer provides for the reader's pleasure. The omission is total; the text can never be completed due to its relationship to historical transcendence. A text, any text, divides itself from the world by a process of selection and negation; in its finitude, it can include a,b,c, but not x,y,z. However, it ought to be open to all that it negates because the material world has no end in its friction against the creating consciousness. And that creating consciousness, in its discursive productivity, ought to posit the world in all its complexity and infinity. So unless one falls back upon a metaphysics to fill all gaps and give an illusion of continuity and consistency

amongst all phenomena, the text, in its ceaseless movement towards a future, in its ever new beginning, can never be completed. Completion is a myth: the story never ends simply because the material world never ends. The economy inherent in Malraux's language of drama and action is therefore not primarily an expression of literary craftmanship, not a gimmick or a puzzle directed at the reader: it constitutes Malraux's world view. The gap is of all that cannot enter into the text but which the text must hypostatise in its openness. Suspension, then, coincides with an ongoing process of interrogation—the open-endedness of consciousness grappling with the world. (pp. 124-27)

This negation of closure is prevalent throughout the text even in passages describing a given synchronic slice. The dialogue with Max Torrès, Malraux's friend from the Spanish Civil War, for example, takes place on Monday, 6 May 1968. In the foreground there is a dialogue of intellectuals exposing some interesting ideas on the relationship between drugs and creativity; in the background, however, this dialogue of intellectuals is criss-crossed by a number of telegrams portraying the progress of the May 1968 student revolution in France. These telegrams in themselves unfold the tragic turn of events and constitute some kind of chorus to the dialogue on creativity. At the same time Malraux glances at the newspaper on his desk; the headlines tell of the student revolution, the Vietnam peace talks and Dubcek's visit to Moscow. In effect, the Malraux—Torrés dialogue takes meaning only in relationship to Vietnam, Dubcek, the student revolution and an infinity of other events which a book in its finitude cannot contain.

Complexity, then, accounts for the denseness of Malraux's language, for the aim is to introduce into the text as much of the material world as possible. The comprehensiveness of the event, the juxtaposition and multiplicity of events show how a consciousness apprehends reality more faithfully than would the telling of the individual event. To return to the above passage relating the palm of a dead hand to the veins of the earth, a realist writer might have reduced the event (by which Malraux attempts to approximate the complexity of reality) to personal grief, centering on it as if it were the only thing happening in the world at the moment; the world would be reduced to the parameters of a hand. Malraux enriches the event by making it more comprehensive: the relationship between the veins of the earth seen from a drifting plane and the palm of a dead hand gives a further dimension to both phenomena; it integrates both in a more complex universe. This complex process of 'relating' reduces divisiveness and separation and promotes solidarity.

The comprehensiveness of the historical event makes for Malraux's basic postulation of otherness and his rejection of individualism, both the ideology and the novelistic form which incorporates it. His concern with man's place in the historical process is already apparent in his first novel, *La Tentation de l'Occident*. . . . [It] is the temptation of the West to forget its individualism and espouse the Eastern merger with the universe, as well as the temptation of the East for Western ways to accede to modern history. This dialogue ends with no definite adoption of either one of the two views of selfhood, rather making each conditional upon the other; that is, it hypostatises the mutual dependence of both. The insertion of an 'other' world view as a counterbalancing force to the Western one emphasises Malraux's departure from an exclusive literary tradition. It emphasises as well his postulation of otherness as the overall ontological structure which conditions being and a corresponding dialogical structure which produces a new literary form. Hence the absence of a protagonist who exists for himself; hence too the absence of a life story—dialogue requires at least two life stories. There are only situations and human beings interacting within these situations. (pp. 128-29)

If De Gaulle and Mao and Senghor have no biography, then what are they? They are simply what Malraux coins 'les hèros de l'histoire'. The role pre-exists the man who fills it; the historical process is filled with such roles, as they arise in specific situations. The dream is already there to be realised. Interestingly enough, Malraux attributes a common predicament to both the historical personage and the fictional protagonist because he posits that history in its process of productivity as text, is a fiction, an intentional relationship to the world incarnated by a given subjectivity. . . . De Gaulle, the historical personage, exists in the Other, in dialogue, and the dialogue is both a dialogue of cultures and a dialogue of individuals. The Malraux-De Gaulle exchange is inscribed within a structure of dialogue which comprises the Malraux-Nehru, the Malraux-Mao, the Malraux-Senghor exchanges, and a multiplicity of other exchanges. These names can be replaced by other names; what remains is the dialogue between two consciousnesses in their confrontation with a given historical reality, be it Black Africa, the Chinese Revolution, the Indian Revolution, the Fourth Republic in France and so on. The dialogical dimension inherent in Malraux's text is the repeated performance of two 'characters' on a stage exchanging views, two characters with no specific individualities. The absence of physical description, or for that matter of narration which has no bearing on the action, points to the non-pertinence of the biography of these individuals. Mao means to the extent that he fulfils the role of 'Mao tse-Tung', the leader of the Chinese Revolution, Senghor, to the extent that he is 'Leopold Senghor', the speaking voice of modern Africa. The dialogical nature of Malraux's text as a whole posits the absence of selfhood in its particularity; it rejects mediation and introspection as the apprehension of self and advances a language of action as the historical dimension of consciousness which creates and is created in its friction against the world. (pp. 130-31)

Malraux's predilection for action implies a rejection of any definition of man in which destiny overtakes intentionality. Rabaud's and Walter Berger's early positions [in *Les Noyers de l'Altenburg*] constitute expressions of two ideologies that look backward for a definition of the future. And if the future is to be transcendental and not figural, man's unconscious or his eternal nature cannot lead to the freedom necessitated by action. Indeed, Rabaud's human nature and Walter Berger's unconscious posit man's definition before he acts on the historical scene; they indicate man's helplessness and lack of courage in the face of destiny, whereas the definition of man as action is an anti-destiny, an ongoing intentional transformation of the material world, a ceaseless metamorphosis. Intentionality and anti-destiny motivate Malraux's main metaphor in this book; the trunks of the walnut trees of Altenburg stand for man's unfailing will to metamorphose the universe: rather than attempting to free themselves from the earth which is intent upon subjugating them, the roots of these trees impose their presence and rectitude on it; they subdue the earth with their massive will. (p. 132)

If indeed man is defined by action, he cannot be an artificial construct made up of a heap of secrets, nor can he be a series of well-ordered events, for he is as he acts and action negates cumulation and linear order. Action does away with chronology which is the main operational concept of the prevalent ideologies of the West. Events do not happen within chronology; actually, they defy it: they are the asperities which spring up upon a rugged historical terrain. Chronology follows the logic of the series which in no way can encompass the complexity of the historical process. Events make up the historical process while threatening its unity and continuity, since they stand up against the background of the non-event, that is, the event which is not intentional, the event which occurs despite itself, the event that cannot be helped.

Malraux's fictional world accommodates a variety of actions; there is the action of the individual as in *La Voix royale,* and the action of the collectivity as in *L'Espoir.* There is the action of the adventurer (Perken, Garine) and the action of the socially committed man (Kyo, Manuel, Katow). There is action geared towards being something, to wit, action directed towards self-fulfilment, and action aimed at social amelioration. Most striking among a plurality of roles are the roles of the adventurer, the revolutionary, the militant, the drifter and the artist. These roles partake in the historical process in qualitatively different ways since they incarnate different ideologies.

An important role in Malraux's fictional gallery is the role of the drifter-dreamer; that is, the escapist as portrayed by Clappique in *La Condition humaine.* Clappique is the gambler who risks both money and life; in choosing to live on the border between dream and reality, Clappique wears a variety of masks which he presents to others in order to escape any definition. . . . The risks he seems to be taking with the shipment of arms do not constitute a commitment to the revolutionary cause. Rather, the revolution is a precarious situation to be exploited in terms of the money that can in turn be spent at the gambling table where destiny is played out. . . . (pp. 134-35)

Despite Clappique's important part in the revolutionary events he is not a positive voice in the novel. The novel is made up of Clappiques as well because the fictional world, like the real one, in its complexity includes Kyos, Katows, Ferrals and Clappiques. Clappique is a mythomaniac who negates life because he lives in a situation to which he refuses to contribute. Clappique is Clappique because he interacts with the revolutionaries, the militants, and the Chinese masses in terms of an intentional ideology of escapism. Clappique is not forced to be Clappique; he 'acts' Clappique.

The adventurer is one of the prime movers in the fight for the new order; indeed, Perken and Garine are committed to the establishment of a new society based on equality and justice, and to a certain extent they succeed in their endeavour. . . . The adventurer is not a dreamer but an active man with a goal. But does this goal coincide with social amelioration? It seems as though the revolution itself is not the end but a means in the hands of the adventurer to realise his own self-fulfilment. The search for power is never the promotion of the social cause: the cause is but a by-product of the adventurer's drive for self-assertion.

Although he ultimately contributes to the revolution, the adventurer restricts his commitment exclusively to his own self which he seeks, in action, after having failed in the bourgeois society from which he originates. The eventual future of the new order for which the adventurer fights is of no consequence: the frenetic present of action is what attracts him. (pp. 135-36)

[The] adventurer is bound to fail because, in the end, he does not realise the self he thought he had when he escaped the solitude of his bourgeois culture. His commitment to action does not lessen his feeling of isolation, because he does not want to create a new self but to keep the old one with all its old values. Rather than letting the situation dictate his role, he dictates his own role to the situation. The adventurer drags his old self with him, and his failure is echoed in his physical downfall. Both Perken and Garine end their lives sick and helpless, and while the defiance of sickness gives them a greater sense of power (in controlling, as it were, their own death), they finally become conscious of their failure. This realisation, however, occurs at the point of no return, when the course of events can no longer be reversed. The true tragedy of the adventurer is in the realisation of his failure and in his struggle with destiny. Both Garine and Perken, ironically enough, become self-conscious . . . through the look of the Other. Garine and Perken are thrown back to their own lonely, diseased bodies by whores who refuse to be made into objects. . . . (p. 136)

The exclusion of the Other in the realisation of self is further elaborated by the revolutionaries who carry the action of the adventurer to its extreme. Self-possession becomes the only drive of Tchen and Hong who forget the cause for which they are fighting; their action is mere terrorism, bordering on anarchism in its negation of the principles and ideas of the parties they so enthusiastically joined in the first place. Both Hong and Tchen represent Western consciousnesses in their obsession with their own self and with the realisation of self through a totally destructive action. (p. 137)

The entanglement with self, and the fascination for terrorism to realise it, bring about a feeling of alienation in Tchen. . . . 'il n'était pas des leurs. Malgré le meurtre, malgré sa présence. S'il mourrait aujourd'hui, il mourrait seul.' Tchen's pursuit of his self finally drives him to self-destruction; his final act is not a heroic one since his true purpose is not the murder of Chang-Kai-Shek but an extreme form of self-possession. Tchen wants to be his own God in giving himself his own death; but even self-possession in death is unrealisable for the final release of the trigger is barely a conscious act, if at all intentional. . . . The revolutionary, then, is an adventurer taken to the extreme; they both negate the cause for which they struggle, and must therefore be transcended if social change is to take place; they both die or disappear from the scene of the novel.

The roles of the adventurer and the terrorist are counterbalanced by the role of the militant. The action of the militant is determined by the social principles which pre-exist him and which he contributes to bring about; the militant is a tool in the hands of a social movement. Kyo and Katow are motivated by social principles which transcend them; their death as individuals in no way effects the course of history and the fight for these principles. The militant struggles for a cause, not his own. . . . The militant is not concerned with the immediate since he constructs a building which takes time and planning; the militant rejects the Apocalypse and builds for the future. (pp. 137-38)

The ultimate failure of the adventurer points to Malraux's postulation of selfhood as the product of a situation which, in the case of the militant, coincides with the ideology and subjectivity with which the party, the social cause, invests the individual. The committed man exists in a network of relationships; he is for-the-others whereas the adventurer seeks self-definition and fulfilment in the arrangement of his own biography. Heroism (the traditional hero) constitutes a chronological laying out of autobiographical facts in a series; that is, the performance of an autobiography. Rather than living out a life-in-situation, in relationship, the adventurer (and the hero) acts out his autobiography.

These roles, it should be noted, are dictated by a historical situation, be it the Chinese Revolution, the Spanish Civil War, or the Second World War, and they are assumed as such by the individuals who embody them. Whether the role is of the escapist, or of the militant or adventurer, they all relate to a situation of social change. (pp. 138-39)

Malraux's conception of the role is [such] that while it cannot describe the role within that future society, it at least points to the possibility and the direction of these roles in a sane social praxis. After all Malraux himself is a product of a welldefined historical period in which the 'adventurer' is still a possible role. Also, the roles of the adventurer and the escapist are residual roles originating in the West. (Discursively they hark back to the Neo-Classical era when the travel and the escape were new productions, for all the literary thematics of the period centre on travel and escape down to the end of the romantic period.) In conformity with the notion of the historical personage, Malraux's conception of role is historically conditioned; it is a meeting place of a social definition and an individual consciousness which chooses freely to incorporate that definition. The role is not a ceremony: it is a genuine social performance geared towards the improvement of the social body as a whole. (p. 140)

In terms of structure, [*Antimémoires*] opposes the cumulative process of traditional autobiographies where one event follows another as if things happen in a linear sequence. Linearity is an artificial construct totally alienated from the event itself. Instead, Malraux proposes a cluster of experiences around which one can situate a self, but his self does not limit phenomena to its own parameters. It is 'relationship' and as such must be considered as an element within a whole. This is precisely why Malraux encounters a personage, for in every relationship the role is primordial. The personage, the persona that is formed from the outside through the combination of a situation and another consciousness is described with detachment; from an angle one can have a perspective on one's acts. Malraux describes the act as if it were not his; this is the point at which fiction and life become one. Those fictive roles coincide with the contingent entity labelled 'André Malraux'. The episodes from the past—and this is a secondary process—are brought back by memory and Malraux simply adds ('rajoute') them to those basic experiences that define him.

Memory is a secondary process—a simple addition—because it is not the primary organising principle of experience. The organising principle is that cluster of experiences to which all other phenomena are functional. The small biographical details attach to those central experiences: they do not constitute an end in themselves. And if they can be done away with, so much the better. The story of a childhood becomes futile since it does not contribute to the basic relationship Malraux wants to establish with the world. But memory does not run in opposition to imagination; it is merely subordinate to it, for certain acts of memory are necessary in the creation of relationships and juxtapositions. Malraux is negating a specific kind of time, not time *per se*. In the writing of *Antimémoires* he is rejecting an individual time which developed in the classical age. But while negating individual time Malraux promotes historical time. Rousseau, we recall, in his rejection of time, gives the effect of a frozen moving picture for he advocated the superposition of the past over the present in the sphere of the individual consciousness. The achievement of eternity in Rousseau—stillness—is the outcome of a transformation of time into space: the frozen image becomes a spatial entity. Not so with Malraux. We are presented in this text with an indefinite series of tableaux interconnecting and interpenetrating one another. It is a horizontal movement, but with an inner dynamic. Time, in Malraux, means the dimension which consciousness achieves in its spreading of itself over the surface of things—a 'counter-memory'. The act of spreading itself is a moving present for, while it moves, consciousness creates itself together with the world—the effect of a series of movies running on the same screen in synchrony.

In effect, then, Malraux achieves two important goals. One is the creation of a new form within the autobiographical tradition (a transformation conforming to a definite discursive shift which Malraux embodies) which has to do with the structure of the book. The other is a rejection of a world view in which the world is reduced to the self. The refusal of chronology in *Antimémoires* means the rejection of introspection, for beyond Malraux's expressed hatred for his own childhood, there is a philosophical statement about the recapture of childhood in general. The introspective process functions on the assumption that one can corner one's self, that one can go back to a basic truth, to something that is there although not apparent at the moment. But in effect one encounters only an image of one's self, and a fleeting one at that. This image cannot be consistent since it changes as time goes on. Catching one's centre is similar to the dog's futile attempt to catch its tail. The recapture of a past individual life that finds meaning in its own irreducible and immediate uniqueness as an entity abstracted from the historical continuum (or in most cases as an escape from that continuum) is what Malraux is attempting to negate in this text. In classical autobiography self is less a negation of the world than an affirmation of its power against the world; self always remains the last resort against all external odds—especially, the Other. This is a conception of self that promotes competitiveness and divisiveness, and opposes integration.

Malraux is offering us an integrated self, a self within-the-world, a self which is pure exteriority. To Malraux, self-knowledge, self-discovery, is an illusion. Self cannot be discovered since it is not there; it is a vacuum to be filled from the outside. It has to be created. Hence the necessity for fiction: there is no truth to be found or discovered in the story of a life; truth must be created. Truth remains a future process, something to look forward to. And if Malraux cannot find his central self (because it does not exist) he must seek his identity in the various fictional selves which he creates. The various masks mediate one another in turn; and each mask is mediated by the outside world—that is, the existing situation and the other consciousnesses partaking in it—while it is enacted.

This conception of self gives a perspective on Malraux's views of Freudianism and the Surrealist movement which he espoused at the beginning of his writing career. Both Freudianism and Surrealism share one basic belief: that one can go back to a primordial reality inherent within the human consciousness. (pp. 141-43)

With Malraux there is nothing to go back to and definition becomes a transcendental movement towards the future. If action replaces introspection, it is because action is the dimension of hope (*L'Espoir*). The man of action, the artist, does not drag a self with him wherever he goes; he creates a fresh one as he moves. . . .

The fact that [Malraux] wrote the book in his seventies does not make him a summariser of past events for Malraux never planned to write his autobiography. He wanted to complete another work of fiction stated early in his career, *La lutte avec l'ange*, but instead, the *Antimémoires* came to him. To Malraux one does not plan an autobiography not because one cannot plan one but because there is nothing to plan, nothing to arrange. Self, then, is the dimension of imagination and not of memory, an entity that must be renewed ceaselessly. The creation of fiction coincides with the remembrance of an imaginary act which is, in effect, an autobiographical act. And those critics who claimed that Malraux was unable to create independent characters and that all his heroes are extensions of his self missed this crucial point.

Denis Boak, for example, claims that 'Malraux has deliberately attempted to create his own life as an artistic entity in its own right', and that 'in all Malraux's characterization the one constant factor is intellectual conception. He does not achieve such richly human characters as Proust or even Martin du Gard.' These statements clearly indicate where Denis Boak stands; his comparative tool is the novel of 'character', the biographical novel. Indeed, if we compare Malraux's heroes to the traditional hero of the Realist novel, they certainly lack substance. But is this an adequate basis of comparison? Forcing this comparison on Malraux's text means inserting it in a literary tradition he rejects, a tradition he writes against. So Tchen, Garine, Perken, Kassner are naked not because Malraux could not grant them more substance but because they are different from the 'complete hero' we often encounter in works of fiction.

The 'complete hero', or in Boak's terms the 'richly human character', purports to be a duplication of a real human being and the truth of this kind of character lies in his realisation of his human counterpart. Such a blurring of the ontological gap between fiction and reality corresponds to an ideology which sees the world as a static phenomenon to be represented in fiction. Such a replication can occur only within the *status quo* which accommodates a static conception of the literary act. (pp. 143-45)

But if the socio-historical reality is dynamic, it cannot be replicated (unless we force duplication on it) as a whole, be that whole an individual or a group. What, therefore, is the ontological status of Malraux's protagonists? Can we talk of pure absences? Indeed, the character as a well-rounded entity with an identity card is non-existent in Malraux's fictional world. His protagonists are personages—personae—incarnated roles. . . . There is no doubt that Malraux's signifying personage has an autonomous life since he acts freely in accordance with his world view; he is independent to the extent that he signifies an idea, incarnates an ideology. At the same time this personage is Malraux's own extension because Malraux provides him with his field of play, the idea to incorporate. It should be noted that the signifying personage is not an abstraction; it is not a pure idea. Between the personage and the idea, there is the role. In other words, we are not dealing with an absence but with a partial presence; the personage does not coincide with the idea because fiction, being a scene that demands performances, cannot accomodate abstracted ideas. In Malraux's view of the form, fiction requests the signifying personage in order to move the idea forward; because fiction constitutes the description of situations, a personage is needed to carry out the actions the situation calls for. The signifying personage is the body of the idea—the minimum physicality incarnation requires. The signifying personage is not fact but value. In contrast to the *nouveau roman,* Malraux's novel is not a novel of absence; it is the novel of a necessary active presence.

The signifying personage exists in the present only; not only are we not exposed to his past but he himself probes his past, if he does so at all, in function of a present preoccupation. The reader is exposed to that present only, to one point of view at a time; if he is to recreate the text, the reader must of necessity enter the consciousness of the personage. (The first scene of *La Condition humaine,* for example, exposes the reader precisely to what Tchen is experiencing at the moment: we see with Tchen the street lights through the window and the shadow of the cat in the room; we feel the wound Tchen inflicts to his arm and the nausea caused by it.) Malraux is no doubt influenced by film techniques, for in film too the viewer is exposed to one point at a time. When the present of a given scene in the Malrucian world becomes past, when the action of a given moment is consumed, then we move to another present. This is not to say that we are confronting here a situation of fragmentation; the lack of connectedness among the scenes of *L'Espoir* or the novels on China is apparent because the scenes do not follow one another in time though they belong to the same reality being portrayed, be it the Spanish Civil War or the Chinese Revolution. And this complex reality affects various personages in various settings. Again, these scenes and settings follow one another in the book because the book is linear in its physical nature; but in Malraux's fictional universe they occur in simultaneity in a multiplicity of times and settings. (pp. 145-47)

Malraux's novel of situation, then, makes all psychological considerations irrelevant. Though autonomous in their actions, his heroes must be, by definition, extensions of himself, incarnations of his ideas. Identical to him, they have no past and nothing to look back to. We should not even use the word 'hero'; like the word 'character', it connotes a well-rounded entity, a finished product, an artificial construct. (p. 147)

What is at stake here is the essence of literature itself, its definition and purpose. With *Antimémoires* as the crowning of his fiction, Malraux is advancing a new conception of literature—a literature that negates psychology; in other words, the negation of the accepted practice of literature. With the rejection of memory, introspection and psychology (all of which point to the same reality in Malraux's view of the literature of yesterday), he is making a statement on what literature ought to be. For given the impossibility of knowing oneself, introspection and psychology become futile: how can one claim to know the Other when one does not know oneself! The Other as a closed entity is non-measurable, a pure unknown. The only realm of exchange and communication is action, for in action the dialectics of the moment is all that counts. And action, in turn, means freedom from memory: not forgetfulness as temporary amnesia (where the possibility of control is still given to the past over the present), but for-getfulness as a radical act eradicating the residues of the past and forcing the present over consciousness. The present is, in essence, a ceaseless beginning, and man renews this present through his continual metamorphosis. Man, the anonymous and impersonal man, the artist of ancient cultures and civilisations, everyman, is the generator of metamorphosis. (p. 148)

To Malraux, art is non-mimetic; it recreates the world in ever-renewed forms. Style is an existing structure which the artist penetrates; it is the artist's own realm of action. Art is an anti-destiny because it rebels against destiny in its recreation of an autonomous reality which is parallel to the world without duplicating it. As Malraux indicates in *Les Voix du silence,* the historical process of artistic creation is dialectical. An artist is always born to a cultural reality, to a particular epistemic configuration, which he assimilates in order to achieve signification and transcendence. The artistic act is inscribed within an artistic discourse the paramaters of which the artist must transcend through the creation of new forms via the permutation of the old ones. Malraux's views on art are consistent with his own literary creation; it would therefore be wrong to assume that he functions within the Realist tradition or within the prevalent autobiographical tradition. It is clear that he transcends both and creates new forms which are more adequate to the expression of our historical situation. His views on the critical activity counter all traditions of positivistic criticism; his conception of the colloquy points to a critical activity based on group effort and dialogue. . . . The Colloquy negates the individual act of the critic centreing on the individual life of the writer. Since an individual life overflows its immediate parameters into an infinity of ramifications, the Colloquy attempts, by a process of approximation, to cover, at least partially, some of these ramifications. Because the author is caught in a network of relations—style, form, culture, country, historical period, ideology, etc.—he can never be exhausted. He exists in these relations only; hence the absurdity of any attempt to grasp the 'writer' or his 'work'. The pluralistic approach of the Colloquy coincides with Malraux's comprehensive and dialectical outlook on phenomena. Like the Malrucian novel, the Colloquy is open-ended; it deals with subjects-in-situations, with the movement of events.

Antimémoires, then, competes with life; it creates a coherent world through a series of permutations of the material world. Again, it is not a historical reconstruction, but a relating to the world through the act of fiction which in itself is biographical. Fiction as an act of relation opposes the spontaneity and satisfaction of the 'story' as it is or was lived. Fiction means the intentional creation of situations where different consciousnesses meet each other and the world, and not the creation of linearly developed monadic individuals. Fiction is a statement of value, and the intentionality of value transcends biographical spontaneity. Literature, then, is the biography of situations pertaining to the human condition. *Antimémoires* is such a depiction through its selection of three of the most instrumental historical events in our century— Gandhi at the head of the Indian masses on the salt march against the British Empire, Mao at the head of his armies crossing the Ta-tu river, and the annihilation of masses of human beings and their values in the Second World War: the entrance of two huge nations on the scene of modern history, and the degradation and humiliation of multitudes because of the loss of faith in human values. The choice of two nations of the East is not gratuitous: it counterbalances the individualism of the West. In the East man is (still) an integrated member in the group, and not an alienated, self-sufficient entity torn from its supportive structures.

But despite the horrors and tragedies recounted by camp survivors and the eulogy to Jean Moulin, the martyred Maquis commander, in the last section of the book, *Antimémoires* remains a celebration of man throughout his historical vicissitudes. Malraux emphasises repeatedly the sacred dimension of human life. Whether he speaks of the old religions and cultures or of recent historical events, Malraux relates to the sacred in man—that part of man which cannot be annihilated by torture or degradation. . . . And this sacredness has nothing whatsoever to do with metaphysics. It is man's ability to prevail in his ongoing metamorphosis of old structures in the creation of new forms. Not by chance does Malraux end the volume with a final visit to the Lascaux caves, for in these caves human destiny throughout the ages is enacted. It is in these caves that history is played out. The Lascaux caves are the dwellings of primitive man, the location of his art; they also provide storage for the arms of the Resistance fighters. An 'incomprehensible bond' links the animals on the walls with the crates of weapons. (pp. 148-51)

Robert Elbaz, "Malraux's 'Antimémoires'," in his The Changing Nature of the Self: A Critical Study of the Autobiographic Discourse, *1987. Reprint by Croom Helm, 1988, pp. 119-51.*

Cormac McCarthy

1933-

American novelist.

McCarthy is regarded as an important contributor to the Southern Gothic tradition as exemplified by William Faulkner, Carson McCullers, and Flannery O'Connor. His novels, which are usually set in his native Tennessee, are praised for their inventive use of Appalachian dialect and archaic diction as well as for their powerful examinations of evil. McCarthy's bleak vision is evidenced in his protagonists, typically grotesque outcasts who suffer cruelty without understanding their fates. Although some critics fault McCarthy for excessively florid prose and a relentlessly pessimistic worldview, others contend that his depiction of the fallen condition of humanity has universal implications. Robert Coles observed: "[McCarthy] writes novels that tell us we cannot comprehend the riddles of human idiosyncrasy, the influence of the merely contingent or incidental upon our lives. He is a novelist of religious feeling who appears to subscribe to no creed but who cannot stop wondering in the most passionate and honest way what gives life meaning."

In his first novel, *The Orchard Keeper* (1965), McCarthy utilizes three narrative perspectives—one from the young protagonist John Wesley Rattner and two from his mentors—to portray the hero's emergence into adulthood in the solitude of the East Tennessee mountains. Through these characters McCarthy examines the conflict between achieving independence and individuality and the need to satisfy civic duties. In his second novel, *Outer Dark* (1968), McCarthy blends myth and naturalism to show the divergent destinies of incestuous siblings Culla and Rinthy Holme. After Rinthy gives birth, Culla, inspired by shame, leaves their son to die in the woods, but the infant is found and nurtured by an old hermit. McCarthy recounts Rinthy's search for her baby and Culla's quest for Rinthy by employing each as first-person narrators of their journeys. Although both characters suffer, Culla's experiences are far worse, suggesting that his misfortunes result not only from committing incest but also from his faithlessness and unsanctified state of being.

Child of God (1974) details Lester Ballard's gradual decline into murder and necrophilia after fellow citizens brand him as a pariah. Although Ballard has descended into total depravity, McCarthy asserts that he is still a "child of God." McCarthy's next novel, *Suttree* (1979), shifts setting from the mountain region of *Child of God* to the city of Knoxville, but retains as its protagonist a similarly debauched outcast. Traumatized by the death of his twin brother in infancy, Suttree, a husband, father, and college graduate from a wealthy family, rejects his past and decides to live among the city's degenerates where he will work as a fisherman in an effort to deny his heritage. Suttree undergoes a spiritual rejuvenation, however, after nearly dying of typhoid fever, and renounces his corrupt ways. In *Blood Meridian; Or, The Evening Redness in the West* (1985), McCarthy parodies values espoused in popular Western films by exaggerating the notion of rugged individuality to the point of demented lawlessness. Although some critics found this novel unreasonably grotesque, Andrew Hislop remarked: "[*Blood Meridian*] is much more than

a counterblast of bloody imagery against more cosy perceptions of the West. It is an exploration, at times explicitly philosophical, of the relationship between culture and violence."

(See also *CLC*, Vol. 4; *Contemporary Authors*, Vols. 13-16, rev. ed.; *Contemporary Authors New Revision Series*, Vol. 10; and *Dictionary of Literary Biography*, Vol. 6.)

THOMAS LASK

Cormac McCarthy's second novel, **Outer Dark,** combines the mythic and the actual in a perfectly executed work of the imagination. He has made the fabulous real, the ordinary mysterious. . . .

The time and place are blurred. We know that it is somewhere in the South, a tucked-away area that has maintained itself free of outside contamination since the first settlements were established. The land and the climate have conquered the people. They move to a rhythm that is seasonal, not diurnal. A listlessness has seeped into every corner of that world.

Their actions have no edge, except when they explode into violence. An unnamable threat hangs over their lives: they are all doom-haunted.

The time, too, is inexact except that it is still a time of dirt roads and narrow trails, when men traveled in mule-team wagons, rode horse and went miles on foot. Their language is soft, musical, courtly, always in contrast to the violence that surrounds them. It sounds like authentic local speech, but like the incidents in the novel, may simply be a product of the author's skill.

In the outline, the story has a Faulknerian profile. In a shack in the woods, a young girl is about to give birth to a child, which she has conceived by her brother. The girl struggles through the delivery without any help except for the fumbling attention of the boy. After the baby is born, the young man exposes it to die in the woods. But a tinker who has been suspicious of what was going on in the cabin, carries the infant off. The girl learns of it and sets off in search of her incestuous son; the boy sets off in search of her. The double quest is the heart of the story.

It is a search made difficult for the boy because also traveling abroad is an unholy trio, who move about like the horsemen of the Apocalypse, bringing fear and death to those they encounter. They are the mindless evil in the world. Because of them suspicion springs up everywhere and the boy learns to be alert and sensitive to every change in mood; to clear out at the first sign of hostility. . . .

The incidents are not only stages in the search but reveal the culture they are a part of. The loose and flexible ways of the law are shown in the boy's trial and sentence after he is caught trespassing. Both the judge and the man who caught him are less interested in the violation than in procuring free labor. . . .

It is a suspicious, watchful, fearful world, close to the earth, with some of the earth's impassivity and indifference to human life and values.

Mr. McCarthy has, however, not merely written a gothic tale. The shadows and dark corners are not only there for atmosphere. A stubborn, impenetrable society lives in the book, one we hoped had long since disappeared. And in it are acted out the old patterns of crime, punishment and sacrifice.

> *Thomas Lask, "Southern Gothic," in* The New York Times, *September 23, 1968, p. 33.*

GUY DAVENPORT

There is a strange awfulness about Appalachia that quickens the imagination. Its traditions are unconscious and deep in the bone. It still believes in fate. The Calvinist still walks there in Bunyanesque starkness. The world is an allegory and no violence however sickening is ever quite unexpected in the course of a day. It bears its poverty with Celtic dignity and looks at life with the Celtic disbelief in its permanence. And in the Tennessee novelist Cormac McCarthy it has found a new storyteller to depict the darkness of its heart and its futile defiance of its luck.

Mr. McCarthy's first novel, *The Orchard Keeper,* won the William Faulkner Foundation Award three years ago. [*Outer Dark*], his second, is even finer. Though it pays its homage to Faulkner's rhetoric and imagery, it is not a Faulknerian novel. It is much leaner, closer in pace and spareness of line to the Gothic masters Gertrud Le Fort and her disciple Isak Dinesen, and lacks Faulkner's sociological dimension. Mr. McCarthy is unashamedly an allegorist. His responsibility as a storyteller includes believing with his characters in the devil, or at least in the absolute destructiveness of evil. . . .

Lucklessness is a dominant theme in the Appalachian mind. Mr. McCarthy's protagonist believes that "a man makes his own luck," and has made his by begetting a child upon his sister. Thereafter, his doom, and his sister's, unfolds with a perfectly logical inevitability that would have earned a gasp from Sophocles. The plot is like the finding by a malevolent hand the thread that knits the world; page by page it plucks the stitches loose until the fabric parts in a catastrophe so awful that one's eyes leave the page by sheer reflex.

The originality of Mr. McCarthy's novel is not in its theme or locale, both of which are impressively ancient. It is his style which compels admiration, a style compounded of Appalachian phrases as plain and as functional as an ax. In elegant counterpoint to this bare-bones English is a second diction taken from that rich store of English which is there in the dictionary to be used by those who can ("his shadow moiled cant," "the tapered spline of the axle").

Surprisingly, so hard-wrought a style is not in the least precious. The bookish diction complements the countrified one. Every word, moreover, is designed to serve Mr. McCarthy's sharply controlled sense of place and action. There is not a page of this novel which does not depict swift and significant action. Nor does Mr. McCarthy waste a single word on his characters' thoughts. With total objectivity he describes what they do and records their speech. Such discipline comes not only from mastery over words but from an understanding wise enough and compassionate enough to dare tell so abysmally dark a story.

> *Guy Davenport, "Appalachian Gothic," in* The New York Times Book Review, *September 29, 1968, p. 4.*

ROBERT COLES

[*The essay excerpted below originally appeared in* The New Yorker, *March 22, 1969.*]

[McCarthy's characters in **Outer Dark**] talk and act like Appalachian highlanders or yeoman farmers, but they seem meant to represent something else, something that stretches beyond the limits of space and time. What matters is not the where and when of McCarthy's story, for all the intricate and lyrical descriptions of rural life, but the feeling that he wants to make his stories suggestive, allegorical, apocalyptic. Plot means little, even this mixture of the sublime and the grotesque, the religious, the rude, and the barbaric. The ground rules are clear: We will be told a story that will frighten and alarm us, but, as in a nightmare, the mood evoked will matter more than details—the mood of darkness and hopelessness that no technological progress, no refinement of psychological analysis, can explain away or (that cool, slippery word of our times) resolve.

Cormac McCarthy's "outer dark" is not that by now cozy unconscious whose wild and irreverent and banal tricks continue to amuse our fashionable novelists. Nor is he interested in becoming a gilded version of the American social scientist, who has a name or a label for everything and wants at all costs to be *concerned* and *involved.* McCarthy's "dark" is not the mind's interior or the world's exterior; it does not deal with the conceits and deceits that are always at work everywhere—even, say, in the White House and the Kremlin. One begins by wondering what McCarthy's psychological and political purposes are. (Everyone, we have discovered, must have such purposes, and be knowingly or unwittingly at their mercy.) Soon, though, we are asked by the author to stay in the presence of this "outer darkness" and suffer what Conrad called "the horror, the horror" or else to dismiss his novel as dense and out-of-date and so muddled with Biblical and Attic overtones that it is the worst of all possible things today—*irrelevant.*

Culla and Rinthy Holme, brother and sister, are lovers, and the parents of a son. Culla delivers his son in a shack no visitor has entered in months, and immediately abandons him to the woods. A tinker whom Culla, shamed, has rebuffed outside the cabin, because Rinthy, inside, is obviously pregnant, discovers the child, gives it to a wet nurse, and goes his way. Rinthy sets out to find her child, because she does not believe Culla's assertion that he is dead. She senses that the tinker may have come upon her child; she may have heard his wagon pass by. Then Culla sets out to find Rinthy. So they pick their way through woods and hills and across swamps and rivers, resting under trees, in houses, in towns that seem deserted. Mostly, because they are wary and haunted, they stalk the land. Who are they and what do they intend, the country folk along the way ask. "I'm a-huntin this here tinker." And why the tinker? Did he steal something? "Well. Somethin belonged to me." What? "It was just somethin." Culla is often assumed to be an outlaw, a rascal on the run, and therefore easily exploited by law-abiding citizens, who can have it both ways—the profit from a desperate man's plight, the pride and power that go with hospitality. Hungry, frightened, driven, Culla and Rinthy never stop anywhere for long. They meet all sorts of obstacles, human and natural, as they move relentlessly on. . . . (pp. 119-21)

It is a hard book to read—a book written with fervor and intensity and concentration, an urgent and at times an inscrutable book. As if to assert timelessness and universality, McCarthy moves from the clear, concrete words of the mountaineer to a soaring, Faulknerian rhetoric of old, stately words, unused words, medieval words. . . . The author uses nature to establish an ironic tone, to comment indirectly on mankind, and to entrance his readers with his flowing and at times stunning descriptions of rats and turtles and spiders and snakes and birds and trees and flowers. . . . (p. 122)

Cormac McCarthy's first novel, *The Orchard Keeper,* won him the William Faulkner Foundation Award and a grant from the Rockefeller Foundation. *Light in August* comes to mind as *Outer Dark* unfolds: the poor white people, the harsh puritanism, the disastrous collision of Instinct with Piety and Custom, and the imagery—of the exiles, the wanderers, the outcasts, all dressed up, though, in rural American habit. . . . In *Outer Dark,* as in Faulkner, we are required to pay close attention. But McCarthy directs our attention to very few people, nor are we allowed to sit back and relax and just laugh, though there are lovely, tender moments and a few eerily comic scenes. McCarthy's handful of characters move from place to place, always going downhill. Their curse is explicit, and the futility of their lives is spelled out: Rinthy finds the bones of the tinker and her child, and Culla

meets a blind man on a road toward a swamp, "a spectral waste out of which reared only the naked trees in attitudes of agony and dimly hominoid like figures in a landscape of the damned." In *Outer Dark,* characters touch, collide, then go on, rather than get to "know" one another; they hurt and are hurt in accordance with unfathomable necessities. They don't analyze themselves or others. They don't have to earn their distinction, their significance. Their origins don't have to be expressed and related to society or "the culture." They are immediately presented as people larger than life, important for reasons everyone can sense. The "action"—again there is the contrast with Faulkner—is swift and unequivocal. One person commits a crime against the gods, then others are drawn into a series of accidents, misfortunes, and, finally, disasters, all of which make for a tragedy whose meaning every reader had better comprehend.

Not for a long time has an American writer—a young one, at that—attempted to struggle with the Fates and with what Plato called their mother: Ananke, or Necessity. On our way to another planet or layer of the unconscious or new "social structure," we of this century don't worry about the dread every man is heir to, nor do we consider envy, passion, and hate things that will always plague man, however lovingly and scientifically he is reared, and in whatever social, political, or economic system. Always it is the next bit of progress, the next device, the next body of knowledge, the next deal or plan that will—what? Make man superman? Free man of himself, of his nature as someone who is born, lives, and dies, and in between, for a second of eternity, tries to flex his muscles, clench his fists, and say "It is me, me amid the outer dark"? Necessarily, said Plato, the Fates can never be thwarted, and they cannot be thwarted today, even by a million computers and consulting rooms. Necessarily, says McCarthy, the dark is out there, waiting for each of us. Necessarily, our lot is assigned; we have to contend with our flaws, live with them, and all too often be destroyed by them.

We do not learn what Rinthy and Culla Holme were like when they were young and perhaps smiled and laughed from time to time. We meet them in Hell, and we keep wondering what they could have done to earn their desperation. At worst, they are a little too stubborn—thick-headed, and unwilling to share themselves with others, to share their vision, their secrets, their temptations, their humanity. Questioned, they demur, they flee. A touch of self-righteousness comes through—brilliantly and subtly arranged by a writer who can bring about emotions in both his characters and his readers without making a whole showy business out of the effort. Then all is scrambling and grumbling; the road turns and one desperately makes the turn, and no fire, no roof, no blanket will work. McCarthy's "outer dark" is austere and bleak and blue and cold and ultimately impassable; his mountains open up only to reveal a foul swamp, a wild river, and yet another mountain. If exiles and fugitives have fascinated writers—who themselves often keep their distance—so have men like McCarthy's tinker. V. K. Ratliff, Faulkner's sewing-machine agent, is a reminder that we the readers are there, with advice and ideas and *our* stories to tell. *Outer Dark's* tinker, who not only sells or repairs kettles and pots but offers everything from food and soap and liquor to gadgets of all kinds, is something else. It is a measure of McCarthy's seriousness that we are allowed no letup. The tinker provides us no alternative, no vision of a better world. What hope and encouragement we do get can come only from a rural landscape that is rich with life, variety, spontaneity, endless possibilities, and an unself-consciousness that Culla and Rinthy Holme will never possess.

The only diversion granted us is in the best sense unintentional; it is the commanding diversion a writer's skill provides. McCarthy works hard to write well and ingeniously, but there are moments in this sad, bitter, literally awesome book when only an exceptionally gifted and lyrical writer could take his audience's continuing attention for granted. . . . **Outer Dark** is arresting and puzzling enough to drive one to distraction, but always to the next surge of reading. It is as if the reader, too, becomes a traveller, and for doing so is rewarded with an astonishing range of language—slow-paced and heavy or delightfully light, relaxed or intense, perfectly plain or thoroughly intricate. Eternal principles mix company with the details of everyday, pastoral life—always under some apocalyptic cloud, though. Errors will be punished, retribution exacted. The blind lead the blind, though some think of themselves as seekers rather than driven, as knowing rather than compelled. And we all must face that final reckoning. Three horsemen ride through **Outer Dark,** looking for someone, covering the brooding countryside with their dark and fierce presence. Cormac McCarthy knows the Revelation of St. John the Divine, who announced that he would set down "all things that he saw" and the "bare record of the word of God." I suppose good writers also come dangerously close to doing that, seeing so much and putting so much down on paper that the universe itself is spread out before us, and the words come near to being the Word—to haunt us and make us pause and wonder for a moment, even though, alas, we keep moving on our particular roads. (pp. 123-26)

> Robert Coles, "The Empty Road," in his Farewell to the South, *Atlantic-Little Brown*, 1972, pp. 119-126.

WALTER SULLIVAN

Outer Dark is a sort of double picaresque, and scene by scene it is written with great force and clarity. The frame is simple enough. Having fathered his sister's child, Culla Holme hides the infant in the woods intending that it should die there. However, the baby is found by an itinerant peddler—a "tinker" in the half-archaic tongue McCarthy's people employ. Rinthy Holme takes to the road in search of her offspring and Culla goes in search of Rinthy. The method of the book is to switch back and forth from brother to sister chronicling for each a series of adventures that seem purposefully isolated. Culla is hungry or finds work, steals a pair of boots and has them stolen from him, is pursued as a murderer, arrested for trespassing, and is almost lynched by a gang of hog drovers for having done nothing at all. Rinthy's lot is easier. She is occupied mostly with fending off the advances of men and answering questions about where she is from and enduring the agony of not being able to find her baby.

There is no way to overstate the power, the absolute literary virtuosity, with which McCarthy draws his scenes. He writes about the finite world with an accuracy so absolute that his characters give the impression of a universality which they have no right to claim. For unlike those of his master, Faulkner, McCarthy's people are drawn from the periphery of the world. In Faulkner, even the most romantic figures—the Sartorises, Sutpen—and the most despicable—Flem Snopes, Popeye—are avatars of those qualities that are most essential in our common personality. It is the way of the good writer to find the universal in the particular, for finally it is the universal that he seeks. McCarthy, on the other hand, seems to

love the singular for its own sake: he appears to seek out those devices and people and situations that will engage us by their very strangeness. Nothing apparently is included for the way in which it relates to the other elements of the novel or for the truth to which it will finally lead us.

So we move through a world of curiously contrived ferries, fat men who live in decaying houses, preachers who attempt to inspire bloodshed, criminals who kill for the joy of killing. The question is not whether these things taken separately exist, but rather what kind of world they come together to create, what kind of unity they make. And the answer is: none; they remain separate features of the surrealist landscape. Time and place remain undefined. From the language we know we are in the South, from the trappings of life we know we are in the past; but where in the South, how far into the past, we have no way of telling. At the end, the novelist discloses his theme: we go blindly through the world and therefore the gods have been unjust to us. I can see how McCarthy might defend his rendering of the public image in terms of our inability, as sightless men, to conceive the circumstances of our mortal journey. But this is a confusion of the physical with the metaphysical, of fate with the solid realities of flesh and stone. There is no way to avoid grappling with the intractable reality that surrounds us. Even someone as extraordinarily gifted as McCarthy must pay the full price that his art demands. (pp. 661-62)

> Walter Sullivan, " 'Where Have All the Flowers Gone?' Part II: The Novel in the Gnostic Twilight," in The Sewanee Review, *Vol. 78, No. 4, Fall, 1970, pp. 654-64.*

JEROME CHARYN

[**Suttree** is] a book with rude, startling power and a flood of talk. Much of it takes place on the Tennessee River, and Cormac McCarthy . . . gives us a sense of river life that reads like a doomed *Huckleberry Finn.* The river has lost its kind edge. It's now "the slow voice of ruin." The sun beating down on it is "like a bunghole to a greater hell beyond." As the river begins to swell and roll down from "the gutted upcountry," it maims and kills. "The fish . . . themselves looked stunned." . . .

At times Mr. McCarthy's picture of hell becomes bloated and strained with thick, gassy language, as "troops of ghost cavalry clashed in an outraged sky, old spectral revenants armed with rusted tools of war colliding parallactically upon each other like figures from a mass grave shorn up and girdled and cast with dread import across the clanging night and down remoter slopes between the dark and darkness yet to come."

But the bombast disappears as quickly as it arrives, and Mr. McCarthy creates images and feelings with the force of a knuckle on the head. Here is Cornelius Suttree, the central "voice" of the novel, thinking of the wife he has abandoned: "Remember her hair in the morning before it was pinned, black, rampant, savage with loveliness. As if she slept in perpetual storm."

Suttree is a fisherman who has a houseboat on the river. The "reprobate" overschooled son of "doomed Saxon clans," he chooses to become a river rat, and the "rats" around him make up the other voices of the novel: gamblers, junkmen, prostitutes, stray boys. (p. 14)

Suttree himself is a lost creature who can find no real hook into this world. He roams about "like a dog" at large. He can touch another human being for a moment, drink beer with a friend, fish, make love, but he has to move on, jump downriver, or hide in the dead, nightmare city. The book comes at us like a horrifying flood. The language licks, batters, wounds—a poetic, troubled rush of debris. It is personal and tough, without that boring neatness and desire for resolution that you can get in any well-made novel. Cormac McCarthy has little mercy to spare, for his characters or himself. His text is broken, beautiful and ugly in spots. Mr. McCarthy won't soothe us with a quiet song. *Suttree* is like a good, long scream in the ear. (p. 15)

> *Jerome Charyn, "Doomed Huck," in* The New York Times Book Review, *February 18, 1979, pp. 14-15.*

DOROTHY WICKENDEN

[*Suttree*] is rife with violence and perversity. The story is macabre, the language strident and ruthlessly explicit, the characters seamy—they belong to the underworld of the dispossessed. *Suttree* is a neo-gothic novel, appalling in its insistent concentration on the grotesque, in its frank portrayal of the unspeakable. Like its 18th-century gothic predecessors, *Suttree* exposes a fragmented existence in which old beliefs and social structures are no longer secure.

The setting is Knoxville, Tennessee, in the early 1950s; the hero, a restless and enigmatic loner, makes his living as a fisherman. Two seething entities, the river and the city, circumscribe his life, each harboring peculiar forms of malevolence. . . .

From the first pages of the novel, when a bloated body is dragged from the river, to one of the closing scenes, when Suttree returns to his houseboat after a prolonged absence and discovers a maggot-infested corpse in his bed, decay and death obsess him. "Death is what the living carry with them. A state of dread, like some uncanny foretaste of a bitter memory. But the dead do not remember and nothingness is not a curse. Far from it." Death and memory, guilt and family bonds mingle confusedly in his imagination. . . .

He has fled to the river to escape his marriage, his heritage, to seek a kind of oblivion. Instead he is drawn into the city's subculture of the unemployed and homeless, the haunt of deviants, drunks, ragmen and whores. They have their own peculiar demands to make of him, and his involvement in their sordid lives gradually undermines his original stance of noncommittal solitude and self-sufficiency. The novel's moral is heavily Christian. McCarthy takes his hero through some moments of extreme deprivation—cold, ravenous hunger, total isolation and a nearly fatal spell with typhoid fever—forcing him to learn a measure of humility and to accept the stubborn fact of mortality.

Although McCarthy's convoluted style can be as oppressive as his themes, he uses language powerfully. His imagery, repellant though it may be, is rich and tactile. The dialogue, in contrast to some of the labored descriptive passages, is pointed, wry and credible. He reveals the idiosyncrasies that are the essence of his characters in scenes of fantastic audacity. . . .

There are many . . . scenes of surreal horror in the novel, too many. Some succeed in creating a queasy fascination with McCarthy's "world beyond all fantasy"; others are gratuitous indulgences of the author. The book is saved by McCarthy's startling sense of humor; the scenes involving Harrogate and his zany schemes to make some fast money are amusing and oddly touching. They relieve what would otherwise be an intolerable dose of sin and retribution, fear, guilt and rage. And Suttree is an absorbing hero with emotional and intellectual depth. But ultimately this is a cruel, unscrupulous novel. You'll put it down feeling tainted and abused along with Suttree and all of his doomed fellows.

> *Dorothy Wickenden, in a review of "Suttree," in* The New Republic, *Vol. 180, No. 10, March 10, 1979, p. 46.*

WALTER SULLIVAN

The main character in Cormac McCarthy's *Suttree* is a lapsed Catholic, but to say this is to pass along merely incidental information. Like all of McCarthy's protagonists Bud Suttree is a renegade citizen, a defector from society, ex-son, ex-nephew, ex-husband, ex-father, a member of the lumpenproletariat whom we see for the first time shortly after he has been released from the penitentiary. The shape of the novel is amorphous, even for McCarthy, whose long suit has never been dramatic structure. One gets the impression that McCarthy walks through the world cramming his brain with experience both actual and vicarious and then goes to work and gives everything back, scene upon scene, the devil take the hindmost. McCarthy is certainly the most talented novelist of his generation. He is the only writer to emerge since World War II who can bear comparison to Faulkner, and he invites such comparison by imitating Faulkner's style. He is capable, as he frequently demonstrates, of unbelievable overwriting. . . . But more often than it fails, McCarthy's Faulknerian prose achieves a lyricism that touches the heart and a dignity which endows some of the ugliest aspects of creation with a certain beauty.

Suttree, for all his shiftless ways, is one of McCarthy's more respectable characters. The old man in *The Orchard Keeper* is fairly tame, but the brother and sister in *Outer Dark* are incestuous lovers and the protagonist in *Child of God* is a necrophiliac. Clifton Fadiman once said that the characters in Carson McCullers's work made those in the Faulkner canon look like "the folks next door," but such tame comparisons are meaningless when one comes to speak of McCarthy's personae. Within the ordinary world where most of us parse out our days—Knoxville, Tennessee, in the case of *Suttree*—McCarthy builds another twilight kingdom, a land of evil and viciousness and dark motivations, an outpost of rebellion both mundane and spiritual against the status quo. Suttree lives on a shanty boat, sets out trotlines for a living, and brawls and loves and drinks his way through life. He is alienated from his family for reasons that we are not told, except that alienation from all customs and attitudes that are traditional to civilization is taken for granted in the kingdom that McCarthy creates. McCarthy's rendition of Knoxville is as foreign to the ordinary citizens of that city as a hamlet in Asia or Africa would be, but when he is not indulging his taste for rhetoric, McCarthy's prose is so sharp and lucid that only the most determined skeptic can remain unconvinced. His detail is clean, accurate, and abundant: he knows the name of everything: parts of automobiles and boats, poisons, diseases, the human anatomy, utensils used at the altar, the equipage of the police. He can describe with the most precise realism the look of a human eye separated from its socket, the smell of a putrefying corpse, the taste of a potion mixed by a voodoo woman.

Suttree comes to life, and for all his faults and the gaps in his history that are never filled, he is a sympathetic figure. He serves his time for having been along when a drugstore was robbed. He makes his bit of money and shares what he has. His friends are gamblers and cheats, prostitutes and marginal business people, and McCarthy succeeds marvelously in the creation of these minor characters. Big John fights continually with, and is finally killed by, the police. Gene Harrogate, whom we first see sexually violating watermelons, is a scrawny outrageous blunderer who steals and begs and connives most shamelessly, but somehow elicits the help of those around him and a grudging acceptance from the reader. At the end of the book Suttree, having lived off the earnings of a lady of ill repute, leaves her when she suffers a mental collapse and leaves Knoxville, his physical departure from this particular place marking a kind of conclusion. But, properly speaking, the book has no beginning and no end: it takes up, it catalogues the outrages and agonies and small gains of this limited segment of humankind, and it stops with nothing solved or put to rest or brought to fruition. Doubtless McCarthy meant for his novel to take this course, and we can comprehend his structure as a reflection of life's meaninglessness. But I, for one, can also deplore what seems to me to be a limited use of an enormous talent. In his almost exclusive concern with the grotesque McCarthy offers a distorted view of creation, fragmented and debauched though that creation now may be. I hope he will read Faulkner again and learn how to broaden his scope and enlarge his image. (pp. 341-43)

> *Walter Sullivan, "Model Citizens and Marginal Cases: Heroes of the Day," in* The Sewanee Review, *Vol. LXXXVII, No. 2, Spring, 1979, pp. 337-44.*

JOHN DITSKY

Born in 1933 in East Tennessee, Cormac McCarthy has demonstrated the abiding fictional potential of his native region—and in the process added to the stature of the American Southern literary tradition—in four remarkable novels: *The Orchard Keeper* (1965), *Outer Dark* (1968), *Child of God* (1973), and *Suttree* (1979). . . . As with *A Death in the Family* by McCarthy's co-regionist James Agee, McCarthy's novels are fitted out with interchapters which accomplish passages of time and increments of action by means of refractive prose—changes in angle of vision. But the comparisons with other Southern writers, chief among them Faulkner, that the novels of Cormac McCarthy bring to mind are beyond our fully considering here; suffice it to observe that in the case of Faulkner, that "Dixie Limited" which, in Flannery O'Connor's memorable phrase (and she having said so much that is pertinent to McCarthy's writing, without mentioning the man, in her essays), comes roaring down on the "mule and wagon" of every other writer from the South who attempts to raise his or her own unique voice, the possibility of comparison with McCarthy does not seem to have inhibited the latter in the least. Dictionally, tonally, McCarthy simply goes *beyond* Faulkner.

It is that journey beyond Faulkner—though without sustaining a continuing reference to the older writer—that I intend to survey in this paper. If the writing of William Faulkner can be called "Gothic," "grotesque," and in diction "florid" or "obscure," "arcane," then Cormac McCarthy has gone him one better. Though doubtless operating under some degree of Faulknerian influence, McCarthy writes as though Faulkner had never existed, as if there were no limits to what language might be pushed into doing in the last half of the twentieth century. The clash between near-incredible erudition and resources of diction and the actual subject matter—the characters, the actions, the settings—of his books creates in McCarthy's work an enormous and disturbing energy and power to move the reader. By means of this energy and power, he is able to carry that reader further into darkness than even Faulkner, seemingly, dared go—to that place where those reside who have rejected the covenant: those "children of the kingdom" mentioned in Matthew 8:12 whose rejection of grace has earned them "weeping and gnashing of teeth." It is this rejection, I should think, that accounts for the titles of two, or perhaps three, of McCarthy's books, and the seemingly motiveless malignancy of certain of his characters that makes their passages through this world seem so chilling—although their portraits, in their extremity, do not become the less familiar (which redoubles the chill).

This arguably Biblical presentation of character is abetted by a similarly Biblical narrative flow; in spite of the resources of diction already mentioned, McCarthy's stories are told with the economy of folk tales. Or parables. They focus in on basics, on the here-and-now, on the earth itself, in a manner which the language used for summing-up, for commentary, makes seem the starker, the more extreme. Here, for instance, is (excluding from consideration the first of the interchapters alluded to earlier) the very first paragraph, entire, of McCarthy's "first" novel, *The Orchard Keeper:*

> For some time now the road had been deserted, white and scorching yet, though the sun was already reddening the western sky. He walked along slowly in the dust, stopping from time to time and bobbling on one foot like some squat ungainly bird while he examined the wad of tape coming through his shoe-sole. He turned again. Far down the blazing strip of concrete a small shapeless mass had emerged and was struggling toward him. It loomed steadily, weaving and grotesque like something seen through bad glass, gained briefly the form and solidity of a pickup truck, whipped past and receded into the same liquid shape by which it came.

This is one of McCarthy's seething monsters afoot, filled with resentments at all who cross his path, cross *him,* making his life futile and filled with bile. . . . If this is the South, it is the South perceived by Vladimir and Estragon.

Yet almost immediately, there is a characteristic switch to a more elaborate diction, descriptive passages creating the image of a Knoxville region where "Clay cracks and splits in endless microcataclysm and the limestone lies about the eroded land like schools of sunning dolphin, gray channeled backs humped at the infernal sky," and where the forest floor "has about it a primordial quality, some steamy carboniferous swamp where ancient saurians lurk in feigned sleep," and where even the shacks of mountaineers can be seen "squatting over their gullied purlieus like great brooding animals rigid with constipation." *Mosquitoes,* yes; but not even Faulkner quite so consistently made up images like these. The "poetic" excess of these passages—McCarthy does become more "restrained" in time—serves as index to this book, and to its author's canon. (pp. 1-3)

The habit of omitting quotation marks around dialogue is but one of the devices by which McCarthy intensifies reader experience of violent action—in this book, for instance, including the collapse of a tavern porch into a gully and the crash of an automobile into a creek. The interplay of present event and memory assists in this process of making experience vivid. But for the most part, McCarthy's achievement—in [*The Orchard Keeper*], which contains a Faulknerian hunt for reputed "treasure" and which ends in contemplation of the peace of the dead, *The Mansion*-like—depends upon his splendid choices of imagery. In mid-novel, for instance, amid a snowy landscape and "brilliant against the facade of pines beyond, a cardinal shot like a drop of blood." And this is the meditation on the dead just alluded to:

> Evening. The dead sheathed in the earth's crust and turning the slow diurnal of the earth's wheel, at peace with eclipse, asteroid, the dusty novae, their bones brindled with mold and the celled marrow going to frail stone, turning, their fingers laced with roots, at one with Tut and Agamemnon, with the seed and the unborn.

It will be argued that this verbal richness is simply flamboyant overwriting, that little is gained by such a purpled and mannered cast. The answer—which cannot, of course, mollify all potential detractors—lies in the reading, in the effects achieved: in the tension mentioned earlier between materials and narrative style.

Moreover, McCarthy's later works shows evidence of increasing care in the lavishing of verbal embellishment (if that is indeed the proper term). Yet "materials," as noted above, continue to attract him; he grounds his language in matter—as any of the quotations already included will attest—like one of Steinbeck's country folk drawing with a stick in the earth while dealing with a problem. *Outer Dark* continues this attention to the material, the vengeance enacted upon its wanderers and those they chance upon augured and adumbrated in the state of nature itself, like the dream with which the novel begins. At once the dreamer, who has committed incest with his sister and fears it will be discovered, is distracted by the noise of a passing tinker and wonders "what new evil this might be." The baby born of this relationship is abandoned in the woods, and the description of its protests echoes those of Benjy Compson:

> It howled execration upon the dim camarine world of its nativity wail on wail while he lay there gibbering with palsied jawhasps, his hands putting back the night like some witless paraclete beleaguered with all limbo's clamor.

What exactly does all this *mean?* It is the poetic flow of a writer who creates a Brothers-Grimm world of uncertain date, one in which a tinker poised upon a bridge brings a troll to mind for the reader, and in which a confused sinner sits on a roadside stone "and with a dead stick drew outlandish symbols in the dust." McCarthy portrays a society reduced again to primitivism—if indeed it has ever emerged—and communicating through barbarous violence and magical runes. When the victim sister seeks out the grave of the infant she has been told is dead, she moves "with quiet and guileless rectitude to stand before a patch of black and cloven earth": good and evil confront one another in stark extremity, again as in fairy tales; evil triumphs, and only death brings peace. The brother flees, found out, and raises "his clenched hands above him threatful, supplicant, to the mute and windy heavens." Naturally there is no answer.

Indeed, the next scene is of the arrival of the three dreadful avengers, who bring horror and death wherever they go; McCarthy daringly likens them to figures in some piece of W.P.A. postoffice art: "parodic figures transposed live and intact and violent out of a proletarian mural and set mobile upon the empty fields . . ." Later in the book, hanged men remind the reader of scenes out of some Breughel painting, the horror thus evoked being timeless, everlasting. Nor is this the limit of language's wizardry in this book where Faulknerian nobles are called "squire"; within a space of three pages, McCarthy uses these three examples of yoked opposites: "static violence," "furious immobility," and "violent constraint." Travelers on their wagon-borne chairs appear, in their "black immobility," like "stone figures quarried from the architecture of an older time." And the sister searching for her child wakens in the woods to see "toy birds with sesame eyes regarding her from their clay nests overhead." But what but fantastic language will serve to describe a world in which violent arguments break out over the making of butter, and in which hanged men are encountered casually, in the middle of a field, attended by a pair of buzzards merely? It is, needless to remark, our world precisely, rendered as dream and thus heightened in effect; hence McCarthy's diction. (pp. 4-5)

McCarthy parallels some of Faulkner's great horse scenes with what must inevitably remind the reader of the Biblical account of the Gadarene swine; the herd of hogs being driven by in *Outer Dark* can carry men along with them, but first there is a discussion in which one character mentions Jewish dietary laws and the other replies, "What's a jew?" What then occurs acquires its power because to these people, it has not happened before: they do not know they are repeating a pattern of possession and atonement. There is some suggestion in the novel, moreover, that the three killers—or at least their leader—are operating out of some sense of the injustice of human destiny; but at once, and abruptly, the child—which moments before had dangled from a man's hands "like a dressed rabbit, a gross eldritch doll with ricketsprung legs and one eye opening and closing softly like a naked owl's"—has its throat slit. The novel ends when the brother, having found that the road he is following ends in a "spectral waste out of which reared only the naked trees in attitudes of agony and dimly hominoid like figures in a landscape of the damned," turns back, wondering why "a road should come to such a place." But on his journey back, he passes a blind man going to the place he has just returned from. He says nothing. He merely notes that "Someone should tell a blind man before setting him out that way."

Well yes; someone should. Denials of responsibility, along with unwarranted assumptions of authority, run through Cormac McCarthy's four novels. *Child of God* is as illustrative of this notion as any of the others, but here the prose has been stripped to its absolute leanest; in its starkness and simplicity of means *Child of God* comes near to being a tour-de-force. In one of those ironic characterizations that nearly give his hand away, McCarthy encapsules his central character on the novel's second page: "A child of God much like yourself perhaps." Said child of God is seen threatening an auctioneer almost immediately; more to the point of McCarthy's presentation of his ordinariness, Lester is soon seen urinating, defecating, and masturbating. The atmosphere, particularly within the abandoned house where Lester takes up residence, is one of rot and decay; man is but another particle within a material nature in this novel. Within a few pages, a fox hunt rushes right through Lester's new home (and later on he witnesses a boar hunt). Life's value is far from assured here. (p. 6)

[For] the most part, the humor is of a black sort, designed to chill and repel. And often, a poetically rendered scene turns sour when Lester intrudes: a girl found sleeping outdoors in her nightgown turns into a feral self-defending beast; a young girl watching fireworks is unwittingly attracted to this dangerous stranger:

> . . . And you could see among the faces a young girl with candyapple on her lips and her eyes wide. Her pale hair smelled of soap, woman-child from beyond the years, rapt below the sulphur glow and pitchlight of some medieval fun fair. A lean skylong candle skewered the black pools in her eyes. Her fingers clutched. In the flood of this breaking brimstone galaxy she saw the man with the bears watching her and she edged closer to the girl by her side and brushed her hair with two fingers quickly.

The young girl's movements sum up the power of McCarthy's style: by combining elaborate diction with terrible deeds, he creates a tension of attraction-repulsion. Evil fascinates with its lurid beauty.

Quentin Compson's protests that he doesn't hate his South (at the end of *Absalom, Absalom!*) would have to be amplified at an even shriller pitch to cover what is depicted in *Child of God.* Within a very few pages, we are shown a blacksmith's ritual of proud and careful effort being ignored by a loutish countryman, an infant chewing the legs off a captured robin, a scene of necrophilia with an element of voyeurism thrown in for good measure, the main character shopping for clothes to deck out his dead beloved, a fire that consumes this favorite corpse and sends the protagonist to a cave to live, and the killing of a fresh beloved (and the leaving of her idiot child to die in another fire). At last, Ballard has created his underground kingdom of the dead in the image of his own graceless soul:

> He followed this course . . . through a tunnel that brought him to his belly, the smell of the water besides him in the trough rich with minerals and past the chalken dung of he knew not what animals until he climbed up a chimney to a corridor above the stream and entered into a tall and bellshaped cavern. Here the walls with their softlooking convolutions, slavered over as they were with wet and bloodred mud, had an organic look to them like the innards of some great beast. Here in the bowels of the mountain Ballard turned his light on ledges or pallets of stone where dead people lay like saints.

It is hard not to draw in the breath at one of these chapter-ending revelations. This is the world beyond good and evil, where only the unbridled intelligence exists, playing God: "Disorder in the woods, trees down, new paths needed. Given charge Ballard would have made things more orderly in the woods and in men's souls." Ballard, who has taken to wearing the clothing of his victims, is even seen telling the snow to fall faster ("and it did"), and wondering "what stuff" the stars were made of, "or himself."

Thus McCarthy has endowed this "child of God," supposedly like overselves, with the capacity to protest his fate, to attempt to rewrite the order of things. We find him saving his corpses from a flood, the heroic effort required seeming mock-Biblical or mock-epical and leaving him "gibbering, a

sound not quite crying that echoed from the walls of the grotto like the mutterings of a band of sympathetic apes." But when a deputy asks an old man if people are meaner than they used to be, the old man replies, "No . . . I don't. I think people are the same from the day God first made one." In Ballard's career human history is telescoped and reversed. Contemplating the fields renewing themselves in the springtime, Ballard drops his head and weeps; later, he dreams a dream of an idyll in nature, riding on muleback and resolved to go on riding, "for he could not turn back and the world that day was as lovely as any day that ever was and he was riding to his death." Fleeing his enemies later, Ballard finds an "ancient ossuary" deep in the bowels of the earth, where there are the bones of "bison, elk," and a jaguar whose eyetooth Ballard takes along. Ascending to the surface of the earth again, Ballard turns himself in to the county hospital, and dies of pneumonia before he can be charged with any crime. His body is reduced to spare parts, like Gary Gilmore's in Norman Mailer's *The Executioner's Song.* . . . (pp. 7-8)

Cormac McCarthy's concise history of mankind takes a more naturalistic turn in his first/fourth novel and most recently published work, *Suttree.* It is, in length and approach, a considerable departure from what has gone before. It is perhaps as long as the other three books put together, and it is an urban novel whereas the other three are rural. It is tied to a specific city, Knoxville, Tennessee, and to a fairly specific time, whereas the others, for all the occasional clues one might find therein, are without time and almost without place too. In a peculiar and doubtless unplanned (or not totally planned) sense, *Suttree* completes the others, makes them a square, takes them into another dimension.

Sheer length and density of presented experience prevent adequate critical consideration of *Suttree* here, but it may be possible to fit the work within McCarthy's canon generally, for certain stylistic traits are in evidence here as much as in the other three novels. For one, McCarthy's handling of dialogue is as superb here as ever—a point difficult to establish without extensive quotation, and one which nevertheless can be cited as common to several of the writers of the American South in our time. We might distinguish Suttree himself as observer and absorber from McCarthy's other protagonists, for his intelligence and articulateness mark him as having the gifts to cope, albeit painfully, with the anguishes of his time, as none of his creator's other characters seem able to do. Indeed, though the novel is set in Knoxville in the Fifties, Suttree himself is nearly a stereotype of the Sixties—a gifted and conscious dropout (as they used to be called) from a rotten society. "Blind slime. As above, so it is below," Suttree comments on the possibility that there are caves below Knoxville. Thus this vision of the world as scarcely created, or as created badly, is what the character Suttree seems to share with McCarthy the author. What persists of the writer's standard "first novel," arguably, is this projection of the self into the figure of the central character—one who, nevertheless, is better at suffering and being there than at acting.

Knoxville has had, arguably, more and better talent devoted to its fictional depiction—James Agee, David Madden, Cormac McCarthy—than any other American city, once size is considered and weighed accordingly. McCarthy's Knoxville is rather akin to Eliot's Waste Land or Unreal City; in McCarthy's case, however, Knoxville becomes the all-too-real city. A fragment of the novel's initial reverie, italics removed, reads:

> . . . Encampment of the damned. Precincts perhaps where dripping lepers prowl unbelled . . . The buildings stamped against the night are like a rampart to a farther world forsaken, old purposes forgot. Countrymen come for miles with the earth clinging to their shoes and sit all day like mutes in the marketplace. The city constructed on no known paradigm, a mongrel architecture reading back through the works of man in a brief delineation of the aberrant disordered and mad. A carnival of shapes . . .

Thus we are not too surprised to find that "the city is beset by a thing unknown" which simply to dwell upon is to invite in. Alas, the thing is human nature, an image of ourselves presented at the gates which we are compelled to take in and worship—and which turns, immediately, into our ruin. (pp. 8-9)

Again, space prevents an adequate consideration of the subject of humor in McCarthy's works, for what strikes the reader as amusing may also serve to judge that reader; long exchanges of dialogue, further demonstrations of how finely tuned McCarthy's ear is, eventually become demonstrations of attitude. As in the fiction of the South generally, laughter is generally accompanied by cruelty—to animals or persons—and pain. But one of the most hilarious passages one might have read anywhere in recent years is surely the section of *Suttree* in which the character Harrogate is introduced. A walking actualization of all our cliches about simple and naive country boys, Harrogate has a secret passion, indulged in the dark of night, that gets him sent to prison: he fornicates with watermelons. It is as if there is no end to the deviltry a clouded human imagination can invent for itself; McCarthy's novels accomplish the non-theological proof of the existence of what once would have been called Original Sin. His characters are wandering harrowers of a present "terrestrial hell"; as the ending of *Suttree* has it,

> Somewhere in the gray wood by the river is the huntsman and in the brooming corn and in the castellated press of cities. His work lies all wheres and his hounds tire not. I have seen them in a dream, slaverous and wild and their eyes crazed with ravening for souls in this world. Fly them.

Thus ending echoes Prologue; the hunter is within the gates.

By avoiding the space-wasting device of plot summary, this essay, it is hoped, may pique the curiosity of readers heretofore unfamiliar with Cormac McCarthy's fiction. By concentrating on the salient features of his style, however, and by attempting to summarize the categories of character and event encountered in that fiction, it may have left the impression that McCarthy is a compiler of horrors merely, an indiscriminate creator of cheap shock effects. Nothing, I feel, could be further from the truth. Nor by this time should it still be possible to dismiss his verbal ingenuity as mere posturing, or as some last gasp of Southern decadence extinguishing itself even as it blazes wildly. Cormac McCarthy may have certain features in common with the early Joyce Carol Oates, the early John Hawkes; yet he is still his own man entirely, indebted neither to such writers as these nor to the shade of William Faulkner, with which we began. "I never worried about the influence of *any* good writer," he has recently written me. "More the better, to my way of thinking."

"The style comes *out* of the place, material, characters, etc." he continues in the same letter, referring to the differences between *Suttree* and the rural novels (his next book is "about Americans in northern Mexico in 1849, which will be a different style again"). "The free-floating anxiety that provides *ambiance* in some of my books is something I have found in the world and so I put it in," he concludes, understandably reluctant to discuss further "the confrontation of evil" in his works (because "then I'd be an essayist, and I aint"). One can hardly blame him: the novels speak eloquently for themselves, and ultimately the reader must go to them, or return there, and accompany this splendid prophet further into darkness. (pp. 10-11)

> *John Ditsky, "Further into Darkness: The Novels of Cormac McCarthy," in* The Hollins Critic, *Vol. XVIII, No. 2, April, 1981, pp. 1-11.*

VEREEN M. BELL

Cormac McCarthy's novels are as innocent of theme and of ethical reference as they are of plot. On the other hand, each of them constitutes a densely created world as authentic and persuasive as any that there is in fiction. The worlds are convincing not because the people in them do normal and recognizable things, or represent us metaphorically, or even inhabit identifiable time and space, but because McCarthy compels us to believe in them through the traditional means of invention, command of language, and narrative art. To enter those worlds and move around in them effectively we are required to surrender all Cartesian predispositions and rediscover some primal state of consciousness prior to its becoming identified with thinking only. There is a powerful pressure of meaning in McCarthy's novels, but the experience of significance does not translate into communicable abstractions of significance. In McCarthy's world, existence seems both to precede and preclude essence, and it paradoxically derives its importance from this fact alone. The vivid facticity of his novels consumes conventional formulae as a black hole consumes light. He is Walker Percy turned inside out—intuitive, unideological, oblivious to teleological fashions, indifferent if not hostile to the social order, wholly absorbed in the strange heterocosm of his own making. Ethical categories do not rule in this environment, or even pertain: moral considerations seem not to affect outcomes; action and event seem determined wholly by capricious and incomprehensible fates. His stories are lurid and simple; they seem oddly like paradigms without reference and are all the more compelling because of that, since the matter of the paradigm does not lose its particularity in abstraction. The characters—without utilitarian responsibilities to well-made plots and unrelated to our bourgeois better natures—are real precisely to the degree that they resist symbolization. (pp. 31-2)

The main characters of McCarthy's four novels, because of their rural isolation and poverty, or because they have chosen isolation and poverty, live a daily hermeneutic adventure, their simple objectives leading them through mystifying disclosures of meaning with which they become continuous. They exist in isolated pockets of experience, intersect with each other briefly, become involved in, or remain auditors of, baroque, wonderful stories of human ingenuity and hardheadedness or of grotesque cruelty. By this strategy human life is revealed through anecdote and incident rather than through thematic patterns, in particulars rather than through types. Rinthy Holm in *Outer Dark* is a prototype of the character who knows things raw, "unshaped by the constructions of a mind obsessed with form." We do not know where she and her brother, Culla, live when the novel opens; we know virtually nothing about her parents, and neither does she. The two of them inhabit an austere, rural void. When Culla, leaving her for a brief period, tells her not to take strangers in, she replies, "They ain't a soul in this world but what is a stranger to me." When she sets out in search of her newborn child, which Culla, its father, has left to die in the woods, she doesn't know whether she is headed toward town or away from it because she's never been there. When she is asked by a suspicious farmer whether she hasn't run off from somewhere she says, "No . . . I ain't even got nowheres to run off from." She says to a doctor later, "I don't live nowhere no more. . . . I never did much. I just go around huntin my chap." Hunting her "chap" entails hunting a malicious tinker who has in fact found and taken the abandoned baby. But she has never seen the tinker and he has never seen her, and she does not even know, until a storekeeper tells her, that there is "more than one kind." She has no reason to choose one road over another since the tinker could be anywhere. Her quest proceeds in a vacuum, intermittently filled by the sympathetic rural people who help her out but seem somehow, though they have homes and families, no less wandering in space than she. She is shrewd and strong and humorous, but she is virtually without thoughts, driven on and sustained by the simple meaning that she makes. She remains unaware of the appalling facts which transpire in the novel's parallel narrative. In that opposing narrative an evil surrealism prevails, the dark inversion of Rinthy's simpleminded, maternalistic grace. Farmers and towns-people are gratuitously murdered, found hung from trees; corpses are dug up from their fresh graves and robbed of their clothes. All of this is phlegmatically perpetrated by three lawless, sadistic nightriders. The last of the victims are the tinker and Rinthy and Culla's child, whose throat the bearded leader slits, before Culla's eyes, as dispassionately as if he were lighting a pipe.

In the beginning of **Outer Dark** Culla has had a strange dream of a prophet who promises cures to all the diseased, lame, and blinded assembly of "human ruin" who attend him, once the sun has gone into and through an eclipse. But in the dream the sun goes into eclipse and does not return, and the crowd waits restlessly in the cold darkness for the promise to be fulfilled. Finally the crowd grows mutinous and turns not upon the prophet but the dreamer, who himself has asked to be cured, and the dreamer is unable to hide, even in the darkness. The dream is a parable of the promise of life— that we may be cured—and the perverse issue of that promise in misery and deprivation. The dreamer is set upon as if he were God, whose broken covenant is grotesquely inverted by those who, rejected, reject him and in doing so make their own darkness. Rinthy represents a fragile human beauty—a promise of sorts—which is merely parallel to the ugliness and inhumanity which prevail elsewhere; this harsh contrast underscores the novel's pervasive concern with the mystifying discontinuities of experience.

> When they had done in the kitchen she followed the woman down the passageway at the rear of the house, the woman holding the lamp before them and so out into the cool night air and across the boardfloored dogtrot, the door falling to behind them and the woman opening the next one and entering, her close behind, a whippoorwill calling from nearby for just as long as they passed through

the open and hushing instantly with the door's closing.

> She opened the door and the night air came upon them again sweetly through the warm reek of the room, the whippoorwill calling more distant, the door closing and the woman's steps fading across the dogtrot and the bird once again more faintly, or perhaps another bird, beyond the warped and waney boards and thin yellow flame that kept her from the night.

> The whippoorwill had stopped and she bore with her now in frenzied colliding orbits about the lamp chimney a horde of moths and night insects.

> She put the lamp on the shelf and sat on the bed. It was a shuck tick and collapsed slowly beneath her with a dry brittle sound and a breath of stale dust. She turned down the lamp and removed her dress and hung it over the brass bedpost. Then she unrolled the shift and put it on and crawled into the bed. . . . When they were all turned in they lay in the hot silence and listened to one another breathing. She turned carefully on her rattling pallet. She listened for a bird or for a cricket. Something she might know in all that dark.

Rinthy is not threatened here. She, in fact, has been taken in by responsive, if laconic, strangers. Nevertheless, the five pages that it takes to get Rinthy from washing up to bed are dense with alternating signals of strangeness, uncertainty, and reassurance. The command of the nuances of speech and narrative rhythm, of sounds and of visible objects, and even of silence, is unfaltering. The un-lurid, almost pastoral occasion is a subtle microcosm, and the whole of the novel is the sum of such occasions. Each episode, the novel as a whole, and the texture of the prose itself express repeatedly a sense of the interwoven beauty and terror of life which is the unassuming beginning and end of McCarthy's vision. What meaning there is remains inseparable from the sensation of experience.

Risking portentousness, one might characterize McCarthy's nihilism as not simply ambiguous but dialectical. There is Rinthy on the one hand, and the evil Magi on the other, the whippoorwill's song and the silence when it ceases, her dreamed child and the real one. There is Lester Ballard's helpless loneliness and hunger for love and the remains of the victims of it, "covered with adipocere, a pale gray cheesy mold common to corpses in damp places, and scallops of light fungus [growing] along them as they do on logs rotting in the forest"; the gothic element in McCarthy refers us to what we contrive to avert our senses from in normal life). During one idle journey along the river [in **Suttree**], Cornelius Suttree witnesses at one point a peaceful baptism ceremony—"total nursin" one of the participants calls it—and hears talk of being saved; at another point he remembers from his own childhood being instructed in killing, near the same spot, by an old turtle hunter and watching a turtle's skull being blown away "in a cloud of brainpulp and bonemeal": "the wrinkled empty skin hung from the neck like a torn sock." At the end of the novel, as Suttree hitchhikes out of Knoxville, he is approached and offered a dipper of cold water by a boy who is carrying water for a road-construction crew (they are building the new expressway): "Suttree could see the water beading coldly on the tin and running in tiny rivulets and drops that steamed on the road where they fell"; he sees himself for an instant in the blue of the child's eyes. Then moments later, after he has been picked up, he looks back and the child is gone. In his place has come an "enormous lank hound . . . sniffing at the spot where Suttree had stood" and he recalls the hounds of the huntsman of one of his feverish dreams, "slaverous and wild and their eyes crazed with ravening for souls in this world." Such juxtapositions are calculated, but they are suggestive rather than schematic. Their disturbing effect is condensed in a story told to Suttree by an old railroad man. Back in the days when he had "used to hobo a right smart" he had been passing through the mountains in Colorado in a slatsided boxcar crouched in a corner against the winter wind. But the car catches fire from a match he has flipped away, and when he is unable to stamp out the flames he leaps from the ascending train into a snowbank; "and what I'm going to tell you you'll think peculiar but it's the god's truth. That was in nineteen and thirty-one and if I live to be a hunnerd year old I don't think I'll ever see anything as pretty as that train on fire going up that mountain and around the bend and them flames lightin up the snow and the trees and the night." This could not seem very peculiar to Suttree, since it is the minimal point of his experience that we dwell inescapably in paradox and should learn to be willing to do so, since things could be a lot worse.

The clear, good water that recurs in the novels is a simple representation of what is desired of the world but is a provisional image only, not a symbol of redemption. When Gene Harrogate, Suttree's hilarious young neighbor, is rescued by Suttree after days of being trapped under debris and sewage in a vast cave under the city, his lunatic plan to blast his way through the foundation of a bank disastrously thwarted, he says first of all, "I hate for anybody to see me like this" and then, "I'd give ten dollars for a glass of icewater. . . . cash money"— thus comically uttering a serious refrain, the story of anyone's life in McCarthy's world. One of the mysteriously affecting moments in **Outer Dark** comes when Rinthy and the farm family that has taken her in stop along the hot road to town to drink from a spring. "That's fine water, the man said. Fine a water as they is in this country. She took the cup from him and dipped it into the dark pool, raised it clear and drank. It was sweet and very cold." Such images and episodes rhyme with each other meaningfully. They also ground and reinforce episodes of greater apparent import. One such is Suttree's wholesomely erotic interlude with the young daughter in a family of mussel-shell gatherers which ends when she is killed beneath a landslide of slate. The small moments are subtly foregrounded and achieve significance because they form a whole with the otherwise dominating spirit in the novels of violence and perversity. The vague dialectic is one point; its irresolution is the other.

In this context something grander Yeats wrote comes to mind: "The human soul would not be conscious were it not suspended between contraries, the greater the contrast the more intense the consciousness." In McCarthy's novels intensity of consciousness is not that of any given character. His technique is to represent characters who are strikingly devoid of consciousness, insofar as we are permitted to see. The intensity of consciousness is the novelist's—or that of the novel itself—and then ours as we are compelled to cross over from our world into his. His daring range of styles is essential to this effect. On the other hand, all of McCarthy's novels are unusual for the high degree of unassimilated raw material they accommodate. His world stands forth vividly. His scrupulous reproduction of detail (reflected in the precision of his language), his casual command of the right names for things—for parts of things, for aspects of various processes, and how things get done—his respect for the taxonomic specificness of the natural world, are like Joyce's in that they give his work a deep cohesion that mere shape and plot cannot. And this method has its point, too—that the raw materiality of the world is both charismatic and overpowering: the ego is as fragile and as transient, and perhaps as illusory, as any imagined form.

The negotiations between the ego and the contrary world are a main issue in **Suttree,** since for its protagonist the nature of identity is a primary, consuming mystery. It is, however, through his friend Harrogate that the point is most affectingly conducted. Known also as country mouse and city rat and—for good reason—as the moonlight melonmounter, Harrogate is oblivious to such morbid distractions as ontological insecurity. He is a resourceful survivor for whom poverty is an exhilarating game. Yet when he is arrested finally, trying to rob a store, and is sent to the state penitentiary, he is made by McCarthy, in a passage of remarkable originality and insight, to seem virtually to disappear. On the train to Brushy Mountain Prison Harrogate is without thoughts; he merely watches from his window, sees things as they pass: a cornfield and the dark earth between dead stalks; flocks of nameless birds; winter trees against a winter sky; a woman tossing a dishpan of water into the yard and wiping her hands on her apron; a little store at a crossing; a row of lighted henhouses; a lighted midnight cafe. Then, abruptly, as the train moves into the dark rainy country, the windows become tearstained, black mirrors: "and the city rat could see his pinched face watching him back from the cold glass, out there racing among the wires and the bitter trees, and he closed his eyes." To think of Harrogate dispersed into the world and then to remember him free, contriving his endless, baroque schemes, is to perceive the real and metaphorical horror of prison life, of passivity and inaction, and to consider how it is that schemes and scheming hold the world at bay. This long, saddening account of Harrogate's journey has begun with the observation—his or the narrator's: "It is true that the world is wide." The dreadful reality within the cliché—that we are not the world nor the world us—would not be likely to occur to Harrogate as a thought, but it has entered his mind, and we experience it his way.

Suttree himself is an educated and reflective character, the anthithesis of freewheeling Harrogate, and he is paralyzingly aware of everything that Harrogate's industry and simplicity shield him from: the true horror of death; the sure corruption and end of all friends, all love, all singular, cherishable things; the impersonal relentlessness of time; the cruel absence of God from the world. He is obsessed also with the arbitrariness of identity, of how even that minimal coherence erodes when reassuring reflectors or the conventions of social roles or homes and families fail. (He is haunted by doppelgängers, especially that of a twin brother who died at birth.) Living on the river off of his trotlines seems to be saturation therapy for him, a way of confronting head-on and dealing with the chaos and violence that he both identifies with and fears, a choice to endure authentically at the risk of both his selfhood and sanity. Insofar as McCarthy's vision and technique allow for anything like an epiphany, a small one seems to issue from Suttree's experience when he irreverently tells the priest who has come to attend his death (Suttree is a genuinely lapsed Catholic, not a fake Burgessite one): "I learned that there is one Suttree and one Suttree only." This means of course that there is only one Suttree lifespan, complete in itself; but it also appears to signify not a realization about identity but a choice—that *a* Suttree of the many possible in a world of anti-form must be made to be. In its minimal way, this is also an affirmation. Not long before his grisly contest with typhoid fever and its accompanying allegorical derangement, Suttree has himself attended the death of the old ragpicker who is the novel's oracular voice of nihilism's despair, cursing life and God, and himself as well (he has tried to contract with Suttree to be soaked in coaloil and burnt on the spot when he dies). Looking upon his body Suttree is moved by his own residual existential stamina to think about him for the first time and to reject him. "You have no right to represent people this way, he said. A man is all men. You have no right to your wretchedness." This intellectual gesture implies a tenuous hold upon purpose and it seems to be a stage in the same subterranean process by which becoming one Suttree becomes a rational goal. It is a product of experience rather than naive faith, since for all the atrocity and deformity, alienation, bone-deep physical pain, and violent death Suttree witnesses and suffers, his various undejected friends have borne him care and have embodied for him a heartening, hell-raising stoicism. So the as yet inchoate one Suttree is fully conscious of the two symbolic acts at the end, drinking the water and fleeing the hounds. Wrenchingly conflicted as this amazing world of McCarthy's is, from which logos has been borne away, even an illusory choice, an illusory transcendence gets one through to the next place in one's life where something bizarre or exhilarating or moving—worth surviving for—obscurely waits. In Cormac McCarthy's novels, adjusting a notion of the self to an understanding of the nature of the world is a baffling and precarious enterprise, since it is the essence of that world, in all the novels, that form and meaning refuse to coincide. Experience, meanwhile, continues to insinuate questions while supplying no answers, leaving the articulate and the inarticulate alike fatefully free. (pp. 35-41)

> *Vereen M. Bell, "The Ambiguous Nihilism of Cormac McCarthy," in* The Southern Literary Journal, *Vol. XV, No. 2, Spring, 1983, pp. 31-41.*

CARYN JAMES

Blood Meridian comes at the reader like a slap in the face, an affront that asks us to endure a vision of the Old West full of charred human skulls, blood-soaked scalps, a tree hung with the bodies of dead infants. But while Cormac McCarthy's fifth novel is hard to get through, it is harder to ignore. Any page of his work reveals his originality, a passionate voice given equally to ugliness and lyricism. Over the past 20 years the brutality of his subjects may have kept readers away, but the power of his writing has earned high critical repute. . . .

This latest book is his most important, for it puts in perspective the Faulknerian language and unprovoked violence running through the previous works, which were often viewed as exercises in style or studies of evil. *Blood Meridian* makes it clear that all along Mr. McCarthy has asked us to witness evil not in order to understand it but to affirm its inexplicable reality; his elaborate language invents a world hinged between the real and surreal, jolting us out of complacency.

Loosely based on historical events, the novel follows a fictitious 14-year-old called only "the kid"—born in 1833, exactly 100 years before the author—as he drifts through the Southwest. He soon joins an outlaw band of Indian hunters who have been hired by a Mexican governor to return Apache scalps at $100 apiece. These misfits—including an ex-priest, a man with initials tattooed on his forehead and a mysterious, erudite judge named Holden—have a taste for blood and death that Mr. McCarthy seems to revel in.

Grotesque descriptions are alleviated by scenes that might have come off a movie screen. Indians pass through the novel like extras in a Fellini film. . . .

The horrifying details stick in our minds, however, while the surreal elements melt away. That imbalance is a problem, for Mr. McCarthy's emphasis is not on the violent set pieces but on the characters' reactions to them. The kid recedes into the background as the judge comes forward, in scene after scene sounding the novel's major themes and hinting at the author's strategy. Half-naked, the judge sits among the others by the fire "like an icon" and pontificates. One who observed a conflict between two enemies "expressed the very nature of the witness and . . . was no third thing but rather the prime, for what could be said to occur unobserved?" Pointing to the surrounding Indian ruins he announces, "Here are the dead fathers" against whom their descendants define themselves.

The kid and the judge are our own dead fathers, whom Mr. McCarthy resurrects for us to witness. He distances us not only from the historical past, not only from our cowboy-and-Indian images of it, but also from revisionist theories that make white men the villains and Indians the victims. All men are unremittingly bloodthirsty here, poised at a peak of violence, the "meridian" from which their civilization will quickly fall. War is a civilized ritual beyond morality for the judge, but not for Mr. McCarthy, who positions his readers to evaluate the characters' moral and philosophical stances. The kid frequently responds to the judge's grandiose speeches by saying, "You're crazy"—a notion so plausible that it effectively undermines the judge's authority.

Mr. McCarthy carefully builds this dialectic only to let us down with a stylistically dazzling but facile conclusion. Years later, in a saloon where a bear dances on stage, the kid encounters the judge, who calls himself a "true dancer" of history, one who recognizes "the sanctity of blood." There is a hint that he kills the kid. Last seen as a towering figure on stage, the judge is "naked, dancing . . . He says that he will never die."

He is denied the last word, though. Mr. McCarthy's half-page epilogue presents a man crossing the plain making holes in the ground, blindly followed by other men who search for meaning in this pattern of holes. The judge's enigmatic dance and the long ordeal of the novel's violence demand more than this easy ambiguity. There are, of course, no answers to the life-and-death issues Mr. McCarthy raises, but there are more rigorous, coherent ways to frame the questions.

> *Caryn James, "Is Everybody Dead around Here?" in* The New York Times Book Review, *April 28, 1985, p. 31.*

TERENCE MORAN

[*Blood Meridian; or, The Evening Redness in the West*] is about cowboys and Indians. It tells the gruesome tale of a nameless drifter, introduced as "the kid," who heads west to Texas in the year 1847 when he is 14 years old. He falls in with bands of marauders, witnesses an immense amount of slaughter, becomes a dazed and psychopathic killer, survives a few massacres, and dies horribly in an outhouse. *Red River* this ain't. The kid's story parodies our popular Westerns; John Wayne's rugged individualism grows here into a crazed licentiousness, and the challenge of starting society anew, epitomized by the well-scrubbed little community in *Shane,* is transformed into the rootless quest for blood, money, loot, and women.

The kid himself acts out nightmarish possibilities of the American dream. He is no buckskinned and baby-faced Alan Ladd, but a monster, a panhandle Caliban. He is unkempt, uncared for, stupid, and mean: "He can neither read nor write and in him broods already a taste for mindless violence." The American West that the kid travels through is both beautiful and hellish, at times a frontier full of promise, at times a stark terrain offering only empty vistas and blind calamity.

McCarthy's landscape is his real protagonist, looming over the kid's story like some perverse deity or idiot narrator, turning horrible and benign in dark mimicry of the trail of destruction that the kid and his companions ride. The wild country is vividly brought to life in McCarthy's highly wrought prose. . . . (p. 37)

Blood Meridian is full of evocative passages. . . . Unfortunately, they're surrounded by the rest of the novel, which is tedious and contrived. There are hundreds of brutal killings in this book. Dying men are sodomized, babies are strung up through their mouths and tied to trees, a tame dancing bear is shot full of holes and bleeds to death in the arms of its little girl keeper. Everyone the kid meets is either a killer, a victim, or a pervert. Everywhere he goes turns into a scene of horrible massacre or sickening degeneracy. None of this grotesquerie earns its place in the landscape, or in the kid's story.

McCarthy, who is a serious and accomplished novelist, has failed in *Blood Meridian* to retell a simple Western in his haunting, original voice. In his previous novels, he wrote authentic high Southern gothic tales, set in the backwoods of the hill country. Although true to their period and landscape, they were imbued with an edginess, a kind of hallucinogenic despair, that felt wholly contemporary.

Outer Dark (1968) and *Child of God* (1973), for example, are chilling and absorbing stories steeped in violence and depravity. But the crimes McCarthy details there grow uncannily, frighteningly out of the closely observed lives of his characters and their surroundings. He writes spare prose rich in the slightly archaic vocabulary of his Appalachian settings, and in his dialogue faithfully recreates the region's language, the cadences and textures of the country's rural poor. McCarthy has lived most of his life outside of Knoxville, Tennessee, and knows the hills and hollows of the mountain country intimately; he also knows the lunatic, hidden places in the hearts and minds of some of the people who live there.

But in *Blood Meridian* he has nearly abandoned these strengths to try his hand at myth and metaphysics. The grim and patient character development, the crisp narration of the earlier novels are junked; what's left is hyperbolic violence, strained surrealism, and pseudo-philosophic palaver, spewed forth from the mouth of the bizarre Judge Holden. . . . (pp. 37-8)

Blood Meridian is McCarthy's grand attempt to extend and deepen his exploration of the beastly potential inherent in the American character, in the vastness of the American continent. But his sharp sensibility for the random destruction the country's "outlaws" can wreak on the society that's passed them by, for the rootlessness and alienation that can turn in a twisted mind into a murderous liberty—this sensibility convinces only when it is acutely dramatized in the lives of small characters and in the empty concreteness of their country.

But in *Blood Meridian,* McCarthy ends up merely toying with his language and ideas. We are neither afraid to look at what he sees, nor moved to think about his vision of America. This novel, despite its chronicling of appalling horros and its straining for apocalyptic effects, is boring. McCarthy should go home, and take another, closer look. He'll find the real devil soon enough there. (p. 38)

Terence Moran, "The Wired West," *in* The New Republic, *Vol. 192, No. 18, May 6, 1985, pp. 37-8.*

Mbongeni Ngema

1955-

South African dramatist and actor.

In his plays, Ngema confronts his country's racial policy of apartheid. Based on actual events and blending such theatrical forms as mime, dance, comedy, and music, Ngema's works generate forceful political statements. Originally an actor and musician in Durban, South Africa, Ngema formed the Committed Artists—a politically involved acting troupe—in response to the murder of activist Msizi Dube in 1983. This company is dedicated to eliminating social inequality by exploring the racial and moral issues facing contemporary South Africa. Critics often express surprise at the Committed Artists' use of humor to convey grave themes, but Ngema explained: "Our oppressors have deprived us of everything but our joy."

Ngema's first play, *Woza Albert!* (1981), was written in collaboration with Percy Mtwa, a fellow South African dramatist and actor. A satirical fantasy set in South Africa concerning the second coming of Jesus Christ, *Woza Albert!* depicts the unsuccessful attempts of the Afrikaaner government to use the Savior for its own political purposes. Although Christ is sentenced to solitary confinement on Robben Island, a high-security penitentiary for black political prisoners, he appears in a graveyard at the play's end to resurrect such black resistance leaders as Albert Luthuli and Stephen Biko. Ngema's next production, *Asinamali!* (1983), was written in honor of Msizi Dube, the black South African who led protest marches with the cry "Asinamali!"—which translates as "We have no money!"—in response to a rent increase in the black township of Lamontville. Upon the debut of *Asinamali!* in South Africa, black supporters of apartheid raided the theater and killed the play's promoter, and one original cast member linked to Dube's protests was arrested. Set in Johannesburg's Leeukop Prison, *Asinamali!* revolves around five black men who reenact the various incidents that led to their arrests. Dressed in khaki and their heads shaved, the characters convey a sense of unity, yet their actions emphasize their uniqueness. In one acclaimed scene, the cast searches the theater for government informers and interrogates an audience member in the manner of South African police. The play ends with a rapid recitation of the names of "the wasted people," those imprisoned or killed as a result of apartheid. Although several critics considered the production polemical, its reception was generally positive, and Mark Abley declared *Asinamali!* "remarkable for its rough and buoyant resilience, its joyful defiance of self-pity."

Ngema's recent production, *Sarafina!* (1987), is based on the Soweto township uprising of 1976, in which 200,000 schoolchildren rejected their government's decree that they learn the Afrikaans language. The ensuing riot resulted in the shooting deaths of hundreds of children, as well as a student boycott of the language that black South Africans consider a suppression of their native culture. Ngema's play celebrates the strength and spirit of South African youth by combining vibrant songs and dances with *Mbaqanga,* a form of music that originated in the country's black townships. Blending traditional Zulu rhythms with such influences as jazz and

reggae, *Mbaqanga* was described by Ngema as "the music of liberation." *Sarafina!* centers upon the attempts of a black high school class to present a concert illustrating their country's lamentable history. Following numerous scenes that include protests, police raids, school pranks, and funerals, the play concludes with the class's joyous concert. Critics praised the play's innovative style, and Clive Barnes observed: "[*Sarafina!*] celebrates man, while dramatizing man's injustice." The American production of the musical is examined in an acclaimed film documentary, *Voices of Sarafina!* (1988).

FRANK RICH

[In *Asinamali!*], five black men sing, dance and shout unceasingly for 90 frenetic minutes—almost as if they feared that to stand still might be to surrender or to die. And that may well be the overriding point of this stunningly performed tapestry of satire, tragedy and reportage from the land of apartheid. What can people do when denied their rights, their dignity, their families, their lives? The men of *Asinamali!* turn not only their harsh experience but also their voices and bodies, their every sound and gesture, into protest art. In this kinetic theatrical event, each rapid-fire breath is a volley of defiance against the repressive state. . . .

[*Asinamali!*] takes its title from a Zulu slogan, meaning "We have no money!," that was the rallying cry of a 1983 rent strike in Lamontville township. The form of the work is simple: The five performers portray prisoners in a South African jail who successively act out the travails that led to their incarceration. The stories told will come as no surprise to anyone remotely familiar with the society under examination. The men of *Asinamali!* have been variously victimized by racist laws, unemployment, forced separation from their families, violent police tactics and a seeming infinity of daily humiliations. . . .

What makes *Asinamali!* special is less the sadly familiar cases it has to recount than the way in which it presents them. Mbongeni Ngema, the author and director, hasn't conceived this work as a living newspaper or any other form of documentary agit-prop drama, but as full-throttle theater. *Asinamali!* is not something one could see on the evening news—even if the South African Government didn't censor the news. Although the world dramatized in this work is real, Mr. Ngema's staging eschews realism for a tightly choreographed melding of indigenous ritual, storytelling and musical theater that goes well beyond *Woza Albert!*, the glancingly similar earlier piece on which he collaborated.

In *Asinamali!*, the cast members, all bald and wearing identical khaki prison costumes, seem to become a single vibrating organism. To call the feat ensemble acting doesn't quite do it justice. Even as the men spin out their individual tales on the undecorated stage, they remain visually connected—a phalanx of humanity that contracts or expands or twists or breaks like a rubber band, as a given scene demands. The oral fabric matches the visual one. Conventional dialogue flows into choral recitations, a cappella songs and sound effects that can alternately suggest the hubbub of contemporary black townships, the characters' deepest cultural roots and the desolate wilderness of the itinerant worker's road.

Some of the images and sequences are unusually upsetting. By miming the act of peering through a cell door's high peephole, the actors evoke the claustrophobia of imprisonment—a feeling that is further heightened when they huddle for warmth while sleeping, their bodies entangled like a pile of rags. In one of several incidents that emphasize the perverse sexual quotient of master-slave relationships, the men undergo an official examination for venereal disease that is every bit the symbolic castration the authorities intend it to be. One is also aware throughout *Asinamali!* that the dancing, however strenuous, has a slightly contorted quality: The splayed limbs and hands clearly belong to men who are shackled, whether in jail or not.

Not all of the piece is at the same imaginative level. Some of the incantatory repetitions are tiresome. A contrived scene in which the cast enters the auditorium to search for "informers" among the audience does not, as intended, show us what it must be like to live among Judases in black South Africa; we're reminded instead of how experimental theater troupes used to whip up orgies of liberal guilt among New York theater-goers in the 1960's. American viewers must also be warned that *Asinamali!* refuses to sacrifice any authenticity for the sake of clarity. Not for nothing are there helpful program notes.

The commitment and intensity of the performance carry one past the troughs, and so, of course, does the compelling, unending history that is retold. It says much about the particular character of this effort that its moving climax is not so much the ritualistic final roll call of famous dissident martyrs ("the wasted people") but a slightly earlier, more typical passage in which the cast recalls the specific protest that led to the creation of the play. In that scene, the men turn the slogan "Asinamali!" into an acrobatic and musical expression of freedom—yet, as soon as they do, the defiant word dies on their lips, their jubilant postures sag, and they become prisoners again. High as *Asinamali!* flies as political theater, it never loses touch with the earthly courage and suffering that gave it birth.

Frank Rich, "South Africa's 'Asinamali!'," *in* The New York Times, *September 12, 1986, p. C3.*

VARIETY

The South African agony is dramatized with throbbing immediacy in *Asinamali!* . . . This dramatic collage by Mbongeni Ngema harnesses the theater's unique power to humanize actuality, and transforms the audience into a collective witness of poor blacks' anguish in an inequitable society.

At the same time *Asinamali!* is a joyous expression of human individuality and the life force that oppression can't extinguish. Playwright Ngema, co-author of *Woza Albert!*, which played the U.S. several years ago, has a sly fondness for low comedy which lightens what is essentially somber material.

Using techniques from the experimental theater and films, *Asinamali!* unfolds as a high-speed ensemble performance in which the actors make grippingly effective use of sound and unison movement to enhance a basic series of dramatic sketches about poor black prison inmates.

The narrative envelope is a rent strike organized by residents of a slum near Durban in 1983 which led to the rallying cry of "Asinamali" (we have no money) and ended in the government-backed murder of the strike's leader. Against that background, the five jailed men act out key events in their pre-prison lives. What emerges is a vivid impression of a fundamentally unjust society.

A kangaroo court trial, the brutality of the white prison guards, the squalor of life in a tiny cell, the discriminatory red tape designed to maintain blacks' economic inferiority, humiliation of a V.D. exam and the eventual rent riot which ended in bloodshed—these and other incidents are woven together in a rapid, seamless piece of "performance theater." . . .

In part because of the actors' unfamiliar accents and their rapid-fire delivery, some of the local factual details whiz by before the ear can assimilate them. But even though some of the issues have changed in South Africa (the passbook law has been repealed) the reality of outrageous injustice sadly remains current, and in fact has worsened.

Perhaps the most powerful moment in this potent piece comes when the characters seem to identify government informers in the audience and boil off the stage into the auditorium to directly confront their observers. It triggers a momentarily alarming release of adrenalin directly into one onlooker's heart, and reminds that this show isn't fiction but very real.

Humm, in a review of "Asinamali!," in Variety, *September 17, 1986, p. 112.*

JACK KROLL

[*Asinamali!* is] a stunning work written and directed by 30-year-old Mbongeni Ngema, one of the young black dramatists who are creating a powerful indigenous black South African theater movement. Not a "play" in any conventional sense, *Asinamali!* is performed by five black actors playing prisoners in a South African jail. In their prison khakis, their heads shaved, moving with galvanic precision from speech to song to dance, these five men become a human kaleidoscope evoking the collective destiny of blacks under the Kafkaesque madness of South African apartheid.

With tragic starkness we are told that one man killed his girl-friend after she had strangled their child. With farcical absurdity another man is whirled through the bureaucratic maze of the infamous pass system. With ribald irony one prisoner describes his liaison with his white boss's wife—whose child, hearing an outburst of ecstatic Zulu in the house, is reassured by her mother that it's only Radio Zulu. Still another prisoner was a cohort of Bro Tony, the master pickpocket who "understood the human body like Dr. Christiaan Barnard." In scenes like strokes of lightning we see the men processed from railroading trials to humiliating VD examinations. The pivotal event is a 1983 mass strike against government-imposed rent increases . . . that resulted in the murder of activist Msizi Dube, one of the "wasted people" whose names are evoked by the actors in an outburst of angry determination.

The show's impact is marred by an excursion into the audience that is ill advised to begin with and pulls its punches in the bargain. But this is a shattering, sophisticated theater piece that is not propaganda but the distillation of a whole people's fatality, pride and power. That pride is not at all geared to the comfort of even the friendliest whites in South Africa or elsewhere.

Jack Kroll, "Cry the Beloved Country," in Newsweek, *Vol. CVIII, No. 12, September 22, 1986, p. 85.*

JOHN SIMON

Asinamali! is a cross between a folk play involving song and dance and a piece of agitprop street theater; indeed, the playwright's troupe, the Committed Players, is modeled on California's El Teatro Campesino. Five performers, who portray five inmates of a South African jail, tell, mime, sing, and dance their diverse but similarly grim stories. (p. 98)

Much of this show is effective in its very detachment, although it tends to be less informative and affecting than the newspaper and television coverage of these events. The use of Zulu chants and stylized dance movements is compelling until it becomes distracting when kept up extensively as background to the action at hand. The performers are deft and appealing (except when they run out into the auditorium to buttonhole and harangue the audience), and most of the scenes progress with judicious speed. The program states that the "primary artistic concern [of the Committed Artists] was the

revelation and ultimate eradication of racial and social inequality." True enough, I'm sure, except for that word "artistic." There is very little art in *Asinamali!;* mostly, it is good, rousing political agitation, kept sensibly in check by humor and disciplined performing. Art's concern is never *primarily* racial or social, but always artistic first and everything else afterward. This is not art.

Yet it might be almost too much to expect theatrical art at the present time, under the current conditions. I can well imagine, however, that even as it is, *Asinamali!* would be tremendously moving and invigorating when staged in South Africa, and it certainly drew standing ovations from the American spectators I saw it with. Still, I am a bit skeptical about such orgies of liberalism when the trouble depicted is a fire many doors away and you can prove your righteousness by merely standing up and applauding in a safe theater. As a document and a call for justice this is powerful stuff—almost cannot help being powerful. But neither its derivative dramatic form nor its simplistic language, neither its underdeveloped characterization nor its metaphysical blankness, can be particularly commended. . . .

Asinamali! is almost all ethics without aesthetics. If art goes in for moralizing before and above all else, it is lost as art; if art is divorced from even secondary moral values, it becomes dehumanized. One of the problems with much of modern art (painting, for example) is that it is "whatever your imagination tells you it is; if you think it's a spider, it's a spider." But if you don't, it's just as readily an octopus or a multinational corporation. Another problem is that it's too often content to peddle easy, unexamined uplift· moral, social, political, religious. The solution is to push aestheticism to the point where it becomes a moral choice, to question and refine morality to the point where it becomes aesthetic. . . . Playing to coteries and pandering to the masses are barren pursuits. Only by the clearest embodiment of private truths can idiosyncrasy become universal, and the one speak to and for the many. (p. 100)

John Simon, "Spiders, Aesthetic and Moral," in New York *Magazine, Vol. 19, No. 38, September 29, 1986, pp. 98, 100.*

MARK ABLEY

One critic has praised Mbongeni Ngema's play *Asinamali!* as "a kaleidoscope of impressions of life in the black South African townships, with breathtaking intensity and epic sweep." Another has called it "sidesplittingly funny and frightening." . . . [The drama] was written in 1983 in honor of the martyred black leader Msizi Dube, who had led protests against rent increases in the township of Lamontville. . . . [Audiences] will find that its political ferocity is matched by an acute sense of fun.

Although books and plays about black South Africans have often idealized their struggles, *Asinamali!*'s portrait of life in South Africa is unflinching. One of the prisoners in the play is a pickpocket who enjoys reminiscing about his thefts. "That's why the play is respected back home," suggested actor Bhoyi Ngema (brother of the writer-director). "*Asinamali!* doesn't censor itself." To the cast, such respect is even more important than the play's international success. . . .

Standing ovations have become routine, even though *Asinamali!* contains some unnerving scenes. At one point, all five actors leap off the stage to search for informers, briefly subjecting the audience to a taste of the fear that is part of daily life in black South Africa. Onstage, the cast members are almost frenetic; offstage, they are plainly exhausted. . . . Cast member Thami Cele explained: "Before the show, we all travel in spirit to South Africa. It's what the playwright told us. We must never forget where we come from. We treat the show with love."

For the performers, *Asinamali!* is not just a piece of theatre. It is also a mirror of their own lives in the crowded townships near Durban. The script grew out of workshops at the time of Dube's rent agitation; the actors told Mbongeni Ngema what they had witnessed in the streets. The performers include a former postal clerk, a former factory worker and a former miner, all of whom belong to the 30-member collective, Committed Artists. . . .

One of the original cast members, whom police linked with Dube's protests, is still in South Africa and currently appealing an eight-year prison sentence. Shortly before leaving their country eight months ago, the actors narrowly escaped murder at the hands of Zulu vigilantes, who hacked the tour's promoter to death and burnt a hall where a performance of *Asinamali!* had just ended. . . .

[Despite the threat of violence], the show remains remarkable for its rough and buoyant resilience, its joyful defiance of self-pity. "There's a saying in Zulu," says Thami Cele in a low, determined voice, "We laugh even though there is death."

Mark Abley, "Acting against Apartheid," in Maclean's Magazine, Vol. 99, No. 45, November 10, 1986, p. 79.

DUMA NDLOVU AND MBONGENI NGEMA [INTERVIEW WITH MARGARET A. NOVICKI AND AMEEN AKHALWAYA]

[*The following excerpt is taken from an interview with Mbongeni Ngema and Duma Ndlovu, co-producer of* Asinamali! *and executive director of* Woza Afrika!]

[Novicki and Akhalwaya]: *Can you tell us about your professional backgrounds that led you to bring the first black South African play to Broadway?*

[Ndlovu]: I worked as a journalist in South Africa for the *World* newspaper first, then for *Drum* and a few other black publications. I came to the U.S. in 1978 after I had left South Africa for political reasons. I have always regarded myself as a cultural nationalist, being a direct offspring of the black consciousness movement and belonging to the cultural wing of organizations like the South African Students Organization. . . . I came to the U.S. more interested in developing my cultural profile than my journalistic instincts.

What made it much easier was the fact that when I got to New York, I found that we had so much in common with the African-American experience. Culturally our expressions and interests were very similar. So I started getting involved with trying to increase the awareness of South African music because we've always believed that any form of South African culture or art is a voice against what is happening in South Africa.

We got an opportunity to bring Miriam Makeba to this country for the first time in seven to 10 years. We started a trend

of commemorating June 16 in this country every year, and also commemorating the death of Steve Biko, which gave us an opportunity to invite not only South African cultural artists like Hugh Masekela, Dollar Brand, and others to participate, but also to invite the larger African-American population. We worked with people like Nina Simone and other culturally conscious people.

In 1984, we got the chance to participate on a larger scale in theater when *Woza Albert!* came to the U.S. When I came to the U.S., *Woza Albert!* had already played here and there were a lot of write-ups about it. Then I went and saw the piece and I was astounded by the energy. I had been a fan of Gibson Kente and of radical black South African theater, but what I saw presented in *Woza Albert!* I identified as a new form of South African theater. . . .

[*Woza Albert!*] was both funny and serious. It was painful. And it was very highly skilled theatrically. So it was a new experience. You could go to a theater and laugh at seriousness and at pain, at the same time leave having been moved. So, we started talking with Mbongeni Ngema and Percy Mtwa, who were the co-creators of *Woza Albert!* . . . [We] got together with them and explained the mission we were embarking on—bringing quality theater to Harlem at affordable prices. (p. 36)

Mbongeni and I started a relationship over the phone between South Africa and here, and by the end of 1985, all the pieces were falling together. In early 1986, we collaborated in bringing *Asinamali!,* which premiered in Harlem. And it proved to be a much stronger play than *Woza Albert!* in the perception of the theater critics here, who thought it was the most astounding piece of work that they had ever seen.

[Ngema]: I started as a musician and then bit by bit, friends called me in to write music for their plays. And in time, I started falling in love with theater. A playwright friend called to ask me to help him with the songs in one of his plays, and then I fell in love with the part of the lead character in the play. When he was on stage, I would mimic him backstage making the other musicians laugh. And then one evening, the actor did not turn up and there was no one to take his part. In the townships, we don't have understudies—it was not in our budget, it's what we get at the door. The play had to go on, it was a performance in Zululand at a sugar cane hostel, where you would not cancel a performance when the people are sitting inside—those guys can be very rough! We had to do a performance. So I volunteered to do the part and half the time I would be backstage playing the guitar and then I would put down the guitar, go on stage, and do the part.

Then the playwright came to me and said, "Let's write a play together." We collaborated on a piece together and I was the lead actor in that piece, too. We became successful on a much smaller scale in the townships. Then, finally I wrote my own piece which I directed myself and wrote the music for. That's how it developed—I became an actor, then a writer and director.

All this happened between 1976-78. Then in 1979, I went to Johannesburg. I had decided that I had to know more about theater. I joined Gibson Kente because I noticed that he had some magic in his productions that I didn't have, and I wanted to find out how he did it. I joined the company and worked with Gibson for over two years, and then left him. That's when I met Percy Mtwa and we started collaborating on *Woza Albert!,* which became a phenomenal success from the time it first opened. And it went on and on for five years. Then I did *Asinamali!*

Can you tell us how you formed your theatrical group, "Committed Artists"?

Ngema: In 1982, when I was touring the West coast of the U.S., I met with a Mexican-American director, Luis Valdez, who has a company called El Teatro Campesino, theater for farm workers. They were interested in our style and they wanted us to come and do some workshops with them. We saw what they were doing which was very exciting. Then he told me the history of that company. They started with Mexican-American farm workers, who after working all day on plantations would stop their trucks at the junctions of the streets on the way home and perform a short play. If it became dark, they would use the other trucks as stage lights. And then audiences gathered.

This idea excited me and I started thinking about what is happening back home. There are a lot of people around Durban who were evicted and live in tents. And they have nothing to console their spirits. No churches, no schools, absolutely nothing. When I got back to South Africa, I was involved with a friend who was running community educational workshops around Durban in such places. And she said, "It would be interesting if you used your skill in helping these people." Then I said, maybe we should start a small group that would allow artists to help in such matters, maybe do benefit performances or have those people participate in our performances. I made a big advertisement and a lot of people came to a meeting—artists, actors, writers, poets, musicians. I explained my ideas. Everybody got excited and said, "What are we going to call it?" Because I kept saying we have to be committed to this, it ended up being "Committed Artists."

We did a lot of things—music, poetry, and dancing. And then I started writing a play about poverty because I had seen what was happening to those people. In the middle of my writing a play, a man in Lamontville, Msizi Dube, who was leading the people against rent increases, was killed. All of us then starting focusing on what was happening in Lamontville. More people were being killed, a funeral was giving birth to another funeral, as the police would come in and shoot more people. We had to forget for a while what was happening in our group and just concentrate on what was just happening in Lamontville. Then I said we should use what is happening here back in our workshop. I had a group of actors that I had started to train, people with no acting skills. I took five of them and said let's do a play about poverty which will also involve what is happening in Lamontville.

So Msizi Dube in **Asinamali!** *was an actual person.*

Ngema: Yes, he's an actual person who died. Most of the people mentioned in the play are real people—like the guy who says his friend was shot by policemen, he's a real person and that's how he died. He was very active in Lamontville township. So if the actors didn't read the lines and get the spirit right, I would say, "Let's go to a funeral in Lamontville, so that we experience running away from tear gas, how it is to be close to death" and bit by bit, they began to understand what I wanted. I didn't want anything more than the true spirit of the people in the play. I know how to deal with technique in terms of training the actors. I wanted technique as well as the truth.

So the actors in the play are not professional actors, but rather local people who got involved in your workshop.

Ngema: Yes. What was the key for me was a play that we could do for people in those tents but that could also be performed on a Broadway stage. It has to be so good technically and artistically that people would not go to see it because it's about politics, or about the poor, black people of South Africa. They should go and see it because it's good theatre. At the same time, it should be about the spirit of our people.

Was **Asinamali!** *written with the intention of performing on Broadway?*

Ngema: No. But I knew it was going to be a good play. I gave myself time to train the guys and I knew it was going to be successful. First of all, I wanted it to be celebrated by the people back home. But I wanted them to get the same kind of quality performance as the people on Broadway, because people in those tents never see good theater. And they can't afford to pay any money for theater.

We opened the play in Lamontville after the death of Msizi Dube. We were supposed to put on one performance for one night. We asked for a donation of one rand from the community to come and see the play. But there were so many people that we ended up doing three performances that night—one performance after the other. And the following night, and then for four days. It just became a people's play. The slogan "Asinamali!" [We have no money!] was Dube's slogan and everybody knew it. People said, "Ah, this is us!" And then on the fourth night, police moved in and arrested some of the actors. One of them came back but the other is doing an eight-year sentence right now. From there, "Committed Artists" started to grow. The success of **Asinamali!** in the U.S. last year made it possible for me to establish it as a real company. Now we've moved to Johannesburg. We've leased a very large building and we accommodate about 30 people in that building—artists from all over South Africa, musicians and actors.

How does the South African government respond to what is clearly political theater?

Ngema: It depends where you are and who you are. There is no logic in that government, for the mere fact that they can pass a law today and tomorrow amend it. They keep patching the holes. In our case, there has not been a direct approach except for when we performed this play in Cape Town, just before we came over here. They came down to censor a scene and they put on an age restriction. We called in our lawyers and finally we won the court case.

How did they censor a scene—they told you to take the scene out?

Ngema: Yes. So, that's as far as they came to us. I don't know how they operate.

Is it because you perform in the townships and too many blacks are involved that they take action? If you were to perform in "legitimate" theaters in the cities, like the Market Theatre, you would be less likely to face problems.

Ngema: Yes, if you perform in the townships, they say you are inciting people. But if you are in a theater in the city, they want to regard it as theater. They know that it's the same thing, but it's hard to define these lines. (pp. 36-8)

Is there a perceptible difference in the responses you have got-

ten to the play between white and black South Africans and white and black Americans?

Ngema: Black South Africans understand everything, so there is definitely a difference. But I think we've found a balance now. It's a matter of sometimes changing a line so that it makes sense to a certain audience. Duma comes to rehearsals and says, "I'm sure that line does not come across to Americans." Then we find a way which will be true to South Africans but also understandable to Americans.

Ndlovu: This would be the wrong play to answer your question in a proper way, because *Asinamali!* is a different piece of work, and I have been very shocked to find blacks and whites responding to it in the same way. In all the years that we have been working with culture, theater, and art, we found that blacks and whites do not react similarly to different pieces of work. There are differences in reactions, but in the case of *Asinamali!,* those differences are indistinct. The reason for that is because there is concentration on the artistic quality of the play, as well as the message. Whereas people go to see a South African play because of its strong political message, this is one play where even if you didn't care about the politics of South Africa, you can go and see five bodies on a stage responding like rubber to a director's command in a manner that even Brecht wouldn't be able to do. So whether you're black or white you are bound to react to the art on stage. (p. 38)

How do white South Africans react to [Asinamali's] political message?

Ndlovu: It's interesting. I remember one day we got four white Afrikaner women who came to the play. I made a special effort to be where I would be able to watch their reactions. And they were just as stunned as everybody else. Of course, there are parts of the play, like the judge who speaks in Afrikaans, which tickled their fancy, but I think they came out equally stunned by the piece. I want to believe that they were as moved as everybody else. And in South Africa, at the Market Theatre, a lot of whites came to see the play and had the same reaction. The white press in South Africa was very, very positive about the play. . . .

What are your plans from here?

Ngema: I've been working on another play for seven months, we've been rehearsing it in Johannesburg for seven months. Hugh Masekela and myself are writing the music. It's a big musical play, which involves 20 kids, from 16-year-olds to about 20 years of age, about schoolchildren in Soweto. It is called *Sarafina.*

Ndlovu: Where do we go from here? *Sarafina* is the next stop. . . . It will be the first South African musical with that intensity. There were others, but they weren't really of the townships. This is a musical with a difference. In terms of the political significance of *Sarafina,* it will be regarded as the first genuine black musical to come out of South Africa with a very strong political message. The next step is that we would like to see people being more and more aware of the situation inside South Africa in this country and all over the world. We want them to support the arts and culture. But if they just come and pay their money and go back home without taking the message, then our mission would not be fulfilled. (p. 39)

Duma Ndlovu and Mbongeni Ngema, in an inter-

view with Margaret A. Novicki and Ameen Akhalwaya, in Africa Report, *Vol. 32, No. 4, July-August, 1987, pp. 36-9.*

ROBERT PALMER

[*Sarafina!* features the] lilting sound of Mbaqanga, South Africa's distinctive black pop music. . . . Six musicians, looking sharp in pressed khaki uniforms, were churning out the music's joyous rhythms, while a seventh player . . . swayed back and forth, embroidering the beat with lightning-fast runs on his electric guitar. The music had a tropical sway, something like reggae but faster, with two trumpets punctuating the light but driving rhythms. The musicians were playing on a stage set behind a high fence topped with barbed wire.

On the other side of the fence, Mbongeni Ngema, a compact, intense young playwright, actor, director and musician from Durban, was taking a group of young South Africans through a complex dance routine. The cast of *Sarafina!,* a new musical from South Africa with songs by Mr. Ngema and Hugh Masekela, . . . was working hard. A visitor remarked that the scene had seemed tight and precise at a preview the night before. . . .

Mr. Ngema had been rehearsing his cast and musicians all day. But after taking only a minute to freshen up he was ready to talk about *Sarafina!* "I knew I wanted to do a show that would capture the sound of Mbaqanga," he said,

> and I started talking about it with Hugh Masekela back in 1984. I went around the compounds, the hostels where the gold miners live, asking about new musicians, because I didn't want to just get somebody from a known band. That's how I found Douglas Mnisi, the guitarist. He was living in the mining compounds, playing with some bands that people look at and say, 'Ah, how can you pay to go and see that kind of thing?' He came from the *real* underground. . . .

A conversation Mr. Ngema had with Winnie Mandela, wife of the imprisoned South African leader Nelson Mandela, convinced the playwright that his show should be about more than Mbaqanga. "We talked about the state of emergency in South Africa and the killing of the children in the townships," Mr. Ngema recalled,

> and we both remarked on the incredible resilience of the children, who are so positive in spite of everything. I decided the show had to celebrate the spirit of the students and the power of Mbaqanga, which I call the music of liberation. The name of the main character, Sarafina, is the title of a tune by Masekela. It's also the name of a lot of township girls.

Mr. Ngema was also able to draw on his own experiences for events in *Sarafina!* He was born in 1955 and grew up in several townships around Durban, where he completed high school and worked as a laborer and a guitarist. A job providing guitar music for plays led to his first acting role; he directed a play of his own in Durban before moving to Soweto in 1979. Two years later, he collaborated with Percy Mtwa and Barney Simon in writing *Woza Albert!,* a play that won international acclaim. After touring the United States with the play, he returned to South Africa and put together a new play, *Asinamali!,* and his own theater company, Committed Artists. (p. H5)

In 1986, after working on the music for *Sarafina!* with Mr. Masekela in London, Mr. Ngema returned to South Africa and set up auditions all over the country. "I wanted a company of 13," he said,

> but there was a tremendous response. So many parents wanted their children to be chosen, we were offering them a traveling school, a free education along with the musical and theatrical training. And there was so much talent! I finally ended up with 24 performers. The average age of the girls is 15, of the boys, 20.

> Committed Artists rented the top floor of an old hotel in Johannesburg and created a rehearsal space and offices, . . . and we lived there together for eight months—me, the kids and the seven musicians. The training covered everything from movement to singing in tune to theater classics. In South Africa, we don't have theaters in the townships, so when *Sarafina!* opened . . . in June 1987, most of the kids had never sat in a theater seat or encountered a live audience.

> In the townships, a police constable can come and close a show and arrest the cast. But if you do the same play in a city like Johannesburg, there you have newspapers, and especially if people identify the play as a play of the people, as they did with *Sarafina!,* you will most likely be left alone. But you never know.

Sarafina! follows a group of students through school days that include army incursions into classrooms, protests and bloody confrontations with the police, as well as games, pranks and lessons. "The student uprisings started in 1976," Mr. Ngema explained,

> when the government decreed that students should learn the Afrikaans language. The students felt the government wanted to train them be servants, and didn't want them to be able to communicate with the rest of the world, so there was an uprising, and many students were killed. The students have never accepted Afrikaans, and there have been riots year after year. Now they have the army in the schools, and policemen coming into the classrooms telling the teachers what they can and can't teach. So all of the incidents in the show were real incidents.

The lyrics to some of the songs reflect the political situation. Others are simply exhortations to dance. (pp. H5, H15)

> Robert Palmer, *"A Musical Born of South African Protest,"* in The New York Times, *October 25, 1987, pp. H5, H15.*

CLIVE BARNES

There is always an irony added to art when it comes out of suffering. . . .

[In *Sarafina!*], you will encounter perhaps the most joyous noise to be heard in New York City. . . .

It is [Mbaqanga], the jazzy folksy music of South African townships, and it combines elements as diverse as African drums, American jazz, and English hymns.

Most important of all, it is a music born, bred, and nurtured from suffering. It comes from South Africa's "days of anger,

the days of panic and fear." Days that have mounted up to lifetimes punctuated with tear-gas, fire, and death.

Song is a potent political protest, and can be an unanswerable instrument in revolutionary strategy. And *Sarafina!* sings and protests with a fervor born of oppression and immortal hope.

Its genesis—and yes, there is a certain biblical tone to the evening—has been much written about. The story has been told how the South African playwright, director, and musician, Mbongeni Ngema, got together with the emigre South Africa jazz trumpet player Hugh Masekela to create this unique slice-of-life musical.

It was Ngema who recruited the adolescent schoolchildren from the townships, took them to Johannesburg, and trained them from scratch, to create this oddly improvised-seeming, cantata-style musical. . . .

Ngema's achievement simply in forging this troupe into a cutting-edged theater force is almost incredible. They all perform with the calculated spontaneity of veteran tradition.

Inspired by an existing Masakela song, *Sarafina!,* which takes a young black girl as a symbol of township sacrifice and resistance, Ngema created this musical inspired by the student protests of 1976 at Morris Isaacson High School in Soweto.

There is a slender story line—which takes some time to emerge—about the students putting on a show about the imaginary return of the apartheid opponent and national hero of the townships, Nelson Mandela.

The show itself—this show within the show—is terrific, ending with a Zulu tribal dance of celebration that sends you whirling out into the street in a state of dizzy exhilaration. Leaving the night air to remind you that the triumph is of the soul not of the body, fiction and not yet fact.

The fact—the oppression, the bigotry, and the torment—never far away in the show, are a constant reminder, as is the barbed-wire enclosure at the back, and the uniformed band playing its music around a government tank, the very symbol of a people's slavery.

But the air of *Sarafina!* is alive with triumph, the music glorious, the performances vibrant. I predict it will do as much to fight the terrible canker of apartheid as any number of half-hearted economic sanctions against the South African government proposed to the UN.

For *Sarafina!* lives—and celebrates man, while dramatizing man's injustice.

> Clive Barnes, *"From Pain, This Hope,"* in New York Post, *October 26, 1987.*

FRANK RICH

Though diligent New York audiences of the 1980's may not learn a lot about the political dynamics of the United States at the theater, they have surely become experts on South Africa. Dissident productions from Johannesburg's Market Theater, urgently telling and retelling the atrocities of apartheid, now reach New York faster than new plays from Louisville or London. Is there a danger that we'll be rendered numb by the oft-told tales of Soweto and Sharpeville? Perhaps, but not as long as South Africa's defiant theater artists revel in the cultural heterogeneity that the South African Government would like to suppress. While there is indeed nothing new in the grim content of Mbongeni Ngema's *Sarafina!*. . . . the show's exuberant form is its own revelation.

[Mr. Ngema] has brought forth a musical that transmutes the oppression of black townships into liberating singing and dancing that nearly raises the theater's roof. *Sarafina!* is a celebration of Mbaqanga, the indigenous township rock music [of South Africa]. . . . In *Sarafina!,* that music, as composed by Mr. Ngema and the celebrated trumpeter Hugh Masekela, is . . . heard straight, undiluted. . . .

Mbaqanga is driving, infectious dance music that seems to express the complex history of a people. If its roots are deeply embedded in Zulu culture, one also hears the latter-day influences of white colonial missionaries, of black American gospel music, of Motown rhythm-and-blues and of metallic, present-day rock. The score of *Sarafina!*—whether driven by timeless drums or jazzy horns or electric guitar—evokes the cacophony of life in a black society both oppressed and defiant, at once sentenced to hard labor and ignited by dreams of social justice. It is a society like no other and yet it is far more plugged into the international pop culture, black and white, than an outsider might have thought.

Fittingly, the evening's numbers are performed by two dozen young people—most of them in their late teens—who are actual participants in township life rather than professional performers. Mr. Ngema found his cast in countrywide auditions, then trained it in singing and dancing. That training produced more virtuosity than ever seen on MTV, because the large *Sarafina!* company becomes a single entity, a rolling human wave—whether forming a choir that sings close harmonies a cappella or a gyrating dance ensemble that flies across the stage in angular leaps coordinated even to the slightest flicks of elbows or index fingers. . . .

As drama, *Sarafina!* is an attenuated, if well-meaning, grab bag. The setting is Morris Isaacson High School, the site of student protests during the Soweto uprising of 1976, and the premise has to do with the students' efforts to create a play out of their tragic history. The blurred vignettes recounting the horrors inflicted by the secret police, from the patrolling of class rooms to the detention of teachers are perhaps presented too accurately in the manner of high-school dramatics: they have an unspecific, generic, playacting feel that blunts their immediacy. In a climactic sequence depicting the massacre of schoolchildren by policemen, one is more conscious of the asphixiating fake smoke and toy machine guns than the real-life history being recounted.

The humorous sketches about the prankish, everyday activities of school kids also lack impact. Neither the writing nor the acting instills the characters with the individuality necessary to sustain such antics. But the character of the music and of the young faces of *Sarafina!* exerts a pull that keeps rescuing the evening from its failures at conventional theatrical tasks. Even as the show's half-hour or so of overlength becomes painfully apparent in Act II, the cast keeps winning back the audience's good will. . . .

Sarafina! is hardly the tidiest evening of South African theater to reach New York, but one wonders if the raging pulsebeat of apartheid's victims has ever seemed so loud or so close.

Frank Rich, "South African 'Sarafina!'" in The New York Times, *October 26, 1987, p. C15.*

JOHN BEAUFORT

Sarafina! more than honors its exclamation point. From rhythmically driving overture to tumultuous finale, the new black South African musical . . . throbs with an energy that reinforces the urgency of its message. The message, of course, is freedom. The method is a collage of song, dance, narration, and dramatic incident performed by a cast of mostly school-age youngsters. . . .

A Playbill note by Duma Ndlovu explains the *Sarafina!* background:

> In April of 1976, children in seven junior high schools in Soweto decided to boycott classes in protest [against the establishment of Afrikaans as the medium of instruction in all South African schools]. . . . On the morning of June 16, 1976, more than 200,000 students gathered at the Morris Isaacson High School and marched toward the outskirts of Soweto. This marked one of the most significant days in the history of the black political struggle in South Africa, and proved to be a catalyst of profound importance. By the end of the year, the police and soldiers killed many hundreds of school children. The first official victim was 11-year-old Hector Peterson and, since then, the educational system has never been the same.

Author-director Ngema has chosen Morris Isaacson as the setting for *Sarafina!* After a tumultuous assembly, the pupils, clad in black school uniforms topped by black bowlers, pass an intimidating identity check. Once in their places, the children are brought more or less to order by Mistress It's a Pity. Their studies of English poetry (Wordsworth), algebra, and black history are punctuated with song and dance. A recital of oil-producing countries is brusquely interrupted by armed soldiers as smoke fills the stage and the theater.

Spontaneously performed and precisely choreographed, the musical numbers provide a running commentary on the children's experiences—the acts of protest, troops and police in the classroom, imprisonment and torture, and the funerals of victims (a particularly moving mimed passage). Inspired by Sarafina (herself detained briefly and tortured) the children decide to create a play to welcome imprisoned activist Nelson Mandela and his wife, Winnie, on the occasion of Mandela's hoped-for release.

Though the text is sometimes difficult to follow, Ngema, Masekela, and their young performers can be equally eloquent, whether the theme is brotherly love or militant protest. . . .

[*Sarafina!*'s] numerous cast raises the roof . . . in what Mr. Ngema described as a musical "to celebrate Mbaqanga music [black South African popular music] and the power of the children."

John Beaufort, "Black South African Musical Brightens Broadway," in The Christian Science Monitor, *October 28, 1987.*

JOHN SIMON

Sarafina! is infectious—not like a disease, but like health when it bubbles with enthusiasm, humor, righteous anger, passion, and unquenchable hope. This musical about black South African high-school children has some undeniable flaws, but also the strength, spirit, and savvy with which to overcome them exultantly.

Written and directed by Mbongeni Ngema—who gave us *Asinamali!*—with songs by Ngema and the trumpet wizard Hugh Masekela, it is a predominantly musical celebration of the power, courage, and endurance of adolescents tragically catapulted into bloodily engulfing adult history. And a celebration, too, of *mbaqanga,* the rocklike music that electrifies and sustains the black townships. These young students were the core of the 1976 Soweto uprising, when 200,000 of them gathered and marched forth from Morris Isaacson High School, where the action of *Sarafina!* is mostly laid. . . .

[The production's] young people, whom Ngema chose from all over his country, are an undiluted joy to watch and listen to. They were given, Ngema says, eight months' training in singing, dancing, and acting, and the glory of it is that they combine the artistry and discipline of a time-tested ensemble with the idiosyncratic sparkle of amateurs bursting into unrehearsed fire. Ngema calls some of the girls world-class beauties; to my view, the beauty of it all is in how ordinary everyone looks, how plainly representative of a large and gallant segment of oppressed humanity. . . .

I don't want to oversell an essentially modest show, intimate despite its big cast and bigger cause. Yet, though I have scant use for rock, I found this *mbaqanga* an engaging and often elating music, zestily orchestrated and compellingly performed by the musicians and singer-dancers alike. In fact, the music is so good that it dwarfs even further the rudimentary book, partly about the horrors of South African history, partly about the Morris Isaacson students enacting a school show about those horrors under the eye of their beloved schoolmistress, who then joins in it. What emerges is perfunctory, indeed awkward—those good musicians cannot properly double as murderous police; part of the bandstand should not look like a funny mock-up of a tank—and lengthens the show unduly. The narration of a cruel incident is less potent than the prowess of these kids and this music, which communicates even with the non-English lyrics, let alone the sweetly or stirringly folklike English ones.

In the second act, we become aware of longueurs, even of a certain sameness in the songs, which may or may not be avoidable. Yet there are high points in this act as well, as when a robust, seemingly crew-cutted young woman with extraordinary vocal and physical expressiveness renders a song that creeps into every part of one's body and soul. . . .

Now and again, *Sarafina!* slips into cliché, as even that unnecessary exclamation point after the heroine's name betokens. Yet it offers, aside from the obvious pleasures, incidental ones, too, such as the way these kids speak the English language. . . . Altogether, English takes on a new lilt here, even as the musical numbers, except for one or two unduly show-bizzy ones, transmute sounds we distantly associate with something familiar into something quite unfamiliar yet surprisingly close. (p. 124)

John Simon, "Out of the Mouth of Babes," in New York Magazine, *Vol. 20, No. 44, November 9, 1987, pp. 124, 128.*

J(ames) F(arl) Powers

1917-

American novelist, short story writer and critic.

Powers is considered one of the foremost satirists of institutional Catholicism. Displaying both humor and compassion, his fiction lampoons materialistic members of the Catholic lay and clergy and illuminates the conflict between religious ideals and the exigencies of the secular world. Critics commend Powers's authentic rendition of Midwestern speech patterns, his use of small details to reveal character, and his economical prose style which includes elements of word-play. Mary Gordon observed: "It is in the close, packed atmosphere of parishes and monasteries that the comedy of Powers grows and flourishes: an odd, rare bloom: satiric, harsh, and yet not condemning, falling with an undisguisable relish upon the clergy's faults yet based upon a tough and weary faith in what these clergymen so ineptly represent. Powers's voice is dry, supremely ironic."

Powers was born into a middle-class Catholic family in the predominantly Protestant town of Jacksonville, Illinois. After graduating from high school in 1935, he moved to Chicago and worked a series of jobs while attending Northwestern University. During the early years of World War II, Powers experienced a spiritual crisis that led him to become a conscientious objector, a moral and political stance for which he spent thirteen months in prison. Much of Powers's first publication, *Prince of Darkness and Other Stories* (1947), was inspired by these experiences and voice his burgeoning social and political conscience.

Powers frequently explores the ironic possibilities in the clergy's dual commitment to the spiritual and the material worlds. "The Forks," collected in *Prince of Darkness,* stages a confrontation between the spiritual realm, represented by the Church and a sanctimonious young priest, and the material realm, represented by a seemingly worldly monsignor and an unscrupulous local company which underpays its employees and distributes its excess profits as charity to members of the clergy. In this story, along with such others as "Priestly Fellowship" and "The Keystone" from Powers's third volume of short fiction, *Look How the Fish Live* (1975), Powers's satire is directed at those members of the clergy whose overweening spirituality conflicts with their service to humanity.

In other stories in *Prince of Darkness,* Powers humorously emphasizes the similarities between religious and secular life. "Prince of Darkness," for example, portrays Father Ernest "Boomer" Burner, a spiritual failure whose love of golf and other secular pursuits interferes with his ambitions within the Church hierarchy. In "Death of a Favorite" and "Defection of a Favorite," from Powers's second collection of short fiction, *The Presence of Grace* (1956), Father Burner is seen through the eyes of a dryly ironic rectory cat. Many of the pieces included in *Look How the Fish Live* humorously depict the power struggles enacted among inhabitants of businesslike church rectories.

A test of faith leading to spiritual rebirth is a recurring motif in Powers's fiction. "Lions, Harts, Leaping Does," a much

anthologized story, concerns Father Didymus, a retired geometry teacher torn between his faith in God and his habitual reliance on logic. Just before his death, the priest loses sense of his corporeal being and becomes infused with the presence of grace. *Morte D'Urban* (1962), Powers's first novel, offers an extended treatment of this theme by depicting the metaphorical death of the worldly Father Urban as necessary to his coming to full spiritual life. In *Wheat that Springeth Green* (1988), Powers's second novel, a zealously pious young priest slowly becomes disillusioned with the efficacy of the Catholic Church's social programs. In middle age, and through the example of a young, unconventional curate's enthusiasm, however, the protagonist's faith in his role as priest is renewed, and he leaves his suburban parish to work in the inner city. Eleanor B. Wymard remarked: "Although Powers has been attacked and defended for his attitudes toward the Roman Catholic priest, the spiritual orientation of his fiction neither rises nor falls on his portrayal of the inner sanctum of the rectory. It provides simply an external structure for his pursuing the deeper problem that our generation is condemning itself to unfulfillment by ceasing to search for Mystery and Truth."

(See also *CLC,* Vols. 1, 4, 8; *Contemporary Authors,* Vols. 1-4, rev. ed.; and *Contemporary Authors New Revision Series,* Vol. 2.)

WILLIAM PRITCHARD

Powers's early stories were admired by readers who looked to discover in fiction the metaphoric, "poetic" qualities of lyric verse—qualities that were present in the work of writers like Katherine Anne Porter and Eudora Welty. Like them, and like his young contemporary Flannery O'Connor, Powers had a genius for capturing some of the ways people talked; much of the pleasure in reading him had to do with the pure satisfactions of American speech accurately rendered. But Powers was also a Midwesterner whose first favorite writer was Sinclair Lewis, who loved Sherwood Anderson's "Triumph of the Egg," whose distinctive subject was the American Catholic clergy.

Powers would say, in an interview in 1964, that he wrote about priests "for reasons of irony, comedy, and philosophy," and that these were compelling reasons because priests "officially are committed to both worlds in the way most people officially are not." Its commitment to sacred as well as spiritual reality meant that the priesthood was a specially good place to observe what Powers called the "intramural dogfights between ascetics and time servers." The typical protagonist in a Powers story has made some sort of choice or compromise between the two worlds; and it is usually an unsatisfactory compromise, since—like the rest of us only more so—priests are the victim of their position.

Such a victim was the hero of Powers's award winning first novel of 1962, *Morte D'Urban.* In that book, he became more expansive—after all, he was writing a novel—and brought an exploratory-creative manner to his study of the get-ahead priest. Throughout the novel Father Urban is both the object and the vehicle of Powers's satire, as he strives to improve the Clementine order and bring about useful accommodations between the Church and the world. But by the end of the book something has happened to make this time server care less about whether or not he represents a "first class outfit." He has become physically weaker but (Powers seems to suggest) spiritually stronger.

The tone of *Morte D'Urban* was more relaxed than the earlier stories, even wayward. A reader couldn't always see exactly how one chapter followed from its predecessor. . . . In shorter works such as **"Keystone"** and **"Farewell"** (from his third collection, *Look How the Fish Live,* which appeared in 1975), a similarly reflective and leisurely spirit kept the narrative from becoming too streamlined. These stories gave the impression that when Powers began them, their endings were not already in sight, waiting on the horizon. (The surprising, wonderfully casual ending of **"Farewell"** provides a nice instance of concluding by not exactly concluding: we're told that the bishop, his car having been sideswiped by a truck, "was in the hospital for a while, doing fairly well for a man of his age, he understood, until he took a turn for the worse.")

Two stories from *Look How the Fish Live,* **"Bill"** and **"Priestly Fellowship,"** now turn up rewritten and expanded.

They are episodes in Powers's extremely funny and satisfying new novel, a long 26 years after *Morte D'Urban. Wheat That Springeth Green* takes its hero, Father Joe Hackett, from a youthful portrait of the priest as young rascal, through his experiences at seminary and as a curate celebrating his first mass, and into his life as the pastor of St. Francis and Clare in suburban Inglenook, out there someplace in Powers's Minnesota. As with his earlier novel, the structure is episodic, the episodes mainly organized to exploit serious matters for comic purposes.

These matters include Joe's sexual awakening (really the first time Powers has dealt with such material, and very successfully); his strivings as a seminary student to become more contemplative by discomforting the flesh with a hair shirt; his principled refusal as a rookie priest to participate in the taking up of a special collection at his first mass. Compared with most of his fellow seminarians, the young Joe Hackett is an "ascetic," unpopular and unbending in the stands he takes on spiritual matters. Powers treats him with an irony that is affectionate and offhand. In fact, the narrative style of the early episodes—and most sustainedly so in the 200 or so pages about Joe's life as a priest (the second and by far the longest of the book's three sections)—is a more racy, idiomatic, and intimate one than that of *Morte D'Urban.* Part of Powers's design, in the earlier novel, was to make us uncertain just how to respond to Father Urban's success as a publicist for the Clementine order and to his prideful irritation at being closeted with intellectual and social inferiors at the Clementine rural retreat. Is Urban a snob, unpriestlike in his pride? Or does he have a right to be furious? Powers never tells us, and his sentences maintained a cool distance from Urban, whose character was more observed than delighted in, more inspected than used as a vehicle through which his creator could perform.

Performance, however, is very much the stuff of *Wheat That Springeth Green.* Powers has said that in writing fiction he thought mainly about giving his readers an experience, that he was a performer, "a little monkey with a cup." The new novel makes its appeal through the variety and charm of its particular performances, to which strong story lines and thematic emphases take a back seat. In one of the best of such sequences we follow Joe on a pilgrimage to a mall where he plans to return an empty beer case and dispose of his nonreturnable empties of the hard stuff (the pastor is a serious drinker). Setting out in his car he nearly collides with a pesky journalist named Brad who, annoyingly, says *"Ciao"* to Joe and addresses him as "padre." After this:

> Approaching Inglenook's period shopping mall—cobblestones, gas lights, board signs—Family Grocer & Fruiterer, Apothecary, Ironmonger, and so on—Joe noticed that the weather ball, from which the mall took its name, Ball Mall, and for which a color code too often appeared in Hub's Column (Hub being Brad's nom de plume) in the Inglenook *Universe—*
>
> > When weather ball's red as fire,
> > Temperature's going higher;
> > When weather ball's white as snow,
> > Down temperature will go;
> > When weather ball's royal blue,
> > Forecast says no change is due;

When weather ball blinks in agitation,
Watch out, folks, for precipitation—
was grey, not working.

If you're not paying full attention to this dense writing, you may miss how the almost-forgotten subject of the sentence ("weather ball") eventually completes itself. When attended to, indeed, when listened to—as we must listen to the voice of Powers's sentences—the effect is masterly.

Joe's motto throughout the book might be said to be, in one of his own formulations, that "the separation of Church and Dreck was a matter of life and death for the world." But Powers is a satirist who, like Flaubert and Joyce before him, feeds off Dreck as the stuff of comic life, and he has a remarkable eye and ear for the marvelous awfulness of American commercial invention. The pride of Ball Mall, for example, is a "discount house with a heart" called the Great Badger, which hires the aged and handicapped and stays open six nights a week until nine, thus outstripping the other Mall stores:

> The Great Badger itself, a forty-foot idol—its enlarged, exposed, red neon heart beating faintly in the sunlight that morning—sat up on its hunkers in the middle of the parking lot and waved a paw at cars going by. Joe did not, though he sometimes did if he had a passenger, wave back.

The portrait of the Badger is memorable enough, but it's that final sentence, so subtly awkward in its construction, that reveals the real force of Powers's art. In their calculated spin, his sentences are the equal of those concocted by satiric contemporaries like Kingsley Amis and Philip Roth.

Powers's dialogue is similarly complicated and energizing. Joe and a fellow priest named Lefty are about to go for a drink in the Little John Lounge (having just dined in the Robin Hood Room) when a woman, "apparently sober," asks them whether they are father and son. Joe, who is shorter and younger-looking, proceeds to the lounge, but Lefty stays to talk with her, and when he rejoins Joe has to confront some questions:

> "O.K. *Father.* What'd you tell that woman?"
>
> "What woman, *Father?*"
>
> "You know what woman. Tell her we're Protestants?"
>
> "Why should I tell her a thing like that?"
>
> "She didn't ask what we were?"
>
> "No."
>
> "O.K., *Father.* What if she *had* asked what we were?"
>
> Joe, silent, waited for Lefty to answer the question.
>
> "Hell, I don't know. Greek Orthodox maybe, or that I was a late vocation."

It is reminiscent of a good stage routine. Some of the best of such dialogue occurs between Joe and the new curate Bill (whose name Joe has to find out by a most circuitous route, in one of the book's funniest sequences). Much of the comedy in their scenes consists of what Joe refers to as "each . . . grinding his generation's ax." Joe grinds his when, on the cu-

rate's first morning at the rectory, Bill appears in jeans and a T-shirt and is told:

> ". . . I don't want to see you got up like that."
>
> "Around the house, I thought . . ."
>
> "No good, Father, No overalls."
>
> "Overalls? You mean jeans."
>
> Joe did, but wouldn't use the word, hating the phony-cozy sound of it. "Look, Father. You may not be able to brighten the corner where you are but why crumb it up? Why go out of the way to look bad? Everybody's doing it, sure, but you're not everybody, Father."

That contempt for the word "jeans" is, of course, Powers's; and it is typical of the tough fastidiousness he lets Joe exercise on the language-Dreck of others (the curate's musical tastes run to "Folk," which—another nice touch—Joe insists on calling "Folks"). There is plenty of animus here, but that has been part of Powers's strength as a writer from the beginning.

His comedy exists most pungently at the level of one-liners that punctuate and make vivid Joe's stream of thought: "People, he was thinking, have a right to be judged by their own standards until these can be raised . . ."; "Joe wasn't a fanatic about education. All he'd wanted was a school where the emphasis was on studies and sports (mens sana, you might say, in corpore sano), where those who failed were not passed, where the boys wore dark green blazers and the girls dark green jumpers ('Down with the daily style show!')"; "These were sobering thoughts to Joe. He got up and made another drink."

By singling out such scenes and sentences I may seem to neglect the novel's moral dimension. In **Morte d'Urban,** Urban's sense of himself and his vocation is altered over the narrative's course. In **Wheat That Springeth Green** (the title is from a medieval carol with the line "Love is come a-gain like wheat that spring-eth green"), an analogous change or discovery seems to occur in the short final section of the novel in which Joe gives up the bottle and makes a change in his pastoral career. But these pages are too elliptical to enact convincingly any spiritual transformation. We simply don't know enough about what the new man—if such he is—is like, or what, if anything, he has learned. Still, rather than thinking of the novel's ending as a failure, we should read it as testimony to how solid has been the affectionate irony with which the hero—a comic hero, surely—is treated in the previous 300 pages.

In fact, the different styles through which Joe is presented—sometimes realistically, in dialogue and relatively straightforward narration, at other times through more artificial and (as in *Ulysses*) distancing techniques—make for a character who eludes and renders irrelevant most of the moral terms by which we might judge him. By this I mean that Powers's fantasies, woven around and through the mind of his protagonist, are stronger and more memorable than our concerns about what will happen to him next, or finally.

An important source of such fantasies and musings is baseball, a game that means a good deal to Joe (as I suspect it does to his creator), and is an excellent vehicle for saying serious things humorously. The fantasy may be simply but deftly spun out, as when Joe pitches a dog's rubber ball ("the official American league ball") at his garage: " 'The Bosox could sure use Father.' '*Any* club could.' He alone, with his knowledge of batters (encyclopedic), his stuff (world of), his control (phenomenal), had made the Twins a constant threat down the years." Those parenthetical insertions make the sequence delightful. Or there is the following explicit comparison between the priesthood and the sport: "As was true of many players, some the best, the history and mystique of the Church evidently meant little to Lefty, as the history and mystique of the Church evidently did to many priests, some of the best." Anyone, we feel, who can think this way, in such an aptly cadenced pattern of wit, should keep on doing what he's doing and form his character. Powers provides his hero with so many splendid formulations that, verbally at least, he can't be improved on.

There is no need, in the case of a writer whose output over 40 years has been as small as J. F. Powers's, to rank his books in relation to one another. But his new novel seems to me the best book he has written. He would perhaps approve of Pope's couplet, "Let the strict Life of graver Mortals be / A long, exact, and serious Comedy." Joe Hackett puts the idea in a different idiom but comes up with something just as true: "Sure, birth was a big deal—after death, the biggest deal—but what was there to say about either of them, after a point?" *Wheat That Springeth Green* says a lot of what there is to be said about the life in between those big deals. (pp. 36-9)

William Pritchard, "Church and Dreck," in The New Republic, Vol. 199, No. 13, September 26, 1988, pp. 36-9.

AUSTIN MacCURTAIN

Though he is known only to a relatively small group of readers, J. F. Powers is one of the wittiest and most exact stylists writing in English. . . .

In [*Wheat that Springeth Green*] as in almost all his work, Powers confines himself to a very small canvas: the daily doings of Roman Catholic priests in Minnesota, usually in their unbuttoned and more profane hours in the presbytery. While there are still some modern novels in which the occasional clergyman drifts in and out of the action, almost none deals expressly with the ecclesiastical profession. A notable exception is John Updike's *A Month of Sundays,* which depicts the sensual indiscretions and theological doubts of an errant Episcopalian priest cast into a therapeutic community of other clerical delinquents of various denominations. But where Updike's Tom Marshfield confronts differing theological views head-on and with pyrotechnical eloquence, Powers's Joe Hackett, as seminarian, curate and pastor in the Church of the one true faith, gropes and bustles his way to ordination and his subsequent responsibilities, experiencing much confusion, but never a doubt—at least, never an acknowledged doubt.

Powers is a master of dialogue and interior monologue couched in the basest cliché. Sports, show-business and political rhetoric provide the language on which his priests draw for their conversations and debates. Their analogies consist of gleanings from a vast stock of consecrated anecdotes, worn smooth by generations of use until they are as indistinguishable as poker chips, items of mortified language used to evoke conditioned responses or no response at all. After all, they are part of the deposit of tradition bequeathed by the great "ad-

venturers of the spirit", and therefore true, even if not quite applicable or proportionate to the situations they address.

The social and moral claustrophobia of the American Catholic outlook, preserved and nourished by an educational system which emphasizes the Church's absolute and, by implication, exclusive possession of truth, is expertly conveyed in this novel. In the United States itself, the most prosperous society in the world, a system, as one of its historians has said, that could with no sense of irony regard itself as founded on perfection and in search of improvement, Catholics had been brought up to believe that they had it "made in the shade". The wisdom of the ages held in the bosom of the Church combined with Lyndon Johnson's Great Society to give many of its priests the sense, only rarely modified by experience, of having a stranglehold on the only truths that really matter.

This somewhat dyspeptic and broadly drawn criticism is, however, nowhere expressed in Powers's compassionate, funny, often hilarious novel; rather it underlies and permeates the book, as the condition in which Joe and his fellow priests have to function. The world about them is respectfully indifferent to their mission, which has declined into a set of building programmes to be paid for by their flocks: school, church, rectory, in that order, with the added Archdiocesan levy or "assessment" of each parish. Riding herd on their parishioners and maintaining their "plant" leaves the priests with a great deal of idle time, which they fill with fussy domestic chores and much eating and drinking, punctuated by bibulous gatherings classified as "priestly fellowship".

Even as he records the conversations of Joe, Lefty, Pot, Conk and Bill, and the scrapes they get into on account of their inchoate suspicions that their Church's attitude to financial and politico-military matters might need some adjustment, Powers is deeply aware of how hopelessly unprepared they are to deal with the complexities and perplexities they must daily address. . . .

Here is Joe, now over forty, after his Sunday nap, sternly forbidding himself another beer and urging himself on:

> The thing is not to let up, the thing is to pour it on, as every champion knows, be he (or she) athlete or saint, and that is what he was doing, pouring it on. Spiritually and physically—let's face it—he'd dropped too many decisions. He was on the way down. But he still had it at times. Call it guts. Call it class. The great ones all had it—Sugar Ray, St John of the Cross, Man o' War. . . .

This is high comedy, but it is not parody. Powers has a perfect ear for the idiom of his priests, and Joe's long bouts of fantasy are subtly placed in the novel to show that he tries, from time to time, and with what resources he has, to retain a distant glimmer of his pristine ideal.

Throughout the book, from being an only child and a pretty one, Joe displays a self-regard, a preoccupation with his "image", a desire to excel in the eyes of those who matter, that thwarts all his best efforts to get it right. The bristling paradox that confronts the priest: called to be a saint and required by his Church to be a banker; to be a successful manager of money and property and simultaneously a witness to a crucified Christ in a Church that insists on being a quantitative success—demands a kind of intellectual and moral equilibrium that is too sophisticated for Joe Hackett.

Finally—and here Powers's irony is at its subtlest—Joe is

driven to think for himself. The Archbishop's decision, for the sake of pleasing some influential parishioners, to admit a group called The Cheerleaders to the solemn blessing of Joe's splendid new rectory, after Joe himself had expressly forbidden them, is too much. Joe climbs down and admits them, but when the Archbishop commends him for his obedience and prudence, Joe replies curtly:

> "That's what I'm afraid of." *Wham!*
>
> The Arch smiled frostily.
>
> Joe had been hoping for more of a response, believing that the separation of Church and Dreck was a matter of life and death for the world; that the Church was the one force in the world with a chance to save it (but first, "Physician, heal thyself!"). . . .

Joe cuts the knot in the only way he decently can. Having sworn off alcohol and stopped trying to justify to himself what he sees in his personal life as unjustifiable, he does the simple thing: he pays the Archbishop a visit. When next we see him, he has been transferred to a poverty-stricken city parish, there to pursue while yet there is time, and with his hard-won handful of spiritual integrity, the ideal which had beckoned to him when he was truly a boy.

It might be objected that this is more a collection of stories than a novel. Joe is the only character; the others, priests and laity, though drawn with loving accuracy, exist as functions of Joe and fill out his world. Poised and subtle in its poker-faced irony, [*Wheat that Springeth Green*] reveals with a combination of affection and exasperation the uphill struggle of decent men caught between the temptation to rebel against the institution that has nourished them and a dead conformism which believes everything because it believes nothing. It is a mark of Powers's own steady belief in the presence of grace that he can bring such serene and clear-sighted compassion and such healing humour to the depiction of their struggles against the terror of unbelief.

> Austin MacCurtain, "The Race for Sainthood," in The Times Literary Supplement, *No. 4465, October 28, 1988, p. 1211.*

AMY EDITH JOHNSON

How rare a subject in fiction, the spiritual life—and yet each of us has one. The realist novel gradually laid claim, in the 18th and 19th centuries, to the varied aspects of our identities—but even from its most sublime practitioners we have had ten thousand Eugène de Rastignacs for every Konstantin Levin, twenty thousand Emma Bovarys for one Maggie Tulliver. In American fiction, the spiritual dimension of character has regularly been passed off as a misnamed facet of the "genuine" psychological reality of the individual.

This secularizing dismissal finds its counterpart in a facile confusion of the spiritual with the religious life and practice. When the religion is Roman Catholicism and the practitioners in question are the American clergy, no eye has been sharper, no ear finer than that of J. F. Powers at discerning the nuances of service to God and mammon. His mastery of our middle-class speech and the elegant economy of his storyteller's gift have long been valued by readers of his three collections of stories and previous novel, *Morte D'Urban,* which won the National Book Award in 1963. Perhaps the publication of this splendid second novel [*Wheat that Springeth Green*] will scandalize the literary establishment into rushing Mr. Powers's earlier works back into print.

Wheat That Springeth Green (a title whose tone is wholly uncharacteristic of the book, from which one hopes it will not discourage readers) is the utterly down-to-earth story of Joe Hackett, a priest with three problems: the world, the flesh, and (but only by implication) the devil. If you've been daunted by our current fictional choices, when revenants, angelic visitations, and high lyricism are commonplaces of the "magic realism" school and lovelessness, monosyllables, and substance abuse constitute the hallmarks of the minimalists—crème de menthe or muscatel, what's your pleasure?—then this sparkling draft of honest incident and clear, cold prose is for you.

The beauty of Mr. Powers's writing lies in its art's being almost invisible. The craft and balance of the novel's literary achievement are discernible in every sentence, but only on second thought, so thoroughly has the author subordinated form to function. No other modern stylist has offered us the faultless colloquialism of Mr. Powers's conversations, and in [*Wheat That Springeth Green*] this perfection is extended to the narrative mode itself: never omniscient (that quality being the prerogative of a silent but ubiquitous character), it rather offers Joe's chronicle through his own perceptions and, though not in his own person, in his own language. The novel's pervasive irony—and what modern novel can afford to be without it?—is therefore Joe's own, which endows it with dignity and generous humor. Even his most callow, craven or pompous moments are lightened by an unpretentious and wry detachment that approaches insight and commands respect.

Seldom have so many of the clichés and idioms that shape our mental and social life been held—lovingly, ruefully—up to the light. Father Hackett, dropping Sunday's collection into the drive-in depository, idly wonders "if there was anything in the idea of reviving the practice of coin washing . . . a small service that banks could perform, and would if they *cared* as much as they said they did in their advertising." J. F. Powers cares deeply about the well-rubbed coin of our verbal exchange, and it brightens under his fingers.

Although it has taken Joe Hackett about 40 years and almost 100 pages to assume the parish of SS. Francis and Clare (but only two months and 15 pages, eventually, to leave it), it is in this pastoral role, during April to November of 1968, that *Wheat That Springeth Green* crucially finds him—and that he finds himself. Mr. Powers lives outside of Minneapolis, and most of the laity—there aren't many—in this novel "speak Minnesotan," but Inglenook, Joe's suburban parish, is no Lake Wobegon. Its economic life is underwritten by "the giant Cones, Casing, Inc." (a conglomerate generating "nose cones for missiles as well as ice cream cones, casings for bombs as well as sausages"); it is variously expressed in the local "period shopping mall" and its flourishing, paternalistic rival, the Great Badger discount house, whose owner, Mr. Brock, forgives the debts of deceased customers and employs "the aged and handicapped." . . .

Tracing Joe Hackett's path to Inglenook, Mr. Powers has sought to depict a life's trajectory, but despite a fine early chapter on a crisis for the future Father as a 9-year-old, the novel doesn't really hit its stride until Joe assumes his vocation "at the sem, when a character sketch of him might have read, 'Bright, good family, dough, but unbalanced on subject of sanctity (also pacifism), gets on your nerves.' " Joe's aspirations to sainthood—variously expressed in adventures with a hair shirt and the recruitment of a short-lived cadre of "spiritual athletes"—discomfit his superiors and fellow students; when, at an evening lecture, he asks, "Father, how can we make sanctity as attractive as sex to the common man?" the hilarity is universal.

Five years as a curate at Holy Faith, under "the only known contemplative in the diocese (among pastors)," and seven more as administrator of Archdiocesan Charities change Joe imperceptibly from a starry-eyed prig into a "good hard worker fond of the sauce." His pessimism and regret, intermittently felt, are more than personal; not only society at large, but the church itself, seems to him debased by preoccupation with image: "We used to stand out in the crowd. We had quality control. We were the higher-priced spread. No more."

Simply to maintain his priestly dignity has become Joe's mock-epic yet genuinely heroic task, as parish assessments, professional fund-raisers and public relations become the distracting and tormenting equivalents of St. Anthony's demons. Flirtations with martyrdom in America's heartland in the year of Our Lord 1968 consist of declining to have public prayers for the passage of a munitions bill beneficial to Cones, Casing; or counseling a local draft resister to follow his conscience. Father Hackett persists in the unsentimental, pedestrian maintenance of his own integrity. (p. 15)

Simultaneously, "a saint for today" ("At last! . . . Blessed Joseph of Inglenook, help of victims of P.R., pray for us!") and an average Joe, Father Hackett deliberates, equivocates and pontificates his way through elating and deflating sitcom quandaries in which his black suit is sometimes incidental: negotiating with a department store for the delivery of a bedroom set; welcoming the new curate whose name no one has thought to tell him; serendipitously foiling, to public acclaim, a heist at the local liquor store where he'd rather his gin purchase pass unnoticed.

These events give Mr. Powers the opportunity to sketch, essentially through dialogue, a couple of dozen minor characters, each marvelously vivid and distinct. Though mostly male and largely clerics, they could be bank officers, policemen, minor politicians; Mr. Powers hears middle America singing. Joe "passes" easily when traveling, on vacation, "in mufti," striking up random conversations: "Duke was in uranium, Joe in life insurance. ('What company?' 'Eternal.') . . . 'Kind of work you do?' 'Oh, office work.' 'Office manager?' 'Yes. Branch office.' 'Big concern?' 'Well, we're multinational.' " Father Hackett is more Everyman than Everypriest.

Wheat That Springeth Green is funny on every page, but it is finally comic in the same sense that inspired Dante to call his visionary account of the Catholic world view "*mia commedia.*" The Christian promise is a happy ending, and it is not despite but because of this that the last word of Mr. Powers's novel is an emphatic "*Cross.*" In the middle of the journey, Joe Hackett sees his early spiritual inquiries with a new perspective. Recalling the incident that made him notorious as a seminarian, he reflects: " 'How can we make sanctity as attractive as sex?' Answer I got was, "Just have to keep trying." Not much of an answer. Nobody remembers it—just the question. Guess it's the answer to all these questions.' "

The novel's title alludes to both Matthew 13:23 and John 12:24—parables of fertility, futurity and the deception perpetrated by despair. "You never knew where you were in the spiritual life; that was the hell of it—only God knew. Joe's hope had to be that he was, without knowing it, a sleeper." (pp. 15-16)

[This novel] expresses, in more than one dimension, the miracle of hope. In *Wheat That Springeth Green*, J. F. Powers has made sanctity as attractive as sex to the common reader. Long may he, in triumph, keep trying. (p. 16)

Amy Edith Johnson, "Bearing the Cross in Inglenook, Minn.," in The New York Times Book Review, *October 30, 1988, pp. 15-16.*

WALTER H. CLARK, JR.

Twenty-six years ago *Commonweal* reviewer Thomas Conley called J. F. Powers's long-awaited first novel, *Morte D'Urban,* the work of a master. *Wheat That Springeth Green,* his second novel, fifth book, is likewise the work of a master and, like *Morte D'Urban,* a comedy of spiritual salvation played out in the story of a priest.

Father Joe Hackett, son of a prosperous coal dealer, thinks of becoming a priest from an early age. The story follows him through seminary and enthusiasm for contemplation, on into the realities of a parish curacy, and a staff position in Diocesan Charities. Looking back at his spiritual development, he worries over the loss of youthful idealism and certainty, " . . . you never knew where you were in the spiritual life; that was the hell of it—only God knew, Joe's hope had to be that he was, without knowing it, a sleeper."

At age forty-four, he is pastor of the Church of Saints Francis and Clare, Inglenook, a comfortable suburban parish, for which he has built a school, convent, and rectory. ("Just as the heart of the church is the altar, he'd say, so the heart of the rectory is, or should be, the office.") He pays for these achievements in loneliness and drink and seems to be headed for spiritual drought.

What saves Joe Hackett, or provides the occasion for his saving himself, is the arrival of his new curate, Father Bill, a priest of the sixties, whose naiveté masks a sweetness and generosity of spirit that rekindle the older man. Father Joe thinks of himself as guiding and instructing Bill, but it is actually through Bill, and his concern for Bill, that Joe comes back into contact with his vocation and his fellow man. (In the words of a habitual telephone pest who identifies himself as Lyndon B. Johnson, "*You* should be *his* assistant.") As the novel ends, we find Joe, having been "gently purged and ardently moved," volunteering for a thorny post in the inner city.

But this is not only a comedy of spiritual salvation. It's full of ridiculous incident, humorous characters, slapstick, and word play. When Monsignor Toohey, a two-bit Chancery ogre, withholds from Father Joe the name of his new curate, Joe's attempts to find out, without revealing what it is he doesn't know, lead to hilarious complications. And Joe's diplomatic endeavors to avoid being drawn into a war between the Mall merchants and the local discount house are worthy of a Kissinger.

As for character, what starts as caricature often ends as portrait, a Powers trademark. Here is Joe's view of Father Felix, who helps out on Sundays:

The monk, whose glasses still needed changing, still held the paper open in front of him, as far away from him as he could, so that it was like the prow of a ship, until his arms gave out and the whole thing came crashing down in his lap—this was hard on the paper. Instead of smoothing it out while waiting for the strength to be restored to his arms, he cocked his head back and read what he could of the text in its collapsed and crumpled condition, the salient items or sentences thereof, noisily wrenching up more, shifting and tightening his grip like a dog with a bone—this was hard on the paper.

The picture is one of charming simplicity, yet Father Felix preaches sermons straight out of the middle-European peasant imagination, spreading panic among impressionable adolescents in the parish. Who is this mild-mannered monk?

Other colorful clergymen come and go, their intrigues and nicknames like decorative threads in a tapestry. Monsignor "Catfish Toohey," Joe's antagonist since grade school, "Lefty Beeman," the eternal curate, forever seeking his own parish, forever affronting the authorities at the wrong moment, "Dollar Bill" Stock, who insists on a special collection at Joe's first Mass, and whose retirement purse is unanimously boycotted by his congregation. Then there is Father Van Slaag (known to his housekeeper as "Slug"), who has "horny grey growths on his knees" from praying, and permits the housekeeper's dog to bite his ankles—which finally persuades young Father Joe that he is not cut out for the contemplative life.

Someone once asked Powers why he restricted himself by writing about Catholic clergy, and he replied that it made for stronger beer. The metaphor seems appropriate for a novelist whose underlying subject is the life of the spirit. The problem Powers sets himself is not so much writing about priests, as writing about spiritual realities in an age that ignores them. Part of his approach is to be up front with the venalities and vulgarities attendant upon institutional religion, while recording without comment unnoticed spiritual changes that take place like movements in the crust of the earth. Amusing as *Wheat* is to read, it has an underlying lapidary toughness, a seriousness of purpose. First impressions and last impressions are quite different things in the reading of Powers's novels, and a Richter scale can be handy. (pp. 592, 594)

Walter H. Clark, Jr., "A Richter Scale Can Be Handy," in Commonweal, *Vol. CXV, No. 19, November 4, 1988, pp. 592, 594.*

JULIAN MOYNAHAN

Wheat That Springeth Green is J. F. Powers's first novel in twenty-five years, his second altogether. The preceding one, *Morte d'Urban,* won the National Book Award; the new book was nominated for the same prize. . . .

The title of the new book, which has perplexed some reviewers, perhaps because it seems uncharacteristically hopeful, is taken from a lyric by J. M. C. Crum (1872-1958) set to medieval French carol music. The words remark how love returns "that with the dead has been," just as the wheat "that in dark earth many days has lain" comes back to life as a "green blade." The title seems appropriate for a work by our leading Catholic novelist, whose faith numbers among its tenets the physical resurrection of Christ from the tomb where he was laid after dying on a cross, and the physical resurrection of

all mankind at the end of the world and of time. How the image of rebirth applies to the book is of course another matter. Perhaps it merely suggests an author who has produced another novel after so long an interval. . . .

In Catholicism there are the joyful and the sorrowful mysteries. *Wheat That Springeth Green* is practically on a line between the two, maybe inclining slightly toward the joyful side. It is the imaginary biography of a Minnesota Catholic, Joe Hackett, son of a prosperous small-town coal and ice merchant, who makes his career in the secular priesthood. That means that he attends a local seminary, does not go on to Rome for advanced study, becomes an assistant in local parishes, and progresses to become a rector or pastor within the same archdiocesan authority. During the long Part Two of the book Joe is rector at Saints Francis and Clare, a surburban parish in Inglenook, Minnesota, where the permanent church structure is still to be built from funds mostly to be raised by Joe. The time is the 1960s, and among Father Hackett's problems are changing suburban mores in an era of burgeoning consumerism, the impact of Vatican II reformism on the attitudes and behavior of the new church assistants, a large assessment from the archdiocesan fund drive that somehow must be raised within the parish, and the quandary of how to advise young men who are being forced to choose between Vietnam War service and some type of draft evasion or resistance.

Joe remains interestingly unpredictable in the views he holds (and sometimes argues at excessive length). He is a conservative on the conciliar reforms yet rejects theological arguments urging the doctrine of the just war, and he therefore advises young men to follow conscience wherever it may lead. When conscience leads the son of a fiercely patriotic family to emigrate to Canada, Joe is fully supportive. He even feels regret at having failed to register as a CO himself during World War II, which he spent in the seminary protected by the standard deferment offered to divinity students. Joe is headstrong and quixotic: after winning a thousand dollars at cards from well-heeled fellow priests during the annual diocesan retreat for rectors, he gives the money to a bookie to bet that Eugene McCarthy will win the Democratic nomination for president, because the staggering odds will pay off the renewal fund assessment at one blow if God arranges for McCarthy to win. But God, as we know now, had other plans.

Wheat That Springeth Green opens in its hero's earliest childhood: we see him at the age of three trying to show off to the adults at his parents' party. Powers is an ironist who rarely shows his hand, but we would be wise to consider the following questions: a) Is there a connection between this early showing off and the "show" of the priest to come as he gestures and chants at the altar during the Mass? b) Is the showing off an early sign of "vocation," as the opening of Joyce's *A Portrait of the Artist* reveals the later vocation for literature in the infant Stephen's absorption in the words of nursery rhymes and his father's bedtime stories? If so, then God is an ironist too, as everything by Powers suggests He is.

In high school Joe is a star athlete and in the seminary (the "sem") he pushes hard during the competitions of ostentatious piety that go on, and there is a wonderful episode about an actual hair shirt that he gets hold of. It begins to dawn on young Father Hackett that a career of ordinary service, rather than one of sanctity, is what the future holds.

One of the difficulties in responding to Father Hackett and to the novel is that Powers is quite elusive in deciding whether Joe is an extraordinary or an ordinary man. That is, does his ordinary manner conceal exceptional spiritual powers? This is a question about what he is "called" to do: no one, least of all the author, is questioning the validity of the calling itself. Part of the difficulty comes from Powers's angle of narration. Joe is always in the foreground, very much a "debating hero," which means that he is mainly seen from his own point of view, and is always given the most to say and the clinching arguments in his discussions with fellow priests, with lay people, and with his ecclesiastical superiors. At the same time, he accepts the ground rules: the Church is divine and may do with his life what it will.

At the end of the book Joe is reassigned from the pleasant suburban parish to a difficult, racially vexed poor parish in the heart of a big midwestern city. We don't follow what becomes of him there—his story breaks off at the end of the 1960s. I suppose Powers is deliberately begging the question I have raised about whether Hackett is ordinary or special or heroic, no doubt for sound theological reasons. For us laity and scoffers this could be translated as "It ain't over till it's over." Sanctification can never be ruled out, and hell forever yawns. One remembers that the priest in Powers's early short masterpiece, **"Prince of Darkness,"** whom Evelyn Waugh called "a magnificent study in sloth," was in fact a compendium of all seven deadly sins (except lust), having accomplished so much without ever rising above the rank of parish assistant.

Joe himself drinks a lot and worries about it in the usual way. He is also shown to be "normal," if that is the word, in sexual development: at age fifteen he takes on at the same time two uninhibited servant girl-waitress types and performs with astounding vigor. At least the girls are impressed. Once this is gotten out of the way sex does not rear its head again, until the mid-1960s when Father Hackett begins among the newly ordained to meet serious young men who dress like hippies, prefer driving VW Beetles to big black sedans, and are not really convinced that a celibate priesthood is a good thing. Joe argues them down on all these points, but certainly on the last he lacks mature experience with women to bring to bear. He is shown spending no time at all with the other sex, or addressing their problems as a pastoral counselor outside the hasty routines of confession. His recreations consist of getting drunk fairly often, eating out with buddies from seminary days or other male friends, and following the Minnesota Twins on television. This is not to say that he fails to put in long hard hours running the parish.

In debate Joe compares the Church to "a big old ship. She creaks, she rocks, she rolls, and at times she makes you want to throw up. But she gets to where she's going. Always has, always will, until the end of time. With or without you." Even for a politician talking about the "ship of state," Joe's complacency, with its edge of quirkiness, would be excessive. The question is, are assumptions that go without saying ever worth holding?

Other propositions and positions Joe regards as self-evident—they are certainly unfalsifiable—are that "people, most people, lay and clerical, just weren't up to much," and that "people might not be able to exercise free will any more, owing to the decline in human intelligence." He faults Vatican II for putting the Church in the direction of "going too far too soon," but fails to indicate whether he is thinking of the vernacular Mass or of more fundamental change. Joe says, in "priestly fellowship," laying this stuff on some polite young curates who wouldn't dream of telling him he's full of hot air, "A few monks saved civilization once. Could be the answer again. Principle's sound." Evidently he has in mind a single-sex civilization of celibate men, saved by other celibate men. Women on the face of it would only get to bring in dinner and mend socks. How the human stock would be replenished is as much in question as it was for the thirteenth-century Albigensians and their nineteenth-century avatars, the Shakers. (pp. 51-2)

The rector of Saints Francis and Clare does better at trying to save his church grounds from invasion by a marching band and pom-pom girls sent over from the nearby shopping center for a photo opportunity with an archepiscopal visitor—although he fails. The effort stems from his belief in "that separation of Church and Dreck [which] was a matter of life and death for the world." There is also the delicious comedy of his bemused interactions with Father Felix, an unworldly yet would-be with-it Franciscan monk who busses in weekends from a monastery eighty miles away to help with confessions and the odd extra Sunday Mass. Felix's sermons stupefy the congregation with minutiae of medieval historical anecdote, cast in a narrative style owing much to Disney films of the *Snow White* era, the moral point of which no one can make out.

The most interesting issues cluster around an incident at Joe's first Mass following his ordination. As he is conducting this service and assisting the same morning at the first Mass of one Toohey, occasions which ought to be so joyous that they might help to sustain a priest through years of dull clerical routine, a problem of conscience comes up that Powers never settles or perhaps would even intend to settle. Instead it persists, casting a casuistical spell on the rest of the novel, a "case" about which arguments might go on and on. Powers's mastery of his materials and of his art is at its height here, for the incident is a high point of comedy even as it establishes a nexus of moral and spiritual issues which Catholicism has a distinctive way of approaching.

What happens is that Fathers Hackett and Toohey are scheduled to celebrate their first Masses in the church of a notorious money-grubber and skinflint named Father Stock. He decides that there is a lot of extra money to be made by having each new priest, as a special object of edification to the pious congregation, pass the collection basket at the other's Mass. Joe is properly appalled and tries to buy his way out by making a five-hundred-dollar donation to Father Stock's general fund. But the rector is adamant, and when he is sent down one aisle, basket in hand, during the collection interval at Toohey's service Joe tries to run out of the church. Toohey on the other hand has no problem with these arrangements. He will go straight on from his first Mass to become a church politician of monsignor rank, working at the chancery and a perpetual thorn in the side of decent rectors of the Father Hackett type.

In the end, Joe caves in and passes the collection basket. He had resisted for the best reasons but he complies because open conflict with greedy Father Stock would cause "scandal." To a non-Catholic this may appear as sheer rationalization. Scandal, however, is a complex notion for Catholics. The old example was that speaking lies or making false accusations about somebody is a great sin, but telling the truth about someone's failings or exposing them may be a greater sin, depending on circumstances, for you may drive a person to do desperate things and, in the end, to the greatest of all sins, which is despair. So one may not want to show up the simoniac rector before his own congregation (and the celebrants' friends and relatives) not only because it makes the Church, which is divine, look bad, but also because Father Stock might go to pieces when his grossness becomes widely known and fall prey to the devil through despair. Whether this analysis is correct by current RC standards of casuistry is hardly the point; what matters is that nobody else in American fiction is capable of making such cases of conscience palpable in the American midlands.

Powers's greatest story may be **"Lions, Harts, and Leaping Does."** In it an old monk dies an ecstatic and beautiful death that is represented through severely restricted imagery—Minnesota imagery—of snow falling on bare frozen fields as night comes, of an ancient high-shouldered canary escaping its cage and out through a window deliberately opened into the icy dark. The monk could be a saint in the making. Joe Hackett is more of a foot soldier, but unlike Toohey he understands his vocation well enough to aspire to a death like that. Powers creates interest in a substantial world and in distinctions and values that matter whether you believe in anything or not. (p. 52)

Julian Moynahan, "Waiting for God in Inglenook,"
in The New York Review of Books, *Vol. 35, No. 19,*
December 8, 1988, pp. 51-2.

TERRY TEACHOUT

A man of one book is easy to figure. So is a man of many books. It is the man of a few good books who is hard to pin down. Take J. F. Powers. By the age of forty-five, Powers had written a grand total of three books: *Prince of Darkness,* published in 1947; *The Presence of Grace,* published in 1956; and *Morte d'Urban,* published in 1962. Still, his gifts were acknowledged by critics ranging from Evelyn Waugh to Gore Vidal, and he was regularly mentioned in tandem with Flannery O'Connor as one of the most promising young Catholic writers in America. When *Morte d'Urban,* Powers's first novel, won the National Book Award in 1963, F. W. Dupee, another critical admirer, rightly remarked that its author enjoyed "an inconspicuous fame."

That fame trailed off to next to nothing in the succeeding quarter century, during which Powers published only one other book, a slender collection of prose sketches and work in progress called *Look How the Fish Live.* No selected essays, no collected letters, no regular appearances on the campus lecture circuit, no groaning casebooks of close readings appeared in the wake of *Morte d'Urban.* Powers allowed his reputation, such as it was, to be sustained solely by four books published roughly a decade apart. Not surprisingly, he soon became a ghostly figure. (p. 69)

But J. F. Powers, though silent, was not forgotten, as the publication [in 1988] of his second novel, *Wheat That Springeth Green,* proved. Profiles and interviews suddenly began appearing in a variety of respectable venues as the word began to get around that Powers, at the age of seventy-one, finally had a new book coming out. The reviews were universally favorable, and a second National Book Award nomination followed in due course. The lackluster reputation of a half-remembered writer had somehow regained its old patina. For

once, a cautionary tale of the literary life had a happy—and well-deserved—ending. (pp. 69-70)

By concentrating on the secular aspects of the priestly life, J. F. Powers avoided the parochialism that has long been the curse of Catholic fiction writers. His tone was even sufficiently urbane for him to publish in *The New Yorker*—a magazine where the blunter, more grotesque parables of Flannery O'Connor were misunderstood and unwelcome. This lightness of touch, coupled with an absence of the more obvious kinds of religious sentimentality, misled some commentators into thinking that Powers's choice of subject matter had nothing to do with his spiritual convictions. "Mr. Powers," Peter De Vries went so far as to suggest in his introduction to a 1963 collection of Powers's short stories about priests, "does not seem to me a religious writer at all. He is undoubtedly a religious man, but that is something else entirely."

J. F. Powers is certainly a religious man, but he is quite clearly a religious (or, if you prefer, spiritual) writer as well. His stories invariably revolve around a single question: How is it that ordinary people, with all their commonplace failings, can do the work of God? Powers approaches this simple but intriguing paradox from a dozen different angles, and the fundamental incongruity which it implies is the source of his richest humor. In **"Prince of Darkness,"** Father Burner, through desultory indulgence in the seven deadly sins, is actually transformed into a devil—the most petty and preposterous of devils, to be sure, but one in whom the transformation is so complete that the reader is even allowed to catch a fleeting glance of diabolic features. ("Father Burner, applying a cloven foot to the pedal, gave it the gas.")

Having found his métier, J. F. Powers had the wit to stick with it. He wrote slowly and carefully, producing an occasional story about secular characters but generally remaining loyal to the dryly comic tone and idiosyncratic subject matter which had served him so well.

Powers's second story collection, *The Presence of Grace,* was more consistent in quality than *Prince of Darkness* but lacked the high points of the earlier volume. ("I agree with you that nothing in this present collection of Powers equals the best in the first," Flannery O'Connor wrote to a friend in 1956. "However, who am I to be saying that in public?") Two of the stories in *The Presence of Grace* which originally appeared in *The New Yorker,* **"Death of a Favorite"** and **"Defection of a Favorite,"** made use of a rectory cat as narrator, a Saki-like device which Powers carried off with ease and charm but which is an unconvincing departure from his customary acerbity.

The Presence of Grace, though engaging, suggested at times that the formula which had brought Powers so much success in *Prince of Darkness* might be reaching a point of diminishing returns. This suspicion was laid to rest with the publication in 1962 of Powers's first novel, *Morte d'Urban.* Installments of the novel, which took Powers more than six years to complete, appeared at intervals in various American magazines between 1956 and 1962, and some critics suggested that it was not a true novel but a succession of short stories unconvincingly stitched together. They were wrong. *Morte d'Urban* is sectional, even picaresque, in its approach. But it holds together brilliantly—so brilliantly, in fact, as to add up to one of the most impressive comic novels written by an American.

Father Urban, "fifty-four, tall and handsome but a trifle loose in the jowls and red of eye," is the quintessential J. F. Powers priest. Having drifted into the priesthood without any obvious vocation, he treats it precisely as he would any other job: with one eye firmly fixed on the main chance. The star preacher of the Clementines, a midwestern order which "labored under the curse of mediocrity," the peripatetic Father Urban, whose thoroughly modern mottos are "Be a winner" and "You may be right," ministers to his flock with hearty sermons and after-dinner speeches. . . . (pp. 71-2)

Morte d'Urban begins when the Father Provincial of the Order of St. Clement, sensing that his star preacher has grown too big for his collar, assigns him to a rundown retreat in the wilds of Minnesota. Father Urban promptly puts his go-getting energies to work and turns the monastery into a four-star lay retreat complete with a beautifully tended golf course. The building of this elaborate institution is used as the occasion for an equally elaborate *tour d'horizon* of small-town life in Minnesota in which Powers divides his satirical potshots between the foibles of the Catholic Church and the vulgarities of middle-class America in the age of Eisenhower. (p. 72)

The fate of Father Urban offers ample opportunity for excesses of religious sentiment, and it is to Powers's credit that he avoids them completely. We are invited, if it suits us, to dismiss Father Urban's "conversion," but the author himself clearly regards it with the utmost seriousness. It is Powers's sense of literary grace that allows him to leave the question unresolved, and he handles with similar reticence the subtle references to the Arthurian legend around which *Morte d'Urban* is built. The tone of *Morte d'Urban* is predominantly comic; Powers's larger purpose is expressed as a discreet undertone of spirituality that gives unexpected resonance to a genuinely touching book. (p. 73)

Wheat That Springeth Green is not as finished an artistic product as *Morte d'Urban*. The old J. F. Powers attacked the vulgarization of the church in America through satire and indirection. *Wheat That Springeth Green* makes the same points in the same way, but Joe Hackett is also allowed to do more than a little complaining of his own, in the course of which one hears a crotchety authorial voice that the younger Powers would have taken care to avoid. ("We used to stand out in the crowd," Joe says of the Catholic Church. "We had quality control. We were the higher-priced spread. No more.") In addition, the charges of slackness wrongly leveled at *Morte d'Urban* are far more applicable to *Wheat That Springeth Green*. The great set pieces of *Morte d'Urban* gain added strength from their context in the complete novel. But the seams that join **"Bill"** and **"Priestly Fellowship"** to the rest of *Wheat That Springeth Green* are perhaps too visible to the naked eye.

In the end, *Wheat That Springeth Green* is likely to strike the reader familiar with Powers's other books as not quite necessary—a trope on *Morte d'Urban,* so to speak, rather than the product of a fresh and fully independent artistic conception. But Powers has not lost his sharp eye for the absurdities of priestly life in a secular society. (What other novelist could extract laughs from a hair shirt?) And if the best parts of *Wheat That Springeth Green* are the chapters which originally appeared in *Look How the Fish Live,* it is still satisfying to see how ingeniously Powers has developed them. *Wheat That Springeth Green,* in short, is no *Morte d'Urban,* but it is a witty and moving book in its own right.

"Some of the new book," Powers said in a recent interview, "might be a little too subtle for a lot of people. It's not the kind of thing I'll clean up on." No doubt. Powers is precisely the kind of minor master whom most American readers (and many American critics) do not understand very well. But within the comparatively narrow framework of what he has tried to do, he is at his best quite nearly perfect. One need not be a skeptic to appreciate his wit; one need not be religious to appreciate his spirituality. And the smallness of his output is redeemed by its exceptional quality. To have written a dozen first-rate short stories and a comic novel comparable to [W. Somerset Maugham's] *Cakes and Ale* or [Evelyn Waugh's] *Black Mischief* requires no apology. It is an unalloyed pleasure to have J. F. Powers back, and one hopes that *Wheat That Springeth Green* will not be his last word on the splendors and miseries of the Roman Catholic Church in Minnesota. (pp. 73-4)

Terry Teachout, "Father Babbit's Flock," in The New Criterion, *Vol. VII, No. 5, January, 1989, pp. 69-74.*

JOHN WAUCK

"Powers's stories," wrote Flannery O'Connor in 1958, "can be divided into two kinds—those that deal with the Catholic clergy and those that don't. Those that deal with the clergy are as good as any stories being written by anybody; those that don't are not so good."

That remains a fair assessment. But what Powers's fiction lacks in quantity and diversity, it has made up for in quality, for he has mostly played to his strengths and stuck to priests. His 1962 novel *Morte d'Urban*—a subtle comedy about a year in the life of Father Urban Roche, a worldly priest driven to an ambiguous sort of holiness—demonstrated what Powers's first collection of stories, *The Prince of Darkness,* had suggested. The author's mastery of the clerical perspective, his dead-on ear for priestly dialogue, his quiet wit, and his flair for creating sublime farce all prompted high expectations for Powers's future. (p. 51)

Like [*Morte D'Urban, Wheat That Springeth Green*] tells the story of a Catholic priest in Powers's native Midwest. But unlike Urban Roche, Powers's new hero, Father Joe Hackett, starts out—after a crude and implausible *ménage à trois* in his neighbor's garage at the age of 15—in hot pursuit of a quite unworldly sanctity. Aspiring to a life of contemplation, he becomes in his seminary the leader of a band of likeminded "spiritual athletes," and even takes to wearing a hair shirt.

Ironically, it is his first parish assignment that punctures his illusions: the demands of parish work and the daunting holiness of his pastor cause Joe to despair of sanctity. He gives himself up to the social demands of his parishioners. Before long he is regularly waking up unsure of exactly when and how he got home.

After a stint as an archdiocesan bureaucrat, he finally gets his own parish (a coup) and a groovy, guitar-playing, Volkswagen-driving curate named Bill (a disappointment). After obligatory frictions, however, the two become friends, and the rest of the novel is the story of Joe's very gradual return to spiritual health.

In the course of the story, perhaps to grind an axe or two gently before signing off, the 71-year-old Powers allows himself, through the mouth of Joe, two formal sermonettes: one on the impossibility of "just war"; the other on what ails today's Catholic Church. The unexpected way in which Powers handles these two issues reveals him to be one of those liberals, nearly extinct by now, who do not allow their politics to change their view of the nature and purpose of the Church. A distrust of money and bourgeois America colors much of Powers's view of Midwestern life; he describes one monument to mammon at the local Badger shopping mall as if it were a sickening mockery of Catholic paintings of the Sacred Heart of Jesus. . . . Yet, for a socially sensitive pacifist, Joe has some harsh things to say about the tenor of post-Vatican II Catholicism: "All this talk of community, communicating, and so on—it was just whistling in the dark. Life's not a cookout by Bruegel and Elder and people know it."

Powers's prose is low-key and economical (he's the sort of writer who slips important plot developments into parenthetical phrases), and the laughs are never loud; his is an art of cumulative comedy. His portrait of parish life is as accurate as ever, though complicated now by the changes of Vatican II. Novelists always face a special challenge in priests—a group of men, neither relatives nor necessarily friends, thrown together not just to do a job but to be and think and feel according to an exacting ideal of personal holiness. Priestly talk can be tortuous. When the proper Christian responses are so familiar that they need hardly be articulated, the normal trajectory of accusation, denial, forgiveness, self-criticism, and rapprochement can be as instantaneous as it sometimes is in marriage. But those genuine Christian responses remain so difficult that one is never sure that they really occur. It is a subtle sort of spiritual one-upsmanship that Powers describes: rectories filled with vague resentments that surface in oblique verbal assaults, possibly innocuous remarks that seem to dare the target to take offense, making him doubt his own charity rather than the charity of the remark.

But the real concern of *Wheat That Springeth Green* is how a trail of failures, near-misses, compromises with evil, and occasional victories vitiated by self-congratulation can add up to a noble life. As Joe puts it to Bill, the priestly life is "not a hundred-yard dash. Not a mile run. . . . It's a sack race." Indeed, although Joe does enjoy a rather sudden release from his drinking problem and rejuvenation toward the end of the novel, his real transformation comes from realizing that it isn't contemplative ecstasy or warm faith but rather humiliating troubles, petty failures, and willing sacrifice that will ultimately forge his sanctification and salvation. The Holy "Cross" is literally the last word of the book—the bottom line. (pp. 51-2)

> John Wauck, "Benefit of Clergy," in National Review, New York, Vol. XLI, March 10, 1989, pp. 51-2.

DEAN FLOWER

[Like William Trevor, another] Irishman under-appreciated in this country is J. F. Powers. He is of course an American, but his ironic stories of Roman Catholic curates and pastors which began appearing in the 1940s, have sometimes seemed closer to Frank O'Connor's or even Joyce's than to anything in the American grain. Put Joyce's "Grace" or O'Connor's Bishop Gallogly stories (e.g., "Achilles Heel" or "Vanity") next to any Powers story, and you will see at once what I

mean. His only popular book, *Morte D'Urban* (1963, National Book Award), was followed by a disappointing story collection, [*Look How the Fish Live*], in 1975. Now I am happy to say he has written the funniest, and most profound book of all, [*Wheat that Springeth Green*] the story of Joe Hackett whose ambition it is to become a true contemplative, not just a pastor but a saint. If he fails in this—and it's not entirely clear that he does—the secular world including the Church and its clergy share richly in the blame.

Joe is the culmination of a lifelong series of Powers characters, from the high-principled young curates like Father Eudex ("The Forks") and the saintly old pastors like Didymus ("Lions, Harts, Leaping Does") to the selfish and sarcastic fathers fresh from seminary, like Father Faber in "A Losing Game" (1955) and the enterprising scapegrace con-men figures like Father Urban. He bears affinities too with Rafferty, the perversely-principled hero of the novel Powers' wife wrote in 1969 (Betty Wahl, *Rafferty and Co.*). What's new about Joe is that he's not just glimpsed in a short story, but given the slow growth and complexity of a novel. Joe came into being in two stories, "Bill" and "Priestly Fellowship" published in *The New Yorker* in the early 1960s. From these one can only conclude that he's perhaps funny and crusty, but essentially a curmudgeon. He doesn't know his new curate's last name and is too stubborn to ask directly. He criticizes his colleagues' priestly small talk, and then feels sorry for himself when he's left out of their company. But this view of Joe turns out to be, in the novel's larger context, quite mistaken.

Powers begins, astonishingly enough, with a Joycean display of technical virtuosity, depicting Joe as a child, a boy, an adolescent, a young man—shifting language and style in each chapter to befit the changing consciousness. For the first time in his work Powers uses explicit sex and a lot of vulgar language, but with such irony and poise as to make one wish for more. Brevity is indeed the soul of Powers' wit. Here is Joe negotiating his first sex with the neighborhood bombshell: "Dora?" "Whut?" "You know what you said." "Whut?" " 'Anytime,' you said." Silence. "Dora." "Whut?" "You know." Silence. "Dora." "Cost ya, kid." "O.K." "Ten dollars." "O.K." "I mean twenty." And so on. Powers has refined to a high art this monosyllabic style of talk, its silences more evocative of the tone (here it's funny, sad, tawdry, ironic) than any ampler style could have made it. Wherever Powers uses this terse colloquial style—in telephone exchanges, pastor-to-curate dickering, conversations at the liquor store, Joe talking with himself—he seems to extend its expressive range. These are breathing lessons every writer should study. At one point when Joe and his curate Bill toss a baseball back and forth, Powers makes the *pop* of Bill's weaker pitch in Joe's glove and the *plunk* of Joe's fastball in Bill's glove carry at least half of their conversation. Powers has never before been so inventive and verbally resourceful as this.

[*Wheat that Springeth Green*] does again what Powers has always done well—expose hypocrisy, cut down the complacent, ridicule the greedy and pretentious, lament the endless secularizations and corruptions of spiritual life. But his portrait of Joe does more than that. Out of all Joe's lapses and failures, he emerges a good man. He makes the value of human goodness shine forth. Perhaps the word is integrity, perhaps what he achieves is grace. Wheat that springeth green. But if it die, it bringeth forth much fruit. Whatever the nature of Joe's goodness may be, Powers manages triumphantly to make it real. Only a very few writers in any generation manage to do that. (pp. 138-40)

Dean Flower, "Barbaric Yawps and Breathing Lessons," in The Hudson Review, *Vol. XLII, No. 1, Spring, 1989, pp. 132-40.*

Thomas (Hunton) Rogers

1927-

American novelist, short story writer, and critic.

Rogers is respected for his comical novels that sympathetically portray young people disenchanted with contemporary American values. His first work, *The Pursuit of Happiness* (1968), which was adapted for film, chronicles the misadventures of William Popper, a rich graduate student and campus radical. Popper accidentally kills a pedestrian with his car and is sentenced to a year in prison, largely for failing to show remorse. Propper's life becomes endangered after he witnesses a murder in prison, impelling him to escape. He flees with his girlfriend to Mexico, where they intend to pursue the happiness they believe is unattainable in the United States. In this novel, Rogers suggests that even individuals who possess cherished American qualities cannot live in their homeland with clear consciences. Richard Gilman commented: "[*The Pursuit of Happiness* is] a fable that at its root carries the gentle, mysterious implication that our experience in and of America has had its ground cut away, has become questionable, not in the details but in its essence."

Rogers's second novel, *The Confession of a Child of the Century by Samuel Heather* (1972), described by the narrator as a "comical historical pastoral," revolves around the conflict between the title character's rebellious paganism and his bishop father's rigid faith. Expelled from Harvard University after a prank, Heather joins the Army, sees action in Korea, and is captured and brainwashed by Chinese Marxists. After the war, Heather marries a Peking Maoist and works a stint in the Central Intelligence Agency before becoming a successful writer of espionage fiction. Ultimately, Heather renounces his past and accepts his father's values, vowing to write books that "will make people better rather than worse." Rogers also authored an autobiographical novel, *At the Shores* (1980), about a midwestern teenager's first experiences with love, sex, and heartbreak. Anatole Broyard observed: "[*At the Shores*] reminds us how wonderful love is before we learn to pride ourselves on outgrowing it."

(See also *Contemporary Authors,* Vols. 89-92.)

IRVING HOWE

Thomas Roger's ***Pursuit of Happiness,*** . . . seems to come from the very center of the new sensibility, a pure fable of alienation and distrust. If the publishers can get the word around to the right universities, this book ought to be a commercial success, for it seems so thoroughly to express the sentiments of a certain brand of campus radicalism—innocent, egocentric, middle-class, and apolitical—that younger readers will feel that here is a book which really speaks for them.

Pursuit of Happiness stays in one's memory, perhaps because it contains a structured action, something like a plot, intended to reveal a cluster of meanings. Its central figure is a young rich boy, William Popper, living at the edge of the University of Chicago, involved with campus radicalism in a free-lance sort of way, and enjoying an affair with a likable girl, Jane Kaufman, daughter of an academic liberal. At once pleasing and feckless, generous and unreflective, they are figures recognizable to anyone who has spent some time on the American campus.

Mr. Rogers entraps them by having William accidentally run over and kill a pedestrian. By refusing the customary little hypocrisies which gain indulgence from judges, William gets himself sentenced to a year in prison. He breaks out, gathers up his Jane, and takes off for Mexico, where they will now lead the uncorrupted life. William feels no regret at having left the U.S. behind him; it's not his kind of country.

As a plot this has a glaring weakness: it makes the clash between William and American culture, meant to suggest an irreconcilable opposition of values, dependent on a mere automobile accident. But as a fable exhibiting the style of alienation, ***Pursuit of Happiness*** seems entirely attuned to the current emotions of "youth culture." When William gets into trouble his very rich grandmother supports his decision to flee the country, while Professor Kaufman, the stuffy liberal who keeps muttering about social responsibilities, proves hostile to the young people. Mr. Rogers never says much on his own, being cool to the point of caginess, but he arranges his material so as to make certain that the liberal—cast, of course, as the main enemy—is never allowed to declare the reasons for his dismay or even to say anything coherent at all. Mr. Rogers is thereby likely to endear himself to those young people who regard liberals as all but indistinguishable from finks; but as a novelist he is taking the easy way out. For he has failed to see that, in a novel dealing with a clash of ideas or political outlooks, it is necessary to endow the opposition with some powers of articulation.

Yet one can't be entirely sure that Mr. Rogers fails to see through the amiable young prig he has created in William. Exiled in Mexico, William soon makes certain that the family trust fund will keep him in groceries and luxuries—and one can foresee a future in which he reads Regis Debray, sneers at the compromises of his social-democratic father-in-law, and keeps a sharp eye on the stock market quotations. This too seems emblematic of a certain strand of New Leftism, and surely Mr. Rogers is too shrewd a writer not to realize that this final and very amusing touch calls into question his novel as a paradigm or defense of youthful estrangement. . . .

Apart from some silly dialogue passed off as student humor, *Pursuit of Happiness* is neatly written. It is likely to "bug" adult readers, but whether Mr. Rogers really wished to settle for so modest an outcome I don't know. Perhaps, like many other academics these days . . . Mr. Rogers wanted to identify himself with the "swingers" yet at the last moment, needled by his intelligence, he had to toss a bone to the bitch goddess of Maturity. (p. 84)

> *Irving Howe, "First Novels: Sweet and Sour," in* Harper's Magazine, *Vol. 236, No. 1416, May, 1968, pp. 83-8.*

RICHARD RHODES

William Popper and Jane Kauffman, the major figures in this quietly ironic first novel, [*The Pursuit of Happiness*] are two of the more sensible people to appear in recent fiction. Graduate students at the University of Chicago, happy lovers, children of good families, they do not picket, march or burn. William has a private income. Jane's father is a prominent economist. Both young people respect their elders. Nothing in their backgrounds obviously prepares us for the moment when they decide that they cannot pursue happiness in the United States of America, and must exile themselves to Mexico.

Thomas Rogers intended our surprise. . . . He must have chosen two young people as basically reasonable as William and Jane to make their defection more startling to readers over thirty, like, my God, even those nice kids next door have given up on the good old U.S. of A.

Jane is willing to stick with William wherever he goes, and William requires more than a little prodding to make him drop out. He gets it when he kills an old lady in a traffic accident one rainy day and finds himself sentenced to a year in prison at Joliet. He is sorry he has killed someone, but the sentence seems absurd to him. He could not have avoided the accident, and even the judge admits there is no evidence of negligence. William visits his victim's home and discovers that her daughter-in-law is glad to have the extra room for the kids. His father's stuffy lawyer demands that William show remorse, but he can feel none. Like the rest of us, he accepts the national traffic toll and sees no reason why he should go to prison for keeping the statistics intact.

Reluctantly in prison, sharing a cell with a chauvinistic politician who is serving time for graft, William befriends a Negro homosexual working on the same coal gang and helps him write a letter to a boy he has fallen in love with. William witnesses his friend's murder in a shower by a jealous rival, and though the prison code demands that prisoners do not inform on each other, he believes he should testify to what he saw. Now in some danger of being knifed himself by the murderer's friends, he drops out of a restroom window on his way to court, picks up Jane in Chicago and takes off for Mexico, a fugitive in permanent exile—but also a young man who has resumed control of his life.

William's family background makes his act more plausible. His fire-breathing grandmother, embattled in her walled castle on Prairie Avenue, fights off with lights and dogs and fire-hoses the Negro children who climb the walls every night. His gentle father hopes to build tree-shaded New Towns and save America by returning it to nature. His artistic mother communicates with her son in fuzzy, mystical letters and is a devotee of Kahlil Gibran. What they have given William, what he has evolved to, is an absolute sense of his own right and ability to make decisions about his life—a deeply American faith, after all. Who would have thought, Mr. Rogers implies, that the final stage of the evolution of the American dream might find our secure, affluent off-spring turning against America itself?

> *Richard Rhodes, "The WASP without a Country," in* Book World—The Washington Post, *June 9, 1968, p. 5.*

MARIAN ENGEL

Thomas Rogers does well to preface [*The Pursuit of Happiness*] with a quotation from the *Nicomachean Ethics:* "There is a general assumption that the manner of a man's life is a clue to what he on reflection regards as the good—in other words happiness." His novel's theme is a narrowly ethical problem, one which pervades America today: the survival of idealistic, well-educated, tough-minded youth in a pragmatic, cynical society whose rules are still Victorian.

William Popper is heir to one of those pragmatic, Victorian fortunes that were once easy to make in Chicago, but as his aunt, the beamish and pervasive Mrs. Thwett, complains, he fails to live up to its reputation. He lives on the South Side near the university, where he is a dilatory student, with Jane Kauffman. They read in bed and live out of tins; and, because she is a professor's daughter, he returns her like a library book to her dormitory at midnight. They are happy in spite of the incursions of Mrs. Thwett and the diffidence of Jane's father. Though they complain that most of the old radicals have graduated and they don't know the new, they are taking a fair swipe at the Good Life and winning.

Until the fatal spring morning when William's car skids in the slush and kills a pedestrian. He carries no insurance and has not seen fit to renew his driver's license. And, as his father's lawyer furiously points out, he has not even seen fit to *cry* as he examines the body of the woman he killed.

William takes it all with bland confidence, putting first things (Jane and decency) first as usual, until he begins to feel the slow grind of the mills of the gods. Then he has to choose between law and freedom. . . .

Jane and William, impervious to convention, indifferent to money once a modicum is there, interested as children in literal truth, are more successful human beings in modern times, but they find that they cannot survive reasonably in American society; for very good reasons, they opt out.

The Pursuit of Happiness is a novel remarkably free of cant considering its subject matter. It is handled almost entirely in dialogue, and as much of the dialogue is as flat as it is witty. The book gains its stature from its honesty, its truth to patterns of speech and feeling, its accurate and free rendering of the conundrums of human relationships. The book represents no technical advances. Its stylistic virtue is its transparency. There is no clumsy exposition; there are no purple passages; nothing is particularly quotable.

In the same way, William Popper glides on nylon casters and one fears at times his guilelessness is stupidity. "We have nothing to worry about," he says after he has served part of his sentence and then escaped from jail, "except the police—and what our parents may say." But one feels that he is an *ur*-character, a source of comment on America today, with his books on philosophy and revolution, his intelligent girl and his funny W. C. Fields voice, his ability to care in a general rather than a family way and yet to love the people who made him, and find them funny as well as insulting. An odd vindication of good values, in fact.

Is it easier when there's an Aunt Thwett to turn up with papers concerning one's income from the Mexican Mutual Fund, or a Mother shipping the washing by parcel post to Canada? Is it moral to waste your life in jail? Is there any good reason to tell lies because it makes the system run?

Mr. Rogers manages to ask a lot of questions in a short and superficially simple book. It's a book for now and a very good one, underdecorated as Shaker furniture: America's best emissary.

Marian Engel, *"Turn In and Opt Out," in* The New York Times Book Review, *July 28, 1968, p. 29.*

JACK RICHARDSON

There is a great deal to admire in [*The Pursuit of Happiness*]: intelligence, humor, several happily drawn minor characters. But what is one to make of the book's hero, William Popper, a young man on the verge of leaving college who, through a series of accidents, finds himself at the book's end an expatriate in Mexico uttering a concise "No" to his aunt's question, "And don't you ever want to live in your country again?" I have little idea just what Mr. Rogers wants us to make of him, though some reviewers have found the young man to be the prototypical youth of his time, morally repulsed by the society which nurtured him. They may be right, but if they are, we are in for a most flaccid form of social protest based on moral egoism and buttressed by an independent income. No, whatever else William Popper may be and whatever battles he engages in with the mores of his country, he is not a social changer nor a representative of a disaffected generation. He is, alas, a good but dim young man, not particularly gifted, with a compulsion to make honest emotive noises no matter what the situation—and this compulsion, as literature profane and sacred has taught us, soon puts one on a collision course with Caesar's laws and the society which is founded on them.

The main narrative event of *The Pursuit of Happiness* is an automobile accident in which William runs over and kills a woman. Suddenly the holy categories of society, which the enlightenment of a university education had taught him to be vague, amusing annoyances, settle upon him with their behavioral demands, to which his response is, like Melville's Bartleby's, "I prefer not to." He will not show suitable grief immediately after the accident; he will not desist from seeing and sleeping with his girl friend; he will visit the dead woman's relatives and announce he doesn't believe in God. When this candor succeeds in earning him a sentence of a year's hard labor, his non-dissembling ways entangle him in a homosexual triangle and an eventual murder. Called upon to testify about the crime, he is caught between the vengeance of the murderer's friends if he tells the truth and self-repugnance if he takes his lawyer's counsel and delivers legally ambiguous testimony at the trial. Pinned between these alternatives, the sense of self-preservation rises in William and he escapes from the courthouse, picks up a few thousand dollars from his grandmother, and takes his girl across the border into Mexico, there to live with his emotional integrity on the earnings from a mutual fund.

Now, had Thomas Rogers written a new *L'Etranger,* a work which pared down human response and pitted a life against the emotional rituals expected of it, one might find his character admirable, perhaps even saintlike in his innocent wonder that truth is not enough in the world. But *The Pursuit of Happiness* is a much smaller book, its scope is meant to include little more than distaste with the curiosities of a particular set of social circumstances, and neither the novel's detail nor design in any way enforces William Popper's "honesty" or makes of it something more than a quaint stubbornness. In the end, William is simply a pleasant person who is going to find a hard time of it so long as he remains on this planet, for if he thinks he has seen a mad society at work, wait until the rich young *gringo* runs over an old lady in Mexico.

There is, of course, another way of looking at Mr. Rogers's book, and that is as pure farce, with William Popper as a sort of modern Alceste—a quiet, well-bred misanthrope with just enough money to indulge his capacity for frankness. However much I would like to think that this was Rogers's intention, there is too much underlying serious approval of William's actions throughout the book to sustain that notion. It is more likely that the author finds American society so absurdly intolerable that even someone so ordinary as William Popper, who has little perception and no imagination, can be turned from it. For it must be said that Rogers, in a kindly, *sotto voce* way, draws up a formidable list of charges against recognizable national types and attitudes. There is a pragmatic lawyer, defender of a legal system based as much on sentimentality as on justice, and an imprisoned political boss, still loyal to his old party and pleased with his old ethics. The desperate stabs by the rich at some form of spiritual life are embodied in William's mother who has left an amiable and good husband to read *The Prophet* and paint; and there are the bourgeois anxieties of the successful academic liberal—in short, a good sampling of the American lie which Rogers, near the book's end, summarizes in an old vagabond William and his girl pick up on their way to Mexico. He is full of mythic braggadocio, a veritable slice of Americana on the road. So long as he is fed and ferried along his way, he remains a tolerable old bluff, spewing out stories of past wars, of adventures in oil fields and other frontiers, and of a half dozen or so ex-wives and children scattered across the land.

However, the old myth turns vicious when the young couple make it plain that they no longer want his company. Even a parting gift of money won't propitiate his rage:

> "Young folks! Got no time for old people. It's all they care about is just themselves, but who kept the country free for you, I'd like to know? We liberated Cuba, and you young folks lost it. Colonel Roosevelt spoke to me personally. He said, *Beat that drum, boy, beat it like hell.* Where's the spirit now, I'd like to know, letting the Japanese decide everything? You ain't married, I can tell. Kids! I'm proud to be an American. Never voted Democratic in my life, and never going to. You'll see, sailing along in that car, breaking all the speed limits. They'll get you."

Although the arrival of such a warped old legend may be a little too pat, it is a good enough way for Rogers to bring his elements together. Where they would have been better met, of course, is in William himself, but here we return to my opening remarks. The young hero does not have enough life for his actions and desires to be more than convenient, generalized responses to what the author has set against him. The great difficulty, of course, is that such a character, who will neither prick nor accept the social order, is forced to make of himself his own society. Since William Popper is far from capable of the imaginative exercise necessary to accomplish this, we are left with the simplistic geographic solution of Mexico. This is unfortunate, for there are many very good things in Rogers's novel that hover about the exasperating emptiness at its center. (pp. 12-13)

> Jack Richardson, "I Don't Want to Go Home," in The New York Review of Books, *Vol. XI, No. 2, August 1, 1968, pp. 12-14.*

RICHARD GILMAN

Thomas Rogers' *The Pursuit of Happiness* is . . . about a crime and about the inability to feel what one is supposed to feel. When William Popper, a well-to-do young graduate student at the University of Chicago, kills a woman with his car in an accident he might have prevented—"I should have honked, but I hate honking at people"—he is drawn into the meshes of moral and legal machinery whose workings he was unprepared for. He is expected to feel sorrow and contrition. " 'This is a very sad thing',," his lawyer tells him, " 'I'm sure you're deeply grieved'." " 'I don't feel anything much right now,' said William. 'I'm sure you're deeply grieved,' said Mr. Lawrence firmly. The full red lips pressed together in a single line."

Largely because of his inability to put on the right, concerned face before the judge, William is convicted of manslaughter and sentenced to a year in the penitentiary. There he feels himself "imprisoned by a chain of circumstances more durable than the walls that surrounded him. If he could only slip the chain and resume some sort of control over life!" Seeing his chance, he simply walks out one day, rejoins his lover, a Jewish girl with whom he had planned, as she says, "to do something . . . to make the world better," gets money from his rich grandmother and flees with his girl to Mexico. . . .

A sort of witty, understated, philosophically uncomplicated Americanization of Camus' *The Stranger*, Rogers' novel is written with an economy that almost never loses hold (the few times it does have mostly to do with the eccentric, rather stock-figurish grandmother), a wry, deft humor that is very rare in present American fiction. If it's almost too bare, too wry, this may be a price it pays for avoiding temptations: to be an indictment of American society, to poke around in moral corners, to be a "portrait" of today's youth. The book is a portrait of a possible world, thin air, empty landscapes, no maps. Without being a major work of fictional art, it's admirable and pleasing, a fable that at its root carries the gentle, mysterious implication that our experience in and of America has had its ground cut away, has become questionable, not in the details but in its essence. (p. 35)

> Richard Gilman, "News from the Novel," in The New Republic, *Vol. 159, No. 7, August 17, 1968, pp. 27-30, 34-6.*

DAVID J. GORDON

A common type of contemporary American novel tells the story of a sensitive, innocent youth, often with an unattractive mother and an attractive father, who becomes so alienated from the society he is about to enter that he takes upon himself the burden of renouncing its values in the name of something better. When such a story is skillfully managed it can dramatize the moral weakness of an entire society. But it often conveys the effect of false pathos or sentimentality.

The best among five or six recent examples of the type is *The Pursuit of Happiness,* a mature first novel by Thomas Rogers. Its hero, William Popper, is a University of Chicago senior, rich, white-Anglo-Saxon-Protestant, securely and vigorously in love, at ease with himself and others, already disillusioned in political causes but still idealistic and capable of moral indignation. Rogers has evidently taken pains to exempt his hero from social grudges and psychological hangups so that the alienation his novel dramatizes will seem as objective as possible. William's immediate circle consists of a saintly father who would like to create a genuine sense of community within the housing development he owns; an equally saintly but more spirited girl friend, Jane Kauffman, who cherishes a similar dream for the University neighborhood; a self-absorbed mother who has run off to New York to mysticize and paint; an aunt who means well but cannot understand how anyone can fail to share her own middle-class values; and two really marvelous eccentrics: fierce Grandma Popper, who maintains her capacious residence in a state of "siege" because it is now the heart of a Negro slum; and Melvin Lasher, the young lovers' zany classmate who "raises offensiveness to new levels of artistry." (pp. 112-13)

Rogers sets his story in motion with one bold push: William's car skids on an icy road, and a woman is run down and killed. It is an accident and, though he is appalled and sorry, William is unable to feel like a criminal. Everyone (except Mr. Popper and Jane) needs to explain the accident, especially William's lawyer who, whatever his private views, stresses the need for presenting to the court an image of a penitent youth of good character in order to combat the prosecutor's likely image of a rich young scofflaw living in sin and professing radical views. Recognizing himself in neither image William "felt himself becoming more and more hopelessly involved in something that made no sense." If William were more willing to play the game or had somewhat better luck, his sentence (one year in prison) would be milder, but he is too sincere and naïve to do the first, and Rogers exercises restraint in mounting circumstances against him. Rogers deftly makes prison society resemble society at large in being supported by hypocrisies, threatened by truth, and in dragging down all associated with it. William seizes an opportunity to escape, fully aware now of his imprudence and its cost, but believing that "being free with the permission of society is no freedom at all." He does not intend to be caught again, and in a sequence of final incidents which underlines both the seriousness of their decision and the moral ugliness they are leaving, William and Jane flee to Mexico. (pp. 113-14)

Rogers's style is so tactful, economical, and charming that we are surprised at the force the novel has quietly gathered behind this abrupt ending. Jane's struggle not to surrender her commitment to causes contributes to this force. She has repeatedly put off marriage because she wants to include something outside of themselves in their happiness. And it costs her hard tears to say, "we thought we could do something," and "the world will stagger along in its terrible way." Mexico of course is no solution. Jane will have a baby, William will write, the rest is uncertain. *The Pursuit of Happiness* is written in two parts called Life and Liberty, making us expect the title phrase in a third part which never comes. William only knows that "I don't have to be a middle-class American boy." He becomes a martyr to a certain idea of possible community. Because of the novel's power it is almost quibbling to object that its hero is made too invulnerable psychologically (especially in view of his oversweet relationship with his father) and too vulnerable socially (for the naïveté that aggravates his trouble with the law does not sort well with his general alertness). William's final decision is impressive enough to rob even Lasher of his accustomed irony: "it's a historic occasion when a genuine Chicago scion has to light out for the frontier." (p. 114)

David J. Gordon, "Some Recent Novels: Styles of Martyrdom," in The Yale Review, Vol. LVIII, No. 1, October, 1968, pp. 112-26.

ANATOLE BROYARD

[*The Confession of a Child of the Century by Samuel Heather*] is a charming book and it's a pity, because Thomas Rogers has shown signs of real talent. If he set his mind to it, he could probably write a genuine novel. I think someone ought to tell him, or he might just go on writing charming books. What is a charming book? It's one in which the author disarms his readers by his unpretentiousness, his comfortable air of casualness. . . .

Samuel Heather, the hero of *The Confession of a Child of the Century,* is the only child of a bishop, and he feels that this puts him into a hopeless sibling rivalry with Jesus Christ. He suffers from another, equally crippling disadvantage: the bishop is a professional father. Other family men are businessmen or dentists or farmers five days a week and fatherly only on occasion. But the bishop fathers his diocese too: he is always on the job. As a result, he has developed the paternal instinct to a monstrous degree.

Once out of his sight, at Harvard, Samuel rebels by blowing up part of the embankment of the Charles River. He uses for the job a stick of dynamite he happens to have about him. He never explains how he got it. Instead, he says: "I have an obscure sense that if an explosion is called for I am provided with explosives." Here is charm caught red-handed: a witty sentence doing duty for a motive. He is talked into blowing

up the embankment by one of his roommates—a piece of shameless expediency on the author's part, for one can't imagine Samuel's arriving at the decision within his own personality.

He is caught and suspended and joins the Army to avoid a jail sentence. The Korean war takes him to the front, and he is captured and interned. In a funny scene that will almost certainly be overestimated, Mr. Rogers pictures President Truman sitting in his bath arriving at the doctrine of voluntary repatriation of prisoners. The North Koreans' response to this means years of prison camp for Samuel, and during this time he is brainwashed, only it is more like having his head scratched. The cadences of Maoist cant recall his father the bishop and the religious impulse in Samuel, which has never found satisfactory expression.

He defects, spends 10 months in China, marries a Chinese girl and returns home—for no better reason than that the falling forward of the book demands it. His wife has a child, and he can't get a job, so he joins the Central Intelligence Agency. He has rationalizations for this, but though I've spent a lifetime listening to rationalizations and feel I should know my way around the field by now, I was not able to get a grip on Samuel's. . . .

When the bishop dies and leaves Samuel a bit of money, he resigns from the C.I.A. and writes three best-selling spy books. Just like that—easy as falling off a log. The books make him independent enough to take time out for his "confession." He has enough leisure, in fact, to enjoy a religious revelation while riding in the Paris Métro. Angels surround him and start telling him what to write: *"Write something that will make people better rather than worse."*

He decides to revise his "confession" and write a final scene in which Samuel and the bishop confess to each other and are reconciled. But not only his publisher objects: his unconscious does, too. He can't disavow the sinful truths of his life. His only alternative, as Mr. Rogers sees it, is to join a church, which he does. The book ends with a prayer, whose last line is "Praise Father, Son and Holy Ghost."

If this is a put-on, it's in bad taste. If it is sincerely intended, it's in bad taste of another sort, by literary standards. I found it impossible to tell which the author has in mind. You see, he's much too charming to be plainspoken about such a touchy subject.

Anatole Broyard, "Charm and Its Limitations," in The New York Times, May 30, 1972, p. 35.

JONATHAN YARDLEY

Thomas Rogers is in his mid-forties; *The Confession of a Child of the Century* is his second novel. At a time when good young writers are popping forth all over the place, bringing new life and excitement to American fiction, one who comes as late to the novelist's craft as Rogers is something of an anomaly—all the more so since in both of his novels his subject has been the generation gap. But his fiction is a powerful argument for the virtues of maturity and experience, for it possesses a depth, compassion and complexity that only the rarest of younger writers commands. (p. 4)

Told in the words of its "author" Samuel Heather, [*The Confession of a Child of the Century*] is an astonishing kaleidoscopic account of coming of age in postwar America, a tour de force but much more—a comic and sympathetic vision of the age-old battle between fathers and sons, a rich, boisterous, satisfying novel that stands confidently on its own as a major accomplishment by, no doubt about it, a major writer.

Samuel Heather calls it a "comical historical pastoral," written in

> a mixed style, both high and low, banal and eloquent, witty and sloppy. Indeed the more mixed the better, for what we aim at in works of this sort is to be all-inclusive. That is why the hero . . . though highly intelligent . . . should display great stupidity and make disastrous errors of judgment that lead to no harm. . . . He should be serious and silly, noble and vulgar, tender and cold. In short he should be a perfect mine of contradictions.

"The plot," Samuel continues, "should be made up of one whole and complete action which appears episodic and wayward. The action, though set in remote times and distant lands, should be described as if it happened yesterday in the backyard."

This all describes Samuel's *Confession* perfectly. As the book opens, in 1949, he is at home in Kansas City on vacation from Harvard, carrying on his running war with his father, the Episcopal bishop of that city: "Father was at heart a Puritan. For all his fashionable High Church practices, his real vision was gymnastic rather than sacramental. He saw life as an obstacle course to be successfully and effortlessly negotiated by those with good habits." Samuel has scarcely a good habit in him. At every turn he resists the virtues his father extolls—"work, discipline, purpose, faith"—and thus the real story of *The Confession* is the conflict between the stern faith of the father and the vague faithlessness of the son.

It is a story that whirls Samuel through a whole earth catalogue of postwar experience. He returns to Harvard and fumbles into an affair with a diminutive daughter of Old Boston whose amorous expertise turns out to be decidedly not Back Bay. Egged on by a roommate . . . Samuel dynamites the Charles River embankment. Sent packing by Harvard, he enlists in the Army to prove (more to Father than to Harvard) "that I was on the path to maturity." To his surprise, however, it turns out to be the path to Korea, where he sees battle briefly, is rather easily captured by the Chinese, and ends up getting a brainwash job from a Maoist whose unbending Marxist moralism sounds suspiciously like his father's unbending Christian moralism.

When the war finally ends, Samuel joins the small band of American P.O.W.'s who choose not to be repatriated; the chance to see China, he thinks, is too good to be missed, and besides it is a way to get back at the Bishop. At Peking University he woos May, a lovely little Maoist, and marries her. . . . He brings her home (to a disastrous reunion with Father), returns briefly to Harvard, becomes a father himself, then is cajoled into translating Chinese documents for the C.I.A. When last we see him, he has abandoned that and embarked on a career writing wildly successful novels in the Ian Fleming mode.

All of this is entirely bizarre, but there is a point to it: After being exposed to all the "moral and religious certainties" of the age, their "killing effect, especially on the young," Samuel, at 40, finds his *modus vivendi:* "If I must carry on then I will make my choice and announce my decision that life on

earth is a conflict, a great war which we must prosecute joyously and lovingly until we are given our final rest. We must fear no one and hate no one, but we must fight all our days against sin and death which have found their way into this world and will never be expelled." His father is by then dead, but Samuel comes to a reconciliation with the Bishop's memory, to an acceptance of the "mercy, forgiveness, and healing" of his faith.

The moral of the tale is a delicious one: "My story showed that even a son of a bishop can live happily ever after, which would perhaps encourage other young men to keep plugging away without giving up life." To put it another way, fathers and sons have more in common than they usually realize, not the least being that sons themselves eventually become fathers—carrying on the same fight, embracing many of the same traditions. Beyond paternal stricture and juvenile rebellion, there is accommodation and understanding.

It is a wise lesson, and Rogers tells it beautifully. He shifts stylistic gears with the skill and exactitude of a Stirling Moss, going back and forth among comedy and slapstick, contemplation and outrage, elegance and slang—splendidly conveying the aspects and moods of Samuel Heather, a bright and befuddled young man teetering along the way to maturity, wise one moment and foolish the next, the perfect hero for a "comical historical pastoral." Samuel is one of the best-realized characters of recent fiction, a "mine of contradictions" who wrestles valiantly with the inanities, insanities and contradictions of the time—a child of the century if ever there was one. Samuel's *Confession* is fiction of great depth and distinction, comedy in the classic sense, the tale of a happy human triumph over the varieties of 20th-century adversity. (pp. 4-5, 32)

> *Jonathan Yardley, in a review of "The Confession of a Child of the Century," in* The New York Times Book Review, *June 11, 1972, pp. 4-5, 32.*

ROGER SALE

The Confession of a Child of the Century by Samuel Heather by Thomas Rogers is, like Olivier's *Hamlet*, about a man who could not make up his mind. Unfortunately the man in question is not the putative author Heather, but the real one, Rogers. It begins fine and familiar and hokey and breezy. Heather, son of the Episcopal Bishop of Kansas City, arrives at Harvard in the late Forties, reads books, sleeps with a girl, is generally unhappy. The confessional habit of the older Heather looking back on all this is not one that encourages us to take it very seriously:

> I took Martha to a tea parlor near Copley Square where we took tea.
>
> "I'm leaving Harvard," I told her. "I'm not getting anything out of the place. I'm going to go to the Far East. Will you miss me?"
>
> She never took my lies seriously. "Will you go?" she asked.
>
> Dull question. Even the most petite charmer can occasionally say the wrong thing.

End of scene. What Heather wants that he is "not getting" at Harvard, how he knows he is lying about going to the Far East, why we are being told this little scene—Heather's manner presumes all these are silly questions. He is a raconteur, amusing us, catching sights and sounds of the familiar and the bygone.

When Heather has a vision, one can be relaxed and charmed about it:

> I saw that happiness was the worst rationalization of all. How dared those miserable old Greeks and Hebrews with their lousy climate and incessant wars and atrocious dooms, how dared they even raise the possibility of men being happy? Socrates talking about the good life! Isaiah putting specious words into the Lord's mouth! *Comfort ye, comfort ye, saith the Lord. Speak ye comfortably to Jerusalem and cry unto her that her warfare is accomplished.*
>
> Ha! Jerusalem's warfare was just getting well underway when Isaiah wrote those words. And yet both Socrates and Isaiah paled into insignificance compared to the Christian message. What a flood of false expectations had been let loose there! I thought of the early Christians, their hearts reeling with love as the Empire collapsed around them and the aqueducts dried up. Ahead stretched more than a thousand years when one could not have even a decent bath, and all they talked about was being washed in the blood of the Lamb. Well, thank God I'd seen through it all early enough so I could go through the rest of my life with a firm, sober, rational understanding that things were just going to get worse and worse.

Ask novels to be like Jane Austen, and this won't do at all; think of Bellow's *Herzog* as sophomoric in his historical insights and Samuel Heather is at best an early adolescent. But it seems to me splendid; a thousand years in his sight are as but a single sentence.

It is fitting that having lied to his girl about going to the Orient Heather does in fact go there, albeit as a soldier to Korea, and when he gets there we have a bouncy account of his induction into battle, actually learning that he is being fired at, actually deciding to fire back. But then Heather is taken prisoner and something happens to the novel. Rogers seems to have decided that at this point the fun and games are over and that he really wants to write a *Bildungsroman*, a *Sons and Lovers* or a *Portrait of the Artist*. In the prison camp Rogers surrounds Heather with a lot of other prisoners who don't like him and, we see, with good reason. But the moment this happens our relation to the book is forced to change, from listening to an entertaining "comical-historical-pastoral," as Heather calls it, to seeing the painful limitations and needs of a spoiled, educated, callow, aggressive young man.

For this new purpose Rogers's original mode is all wrong. All might have been well had Rogers tried to drop the chatty tone and thereby indicate that such tones are possible only to the breezy young. But though the tone does get more somber and strident, the superficiality of Heather's vision of himself defeats whatever changes in tone Rogers was trying to dramatize. When Heather decides to defect to China, for instance, after giving us a slambang account of how Truman came to believe in voluntary repatriation, he says it was the decision of a moment. The trouble is that we have too little to go on to see it as anything other than a whim, a novelistic signal for new adventures, a petulant judgment by Heather against the other prisoners, perhaps, or a dimly understood retaliation against Daddy or Harvard. Then when Daddy becomes im-

portant in the novel, we are asked to believe that Heather's whole problem is being the son of a man who serves The Son, but we have no private or personal Heather on whom this possibility can register as anything other than a joke.

Finally, when Heather goes to China and meets and falls in love with a Chinese girl, we are told we will hear nothing of their private life because Heather eventually marries the girl and she, Mrs. Heather, doesn't want personal affairs discussed in her husband's public confession. You can get away with that kind of nonsense in a raconteur novel, maybe, but when we are being asked to figure out what happened to Samuel Heather, we can only be affronted by the presence of a censoring Mrs. Heather in a novel by Thomas Rogers.

Thus it is that for long stretches in the second half of the novel one longs to help Rogers, to see that the tone is just right after all, to deny that the novelist is trapped. But it won't do:

> I feel I am not giving my girls a sufficiently impressive image of fatherhood to get through life with. And certainly they're not going to get much from the young men I see around these days, urban rubes with their hair in a braid. One of the main reasons we're going to Paris is to get the girls away from American boys for a while. Keeping children virginal is a mighty task. I've begun to appreciate Father's efforts along these lines. His argument seems to me more and more irrefutable. One cannot give oneself to everyone. It's both foolhardy and vain.

This comes at the very end, where we will know how to read rightly, if we ever will. One sees immediately the bankruptcy of this voice: Heather is involved in sexual competition with the potential seducers of his daughters; he is afraid and in flight; he cannot begin to remember accurately the conversations he had with his father about sex; he is pompous, and so foolhardy and vain himself. But we can only guess if Rogers wants us to share this view, and my guess is that, on the contrary, he would like us to be both convinced and amused by Heather as much at the end as at the beginning. Even if Rogers does want us to see Heather's bankruptcy and blindness, he has long since given up finding ways to make him interesting, whether as raconteur or defeated and pathetic hero. The sadness is that after a fine beginning we gradually cease to care. (pp. 28-9)

Roger Sale, "I Am a Novel," in The New York Review of Books, *Vol. XVIII, No. 12, June 29, 1972, pp. 28-31.*

JOHN GREENYA

Samuel Heather, author of the novel within this novel, was born in 1930 and " . . . actuarially speaking I am due to cease upon the midnight with no pain at the beginning of the year 2000 . . ." hence the title [*The Confession of a Child of the Century by Samuel Heather*]. Heather is, pardon me in advance, a son of a bishop. But credit Thomas Rogers that although he sets up that musty gag by making his hero the male child of the Episcopalian bishop of Kansas City, he never comes right out and says it until the very end. Nor, in fact, does he use gags per se at all, yet he has managed to write a book so filled with comedy that the covers should bulge.

In 1968, Thomas Rogers' first novel, *The Pursuit of Happi-*

ness, was a rather surprising nominee for the National Book Award, surprising both because of the plain-faced humanity of an over-40 novelist writing about young graduate students, and because of the poignant comedy in it, at a time of brutal national wrenchings. In this new book he goes against the grain again and writes a tale that is clean, sentimental, simple and, though irreverent, politely so. It's an intentional anachronism. Here's Samuel on his early home life, paterfamilias in particular:

> Father was bishop of Kansas City. "What is it like to have a bishop for a father?" people ask. Well, it's hell. Most fathers are terrible (most sons are terrible too) but a bishop father is worse than most. He is a professional father. His diocese is his family. He delivers homilies and distributes advice. He gets into the habit of being a father, whereas most fathers are fatherly only on occasion. Their daily work is to be businessmen or dentists or farmers. My father's daily work was to be a father. It was excruciating.
>
> Dinners had the mixed character of a sacred repast and a gladiatorial combat. The Episcopal palace of Kansas City (actually a ten-room McKinley Administration house) was far from cheerful. There was more stained glass than one wants in a home. The downstairs rooms were too lofty for small talk and the halls too narrow for comfort. The bedrooms were like old-fashioned Pullman cars, all green and hard. It was really a terrible place to live.

So Samuel Heather left Kansas City to begin his life as a child of the century which he expected would blossom at Harvard. But he found that a terrible place to live too, and managed to get himself expelled for what used to be called a "prank," though blowing up a section of the Charles River bank is prankishness with a modern flavor. (p. 35)

Heather leaves Harvard, enlists, finds himself in Korea, and after a battle on his very first day is captured. When he is finally released, his natural inclination to do the unexpected leads him to accept the Red Chinese offer to go there and study. What takes place when the news of this "un-American" act descends in its full horror on Kansas City and its Episcopal bishop is both funny and humane, and is followed by news of his choice of a Communist wife and his subsequent decision to leave China, come home, and to go to work for what else?—the CIA.

Eventually Heather leaves the CIA and becomes a best-selling author of mystery stories with a hero named Dalton Smed. Perhaps it is only natural that having failed at Episcopalianism, Harvard, the United States Army and even communism, he should succeed at spying and making up stories. To Samuel it's all of a piece; he had experienced the emptiness of the Right Way and the Good Life, but found pleasure and even monetary reward by doing just what people didn't want him to do—a true child of the century. (pp. 35-6)

> *John Greenya, "Up-To-Date in Kansas City," in*
> The New Republic, *Vol. 167, No. 8, September 2, 1972, pp. 35-6.*

ANATOLE BROYARD

In *At the Shores,* Thomas Rogers gives us a definition of adolescence as it was 30 years ago. Mr. Rogers isn't afraid to be grotesque either; his adolescent hero is happy. He loves his mother, his father, *and* his sister. At crucial moments in Jerry's life, his mother gets an "alert" expression on her face, which is a wonderful way for a mother to be—alert, converting love into concentrated attention.

When Jerry is in ninth grade, he begins to feel, for the first time, that there is a sharp dividing line between himself and girls. He has to touch them to make sure of who and what they are. When he and his friends see their first pornographic film, he feels that the dividing line between himself and girls has somehow been blurred or smeared, and it makes him very anxious. . . .

When at the age of 17, Jerry falls in love with Rosalind, he is amazed to find that she loves him, too. Perhaps the truly loved one is always amazing. But Rosalind is rich and her love isn't as hungry as other girls; it is just one more luxury to her. Rosalind is beautiful and intelligent, but she lacks a sense of adventure. She can't understand why, when she and her family were away, Jerry broke into their house to kiss her bathing suit and bite her sandals. . . .

Like every other adolescent boy, Jerry is puzzled by the mystery of attractiveness, why one girl is attractive and another is not, and he has the decency to grieve over this random distribution of luck. He feels, as so many boys of his time must have felt, that he and Rosalind belong to two different but closely related species. His species seems to have animal instincts where hers has social instincts.

Mr. Rogers reminds us what an educational experience first love is, like our first serious reading, listening to music or looking at paintings. Rosalind is the first female Jerry ever loved who was not a mother or a sister. She is a sudden lesson in the complexity of love, in the uses of frustration.

At the end of *At the Shores,* when Rosalind has broken Jerry's heart, he discovers that he is not really harmed by his broken heart. Adolescent hearts are so strenuous that perhaps they have to be broken, just as horses have to be broken, if one is to do anything with them. An unbroken heart may be incompatible with the second half of the 20th century.

Mr. Rogers says of Jerry that he still "thought of girls as a kind of blessing." Sometimes books are a kind of blessing, too. *At the Shores* is a blessing on the beginnings of love. It reminds us how wonderful love is before we learn to pride ourselves on outgrowing it.

> *Anatole Broyard, in a review of "At the Shores," in*
> The New York Times, *November 1, 1980, p. 23.*

EVAN CONNELL

Several years ago Thomas Rogers wrote *The Confession of a Child of the Century,* providing some of the funniest passages in recent American literature. The book began to disintegrate, as I recall, when Mr. Rogers thought he had been amusing long enough and decided to get serious. It was a mistake. Except for that miscalculation he might have delivered something as outrageous and unforgettable as *Lolita.* In any case, quite a few readers will open his new novel with the expectation of more such raucous comedy; and although a misty humor does permeate *At the Shores,* it does not even resemble the inspired lunacy of his previous creation. (p. 15)

What we have this time is a deliberate account of an altogether natural boy growing toward manhood—which is to say that for most of his youth he thinks about nothing except girls. Oh, there are interludes when one thing or another occurs to him, then it's hippety-hop back to that marvelous, strangely foreign stuff.

His name is Jerry Engels and he grows up on the edge of Lake Michigan, first in the town of Whiting, Ind., later in Chicago. Nothing extraordinary happens. Perhaps he is closer than normal to his sister, yet not pathologically so. He imagines himself with a squadron of girls, though there is little enough action—apart from one visit to a Michigan City whorehouse—until he entangles himself with Rosalind. This sandy hillside idyll ends the moment she tells her mother; she is packed off to Miss Chapin's school in New York, leaving Jerry so desolate that he resolves to drown himself. Halfway to eternity he changes his mind, oppressed by a conviction that he must go on living; he swims to shore and by the end of the book we understand that he will soon go galloping after another nubile classmate.

The fact that nothing unusual happens throughout the story is of itself unusual and is a credit to Mr. Rogers, considering that most writers depend on specious drama. What is disappointing, apart from the sparkling promise of his first book, is the absence of anything vital or fresh. The author seems to have combed the memory of his own adolescence for details: Scammons Gardens, the Shoreland Hotel, the Tri-City sailboat race, Horton's Dock, the 49th Street block of Woodlawn, Stineway's, the Junior Night party at U-High, popular singers and songs: "Amapola," "Begin the Beguine" and so on. Much of this is required to establish time and place, without which an honest novel has less specific gravity than science fiction. But along with such particularities we ask for the author's insight, for an interpretation—however indirect—of the events he describes; we ask for the development of characters whose form and behavior will remain with us after we finish reading.

Instead, we are given an almost interminable transcript of accurate but insignificant teenage reflections and dialogue. . . . (pp. 15, 26)

Once in a while Rogers breaks through this crust to write with grace and sensibility. Now and then, there are wonderful moments. . . .

But all too soon the beat goes on. . . . (p. 26)

It's curious and puzzling. But like a large body of water a writer will display crests and troughs; we shall see what Mr. Rogers brings to the surface next. (p. 27)

> Evan Connell, "Girl Crazy," in The New York Times Book Review, November 23, 1980, pp. 15, 26-7.

JOSH RUBINS

Like [Gilbert Sorrentino's] *Aberration of Starlight*, [*At the Shores*] too is a memory-book, palpably autobiographical, reaching back to the late 1940s. The setting is also a lakeside vacation spot, though Rogers's summer cottages at Indiana Shores, thirty miles across Lake Michigan from Chicago, have little in common with the Reccos' drab boarding-house accommodations. Again the scope is small—a single summer, a crucial time for a kid who'll probably grow up to be a writer. But while Sorrentino holds an inquisition on memory, testing for frailty and impurities with every probing, frag-

menting shake-down device he knows, Rogers intends to embrace every bit of the past—and even, in fact, improve on it—through the deft marshaling of all the storytelling artillery at his command.

Adolescence. First love. First sex. First "broken heart." First twistings away from the comfortable family niche. Jerry Engels, in the summer between his junior and senior years of high school, is going to brush up against each of those milestones, and Rogers means for it all to be . . . well, beautiful. But idealizations of common experience are likely to meet resistance unless they're carried out somewhat surreptitiously; we have to be half-convinced that "this is how it was" before we'll let ourselves be fully seduced by "this is how it should have been." And the traditional central feature of an idealized coming-of-age—an insistence on fundamental innocence, a denaturing of actual sexuality—won't convince readers in 1980, when television toddlers in designer jeans seem to know everything that Judge Hardy could never quite manage to tell Andy.

So if Jerry Engels's summer is to be better-than-real but never risible, Rogers needs to find a stretch of adolescent sand somewhere between *Ah, Wilderness!* and *Endless Love*. For every archetypal gesture he makes, he needs to make a dozen that plant Jerry on rough, specific, verifiable ground. One false move and the whole idyllic confection will turn into treacle. Fortunately, Rogers has the narrative abilities required for such a chancy proposition, and his near-fable has the textured authenticity of a photo-essay.

The too-true-to-be-goodness is tempered—but never negated—by the kinks in Jerry's character: his narcissism, his flirtatiousness, his passion for women of all ages (with just the slightest dark shadow over his attachment to his older sister Anne). Operatic flights are brought down to size, tenderly, with moments that capture the drifty, fickle nature of adolescent attention: in the midst of a careening life-and-death meditation, Jerry finds himself face to face with a blueberry bush and happily transfers his energy to a burst of berry-picking; Jerry's lyrical suicide attempt (after his heart has been duly broken by guilt-ridden girlfriend/lover Rosalind) is cut short when he thinks of the lambswool suit just bought at Marshall Fields. . . . And, most importantly, the dangers of free-floating romanticism are averted by some genuine eroticism and concrete sexual detail, though the fierce selectivity here does tend to draw attention to the idealizing process. (There are no dirty words in Jerry's sexual world, and only the most reluctant, oblique references to masturbation.)

Again and again Rogers's substantial gifts—comic, intuitive, evocative—neatly conspire to bring Andy Hardy and O'Neill's Richard Miller thoroughly up to date. When Jerry's near-perfect mother attempts to comfort her mysteriously mopey son, Rogers tells us that Jerry "felt like throwing himself into her arms and sobbing out, 'Oh Mom, I'm so horny.'" That's a lesson in how to revalidate an archetypal scene with one piercingly specific, immaculately chosen detail.

A lot of readers will no doubt welcome *At the Shores* as realistic fiction—simply one young man's story vividly remembered and re-created. Rogers is, after all, a far gentler juggler of conventions than Sorrentino, but for both of them writing a novel seems to have become the equivalent of taking a dare. You'd think that would be true of most any novelist; it isn't.

These two books have an inner motion, a sense of risk, that you'll find in very little recent fiction. (p. 64)

Josh Rubins, "Balancing Act," in The New York Review of Books, *Vol. XXVII, No. 20, December 18, 1980, pp. 63-4.*

Jerome Rothenberg

1931-

American poet, editor, and translator.

Rothenberg's interest in such Modernist experiments with language as Dadaism and Surrealism led to his conception of poetry as a non-rational expression of the subconscious. His poetics, known as "deep image theory," describes the belief that images from the poet's subconscious should be the fundamental substance of poetry. Rothenberg's numerous collections and influential anthologies of ancient and primitive verse challenge the traditional definition of poetry. His theory of total translation, which emphasizes the circumstances surrounding a poem's presentation, including ritual, music, and pictograph, evinces his belief that poetry is an expression of the collective unconscious of a culture. Rothenberg's own verse is commended for its technical daring and its unusual and evocative imagery.

Rothenberg's early volumes, which include *White Sun Black Sun* (1960), *The Seven Hells of Jigoku Zoshi* (1962), and *Poems 1964-1967* (1968), work through the influence of Federico Garcia Lorca, Gertrude Stein, and abstract artist Arshile Gorky on his imagination. For example, in *The Gorky Poems* (1966), reprinted as one section of *Poems 1964-1967,* Rothenberg creates linguistic analogues to Gorky's experiments with collage, relying for meaning on aural effects and the juxtaposition of words and images. His association with the deep image movement of the late 1950s contributed the attempt in many of these early pieces to garner images from the poet's unconscious which speak directly to the unconscious of the reader.

Rothenberg's interest in the non-rational led him to study ethnological records of native cultures from many countries. While editing and translating several compendia of native poetry, legends, chants, and rituals in the late 1960s and early 1970s, he developed the concept of total translation, which, he has stated, "takes into account any or all elements of the original [poem] beyond the words." The extensive notes and commentary which conclude such anthologies as *Technicians of the Sacred: A Range of Poetries from Africa, America, Asia, and Oceania* (1968), *Shaking the Pumpkin: Traditional Poetry of the Indian North Americas* (1972), and *America a Prophecy: A New Reading of American Poetry from Pre-Columbian Times to the Present* (1973), emphasize the original culture and ritual that produced each poem and identify such contemporary, often avant-garde, analogues as concrete poetry, prose poems, and projective verse. These works have influenced the study of both poetry and anthropology. Although some anthropologists question the authenticity of Rothenberg's translations, these anthologies are universally praised for printing previously inaccessible material.

Rothenberg's work with Native American poetry has directed the focus of his own verse away from the individual unconscious toward the collective unconscious. *A Seneca Journal* (1978), which was originally published in three volumes in 1973, 1975, and 1978, chronicles Rothenberg's initiation into Native culture during an extended sojourn at the Allegany Seneca Indian Reservation in the early 1970s. The poems col-

lected in this compilation explore similarities between Seneca traditions and rituals and those of his own Polish-Jewish heritage. *Poland/1931* (1974), often considered Rothenberg's most successful collection of his own verse, further examines the impact of ethnicity, religion, time, and place on the formation of a stable identity. Rothenberg also correlates the experiences of European Jews and Jewish immigrants in America. A series of extended verbal collages, these poems incorporate such sacred and secular texts of the European Jewish culture as the Bible, Yiddish literature, numerology, folktales, and the Cabala.

(See also *CLC,* Vol. 6; *Contemporary Authors,* Vols. 45-48; *Contemporary Authors New Revision Series,* Vol. 1; and *Dictionary of Literary Biography,* Vol. 5.)

KEVIN POWER

[Rothenberg's *Deep Image* theory & Charles Olson's *Projective Verse*/concept] share a larger area of common ground than was evident at the time. They both refuse any interpretation which focuses meaning on a third party outside the text, & both return towards Pound's definition of the image as "an emotional & intellectual complex in an instant of time." Rothenberg's concern with process as a "chain of images" is markedly similar to Olson's notion of a "chain of perceptions." Both men view the poem as a high-energy construct—an extension of Pound's idea of the image as an energy cluster—but while Olson dances with the eye making the poem into a mosaic of life's surface & of man's presence on it as the ordering perception, Rothenberg prefers the more exotic voyage inwards where the eye fumbles in the darkness seeking clarity in the form of revelation. Both Olson & Rothenberg are profoundly concerned with communication—Olson, perhaps, primarily in the sense of a code of action, & Rothenberg, above all, of discovering the images that constitute the 'deep structures' or organising forms behind the life of a community. Rothenberg seeks to move both poet & poem back towards a more significant role at the centre of society, & the 'deep image' forms the essence of the emotive code man unconsciously uses to structure his capacity for & his need of interrelating. On one level, the deep image is a process that leads to the discovery of a universal language.

> I connect "deep image" with perception as an instrument of vision ie a visionary consciousness opening up through the senses, grasping the phenomenal world, not only for its outward form (though this also, of necessity) but winning from a compassionate comprehension of that world a more acute, a more agonising view of reality than by rational interpretation. (Rothenberg)

The image was the prima materia. It fused those words that were extensions of man's daily presence—words that were there at the end of his arm either as tools or as constants of his imagination—into revelations of larger meanings. The 'deep image' as it emerges is a definition of that sensed awareness we all share. It belongs to the category of vision because it reveals what is there. Its field is that of a permanent present. It depends on the cumulative effect of the build-up of images, their cutting edge, their suggestive capacity, their penetration, & the flash of recognition. The action & interaction of the images move the poem towards revelation, & the keys to such movement are found in tension & reverberation. The image is not, therefore, a static picture or an object to be viewed but the active constituent of vision. The 'deep image' can be read as the sensation which emerges from this process & transfers itself as 'a flash of recognition' without any sharply delineated outline. (pp. 154-55)

Grammar exists here to present the image not the word. The phrase is the basic unit with the noun being its dominant member. In primitive poetry the power of naming carries immense weight, it signifies decisions made, knowledge acquired, & choices taken. Rothenberg exploits this more fully in his later poetry but at this point he was concerned with the power of the noun to accrue new meanings to it. Such a role extends well beyond the simple code of noun + associations. Rothenberg uses the noun to ring up how a man lives, the nature & implications of his daily routine, the nailing of a pattern of life. The images are transcultural to the extent they imply specific sources rather than just simply common contexts. This is a vital activity & one that distinguishes between image as ornament & image as agent for change. Rothenberg's early poems were a powerful counter-balance to a climate that suspected the image & underestimated its effect to

be 'powerfully present.' The equation of action/affirmation as equally truth was over facile & undervalued both 'experience recollected' & epiphany as the hard-won measure of experience. Energy controlled rather than casually exhibited is, of course, the essential factor. The poems in **White Sun Black Sun** belong to a powerful current that includes Char, Trakl, Vallejo, Lorca, Neruda, & the French Surrealists, but Rothenberg directs these poems towards the articulation of the American experience:

> the giant waits on the beach
> for the sand to turn pink with the blood
> from the star in his throat

Rothenberg's early poems have clear affinities with Surrealism. He uses sharp images as juxtapositions to the fuzzy outlines of bourgeois life. . . . Rothenberg uses the image not simply in the sense of an exploration of the individual psyche but rather in the Jungian terms of penetrating the collective unconscious. He deals not so much with the mind's capacity to invent as its power to reveal. His search is for the myth that socialises the human into a community. The Surrealists used the image as a means of provocation. Desnos shows that his purpose was to get beyond automatism into the political arena: 'beyond automatism there is the intentional, beyond poetry there is the poem, beyond poetry received there is poetry imposed, beyond free poetry there is the free poet.' Rothenberg would, I suspect, sympathise with this view but it's not his essential objective. His inclinations lay more with the 'organic surrealism' of Lorca & Neruda, even if he remains:

> a city boy lost in the country, a
> wound in the hand was all I knew about willows.

Rothenberg was well aware of the dangers of romanticism inherent in such a view but he shares Cassirer's belief in life as a continuous unbroken form. The problem here lies in attempting to define the exact nature of the image's roots in its language. Neruda & Lorca speak against a backcloth of an essentially unchanging culture, Rothenberg speaks from within a continuously shifting culture that resists meaning, roots, or definition. . . . The history, the context, provide the image with the materials for myth. Lorca could truly collect his images from the voices in the fields, catch their reverberations in the wind, & intimately feel what naming meant to the voice. There is a circular process where the image can emerge, disappear, & re-emerge. This is not a situation where the American poet can feel at ease but Rothenberg was aware of the importance of recovering some of these fundamental links between image & language/man & society. . . .

The iconography of [Rothenberg's] early poems recalls a Magritte or Dali world of eggs full of hours, trains, umbrellas, gloves, glasses of white chalk, & mirrors—words that are emotively charged, already contextualised in a revenant urban landscape. It is not easy to control their emergence as demands of a real occasion, & there is always the temptation to use them as stimuli to provide occasion. Rothenberg accepts the risk & admits the power to freely associate perceptions. Bly termed this 'negative surrealism,' products of the mind, but he misses the point that an urban environment of pressurized work patterns, full-blooded consumerism, & of social & political crises produces 'organically' twisted & uprooted images as a natural consequence of its malfunctioning:

> You were trying to dream.
> An icicle broke from the sky

> & entered my heart.
> The moon was a spider.

These are not indulgences of the imagination, not a play of mind at the expense of feeling, but the mind in a corner deprived of both landscape & object as natural extensions of its full self. (pp. 155-57)

For Rothenberg the source of the image is the common particular whose associations carry both reader & poet into the depths of the unconscious. As a *choseiste* he's the exact opposite of Robbe-Grillet since his objects send back radar signals of man's emotions. But clearly mere image is insufficient. The image of itself is only an object if it does not move. Tension, resonance, reverberation, silence are the techniques of such movement. 'The fundamental rhythm of the poem is the rhythm of the images; their texture, their contents offer supplementary rhythms' (Kelly). But sheer multiplicity of image is no use unless the jumps between the images are clearly part of the process of discovering identity. Tension comes from making the jump as large as possible without breaking the unity. The image, for Rothenberg, discovers its being through its function. . . . (pp. 158-59)

> Basically the fullest force is possible only by means of the successful employment of one image's position in a context of other images, after its first appearance as dark sound still lingers on as resonance. This resonance must be controlled, & the effective means of control are the acoustics of space intervening between one image & the next. The subsequent image is conditioned, made to work, by the image that precedes it, & conditions as it is finally conditioned by, the image that follows it: through the whole poem (Kelly).

Kelly acknowledges his indebtedness to Lorca's idea of the darkness surrounding all things. Rothenberg similarly emphasises that sound is not the only element in the music of the word, the tension between speech & meaning is of compatible force. This music activates silences of the poem which have functions parallel to the blanks in a Cezanne watercolour or the areas between Noguchi's stone. Spicer has said that he would like to make a poem that has no sound but the pointing of a finger. The 'deep image' theories are such pointings. (p. 159)

The problem of defining a process towards revelation was that Rothenberg found himself, to some extent, trapped in a language of vision—key words that easily became a code, putting visions on tap with their associations & complexes of meanings already cemented in. Rothenberg was, finally, threatened by the process as the Abstract Expressionists had been, threatened by the sense that it was dangerously open to imitation. Vision could easily succumb to the mirror of its surface. I also feel that Rothenberg felt that the exigences of the image limited the attacks he wanted to make on syntax. Whorf has stated that the grammatical & syntactical rules that characterise a language reflect the structures of the society it belongs to. Rothenberg in **Sightings,** "Further Sightings," & "Steinbook & More" has as part of his intention the revealing of deep structures in language for the purpose of undermining them.

Rothenberg opens the **Gorky Poems** with a quote from Gorky's journals: 'I like the heat, the tenderness, the edible, the lusciousness, the song of a single person, the bathtub full of water to bathe myself beneath the water.' & Gorky had continued: 'I like the wheat fields, the plough, the apricots,

the shape of apricots, these flirts of the sun.' Rothenberg's imagery in these poems contains this same mixture of succulence & sensuality. He uses the same wide brush-strokes, the same ambiguity of image that could be vagina, earth furrow, or the breaking open of ripe fruit.

This was a truly felicitous meeting. They share similar cultures, & they both use them as active transforming agents, as makers of words & images. Rothenberg's poems are, he says, a matter of convergences: these would include the use of rich oil textures, a multiplicity of focus, the sudden peaking of an image, & the use of chance techniques as a means of discovery rather than as an end in itself. Both Rothenberg & Gorky work from a confusion of perspectives where vision is altered by emotion. The poems, like the paintings, are organic interiors where their landscapes can grow. *Charred Beloved* presents a deep psychological world, a cloudy space where insistent shapes or images tie one to unconscious memories. Gorky was able to push off from the haphazard forms made by one grass blade against another, using them as prototypes for the fantasy of forms that fill his canvases. Rothenberg in the same way pushes off from his impressions of the painting, using their unity as a filter for the flow of images. There's a density, an aggressiveness, a continuous underswell of passion that is so true of lives regulated by short-seasoned bursts of color. The eroticism is earthy & violent, the plums heavy on the branch: to yield is also to want. (pp. 159-60)

Rothenberg shows his concern for the felt intuited truth—the truth which lies at some central meeting place: the place where naming is not an act of generalised meaning but the seeing through in the moment of need. Rothenberg merges, as Gorky does, the ambiguity of image & meaning. He produces multiple images, or what Breton called referring specifically to Gorky 'hybrid forms.' Rothenberg sets out the terms of a universal morphology—one where 'lobster & spider' can be forced into the same sack. His eye finds the similarities of form between apparently unrelated structures. Shapes or meanings have a multiplicity of reference, this is partly a surreal throw-back to categories of things. Generic differences are ignored for form metaphors, so that any given image can be an amalgam of various sources & have a multiplicity of sources. . . . (pp. 160-61)

It was Stein's completion to 'a rose is a rose is a rose' that made her point: '& then later I made that into a ring, I made poetry & what did I do I caressed, completely caressed & addressed a noun.' This then is the function of repetition to make the ordinary extraordinary, to lift the word above its first sound, above its primary meaning. The repetition is an insistence, a clarification, & finally what is so especially interesting to Rothenberg, *a revelation*. In any case there is no such thing as repetition, 'existing in human terms . . . is never repetition.' Saying again is always adding. Stein's point is an access to Rothenberg's work, 'remembering is the only repetition,' just as 'remembering is the only confusion.' Stein writes of Picasso 'he tried to express things seen not as one knows them but as they are when one sees them without remembering,' & this is precisely what Rothenberg tries to do. His early poems offer new ways of seeing, behind them is the assumption that nothing changes except the form under which it is articulated. The image is a means of glimpsing at eternal & inarticulatable truths.

Rothenberg's work shows this peculiar indebtedness to Stein, he saw her early on in the game as a poet. He finds in her the same passion for naming. Naming in order to define the limits of one's life & naming in order to make it new. They both insist that the noun is the Word. Stein offers Rothenberg a methodology to test the structures of the language game & to play on the peripheries of what's possible: 'So I say poetry is essentially the discovery, the love, the passion for the name of anything.' She underlines the significance of what for him was a sacred event. This breaking into silence that is both mysterious & powerful, the rich surprise of making contact. The noun can be exploited poetically, commercially, or politically—& abuse on the grand scale is an American miracle (Watergate, Exxon's ecology adverts, Kissinger's peace missions are all abuses of language). The integrity of Rothenberg's poetry is what the fight is about. He knows that in the face of a continually self-renewing reality we must retain an ever renewed sense of wonder. . . .

The poet's joy is this instant of recognition, of giving name to what he sees & feels, it's always a unique occasion & the names have to be discovered:

> *The names*
>
> A glass ring:
> images beyond suspicion:
> not beyond names

There is no separation between act & referent, no prior knowledge, the name is there in the recognition. Memory & knowledge are hindrances to seizing this instant. Seeing moves both inwards & outwards. Comparable impressions can only dull the particular perceptual instant. Naming realises the present. (pp. 161-62)

Rothenberg also makes use of Stein's explorations into language games & syntactical possibilities. He has learnt from the way she demonstrates the building up of grammatical units or how to illustrate the function of a particular word:

> the sisters
>
> made promises
> made electricity
> made light

The puns are multiple & the tension dramatic. Like Stein he has that fine instinct to know what can & what can't be used. 'I was overcome with remorse. It was my fault that my wife did not have a cow. This sentence they cannot use.' But Rothenberg's poetry shows consistently that he knows where the real risks are, & earns, as Stein, the right to talk of use. (p. 163)

> *Kevin Power, "An Image Is an Image Is an Image,"*
> *in* Vort, *Vol. 3, No. 1, 1975, pp. 153-63.*

HARRIS LENOWITZ

Rothenberg does to Jewish materials just about what he does with the "primitive" materials (in *Technicians of the Sacred, Shaking the Pumpkin,* etc.): collects fragments and assembles them. His authenticity, in either case, is a result of his selectional criteria and his assembling scheme. The materials must fit together, regardless of authenticity, and the scheme must be comprehensive. For the result to be "authentic" though it must be comprehensive of all the items assembled and structured in such a way that new items and their situation in the scheme can be predicted, or, having been found, can be located in the assembly structure (be meaningful). The Jewish materials are all the bits of Jewish history and their

meaning in a cosmos driven by the Jewish god; the history of God interacting with a peculiar people. Of all previous assembly systems (from that in which the god is materially beneficent, as in the conquest of the Promised Land, to that in which the god uses history as a teacher's cane) it appears that only two remain operative: the esoteric line, that might as well be called kabala (which plays an important part in Rothenberg's rules, but which I can't deal with here); and the tribal cult, which primarily concerns itself with matters of feature distinction. Rothenberg utilises a system that is a composite of these two systems of meaning, which are pre-Exilic; his system is shown as comprehensive enough to deal with the new facts of Jewish life in America, movement to this new life from Eastern Europe and existence in Eastern Europe, the mythologised ancestral beginning, viewed as continuous with the new life.

All of Rothenberg's Jewish poetry is in *Poland/1931.* In this magnificent collection Rothenberg brings his Jewish imaging to bear on the process of removal and continuation; from Jewish life in Poland to Jewish life in America. In his vision nothing is lost in process; the relationship he sees as organising all Jewish experience, and particularly the Jewish experience of dispersion and resettlement, is that of desire and control. This relationship is expressed in the dominant symbol of blood.

Blood and its nature have been Jewish cultic concerns from the beginning. First, blood is a type of fluid; the control of fluid is the most difficult control to achieve since fluids are so instantaneously responsive to gravity and so irredeemably commingling. It is for this reason that myths of the origin of cosmos have so regularly symbolised the creation ground as wet; for in overcoming fluid, even temporarily, differentiation begins and the process which culminates in the "myriad things."

Then, blood is a type of fluid peculiar to living beings. It is the chaotic sea, continually setting the world of human-animal relationships awash, renewing chaos with every uncontrolled drip, gush, spot. For this reason the systematic ("divine") conquest of watery chaos must continue into the animate field to be complete and organise the world of life, control blood. Confusion is blood's design: in the ordering of this desire, tension results which is the peculiar state of human existence, still an arena for the prime battle. Total formality results in the destruction of life, just as a surgeon's slicing Siamese twins apart at the heart must kill both . . . ; total chaos will mean reversion to pre-vital dissolution. The tension must continue, and is the war of Rothenberg's epic.

The oldest Poland-of-the-Jews and newest America-of-the-Jews are linked in this struggle through adherence to "The Code of Jewish Law," which is both Rothenberg's poem on this, and the title of the book from which he gathered the fragments (an English translation of the abbreviated "Shulhan 'arukh" by mystic-legalist Joseph Karo). Probably, so you shouldn't think that all these adhering Jews, Polish and American, *observe* the restrictions of the Code, I should say that for *all* of us awareness of the system presented in the Code is adherence, whether we follow the rules as given, reinterpret them or choose to oppose them altogether. (pp. 179-80)

Section 2 of the Code as it appeared in the original *Tree* publication has been redone and appears in the poem **"The Grandmothers."** The section originally focussed very tightly on the mikva. In it, the blood of woman which signs her relationship to Tiamat (ancient sea goddess, the chaos 'Elohim-Marduk must control) is scrubbed from the earth, fanatically, meticulously, and returned to the watercourse, making the connection between human blood and the ichor of chaos. . . .

[The] connection between woman and chaos is asserted in the relationship of the two female fluids, milk and blood, which must be kept separate, totally, since any proportion of blood totally assimilates the milk, force of continuing generation. (pp. 180-81)

Jews in Rothenberg are nearly co-terminous with their God. (The "nearly" is where all the mysticism comes in, that's too much to write about here.) They are God's army in the chaos war. They still are in places they no longer live; They have been to places they've never been; They are always the same, with the same problem of graduating chaos-fluid-blood; They engage the fluids, again and again, with heroism, especially in the bloody desires of their lives; lust for sex, for food, for taste, for blood itself; They've been driven out of Poland and They will never leave:

> such men are jews
> just as other men are not jews
> not mad
> don't call you by your polish name
> or ride the train to lodz
> if there are men who ride the train to lodz
> there are still jews
> just as there are still oranges
> & jars
> (from **"The Connoisseur of Jews"**)

The Baal Shem Tov comes to America and mixes with the American West, and brings East Europe with him, in **"The Cokboy:"**

> how vass I lost tzu get here
> am a hundred men
> a hundred fifty different shadows
> jews & gentiles
> who bring the Law to the Wilderness
> (he says)   this man
> is me   my grandfather
> & other men-of-letters
> men with letters carrying the mail
> lithuanian pony-express riders

They are always the same, in the same struggle, which is mostly the point of the "American" poem, **"The Immigrant"** and the "Polish" poem, **"The Wedding"** and the Polish-American poem, **"The Fathers."**

Heroism, in the engagement. Here is where Rothenberg's system comes to life for me (oddly, the life is a lot like that in the writings of that arch-anti-semite Celine). I know it personally: a week ago I had to address a high-school audience in a particularly stupid area of our city on a subject about which they knew nothing: Judaism. The first question I was asked was about whether the Jews believed in Christ. After making the usual disclaimers (no such thing as Jews) I felt the mantle of Shylock and Ahasuerus descend about my shoulders, and the desire to be the absolute worst thing Christians ever thought about Jews overcame me. I became Christ-killer. Told them all about how there was absolutely no contemporary historical evidence, from outside the Jesus cult, that Jesus ever lived. Here, in Rothenberg, this lust to come at the worst, the realm of the forbidden, to engage blood on its own terms, explodes into life. The lust for sex:

> visitor to Warsaw
>   old man with open fly
> flesh girls could suck
>   mothers would die to catch sight of
>   (**"Portrait of a Jew Old Country Style"**)

for food:

> let us tread thy markets where thy sausages grow
>   ripe & full
> let us bite thy peppercorns let thy oxen's dung be
>   sugar to thy dying jews
>   (**"The Wedding"**)

for taste:

> "snuff too weak" you
> soak in whiskey
> you mix with fine pepper
> your nose grows warm
> & fat from it
> you become a wealthy man
> by sneezing
> everybody says "god bless you"
> the hairs inside your nose
> grow hairs
>   (**"A Polish Anecdote"**)

for blood itself; here the paradoxical closeness-to-thy-enemy is hardest at work, and is ultimately, the strongest link between the old and new world, between hate and love, form and chaos, life and death. In Poland the poem is **"The Slaughterer's Testimony,"** which you must read whole; in America, it is **"The Murder, Inc. Sutra."** . . . (pp. 182-83)

The overall thrust in *Poland/1931* is towards acceptance of fluidity, sex, violence, etc., with all its felt dangers. (The Baal Shem becomes **"Cokboy"** though he suffers the becoming in a still hostile gentile world, in which he shares the death of native Americans and other tribal people.) This thrust in Rothenberg begins to appear much earlier, in the Gorky poem **"The Water of the Flowery Mill"** for example: "He is blood, himself / the killer / is where the sun goes down." Then becomes located in the Jewish experience. And continues as theme in the *Seneca Journal* to which **"Cokboy"** serves as an introduction. (p. 184)

Harris Lenowitz, "Rothenberg: The Blood," in Vort, *Vol. 3, No. 1, 1975, pp. 179-84.*

WILLIAM M. CLEMENTS

When confronted with the task of converting the products of oral performance into printed documents, the translator faces a dilemma. On one hand, he may attempt a holistic re-creation of the oral performance by such methods as extensive description of context, stage directions, labanotation or some other technique for representing body movements, and diagrams; in the process, though, he burdens the reader with so much detail that the artistry in the performance may escape notice. On the other hand, the translator may concentrate on one aspect of the oral performance—usually the words of the performed message; thus he creates some sort of artistic experience for the reader, but one which lacks many of the dimensions of the oral original. This dilemma is compounded when the oral performance occurs in a language and arises out of a cultural milieu unfamiliar to the intended reader. Attempts to make Native American oral poetry accessible to Euro-American readers provide excellent evidence of how unresponsive the dilemma is to easy resolution. Yet translators have been making attempts at translating Native American oral poetry for two centuries.

Perhaps the most visible and influential of those translators during the past decade and a half has been Jerome Rothenberg, whose anthologies of oral poetry have become staples in libraries, in college classrooms, and on readers' personal shelves. Both *Technicians of the Sacred* and *Shaking the Pumpkin* have tried to present oral poetry (exclusively Native American in the latter book) in "total translation . . . that takes into account any or all elements of the original [oral poetry] beyond the words." The results have been some effective, challenging, and possibly accurate representations of the full texture of the oral event. But ultimately, *Shaking the Pumpkin,* singled out here because of its Native American focus, is a dangerous book, which perpetrates alarming misconceptions about the nature of Native American verbal art and sets an unacceptable precedent for those who wish to translate that art.

Shaking the Pumpkin appeared to generally favorable reviews in the spring of 1972. Though some quibblers groused that Rothenberg might have limited the anthology's scope to fewer tribal groups and thus allowed himself space to present some cultural context, reviews in a wide range of periodicals praised the book. (pp. 193-94)

The only major negative response to *Shaking the Pumpkin* appeared in an essay by William Bevis in *College English.* Bevis lamented that "recently a number of 'editors' with little or no knowledge of Indian languages have rewritten older translations and published their revised versions as anthologies of Indian poetry." He doubted "the quality of the material available to meet the growing demand for things Indian." As far as *Shaking the Pumpkin,* one of several anthologies treated in Bevis' article, is concerned, those doubts are well founded. Very little in the book is actually translated from original Native American languages. Instead, Rothenberg has taken the translations of such notable predecessors as the ethnologist James Mooney and the ethnomusicologist Frances Densmore and reworked them. The results seem to reflect what Jerome Rothenberg feels Native American oral poetry should be rather than what it actually is or was, at least as far as available evidence can demonstrate. Moreover, Rothenberg violates even the most fundamental rules of sound scholarship when presenting the words and ideas of others. Except in the poems which Rothenberg or another translator worked out with the assistance of Native American performers, *Shaking the Pumpkin* does not measure up to its subtitle, *Traditional Poetry of the Indian North Americas.* Readers of this anthology should be cognizant of four major problems with the book: misquotation of sources, substitution of intuition for available evidence, misrepresentation of presented material, and failure to achieve the goal of "total translation" through unnecessary selectivity and typographic gimmickry.

A basic principle of scholarship, journalism, anthologizing— of any of the arts which sometimes require the reproduction of the spoken or written words of others—is the sanctity of those words. Tampering with them through changing word choice or sentence structure, through shifting of emphasis, through omitting without proper ellipsis, or through adding without proper bracketing constitutes fraud. The source of the misquoted material suffers from the fraud since he or she may be made to say or write something other than what was intended. The reader of the misquoted material suffers from the fraud since he assumes unquestioningly that quotation must be accurate and may thus be completely misled about the nature of the source's intentions. In several places in *Shaking the Pumpkin,* Jerome Rothenberg has perpetrated the fraud of misquotation. . . . For example, the last selection in *Shaking the Pumpkin* is "Three Ghost Dance Songs," at the end of which the editor makes a clear attribution of source: *"Translations by James Mooney."* The originals of Mooney's translations appear in his major work on the Ghost Dance which came out in the Bureau of American Ethnology's *Annual Report for* 1892-1893. The first song, an Arapaho text, was translated by Mooney as follows:

> My children, when at first I liked the whites,
> My children, when at first I liked the whites,
> I gave them fruits,
> I gave them fruits.

Rothenberg's text, supposedly quoted from Mooney, appears thusly:

> My children,
> when at first I liked the whites,
> I gave them fruits,
> I gave them fruits.

Not only has Rothenberg reset the lines from Mooney's translation, but he has omitted one line without indicating so by means of ellipsis. Rothenberg's product may be slightly better poetry, but it is not what it purports to be: the reproduction of a translation by the pioneer American ethnologist James Mooney. (pp. 195-96)

Rothenberg also misquotes in the commentaries on the poems included in *Shaking the Pumpkin.* These commentaries, often the only guide which the reader has to cultural and performance contexts for the poems, should relate clearly and accurately the data they convey. Yet Rothenberg chooses to change his sources' words in order to reinforce his own ideas about the material. For instance, in his notes to a reworking he has done of a Cherokee formula for effecting death, he attributes the following to James Mooney:

> As the purpose of the ceremony is to bring about the death of the victim, everything spoken of is symbolically colored black. . . . The declaration at the end, "It is blue," indicates that the victim now begins to feel the effects of the incantation, & that as darkness comes on, his spirit will shrink & gradually become less until it dwindles away to nothingness

Yet the source of the quotation, another Bureau of American Ethnology *Annual Report,* reads as follows:

> As the purpose of the ceremony is to bring about the death of the victim, everything spoken of is symbolically colored black. . . . The declaration near the end, "It has become blue," indicates that the victim now begins to feel in himself the effects of the incantation, and that as darkness comes on his spirit will shrink and gradually become less until it dwindles away to nothingness.

The slight change in wording may seem at first glance a minor point, but it leads into another major problem with *Shaking the Pumpkin,* Rothenberg's use of his own Euro-American intuition as the guide to how Native American poetry should be translated. And, of course, any misquotation is to be frowned upon.

The basis for the poem which is elucidated by the commentary quoted above is Mooney's paper "The Sacred Formulas of the Cherokees." Therein he reproduces in phonetic Cherokee and free translation a number of ritual incantations preserved in the Swimmer Manuscript, a "small day-book of about 240 pages . . . about half filled with writing in the Cherokee characters." Mooney's translation of the relevant poem, entitled "To Destroy Life" in his paper, follows:

> Listen! Now I have come to step over your soul. You are of the (wolf) clan. Your name is (A'yû'ini). Your spittle I have put at rest under the earth. Your soul I have put at rest under the earth. I have come to cover you over with the black rock. I have come to cover you over with the black cloth. I have come to cover you with the black slabs, never to reappear. Toward the black coffin of the upland in the Darkening Land your paths shall stretch out. So shall it be for you. The clay of the upland has come (to cover you. (?) [sic] Instantly the black clay has lodged there where it is at rest at the black houses in the Darkening Land. With the black coffin and the black slabs I have come to cover you. Now your soul has faded away. It has become blue. When darkness comes your spirit shall grow less and dwindle away, never to reappear. Listen!

Rothenberg has taken Mooney's translation and reworked it into a poem called "The Killer":

> Careful: my knife drills your soul
>   listen, whatever-your-name-is
>   One of the wolf people
> listen   I'll grind your saliva into the earth
> listen   I'll cover your bones with black flint
> listen   " " " " " " feathers
> listen   " " " " " " rocks
> Because you're going where it's empty
>   Black coffin out on the hill
> listen   the black earth will hide you, will
>   find you a black hut
>   Out where it's dark, in that country
> listen   I'm bringing a box for your bones
>   A black box
>   A grave with black pebbles
> listen   your soul's spilling out
> listen   it's blue

In this marked recasting of Mooney's original, there is no serious breach of professionalism since Rothenberg indicates that it is his own *"working, after James Mooney."* But serious questions may be raised about how Native American the result really is. We have absolutely no evidence of how this formula was performed orally. The Swimmer Manuscript, written in the Cherokee syllabary, is the closest document to the oral performance, but one must not expect such a document to convey much more than the bare text. Mooney, in translating from the manuscript, admitted that his efforts were at best "free renderings of the spirits of the originals." Working from Mooney's "free renderings" of manuscript materials, Rothenberg has created what he must think the oral performance should have been. But he does not draw from firsthand knowledge of Cherokee culture and language; he is guessing. "The Killer" is an admittedly effective poem, but it is Jerome Rothenberg's poem, not a Native American poem. Mooney is probably much closer to Native American art since at least he knew the language he was translating from. Note also that Rothenberg by misquoting Mooney in the commentary for the poem may be trying, in effect, to enlist Mooney's unknowing support for his own reworking by attributing his own translation of the last line to the ethnologist.

Another instance of Rothenberg's metamorphosis of previously translated material into his own "working" occurs in the Winnebago "Peyote Visions," which are designated as *"Jerome Rothenberg's working, after Paul Radin."* The source for the five texts in this series of poems is Radin's edition of *The Autobiography of a Winnebago Indian,* the forerunner of the famous Winnebago autobiography *Crashing Thunder.* The earlier work was written in the Winnebago syllabary script by S[am] B[lowsnake] (alias Crashing Thunder, alias Big Winnebago). According to Radin, "The translation was made by the author [i.e., Radin] on the basis of a rendition from his interpreter." . . . Rothenberg makes some major changes when he reworks this account of a personal experience. . . .

As with the Cherokee formula, Rothenberg seems to presume an intuitive right to represent how the material should be orally performed, even though no evidence for that performance exists. Rothenberg's repeated substitutions of his own poetic intuition for the insight of Native American sources or of the ethnologists who studied the relevant cultures firsthand undermines the authenticity of *Shaking the Pumpkin* as a representative collection of Native American oral poetry.

A third problem with the material in this anthology arises out of the second. For not only does Rothenberg imply that his workings of ethnologists' translations surpass their renderings from the original languages, but he also seems to suggest that he knows what constitutes Native American poetry better than the ethnologists or the Native performers. Rothenberg frequently misrepresents the texts in *Shaking the Pumpkin* in order to suit his apparent preconceptions about the nature of all Native American verbalization. He seemingly opines that anything said by a Native American is poetic. But this romantic notion that the Noble Savage living harmoniously with Nature automatically articulates in poetic forms has no substance. Though one may agree with Rothenberg that prose is directly tied to the written word and serves as a poor vehicle for conveying the nature of oral performance, he must realize that Native Americans, like everyone else, recognize a distinction between verbal art and everyday verbalization. For example, a Winnebago, even one who narrated his life story orally, would not consider what he said necessarily to be poetic; he would differentiate artistic speech from the mere communication of information. Yet Rothenberg represents verbalizations—even written documents—by Native Americans as poetic even when the intent of the communicator was not to be so. The anthologist's own predilections assume precedence over legitimate presentation of Native American oral performance. (pp. 197-202)

The fourth problem with Rothenberg's work involves his response to the translator's dilemma which introduced this essay. In short, Rothenberg has failed to achieve his objective of presenting the experience of oral communication in print. Such an objective may indeed be so elusive as ultimately to defy success, but Rothenberg could have approached his goal more nearly if he had not exercised unnecessary selectivity in the kinds of data he chose to reproduce and if he had devised a meaningful typographic system for capturing oral performance.

Of course, some selectivity is essential. It would certainly be unfair to expect Rothenberg to bury his poems amid masses of ethnographic commentary, but one should expect the inclusion of the most obvious elements of the oral performance. For example, the treatment of the Chippewa "Songs & Song Pictures" in *Shaking the Pumpkin* omits at least one vital element in their performance. This material, collected and originally published by Frances Densmore, consists of several songs performed primarily at ceremonies of the Mide Society, the major Chippewa religious organization. When Densmore presented each song, she included the Chippewa words, her translation, the reproduction of a birchbark drawing associated with the song, the melody, and some information on the song's precise ritual context. Rothenberg, though, provides only a "working" of the original translation and the picture for each of the twenty songs taken from Densmore's work. Perhaps Rothenberg decided the comments about ritual occasions for the songs would encumber the artistry of the material, but his deletion of the melodies cannot be so easily explained away. These texts are indeed songs; as such, their melodies are as vital as their words. The absence of any musicological indications prevents the reader from appreciating the integrity of the performance of this material as song. One can certainly make no claims of having achieved "total translation" when elements essential to depicting the nature of oral performance are ignored.

The omission of such essential details from the presentations of the poems is not the only way in which Rothenberg has failed to capture oral performance in print. The device by which he attempts to achieve this difficult goal lies primarily in typographic manipulation. Many of his translations and workings appear in highly unconventional formats, often approaching concrete poetic forms. In using departures from standard typographic patterns such as those employed in "The Killer" and "Peyote Vision 1," Rothenberg alerts the reader that the material is not conventional poetry in the Euro-American sense. But his typography accomplishes little beyond this. The reader may understand that the poetry is unconventional and even that its basic difference from other poetry he has read relates to its oral nature; yet Rothenberg's settings for the material do nothing to convey how that oral nature manifests itself in performance. . . . Rothenberg's settings create what amounts to a more intense *visual* experience for the reader, not appreciative insight into oral performance.

These problems with *Shaking the Pumpkin* as a reputable anthology of Native American verbal art should not blind the reader to the worthwhile poetry by Rothenberg and others that appears in the volume. But so much of the book has so little that is truly Native American. We may lament that the records of Native American verbal art which were garnered in the late 1800s and early in this century fail to convey its richness, but we can do little about those records now. Certainly we should not change them to suit our current attitudes, and least of all should changes be made by a Euro-American with no direct knowledge of the material he is changing. We must content ourselves with the material collected by Cushing, Boas, Benedict, Fewkes, Michelson, and all the other early figures in Native American studies. By taking liberties with their material, *Shaking the Pumpkin* destroys the images of Native American verbal art which their material is able to convey. The "total translation" espoused by Jerome Rothenberg is a worthy goal, but one that can be approached only under certain conditions: the translator's first-hand experience of the verbal performance, his close rap-

port with the performer, his sincere attempt to understand the matrices from which the performance arises, and his deep respect for culture and performer and performance. Total translation without these conditions becomes gimmicky, ersatz, and counterproductive. (pp. 202-04)

William M. Clements, "Faking the Pumpkin: On Jerome Rothenberg's Literary Offenses," in Western American Literature, Vol. XVI, No. 3, November, 1981, pp. 193-204.

MARJORIE PERLOFF

Technicians of the Sacred, originally published in the milestone year 1968 and now extensively revised, primarily by the addition of European (Mesopotamian, early Greek and Roman, Celtic, Anglo-Saxon, etc.) texts, has aroused a good deal of controversy. In the late sixties a score of poets hailed it as, in the words of Richard Kostelanetz, "the single most influential literary anthology of the past decade." And in a recent discussion of ethnopoetics in *Parnassus,* Judith Gleason, herself a performance artist and "ethnopoet," explains: . . .

> Rothenberg's "dream of a total art—and of a life made whole," far from being an idle vision, is, rather that of an indefatigable worker, uniting us in his traces. Stakhonovite of the sacred, like one of Rilke's bees of the invisible he goes about extracting the sweetness from meadows distant and close to home. . . . Thus *Technicians of the Sacred,* surely the outstanding anthology of our time, along with *Shaking the Pumpkin,* is already serving our contemporary sensibilities as once the comparable ardor of the brothers Grimm nourished those of our romantic ancestors.

At the same time, Ethnopoetics in general and Rothenberg's "dream of a total art" in particular have come in for criticism by those who argue that, in his cult of the "primitive" and the remote, Rothenberg betrays his own nostalgia for origins, for an ethic of archaic and natural innocence and for a transcendent harmony and metaphysical wholeness at odds with late twentieth-century thought. And further, Rothenberg's project has been criticized as a fuzzily Romantic claim to recuperate the "primitive" Other, an Other that by definition eludes our grasp and denies our appropriation. Thus, when Rothenberg declares, in "Pre-Face 1984," that "Our ideas of poetry—including, significantly, our idea of the poet—began to look back *consciously* to the early & late shamans of those other worlds: not as a title to be seized but as a model for the shaping of meanings & intensities through language. As the reflection of our yearning to create a meaningful ritual life," Post-Structuralist readers are likely to respond that we cannot, in 1985, recreate the "meaningful ritual life" of the Aztecs or the Basuto of Africa, that indeed the versions of "primitive ritual" anthologized in *Technicians of the Sacred* fail to recuperate the spirit of the originals.

But then how close to the "real" China of Li Po is Ezra Pound's *Cathay?* And how close do we want it to be? Like all of Rothenberg's extraordinary anthologies, *Technicians of the Sacred* must be understood less as a gathering of poems by others—in this case, a gathering of "primitive" poems from around the world—than as a long and complex poetic text by Rothenberg himself. The clue to Rothenberg's method is found in the "Pre-Face" to the first edition of *Technicians* in which he remarks:

Like any collector, my approach to delimiting & recognizing what's a poem has been by analogy: in this case . . . to the work of modern poets. Since much of this work has been revolutionary & limit-smashing, the analogy in turn expands the range of what "we" can see as primitive poetry.

This generalization is followed by an elaborate tabulation of analogies: for example, the " 'pre'-literate situation of poetry composed to be spoken, chanted or, more accurately sung" is compared to our own "post-literate" situation (McLuhan's phrase) in which public readings and performance poetry have come to the fore. Or again, the "image-thinking" of "primitive" poetry is related to the deep-image poetry of the sixties, while the "minimal art of maximal involvement" of primitive cultures, an art that leaves "plenty of room for fill-in" by the spectator as ritual participant, is compared to post-modern concrete poetry on the one hand and the happening or "total theater" on the other.

But, as D.H. Lawrence might have put it, "Never trust the editor, trust the anthology." For the analogical relationships Rothenberg establishes are more difficult and unsettling than he seems to realize. In his "Pre-Faces," Rothenberg refers repeatedly to the "world that they & we share," but the actual format of the book stresses difference as much as likeness. Four-hundred thirty pages of "The Texts" are followed by almost two-hundred pages of "The Commentaries." The latter include bibliographical material, indicating the source of each text, Rothenberg's commentary on the given text, and then "Addenda," which is to say a series of paratexts that include quotations from history or anthropology books, related foreign texts, contemporary poems, and so on. But the cited poems by Gary Snyder or Jackson Mac Low, the "calligrammes" by Apollinaire and August de Campos, the translations of Aimé Césaire and Pablo Neruda—are not so much "analogues" of their "primitive" counterparts as they are ironized and problematized versions. The resulting collage composition is itself a working-out of the title's oxymoron: it shows us what it means to be a *technician* of the sacred.

Consider, for example, the text called "Bantu Combinations" under the heading "Origins & Namings." The "primary text" itself takes up less than a page:

1.

> *I am still carving an ironwood stick.*
> *I am still thinking about it.*

2.

> *The lake dries up at the edges.*
> *The elephant is killed by a small arrow.*

3.

> *The little hut falls down.*
> *Tomorrow, debts.*

4.

> *The sound of a cracked elephant tusk.*
> *The anger of a hungry man.*

5.

> *Is there someone on the shore?*
> *The crab has caught me by one finger.*

6.

> *We are the fire that burns the country.*
> *The Calf of the Elephant is exposed on the plain.*
>   (Africa)

The Commentary on these six small couplets takes up almost

three pages. First, a reference to Rothenberg's source (Henri A. Junod's *Life of a South African Tribe*), then an elucidation as to how to read these gnomic Bantu verses:

> Examples of plot-thickening in the area of "image": a conscious placing of image against image as though to see-what-happens. Apart from its presence in song, this juxtaposing of images turns up all over in the art, say, of the riddle—of which several of these "combinations" are, in fact, examples. Poem as opposition or balance or two or more images is also the basis of the haiku, less clearly of the sonnet. In all these the interest increases as the connection between the images becomes more and more strained, barely definable.

Note that this is by no means a factual account. The phrase "plot-thickening,' for example, refers to a specific Zen parable. In John Cage's account in *Silence*, "Sri Ramakrishna was once asked, 'Why if God is good, is there evil in the world?' He said, 'In order to thicken the plot.' " Again, the evident pleasure Rothenberg takes in the "conscious placing of image against image as though to see-what-happens" has to do with his own poetic rather than with the sonnet mode, the sonnet being a form traditionally more dependent upon rhetoric and the structure of argumentation than upon the juxtaposition of vivid images. For Rothenberg, the "Bantu Combinations" become forerunners of the Dada and Surrealist collusion of disjunctive images, of "strained, barely definable" associations. "Not subtlety . . . but *energy*: the power of word & image" that produces "vision." And he cites the following "Modern" analogues:

> (1) *Now I a fourfold vision see*
>   *And a fourfold vision is given to me*
>   *Tis fourfold in my supreme delight*
>   *And three fold in soft Beulahs night*
>   *And twofold Always. May God us keep*
>   *From Single vision & Newtons sleep*
>   —William Blake (1802)

> (2) The image cannot spring from any comparison but from the bringing together of two more or less remote realities. . . .

> The more distant and legitimate the relation between the two realities brought together, the stronger the image will be . . . the more emotive power and poetic reality it will possess.
>   —Pierre Reverdy

> (3) The African image is not an image by equation but an image by *analogy*, a surrealist image. Africans do not like straight lines and false *mots justes*. A two and two do not make four, but five, as Aimé Césaire has told us. . . . African surrealism is mystical and metaphysical. . . .
>   —Léopold Sédar Senghor

Having presented the case against what Blake calls "Single vision" and Senghor the "straight line," Rothenberg gives us seven "Contemporary Combinations," analogous to the "Bantu Combinations," arranged in roughly chronological order. The first is Phillipe Soupault's "A church leaped up / exploding / like a bell," the second, a single line by Paul Eluard & Benjamin Peret: "Elephants are contagious." Then Gertrude Stein's one-line aphorism from *Tender Buttons*: "A white hunter is nearly crazy," and Kenneth Koch's five-word poem "In the Ranchhouse at Dawn," which reads: "O corpuscle! / O wax town!" And finally, the following three contemporary minimalist works:

WOOD

I repeated it.
                                    —Clark Coolidge

A man torments the sun.
Cows are disturbed by their calves.
                                    —Barrett Watten

        the last days like this
        a red stone
        all we know of fire

                                    —Robert Kelly

Kelly's tercet is in fact the last of six stanzas of a poem called "New Moon Over Whaleback," which appeared in *Lunes* (1965). In the first edition of *Technicians,* Rothenberg reproduced the entire poem as a specific modern analogue to the Bantu Combinations. Kelly's poem begins with the stanza "this new moon low down / a plain sky / holding it in place," and proceeds to relate the moon rim in the black sky to the loss of the poet's beloved. In revising the Commentaries, Rothenberg evidently found "New Moon Over Whaleback" too coherent—a nice enough but fairly unexceptional sixties "deep image" poem. Accordingly, in the new edition he opts for the final tercet, inexplicable as that tercet is when taken out of context. The mystery of the image is thus a function, not of Kelly's own poetic structuring, but of Rothenberg's creative collage cut.

Collage composition is further complicated by placing the Kelly tercet, with its reference to "red stone" and "fire," next to Watten's line, "A man torments the sun," with its alogically connected corollary, "Cows are disturbed by their calves." Or again, Gertrude Stein's "white hunter" is given new life by its proximity to Kenneth Koch's "wax town," while Soupault's exploding church coexists with Eluard and Peret's contagious elephants. All these passages belong to larger wholes from which they are wrenched, the exception being Clark Coolidge's "Wood," whose single line, "I repeated it," can be taken to refer to chopping wood, or the "repeat" (grain) in the wood, or the repetition of identical trees in the "wood," and so on.

How do such minimalist works relate to the "Bantu Combinations" themselves? My own sense is that the latter are not as inexplicable or as "visionary" as Rothenberg would have us think. The Bantu speaker who says, "I am still carving an ironwood stick," no doubt a necessary item in a specific ritual, adds, not surprisingly, "I am still thinking about it." In #2, we have two parallel instances of decay and death: the lake drying up at the edges and the elephant killed by a small arrow. In #3, the projected "debts" are the consequence of the fact that "The little hut falls down." In #4, "The sound of a cracked elephant tusk" is compared quite logically to another sound, "The anger of a hungry man." In #5, the question "Is there someone on the shore?" is the cry for help of a man whose finger has been caught by a crab. And in the final Combination, the "fire that burns the country" inevitably strikes "The Calf of the Elephant [which is] exposed on the plain."

Taken as a whole, moreover, the six-couplet "poem" contains the skeleton of a narrative: it relates the story of the carving of an arrow by a "hungry man," who has lost his "little hut" and is in debt, to be used to kill an elephant, a killing regarded as an inevitable ritual: "We are the fire which burns the country."

Does this mean that Rothenberg is somehow cheating the reader? Not at all. For one thing, the Bantu texts have a sophistication that lends credence to Rothenberg's central thesis that " 'primitive' means complex." To compare the angry howling of a hungry man to "The sound of a cracked elephant tusk" is hardly naive. Secondly, Rothenberg uses these "primitive" analogues to create his own poetic text. Soupault's church that "leaped up / exploding / like a bell" has affinities to the elephant "killed by a small arrow," and the line "Elephants are contagious" can be inserted into the Bantu text itself so as to create resonance. Add to the African landscape a "White Hunter" who is "nearly crazy," a "Ranchhouse at Dawn," and the presence of "Wood" where an unknown "I" "repeated it," and we have what John Ashbery has called "an open field of narrative possibilities." Both the "primitive" and the "contemporary" text end, in any case, with the apocalyptic appearance of fire, the emblem of "last days." No wonder Robert Kelly's first five stanzas were eliminated.

"An assemblage like this one," says Rothenberg in his "Pre-Face (1984)," "is by its nature an anthology of *versions.* " Precisely, and the "versions" are Rothenberg's own: it is, he, after all, who is the "technician of the sacred." Consider, for example, his startling conjunctions of Navajo and American Shaker sound poems to Hugo Ball's Dada sound poem "Gadji Beri Bimba." Or the ritual naming poems of the Egyptians to Gertrude Stein's quite different speculations on the naming process in *Lectures in America.* Or the structure of Aztec Definitions, as recorded in the so-called Madrid and Florence Codices, to a postmodern definition poem like David Antin's "Definitions for Mendy." Or the rhythms of Eskimo Magic Songs to Rochelle Owens's "Song of Meat, Madness & Travel."

Indeed, *Technicians of the Sacred* can be understood as a gold mine of poetic forms and genres that can be (and have been) adapted by contemporary poets. Ritual naming song, shamanic chant, spell, visual poem, hieroglyph, definition poem, fragment, praise poem, quest romance—all these are paraded before the charmed reader's eyes as possibilities for writing in the present. The section called "The Book of Events" contains descriptions of rituals from around the world (e.g., the "Forest Event" from Hungary, the "Stone Fire Event" from Australia) that provide us with paradigms for the happenings of the sixties (Alison Knowles, La Monte Young, Carolee Schneemann, Alan Kaprow) as well as the more explicitly poetic performance works of the seventies like Vito Acconci's "Security Zone," Linda Montano's "Mitchell's Death," and Joseph Beuys's "Coyote: I Like America & America Likes Me."

As in the case of the "Bantu Combinations," Rothenberg's versions of primitive "Events" are purposely presented so as to illuminate their contemporary counterparts. "The editor," Rothenberg explains, "has taken a series of rituals & other programmed activities from a wide geographical area & has, as far as possible, suppressed all reference to accompanying mythic or 'symbolic' explanations." Such "distortion," he argues, "can have a value in itself. Like seeing Greek statues without their colors."

An especially interesting example of the value such "distortion" may have is found in Rothenberg's commentary on "The Girl of the Early Race who made the Stars," an African Bushman origin poem narrated by the so-called "//Kaboo," a name which literally means "dream." It begins:

My mother was the one who told me that the girl arose; she put her hands into the wood ashes; she threw up the wood ashes into the sky. She said to the wood ashes: "The wood ashes which are here, they must altogether become the Milky Way. They must white lie along in the sky, that the Stars may stand outside of the Milky Way, while the Milky Way is the Milky Way, while it used to be wood ashes." They the ashes altogether become the Milky Way. The Milky Way must go round with the stars; while the Milky Way feels that, the Milky Way lies going around; while the stars sail along; therefore the Milky Way lying, goes along with the Stars.

The source used here is Wilhelm H.I. Bleek and Lucy C. Lloyd's *Specimens of Bushman Folklore* (1911); Rothenberg calls their workings "the best examples the editor knows of how a 'literal' translation, when handled with respect for the intelligence & sense of form of the original maker, can point to the possibility of new uses in the translator's own language." Specifically, these translations, so Rothenberg suggests, "call into question the distinction (still strong among us) between poetry & prose." Since primitive prose is based on the art of oral delivery and is, accordingly, more closely related to modern oratory than to printed literary style, its rhythms are much closer to what we consider "poetry" than to "normal" prose. "Today, too," says Rothenberg, "poetry & prose are coming to a place-of-meeting in the spoken language—& the distinctions made by previous centuries have come to mean much less." And he reads "The Girl of the Early Race who made the Stars" against Gertrude Stein's play *Listen to Me* (1936), which has a whole scene constructed from permutations on the sentences "No dog barks at the moon," "The moon shines and no dog barks," and "Because there are so many lights anywhere."

The "place-of-meeting" of "poetry" and "prose" that Rothenberg discovers in the translation of the African Bushman text and relates to Gertrude Stein's admittedly quite different text *Listen to Me,* is a confluence increasingly prominent in the poetry of the eighties. (pp. 41-4)

Marjorie Perloff, "Soundings: Zaum, Seriality, and the Recovery of the 'Sacred'," in The American Poetry Review, *Vol. 15, No. 1, January-February, 1986, pp. 37-46.*

LARRY LEVIS

In his "Pre-Face" to **New Selected Poems,** Rothenberg admits that this "is not a selected poems in the usual sense but an attempt to isolate in the work of the last 15 years . . . the thread of a single long poem or sequence that the individual books . . . may have tended to obscure." If the animating editorial desire of such a project is coherence, the "thread," rather than the *prima facie* authenticity of mere artifact, then the whole collection seems a little imbued with futility. Rothenberg himself almost suggests as much by way of concluding his introductory prose; his "thread" seems to be a totality of experience after all: "That all includes the world, the present, as it comes and goes. I am a witness to it like everyone else, & all the experiments for me . . . are steps toward the recovery/discovery of a language for that witnessing. . . . Everything & everyone around here are welcome to come into the poem. . . ."

Nevertheless, coherence may abide within an "all" if that "all" is given enough shape by the poet's psyche and craft. But after the fine overture to the whole, the poem **"Poland/1931,"** the project that begins and that occupies most of this collection is trivializing and careless. Because of such neglect of craft, and such lack of a truly shaping spirit, the obsessions never become clearly realized nor compelling enough to sustain my attention. Nor does the absence of characterization help in such circumstances. When Gary Snyder, in *Myths & Texts,* took up a similarly difficult mythic task, he retained an almost Whitmanian reverence for the real: the Indians, loggers, firefighters and others who lived in those pages and did so without being molested and transmuted into abruptly symbolic shapes. I miss this in Rothenberg's work. Too often the characters here, "Cokboy" and others, are stereotyped contrivances amounting in sum to a cardboard populace. (p. 14)

There is, in the chosen forms here, a Post-Modernist satirical bravado reminiscent of some of Ginsberg's work but lacking Ginsberg's early passionate renewal of Whitmanian oratorical modes. In style, the sheer amount of seemingly unexamined, unedited repetition of such techniques deadens much of this.

> American is born
> the Baal Shem is a beaver
> (happened while the Indian talked
> changed behind Cody
> the mad jew slid to life
> past pink styrofoam snow of her body's
> channels
> the freaky passageways
> unlit unloved
> like gums of an old woman
> teeth were ripped from
> ages gone) into

That simile, "like gums of an old woman," does little to inform the scene here, and throughout, all this giddy, windy zeal adds up not to an epic as much as it does to epic self-indulgence, a lazy craftsmanship in which most lines are broken on a unit of syntax or image, or, when Rothenberg unnecessarily decides to emphasize something, on a word: "channels."

The quest for a renewing myth, a minor Modernism here, is gratuitous in its choices because the poet has not assimilated it deeply enough into his psyche so that it speaks for the mind of a people as a whole:

> delights old Beaver man gathers
> descendants around him
> he stands on the water
> hard with his tail (sez)
> "Old Enemy
> "Otter
> "in the name of Longhouse the Great
> "Rabbinical Council
> "mammals the longbeards of
> "Zion America
> "I have lived my last under the earth
> "into a new sun I skitter
> "tribal equivalent (sez Beaver)

The Beaver's *agon* with the Otter doesn't distinguish itself much from Disney, and whatever referential difficulties of source and "text," which might have become the richness of the work, are here so lost in their appropriation by Rothenberg that they wither away unattended. (pp. 14-15)

It comes as no surprise, given the craft here, that a later series of poems in the collection attempts to resuscitate Dadaism. But in the 1980s such a rebellious Modernist aesthetic is unequipped to do more than appear tawdry and docile. For Tzara's project never presumed a perennial recurrence; in fact, its aesthetic willfullness was a reaction against such notions of permanence and, if anything, Dada's ambition (to use an oxymoron of sorts) would have been an existence in an eternally obliterating *present,* something as uncompromisingly impossible as Dada itself. Its rebirth here is unrenewed especially in the innocence of Rothenberg's embrace of it; he appears to have discovered Dada about two weeks ago (although this is untrue and unfair as a remark if only because I suspect he has *attempted* to make Dada's influence upon him appear this abundantly fresh). (p. 15)

Rothenberg's **"The Holy Words of Tristan Tzara"** is the reintroduction of a mode (and its poet) which, for all its charm, is lacking in purpose and serves mostly to anthologize this older mode while perhaps presuming its lasting importance to any *avant-garde* thinking in the present. Which is assuming quite a bit, given the circumstances just now.

    dada
    dada ice
    dada piano
    dada flowers
    dada tears
    dada pendulum
    dada vanilla
    dada don quixote
    dada humid

If Rothenberg's epic fails through formal incompetence and a self-aggrandizing impulse, the final section of this book *is* both valuable and radical. The hilarious **"Visions of Jesus"** and the austere scrupulousness of **"15 Flower World Variations"** are superior to everything else that precedes them except, perhaps, **"Poland/1931"** and part of **"Vienna Blood."** These final poems from a collection of too much are, to my mind, a truer indication of this poet's abidingly significant and generative presence in our poetry.

                Ponca City
    Jesus. Pawnee Jesus.
    He is staring at the eyes of Jesus
    staring into his.
    Their eyeballs spin around
    like planets.
    Visions of Jesus everywhere.
    Gambler Jesus.
    Banker Jesus.
    Flatfoot Jesus with a floy floy.
    Jesus shuffling.
    The soldiers guard his silent fan,
    tacked up, beside his rattle.

The passage above, timely and curative, is not the restoration of any myth, and frankly I am glad to be free of that project; the passage above is the restoration of humor and of sense by which any mythology might be understood. (pp. 15-16)

Larry Levis, "Not Life So Proud to Be Life: Snodgrass, Rothenberg, Bell, and the Counter-Revolution," in The American Poetry Review, Vol. 18, No. 1, January-February, 1989, pp. 9-20.

PAUL CHRISTENSEN

Postmodern poetry began at different points of the political spectrum, but all agreed that a system of ideas was in decay and the initiation of their poems described the process, emotional and intellectual, by which selfhood underwent a transformation of identity—from a sense of its absolute autonomy in the social realm to being an extension of a collective imagination whose boundaries extended into the core of nature. Hence Olson's depiction of society as a "polis," a civil collective, in which individuals within it were not "I's" but "eyes," the individualized sensory awareness of organisms who looked out and brought the world into the social midst.

But almost any aspect of a "group" was suspect in the political thinking of the 1950s; group-centrality posed a threat to political authority as well as to ideological principles. The fear of Communism, Socialism, ethnic blocs, racial subgroups, was inspired not so much by alien political visions as by potential conspiratorial motives, the sinister powers of group-loyalty. Self-denial, such as in the mythical images of the kamikaze pilot or the ferocious rage of Mau-Mau tribesmen, possessed an irrational, terrifying strength incommensurate with the actual potentials of the individual. The fifties was a decade oddly obsessed with the surveillance of groups and their supposed agents who jeopardized the workings of American institutions and government agencies.

But it was Ginsberg's *Howl* of 1955 that seized on the rebellious youth of the era as the victims of an imperial government. The "witch-hunts" conducted by the F.B.I. and the McCarthy hearings suggested a move by federal authority to suppress insurrectionist hordes. Ginsberg's poem tapped a general guilt about racial conflict in American history, from Indian wars to Slave Laws and segregation battles of the "civil rights" era, as well as about past colonial wars, when he identified government as the persecutor of the nation's youth. His mystics, addicts, prophets, saints, and rebels stood for a long history of conflict between alien races and Anglo-Saxon expansion; youth represented a vast undeclared tribal subculture whose altered consciousness (by drugs, sexual freedom, exotic religions, criminality) was being systematically destroyed by Moloch, the imperial arm of the state.

If the beginning of Postmodernism lay in the collapse of European and English empires at mid-century it marked, in Rothenberg's phrase, "a desire for a new beginning . . . the return of what Blake called 'our antediluvian energies,' " or what Michael McClure described as "a *massive* return to 'instinct and intuition.' " Olson posed the central question to poets: What could be gained by transfer of belief to the "other" side, to the native cultures both at home and among the ex-colonies of the new age? (pp. 138-39)

The roots of Olson's question go back to Picasso's *Les Desmoiselles D'Avignon* of 1907, the inaugural Cubist study in which stark young women, prostitutes of a Barcelona café, stare from the eye-holes of Zairean ritual masks, and to the primitive studies of nudes by Matisse. Olson left to others the task of collecting the art of primitive traditions, the folkways, oral literature, rites and myths of systems outside or "under" Western control that would form the aesthetic bases of new writing at home.

For a time after the publication of Donald Allen's anthology *The New American Poetry 1945-1960* (Grove Press 1960), the mainstream of post-modern writing seemed to recede behind the tumultuous public events of the "hippie" years. In the second wave of responses to the end of the imperialist age, youths wore the symbols and costumes of so-called primitive people, formed communes, and practiced basic crafts and rudimentary agriculture, adopted native customs and religions, or found expression through the ritualistic performances of certain rock groups. . . . The 1960s marked the point at which youths discovered the political power of group activism. The mystique of the group or tribe had come to stand for the counter to individualism, an alternative ideological principle. Not only had "group therapy" become a popular form of rehabilitation for the beleaguered individuals of mass society, but others began applying the function of group identity to corporate structure. . . . (pp. 139-40)

Technicians of the Sacred captured the spirit of the 1960s with its restless search for alternatives to Western modes of conduct, belief, and understanding. Here were all the denied or exploited cultures of imperialism—African, Asian, Amerindian—given reverence as complex, sophisticated modes of language; Rothenberg reversed the usual condescension and detachment of orthodox ethnography and offered up his world text as evidence of an equal but opposite order of imagination. "Primitive," Snyder wrote in "The Politics of Ethnopoetics," "is not a word that means past, but *primary,* and *future.*" The term describes the orders of thought by which one possesses knowledge "in community with the other people—non-human included—brothers and sisters." A poetry of individual mind is merely one "line of thinking in the West," an Athenian poetics that should not stand for all that has occurred in occidental art. By careful discriminations, one can reveal the primitive origins of European ethnicity, as Rothenberg sets out to do in his revised edition of *Technicians,* and thus further isolate an Athenian branch of abstract reason that set in motion Western monocultural drift. (p. 141)

Imperialism split not only the geopolitical scheme of nations but the sensibility of the imperators as well—a split between "lower" and "higher" functions, genital and mental centers of awareness. "We," i.e., American whites, Rothenberg says in his preface to *Shaking the Pumpkin,* "will never be whole without a recovery of the 'red [Amerindian] power' that's been here from the beginning. The true integration must begin & end with a recognition of all such powers . . . we're doomed without his tribal & matrilocal wisdom, which can be shared only among equals who have recognized a common lineage from the Earth." Ethnopoetics is not only a poetic but also a therapy. (p. 142)

An "*ethno*poetics" is, as Rothenberg describes it, "the 'attempt to define a primary human potential.' " The therapeutic value of rediscovering other cultures lies, he says, in overcoming "a mindless mechanization that has run past any uses it may once have had." The anthology [*Symposium of the Whole*] is a kind of herbal medicine, for its contents have been missing from the Western intellectual diet. "In such a new 'totality,' "—here Rothenberg quotes Robert Duncan—" 'all the old excluded orders must be included.' " Duncan goes on to list a menu of reformist programs in the post-WWII era: "The female, the proletariat, the foreign; the animal and vegetative; the unconscious and the unknown; the criminal and failure—all that has been outcast and vagabond must return to be admitted in the creation of what we consider we are." Here, then, are vials of animacy, magic, charms, spells, incantations, visions, dreams, and fantasies scrapped from thought

in the philosophical upheavals of European evolution. (pp. 142-43)

Technicians and *Symposium of the Whole,* along with their companion anthologies by Allen, *The New American Poetry* and *The Poetics of the New American Poetry,* take up only a half-foot on the library shelf but enclose a mid-century debate on poetry, from both sides of the imperial question: domestic poetry and ideas, a range of alien literature coming into Western consciousness. In none of them will you find defenders of the old Anglo alliance or its literary tradition. They are outsider anthologies whose figures were, until recently, left out of the standard textbook anthologies that students lug to their survey classes throughout the U.S. In the *Symposium,* the Rothenbergs seized the opportunity to legitimize this alternative body of writing: The book is an "intersection between poetry and anthropology," with sober field studies by Bronislaw Malinowski, Paul Radin, Ruth Finnegan, Stanley Diamond, and Ramón Medina Silva corroborating the speculations of the poets. (p. 144)

To these activities one must add Rothenberg's work in other anthologies and journals; *Shaking the Pumpkin; America: A Prophecy,* edited with George Quasha (1973); the ten-year run of *Alcheringa,* co-edited with the anthropologist Dennis Tedlock (1970-1980); the ongoing *New Wilderness Letter;* fifteen volumes of his own poetry; half a dozen translations, recordings, and so on. In the late 1960s Rothenberg turned to himself as subject, as Jew in the era of the Holocaust, as member of a victimized race, a "tribe." This conception of himself as "other" closed a gap between his critical interests and his own writing. The result was the poem *Poland/1931* (1974), a fusion of surrealism with his experiments in "performance pieces." The title makes a node of his interests: the Poland of his parents' youth, the site of Nazi persecution, a Poland of ancestry and traditions called up through chanting. In a Pre-Face to *New Selected Poems,* Rothenberg notes that work on *Technicians of the Sacred* led him "to my own reserves as a person of a certain culture, summoning images from an ancestral past . . . & trying to set those down without the sentimentality & nostalgia that such a search has sometimes encouraged." . . . Rothenberg's voice shifts fluidly through various identities, including the archaic "thy" of a guest at the old Polish weddings; the repetitions combine here the incantatory language of rituals and the moving tempos of a modern lamentation over a violent history. The imagery forms a kaleidoscope of impressions, memories, associations, and racial caricatures, but there is a wry surrealistic humor threading through the language, the kind of satiric wit and sincerity one finds in Marc Chagall's similar reveries over his Romanian roots.

Rothenberg's would not be another immigrant tale of pathos and assimilation, but a celebration of ethnic identity. There followed a new anthology, *A Big Jewish Book,* 633 pages of the Jewish imagination "from Tribal Times to Present." In a parallel exploration, Rothenberg spent a year on the Allegheny Seneca Reservation, where he recorded *A Seneca Journal* (1978), in which the dichotomy of the personal and tribal is explored in a mixture of serious and whimsical lyrics. A portion of the *Seneca Journal* takes up part II of *New Selected Poems,* making a tacit connection between Rothenberg's Jewishness and Amerindian culture. In "Seneca Journal I," an old Senecan tale of a child and his friendship with animals recalls "a memory of my own,"

. . . grandfathers

not as hunters in the woods but on the edge of
   old world
forests men & women walked by on the way
   to markets
public baths went berrying in summer chased by
   wolves in
winter past   the huts where mushrooms hung to
   dry the
old   women of the woods lived   heavy in grey dresses
chin hairs bristling into gentile beards their
   own   familiar
dogs & cats beside them had   the master of the
   good name
learned from these the speech   of animals   this   is
the secret all men have retained that greater
   language of
what   biological fellowhood   will open   to us once
again

   ethnology the visions
   of McClure & Chomsky all
   the speakers of deep tongues point
   a route this generation
   will be privileged to assume
   a universal speech
   in which the kingdoms of the world
   are one
   the kingdoms of the world are one

The spacings between phrases score the language and give a visual tempo. Oral or "performance" poetry is structured into fluid phrases punctuated as breath units, which may also serve as the points at which the performer may either turn, rest, or reposition himself/herself in a dance-recitation. The silences are, in the old sense, the turning points of verse, the boundaries of the stage on which the performer recites. The act of versing his narrative brings Rothenberg back to origins of drama, to its prehistoric background in rituals and tribal ceremonies. This is the "biological fellowhood" one regains by returning to one's artistic roots in the deep past. Though Chomsky and McClure may view the past differently, in Rothenberg's view they draw the same conclusions about the Paleolithic mind. Chomsky's "language universals" underlie all languages and are the "deep structure" of roots from which linguistic differentiations flower. Rothenberg's earlier conception of the "deep image," the archetypal image, was an experimental equivalent of the "language universal," a psychological datum the species held in common. McClure's dithyrambs over the "beast spirit" and "bio-alchemical consciousness" are hymns to chthonic gods, another form of "universal speech." Rothenberg's visions point toward a Jungian universe of mind, the collective and universal mental functions of a species on which to base a political world system, the merged "kingdoms of the world."

The winnowings of fifteen years of writing are compressed into *New Selected Poems* and build on the narrative of identity in *Poland/1931.* The poems use a wide range of techniques in twentieth-century poetry, from brief unrhymed quatrains to exploded stanzas, to zigzagging triplets and a mélange of prose and long-lined strophes in the poem **"Galician Nights, or a Novel in Progress,"** which closes on a passage that runs down the page like a chant from "Song of Myself," each line beginning with the word "Circumstances." The Rothenberg voice is always present, whether the language is cramped into brief stanzas or sprawls out over the page like an Olson poem. The full panoply of experimental poetics is brought into the act of fleshing out a contemporary voice. Diversity of style tests the limits, the durability, and the resilience of that cen-

tral figure, whose drama in the five sections of the book takes him from recollections of his ethnic and racial roots in Poland, to identification with the Seneca Indians, and from this tribal context to a study of Jewish artists and tradition at home and in Europe. The poems explore the limits of Jewish identity, from the remote but personal past of Rothenberg's Polish ancestry to the artists whose influence bears directly on his own imagination; part V, the closing section, seems reserved for a demonstration of his own view of the world—though by now one feels he has become the concatenation of all the influences and memories he has demonstrated previously. The voice we hear throughout *New Selected Poems* is that of the earthy, street-talking Jewish immigrant, a figure clothed in the culture around him but who remains the outsider, the rejected race. The poems develop a figure whose expanding identity finds fellowship among other outcasts who cke out an existence in one civilization while keeping alive their own myths and visions. This "otherness" that Rothenberg's persona links himself to is the other tradition Western thought has pushed aside; the sheer variety of poetic forms ultimately calls attention to the constant presence of others in whom a coherent but alienated cultural tradition remains vigorously alive. (pp. 145-48)

In **"The Serpent"** and other poems of part II of *New Selected Poems,* darkness, evil, and other aspects of Western fear are taken up and reinvestigated from the point of view of their mythological functions. In **"The Serpent,"** the dreadful "monster" discovered in 1937, which reappears in other creation myths as a source of trouble in the world, is seen slithering into "the eddy called 'deep water' / or 'deep hole,' " which catches the moment of the human schism, the parting of light and dark, rational and irrational. ". . . One heavy serpent / slid down the hill astride a log / while men shot arrows after it." But in the second movement of the poem, Rothenberg takes up the defense of this maligned aspect of human nature:

   in denial of its beauty
   the story so modified by time
   few would remember
   the shining lines of snake flesh
   pale blue in the water
   blue & green
   "the woman who loved a snake"

The poem **"The Structural Study of Myth"** makes a brief summary of the kind of mythic concurrences on which Rothenberg's poetry now turns. Archetypal heroes are variations upon some core of human identity, as in this case, the overlaying of heroic models among Jesus, Coyote/Trickster, the "old story" of how "the thief became the rabbi," the "stories of . . . magic" contained within the long tradition of Jewish folklore. The poem gets to the gist of ethnopoetics, its goal being to connect with an undercurrent of shared mythologies, the key mythology running throughout human consciousness as a kind of central lode of the species. In **"Visions of Jesus,"** Rothenberg takes on the central protagonist of Western vision, and by a series of comic deflations negates some aspects of Christ to reveal others, those overlapping facets of godhead that link Christ to all the other Christ-gods of mythology. Hence the process by which an abstraction of mind is drenched in "the raw, brute sewage and liquid deliciousness of reality," to borrow from Rothenberg's colleague, Armand Schwerner. Hence, Christ as "Cokboy," father of numerous unidentified children, dancer, swaggering outcast, etc., though by the end of these "vaudeville" takes, the jokes have turned Christ into a shaman. "Coyote Jesus . . . Pawnee Jesus," or "Mother Jesus," "Alfalfa Jesus," and "Jesus / in a feathered skull cap." Jesus as "the voice / of renegades & preachers . . . Wordless in peyote . . . The freaky Jew." Rothenberg closes his book on **"Visions"** as the signal that his own transformation occurs in the repossession of abstract gods whom he returns to elemental energy, as hunger, instinct, desire, intelligence. (pp. 153-54)

Paul Christensen, "Some Bearings on Ethnopoetics," in Parnassus: Poetry in Review, *Vol. 15, No. 1, 1989, pp. 125-62.*

Alan Sillitoe

1928-

English novelist, short story writer, poet, translator, and author of children's books.

One of England's most prolific contemporary authors, Sillitoe is renowned for his candid, compassionate depictions of British working-class life. Often set in or around the industrial city of Nottingham in the British Midlands, Sillitoe's fiction features spirited protagonists whose struggles for survival take place outside the mainstream of society and often serve to attack Great Britain's class system. Although he usually portrays disillusioned characters who are unemployed or trapped in unskilled occupations, Sillitoe avoids cynicism through his realistic approach, and the emotions and concerns he addresses are often considered universal. John Mellors commented: "[The] great strength of Sillitoe's writing seems to lie in his tenderness. To the movements of feeling behind the roughness of behaviour Sillitoe is endlessly gentle."

Sillitoe's fiction is frequently based on his personal life. The son of a functionally illiterate man, Sillitoe was raised in Nottingham, where unemployment was widespread prior to World War II. To help ease his family's financial burden, Sillitoe left school at age fourteen to work in a bicycle plant then escaped the tedium of factory work by joining the Royal Air Force four years later. He served as a wireless radio operator in Malaya prior to contracting tuberculosis. Two years after he returned to England, Sillitoe married American poet Ruth Fainlight and relocated to France, where he found the necessary detachment to write about the social injustices in his country.

Upon the publication of his first two major works, the novel *Saturday Night and Sunday Morning* (1958) and the short story collection *The Loneliness of the Long Distance Runner* (1959), critics associated Sillitoe with the Angry Young Men, a group of writers whose literary output reflected the social consciousness of post-World War II England. Reviewers contended that both books powerfully evoke the country's prosperous yet bitter postwar atmosphere. Sillitoe's best-known characters, the Seatons, mirror his own family and are instilled with the resilient spirit Sillitoe acquired during his harsh childhood. *Saturday Night and Sunday Morning* follows the life and loves of Arthur Seaton, a bored young factory worker whose life is comprised of good wages, sexual adventures, and wild weekends at the neighborhood pub. His fishing excursions and retreats to the countryside, as well as his rebellious nature and refusal to be worn down by an unfair system, save Arthur from embracing a wholly destructive lifestyle. His vivacious nature belies his hapless situation, and many critics agree that Arthur emerges as a sincere, absorbing character. The title story of *The Loneliness of the Long Distance Runner,* a collection for which Sillitoe received the Hawthornden Prize, is regarded by many critics as a masterpiece of short fiction. Set in a boys reformatory, this piece revolves around a cross-country race that becomes a battle between subjection and independence. The story's adolescent narrator, Colin, seeks victory until he realizes that the race was conceived to flaunt the reformatory's rehabilitation pro-

gram to the region's governor. Although winning would gain Colin social acceptance, he intentionally loses the race and retains his self-respect. Both "The Loneliness of the Long Distance Runner" and *Saturday Night and Sunday Morning* were adapted for film.

Although critics first identified Arthur Seaton as Sillitoe's fictional counterpart, the author actually expressed an affinity with Brian Seaton, Arthur's older brother. The novel *Key to the Door* (1961), concentrates on Brian's military experiences in Malaya, where he is gripped with uncertainty about the war and repelled by England's political system. This protagonist also appears in several short stories. One collection, *The Ragman's Daughter and Other Stories* (1963), includes the piece "The Firebug," an enlarged passage from *Key to the Door* which examines young Brian Seaton's pyromaniacal tendencies. In 1989, Sillitoe published *The Open Door,* a continuation of Brian's story written as a stream-of-consciousness narrative. Returning to Nottingham from Malaya, Brian is hospitalized with tuberculosis and begins writing fiction to pass the time. Emotionally isolated, Brian's social consciousness develops to the point where he can no longer accept his country's social incongruities, and he moves to France to continue his writing career. Critics commended Sillitoe's humorous, perceptive portrait of his protagonist. Brian

Morton asserted: "*The Open Door* is an extraordinary, almost symphonic development of deceptively familiar materials, and confirms [Sillitoe's] standing as one of Britain's most powerful and sophisticated fiction-writers."

The Death of William Posters (1965) is the first book of Sillitoe's trilogy about the personal insurrection of Frank Dawley. In response to signs marked "Bill Posters Will Be Prosecuted," Dawley invents a character named William Posters, who symbolizes the working-class struggle for equality and freedom. Dawley soon resigns from his job, abandons his wife and children, and assumes the persona of William Posters. He deems the identity unnecessary, however, after enlisting to fight in the Algerian rebellion against France. In *A Tree on Fire* (1967), Dawley returns to England following his adventures in the Algerian army and is recruited by a radical organization to help establish a utopian society. *The Flame of Life* (1974) explores the group's unsuccessful efforts to rectify Britain's rigid social structure due to their own petty quibbling.

Sillitoe once again examines the theme of self-reformation in his picaresque novel, *A Start in Life* (1970). This work centers upon Michael Cullen, a nihilist who journeys to London to escape the wrath of his pregnant girlfriend. In the city, he becomes involved in a smuggling ring and is ultimately imprisoned. Upon his release, Cullen moves to the country, where he vows to live as a respectable gentleman. In the sequel, *Life Goes On* (1985), however, Cullen becomes bored with his new lifestyle and drifts back to delinquency. He discovers that his father is ghost-writing the memoirs of Claude Moggerhanger, the leader of his old smuggling ring. Moggerhanger enlists Cullen as a courier in a heroin trafficking operation bound for the Soviet Union, and the remainder of the novel largely revolves around the stories of the degenerate criminals he meets.

In *Her Victory* (1982), Sillitoe offers a female perspective to the theme of the individual's search for identity. Pam, a middle-aged housewife, leaves her abusive husband and is rescued from suicide by Tom, a man who soon becomes her lover. This friendship leads Pam into an unconventional lifestyle and a brief lesbian liaison. The novel's conclusion, in which Pam returns pregnant and subservient to Tom, elicited negative critical reaction. Several reviewers considered *Her Victory* to be a chauvinistic treatment of the feminist movement, impugning the lack of emotional growth in an "emancipated" character. In his next work, *Down from the Hill* (1984), Sillitoe compares the liberalized England of the 1940s to its current conservatism under Margaret Thatcher's rule by paralleling two excursions taken by Paul Morton, the story's narrator. Morton takes a cycling tour through the Midlands in 1945 at age seventeen and duplicates the journey forty years later by automobile. Critics applauded both the novel's nostalgic portraits and strong political statements. *Out of the Whirlpool* (1987) recounts the story of Peter Granby, an orphan whose life is changed after he comforts a dying elderly woman and is employed as a caretaker by her wealthy middle-aged daughter, Eileen. When Granby reluctantly becomes Eileen's lover, he is forced to come to terms with his own emotionally disturbed life.

Sillitoe's short fiction often shares the recalcitrant characters and humane concerns of his novels. Although his later collections have not achieved the enormous success of *The Loneliness of the Long Distance Runner*, Sillitoe's short stories are usually considered superior to his longer works of fiction.

Eric Moon asserted: "The background of Sillitoe's stories is generally as unrelieved as that of his novels, but in the stories he is more able to vary his pace and his attitudes. He often reveals humor and a greater compassion, and sometimes he achieves a curiously convincing blending of his usual realism and passion with a lyrical romanticism." The collection *Guzman, Go Home and Other Stories* (1968) examines the impossibility of escaping social malaise. In the story "Chicken," for example, a man catches and decapitates a stray hen to feed his family, but the fowl escapes, runs headless into a neighbor's kitchen, collapses in a salad, and is claimed as property by the neighbor. "Guzman, Go Home" concerns an English painter who vacations in Spain to escape the political corruption of the art world but meets an exiled Nazi war criminal. *The Second Chance and Other Stories* (1980) continues Sillitoe's fascination with the struggle for personal identity in a malevolent society. In the title story, an elderly couple meet a young man who exactly resembles their dead son. The grief-stricken couple ask the stranger to live with them, unaware that he is a sociopathic criminal who plans to rob them. "A Scream of Toys," an uncomplicated story set during World War II, describes the friendship of an English working-class girl and an Italian prisoner-of-war. Numerous reviewers praised Sillitoe's rendering of everyday events and the tense interactions between the girl and her alcoholic parents.

In addition to his novels and short stories, Sillitoe has also published several collections of poetry, including *Love in the Environs of Vorenezh and Other Poems* (1968) and *Snow on the North Side of Lucifer* (1979), an acclaimed modern interpretation of Satanic legend. Sillitoe is also the author of such children's books as *The City Adventures of Marmalade Jim* (1967) and *The Incredible Fencing Fleas* (1978).

(See also *CLC*, Vols. 1, 3, 6, 10, 19; *Contemporary Authors*, Vols. 9-12, rev. ed.; *Contemporary Authors New Revision Series*, Vols. 8, 26; *Contemporary Authors Autobiography Series*, Vol. 2; and *Dictionary of Literary Biography*, Vol. 14.)

STANLEY S. ATHERTON

For Alan Sillitoe's heroes, to live at all is to fight, and this belligerence defines their existence in the English working-class world that they inhabit. Their struggles, while reflecting the difficulties of individual protagonists, are primarily class conflicts echoing the author's disillusion with contemporary English society. . . . The battles of his heroes, whether they are visceral or cerebral, internal or external, idealistic or pragmatic, are all fought to achieve Sillitoe's utopian dream of a better world.

The central campaigns in Sillitoe's war are aimed at toppling a social structure built on inequality and characterized by haves and have-nots. The early fiction makes it clear: the two groups are enemies. Smith, the Borstal boy in **"The Loneliness of the Long-Distance Runner,"** talks of "them" and "us" and reveals that "they don't see eye to eye with us and we don't see eye to eye with them." His thoughts on the lonely practice-runs over the early-morning countryside lead him to conclude that "by sending me to Borstal they've shown me the knife, and from now on I know something I didn't know before: that it's war between me and them. . . . I know who my enemies are and what war is." The enemies, according to

Smith, are generically called "bastard-faced In-Laws" as opposed to Out-Laws) and the species includes "pig-faced snotty-nosed dukes and ladies", "cops, governors, posh whores, pen-pushers, army officers, Members of Parliament." Arthur Seaton, the protagonist of **Saturday Night and Sunday Morning,** includes "landlords and gaffers [bosses], coppers, army, government" in the list of enemies he plans to be "fighting every day until I die."

All these groups are targets for Sillitoe, for they are the bastions of an established order which he rejects. The army is particularly singled out for attack because it is a clearly visible instrument of reactionary government. Arthur Seaton makes this clear in his commentary on rifle practice during his annual fifteen-day training period: "When . . . I lay on my guts behind a sandbag shooting at a target board I know whose faces I've got in my sights every time the new rifle cracks off. Yes. The bastards that put the gun into my hands . . . [and who plan] how to get blokes into khaki and fight battles in a war that they'll never be in."

Hatred of the army is often focussed on the uniform. In **Saturday Night and Sunday Morning,** for instance, Arthur Seaton gets caught up in a street incident in which order is represented by a young woman "wearing an army uniform—the colour of which immediately prejudiced him." His brother Brian, the hero of **Key to the Door,** is conscripted for the post-war occupation of Malaya yet remains a rebel by wearing his uniform only to collect his pay, and by showing a class-formed contempt of such "good" soldiers as Baker, who "had been to a public school, was hidebound and . . . mutinous only within the limits of King's Regulations." The pervasiveness of this attitude is seen in the Seaton family in which "out of a dozen able-bodied men in all remotely connected branches of the family, only two went into the army and stayed" during the Second World War.

This collective rebellion may be partly explained by the working-class feeling that the government (seen in its visible manifestations of army, police, and parliamentarians) simply does not care about the individual. And the English working classes, possibly because they have had little wealth to lose, have traditionally fostered a fierce sense of personal independence. Sillitoe shows his awareness of this phenomenon by showing us a class solidarity which finds its expression in individual (rather than collective) rejections of authority. Brian Seaton, for example, has regarded the police as enemies since his childhood reading of *Les Misérables* which he found "an epic of reality . . . a battle between a common man and the police who would not let him free because he had once stolen a loaf of bread." . . . (pp. 324-25)

Distrust of government is also characterized by a rejection of both major parties, and although there is some wavering sympathy for Labour as the socialist or egalitarian party, political affiliations are not encouraged in Sillitoe's working-class world. The Tories as representatives of tradition, position, and privilege are thoroughly damned. Brian Seaton, reminiscing about his childhood, thinks: "Conservative—it was an official word to be distrusted, hated in fact." Smith remembers turning the sound down on television political announcements. . . . And Arthur Seaton condemns both Tory and Labour for their lack of sympathy with the working class: "I ain't a communist, I tell you. I like 'em though, because they're different from these big fat Tory bastards in Parliament. And them Labour bleeders too. They rob our wage packets every week with insurance and income tax and try to tell us it's all for our own good."

The angry protest remains only an impotent expression of disillusion. . . . Their rebellion is visceral. So when Arthur Seaton hears a shop window being smashed and finds that the sound of breaking glass "synthesized all the anarchism within him," the anarchism remains only an urge. A substitute for action is the anarchistic dream. Like romantic guerillas in some hillside hide-away, the Seaton men dream of destroying the power structure of the established order, of blowing up factories and the Houses of Parliament because, as Arthur puts it, "that'd be something worth doing." He is never quite lucid, however, about why it is worth doing, and it never gets done. Lacking a rational stimulus, the working-class protest in the Seaton novels is never translated into effective action.

What these novels offer, instead, is a many-faceted description of working-class anger in which the exuberant characters of Sillitoe's world come alive through the processes of revolt. Their belligerence is the dominant quality of their being from childhood through courtship and in the day-to-day struggles of married life. In **"The Decline and Fall of Frankie Buller,"** an autobiographical short story, Sillitoe writes of his early allegiance to the leader of a slum gang, "a full-bown centurion with his six foot spear-headed railing at the slope, and his rusty dust bin lid for a shield . . . marching to war, and I was part of his army." To young Brian Seaton in **Key to the Door,** a good-night kiss between his sister Lydia and her boyfriend Tom "looked like a more desperate combat than that which was supposed to have taken place between St. George and the dragon." And in the family of "shuttlecocked Seaton and battledored Vera" the growth to manhood of the boys created "a balance of power that kept the house more or less peaceful"; yet even this was shattered by Vera's jealousy of Harold's flirtation with the "black-haired inscrutable Millie from Travers Row . . . [when] the house witnessed pitched battles that even made the money quarrels of the dole days look like the pleasant tit-for-tat of a lively courtship."

Belligerence is also evident in the religious attitudes of Sillitoe's characters. An atheist himself, Sillitoe attempts in the Seaton novels to establish an atheistic tradition for his working-class heroes. [In **Key to the Door**], Harold Seaton's father-in-law, the blacksmith Merton, shocks his wife Mary with his heretical outbursts, and Harold himself replies to his wife Vera's remonstrance "God will pay you out" with "What bastard God? . . . There ain't no bastard God." His sons carry on the tradition. Arthur refuses to believe in God. Brian as a child associates God with garbage, thinking the Sanitation Department incinerator is "like the inside of a church"; he later concludes that "there ain't no God." Such irreverent outbursts serve to reinforce the working-class attitude of angry protest against a world that for them turns on social inequality and injustice.

Sillitoe, in speaking of the phenomenon of protest in recent English fiction, described the writers as

> taking society to pieces and trying to show what it was made of. Perhaps after they had taken off the outer casing, found out more or less what made society tick and shown this in all its detail, these writers or new writers after them would not only express anger and protest, but would be able to show the positive way out.

(pp. 325-27)

Sillitoe's persistent emphasis on the revolutionary activities of his heroes points up his concern with what Denis Donoghue calls "the ordinary universe." He continues to feel it worthwhile to criticize society; and because he is one of the few serious writers today who has not disowned society for the autonomy of the imagination, he makes a legitimate and significant claim on our attention. His fiction reminds us that the tradition of social commitment in literature is not dead, for like William Blake he exults in the reformer's battle-cry:

> I will not cease from mental fight,
> Nor shall my sword sleep in my hand,
> Till we have built Jerusalem
> In England's green and pleasant land.

(p. 331)

Stanley S. Atherton, "Alan Sillitoe's Battleground," in The Dalhousie Review, *Vol. 48, No. 3, Autumn, 1968, pp. 324-31.*

THE TIMES LITERARY SUPPLEMENT

As in his earliest work, Alan Sillitoe's narrators [in *Guzman, Go Home and Other Stories*] maintain a dour rhetoric, exhilarating if sometimes undisciplined, and a grim pleasure in facing ugly facts not only about society but also about themselves. In the first of these stories, **"Revenge"**, a Nottingham man of forty marries late, fights his wife until he is reduced to accepting psychiatric care and then, finding that the doctors are as untrustworthy and contemptuous of him as other authorities are, he fights the doctors and walks out, proud, self-reliant and mean. The same kind of man again—but young, long-haired, stoned in Greece and peddling cannabis—recalls his Nottingham past, the thefts, the imprisonment and the lost girl, in a story called **"The Rope Trick"** which bridges the supposed gap between the angry 1950s and the swinging 1960s. The principal character in **"Isaac Starbuck"** is not strictly the narrator, but he talks so much that he might as well be. Characteristic is a brief memory of schooldays when a boy, thinking his forename Jewish, asks: "Who killed Christ?" Little Isaac replies: "That's right, I did", and follows up with "a savage bash into the middle of next week". That is Isaac's style. Pursued by his "search-party brother-in-law" on his "tin-pot push-button people's bike", this reluctant husband stands observing the street names of Nottingham:

> Rifle Street, Gatling Street, Bastion Street, Redoubt Street, Citadel Street—fighting monickers made up by some fat and comfortable swine who'd never heard a bomb or had a fist in his face . . . I'd name them Love Street, Vagina Row, Womb Lane.

This "make love, not war" principle is agreeable to the higher feelings of Sillitoe's narrators; but they hardly seem the right people to put it into operation. Their love-making tends to involve punch-ups with husbands.

The merriest of these tales is [**"Chicken"**], an anecdote about a stolen chicken which, after being beheaded, runs spouting blood into a neighbour's house, landing on the butter and trifle, still bleeding and scratching. There is much ill-feeling here, for the neighbour won't give it back and, evidently, everybody is going to hold the incident against everyone else for a long time. These are bloody-minded tales, all of a piece, leading up to the unexpected title story [**"Guzman, Go Home"**], in which the principal narrator, Guzman, is a German war criminal and former artist, now living in Spain as

a prosperous garage proprietor. Here the ungenerous self-reliance of the Nottingham narrators is presented more objectively, without charm. This narrative is an excellent feat of impersonation and the story acts as a kind of critique of the philosophy expressed by Sillitoe's other characters. The conclusion points to the inefficiency, rather than the immorality, of excessive individualism.

"Love and War," in The Times Literary Supplement, *No. 3478, October 24, 1968, p. 1193.*

RICHARD CLARK STERNE

Alan Sillitoe is a Chekhovian Robin Hood. His heart is with the English working class, from which he comes, and his wry, virile stories tell chiefly of the aborted or frustrated passions, compassions and rebellions of laborers and marginal bourgeois, chiefly in and around Nottingham. . . . Sillitoe (who has published several novels, as well as a few volumes of poetry) is actually at his best in shorter fictions that have not received cinematic consecration. **"The Fishing-Boat Picture,"** **"On Saturday Afternoon,"** and **"The Disgrace of Jim Scarfedale"** [in *The Loneliness of the Long Distance Runner*]; **"The Firebug," "The Magic Box,"** and the title piece of the book that includes them, *The Ragman's Daughter;* and the first three stories in *Guzman, Go Home* are all resonant and moving.

The first-person narrator of **"Revenge,"** whose language obscurely troubles us from the beginning, is, we gradually learn, schizophrenic. His propensity to see himself from outside, as an object, while experiencing intense fear and resentment of other persons, seems frighteningly symbolic of widespread tendencies in our technological—Sillitoe might say capitalistic—culture. "Airplanes," the narrator remarks, "are so much more perfect than men, and more useful." The psycho-sociological categories of "alienation" and "reification" could hardly be brought more vividly alive than they are in this story.

"Chicken" is a brief masterpiece about a foundry worker who picks up a stray hen while biking on a country road, brings it home and decapitates it so that he and his mother and two brothers can have it for dinner next week. Trouble is that the headless hen, now knowing it's kaput, cuts out of the back yard and into a neighbor's kitchen, where it eventually falls "dead in the salad, greenery dwarfed by snowing feathers and flecks of blood." The irate neighbor, armed with a poker, immediately asserts property rights in the hen, whose captor-murderer is forced to beat a humiliating retreat.

In **"Canals"** a London schoolteacher who has gone home to Nottingham to be with his dying father suddenly decides after the father's death to visit a former girl friend he hasn't seen in fifteen years. His highest ambition had once been to be a good toolsetter, but in the army he had "discovered that he was intelligent in a more worldly sense," and had also become unable to accept Marian's inarticulate, unsubtle, complete love. Now, he is married and has three children. She, living in the same old place, working at the same stocking factory, has a son by a husband whom she has refused to see since he was jailed for house-breaking. Delighted that her former lover has visited her, she is more clear-sighted than he about their past:

You said you wanted to stay in the army for good, and so getting married wouldn't be fair to either of us. I remember all of it clearly. But I could see that that wasn't it at all, though. You'd just lost interest. There was nowt else you could get to know about me, after all the times we had. We didn't even fall out with each other. I didn't know what to tell the girls at work when they asked about you.

What these three superb stories have in common with three others in the book that are extremely good, and with one diffuse but interesting piece (**"Isaac Starbuck"**), is a concern with the link between personal anguish and the social system of which persons are a part. Sillitoe does not blame "society" for all his characters' ills and misfortunes. But one character's remark that "if some new system of social life came to involve him deeply then this piece of stupid personal confusion might bother him less than it did" seems pertinent to most of the people Sillitoe creates.

This includes the Nazi war criminal in the virtuoso story **"Guzman, Go Home."** Hitler and his New Order had temporarily resolved all of "Guzman's" confusions, but since 1945 he has lived in exile in Spain, believing in absolutely nothing except the mechanical virtues of the Volkswagen. Sillitoe's point is unmistakable: our personal confusions may be mitigated by any "system of social life" that comes "to involve us deeply," but there are hideous systems and involvements as well as humane ones. Through his art, Sillitoe asks us to make a choice.

> *Richard Clark Sterne, in a review of "Guzman, Go Home and Other Stories," in* Saturday Review, *Vol. LII, No. 47, November 22, 1969, p. 86.*

ALAN HISLOP

Guzman, Go Home takes us back, in most of the stories, to Alan Sillitoe's Nottingham, where nothing is much better or worse than it was in his two previous collections, *The Loneliness of the Long Distance Runner* and *The Ragman's Daughter.* The people aren't quite as poor, but their frustrations and disappointments, their failing marriages and dying hopes are familiar, and they retain the crafty independence and pride that makes them so appealing, even at their worst.

If the stories lack the force of those in his earlier volumes, that is because Sillitoe mapped out his territory so well. He isn't repeating himself; we are simply seeing some new parts of his world.

His characters are often sad and bitter and discontented with "the system," but Sillitoe doesn't patronize them as victims. "Life is long, long enough always to start again. The black pitch of energy is inexhaustible in the barrel . . . Nothing can stop it, not in me," says the hero of **"Revenge,"** and he could be speaking for everyone in this book.

The title story [**"Guzman, Go Home"**] deals with the relationship between art and politics. A young English painter and his wife and child, driving through Spain on their way to Morocco and self-imposed exile from "the political atmosphere that saturated English artistic life," meet Guzman, garage mechanic and artist *manqué*, an ex-Nazi being pursued for war crimes. Guzman's reminiscences make up the body of the story, a parable to the effect that if you're going to mix art with politics, you'd better have a successful recipe—

although the story doesn't indicate what it might be. Guzman is a compelling figure in a memorable story. (p. 45)

> *Alan Hislop, "Life as a Series of Lost Directions," in* The New York Times Book Review, *December 14, 1969, pp. 44-5.*

ANNA RYAN NARDELLA

Alan Sillitoe is primarily concerned with the age-old problem of man's identity—man's attempt to define himself as *being* or *nonbeing* in a chaotic, disturbed universe where life and identity are constantly threatened by personal and/or impersonal forces—where man faces the chasm of nothingness, sapped of his vitality by monotonous ritualistic routine and meaningless institutions that first incarcerate, then deaden the soul *unless* there is the conscious attempt to throw aside these entrapments to find self. For Sillitoe, finding the *vital self* necessarily means casting aside the traditional values, values which can no longer prove functional in a post-Kantian world, in a world where all verities have come under question, in a world where God is dead and wars continue with, as Sillitoe says, "impending bourgeois atomic juggernaut," momentarily possible. With World War I serving historically as the breaking point between a positive, ordered view of the universe and a nihilistic, chaotic view of the universe, each individual must now define himself for himself. But often his quest to do so is a futile quest, for there is only momentary peace, if any at all, since death is the only permanent value. Sillitoe's characters must constantly persuade themselves "that life has some significance otherwise [they] sink into the morass of the living dead." Sillitoe's characters recognize the meaninglessness of life, the *nada* permeating all actions, but yet they must find some way to live with the nothingness. (p. 469)

[In *Saturday Night and Sunday Morning*], Arthur Seaton, the novel's working-class hero, is fighting the forces of dehumanization. . . . [He must] learn to cope with the mechanistic routine of life in post-World War II England; and though the English economic system now is better than ever before, Seaton must find his escapes so that he "won't knuckle under" to the routine of the bicycle factory. Thus, he drinks heavily, manages affairs with two married women, and longs to retreat into nature.

That Seaton lives in an existential universe is quite clear throughout the novel, for he is constantly fighting to be human in a highly mechanistic environment. As a capstan lathe operator in the bicycle factory, Seaton knows the value of his weekly productivity. He knows that he can produce only so many parts per day without his quota being increased. He paces himself, taking great pleasure in doing his work neatly and accurately. . . . Arthur works day by day amid the noise and smells "of oil-suds, machinery, and shaved steel." His life is hard, and his only reward is the good wages which can buy him some momentary pleasures; but the money itself, like all other things, has no intrinsic value because there is the constant threat of nothingness:

> it was no use saving your money year after year. A mug's game, since the value of it got less and less and in any case you never knew when the Yanks were going to do something daft like dropping the H. bomb on Moscow. And if they did then you could say *ta-ta* to everybody, burn your football

coupons and betting-slips, and ring-up Billy Graham. If you believe in God, which I don't.

There is for Arthur only the daily, weekly, and monthly repetition of toil. Every Monday morning he clocks in; yet the "bright Monday-morning ring of the clocking-in machine [makes] a jarring note, different from the tune that [plays] inside Arthur." He tries on the weekends to reassert his humanity. He escapes his mechanical routine at the lathe by drinking excessively, for alcohol is the anodyne that dulls the pain of life. Arthur is always shouting for a pint, "the only sufficient liquid measure that can begin to swill away the tasteless ash-like thirst." Arthur's "ash-like thirst" is the thirst of a wastelander—a man trying to exert his existence in a meaningless universe. In the opening scene of the novel Arthur is roaringly drunk. He falls down a flight of stairs and then vomits upon two people. His nausea is the existential nausea—a sickness produced by the vacuity of life.

Arthur also tries to proclaim his *being* by having affairs with two married women—Brenda, the wife of a fellow worker at the factory, and her sister Winnie. Arthur deceives both husbands for a time only to be beaten badly later by Winnie's soldier husband and his "swaddie" friend. Throughout the escapades with both women, Arthur is testing himself to prove himself. He is desperately seeking momentary pleasure, although he is constantly aware of the risks involved. The risks, however, make his life exciting, proving his existence. He can for a time control the risks and balance the forces, but he knows that "the winner takes nothing." The value is in preventing "the world's gigantic wheels from crushing one" for just a while longer. The value is in maintaining discretion for as long as possible so that "the tight-rope neither [sags] nor [weakens]." (pp. 470-71)

To escape the deadening routine of his life at the factory, Arthur longs to retreat into nature, for he finds there a momentary happiness, a kind of "separate peace." He takes Brenda into the woods one evening for lovemaking, and their pleasure from the act performed in nature is comparable to that described in Hemingway's *For Whom the Bell Tolls* when Maria and Robert Jordan feel "the earth move out to nowhere and time stand still" as they make love in a mountain field. Arthur does find pleasure in Brenda's bed, but his pleasure is intensified in nature. He desires to become once again reunited with nature, for a closeness with nature seemingly establishes identity:

> Arthur sweated at his lathe, working at the same fast pace as in winter to keep the graph-line of his earnings level. Life went on like an assegai into the blue, with dim memories of the dole and school-days behind, and a dimmer feeling of death in front, a present life punctuated by meetings with Brenda on certain beautiful evenings when the streets were noisy and the clouds did a moonlight-flit over the rooftops.

Arthur's love of fishing is also symbolic of his desire to return to nature. He feels cleansed for a time by fishing, for "the only peace you [get is] when you [are] away from it all, sitting on the osier-lined banks of a canal waiting for fish to bite, or lying in bed with a woman you loved."

Arthur's values are simple ones really: he drinks, loves, and fishes. He rebels in his way, but he finally surrenders to the forces of domesticity. He decides to marry Doreen and become a "regular bloke," accepting a way of life which he has

previously viewed as stifling and narrow. He apparently gives up the struggle to define himself for himself against the forces of life crushing him. He has fought hard: "I'm me and nobody else; and whatever people think I am or say I am, that's what I'm not, because they don't know a bloody thing about me." He has been a rebel believing it best to be a rebel "so as to show 'em it don't pay to try to do you down." Nonetheless, Arthur surrenders to what he hates, to that which appears to be contrary to his nature. He does so because he is tired of the fight and he recognizes the futility of the fight. He desires a kind of peace, even if won at the expense of himself.

After being beaten by Winnie's soldier husband and his friend, Arthur lies in bed for a long time "in an apathetic state . . . sitting up to move his pillow, [staring] without recognition at the pink wall of the bedroom." His pain is not merely physical pain from the beating. His pain is the mental anguish of the human condition, and Arthur Seaton comes to a full recognition of the nature of life while lying in bed: "He didn't much care whether he lived or died. The wheels of change that were grinding their impressive tracks through his mind did not yet show themselves off in him to advantage." The fight serves as a symbol to Arthur, as a pivotal point in his life: "He sensed that though he had merely been beaten up by two swaddies—not a very terrible thing, and not the first time he had been in a losing fight—he felt like a ship that had never left its slipway suddenly floundering in mid-ocean." He realizes his own insecurity in an insecure world: "No place existed in all the world that could be called safe, and he knew for the first time in his life that there had never been any such thing as safety, and never would be, the difference being that now he knew it as a fact, whereas before it was a natural unconscious state." Arthur's is an existential recognition. He now knows that he lives in a cave in the middle wood where he is not safe. He describes his dream of falling from a cliff, but never landing—until one day he hits the bottom without knowing it, "like a bubble bursting when it touches something solid, and [he was] dead, out like a light in a Derbyshire gale." Arthur has always feared isolation, and his raucous life has been a hedge against isolation: "To be alone seemed a continuation of his drugged life at the lathe. He wanted noise, to drink and make love." Now, after the beating, he fears isolation even more, seeing every man as his own enemy caught up in his own isolation. Arthur has now come to an articulation of the existential nature of the human condition, and he is scared. So, in his insecurity he seeks some kind of permanent value—and that seems to be marriage to Doreen. He has now quit fighting himself and those things he cannot change. He will now turn his attacks against "the capital G of Government" while "accepting some of the sweet and agreeable things of life."

Once Arthur realizes man's true position in the universe, he becomes Doreen's young man and takes her into nature where they lie down together in "a deathly and irresistible passion." Before their lovemaking, however, they walk the fields on a timeless day with the trees budding. They are viewed as a courtin' couple, and a vendor exclaims to Arthur that "the fishes can rest in peace from now on," to which Arthur responds, "there'll still be time for fishin'." Indeed, there will be time for fishing. There *must* be time for fishing, for nature provides man solace. (pp. 471-73)

[Sillitoe's] works are existential renderings of man caught in a chaotic world where he must make his own meanings and find his own freedom until death ends all. Sillitoe's man "doesn't knuckle under," as Arthur Seaton says, but continues, against all odds, to exert himself as *Being,* avoiding always those forces that seek to nullify that *Being.* (p. 481)

Anna Ryan Nardella, "The Existential Dilemmas of Alan Sillitoe's Working-Class Heroes," in Studies in the Novel, *Vol. V, No. 4, Winter, 1973, pp. 469-82.*

JOHN LUCAS

When Kingsley Amis recently brought out his *Collected Short Stories* he provided an introduction in which he said that he thought of the collection as "really one of chips from a novelist's work-bench". I doubt if Alan Sillitoe would want to say the same about the stories that make up his new collection. *The Second Chance.* After all, Sillitoe has always written short stories and he has several previous volumes to his credit. Yet it would be interesting to know what he thinks of the short story as an art form, what he considers its demands to be, and in what ways, if any, they differ from those made by the novel. For there is a sense in which Sillitoe's stories seem peculiarly artless. This is perhaps to say only that even the best of them work in a manner that is unusual or unorthodox. There seem to be at least two formal orthodoxies for the modern short-story. . . . By and large, they follow either the pattern of the figure in the carpet, the half-hidden thread that can be traced through discreet symbol, verbal echo, juxtaposed episodes, or any combination of these; or they rely on the epiphanic, the moment of wild strawberries that suddenly makes sense of character, or characters, and that explains motive or behaviour.

Sillitoe's short stories do not follow either of these patterns. Moreover, although some of them are anecdotal in a way that recalls Arnold Bennett, none is particularly strong on plot. And those which do rely on it are nearly always the weakest. In the present volume, for example, **"The Meeting"** and **"Confrontation"** are slight, would-be slick tales that hardly earn their keep: they seem to be written for the kind of magazine and audience which started up during the Edwardian period and which ceased to exist some time ago.

["The Second Chance"] is clearly an ambitious and very differently conceived tale, but seems to me a complete failure. It is about a young wastrel who finds himself befriended by a Major Baxter, an elderly retired officer, and who, at his request, acts out the part of his son, to whom he bears a close resemblance. The son had been killed in the war and his mother has been unable to accept the fact. It is a complicated story and potentially a very interesting one, but Sillitoe cannot do much with it because he cannot really imagine his subject. This is how he writes of the elderly couple.

> Forever locked into each separate fire of deliberate forgetfulness was their only way of never putting [their son] out of their minds for a single instant, and kept him more alive than if they had gone through endless seasons of grieving together.

How can you be locked into a fire, what on earth is a fire of deliberate forgetfulness, and how can such a fire make for memory ("kept him more alive")? As you read through **"The Second Chance"** it comes more and more to have the feel of something that came out of what seemed at the time a good idea. It has about it the air of having been willed into existence, and like all acts of will it is grotesquely unnatural. It is not merely that the narrative is awkwardly written; the dialogue is wooden, inauthentic, as though Sillitoe had never listened to the speech rhythms of the kinds of people he writes about here.

Yet there is a quite different Sillitoe, one who is represented in this volume by such stories as **"A Scream of Toys"** and **"A Time to Keep"**. I do not think that either story is as good as the very best Sillitoe, but that hardly matters. For both stories show that unique ability which Sillitoe perhaps first demonstrated in the remarkable **"Loneliness of the Long-distance Runner"** and in another early story **"To Be Collected"**, which, if less well-known, is almost as fine. It is in stories such as these that Sillitoe's cherishable characteristics appear: an extraordinarily keen eye and ear for the ways in which certain people move and speak, and more than that, a surprisingly tender, uncondescending knowledge of the constraints within which they live.

"A Scream of Toys" seems on the face of it a very old-fashioned piece of naturalism, a rough-cut slice of life. Set in Nottingham during the second world war, it is about a young working-class Nottingham girl who by chance meets and befriends an Italian POW. Sillitoe is good on the semi-formality of their relationship, good also on the girl's uneasy relationship with her semi-drunken parents. But what makes the story so impressive is Sillitoe's awareness of, and his ability to communicate, the emotional tension that lies under the surface of, for example, the girl's monosyllabic talk with her parents. And he marvellously shows how such tensions are increased by trivial domestic happenings, and finally break out in violence.

It is in the tale's strange, drifting, rhythm that one notes Sillitoe's apparent artlessness, and the real worth of his art. For nothing happens: there is no revelation, the story hardly seems to be a story at all. Yet in fact it has a completeness that sets it quite apart from and above such clumsy constructions as **"The Second Chance"** or **"The Meeting"**. The same is true of a handful of other stories in the present volume, including **"The Fiddle"**, and **"The Sniper"**, both of which return Sillitoe to the familiar ground of Nottingham working-class life, but both in unfamiliar ways. It might be thought that in so often returning to this material Sillitoe is in danger of parodying himself. In fact, the parodies occur only on those occasions when he tries to produce a well-made story.

John Lucas, "The Art of Artlessness," in The Times Literary Supplement, *No. 4060, January 23, 1981, p. 76.*

D. M. ROSKIES

In noticing its more marked felicities and shortcomings, almost all the reviewers and interpreters of Alan Sillitoe's oeuvre are unanimous. Subcutaneous penetration is his strong suit, a matchless capacity for involving his reader, unsentimentally and with a rare degree of empathy. . . . On frequent exhibit as well is a talent for conveying the feel and smell of semi-skilled labour and subsistence-level scrounging in Nottingham, the author's favoured terrain as well as elected literary ambient. The town and its environs compose a country of the mind as well as an intimately known human ecology, and from among its inhabitants he finds the characters he most admires—the felon, the poacher, the juvenile tearaway, the chronic deserter from the Forces, schismatics all, sensing themselves quarantined in the workings of the system (when not altogether outside it) and spoiling for a fight. It is a further, if not always noticed, mark of Sillitoe's skill and range that the shape and condition of life in Nottingham's lower echelons—not just its fundamental poverty but its fundamental insubordination—should seem entirely typical of working-class life in England in mid-century. (p. 308)

Sillitoe is least happy within the ramifications of the traditional full-length novel, that species of creative effort which, for its effect, crucially depends on a knack, acquired or intuitive, for linking scene with scene and sequence in a grand and necessary design, with the aim of conveying a tension plausibly located in intricate links of moral cause and effect. His imagination, rather, is instinctively lapidary in operation; it is seen to best advantage within the compressed and miniaturised confines of the short story and novella, where the demand is for a concentration of resources upon a critical event, or series of events, in which individual character is made to reveal its constitution and quality. This is why *Saturday Night and Sunday Morning* (1957) his first and best known novel, succeeds. Anecdotal in conception, it is unitary in effect. . . . It is on the intense small scale that the consensus finds [Sillitoe] best able to exercise to the full his faculty for expressing sentiments of class-solidarity, separateness, violence and dichotomy, in situations dramatically contrived to justify their explosion, verbal or physical. The pieces collected in *The Loneliness of the Long Distance Runner* (1959), *The Ragman's Daughter* (1963), *Guzman, Go Home* (1968), and, latterly, in *Men, Women and Children* (1973) are in this regard the crown of his achievement to date. (pp. 308-09)

Where critical opinion has proven less than adequate is in accounting for the concrete display of such a talent, as well as its considered intellectual basis. A writer of Sillitoe's provenance and concerns invariably invites a certain analytical lethargy, the tendency being to assume that such eccentricity of perspective is so self-evident as to require no detailed scrutiny. So it is well to ask, just *how* does the trick come off? How does Sillitoe manage, and manage to sustain, so self-authenticating an inwardness; to what aesthetic ends; and with what notions in mind of character and conduct? . . . The proper response to the issue of point of view, social or narrative, and its reputed independence from received ways of seeing and judging, must take as its point of departure an intimate inspection of the writer's chosen expressive manner. (p. 309)

A hard look at the technical format of Sillitoe's narration makes a good beginning. This, in stories like the preceding, in *Saturday Night,* and in many of the sections revolving around Brian Seaton in *Key to the Door,* is the informal vernacular monologue, addressed by the narrator to an audience of compeers in whom the reader by fictional grace is included. Variously ranging in manner from the colloquial soliloquy (**"The Disgrace of Jim Scarfedale"**) to the backyard or on-the-job confessional (**"The Bike"**), to the colloquialized stream-of-consciousness (*Saturday Night*), these monologues are conceived with the requirements of "the ideal story" in mind, a form which, in Sillitoe's view, stops and starts up again, making room for flourishes of comment and leisurely digression, seemingly unconcerned with effects of accumulation and foreshortening, counting on the tacit participation of an audience. (pp. 309-10)

[Sillitoe's narrative style makes use of] a speech-register based on a colloquial diction and an informal delivery. In this respect Sillitoe represents a distinctive meeting of the self-consciously literary impulse with that "immemorial tribal instinct of ghetto and village" he prizes as the spur to storytelling. Lean and artfully self-sufficient in its lexical limitations, impudently importunate or fraternally confiding, frequently assuming the character of rasping conferences between beleaguered comrades united in the democracy (or in the conspiracy) of a shared condition, it is a speech that incarnates a particular kind of social psychology. Its features are designed to reproduce the working of a restless, fractious, untutored mind, inclined to shuffle between polar emotions, ever ready to visit retribution upon its antagonists, but ready also to look sidelong in amusement at itself and at the temerity of its own self-expression. Its typical effect is one of carefully managed variety: the staggered rhythms of off-the-cuff talk, with its sudden rests, its fumbling pauses, its exercising of leave to correct and supplement itself in midstream, its depreciation of the lengthily analytical explanation in favour of the richly contumacious self-justification. Insofar as the speaker is directly involved in or able to authoritatively report back on the matter described, he usually is, or has recently been, in transit: in full flight from "those who hold the whip-hand" (like Smith in **"The Loneliness of the Long Distance Runner"**); "in a police cell, stretched full length on the floor and packed in with eleven others" ("I" in **"The Good Women"**). And because he is usually physically "dead to the wide", or emotionally "fed-up", or simply fidgetingly at loose ends between jobs or after work, he speaks extemporaneously, in a verbally defensive posture, hewing close to a line of particulars as if material reality is all that can be trusted to provide potential haven, if haven be needed. Lacking the time or the inclination to distribute the events he recounts in synthetic sequence, he speaks as the spirit moves him, asking rhetorical questions, doubling back to account for his lapses of memory, his speech widdershins but never wandering in sense, unified as it is by the consistency of voice-pitch and the speaker's awareness of his audience. Those of Sillitoe's fictions given over to a first-person narrator are therefore among his most fluent and finished creations. Everything in them, including the element of suspense, depends on the tactics of the dominating voice, its ability to improvise or conjure up tentative approximations of the speaker's responses, to transmit fresh and undisturbed the subjective feel of the workaday world in which the account is set. . . . [The] novelist is convincingly omniscient in proportion as he contrives to enter the subject's mind at the level of mental speech, then to weave about within the given train of thought, moving from overt vernacular reflection to vernacularized summary of thought. . . . (pp. 310-11)

Two examples of Sillitoe's prose-style bearing his characteristic signature and used as the basis of technical address, will suffice to illustrate the preceding. The first is from the title-story of *The Ragman's Daughter;* the second from *Key to the Door:*

> I was walking home with an empty suitcase one night, an up-to-date pigskin zip job I was fetching back from a pal who thought he'd borrowed it for good, and two plain-clothed coppers stopped me. They questioned me for twenty minutes, then gave up and let me go. While they had been talking to me, a smash-and-grab had taken place around the corner, and ten thousand nicker had vanished in the wide open spaces of somebody who needed it.

> That's life. I was lucky my suitcase had nothing but air in it. Sometimes I walk out with a box of butter

and cheese from the warehouse I work at, but for once that no-good God was on my side—trying to make up for the times He's stabbed me in the back maybe. But if the coppers had had a word with me a few nights later they'd have found me loaded with high-class provision snap.

[**"The Ragman's Daughter"**]

Most of the foremen and chargehands had been at Robinson's anything from twenty to forty years . . . Brian laughed to think of it. Thank God there was a war on: I can allus go somewhere else if they try to come the hard gaffer with me, though I'm not much of a lad at swapping jobs and would rather stay at one place a couple of years to get my hand in and make a few pals. I can't understand people being here forty years—worse than a life sentence—especially when they can get better money at other places. And what do they end up wi' if they hold on here for that long? A cup o' cocoa, a copy of the Bible and a five-bob pocket-watch to time out the days of idleness left to them. Not even that though: I'm making it up. They're lucky to get a thank you, and become hot and bothered with gratitude if they do, or only spit the smell of thank you out when it's too late to do much else about it, such as drop a nub-end on a heap of parra-fin rags, to trip one of the gaffers into a manhole. It's too late then, to matter how they feel. Earlier on they thought they'd got a trade and wouldn't turn to labouring—put up with blood-tubs telling 'em what to do as if they was skivvies. But forty years is a lifetime, a waste of breathing in which you could have lived in every country in the world, seen everything, done everything, instead of staying a cap-touching loon in Robinson's rat-warren.

Talking to Bob Thorpe the other day I said that old Robinson was a Bible-backed slave-driver, a two-faced twisting dead-head who'd sell his grandmoth-er wholesale if they came more than two at a time. Old Thorpe said I shouldn't talk like that, and had better not let Robinson or any of the other gaffers hear it. "What would happen if they did?" I asked, laughing to myself. "Why," he said, an almost ter-rified look on his long face, "you'd get the sack." He's a pasty little bloke of sixty. "That'd be terri-ble," I said. "I'd have to get another job, wouldn't I?" Then he brightened up and said: "You won't be so cocky after the War when jobs is hard to get again." "Don't bother," I said, quick off the mark, "Old Fatguts with the big cigar will be out when the War's over, on his neck with the rest of his gov-ernment. It wain't be the same again. Them days is over." At least they'd better be. Yet nobody could be sure, and neither was Brian, despite the look of dead certainty on his face; for he dreaded the return of his father's means-test fate on himself. I'll shoot myself first, he thought. No, better shoot the other bastards, then maybe it'll alter before I do it to myself.

[*Key to the Door*]

The speaker in the first passage is Tony, now "going straight . . . working in the warehouse where they store but-ter and cheese," yet poised to recall the illegal escapades of his youth from the vantage point of approaching middle age. In the second it is Brian Seaton, aged 15, set to cleaning flues in a cardboard factory, contemplating the progress of the on-going war; his duties as "an odd-job lad, . . . running errands and sweeping up;" and his father's admonition to "volunteer for out, . . . not even a Christmas club, not two pieces of ef-

fing string." The difference in age and condition should not obscure the features their respective deliveries share in com-mon. In neither passage are we to look for words as separate verbal integers, sufficient unto themselves, objects to be ex-amined or probed for their covert or symbolic reverberations. Instead we are expected to attend to the accents, the percus-sive beat, of a voice, formulating its statement in discrete units composed of nouns moved by gerundives or participles enhanced by neutral frames of conjunctions and copulas. . . . Both passages observe loose sequences of thought, the first marking time, so to speak (after "That's life") while locating the next set of ideas, the second conceal-ing amid its loquacious flow a number of semantic dead spots and lulls where, as the meaning clouds over somewhat ("Not even that, though;" "it's too late then, no matter how they feel;" "forty years is a lifetime") the speaker is left to follow a random thought through thickets of private assoc-iation. . . . Neither passage is pure vernacular: there is no stockpiling of dialectal oddities, no malapropisms, or deliber-ate typographical distortions (the only irregularities, in them-selves hardly distracting, are "wain't", "allus", "o' ", and "wi' "); no effort on the part of the prose to assert its lexical oddness. What we are offered is vernacular material managed with a view to achieving a warm interiority, the phraseology and vocal patterns of working-class speech (in its North Country register) monitored by an author aware of standard prose but systematically deferring to modified colloquial practice; enticing the reader to follow, with a minimum of an-alytical backtrack, the small shifts of statement, the sudden shifts of emphasis and intonation, the very threads of banali-ty, that intensify the illusion of unmediated reality. And the intensification of that illusion is inseparable from the intensi-fication of artifice. Sillitoe's dealings with language, then, are substantially the same as his approach to character can be said to be. There is a subtle foiling of expectation, an insis-tence that the reader, in the very ease of the reading, must work more diligently than he might have expected in order to apprehend the affective context evoked by the words and the sentences; an insistence on the ability of a lexically re-stricted, unpolished vocabulary to generate a complex emo-tional economy where "simple" feeling might have been sus-pected. (pp. 311-13)

A prose of veraciousness; . . . Sillitoe's is also a prose of anger and affirmation; its very stylistic inflexions are instinct with qualities of class-separateness and wrath . . . [Sillitoe's characters] are always free—always claim the right—to talk: to recount anecdotes to themselves and to each other, in alle-viation of their ill-humour; to comment wryly or with bravu-ra insouciance on the varieties of defensive combat in which they find themselves caught up. Resentful at, and feeling hemmed in on all sides by, "those who tell you what to do, . . . pay your wages, collect your rent and telly dues, read the news on the wireless . . . hand you the dole . . . the shopkeeper, copper, schoolteacher," they unfetter themselves through truculently vernacular introspection, and compensate for their relative powerlessness by metaphorically elaborate punitive imaginings. Button-holing their fellows, eavesdrop-ping upon them, confiding in them, they flaunt their rooted-ness even while proclaiming their irredeemably "outside" sta-tus vis-à-vis "Them". And in all this they show themselves to be not so much overtly revolutionary (as has sometimes been alleged) as capable, given the right provocation, of act-ing *as if* they were revolutionaries; as containing within them-selves the shards and remnants from which a revolutionary militancy might be grafted.

Lightheartedly, and in a way that subsumes the preceding observations about language and style, this propensity is pointed up in **"The Disgrace of Jim Scarfedale,"** where "I" states his case—scored brilliantly for a single voice—with an insolent verve that brooks no riposte:

> I'm easily led and swung, my mind like a weathervane when somebody wants to change it for me, but there's one sure rule I'll stick to for good, and I don't mind driving a nail head first into a bloody long rigmarole of a story to tell you what I mean.
>
> Jim Scarfedale.
>
> I'll never let anybody try and tell me that you don't have to swing your hook as soon as you get to the age of fifteen. You ought to be able to do it earlier, only it's against the law, like everything else in this poxetten land of hope and glory.

After this swaggering declaration, the account of Jim's shaming—eventually made public through his arrest on a charge of child molestation—might seem a trifle superfluous. Uxorious and womanishly acquiescent, incapable, so we are informed, of telling "the difference between an apron string and a pair of garters", his weak-kneed character, which sends him rebounding hotfoot from a "brand-new almost-beautiful wife" is fully established and condemned from the start. But this is as it should be. The ensuing elaboration of his haplessness is only a foil for, a convenient contrast to and illumination of, "I's" own vaunted independence and brash disdain for the bloodlessness Jim exemplifies. The reader's attention is drawn less to the fact of Jim's dismantled will, less, even, to the narrator's jubilation at being "thin-rapped enough to squeeze myself along and listen-in" to the affairs of the Scarfedale household while perched on "a ledge between the factory roof and the scullery window," than to the values which govern his amazement at Jim's emasculation; and to the values which serve to distinguish this amazement from backyard *schadenfreude*. For in surreptitiously contracting a marriage, Jim has chosen to defect from his possessive matriarch, with her disabling maxims of filial piety and her delight in exacting a venerative submissiveness from her son—only to discover himself similarly entangled with a "posh missus", who

> Had some ideas that a working bloke like myself was good an honest and all that sort of thing . . . she used to say that it was a treat to be able to marry and live with a bloke like myself who used his bare hands for a living, . . . at night she used to talk about politics and books, saying how the world was made for blokes like me, and that we should run the world and not leave it to a lot of money-grubbing capitalist bastards. . . .

And so it comes to no surprise to learn that, as the knowledge of his insipidity dawns upon her, the "missus" relinquishes romantic adulation for the patronizing sneer, passing thence to an undisguised contempt for her invertebrate "noble savage" and, in a final accession of disgust, abandoning him to his abject domesticities—"listening to the wireless and reading the paper in peace." By turns coddled and bullied, he is only partly responsible for his eventual undoing. And the story relies for its suspense upon the comeuppance the reader is encouraged to wish upon Mrs. Scarfedale, as she hands out a drubbing to her son in a way that—filtered through, and distorted by, "I's" censorious glee—both reveals and slyly in-

culpates her hunger to be thought well of, a hunger of which she has become the very enbodiment:

> Courting on the sly like that . . . Ungrateful, after all she'd done for him, bringing him up so well, . . . Think of all the times she'd slaved for him! Think of it! Just think of it! (Jesus, you should have heard her.) . . . Fair would you say it was—she sobbed her socks off—after all I've struggled and sweated, getting you up for school every morning when you was little and sitting you down to porridge and bacon . . . which was more than the other little ragbags in the yard wore because their dads and mums boozed the dole money (she said this, she really did, because I was listening from a place where I couldn't help but hear it—and I'll swear blind our dad never boozed a penny of his dole money and we were still clambed half to death on it . . .) And I think of all the times when you was badly and I fetched the doctor, she went on screaming. Think of it. But I suppose you're too self-pinnyated to think, which is what my spoiling's done for you? Eh?

To submit, like Jim, to the ethics of deference so jubilantly (even smugly) derided here is ultimately to "go the same way," where "I" is concerned. Quite how the spectacle of the upbraiding connects in sequence with "I's" surly chafing at the bit and with his newly-formed ambition to thieve, may seem at first unclear. Yet the semi-humorous vindication of outlawry—Jim's crime, we are told is venial as compared with "deserting, setting fire to buildings . . . running up big debts for wirelesses . . . and then selling them, . . . and all sorts of larks that didn't mean much"—conceals a serious effort to come to terms with one species of moral weakness associated with, but by no means restricted to, "our yard". And it conceals as well a shrewd appraisal of the penalties incurrable for setting about challenging the established order with insufficient hardihood and gumption—a failure embodied through Jim. His bid for emancipation is less mishandled than misconceived. Gratefully truckling to the conventions while making show of renouncing them, he has merely exchanged one servitude for another. Overheard by "I", Jim's admonishment ostensibly clinches the former's decision to cut free from a community capable of producing such as the Scarfedales, the son impotent and kow-towing, the mother as imperious as the neighbouring "iron presses slamming as if they was trying to burst through the wall." Indifferent, we might suppose, to the ways of "our terrace" and to its inhabitants, the narrator will opt out of anything but selfish pleasures pursued in solitude. But in fact the point of this droll little morality has less to do with "I's" need to "see a way of making-off—even if I have to rob gas-meters" than with his awareness of the manifold varieties of deprivation and subjugation, moral as well as material. And the tale hinges upon his novel resolve to apply himself perciently as well as diligently, with zeal and spunk and guarding against backsliding, where Jim has been both lackwit and nerveless. The awakened refusal to let others, regardless of position or rank, in the community and outside it, control one's life is far from being immaturely escapist. It is nourished by a sense of rootedness of life in "our terrace". And paradoxically, it draws sustenance from a witty confraternal admiration for "Jim's Mam", who "lived . . . in a house like our own" and "usually got what she wanted and knew what she wanted was right". The mood of the telling is waggishly affectionate and its manner saucily tongue-in-cheek. But it wants only a slight twist of situation for "I" to become Smith, in **"The Long Dis-**

tance Runner", stumbling toward a revolutionary outlook, impelled by his decision to "rather be like I am—always on the run and breaking into shops for a packet of fags and a jar of jam." In both cases—and generally in the early stories and novels—the rebellious urge has finally less to do with evasion, much less with the assumption of political causes, than with the preservation of autonomy of choice. And autonomy of choice, in turn, is predicated on an understanding of the moral difference between victim and rebel, prisoner and insurgent; is at least always clear-cut. It is the difference between those, like Jim, who all too disastrously "know their place;" and those, like "I", chafing at the bit and craving for action, who will, ominously, go on knowing their place until they can get out of it on their own terms. Stirred to such knowledge, he is stirred to impertinent narration; moved to create a drama of expressive self-assertion. And the impulse to create such a drama is one of the main sources of character in Sillitoe's writings: character here indicating personal energy and a certain fricative pride of class being, bound together in a symbiotic knot.

In this connection **"The Loneliness of the Long Distance Runner"** is the most quintessential, and also the most complex and intriguing, of Sillitoe's creations. Considerations of space forbid, of course, the protracted discussion needed to support such a claim, but the foregoing may perhaps serve to indicate the discoveries that lie in wait for the discerning reader. The recreant Smith's arrival, through trial and error, at an unshakable resolution to be "honest" after his own fashion and that of his mates—a resolution which leads him to throw the race and symbolically repudiate the competitive, materialistic values it represents—records another, more subtle passage from a jejune and footling disobedience to a mature grasp of rebellion as a moral-political act founded upon considered preference, and so segregated from mere ornery contrariness. Analysis might go further, however, in uncovering the planned artlessness of the telling, in showing how this transition is described in a language—never more strongly sinewed than when offhand, deadpan and self-deprecating—which serves Smith, in its pain and candour, as a kind of substitute territory, doing duty for the practical absence of power and of opportunities for effective management of one's public destiny. At the same time it would demonstrate how the unmediated prose provides the narrator with an unrivalled coign of vantage from which to assess, trenchantly and without illusion, the depth of his disaffiliation from "their" mores; how the prose is implicitly designed to break down and dislodge a tyrannic repertoire of regimenting, homogenising images condoned and propagated by "Them". It would remark how Sillitoe ransacks the metaphor for the paradoxes and tensions implicit within it, exploiting its dualisms to the full and so establishing an angle of vision in perfect rapport with a character incontrovertibly persuaded that "they don't see eye to eye with us, and we don't see eye to eye with them, and that's how it'll always be." And it would reveal that while the story is all but perfectly organised—structurally by the race, thematically by the recurrent problems, liberation and servitude chief among them—its natural sense of ensemble is really a function of a concinnity that is unaware of itself. The seemliness and logic of the delivery have closely to do with the permission granted to a principal allowed to speak spontaneously in his own graceless unrevised idiom with exclusive authority and with a mordant involving frankness.

The conclusion of such an analysis will, however, be the same as that reached here: that Sillitoe's commitment is never more

splendidly available than when conveyed through a prose manner whose very torsions and tensions are the product of a maximum engagement with his subjects, those "harried by persecutions" and "outside the habits of literacy". Hence the capacity of that prose to tender an unassailable guarantee of its own credibility and validity. In a classic statement on the relations between literature and society ["Genetic Structuralism"], Lucien Goldmann argues that a writer becomes significant when pledged to "working out of rough categories (of social life) and of the connections between them"; and that he is to be judged according to his "capacity to take them much further than other members of his group have, but only within the world he has created." This is as good a summary as one could wish for of Sillitoe's eccentric achievement: a maverick one, as the critics keep insisting, perhaps understanding more than they let on. (pp. 314-18)

> D. M. Roskies, " 'I'd Rather Be Like I Am': Character, Style, and the Language of Class in Sillitoe's Narratives," in Neophilologus, Vol. LXV, No. 2, April, 1981, pp. 308-19.

JULIAN MOYNAHAN

The Second Chance is a gathering of short and novella-length narratives written during the past 20 years or so by [Mr. Sillitoe]. . . . *"No Name in the Street"* previously appeared in *The New Yorker,* and most of the other pieces in assorted English periodicals. This is Mr. Sillitoe's 25th book in a fruitful career that goes back to the mid-1950's. (p. 6)

Mr. Sillitoe is working class, his fiction remarkable in the time it spans, from the starveling period of the dole to the present era of indexed welfare benefits and mass unemployment under Margaret Thatcher. And he writes with particular insight about military men, as in his superb novel *The Widower's Son* (1978), the story of a career in the British Artillery that proceeded honorably for 30 years, only to end in a nervous breakdown after retirement.

[**"The Second Chance"**], set in southern England, is about an older couple, the Baxters, who lost their son Peter, a Spitfire pilot, in the Battle of Britain. Helen Baxter has been in a state of near-catatonic grief for decades when her husband, George, fetches home a new Peter, a young man encountered in a hotel bar who bears a startling resemblance to the dead son. The Baxters need a "second chance" to get their lives on track, and so does Peter. He is a sociopath who has just completed a short jail sentence for passing bad checks, and he regards the Baxters, proprietors of a household filled with valuable rare books and handmade shotguns, as sheep ready for the shearing.

Through the ensuing beautifully and tightly plotted charade, things don't quite work out that way. In this very English story it swiftly becomes clear that each character has played out his assigned roles, and can only go forward if these roles are drastically expanded and revised. Someone will have to die so that someone else—the mother, and perhaps even the dead pilot—can come back to life. Who will get his quittance, the interloping Peter or George, the orchestrator of the risky plot. Suspense is maintained until the unexpected resolution of this fascinating tale, which owes something to Harold Pinter and reflects English class feelings and infighting in their most convoluted form.

Very different but just as good is **"The Sniper,"** the last story in the collection. It explores the mind and career of a Nottingham worker in 1914 who disappeared into the army after secretly murdering his wife's lover. Made preternaturally alert by the constant expectation that his crime will be detected, this man develops into an excellent infantry soldier, eventually becoming a sniper assigned to shoot Germans from a hidden but risky vantage point on the Allied side of no man's land.

Mr. Sillitoe's account of the sniper's routines is absolutely riveting, as good as his best stuff on gunnery in *The Widower's Son.* Though crawling with trench lice, he must not move, lest his location be pinpointed and targeted for heavy retaliatory fire. And he must not be tricked into shooting at false targets for the same reason. At times the sniper imagines that he sees the man he murdered wandering between the lines in civilian clothes. But he retains sufficient composure not to waste bullets on this apparition. With its great insight into the feelings of this solitary figure, doubly cut off from his fellow men by his great crime and by the strange, bloody work he has been given to do, and with its detailed knowledge of the travails of war, this is a story that only Alan Sillitoe could have written.

Yet he can write with comparable knowledge and insight about the hard ordinary life of a Notts working girl—"deep dark Edie Clipston at her sewing and seaming machine earning fifty bob a week." This description occurs in **"A Scream of Toys,"** which, despite a weak ending, is my favorite story in the collection. We follow Edie through her recollections of a childhood during the Depression, when she played in the littered street and dreamed of toys that never came, to her first job, when she walks out with an Italian POW and tries to win a measure of independence from her hard-bitten parents, both munitions workers who are not above kicking Edie around the room when they come in tipsy from the pub on weekend nights.

Mr. Sillitoe's sense of the conditions of English working-class life is that they are bad and not likely to get better. The people, nevertheless, especially the young, have spirit, toughness, humor and a feeling for the countryside into which they occasionally escape for picnics or lovemaking. The remainder of the stories are divided between middle-class situations (**"The Meeting," "Confrontation"** and **"The Gate of a Great Mansion"**) and further explorations of working lives (**"A Time to Keep," "The Fiddle,"** and **"Ear to the Ground"**). Alan Sillitoe has a head for both milieus, but who can doubt where his heart is? (pp. 6, 25)

Julian Moynahan, "What Life is Really Like in England," in The New York Times Book Review, *April 19, 1981, pp. 6, 25.*

KATE CRUISE O'BRIEN

Pam, the heroine of Alan Sillitoe's ambitious new novel [*Her Victory*], leaves her nasty husband George. 'If someone asked why she had left her husband she wouldn't have said anything because the answer she had been born with was embedded like a stone, not to be pulled prematurely into the glare of day without ripping her to pieces.' Pam may not know who she is, but she is fortunate in other respects. Women who attempt to leave their husbands have been known to turn back when they remember that they don't have any money and they do have children. But Pam has access to the joint bank account and her son has left home. So Pam takes out £400 and is free to gaze at her reflection in a full-length mirror in a squalid bedsitter. She can go to bed when she likes, eat when she likes, even spill beer if she likes. But it is all too much, so Pam tapes up the windows and turns on the gas.

All is not lost. Along comes Tom, a middle-aged-orphan-Merchant-Navy-man and turns off the gas. The lonely couple go off to live in the flat of Tom's dead Aunt Clara. They rummage through boxes simply crammed with clues to Tom's missing identity. They are joined by their lesbian friend Judy and everyone makes love to everyone else, sustained by the £300,000 left by good old Clara. Pam gets pregnant—her ever-precarious identity is again threatened. Tom goes to Israel where his Jewish identity is. Pam decides to join him, still hedging her bets. 'I'm too free a person to commit myself,' she reminds us.

Pam's victory could be seen as this noble attempt by a man to understand the consciousness of woman. But Pam is simply too lucky to be representative. Most women are confined and constrained by financial considerations. Few of us awake from suicide attempts to find single strangers waiting with fortunes in their pockets.

Kate Cruise O'Brien, "Breaking Down," in The Listener, *Vol. 108, No. 2786, November 11, 1982, p. 27.*

ALAN CHEUSE

Nearly 25 years ago in a review of *Saturday Night and Sunday Morning* the English critic Anthony West declared that Alan Sillitoe, then a 31-year-old fiction writer from Nottingham, had with this one book "assured himself a place in the history of the English novel." Blessed with such high praise and early success, Mr. Sillitoe went on to produce nearly 20 more works of fiction, almost a dozen of them novels. But with the exception of his second book, the stories gathered together under the title of *The Loneliness of the Long-Distance Runner,* nothing else he wrote captured either the extraordinary reviews or the broad readership of his first novel. (p. 15)

With the publication of *Her Victory,* a long, sometimes sluggish but almost always engrossing new novel, Mr. Sillitoe may be about to win back his wider audience and even add to its numbers from among the devotees of the fiction of Doris Lessing and Margaret Drabble.

In fact, Pam, the unhappily married, 40-year-old Nottingham woman who serves as one of the two main characters in *Her Victory,* resembles so closely the heroines of a number of recent English and American feminist novels that the reader of Mr. Sillitoe's new book will work his—or her—way through the early pages with some misgiving. Can it be that the creator of Arthur Seaton, the working-class hero of *Saturday Night and Sunday Morning* (for whom in his more tolerant moments "women were more than ornaments and skivvies . . . they were warm wonderful creatures that needed and deserved to be looked after"), has decided to tackle those volatile and controversial themes that we sometimes lump together under the heading of "women's liberation"? He has done precisely this—and the results are more interesting and affecting than anything else he has published in years.

Pam's rebellion against a debilitating 20-year marriage begins where the revolt of Ibsen's Nora leaves off. We first meet her at breakfast with her husband, George, a foul-mouthed, bitter-tempered bloke of a toolmaker whose only difference from his loutish, often down-and-out trio of brothers, Bert, Alf and Harry, is that he has worked his way up to the ownership of a small, local tool factory. The old Sillitoe is present in the scenes of brutal horseplay among the brothers, in the awful account of how Harry accosts Pam on her wedding day and later in the vile way that George humiliates her at the breakfast table, so vile, in fact, that she attempts to come at him with a knife and receives in turn a punch in the face. When George leaves for the factory Pam packs and leaves for London, where in a cold, filthy bed-sitting room she concludes the novel's opening section by turning on the gas. "The only victory is in being alive," she thought to herself just before she ran off, but apparently she didn't much believe that.

The plot turns ponderously on its axis as the gas builds up in the unconscious Pam's bed-sitting room. Up the steps from the street comes 50-year-old, newly retired merchant seaman Tom, a rough-and-ready, ginger-haired isolate who was raised in an orphanage and, with the exception of his own bed-sitting room on the same floor and his now dead Aunt Clara's apartment in Brighton, never had anything to call home but ships at sea. Tom sniffs the gas, breaks down Pam's door and rescues her—and then whisks her off to Aunt Clara's place at Brighton, where they walk the beach, eat out and make vigorous, triumphant love.

Echoes of Conrad's *Victory* abound as third-mate Tom takes Pam in his arms and carries her out of the lonely place in London in which he discovered her. And when, while digging his way through the notebooks in Aunt Clara's closet, Tom learns that not only was he born out of wedlock but he is also, it seems, Jewish, some readers may see grand allusions to Dickens and to George Eliot's *Daniel Deronda*. But no amount of allusiveness to the realistic tradition in which Anthony West awarded Mr. Sillitoe a place nearly a quarter of a century ago can make a novel work if it doesn't have a life of its own (and you don't have to travel further than a copy of Mr. Sillitoe's own homage to Fielding, **A Start in Life,** or his Swiftian satire, **Travels in Nihilon,** to discover that fact). However, the leisurely but vital second half of this book builds on the rough authority of its opening sections, showing us quite persuasively how Pam and Tom reconstitute themselves as a couple.

Mr. Sillitoe takes his time developing all this. But the time he takes resembles the "endless time" that Tom seems to understand comes with the onset of middle age ("where it had formerly seemed hardly worth waiting for and living through"). Mr. Sillitoe takes his sweet narrative time and tells a story like the tale of his origins that Tom reconstructs for Pam during their stay in Brighton after he goes through Aunt Clara's possessions, a story whose unfolding is more like "the assembling of a mosaic rather than an ordinary account which would have been finished too quickly and thereby diminished in the telling for him, and been less absorbing in the hearing of it for her."

Several gaps exist in this assemblage, particularly in a section devoted to Pam's early life and in the pages about the response to her flight from Nottingham by her 18-year-old son. But this simply means that I didn't wish Mr. Sillitoe's victorious—and, in an odd, compelling way, neo-Victorian—novel to end too quickly. (pp. 15, 28)

Alan Cheuse, "Creating a Couple," in The New York Times Book Review, *December 12, 1982, pp. 15, 28.*

STEPHEN BANN

What makes the novels of Alan Sillitoe infinitely superior . . . is the abiding sense that the strong narrative line, though traditionally conceived and carried through, is at the same time a vehicle for allegory or, if that is too strong a word, anagogical reading of the author's own attitude to his art. Kipling chose to picture the great novel which he never wrote as a ship, 'a veritable three-decker out of chosen and long-stored timber—teak, green-heart, and ten-year-old oak knees—each curve melting deliciously into the next . . .' Sillitoe's evidently well-informed portrayal of **The Lost Flying Boat** goes beyond the reminiscences of the former member of the [Royal Air Force], who has done his homework, and evokes a more general analogy with the ethos of humane craftsmanship:

> A flying boat is built by people who guide each strut, float, stringer, tailplane, aileron and leading edge into place, I said. The anatomical diagram is adhered to as a blueprint for every component from a tiny screw to the whole engine. After launching, the flying boat retains the touch of human hands. Even if few felt that they were creating a work of beauty, it justified what I was trying to say—which Nash admitted might be true enough.

The 'loss' of the flying boat, for which we are prepared in the title, is therefore compensated on the symbolic level by the narrator's closing vision: 'All parts intact, its beautiful form flew just above the sea, belly glistening in the sun.' And this rehabilitation of the lost object is achieved precisely because the narrator is, by his own recognition, a communicator: a wireless operator for whom 'Reality was when I twiddled the tuning knob of the radiogram and heard morse chirping from the speaker.' It is at this closing stage of the novel that we begin to sense the many overtones of what has been, up to that point, a gripping adventure story, and our retrospective view of the action is greatly enriched.

Even such an elliptical comment on **The Lost Flying Boat** prepares us for the likelihood that this will remain an important novel in Sillitoe's later career. The dedication lets slip the information that it was 'promised a long time ago', and it is evident that the superb command of aeronautical detail has been carried over from the time when Sillitoe himself was a radio operator, before he was invalided out of the service and became a writer. No doubt the experience was stored until it could be utilised to create, not a mere adventure story, but a fable about the warring principles of communication and action, art and authority. Bennett, the obsessional captain of the rogue flying boat, is the only character who usurps, for one brief section, the narrator's otherwise consistent point of view. It is Bennett who creates the wireless operator/narrator's central dilemma, which is whether or not to send out false signals as a necessary safeguard for the illegal expedition, and thereby break the iron laws of his profession. But by setting up this dilemma, Bennett does not bind his communicator to him in unreserved loyalty:

> I would have stayed in any case, acceptance being composed of pride, tradition, greed, honour and a desire to explore my nature to the utmost. There was nothing more attractive to me at that time. I

thought of fate as the unbreakable spider's web, but did not know whether by being drawn to it I was the spider or the victim. In my imaginary conversation I told Bennett none of this.

The Lost Flying Boat has a wealth of poignant implications that distinguish it as a work of mid to late career. (pp. 12-13)

Stephen Bann, "Mystery and Imagination," in London Review of Books, *Vol. 5, No. 21, November 17-30, 1983, pp. 12-13.*

BARBARA HARDY

[*Down from the Hill*] is an entirely individual novel. Nothing in it could be replaced out of the common box of fashionable spare parts. It is skillfully crafted but looks as natural as leaves on the tree. It refreshes myth through imagination, not cold imitation. It contemplates love and hostility, inventiveness and flatness, social hope and cynicism, through an intelligent medium which shifts under your eyes, as real art does. It actually seems to have been written out of the self-delighting impulse to think and feel in the language of fiction.

This is a memory novel which doubles the act of memory in a story of two journeys, one in 1945, one nearly forty years later. The un-Proustian research into time past discovers that a journey can't be recovered, though the novelist proves this by imagining both trips and setting them side by side in loving and ironic contrast. The young Paul Morton, a first-person narrator, and his middle-aged self, presented in the third person, are manipulated by the authorial imagination, which can return. Despite the neat antithetical balance, the structure allows for a variety of flashback. The young man remembers, though he does a lot of anticipating. The older man looks ahead a bit, though he has more to remember. The acts of recall aren't simple and single, but manifold. Consciousness is presented as a temporal hodge-podge. The first part of the novel is especially good at the difficult job of presenting time present, through the elated, open, exposed awareness of the seventeen-year-old boy, cycling for dear life through the postwar Midlands landscape.

Alan Sillitoe is very good at the motions and maps of journeys, on foot, in flight, or as here, by bike and car. The bike trip covers the miles slowly, the car moves fast. Both are aptly and wittily varied vehicles for meditation and fantasy. The form is ancient, but it never looks over its shoulder with bookish evocation of odysseys, quixotic trails, or pilgrims' progress. Like Ulysses and Huck Finn, Paul is a story-teller who deals with the people he meets on the road by making up identities for himself and for them. Strangeness is a great stimulus to invention, and imaginary stories are fitted to real people as fast as imaginary people spring into life at a hint from a stab of feeling or a name of a place. Moreover, the other travellers are also story-tellers, like the people encountered by Tom Jones and Nicholas Nickleby. The story is comically and richly faithful to its great tradition, crammed with narratives which are socially revealing models, funny and pathetic anecdotes, and images of the hero's consciousness and art. The young Paul creates as he breathes. He is to become the older Paul, writer of screenplays, assertive in his non-stop fantasies and convincingly touched in as a professional. Some of the stories are briefly brilliant, like the fantasies about a vampire or a jealous husband, the latter figment realized in a stroke of style, "And for God's sake get my dinner on the table. I'm bloody starving."

It's a story about stories. Paul knows that he constructs reality out of lies. Both young and older Paul dream their dreams of fair women, for the story is also about love. Fantasy and reality blur. A real girl called Alice Sands is no more real than a playfully invented one called after a place, Edith Weston. Both stand for an early, pure, and romantically unconsummated love, but they are created and regarded with irony as well as desire, known to be futures as unreachable as the past. Both young and older Paul are open to love and the erotic fantasies and erotic acts are done with delicacy and the right touch of roughness.

Down from the Hill both is and is not a novel about politics. The young Paul observes that "All times were historic." The book suggests that some times are more historic than others in its focus on 1945, after the Labour landslide, and 1983, after Mrs Thatcher's second victory. . . . The older Paul speaks out of a political, as well as an emotional loss; his brief observations are effective metonymies, like the mention of anti-semitism, but there is a gap the novel never fills in, between the middle-aged disguised man and the apolitical young Paul. The rest of the life between the journeys is there, in its professional, familial, and amorous implications, but the story is left backgrounded and incomplete. Fair enough, perhaps. It is a novel, not a history; an uncomfortable one.

Barbara Hardy, "Vehicles for Meditation," in The Times Literary Supplement, *No. 4259, November 16, 1984, p. 1301.*

D. A. N. JONES

[*Down from the Hill* is a] novel about discontented middle-aged reminiscence. The narrator of the first section is a 17-year-old factory worker from Nottingham describing a long bicycle-ride through the Midlands, 250 miles, stopping at a Youth Hostel and a bed-and-breakfast place for building-workers. This took place in 1945, during the General Election with its surprising and exciting Labour victory, but the story is as fresh as if the boy had written it yesterday. The cyclist, Paul Morton, is expecting to leave his factory and become an air-traffic control assistant, but he is worried about a medical report which may prove him to be tubercular. The dust-cover biography of Alan Sillitoe suggests that the story may be partly autobiographical. The second section, a quarter of the length, gives us Paul Morton (in the third person, no longer narrating) in a boring motor-car, following the same route, trying unsuccessfully to recapture his youthful enjoyment. He is now a middle-aged television playwright, disillusioned by the trendier sort of left-wing politics but more deeply indignant at the present Conservative Government and the deliberate creation of unemployment and 'redundancy'.

The young narrator is a rather dour sort of boy, defensively guarding the loneliness of his long-distance ride. Another cyclist wants to ride alongside him, but he is rather a posh boy, with a Conservative family. Then there is a middle-aged man on a heavy, tank-like bike who shouts eccentric opinions like: 'The British are a nation of slaves!' He, too, must be left behind. Paul finds the girl he was looking for: he had met her with his mate Albert in Stafford and she is sorry he has not brought Albert with him, for her friend, Gwen. He meets a Ukrainian working for (quarrelling with, perhaps living with) a female farmer who sports a mannish shirt and tie. He feels more comfortable with three North Country boys, amiably dim, making no demands, and with the building-workers who suggest he should become their tea-boy. It is better to work out of doors, on building-sites, than in a factory, they suggest.

The idea of being a tea-boy crops up again in the second section, when the middle-aged Paul gives a lift to an unemployed man travelling the country, moving south from Liverpool, looking for work: 'On a building site, if I can. Even as a tea-lad, if they'll have me.' Paul, as a playwright, begins to dream up a television script about this hitchhiker, a sort of thriller, but the man starts talking about Handel, listening to *Israel in Egypt* on the car radio: he had been in a choral society before he was made redundant. They talk of the prophet Isaiah and Paul is moved to think: 'The television set lives for us, now that we have sold our birthright to the computers.' He has been led to this thought by a conversation with an old man he met in Stafford. Paul had asked him about his former girlfriend and her family: the old man knew all about them but wanted to talk only about the plot of a television serial and the behaviour of one Muriel Fletcher (for whom Paul had written scripts), as if her television life were more real than that of the old man's neighbours. There is not much of a plot to this novel. It is more like Priestley's *English Journey*, a travel book with stern thoughts. 'We've got everything to fight for, but we don't believe in God, so we can't.' Or, still using religious language: 'If he had work, he was one of the elect. If he had no work, he was one of the damned—not even in Limbo.' (p. 19)

D. A. N. Jones, "Manliness," in London Review of Books, *Vol. 6, No. 24, December 20-January 24, 1985, pp. 19-20.*

ALASTAIR NIVEN

[*Down from the Hill*] is an unashamed exercise in nostalgia. It looks back to the year in which the Second World War ended, to the week when the socialists came to power and England stood on the threshold of a welfare state. This was an England in which local culture was made up of friendly tea-shops and bicycle journeys round sunny shires, rather than football vandalism and television. Alan Sillitoe is presumably recalling a trip he made himself since he would have been seventeen at the time, like his 'hero' Paul Morton. Is the name supposed to evoke Lawrence's Paul Morel? We are in the same area of England and this novel is as much concerned as *Sons and Lovers* with sexual awakening and the development in its central character of a kind of social scepticism. It is a much thinner novel, however, with touches of heavy-handed floridity in the prose: 'Rolls of cloud looked like curlers in the hair of a woman who'd had nothing but worry all her life'. . . .

During his cycling trip round the Trent valley and its environs Paul meets a variety of other cyclists and tea-shop, pub and hostel proprietors. He thinks obsessively of a girl called Alice Sands. He moves in and out of gentle comic observations and moments of a more shadowed reflectiveness. All this Sillitoe brings before us with low-key irony and the most restrained kind of melancholy. Until, that is, the brief second part of the novel when Paul retraces his journey today in a car. This is Thatcher's Britain, a less friendly place in every way. People seem wary, towns have been transformed by concrete. The political edge in this section is more overt than in the 1945 chapters, perhaps because the cautious optimism of that period has been replaced by something much bleaker.

Yet Paul still fantasizes—he has become a film-maker in the intervening years—and the sun still shines on the incorruptible natural beauties of England. ***Down from the Hill*** is a book that anyone who recognizes nostalgia as something different from sentimentality will want to read. It is not a masterpiece or anything near one, but if you care for England and what is becoming of it now, . . . then it will strike many chords in you, as it did in me.

Alastair Niven, in a review of "Down from the Hill," in British Book News, *April, 1985, p. 237.*

PATRICK PARRINDER

Life goes on is a sequel to ***A Start in Life*** (1970). . . . In the earlier book Michael Cullen left working-class Nottingham for the metropolis, fell into the proverbial bad company, and ended up as a convicted gold-smuggler. Now, having been abandoned by his wife after ten years of idleness in the Cambridgeshire village of Upper Mayhem, he needs very little persuasion to get back on the road. 'If I'm not on the move, I'm not living,' he thinks. Soon this first-person narrator endowed with Sillitoe's fine storytelling talents is not merely on the road but on the run.

Cullen, who thinks of his novelist-father as a 'randy old prick-head' and 'walking penis', is himself a chip off the old block. Once back in London, he discovers that his father is ghosting the memoirs of Claude Moggerhanger, who used to be his—Michael's—gold-smuggling boss and is now an eminent peer. Moggerhanger's latest business, it transpires, is to supply the Soviet Union with consignments of high-grade heroin laundered through the British Isles but originally grown on collective farms in (you guessed it) the Soviet Union. Lord Moggerhanger is looking for a new chauffeur and courier. Protest as he may about keeping his hands clean, Cullen is the sort of permanent adolescent who (having failed to become a sailor, a pilot or an engine-driver) would do almost anything to get behind the wheel of another man's Rolls Royce. Naturally he cannot resist Lord Moggerhanger's offer, and (apart from the occasional trip by sea, rail or air for variety's sake) the heart of his narrative consists of dashes and dodges in the yellow Roller up and down the motorways which currently criss-cross pastoral England. One would have to go back to the days of John Buchan to find an English fictional hero capable of squeezing so much fun out of driving a car.

Should Cullen blow the gaff on Lord Moggerhanger's exploits? And could the British social fabric survive their exposure? ***Life goes on*** has a plot which hinges on these and similar questions, but the thriller material sits lightly on the framework of a picaresque novel in which hitchhikers, lay-bys, motorway cafés and petrol stations take the place of the genre's traditional quota of fellow travellers, gipsy encampments, roadside inns and changes of horses. Cullen, who likes to think of himself as a hard-boiled rogue, has a soft spot for almost any waif, stray or female under sixty who crosses his path. The waifs and strays are, as often as not, billeted on his father or dispatched to Upper Mayhem to keep the home fires burning; while errant females are bedded and discarded at the rate of approximately one every fifty pages.

No contemporary novelist has a stronger sense than Sillitoe of the wool-gathering, homespun poetry of the masculine adventurer, the free-born Englishman for whom (in one of Cullen's striking anachronisms) this is still a 'cosy and exciting country to live in'. Sillitoe has a nice ear for English place-names: there are high jinks at Doggerel Bank, Back Enderby, Peppercorn Cottage and Upper Mayhem, all (appropriately) dens of thieves. Local patriotism is in plentiful supply, since so many of the companions Cullen picks up are, like himself, 'all-knowing bottom-dog Nottingham' types, sentimental Sherwood Foresters torn between the bleak romantic thrill of setting off at dawn up the Great North Road and the domestic attractions of a spot of hearthrug pie or a strong pot of jollop.

English novelists, Cullen's father tells us, have always been attracted by the demotic—which is evidence that Sillitoe is well aware of one of his main sources of strength. Conversely, *Life goes on,* like most fiction nowadays, is not free of the heavy hand of writerly self-consciousness. Virtually every (male) character here is at once an actual rogue and a potential writer. Cullen in his less frenetic moments sits down to write a novel on his father's behalf which brings home the prestigious Windrush Prize. His friend Bill Straw, an ex-soldier, manages to churn out a full-length thriller—a feat which not even his faith in the 'old infantry training' as a standby in any emergency can do much to explain. Finally, Sillitoe rounds off this bubbling entertainment with a hint that he might consider a further installment. At the end Cullen's charmed life has once more left him a married man, on the straight and narrow, with a job in an advertising agency. It is hard to believe that he is meant to stay there. (p. 22)

Patrick Parrinder, "Was Carmen Brainwashed?" in London Review of Books, *Vol. 7, No. 21, December 5, 1985, pp. 22-3.*

PHILIP SMELT

Fifteen years ago, Alan Sillitoe introduced Michael Cullen to *A Start in Life.* Now settled in the disused Cambridgeshire railway station of Upper Mayhem, Cullen picks up the thread of his yarn to show how *Life Goes On.* In the old days Cullen was smuggling bars of gold for Jack Leningrad, a criminal who protected his identity by living in an iron lung and speaking to the outside world by telephone. But after a spell in prison and a reasonably happy marriage, Cullen takes up with the recently ennobled Lord Claud Moggerhanger—a racketeer and, according to Cullen's demonology, a big, rich bastard "which made him more effective than a poor bastard like me". Cullen's view of these matters is charmingly idiosyncratic:

> I used to be a 22-carat no-good bastard, in the opinion of friends as well as enemies, but since my father married my mother twenty or so years after the event, I have only been a bastard to myself, which isn't saying much, because I am too fond of my own skin to be more of a bastard than is absolutely necessary.

Like the earlier novel, *Life Goes On* records the improbable doings and reunions of a shifting population of prostitutes, poets, tramps and hoodlums—a rich mixture of ne'er-do-wells such as Jericho Jim, the bruiser; Almanack Jack, the destitute encyclopedia-salesman; [and] Polly Moggerhanger, ravishing and ravished daughter of the drug-smuggling peer. . . . Each character tells his or her own lengthy story with Chaucerian wit and style "because", as Cullen asked in *A Start in Life,* "who isn't still gripped by tales of medieval

jealousy, mother-love, and spite, even though it can be seen as rockingly funny?"

Clearly Sillitoe is still gripped by this device, but towards the end of *Life Goes On* its hold weakens. As well as featuring more sex and violence, his new novel reveals a preoccupation with literary technique. Cullen's father, Gilbert Blaskin, is a famous and serious novelist who also churns out trashy thrillers under the pseudonym of Sidney Blood to help prop up his shaky finances, which are undermined by the usual literary vices—drink and women. The uneducated but worldly-wise Cullen scoffs at these sensational pot-boilers but he agrees to help his father by writing one that will satisfy an unwanted publishing contract. The result might not have disgraced Sillitoe himself. Reviewing the progress of this novel within a novel, Cullen observes that "I could end the book any time because there were two hundred pages on the table, but I went on and on". Ironically the bastard-book becomes a best seller and the delighted publishers want to nominate it for the "Windrush Prize".

Life Goes On is a long-distance saga with considerable pace, but it lacks staying power, and there is a feeling that Sillitoe has given up before the finishing line.

Philip Smelt, "The Bastard's Tale," in The Times Literary Supplement, *No. 4314, December 6, 1985, p. 1407.*

ROSALIND WADE

[In *Out of the Whirlpool*], Alan Sillitoe has not only returned to the background of some of his early successes but has sought to re-write the mood and characters of *Saturday Night and Sunday Morning* without necessarily having anything new to say about them. Thus we have the disorientated and disgruntled Peter Granby who, caught in the trap of the industrial Midlands in a crude home provided by his grandmother and her 'live-in' friend, Len, has never had a chance to improve his way of life. But when, by the merest chance, he meets Eileen Farnsfield, a widow and a wealthy woman in her own right, he is at last on the way up; appointed manager and caretaker of a group of holiday bungalows on the bleak part of the Essex coast and with the opportunity to drive his employer's car. His experiences are rich with humour. Peter Granby lacks even rudimentary table manners so that it is fine sport for the affluent Eileen to teach her protégé a veneer of social good behaviour; and, as she has been sexually deprived since the death of her elderly husband, it comes as no surprise that the two lonely though disparate souls are soon to enjoy a passionate physical relationship. But before long, Eileen tires of her unsophisticated partner, seeking another lover more polished and well-positioned. Whereupon, stripped of both income and living quarters, Peter Granby is no better off than when he first encountered Eileen. He attempts a return to his old home and mode of living, only to learn that Granny is dead and Len in hospital. (Yes, we are back in the all-too-familiar world of hospital wards and day-rooms). His self-confidence rapidly evaporates and he gets the worst of a meaningless brawl. As a result he is blinded—or isn't he? It is difficult to be certain, for once again the need for a quick finish leaves the *dénouement* ambiguous and unresolved.

Rosalind Wade, in a review of "Out of the Whirlpool," in Contemporary Review, *Vol. 251, No. 1461, October, 1987, p. 214.*

ANN SLEEPER

[Sillitoe's *Out of the Whirlpool*] is a stunning distillation of his literary hallmarks: the unsophisticated working-class hero and the theme of man's isolation—presented in this story as the urge to uproot oneself battling against the need to belong. Every beautifully crafted sentence and image characteristically startles or mesmerizes in turn.

Peter Granby, an orphan at 18, working in a furniture factory, is a frustrating, appealing, and ultimately tragic mix of opposites: the limited truisms of his mother and grandmother echo against his own vague yearnings. Satisfaction with each piecemeal proof of his gift for repairs is undermined by his constant search for the next item to fix. A studied outward toughness contests with a vulnerable spot for women. When Peter helps an elderly lady who collapses outside the factory, he is rewarded with a standing offer from the woman's daughter to repay the favor. The idea strikes his humble side as ludicrous, but desperation and his unconscious aspirations later change his mind.

Eileen employs Peter as her caretaker and plaything, and Peter is an apt, if ambivalent apprentice. The steady swim out of his personal whirlpool intensifies his duelling nature, as he swings ever more wildly between inferiority and feelings of power, between patient scheming around Eileen's needs and uncontrollable rage at her rebukes. What saves the story from being a formulaic morality tale is the rhythmic, often surprising language that carefully exposes Peter's growing needs and his attempts to understand them, the methodical yet increasingly desperate strokes that propel his own fate. "She looked as if she owned him absolutely. 'At least I've got you.' There was nothing he could say to that, but she seemed to mean it, so he peeled her an orange."

Ann Sleeper, "Spring Collection," in Book World— The Washington Post, *April 13, 1988, p. 8.*

DONOVAN FITZPATRICK

[*Out of the Whirlpool* features] Peter Granby, age 18, a dropout, doomed to fetch and carry in a furniture factory in Nottingham, England. Mother dead of cancer, father long gone off with a "fancy woman." There seems little in the lad's future, but his needs are few and his wants modest. Suddenly, in the best Horatio Alger tradition, Peter's life is transformed when he goes to the aid of an old woman who collapses and dies on the street. The woman's daughter, Eileen Farnsfield, an affluent widow pushing 40, rewards him with five pounds and the promise that "if ever you need help from me, you've only to let me know." And so, when Peter is hurt badly in a mugging, he calls Eileen. True to her word, she takes him into her home, nurses him back to health, and offers him a job as a chauffeur and caretaker. Thus the Alger story segues into *Lady Chatterley's Lover.* But the affair comes to an explosive end when he finds his beloved in bed with her accountant. In *Out of the Whirlpool,* . . . , Alan Sillitoe's hero occasionally steps out of character, and some of the book's passages are disturbingly elliptical. But as he demonstrated in *The Loneliness of the Long Distance Runner,* Mr. Sillitoe is an expert observer of lower-class British life, a writer deeply sympathetic to its frustrations and boredom.

Donovan Fitzpatrick, in a review of "Out of the Whirlpool," in The New York Times Book Review, *April 24, 1988, p. 34.*

ELAINE FEINSTEIN

It is some 30 years now since Alan Sillitoe's *Saturday Night. Sunday Morning* introduced us to the Seaton family and a town-based working class that owed little to Lawrence. [*The Open Door*] is the third in a trilogy of books around that family, and is set just after the Second World War, when Arthur, the rumbustious protagonist of the first book, is still at school. The England of *The Open Door* is seen through the eyes of Arthur's elder brother Brian, returning from Malaya with X-rays showing TB; an experience Brian shares with his author, along with a preoccupation with writing.

Displaced by service life, Brian perceives the class differences of those days as a violent shock to the senses. Times had been worse before the war (indeed rationing had been a boon to families often short of basic food). But in his own familiar streets people still had bad teeth, short sight, blue veins, drab skin, thin hair, sunken cheeks, and were recognizable as working class by stance, clothes, and voice. Sillitoe's knowledge of the impoverished options to which Brian is returning in civilian life makes him sympathetic to Brian's distinctive and disgusted refusal to replace himself inside the class system, when his communist friend tries to fill him with his own enthusiasm for things Soviet. This knowledge of Brian's likely expectation gives the hospital to which he is sent for treatment the air of a refuge, even though the threat of early death from TB is hideously real. And it adds another dimension to the awakening sense of literary ambition that is the emotional plot.

It is an ambition always hard to make effective; but Sillitoe makes it seem not just moving but significant, because he is so grittily honest; Seaton's decision to live as a writer would have been hard to realize without the disability pension which enables him to go off and learn his craft. The novel ends as that particular door opens in the sunshine of France; but we have watched Brian's consciousness developing. His finest passion goes into that; the breakup of his soulless first marriage hardly touches him; and his affairs with two loving nurses and a poignant girl from his own town also suffering from TB are the unreliable affections of a young man. Ultimately only his precociously streetwise brother Arthur remains as a representative of English life that Brian seems reluctant to leave.

Elaine Feinstein, "Making a Living as a Writer," in The Times, London, *February 23, 1989, p. 19.*

MARTIN SEYMOUR-SMITH

I confess that before I read *The Open Door* I had not rated Alan Sillitoe highly. . . . I still valued some of the short stories, and came to agree with the late George Fraser's judgment: "the short story is his proper length".

I was wrong: *The Open Door* has the rare virtue of illuminating its author's previous work, even of giving some of it a significance that it did not possess when it was first issued. It is a shocking book in the best sense: every word and sentence and paragraph in it is just right, and, furthermore, it tells the story (among other stories) of how this has been achieved. It is by a long chalk Sillitoe's most profound book; and it offers a lesson in the paradox that, exactly at the point when a writer becomes truly aware of his limitations, so can he transcend them.

It is the third (and last) of the Seaton books. ***Saturday Night and Sunday Morning*** dealt with Arthur Seaton, who was at least convincing enough for no one to want to know what happened to him after he had accepted his lot in life (there are a few glimpses of him here as a 15-year-old). ***Key to the Door*** dealt with Brian Seaton, Arthur's elder brother, and with his service as an RAF wireless operator in Malaya. . . .

In ***The Open Door*** the story of Brian Seaton is continued. He returns from the jungle to be demobbed, but is found to have tuberculosis. He remains in the RAF, but in hospital (with spells of leave). By the end he is cured, has been deserted by his wife, has had three—nearly four—love affairs, and is on his way to France, alone, to try to become a writer.

Of course this is what is called "autobiographical". Sillitoe did his national service in Malaya as a wireless operator, and then spent two more years in the service, mostly on his back, being cured of tuberculosis. But it is well to point out that there are differences between Brian Seaton and his creator— and, more important, that Sillitoe is well aware of them. Apart from the fact that Brian has a cow-like wife, Pauline— he married her before he went into the RAF because he got her pregnant—there are other and subtler differences, each of which is exploited to the hilt. However, there are some less than subtle differences between this Brian and the Brian of ***Key to the Door.*** The Malayan communists, for example, have faded in his memory with remarkable rapidity. Is this Brian's or Sillitoe's own "retrospective falsification"? It hardly matters: ***The Open Door*** is so superior to ***Key to the Door*** that it would be worth destroying all trace of the latter. Indeed, Sillitoe may well have delivered himself of the autobiography of his immaturity in his account of Arthur Seaton.

In this progress of Brian Seaton from ignorant bastard to fledging writer, we see the doggedness that has led his creator to make so many errors, and now to be able to correct the more vital of them in one splendid fell swoop. Brian is unlikeable at first, but his growing awareness of what he does not like in himself will lead most readers to like him more by the end of this admittedly dour but certainly triumphant saga.

The Open Door is written in a sensibly modified, stream-of-consciousness style—including some reported speech— interspersed with excellently authenticated dialogue. Brian recognises that "all the mistakes in his life had been because he hadn't spoken"; this is reflected in this terse, laconic record—almost entirely without laughter except for some details of a Nottingham literary group—which says just enough to allow Brian to slip through, at last, as a potentially complete human being who no longer needs to make the most fatal mistake of all: of being too shut-up within himself to be capable of putting himself in someone else's place. But he discovers this only at the expense of his betrayal of one woman and his rejection at the hands of another.

Central to ***The Open Door*** is an image of the summit of Gunong Barat, a height Brian failed to scale while he was in Malaya. Sillitoe, with beautifully judged artistry, inserts into the text an account Brian wrote of the attempt while he was making it: this narrative is both awkward and gifted. The unobtrusiveness of this nevertheless all-pervading symbol has the effect of magnificent poetry, in a generous, courageous, moving and finely-made novel that is all the more delightful for coming as such a surprise.

Martin Seymour-Smith, "A Last, Fine Careful Rap-

ture," in The Sunday Times, *London, February 26, 1989, p. G6.*

PHILIP OAKES

Alan Sillitoe has either a phenomenal memory or a fund of well-filled notebooks. Probably both. His new novel [***The Open Door***] is the third and last (or so the publishers think) in his sequence about the Seatons of Nottingham. . . . Twenty-eight years seems a long interval before resuming the tale, but the continuity holds. Even more remarkable is the energy with which it peels off the page.

The year is 1949 and Brian Seaton (Arthur's elder brother) is home from Malaya where he has been serving with the RAF as a wireless operator. "You left England one person and came back another," he reflects and the most significant change in his own condition is that he has contracted TB. His marriage to slatternly Pauline is at an end. He has dreams of becoming a writer and, confined to a hospital bed, he speeds his self-improvement by reading *King Lear,* listening to Beethoven and learning French from a tuppenny primer.

Naturally, he finds time for sex. Nice nurse Rachel drops him after her parents object to a proposed dirty weekend at Ilfracombe and she is replaced by Sister Nora, an older woman who wears corsets and has a cottage in Kent. Convincingly, Seaton sees them both as brief chapters in his sentimental education. His affair with Lillian, a tubercular girl from the next street, ends with her suicide. And when last sighted, Seaton is bound for the south of France ("where artists don't need much to live on"), pen poised over notebook, Remington portable at the ready.

The Open Door is nakedly autobiographical. In its substance and spirit—which is coltish, and candid—it is also a young man's book. But it is never ingenuous. Sillitoe shuns capital letters and though his theme is, unashamedly, The Making of a Writer his attention to time and place gives it the perspective that essays into literary salad days usually lack. . . .

Politically, he chooses to remain disengaged, because it suits him as a writer. Communists who come doorstepping for support are given short shrift because he finds the workers in the party literature they proffer are no more than pious cut-outs. The demands of art and pragmatism coincide. Enlightened self-interest requires that he goes it alone. How ironic that the qualities which, 30 years ago, signalled an outsider should now slot neatly into the canons of Thatcherism.

Sillitoe's novel is well-remembered and decently rendered. He deals in a kind of sad poetry, especially effective in his Midlands vignettes in which anglers stand by slow rivers, "their floats twitching in mid-stream", and cyclists ride across fields between rubbish tips, "their arms horizontal like circus performers". It is a landscape done in monochrome, haunted by the ghosts of spaghetti junctions to come. Few writers could travel through it hopefully. It would be interesting to know what Brian Seaton thought of it now. But he did well to get out.

Philip Oakes, "The Making of a Writer," in New Statesman & Society, *Vol. 2, No. 40, March 10, 1989, p. 36.*

BRIAN MORTON

The Open Door takes up exactly where *Key to the Door* left off, with Brian Seaton's return to England from signals service in the Air Force in Malaya. There is no question but that *The Open Door* is more self-consciously "written" than its predecessor (there are reasons for this), and that Sillitoe's processing of memory—if memories they strictly are—has become attenuated over time and distance.

The Nottingham background, always seen as Sillitoe's great forte, is more diffuse now, but that is largely because Brian is multiply alienated from it. The jungle and the Communist "menace" suggest both a metaphor for the society he has returned to and a solution to its ills. The experience also suggests ways in which life can be distanced and insulated through writing and ideas; there is a long interpolated narrative, convincingly stilted, of a pointless expedition to Gunong Barat, reminiscent of the ascent of Mount Anaka in Mailer's *The Naked and the Dead*.

Brian's own ills are no easier than those of society, though every bit as susceptible to literary response. A dockside medical consigns him to a sanatorium, lungs scarred by tubercules. Henceforward, his life and his life-story are haunted by a small, red-bearded man from Eastwood, similarly afflicted, similarly possessed of a compulsion to redeem society by giving things their right names. The language at least is post-*Chatterley* (the most immediate difference from *Key to the Door*) and amazingly precise, even where Brian's own use of it betrays a too self-conscious desire to chime with the Nottingham literati whose company he alternately pursues and rejects. They, needless to say, are more interested in his x-rays and his vowels than in his stories of Kota Libis.

When one of them, unhappily married, kisses him, he is quick to recognize and disappoint her desire for "infection". It's a fleeting and ambiguous moment and thus typical of Brian's encounters with women, which are very much in the East-wood mould. His sentimental education seems to be undertaken under some accelerated provision of the 1944 Act. Where his brother Arthur—hero of *Saturday Night and Sunday Morning,* who appears here duly miniaturized in a younger self—is all raw appetite, Brian treats all encounters, sexual and otherwise, as successive drafts in a process of self-identification, as easily discarded as his teenage wife, Pauline. After a hurried return-of-the soldier coupling, she disappears from the scene, conveniently unwilling to expose their infant boy to the infected air of the sanatorium. Brian's three mistresses are all in some way adapted to that constrained environment and atmosphere, surrounded by death, marked or bereaved by it, and yet curiously in command of it even as their perceptions are narrowed by its presence.

Each woman is progressively nearer to mortality. Rachel, a middle-class nurse with a background of loss, turns her own past into a soft-focus idyll, no more real than Brian's soldierly lies and inventions. Nora Middleton, older and one-eyed, is full of passion (identified at first as compassion), but offers only a suspiciously astigmatic and monocular view of Brian's first attempts at writing. Finally, back in Radford on home leave, there is the consumptive Lillian, denied any fuller contact with life than voices outside her sickroom window until Brian "cures" her sexually (the most self-consciously ironic nod at Lawrence); she responds to rejection by cutting her throat—another page neatly torn across.

As in *The Storyteller,* Sillitoe treats the narrative instinct as a defence against violence and loss. *The Open Door* is an extraordinary, almost symphonic development of deceptively familiar materials, and confirms his standing as one of Britain's most powerful and sophisticated fiction-writers.

Brian Morton, "Coming Closer to Mortality," in The Times Literary Supplement, *No. 4488, April 7-13, 1989, p. 364.*

Charles (Paul) Simmons

1924-

American novelist, short story writer, editor, and critic.

In his fiction, Simmons shuns conventional narrative techniques, opting to relate the vicissitudes of contemporary society in a style that combines a loosely structured format with free association, humor, and pathos. Critics generally agree that the appeal of Simmons's works stems from his informal treatment of familial and sexual concerns of everyday life. The themes of Simmons's novels often revolve around the impermanence of many aspects of human existence, and his characters frequently reveal their psychological responses to transitions in their lives.

Simmons's initial work, *Powdered Eggs* (1964), which won the PEN/Faulkner Award for best new novel, takes place during the summer following a cynical New Yorker's college graduation. Comprising letters written to a friend, the book relates anecdotes about sex and society while sardonically attempting to explain the meaning of life. Because the unnamed protagonist is an ex-Catholic and his friend is a Protestant Jew, the letters often satirize religion. Reviewers lauded Simmons's observations as humorously unerring, and Anthony Burgess commented: "It is the combination of wit and innocence which makes this book a very acceptable piece of post-Salingerism." Critics were generally disappointed with Simmons's next novel, *An Old-Fashioned Darling* (1971). Tired of hiding from angry husbands, Oliver Bacon, a heedless, libidinous bachelor and assistant editor with *Quiff* magazine, realizes that he is no longer interested in women and decides to give them up entirely. This drastic change allows Oliver to witness society's sexual wars as a neutral spectator for the first time.

Wrinkles (1978) is a highly lauded psychological exploration written in a stream-of-consciousness mode. In each of the book's forty-four short chapters, the anonymous narrator introduces a random thought and offers perspectives from childhood, young adulthood, and old age. In a section on woodworking, for example, the protagonist begins with a recollection of the homemade boats he sailed as a child, continues with a discussion of the toys that he created for his daughters while a young man, and concludes by revealing his hobby of building tables and reminiscing about his deceased father while the varnish dries. Webster Schott remarked: "Reading *Wrinkles* you are likely to feel that . . . Charles Simmons has been reading your history, waiting until this instant to report back to you on your struggles for certainty, your fractured morality, and your great yearning to be loved, flawed as you are."

Simmons's recent novel, *The Belles Lettres Papers* (1987), satirizes New York's literary scene through its account of a small magazine's takeover by a business conglomerate. The periodical, *Belles Lettres,* is assigned a new editor, Newbold Press, who discerns no difference between literary and industrial business. The magazine's reviewers plot to oust Press by perpetrating a scheme involving the discovery of nine previously unknown sonnets that supposedly prove the homosexuality of William Shakespeare. The editor's naive belief in the

hoax ultimately leads to his downfall. Simmons spent thirty-three years as an editor with *The New York Times Book Review,* and the *Belles Lettres* offices are occupied by characters who closely resemble his former colleagues. Referred to as a "revenge novel" by several critics, *The Belles Lettres Papers* was praised for its droll tone. In addition to his novels, Simmons has contributed literary criticism and short stories to such periodicals as *Esquire, The Saturday Review,* and *The New York Times Magazine.*

(See also *Contemporary Authors,* Vols. 89-92.)

THE TIMES LITERARY SUPPLEMENT

> Purporting to be a series of letters from one young man to another during the summer and early fall following their graduation from college, it is no more than hastily written and often foul anecdotes intermixed with vague and pretentious observations about life,

says Mr. Simmons with some measure of accuracy in a fake review of his own book [***Powdered Eggs***], which is also, it is

404

only fair to add immediately, one of the liveliest, funniest and most intelligent performances in the hipster-young-man-not-quite-comprehending-society line we have had for some time. And a performance it is. For a good deal of the book Mr. Simmons is showing off. There is a novel within the novel which is about an invisible man. There are interspersed "didactic stories", meant to explain "the true nature of the universe". There is an ebullience of tone and attack which is not, though it might have been, annoying, but is, when it ought not to be, occasionally stagy.

The young hero is an ex-Catholic who is writing to a Protestant-Jewish friend. This gives rise to a good deal of religious by-play, mockery and bawdy. What saves Mr. Simmons from being a common kind of bore is that he is frequently accurate and often funny. The young man's account of the confession he made to please his Catholic girl-friend is an example: preposterous, but written from intimate knowledge of the drill.

The events of the summer are lively enough, though they do not, of course, constitute a plot. Our hero's father dies. Though apparently left some money he goes to work for the Modern Universal International Encyclopedia, first as a writer . . . , then as a salesman whose name is printed into his sample as an editorial adviser. Naturally some adventures, including one with an avid widow, befall him in the course of salesmanship. He gets engaged first to his chaste Catholic girl-friend, then to another girl who turns out to be pregnant by somebody else. Still wanting to marry her he unsuccessfully pursues her to Italy and here more or less the book ends. In the meantime, of course, he has been reflecting about America, sex, Catholicism and society. Anecdotes, literary interpolations and reflections add up to an unusual, engaging and promising first production which has just won the William Faulkner Award for the best novel of 1964.

"Cracks," in The Times Literary Supplement, *No. 3292, April 1, 1965, p. 249.*

HARRY CREWS

An Old-Fashioned Darling records the sexual wars of all of us with joy and unrestrained delight. The novel takes place between navel and knee—and that is not meant as a pejorative statement. Keepers of the public morals notwithstanding, there is subject enough between navel and knee to test the art of the most talented writer. The readers of Charles Simmonss's first novel, *Powdered Eggs,* already know that he is a talented writer—know, in fact, that his is one of the finest comic voices to appear anywhere in years.

Does that mean then that in his new novel his art was equal to the subject? Not entirely. Unfortunately, he abandons his real subject in the middle of the book, loses the focus of what he is dealing with. Because of this loss, *An Old-Fashioned Darling* is not the book it could have been.

The novel opens on the life and loves of young Oliver Bacon, assistant editor of a magazine called *Quiff,* edited by a rather difficult man named Ernest Mather (who is "descended from the Puritan clergyman Increase Mather, and had no feeling whatever for the kind of thing *Quiff* dealt in. Some people claimed that he got the job originally because the organization needed a respectable front for a girlie magazine.") Oliver makes $300 a week, has a good bachelor pad and a friend named Arf who helps him into and out of all sorts of trouble. So what's the problem? The problem is that he spends every

waking moment jumping into bed with a whole covey of quail, three of whom are named—or, at least, called—Long Island, Florida and Brooklyn. Long Island and Florida are married so poor Oliver is continually dodging husbands, avoiding beatings, and dealing with almost constant domestic crises.

The logistics of the pursuit of women becomes overwhelming. One day . . . Oliver admits he doesn't really want what he has been spending all his time getting. He decides to give up girls entirely. And thereby hangs the tale. Or ought to.

The characters of the girls are carefully and fully drawn. As for Oliver, he is not only alive, he is also kicking and screaming and conniving and engaging us in laughter and tears in the same moment. At the point Oliver decides to give up girls, we are only on page 49. The whole book lies before us. But the story that remains to be told does not really deal with the consequences of that decision, as we have every right to expect. It is true that Arf is shocked and dismayed at Oliver's decision. It is also true—and hilariously so—that Oliver's pool game and his tennis game dramatically improve as the apparent result of his action, or as is the case, his lack of it.

But the whole middle of the book is taken up with the workings of the magazine *Quiff.* There is a long, long section devoted to a weekend on Long Island—the place, not the girl—during which time Arf and Oliver and the editor of *Quiff* try to shoot a series of erotic pictures. The local police raid them. The editor of *Quiff* (the man named Mather but unaffectionately called Mother) is fired; and Oliver gets Mother's job, only to lose it after two days. This part of the story is funny and inventive enough—but the personality of Oliver Bacon and the essential problem of the book all but disappear while it is taking place. And that blurs the focus. Or at least it does for me.

I said earlier that Mr. Simmons's novel is not the book it could have been. The obvious reaction to such a statement is that no book is ever the book it could have been. In spite of my reservations, *An Old-Fashioned Darling* is enough book to be tremendously excited about. Its author does so many things so well that his flaws are more enjoyable than many writers' successes.

Harry Crews, "The Aftermaths of Sex," in The New York Times Book Review, *November 21, 1971, p. 6.*

EARL SHORRIS

Charles Simmons and I are friends. We talk often about writing, including his work and mine. Mostly we talk about other writers. He enjoys talking about Chekhov and the suspense of Latin sentence structure; I answer with Latin American novels and political philosophers. It is a good friendship: we do not have to gossip very much. (p. 320)

One learns nothing about a novel from knowing the novelist; the graduate students are wrong: the context is language, not biography; and any intent, any teleology beyond the will to make a novel can only degrade the work. If the writer goes about his work seriously, as Simmons has, the novel will not be an alibi for a life, and the distance between the beginning and the end will be far less than the distance between personal history and the words chosen and ordered on the page.

Have you heard any good definitions of the novel lately? I

once heard a stupid woman say, speaking of an unfashionable work, "This is not a novel." A corrupted woman, she became an editor by accepting the theory that the novel had died in England in the 19th century when the pound was firm. Simmons has made a form in opposition: a Catholic novel, formally Aristotelian; compressed, it opposes invention to expansion.

Forty-four categories in apposition comprise *Wrinkles.* In each category the hero's life passes before the reader, beginning in childhood and ending in speculation about old age. The present time of the hero is the middle of middle age, a vantage point from which the not quite omniscient narrator looks both ways.

The first category is numbers, a birth of abstract thinking, beginning with the number one (Joyce's moocow, Sartre's words, Augustine's sin, the convention of the writer who does not spare himselfc); and the last category tells not of death but of the fear of death. In every category the hero grows close to death, his death is implied; and on the following page he begins again. The tension of the novel lies in the turning of the page, between death and resurrection. (pp. 320-21)

Like St. Augustine in *The Confessions* struggling against the seemingly ostensible truth of Manes, the hero, who has no name but the appropriate pronoun, seeks relief from the terrible dualities of this life. Born, become conscious, he encounters a world divided by the opposition between good and evil, but he cannot be certain of what they are, for they are always shifting. No Augustinian reconciliation in God and love comes to the 19th-century hero. A marriage fails, a second blooms in all but certainty. He is born, he ages, he is born again, " . . . as waking follows sleeping." No other answer can be offered through the life of the hero, only the metaphor of the form; he is otherwise content to have lived, to live, as if in the process itself that reconciliation may have been made.

Within the dogma of the form, under the implied words printed in red above each category, a twice-invented life occurs abstracted, then reified by category. The language is as tight-lipped as a schoolman's argument, even while it says love, irony or relieves the tension in occasional sentimentality:

> When his wife asked him to leave home he told his children that he and their mother would no longer be husband and wife but that he would always be their father. The children watched him carefully; he wept throughout the talk. Before he moved out the younger child drew for him a picture of herself sad. He gave it to his mother, whose eyesight was failing; she said it was very nice and hung it in her bedroom.

Nothing trendy happens in the novel: the hero visits no boutiques, takes no notice of the space program, offers no gossip about political figures or the lords of academia; he doesn't even jog. The discipline of the form permits only the inclusion of the thoughts and things essential to the particular life. There are no cosmic disappointments, only a recurring quietness, as in awe, at the winding down of a life (the predictions of the time following middle age are almost always said in softer words, the consonants somehow made to seem silent).

The arrangement of the categories offers as much commentary on the life of the hero as does the text itself:

       regrets
      birthdays
      children
        love
       anger

    . . . .

      authority
      animosity
      charity

    . . . .

    appearances
  companionship
     duties
   gratifications
   fear of death

Yet, a novel could not be more quotidian, more mortal, telling of coins, sweets, the frustrations of jobs, summerhouses, fabrics, movies, woodworking, dogs, tricycles, peeing, ministering to the nights of infant children, jokes, schooldays, sex, infatuations and disillusionments in all the stages of a life; and always darkening, as if seen through the closing lens of an eye. If the novel did not bloom after the reading, it would be wound too tightly in the form and the prose, the compression would be too great; were it not for the implications of the verbs, the lack of adjectives would have left the novel thin. Were it not for the timelessness of form, *Wrinkles* would be unbearably mortal; art demands that the contemplation of death be tempered with births. Simmons has kept his direction in the novel, driving the horses of form and content with balance, composing a novel as clear as ancient music, and playing it remarkably well.

In the aftermath of reading, the best novels leave the reader with something more than the vicarious experience. *Wrinkles* offers the Catholic and treasurable advice that nothing is final but forgiveness; and perhaps that is not, after all, so far from Augustine's answer. (pp. 321-22)

Earl Shorris, "Looking Both Ways," in The Nation, *New York, Vol. 227, No. 10, September 30, 1978, pp. 320-22.*

WEBSTER SCHOTT

Wrinkles is funny and sad, innocent and knowing, and pertinent to the point of pain. It is a novel about change.

Reading *Wrinkles* you are likely to feel that someone, Charles Simmons, has been reading your history, waiting until this instant to report back to you on your struggles for certainty, your fractured morality, and your great yearning to be loved, flawed as you are.

Wrinkles is a nearly perfect novel of psychological exploration. I have never read anything like it and can think of parallels only in René Char's prose poetry or Bach's cantatas.

Charles Simmons plays with the physical and emotional life of his hero as if handling an opal, turning the man this way and that way to reflect still another mood or discovery. He gives us a complete life. We learn everything we want or need to know about him to recognize him. There are parts of him that are all of us. But these parts become a whole and unique human being in Simmons' hands.

Simmons' hero has no name. He is simply "He" and is at the center of each of the novel's 44 short chapters. They range in length from around 700 words to 1000 words. There's an idea, a place, a person, a puzzle at the start of each chapter. For instance, the magic of numbers, Aunt Mae, grammar school, belief in God, and his childhood home trigger the first five chapters. Each takes a similar, extraordinary form. Each chapter begins at a point in the hero's early childhood. Then it moves to adolescence, young adulthood, middle age. Every chapter closes with old age and anticipating the hero's death.

While there is no linear story line, no formal portraiture, and no dramatic crisis or dénouement to *Wrinkles,* all are here in disguise. They are disguised by the process of aging that colors and alters everything Charles Simmons and his autobiographical hero once thought or believed.

Simmons' hero suffers the whole catastrophe of 20th-century life in an advanced society. He grows up Catholic and discovers that God is not in charge of the world. He goes to war and cannot fight. He marries without experience (his childhood sweetheart) and has children. He has affairs. He develops "a taboo against sleeping with a woman he liked nothing about," and falls in love with a woman much younger than he. He divorces and sees his children reject his values. He too, of course, gives up these values along the way because they don't work. He's about 56 as the novel is written and is seeking new bedrock as he anticipates death. He settles for consolations like having a doctor older than himself because of "the appeal of having an expert between oneself and death." . . .

He retreats into his sensibilities, which is importantly what *Wrinkles* is about. He understands that choice in his life, with time passing, is divided between those who help him achieve his most immediate needs and those who please him because they cater to his preferences: "Less and less will he think of people as good or bad; rather it will seem to him that benefactors will look good to the beneficiaries, injurers bad to the injured, and that the rest is taste."

Much of *Wrinkles* is about sex because sex ties us to youth and is the last drive to go before the drive to stay alive. More of *Wrinkles* is about surrendering hope, accepting that youth cannot fulfill its expectations. Not knowing is a condition of believing. Disappointment is the slate upon which age writes our names.

If I've suggested that Charles Simmons' novel is more dark than light, that's because it reads that way, and such may be its flaw. Horace Walpole said those who think are likely to find life comic; and those who feel will find life tragic. Simmons knows both. The brilliance of his exposition illuminates everything, even darkness.

Episodes and events focus Simmons' vignettes on the ordinary transactions of life. But the reflective mind of Simmons' hero gives them meaning. B. F. Skinner has remarked that science is another way of looking at life. Charles Simmons in *Wrinkles* shows us once more—in case we've been seduced by journalism, clinical history, or enriched gossip—that the art of fiction is also a way of looking at life.

Science generalizes. Art specifies. Both have in common the possibility of finding in the individual that which is near-universal. Taking the life of one man, examining it with care and patience, Simmons shows us the life of many men and women. Looking at one life we see ourselves, deeper and more intensely than before. The crucial transaction of art takes place in *Wrinkles* in all its majesty.

> Webster Schott, "Turning the Kaleidoscope of Memory," in Book World—The Washington Post, November 12, 1978, p. E5.

DAVID EVANIER

Wrinkles has far more humor and concreteness than Sherwood Anderson, more believability, vulnerability, and real sexuality than Hemingway. Yet it has things in common with both of them: crystalline prose, sharp compression, a strong tactile sense, and, most importantly, a new and probably unduplicable prose form.

Simmons wrote an earlier comic delight, *Powdered Eggs,* which was the angry young artist's book. *Wrinkles* is about what its title implies: physical aging and loss, and the growing moral ambiguity of middle age. When he was young, "Often he carried a book with him. At its most powerful the right book he felt would save him from death or see him through death without panic or despair. His favorites were small editions of Herrick, Catullus, Lucretius, and *Antony and Cleopatra.*" Later:

> Although he travels with personal equipment—pen, keys, wallet—nothing material has saving significance for him now. Soon he will feel that the quality of immutability, which once attracted him to certain objects, is worthless. . . . Less and less will he think of people as good or bad; rather it will seem to him that benefactors look good to the beneficiaries, injurers bad to the injured, and that the rest is taste.

Simmons has organized each chapter by a common subject, attitude, or feeling (which is not explicit, however): the old neighborhood, numbers, school, religion, the summer house, regrets, clothes, birthdays, fatherhood, love, fighting, doctors, cheating, movies, wood, firearms, animals, vehicles, homosexuality, authority, animosity, [and] sex. . . . (p. 108)

In his vehicles chapter, he deals chronologically with wicker baby carriages, toy autos, tricycles, roller skates, surfboards, slides and swings, sailboats, ice skates, horseback riding, and cars. . . . In his chapter on wood, the narrator proceeds from his father's making benches, porches, awnings, walks, steps, railings, while the narrator made toy boats, to the narrator's own fatherhood: "He liked to take his daughters walking in parks and from fallen or new-cut branches make them walking sticks on which he carved designs by stripping the bark in spirals and crosses." When he is divorced and alone, "He made more tables than he had room for and gave the excess like kittens to friends. When a table came out well he sometimes sat up drinking, waiting for the varnish to dry, and wished his father were alive to see it." Among the things from my own childhood I recognized was the narrator's apartment house, with its garden at the entrance where "in the center, under an arched bridge was a pond. Goldfish swam there in the summer; in winter the pond was drained." Exactly like the narrator, I "wondered where the goldfish were kept in the winter."

So the chapters go, working forward in free association reined in by a discerning control. The result is a portrait that is so universal that no reader will feel he is not a part of it. The summaries could easily have left out the juice, the vital matter that essentially determines whether a novel is alive or not. Simmons has delicately sketched in the precise detail, the single line of dialogue that tells it all. In his clothing segment, he writes that, at the end of the narrator's life, "suits he will continue to buy singly, except on one occasion when he will buy two, a sporty herringbone ('The older the bird the brighter the plumage,' he will say to the salesman) and the other dark blue." The things of the earth are recorded here, along with the people, the places, in a revolving mosaic. Above all, *words* are embodied here. Their meanings are looked at as if for the first time, by the book's form. It is as if a dictionary had sprung to life.

I was around at the genesis of this book, and it may be pertinent to mention that occasion. When I was a copyboy at the *Times Book Review* in 1967-68, Simmons took me under his wing. He had finished **Powdered Eggs** and was looking for a way of saying what he wanted to say now; the attitudes of youth that prompted the first book would not do again. The feelings, the perceptions, were different.

I remember conversations about Dickens, about long books and how things could now be said in a paragraph that took hundreds of pages for the Victorian writers. A wonderful talker, Simmons was searching for a great title and a new form for a book. I remember his interest in aphorisms and in words—the meanings of words—and how, one day while we walked down 43rd Street, he talked about starting with the dictionary, taking one word at a time and exploring its meaning in one's life. I recall thinking, filled with myself, that his idea was both too grandiose and too abstract. I did not really hear what he was saying.

Wrinkles is a triumph. (pp. 108-09)

> David Evanier, "A Triumphant Original," in National Review, *New York, Vol. XXXI, January 19, 1979, pp. 108-09.*

NOLAN MILLER

Rarely does any novel, when a reading is finished, seem unfinished unless immediately read again. [*Wrinkles*] is such a novel. (p. 243)

Each section is a measure of experience unmarked by obtrusively progressive years. Dates and years are of greater service to historians or tax-collectors than to novelists—at least to the author of this one, with his knowledge that there is no fixed reality except in the consanguineous flow of an individual and private memory.

We begin with a child learning numbers from his mother, as one by one he unfolds the fingers of his fists. "He had different feelings about each digit. One was perfect and friendly. Two looked more complicated than it was. . . . Three was pleasing; its three points made it easy to understand and remember." And so on.

We conclude. The man who was the child feels certain he has throat cancer, although assured both by his psychiatrist and his physician that he does not. He spends his time playing games with newspaper obituaries, making guesses about the age at which he may or may not die and under what circumstances. The final sentence is this: "As he gets older he will sometimes try to enquire into his deepest wishes, hoping to find a weariness with life that would make death less fearsome, but can't." Life is never less than amazing, even awe-some. But death is never less than fearsome. A man ages, becoming day after day more and more wrinkled, and then dies.

Here, then, in these spare pages, we have a life, the memories of a husband, a father, a writer, a man never spectacularly a success nor, on the other hand, a failure. It is a life of moment following moment, each entangled in memories of the past, haunted by the unknown future. It is life that cannot be summed up, cannot be plotted, cannot, being lived, have the novel's required simulation of any beginning, middle, and end. Nothing can be plucked clean to be called a naked story. No one event in the continuum of these moments of existence can be tagged as a climax. Little seems to be what can be called fiction, unless one argues that the very facts of existence are fictions.

Yet this is a novel, one so original in conception that form and content have become inseparable. There can be no other novel like it because the innumerable and distinctive details of the life here represented are unique. *Wrinkles* is important. To miss reading it is to miss what may be a landmark in American literature. (pp. 243-44)

> Nolan Miller, in a review of "Wrinkles," in The Antioch Review, *Vol. 37, No. 2, Spring, 1979, pp. 243-44.*

JOHN BLADES

If you stay tuned to literary channels, you surely know Skippy Overleaf. He was the innovative, radical editor of Belles Lettres, the weekly book review whose history Charles Simmons breezily recaps in **The Belles Lettres Papers.** At the point in his mayfly career that Simmons catches [or impales] him, Skippy was the "current wonderchild of American journalism": not only editor of *Belles Lettres* but a critic, author and freelance hustler, who has "produced so much of such high quality," Simmons writes, "that Wilfrid Sheed once accused him of being twins."

Okay, so you don't know Skippy Overleaf. And you've never heard of *Belles Lettres* either. But there's no reason to feel illiterate, since they're both fictitious creatures, figments of Simmons' deviously satirical imagination. But because Simmons has make Skippy [and everyone else in his novel] such a facetious caricature is not to assume he has no basis in reality. In fact, he bears a canny resemblance to John Leonard, who used to be the editor of the *New York Times Book Review.* . . .

Like Nora Ephron's *Heartburn* and Erica Jong's *Parachutes & Kisses,* Simmons' book [**The Belles Lettres Papers**] belongs to one of our most cherished and ignoble genres: the revenge novel. Though he's frothy and irreverent, a cultured Perelman, Simmons isn't just content to lampoon and burlesque the New York literati, which he does with ease. He's also out to settle some old scores, which gives his book a nice malicious kick.

At the outset, Simmons includes a cast of his fictional characters, who are assigned such Perelmanesque appellations as Samuel Serif, Selma Watermark, Barry Vellum, Aubrey Buckram, Bobby Quarto and Lou Bodoni. More to the point, he might have provided a cast list of real people who served as their models, though the capos of New York publishing (for whose amusement and chagrin this book is principally intended) should have no difficulty recognizing them—or themselves. Even more flagrant than Overleaf/Leonard, for instance, is S. Sewnbound, the book's "premier Shakespearean scholar," who has at least a patronymic resemblance to the real Shakespearean scholar, S. Schoenbaum.

Sewnbound plays a small but crucial role in **The Belles Lettres Papers;** he's the expert who's duped into authenticating nine newly discovered Shakespeare sonnets, which are submitted as conclusive proof that the Bard was gay. This turns out to be a hoax engineered by an ex-copy boy, Art Folio, who was fired for selling review copies of books, and other vengeful *Belle Lettres* employees, in order to sabotage the magazine's new editor, Newbold Press.

The "semisimian" Newbold Press has been hired away from the Rupert Murdoch empire to popularize *Belles Lettres* (a composite of the *New York Review of Books* and the *New York Times Book Review*). To do so, the philistine editor resorts to such practices as drawing up a list of America's 25 greatest writers and promoting a heavyweight match between Saul Bellow and John Irving, not to mention the publication of the bogus Shakespeare sonnets, which is what finally brings down Newhouse—make that Newbold.

But never mind the plot—it's as fragile as onionskin and as transparent as laughing gas. What counts here are the incestuous jokes, the defamation of characters both real and imaginary, the delightful slurs against book reviewing, a profession, as some of us will gladly testify, that is not always so gentlemanly [or ladylike] as outsiders suppose. As one *Belles Lettres* editor says, "Book reviewing is a mug's game when done regularly." After reading Simmons' novel, a lot of book reviewers, editors and publishers are going to feel as if they've been mugged.

John Blades, *"A Wicked Satirist Turns Tables on Book Reviewers,"* in Chicago Tribune—Books, *April 19, 1987, p. 3.*

STEPHEN SCHIFF

In some fictions the milieu is all; you read them not for rich characterizations or provocative themes, but for a taste of life in the fashion industry or the Mafia or the neon demimonde today's young coke-heads inhabit. **The Belles Lettres Papers** is a rather classy example of the genre, but, as milieu novels go, it aims for a strangely select audience. Its author, Charles Simmons, was for many years an editor at the book review you are now reading, and its setting is a magazine called *Belles Lettres,* which turns out to be very like the book review you are now reading. The tone is knowing and satirical, with a vengeful edge, and the jokes are of the "in" variety—lots of references to authors and critics known mainly to other authors and critics, lots of keenly honed barbs and jingling *clefs.*

Lovers of literary quizzes will savor Mr. Simmons' wordplay: the characters have names like Folio and Serif, and when an editor is asked to examine an impenetrable review of Graham Greene's latest, he promises he'll get to the heart of the matter. Mr. Simmons has even composed nine hilarious "undiscovered" Shakespeare sonnets, all of them shapelier and more Elizabethan than the "Shall I die? Shall I fly?" travesty (so reminiscent of Edward Lear on a groggy day) that some scholars allege to be the most recently unearthed Shakespearean shard. . . .

Despite all its vim and gossip value, **The Belles Lettres Pa-**

pers is cracker-thin and brittle. Its hero, a young editor named Frank Page, has been hired right out of college by the saintly (if long-winded) editor in chief, Jonathan Margin, and the novel follows Page's progress as his mentor battles the termagant wife of the magazine's owner, only to be replaced by a corporate thug. Sopping wet behind the ears, Page nevertheless proves to be a bottomless gusher of wit and wisdom, the source of nearly every good idea at the magazine, nearly every adroit business and political maneuver. Any office in the real world would instantly mark him as an insufferable brown-noser, yet the staff at *Belles Lettres* trusts and adores him unquestioningly.

But if Page is designed to let the author give his own back a hearty thump, Mr. Simmons' chief intent seems to be to scandalize: You think the administration of this book review is all probity and unswerving idealism? Well, get a load of this. Unfortunately, the loads Mr. Simmons plops before us don't kick up much dust. Are we shocked to discover an editor consulting a reference book to come up with a list of the 25 best American writers? Are we horrified to learn that the philistine new editor in chief doesn't know how to pronounce Alfred Knopf's name? The novel's only sizable brouhaha involves the sale of places on the best-seller list, but this disturbance, like nearly every other in the book, no sooner befouls the atmosphere than it departs, meekly, by the back door.

The Belles Lettres Papers has a lazy aura; one wishes Mr. Simmons had crashed beyond the book review's walls to tackle the byzantine relations between the magazine and the wider—and perhaps more scurrilous—literary world. That might not have made for such sweet revenge, but it certainly would have juiced up this novel's tiny milieu.

Stephen Schiff, *"Anyone We Know?,"* in The New York Times Book Review, *May 24, 1987, p. 10.*

ANGELA RINALDI

The book publishing industry has always been a source of fascination to many. Lately, it has reached an even larger scale of interest as what was once regarded as a gentlemanly profession has become the target of corporate takeovers and the stuff of which front-page business sections stories are now made. Authors make headlines when their several million-dollar advances break records. Agents appear in the likes of *People* magazine. The memoirs of a 29-year-old game show hostess reflects the public's taste. Presidents and CEOs of major publishing houses show up in the Wall Street Journal with the Journal's prestigious line drawing portrait set into the article while at the same time the same face appears in a full-color, double-page ad for a state-of-the-art printing process.

While all this goes on, the everyday life of the publishing industry is seldom chronicled. The real drama and politics never reach daylight. No one would ever suspect that the people least talked about—editors—are the people who give the industry the most color. No one except any editor that has ever worked in a publishing house or for a powerful literary review.

Several former editors have tried their hand at characterizing editorial staffs in commercial novels or publishing histories. But none has succeeded in capturing this scene with the wit and insight of Charles Simmons. . . .

Simmons' novel *The Belles Lettres Papers* details the daily machinations of a powerful literary review called *Belles Lettres*. Its narrator, Frank Page, is a young staff member. Sound familiar? "Frank Page" was the pseudonymous author of the chapters of *The Belles Lettres Papers* when they first appeared in the *Nation* and the *New Republic*. Any resemblance between Frank Page and Charles Simmons is, ahem, coincidental. Any resemblance between the novel's characters and the real-life characters that populate the industry is not coincidental. (p. 2)

An obviously "in" novel for the literati, *The Belles Lettres Papers* crosses several audiences. It will be devoured by editors who will boast that they were involved in some of the antics. Self-respecting book reviewers will cringe at the reviewer selection process. Of course, authors will eat it up; Norman Mailer will love the following description of [his novel] *Ancient Evenings* recited at a weekly assignment meeting—"The Old Testament written by Mel Brooks, *The Iliad* written by Woody Allen." If you're interested in a publishing career, here's your chance to reconsider. Devoted fans of book review sections can learn if book editors read all the books they assign, dictate to book reviewers what to say, select reviewers they hope will be friendly (or the reverse).

Finally, Simmons has written a novel in which anyone who has ever worked for a social-climbing tyrant can identify with. Anyone would sympathize with editor Jonathan Margin as he loses his job to Newbold Press, a corporate hit man brought in to clean house. Press thinks his inherited editorial staff should be working on scrolls instead of reviewing manuscripts. He underestimates their powers of endurance and their innate survival instincts as they rally to a diabolically plotted finish for Press. One turns the last page applauding their genius. (p. 11)

> *Angela Rinaldi, in a review of "The Belles Lettres Papers," in* Los Angeles Times Book Review, *July 19, 1987, pp. 2, 11.*

STANLEY REYNOLDS

Surprising to see just who among the so many literary Limeys plying the Atlantic trade are considered the hot-shots by the Yanks. There are, of course, Alexander Cockburn and Wilfrid Sheen but these two exiles have been so long in America that they are taken to be, if not genuine Americans, at least hundred per cent New Yorkers. But which of the hopefuls who have knocked at the golden door have found it swinging open for them? It is not a very satisfactory list. It is composed only of V. S. Pritchett and Anthony Burgess. Of these, it is Pritchett who is seen as incorruptible. Anthony is thought soft. That is, Burgess is considered a soft reviewer and the Yanks are extremely puritanical about the taint or even hint of corruption in their book reviewing (they, apparently, do not sell review copies!). Book reviewing, that's what this slim and very funny novel [*The Belles Lettres Papers*] is all about.

The author is a former editor of the *New York Times Book Review*. But the target here is not that millstone of the East Coast Establishment. He is after something more akin to the *New York Review of Books*. He calls it *Belles Lettres* and it is supposed to be one of those rather precious little literary monthlies which falters and is bought up by a publishing giant. Here is the kindly old editor and his staff fighting against a former Rupert Murdoch-man who has been

brought in to Hoover the joint. . . . The satire is against the new savages of contemporary journalism who see no difference whatsoever between literature and any other business.

Do not be put off by thinking it will be too insider-New York and Yank. We do have the same sort of thing right here in London. *Belles Lettres* will ring unpleasant bells with anyone working in any sort of office anywhere. Suck-ups, sneaks, time-servers, dead-wood and the new hit-men of modern business practices get an airing. But, unlike real life, it all ends happily, with the dreadful Murdoch mobster getting his just deserts. (pp. 54-5)

> *Stanley Reynolds, "It Can't Happen Here," in* Punch, *Vol. 292, No. 7650, August 12, 1987, pp. 54-5.*

TINA BROWN

In the era of the Big Book, few American novelists have the courage to be slight. Literary earnestness is so intense, it's almost unpatriotic to want to be "amusing". It's certainly deeply un-American; which is why Charles Simmons's spoof of the world of book-reviewing is such a curiosity. And Simmons strives not only to be amusing; he is satisfied with nothing less than fine irrelevance.

The action takes place in the office of *Belles Lettres,* a literary magazine that lost its hyphen in 1960. The narrator is a sound young assistant editor, Frank Page, whose role is to try to pilot his good-egg editor Jonathan Margin through the storm of progress unleashed by the brashly commercial stewardship of Cyrus Tooling. He fails and Margin is replaced by Newbold Press, an editor as crass as his proprietor. In the end, Press is brought down by succumbing to a hoax discovery of some Shakespeare sonnets that prove the Bard was gay.

It's a weak dénouement and one wishes that, in general, Simmons had been a bit more inventive with the plot. At first it seems as though this might be another *Scoop*, or a literary *Billy Liar*, but Simmons is too easy with himself: comic names are always a bad sign and there is a rash of them here, most of them derived from typography and publishing.

By far the best part of *The Belles Lettres Papers* is the opening chapter, which traces the pedigree of the magazine from rich man's plaything under Aubrey Buckram to media property under Cyrus Tooling, and sketches the lineage of editors. The worthy idealist Samuel Serif gives it a faltering start; the visionary Xavier Deckle launches it into the literary stratosphere; the humdrum professional Effie Backstrip (beloved by the publishing world as "a real bookman") consolidates the success; flaming wunderkind Skippy Overleaf rocks the boat; and the sane gentleman-hack Jonathan Margin returns the pendulum to dead centre. "Unlike Backstrip, he was a literary bloke. Unlike Overleaf he was not a wonderchild." Names apart, the sequence is litcom at its most authentic. . . .

The Belles Lettres Papers is, on the whole, a droll disappointment. The revelations as well as the satire are simply too polite—rather as if Mr Pooter had written *Answered Prayers*. When it appeared in the United States it caused a small stir and Simmons resigned his job on the *New York Times Book Review* shortly afterwards. A slight satisfaction. Or perhaps a little lump of yeast.

> *Tina Brown, "Irrelevant Finesse," in* The Times

Literary Supplement, *No. 4415, November 13-19, 1987, p. 1249.*

Andrei Voznesensky

1933-

Russian poet, fiction writer, and memoirist.

One of the Soviet Union's most prestigious contemporary poets, Voznesensky combines vibrant imagery with technological metaphors and allusions to create complex, experimental verse. He is a protegé of author Boris Pasternak, whose novels and poetry revolve around the loss of identity and the alienation of individuals in an industrial society. In his work, Voznesensky reiterates the concerns and lyrical qualities of his mentor, whom he describes as "my god, my father, and for a long time, my university." While Voznesensky's linguistic dexterity has occasionally been faulted for overshadowing content, his poetry is generally regarded as a formidable contribution to Soviet postwar literature for its unrelenting boldness. W. Gareth Jones commented: "Brittleness, brashness, technical brilliance are not merely qualities of Voznesensky's verse but an integral part of what he has to say about his existence. Face to face with a world in which existence may appear gratuitous and obscene, Voznesensky on the one hand gives acute expression to this human predicament while simultaneously wrestling with it and attempting to bring his world to a tense, dynamic equilibrium."

Voznesensky's poetry and public readings have provoked much controversy and commentary. While his works often profess a profound love for Russia, they express opposition toward its repressive government, revealing an ambivalent relationship between Voznesensky and his country. Such early collections as *Mozaika* (1960), *Parabola* (1960), and *Pishetsya kak lyubitsya* (1963) produced charges of obscurantism, and former Soviet Premier Nikita Khrushchev renounced Voznesensky as a "bourgeois formalist." By 1969, Soviet literary journals were refusing to publish Voznesensky's work. In 1979, he further angered the Soviet government when he and several other writers published *Metropol,* an intellectual magazine that challenged the prevailing political control of arts and letters. Voznesensky's outspokenness has also prompted Russian officials to deny him the right to appear at poetry readings in the United States, yet his work remains immensely popular in the Soviet Union and has been translated into more than a dozen languages.

In his first two major translated volumes, *Antimiry* (1964; *Antiworlds*) and *Voznesensky: Selected Poems* (1966), Voznesensky stresses the importance of human values through works of irony and eroticism. In one of his most celebrated poems, "I Am Goya," Voznesensky expounds on the destruction and wars that have ravaged Russia by utilizing the persona of Francisco de Goya (1746-1828), the Spanish painter whose works reflect the political and social upheavals of his time. Voznesensky shifts from a political to a personal exploration of this theme in "Someone Is Beating a Woman," the discordant power of which evoked widely varied reactions. Loss of identity is explored in "Monolog Merlin Monro" and "Oza" through two distinctly different techniques. The first poem, a discussion of ill-fated actress Marilyn Monroe, shows how the manipulative power of society can turn individuals into objects, while "Oza," a spoof of Edgar Allan Poe's "The

Raven," examines the bewilderment of artists in a technocratic world.

Avos (1974; *Story under Full Sail*) is a long narrative poem based on an actual love story. In 1805, a Russian nobleman traveled to America, where he met and fell in love with a sixteen-year-old girl. While returning to Russia to obtain permission from the Tsar to marry, he died in Siberia, and the girl waited thirty-five years for his return before entering a convent. In 1981, Voznesensky transformed this poem into a highly successful rock opera, *Juno and Avos. Nostalgia for the Present* (1978) contains satirical poems in which Voznesensky contemplates the changing concerns and attitudes of the Soviet Union. Critics noted that the potency of Voznesensky's opinions are ironically weakened as a result of the restrictions placed on Soviet literature.

Voznesensky's later works have benefitted from the increased artistic freedom permitted under the rule of Soviet Premier Mikhail Gorbachev. Critics assert that Voznesensky's contemporary poems are more thoughtful, direct, and dynamic than his earlier verse. *The Ditch: A Spiritual Trial* (1986) is a collection of candid poetry and prose, with the title work focusing on the 1941 Nazi massacre of twelve thousand Soviet Jews. Voznesensky also comments on such modern problems as Siberia's water pollution and the Chernobyl nuclear disaster. *An Arrow in the Wall: Selected Poetry and Prose* (1987) probes humanity's pretensions through extensive use of irony. The acclaimed prose memoir "I Am Fourteen" recalls Voznesensky's boyhood friendship with Pasternak. The title of this work refers not to Voznesensky's age but to the only age Pasternak ever mentioned in his poetry. Reviewers lauded the volume's humor and sincerity, and Anne Leaton contended: "[The] best of Voznesensky is the confluence of energetic emotion, precise, compelling, often bizarre imagery, political innuendo, and the fluid colloquialism of his voice."

(See also *CLC*, Vols. 1, 15 and *Contemporary Authors*, Vols. 89-92.)

PAUL WOHL

The Soviet postwar generation is currently being interpreted to Americans by the Russian poet Andrei Voznesensky, who also speaks for Russia past and present with its love, anguish, and daring, its elemental power and sensitivity. But most of all, for Russia-about-to-become, with its new and wondrous sense of transition.

Voznesensky is essentially the poet of the new elite educated in the natural sciences. More than any other avant-garde poet he voices the visions of the youth of what Yugoslavia's Milovan Djilas has called "the new class." . . .

What comes through in translation as well as in the original, is the poet's relentless sincerity, a compassion and spiritual strength which enable him to reach out to the living core of things.

Russia's age-old oral culture in which the poet, like the ancient bard, becomes seer, way-shower, and interpreter of the secrets of life, seems to have remained unaffected by the streams of stereotype copy which the party press pours over the land.

The English writer Herbert Marshall in his introduction to the latest and most complete volume of Voznesensky's poems—*Voznesensky: Selected Poems*—traces Voznesensky to Alexander Blok and Boris Pasternak, symbolist poets related to the surrealists.

While calling Pasternak his "father and god," Voznesensky went beyond his model and developed an imagery which foretells the 21st century. No other major Russian poet of the postwar generation is as fascinated by modern technology, electronics, nuclear physics and interplanetary prospects as this son of an electrical engineer.

It has been said that he projects a montage of conflicting images and mathematical metaphors and allusions without a narrative line or overt connections. Yet his poetry can have warmth and immediacy. It can come as close to nature as the lines in his poem **"Autumn"** where he sees life fermenting "in the hollow of oaks, in meadows, in houses, in windswept woods."

The metaphysical streak in Voznesensky's poetry manifests itself in his **"Ballad of the Full-Stop,"** which deals with the violent shooting of many of Russia's most brilliant poets from Pushkin to Mayakovsky. The ballad—as translated by Mr.

Marshall—ends: "There are no deaths. No full-stops, / There's bullet's trajectory / And just as straight is the second projection. / There's no full-stop in the estimate of nature. / We'll be immortal. And that's for sure."

The United States fascinates Voznesensky. He has composed a fine poem on New York's Kennedy Airport. Of the city itself he has written:

> I'm on the roofs like a gnome, over New
> York's planning perched.
> On my little finger your sun glows like a
> lady bird. . . .

Although Soviet poets on tour abroad usually get a build-up in their own press, *Komsomolskaya Pravda*, the daily of the Communist Youth Organization with more than 20,000,000 members, obliquely criticized Voznesensky the day following his second appearance in New York. The poet was accused of projecting his heroes into "supranatural states" and evoking "exotic situations for self-revelation." "One would like to see in Andrei Voznesensky . . . something of the anti-unexpected," wrote the regime critic Vladimir Turbin. In other words, he is admonished to be more commonplace, more easily understandable, closer to folk art, more "unpretentious."

Paul Wohl, "He Speaks for the 'New Elite'," in The Christian Science Monitor, *April 1, 1966, p. 9.*

ERNEST J. SIMMONS

There are several young contemporary American and Western European poets who compare favorably with Andrei Voznesensky in poetic talent and accomplishment without enjoying anything like his national and international reputation. This fact is not unconnected with cold-war exploitation in the West of the so-called "angry young men" among Soviet writers, as well as with the amazing popularity of Soviet poetry readings, often by consummate performers (including Voznesensky) who appear to compose verse with an ear attuned to the public response to recitation.

These extra factors of reputation-building are lacking in the case of Soviet poets of superb merit such as Boris Slutsky and Leonid Martynov, whose names are almost totally unknown in the West. Already collections of Voznesensky's verse have been published in German, Italian, and British translations, and various renderings of separate poems have appeared in foreign anthologies and in several well-known American magazines and reviews.

These two new volumes of translations [*Antiworlds* and *Voznesensky: Selected Poems*] may well add to Voznesensky's special kind of reputation among English readers without necessarily convincing them that he is a major poet. But then he is still young, only 33, although one may hope that he will not be among those Soviet poets who remain young too long. There is just a suggestion of arrested development in Voznesensky's latest and most ambitious effort, the long poem **"Oza,"** which is included in *Antiworlds*. . . . This work, in which one had a right to expect some comprehensive development of Voznesensky's hard core of thought, is quite ambiguous in meaning and leaves me . . . frankly baffled.

If the more objective Soviet critics see much "froth" in Voznesensky, they also see much talent. W. H. Auden, in a brief Foreword to *Antiworlds*, is content to describe him as "a good poet" and to note his craftsmanship, effective use of rhythm, rhyme, assonance, slang, contrasts in diction, and his wide range of subject matter. This Foreword, in its commonsense humility so unlike the cold-war-ridden Introductions to both of these volumes, wisely reminds English readers that every word Voznesensky writes, even in a critical way, "reveals a profound love for his native land and its traditions." For Mr. Auden recognizes the danger of misunderstanding him "by looking for ideological clues instead of reading his poems as one would read any poet who is a fellow countryman." (pp. 6-7)

Voznesensky has learned much about imagery from his master Pasternak, who declared that in his art man is always silent and only the image speaks. For Voznesensky, however, "metaphor is the motor of form," but often the motor sputters and coughs: "My shout / On a tape recorder rolled, / Like a crimson tongue ripped out!"; "And fingers in hangnails rusty / almost shuffle over one's heart"; "and like flames of cigarette lighters / the silent tongues of sheep dogs glow."

In poetry—Voznesensky asserts in a note—"the best tradition is novelty." And he pursues it sometimes with notable effect as in **"New York Airport at Night."** . . . Here the poet boldly identifies himself with the huge glass structure which in the end inspires an outpouring of almost mystical transports. Arresting, too, is the long poem **"The Masters,"** on the building of St. Basil's Cathedral. . . . To appreciate the novelty of the poem, one must read the conclusion with its amazing fusion of the craftsmen of the time of Ivan the Terrible with those of the Soviet Union, with whom Voznesensky symbolically identifies himself in celebrating his country's progress.

Equally impressive in its novelty is **"The Skull Ballad,"** in which the decapitated head of Peter the Great's unfaithful mistress speaks out in defense of her conduct to the Czar, who is present at the execution. . . .

The search for novelty leads Voznesensky astray at times, as in **"Someone Is Beating a Woman"** with its thudding alliterations in the first stanza (*byut / blestit / belok / buytsyabetye*). . . . [The] unexplained, merciless beating of the woman leaves the reader about as detached from its horror as the poet seems to be. It strikes one as an effort in poetic sensation.

Some of the poems, and their translations in these collections, reach the reader readily enough, such as **"I Am Goya,"** **"The Cashier,"** **"My Achilles Heart,"** **"Dead Still,"** **"Hunting a Hare,"** . . . and **"First Frost"** which is wonderfully effective in its simplicity. But other poems seem banal or as naive and ambiguous in their communication as a child's smudged finger paintings.

Nor, after perusing the originals, can one always agree with the assertion of the editors of **Antiworlds** that Voznesensky's modernist use of language is always disciplined and devoid of the tendency of lesser poets to flaunt their emancipation in this respect. Though he no doubt possesses a mastery of his medium, Voznesensky's employment of scientific and technological terms is excessive, and his effects in language in general and in poetic devices are at times overdone and patently contrived. But there can be no question of his talent or that his poetry—as Auden puts it—has much to say to foreign readers as well as to Russians. (p. 7)

Ernest J. Simmons, "A Good, Young Poet," in The

New York Times Book Review, *June 19, 1966, pp. 6-7.*

NEWSWEEK

At 33 poet Andrei Voznesensky is one of the most celebrated and controversial citizens of the Soviet Union. His books, in editions of 100,000 copies, sell out as soon as they are published. His public readings are attended by stadiums-full of eager Russians. Along with Evgeny Evtushenko and others, he is one of the generation of young poets who have jumped the spark gap between East and West and helped to turn the cold war into the beginning of a warm contact between brains and hearts. He has been berated by the vicious scolds of the vestigial and neo-Stalinists; but his continued relative freedom to travel, speak and write is a portent of a future that is bound to come.

At Voznesensky's recent readings in New York, Chicago and Washington it was heartening—viscerally, intellectually and ideologically—just to see and hear him. He is a slight, blond figure with a boyish, open face, a strong actor's voice, Stanislavsky shrugs and an eloquent Adam's apple, who rolls his famous assonances off his tongue like the bells in **"Boris Godunov"**: "*Ya Góya . . . nagóya . . . ya górye . . . ya gólos . . . góda . . . ya gólod . . . ya górlo . . . góloi . . .*"

Those booming O's are from Voznesensky's most famous poem, **"I Am Goya,"** in which he most powerfully assumes his characteristic role, that of the witness to his time. In this case he speaks through the mouth of one of the most relentlessly clear-eyed witnesses in human history:

> I am Goya / of the bare field, by the enemy's beak gouged / till the craters of my eyes gape / I am grief / I am the tongue / of war, the embers of cities / on the snows of the year 1941 / I am hunger / I am the gullet / of a woman hanged whose body like a bell / tolled over a blank square / I am Goya . . .

Not many Western poets would risk such straight-out bardic basso profundo, but one of the bracing things about Voznesensky and his young compatriots is this almost ingenuous straightforwardness, this athleticism of voice and mind which is not afraid to leap strongly, spin gracefully and pose starkly in a brilliant gymnastics of the poetic impulse.

English-speaking readers can watch Voznesensky in action through two important new books [**Antiworlds** and **Voznesensky: Selected Poems**] which take on the impossible task of translating an original and idiosyncratic poet. . . .

The results are some brave misses but some brilliant "overchanges," as Ezra Pound called translations. These catch the gallant bite of Voznesensky's voice and mind, the crisply rhapsodic, vauntingly no-nonsense way in which he turns experience into lyrics flashing with the happy magic of a young man who feels he can outfox a grim-looking future. "We were not born to survive, alas / But to step on the gas," he writes. (p. 93)

In America, "godless / baseball-crazy / gasoline-hazy / America!" he sees the airport, the "crystal giant" with its "Duralumined plate glass . . . / Like an X-ray of the soul"; the ubiquitous beatnik, whom he tells to "Flee into yourself, to the Church, to the john, to Egypt, to Haiti—flee!"; the Negroes, "Homeric tom-toms with doleful eyes," and "The blaze of your buildings, shooting up to the stars, to heaven's outskirts!" He knows that both countries are united in a massively ordered stampede toward precision, and that this is more exciting and dangerous than the refrigerated ideological leftovers of the cold war.

He speaks his contempt for the "Home-bred Iagos" who try to keep the chill on in Russia, but he knows that "folly's world-wide wind" blows everywhere. Voznesensky rides that wind on every supersonic Pegasus he can find. He trained as an architect, "Yet poetry was flowing in me like a river under the ice." The ice melted when the Moscow Architectural Institute burned down and he became Pasternak's protégé. "Pasternak was my god, my father and for a long time my university. When he died I felt that someone had come out of myself. I felt utterly alone. I wanted to die. Then I thought, someone must continue Pasternak's work. And now I'm no longer alone."

Voznesensky thinks of himself as a "patriot of poetry" whose

> prophetic mission in the world . . . is to look deep inside man. When I read my poetry to a great number of people, their emotional, almost sensual, expression of feeling seems to me to reveal the soul of man—now no longer hidden behind closed shutters, but wide open like a woman who has just been kissed.

Voznesensky is a young man with an open heart and a fierce love of language as the carrier of thought and feeling and the connector of people. He and his friends, risking their "Achilles hearts," are trying to bring together again the most private and public energies of what he rightly calls Russia's "national art." (pp. 93-4)

> " 'Step on the Gas'," in Newsweek, *Vol. LXVIII, No. 2, July 11, 1966, pp. 93-4.*

M. L. ROSENTHAL

One of the things that comes through beautifully in [*Antiworlds* and *Selected Poems*] is the erotically charged character of many of the poems. Voznesensky finds woman, in the flesh and in what she symbolizes, not only "interesting" in the normal romantic and sensual ways but irresistibly touching. He is very much like his master Pasternak in this matter, though I think far less subtle. . . . [**"Autumn"**] has to do with the hopeless illicit involvement of lovers whose affair can have no future. [**"First Frost"**] is a winter closeup of a young girl "freezing in a telephone booth"—the freezing is a matter both of weather and of her humiliation, "a beginning of losses". In **"The Last Train to Malakhovka,"** a sequel to this poem, Voznesensky tells of reciting it to a crowd of tough youngsters on the train. It doesn't seem to take, until one of the youngsters, a girl with "that soggy used-up look" whose "blouse records the fingerprints / Of half the boys in Malakhovka", begins to cry stormily and astounds everyone by leaping from the train, "purer than Beatrice". (p. 41)

I cannot, of course, discuss every interesting facet of Voznesensky in so brief a review. He is a satirist (**"Oza,"** *Antiworlds*) who is against the computerization of the soul. He's like us! He can be bitter, "disillusioned", and self-ironic. Like us! Born in 1933, he could not be a revolutionary in the sense that Mayakovsky was, but he is an independent spirit and at the same time deeply immersed in Russian tradition.

> Russia, my country, home of beauty,
> Land of Rublev, Blok, and Lenin,
> Where the snow falls enchantingly. . . .

The fourteenth century painter of ikons, the poet who was so thrilled and shocked at once by the power of the Revolution, and the genius of the Revolution are symbolic dimensions of an idealized vision of national political destiny in which the past, the spirit of poetry, and the most determined political activism are seen to be aspects of a single romantic perspective. Voznesensky is not primarily a political poet, but in a poem like **"I Am Goya"** catches the essence of national tragedy and in **"Oza"** trains his guns on the technocratic-bureaucratic antihumanism of modern life (partly through an exquisitely ludicrous, randy parody of Poe's "The Raven". He hits out sharply at his critics and at those who pry into his doings and affairs, as well as at the cult of Stalin. A slight figure physically—one imagines him proudly holding off the bullies. From an American standpoint, too, there is something archaically engaging about his struggle for feeling as opposed to *efficiency.* That is a privilege of the popular poet, unselfconsciously acting out a poet's role for his hundreds of thousands of readers and hearers. But the imagination is unique and fresh, a function of deeprooted, magnetic personal feeling. (pp. 41-2)

> *M. L. Rosenthal, "Voznesensky in Translation," in* Poetry, *Vol. CX, No. 1, April, 1967, pp. 40-2.*

THE TIMES LITERARY SUPPLEMENT

[Voznesensky's *Antiworlds*] has a notable, and in the end not quite satisfactory, long poem. **"Oza"**, written in alternations of verse and prose, and in a fine variety of metres which at one point parodies Poe's "The Raven", explores the feelings of an artist in a world of science. In one delicate and moving section, already famous, the central theme of protecting gentle and intuitional human values against the encroachments of cybernetics is floated into the image of a pair of woman's slippers, empty but still warm from the feet, lying askew and helpless "like doves perched in the path of a tank". Voznesensky can say "I love Dubna" (the atomic research centre), yet remain deeply suspicious of the research his scientific friends are engaged in: the fragmented body of the poem reflects divisions and uncertainties in his own mind. Is one wrong to be disappointed that such a fine sensibility as his should seem to be adding his voice to the anti-science brigade? He refers to Russia as the land "of Rublev, Blok, and Lenin", which brings together art, poetry, and politics. But Russia is also Lomonosov, Mendeleyev, and Gagarin, and there is nothing to be ashamed of in that.

"Oza" is one of the poems included (in a slightly different version) in *Akhillesovo serdtse.* This rich and pungent volume also prints two other long poems, or poem-cycles, the early **"Master-Craftsmen"** and the poem on Lenin, **"Longjumeau"**, in addition to a wide selection of favourites from previous books and some poems written in 1965 and 1966. The "Achilles heart" of the title is found in one of these recent poems . . . and it is a recurrent theme: if the poet is attacked—if poetry is attacked—the Achilles heel is the heart, secret, suffering, a natural target, yet for all that it would not be fine not to have one. Our effort should be to keep it hard to locate, "as a bird diverts the hunters from its nest".

> *"Siberian Dam and Achilles Heart," in* The Times

Literary Supplement, *No. 3427, November 2, 1967, p. 1039.*

W. GARETH JONES

Andrey Voznesensky has come to be acknowledged as one of the most exciting and talented of contemporary Russian poets. The brilliant sound of his verse, the breathtaking rhythms and rhymes, the sophistication of his visual imagery; in a word, the virtuoso technique of the poet is admitted. Yet praise is given grudgingly. Critics seem to suspect the glitter on the surface of the verse, and its captivating but occasionally strident sound. Can it be that the reader is being hoodwinked by a manipulative technician, and that there is little substance beneath the brilliant surface? (p. 75)

My aim here is to show that Voznesensky has a grasp of life and has something to say about it. To find out what he has to say, the motifs making up his poetic universe must be examined closely, and in particular those recurring images and themes which re-echo throughout his work and are productive of others. Voznesensky's poems should not be read in isolation: the significance of a poem such as **"Parabolicheskaya ballada"** may be distorted, as I shall seek to show, by being treated as an isolated poem. In his collection *Antimiry* the prelude of three poems, **"Monolog rybaka"**, **"Monolog Merlin Monro"**, **"Rublyovskoye shosse,"** which are later repeated, suggests to the reader that this is not a collection of separate lyrics, but a book of poetry to be read as a book. And this work is held together by motifs which appear again and again. The mere statistical recurrence in poetry of certain themes, of course, is not in itself significant. What is important is their weight, their complex of significance, their organising power within a poem and their power to produce new themes. (pp. 75-6)

> It is unbearable when undressed
> in all the posters, in all the papers
> having forgotten,
>   that there is a heart in the centre,
> they wrap herrings in you,
> eyes crumpled,
>   face torn
> (how terrible to recall in
> 'France-Observer'
> one's own photo with its mug
>   self-confident
> on the other side of the dead Marilyn).

Here in **"Monolog Merlin Monro"** is the mainspring of Voznesensky's poetry; the anguished sense of self, abandoned in an indifferent or hostile world, subjected to looks which make one an object. This terrible sense of being looked at, of being an object in a world of contingency is at the centre of the monologue. (p. 76)

Conscious of himself as a hideous object side by side with dead herrings, the poet identifies himself with Marilyn Monroe and chooses her—a thing observed by others—as the symbol of the human condition. As a cinema star, controlled and objectivised by director and producer, she is the extreme case of the human-object stared at by others. On the 100-metre screen in a drive-in cinema she is looked at not by people even, but by motor cars. . . . What drives Marilyn Monroe to suicide is this sense of being watched and contemplated on advertisements in underground, trolleybus and shop, on prairie billboards, a draining of her personality by others

presaged at the beginning of the poem by the heavy tread of *'Komu? S kem? Kto?'*

Again the same horror at being watched is expressed in the poem **"V Amerike, propakhshey mrakom"** . . . with a grim and almost hysterical humour where Voznesensky describes his pursuit by 17 FBI cameras which again capture him in a series of absurd photographic stills, *'Kak plenniki v igre "zamri"!'* The same agony before the crimson eye, 'the staring eyes of Freedom' is felt again and a hint given of the Passion story:

> What torment to be crucified,
>   through every birth-mark,
> When into you from head to toe,
> eyes are lodged like bullets!

(pp. 76-7

Not always is the feeling of being observed expressed with such bitterness. There is wry humour in **"Marshe O Pyus"** where the poet is aware of himself as just another obsolescent object viewed by a Picasso figure with a ball-bearing eye, and in **"N'yu-yorkskaya ptitsa"** where he is under the gaze of a mysterious robot-bird. The gaze may be lyrical in feeling as in **"Lezhat velosipedy"** . . . where the look emanates from the wheels of a pair of bicycles which are a symbol of lovers' bodies. Often this self-consciousness at being watched is linked with an awareness of nakedness. This is an example of the way in which a key theme becomes dominant in its expansion: the sense of being observed is heightened by the expansion of the motif to take in nakedness and is given a strong sense of eroticism. (pp. 77-8)

Despite the horror of being watched, Voznesensky is acutely aware that only in others' eyes does our self have a mould and that we cannot escape this, as we learn in **"Kto my,—fishki ili velikiye?":**

> What are you? What?!—You look with longing
> Into books, through windows—but where are you
>   there?—
> You press as against a telescope,
> against men's immobile eyes!

In this awareness of the other's gaze, there is also an awareness of the distance between you and him, a sense of space. . . . In Voznesensky a key motif expressing this spatiality is that of movement in a restricted line by vehicle—train, motor cycle or car where the passenger, despite the movement, is separated from the natural world and isolated from his fellows. Yet paradoxically in this isolation he is not an individual but part of the mass of an automobile civilisation. This motif interweaves with that of being-looked-at in the drive-in cinema of **"Monolog Merlin Monro"** where the actress is eyed by cars. Merely cutting a way through space without organising it in any way, the apparent determined motion of vehicles, is, in fact, aimless: in this sense suiciders are motor cycle riders. (p. 78)

In his poetry Voznesensky seeks to break free from the shackles of being an object in the world, in order to refashion the world: to volatilise the density of his universe, to lighten its opacity, to regroup the scattered things, and curb its viscosity. And through this apparent paradoxical movement Voznesensky achieves a dynamic equilibrium in his verse.

He faces the world with a hard look. In Voznesensky's poetry neither beauty nor reality lies passively in the eye of the beholder. If he himself is made a victim of another's eyes, then he will turn his own look against the world. It is an intense visual awareness of the universe which is at the base of his work, and it is not surprising that Voznesensky is a graduate of the Moscow Institute of Architecture, does a lot of painting and feels that Andrey Rublyov, Joan Miró and the later Le Corbusier have given him more than Byron. Other artists figure in his poetry: Picasso, Rubens, Raphael, Modigliani. The fascination of the theme of the sequence **"Mastera"** for Voznesensky, perhaps, is that the architects had their artistic life extinguished by having their eyes put out.

We have seen how the poet is observed as an object, and how this motif is interwoven with an awareness of his own body and may be given a specific sexual characteristic. Voznesensky retains the same complex motif when he puts himself into the role of voyeur. In **"Sibirskiye bani"** he plays the faun, observing women leaping naked into the snow from a steaming bath-house (although it is worth noticing how the motif is kept in equilibrium here when one of the women at the close of the poem turns, and by throwing a snowball demonstrates her own ability to objectify another person). In **"Tayga"** the sexual relationship of the watcher and the watched is conveyed by showing a girl caught upside down like a Thomasina Thumb in thousands of dewdrops: she is taken in a look multiplied over and over again in the reflection of the drops. The attack of the watcher is not always playful. It may be cruel as in **"Striptiz"** with its insistent rock'n'roll rhythm and the watching eyes swelling like leeches, although again the motif is kept in equilibrium as the watcher at the end of the poem falls back into the embarrassment and shame of the watched, as the stripteaser faces him, mocks his accent and uses him to order a drink. (p. 80)

Nakedness is an ambiguous quality in Voznesensky. Just as a look can turn him into a mere object, but also enable him to see the world without its false trappings, so nakedness suggesting shame, embarrassment and the selfconsciousness of self may also paradoxically suggest innocence and delight in a dense world made light and fluid. . . . It is through this ambiguity that Voznesensky's motifs are kept in equilibrium.

Undressing an object with an aggressive look is not sufficient in itself to desolidify a dense world. An object remains an object and the voyeur remains impotent. But it is interesting to note that a naked object (or an object in which the body is indicated by fetishist details) often merges with, and drifts into a sensual image of water. Thus the 'plashing' of the girl's clothes in **"Rublyovskoye shosse"** dissolves a solid picture. In **"Tayga"** the lover who is content to observe the girl at a distance in the dewdrops, is aware of the precious instability of the myriad drops of water. Women in these poems (and sometimes their eyes as in **"Pel Tvardovsky v nochnoy Florentsii, B'yut zhenshchinu"**) are often metamorphosed into water as in **"Gornyy rodnichok"** where a girl runs to a mountain spring with her skirt seen as a spraying watering can, so that Voznesensky is able to see two miraculous streams in which it is impossible to say which is the girl and which the spring, so triumphantly are the solid objects of his world dissolved. In this water, of course, one is able to immerse oneself while maintaining one's innocence and integrity: there is a sense of baptism in these water images, the sense that one can fall into the world, and yet save oneself. Thus the beatniks in **"Monolog bitnika"** to save themselves from the 'rapacious things of the age' dive naked into water. (p. 82)

If the solid world can be made to run away in cleansing water, then it is also possible for its opaqueness to be dispelled in fire

and light. . . . Salutes blazing like searchlights across the dark Moscow sky are recalled in **"Gruzinskiye beryozy"** where it is the transparency of the birches that inspires the poet. And again they dispel the solid opacity of the world and achieve a kind of innocence:

> I love their weightlessness
> their most high form
> I check my conscience
> against their white purity.

The blaze of light, which we experience again in **"Reportazh s otkrytiya GES"** is rare in Voznesensky. More usual is the soft transparency or steady translucency which suffuse many of his poems. It is what remains when the poet's aggressive look has stripped away the heaviness of the world. . . . Translucency is sought by the poet, conscious of his own unclothed body in **"Vozvrashcheniye v Siguldu."** He consciously sees his cottage through the hills, as its fertile stone can be seen through the flesh of a plum:

> And our cottage with its three windows
> through the hill among the blocks of forest
> shows, as a stone
> shows through a plum.

Here the idea of translucency expands the cottage into a fertile image. We ourselves are seeds in the greenery drawing thoughts like juices from the earth. The solid oppressiveness of the world dissolves as the cottage windows open their shutters and suck in lilac, a flower which is light, fragmented, yet whose fragmentation is contained within a definite form: this is a recurring image in Voznesensky's poetry. . . . (pp. 83-4)

Lilac, green, the blue of the sky, the silver of birch, the red of plum and cherry: these are Voznesensky's key colours creating the translucency and luminosity which breaks down the oppressive solidity of his world of doubt.

When Voznesensky indicated Andrey Rublyov as an artist with whom he was in sympathy, no doubt he had in mind the characteristic luminosity and exceptional transparency of the great icon painter's palette whose colour range too is similar to Voznesensky's. Rublyov used colour to create an illusion of lightness and airiness within a solid design: in this way he sought to show grace, innocence and spirituality through the material. It is this tradition that Voznesensky follows in breaking down the density of his world by the luminosity and translucency of his images. . . . (p. 84)

We have traced then the main outlines of Voznesensky's verse. He is acutely aware of himself, of his own body and embarrassed by the sense of being yet another object in a world of valueless objects, a world at times oppressive in its heaviness and density and at times frightening in its fugitive fragmentariness. This is his sense of fallenness, his metaphysical doubt. But Voznesensky does not rest there. As an artist, he is able to attack the world and affirm himself. The seen becomes the seer. The object becomes the triumphant subject. He volatilises the density of the world and lightens its darkness so that in the luminosity of what has been made transparent true existence becomes apparent. And he gives shape and life to a drifting fragmentary universe by his dynamic curves and parabolas.

Voznesensky is also a civic poet who has written a number of poems on the theme of Lenin. What is interesting in these poems is to see how Lenin is placed firmly within the general topography of Voznesensky's poetry (and it is, therefore, difficult to agree with Sir Maurice Bowra [in his *Poetry and Politics, 1900-1960*] that **"Lonzhyumo"** is a poem 'which, despite considerable eloquence and ingenuity, is profoundly conformist at heart.') Lenin appears in these poems not in any social or historical situation, but within that condition of metaphysical doubt felt by the objectified person. (pp. 86-7)

[As] the poet and artist is able to use his eyes to refashion his universe, so is Lenin:

> Direct and with a large forehead like a lens,
>   he gathered into an angry focus,
> what the hall thought.

Even in death, Lenin looks through people like an X-ray in his mausoleum. In the Russian game of gorodki (where the aim is to hit wooden chocks piled in certain patterns out of an area with a wooden stave) we see Lenin screwing up his eyes in order to attack with them. . . . Just as the poet's eye attacks the solidity of his world, so the Leninist eye aims to shatter the geometrical solidity of the chock patterns within the contingency of the game. For the player the disarray of the chocks, the destruction of the careful pattern signifies something positive. The scattered blocks of wood in their random positions signify paradoxically that the player is 'scoring in the game'. It is in this way that Leninism scatters the conventional geometrical shapes of imperialism, clericalism, and fascism. Out of these conventional shapes comes a creative randomness. Lenin, like the artist, dissipates and dissolves things but the destruction is kept in equilibrium and we become the witnesses of creative metamorphoses. (pp. 87-8)

Brittleness, brashness, technical brilliance are not merely qualities of Voznesensky's verse but an integral part of what he has to say about his existence. Face to face with a world in which existence may appear gratuitous and obscene, Voznesensky on the one hand gives acute expression to this human predicament while simultaneously wrestling with it and attempting to bring his world to a tense, dynamic equilibrium. In this he evokes the aid of artists, and, more boldly, Lenin who is less of an historical than an existential Lenin set firmly within the topography of Voznesensky's poetical universe. (p. 90)

> *W. Gareth Jones, "A Look Around: The Poetry of Andrey Voznesensky," in* The Slavonic and East European Review, *Vol. XLVI, No. 106, January, 1968, pp. 75-90.*

EDWIN MORGAN

[The following excerpt originally appeared in a slightly different form in Vol. I of Scottish International, *January, 1968.]*

The honour of a poet may be said to subsist in a double commitment. Towards defined values he reacts with a vigilant curiosity that can still acknowledge dependence, kinship, stance, era. For undefined values he reserves his deepest receptiveness, prepared to take on boarders, fight fires, or abandon ship as the case may direct. (p. 71)

A poet may have to bury and hide himself like a bulb, for anything to grow. Distraction is continuous, enormous, fascinating, and frightening. Roles are adopted and discarded. The self shrinks, shudders, makes covert decisions, asks terrible questions. A poetry which wants meaningfully to interlock with this age must be prepared to be vulnerable, fluid, various, adventurous, and searching. It is in connection with such

speculations and demands as these that the poetry of Andrei Voznesensky seems to be both diagnostically and absolutely of great interest. I would like to start discussing it from an example, an extract from a long poem included in his volume *Akhillesovo serdtse* (1966):

> Everything flows. Everything changes.
> One thing passes into another.
> Squares go slipping into ellipses.
> Nickel-plated bedstead-ribs
> flow like boiling macaroni.
> Dungeon portcullises dangle
> like pretzels or shoulder-knots.
>
> Henry Moore
> red-cheeked English sculptor,
> drifted over the billiard-cloth
> of his well-trimmed lawns.
> The sculptures gleamed like billiard-balls,
> but sometimes they swam off like a flux, and sometimes
> took jewel-shapes of pelvic joints.
> 'Stay still!' Moore cried. 'You are beautiful! . . . '
> They never stayed still though.
>
> A flock of smiles swam through the streets.
>
> In the world's ring, two wrestlers embraced panting.
> Orange and black.
> Their breasts pressed hard together. They stood moving
>   sideways
> on vertical pliers.
>
> Bu-ut how horrible!
> Menacing black stains began to spread on the orange back.
> Something was seeping through.
> With a neat ruse, orange twisted his rival's ear
> and howled with pain—
> from his own ear.
> It had flowed across to its antagonist.
>
> Sentences unstable. Wordspressedtogetherinonephrase.
> Consonants dissolving.
> Only vowels left now.
> 'Oaue aoie oaaoeaia! . . . '
>
> That's what I'm screaming.
> They wake me up. They thrust the icy thermometer under
>   my armpit.
>
> I look up in terror at the ceiling.
> It's square.
>
> **("Sketch of a Long Poem")**

Voznesensky's concern with the theme of metamorphosis, which this passage brings out fairly clearly, has three aspects. It reflects the quite real blurring, overlap, interchange, and evolution of forms which fast travel, cinema and television, modern art, and newspaper and advertising techniques have made a familiar part of experience; it has, in its Russian context, a quasi-Aesopian function in that without lifting the blunt instrument of allegory it helps to recommend disavowal of the monolithic; and perhaps most important, it tries to resurrect the creative imagination through a development of that linguistic *ostranenie* ('dislodgement', 'alienation', 'making strange') which the Russian formalist critics of the 1920s saw as central to poetic vigour. In the poem, instability and paradox are shown as features of modern life that are at least as unavoidable (if one is open to the signs of change) as dogma and explanation. This is expressed partly by hyperbolic and often comic imagery (metal bedsteads flowing like macaroni), and also by the references to art and ideology. The name of Henry Moore is carefully chosen—the English words having a functional 'strangeness' in their Russian context, his works having that combination of 'flow' and hardness which the poem is concerned with, and Moore being recognized as an influence on a Soviet sculptor like Neizvestny whom Voznesensky and other poets admire despite official disapproval. Many of Moore's sculptures are usually variable as you walk round them, and photographs of them taken from different angles can be almost unrelatable. Voznesensky presents the sculptor himself as being humorously exasperated, but also pleased, by this fluidity, and one remembers the rather similar attitude of the poet himself to architectural forms in his poem **"New York Airport at Night"**, where he talks in terms of a 'mastery of immaterial structures', and sees the airport as advancing far beyond the beauty of stone. . . . [One] is aware of how often the theme of America recurs in his poetry, and of how deep and confused his feelings about America are. The politically dangerous metamorphosis of becoming what you begin by sympathetically observing is what lies behind some Soviet criticisms of Voznesensky's American poems. It might be all right to have airports like New York's, but not the beatniks and striptease as well, though the poet presents these with equal vividness. This criticism is misplaced, since if Voznesensky trails his American coat a little, this is done largely as part of a broader strategy, in which he can see himself and Robert Lowell, and poets in other countries too, as the necessary gnoseologists of 'this age' in its non-ideological aspect, post-Stalin but also post-Kennedy, post-Hiroshima but also post-Sputnik, post- so many things that for all its baffling malaise and hideous Vietnams it seems like an age about to be one of extraordinary beginnings. (pp. 71-4)

But not easily, not obviously. 'Words strain, / Crack and sometimes break, under the burden . . . / Will not stay still.' It is both ironic and yet only true that Voznesensky of all people—a master of poetic language—should claim to find words failing him ('only vowels left now') when he tries to make language accompany and define the transformations of the world. Perhaps, like Kafka's Gregor Samsa, the speaker is 'sick', but he does not wake up one morning transformed into a gigantic insect—he is wakened from a nightmare of the dissolution of language into the simple daylight terror of looking up at a square ceiling. The terror of the rational square is worse than the irrational metamorphoses of bedsteads, sculptures, ears, sentences, and words.

This would suggest that 'flowing' is almost a metaphor for change, seen under the double aspect of the upsettingness of anything new and the attractiveness of any reversal of roles. On balance, the attraction is greater than the upset, because of the rigid cultural context the poet works in and seeks to prise open through exaggeration and fantasy.

Many poems take up this 'prising open' process, from different angles. In the simplest ones, a slightly startling but naturalistically based analogy is used. The leather-clad Amazon of **"Motorcycle Stunts on the Vertical Wall"** is bored with 'living vertically' on the ground and as soon as she steps off her motorcycle her eyes are filled with 'horizontal nostalgia'. Here, the hazardous but thrilling human displacement of the wall-of-death ride is allowed to reverberate as an idea without being pushed into any statement about the restricting verticality or uprightness of conventional life. The rider has been metamorphosed, through habit, into a creature living at right angles to the norm, but the poem surrounds her with a grotesque humour which salts away any straightforward recommendations.

In **"Wings"**, a similar idea is developed farther.

> The gods are dozing like slummocks—
> Clouds for layabouts!
>   What hammocks!
>
> The gods are for the birds.
> The birds are for the birds.
>
> What about wings,
> all that paraphernalia?
> It's too weird, I tell you.
> What did the ancients see in these things?
> Nearer
>   and nearer
>   to the fuselage
> clouds press them in,
>   to a vestige-
> ality of winginess on our things,
> our marvel-machines, strange
> to them. Men have unslung
> something new, men don't hang
> out wings, men are with it, bang.
> Man, men are winged!

In the ages of time, men become the gods they once adumbrated. The wings they gave deities they take to themselves, but in the process of becoming truly 'winged', men go through the metamorphoses—from Leonardo to the Wright Brothers to Gagarin—of inventing, developing, and then discarding actual wings. The light, buoyant tone of the poem is not too light to conceal the joy of tracing an enormous, but enormously slow, change in human exploratory capability. And who is to say whether Gagarin was living vertically or horizontally?

In two poems, **"Foggy Street"** and **"Earth"**, Voznesensky presents first a naturally and then an imaginarily transformed environment. In the former poem, the poet delights in the confusions and errors induced by fog—bumping into people, mistaking men for women, interpreting or misinterpreting disembodied objects like car-lights, a glimpse of a cheek or a moustache, everything "in pieces, disconnected as delirium'. At the end rationality returns and he wishes he could send the fog packing, but only after he has given us, in the main picture, the pleasures of distorted perception. **"Earth"**, on the other hand, combines a strong feeling for the actuality and thinginess and inescapability of our planet as it is, with a Chagall-like dream of what it might be. The second half of the poem projects two futures—or perhaps they are the same future, seen in a science-fiction aspect—in which change is beautifully balanced between surreal fantasy and scientific progress, but in both cases tied to and emerging from and acknowledging the familiar and the old. Man transforms both himself and his world, and what characterizes Voznesensky is the joy he takes in envisaging the transformations; but there is nothing vapidly optimistic about the joy. Wherever he goes and whatever he does, man takes with him his handful of earth, his handful of pain, of history and remembrance.

> An earth in dreams appeared to me, without trenches and
>   chains,
> without detonation of mines: a dream of telescopes,
> of lime-trees, eucalyptus, peacock rain-
> bows, lifts on crazy ropes
> and showers of aluminium!
> A world of seas, of trains, of women—
> a world all puffing and
> fructifying,
> marvellous as man! . . .

Somewhere on Mars he goes, a visitor from Earth.
He walks. He smiles. He takes out a handful of earth—
a tiny handful of that burning,
half-bitter, homely,
far-whirling,
heart-catching earth!

Transformation of environment can of course be used for satirical purposes, and Voznesensky is not lacking in satire. But he has evolved a peculiar brand of metasatire where the social, aesthetic, or moral criticism is so closely plaited with comic, lyric, and hallucinatory elements that to speak of reformism or didacticism would be well off the mark. In **"Paris without Rhyme"** he starts off by observing how clean Paris is becoming, building after building being sandblasted under M. Malraux's instructions until a new city seems to be emerging. But why stop there? Why not blast the walls away altogether, see what the city is really like under the protective shell of architecture? So there is a sudden transformation-scene: Notre Dame minus its walls is only a rose-window hanging over the square like a traffic-sign, in a room a teapot-shaped mass of tea stands without a pot, people whose heads have been screwed off walk about with their thoughts 'whistling there like birds in wire cages', an OAS man's mad pate holds Sartre smouldering away in a frying-pan, a striptease girl starts to peel off not her clothes but her skin until the poet is sent shuddering back to normality at the moment of horror when he sees nothing but the whites of her eyes 'dead and blank like insulators, in that dreadful howling burning face'. He is sitting in the world of solid walls; with his friends; eating a melting ice. Yet the poem ends with a curiously disturbing transfusion of Hieronymus Bosch into the normal city of 1962:

> But through the window and through the centuries
> motorcyclists race
>   in their white helmets
> like fiends from hell with chamber-pots.

This extraordinary poem, reminding us of some of the difficulties of interpreting Swift's 'woman flayed', shows a complex irony at work, and also something which is not irony at all. The woman peeling off her skin 'like tights' is beyond being a comment on the decadence of striptease, even though the juxtaposition of 'dead eyes' and 'howling face' at once suggests some such deadening of the spirit, a silent screaming from some accepted indignity that only a poet can hear and report. Since the poem runs the gamut from playfulness to horror, it may be that Voznesensky, like Swift, is pointing out both the necessity and the dangers of 'stripping off appearances' and trying to reach the raw truth. The woman was screaming, certainly; but why should Mass not be celebrated in a cathedral without walls?

In a sensitive and beautiful love-poem, **"Autumn in Sigulda"**, Voznesensky describes a parting and separation, and in doing so he makes metamorphosis a central feature of the interdependence of life—

> but o you are going away, going away,
> as a train goes, you are going away,
> out from my empty pores you are going away,
> each of us goes, we separate, we go on our way,
> was this house wrong for us, who can say?
>
> you are near me and somewhere far off,
> Vladivostok is no farther off,
> I know our lives come round again
> in friends and lovers, grass and grain,

changed into that, and those, and this,
nature abhorring emptiness . . .

the old saw about nature reflecting here a Pasternakian sense of the dissolving of the artist into the lives of others, a perpetual renewal under perpetual conditions of change, the lost and mysterious seeds of the personal life transformed into a general standing grain in the fullness of time. Not only from, but to, everything flows. (pp. 75-8)

> *Edwin Morgan, "Heraclitus in Gorky Street: The Theme of Metamorphosis in the Poetry of Andrei Voznesensky," in his* Essays, *Carcanet New Press Ltd., 1974, pp. 71-8.*

CLIVE JAMES

[Voznesensky] is blessed with such a way of putting things that he can vault the language barrier as if it were a low fence. In a poem called **"Winter at the Track"** he talks of a frozen bird hanging in the air like an ornament, and a dead horse on its back with its soul sticking up out of its mouth like a corkscrew from a penknife. All he means is that the temperature is forty-five below zero centigrade, but somehow the simplest statement comes out like a burst of colored lights. Going overboard about Voznesensky seems, at first reading, the only decent thing to do.

But after intoxication comes the hangover. Viewed soberly, Voznesensky's poetry has the same limitations as most other Soviet literature which has ever been officially published, except that in his case the limitations are even more glaring. Lesser talents might profit from not being allowed to speak out directly: they can palm off evasiveness as ambiguity. But Voznesensky is transparently a case of the poet who, in Mayakovsky's famous phrase, stands on the throat of his own song.

With good reason, Voznesensky is a hero to all those in the Soviet Union who want their poets to tell them the truth. But at the risk of his career, freedom, and perhaps even his life, he has never been able to do much more than drop hints. Reading his work through from the beginning, you can see that what ought to be his main subject matter is hardly there. When the subject is the history of his own country, everything he has to say is tangential. And eventually, because he is unable to state the plain truth about his own time and place, he is unable to state the plain truth about any other time and place. The result is a kind of false complexity, a string of profundities that do not add up to much. (p. 14)

[The] truly subversive moments in *Antiworlds* are all indirect. Instead of condemning Stalin he comes out with a no-holds-barred, knock-down-and-drag-out assault on Peter the Great. Peter the Great is portrayed as a monster engaged in butchering his erstwhile favorite, Anna Mons. (pp. 14-15)

I am afraid that *Nostalgia for the Present* has all the disappointing aspects of *Antiworlds* plus a few new ones. But first we should remind ourselves that Voznesensky remains a talent of the first class. His books are important, whatever use he might be making of his gifts. . . . Voznesensky's verbal facility still seems unimpaired.

Beginners with Russian should beware of falling for what sounds like musicality: they could be making the same mistake as all those Frenchmen who thought that Poe wrote subtle verse. But even the fledgling can tell that Voznesensky's tricks with alliteration are something better than mere echolalia. He has an effortless mimetic knack. The humbler translators have done their best to transmit some of this, but even when they despair of the attempt there is still a lot of straightforward imagery which would be fascinating in any language. Those without any Russian will find plenty to enjoy. All they will need is a receptive heart for the poet's unbounded charm. In **"From a Diary"** we find him lying on a bed with a young lady citizen of New York.

> Who in his right mind would have thought
> That here in New York we'd lie upon
> This pillow one day, opened out
> Like a Russian-English lexicon?

No wonder the girls go crazy about him. There is more of the same in **"Christmas Beaches,"** where yet another young lady is to be found prostrated on a bed beside the poet, with the shadow of the shutters lying on her "like a striped sailor's shirt." (p. 15)

[*Nostalgia for the Present*] is rich with fine conceits. By now Voznesensky has been hailed as a cultural hero all over the world. He hails the world right back. He loves Paris in the springtime, he loves San Francisco in the fall.

But again he has not very much specific to say about the Soviet Union. Sloth, bribery, and regimentation all get it in the neck. He mocks the thousands of geniuses who make up the Writers' Union. There is a deserved hymn, with no sensitive names mentioned, to the Russian intelligentsia as the collective guardian of human values. But that's about it. All other criticisms are indirect at best. More often they are just vague.

Arthur Miller, in his introductory note, gets it exactly wrong when he talks about poems that "cut close to the bone on sensitive public issues." The sensitive public issues remain safe when knives are as blunt as these. In **"On the Death of Shukshin"** Voznesensky mourns the famous writer/actor as "the conscience of the nation." But Shukshin died of natural causes and his quarrel with authority was about the pollution of Lake Baikal. (pp. 15-16)

"Ice Block" is a poem about "man's guilt before nature." It appears that man should feel particularly guilty about—Dachau. Of Vorkuta or Karaganda, no mention. The inevitable effect is to deprive Dachau of some of its context and therefore of much of its meaning. In **"Darkmotherscream"** Marina Tsvetaeva gets in very obliquely, and it is hard to avoid the conclusion that it is possible to mention her only because she killed herself, and was not, on the face of it anyway, killed by somebody else. (Tsvetaeva committed suicide in Yelabuga concentration camp in 1941. Several of Voznesensky's contemporaries, most notably [Bella] Akhmadulina, have written poems about her, but always without going into much detail about what brought her to such a pass.) . . .

All these hints and evasions are unsatisfactory but you can't ask the man to put his head on the block. The culprit is the Soviet Union, not Voznesensky. Alas, there are other sad aspects of the book in which the culprit is Voznesensky and not the Soviet Union. The star status which Voznesensky has enjoyed on his trips to the West might not have swelled his head, but it has certainly inflated his rhetoric. In numerous poems about his junkets abroad he almost achieves the difficult feat of sounding as fatuous as Yevtushenko. In an awful poem called **"Lines to Robert Lowell"** he apostrophizes History ("You, history, are the moan / of crucified prophets"),

congratulates the Poet for his propensity to suffer ("The poet thrusts his body / like a tolling bell / against the dome of insults"), and holds a meaningful dialogue with his means of transport ("And you, my plane, where are you flying / in this darkness?"). . . .

There is worse to come. Aping Lowell's portentousness, Voznesensky is at least in no danger of slumming. Unfortunately he is equally thrilled by the profundities of Allen Ginsberg, as in **"American Buttons."**

> I love Greenwich Village
> with its sarcastic buttons.
> Who's the shaggy one who showed up
> cock & balls in dark glasses?
> It's Allen, Allen, Allen!
> Leap over Death's carnival,
> Allen, in your underwear!

(p. 16)

It is not because of jet-lag, hash, or willing American maidens that Voznesensky can so readily pick a side in such an inane debate. Nor, I think, is it a result of the parochialism from which even the most astute artists in a closed society are bound to suffer. He ends up making empty remarks about the US because he started making empty remarks about the USSR. The more he travels, the less he has to say. There is no mystery about the reason. Had he tried to say anything definite, the Soviet authorities would have arranged a different form of travel for him, within the borders of his own country.

There is something terrible about hearing a poet of Voznesensky's ability say vaporous things about world merchants of death, etc. Nobody ever expected Yevtushenko to become a mature artist. But of Voznesensky it was the least we could expect. Yet on this showing he has not done so. The fact is sad but not surprising. For a poet, to be denied one word means that all the others are not enough. Voznesensky has been denied the most fundamental truths about the country in which he grew up. Unable to be frank about those, he is unable to be frank about anything else either. Without the possibility of frankness there can be no true ambiguity, obliqueness, subtlety, or depth. There can only be obfuscation.

People should give up talking as if in the case of the Soviet Union the second law of thermodynamics has been suspended. The notion that poetry benefits from repression is essentially vulgar: it is a version of the equally vulgar idea that politics are not real unless they are extreme. The mass audience for poetry in the Soviet Union exists only because of the fleeting possibility that in poems some elementary truth might be mentioned, or at least alluded to, or anyway not denied outright. Poetry which exhausts most of its energy hinting at some forbidden topic is inevitably trivial. It is balderdash to suggest that the Soviet authorities repress poetry because they take it seriously. All they take seriously is what poetry might bring with it—open discussion of the historical facts. (pp. 16-17)

For the moment Voznesensky has had most of his privileges suspended by the Soviet authorities. While he has made brief trips abroad, he has been denied permission to give readings at home—for a Soviet poet, no light punishment. The immediate cause of all this disfavor was Voznesensky's temerity in publishing a cluster of unofficial poems in the *samizdat* magazine *Metropol*. It could be that I am missing some hidden meanings, but as far as I can see these unofficial poems are not very different from his official ones. The most subversive poem of the bunch seems to be the one addressed to Derzhavin, the favored court poet in Catherine the Great's time. Voznesensky puns on his name (which is like one of the words for "power"), compares the old boy to a double-headed eagle (the imperial symbol), and congratulates him on at least being able to talk to himself.

The implication is that a poet of the present day can't be frank even when alone. What we have to imagine is a country where to write such a poem is correctly regarded as an act of daring not just by the authorities, but by the poet himself. . . .

Unofficial poetry is a brave try. But most of it is written by official poets leading double lives, with the implication that their official lives are fake. Worse circumstances for the production of poetry would be hard to imagine. Poetry is not just facts, but it can't start without them. It is no use saying that Voznesensky might simply be an apolitical poet. If he can't *choose* to be apolitical, we can never tell. In a long and scrappy poem called **"Story Under Full Sail,"** printed near the end of *Nostalgia for the Present,* Voznesensky gives the game away.

> It's shameful to spot a lie and not
> to name it,
> shameful to name it and then to
> shut your eyes,
> shameful to call a funeral a
> wedding
> and play the fool at funerals
> besides.

The speaker is the nineteenth-century buccaneering court chamberlain Rezanov, but it might as well be the poet himself. . . . With typical obliqueness, but this time with real point, Voznesensky is saying that the Soviet Union must face the truth about its past. Until that happens, every aspect of Soviet life will go on being distorted, the arts not least. When the alternatives are death, exile, or silence, we should be glad that Voznesensky has settled for stardom. But he could have had stature, if only things had been different. (p. 17)

> Clive James, "Voznesensky's Case," in The New York Review of Books, Vol. XXVI, No. 13, August 16, 1979, pp. 14-17.

ANDREI VOZNESENSKY [INTERVIEW WITH **QUENTIN VEST** AND **WILLIAM CRAWFORD WOODS**]

[Vest and Woods]: *I wonder if you think there is a connection between poetry and alcohol, or drugs, or more specifically between poetry and what [Arthur] Rimbaud called derangement of the senses.*

[Voznesensky]: There is some connection. But if you drink a lot it's not so good, because it's *instead* of. I see more of a connection with sex. Flesh and blood. When you are tired after sex, it's very hard to make a reading. I'm not an actor. I only try to repeat my way of writing poetry, you see. I remember my feelings, and I remember the circumstances. If I sometimes change the style of one or another poem, it's because I'm not a machine, I'm not a robot. Giving a reading gives me physical pleasure. And when the audience is good to you, you get to read better; they are coming to you and you

to them—another example of the connection between sex and reading. But I tried marijuana here, as an experiment, when I was very close to Allen Ginsberg.

Other drugs too?

Allen once gave me one he said was a little bit like LSD but something new. It was a white drug and I became very ill after. It was very strange. I took this drug when I was staying at the Chelsea Hotel; Allen gave me this drug and went away. I spent most of the day in a blackout. But I later had to get up and go read in Town Hall. I was a little high. I thought, "People will think I am drunk." I was in a strange mood. For the first time in my life I forgot my lines, and didn't know why I was there. But when I saw the audience and after Robert Lowell (I think) introduced me, my old reflexes began working again. I was like a reading machine. It was very difficult for me to come on to the music of poetry because of this drug experience. I read the first poem by instinct; the second poem was hard but then it got better and better as the poetry took over and the drug went away. And I forgot about the drug. One doctor told me that it was very good; I was destroyed after the reading; I was not longing for more drugs. Drugs don't help poetry. When you try to write on pot, you think it's very good, but you are false because you have no real feelings. You think it is very good, but later when you read it, it's bullshit.

Do you like Ginsberg's poetry?

Yes, I like his "Howl." I love "Howl" and "Kaddish." He came to see me in the Soviet Union, and people thought he was mad. He went to Mayakovsky's grave and fell down crying and weeping and praying to him. He is very interesting. I feel he is a type of guru. We had a very good reading together on a ferryboat in New York. I read my poems and he read translations. But I'm very sad that at another reading, somebody I don't know personally said, "Please don't ask Allen to come to the stage, because so-and-so will be upset, they don't approve of him." I was upset and I repeated this to Allen who said, "Oh, Andrei, don't start anything please. I'll be here in the hall, in the auditorium. I'll be happy." But I like to read together with him, because he is a great performer. We read in a church once, for Bangladesh.

Stepping into the middle of our literary wars must seem strange to you.

It is a little bit strange, yes. But you see, I'm not a chauvinist. I would not say only good words about my country, only good words about our poets. There's a lot of backstage intrigue among some of our poets. They too are jealous of one another. And I hate this jealousy. You ask one of our poets about another, and he says, "Oh, no—he's not—well, he's nice of course—but he's a piece of shit." I hate it. (pp. 100-02)

Do you think your background in architecture has a great deal to do with your poetry?

Yes. The essential question in either case is one of structure. When I first began writing, I was condemned as a formalist. In Russia, that's a dirty word, certainly according to socialist critical dogma at that time: Pasternak was considered a formalist. But I had to think of structure, of form. I think it's man's duty to be accurate. Man can't just be blah, blah, blah, without end. When you make a building, the form must be sound—sound forever. And I think it is the same in poetry. Yes? It is like architecture. You need a style as much as a bathroom. If the construction is good for your time, it will be good for all time.

Is there anybody in particular you trust to tell you when a poem's no good?

Not really. I test my work on friends, but I never do as they advise me. Poems have their own fates, like children. You have only to give birth to them. Certainly, you struggle for them: to publish, to get them read and heard. But I'm a little fatalistic about the destiny of a given poem.

Do you feel separated from a poem, once you've completed it?

Yes. Although I can make a new connection in a public performance, particularly with my most recent work. That's why I feel sad not to have been able to read my very new poems on this tour; there's been no time to have them translated. In a performance in Russia, I read for two or three hours without a break; the first hour is all new stuff. After that, the audience sends up requests. Sometimes they set up questions—they try to turn the reading into a press conference, which I don't like, though some of my friends like that kind of thing. Yevtushenko likes it very much. He loves public meetings, speeches, discussions. I don't like to mix that up with readings. It breaks the mood, like jokes after church. (pp. 104-05)

Sometimes when you perform the same poem—a very famous poem like "Goya," say—over and over again, does it lose meaning for you? Or change meaning?

I never read **"Goya"** in Russia anymore. And I try not to read it here. Still, I think it brings me luck because it was the first poem I read in the West. And, yes, it does change. A poem like **"Master Craftsmen"**—the one with all the Russian bell sounds in it—changes even more. American bells aren't Russian bells. The readings at public performances are different than what are on the records. On stage, I'm another person, I do everything by instinct—maybe in Russia more than here, because here the program is more rigid. I'm always afraid to give a dead performance, to make a dead thing. In Russia, I never know what poem I'll read. Even here, I never know what mood I'll be in. Readings are irrational, instinctive, gut. They melt analysis and intellect from the printed poem. Not like when you read the page—then you have time for intellectual analysis. (pp. 105-06)

Have you had to field a lot of political questions on this American tour?

Not so much. Perhaps they've wanted to protect me. In any case, whatever I want to express politically, I express in my poetry. A poet can't give you opinions—he can only give you a way of thinking, a method. Isn't it more important to teach people how to think than tell them what to think? My poetry is complex, but I like to think that it is a key that opens up other questions: to sexual life, social life, political life. It's more important that I do *that* than that I answer, as a poet, specific political questions—like, say, should Sadat go to Israel. Certainly, I have my opinion about that as a man. But as a poet, we have only to give a key. A crystal of harmony. (p. 106)

Are there moments when you're afraid you won't be able to write anymore?

Yes. I am afraid. Because I am full of Russian superstition. You have the same myths in your country: a poet writes only when he is young and sexy and he's got it all together. I'm afraid that one day it will stop coming, because for me it all depends on gut, on instinct. Yes, certainly I am afraid that one day I will stop like many poets long before my time. Where is wood? I want to knock on wood.

But you had for yourself the example of Pasternak. You knew him when he was very old, and he didn't stop.

Pasternak was fantastic. He was a great poet. He stopped writing poetry because of Stalin. That was before the war—he said he didn't want to write any more poetry. But he couldn't say that openly. There's a story; I don't know all the details. The sense of the story is that after Stalin declared that Mayakovsky was the greatest Soviet poet of the age, Pasternak wrote Stalin a letter. This was a very dangerous thing to do, but Pasternak was careless about his safety. In his letter he said that if Stalin believed that Mayakovsky was the greatest poet of the age, that was very good; but he, Pasternak, would now drop a burden from his shoulders: the fate of Russian poetry. After that, he only did translations, the Shakespeare plays. And he refused to take part in his own anniversary celebrations. He refused all honors, everything. Pasternak never wrote any primitive, official poems, and yet he was not arrested. Perhaps it was because of that letter people say he wrote to Stalin. It was rumored that Stalin said that Pasternak was a holy fool and should be left alone. Then, during the war, it was as if Pasternak had been born again. He began to write great poetry, in a new style for him, very classical. I had first met him when I was a child, a boy of fourteen. Perhaps Pasternak's example helps me in my life.

When you're not on tour, when you're at home, do you have a regular working schedule? (pp. 107-08)

I don't schedule. Nobody does. In Russia, everything is improvisation. Nobody can tell where he'll be on Friday night. Let me give you an example. When I came to America, I wanted very much to visit my dear friend Robert Lowell's grave. We drove out from Boston in the late afternoon—a dinner had been arranged for that evening. It was dark by the time we found the grave in the forest. I was with a young poet from Boston, and I said to him, "Please, I'm sorry, excuse me, it is impolite, but leave me alone, go to your car, I want half-an-hour alone." Then I began to write poetry. Later I asked him to find a phone and call the people and tell them we wouldn't come to dinner. They were all friends of Lowell's and they were very upset with me. But how could I have gone to a dinner party and broken the mood of that encounter? Even if I hadn't been writing a poem, I couldn't have gone to a party after that visit to his grave. (pp. 108-09)

[In America] there are more people claiming to be poets than there are buying books of poetry.

In Russia, the same problem. Poetry is as popular as rock music is here. Everybody writes poetry. Everybody wants to be a poet. It's frightening. It might be possible for a nation to have ten or twenty gifted poets. It might be possible to have a hundred. But several thousand? The mathematics are alarming. But I don't know. Maybe there will come a time on earth when everybody *can* write poetry. A genetic change. After all, we all carry the gene of poetry. (p. 109)

Andrei Voznesensky, Quentin Vest and William Crawford Woods, in an interview in The Paris Review, *Vol. 22, No. 78, Summer, 1980, pp. 94-109.*

MICHAEL BINYON

[Vosnesensky] is virtually a household name throughout the Soviet Union. He first burst into print in 1960 during the turbulent Khrushchev years and has never since been far from controversy. A disciple of Pasternak, whom he recently honoured in an impressive memoir that for the first time brought the poems from *Dr Zhivago* into public print, he is an arresting, lyrical poet, an avowed modernist of intensely expressed emotion and complex imagery. His works have been translated into a dozen languages.

Poetry in Russia has always appealed to a wider audience than in most countries. But Voznesensky has built up a mass following that is astonishing, especially in view of his abstruse metaphors and intellectual challenge. . . .

He is called the voice of his generation—a compliment he dislikes as he feels it limits his poetry to a certain time and place. He has come under intense political pressure to express the correct political message—though thanks to well-timed silences he remains one of the few writers, officially still in favour, who has never compromised.

But the paradoxical advantage is that he has been able to stay an individual.

> Only an individual expressing his individuality can give anything to the ordinary person. You believe in yourself if you know millions are waiting for your voice. I cannot give people any answers. But I can put the questions, suggest ways of looking at things, help people to be brave and analyse their feelings.

His poetry reflects the changing concerns of Soviet society. As an outspoken and often wild young man—he once blew his entire foreign royalties on a reckless week's spree in Rome—he mirrored the hopes and naivety of the post-Stalin thaw. Now he is more cautious—as he says, "more cautious—as he says, "more classical"—but at the same time has taken up new and typical obsessions: the search for the mystical in a cynical and disillusioned age, interest in the occult and extrasensory forces.

He has also turned increasingly to pop music. He wrote the words for **"Drum"**, a number one hit last year, and this summer turned one of his longer narrative poems into a rock opera that began its run last week in a theatre besieged by eager fans.

Voznesensky was amused at one recent poetry reading to find all the questions were about his next pop song: he writes pop lyrics for a joke. But it is one he takes half seriously, believing that pop music, the mass culture of today, can lead people to more profound poetry.

Michael Binyon, "Prime Time Poet Who Spurns the Party Line," in The Times, *London, November 2, 1981, p. 8.*

ANNE CHISHOLM

Poets in Russia, if not banned or exiled, are regarded as romantic, visionary characters. Recently, one of the most romantically famous, Andrei Voznesensky, was in London in connection with a British TV production of a remarkable rock opera, **Juno and Avos,** based on a true love story between a Russian nobleman and a Spanish-American girl. . . .

For the past two years, the rock opera for which he wrote the libretto, has been packed out at every performance in Moscow. Tickets change hands at high prices on the black market. Why, in his view, is it such a huge success, especially with the young?

'I think first because it is a real love story,' said Voznesensky, without hesitation. He speaks good English. 'Romeo and Juliet is fiction. This is reality.'

The opera is based on the romance between Count Rezanov, a 42-year-old Russian soldier and explorer, and Conchita, a 16-year-old daughter of the Spanish governor of California. They met in 1805, when Rezanov arrived as the Tsar's envoy in San Francisco looking for trade and a strategic foothold. They were betrothed, despite her parents' opposition, but Rezanov then had to return to Moscow to obtain permission from the Tsar for himself and a dispensation from the Pope for Conchita.

On this journey he died in the wastes of Siberia. Conchita waited for him for 35 years. Eventually she entered a Dominican convent and lived as a nun until her death in 1857.

Voznesensky came across the story—well-known in the United States—on a trip to Canada, and wrote a long poem about it. Back in Moscow, he discovered—contemporary records about the episode lying neglected in the archives. . . .

At the end of the show, the chorus begs for peace in the world. 'Then most of the younger people in the audience are in tears,' says Voznesensky. 'Not just for the lovers, not for political reasons—I think it is difficult to make tears for political reasons. I wrote it during détente. Today, the world is more dangerous. I think the tears are a nostalgia for détente.'

Andrei Voznesensky was born in Moscow; his father was a professor of engineering and his mother read poetry to him as a child. He studied architecture but turned to poetry; his hero and mentor was Pasternak, to whom he sent his early poems. Like Pasternak, Voznesensky's underlying theme has always been the potentially subversive conviction that the lives and feelings of individuals matter more than governments and theories.

He has managed to work within the Russian system, sometimes more easily than at other times; he became famous during the early post-Stalin years, then incurred Khrushchev's anger. His answer to questions about his attitude to censorship and freedom of speech in Russia is to show a photograph of himself at a rostrum with Khrushchev glowering in the background. Since then, he has sustained the tricky balance between challenge and conformity.

Both in the original poem, and in the opera, he brings in the figure of the Virgin Mary—not in the familiar, idealised, a-sexual way, but as a woman sympathetic to passionate love. He wanted to question the usual image of the Virgin, to suggest that Christian tradition has reduced her to a useful stereotype. 'I do not like anyone to be just used,' he said.

Anne Chisholm, "Poet Superstar," in The Observer, *December 4, 1983, p. 27.*

PHILIPPE RADLEY

"In our age," Andrei Voznesensky once answered an inquiring journalist, "when technology more and more dominates the world, standardization is a clear menace. To save ourselves from mechanization, we must turn to poetry as often as possible. I am convinced that poetry will save man from the danger of being a slave to the machine." Such ambitious pronouncements are an indication of the seriousness with which Russians approach poetry. They suggest that the idea of the poet as a truth seeker—a clear echo of the romantic era—is still alive, at least in Russia.

To Americans, this smacks of the exotic: we are familiar with the hit pop star, but only they know the hit pop poet. And so we have fallen into the habit of lionizing Voznesensky and Yevtushenko, his more political clone, on their tours of the United States. Poetry readings, province of the scholarly and the well-read as a rule, are genuine entertainment events when the Russian stars perform—complete, as in a recent Carnegie Hall performance of both, with music and costume. No matter that neither poet does more than declaim (and forget lines) and shout. This is serious business; this is poetry.

In confirmation of this seriousness, the Soviets have now issued [*Sobranie sochinenii*] a three-volume set of Voznesensky's poetry, from the early histrionics such as **"Parabolas"** and **"Goya,"** to the shadow rhythms of **"The Shadow of Sound"** and **"The Three-Cornered Pear,"** to the more recent **"I feel, therefore I exist"** and **"Prose Rhythms."** Everything is infused with Voznesensky's pyrotechnics, which have even been discussed in excellent essays by some of our universities' most capable scholars.

The third volume contains an interesting essay written between 1972 and 1982, **"Archistichs,"** which discusses the parallels between architecture (Voznesensky's first chosen profession, which he abandoned, according to legend, because Pasternak told him to be a poet) and poetry: both the poet and the architect *build*. And if building means creating new words and verse forms, the poet here shows us how: giving us visual verse, approximate rhymes, unclassical meters. The reader not only reads that the crow crows, but is treated to grunting sound effects (whose layout suggests a bird). To the imagined retort from some reader that this is senseless, Voznesensky snaps that poetry can sometimes be "stupid." It is his ars poetica.

Bewildering, wild, inventive this kind of writing is. But what does it mean? More and more this seems like sound effects and gestures, but little else. Is it?

> *Philippe Radley, in a review of "Sobranie sochinenii," in* World Literature Today, *Vol. 60, No. 2, Spring, 1986, p. 328.*

PHILIP TAUBMAN

The poet Andrei Voznesensky has published a major new article commemorating the suffering of Soviet Jews during World War II, a subject long suppressed by the authorities.

The powerful work of prose and poetry, which is also an indirect attack on Soviet anti-semitism, has stirred public debate but so far generated no criticism from the Government.

It is called *The Ditch: A Spiritual Trial.* The subject is a 1941 Nazi massacre of 12,000 Soviet citizens in the Crimea, the Black Sea peninsula, and the recent plundering of their mass graves by Soviet citizens. Most of the victims were Jews.

Taking advantage of increased artistic freedom under Mikhail S. Gorbachev, Mr. Voznesensky reflects at length in the piece on the long-forgotten massacre and the callous behavior of the grave robbers and the authorities who tolerated their crimes.

Mr. Voznesensky makes clear that most of the victims were Jews, and, without stating so explicitly, suggests that the looting was tolerated for that reason.

By implication, the work is an indictment of the official Soviet recollection of the war, which treats the killing of Soviet Jews as a minor chapter and discounts the anti-Semitic character of Nazi atrocities.

Friends of Mr. Voznesensky said he considered the work to be a clear protest against anti-Semitism that is widespread in the Soviet Union but did not feel free, even in the more relaxed literary climate under Mr. Gorbachev to make a frontal attack.

Mr. Voznesensky describes his horror at finding the looted grave earlier this year, surrounded by the unearthed detritus of the dead, including blackened skulls, clothing and hair.

The grave is located outside Simferopol, the Crimean capital.

"Tired from the sun, we walked slowly away from the highway," he wrote in an opening section he called the afterword.

"And suddenly, what is this? On the path through the green field, there is a black rectangle of a freshly dug well. The earth is still damp. Beyond it is another. Around them are heaps of smoke-blackened bones, rotten clothing."

Mr. Voznesensky said in an interview that he had received hundreds of letters from readers since the work appeared in the July issue of *Yunost,* a youth magazine.

"A year ago, it would have been impossible to publish this work," Mr. Voznesensky said. . . .

The Ditch includes 27 poems, many of which take off from the subject of the massacre to deal with contemporary themes like high-level corruption, the pollution of Lake Baikal in Siberia and the disaster at the Chernobyl nuclear power plant.

> *Philip Taubman, "Soviet Poet Looks Hard at Suffering of the Jews," in* The New York Times, *October 20, 1986, p. A10.*

ANNE LEATON

"Poets in [England and America]," W. H. Auden wrote in 1966, introducing Andrei Voznesensky to a Western audience in the foreword to *Antiworlds*—"have never been considered socially important enough for the state to take any notice of them . . . whereas in Russia, whatever the regime, they have been taken seriously."

Voznesensky himself is a case in point: The object of Khrushchev's special wrath in the infamous attack upon modern painters and poets at the Manege exhibition in Moscow in 1963, he was vilified and unpublished for seven anguished months—part of an attempt by the state to renew a Stalinist control over its artists. This effort failed, not least because of the immense popularity of poets like Voznesensky, Yevgeny

Yevtushenko and Bella Akhmadulina: 100,000 subscribed to Voznesensky's *The Triangular Pear;* press runs of 300,000 to a half million for the new work of young Russian poets sell out.

In 1962, a crowd that would only gather in this country for an athletic contest came together 14,000-strong in a Moscow stadium to hear Voznesensky read. Why? For one thing, he reads magnificently, by all accounts (and the accounts are worldwide): like music, it is said. People in his audience follow the text as they would a score. The stretched, resonanting vowels, the assonance, the modulations of pitch, the extraordinary intensity. . . .

But, finally, it wouldn't matter how magically he read or with what moral vigor his work was infused if the poems themselves were inferior. Against such a judgment, *An Arrow in the Wall* is proof. This bilingual edition contains poems from two earlier American collections, *Antiworlds* and *Nostalgia for the Present,* along with a selection of new poems and two prose pieces.

"I am Fourteen" is a memoir of Voznesensky's first schoolboy meeting with Pasternak in the mid-'40s and their continuing relationship. There are memorable scenes of life at Pasternak's death in Peredelkino; illuminating replications of the style and content of the elder poet's speech: revealing anecdotes, some of which disclose an occasionally unattractive Pasternak.

The title of the essay does not refer to the age at which Voznesensky first met the famous poet and novelist. "Bunin and Nabokov have the clarity of early autumn; they are always forty. But Pasternak is an eternal adolescent . . . Only once in his poetry does he give his age: 'I am fourteen.' Once and for all."

In the second prose selection, **"O,"** Voznesensky moves fluidly, almost cinematically among impressions of Pasternak, Henry Moore, Picasso, and the architect L. N. Pavlov. At the heart of (O) is a revealing tale of Voznesensky himself, hung upon the skeleton of these luminaries.

Now, the poems. No one writes like this in America today: the surreal, the declamatory, the political subtext . . . the *noisy* poem.

The jivey, colloquial poem, bequest of Mayakovsky (who painted roses on his cheeks before he read to his bedazzled, post-Revolutionary audience): "We were not born to survive, alas, / But to step on the gas." The satirical poem: "Of Stalin do not sing: / That is no simple song . . . " The "political" poem, raised buildings high above mere politics: "In these days of unheard-of suffering / One is lucky indeed to have no heart. / Crack shots plug me again and again, / But have no luck." The elegiac: Do not overlook the very fine **"Saga"** with its sorrowing, recurring "I shall not see you anymore." The lyric: "In a world of metal, on a planet of black, / Those silly shoes look to me like / Doves perched in the path of a tank, frail / And dainty, as delicate as eggshell."

The range is considerable. But the best of Voznesensky is the confluence of energetic emotion, precise, compelling, often bizarre imagery, political innuendo, and the fluid colloquialism of his voice. Listen to the opening lines of **"At Hotel Berlin"** (from the long, ambitious, **"Oza"**): "You are celebrating your birthday today—the 16th—in the banquet room of the Berlin. The ceiling there has a mirror." From these, Voznesensky constructs a sustained metaphor of the antiworld/antihero motif central to his work: "Under this world suspended on the ceiling, there is a second world, an upside down one . . . they are counterpoised like the two halves of an hourglass. . . . " Extraordinary similes, scattered throughout, stretch the center of the poem ("the partings of well-groomed hair shine like the slits in piggy banks" . . . "You sitting there next to me, but you are splendidly remote, like a gift wrapped in cellophane"). . . .

It is good to have such a large body of Voznesensky's work available to us at last, and under one cover. For these words of Auden's are indisputably true: "I am certain that Voznesensky is a good poet because though I know no Russian and have never been to Russia, his poems, even in English translation, have much to say to me."

Anne Leaton, in a review of "An Arrow in the Wall," in Los Angeles Times Book Review, *March 29, 1987, p. 6.*

JOHN BAYLEY

I remember, way back in the 1960's, hearing Andrei Voznesensky read his poems at Oxford. It was certainly a memorable experience. A slight young man, compact and relaxed rather than intense, he seemed to fly upward on the wings of the Russian vowels, putting his whole being into them, so that the separate sound of each survived in the hall as a permanent humming resonance. He has himself observed that there is "a kind of drawn-out music in Russian speech that comes from the great distances of the Russian steppes. This cello-like note resounds in the lengths of our names—in our surnames and patronymics. Language is the music of thought, it is what our ancestors called the soul."

That sort of remark is perhaps not entirely reassuring for its audience. It suggests a poetry more concerned with sound than with sense, with the appearance of being poetry rather than with the compression and surprise of a new meaning. And it is true that the first poem in [*An Arrow in the Wall*], **"I Am Goya"**—one of Mr. Voznesensky's earliest and most famous—works through a series of interrelated sounds, variations on the name of the painter, which echo through the brief poem in a series of desolate crashes—*gore* (grief), *golos* (voice), *gorod* (town), *golod* (hunger). Tolling out like deep bells ("I am the gullet / of a woman hanged whose body like a bell / tolled over a blank square"), the syllables convey a powerful impression of war and ruin and nightmare, the nightmare of the German invasion in 1941, when Mr. Voznesensky was a young child and his father, an engineer engaged in evacuating factories from Leningrad, brought him home a volume of Goya's etchings.

Mr. Voznesensky's recitation of this poem was electrifying, but it may be that the element of performance bulked necessarily larger than the poem's emotional impact. Russian poetry has always inspired recitation and a rapt response from the reciter's audience, but Mr. Voznesensky, and his contemporary Yevgeny Yevtushenko, are perhaps the first Russian poets to exploit this in the actual process of composition—to write poems specifically for performing, as pop songs are written for electronic transmission by singers and band. This exploitation of Russian sounds is in marked contrast to modern Polish poetry, which depends on a quiet, pellucid precision, the voice never being raised. . . .

When Mr. Voznesensky showed one of Auden's translations of his poems to the Russian poet and novelist Kornei Chukovsky, who was himself an excellent translator, the latter remarked admiringly: "One madman has understood another." Something of the same element of understanding was implied in a remark of Mr. Voznesensky that Auden himself might have made: "The poet is two people. One is an insignificant person, leading an insignificant life, but behind him, like an echo, is the other who writes the poetry." We have the impression, oddly enough, that it is the two "insignificant" persons who met when Auden translated a Voznesensky poem, as if the two poets could afford to cancel each other out, and become a single human being.

This occurs in the poem **"Hunting a Hare,"** in which pity and guilt—pity for the hare and guilt about shooting it—are so straightforward as to seem the feelings of the "insignificant person" rather than of the poet:

> Something is wrong, I know,
> When a glassful of living blood has to fly
> In terror across the snow.

The cunning rhyme on "snow" and "glass" (*snegam / stakan*) shows the poet in charge, but the feeling of horror at the hare's cry in the silence of nature has a penetrating simplicity and appeal about it. There is no Western equivalent of this sort of Russian poetry, whose tradition is at once both very sophisticated and very direct. Songs or blues, which do not count as "poetry," would be as close as we come to it, and to the comparison of the hunter's faces to red traffic lights as they rush home by car through the dark. At the same time there are references in these poems from a stock of images that goes back beyond Pushkin—such as the one in **"I Am Goya"** to Dmitri the Pretender, Czar in the Time of Troubles, whose ashes were fired from a cannon in Moscow defiantly toward the west.

Nonetheless, Mr. Voznesensky was out with all the trappings of the chase—snowmobiles and so on—hunting this hare and afterward making a poem about it. There is a somewhat uneasy paradox here, referred to in a thoughtful introduction to **An Arrow in the Wall** by William Jay Smith. He mentions the 1979 attack on the poet by Clive James in The *New York Review of Books* [see excerpt above] a formidable indictment that amounted to saying there was something fatally facile about the poet and his poetry, because he could not tell the whole and direct truth about things in Russia. In the absence of that truth, all his poems were subtly untruthful.

Mr. James seemed to be saying that success and survival were themselves symptoms of dishonesty and that because Mr. Voznesensky had not been killed in a duel like Pushkin or hanged himself like Tsvetayeva, or had not been persecuted like Pasternak or sent to a camp like Irina Ratushinskaya, he could not be taken seriously. The case of Pushkin is in fact the best refutation of this argument, for his attitude to the Czar's regime was much the same as that of Mr. Voznesensky to the Soviet. In poems like "The Bronze Horseman" the great poet covertly criticized czardom—as Mr. Voznesensky has done in **"The Driver,"** his poem about Stalin as Caesar, or in **"Old Song,"** where he seems to be writing about Turkish janizaries but is really expressing his feelings about the Soviet invasion of Czechoslovakia.

The poet as secret and alternative truth-teller is an old Russian tradition, and it goes with the passionate love of his country Pushkin displayed. . . .

Pushkin himself would have enjoyed the quality of Mr. Voznesensky's humor, often so similar to his own.

> Over a dark and quiet empire
> alone I fly—and envy you,
> two-headed eagle who at least
> have always yourself to talk to.

The reference is to the old imperial symbol, inherited from Byzantium, the eagle whose heads face east and west. Mr. Voznesensky implies in his reference the continuity of imperial Russia and the Soviet Union, as he fills another poem, **"Does a High Wind Make Me Reel?"** with references to Stalin, whose "great mustaches of state," stained red, hovered over the land like "the wings of a bird of prey." Equally irreverent about all past tyrants, the poet notes only that they are "over" (*bilo*), in a single-word sentence.

The poems with an international flavor are less good, for, although he is a traveler who knows his West very well, Mr. Voznesensky tends to produce smart verbal fantasies about the West, hardly to be distinguished from most cosmopolitan writing. Nor is his prose as good as his poetry, although it is well translated by Antonina W. Bouis. His account of getting to know Pasternak, in **"I Am Fourteen,"** has a breathless and sentimental charm, sticky with hero worship: " 'It's Pasternak on the telephone. For you!' My dumbfounded parents stared at me. When I was still a schoolboy, without a word to anyone, I wrote to him and sent my poems. This first decisive action was to shape my life." There is a vulgarity about this piece never wholly absent in Mr. Voznesensky's work. The other prose piece, called simply **"O"** (Russian for "about"), is a personal meditation containing accounts of meetings with Picasso and Henry Moore, the sculptor.

John Bayley, " 'Over a Dark and Quiet Empire',"
in The New York Times Book Review, *March 29,*
1987, p. 7.

ELAINE FEINSTEIN

The most significant idea in the lyrics of Voznesensky . . . an ironic questioning of the desirability of taking man as the measure of all things, runs throughout his [**An Arrow in the Wall: Selected Poetry and Prose**].

A bitterness in this questioning makes him an altogether less ebulliently personal writer than Yevtushenko. "We've lived shamefully. Pettily," he writes in **"A Conversation in Rome."** Perhaps for this reason, it is language rather than thought or feeling that has dominated his responses. Throughout the extremely varied poems in his **Selected Poetry,** we are always conscious of the literature of the past. We can hear echoes of Paul Eluard and García Lorca alongside early Mayakovsky, and unmistakable notes of Whitman:

> I exalt what is common.
>   I discover, wheezing,
> In America—America.
> Me—
>   in myself.

Perhaps it is in the freshness of his impressions of America that we are most conscious of Voznesensky's experience of the present, but that is a matter to which I shall return. He can write equally movingly of a hare crying out before death or a girl freezing in a telephone booth, huddled in her flimsy coat, her face stained by tears. . . .

He enjoys the conceptually fanciful, and is for that reason intrigued by bizarre lives that can generate fanciful imagery. Where he writes about an Amazonian motorcyclist riding around a **"Wall of Death,"** of the kind used in the Moscow circus, what interests him is her "longing / for the horizontal" as "her orbit whirls her round the wall." The absurd thought occurs to him that

> It's the plight
> only of vestal virgin and suburbanite
> to live vertical and upright.

He takes a sharply sensual pleasure in visions of extremity: a czar's wife's head, cut off by her husband's ax, is held up like a red-topped turnip root. We are asked to smell borscht and peas as the czar is rocked by the passion that speaks from her dead lips. At his best, the everyday world is transfigured by resemblances that demand no further explanation, as when he sees the floor of a garage as a "trout's back stippled with light." (p. 36)

Ironically, a reader of this volume faces as much difficulty in making the transition from the Sixties to the present day as from Russian to English. I've already spoken of Voznesensky's eager seizing upon his experiences in the West, and particularly those in the United States. It is a problem. Yevtushenko, essentially, brought the Soviet Union to us. He spoke for Russia, perhaps even Siberia—in any case for a peasant world. Voznesensky seems instead to have been ensnared by his observation of the details of our style and behavior. As a result many of these poems express the thoughts and occasionally the slogans of an age—the Sixties—that has gone, one we observe more coolly because we can place it even as we may regret its innocence.

Of Voznesensky's poems in this vein, one of the most telling is **"American Buttons,"** translated here with some verve by Lawrence Ferlinghetti. The word *button* for a bell to be pressed for admission is exotic in Russian, and perhaps for that reason it leads Voznesensky to explore assonances that leave Ferlinghetti with a trail of much less evocative associations. What Voznesensky is doing is making a game out of American references, and teasing his Russian readers with their strangeness. He is taking the world of Allen Ginsberg and hippie slogans back to the country of Mayakovsky. It's almost impossible for a translator to cope with these ironies:

> Buttons flash over yawns.
> The funnier they are, the more
>   terrifying
> And like bull's-eyes for bullets.
>
> GOD HAS MOVED TO 43 AVENUE
>   OF PEACE.
> RING TWICE.

Voznesensky's prose is more difficult to assess. It is likely to strike most contemporary Western readers as pretentious. The influences upon it seem to belong to another part of the century, to a modernism now bypassed. We have never lived in the situation of enforced Socialist Realism, and so it is difficult for us to understand the seduction of this kind of modern experiment.

Of the two prose pieces, the one on Pasternak is more interesting because of its subject matter. . . .

[Voznesensky's] insights are more human. He reflects on Pasternak's generous interest in his own early poetry, and the

pleasure he took in listening to Pasternak read his own poetry aloud. "Perhaps what he liked in me was himself, who had run to Scriabin as a schoolboy. He was drawn to his childhood. The call of childhood never died in him." There are passages describing Pasternak's talk in which we can almost hear the stumbling voice of the poet himself. There is a diversion about a vividly observed secondhand bookseller, to whom Pasternak had introduced him, who keeps a first edition of Tsvetayeva's *Versts* in a dusty glass case. And, best of all, there are vivid pictures of Pasternak striding about Moscow, with his coat open and his hat on one side, with the snow just beginning to melt, talking about the importance of losing things, and claiming to have lost a third of what he had done without regret.

There is another, more surreal, vision of the poet, approaching from the other side of Peredelkino pond, and seeming to soar above it supernaturally because his trousers blend with the color of the boards of a bridge. Voznesensky describes him as floating on the waters with a "childlike smile of puzzlement and delight on his face." Something in Pasternak touched the homages that were written to him with a sense of his being more than human; Bella Akhmadulina's tribute to him has a similar quality. It is as if in writing about him, Russian poets were honoring something close to an ideal of poetry itself.

The second piece of prose here—**"O"**—is an occasion to explore other memories; it consists of sharp, quick sketches and fancies, often a matter of only a few lines. There is a portrait of Akhmadulina reading with "her crystal chin so high that neither her lips nor her face is visible, her face is in shadow [so that] all we can see is her defenselessly open neck with the pulsing, unearthly, chilling sound of convulsive breathing." A black hole flies into Voznesensky's room in the writers' colony and ironically claims to be his lost civilization. He makes a kind of pet of it and comments, "I learned that black holes are clots of compressed memory." The O that gives this piece its title is playfully used to string together reflections about meetings with Henry Moore, Picasso, and many others. Voznesensky is more interested in language than he is in anecdote. (p. 37)

> *Elaine Feinstein, "Ringing the Button," in* The New York Review of Books, *Vol. XXXIV, No. 19, December 3, 1987, pp. 36-7.*

SAM DRIVER

It is time for another collection of Andrei Voznesensky's poetry in English translation. Although critical opinion remains still very sharply divided, one tends to agree with [William Jay Smith and F. D. Reeve, the editors of ***An Arrow in the Wall: Selected Prose and Poetry***] that the poet has not always been fairly treated. Voznesensky is one of the best-known poets in the Soviet Union and certainly one of the best-known Soviet poets in the United States. An earlier volume of translations appeared in the sixties, when Voznesensky was becoming established, and another in the late seventies. One advantage of [***An Arrow in the Wall***] is that it incorporates selections from the earlier ones and also provides a large number of poems from more recent work. . . .

The volume concludes with two of Voznesensky's longer prose pieces. The first is more or less autobiographical, focusing on Pasternak and the adolescent poet's relationship to the master; fortunately, the political topicality of the work has been blunted by developments in recent years, and it can be judged on its own very considerable merits. The other prose selection is likely to have a much narrower appeal. A cut-down version of a longer work entitled **"O,"** with the several meanings and connotations of the word in Russian, it is the type of prose which is often lumped under the catchall term *experimental,* although the experiments it brings to mind have a definite flavor of the 1920s. Perhaps Voznesensky intended this, but we are given no hint as to why.

Perhaps the most satisfying part of the volume is the third section, **"Release the Cranes,"** poems mostly from the eighties. There is no sharp departure in manner or style from the earlier poems—Voznesensky is really very consistent in this regard—but there is notably less stridency, more reflection. A visual image occurs and is apposite: Voznesensky at a poetry reading last year during his most recent U.S. tour. The poet, now edging toward middle age and tending a bit toward mature solidity, read again the poems he had belted out a quarter-century ago as a skinny, taut-necked young Turk of the early sixties. One must say that both the older man and the older man's poems are a great deal more sympathetic.

Sam Driver, in a review of "An Arrow in the Wall," in World Literature Today, *Vol. 62, No. 2, Spring, 1988, p. 301*

Marianne Wiggins

1948-

American novelist and short story writer.

Wiggins's often comic fiction examines the psychological characteristics of women who assert their individuality and challenge social conventions. Her first novel, *Babe* (1975), centers on a young divorcée's struggle to raise her child and pursue her ambitions, and *Went South* (1980) chronicles the emotional progress of a young mother whose second marriage is dissolving. *Separate Checks* (1984), the novel which generated Wiggins's first significant critical attention, relates the turbulent history of an all-female family. From a psychiatric hospital where she is recovering from a nervous breakdown, protagonist Ellery McQueen recounts the exemplary triumphs and comic transgressions of her female forbears. Although some reviewers considered Wiggins's narrative unbalanced and often sensational, many commended her witty investigation of family bonds. Richard Eder remarked: "[Wiggins] writes beautifully about women. She mines fortitude and ferocity out of them along with grace and fatuousness. Sometimes she uses too much dynamite for the dislodging, and she is awkward at fitting the pieces together; but there is an inspired insight at work, and a perilous talent."

Wiggins presents various female perspectives on romance and estrangement in her short story collection *Herself in Love* (1987). While some critics considered her symbolic connections opaque and extreme, most commented that Wiggins almost faultlessly renders place and dialect in stories set in Nairobi, London, and America's Deep South. Michiko Kakutani observed: "The down-home twang of an aging small-town couple; the knowing sarcasm of New York sophisticates; the alternating anger and sentimentality of a woman involved in a lousy affair—the voices of these disparate people are all captured with precision and wit by Ms. Wiggins, who combines the writerly gifts of observation with the magical abilities of a finely trained actress and ventriloquist." Many reviewers praised "Stonewall Jackson's Wife," a recreation of the Confederate general's funeral as witnessed by the ghost of his first wife. The narrator's identity is gradually revealed as she interrupts observations of the somber event with acerbic comments on the general's second wife and nostalgic musings on her own marriage to a younger, more modest Jackson. Critics admired Wiggins's investigation into the union of love and memory and lauded her incisive depiction of female rivalry.

Wiggins's next novel, *John Dollar* (1988), satirizes such institutions of Western civilization as imperialism, patriarchy, and Christianity. The narrative opens in the 1980s with the burial of protagonist Charlotte Lewes, and, through an extended flashback, reveals her traumatic and mysterious past. As a strong-willed schoolteacher among the English colonists of Burma just after World War I, Charlotte defies social mores and takes the sailor John Dollar as her lover. The couple accompanies the colonists on an imprudent voyage to a remote island in the Bay of Bengal that the English wish to claim in honor of King George. After disembarking, the landing party is beset by violent storms and attacked by native cannibals. A tidal wave then strands a paralyzed John Dollar alone with eight bewildered schoolgirls. After surrep-

titiously watching as cannibals cooked their parents' corpses, the frenzied girls gradually form their own barbarous social order, complete with religious rituals involving the eucharistic consumption of John Dollar's flesh. Like William Golding's *Lord of the Flies,* in which marooned boys revert to savagery as a means of survival, *John Dollar* examines basic human motivation. While some critics considered the novel's disturbing episodes sensationalistic, others commented that these elements elucidate both the depths of the female psyche and the sanguinary origins of religious myth. Anne Tyler concluded: "When you set aside *John Dollar,* what hangs on is not the horror of the story but the pleasure in the way it was told, and an abiding respect for a next-to-impossible task most elegantly accomplished."

MARTIN LEVIN

" 'Babe,' my father used to say, 'babe: If it hurts, it's real.' " . . .

Babe, who has grown up to be a young divorcée named Maggie Novak [in Marianne Wiggins' **Babe**], remembers her father's aphorisms fondly and uses them with a frequency that irritates her lover, a married securities broker with personal problems. She also has made natural childbirth a metaphor for coping with life. ("Remember the procedure: don't push until the head comes free.") Plus she insists on lecturing the reader as though he were an audience at Town Hall. ("I believe the pervasive social unwholesomeness is certainly causant to many of our individual ills.")

Some of this static notwithstanding, Marianne Wiggins does get on the reader's wave-length long enough to tell him/her what it is like to be a woman on her own (no alimony), with a job to pursue, a 5-year-old to raise, a calling to follow and a husband to steal. Along with the homilies, Babe's father evidently gave his daughter a liking for being herself, which bubbles up happily through the rhetoric.

Martin Levin, in a review of "Babe," in The New York Times Book Review, *May 11, 1975, p. 22.*

KIRKUS REVIEWS

In spite of an initial air of inflated import (talk of "Crystal souls" and hunting for "heroism within herself"), [**Went South**] is essentially an upbeat, often comic, domestic free-for-all romance. Once-divorced Megan is now married to Mel Rosen—a New Jersey insurance man of loutish sensibilities who calls her "miss," tells doo-doo jokes, and says "very tasty" after any meal. So naturally Megan's first glimpse of Charlie Olsen, her daughter Leda's fifth-grade teacher, is arresting—he's got hair like Prince Val, and he walks with giant strides, waving his arms over his head. And, despite Charlie also being wed (to grim, rich Stephanie), discreet foreplay (during a class movie-project) leads to an affair and to dreams of escape from those two lumpy spouses. But Megan has her worries and miseries. Mel's awful son Doug has incinerated her car (which contained the one copy of her all-important novel); and Megan does love their New Jersey farm with a pony, goats, and geese. Still, she attempts to break with Mel, who gets revenge by breaking his leg and then becomes a monstrous Elmer Fudd—ranting and raving, assaulting Megan and forcing Charlie to eat manure. Clearly, Charlie and Megan are bunglers in the divorce game—but they make it at last. . . . With some corny happy-ending stuff at the close—pretentious at the edges, but soft and often funny at the center. (pp. 675-76)

A review of "Went South," in Kirkus Reviews, *Vol. XLVIII, No. 10, May 15, 1980, pp. 675-76.*

PUBLISHERS WEEKLY

This clear-eyed novel [**Went South**], Wiggins's second, introduces a contemporary woman coming of age, showing us how Megan Rosen at last learns to take charge of her life. Megan, 31, is pretty; she's done what's expected of pretty girls—she has married (twice), and had a child, "tried to be like everyone else." But deep down she wants something more, and heeds "the haunting call toward heroism in herself." Her comfortable exurban New Jersey minifarm has become a prison to her, as has her marriage to an impossible man whose be-all and end-all is money. In fact, Megan admits she hates the '70s, "all of it," from "public discussion of what used to be private" to television, to the way people talk, costume themselves, act. She misses "the heroes and the hero-

ines," those who dare. South here means "Away. Xanadu. Over the rainbow. Fishin'." and Megan herself eventually dares on her own. The portrait of this wife and mother beset, the bonds she struggles against, the small risks that lead to bigger ones, is sharply and perceptively drawn. Wiggins captures the feelings, the talk, the way it is wonderfully well, as, surprisingly well, Megan Rosen indeed "goes South."

A review of "Went South," in Publishers Weekly, *Vol. 217, No. 23, June 13, 1980, p. 66.*

RICHARD EDER

In the Christian tradition, sainthood comes only after death. In the literature of post-Salinger sensibility, it requires a nervous breakdown. The narrator of **Separate Checks** has her status as seer confirmed by temporary passage through a psychiatric clinic.

Ellery McQueen (the *Ellery* was conferred by her flighty, mystery-writing mother) constructs—for her recovery and our instruction—a cosmogony of women. There have been about 6.8 billion women since the dawn of history, she reflects, or enough to stretch more than 5 million miles. Instead of stretching she compresses, distilling them, in her imagination, through the women of her own family: her grandmother, mother, four aunts, five cousins and three nieces.

She fashions glimpses of these women, or whole stories, which, like Scheherazade's, serve to save her life. Through them she seeks to discover who she is and the shape of the galaxy. Men are singularly not there.

"We ate them," she writes, setting up the book's stormy and comic tone and a quality that veers between the dazzling and the contrived. Indigestable or half-digested, the men return as bad dreams or burps. They are ghosts, brutalizers, splendors or monsters. Like weather, they happen to the women, while nothing really happens to them. The only human ones are marginal: a priest, a taxi driver, a Mexican farm worker. The others are one great crawling Georgie Porgie, the bothersome fellow who erupts only to kiss the girls and make them cry.

Marianne Wiggins makes Ellery not so much a point of view as an urgency, a heightened voice that turns the puzzling-out of her family into a life-and-death matter. The doctors have ordered her to write about herself, and she, an actress, whose job is to wield emotions and who has lost hold of them, cannot see herself. So she looks to her fellow sojourners, her cousins and her aunts.

Her grandmother, known variously as Gritty and the Old Bitch, was a fierce woman who gave her daughters no tenderness but worked to get them an education and a grip on the world. They turned out special: Jahnna became an aviator; Henrietta, an anthropologist; Sydna, a high-level government official; Mavis, a writer, and—special in humiliation—Willa married a painter who beat, abused and abandoned her for other women and world fame. (pp. 1, 5)

Ellery begins by addressing the mysterious pain, the mixture of love and betrayal, transmitted from mothers to daughters. Nobody in her hyperactive family takes life lying down. Mavis, her mother, insists she learn how to drive and then, distracted by martinis and a male friend, leaves her marooned at poolside. Years later, Mavis interrupts Ellery's performance in a play to announce she needs to see her. Afterward, Ellery charges over, ready to murder, only to find that Mavis is dying of cancer.

When Willa runs off with the painter instead of going to college, Gritty proclaims that she is "dead." Sydna (who later joins the Roosevelt Administration, does wartime intelligence work, has women lovers and turns into a grand, kind old woman) takes this literally. And when she realizes that the phrase is simply a moral judgment, she goes for Gritty with a kitchen knife. When the painter beats Willa, their daughter, Belle, sides with him and would like to beat her as well.

"These are awful feelings to admit," Ellery writes. "Mothers do not set out to make their children hate them." The fault, she continues, can't be with mothers. It must be with "awful children."

This is not ironic, exactly. Nor is it willful blindness. This is blindness produced by the pain that surrounds us. Where does pain come from? Why can we never be rid of it but, at most, accept it partway, as Ellery will do when she writes herself out?

There is rape and murder and a melodramatic cast to some of the plotting. Wiggins' women tend to be exemplars and set at the extremes. She has created some remarkable characters; they shine brightly, but the polishing can be over-evident. Wiggins is so determined that we shall be moved by them that sometimes she forces things.

But it has been a real war. Wiggins, apart from a mannerism or two, writes beautifully. Of the eccentric Sydna, for example: "Trying to hold a conversation with her was like trying to hold the sense of a landscape from the lights one sees from a train in the dark." More important, she writes beautifully about women. She mines fortitude and ferocity out of them along with grace and fatuousness. Sometimes she uses too much dynamite for the dislodging, and she is awkward at fitting the pieces together; but there is an inspired insight at work, and a perilous talent. (p. 5)

> Richard Eder, "Woman Must Survive, a Man Is Marginal," in Los Angeles Times Book Review, April 1, 1984, pp. 1, 5.

JUDY BASS

Separate Checks resembles Sylvia Plath's *The Bell Jar* gone haywire. Both involve female protagonists combating nervous breakdowns, but *Separate Checks* lacks cohesion, lucidity and poignancy. Ellery McQueen, a 33-year-old actress, has had a life conducive to instability. Her mother, Mavis, stifled Ellery emotionally, her father committed suicide, and when her fiancé is murdered, she finally crumbles. At the Lucy Hastings Clinic, doctors advise Ellery to write down her thoughts as therapy. The narrative she produces is a more accurate replication of lunacy than Marianne Wiggins might have intended. Much of the book describes Ellery's aunts and female cousins—the men in her lineage aren't included because, Ellery insists, "We ate them." Cannibalism aside, her relatives are a daft bunch from whom she could easily have inherited some mental aberrations. Her second cousin Cathy is obsessed with discovering what lies on the other side of the universe (Ellery wryly suggests New Jersey). . . .

Cousin Belle had four abortions, committed murder, then poisoned herself in prison. *Separate Checks* is a collage of unfused episodes about Ellery and her family; sentences like "She . . . sat back to consider if the geodesic dome is womb fantasy or trinity made spheroid" only exacerbate the confusion. At one point Ellery says, "I want you very much to like me and to like this story," but that is asking too much. (pp. 20-1)

> Judy Bass, in a review of "Separate Checks," in The New York Times Book Review, April 8, 1984, pp. 20-1.

MARY KATHLEEN BENET

War and famine don't seem to be within the experience of the new generation of American women writers; pestilence (cancer, madness) and death (murder, suicide), however, are just their meat. These two books [*Separate Checks* and Susan Kenney's *In Another Country*] share not only this subject matter, but also a format: both are collections of stories about a family, united by the point of view of a single narrator.

Superficially this can seem to resolve many problems of construction, but in fact *Separate Checks,* the better of the two, is fatally unbalanced; we are led to expect that the female cousins in the book will receive even-handed treatment, but half the narrative is taken up by a single story, so that in the end we wonder who the book is about: Ellery McQueen, the teller (her mother was a mystery writer), or Aunt Belle, her favourite subject. Ellery is writing the stories as therapy after a nervous breakdown; she is trying to make sense of her family. Why are there no men in this family? "We ate them", she coolly replies; but most of the women here are excessively unliberated. The centrepiece, about Belle and Kit, is a sort of Marilyn Monroe-meets-Carlos Castaneda tale, and the heroine doesn't seem to mind that the hero's pet name for her is Bazooms. Finally his drinking and womanizing get out of hand and she shoots him, then kills herself in prison.

This is not the only lurid tale. There is the triangle of Belle's dim mother, artist father, and lesbian stepmother; the coming of age of Cathy and Scooter, two cousins raised like sisters; the long-distance love affair of Millie and Hesh. We understand, after learning about Belle, why her baby Cathy is the most vulnerable of the cousins, the one "who, in a legion of the lost sex, is doubly lost". There is no story about Ellery, but one of the aunts craftily suggests that perhaps all the stories are really about Ellery.

The frame of the book is a luncheon to which Scooter invites them all to announce her engagement. The cousin's attachment to each other, and their nervousness about actually meeting, are well described; Scooter's brainlessness and the reactions of Iris's young children to their father's desertion are compelling. The writing is modern and knowing: Scooter's winsome look is her "Sandra Dee has moved her little bowels" expression. Characters pop up and disappear, but the ones we care about make it in the end, so that's not really disturbing: we can callously say, as Ellery does on hearing of her mother's illness, "What is this, a Bette Davis movie?" Actually, with its references to the Kennedy assassination, old movies, pop songs and vintage cars, it's more like a game of Trivial Pursuit. There is one question, though, that even the most adept players would be hard put to it to answer: why does Wiggins insist on writing "w/" for "with"? It is the only word treated in this shorthand fashion, and after a while you begin looking through the text alertly for any she has missed. . . .

The fashion for writing about divorce and hating your children seems, from the evidence of the both these books, to be on the wane, like the fashion for a Didionesque lack of feeling. Children's misbehaviour is traced to family emotional crisis, and families are broken apart by external, not internal, forces. There is a longing for the home as a centre of values, though in *Separate Checks* the warmest and most welcoming home is that of the priest who befriends Kit and Belle. . . . [In these two books, people] have to get through their lives with whatever wisdom they have managed to accumulate, and there are no short cuts. Religion is not the answer: it simply turns people into Jesus freaks and destroys tolerance. Shock treatment and drugs can re-route the train, but they can't construct whole new sections of railway. The only sources of forgiveness are other people, especially those to whom you are indissolubly connected.

Mary Kathleen Benet, "Family Feelings," in The Times Literary Supplement, No. 4257, November 2, 1984, p. 1239.

NIGELLA LAWSON

Ellery McQueen, actress daughter of famous thriller-writer mother, has had a nervous breakdown. This book [*Separate Checks*] is what she writes to help her get over it, help her make sense of her monstrous, wayward, all-women family. The biggest chunk of narrative goes to Aunt Belle, the father-fixated daughter of a famous artist . . . [who] ends up with famous writer, Kit, whom she eventually kills. The mood of the writing swoops up and down from the swaggering to the vulnerable. The tone is colloquial, intimate, confiding, with the cadences of American speech rhythms. Laconically witty and often searing, with some memorable phrase-making.

Nigella Lawson, in a review of "Separate Checks," in Books and Bookmen, No. 358, August, 1985, p. 31.

JOHN CLUTE

In the longest and loosest of the stories collected in *Herself in Love,* a young married man flees westward across contemporary America by old-fashioned train, only to find that the end of his journey in Los Angeles is also the end of his tether. There is no Wilderness to hide in. He boards the next train back to New York. But **"Gandy Dancing"** ends before its failed Huckleberry Finn reaches home again, where he must begin to live out the consequences of his doomed fugue, and that may be the reason why this story, despite its dark felicities of observation and its loving knowledge of the terminal days of Amtrak, lacks the touchy complexity of Marianne Wiggins's best work.

The best and most excruciating stories in this fine book deal with survivors at the other end of travel, men and women whose moment of significant journeying has passed. Most of Wiggins's protagonists are internally exiled, and several of them are literal expatriates. The author is herself an American living in England, and a vivid sense of the tightrope-walk of exile focuses the sharpest of her tales. Dense, spiky, guarded and extremely competent, these tales speak in barbed, self-sufficient rhythms of making a life in strange surroundings.

This alienated territory may be England for an American, as in **"Herself in Love"**, or old age for a passionate heart, as in **"Among the Impressionists"** or **"Ridin' up Front with Carl and Marl"**, but displacement is always central.

There can be no avoiding the sense that there is something bleak and chilling about the estrangement that moulds these expatriate lives. At the same time, though none of the stories in *Herself in Love* could be described as markedly joyous, an almost ribald bravery and grace does infuse Wiggins's hard-etched portraits. Her protagonists dive into their loves and jealousies, and succumb to the stranglehold of passion, with a defiant *sprezzatura* that helps make reading her remarkable stories a decidedly bracing experience. This is an intensely active book.

At times it is too active. There are moments of pugnacious overwriting; the narrative present tense is applied too facilely and too often, and becomes a kind of stylistic bludgeon quite unsuited to the complex patterns of a story like **"Ridin' up Front with Carl and Marl"**; at times the urge to create tales of a self-sufficient compression leaves a sense of almost inextricable knottedness, or of a sleight-of-hand virtuosity that demands re-reading without necessarily rewarding it. But these are cavils. **"Stonewall Jackson's Wife"** is one of the finest ghost stories of recent years, not only a technical triumph but a vision of the family, of love and solitude, and of the milieu of the American Civil War, whose difficulty is absolutely essential to the reality conveyed. **"3 Geniuses"** may be too knotty, but on reflection unfolds into a sequence of parables whose implications swell richly in the mind. **"The Gentleman Arms"**, a monitory tale of exile and of the cost of ageing, becomes, in its brilliant final paragraphs, a quiet but deeply chastening statement of our shared human condition. **"Herself in Love"** is desperately and comically acute. . . . [This collection of stories] has presence, weight and toughness, and is likely to endure.

John Clute, "At the Other End of Travel," in The Times Literary Supplement, No. 4390, May 22, 1987, p. 558.

RICHARD EDER

I do not like all the stories in *Herself in Love.* There are one or two I only partly understand, and one or two others whose understanding I can manage only on a second reading. Wiggins is knotty and erratic. She careens. And then, she takes us with her on a course we have never thought of but recognize at once.

Her subject is women's pain. You could call her one of our most remarkable feminist writers, but it would be misleading. She writes of women as James Joyce wrote of the citizens of Dublin; as if they were a local phenomenon so thoroughly seen, and seen through, that they serve as universal ways of being human, and not only female.

Estrangement between the sexes comes not because men and women fail to recognize each others' crippled longings but because they *do* recognize them. And they turn away because they can't mend them. Their shared exile separates Adam and Eve more than it unites them.

Wiggins performs the estrangement in a whole variety of ways: tender, frightening, surreal. For the first, made crisp by wit, there is [**"Herself in Love"**]. "Herself," the third-person narrator—if such a thing can exist—is a busy woman, neither naive or unmarked, who quite reluctantly falls in love with a young carpenter.

Killebrew, awkward and indirect, stumbles into a declaration while having several cups of coffee in Herself's kitchen. Their affair, 10 days old and still indeterminate, would be the most banal of events if it were not for Wiggins' discourse about the mysteries of such a thing.

Herself has a hopeless mix of feelings. "Killebrew, that bastard couldn't put two things together without causing one of them to break out in a rash. Herself was decent, ordered, sedulous, just. Killebrew was seepage," she reflects. "Killebrew appeared from time to time like water on the floor inside the house."

That is before. After, comes the meditation on what women like about men. "They think of men not so much as objects of their love but as a project that comes wrapped at Christmas, disassembled." In other words, it is the particular parts, not the whole, that women fix upon. "They say, 'He has spaces between his fingers. He has fine hairs along his shoulders. He has toes.' " (p. 3)

"Stonewall Jackson's Wife" is a wilder and more difficult story, and one that shows Wiggins' power at its nerve-racking best. It begins in the Confederate general's home when word comes of his fatal injury. Mary Ann, whom he married after becoming a widower, goes to his deathbed and to the mournful funeral procession that winds through the remote hamlets of Virginia.

The heart of the story is the narration. It is erratic, full of unexplained rancors and regrets. Only gradually do we realize that the narrator is the ghost of Jackson's first wife, Eleanor.

It is an appropriately haunting protest about what life does to men and women. Eleanor remembers her young Jackson, who loved her and life before he became obsessed with his mission of fighting for the Confederacy. She shows withering contempt for Mary Ann, more nursemaid than wife to the fads, fasts and vigils of the Great Man, who has aged out of the man, pure and simple, whom Eleanor knew. At the funeral, while Mary Ann is playing dignified grief, the ghostly Eleanor is fiercely urging the military honor guard to desert.

Women, Wiggins is writing once again, cherish men's particulars—the fine hairs, the appetite for raspberries—and not the generality—the work, the mission—to which these particulars are sacrificed. The theme is very dark, here; desperation replaces the ruefulness of ["Herself in Love"]. (pp. 3, 15)

In some of the other stories, the men are there mainly as obsessions. **"Kafkas"** is a chilling and wonderfully terse portrait of a woman unhinged by abstraction—she is a Ph.D., probably in literature—who telephones cities all around the country looking for single men surnamed Kafka. Her first name is Fran and she wants to be Fran Kafka. It is an utterly cuckoo way to become, in a manner of speaking, a great writer. Wiggins takes a play on words and makes it the instrument of nightmare.

"Pleasure" is a piece of symbolism so extravagant that, by all rights, it ought not to work. A woman, tormented by guilt about her promiscuity, is at the beach with her children when a dying whale rams up onto the sand. She struggles to push it back in. It seems absurd to have this maimed intruder stand for the ungovernable and alien passion that has taken over the woman's life; it is absurd except that, emotionally, it works wonderfully well.

In **"Greedy Park,"** the precarious tie between a woman and her married lover is portrayed with great erotic tension in a scene in which he languorously shaves her body hair while she is bathing. Later, after he leaves her for his wife, the protagonist goes to a London park where she used to meet the lover and plants flower bulbs on their trysting places. Once more, such a summary sounds ridiculously far-fetched, yet the story has a faultless, magical power. . . . There is broken ground between Wiggins' power to charm and to terrify. It can be awkward, yet the jolts themselves are often revelations. The estrangement of her women is profound, even total, in every respect except one. The writer's unpredictable artistry catapults us into the heart of the estrangement and makes it an odd species of communion. (p. 15)

Richard Eder, in a review of "Herself in Love and Other Stories," in Los Angeles Times Book Review, *August 16, 1987, pp. 3, 15.*

MICHIKO KAKUTANI

In the finely wrought title story of *Herself in Love,* a man writes a long letter to a woman he once knew in the third grade. The letter is an attempt to explain his life, and in it, he tells her how he'd moved away from Buffalo, how he'd gotten married, dodged the draft and had a son. How his marriage had broken up, how he'd moved around and eventually followed his estranged wife and their son to a small town by the sea. "That seemed to sum it up," he writes, "except that that suggested a black vacuum at the center of his life into which his past, his present and his future seemed to float. And maybe that was why he was sitting down to try to write these things. To try to find out where the emptiness came from."

Other characters in this volume suffer from a similar feeling of loss, a feeling that somehow, somewhere, they made a mistake, misplaced something important or passed by an opportunity that might have changed their lives.

In **"Ridin' Up Front With Carl and Marl,"** the characters talk about cherishing an image of some specific, faraway heaven, far removed from the mundane rituals of daily life; to one, that place is Tahiti, to another, "that little dot by that blue lake on the map." In **"The Gentleman Arms,"** a man tracks down the woman who had been his teen-aged girlfriend after 20 years, and they meet in England "to forget and to remember and to test the threads like tightrope walkers or red spiders."

In **"Gandy Dancing,"** the hero similarly attempts to investigate a path not taken: having felt increasingly suffocated at home, he decides he wants to see the country, the whole wide stretch of America, and that afternoon, he leaves New York, flies to Atlanta and hops a train bound for California. He will "be back home before the kids and Terry would have time to notice. The trip would take eight days. Which wasn't much, when you stop to think about it."

Time plays tricks on Ms. Wiggins's characters: it creeps by with the stubborn lethargy of insomnia, only to speed up, surreptitiously, leaving its victims reeling with the abrupt realization that everything has changed, that their future has slipped away. A rejected girlfriend of Stonewall Jackson recalls, in the wake of his death, his pledge of love, delivered as a young man. And Redcar, the man who hops the train to California, comes home one evening to discover that "his house wasn't there." The furniture looks familiar enough, but everywhere there are signs of aging and transformation. "The paint peeled. Window panes rooted fissures. Seismographic traces surfaced through plaster." . . .

Other stories in this collection takes place in London, New York, Nairobi and the backwaters of the South, they attest not only to Ms. Wiggins's unerring sense of place, but also to her ear for language and the idiosyncrasies of expression. The down-home twang of an aging small-town couple; the knowing sarcasm of New York sophisticates; the alternating anger and sentimentality of a woman involved in a lousy affair—the voices of these disparate people are all captured with precision and wit by Ms. Wiggins, who combines the writerly gifts of observation with the magical abilities of a finely trained actress and ventriloquist.

Several of the weaker stories, such as **"Quicksand"** and **"3 Geniuses,"** tend to be little more than clever showcases for these talents. They display the author's ability to impersonate a variety of characters (a jealous husband, a savvy, no-nonsense waitress, a demented man who asserts that the voice of God is contained in a clay pot), but fail to turn those characters' dilemmas into more than comic sketches. . . .

What distinguishes the best of these stories is that Ms. Wiggins manages to render such heightened behavior both believable and sympathetic. As she writes as one heroine, she is "not strange in any way that you could say, 'Oh, you know, all she eats is seeds and berries,' or, 'You know, she claims she can make her palms bleed . . . ' She's strange the way a day can seem real strange because of a real low pressure—strange the way an old unoccupied house can feel real strange." That sort of "strangeness," of course, is something we can all recognize; and it remains one of Ms. Wiggins's most striking achievements that in making us see her characters' humanity, she also compels us to acknowledge our shared yearnings and sense of loss.

> *Michiko Kakutani, in a review of "Herself in Love," in* The New York Times, *August 19, 1987, p. C20.*

MARK LAMBERT

The energy and ambition of **Herself in Love** . . . are most strikingly exhibited in the book's variety of styles and situations. A waitress in one story convinces an obnoxious customer that he has eaten a meal which he hasn't. Another one is about an amphora from Cairo with God's voice recorded on it. In a parable called **"Pleasure"**, a woman urges a beached whale to return to the sea; **"Kafkas"** presents Fran, who late at night makes long-distance phone-calls to men named Kafka, hoping to marry one of them and change her own name to Fran Kafka. And then there are the styles. The amphora-from-Cairo story displays comic-tradition Brooklyn speech:

> It's an *amphora!* You don't know what an *amphora* is? Dummy! It's a clay pot! . . . Run a needle right through here. Listen, Here that? God's Voice! Is That a Voice?! What a Voice He Had!

Wiggins also works the possibilities of dialogue literally translated from the French, and of a Southern poor-white narrative style: 'There's this European painter that paints people with big holes in them, holes as big as windows where you see the clear blue sky and white clouds through their thoracic regions, though Marl couldn't begin to tell you this ol' painter's name.'

Not all the stories in **Herself in Love** work with situations which are Clever Ideas, and not all of Wiggins's styles entertain with dialect, but it is the gimmicky and the jokey which one most notices in this book: the author's basic concern, one feels, is not really with what the dust-jacket describes as the 'average passions', and yet she does not seem to have a very sophisticated interest in the formal qualities of fiction either. One has the sense, perhaps, that this book's ambitions, broader than they are deep, appear mostly as a naive virtuosity. Nevertheless, it also contains one story which seems to me quite beautiful. This piece, **"Stonewall Jackson's Wife"**, has to do with the death of, and the mourning of, General Thomas J. Jackson, the Confederate general who has had a sort of quiet following over the years among men and boys (I was one of these boys myself in the Fifties, in New York). He was a dignified and shadowed figure. We knew him to be a bravely religious man who—which seemed part of the same thing—was to be fatally and accidentally shot by his own men. He could not be moved when he came to hold a position: the exclamation 'There stands Jackson like a stonewall!' gave him his sobriquet. He refreshed himself in battle by sucking on lemons. Admiration for Jackson was, I suppose, a male thing. His reported last words gave Hemingway the title *Across the River and into the Trees,* and 'stonewall' became a verb in the macho vocabulary of the Watergate conspirators. With all this as background, it is not surprising that a story of the 1980s finds Stonewall Jackson a decidedly imperfect hero. The narrator of the story, which takes as its main focus, not the general himself, but his family and servants, encourages a slave to strike back at her mistress, and encourages volunteers to desert: she sees Jackson himself as a crazy. Nothing surprising about that for a story written in our time, and when one adds that the narrator is, as we eventually figure out, the spirit of Jackson's dead but still loved first wife, we might seem to have a story primed with the right sentiments and with one more dubious gimmick. All the same, it works, and to my mind splendidly. What Wiggins has done here is to combine two ideas from high romance: the dying hero, and the great undying love of lovers who are at once a single self and complementary parts of a whole. This combination of ideas allows us to feel both a wrongness in Jackson himself and a goodness around him (female-located in this first wife, and then in the baby daughter towards whom love for Jackson is shifted). In other words, the story finds a way to make mythical sense of our admiration for dangerously archaic virtues. (p. 19)

> *Mark Lambert, "Adele Goes West," in* London Review of Books, *Vol. 9, No. 16, September 17, 1987, pp. 19-21.*

BARBARA RICH

[How] is one to define Marianne Wiggins? As a novelist perhaps, who, having tackled the short story form for the first time, comes up too short? **Herself in Love** is a disappointment for someone who read two of her three novels and liked them. **Went South,** is a joyous book, as full of substance as it is of substantial characters; **Separate Checks,** written four years later, is less meaty but still nourishing.

The thirteen stories in *Herself in Love* leaves one famished, although a very few are capable of warding off severe hunger pangs until a fortifying trip can be made to the nearest bookstore or library. The collection gives new meaning to the word "opaque." Most readers, whether of a serious literary bent or not, like to have some illumination guiding them along on their path to character comprehension—a ray of light, if you will, particularly on the kind of finite journey occasioned by a short story.

Wiggins seems to take an almost perverse delight in turning off as many switches as possible: switches that might lead to glimmers of enlightenment. From **"Quicksand"**:

> "Do married couples rate as one or two these days? Or do they rate as three? Three is such a busy little number. One plus two is three. Or maybe a man and wife just rate as zero nowadays."
>
> She is wound as tight as a propeller on a boy's model airplane. "Don't spoil my little party, Fanny," Richard asks her gently.
>
> "Have I ever?"
>
> "No."

What could have been a devastating story about a wife discovering that her husband and his best friend have been lovers, disintegrates into an oblique dénouement—telling us precious little of the three people who've been engaged in play-acting.

And yet, Wiggins is capable of such observations as "For another thing, she's pale and cloudy as ammonia," and when describing a state of body and mind in which an emotional melange of religion, love and passion are evoked, "It's a longing for another's limbs, it's sensing fingers through a fin or navigating through a realm of magic by one's skin." And:

> Herself had had that kind of bliss and "You can keep it" was her attitude. Herself had said "No more." No more love for her. No more staring pie-eyed at the farthest wall, no more starving, no more feasting, no more fast breaks from routine. The work at hand was far too arduous *a menos de amor.* The work at hand was Living.
>
> In walked Killebrew.

This last is from [**"Herself in Love"**], which presents us with two people: Killebrew and Herself. Although we may not know them as well as we would like to, within the confines of a few pages we understand why they came together, and we wish them well. Not seeking, they have found; not planning, changes have taken place. **"Herself in Love"** is a story that illustrates both the fragility and unpredictability of life, and even if the message is not new, its telling is the sort that refreshes.

Wiggins, an American, has lived in several European cities, and resides now in London. Another successful story—**"The Gentleman Arms"**—is about a reunion in that city: the reunited being Emily, an American expatriate, and William, on a business trip to England.

> After more than 20 years of wanting to be lovers, she and her old boyfriend meet for one long day four thousand miles away from home and hold to one another in the shadow of their youth, their lovemaking projects on this, the shortest night of the year.

The end of the story is wonderful: a combination of the poignant and the ironic. Emily and William are having a lovely cream tea in the garden of the Gentleman Arms; he is to fly back to his wife that evening. The kindly proprietor, mistaking the two for newlyweds, tells them about her 40-year "romance" with an American soldier, and even as "a rare sun breaks through the clouds," the scene is transformed into an icy tableau.

Unfortunately, these two stories are respites—oases of clarity and intimacy in a dense, verbal desert. **"Kafkas"** tells us nothing about disturbed Fran, living with her sister and brother-in-law and given to running up huge phone bills. She calls operators in various regions of the country, asking them to supply her with the numbers of men named Kafka. And why does she do this? "Cause then I'll be Fran Kafka." It isn't enough—Fran has the makings of a real story, and Wiggins didn't bother to develop it. Instead, she leaves us with a quirky device, and we turn the last page with a sigh of relief.

Perhaps **"Pleasure"** comes closest to working in the abstract style Wiggins appropriates for the telling of these stories. Without dialogue, but wrapped in near-lyrical prose, the mood of **"Pleasure"** is in inverse proportion to its title. The central character, a nameless woman, stands on a nameless shore. She believes that her unhappiness has attracted death—in the form of a beached whale—to her side. Purposeful impenetrability is right and proper to this story, but one makes a collection out of this style of writing at the peril of losing readers' patience.

As Wiggins has proven in her novels, she is skilled at the art of drawing word-pictures of women who capture the imagination. . . . But in *Herself in Love,* Wiggins has allowed herself to embrace minimalism with an excessive show of affection. This is not necessarily a fatal flaw; Ann Beattie, among others, has been doing it for years. However, one may embrace without falling madly in love, which is what Wiggins appears to have done, to the point where her drawings become frustrating sketches. Perhaps she can conquer this tendency toward reduction only in the more expansive space of a novel.

Barbara Rich, "Miniaturists at Work," in The Women's Review of Books, *Vol. V, No. 6, March, 1988, p. 20.*

NICCI GERRARD

Take your Hobson's choice: a tale about girls eating a man, or a tale about a man eating a woman. Whether the cannibalistic rituals take place on an island off Burma in 1918, or in a squalid south London bedsit in the 1980s, they make gruesome reading.

Marianne Wiggins uses the unappetising image [in *John Dollar*] to show how human beings, released into "nature", can disintegrate into unimaginable excesses, while Helen Hodgman's outrageously low-key description of cannibalism [*Broken Words*] suggests that nauseous acts of violence go on around us every day. But neither woman implies that her characters turn to cannibalism because they have sunk into gross disorder. Rather, they have become fetishistic; eating people is simply part of the ghastly hierarchy they create for themselves out of their imperfect (or too perfect) understanding of the order they have lost. Both *John Dollar* and *Broken*

Words are, in their different ways, horribly literal readings of our "civilised" worlds.

I suppose a female version of William Golding's *Lord of the Flies* was inevitable; the surprise is how Marianne Wiggins rivets the reader with her gruesome tale. It is 1918 and three ships set off from Rangoon harbour to chart a small island off the coast of Burma. Several schoolgirls, their teacher Charlotte Lewes and her enigmatic lover John Dollar, are among the passengers and, when the ships are hit and broken by a wave, they are the only survivors. They are tipped into an unfamiliar world (flies and blistering heat and no adult except the broken-spined John Dollar) which they immediately attempt to organise.

They make up rules that are jumbled together from the Ten Commandments, the Gentlemen's Club and their own infantile and inappropriate childish desires. They quickly arrange their own hierarchy—there are the bullies, the condoners and the victims. They build up elaborate rituals and roles, around which their lives collapse into strange shapes with a chilling inevitability. Their language becomes fragmented and formal, warped by quotations from their former lives and by foreign words. Even the final act of cannibalism is performed like Holy Communion, and act of female revenge and worship. The dwindling band of survivors become, not unfamiliar savages, but parodies of adults.

John Dollar has its flaws but the prose is flexible enough to ride any bumps. Marianne Wiggins pours poetry over horror, scatters adjectives around like confetti and pulls back from the brink of pretension into sobriety. Even when she is irritating, she compels attention.

Nicci Gerrard, "Eating People," in New Statesmen & Society, *Vol. 2, No. 36, February 10, 1989, p. 39.*

MICHAEL GORRA

On the shelves of their club library in Rangoon, the characters in Marianne Wiggins's provocative novel [*John Dollar*] would have had the great 11th edition of the *Encyclopedia Britannica*, the 1910-11 version that still sets the standard for what such a work should be. If they had used it to look up the Andaman Islands, in the middle of the Bay of Bengal, they would have found that the islands are "the abode of savages as low in civilization as almost any known on earth," a people so primitive that they do not know how to renew a spent fire, whose adults are in intelligence comparable "with the civilized child of ten or twelve" and of about the same height as well. But, *Britannica* adds, the "traditional charge of cannibalism . . . is now and probably always has been untrue."

It's to the Adamans that a group of British families sets out in 1919, bound for a holiday on the one Marco Polo called "The Island of Our Outlawed Dreams," patriotically determined to rename it in honor of King George. What happens when they get there makes *John Dollar* one of the most disturbing new novels I've read in years.

But Ms. Wiggins, an American writer now resident in London, opens her fourth novel in Cornwall, some 60 years after the island journey, with the image of an old Indian servant woman burying the body of her mistress Charlotte. For those six decades the two women have had a sort of death in life on the Cornish coast: "Year after year they refused to forget, to look forward, look inward, look anywhere, but to sea. . . . Nothing progressed. Nothing changed." Now Charlotte has died in actual fact. And as she digs, the Indian—her name is Menaka, called Monkey by the British—remembers another digging. Remembers how "she and Charlotte had killed them . . . [and] had dragged their two bodies down to the sea for the vultures and sharks," and then dug a grave for another body, puzzling its bones "out in the earth till they looked like a man."

It's no small praise to say that what follows makes the *frisson* of that opening seem something more than merely sensational. Ms. Wiggins cuts from Cornwall back to Burma, where in 1917 Charlotte, a war widow, has come to teach. Once there she begins to wear Burmese clothes and soon takes as a lover the sailor John Dollar, whose "hands were used to halyard but not unused to women," a force of nature whom she first sees as a "dolphin running upright, taking off his shirt and running toward her on his legs" as she swims in a lagoon one morning. Ms. Wiggins has some fun contrasting the liveliness of John and Charlotte to the conventionality of the rest of the British, whom she describes, with a pellucid irony, as taking "their quinine like religion, like the eucharist it was," and for whom "the differences between working for one's God or working for one's Country were very subtle."

But John and Charlotte remain enough a part of the community to go along when the British merchants of Rangoon decide to celebrate their Britishness with a trip to the Adamans. They set out in three boats. . . . And on landfall they see themselves as latter-day Robinson Crusoes, cast up on a deserted shore with everything they need to make a civilization, right down to their loyal Burmese Fridays and the Royal Worcester off which they'll eat their celebratory dinner.

But their safe social ritual is not to be: after dinner the ocean begins to glow "bright green, a lurid sort of yellow." . . .

The next day most of the men sail off to another island to hunt, and some of the girls find what they take to be a monkey's skull, but isn't. On the second night one of the boats comes adrift. When he goes to investigate, John finds flies buzzing in the hold and blood everywhere—"the bunks were gashed, the sheets were scarlet mats"—but no bodies. Then, as if the whole natural world itself has risen up in protest, he feels a tremor in the sea beneath him. And as he reaches the deck, he sees an earthquake-born wall of water heading toward both him and the ship on which Charlotte and the girls lie sleeping.

The astringency with which Ms. Wiggins sees her characters reminds me less of the mixed guilt and anger most Western writers about imperialism display than it does of Angela Carter's demythologizing of the historical and literary fictions of the past. And her prose has a quirky brilliance that's similar to Ms. Carter's as well, a prose simultaneously spare and lush, as precisely opulent as a diamond solitaire—darting, telegraphic, cutting quickly from one scene, one tense, one point of view to another. That style gives the novel an almost cinematic speed and objectivity. But it also makes it hard to tell just how, once past Ms. Wiggins's critique of imperial history, we're supposed to take the action she describes.

For when the giant wave sends John, Charlotte and the girls crashing onto the beach, *John Dollar* becomes something more than an expertly ironic period piece, and the relentlessness of their fate leaves the reader feeling drained and hopeless. Ms. Wiggins's attention here, halfway through the novel, switches to the schoolgirls, Monkey above all, who wakes on the beach, her lips "soldered with salt," and realizes that while she sees her classmates around her, there are no boats or adults in sight. Slowly the girls revive and try to find a way to survive, waiting on the beach for the parents they don't know yet will never come to rescue them. . . . Then they find John—alive, but comatose and paralyzed below the waist. When they revive him, he remembers those "scarlet mats" and makes the girls go into hiding. But one day two outriggers come ashore, manned by "tiny naked people— what they thought were children," with a cargo of Europeans, the girls' fathers, caught on their hunting expedition. And as the girls watch from their hiding place, those other "children" build a cooking fire. . . .

The sight drives some of the girls mad. I'll leave readers to discover the brutal consequences of that madness, though I will note that in reading the last 30 pages I seemed to feel an almost malarial series of hot and cold flashes, as I was drawn on by the horror of the novel's action. But I was also troubled by the conclusion of *John Dollar,* and in more than the obvious way.

For one thing, Ms. Wiggins's reliance on the myth of the Andaman Islanders' cannibalism is at odds with the historical scrupulousness she seems to have observed in the first part of the novel. I can only conclude she felt she needed it for what at this point in the novel becomes something like an allegory—though of what isn't immediately clear. One thinks of *Lord of the Flies,* this time with little girls, but rejects the thought, for what Ms. Wiggins is up to is by no means so neat as that tidy parable about original sin. And in fact one wonders what could motivate such a grim novel, which seems so far removed in both time and place from the author's experience, and for which nothing in her fine 1987 collection, *Herself in Love,* has prepared us. The combination of her subject with the cold, slippery objectivity of her style, in fact, makes me briefly wonder if *John Dollar* is simply a tour de force, a deliberately showy shocker,

But I think it's something much more than that. After the Andaman Islanders leave, the girls in their increasingly violent madness begin to acquire the vestiges of civilization— fire, a social order and a religion to replace the Christianity they've lost. Civilization itself begins here in barbarism and madness, and the question of good and evil, into which Robinson Crusoe so neatly divided his experience, starts to seem like a construct to hide our amorality from ourselves.

A familiar enough idea by now, when we find it in Nietzsche or Freud. And yet seeing it enacted in fiction, embodied in characters about whom one has come to care, it still has a terrible power to disturb, a power reinforced by the pitiless and brilliant prose with which Marianne Wiggins evokes "The Island of Our Outlawed Dreams."

> *Michael Gorra, "Washed Ashore without Parents,"
> in* The New York Times Book Review, *February
> 19, 1989, p. 3.*

PETER S. PRESCOTT

Just as religious converts are said to be the most devout believers, American expatriates living in London write the most fiercely British novels. . . . *John Dollar* is flawlessly English; moreover, it extends a venerable British literary tradition. That's the tradition which began with *Robinson Crusoe,*

peaked with *Lord of the Flies* and asks a question central to understanding the empire: when cast away upon an island, how does the proper Englishman govern himself? Defoe found a complacent answer; William Golding, a nightmare of reversion to savagery.

Wiggins sets out to do for girls what Golding did for boys. The first half of her story concerns a young war widow, Charlotte Lewes, who in 1917 sails out to Rangoon to teach the children of the Raj. Appalled by the cocoon that the British have spun to isolate themselves from the country and its people, Charlotte adopts native clothes and lives in a Burmese house. She begins an affair with a raffish sort of sailor, John Dollar, of whom little will ever be known. In honor of the king's birthday, the British residents decide to rename for him an uninhabited island—and to make the occasion a three-day excursion, sailing out with children, native bearers and raffia trunks loaded with crystal and silver. The event conveyed, Wiggins writes, a "sense of exhilaration which comes when one's life bears a likeness to the fictions that one's dreamed; plus there was the weighty thrill of bringing light, the torch of history, into one more far-flung reach of darkness."

Having satirized the empire at its most preposterous and exposed, Wiggins abruptly changes tone. Catastrophe and melodrama will carry her story to its end, a descent into the improbable that works surprisingly well. What happens next is this: marauding natives board one of the English boats by night to murder the little boy heirs-to-empire. Then a tidal wave sweeps the little girl heirs from another boat to a remote beach.

Eight girls on the cusp of puberty—seven from the ruling Anglo-Saxon race and one dusky Burmese—assemble around the immobile body of John Dollar. He has a broken spine. Charlotte is not in view. Like Golding, Wiggins knows that if you want to show children degenerating quickly, you must keep competent adults away. The girls make laws and claim exclusions. Hierarchies and alliances spring up, and in the subsequent struggle for survival unnecessary deaths occur.

The problem Wiggins faces with this story is that Golding got there first. The horrors of social regression in these particular circumstances belong to him. Wiggins can only say: look, I'm working with girls, and believe me, girls can be worse. She proves her case. [*John Dollar*] is a truly horrifying story, melodrama wrought with an elegant style.

> *Peter S. Prescott, "Stylish Tales of Castaways," in*
> Newsweek, *Vol. CXIII, No. 8, February 20, 1989,
> p. 64.*

MICHAEL DIRDA

John Dollar rivals a James Beard cookbook in its obsession with food. Nearly every page talks about eating or hunger, starting with the deprivations of its heroine, Charlotte Lewes, in post-World War I England and ending with a heart-rending act of cannibalism on a deserted tropical island.

John Dollar is also a novel that will inevitably be compared to William Golding's *Lord of the Flies,* since its second half focuses on the moral degeneration of a group of marooned English schoolchildren, this time young girls. But whereas Golding simply plunked readers down immediately on his island with Ralph, Piggy and the others, Wiggins builds slowly to her central act of horror, making the first half of her novel both an account of a lonely woman finding love and a satirical group portrait of British colonials and their entourages.

The writing throughout is masterly, but readers have come to expect that from Wiggins. Her short stories—collected in *Herself in Love*—displayed an astonishing range of tones and voices: From the down home **"Ridin' Up Front with Carl and Marl"** to the allusive postmodern fables of **"3 Geniuses"** and the hip New York angst, present tense and all, of **"Kafkas,"** the tale of Fran Koslow who telephones single men named Kafka and proposes marriage so that she can be called Fran Kafka.

Wiggins' humor and her understanding of people, especially lonely women, both shine in *John Dollar.* Her prose is clear and nicely cadenced, she captures perfectly the speech of sailors, toddlers, servants, supercilious colonels and worn-out wives; almost any sentence may be shot through with wonderful phrases bright as tracer bullets. . . . (p. 3)

A good novelist makes every word do double duty: telling the reader something immediately and preparing him, subtly, unconsciously, for events to come. . . . Charlotte's bleak, cold world will vanish in the bright sunshine and sensuality of the tropics, but the quietly embedded references to embers, fires, bones and death, even that frost of white, will blossom into ominous leitmotifs.

As will references to cannibalism. After being posted to Rangoon as a teacher, Charlotte falls in love with an easy-going, capable sailor named John Dollar. Together with the British colonial community, the passionate couple sail to a little-known island to rename it in honor of King George, as part of a special birthday celebration. Like Ronald Firbank or Henry Green, Wiggins includes pages where people simply converse—without any "he says" or "she replies"—and here she lets her humor, sometimes satirical but usually just high-spirited, enjoy full rein. Only in retrospect do we see the darker implications: an allusion to the riddle of the Cannibals and Christians, anecdotes about the strange things people have devoured ("It's impossible to eat a python properly without vermouth"), a telling of *Hansel and Gretel,* the nipping and biting of love-making secretly overseen by mesmerized 9-year-old girls who mistake "the sad echo of extreme joy for a noise of an ungodly agony."

At the climax of the excursion—following a feast to match dinner at Trimalchio's—occurs a wholesale massacre of sea turtle eggs by island lizards, a dog and many members of the holiday party. This brutal event—scarcely described and consequently all the more horrific—signals a change in the novel's direction. The picnic fun is over; prepare to sup on horrors. (pp. 3, 10)

To tell more of the story would be to mar a reader's pleasure. Some of the action is grim—in **"Kafkas,"** Wiggins reminds us that Schopenhauer called cannibalism the epitome of moral wrong—but the sheer beauty of the storytelling somewhat mitigates our revulsion. Besides we have grown used to many of these matters: the heartlessness of children, the thin veneer of civilized behavior, moral cannibalism as preparation for actual omophagis, sex as voracious and sadistic to young eyes (Freud's primal scene), the eating of flesh as a mockery of Christian communion. Wiggins nonetheless makes her fable seem bright and new, even for admirers of similar books such as Richard Hughes' *A High Wind in Ja-*

maica, Golding's classic and Harlan Ellison's *A Boy and His Dog.*

Wiggins also resorts to a few too many narrative coincidences—for instance, the double disaster that sets the tragedy in motion and the reemergence of Charlotte at its end. But these are minor flaws in an otherwise superb novel, hypnotic, disturbing and artful. Sadly, though, just when Wiggins ought to be enjoying a triumph, the maelstrom of political attention engulfing her husband, the novelist Salman Rushdie, surely has made the success of *John Dollar* among the least of her concerns. (p. 10)

> *Michael Dirda, "Marooned on the Island of Out-lawed Dreams," in* Book World—The Washington Post, *February 26, 1989, pp. 3, 10.*

CARYN JAMES

After a bookstore in Washington sold out of Salman Rushdie's *Satanic Verses,* Marianne Wiggins's new novel, *John Dollar,* appeared in the window instead. "If you can't read the husband's book," said a sign above the display, "read the wife's." . . .

Until *John Dollar,* Ms. Wiggins's writing closely charted the surface, though not the depths, of her own life and times. . . . When her first novel, *Babe,* appeared in 1978, she . . . moved to Martha's Vineyard, where she turned out two more novels—*Went South* and *Separate Checks*—and a highly esteemed story collection, *Herself in Love.* They constitute one long, wry, savvy look at motherhood, divorce and contemporary women in love.

Separate Checks, published in 1984, is a profuse, cockeyed look at three generations of women in one family. Their stories are written from a psychiatric hospital by the heroine, whose mystery-writer mother has named her Ellery McQueen. Ms. Wiggins tweaks religion in her title, which Ellery lifts, from a Mel Brooks movie. (A waiter at the Last Supper: "Are you all together or is this going to be on separate checks?") And Ellery offers two theories why there are no men in her stories. "The first is that males born into our family were exposed at birth; and the second theory is we ate them." These jokes have their serious comeuppance in *John Dollar.*

Set in Burma just after World War I, Ms. Wiggins's new novel concerns a group of British schoolgirls stranded on an island with a paralyzed sailor named John Dollar. It ends in cannibalism and is being described, in another instance of inadequate short-hand, as a female *Lord of the Flies.* Ms. Wiggins's most ambitious and accomplished novel, it is a lyrical and effectively savage critique that means to undermine some foundations of Western civilization—patriarchy, imperialism, colonialism, and the rituals of Christianity. Though it is possible to see Mr. Rushdie's influence in these huge cultural themes, *John Dollar* is as spare as Mr. Rushdie's work is extravagant.

The novel, whose working title was *Eucharist,* is replete with mock sacraments, as John Dollar, the symbol of British male supremacy, becomes the girls' false god. They bathe him in wine; they place white quinine tablets on his tongue. Two small girls—one of them a minister's pious daughter—eat his flesh, shaving off bits of his leg in a daily religious ritual. In an interview published not long before Mr. Rushdie's life was threatened, Ms. Wiggins told The Sunday *Times* of London that cannibalism "is the ultimate taboo masked in all our religious rituals, particularly Christianity, the body of Christ, taking the bread and wine. The men who thought up religion knew exactly what they were doing, playing on people's deepest fears."

Ms. Wiggins's novel is far less explosive than Mr. Rushdie's, though. Her iconoclasm seems bound to its historical moment, safely tucked away in the past: and it is the sort of critique of institutional religion that Christians have heard often enough.

Although the cannibalism is too extreme a symbol, *John Dollar* soars beyond the deft but shallow observations of Ms. Wiggins's earlier works. (pp. C17, 23)

> Caryn James, *"The Ayatollah's Other Victim,"* in The New York Times, *February 28, 1989, pp. C17, C23.*

RICHARD GEHR

Marianne Wiggins's ironic fate is to have written [*John Dollar,*] a novel vastly more blasphemous toward the Church of England than her husband Salman Rushdie's *Satanic Verses* is to Islam. Lucky for her, England's religious right is somewhat less volatile than Iran's mullahs, and lacks the obsessive fervor necessary to mount days of rage and post bounties. If Rushdie unwittingly condemned himself to a life of extreme caution for satirically implying that Mohammed's wives were prostitutes, imagine how Christian zealots would react to the eucharistic feasting of nice English girls upon the living body of a paralyzed Christ figure.

Wiggins's fourth novel—reportedly a single-draft effort, first titled *Eucharist*—takes place primarily on The Island of Our Outlawed Dreams, where a tsunami has beached eight little girls, all daughters of Rangoon's British squirarchy. *John Dollar* could be called *Our Lady of the Flies*—it's like a particularly horrifying season of *Gilligan's Island*—wherein Wiggins links Rushdian extraterritorial and colonial concerns to often acute reflections on the byways of female consciousness. Neither as carefully structured as Wiggins's charming 1984 novel *Separate Checks* nor as casually self-conscious as her 1985 short-story collection *Herself in Love,* *John Dollar* reads like a feverish, escalating meditation on transgressions of sexuality, religion, and class amid the declining British raj.

The book begins and ends as the story of 25-year-old Charlotte Lewes, an "undersexed," passionless WWI widow desiring "that death that takes a person somewhere else." Solving that problem by taking a position as a Rangoon schoolteacher, she becomes purified and resexualized by the region's "Lassitude" and her "Sudden Loss of Language" (seemingly unmotivated caps and marginalia pepper the book, suggesting a forgotten classic but not much else). Her Burmese life brings out an ambiguous duality; she becomes "neither one thing nor the other, not a gill-fitted English woman who'd gone troppo nor an indigenous inhabitant of the native land." Her lover, the sailor, John Dollar, embodies passion transcending the lexicon of love. . . .

Nature and culture, and love and death, flipflop throughout the novel, so that Wiggins's more obvious symbolism collides with her subtler perceptions (missing in action is the writer's nimble wit). The apocalyptic tsunami that strands the group might be nature punishing the girls' fathers for having ravished freshly laid turtles' eggs during the party's first predisaster night on the island. But it may also have been caused by the spectacle of Charlotte and John's lovemaking as witnessed by the prepubescents, who interpreted it as agony.

Having fallen into a new world, by their standards a nonworld, the girls feel deserted, punished, and guilty. Lacking practical responses to their situation (the novel at times suggests a parodistic post-colonial *Robinson Crusoe*), they first mimic patriarchal order by writing new laws, renaming the world around them, and reestablishing authority—resolutions that quickly degenerate into a negative version of the torpor and linguistic dissolution that reawakened Charlotte upon her arrival in Burma. *John Dollar* reverberates with such repetitions and variations between generations; the presence of a French translation of *The Notebooks of Leonardo Da Vinci*—John Dollar's beach reading—suggests the problem is one of *proportion* between young and old, impotent and empowered, colonized and colonizer. No surprise that the lone survivors, as we learn early on, will be dualistic Charlotte and resourceful "Monkey," the half-Indian bastard daughter of a British philanderer. An apotheosis of the noble savage is thankfully never suggested.

Marianne Wiggins's writing, with its intermittent fireworks and elegant depictions of otherness, suggests Ellen Gilchrist crossed with Paul Bowles (although she possesses an utter tin ear for working-class speech). Wiggins wrestles with phallocentric discourse, man's language; but among this savage little tribe of deracinated—or reracinated—primitives, only silence remains to say good night to the old rules because "theirs is a failure of community." Structured as an immense flashback, *John Dollar* suggests an endlessly tragic replay of eucharistic rituals as a doomed attempt at group preservation. In other words, the culture that prays together, slays together.

> Richard Gehr, *"Sins of the Flesh Eaters,"* in The Village Voice, *Vol. XXXIV, No. 12, March 21, 1989, p. 50.*

ANNE TYLER

Until now, Marianne Wiggins has seemed a quintessentially American writer. Her previous books—among them a delightful novel, *Separate Checks,* and a short-story collection, *Herself in Love*—had a broad streak of zany humor and a distinctively Western, easy-going swagger.

But Wiggins currently lives in England, having married the Indian-born British author Salman Rushdie (which, in light of recent developments, must have given her a number of fresh insights into human behavior worldwide). And *John Dollar,* her fourth novel, is as English as a book can get: delicate in tone, tripping rather than sauntering, coolly understated. It's full of words like "tiffing" and "fishballs" and " 'round" (as opposed to "around"). Above all, it is ironic—although, since the irony is often directed at the British notion of empire, one wonders whether a born Englishwoman would have managed to wrench the same amount of comedy from her material.

Comedy, you ask? Comedy, in a book that's in many ways a female version of *Lord of the Flies?* Well, yes, believe it or not. Oh, *John Dollar* is a grisly story, all right. It's the kind where you're reading cheerily along and you suddenly say, Wait. They did *what?* And you go back and read again to make sure, and the truth finally hits you with a sickening punch to the stomach. But precisely what gives the punch its oomph is that you were, indeed, reading *cheerily* along, up until that unexpected moment. *Lord of the Flies* was more predictable, more relentless; it was, in my opinion, not half as thoughtful a piece of work.

For one thing, *Lord of the Flies* began when its young characters had already been cast upon their tropical island. The main thread of **John Dollar** begins when its characters are still settled comfortably within their matrix of Englishness and Empire and White Man's Burden. Therefore, the reader's focus is directed not to human beings' basic uncivilized instincts but rather to the nature of so-called civilization itself—to its irrelevance and laughable impracticality, its willful blindness. (p. 35)

The English in Rangoon in 1917 are stuffy and complacent. They plant petunias where frangipani once grew, they read London newspapers two weeks out of date, they take their quinine "like religion, like the eucharist it was." Supposedly, Charlotte [the heroine] will marry into this community (why else would an Englishwoman travel so far?) and devote the rest of her days to family and to Christian charities. But she doesn't. Instead, she finds herself slowly thawing. She discovers that she is not content to remain aloof from the real life of Burma. . . . (pp. 35-6)

So Charlotte "goes native." She moves to a hut on stilts, adopts a sarong, and takes for her lover a seaman of mysterious origins named John Dollar. But she doesn't entirely give up her place among the English. She continues to teach their little girls, and when three boats full of English families set out for a jaunt to one of the Andaman Islands, planning to rename it in honor of King George's birthday, she agrees to come along.

This outing, which sets the stage for all the terrors that follow, provides the book's funniest moments. Even the participants' names are funny: The seven earnest Boy Scouts are named Edward, Edward, Charles, Charles, George, George, and Nigel. The servants (who in actuality bear such names as Ningyan and U Thet) are referred to as Sat, Sun, Tuesday, Wednesday, and Friday, which leads to such odd locutions as "Three days of the week collected the soiled china." It's agreed that the English should be the first to set foot upon the island, but there are all those aubergines, Stilton cheeses, sponge cakes, and so on to be unloaded beforehand, so the servants disembark first but remain discreetly below the high-tide mark, sitting on their crates and smoking while they wait for the official landing party.

So we're lulled. We smile, we lean back. And then neatly, almost daintily, people begin to fall away. An earthquake, a tidal wave, a bloody attack upon one of the boats—and all at once the island's only visible inhabitants are eight little girls and John Dollar, who's been left paraplegic and comatose.

Surely it's no accident that all of Wiggins's castaways—all those who can function, at any rate—are girls, while all of William Golding's were boys. There is a distinct difference in the girls' approach to their situation. They're generally better at caretaking, although sometimes this disintegrates into elaborate, empty ritual; and they show little of the Golding characters' zest for the hunt or for territoriality. Ultimately, their behavior is far more shocking, although this may be less a matter of gender than of circumstances. (One particular scene they're forced to witness effectively drives them all insane.)

While the rescuer in *Lord of the Flies* was appalled that *British* children should have managed so poorly, the gradually awakening John Dollar seems disappointed precisely by that which is most British in his young companions—by their salvaging a box of tea, say, instead of something useful like rope or poles. (Although it could be argued that their femaleness is what he finds exasperating—their frivolity, their preference for constructing pretty necklaces rather than shelters. Or just their childishness; it's hard to say for sure.) Those who are less British than the others—a half-Indian girl, for instance—tend to fare better. In fact, there are moments when the book comes perilously close to sentimentalizing all that is "native"; it seems a bit too pat that the half-Indian girl is apparently the only one with a genuinely loving mother.

John Dollar is made up of crisp, firm, authoritative sentences, and the effect is one of great certitude. We can tell we're heading toward a definite goal—toward something dreadful, maybe even unbearable. But that's where Wiggins shows her skill. At the end of the book, when we're left feeling hammered and bruised by all that's happened, we start thinking about the start of the book, which offered us a glimpse of Charlotte and one of the castaways some 60 years after the events on the island. All at once that scene begins to make more sense; we turn back to read it once more. So the book is, finally, a circular experience, and oddly healing. When you set aside **John Dollar,** what hangs on is not the horror of the story, but the pleasure in the way it was told, and an abiding respect for a next-to-impossible task most elegantly accomplished. (p. 36)

Anne Tyler, "Burmese Days," in The New Republic, *Vol. 200, No. 13, March 27, 1989, pp. 35-6.*

☐ Contemporary Literary Criticism

Indexes

Literary Criticism Series
   Cumulative Author Index
Cumulative Nationality Index
      Title Index, Volume 57

This Index Includes References to Entries in These Gale Series

Contemporary Literary Criticism

Presents excerpts of criticism on the works of novelists, poets, dramatists, short story writers, scriptwriters, and other creative writers who are now living or who have died since 1960. Cumulative indexes to authors and nationalities are included, as well as an index to titles discussed in the individual volume.

Twentieth-Century Literary Criticism

Contains critical excerpts by the most significant commentators on poets, novelists, short story writers, dramatists, and philosophers who died between 1900 and 1960. Cumulative indexes to authors, nationalities, and titles discussed are included in each new volume.

Nineteenth-Century Literature Criticism

Offers significant passages from criticism on authors who died between 1800 and 1899. Cumulative indexes to authors, nationalities, and titles discussed are included in each new volume.

Literature Criticism from 1400 to 1800

Compiles significant passages from the most noteworthy criticism on authors of the fifteenth through eighteenth centuries. Cumulative indexes to authors, nationalities, and titles discussed are included in each new volume.

Classical and Medieval Literature Criticism

Offers excerpts of criticism on the works of world authors from classical antiquity through the fourteenth century. Cumulative indexes to authors, titles, and critics are included in each volume.

Short Story Criticism

Compiles excerpts of criticism on short fiction by writers of all eras and nationalities. Cumulative indexes to authors, nationalities, and titles discussed are included in each new volume.

Children's Literature Review

Includes excerpts from reviews, criticism, and commentary on works of authors and illustrators who create books for children. Cumulative indexes to authors, nationalities, and titles discussed are included in each new volume.

Contemporary Authors Series

Encompasses five related series. *Contemporary Authors* provides biographical and bibliographical information on more than 92,000 writers of fiction, nonfiction, poetry, journalism, drama, motion pictures, and other fields. Each new volume contains sketches on authors not previously covered in the series. *Contemporary Authors New Revision Series* provides completely updated information on active authors covered in previously published volumes of *CA*. Only entries requiring significant change are revised for *CA New Revision Series*. *Contemporary Authors Permanent Series* consists of updated listings for deceased and inactive authors removed from the original volumes 9-36 when these volumes were revised. *Contemporary Authors Autobiography Series* presents specially commissioned autobiographies by leading contemporary writers. *Contemporary Authors Bibliographical Series* contains primary and secondary bibliographies as well as analytical bibliographical essays by authorities on major modern authors.

Dictionary of Literary Biography

Encompasses three related series. *Dictionary of Literary Biography* furnishes illustrated overviews of authors' lives and works and places them in the larger perspective of literary history. *Dictionary of Literary Biography Documentary Series* illuminates the careers of major figures through a selection of literary documents, including letters, notebook and diary entries, interviews, book reviews, and photographs. *Dictionary of Literary Biography Yearbook* summarizes the past year's literary activity with articles on genres, major prizes, conferences, and other timely subjects and includes updated and new entries on individual authors. A cumulative index to authors and articles is included in each new volume.

Concise Dictionary of American Literary Biography

A six-volume series that collects revised and updated sketches on major American authors that were originally presented in *Dictionary of Literary Biography*.

Something about the Author Series

Encompasses three related series. *Something about the Author* contains heavily illustrated biographical sketches on juvenile and young adult authors and illustrators from all eras. *Something about the Author Autobiography Series* presents specially commissioned autobiographies by prominent authors and illustrators of books for children and young adults.

Yesterday's Authors of Books for Children

Contains heavily illustrated entries on children's writers who died before 1961. Complete in two volumes.

Literary Criticism Series
Cumulative Author Index

This index lists all author entries in the Gale Literary Criticism Series and includes cross-references to other Gale sources. References in the index are identified as follows:

AAYA: *Authors & Artists for Young Adults,* Volumes 1-2
CAAS: *Contemporary Authors Autobiography Series,* Volumes 1-10
CA: *Contemporary Authors (original series),* Volumes 1-129
CABS: *Contemporary Authors Bibliographical Series,* Volumes 1-2
CANR: *Contemporary Authors New Revision Series,* Volumes 1-28
CAP: *Contemporary Authors Permanent Series,* Volumes 1-2
CA-R: *Contemporary Authors (revised editions),* Volumes 1-44
CDALB: *Concise Dictionary of American Literary Biography,* Volumes 1-4
CLC: *Contemporary Literary Criticism,* Volumes 1-57
CLR: *Children's Literature Review,* Volumes 1-19
CMLC: *Classical and Medieval Literature Criticism,* Volumes 1-4
DLB: *Dictionary of Literary Biography,* Volumes 1-90
DLB-DS: *Dictionary of Literary Biography Documentary Series,* Volumes 1-7
DLB-Y: *Dictionary of Literary Biography Yearbook,* Volumes 1980-1988
LC: *Literature Criticism from 1400 to 1800,* Volumes 1-12
NCLC: *Nineteenth-Century Literature Criticism,* Volumes 1-25
SAAS: *Something about the Author Autobiography Series,* Volumes 1-8
SATA: *Something about the Author,* Volumes 1-57
SSC: *Short Story Criticism,* Volumes 1-4
TCLC: *Twentieth-Century Literary Criticism,* Volumes 1-35
YABC: *Yesterday's Authors of Books for Children,* Volumes 1-2

Bellow, Saul
  1915- ..... **CLC 1, 2, 3, 6, 8, 10, 13, 15, 25, 33, 34**
  See also CA 5-8R; CABS 1; DLB 2, 28; DLB-Y 82; DLB-DS 3; CDALB 1941-1968

Belser, Reimond Karel Maria de 1929-
  See Ruysiinck, Ward

Bely, Andrey 1880-1934........... **TCLC 7**
  See also CA 104

Benary-Isbert, Margot 1889-1979... **CLC 12**
  See also CLR 12; CANR 4; CA 5-8R; obituary CA 89-92; SATA 2; obituary SATA 21

Benavente (y Martinez), Jacinto
  1866-1954 .... **TCLC 3**
  See also CA 106

Benchley, Peter (Bradford)
  1940- .... **CLC 4, 8**
  See also CANR 12; CA 17-20R; SATA 3

Benchley, Robert 1889-1945 .... **TCLC 1**
  See also CA 105; DLB 11

Benedikt, Michael 1935- .... **CLC 4, 14**
  See also CANR 7; CA 13-16R; DLB 5

Benet, Juan 1927-................ **CLC 28**

Benet, Stephen Vincent
  1898-1943 .... **TCLC 7**
  See also YABC 1; CA 104; DLB 4, 48

Benet, William Rose 1886-1950 ... **TCLC 28**
  See also CA 118; DLB 45

Benford, Gregory (Albert) 1941-.... **CLC 52**
  See also CANR 12, 24; CA 69-72; DLB-Y 82

Benn, Gottfried 1886-1956......... **TCLC 3**
  See also CA 106; DLB 56

Bennett, Alan 1934-.............. **CLC 45**
  See also CA 103

Bennett, (Enoch) Arnold
  1867-1931 .... **TCLC 5, 20**
  See also CA 106, DLB 10, 34

Bennett, George Harold 1930-
  See Bennett, Hal
  See also CA 97-100

Bennett, Hal 1930-.............. **CLC 5**
  See also Bennett, George Harold
  See also DLB 33

Bennett, Jay 1912-............... **CLC 35**
  See also CANR 11; CA 69-72; SAAS 4; SATA 27, 41

Bennett, Louise (Simone) 1919-..... **CLC 28**
  See also Bennett-Coverly, Louise Simone

Bennett-Coverly, Louise Simone 1919-
  See Bennett, Louise (Simone)
  See also CA 97-100

Benson, E(dward) F(rederic)
  1867-1940 .... **TCLC 27**
  See also CA 114

Benson, Jackson J. 1930-......... **CLC 34**
  See also CA 25-28R

Benson, Sally 1900-1972 .... **CLC 17**
  See also CAP 1; CA 19-20; obituary CA 37-40R; SATA 1, 35; obituary SATA 27

Benson, Stella 1892-1933........ **TCLC 17**
  See also CA 117; DLB 36

Bentley, E(dmund) C(lerihew)
  1875-1956 .... **TCLC 12**
  See also CA 108; DLB 70

Bentley, Eric (Russell) 1916-...... **CLC 24**
  See also CANR 6; CA 5-8R

Berger, John (Peter) 1926- ...... **CLC 2, 19**
  See also CA 81-84; DLB 14 ◄

Berger, Melvin (H.) 1927-......... **CLC 12**
  See also CANR 4; CA 5-8R; SAAS 2; SATA 5

Berger, Thomas (Louis)
  1924- .... **CLC 3, 5, 8, 11, 18, 38**
  See also CANR 5; CA 1-4R; DLB 2; DLB-Y 80

Bergman, (Ernst) Ingmar 1918-..... **CLC 16**
  See also CA 81-84

Bergson, Henri 1859-1941 .... **TCLC 32**

Bergstein, Eleanor 1938-........... **CLC 4**
  See also CANR 5; CA 53-56

Berkoff, Steven 1937-............. **CLC 56**
  See also CA 104

Bermant, Chaim 1929-............ **CLC 40**
  See also CANR 6; CA 57-60

Bernanos, (Paul Louis) Georges
  1888-1948 .... **TCLC 3**
  See also CA 104; DLB 72

Bernhard, Thomas 1931-1989 .... **CLC 3, 32**
  See also CA 85-88

Berriault, Gina 1926-............. **CLC 54**
  See also CA 116

Berrigan, Daniel J. 1921-.......... **CLC 4**
  See also CAAS 1; CANR 11; CA 33-36R; DLB 5

Berrigan, Edmund Joseph Michael, Jr.
  1934-1983
  See Berrigan, Ted
  See also CANR 14; CA 61-64; obituary CA 110

Berrigan, Ted 1934-1983 .... **CLC 37**
  See also Berrigan, Edmund Joseph Michael, Jr.
  See also DLB 5

Berry, Chuck 1926- .... **CLC 17**

Berry, Wendell (Erdman)
  1934- .... **CLC 4, 6, 8, 27, 46**
  See also CA 73-76; DLB 5, 6

Berryman, John
  1914-1972 ..... **CLC 1, 2, 3, 4, 6, 8, 10, 13, 25**
  See also CAP 1; CA 15-16; obituary CA 33-36R; CABS 2; DLB 48; CDALB 1941-1968

Bertolucci, Bernardo 1940- .... **CLC 16**
  See also CA 106

Besant, Annie (Wood) 1847-1933 ... **TCLC 9**
  See also CA 105

Bessie, Alvah 1904-1985.......... **CLC 23**
  See also CANR 2; CA 5-8R; obituary CA 116; DLB 26

Beti, Mongo 1932-.............. **CLC 27**
  See also Beyidi, Alexandre

Betjeman, (Sir) John
  1906-1984 .... **CLC 2, 6, 10, 34, 43**
  See also CA 9-12R; obituary CA 112; DLB 20; DLB-Y 84

Betti, Ugo 1892-1953 .... **TCLC 5**
  See also CA 104

Betts, Doris (Waugh) 1932-.... **CLC 3, 6, 28**
  See also CANR 9; CA 13-16R; DLB-Y 82

Bialik, Chaim Nachman
  1873-1934 .... **TCLC 25**

Bidart, Frank 19??-.............. **CLC 33**

Bienek, Horst 1930-............ **CLC 7, 11**
  See also CA 73-76; DLB 75

Bierce, Ambrose (Gwinett)
  1842-1914? .... **TCLC 1, 7**
  See also CA 104; DLB 11, 12, 23, 71, 74; CDALB 1865-1917

Billington, Rachel 1942-........... **CLC 43**
  See also CA 33-36R

Binyon, T(imothy) J(ohn) 1936- .... **CLC 34**
  See also CA 111

Bioy Casares, Adolfo 1914-.... **CLC 4, 8, 13**
  See also CANR 19; CA 29-32R

Bird, Robert Montgomery
  1806-1854 .... **NCLC 1**

Birdwell, Cleo 1936-
  See DeLillo, Don

Birney (Alfred) Earle
  1904- .... **CLC 1, 4, 6, 11**
  See also CANR 5, 20; CA 1-4R

Bishop, Elizabeth
  1911-1979 ...... **CLC 1, 4, 9, 13, 15, 32**
  See also CANR 26; CA 5-8R; obituary CA 89-92; CABS 2; obituary SATA 24; DLB 5

Bishop, John 1935-.............. **CLC 10**
  See also CA 105

Bissett, Bill 1939-................ **CLC 18**
  See also CANR 15; CA 69-72; DLB 53

Bitov, Andrei (Georgievich) 1937-... **CLC 57**

Biyidi, Alexandre 1932-
  See Beti, Mongo
  See also CA 114, 124

Bjornson, Bjornstjerne (Martinius)
  1832-1910 .... **TCLC 7**
  See also CA 104

Blackburn, Paul 1926-1971 ...... **CLC 9, 43**
  See also CA 81-84; obituary CA 33-36R; DLB 16; DLB-Y 81

Black Elk 1863-1950 .... **TCLC 33**

Blackmore, R(ichard) D(oddridge)
  1825-1900 .... **TCLC 27**
  See also CA 120; DLB 18

Blackmur, R(ichard) P(almer)
  1904-1965 .... **CLC 2, 24**
  See also CAP 1; CA 11-12; obituary CA 25-28R; DLB 63

Blackwood, Algernon (Henry)
  1869-1951 .... **TCLC 5**
  See also CA 105

Blackwood, Caroline 1931- .... **CLC 6, 9**
  See also CA 85-88; DLB 14

Blair, Eric Arthur 1903-1950
  See Orwell, George
  See also CA 104; SATA 29

Blais, Marie-Claire
  1939- .... **CLC 2, 4, 6, 13, 22**
  See also CAAS 4; CA 21-24R; DLB 53

Coover, Robert (Lowell)
1932- . . . . **CLC 3, 7, 15, 32, 46**
See also CANR 3; CA 45-48; DLB 2;
DLB-Y 81

Copeland, Stewart (Armstrong)
1952- . . . . **CLC 26**
See also The Police

Coppard, A(lfred) E(dgar)
1878-1957 . . . . **TCLC 5**
See also YABC 1; CA 114

Coppee, Francois 1842-1908 . . . . . . **TCLC 25**

Coppola, Francis Ford 1939- . . . . **CLC 16**
See also CA 77-80; DLB 44

Corcoran, Barbara 1911- . . . . **CLC 17**
See also CAAS 2; CANR 11; CA 21-24R;
SATA 3; DLB 52

Corman, Cid 1924- . . . . **CLC 9**
See also Corman, Sidney
See also CAAS 2; DLB 5

Corman, Sidney 1924-
See Corman, Cid
See also CA 85-88

Cormier, Robert (Edmund)
1925- . . . . **CLC 12, 30**
See also CLR 12; CANR 5, 23; CA 1-4R;
SATA 10, 45; DLB 52

Corn, Alfred (Dewitt III) 1943 . . . . . **CLC 33**
See also CA 104; DLB-Y 80

Cornwell, David (John Moore)
1931- . . . . **CLC 9, 15**
See also le Carre, John
See also CANR 13; CA 5-8R

Corso, (Nunzio) Gregory 1930- . . . **CLC 1, 11**
See also CA 5-8R; DLB 5, 16

Cortazar, Julio
1914-1984 . . . . . **CLC 2, 3, 5, 10, 13, 15,
33, 34**
See also CANR 12; CA 21-24R

Corvo, Baron 1860-1913
See Rolfe, Frederick (William Serafino
Austin Lewis Mary)

Cosic, Dobrica 1921- . . . . **CLC 14**
See also CA 122

Costain, Thomas B(ertram)
1885-1965 . . . . **CLC 30**
See also CA 5-8R; obituary CA 25-28R;
DLB 9

Costantini, Humberto 1924?-1987. . . **CLC 49**
See also obituary CA 122

Costello, Elvis 1955- . . . . **CLC 21**

Cotter, Joseph Seamon, Sr.
1861-1949 . . . . **TCLC 28**
See also DLB 50

Couperus, Louis (Marie Anne)
1863-1923 . . . . **TCLC 15**
See also CA 115

Cousteau, Jacques-Yves 1910- . . . . . . **CLC 30**
See also CANR 15; CA 65-68; SATA 38

Coward, (Sir) Noel (Pierce)
1899-1973 . . . . **CLC 1, 9, 29, 51**
See also CAP 2; CA 17-18;
obituary CA 41-44R; DLB 10

Cowley, Malcolm 1898-1989 . . . . **CLC 39**
See also CANR 3; CA 5-6R; DLB 4, 48;
DLB-Y 81

Cowper, William 1731-1800. . . . . . . **NCLC 8**

Cox, William Trevor 1928- . . . . . . **CLC 9, 14**
See also Trevor, William
See also CANR 4; CA 9-12R

Cozzens, James Gould
1903-1978 . . . . **CLC 1, 4, 11**
See also CANR 19; CA 9-12R;
obituary CA 81-84; DLB 9; DLB-Y 84;
DLB-DS 2; CDALB 1941-1968

Crane, (Harold) Hart
1899-1932 . . . . **TCLC 2, 5**
See also CA 104; DLB 4, 48

Crane, R(onald) S(almon)
1886-1967 . . . . **CLC 27**
See also CA 85-88; DLB 63

Crane, Stephen
1871-1900 . . . . **TCLC 11, 17, 32**
See also YABC 2; CA 109; DLB 12, 54, 78;
CDALB 1865-1917

Craven, Margaret 1901-1980. . . . . . . **CLC 17**
See also CA 103

Crawford, F(rancis) Marion
1854-1909 . . . . **TCLC 10**
See also CA 107; DLB 71

Crawford, Isabella Valancy
1850-1887 . . . . **NCLC 12**

Crayencour, Marguerite de 1913-
See Yourcenar, Marguerite

Creasey, John 1908-1973. . . . . **CLC 11**
See also CANR 8; CA 5-8R;
obituary CA 41-44R

Crebillon, Claude Prosper Jolyot de (fils)
1707-1777 . . . . **LC 1**

Creeley, Robert (White)
1926- . . . . **CLC 1, 2, 4, 8, 11, 15, 36**
See also CANR 23; CA 1-4R; DLB 5, 16

Crews, Harry (Eugene)
1935- . . . . **CLC 6, 23, 49**
See also CANR 20; CA 25-28R; DLB 6

Crichton, (John) Michael
1942- . . . . **CLC 2, 6, 54**
See also CANR 13; CA 25-28R; SATA 9;
DLB-Y 81

Crispin, Edmund 1921-1978. . . . . . . **CLC 22**
See also Montgomery, Robert Bruce

Cristofer, Michael 1946- . . . . **CLC 28**
See also CA 110; DLB 7

Crockett, David (Davy)
1786-1836 . . . . **NCLC 8**
See also DLB 3, 11

Croker, John Wilson 1780-1857 . . **NCLC 10**

Cronin, A(rchibald) J(oseph)
1896-1981 . . . . **CLC 32**
See also CANR 5; CA 1-4R;
obituary CA 102; obituary SATA 25, 47

Cross, Amanda 1926-
See Heilbrun, Carolyn G(old)

Crothers, Rachel 1878-1953. . . . . . . **TCLC 19**
See also CA 113; DLB 7

Crowley, Aleister 1875-1947 . . . . **TCLC 7**
See also CA 104

Crowley, John 1942-
See also CA 61-64; DLB-Y 82

Crumb, Robert 1943- . . . . **CLC 17**
See also CA 106

Cryer, Gretchen 1936?- . . . . **CLC 21**
See also CA 114, 123

Csath, Geza 1887-1919. . . . . **TCLC 13**
See also CA 111

Cudlip, David 1933- . . . . **CLC 34**

Cullen, Countee 1903-1946 . . . . **TCLC 4**
See also CA 108, 124; SATA 18; DLB 4,
48, 51

Cummings, E(dward) E(stlin)
1894-1962 . . . . **CLC 1, 3, 8, 12, 15**
See also CA 73-76; DLB 4, 48

Cunha, Euclides (Rodrigues) da
1866-1909 . . . . **TCLC 24**
See also CA 123

Cunningham, J(ames) V(incent)
1911-1985 . . . . **CLC 3, 31**
See also CANR 1; CA 1-4R;
obituary CA 115; DLB 5

Cunningham, Julia (Woolfolk)
1916- . . . . **CLC 12**
See also CANR 4, 19; CA 9-12R; SAAS 2;
SATA 1, 26

Cunningham, Michael 1952- . . . . **CLC 34**

Currie, Ellen 19??- . . . . **CLC 44**

Dabrowska, Maria (Szumska)
1889-1965 . . . . **CLC 15**
See also CA 106

Dabydeen, David 1956?- . . . . **CLC 34**
See also CA 106

Dacey, Philip 1939- . . . . **CLC 51**
See also CANR 14; CA 37-40R

Dagerman, Stig (Halvard)
1923-1954 . . . . **TCLC 17**
See also CA 117

Dahl, Roald 1916- . . . . **CLC 1, 6, 18**
See also CLR 1, 7; CANR 6; CA 1-4R;
SATA 1, 26

Dahlberg, Edward 1900-1977. . . **CLC 1, 7, 14**
See also CA 9-12R; obituary CA 69-72;
DLB 48

Daly, Elizabeth 1878-1967. . . . . **CLC 52**
See also CAP 2; CA 23-24;
obituary CA 25-28R

Daly, Maureen 1921- . . . . **CLC 17**
See also McGivern, Maureen Daly
See also SAAS 1; SATA 2

Daniken, Erich von 1935-
See Von Daniken, Erich

Dannay, Frederic 1905-1982
See Queen, Ellery
See also CANR 1; CA 1-4R;
obituary CA 107

D'Annunzio, Gabriele 1863-1938. . . . **TCLC 6**
See also CA 104

Danziger, Paula 1944- . . . . **CLC 21**
See also CA 112, 115; SATA 30, 36

Dario, Ruben 1867-1916 . . . . **TCLC 4**
See also Sarmiento, Felix Ruben Garcia
See also CA 104

Darley, George 1795-1846. . . . . **NCLC 2**

Daryush, Elizabeth 1887-1977. . . . **CLC 6, 19**
See also CANR 3; CA 49-52; DLB 20

Author Index

Author Index

Simmons, James (Stewart Alexander)
1933- .... CLC 43
See also CA 105; DLB 40

Simms, William Gilmore
1806-1870 .... NCLC 3
See also DLB 3, 30

Simon, Carly 1945-............. CLC 26
See also CA 105

Simon, Claude (Henri Eugene)
1913- ....CLC 4, 9, 15, 39
See also CA 89-92

Simon, (Marvin) Neil
1927- .... CLC 6, 11, 31, 39
See also CA 21-24R; DLB 7

Simon, Paul 1941- .... CLC 17
See also CA 116

Simonon, Paul 1956?-
See The Clash

Simpson, Louis (Aston Marantz)
1923- ....CLC 4, 7, 9, 32
See also CAAS 4; CANR 1; CA 1-4R;
DLB 5

Simpson, Mona (Elizabeth) 1957-... CLC 44
See also CA 122

Simpson, N(orman) F(rederick)
1919- .... CLC 29
See also CA 11-14R; DLB 13

Sinclair, Andrew (Annandale)
1935- .... CLC 2, 14
See also CAAS 5; CANR 14; CA 9-12R;
DLB 14

Sinclair, Mary Amelia St. Clair 1865?-1946
See Sinclair, May
See also CA 104

Sinclair, May 1865?-1946 ...... TCLC 3, 11
See also Sinclair, Mary Amelia St. Clair
See also DLB 36

Sinclair, Upton (Beall)
1878-1968 ....CLC 1, 11, 15
See also CANR 7, CA 5-8R;
obituary CA 25-28R; SATA 9; DLB 9

Singer, Isaac Bashevis
1904- .... CLC 1, 3, 6, 9, 11, 15, 23, 38;
SSC 3
See also CLR 1; CANR 1; CA 1-4R;
SATA 3, 27; DLB 6, 28, 52;
CDALB 1941-1968

Singer, Israel Joshua 1893-1944 ... TCLC 33

Singh, Khushwant 1915-........... CLC 11
See also CANR 6; CA 9-12R

Sinyavsky, Andrei (Donatevich)
1925- .... CLC 8
See also CA 85-88

Sirin, V.
See Nabokov, Vladimir (Vladimirovich)

Sissman, L(ouis) E(dward)
1928-1976 .... CLC 9, 18
See also CANR 13; CA 21-24R;
obituary CA 65-68; DLB 5

Sisson, C(harles) H(ubert) 1914-..... CLC 8
See also CAAS 3; CANR 3; CA 1-4R;
DLB 27

Sitwell, (Dame) Edith 1887-1964... CLC 2, 9
See also CA 9-12R; DLB 20

Sjoewall, Maj 1935-
See Wahloo, Per
See also CA 61-64, 65-68

Sjowall, Maj 1935-
See Wahloo, Per

Skelton, Robin 1925-............. CLC 13
See also CAAS 5; CA 5-8R; DLB 27, 53

Skolimowski, Jerzy 1938- .... CLC 20

Skolimowski, Yurek 1938-
See Skolimowski, Jerzy

Skram, Amalie (Bertha)
1847-1905 .... TCLC 25

Skrine, Mary Nesta 1904-
See Keane, Molly

Skvorecky, Josef (Vaclav)
1924- .... CLC 15, 39
See also CAAS 1; CANR 10; CA 61-64

Slade, Bernard 1930- .... CLC 11, 46
See also Newbound, Bernard Slade
See also DLB 53

Slaughter, Carolyn 1946-.......... CLC 56
See also CA 85-88

Slaughter, Frank G(ill) 1908- ...... CLC 29
See also CANR 5; CA 5-8R

Slavitt, David (R.) 1935- .... CLC 5, 14
See also CAAS 3; CA 21-24R; DLB 5, 6

Slesinger, Tess 1905-1945 .... TCLC 10
See also CA 107

Slessor, Kenneth 1901-1971 .... CLC 14
See also CA 102; obituary CA 89-92

Slowacki, Juliusz 1809-1849 ..... NCLC 15

Smart, Christopher 1722-1771........ LC 3

Smart, Elizabeth 1913-1986......... CLC 54
See also CA 81-84; obituary CA 118

Smiley, Jane (Graves) 1949-....... CLC 53
See also CA 104

Smith, A(rthur) J(ames) M(arshall)
1902-1980 .... CLC 15
See also CANR 4; CA 1-4R;
obituary CA 102

Smith, Betty (Wehner) 1896-1972... CLC 19
See also CA 5-8R; obituary CA 33-36R;
SATA 6; DLB-Y 82

Smith, Cecil Lewis Troughton 1899-1966
See Forester, C(ecil) S(cott)

Smith, Charlotte (Turner)
1749-1806 .... NCLC 23
See also DLB 39

Smith, Clark Ashton 1893-1961 .... CLC 43

Smith, Dave 1942- .... CLC 22, 42
See also Smith, David (Jeddie)
See also CAAS 7; CANR 1; DLB 5

Smith, David (Jeddie) 1942-
See Smith, Dave
See also CANR 1; CA 49-52

Smith, Florence Margaret 1902-1971
See Smith, Stevie
See also CAP 2; CA 17-18;
obituary CA 29-32R

Smith, John 1580?-1631............. LC 9
See also DLB 24, 30

Smith, Lee 1944-................. CLC 25
See also CA 114, 119; DLB-Y 83

Smith, Martin Cruz 1942-......... CLC 25
See also CANR 6; CA 85-88

Smith, Martin William 1942-
See Smith, Martin Cruz

Smith, Mary-Ann Tirone 1944-..... CLC 39
See also CA 118

Smith, Patti 1946- .... CLC 12
See also CA 93-96

Smith, Pauline (Urmson)
1882-1959 .... TCLC 25
See also CA 29-32R; SATA 27

Smith, Rosamond 1938-
See Oates, Joyce Carol

Smith, Sara Mahala Redway 1900-1972
See Benson, Sally

Smith, Stevie 1902-1971.... CLC 3, 8, 25, 44
See also Smith, Florence Margaret
See also DLB 20

Smith, Wilbur (Addison) 1933-..... CLC 33
See also CANR 7; CA 13-16R

Smith, William Jay 1918- .... CLC 6
See also CA 5-8R; SATA 2; DLB 5

Smollett, Tobias (George) 1721-1771 .. LC 2
See also DLB 39

Snodgrass, W(illiam) D(e Witt)
1926- ....CLC 2, 6, 10, 18
See also CANR 6; CA 1-4R; DLB 5

Snow, C(harles) P(ercy)
1905-1980 .... CLC 1, 4, 6, 9, 13, 19
See also CA 5-8R; obituary CA 101;
DLB 15

Snyder, Gary (Sherman)
1930- .... CLC 1, 2, 5, 9, 32
See also CA 17-20R; DLB 5, 16

Snyder, Zilpha Keatley 1927-...... CLC 17
See also CA 9-12R; SAAS 2; SATA 1, 28

Sodergran, Edith 1892-1923....... TCLC 31

Sokolov, Raymond 1941-........... CLC 7
See also CA 85-88

Sologub, Fyodor 1863-1927........ TCLC 9
See also Teternikov, Fyodor Kuzmich
See also CA 104

Solomos, Dionysios 1798-1857 ... NCLC 15

Solwoska, Mara 1929-
See French, Marilyn
See also CANR 3; CA 69-72

Solzhenitsyn, Aleksandr I(sayevich)
1918- ... CLC 1, 2, 4, 7, 9, 10, 18, 26, 34
See also CA 69-72

Somers, Jane 1919-
See Lessing, Doris (May)

Sommer, Scott 1951- .... CLC 25
See also CA 106

Sondheim, Stephen (Joshua)
1930- .... CLC 30, 39
See also CA 103

Sontag, Susan 1933-... CLC 1, 2, 10, 13, 31
See also CA 17-20R; DLB 2

Sophocles c. 496?-c. 406?........ CMLC 2

Sorrentino, Gilbert
1929- .... CLC 3, 7, 14, 22, 40
See also CANR 14; CA 77-80; DLB 5;
DLB-Y 80

Strachey, (Giles) Lytton
　1880-1932 .... **TCLC 12**
　See also CA 110

Strand, Mark　1934- .... **CLC 6, 18, 41**
　See also CA 21-24R; SATA 41; DLB 5

Straub, Peter (Francis)　1943- ...... **CLC 28**
　See also CA 85-88; DLB-Y 84

Strauss, Botho　1944- .... **CLC 22**

Straussler, Tomas　1937-
　See Stoppard, Tom

Streatfeild, (Mary) Noel　1897- ..... **CLC 21**
　See also CA 81-84; obituary CA 120;
　SATA 20, 48

Stribling, T(homas) S(igismund)
　1881-1965 .... **CLC 23**
　See also obituary CA 107; DLB 9

Strindberg, (Johan) August
　1849-1912 .... **TCLC 1, 8, 21**
　See also CA 104

Strugatskii, Arkadii (Natanovich)
　1925- .... **CLC 27**
　See also CA 106

Strugatskii, Boris (Natanovich)
　1933- .... **CLC 27**
　See also CA 106

Strummer, Joe　1953?-
　See The Clash

Stuart, (Hilton) Jesse
　1906-1984 .... **CLC 1, 8, 11, 14, 34**
　See also CA 5-8R; obituary CA 112;
　SATA 2; obituary SATA 36; DLB 9, 48;
　DLB-Y 84

Sturgeon, Theodore (Hamilton)
　1918-1985 .... **CLC 22, 39**
　See also CA 81-84; obituary CA 116;
　DLB 8; DLB-Y 85

Styron, William　1925- .. **CLC 1, 3, 5, 11, 15**
　See also CANR 6; CA 5-8R; DLB 2;
　DLB-Y 80

Sudermann, Hermann　1857-1928 .. **TCLC 15**
　See also CA 107

Sue, Eugene　1804-1857 .... **NCLC 1**

Sukenick, Ronald　1932- ..... **CLC 3, 4, 6, 48**
　See also CA 25-28R; DLB-Y 81

Suknaski, Andrew　1942- .... **CLC 19**
　See also CA 101; DLB 53

Sully-Prudhomme, Rene
　1839-1907 .... **TCLC 31**

Su Man-shu　1884-1918 .... **TCLC 24**
　See also CA 123

Summers, Andrew James　1942-
　See The Police

Summers, Andy　1942-
　See The Police

Summers, Hollis (Spurgeon, Jr.)
　1916- .... **CLC 10**
　See also CANR 3; CA 5-8R; DLB 6

Summers, (Alphonsus Joseph-Mary Augustus)
　Montague　1880-1948 .... **TCLC 16**
　See also CA 118

Sumner, Gordon Matthew　1951-
　See The Police

Surtees, Robert Smith
　1805-1864 .... **NCLC 14**
　See also DLB 21

Susann, Jacqueline　1921-1974 ...... **CLC 3**
　See also CA 65-68; obituary CA 53-56

Suskind, Patrick　1949- .... **CLC 44**

Sutcliff, Rosemary　1920- .... **CLC 26**
　See also CLR 1; CA 5-8R; SATA 6, 44

Sutro, Alfred　1863-1933 .... **TCLC 6**
　See also CA 105; DLB 10

Sutton, Henry　1935-
　See Slavitt, David (R.)

Svevo, Italo　1861-1928 .... **TCLC 2, 35**
　See also Schmitz, Ettore

Swados, Elizabeth　1951- .... **CLC 12**
　See also CA 97-100

Swados, Harvey　1920-1972 .... **CLC 5**
　See also CANR 6; CA 5-8R;
　obituary CA 37-40R; DLB 2

Swarthout, Glendon (Fred)　1918- ... **CLC 35**
　See also CANR 1; CA 1-4R; SATA 26

Swenson, May　1919-1989 .... **CLC 4, 14**
　See also CA 5-8R; SATA 15; DLB 5

Swift, Graham　1949- .... **CLC 41**
　See also CA 117, 122

Swift, Jonathan　1667-1745 .... **LC 1**
　See also SATA 19; DLB 39

Swinburne, Algernon Charles
　1837-1909 .... **TCLC 8**
　See also CA 105; DLB 35, 57

Swinfen, Ann　19??- .... **CLC 34**

Swinnerton, Frank (Arthur)
　1884-1982 .... **CLC 31**
　See also obituary CA 108; DLB 34

Symons, Arthur (William)
　1865-1945 .... **TCLC 11**
　See also CA 107; DLB 19, 57

Symons, Julian (Gustave)
　1912- .... **CLC 2, 14, 32**
　See also CAAS 3; CANR 3; CA 49-52

Synge, (Edmund) John Millington
　1871-1909 .... **TCLC 6**
　See also CA 104; DLB 10, 19

Syruc, J.　1911-
　See Milosz, Czeslaw

Szirtes, George　1948- .... **CLC 46**
　See also CA 109

Tabori, George　1914- .... **CLC 19**
　See also CANR 4; CA 49-52

Tagore, (Sir) Rabindranath
　1861-1941 .... **TCLC 3**
　See also Thakura, Ravindranatha
　See also CA 120

Taine, Hippolyte Adolphe
　1828-1893 .... **NCLC 15**

Talese, Gaetano　1932-
　See Talese, Gay

Talese, Gay　1932- .... **CLC 37**
　See also CANR 9; CA 1-4R

Tallent, Elizabeth (Ann)　1954- ..... **CLC 45**
　See also CA 117

Tally, Ted　1952- .... **CLC 42**
　See also CA 120, 124

Tamayo y Baus, Manuel
　1829-1898 .... **NCLC 1**

Tammsaare, A(nton) H(ansen)
　1878-1940 .... **TCLC 27**

Tanizaki, Jun'ichiro
　1886-1965 .... **CLC 8, 14, 28**
　See also CA 93-96; obituary CA 25-28R

Tarkington, (Newton) Booth
　1869-1946 .... **TCLC 9**
　See also CA 110; SATA 17; DLB 9

Tasso, Torquato　1544-1595 .... **LC 5**

Tate, (John Orley) Allen
　1899-1979 .... **CLC 2, 4, 6, 9, 11, 14, 24**
　See also CA 5-8R; obituary CA 85-88;
　DLB 4, 45, 63

Tate, James　1943- .... **CLC 2, 6, 25**
　See also CA 21-24R; DLB 5

Tavel, Ronald　1940- .... **CLC 6**
　See also CA 21-24R

Taylor, C(ecil) P(hillip)　1929-1981 .. **CLC 27**
　See also CA 25-28R; obituary CA 105

Taylor, Edward　1644?-1729 .... **LC 11**
　See also DLB 24

Taylor, Eleanor Ross　1920- .... **CLC 5**
　See also CA 81-84

Taylor, Elizabeth　1912-1975 ... **CLC 2, 4, 29**
　See also CANR 9; CA 13-16R; SATA 13

Taylor, Henry (Splawn)　1917- ...... **CLC 44**
　See also CAAS 7; CA 33-36R; DLB 5

Taylor, Kamala (Purnaiya)　1924-
　See Markandaya, Kamala
　See also CA 77-80

Taylor, Mildred D(elois)　1943- ...... **CLC 21**
　See also CLR 9; CANR 25; CA 85-88;
　SAAS 5; SATA 15; DLB 52

Taylor, Peter (Hillsman)
　1917- .... **CLC 1, 4, 18, 37, 44, 50**
　See also CANR 9; CA 13-16R; DLB-Y 81

Taylor, Robert Lewis　1912- .... **CLC 14**
　See also CANR 3; CA 1-4R; SATA 10

Teasdale, Sara　1884-1933 .... **TCLC 4**
　See also CA 104; SATA 32; DLB 45

Tegner, Esaias　1782-1846 .... **NCLC 2**

Teilhard de Chardin, (Marie Joseph) Pierre
　1881-1955 .... **TCLC 9**
　See also CA 105

Tennant, Emma　1937- .... **CLC 13, 52**
　See also CAAS 9; CANR 10; CA 65-68;
　DLB 14

Teran, Lisa St. Aubin de　19??- ..... **CLC 36**

Terkel, Louis　1912-
　See Terkel, Studs
　See also CANR 18; CA 57-60

Terkel, Studs　1912- .... **CLC 38**
　See also Terkel, Louis

Terry, Megan　1932- .... **CLC 19**
　See also CA 77-80; DLB 7

Tertz, Abram　1925-
　See Sinyavsky, Andrei (Donatevich)

Tesich, Steve　1943?- .... **CLC 40**
　See also CA 105; DLB-Y 83

Tesich, Stoyan　1943?-
　See Tesich, Steve

Turner, Frederick 1943-.......... **CLC 48**
See also CANR 12; CA 73-76; DLB 40

Tutuola, Amos 1920- .... **CLC 5, 14, 29**
See also CA 9-12R

Twain, Mark 1835-1910.... **TCLC 6, 12, 19**
See also Clemens, Samuel Langhorne
See also DLB 11, 12, 23, 64, 74

Tyler, Anne 1941-.... **CLC 7, 11, 18, 28, 44**
See also CANR 11; CA 9-12R; SATA 7;
DLB 6; DLB-Y 82

Tyler, Royall 1757-1826......... **NCLC 3**
See also DLB 37

Tynan (Hinkson), Katharine
1861-1931 .... **TCLC 3**
See also CA 104

Tytell, John 1939- .... **CLC 50**
See also CA 29-32R

Tzara, Tristan 1896-1963......... **CLC 47**
See also Rosenfeld, Samuel

Uhry, Alfred 1947?-.............. **CLC 55**
See also CA 127

Unamuno (y Jugo), Miguel de
1864-1936 ....**TCLC 2, 9**
See also CA 104

Underwood, Miles 1909-1981
See Glassco, John

Undset, Sigrid 1882-1949......... **TCLC 3**
See also CA 104

Ungaretti, Giuseppe
1888-1970 .... **CLC 7, 11, 15**
See also CAP 2; CA 19-20;
obituary CA 25-28R

Unger, Douglas 1952-............ **CLC 34**

Unger, Eva 1932-
See Figes, Eva

Updike, John (Hoyer)
1932- ...... **CLC 1, 2, 3, 5, 7, 9, 13, 15,**
23, 34, 43
See also CANR 4; CA 1-4R; CABS 2;
DLB 2, 5; DLB-Y 80, 82; DLB-DS 3

Urdang, Constance (Henriette)
1922- .... **CLC 47**
See also CANR 9, 24; CA 21-24R

Uris, Leon (Marcus) 1924-....... **CLC 7, 32**
See also CANR 1; CA 1-4R; SATA 49

Ustinov, Peter (Alexander) 1921-.... **CLC 1**
See also CANR 25; CA 13-16R; DLB 13

Vaculik, Ludvik 1926- .... **CLC 7**
See also CA 53-56

Valenzuela, Luisa 1938-........... **CLC 31**
See also CA 101

Valera (y Acala-Galiano), Juan
1824-1905 .... **TCLC 10**
See also CA 106

Valery, Paul (Ambroise Toussaint Jules)
1871-1945 .... **TCLC 4, 15**
See also CA 104, 122

Valle-Inclan (y Montenegro), Ramon (Maria)
del 1866-1936.............. **TCLC 5**
See also CA 106

Vallejo, Cesar (Abraham)
1892-1938 .... **TCLC 3**
See also CA 105

Van Ash, Cay 1918-.............. **CLC 34**

Vance, Jack 1916?-.............. **CLC 35**
See also DLB 8

Vance, John Holbrook 1916?-
See Vance, Jack
See also CANR 17; CA 29-32R

Van Den Bogarde, Derek (Jules Gaspard
Ulric) Niven 1921-
See Bogarde, Dirk
See also CA 77-80

Vanderhaeghe, Guy 1951- .... **CLC 41**
See also CA 113

Van der Post, Laurens (Jan) 1906-... **CLC 5**
See also CA 5-8R

Van de Wetering, Janwillem
1931-...................... **CLC 47**
See also CANR 4; CA 49-52

Van Dine, S. S. 1888-1939....... **TCLC 23**

Van Doren, Carl (Clinton)
1885-1950 .... **TCLC 18**
See also CA 111

Van Doren, Mark 1894-1972..... **CLC 6, 10**
See also CANR 3; CA 1-4R;
obituary CA 37-40R; DLB 45

Van Druten, John (William)
1901-1957 .... **TCLC 2**
See also CA 104; DLB 10

Van Duyn, Mona 1921-.......... **CLC 3, 7**
See also CANR 7; CA 9-12R; DLB 5

Van Itallie, Jean-Claude 1936- ...... **CLC 3**
See also CAAS 2; CANR 1; CA 45-48;
DLB 7

Van Ostaijen, Paul 1896-1928..... **TCLC 33**

Van Peebles, Melvin 1932-...... **CLC 2, 20**
See also CA 85-88

Vansittart, Peter 1920-........... **CLC 42**
See also CANR 3; CA 1-4R

Van Vechten, Carl 1880-1964 ..... **CLC 33**
See also obituary CA 89-92; DLB 4, 9, 51

Van Vogt, A(lfred) E(lton) 1912-..... **CLC 1**
See also CA 21-24R; SATA 14; DLB 8

Varda, Agnes 1928- .... **CLC 16**
See also CA 116, 122

Vargas Llosa, (Jorge) Mario (Pedro)
1936- .... **CLC 3, 6, 9, 10, 15, 31, 42**
See also CANR 18; CA 73-76

Vassilikos, Vassilis 1933-........ **CLC 4, 8**
See also CA 81-84

Vazov, Ivan 1850-1921.......... **TCLC 25**
See also CA 121

Veblen, Thorstein Bunde
1857-1929 .... **TCLC 31**
See also CA 115

Verga, Giovanni 1840-1922 .... **TCLC 3**
See also CA 104, 123

Verhaeren, Emile (Adolphe Gustave)
1855-1916 .... **TCLC 12**
See also CA 109

Verlaine, Paul (Marie) 1844-1896.. **NCLC 2**

Verne, Jules (Gabriel) 1828-1905 ... **TCLC 6**
See also CA 110; SATA 21

Very, Jones 1813-1880.......... **NCLC 9**
See also DLB 1

Vesaas, Tarjei 1897-1970.......... **CLC 48**
See also obituary CA 29-32R

Vian, Boris 1920-1959 .... **TCLC 9**
See also CA 106; DLB 72

Viaud, (Louis Marie) Julien 1850-1923
See Loti, Pierre
See also CA 107

Vicker, Angus 1916-
See Felsen, Henry Gregor

Vidal, Eugene Luther, Jr. 1925-
See Vidal, Gore

Vidal, Gore
1925- .... **CLC 2, 4, 6, 8, 10, 22, 33**
See also CANR 13; CA 5-8R; DLB 6

Viereck, Peter (Robert Edwin)
1916-....................... **CLC 4**
See also CANR 1; CA 1-4R; DLB 5

Vigny, Alfred (Victor) de
1797-1863 .... **NCLC 7**

Villiers de l'Isle Adam, Jean Marie Mathias
Philippe Auguste, Comte de,
1838-1889 .... **NCLC 3**

Vinci, Leonardo da 1452-1519....... **LC 12**

Vine, Barbara 1930-............. **CLC 50**
See also Rendell, Ruth

Vinge, Joan (Carol) D(ennison)
1948-...................... **CLC 30**
See also CA 93-96; SATA 36

Visconti, Luchino 1906-1976...... **CLC 16**
See also CA 81-84; obituary CA 65-68

Vittorini, Elio 1908-1966...... **CLC 6, 9, 14**
See also obituary CA 25-28R

Vizinczey, Stephen 1933 .... **CLC 40**

Vliet, R(ussell) G(ordon)
1929-1984 .... **CLC 22**
See also CANR 18; CA 37-40R;
obituary CA 112

Voight, Ellen Bryant 1943- .... **CLC 54**
See also CANR 11; CA 69-72

Voigt, Cynthia 1942- .... **CLC 30**
See also CANR 18; CA 106; SATA 33, 48

Voinovich, Vladimir (Nikolaevich)
1932-.................... **CLC 10, 49**
See also CA 81-84

Von Daeniken, Erich 1935-
See Von Daniken, Erich
See also CANR 17; CA 37-40R

Von Daniken, Erich 1935-......... **CLC 30**
See also Von Daeniken, Erich

Vonnegut, Kurt, Jr.
1922- .... **CLC 1, 2, 3, 4, 5, 8, 12, 22, 40**
See also CANR 1; CA 1-4R; DLB 2, 8;
DLB-Y 80; DLB-DS 3

Vorster, Gordon 1924-............ **CLC 34**

Voznesensky, Andrei 1933-... **CLC 1, 15, 57**
See also CA 89-92

Waddington, Miriam 1917- .... **CLC 28**
See also CANR 12; CA 21-24R

Wagman, Fredrica 1937-........... **CLC 7**
See also CA 97-100

Wagner, Richard 1813-1883....... **NCLC 9**

Wagner-Martin, Linda 1936-....... **CLC 50**

Author Index

CLC Cumulative Nationality Index

Nationality Index

Nationality Index

CLC-57 Title Index

Title Index